Blackstone's Statutes on
Family Law

2014–2015

23rd edition

edited by

Mika Oldham

MA, PhD
Fellow of Jesus College, Cambridge

OXFORD
UNIVERSITY PRESS

OXFORD
UNIVERSITY PRESS

Great Clarendon Street, Oxford, OX26DP,
United Kingdom

Oxford University Press is a department of the University of Oxford.
It furthers the University's objective of excellence in research, scholarship,
and education by publishing worldwide. Oxford is a registered trade mark of
Oxford University Press in the UK and in certain other countries

This selection © Mika Oldham 2014

The moral rights of the author have been asserted

First published by Blackstone Press 1990
Twentieth edition 2011
Twenty-first edition 2012
Twenty-second edition 2013
Twenty-third edition 2014

Impression: 1

Public sector information reproduced under Open Government Licence v1.0
(http://www.nationalarchives.gov.uk/doc/open-government-licence/open-government-licence.htm)

Crown Copyright material reproduced with the permission of the
Controller, HMSO (under the terms of the Click Use licence)

Published in the United States of America by Oxford University Press
198 Madison Avenue, New York, NY 10016, United States of America

British Library Cataloguing in Publication Data

Data available

ISBN 978–0–19–870948–0

Printed in Great Britain by
Bell & Bain Ltd, Glasgow

Editor's preface

Many important changes have occurred since the last edition of *Blackstone's Statutes on Family Law*. This twenty-third edition includes amendments—some groundbreaking—to key areas such as marriage, succession, adoption and other important aspects of child law. Primary legislation introducing these changes includes, inter alia, the Marriage (Same Sex Couples) Act 2013, the Enterprise and Regulatory Reform Act 2013, the Children and Families Act 2014, the Anti-social Behaviour, Crime and Policing Act 2014 and the Inheritance and Trustees' Powers Act 2014. Also of relevance to family law are several Bills currently before Parliament; links to these Bills are available via the OUP Online Resource Centre.

As with earlier editions, statutes are included in chronological order and amendments incorporated directly into the relevant text. In line with usual teaching convention, statutes are treated as fully in force once Royal Assent is received. I would like once again to express my gratitude to colleagues and students both here and in other institutions whose helpful comments and suggestions have assisted in the preparation of this edition. As always, any further comments or suggestions would be welcome. I am indebted to the staff at OUP and at the Squire Law Library for their unfailing friendliness and willingness to help, and to my students, whose enquiring minds and enthusiasm are an inspiration.

Mika Oldham
April 2014

New to this edition

The twenty-third edition of *Blackstone's Statutes on Family Law* has been fully revised and updated with all changes effected by relevant legislation through to April 2014 including:

- Inheritance and Trustees' Powers Act 2014
- Children and Families Act 2014
- Anti-social Behaviour, Crime and Policing Act 2014
- Marriage (Same Sex Couples) Act 2013
- Enterprise and Regulatory Reform Act 2013

Contents

Chronological contents

x   Chronological contents

Alphabetical contents

Statutes 1837–2014

Wills Act 1837

(7 Will. 4 & 1 Vict., c. 26)

3 All property may be disposed of by will

It shall be lawful for every person to devise, bequeath, or dispose of, by his will executed in manner hereinafter required, all real estate and all personal estate which he shall be entitled to, either at law or in equity, at the time of his death, and which if not so devised, bequeathed, or disposed of would devolve upon his executor or administrator; and the power hereby given shall extend to all contingent, executory, or other future interests in any real or personal estate, whether the testator may or may not be ascertained as the person or one of the persons in whom the same respectively may become vested, and whether he may be entitled thereto under the instrument by which the same respectively were created or under any disposition thereof by deed or will; and also to all rights of entry for conditions broken, and other rights of entry; and also to such of the same estates, interests, and rights respectively, and other real and personal estate, as the testator may be entitled to at the time of his death, notwithstanding that he may become entitled to the same subsequently to the execution of his will.

7 No will of a person under age valid

No will made by any person under the age of eighteen years shall be valid.

9 Signing and attestation of wills

No will shall be valid unless—

(a) it is in writing, and signed by the testator, or by some other person in his presence and by his direction; and

(b) it appears that the testator intended by his signature to give effect to the will; and

(c) the signature is made or acknowledged by the testator in the presence of two or more witnesses present at the same time; and

(d) each witness either—

(i) attests and signs the will; or

(ii) acknowledges his signature, in the presence of the testator (but not necessarily in the presence of any other witness),

but no form of attestation shall be necessary.

...

18 Will to be revoked by marriage

(1) Subject to subsections (2) to (4) below, a will shall be revoked by the testator's marriage.

(2) A disposition in a will in exercise of a power of appointment shall take effect notwithstanding the testator's subsequent marriage unless the property so appointed would in default of appointment pass to his personal representatives.

(3) Where it appears from a will that at the time it was made the testator was expecting to be married to a particular person and that he intended that the will should not be revoked by the marriage, the will shall not be revoked by his marriage to that person.

(4) Where it appears from a will that at the time it was made the testator was expecting to be married to a particular person and that he intended that a disposition in the will should not be revoked by his marriage to that person,—

(a) that disposition shall take effect notwithstanding the marriage; and

(b) any other disposition in the will shall take effect also, unless it appears from the will that the testator intended the disposition to be revoked by the marriage.

18A   Effect of dissolution or annulment of marriage on wills

(1) Where, after a testator has made a will, a decree of a court of civil jurisdiction in England and Wales dissolves or annuls his marriage or his marriage is dissolved or annulled and the divorce or annulment is entitled to recognition in England and Wales by virtue of Part II of the Family Law Act 1986,—

(a) provisions of the will appointing executors or trustees or conferring a power of appointment, if they appoint or confer the power on the former spouse, shall take effect as if the former spouse had died on the date on which the marriage is dissolved or annulled, and

(b) any property which, or an interest in which, is devised or bequeathed to the former spouse shall pass as if the former spouse had died on that date,

except in so far as a contrary intention appears by the will.

(2) Subsection (1)(b) above is without prejudice to any right of the former spouse to apply for financial provision under the Inheritance (Provision for Family and Dependants) Act 1975.

18B   Will to be revoked by civil partnership

(1) Subject to subsections (2) to (6), a will is revoked by the formation of a civil partnership between the testator and another person.

(2) A disposition in a will in exercise of a power of appointment takes effect despite the formation of a subsequent civil partnership between the testator and another person unless the property so appointed would in default of appointment pass to the testator's personal representatives.

(3) If it appears from a will—

(a) that at the time it was made the testator was expecting to form a civil partnership with a particular person, and

(b) that he intended that the will should not be revoked by the formation of the civil partnership,

the will is not revoked by its formation.

(4) Subsections (5) and (6) apply if it appears from a will—

(a) that at the time it was made the testator was expecting to form a civil partnership with a particular person, and

(b) that he intended that a disposition in the will should not be revoked by the formation of the civil partnership.

(5) The disposition takes effect despite the formation of the civil partnership.

(6) Any other disposition in the will also takes effect, unless it appears from the will that the testator intended the disposition to be revoked by the formation of the civil partnership.

18C   Effect of dissolution or annulment of civil partnership on wills

(1) This section applies if, after a testator has made a will—

(a) a court of civil jurisdiction in England and Wales dissolves his civil partnership or makes a nullity order in respect of it, or

(b) his civil partnership is dissolved or annulled and the dissolution or annulment is entitled to recognition in England and Wales by virtue of Chapter 3 of Part 5 of the Civil Partnership Act 2004.

(2) Except in so far as a contrary intention appears by the will—

    (a) provisions of the will appointing executors or trustees or conferring a power of appointment, if they appoint or confer the power on the former civil partner, take effect as if the former civil partner had died on the date on which the civil partnership is dissolved or annulled, and

    (b) any property which, or an interest in which, is devised or bequeathed to the former civil partner shall pass as if the former civil partner had died on that date.

(3) Subsection (2)(b) does not affect any right of the former civil partner to apply for financial provision under the Inheritance (Provision for Family and Dependants) Act 1975.

…

33   Gifts to children or other issue who leave issue living at the testator's death shall not lapse

(1) Where—

    (a) a will contains a devise or bequest to a child or remoter descendant of the testator; and

    (b) the intended beneficiary dies before the testator, leaving issue; and

    (c) issue of the intended beneficiary are living at the testator's death,

then, unless a contrary intention appears by the will, the devise or bequest shall take effect as a devise or bequest to the issue living at the testator's death.

(2) Where—

    (a) a will contains a devise or bequest to a class of persons consisting of children or remoter descendants of the testator; and

    (b) a member of the class dies before the testator, leaving issue; and

    (c) issue of that member are living at the testator's death,

then, unless a contrary intention appears by the will, the devise or bequest shall take effect as if the class included the issue of its deceased member living at the testator's death.

(3) Issue shall take under this section through all degrees, according to their stock, in equal shares if more than one, any gift or share which their parent would have taken and so that (subject to section 33A) no issue shall take whose parent is living at the testator's death and so capable of taking.

(4) For the purposes of this section—

    (a) the illegitimacy of any person is to be disregarded; and

    (b) a person conceived before the testator's death and born living thereafter is to be taken to have been living at the testator's death.

33A   Disclaimer or forfeiture of gift

(1) This section applies where a will contains a devise or bequest to a person who—

    (a) disclaims it, or

    (b) has been precluded by the forfeiture rule from acquiring it.

(2) The person is, unless a contrary intention appears by the will, to be treated for the purposes of this Act as having died immediately before the testator.

(3) But in a case within subsection (1)(b), subsection (2) does not affect the power conferred by section 2 of the Forfeiture Act 1982 (power of court to modify the forfeiture rule).

(4) In this section 'forfeiture rule' has the same meaning as in the Forfeiture Act 1982.

…

Married Women's Property Act 1882

(45 & 46 Vict., c. 75)

11   Moneys payable under policy of assurance not to form part of estate of the insured

A married woman may effect a policy upon her own life or the life of her husband for her own benefit; and the same and all benefit thereof shall enure accordingly.

A policy of assurance effected by any man on his own life, and expressed to be for the benefit of his wife, or of his children, or of his wife and children, or any of them, or by any woman on her own life, and expressed to be for the benefit of her husband, or of her children, or of her husband and children, or any of them, shall create a trust in favour of the objects therein named, and the moneys payable under any such policy shall not, so long as any object of the trust remains unperformed, form part of the estate of the insured, or be subject to his or her debts: Provided, that if it shall be proved that the policy was effected and the premiums paid with intent to defraud the creditors of the insured, they shall be entitled to receive, out of the moneys payable under the policy, a sum equal to the premiums so paid.

…

17   Questions between husband and wife as to property to be decided in a summary way

In any question between husband and wife as to the title to or possession of property, either party may apply by summons or otherwise in a summary way to the High Court or the family court and the court may, on such an application (which may be heard in private), make such order with respect to the property as it thinks fit.

In this section 'prescribed' means prescribed by rules of court.

Law of Property Act 1925

(15 & 16 Geo. 5, c. 20)

37   Rights of husband and wife

A husband and wife shall, for all purposes of acquisition of any interest in property, under a disposition made or coming into operation after the commencement of this Act, be treated as two persons.

53   Instruments required to be in writing

(1) Subject to the provisions hereinafter contained with respect to the creation of interests in land by parol—

    (a) no interest in land can be created or disposed of except by writing signed by the person creating or conveying the same, or by his agent thereunto lawfully authorised in writing, or by will, or by operation of law;

    (b) a declaration of trust respecting any land or any interest therein must be manifested and proved by some writing signed by some person who is able to declare such trust or by his will;

    (c) a disposition of an equitable interest or trust subsisting at the time of the disposition, must be in writing signed by the person disposing of the same, or by his agent thereunto lawfully authorised in writing or by will.

(2) This section does not affect the creation or operation of resulting, implied or constructive trusts.

184   Presumption of survivorship in regard to claims to property

In all cases where, after the commencement of this Act, two or more persons have died in circumstances rendering it uncertain which of them survived the other or others, such deaths shall (subject to any order of the court), for all purposes affecting the title to property, be presumed to have occurred in order of seniority, and accordingly the younger shall be deemed to have survived the elder.

Administration of Estates Act 1925

(15 & 16 Geo. 5, c. 23)

PART IV DISTRIBUTION OF RESIDUARY ESTATE

46 Succession to real and personal estate on intestacy

(1) The residuary estate of an intestate shall be distributed in the manner or be held on the trusts mentioned in this section, namely:—

    (i) If the intestate leaves a spouse or civil partner, then in accordance with the following Table:

TABLE	
(1) If the intestate leaves no issue:	The residuary estate shall be held in trust for the surviving spouse or civil partner absolutely.
(2) If the intestate leaves issue:	(A) the surviving spouse or civil partner shall take the personal chattels absolutely;
	(B) the residuary estate of the intestate (other than the personal chattels) shall stand charged with the payment of a fixed net sum, free of death duties and costs, to the surviving spouse or civil partner, together with simple interest on it from the date of the death at the rate provided for by subsection (1A) until paid or appropriated; and
	(C) subject to providing for the sum and interest referred to in paragraph (B), the residuary estate (other than the personal chattels) shall be held—
	(a) as to one half, in trust for the surviving spouse or civil partner absolutely, and
	(b) as to the other half, on the statutory trusts for the issue of the intestate.

    The amount of the fixed net sum referred to in paragraph (B) of case (2) of this Table is to be determined in accordance with Schedule 1A.

...

    (ii) If the intestate leaves issue but no spouse or civil partner, the residuary estate of the intestate shall be held on the statutory trusts for the issue of the intestate;

    (iii) If the intestate leaves no spouse or civil partner and no issue but both parents, then the residuary estate of the intestate shall be held in trust for the father and mother in equal shares absolutely;

    (iv) If the intestate leaves no spouse or civil partner and no issue but one parent, then the residuary estate of the intestate shall be held in trust for the surviving father or mother absolutely;

    (v) If the intestate leaves no spouse or civil partner and no issue and no parent, then the residuary estate of the intestate shall be held in trust for the following persons living at the death of the intestate, and in the following order and manner, namely:—

First, on the statutory trusts for the brothers and sisters of the whole blood of the intestate; but if no person takes an absolutely vested interest under such trusts; then

Secondly, on the statutory trusts for the brothers and sisters of the half blood of the intestate; but if no person takes an absolutely vested interest under such trusts; then

Thirdly, for the grandparents of the intestate and, if more than one survive the intestate, in equal shares; but if there is no member of this class; then

Fourthly, on the statutory trusts for the uncles and aunts of the intestate (being brothers or sisters of the whole blood of a parent of the intestate); but if no person takes an absolutely vested interest under such trusts; thenFifthly, on the statutory trusts for the uncles and aunts of the intestate (being brothers or sisters of the half blood of a parent of the intestate);

(vi) In default of any person taking an absolute interest under the foregoing provisions, the residuary estate of the intestate shall belong to the Crown or to the Duchy of Lancaster or to the Duke of Cornwall for the time being, as the case may be, as bona vacantia, and in lieu of any right to escheat.

The Crown or the said Duchy or the said Duke may (without prejudice to the powers reserved by section nine of the Civil List Act 1910, or any other powers), out of the whole or any part of the property devolving on them respectively, provide, in accordance with the existing practice, for dependants, whether kindred or not, of the intestate, and other persons for whom the intestate might reasonably have been expected to make provision.

(1A) The interest rate referred to in paragraph (B) of case (2) of the Table in subsection (1)(i) is the Bank of England rate that had effect at the end of the day on which the intestate died.

(2) A spouse or civil partner shall for all purposes of distribution or division under the foregoing provisions of this section be treated as two persons.

(2A) Where the intestate's spouse or civil partner survived the intestate but died before the end of the period of 28 days beginning with the day on which the intestate died, this section shall have effect as respects the intestate as if the spouse or civil partner had not survived the intestate.

...

(4) The interest payable on the fixed net sum payable to a surviving spouse or civil partner shall be primarily payable out of income.

(5) In subsection (1A) 'Bank of England rate' means—

(a) the rate announced by the Monetary Policy Committee of the Bank of England as the official bank rate, or

(b) where an order under section 19 of the Bank of England Act 1998 (reserve powers) is in force, any equivalent rate determined by the Treasury under that section.

(6) The Lord Chancellor may by order made by statutory instrument amend the definition of 'Bank of England rate' in subsection (5) (but this subsection does not affect the generality of subsection (7)(b)).

(7) The Lord Chancellor may by order made by statutory instrument—

(a) amend subsection (1A) so as to substitute a different interest rate (however specified or identified) for the interest rate for the time being provided for by that subsection;

(b) make any amendments of, or repeals in, this section that may be consequential on or incidental to any amendment made by virtue of paragraph (a).

(8) A statutory instrument containing an order under subsection (6) is subject to annulment pursuant to a resolution of either House of Parliament.

(9) A statutory instrument containing an order under subsection (7) may not be made unless a draft of the instrument has been laid before and approved by a resolution of each House of Parliament.

46A   Disclaimer or forfeiture on intestacy

(1) This section applies where a person—

(a) is entitled in accordance with section 46 to an interest in the residuary estate of an intestate but disclaims it, or

(b) would have been so entitled had the person not been precluded by the forfeiture rule from acquiring it.

(2) The person is to be treated for the purposes of this Part as having died immediately before the intestate.

(3) But in a case within subsection (1)(b), subsection (2) does not affect the power conferred by section 2 of the Forfeiture Act 1982 (power of court to modify the forfeiture rule).

(4) In this section 'forfeiture rule' has the same meaning as in the Forfeiture Act 1982.

47 Statutory trusts in favour of issue and other classes of relatives of intestate

(1) Where under this Part of this Act the residuary estate of an intestate, or any part thereof, is directed to be held on the statutory trusts for the issue of the intestate, the same shall be held upon the following trusts, namely:—

(i) In trust, in equal shares if more than one, for all or any of the children or child of the intestate, living at the death of the intestate, who attain the age of eighteen years or marry under that age or form a civil partnership under that age, and for all or any of the issue living at the death of the intestate who attain the age of eighteen years or marry, or form a civil partnership, under that age of any child of the intestate who predeceases the intestate, such issue to take through all degrees, according to their stocks, in equal shares if more than one, the share which their parent would have taken if living at the death of the intestate, and so that (subject to section 46A) no issue shall take whose parent is living at the death of the intestate and so capable of taking;

(ii) The statutory power of advancement, and the statutory provisions which relate to maintenance and accumulation of surplus income, shall apply, but when an infant marries, or forms a civil partnership, such infant shall be entitled to give valid receipts for the income of the infant's share or interest;

...

(iv) The personal representatives may permit any infant contingently interested to have the use and enjoyment of any personal chattels in such manner and subject to such conditions (if any) as the personal representatives may consider reasonable, and without being liable to account for any consequential loss.

(4A) Subsections (2) and (4) are subject to section 46A.

(4B) Subsections (4C) and (4D) apply if a beneficiary under the statutory trusts—

(a) fails to attain an absolutely vested interest because the beneficiary dies without having reached 18 and without having married or formed a civil partnership, and

(b) dies leaving issue.

(4C) The beneficiary is to be treated for the purposes of this Part as having died immediately before the intestate.

(4D) The residuary estate (together with the income from it and any statutory accumulations of income from it) or so much of it as has not been paid or applied under a power affecting it is to devolve accordingly.

(2) If the trusts in favour of the issue of the intestate fail by reason of no child or other issue attaining an absolutely vested interest—

(a) the residuary estate of the intestate and the income thereof and all statutory accumulations, if any, of the income thereof, or so much thereof as may not have been paid or applied under any power affecting the same, shall go, devolve and be held under the provisions of this Part of this Act as if the intestate had died without leaving issue living at the death of the intestate;

(b) References in this Part of this Act to the intestate 'leaving no issue' shall be construed as 'leaving no issue who attain an absolutely vested interest';

(c) References in this Part of this Act to the intestate 'leaving issue' or 'leaving a child or other issue' shall be construed as 'leaving issue who attain an absolutely vested interest.'

(3) Where under this Part of this Act the residuary estate of an intestate or any part thereof is directed to be held on the statutory trusts for any class of relatives of the intestate, other than issue

of the intestate, the same shall be held on trusts corresponding to the statutory trusts for the issue of the intestate (other than the provision for bringing any money or property into account) as if such trusts (other than as aforesaid) were repeated with the substitution of references to the members or member of that class for references to the children or child of the intestate.

(4) References in paragraph (i) of subsection (1) of the last foregoing section to the intestate leaving, or not leaving, a member of the class consisting of brothers or sisters of the whole blood of the intestate and issue of brothers or sisters of the whole blood of the intestate shall be construed as references to the intestate leaving, or not leaving, a member of that class who attains an absolutely vested interest.

...

48 Powers of personal representative in respect of interests of surviving spouse

(2) The personal representatives may raise—

(a) the fixed net sum or any part thereof and the interest thereon payable to the surviving spouse or civil partner of the intestate on the security of the whole or any part of the residuary estate of the intestate (other than the personal chattels), so far as that estate may be sufficient for the purpose or the said sum and interest may not have been satisfied by an appropriation under the statutory power available in that behalf;

and the amount, if any, properly required for the payment of the costs of the transaction.

49 Application to cases of partial intestacy

(1) Where any person dies leaving a will effectively disposing of part of his property, this Part of this Act shall have effect as respects the part of his property not so disposed of subject to the provisions contained in the will and subject to the following modifications:—

(b) the personal representative shall, subject to his rights and powers for the purposes of administration, be a trustee for the persons entitled under this Part of this Act in respect of the part of the estate not expressly disposed of unless it appears by the will that the personal representative is intended to take such part beneficially.

...

PART V SUPPLEMENTAL

55 Definitions

In this Act, unless the context otherwise requires, the following expressions have the meanings hereby assigned to them respectively, that is to say:—

(1) ...

(vi) 'Intestate' includes a person who leaves a will but dies intestate as to some beneficial interest in his real or personal estate:

(x) 'Personal chattels' means tangible movable property, other than any such property which—

consists of money or securities for money, or

was used at the death of the intestate solely or mainly for business purposes, or

was held at the death of the intestate solely as an investment:

...

(2) References to a child or issue living at the death of any person include a child or issue en ventre sa mère at the death.

...

SCHEDULE 1A DETERMINATION OF THE
FIXED NET SUM

1.—This Schedule has effect for determining the fixed net sum referred to in paragraph (B) of case (2) of the Table in section 46(1)(i).

2.—On the coming into force of this Schedule, the amount of the fixed net sum is the amount fixed by order under section 1(1)(a) of the Family Provision Act 1966 immediately before the coming into force of this Schedule.

3.—(1) The Lord Chancellor may from time to time by order made by statutory instrument specify the amount of the fixed net sum.

(2) An order under sub-paragraph (1) relates only to deaths occurring after the coming into force of the order.

(3) The first order under sub-paragraph (1) supersedes paragraph 2 of this Schedule.

(4) A statutory instrument containing an order under sub-paragraph (1) is subject to annulment pursuant to a resolution of either House of Parliament.

(5) Sub-paragraph (4) does not apply in the case mentioned in paragraph 6(3), or in the case of an instrument which also contains provision made by virtue of paragraph 8.

4.—(1) This paragraph applies where—
  (a) a figure for the consumer prices index for a month has become available, and
  (b) the consumer prices index for that month is more than 15% higher than the consumer prices index for the base month.

(2) The Lord Chancellor must, before the end of the period of 21 days beginning with the day on which the figure mentioned in sub-paragraph (1)(a) becomes available ('the publication date'), make an order under paragraph 3(1).

(3) But if the Lord Chancellor determines under paragraph 6 that the order should specify an amount other than that mentioned in paragraph 6(1), the Lord Chancellor is to be taken to have complied with sub-paragraph (2) if, within the period of 21 days beginning with the publication date—
  (a) a draft of a statutory instrument containing the order is laid before each House of Parliament, and
  (b) paragraph 6(4) is complied with.

(4) In this paragraph—
'the base month' means—
  (a) the month in which this Schedule came into force, or
  (b) if one or more orders under paragraph 3(1) have been made before the publication date, the most recent month for which a figure for the consumer prices index was available when the Lord Chancellor made the most recent of those orders;
'consumer prices index' means—
  (a) the all items consumer prices index published by the Statistics Board, or
  (b) if that index is not published for a relevant month, any substituted index or index figures published by the Statistics Board.

5.—The Lord Chancellor must ensure that the power under paragraph 3(1) is exercised in such a way that an order is made—
  (a) before the end of the period of 5 years beginning with the date this Schedule comes into force, and then
  (b) before the end of the period of 5 years since the date on which the last order under paragraph 3(1) was made, and so on.

6.—(1) Unless the Lord Chancellor otherwise determines, an order under paragraph 3(1) must specify the amount given by paragraph 7(2) or (as the case requires) 7(3).

(2) If the Lord Chancellor does otherwise determine—
  (a) an order under paragraph 3(1) may provide for the fixed net sum to be of any amount (including an amount equal to or lower than the previous amount), and
  (b) the Lord Chancellor must prepare a report stating the reason for the determination.

(3) A statutory instrument containing an order under paragraph 3(1) that specifies an amount other than that mentioned in sub-paragraph (1) of this paragraph may not be made unless a draft of the instrument has been laid before and approved by a resolution of each House of Parliament.

(4) The Lord Chancellor must lay the report before Parliament no later than the date on which the draft of the instrument containing the order is laid before Parliament.

7.—(1) The amount mentioned in paragraph 6(1) is found as follows.

(2) If the consumer prices index for the current month is higher than that for the base month, the amount to be specified in the order is found by—

(a) increasing the amount of the previous fixed net sum by the same percentage as the percentage increase in the consumer prices index between the base month and the current month, and

(b) if the resulting figure is not a multiple of £1,000, rounding it up to the nearest multiple of £1,000.

(3) If the consumer prices index for the current month is the same as, or lower than, that for the base month, the amount specified in the order is to be the same as the amount of the previous fixed net sum.

(4) In this paragraph—

'the base month' means—

(a) in the case of the first order under paragraph 3(1), the month in which this Schedule came into force, and

(b) in the case of each subsequent order, the month which was the current month in relation to the previous order;

'the current month' means the most recent month for which a figure for the consumer prices index is available when the Lord Chancellor makes the order;

'consumer prices index' has the same meaning as in paragraph 4.

8.—(1) The Lord Chancellor may by order made by statutory instrument amend paragraphs 4 and 7 so as to—

(a) substitute for references to the consumer prices index (as defined) references to another index, and

(b) make amendments in those paragraphs consequential on that substitution.

(2) A statutory instrument containing an order under sub-paragraph (1) may not be made unless a draft of the instrument has been laid before and approved by a resolution of each House of Parliament.

Children and Young Persons Act 1933

(23 Geo. 5, c. 12)

PART I PREVENTION OF CRUELTY AND EXPOSURE TO MORAL AND PHYSICAL DANGER

Offences

1 Cruelty to persons under sixteen

(1) If any person who has attained the age of sixteen years and has responsibility for any child or young person under that age, wilfully assaults, ill-treats, neglects, abandons, or exposes him, or causes or procures him to be assaulted, ill-treated, neglected, abandoned, or exposed, in a manner likely to cause him unnecessary suffering or injury to health (including injury to or loss of sight, or

hearing, or limb, or organ of the body, and any mental derangement), that person shall be guilty of a misdemeanour, and shall be liable—

    (a) on conviction on indictment, to a fine, or alternatively, or in addition thereto, to imprisonment for any term not exceeding ten years;

    (b) on summary conviction, to a fine not exceeding the prescribed sum, or alternatively, or in addition thereto, to imprisonment for any term not exceeding six months.

(2) For the purposes of this section—

    (a) a parent or other person legally liable to maintain a child or young person, or the legal guardian of a child or young person, shall be deemed to have neglected him in a manner likely to cause injury to his health if he has failed to provide adequate food, clothing, medical aid or lodging for him, or if, having been unable otherwise to provide such food, clothing, medical aid or lodging, he has failed to take steps to procure it to be provided under the enactments applicable in that behalf;

    (b) where it is proved that the death of an infant under three years of age was caused by suffocation (not being suffocation caused by disease or the presence of any foreign body in the throat or air passages of the infant) while the infant was in bed with some other person who has attained the age of sixteen years, that other person shall, if he was, when he went to bed, under the influence of drink, be deemed to have neglected the infant in a manner likely to cause injury to its health.

(3) A person may be convicted of an offence under this section—

    (a) notwithstanding that actual suffering or injury to health, or the likelihood of actual suffering or injury to health, was obviated by the action of another person;

    (b) notwithstanding the death of the child or young person in question.

...

17 Interpretation of Part I

(1) For the purposes of this Part of this Act, the following shall be presumed to have responsibility for a child or young person—

    (a) any person who—

        (i) has parental responsibility for him (within the meaning of the Children Act 1989); or

        (ii) is otherwise legally liable to maintain him; and

    (b) any person who has care of him.

...

(2) A person who is presumed to be responsible for a child or young person by virtue of subsection (1)(a) shall not be taken to have ceased to be responsible for him by reason only that he does not have care of him.

...

PART III PROTECTION OF CHILDREN AND YOUNG PERSONS IN RELATION TO CRIMINAL AND SUMMARY PROCEEDINGS

Principles to be observed by all courts in dealing with children and young persons

44 General considerations

(1) Every court in dealing with a child or young person who is brought before it, either as an offender or otherwise, shall have regard to the welfare of the child or young person and shall in a proper case take steps for removing him from undesirable surroundings, and for securing that proper provision is made for his education and training.

Law Reform (Married Women and Tortfeasors) Act 1935

(25 & 26 Geo. 5, c. 30)

PART I CAPACITY, PROPERTY, AND LIABILITIES OF MARRIED WOMEN: AND LIABILITIES OF HUSBANDS

1 Capacity of married women

Subject to the provisions of this Part of this Act, a married woman shall—
- (a) be capable of acquiring, holding and disposing of, any property; and
- (b) be capable of rendering herself, and being rendered, liable in respect of any tort, contract, debt, or obligation; and
- (c) be capable of suing and being sued, either in tort or in contract or otherwise;
- (d) be subject to the law relating to bankruptcy and to the enforcement of judgments and orders,

in all respects as if she were a feme sole.

2 Property of married women

(1) Subject to the provisions of this Part of this Act all property which—
- (a) immediately before the passing of this Act was the separate property of a married woman or held for her separate use in equity; or
- (b) belongs at the time of her marriage to a woman married after the passing of this Act; or
- (c) after the passing of this Act is acquired by or devolves upon a married woman,

shall belong to her in all respects as if she were a feme sole and may be disposed of accordingly.

3 Abolition of husband's liability for wife's torts and ante-nuptial contracts, debts and obligations

Subject to the provisions of this Part of this Act, the husband of a married woman shall not, by reason only of his being her husband, be liable—
- (a) in respect of any tort committed by her whether before or after the marriage, or in respect of any contract entered into, or debt or obligation incurred, by her before the marriage; or
- (b) to be sued, or made a party to any legal proceeding brought, in respect of any such tort, contract, debt, or obligation.

Marriage Act 1949

(12 & 13 Geo. 6, c. 76)

PART I RESTRICTIONS ON MARRIAGE

1 Marriages within prohibited degrees

(1) A marriage solemnized between a person and any person mentioned the list in Part 1 of Schedule 1 shall be void.

(2) Subject to subsection (3) of this section, a marriage solemnized between a person and any person mentioned in the list in Part 2 of Schedule 1 shall be void.

(3) Any such marriage as is mentioned in subsection (2) of this section shall not be void by reason only of affinity if both the parties to the marriage have attained the age of twenty-one at the time of the marriage and the younger party has not at any time before attaining the age of eighteen been a child of the family in relation to the other party.

2 Marriages of persons under sixteen

A marriage solemnized between persons either of whom is under the age of sixteen shall be void.

3 Marriages of persons under eighteen

(1) Where the marriage of a child, not being a widower or widow or a surviving civil partner, is intended to be solemnized on the authority of a certificate issued by a superintendent registrar under Part III of this Act, whether by licence or without licence, the consent of the appropriate persons shall be required.

Provided that—

(a) if the superintendent registrar is satisfied that the consent of any person whose consent is so required cannot be obtained by reason of absence or inaccessibility or by reason of his being under any disability, the necessity for the consent of that person shall be dispensed with, if there is any other person whose consent is also required; and if the consent of no other person is required, the Registrar General may dispense with the necessity of obtaining any consent, or the court may, on application being made, consent to the marriage, and the consent of the court so given shall have the same effect as if it had been given by the person whose consent cannot be so obtained;

(b) if any person whose consent is required refuses his consent, the court may, on application being made, consent to the marriage, and the consent of the court so given shall have the same effect as if it had been given by the person whose consent is refused.

(1A) The appropriate persons are—

(a) if none of paragraphs (b) to (h) apply, each of the following—
    (i)   any parent of the child who has parental responsibility for him; and
    (ii) any guardian of the child;

(b) where a special guardianship order is in force with respect to a child, each of the child's special guardians, unless any of paragraphs (c) to (g) applies;

(c) where a care order has effect with respect to the child, the local authority designated in the order, and each parent, guardian or special guardian (in so far as their parental responsibility has not been restricted under section 33(3) of the Children Act 1989), unless paragraph (e) applies;

(d) where a child arrangements order to which subsection (1C) applies has effect with respect to the child, the persons with whom the child lives, or is to live, as a result of the order, unless paragraph (e) applies,

(e) where an adoption agency is authorised to place the child for adoption under section 19 of the Adoption and Children Act 2002, that agency or, where a care order has effect with respect to the child, the local authority designated in the order;

(f) where a placement order is in force with respect to the child, the appropriate local authority;

(g) where a child has been placed for adoption with prospective adopters, the prospective adopters (in so far as their parental responsibility has not been restricted under section 25(4) of the Adoption and Children Act 2002), in addition to those persons specified in paragraph (e) or (f);

(h) where none of paragraphs (b) to (g) apply but a child arrangements order to which subsection (1C) applies was in force with respect to the child immediately before he reached the age of sixteen, the persons with whom he lived, or was to live, as a result of the order.

(1B) In this section—

'guardian of a child', 'parental responsibility', 'child arrangements order', 'special guardian', 'special guardianship order' and 'care order' have the same meaning as in the Children Act 1989;

'adoption agency', 'placed for adoption', 'placement order' and 'local authority' have the same meaning as in the Adoption and Children Act 2002;

'appropriate local authority' means the local authority authorised by the placement order to place the child for adoption.

(1C) A child arrangements order is one to which this subsection applies if the order regulates arrangements that consist of, or include, arrangements which relate to either or both of the following—

    (a) with whom the child is to live, and

    (b) when the child is to live with any person.

(2) Subsection (1) shall apply to marriages intended to be solemnized on the authority of a common licence, with the substitution of references to the ecclesiastical authority by whom the licence was granted for references to the superintendent registrar, and with the substitution of a reference to the Master of the Faculties for the reference to the Registrar General.

(3) Where the marriage of a child not being a widower or widow, is intended to be solemnized after the publication of banns of matrimony then, if any person whose consent to the marriage would have been required under this section in the case of a marriage intended to be solemnized otherwise than after the publication of the banns, openly and publicly declares or causes to be declared, in the church or chapel in which the banns are published, at the time of the publication, his dissent from the intended marriage, the publication of banns shall be void.

(4) A clergyman shall not be liable to ecclesiastical censure for solemnizing the marriage of a child after the publication of banns without the consent of the parents or guardians of the child unless he had notice of the dissent of any person who is entitled to give notice of dissent under the last foregoing subsection.

(5) For the purposes of this section, 'the court' means the High Court or the family court, and rules of court may be made for enabling applications under this section—

    (a) if made to the High Court, to be heard in chambers;

    ...

    (c) if made to the family court, to be heard and determined otherwise than in open court, and shall provide that, where an application is made in consequence of a refusal to give consent, notice of the application shall be served on the person who has refused consent.

(6) Nothing in this section shall dispense with the necessity of obtaining the consent of the High Court to the marriage of a ward of court.

PART II MARRIAGE ACCORDING TO RITES OF THE CHURCH OF ENGLAND

Preliminary

5 Methods of authorising marriages

A marriage according to the rites of the Church of England may be solemnized—

    (a) after the publication of banns of matrimony;

    (b) on the authority of a special licence of marriage granted by the Archbishop of Canterbury or any other person by virtue of the Ecclesiastical Licences Act 1533 (in this Act referred to as a 'special licence');

    (c) on the authority of a licence of marriage (other than a special licence) granted by an ecclesiastical authority having power to grant such a licence (in this Act referred to as a 'common licence'); or

    (d) on the authority of certificates issued by a superintendent registrar under Part III of this Act,

except that paragraph (a) of this section shall not apply in relation to the solemnization of any marriage mentioned in subsection (2) of section 1 of this Act.

5A Marriages between certain persons related by affinity

No clergyman shall be obliged—

    (a) to solemnize a marriage which, apart from the Marriage (Prohibited Degrees of Relationship) Act 1986 or the Marriage Act 1949 (Remedial) Order 2007, would have been void by reason of the relationship of the persons to be married; or

(b) to permit such a marriage to be solemnized in the church or chapel of which he is the minister.

5B Marriages involving person of acquired gender

(1) A clergyman is not obliged to solemnise the marriage of a person if the clergyman reasonably believes that the person's gender has become the acquired gender under the Gender Recognition Act 2004.

(2) A clerk in Holy Orders of the Church in Wales is not obliged to permit the marriage of a person to be solemnised in the church or chapel of which the clerk is the minister if the clerk reasonably believes that the person's gender has become the acquired gender under that Act.

Marriage by banns

6 Place of publication of banns

(1) Subject to the provisions of this Act, where a marriage is intended to be solemnized after the publication of banns of matrimony, the banns shall be published—

(a) if the persons to be married reside in the same parish, in the parish church of that parish;

(b) if the persons to be married do not reside in the same parish, in the parish church of each parish in which one of them resides:

Provided that if either of the persons to be married resides in a chapelry or in a district specified in a licence granted under section twenty of this Act, the banns may be published in an authorised chapel of that chapelry or district instead of in the parish church of the parish in which that person resides.

...

(4) Banns of matrimony may be published in any parish church or authorised chapel which is the usual place of worship of the persons to be married or of one of them although neither of those persons resides in the parish or chapelry to which the church or chapel belongs;

Provided that the publication of the banns by virtue of this subsection shall be in addition to and not in substitution for the publication of banns required by subsection (1) of this section.

7 Time and manner of publication of banns

(1) Subject to the provisions of section nine of this Act, banns of matrimony shall be published on three Sundays preceding the solemnization of the marriage during either the principal service or both the principal service and another service.

(1A) In subsection (1) of this section 'principal service' means the service at which, in the opinion of the clergyman or other person who, under section 9 of this Act, has the responsibility for publishing banns of matrimony, the greatest number of persons who habitually attend public worship are likely to attend.

(1B) Where banns of matrimony are published on a Sunday during both the principal service and another service, both of those occasions shall be deemed to be the same time of asking for the purposes of the form of words referred to in subsection (2) of this section.

(2) Banns of matrimony shall be published in an audible manner and in accordance with the form of words prescribed by the rubric prefixed to the office of matrimony in the Book of Common Prayer or set out in section 2 of the Church of England Marriage (Amendment) Measure 2012, and all the other rules prescribed by the said rubric concerning the publication of banns and the solemnization of matrimony shall, so far as they are consistent with the provisions of this Part of this Act, be duly observed.

(3) The parochial church council of a parish shall provide for every church and chapel in the parish in which marriages may be solemnized, a register book of banns made of durable materials and marked in the manner directed by section fifty-four of this Act for the register book of marriages, and all banns shall be published from the said register book of banns by the officiating clergyman, and not from loose papers, and after each publication the entry in the register book shall be signed by the officiating clergyman, or by some person under his direction.

8   Notice to clergyman before publication of banns

No clergyman shall be obliged to publish banns of matrimony unless the persons to be married, at least seven days before the date on which they wish the banns to be published for the first time, deliver or cause to be delivered to him a notice in writing, dated on the day on which it is so delivered, stating the Christian name and surname and the place of residence of each of them, and the period during which each of them has resided at his or her place of residence.

…

10   Publication of banns commenced in one church and completed in another

(1) Where the publication of banns of matrimony has been duly commenced in any church, the publication may be completed in the same church or in any other church which, by virtue of the Union of Benefices Measure 1923 or the New Parishes Measure 1943, has at the time of the completion taken the place of the first-mentioned church for the purpose of publication of banns of matrimony either generally or in relation to the parties to the intended marriage.

…

11   Certificates of publication of banns

(1) Where a marriage is intended to be solemnized after the publication of banns of matrimony and the persons to be married do not reside in the same parish or other ecclesiastical district, a clergyman shall not solemnize the marriage in the parish or district in which one of those persons resides unless there is produced to him a certificate that the banns have been published in accordance with the provisions of this Part of this Act in the parish or other ecclesiastical district in which the other person resides.

(2) Where a marriage is intended to be solemnized in a church or chapel of a parish or other ecclesiastical district in which neither of the persons to be married resides, after the publication of banns therein by virtue of subsection (4) of section six of this Act, a clergyman shall not solemnize the marriage unless there is produced to him—

    (a) if the persons to be married reside in the same parish or other ecclesiastical district, a certificate that the banns have been published in accordance with the provisions of this Part of this Act in that parish or district; or

    (b) if the persons to be married do not reside in the same parish or other ecclesiastical district, certificates that the banns have been published as aforesaid in each parish or district in which one of them resides.

…

(4) Any certificate required under this section shall be signed by the incumbent or minister in charge of the building in which the banns were published or by a clergyman nominated in that behalf by the bishop of the diocese.

12   Solemnization of marriage after publication of banns

(1) Subject to the provisions of this Part of this Act, where banns of matrimony have been published, the marriage shall be solemnized in the church or chapel or, as the case may be, one of the churches or chapels in which the banns have been published.

(2) Where a marriage is not solemnized within three months after the completion of the publication of the banns, that publication shall be void and no clergyman shall solemnize the marriage on the authority thereof.

…

Marriage by common licence

15   Places in which marriages may be solemnized by common licence

(1) Subject to the provisions of this Part of this Act, a common licence shall not be granted for the solemnization of a marriage in any church or chapel other than—

    (a) the parish church of the parish, or an authorised chapel of the ecclesiastical district, in which one of the persons to be married has had his or her usual place of residence for fifteen days immediately before the grant of the licence; or

(b) a parish church or authorised chapel which is the usual place of worship of the persons to be married or of one of them.

(2) For the purposes of this section, any parish in which there is no parish church or chapel belonging thereto or no church or chapel in which divine service is usually solemnized every Sunday, and any extra-parochial place which has no authorised chapel, shall be deemed to belong to any adjoining parish or chapelry.

16   Provisions as to common licences

(1) A common licence shall not be granted unless one of the persons to be married has sworn before a person having authority to grant such a licence—

(a) that he or she believes that there is no impediment of kindred or alliance or any other lawful cause, nor any suit commenced in any court, to bar or hinder the solemnizing of the marriage in accordance with the licence;

(b) that one of the persons to be married has had his or her usual place of residence in the parish or other ecclesiastical district in which the marriage is to be solemnized for fifteen days immediately before the grant of the licence or that the parish church or authorised chapel in which the marriage is to be solemnized is the usual place of worship of those persons or of one of them;

(c) where one of the persons to be married is a child and is not a widower or widow, that the consent of the person or persons whose consent to the marriage is required under section three of this Act has been obtained, that the necessity of obtaining any such consent has been dispensed with under that section, that the court has consented to the marriage under that section, or that there is no person whose consent to the marriage is so required.

(1A) A common licence shall not be granted for the solemnization of a marriage mentioned in subsection (2) of section 1 of this Act unless—

(a) the person having authority to grant the licence is satisfied by the production of evidence that both the persons to be married have attained the age of twenty-one; and

(b) he has received a declaration in writing made by each of those persons specifying their affinal relationship and declaring that the younger of those persons has not at any time before attaining the age of eighteen been a child of the family in relation to the other.

(2) Subject to subsection (2A) of this section, if any caveat is entered against the grant of a common licence, the caveat having been duly signed by or on behalf of the person by whom it is entered and stating his place of residence and the ground of objection on which the caveat is founded, no licence shall be granted until the caveat or a copy thereof is transmitted to the ecclesiastical judge out of whose office the licence is to issue, and the judge has certified to the registrar of the diocese that he has examined into the matter of the caveat and is satisfied that it ought not to obstruct the grant of the licence, or until the caveat is withdrawn by the person who entered it.

(2A) Where in the case of a marriage mentioned in subsection (2) of section 1 of this Act a caveat is entered under subsection (2) of this section on the ground that the persons to be married have not both attained the age of twenty-one or that one of those persons has at any time before attaining the age of eighteen been a child of the family in relation to the other, then, notwithstanding that the caveat is withdrawn by the person who entered it, no licence shall be issued unless the judge has certified that he has examined into that ground of objection and is satisfied that the ground ought not to obstruct the grant of the licence.

(2B) In the case of a marriage mentioned in subsection (2) of section 1 of this Act, one of the persons to be married may apply to the ecclesiastical judge out of whose office the licence is to issue for a declaration that, both those persons having attained the age of twenty-one and the younger of those persons not having at any time before attaining the age of eighteen been a child of the family in relation to the other, there is no impediment of affinity to the solemnization of the marriage; and where any such declaration is obtained the common licence may be granted notwithstanding that no declaration has been made under the said subsection (1A).

(3) Where a marriage is not solemnized within three months after the grant of a common licence, the licence shall be void and no clergyman shall solemnize the marriage on the authority thereof.

...

Marriage under superintendent registrar's certificate

17   Marriage under superintendent registrar's certificate

A marriage according to the rites of the Church of England may be solemnized on the authority of certificates of a superintendent registrar in force under Part III of this Act in any church or chapel in which banns of matrimony may be published or in the case of a marriage in pursuance of section 26(1)(dd) of this Act the place specified in the notices of marriage and certificates as the place where the marriage is to be solemnized.

Provided that a marriage shall not be solemnized as aforesaid in any such church or chapel without the consent of the minister thereof or wherever the marriage is solemnized by any person other than a clergyman.

...

Miscellaneous provisions

22   Witnesses

All marriages solemnized according to the rites of the Church of England shall be solemnized in the presence of two or more witnesses in addition to the clergyman by whom the marriage is solemnized.

...

24   Proof of residence not necessary to validity of marriage by banns or common licence

(1)   Where any marriage has been solemnized after the publication of banns of matrimony, it shall not be necessary in support of the marriage to give any proof of the residence of the parties or either of them in any parish or other ecclesiastical district in which the banns were published, and no evidence shall be given to prove the contrary in any proceedings touching the validity of the marriage.

(2)   Where any marriage has been solemnized on the authority of a common licence, it shall not be necessary in support of the marriage to give any proof that the usual place of residence of one of the parties was for fifteen days immediately before the grant of the licence in the parish or other ecclesiastical district in which the marriage was solemnized, and no evidence shall be given to prove the contrary in any proceedings touching the validity of the marriage.

25   Void marriages

(1)   A marriage shall be void in any of the following cases.

(2)   Case A is where any persons knowingly and wilfully intermarry according to the rites of the Church of England (otherwise than by special licence)—

(a)   Except in the case of a marriage in pursuance of section 26(1)(dd) of this Act, in any place other than a church or other building in which banns may be published;

(b)   without banns having been duly published, a common licence having been obtained, or certificates having been duly issued under Part III of this Act by a superintendent registrar to whom due notice of marriage has been given; or

(c)   on the authority of a publication of banns which is void by virtue of subsection (3) of section three or subsection (2) of section twelve of this Act, on the authority of a common licence which is void by virtue of subsection (3) of section sixteen of this Act, or on the authority of certificates of a superintendent registrar which are void by virtue of subsection (2) of section thirty-three of this Act;

(d)   in the case of a marriage on the authority of certificates of a superintendent registrar, in any place other than the church building or other place specified in the notices of marriage and certificates as the place where the marriage is to be solemnized,

(3) Case B is where any persons knowingly and wilfully consent to or acquiesce in the solemnization of a Church of England marriage between them by a person who is not in Holy Orders.

(4) Case C is where any persons of the same sex consent to or acquiesce in the solemnization of a Church of England marriage between them.

(5) In subsections (3) and (4) 'Church of England marriage' means a marriage according to the rites of the Church of England.

PART III MARRIAGE UNDER SUPERINTENDENT REGISTRAR'S CERTIFICATE

Issue of certificates

26 Marriage of a man and a woman; marriage of same sex couples for which no opt-in necessary

(1) The following marriages may be solemnized on the authority of two certificates of a superintendent registrar—

   (a) a marriage of a man and a woman, in a building registered under section 41, according to such form and ceremony as the persons to be married see fit to adopt;

   (b) a marriage of any couple in the office of a superintendent registrar;

   (bb) a marriage of any couple on approved premises;

   (c) a marriage of a man and a woman according to the usages of the Society of Friends (commonly called Quakers);

   (d) a marriage between a man and a woman professing the Jewish religion according to the usages of the Jews;

   (dd) a qualifying residential marriage;

   (e) a marriage of a man and a woman according to the rites of the Church of England in any church or chapel in which banns of matrimony may be published.

(2) In this section 'qualifying residential marriage' means—

   (a) the marriage of a man and a woman (other than a marriage in pursuance of subsection (1)(c) or (d) above), one or each of whom is house-bound or a detained person, at the usual place of residence of the house-bound or detained person or persons, or

   (b) the marriage of a same sex couple (other than a marriage according to the rites of the Church of England or other religious rites or usages), one or each of whom is house-bound or a detained person, at the usual place of residence of the house-bound or detained person or persons.

26A Opt-in to marriage of same sex couples: places of worship

(1) A marriage of a same sex couple in an appropriately registered building according to such form and ceremony as the persons to be married see fit to adopt may be solemnized on the authority of two certificates of a superintendent registrar.

(2) For the purposes of this section 'appropriately registered building' means a building which has been registered under section 43A.

(3) An application for registration of a building under section 43A may not be made unless the relevant governing authority has given written consent to marriages of same sex couples.

(4) For that purpose, in relation to a building—

'relevant governing authority' means the person or persons recognised by the members of the relevant religious organisation as competent for the purpose of giving consent for the purposes of this section;

'relevant religious organisation' means the religious organisation for whose religious purposes the building is used.

(5) Nothing in this section is to be taken to relate or have any reference to marriages solemnized according to the rites of the Church of England.

(6) This section is subject (in particular) to sections 44A to 44C (registration of shared buildings for marriage of same sex couples) and regulations made under any of those sections.

26B   Opt-in to marriage of same sex couples: other religious ceremonies

(1) A marriage may, in any of the following cases, be solemnized on the authority of two certificates of a superintendent registrar.

(2) Case A is where—

(a) the marriage is of a same sex couple according to the usages of the Society of Friends (commonly called Quakers), and

(b) the relevant governing authority has given written consent to such marriages of same sex couples.

(3) For that purpose 'relevant governing authority' means the recording clerk for the time being of the Society of Friends in London.

(4) Case B is where—

(a) the marriage is of a same sex couple professing the Jewish religion according to the usages of the Jews, and

(b) the relevant governing authority has given written consent to such marriages of same sex couples.

(5) For that purpose the meaning of 'relevant governing authority' is to be determined in accordance with this table—

The 'relevant governing authority' is...	...if the marriage falls to be registered by...
the Chief Rabbi of the United Hebrew Congregations of the Commonwealth	the secretary of a synagogue certified under paragraph (a) of the relevant definition (certification by the President of the Board of Deputies)
the person or persons duly recognised by the members of— (i) the West London Synagogue of British Jews ('the West London Synagogue'), and (ii) the other synagogues that are constituents of or affiliated to the Movement for Reform Judaism	— either the secretary of the West London Synagogue, as certified under paragraph (b) of the relevant definition — or the secretary of another synagogue in a case where: (i) the secretary is certified under paragraph (d) of the relevant definition by the secretary of the West London Synagogue, and (ii) the synagogue is one of those which are constituents of or affiliated to the Movement for Reform Judaism
the person or persons duly recognised by the members of— (i) the Liberal Jewish Synagogue, St. John's Wood ('the St. John's Wood Synagogue'), and (ii) the other synagogues that are constituents of or affiliated to Liberal Judaism	— either the secretary of the St. John's Wood Synagogue, as certified under paragraph (c) of the relevant definition — or the secretary of another synagogue in a case where: (i) the secretary is certified under paragraph (d) of the relevant definition by the secretary of the St. John's Wood Synagogue, and (ii) the synagogue is one of those which are constituents of or affiliated to Liberal Judaism

The 'relevant governing authority' is...	...if the marriage falls to be registered by...
the person or persons duly recognised by the members of the synagogue by whose secretary the marriage falls to be registered	the secretary of a synagogue certified under paragraph (d) of the relevant definition (certification by the secretary of the West London Synagogue or the secretary of the St. John's Wood Synagogue) in a case where the synagogue is not one of those which are constituents of or affiliated to: (i) the Movement for Reform Judaism, or (ii) Liberal Judaism

In that table—

  (a) 'relevant definition' means the definition of 'secretary of a synagogue' in section 67;

  (b) a reference to a person or persons being duly recognised is a reference to the person or persons being recognised for the purpose of giving consent for the purposes of this section.

(6) Case C is where—

  (a) the marriage is of a same sex couple according to religious rites or usages (other than the rites of the Church of England),

  (b) one or each of the couple is house-bound or a detained person,

  (c) the marriage is at the usual place of residence of the house-bound or detained person or persons, and

  (d) the relevant governing authority has given written consent to marriages of same sex couples according to those religious rites or usages.

(7) For that purpose—

'relevant governing authority' means the person or persons recognised by the members of the relevant religious organisation as competent for the purpose of giving consent for the purposes of this section;

'relevant religious organisation' means the religious organisation according to whose rites or usages the marriage is to be solemnized.

(8) Subsection (6) does not authorise a marriage that may be solemnized under subsection (2) or (4).

27 Notice of marriage

(1) Where a marriage is intended to be solemnized on the authority of certificates of a superintendent registrar, notice of marriage in the prescribed form shall be given—

  (a) if the persons to be married have resided in the same registration district for the period of seven days immediately before the giving of the notice, by each of those persons to the superintendent registrar of that district;

  (b) if the persons to be married have not resided in the same registration district for the said period of seven days as aforesaid, by either of those persons to the superintendent registrar of the registration district in which he or she resided for that period.

(3) A notice of marriage shall state the name and surname, occupation, place of residences and nationality of each of the persons to be married, whether either of them has previously been married or formed a civil partnership and, if so, how the marriage or civil partnership ended and in the case of a marriage intended to be solemnized at a person's residence in pursuance of section 26(1)(dd) of this Act, which residence is to be the place of solemnization of the marriage and, in any other case, the church or other building or premises in or on which the marriage is to be solemnized and—

  (a) shall state the period, not being less than seven days, during which each of the persons to be married has resided in his or her place of residence;

(4) The superintendent registrar shall file all notices of marriage and keep them with the records of his office, and shall subject to section 27A of this Act also forthwith enter the particulars given in every such notice, together with the date of the notice and the name of the person by whom

the notice was given, in a book (in this Act referred to as 'the marriage notice book') furnished to him for that purpose by the Registrar General, and the marriage notice book shall be open for inspection free of charge at all reasonable hours.

(4A) The duty imposed by subsection (4) to enter information in the marriage notice book may be discharged by entering the information in an approved electronic form; and information so entered must be made available for inspection free of charge at all reasonable hours.

(5) If the persons to be married wish to be married in the presence of a registrar in a registered building for which an authorised person has been appointed, they shall, at the time when notice of marriage is given to the superintendent registrar under this section, give notice to him that they require a registrar to be present at the marriage.

...

27A   Additional information required in certain cases

(1) This section applies in relation to any marriage intended to be solemnized at a person's residence in pursuance of section 26(1)(dd) or 26B(6) of this Act, and in the following provisions of this section that person is referred to as 'the relevant person'.

(2) Where the relevant person is not a detained person, each notice of marriage required by section 27 of this Act shall be accompanied by a medical statement relating to that person made not more than fourteen days before the date on which the notice is given.

(3) Where the relevant person is a detained person, each notice of marriage required by section 27 of this Act shall be accompanied by a statement made in the prescribed form by the responsible authority not more than twenty-one days before the date on which notice of the marriage is given under section 27:—

    (a) identifying the establishment where the person is detained; and

    (b) stating that the responsible authority has no objection to that establishment being specified in the notice of marriage as the place where that marriage is to be solemnized.

(4) Each person who gives notice of the marriage to the superintendent registrar in accordance with section 27 of this Act shall give the superintendent registrar the prescribed particulars, in the prescribed form, of the person by or before whom the marriage is intended to be solemnized.

(5) The superintendent registrar shall not enter the particulars given in the marriage notice book, or in an approved electronic form by virtue of section 27(4A), until he has received the statement and the particulars required by subsections (2) or (3) and (4) of this section.

(6) The fact that a superintendent registrar has received a statement under subsection (2) or (as the case may be) (3) of this section shall be entered in the marriage notice book together with the particulars given in the notice of marriage and any such statement together with the form received under subsection (4) of this section shall be filed and kept with the records of the office of the superintendent registrar or, where notice of marriage is required to be given to two superintendent registrars, of each of them.

(6A) Where the particulars given in the notice of marriage are to be entered in an approved electronic form by virtue of section 27(4A), the duty imposed by subsection (6) to enter the statement in the marriage notice book is to be discharged by entering the statement in an approved electronic form.

(7) In this section:—

'medical statement', in relation to any person, means a statement made in the prescribed form by a registered medical practitioner that in his opinion at the time the statement is made:—

    (a) by reason of illness or disability, he or she ought not to move or be moved from the place where he or she is at the time, and

    (b) it is likely that it will be the case for at least the following three months that by reason of the illness or disability he or she ought not to move or be moved from that place; and

'registered medical practitioner' has the meaning given by Schedule 1 to the Interpretation Act 1978; and

'responsible authority' means:—

    (a) if the person is detained in a hospital (within the meaning of Part II of section 145(1) of that Act); or

(b) if the person is detained in a prison or other place to which the Prison Act 1952 applies, the governor or other officer for the time being in charge of that prison or other place.

27B Provisions relating to section 1(3) marriages

(1) This section applies in relation to any marriage mentioned in subsection (2) of section 1 of this Act which is intended to be solemnized on the authority of certificates of a superintendent registrar.

(2) The superintendent registrar shall not enter notice of the marriage in the marriage notice book, or in an approved electronic form by virtue of section 27(4A), unless—

(a) he is satisfied by the production of evidence that both the persons to be married have attained the age of twenty-one; and

(b) he has received a declaration made in the prescribed form by each of those persons, each declaration having been signed and attested in the prescribed manner, specifying their affinal relationship and declaring that the younger of those persons has not at any time before attaining the age of eighteen been a child of the family in relation to the other.

(3) The fact that a superintendent registrar has received a declaration under subsection (2) of this section shall be entered in the marriage notice book together with the particulars given in the notice of marriage and any such declaration shall be filed and kept with the records of the office of the superintendent registrar or, where notice of marriage is required to be given to two superintendent registrars, of each of them.

(3A) Where the particulars given in the notice of the marriage are to be entered in an approved electronic form by virtue of section 27(4A), the duty imposed by subsection (3) to enter in the marriage notice book the fact concerned is to be discharged by entering the fact in an approved electronic form.

(4) Where the superintendent registrar receives from some person other than the persons to be married a written statement signed by that person which alleges that the declaration made under subsection (2) of this section is false in a material particular, the superintendent registrar shall not issue a certificate unless a declaration is obtained under subsection (5) of this section.

(5) Either of the persons to be married may, whether or not any statement has been received by the superintendent registrar under subsection (4) of this section, apply to the High Court or the family court for a declaration that, both those persons having attained the age of twenty-one and the younger of those persons not having at any time before attaining the age of eighteen been a child of the family in relation to the other, there is no impediment of affinity to the solemnization of the marriage; and where such a declaration is obtained the superintendent registrar may enter notice of the marriage in the marriage notice book, or in an approved electronic form by virtue of section 27(4A), and may issue a certificate whether or not any declaration has been made under subsection (2) of this section.

(6) Section 29 of this Act shall not apply in relation to a marriage to which this section applies, except so far as a caveat against the issue of a certificate for the marriage is entered under that section on a ground other than the relationship of the persons to be married.
…

27D Additional information required for certain marriages of same sex couples

(1) This section applies in relation to any marriage intended to be solemnized in pursuance of section 26B(2), (4) or (6) (marriage of same sex couples: Quaker marriage, Jewish marriage, marriage of house-bound or detained person).

(2) The superintendent registrar to whom notice of such a marriage is given under section 27 may require the relevant governing authority to provide a copy of the consent mentioned in section 26B(2)(b), (4)(b) or (6)(d).

(3) In this section, 'relevant governing authority', in relation to an intended marriage under section 26B(2), (4) or (6), has the same meaning as in that provision.

28   Declaration to accompany notice of marriage

(1)   No certificate for marriage shall be issued by a superintendent registrar unless the notice of marriage is accompanied by a solemn declaration in writing, in the body or at the foot of the notice, made and signed at the time of the giving of the notice by the person by whom the notice is given and attested as mentioned in subsection (2) of this section—

  (a)   that he or she believes that there is no impediment of kindred or alliance or other lawful hindrance to the marriage;

  (b)   that the persons to be married have for the period of seven days immediately before the giving of the notice had their usual places of residence within the registration district or registration districts in which notice is given;

  (c)   where one of the persons to be married is a child and is not a widower or widow, that the consent of the person or persons whose consent to the marriage is required under section three of this Act has been obtained, that the necessity of obtaining any such consent has been dispensed with under that section, that the court has consented to the marriage under that section, or that there is no person whose consent to the marriage is so required.

(2)   Any such declaration as aforesaid shall be signed by the person giving the notice of marriage in the presence of the superintendent registrar to whom the notice is given or his deputy, or in the presence of a registrar of births and deaths or of marriages for the registration district in which the person giving the notice resides or his deputy, and that superintendent registrar, deputy superintendent registrar, registrar or deputy registrar, as the case may be, shall attest the declaration by adding thereto his name, description and place of residence.

28A   Power to require evidence

(1)   A superintendent registrar to whom a notice of marriage is given under section 27, or any other person attesting a declaration accompanying such a notice, may require the person giving the notice to provide him with specified evidence—

  (a)   relating to that person; or

  (b)   if the superintendent registrar considers that the circumstances are exceptional, relating to each of the persons to be married.

(1A)   In the case of an intended marriage to which section 27D applies, the superintendent registrar to whom the notice of the marriage is given may require the relevant governing authority to produce evidence relating to the consent mentioned in section 26B(2)(b), (4)(b) or (6)(d).

(2)   A requirement under subsection (1) or (1A) may be imposed at any time—

  (a)   on or after the giving of the notice of marriage; but

  (b)   before the superintendent registrar issues his certificate under section 31.

(3)   'Specified evidence', in relation to a person, means such evidence as may be specified in guidance issued by the Registrar General—

  (a)   of the person's name and surname,

  (b)   of the person's age,

  (c)   as to whether the person has previously been married or formed a civil partnership and, if so, as to the ending of the marriage or civil partnership, and

  (d)   of the person's nationality.

29   Caveat against issue of certificate or licence

(1)   Any person may enter a caveat with the superintendent registrar against the issue of a certificate for the marriage of any person named therein.

(2)   If any caveat is entered as aforesaid, the caveat having been signed by or on behalf of the person by whom it was entered and stating his place of residence and the ground of objection on which the caveat is founded, no certificate shall be issued until the superintendent registrar has examined into the matter of the caveat and is satisfied that it ought not to obstruct the issue of the certificate, or until the caveat has been withdrawn by the person who entered it; and if the

superintendent registrar is doubtful whether to issue a certificate he may refer the matter of the caveat to the Registrar General.

(3) Where a superintendent registrar refuses, by reason of any such caveat as aforesaid, to issue a certificate, the person applying therefore may appeal to the Registrar General who shall either confirm the refusal or direct that a certificate shall be issued.

(4) Any person who enters a caveat against the issue of a certificate on grounds which the Registrar General declares to be frivolous and to be such that they ought not to obstruct the issue of the certificate, shall be liable for the costs of the proceedings before the Registrar General and for damages recoverable by the person against whose marriage the caveat was entered.

(5) For the purpose of enabling any person to recover any such costs and damages as aforesaid, a copy of the declaration of the Registrar General purporting to be sealed with the seal of the General Register Office shall be evidence that the Registrar General has declared the caveat to have been entered on grounds which are frivolous and such that they ought not to obstruct the issue of the certificate.

30   Forbidding of issue of certificate

(1) Any person whose consent to a marriage intended to be solemnized on the authority of certificates of a superintendent registrar is required under section three of this Act may forbid the issue of such a certificate by writing, at any time before the issue of the certificate, the word 'forbidden' opposite to the entry of the notice of marriage in the marriage notice book, and by subscribing thereto his name and place of residence and the capacity, in relation to either of the persons to be married, in which he forbids the issue of the certificate; and where the issue of a certificate has been so forbidden, the notice of marriage and all proceedings thereon shall be void:

Provided that where, by virtue of paragraph (b) of the proviso to subsection (1) of the said section three, the court has consented to a marriage and the consent of the court has the same effect as if it had been given by a person whose consent has been refused, that person shall not be entitled to forbid the issue of a certificate for that marriage under this section, and the notice of marriage and the proceedings thereon shall not be void by virtue of this section.

(2) Where the particulars given in the notice of marriage have been entered in an approved electronic form by virtue of section 27(4A), a person (P) wishing to exercise the power conferred by subsection (1) to forbid the issue of the certificate may do so only by—

(a) attending upon the superintendent registrar at his office, and

(b) requesting him to record that P forbids the issue of the certificate.

(3) The superintendent registrar must, on a request made by virtue of subsection (2), enter in an approved electronic form that P forbids the issue of the certificate, P's name and place of residence and the capacity, in relation to either of the persons to be married, in which P forbids the issue of the certificate.

31   Marriage under certificate without licence

(1) Where a marriage is intended to be solemnized on the authority of certificates of a superintendent registrar, the superintendent registrar to whom notice of marriage has been given shall suspend or affix in some conspicuous place in his office, for 15 successive days next after the day on which the notice was entered in the marriage book, the notice of marriage, or an exact copy signed by him of the particulars thereof as entered in the marriage notice book.

(1A) Where the notice was entered in an approved electronic form by virtue of section 27(4A) ('the approved form'), the duty imposed by subsection (1) is to be discharged by the superintendent registrar—

(a) arranging for the notice to be displayed for 15 successive days beginning with the day after the day on which the notice was entered in the approved form, in an approved electronic form, or

(b) suspending or affixing as described in subsection (1), for 15 days beginning with the day after the day on which the notice was entered in the approved form—

(i)   the notice of the marriage, or

(ii) an exact copy, signed by the superintendent registrar, of the particulars of that notice as entered in the approved form.

(2) At the expiration of the said period of 15 days the superintendent registrar, on the request of the person by whom the notice of marriage was given, shall issue a certificate in the prescribed form unless—

(a) the superintendent registrar is not satisfied that there is no lawful impediment to the issue of the certificate; or

(b) the issue of the certificate has been forbidden under the last foregoing section by any person authorised in that behalf.

...

(4) No marriage shall be solemnized on the production of certificates of a superintendent registrar until after the expiration of the waiting period in relation to each notice of marriage.

...

(4A) 'The waiting period', in relation to a notice of marriage, means—

(a) the period of 15 days, or

(b) such shorter period as may be determined by the Registrar General under subsection (5A) or by a superintendent registrar under any provision of regulations made under subsection (5D),

after the day on which the notice of marriage was entered in the marriage notice book, or in an approved electronic form by virtue of section 27(4A).

...

(5A) If, on an application made to the Registrar General, he is satisfied that there are compelling reasons for reducing the 15 day period because of the exceptional circumstances of the case, he may reduce that period to such shorter period as he considers appropriate.

(5B) 'The 15 day period' means the period of 15 days mentioned in subsections (1) to (2).

(5C) If the Registrar General reduces the 15 day period in a particular case, the reference to 15 days in section 75(3)(a) is to be treated, in relation to that case, as a reference to the reduced period.

...

31A Appeal on refusal under section 31(2)(a)

(1) If, relying on section 31(2)(a), a superintendent registrar refuses to issue a certificate, the person applying for it may appeal to the Registrar General.

(2) On such an appeal, the Registrar General must—

(a) confirm the refusal; or

(b) direct that a certificate be issued.

(3) If—

(a) relying on section 31(2)(a), a superintendent registrar refuses to issue a certificate as a result of a representation made to him, and

(b) on an appeal against the refusal, the Registrar General declares the representation to have been frivolous and to be such that it ought not to obstruct the issue of a certificate,

the person making the representation is liable for the costs of the proceedings before the Registrar General and for damages recoverable by the applicant for the certificate.

(4) For the purpose of enabling a person to recover any such costs and damages, a copy of the declaration of the Registrar General purporting to be sealed with the seal of the General Register Office is evidence that the Registrar General has declared the representation to have been frivolous and to be such that it ought not to obstruct the issue of a certificate.

33 Period of validity of certificate

(1) A marriage may be solemnized on the authority of certificates of a superintendent registrar at any time within the period which is the applicable period in relation to that marriage.

(2) If the marriage is not solemnized within the applicable period—

(a) the notices of marriage and the certificates are void; and

(b) no person may solemnize the marriage on the authority of those certificates.

(3) The applicable period, in relation to a marriage, is the period beginning with the day on which the notice of marriage was entered in the marriage notice book or in an approved electronic form by virtue of section 27(4A) and ending—

(a) in the case of a marriage which is to be solemnized in pursuance of section 26(1)(dd), 37 or 38, on the expiry of three months; and

(b) in the case of any other marriage, on the expiry of twelve months.

(4) If the notices of marriage given by each person to be married are not given on the same date, the applicable period is to be calculated by reference to the earlier of the two dates.

34 Marriages normally to be solemnized in registration district in which one party resides

Subject to section 35, a superintendent registrar may not issue a certificate for the solemnization of a marriage elsewhere than within a registration district in which one of the persons to be married has resided for seven days immediately before the giving of the notice of marriage.

35 Marriages in registration district in which neither party resides

(1) A superintendent registrar may issue a certificate for the solemnization of a marriage in a registered building which is not within a registration district in which either of the persons to be married resides, where the person giving the notice of marriage declares by endorsement thereon in the prescribed form—

(a) that the persons to be married desire the marriage to be solemnized, according to a specified form, rite or ceremony, being a form, rite or ceremony of a body or denomination of Christians or other persons meeting for religious worship to which one of them professes to belong;

(b) that, to the best of his or her belief, there is not within the registration district in which one of them resides any registered building in which marriage is solemnized according to that form, rite or ceremony;

(c) the registration district nearest to the residence of that person in which there is a registered building in which marriage may be so solemnized; and

(d) the registered building in that district in which the marriage is intended to be solemnized;

and where any such certificate is issued in respect of each of the persons to be married, the marriage may be solemnized in the registered building stated in the notice.

(2) A superintendent registrar may issue a certificate for the solemnization of a marriage in a registered building which is the usual place of worship of the persons to be married, or of one of them, notwithstanding that the building is not within a registration district in which either of those persons resides.

(2A) A superintendent registrar may issue a certificate for the solemnization of a marriage in the office of another superintendent registrar, notwithstanding that the office is not within a registration district in which either of the persons to be married resides.

(2B) A superintendent registrar may issue a certificate for the solemnization of a marriage on approved premises, notwithstanding that the premises are not within a registration district in which either of the persons to be married resides.

(3) A superintendent registrar may issue a certificate for the solemnization of a marriage in any parish church or authorised chapel which is the usual place of worship of the persons to be married, or of one of them, notwithstanding that the church or chapel is not within a registration district in which either of those persons resides.

(4) A superintendent registrar may issue a certificate for the solemnization of a marriage according to the usages of the Society of Friends or in accordance with the usages of persons professing the Jewish religion, notwithstanding that the building or place in which the marriage is to be solemnized is not within a registration district in which either of the persons to be married resides.

(5) Where a marriage is intended to be solemnized on the authority of certificates of a superintendent registrar issued under subsection (2) or subsection (3) of this section, each notice of

marriage given to the superintendent registrar and each certificate issued by the superintendent registrar shall state, in addition to the description of the registered building or, as the case may be, the parish church or authorised chapel, in which the marriage is to be solemnized, that it is the usual place of worship of the persons to be married or of one of them and, in the latter case, shall state the name of the person whose usual place of worship it is.

...

39A   Marriage of former civil partners one of whom has changed sex

(1) This section applies if—

    (a) a court—

        (i) makes final a nullity order which annuls a civil partnership on the ground that an interim gender recognition certificate has been issued to one of the civil partners, or

        (ii) ...

    and, on doing so, issues a full gender recognition certificate (under section 5A(1) of the Gender Recognition Act 2004) to that civil partner, and

    (b) the former civil partners wish to marry each other in England or Wales in accordance with this Part without being delayed by the waiting period.

(2) For the purposes of this section the relevant period is the period—

    (a) beginning with the issue of the full gender recognition certificate, and

    (b) ending at the end of 1 month from the day on which it is issued.

(3) If either of the former civil partners—

    (a) gives notice of marriage in accordance with this Part during the relevant period, and

    (b) on doing so, makes an election under this section,

this Act applies with the modifications set out in subsections (4) to (6).

(4) In section 31 (marriage under certificates)—

    (a) omit subsections (1), (4), (4A) and (5A) to (5I), and

    (b) in subsection (2), for 'At the expiration of the said period of 15 days', substitute 'As soon as notice of marriage has been given,'.

(5) For section 33(3) (period of validity of certificate: applicable period) substitute—

'(3) The applicable period, in relation to a marriage, is the period of 1 month beginning with the day on which the notice of marriage was entered in the marriage notice book.'

(6) In section 75 (offences relating to solemnization of marriages), omit subsections (2)(d), (2A) and (3)(a).

(7) ...

(8) In subsection (1)(b), 'the waiting period' has the meaning given by section 31(4A).

...

Marriages in registered buildings

41   Registration of buildings: marriage of a man and a woman

(1) Any proprietor or trustee of a building, which has been certified by law as a place of religious worship may apply to the superintendent registrar of the registration district in which the building is situated for the building to be registered for the solemnization of marriages therein.

(1A) A reference in this section to the solemnization of marriage is a reference to the solemnization of marriage of a man and a woman.

(2) Any person making such an application as aforesaid shall deliver to the superintendent registrar a certificate, signed in duplicate by at least twenty householders and dated not earlier than one month before the making of the application, stating that the building is being used by them as their usual place of public religious worship and that they desire that the building should be registered as aforesaid, and both certificates shall be countersigned by the proprietor or trustee by whom they are delivered.

(3) The superintendent registrar shall send both certificates delivered to him under the last foregoing subsection to the Registrar General who shall register the building in a book to be kept for that purpose in the General Register Office.

(3A) The duty imposed by subsection (3) to register the building in a book may be discharged by registering the building in an approved electronic form.

...

43 Buildings registered under section 41: appointment of authorised persons

(1) For the purpose of enabling marriages to be solemnized in a building registered under section 41 without the presence of a registrar, the trustees or governing body of that building may authorise a person to be present at the solemnization of marriages in that building and, where a person is so authorised in respect of any building registered under section 41, the trustees or governing body of that building shall within the prescribed time and in the prescribed manner, certify the name and address of the person so authorised to the Registrar General and to the superintendent registrar of the registration district in which the building is situated.

...

43A Registration of buildings: marriage of same sex couples

(1) A building that has been certified as required by law as a place of religious worship may be registered under this section for the solemnization of marriages of same sex couples.

(2) Any application for registration of a building under this section is to be made—
  (a) by a proprietor or trustee of the building;
  (b) to the superintendent registrar of the registration district in which the building is situated.

(3) An application for registration of a building under this section must be accompanied by—
  (a) a certificate, given by the applicant and dated not earlier than one month before the making of the application, that the persons who are the relevant governing authority in relation to the building have given written consent to marriages of same sex couples as mentioned in section 26A(3),
  (b) a copy of that consent, and
  (c) if the building is not already registered under section 41, a certificate of use for religious worship.

(4) The superintendent registrar must send to the Registrar General—
  (a) the certificate or certificates, and
  (b) the copy of the consent,
which accompany an application under this section.

(5) The Registrar General must then register the building.

(6) A building may be registered for the solemnization of marriages under this section whether it is a separate building or forms part of another building.

(7) In this section, in relation to an application under this section, 'certificate of use for religious worship' means a certificate given by at least twenty householders and dated not earlier than one month before the making of the application, stating that they—
  (a) use the building as their usual place of public religious worship, and
  (b) wish the building to be registered under this section.

43B Buildings registered under section 43A: appointment of authorised persons

(1) For the purpose of enabling marriages to be solemnized in a building registered under section 43A without the presence of a registrar, the trustees or governing body of that building may authorise a person to be present at the solemnization of marriages in that building.

(2) Where a person is so authorised in respect of any building registered under section 43A, the trustees or governing body of that building must certify the name and address of the person so authorised to—

    (a) the Registrar General, and

    (b) the superintendent registrar of the registration district in which the building is situated.

(3) The power conferred by this section may only be exercised after the end of the relevant one year period (and, if that period has ended before the date of the registration under section 43A, the power may accordingly be exercised immediately).

(4) The relevant one year period is the period of one year beginning with the date of the registration of the building under section 43A (the 'new registration').

...

44   Solemnization of marriage in registered building

(1) Subject to the provisions of this section, where the notices of marriage and certificates issued by a superintendent registrar state that a marriage between the persons named therein is intended to be solemnized in a registered building, the marriage may be solemnized in that building according to such form and ceremony as those persons may see fit to adopt:

Provided that no marriage shall be solemnized in any registered building without the consent of the minister or of one of the trustees, owners, deacons, or managers thereof, or in the case of a registered building of the Roman Catholic Church, without the consent of the officiating minister thereof.

(2) Subject to the provisions of this section, a marriage solemnized in a registered building shall be solemnized with open doors in the presence of two or more witnesses and in the presence of either—

    (a) a registrar of the registration district in which the registered building is situated, or

    (b) an authorised person whose name and address have been certified in accordance with section 43 (in the case of the marriage of a man and a woman), or section 43B (in the case of the marriage of a same sex couple), by the trustees or governing body of that registered building or of some other registered building in the same registration district.

(3) Where a marriage is solemnized in a registered building each of the persons contracting the marriage shall, in some part of the ceremony and in the presence of the witnesses and the registrar or authorised person, make the following declaration:—

'I do solemnly declare that I know not of any lawful impediment why I, *AB,* may not be joined in matrimony to *CD*'

and each of them shall say to the other:—

'I call upon these persons here present to witness that I, *AB,* do take thee, *CD,* to be my lawful wedded wife [*or* husband]':

(3A) As an alternative to the declaration set out in subsection (3) of this section the persons contracting the marriage may make the requisite declaration either—

    (a) by saying 'I declare that I know of no legal reason why I [*name*] may not be joined in marriage to [*name*]'; or

    (b) by replying 'I am' to the question put to them successively 'Are you [*name*] free lawfully to marry [*name*]?'

and as an alternative to the words of contract set out in that subsection the persons to be married may say to each other 'I [*name*] take you [*or* thee] [*name*] to be my wedded wife [*or* husband]'.

...

Registration of shared buildings for marriage of same sex couples

44A   Building subject to Sharing of Church Buildings Act 1969: registration

(1) This section applies to a registration application relating to a building that is—

    (a) subject to a sharing agreement, or

    (b) used as mentioned in section 6(4) of the 1969 Act.

(2) The registration application must be made in accordance with section 43A (as read with section 26A(3)).

(3) But those provisions have effect subject to the following provisions of this section.

(4) Each of the sharing churches is a relevant religious organisation for the purposes of section 26A(3).

(5) A consent given under section 26A(3) (a 'consent to marriages of same sex couples') by the relevant governing authority of any of the sharing churches is therefore sufficient for the registration application to be made in compliance with section 26A(3) (and references to the consent of the relevant governing authority in section 43A are to be read accordingly).

(6) But the registration application may not be made unless the relevant governing authorities of each of the sharing churches (other than those which have given consents to marriages of same sex couples) have given a separate written consent to the use of the shared building for the solemnization of marriages of same sex couples (a 'consent to use').

(7) The registration application must also be accompanied by—

    (a) a certificate, given by the applicant and dated not more than one month before the making of the application, that the relevant governing authorities mentioned in subsection (6) have given written consents to use, and

    (b) copies of those consents.

(8) The superintendent registrar must also send to the Registrar General—

    (a) the certificate, and

    (b) the copies of the consents,

which accompany the application in accordance with subsection (7).

(9) The Registrar General must not register the shared building unless and until subsection (8) and the requirements of section 43A have been complied with.

(10) The Secretary of State may by statutory instrument make regulations containing such provision supplementing this section as the Secretary of State thinks appropriate.

…

Marriages in register offices

45 Solemnization of marriage in register office

(1) Where a marriage is intended to be solemnized on the authority of certificates of a superintendent registrar, the persons to be married may state in the notices of marriage that they wish to be married in the office of the superintendent registrar or one of the superintendent registrars, as the case may be, to whom notice of marriage is given, and where any such notices have been given and the certificates have been issued accordingly, the marriage may be solemnized in the said office, with open doors in the presence of the superintendent registrar and a registrar of the registration district of that superintendent registrar and in the presence of two witnesses, and the persons to be married shall make the declarations and use the form of words set out in subsection (3) or (3A) of the last foregoing section in the case of marriages in registered buildings.

(2) No religious service shall be used at any marriage solemnized in the office of a superintendent registrar.

45A Solemnization of certain marriages

(1) This section applies to marriages solemnized, otherwise than according to the rites of the Church of England, in pursuance of section 26(1)(dd) or 26B(6) of this Act at the place where a person usually resides.

(2) The marriage may be solemnized according to a relevant form, rite or ceremony in the presence of a registrar of the registration district in which the place where the marriage is solemnized is situated and of two witnesses and each of the persons contracting the marriage shall make the declaration and use the form of words set out in subsection (3) or (3A) of section 44 of this Act in the case of marriages in registered buildings.

(3) Where the marriage is not solemnized in pursuance of subsection (2) of this section it shall be solemnized in the presence of the superintendent registrar and a registrar of the registration district in which the place where the marriage is solemnized is situated and in the presence of two witnesses, and the persons to be married shall make the declarations and use the form of words set out in sub section (3) or (3A) of section 44 of this Act in the case of marriages in registered buildings.

(4) No religious service shall be used at any marriage solemnized in the presence of a superintendent registrar.

(5) In subsection (2) of this section a 'relevant form, rite or ceremony' means a form, rite or ceremony of a body of persons who meet for religious worship in any registered building being a form, rite or ceremony in accordance with which members of that body are married in any such registered building.

46   Register office marriage followed by religious ceremony

(1) If the parties to a relevant marriage desire to add the religious ceremony ordained or used by the church or persuasion of which they are members, they may present themselves, after giving notice of their intention so to do, to the clergyman or minister of the church or persuasion of which they are members, and the clergyman or minister, upon the production of a certificate of their marriage before the superintendent registrar and upon the payment of the customary fees (if any), may, if he sees fit, read or celebrate in the church or chapel of which he is the regular minister the marriage service of the church or persuasion to which he belongs or nominate some other minister to do so.

(1A) In this section 'relevant marriage' means—
   (a) the marriage of a man and a woman solemnized in the presence of a superintendent registrar,
   (b) the marriage of a same sex couple solemnized in the presence of a superintendent registrar, and
   (c) a marriage which arises from the conversion of a civil partnership under regulations under section 9 of the Marriage (Same Sex Couples) Act 2013.

(1B) This section does not authorise the marriage service of the Church of England to be read or celebrated in the case of a relevant marriage of a same sex couple.

(1C) This section does not authorise any other marriage service to be read or celebrated in the case of a relevant marriage of a same sex couple unless the relevant governing authority has given written consent to the reading or celebration of that service in the case of such marriages.

(1D) For that purpose—
'relevant governing authority' means the person or persons recognised by the members of the relevant religious organisation as competent for the purpose of giving consent for the purposes of this section;
'relevant religious organisation' means the religious organisation whose marriage service is to be read or celebrated.

(2) Nothing in the reading or celebration of a marriage service under this section shall supersede or invalidate any marriage previously solemnized in the presence of a superintendent registrar, and the reading or celebration shall not be entered as a marriage in any marriage register book kept under Part IV of this Act.

(3) No person who is not entitled to solemnize marriages according to the rites of the Church of England shall by virtue of this section be entitled to read or celebrate the marriage service in any church or chapel of the Church of England.

Marriages on approved premises

46A   Approval of premises

(1) The Secretary of State may by regulations make provision for and in connection with the approval by local authorities of premises for the solemnization of marriages in pursuance of section 26(1)(bb) of this Act.
   ...

46B Solemnization of marriage on approved premises

(1) Any marriage on approved premises in pursuance of section 26(1)(bb) of this Act shall be solemnized in the presence of—

    (a) two witnesses, and

    (b) the superintendent registrar and a registrar of the registration district in which the premises are situated.

(2) Without prejudice to the width of section 46A(2)(e) of this Act, the Secretary of State shall exercise his power to provide for the imposition of conditions as there mentioned so as to secure that members of the public are permitted to attend any marriage solemnized on approved premises in pursuance of section 26(1)(bb) of this Act.

(3) Each of the persons contracting such a marriage shall make the declaration and use the form of words set out in section 44(3) or (3A) of this Act in the case of marriages in registered buildings.

(4) No religious service shall be used at a marriage on approved premises in pursuance of section 26(1)(bb) of this Act.

Marriages according to usages of Society of Friends

47 Marriages according to usages of Society of Friends

(1) No person who is not a member of the Society of Friends shall be married according to the usages of that Society unless he or she is authorised to be so married under or in pursuance of a general rule of the said Society in England.

(2) A marriage solemnized according to the said usages shall not be valid unless either—

    (a) each person giving notice of marriage declares, either verbally or, if so required, in writing, that each of the parties to the marriage is either a member of the Society of Friends or is in profession with or of the persuasion of that Society; or

    (b) there is produced to the superintendent registrar, at the time when notice of marriage is given, a certificate purporting to be signed by a registering officer of the Society of Friends in England to the effect that any party to the marriage who is not a member of the Society of Friends or in profession with or of the persuasion of that Society, is authorised to be married according to the said usages under or in pursuance of a general rule of the said Society in England.

(3) Any such certificate as aforesaid shall be for all purposes conclusive evidence that any person to whom it relates is authorised to be married according to the usages of the said Society, and the entry of the marriage in a marriage register book under Part IV of this Act, or a certified copy thereof made under the said Part IV, shall be conclusive evidence of the production of such a certificate.
...

Miscellaneous provisions

48 Proof of certain matters not necessary to validity of marriages

(1) Where any marriage has been solemnized under the provisions of this Part of this Act, it shall not be necessary in support of the marriage to give any proof—

    (a) that before the marriage either of the parties thereto resided, or resided for any period, in the registration district stated in the notices of marriage to be that of his or her place of residence;

    (b) that any person whose consent to the marriage was required by section three of this Act had given his consent;

    (c) that the registered building in which the marriage was solemnized had been certified as required by law as a place of religious worship;

    (d) that that building was the usual place of worship of either of the parties to the marriage;

    (da) that, in the case of a marriage under section 26B(2), (4) or (6), the relevant governing authority had given consent as mentioned in section 26B(2)(b), (4)(b) or (6)(d);

(e)   that the facts stated in a declaration made under subsection (1) of section thirty-five of this Act were correct: or

(ea) that, in the case of a marriage under section 26A, the relevant governing authority had given consent as mentioned in section 26A(3);

nor shall any evidence be given to prove the contrary in any proceedings touching the validity of the marriage.

(2) A marriage solemnized in accordance with the provisions of this Part of this Act in a registered building which has not been certified as required by law as a place of religious worship shall be as valid as if the building had been so certified.

49   Void marriages

If any persons knowingly and wilfully intermarry under the provisions of this Part of this Act—

(a) without having given due notice of marriage to the superintendent registrar;

(b) without a certificate for marriage having been duly issued, in respect of each of the persons to be married, by the superintendent registrar to whom notice of marriage was given;

(d) on the authority of certificates which are void by virtue of subsection (2) of section thirty-three of this Act;

(e) in any place other than the church, chapel, registered building, office or other place specified in the notices of marriage and certificates of the superintendent registrar;

(ee) in the case of a marriage purporting to be in pursuance of section 26(1)(bb) of this Act, on any premises that at the time the marriage is solemnized are not approved premises;

(f) in the case of a marriage in a registered building (not being a marriage in the presence of an authorised person), in the absence of a registrar of the registration district in which the registered building is situated;

(g) in the case of a marriage in the office of a superintendent registrar, in the absence of the superintendent registrar or of a registrar of the registration district of that superintendent registrar;

(gg) in the case of a marriage on approved premises, in the absence of the superintendent registrar of the registration district in which the premises are situated or in the absence of a registrar of that district; or

(h) in the case of a marriage to which section 45A of this Act applies, in the absence of any superintendent registrar or registrar whose presence at that marriage is required by that section;

the marriage shall be void.

49A   Void marriages: additional provision about same sex couples

(1) If a same sex couple knowingly and wilfully intermarries under the provisions of this Part of this Act in the absence of the required consent, the marriage shall be void.

(2) In this section, in relation to a marriage of same sex couple, 'required consent' means consent under—

(a) section 26A(3), in a case where section 26A applies to the marriage (but section 44A does not apply to it);

(b) section 26A(3) and section 44A(6), in a case where section 26A and section 44A apply to the marriage;

(c) section 26B(2)(b), in a case where section 26B(1), (2) and (3) apply to the marriage;

(d) section 26B(4)(b), in a case where section 26B(1), (4) and (5) apply to the marriage;

(e) section 26B(6)(d), in a case where section 26B(1), (6) and (7) apply to the marriage.

50   Person to whom certificate to be delivered

(1) Where a marriage is intended to be solemnized on the authority of certificates of a superintendent registrar, the certificates shall be delivered to the following person, that is to say:—

(a) if the marriage is to be solemnized in a registered building or at a person's residence in the presence of a registrar, that registrar;

(b) if the marriage is to be solemnized in a registered building without the presence of a registrar, the authorised person in whose presence the marriage is to be solemnized;

(c) if the marriage is to be solemnized in the office of a superintendent registrar, the registrar in whose presence the marriage is to be solemnized;

(cc) if the marriage is to be solemnized on approved premises, the registrar in whose presence the marriage is to be solemnized;

(d) if the marriage is to be solemnized according to the usages of the Society of Friends, the registering officer of that Society for the place where the marriage is to be solemnized;

(e) if the marriage is to be solemnized according to the usages of persons professing the Jewish religion, the officer of a synagogue by whom the marriage is required to be registered under Part IV of this Act;

(f) if the marriage is to be solemnized according to the rites of the Church of England, the officiating clergyman.

...

(3) Where a marriage is solemnized in a registered building without the presence of a registrar, the certificates shall be kept in the prescribed custody and shall be produced with the marriage register books kept by the authorised person under Part IV of this Act as and when required by the Registrar General.

...

52 Provision for marriages in Welsh language

The Registrar General shall furnish to every registrar in Wales and in every place in which the Welsh language is commonly used a true and exact translation into the Welsh language of the declarations and forms of words required to be used under section forty-four of this Act, and the said translation may be used in any place in which the Welsh language is commonly used in the same manner as is prescribed by the said section forty-four for the use of the declarations and forms of words in the English language.

PART IV REGISTRATION OF MARRIAGES

53 Persons by whom marriages are to be registered

Subject to the provisions of Part V of this Act, a marriage shall be registered in accordance with the provisions of this Part of this Act by the following person, that is to say,—

(a) in the case of a marriage solemnized according to the rites of the Church of England, by the clergyman by whom the marriage is solemnized;

(b) in the case of a marriage solemnized according to the usages of the Society of Friends, by the registering officer of that Society appointed for the district in which the marriage is solemnized;

(c) in the case of a marriage solemnized according to the usages of persons professing the Jewish religion—

(i) where the parties to the marriage are both members of the same synagogue, the marriage shall be registered by the secretary of that synagogue; and

(ii) where the parties to the marriage are members of different synagogues, the marriage shall be registered by the secretary of whichever of those synagogues the parties to the marriage nominate,

(d) in the case of a marriage solemnized in a registered building or at a person's residence in the presence of a registrar, by that registrar;

(e) in the case of a marriage solemnized in a registered building without the presence of a registrar, by the authorised person in whose presence the marriage is solemnized;

(f) in the case of a marriage solemnized in the office of a superintendent registrar by the registrar in whose presence the marriage is solemnized;

(g) in the case of a marriage solemnized on approved premises in pursuance of section 26(1)(bb) of this Act, by the registrar in whose presence the marriage is solemnized.

...

55   Manner of registration of marriages

(1) Every person who is required under this Part of this Act to register a marriage shall, immediately after the solemnization of the marriage, or, in the case of a marriage according to the usages of the Society of Friends, as soon as conveniently may be after the solemnization of the marriage, register in duplicate in two marriage register books the particulars relating to the marriage in the prescribed form:

…

63   Searches in register books

(1) Every incumbent, registering officer of the Society of Friends, secretary of a synagogue and registrar by whom a marriage register book is kept shall at all reasonable hours allow searches to be made in any marriage register book in his keeping, and shall give a copy certified under his hand of any entry in such a book, on payment of the following fee, payable, in the case of a fee previously payable to an incumbent, to the parochial church council of the parish, that is to say—

    (b) Certified copy of entry issued under that subsection

        (i)   when application is made at the time of registering or to a registrar the sum of £3.50,

        (ii)   in any other case, the sum of £7.00.

(2) The last foregoing subsection shall apply in the case of a registered building for which an authorised person has been appointed with the substitution for the reference to the incumbent of a reference to the person having the custody of a marriage register book in accordance with regulations made under section seventy-four of this Act.

64   Searches of indexes kept by superintendent registrars

(1) Every superintendent registrar shall cause indexes of the marriage register books in his office to be made and to be kept with the other records of his office, and the Registrar General shall supply to every superintendent registrar suitable forms for the making of such indexes.

(2) Any person shall be entitled at any time when the register office is required to be open for the transaction of public business to search the said indexes, and to have a certified copy of an entry in the said marriage register books under the hand of the superintendent registrar, on payment to the superintendent registrar of the following fee, that is to say:

    (a) for every general search, the sum of £18.00,

    (b) for every certified copy, the sum of £7.00.

65   Searches of indexes kept by Registrar General

(1) The Registrar General shall cause indexes of all certified copies of entries in marriage register books sent to him under this Part of this Act to be made and kept in the General Register Office.

(2) Any person shall be entitled to search the said indexes at any time when the General Register Office is open for that purpose, and to have a certified copy of any entry in the said certified copies of marriage register books, on payment to the Registrar General or to such other person as may be appointed to act on his behalf of the following fee, that is to say:—

    (c) for every certified copy, the sum of £7.00.

(3) The Registrar General shall cause all certified copies of entries given in the General Register Office to be sealed or stamped with the seal of that Office; and any certified copy of an entry purporting to be sealed or stamped with the said seal shall be received as evidence of the marriage to which it relates without any further or other proof of the entry, and no certified copy purporting to have been given in the said Office shall be of any force or effect unless it is sealed or stamped as aforesaid.

…

67   Interpretation of Part IV

In this Part of this Act, except where the context otherwise requires, the following expressions have the meanings hereby respectively assigned to them, that is to say:—

'general search' means a search conducted during any number of successive hours not exceeding six, without the object of the search being specified;

'particular search' means a search of the indexes covering a period not exceeding five years for a specified entry;

'registering officer of the Society of Friends' means a person whom the recording clerk of the Society of Friends certifies in writing under his hand to the Registrar General to be a registering officer in England of that Society;

'secretary of a synagogue' means—

(a) a person whom the President of the London Committee of Deputies of the British Jews certifies in writing to the Registrar General to be the secretary of a synagogue in England of persons professing the Jewish religion;

(b) the person whom twenty householders professing the Jewish religion and being members of the West London Synagogue of British Jews certify in writing to the Registrar General to be the secretary of that Synagogue;

(c) the person whom twenty householders professing the Jewish religion and being members of the Liberal Jewish Synagogue, St. John's Wood, certify in writing to the Registrar General to be the secretary of that Synagogue;

(d) a person whom the secretary of either the West London Synagogue of British Jews or the Liberal Jewish Synagogue, St. John's Wood, certifies in writing to be the secretary of some other synagogue of not less than twenty householders professing the Jewish religion, being a synagogue which is connected with the said West London Synagogue or with the said Liberal Jewish Synagogue, St. John's Wood, as the case may be, and has been established for not less than one year.

'superintendent registrar' means—

(a) in the case of a marriage registered by a clergyman, the superintendent registrar of the registration district in which is situated the church or chapel of which the incumbent keeps the marriage register book in which the marriage is registered;

(b) in the case of a marriage registered by a registering officer of the Society of Friends, the superintendent registrar of the registration district which is assigned by the Registrar General to that registering officer;

(c) in the case of a marriage registered by the secretary of a synagogue, the superintendent registrar of the registration district which is assigned by the Registrar General to that secretary;

(d) in the case of a marriage registered by an authorised person, the superintendent registrar of the registration district in which the registered building in which the marriage was solemnized is situated;

(e) in the case of a marriage registered by a registrar, the superintendent registrar of the registration district within which that registrar was appointed to act.

...

PART VI GENERAL

72 Supplementary provisions as to marriages in usual places of worship

(1) For the purposes of the following provisions of this Act, that is to say, subsection (4) of section six, paragraph (b) of subsection (1) of section fifteen and subsection (3) of section thirty-five, no parish church or authorised chapel shall be deemed to be the usual place of worship of any person unless he is enrolled on the church electoral roll of the area in which that church or chapel is situated, and where any person is enrolled on the church electoral roll of an area in which he does not

reside that enrolment shall be sufficient evidence that his usual place of worship is a parish church or authorised chapel in that area.

(2) Persons intending to be married shall have the like but no greater right of having their banns published and marriage solemnized by virtue of the said provisions in a parish church or authorised chapel which is the usual place of worship of one or both of them as they have of having their banns published and marriage solemnized in the parish church or public chapel of the parish or chapelry in which they or one of them resides.

(3) Where any marriage has been solemnized by virtue of the said provisions it shall not be necessary in support of the marriage to give any proof of the actual enrolment of the parties or of one of them on the church electoral roll of the area in which the parish church or authorised chapel in which the marriage was solemnized was situated, nor shall any evidence be given to prove the contrary in any proceedings touching the validity of the marriage.

...

75   Offences relating to solemnization of marriages

(1) Any person who knowingly and wilfully—

...

    (b)   solemnizes a marriage according to the rites of the Church of England without banns of matrimony having been duly published (not being a marriage solemnized on the authority of a special licence, a common licence, or certificates of a superintendent registrar);

    (c)   solemnizes a marriage according to the said rites (not being a marriage by special licence or a marriage in pursuance of section 26(1)(dd) of this Act) in any place other than a church or other building in which banns may be published;

    (d)   solemnizes a marriage according to the said rites falsely pretending to be in Holy Orders;

shall be guilty of felony and shall be liable to imprisonment for a term not exceeding fourteen years.

(2) Any person who knowingly and wilfully—

    (a)   solemnizes a marriage (not being a marriage by special licence, a marriage according to the usages of the Society of Friends or a marriage between two persons professing the Jewish religion according to the usages of the Jews) in any place other than—

      (i)   a church or other building in which marriages may be solemnized according to the rites of the Church of England, or

      (ii)   the registered building, office, approved premises or person's residence specified as the place where the marriage was to be solemnized in the notices of marriage and certificates required under Part III of this Act;

    (aa) solemnizes a marriage purporting to be in pursuance of section 26(1)(bb) of this Act on premises that are not approved premises;

    (b)   solemnizes a marriage in any such registered building as aforesaid (not being a marriage in the presence of an authorised person) in the absence of a registrar of the district in which the registered building is situated;

    (bb) solemnizes a marriage in pursuance of section 26(1)(dd) or 26B(6) of this Act, otherwise than according to the rites of the Church of England, in the absence of a registrar of the registration district in which the place where the marriage is solemnized is situated;

    (c)   solemnizes a marriage in the office of a superintendent registrar in the absence of a registrar of the district in which the office is situated;

    (cc) solemnizes a marriage on approved premises in pursuance of section 26(1)(bb) of this Act in the absence of a registrar of the district in which the premises are situated;

    (d)   solemnizes a marriage on the authority of certificates of a superintendent registrar before the expiry of the waiting period in relation to each notice of marriage; or

    (e)   solemnizes a marriage on the authority of certificates of a superintendent registrar after the expiration of the period which is, in relation to that marriage, the applicable period for the purposes of section 33 of this Act; shall be guilty of felony and shall be liable to imprisonment for a term not exceeding five years.

(2A) In subsection (2)(d) 'the waiting period' has the same meaning as in section 31 (4A).

(3) A superintendent registrar who knowingly and wilfully—

(a) issues any certificate for marriage before the expiry of 15 days from the day on which the notice of marriage was entered in the marriage notice book, or in an approved electronic form by virtue of section 27(4A);

(b) issues any certificate for marriage after the expiration of the period which is, in relation to that marriage, the applicable period for the purposes of section 33 of this Act;

(c) issues any certificate the issue of which has been forbidden under section thirty of this Act by any person entitled to forbid the issue of such a certificate; or

(d) solemnizes or permits to be solemnized in his office or, in the case of a marriage in pursuance of section 26(1)(bb) or (dd) or 26B(6) of this Act, in any other place, any marriage which is void by virtue of any of the provisions of Part III of this Act;

shall be guilty of felony and shall be liable to imprisonment for a term not exceeding five years.

(4) No prosecution under this section shall be commenced after the expiration of three years from the commission of the offence.

…

76   Offences relating to registration of marriages

(1) Any person who refuses or without reasonable cause omits to register any marriage which he is required by this Act to register, and any person having the custody of a marriage register book or a certified copy of a marriage register book or part thereof who carelessly loses or injures the said book or copy or carelessly allows the said book or copy to be injured while in his keeping, shall be liable on summary conviction to a fine not exceeding level 3 on the standard scale.

(3) Any registrar who knowingly and wilfully registers any marriage which is void by virtue of any of the provisions of Part III of this Act shall be guilty of felony and shall be liable to imprisonment for a term not exceeding five years.

(6) No prosecution under subsection (3) of this section shall be commenced after the expiration of three years from the commission of the offence.

…

78   Interpretation

(1) In this Act, except where the context otherwise requires, the following expressions have the meanings hereby respectively assigned to them, that is to say—

'approved electronic form' has the meaning given by section 74(2);

'approved premises' means premises approved in accordance with regulations under section 46A of this Act as premises on which marriages may be solemnized in pursuance of section 26(1)(bb) of this Act;

'authorised chapel' means—

(a) in relation to a chapelry, a chapel of the chapelry in which banns of matrimony could lawfully be published immediately before the passing of the Marriage Act 1823, or in which banns may be published and marriages may be solemnized by virtue of section two of the Marriages Confirmation Act 1825, or of an authorisation given under section three of the Marriage Act 1823;

(b) in relation to an extra-parochial place, a church or chapel of that place in which banns may be published and marriages may be solemnized by virtue of section two of the Marriages Confirmation Act 1825, or of an authorisation given under section three of the Marriage Act 1823, or section twenty-one of this Act;

(c) in relation to a district specified in a licence granted under section twenty of this Act, the chapel in which banns may be published and marriages may be solemnized by virtue of that licence;

'authorised person' means—

    (a) in relation to a building registered under section 41, a person whose name and address have been certified in accordance with section 43;

    (b) in relation to a building registered under section 43A, a person whose name and address have been certified in accordance with section 43B;

'brother' includes a brother of the half blood;

'child', except where used to express a relationship, means a person under the age of eighteen;

'child of the family' in relation to any person, means a child who has lived in the same household as that person and been treated by that person as a child of the family;

'clergyman' means a clerk in Holy Orders of the Church of England;

'common licence' has the meaning assigned to it by section 5 of this Act;

'ecclesiastical district,' in relation to a district other than a parish, means a district specified in a licence granted under section 20 of this Act, a chapelry or an extra-parochial place;

'England and Wales legislation' has the same meaning as in the Marriage (Same Sex Couples) Act 2013;

'marriage notice book' has the meaning assigned to it by section 27 of this Act;

'parish' means an ecclesiastical parish and includes a district constituted under the Church Building Acts 1818 to 1884, notwithstanding that the district has not become a new parish by virtue of section fourteen of the New Parishes Act 1856 or section five of the New Parishes Measure 1943, being a district to which Acts of Parliament relating to the publication of banns of matrimony and the solemnization of marriages were applied by the said Church Building Acts as if the district had been an ancient parish, and the expression 'parish church' shall be construed accordingly;

'prescribed' means prescribed by regulations made under section 24 of this Act;

'registered building' means a building registered under section 41 or section 43A of this Act;

'registrar' means a registrar of marriages;

'Registrar General' means the Registrar General of Births, Deaths and Marriages in England;

'registration district' means the district of a superintendent registrar;

'sister' includes a sister of the half blood;

'special licence' has the meaning assigned to it by section 5 of this Act;

'superintendent registrar' means a superintendent registrar of births, deaths and marriages;

'trustees or governing body,' in relation to Roman Catholic registered buildings, includes a bishop or vicar general of the diocese.

(2) Any reference in this Act to the Church of England shall, unless the context otherwise requires, be construed as including a reference to the Church in Wales.

(3) For the purposes of this Act a person is house-bound if—

    (a) each notice of his or her marriage given in accordance with section 27 of this Act is accompanied by a medical statement (within the meaning of section 27A(7) of this Act) made, not more than fourteen days before the date on which that notice was given, in relation to that person; and

    (b) he or she is not a detained person.

(4) For the purposes of this Act a person is a detained person if he or she is for the time being detained—

    (a) otherwise than by virtue of section 2, 4, 5, 35, 36 or 136 of the Mental Health Act 1983 (short term detentions), as a patient in a hospital; or

    (b) in a prison or other place to which the Prison Act 1952 applies, and in paragraph (a) above 'patient' and 'hospital' have the same meanings as in Part II of the Mental Health Act 1983.

(5) For the purposes of this Act a person who is house-bound or is a detained person shall be taken, if he or she would not otherwise be, to be resident and usually resident at the place where he or she is for the time being.

(6) If, for the purpose of any provision of this Act, a relevant governing authority has given written consent to marriages of same sex couples, the validity of that consent is not affected only because there is a change in the person or persons constituting that relevant governing authority.

SCHEDULE 1 KINDRED AND AFFINITY

PART 1 PROHIBITED DEGREES: KINDRED

1.—(1) The list referred to in section 1(1) is—

Adoptive child	Grandchild
Adoptive parent	Parent
Child	Parent's sibling
Former adoptive child	Sibling
Former adoptive parent	Sibling's child
Grandparent	

(2) In the list 'sibling' means a brother, sister, half-brother or half-sister.

PART 2 DEGREES OF AFFINITY REFERRED TO IN SECTION 1(2) AND (3)

2. The list referred to in section 1(2) is as follows—

Child of former civil partner	Former spouse of grandparent
Child of former spouse	Former spouse of parent
Former civil partner of grandparent	Grandchild of former civil partner
Former civil partner of parent	Grandchild of former spouse

Maintenance Orders Act 1950

(14 Geo. 6, c. 37)

PART II ENFORCEMENT

16 Application of Part II

(1) Any order to which this section applies (in this Part of this Act referred to as a maintenance order) made by a court in any part of the United Kingdom may, if registered in accordance with the provisions of this Part of this Act in a court in another part of the United Kingdom, be enforced in accordance with those provisions in that other part of the United Kingdom.

(2) This section applies to the following orders, that is to say—

- (a) an order for alimony, maintenance or other payments made or deemed to be made by a court in England under any of the following enactments:—
  - (i) sections 15 to 17, 19 to 22, 30, 34 and 35 of the Matrimonial Causes Act 1965, and sections 22, 23(1), (2) and (4) and 27 of the Matrimonial Causes Act 1973 and section 14 or 17 of the Matrimonial and Family Proceedings Act 1984;
  - (ii) Part I of the Domestic Proceedings and Magistrates' Courts Act 1978;
  - (iii) Schedule 1 to the Children Act 1989;
  - (iv) paragraph 23 of Schedule 2 to the Children Act 1989 or section forty-three of the National Assistance Act 1948;
  - (v) paragraph 23 of Schedule 2 to the Children Act 1989;
  - (vi) section 18 of the Supplementary Benefits Act 1976;
  - (viii) section 106 of the Social Security Administration Act 1992.
  - (ix) Part 1, 8 or 9 of Schedule 5 to the Civil Partnership Act 2004, Schedule 6 to that Act or paragraph 5 or 9 of Schedule 7 to that Act;

...

17   Procedure for registration of maintenance orders

...

(2) If upon application made as aforesaid by or on behalf of the person entitled to payments under a maintenance order it appears that the person liable to make those payments resides in another part of the United Kingdom, and that it is convenient that the order should be enforceable there, the appropriate authority shall cause a certified copy of the order to be sent to the prescribed officer of a court in that part of the United Kingdom in accordance with the provisions of the next following subsection.

(3) The court to whose officer the certified copy of a maintenance order is sent under this section shall be—

    (a) where the maintenance order was made by a superior court, the Senior Courts, the Court of Session or the Court of Judicature, as the case may be;

    (b) in any other case—

        (i)   where the defendant appears to be in England and Wales, the family court; ...

(4) Where the prescribed officer of any court receives a certified copy of a maintenance order sent to him under this section, he shall cause the order to be registered in that court in the prescribed manner, and shall give notice of the registration in the prescribed manner to the prescribed officer of the court which made the order.

(5) The officer to whom any notice is given under the last foregoing subsection shall cause particulars of the notice to be registered in his court in the prescribed manner.

(6) Where the sums payable under a maintenance order, being an order made by the family court or a court of summary jurisdiction in Northern Ireland, are payable to or through an officer of any court, that officer shall, if the person entitled to the payments so requests, make an application on behalf of that person for the registration of the order under this Part of this Act; but the person at whose request the application is made shall have the same liability for costs properly incurred in or about the application as if the application had been made by him.

(7) An order which is for the time being registered under this Part of this Act in any court shall not be registered thereunder in any other court.

18   Enforcement of registered orders

(1) Subject to the provisions of this section, a maintenance order registered under this Part of this Act in a court in any part of the United Kingdom may be enforced in that part of the United Kingdom in all respects as if it had been made by that court and as if that court had had jurisdiction to make it; and proceedings for or with respect to the enforcement of any such order may be taken accordingly.

(1A) A maintenance order registered under this Part of this Act in the family court or a court of summary jurisdiction in Northern Ireland shall not carry interest; but where a maintenance order so registered is registered in the High Court under section 36 of the Civil Jurisdiction and Judgments Act 1982, this subsection shall not prevent any sum for whose payment the order provides from carrying interest in accordance with section 11A of the Maintenance and Affiliation Orders Act (Northern Ireland) 1966.

...

20   Arrears under registered maintenance orders

(1) Where application is made for the registration of a maintenance order under this Part of this Act, the applicant may lodge with the appropriate authority—

    (a) if the payments under the order are required to be made to or through a court or an officer of any court, a certificate in the prescribed form, signed by an officer of that court or (as the case may be) that officer, as to the amount of any arrears due under the order;

    (b) in any other case, a statutory declaration or affidavit as to the amount of those arrears;

and if a certified copy of the maintenance order is sent to the prescribed officer of any court in pursuance of the application, the certificate, declaration or affidavit shall also be sent to that officer.

...

21 Discharge and variation of maintenance orders registered in superior courts

(1) The registration of a maintenance order in a superior court under this Part of this Act shall not confer on that court any power to vary or discharge the order, or affect any jurisdiction of the court in which the order was made to vary or discharge the order.

22 Discharge and variation of maintenance orders registered in summary or sheriff courts

(1) Subject to subsection (1ZA) where a maintenance order is for the time being registered under this Part of this Act in the family court, a court of summary jurisdiction in Northern Ireland or a sheriff court, that court may, upon application made in the prescribed manner by or on behalf of the person liable to make periodical payments under the order or the person entitled to those payments, by order make such variation as the court thinks fit in the rate of the payments under the maintenance order; but no such variation shall impose on the person liable to make payments under the maintenance order a liability to make payments in excess of the maximum rate (if any) authorised by the law for the time being in force in the part of the United Kingdom in which the maintenance order was made.

(1ZA) The power under subsection (1) to vary the rate of payments may not be exercised where paragraph 9(2) of Schedule 6 to the Civil Jurisdiction and Judgments (Maintenance) Regulations 2011 applies (restriction on modifying maintenance decision where creditor remains habitually resident in the part of the United Kingdom in which the decision was made).

(1A) The family court may exercise the same powers in relation to an order registered in the family court under this Part of this Act as are exercisable by the family court under section 1 of the Maintenance Enforcement Act 1991 in relation to a qualifying periodical maintenance order (within the meaning of that section) which has been made by the family court, including the power under subsection (7) of that section to revoke, suspend, revive or vary any means of payment order (within the meaning of that subsection) made by virtue of this subsection.

...

24 Cancellation of registration

(1) At any time while a maintenance order is registered under this Part of this Act in any court, an application for the cancellation of the registration may be made in the prescribed manner to the prescribed officer of that court by or on behalf of the person entitled to payments under the order; and upon any such application that officer shall (unless proceedings for the variation of the order are pending in that court), cancel the registration, and thereupon the order shall cease to be registered in that court.

...

(4) Except as provided by subsection (5) of this section, the cancellation of the registration of a maintenance order shall not affect anything done in relation to the maintenance order while it was registered.

(5) On the cancellation of the registration of a maintenance order, any order made in relation thereto under subsection (2) of section nineteen of this Act shall cease to have effect; but until the person liable to make payments under the maintenance order receives the prescribed notice of the cancellation, he shall be deemed to comply with the maintenance order if he makes payments in accordance with any order under the said subsection (2) which was in force immediately before the cancellation.

(5A) On the cancellation of the registration of a maintenance order registered in the family court in England and Wales, any order—

(a) made in relation thereto by virtue of the powers conferred by section 22(1A) of this Act, and

(b) requiring payment to the family court (whether or not by any method of payment falling within section 1(5) of the Maintenance Enforcement Act 1991), shall cease to have effect; but until the person liable to make payments under the maintenance order receives the prescribed notice of the cancellation, he shall be deemed to comply with the maintenance order if he makes payments in accordance with any such order which was in force immediately before the cancellation.

...

Intestates' Estates Act 1952

(15 & 16 Geo. 6 & 1 Eliz. 2, c. 64)

PART I AMENDMENTS OF LAW OF INTESTATE SUCCESSION

5 Rights of surviving spouse or civil partner as respects the matrimonial or civil partnership home

The Second Schedule to this Act shall have effect for enabling the surviving spouse or civil partner of a person dying intestate after the commencement of this Act to acquire the matrimonial or civil partnership home.

Section 5   SCHEDULES

SECOND SCHEDULE

Rights of surviving spouse or civil partner as respects the matrimonial or civil partnership home

1.—(1) Subject to the provisions of this Schedule, where the residuary estate of the intestate comprises an interest in a dwelling-house in which the surviving spouse or civil partner was resident at the time of the intestate's death, the surviving spouse or civil partner may require the personal representative, in exercise of the power conferred by section forty-one of the principal Act (and with due regard to the requirements of that section as to valuation) to appropriate the said interest in the dwelling-house in or towards satisfaction of any absolute interest of the surviving spouse or civil partner in the real and personal estate of the intestate.

(2) The right conferred by this paragraph shall not be exercisable where the interest is—

    (a) a tenancy which at the date of the death of the intestate was a tenancy which would determine within the period of two years from that date; or

    (b) a tenancy which the landlord by notice given after that date could determine within the remainder of that period.

(3) Nothing in subsection (5) of section forty-one of the principal Act (which requires the personal representative, in making an appropriation to any person under that section, to have regard to the rights of others) shall prevent the personal representative from giving effect to the right conferred by this paragraph.

...

(5) Where part of a building was, at the date of the death of the intestate, occupied as a separate dwelling, that dwelling shall for the purposes of this Schedule be treated as a dwelling-house.

2.—Where—

    (a) the dwelling-house forms part of a building and an interest in the whole of the building is comprised in the residuary estate; or

(b) the dwelling-house is held with agricultural land and an interest in the agricultural land is comprised in the residuary estate; or

(c) the whole or part of the dwelling-house was at the time of the intestate's death used as a hotel or lodging house; or

(d) a part of the dwelling-house was at the time of the intestate's death used for purposes other than domestic purposes,

the right conferred by paragraph 1 of this Schedule shall not be exercisable unless the court, on being satisfied that the exercise of that right is not likely to diminish the value of assets in the residuary estate (other than the said interest in the dwelling-house) or make them more difficult to dispose of, so orders.

3.—(1) The right conferred by paragraph 1 of this Schedule—

(a) shall not be exercisable after the expiration of twelve months from the first taking out of representation with respect to the intestate's estate;

(b) shall not be exercisable after the death of the surviving spouse or civil partner;

(c) shall be exercisable, except where the surviving spouse or civil partner is the sole personal representative, by notifying the personal representative (or, where there are two or more personal representatives of whom one is the surviving spouse or civil partner, all of them except the surviving spouse or civil partner) in writing.

(2) A notification in writing under paragraph (c) of the foregoing sub-paragraph shall not be revocable except with the consent of the personal representative; but the surviving spouse or civil partner may require the personal representative to have the said interest in the dwelling-house valued in accordance with section forty-one of the principal Act and to inform him or her of the result of that valuation before he or she decides whether to exercise the right.

(3) The court may extend the period of 12 months referred to in sub-paragraph (1)(a) if the surviving spouse or civil partner applies for it to be extended and satisfies the court that a period limited to 12 months would operate unfairly—

(a) in consequence of the representation first taken out being probate of a will subsequently revoked on the ground that the will was invalid, or

(b) in consequence of a question whether a person had an interest in the estate, or as to the nature of an interest in the estate, not having been determined at the time when representation was first taken out, or

(c) in consequence of some other circumstances affecting the administration or distribution of the estate.

(4) For the purposes of the construction of the references in this paragraph to the first taking out of representation, there shall be left out of account—

(a) a grant limited to settled land or to trust property,

(b) any other grant that does not permit any of the estate to be distributed,

(c) a grant limited to real estate or to personal estate, unless a grant limited to the remainder of the estate has previously been made or is made at the same time,

...

4.—(1) During the period of twelve months mentioned in paragraph 3 of this Schedule the personal representative shall not without the written consent of the surviving spouse or civil partner sell or otherwise dispose of the said interest in the dwelling-house except in the course of administration owing to want of other assets.

(2) An application to the court under paragraph 2 of this Schedule may be made by the personal representative as well as by the surviving spouse or civil partner, and if, on an application under that paragraph, the court does not order that the right conferred by paragraph 1 of this Schedule shall be exercisable by the surviving spouse or civil partner, the court may authorise the personal representative to dispose of the said interest in the dwelling-house within the said period of twelve months.

(3) Where the court under sub-paragraph (3) of paragraph 3 of this Schedule extends the said period of twelve months, the court may direct that this paragraph shall apply in relation to the extended period as it applied in relation to the original period of twelve months.

(4) This paragraph shall not apply where the surviving spouse or civil partner is the sole personal representative or one of two or more personal representatives.

(5) Nothing in this paragraph shall confer any right on the surviving spouse or civil partner as against a purchaser from the personal representative.

5.—(1) Where the surviving spouse or civil partner is one of two or more personal representatives, the rule that a trustee may not be a purchaser of trust property shall not prevent the surviving spouse or civil partner from purchasing out of the estate of the intestate an interest in a dwelling-house in which the surviving spouse or civil partner was resident at the time of the intestate's death.

(2) The power of appropriation under section forty-one of the principal Act shall include power to appropriate an interest in a dwelling-house in which the surviving spouse or civil partner was resident at the time of the intestate's death partly in satisfaction of an interest of the surviving spouse or civil partner in the real and personal estate of the intestate and partly in return for a payment of money by the surviving spouse or civil partner to the personal representative.

6.—(1) Where the surviving spouse or civil partner lacks capacity (within the meaning of the Mental Capacity Act 2005) to make a requirement or give a consent under this Schedule, the requirement or consent may be made or given by a deputy appointed by the Court of Protection with power in that respect or, if no deputy has that power, by that court.

(2) A requirement or consent made or given under this Schedule by a surviving spouse or civil partner who is an infant shall be as valid and binding as it would be if he or she were of age; and, as respects an appropriation in pursuance of paragraph 1 of this Schedule, the provisions of section forty-one of the principal Act as to obtaining the consent of the infant's parent or guardian, or of the court on behalf of the infant, shall not apply.

7.—(1) Except where the context otherwise requires, references in this Schedule to a dwelling-house include references to any garden or portion of ground attached to and usually occupied with the dwelling-house or otherwise required for the amenity or convenience of the dwelling-house.

(2) This Schedule shall be construed as one with Part IV of the principal Act.

Births and Deaths Registration Act 1953

(1953 c. 20)

PART I REGISTRATION OF BIRTHS

1 Particulars of births to be registered

(1) Subject to the provisions of this Part of this Act, the birth of every child born in England or Wales shall be registered by the registrar of births and deaths for the sub-district in which the child was born by entering in a register kept for that sub-district such particulars concerning the birth as may be prescribed; and different registers shall be kept and different particulars may be prescribed for live-births and still-births respectively:
...

(2) The following persons shall be qualified to give information concerning a birth, that is to say—

(a) the mother of the child;

(aa) the father of the child where—

    (i) the child is one whose father and mother were married to each other at the time of the child's birth, or

    (ii) the father is a qualified informant by virtue of subsection (2)(a) of section 10 (registration of father where parents not married or of second female parent where parents not civil partners) or by virtue of regulations under subsection (6)(b) of section 2E (scientific tests);

(b) the occupier of the house in which the child was to the knowledge of that occupier born;

(c) any person present at the birth;

(d) any person having charge of the child;

(e) in the case of a still-born child found exposed, the person who found the child.

(3) In subsection (2)(aa)—

(a) the first reference to the father is, in the case of a child who has a parent by virtue of section 42 or 43 of the Human Fertilisation and Embryology Act 2008, to be read as a reference to the woman who is a parent by virtue of that section;

(b) the reference in sub-paragraph (ii) to the father being a qualified informant by virtue of section 10(2)(a) is, in the case of a child who has a parent by virtue of section 43 of that Act, to be read as a reference to that parent being a qualified informant by virtue of section 10(2A)(a).

(4) In this Part, references to a child whose father and mother were, or were not, married to each other at the time of the child's birth are to be read in accordance with section 1 of the Family Law Reform Act 1987 (which extends the cases in which a person is treated as being a person whose father and mother were married to each other at the time of the person's birth).

2   Information concerning birth of child whose parents are married

(1) In the case of every birth of a child whose father and mother were married to each other at the time of the child's birth it shall be the duty—

(a) of the father and mother of the child; and

(b) in the case of the death or inability of the father and mother, of each other qualified informant,

to give to the registrar, before the expiration of a period of forty-two days from the date of the birth, information of the particulars required to be registered concerning the birth, and in the presence of the registrar to sign the register:

Provided that—

    (i) the giving of information and the signing of the register by any one qualified informant shall act as a discharge of any duty under this section of every other qualified informant;

    (ii) this section shall cease to apply if, before the expiration of the said period and before the birth has been registered, an investigation is conducted under Part 1 of the 2009 Act, other than one that is discontinued under section 4 of that Act (cause of death revealed by post-mortem examination), in the course of which the child is found to have been still-born.

(2) In the case of a child who has a parent by virtue of section 42 or 43 of the Human Fertilisation and Embryology Act 2008, the references in subsection (1)(a) and (b) to the father of the child are to be read as references to the woman who is a parent by virtue of that section.

2A   Information concerning birth of child whose parents are not married

(1) In the case of every birth of a child whose father and mother were not married to each other at the time of the birth, it shall be the duty—

(a) of the mother of the child, and

(b) in the case of the death or inability of the mother, of each qualified informant falling within section 1(2)(b) to (e), to give to the registrar, before the expiration of a period of 42 days from the date of the birth, information of the particulars required to be registered concerning the birth, together with any other information required by section 2B(1), and in the presence of the registrar to sign the register.

(2) The giving of information and the signing of the register by any one qualified informant shall act as a discharge of any duty under this section of every other qualified informant, but this does not affect—

    (a) any duty of the father by virtue of regulations under section 2C (confirmation of parentage information given by mother), or

    (b) any duty by virtue of regulations under section 2E (scientific tests).

    ...

(4) In the case of a child who has a parent by virtue of section 43 of the Human Fertilisation and Embryology Act 2008, the reference in subsection (2)(a) to the father is to be read as a reference to the woman who is a parent by virtue of that section.

2B   Duties of unmarried mother when acting alone

(1) Where no request for the entry of a person's name as the father of the child is made by virtue of any of paragraphs (a) to (g) of section 10(1) (registration of father where parents are not married) or by virtue of regulations under section 2E (scientific tests), the information to be given under section 2A(1) by the mother includes such information relating to the father as may be prescribed for the purposes of this subsection by regulations made by the Minister, which may include information that is not intended to be entered on the register.

(2) The Registrar General may by regulations authorise or require the information relating to the father to be provided in a prescribed form or manner.

(3) Subsection (1) does not require the mother to provide information relating to the father if she makes in the presence of the registrar a declaration in the prescribed form stating that one or more of the following conditions is met.

(4) Those conditions are—

    (a) that by virtue of section 41 of the Human Fertilisation and Embryology Act 2008 the child has no father,

    (b) that the father has died,

    (c) that the mother does not know the father's identity,

    (d) that the mother does not know the father's whereabouts,

    (e) that the father lacks capacity (within the meaning of the Mental Capacity Act 2005) in relation to decisions under this Part,

    (f) that the mother has reason to fear for her safety or that of the child if the father is contacted in relation to the registration of the birth, and

    (g) any other conditions prescribed by regulations made by the Minister.

(5) Subsection (1) does not apply—

    (a) in the case of a still-birth,

    (b) if the child has died, or

    (c) if the mother acknowledges in accordance with regulations made by virtue of subsection (2)(b) of section 2D (declaration before registration by person claiming to be other parent) that a person who has previously given notice by virtue of subsection (2)(a) of that section is the other parent of the child.

(6) The Minister may by regulations provide that, except in such cases as the regulations may prescribe, where the mother is required by subsection (1) to give information relating to the father—

    (a) the mother's duty under section 2A to sign the register is to have effect as a duty to sign a declaration in such form as may be so prescribed,

    (b) the registrar is not to register the birth of the child until such time as may be determined in accordance with the regulations, and

    (c) the entry in the register is to be taken for the purposes of this Act to have been signed by the person who signed the declaration.

(7) No information relating to the father is to be entered in the register merely because it is given by the mother by virtue of subsection (1).

(8) In the case of a child who has a parent by virtue of section 43 of the Human Fertilisation and Embryology Act 2008—

(a) references in this section to the father are to be read as references to the woman who is a parent by virtue of that section,

(b) the reference in subsection (1) to paragraphs (a) to (g) of section 10(1) is to be read as a reference to paragraphs (a) to (f) of section 10(1B), and

(c) paragraphs (a) and (c) of subsection (4) do not apply.

2C   Confirmation of parentage information given by mother

(1) The Minister may by regulations provide for a procedure under which a person may be registered as the father of a child in a case where information relating to that person is given by virtue of section 2B(1) by the mother of the child and is subsequently confirmed by that person.

(2) Regulations under this section may in particular—

(a) enable or require the registrar by notice to require the person in relation to whom information has been given by virtue of section 2B(1) by the mother ('the alleged father') to state whether or not he acknowledges that he is the father of the child,

(b) where the alleged father acknowledges that he is the father of the child, require the alleged father to give prescribed information to the registrar,

(c) where the alleged father gives that information to the registrar, require the registrar to enter the alleged father's name in the register as the father of the child or, where the birth has already been registered, to re-register the birth so as to show the alleged father as the father, and

(d) provide that in prescribed cases where the alleged father is not required by the regulations to sign the register, the entry in the register is to be taken for the purposes of this Act to have been signed by the alleged father.

(3) In the case of a child who has a parent by virtue of section 43 of the Human Fertilisation and Embryology Act 2008, references in subsection (1) or (2) to the father are to be read as references to the woman who is a parent by virtue of that section (and references to the alleged father have a corresponding meaning).

…

2D   Declaration before registration by person claiming to be other parent

(1) The Minister may by regulations provide for a procedure under which a person may be registered as the father of a child whose father and mother were not married to each other at the time of the child's birth, on the basis of information that is—

(a) given by that person (in the absence of the mother) before the birth is registered, and

(b) confirmed by the mother when she provides information of the particulars required to be registered concerning the birth.

(2) Regulations under this section may in particular—

(a) enable a person who believes himself to be the father of a child to make a declaration to that effect to the registrar before the birth of the child is registered,

(b) require the mother of the child, on giving information concerning the birth of the child or in such other circumstances as may be prescribed, to state whether or not she acknowledges that the person is the father of the child,

(c) where the mother acknowledges that the person is the father of the child, require the registrar to enter the person's name in the register as the father of the child, and

(d) provide that in prescribed cases where the person is not required by the regulations to sign the register, the entry in the register is to be taken for the purposes of this Act to have been signed by the person.

(3) In the case of a child who has a parent by virtue of section 43 of the Human Fertilisation and Embryology Act 2008, references in subsections (1) and (2) to the father (except in the reference

in subsection (1) to a child whose father and mother were not married to each other at the time of the child's birth) are to be read as references to the woman who is a parent by virtue of that section.

...

2E   Use of scientific tests with consent of parties

(1) The Minister may by regulations make provision enabling a report of a qualifying scientific test to be used in connection with the registration or re-registration under this Act of the birth of a child in cases where—

(a) the birth has not been registered under this Act, or

(b) the birth has been registered but no person has been registered as the father of the child (or as a parent of the child by virtue of section 42, 43 or 46(1) or (2) of the Human Fertilisation and Embryology Act 2008).

(2) A qualifying scientific test is a scientific test that complies with prescribed requirements and is carried out by a person who is accredited by the Minister for the purposes of this section in accordance with the regulations.

(3) The regulations may not require any person to participate in a qualifying scientific test.

(4) The regulations may not enable or require a report of a qualifying scientific test to be used as mentioned in subsection (1) unless, before the test is carried out, the mother and the man to whom the test relates—

(a) consent to the carrying out of the test, and

(b) agree in the prescribed manner that if the report of the test is positive the man's name will be entered in the register as the father of the child.

(5) For the purposes of this section, the report of a qualifying scientific test is positive if the report states that the result of the test indicates to a prescribed degree of certainty that the man concerned is the father of the child.

(6) Regulations under this section may—

(a) enable or require the mother or the man, if the report of the qualifying scientific test is positive, to apply for the registration (or re-registration) of the birth so as to show the man as the father,

(b) provide that where the regulations enable or require the man to apply for registration, the man is to be treated for the purposes of this Part as a qualified informant concerning the birth of the child,

(c) impose obligations on the registrar in relation to the registration (or re-registration) of the birth,

(d) require anything to be done in a prescribed form or manner or in the presence of the registrar,

(e) make provision as to the time within which anything is required or authorised to be done.

(7) The regulations may not require the registrar to enter a man's name in the register as the father of a child if it appears to the registrar that by virtue of any provision of sections 35 to 47 of the Human Fertilisation and Embryology Act 2008 the man is not the father of the child.

...

10   Registration of father where parents not married or of second female parent where parents not civil partners

(1) In the case of a child whose father and mother were not married to each other at the time of the child's birth, no person shall as father of the child be required to give information concerning the birth of the child except by virtue of regulations under section 2C or 2E, and the registrar shall not enter in the register the name of any person as father of the child except—

(a) at the joint request of the mother and the person stating himself to be the father of the child (in which case that person shall sign the register together with the mother); or

(b) at the request of the mother on production of—

        (i)   a declaration in the prescribed form made by the mother stating that that person is the father of the child; and

        (ii) a declaration in the prescribed form which is made by that person, states himself to be the father of the child, and is countersigned by a prescribed person; or

  (c) at the request of that person on production of—

        (i)   a declaration in the prescribed form by that person stating himself to be the father of the child; and

        (ii) a declaration in the prescribed form which is made by the mother, states that that person is the father of the child, and is countersigned by a prescribed person; or

  (d) at the request of the mother or that person on production of—

        (i)   a copy of any agreement made between them under section 4(1)(b) of the Children Act 1989 in relation to the child; and

        (ii) a declaration in the prescribed form by the person making the request stating that the agreement was made in compliance with section 4 of that Act and has not been brought to an end by an order of a court; or

  (e) at the request of the mother or that person on production of—

        (i)   a certified copy of an order under section 4 of the Children Act 1989 giving that person parental responsibility for the child; and

        (ii) a declaration in the prescribed form by the person making the request stating that the order has not been brought to an end by an order of a court; or

  (f) at the request of the mother or that person on production of—

        (i)   a certified copy of an order under paragraph 1 of Schedule 1 to the Children Act 1989 which requires that person to make any financial provision for the child and which is not an order falling within paragraph 4(3) of that Schedule; and

        (ii) a declaration in the prescribed form by the person making the request stating that the order has not been discharged by an order of a court; or

  (g) at the request of the mother or that person on production of—

        (i)   a certified copy of any of the orders which are mentioned in subsection (1A) of this section which has been made in relation to the child; and

        (ii) a declaration in the prescribed form by the person making the request stating that the order has not been brought to an end or discharged by an order of a court; or

  (h) in accordance with regulations made under section 2C (confirmation of parentage information given by mother), section 2D (declaration before registration by person claiming to be other parent) or section 2E (scientific tests).

(1A) The orders are—

  (a) an order under section 4 of the Family Law Reform Act 1987 that that person shall have all the parental rights and duties with respect to the child;

  (b) an order that that person shall have custody or care and control or legal custody of the child made under section 9 of the Guardianship of Minors Act 1971 at a time when such an order could only be made in favour of a parent;

  (c) an order under section 9 or 11B of that Act which requires that person to make any financial provision in relation to the child;

  (d) an order under section 4 of the Affiliation Proceedings Act 1957 naming that person as putative father of the child.

(1B) In the case of a child to whom section 1(3) of the Family Law Reform Act 1987 does not apply, no woman shall as parent of the child by virtue of section 43 of the Human Fertilisation and Embryology Act 2008 be required to give information concerning the birth of the child except by virtue of regulations under section 2C, and the registrar shall not enter the name of any woman as a parent of the child by virtue of that section except—

  (a) at the joint request of the mother and the person stating herself to be the other parent of the child (in which case that person shall sign the register together with the mother); or

(b) at the request of the mother on production of—
  (i) a declaration in the prescribed form made by the mother stating that the person to be registered ('the woman concerned') is a parent of the child by virtue of section 43 of the Human Fertilisation and Embryology Act 2008; and
  (ii) a declaration in the prescribed form which is made by the woman concerned, states herself to be a parent of the child by virtue of section 43 of that Act, and is counter-signed by a prescribed person; or
(c) at the request of the woman concerned on production of—
  (i) a declaration in the prescribed form made by the woman concerned stating herself to be a parent of the child by virtue of section 43 of the Human Fertilisation and Embryology Act 2008; and
  (ii) a declaration in the prescribed form which is made by the mother, states that the woman concerned is a parent of the child by virtue of section 43 of that Act, and is countersigned by a prescribed person; or
(d) at the request of the mother or the woman concerned on production of—
  (i) a copy of any agreement made between them under section 4ZA(1)(b) of the Children Act 1989 in relation to the child; and
  (ii) a declaration in the prescribed form by the person making the request stating that the agreement was made in compliance with section 4ZA of that Act and has not been brought to an end by an order of a court; or
(e) at the request of the mother or the woman concerned on production of—
  (i) a certified copy of an order under section 4ZA of the Children Act 1989 giving the woman concerned parental responsibility for the child; and
  (ii) a declaration in the prescribed form by the person making the request stating that the order has not been brought to an end by an order of a court; or
(f) at the request of the mother or the woman concerned on production of—
  (i) a certified copy of an order under paragraph 1 of Schedule 1 to the Children Act 1989 which requires the woman concerned to make any financial provision for the child and which is not an order falling within paragraph 4(3) of that Schedule; and
  (ii) a declaration in the prescribed form by the person making the request stating that the order has not been discharged by an order of a court; or
(g) in accordance with regulations made under section 2C (confirmation of parentage information given by mother) or section 2D (declaration before registration by person claiming to be other parent).

(1C) Subsections (1) and (1B) have effect subject to section 10ZA.

(2) Where, in the case of a child whose father and mother were not married to each other at the time of his birth, a person stating himself to be the father of the child makes a request to the registrar in accordance with paragraph (c) to (g) of subsection (1) of this section—
  (a) he shall be treated as a qualified informant concerning the birth of the child for the purposes of this Act; and
  (b) the giving of information concerning the birth of the child by that person and the signing of the register by him in the presence of the registrar shall act as a discharge of any duty of any other qualified informant under section 2A of this Act.

(2A) Where, in the case of a child to whom section 1(3) of the Family Law Reform Act 1987 does not apply, a person stating herself to be a parent of the child by virtue of section 43 of the Human Fertilisation and Embryology Act 2008 makes a request to the registrar in accordance with any of paragraphs (c) to (f) of subsection (1B)—
  (a) she shall be treated as a qualified informant concerning the birth of the child for the purposes of this Act; and

(b) the giving of information concerning the birth of the child by that person and the signing of the register by her in the presence of the registrar shall act as a discharge of any duty of any other qualified informant under section 2A of this Act.

10ZA Registration of father or second female parent by virtue of certain provisions of Human Fertilisation and Embryology Act 2008

(1) Notwithstanding anything in the foregoing provisions of this Act, the registrar shall not enter in the register—

(a) as the father of a child, the name of a man who is to be treated for that purpose as the father of the child by virtue of section 39(1) or 40(1) or (2) of the Human Fertilisation and Embryology Act 2008 (circumstances in which man to be treated as father of child for purposes of registration of birth where fertility treatment undertaken after his death); or

(b) as a parent of the child, the name of a woman who is to be treated for that purpose as a parent of the child by virtue of section 46(1) or (2) of that Act (circumstances in which woman to be treated as parent of child for purposes of registration of birth where fertility treatment undertaken after her death),

unless the condition in subsection (2) below is satisfied.

(2) The condition in this subsection is satisfied if—

(a) the mother requests the registrar to make such an entry in the register and produces the relevant documents; or

(b) in the case of the death or inability of the mother, the relevant documents are produced by some other person who is a qualified informant.

(3) In this section 'the relevant documents' means—

(a) the consent in writing and election mentioned in section 39(1), 40(1) or (2) or 46(1) or (2) (as the case requires) of the Human Fertilisation and Embryology Act 2008;

(b) a certificate of a registered medical practitioner as to the medical facts concerned; and

(c) such other documentary evidence (if any) as the registrar considers appropriate.

10A Re-registration where parents neither married nor civil partners

(1) Where there has been registered under this Act the birth of a child whose father and mother were not married to each other at the time of the birth, but no person has been registered as the father of the child (or as a parent of the child by virtue of section 42, 43 or 46(1) or (2) of the Human Fertilisation and Embryology Act 2008), the registrar shall re-register the birth so as to show a person as the father—

(a) at the joint request of the mother and that person; or

(b) at the request of the mother on production of—

(i) a declaration in the prescribed form made by the mother stating that that person is the father of the child; and

(ii) a declaration in the prescribed form which is made by that person, states himself to be the father of the child, and is countersigned by a prescribed person; or

(c) at the request of that person on production of—

(i) a declaration in the prescribed form by that person stating himself to be the father of the child; and

(ii) a declaration in the prescribed form which is made by the mother, states that that person is the father of the child, and is countersigned by a prescribed person; or

(d) at the request of the mother or that person on production of—

(i) a copy of any agreement made between them under section 4(1)(b) of the Children Act 1989 in relation to the child; and

(ii) a declaration in the prescribed form by the person making the request stating that the agreement was made in compliance with section 4 of that Act and has not been brought to an end by an order of a court; or

(e) at the request of the mother or that person on production of—
  (i) a certified copy of an order under section 4 of the Children Act 1989 giving that person parental responsibility for the child; and
  (ii) a declaration in the prescribed form by the person making the request stating that the order has not been brought to an end by an order of a court; or
(f) at the request of the mother or that person on production of—
  (i) a certified copy of an order under paragraph 1 of Schedule 1 to the Children Act 1989 which requires that person to make any financial provision for the child and which is not an order falling within paragraph 4(3) of that Schedule; and
  (ii) a declaration in the prescribed form by the person making the request stating that the order has not been discharged by an order of a court; or
(ff) in the case of a man who is to be treated as the father of the child by virtue of section 39(1) or 40(1) or (2) of the Human Fertilisation and Embryology Act 2008, if the condition in section 10ZA(2) of this Act is satisfied; or
(g) at the request of the mother or that person on production of—
  (i) a certified copy of any of the orders which are mentioned in subsection (1A) of this section which has been made in relation to the child; and
  (ii) a declaration in the prescribed form by the person making the request stating that the order has not been brought to an end or discharged by an order of a court.
but no birth shall be re-registered under this section except in the prescribed manner and with the authority of the Registrar General.

(1A) The orders are—
(a) an order under section 4 of the Family Law Reform Act 1987 that that person shall have all the parental rights and duties with respect to the child;
(b) an order that that person shall have custody or care and control or legal custody of the child made under section 9 of the Guardianship of Minors Act 1971 at a time when such an order could only be made in favour of a parent;
(c) an order under section 9 or 11B of that Act which requires that person to make any financial provision in relation to the child;
(d) an order under section 4 of the Affiliation Proceedings Act 1957 naming that person as putative father of the child.

(1B) Where there has been registered under this Act the birth of a child to whom section 1(3) of the Family Law Reform Act 1987 does not apply, but no person has been registered as a parent of the child by virtue of section 42, 43 or 46(1) or (2) of the Human Fertilisation and Embryology Act 2008 (or as the father of the child), the registrar shall re-register the birth so as to show a woman ('the woman concerned') as a parent of the child by virtue of section 43 or 46(1) or (2) of that Act—
(a) at the joint request of the mother and the woman concerned; or
(b) at the request of the mother on production of—
  (i) a declaration in the prescribed form made by the mother stating that the woman concerned is a parent of the child by virtue of section 43 of the Human Fertilisation and Embryology Act 2008; and
  (ii) a declaration in the prescribed form which is made by the woman concerned, states herself to be a parent of the child by virtue of section 43 of that Act, and is countersigned by a prescribed person; or
(c) at the request of the woman concerned on production of—
  (i) a declaration in the prescribed form made by the woman concerned stating herself to be a parent of the child by virtue of section 43 of the Human Fertilisation and Embryology Act 2008; and
  (ii) a declaration in the prescribed form which is made by the mother, states that the woman concerned is a parent of the child by virtue of section 43 of that Act, and is countersigned by a prescribed person; or

(d) at the request of the mother or the woman concerned on production of—
  (i) a copy of an agreement made between them under section 4ZA(1)(b) of the Children Act 1989 in relation to the child; and
  (ii) a declaration in the prescribed form by the person making the request stating that the agreement was made in compliance with section 4ZA of that Act and has not been brought to an end by an order of a court; or

(e) at the request of the mother or the woman concerned on production of—
  (i) a certified copy of an order under section 4ZA of the Children Act 1989 giving the woman concerned parental responsibility for the child; and
  (ii) a declaration in the prescribed form by the person making the request stating that the order has not been brought to an end by an order of a court; or

(f) at the request of the mother or the woman concerned on production of—
  (i) a certified copy of an order under paragraph 1 of Schedule 1 to the Children Act 1989 which requires the woman concerned to make any financial provision for the child and which is not an order falling within paragraph 4(3) of that Schedule; and
  (ii) a declaration in the prescribed form by the person making the request stating that the order has not been discharged by an order of a court; or

(g) in the case of a woman who is to be treated as a parent of the child by virtue of section 46(1) or (2) of the Human Fertilisation and Embryology Act 2008, if the condition in section 10ZA(2) of this Act is satisfied.

(2) On the re-registration of a birth under this section—
  (a) the registrar shall sign the register;
  (b) in the case of any of the following requests—
    (i) a request under subsection (1)(a) or (b) or subsection (1B)(a) or (b);
    (ii) a request under subsection (1)(d), (e), (f) or (g) or subsection (1B)(d), (c) or (f) made by the mother of the child,
    the mother shall also sign the register;
  (bb) in a case within subsection (1)(ff) or (1B)(g), the mother or (as the case may be) the qualified informant shall also sign the register;
  (c) in the case of a request made under subsection (1)(a) or (c) or a request made under subsection (1)(d), (e), (f) or (g) by the person requesting to be registered as the father of the child, that person shall also sign the register;
  (cc) in the case of a request made under subsection (1B)(a) or (c) or a request made under subsection (1B)(d), (e) or (f) by a woman requesting to be registered as a parent of the child by virtue of section 43 of the Human Fertilisation and Embryology Act 2008, that woman shall also sign the register; ...

10B   Re-registration after sole registration: information provided by other parent and confirmed by mother

(1) The Minister may by regulations make provision for the re-registration of a birth to show a person as the father of a relevant child, on the basis of information given by that person after the birth is registered and confirmed by the mother.

(2) In this section a 'relevant child' means a child—
  (a) whose father and mother were not married to each other at the time of the child's birth, and
  (b) whose birth has been registered before or after the commencement of this section without any person being registered as the father of the child (or as a parent of the child by virtue of section 42, 43 or 46(1) or (2) of the Human Fertilisation and Embryology Act 2008).

(3) Regulations under subsection (1) may—
  (a) enable a person who believes himself to be the father of a relevant child to make a declaration to that effect to the registrar,

(b) enable or require the registrar by notice to require the mother to state whether or not she acknowledges that the person is the father of the child, and

(c) where the mother acknowledges that the person is the father, require the registrar to re-register the birth so as to show the person as the father.

(4) In the case of a child who has a parent by virtue of section 43 of the Human Fertilisation and Embryology Act 2008, references in subsections (1) and (3) to the father are to be read as references to the woman who is a parent by virtue of that section.

...

10C   Re-registration after sole registration: information provided by mother and confirmed by other parent

(1) The Minister may by regulations make provision for the re-registration of a birth to show a person as the father of a relevant child, on the basis of information given by the mother after the birth is registered and confirmed by that person.

(2) In this section a 'relevant child' means a child—

(a) whose father and mother were not married to each other at the time of the child's birth, and

(b) whose birth has been registered before or after the commencement of this section without any person being registered as the father of the child (or as a parent of the child by virtue of section 42, 43 or 46(1) or (2) of the Human Fertilisation and Embryology Act 2008).

(3) Regulations under subsection (1) may—

(a) enable the mother of a relevant child to make a declaration to the registrar stating that a specified person ('the alleged father') is the father of the child,

(b) enable or require the registrar by notice to require the alleged father to state whether or not he acknowledges that he is the father of the child,

(c) where the alleged father acknowledges that he is the father of the child, require the alleged father to give prescribed information to the registrar, and

(d) where the alleged father gives that information to the registrar, require the registrar to re-register the birth so as to show the alleged father as the father.

(4) In the case of a child who has a parent by virtue of section 43 of the Human Fertilisation and Embryology Act 2008, references in subsections (1) and (3) to the father are to be read as references to the woman who is a parent by virtue of that section (and references to the alleged father have a corresponding meaning).

(5) Regulations under this section may—

(a) require anything to be done in a prescribed form or manner or in the presence of the registrar,

(b) make provision as to the time within which anything is required or authorised to be done.

(6) Regulations under this section may not provide for any birth to be re-registered except with the authority of the Registrar General.

(7) In this section 'prescribed' means prescribed by regulations made under this section by the Minister.

...

Matrimonial Causes (Property and Maintenance) Act 1958

(6 & 7 Eliz. 2, c. 35)

7 Extension of section 17 of Married Women's Property Act 1882

(1) Any right of a wife, under section seventeen of the Married Women's Property Act 1882 to apply to a judge of the High Court or of the family court in any question between husband and wife as to the title to or possession of property, shall include the right to make such an application where it is claimed by the wife that her husband has had in his possession or under his control—

(a) money to which, or to a share of which, she was beneficially entitled (whether by reason that it represented the proceeds of property to which, or to an interest in which, she was beneficially entitled, or for any other reason), or

(b) property (other than money) to which, or to an interest in which, she was beneficially entitled,

and that either that money or other property has ceased to be in his possession or under his control or that she does not know whether it is still in his possession or under his control.

(2) Where, on an application made to a judge of the High Court or of the family court under the said section seventeen, as extended by the preceding subsection, the judge is satisfied—

(a) that the husband has had in his possession or under his control money or other property as mentioned in paragraph (a) or paragraph (b) of the preceding subsection, and

(b) that he has not made to the wife, in respect of that money or other property, such payment or disposition as would have been appropriate in the circumstances, the power to make orders under that section shall be extended in accordance with the next following subsection.

(3) Where the last preceding subsection applies, the power to make orders under the said section seventeen shall include power for the judge to order the husband to pay to the wife—

(a) in a case falling within paragraph (a) of subsection (1) of this section, such sum in respect of the money to which the application relates, or the wife's share thereof, as the case may be, or

(b) in a case falling within paragraph (b) of the said subsection (1), such sum in respect of the value of the property to which the application relates, or the wife's interest therein, as the case may be,

as the judge may consider appropriate.

(4) Where on an application under the said section seventeen as extended by this section it appears to the judge that there is any property which—

(a) represents the whole or part of the money or property in question, and

(b) is property in respect of which an order could have been made under that section if an application had been made by the wife thereunder in a question as to the title to or possession of that property,

the judge (either in substitution for or in addition to the making of an order in accordance with the last preceding subsection) may make any order under that section in respect of that property which he could have made on such an application as is mentioned in paragraph (b) of this subsection.

(5) The preceding provisions of this section shall have effect in relation to a husband as they have effect in relation to a wife, as if any reference to the husband were a reference to the wife and any reference to the wife were a reference to the husband.

(6) Any power of a judge which is exercisable on an application under the said section seventeen shall be exercisable in relation to an application made under that section as extended by this section.

(7) For the avoidance of doubt it is hereby declared that any power conferred by the said section seventeen to make orders with respect to any property includes power to order a sale of the property.

Maintenance Orders Act 1958

(6 & 7 Eliz. 2, c. 39)

PART I REGISTRATION, ENFORCEMENT AND VARIATION OF CERTAIN MAINTENANCE ORDERS

1 Application of Part I

(1) The provisions of this Part of this Act shall have effect for the purpose of enabling maintenance orders to which this Part of this Act applies to be registered in the family court and, subject to those provisions, while so registered to be enforced in like manner as an order made by the family court and to be varied by that court.

(1A) In the following provisions of the Act 'maintenance order' means any order, decision, settlement, arrangement or instrument specified in Schedule 8 to the Administration of Justice Act 1970.

(2) For the purposes of subsection (1) above, a maintenance order made by a court in Scotland or Northern Ireland and registered in the High Court under Part II of the Maintenance Orders Act 1950 shall be deemed to have been made by the High Court.

(2A) This Part of this Act applies—

  (a) to maintenance orders made by the High Court, other than orders registered in Scotland or Northern Ireland under Part II of the Maintenance Orders Act 1950, and

  (b) to maintenance orders made by a court in Scotland or Northern Ireland and registered in the High Court under Part II of the Maintenance Orders Act 1950.

...

2 Registration of orders

(1) A person entitled to receive payments under a High Court order may apply to the High Court for registration of the order in the family court, and the High Court may, if it thinks fit, grant the application.

(2) Where an application for the registration of such an order is granted—

  (a) no proceedings shall be begun, and no writ, warrant or other process shall be issued, for the enforcement of the order before the registration of the order or the expiration of the prescribed period from the grant of the application, whichever first occurs; and

  (b) the High Court shall, on being satisfied within the period aforesaid by the person who made the application that no such proceedings or process begun or issued before the grant of the application remain pending or in force, cause a certified copy of the order to be sent to the family court;

but if at the expiration of the period aforesaid the High Court has not been so satisfied, the grant of the application shall become void.

...

(5) An officer of the family court who receives a certified copy of an order sent to the court under this section shall cause the order to be registered in that court.

...

(6ZA) Where a High Court order is registered under this Part of this Act in the family court, then—

  (a) if a means of payment order (within the meaning of section 1(7) of the Maintenance Enforcement Act 1991) has effect in relation to the order in question, it shall continue to have effect after registration; ...

(6ZC) Where by virtue of the provisions of this section payments under an order cease to be or become payable to the family court, the person liable to make the payments shall, until he is given the prescribed notice to that effect, be deemed to comply with the order if he makes payments in accordance with the order and any order under subsection (6ZA)(b) of this section of which he has received such notice.

(6A) In this section—

'High Court order' includes a maintenance order deemed to be made by the High Court by virtue of section 1(2) above,

...

3 Enforcement of registered orders

(1) Subject to the provisions of section 2A of this Act and this section, a registered order shall be enforceable in all respects as if it had been made by the court of registration and as if that court had jurisdiction to make it; and proceedings for or with respect to the enforcement of a registered order may be taken accordingly.

...

(3) Where an order remains or becomes registered after the discharge of the order, no proceedings shall be taken by virtue of that registration except in respect of arrears which were due under that order at the time of the discharge and have not been remitted.

(4) Except as provided by this section, no proceedings shall be taken for or with respect to the enforcement of a registered order.

4 Variation of orders registered in magistrates' courts

(1) The provisions of this section shall have effect with respect to the variation of High Court orders registered in the family court, and references in this section to registered orders shall be construed accordingly.

(2) Subject to the following provisions of this section—

    (a) the family court may exercise the same jurisdiction to vary any rate of payments specified by a registered order (other than jurisdiction in a case where a party to the order is not present in England when the application for variation is made) as is exercisable, apart from this subsection, by the High Court; and

    (b) a rate of payments specified by a registered order shall not be varied except by the family court or any other magistrates' court to which the jurisdiction conferred by the foregoing paragraph is extended by rules of court.

...

(4) If an application is made by virtue of subsection (2) of this section for the variation of a rate of payments specified by a registered order and it appears to the family court that it is for any reason appropriate to remit the application to the High Court, the family court shall so remit the application and the High Court shall thereupon deal with the application as if the order were not registered.

(5) Nothing in subsection (2) of this section shall affect the jurisdiction of the High Court to vary a rate of payments specified by a registered order if an application for the variation of that rate is made to that court—

    (a) in proceedings for a variation of provisions of the order which do not specify a rate of payments; or

    (b) at a time when a party to the order is not present in England.

(6) No application for any variation of a registered order shall be made to any court while proceedings for any variation of the order are pending in any other court.

...

(6B) No application for any variation of a registered order shall be made to the family court in respect of an order for periodical or other payments made under Part III of the Matrimonial and Family Proceedings Act 1984 or under Schedule 7 to the Civil Partnership Act 2004.

4A   Variation etc. of orders registered in the family court

...

(2) The family court may exercise the same powers in relation to a registered order as are exercisable by the family court under section 1 of the Maintenance Enforcement Act 1991 in relation to a qualifying periodical maintenance order (within the meaning of that section) which has been made by the family court, including the power under subsection (7) of that section to revoke, suspend, revive or vary—

...

> (b) any means of payment order (within the meaning of section 1(7) of that Act of 1991) made by virtue of the provisions of this section.

5   Cancellation of registration

(1) If a person entitled to receive payments under a registered order desires the registration to be cancelled, he may give notice under this section.

(2) Where the original court varies or discharges an order registered in the family court, the original court may, if it thinks fit, give notice under this section.

...

(4) Notice under this section shall be given to the court of registration; and where such notice is given—

> (a) no proceedings for the enforcement of the registered order shall be begun before the cancellation of the registration and no writ, warrant or other process for the enforcement thereof shall be issued in consequence of any such proceedings begun before the giving of the notice;
>
> (b) ...; and
>
> (c) the court of registration shall cancel the registration on being satisfied in the prescribed manner—
>
> > (i)   that no process for the enforcement of the registered order issued before the giving of the notice remains in force; and
> >
> > (ii) in the case of an order registered in the family court, that no proceedings for the variation of the order are pending in the family court.

(4A) For the purposes of a notice under subsection (2) or (3) above—

'court of registration' includes any court in which an order is registered under Part II of the Maintenance Orders Act 1950, and

'registration' includes registration under that Act.

(5) On the cancellation of the registration of a High Court order—

> (a) any order which requires payments under the order in question to be made by any method of payment falling within section 1(5) of the Maintenance Enforcement Act 1991 (standing order, etc), other than an order which requires payments to be made to the family court, is to continue to have effect, and
>
> (b) any order which requires payments under the order in question to be made to the family court (whether or not by any method of payment falling within section 1(5) of the Maintenance Enforcement Act 1991) is to cease to have effect;

but, in a case falling within paragraph (b) of this subsection, until the defendant receives the prescribed notice of the cancellation he shall be deemed to comply with the High Court order if he makes payment in accordance with any such order as is referred to in paragraph (b) of this subsection which was in force immediately before the cancellation and of which he has notice.

...

(7) In subsection (5) of this section 'High Court order' shall be construed in accordance with section 2(6A) of this Act.

…

Marriage (Enabling) Act 1960

(8 & 9 Eliz., c. 29)

1   Certain marriages not to be void

(1) No marriage hereafter contracted (whether in or out of Great Britain) between a man and a woman who is the sister, aunt or niece of a former wife of his (whether living or not), or was formerly the wife of his brother, uncle or nephew (whether living or not), shall by reason of that relationship be void or voidable under any enactment or rule of law applying in Great Britain as a marriage between persons within the prohibited degrees of affinity.

(2) In the foregoing subsection words of kinship apply equally to kin of the whole and of the half blood.

(3) This section does not validate a marriage, if either party to it is at the time of the marriage domiciled in a country outside Great Britain, and under the law of that country there cannot be a valid marriage between the parties.

Law Reform (Husband and Wife) Act 1962

(10 & 11 Eliz. 2, c. 48)

1   Actions in tort between husband and wife

(1) Subject to the provisions of this section, each of the parties to a marriage shall have the like right of action in tort against the other as if they were not married.

(2) Where an action in tort is brought by one of the parties to a marriage against the other during the subsistence of the marriage, the court may stay the action if it appears—

    (a) that no substantial benefit would accrue to either party from the continuation of the proceedings; or

    (b) that the question or questions in issue could more conveniently be disposed of on an application made under section seventeen of the Married Women's Property Act 1882 (determination of questions between husband and wife as to the title to or possession of property);

and without prejudice to paragraph (b) of this section the court may, in such an action, either exercise any power which could be exercised on an application under the said section seventeen, or give such directions as it thinks fit for the disposal under that section of any question arising in the proceedings.

…

3   Short title, interpretation, saving and extent

(3) The reference in subsection (1) of section one of this Act to the parties to a marriage include references to the persons who were parties to a marriage which has been dissolved.

Matrimonial Causes Act 1965

(1965 c. 72)

PART I DIVORCE, NULLITY AND OTHER MATRIMONIAL SUITS

Divorce

8 Remarriage of divorced persons

(2) No clergyman of the Church of England or the Church in Wales shall be compelled—

(a) to solemnize the marriage of any person whose former marriage has been dissolved and whose former spouse is still living; or

(b) to permit the marriage of such a person to be solemnized in the church or chapel of which he is the minister.

...

Civil Evidence Act 1968

(1968 c. 64)

PART II MISCELLANEOUS AND GENERAL

12 Findings of adultery and paternity as evidence in civil proceedings

(1) In any civil proceedings—

(a) the fact that a person has been found guilty of adultery in any matrimonial proceedings; and

(b) the fact that a person has been found to be the father of a child in relevant proceedings before any court in England or Wales or Northern Ireland or has been adjudged to be the father of a child in affiliation proceedings before any court in the United Kingdom;

shall (subject to subsection (3) below) be admissible in evidence for the purpose of proving, where to do so is relevant to any issue in those civil proceedings, that he committed the adultery to which the finding relates, or, as the case may be, is (or was) the father of that child, whether or not he offered any defence to the allegation of adultery or paternity and whether or not he is a party to the civil proceedings; but no finding or adjudication other than a subsisting one shall be admissible in evidence by virtue of this section.

(2) In any civil proceedings in which by virtue of this section a person is proved to have been found guilty of adultery as mentioned in subsection (1)(a) above or to have been found or adjudged to be the father of a child as mentioned in subsection (1)(b) above—

(a) he shall he taken to have committed the adultery to which the finding relates, or as the case may be, to be (or have been) the father of that child, unless the contrary is proved; and

(b) without prejudice to the reception of any other admissible evidence for the purpose of identifying the facts on which the finding or adjudication was based, the contents of any document which was before the court, or which contains any pronouncement of the court in the other proceedings in question shall be admissible in evidence for that purpose.

(3) Nothing in this section shall prejudice the operation of any enactment whereby a finding of fact in any matrimonial or affiliation proceedings is for the purposes of any other proceedings made conclusive evidence of any fact.

...

(5) In this section—

'matrimonial proceedings' means any matrimonial cause in the High Court or family court in England and Wales ... or any appeal arising out of any such cause or action;

'relevant proceedings' means—

(a) proceedings on a complaint under section 42 of the National Assistance Act 1948 or section 26 of the Social Security Act 1986;

(b) proceedings under the Children Act 1989;

...

Privilege

14   Privilege against incrimination of self or spouse or civil partner

(1) The right of a person in any legal proceedings other than criminal proceedings to refuse to answer any question or produce any document or thing if to do so would tend to expose that person to proceedings for an offence or for the recovery of a penalty—

(a) shall apply only as regards criminal offences under the law of any part of the United Kingdom and penalties provided for by such law; and

(b) shall include a like right to refuse to answer any question or produce any document or thing if to do so would tend to expose the spouse or civil partner of the person to proceedings for any such criminal offence or for the recovery of any such penalty.

...

Family Law Reform Act 1969

(1969 c. 46)

PART I   REDUCTION OF AGE OF MAJORITY AND RELATED PROVISIONS

1   Reduction of age of majority from 21 to 18

(1) As from the date on which this section comes into force a person shall attain full age on attaining the age of eighteen instead of on attaining the age of twenty-one; and a person shall attain full age on that date if he has then already attained the age of eighteen but not the age of twenty one.

(2) The foregoing subsection applies for the purposes of any rule of law, and, in the absence of a definition or of any indication of a contrary intention, for the construction of 'full age,' 'infant,' 'infancy,' 'minor,' 'minority' and similar expressions in—

(a) any statutory provision, whether passed or made before, on or after the date on which this section comes into force; and

(b) any deed, will or other instrument of whatever nature (not being a statutory provision) made on or after that date.

...

(7) Notwithstanding any rule of law, a will or codicil executed before the date on which this section comes into force shall not be treated for the purposes of this section as made on or after that date by reason only that the will or codicil is confirmed by a codicil executed on or after that date.

8   Consent by persons over 16 to surgical, medical and dental treatment

(1) The consent of a minor who has attained the age of sixteen years to any surgical, medical or dental treatment which, in the absence of consent, would constitute a trespass to his person, shall be as effective as it would be if he were of full age; and where a minor has by virtue of this section given an effective consent to any treatment it shall not be necessary to obtain any consent for it from his parent or guardian.

(2) In this section 'surgical, medical or dental treatment' includes any procedure undertaken for the purposes of diagnosis, and this section applies to any procedure (including, in particular, the administration of an anaesthetic) which is ancillary to any treatment as it applies to that treatment.

(3) Nothing in this section shall be construed as making ineffective any consent which would have been effective if this section had not been enacted.

9   Time at which a person attains a particular age

(1) The time at which a person attains a particular age expressed in years shall be the commencement of the relevant anniversary of the date of his birth.

(2) This section applies only where the relevant anniversary falls on a date after that on which this section comes into force, and, in relation to any enactment, deed, will or other instrument, has effect subject to any provision therein.

12   Persons under full age may be described as minors instead of infants

A person who is not of full age may be described as a minor instead of as an infant, and accordingly in this Act 'minor' means such a person as aforesaid.

19   Policies of assurance and property in industrial and provident societies

(1) In section 11 of the Married Women's Property Act 1882 (policies of assurance effected for the benefit of children) the expression 'children' shall include illegitimate children.

…

PART III PROVISIONS FOR USE OF SCIENTIFIC TESTS IN DETERMINING PARENTAGE

20   Power of court to require use of scientific tests

(1) In any civil proceedings in which the parentage of any person falls to be determined, the court may, either of its own motion or on an application by any party to the proceedings, give a direction—

  (a) for the use of scientific tests to ascertain whether such tests show that a party to the proceedings is or is not the father or mother of that person; and

  (b) for the taking, within a period specified in the direction, of bodily samples from all or any of the following, namely, that person, any party who is alleged to be the father or mother of that person and any other party to the proceedings;

and the court may at any time revoke or vary a direction previously given by it under this subsection.

(1A) Tests required by a direction under this section may only be carried out by a body which has been accredited for the purposes of this section by—

  (a) the Lord Chancellor, or

  (b) a body appointed by him for the purpose.

(2) The individual carrying out scientific tests in pursuance of a direction under subsection (1) above shall make to the court a report in which he shall state—

  (a) the results of the tests;

  (b) whether any party to whom the report relates is or is not excluded by the results from being the father or mother of the person whose parentage is to be determined; and

(c) in relation to any party who is not so excluded, the value, if any, of the results in determining whether that party is the father or mother of that person;

and the report shall be received by the court as evidence in the proceedings of the matters stated in it.

(2A) Where the proceedings in which the parentage of any person falls to be determined are proceedings on an application under section 55A or 56 of the Family Law Act 1986, any reference in subsection (1) or (2) of this section to any party to the proceedings shall include a reference to any person named in the application.

(3) A report under subsection (2) of this section shall be in the form prescribed by regulations made under section 22 of this Act.

(4) Where a report has been made to a court under subsection (2) of this section, any party may, with the leave of the court, or shall, if the court so directs, obtain from the tester a written statement explaining or amplifying any statement made in the report, and that statement shall be deemed for the purposes of this section (except subsection (3) thereof) to form part of the report made to the court.

...

21   Consents, etc., required for taking of bodily samples

(1) Subject to the provisions of subsections (3) and (4) of this section, a bodily sample which is required to be taken from any person for the purpose of giving effect to a direction under section 20 of this Act shall not be taken from that person except with his consent.

(2) The consent of a minor who has attained the age of sixteen years to the taking from himself of a bodily sample shall be as effective as it would be if he were of full age; and where a minor has by virtue of this subsection given an effective consent to the taking of a bodily sample it shall not be necessary to obtain any consent for it from any other person.

(3) A bodily sample may be taken from a person under the age of sixteen years, not being a person as is referred to in subsection (4) of this section,

(a) if the person who has the care and control of him consents; or

(b) where that person does not consent, if the court considers that it would be in his best interests for the sample to be taken.

(4) A bodily sample may be taken from a person who lacks capacity (within the meaning of the Mental Capacity Act 2005) to give his consent, if consent is given by the court giving the direction under section 20 or by—

(a) a donee of an enduring power of attorney or lasting power of attorney (within the meaning of that Act), or

(b) a deputy appointed, or any other person authorised, by the Court of Protection,with power in that respect.

(5) The foregoing provisions of this section are without prejudice to the provisions of section 23 of this Act.

...

23   Failure to comply with direction for taking bodily samples

(1) Where a court gives a direction under section 20 of this Act and any person fails to take any step required of him for the purpose of giving effect to the direction, the court may draw such inferences, if any, from that fact as appear proper in the circumstances.

(2) Where in any proceedings in which the parentage of any person falls to be determined by the court hearing the proceedings there is a presumption of law that that person is legitimate, then if—

(a) a direction is given under section 20 of this Act in those proceedings, and

(b) any party who is claiming any relief in the proceedings and who for the purpose of obtaining that relief is entitled to rely on the presumption fails to take any step required of him for the purpose of giving effect to the direction, the court may adjourn the hearing for such period as it thinks fit to enable that party to take that step, and if at the end of that period he has failed without reasonable cause to take it the court may, without prejudice to subsection (1) of this section, dismiss his claim for relief notwithstanding the absence of evidence to rebut the presumption.

(3) Where any person named in a direction under section 20 of this Act fails to consent to the taking of a bodily sample from himself or from any person named in the direction of whom he has the care and control, he shall be deemed for the purposes of this section to have failed to take a step required of him for the purpose of giving effect to the direction.

24   Penalty for personating another, etc., for purposes of providing bodily sample

If for the purpose of providing a bodily sample for a test required to give effect to a direction under section 20 of this Act any person personates another, or proffers a child knowing that it is not the child named in the direction, he shall be liable—

(a) on conviction on indictment, to imprisonment for a term not exceeding two years, or

(b) on summary conviction, to a fine not exceeding the prescribed sum.

25   Interpretation of Part III

In this Part of this Act the following expressions have the meanings hereby respectively assigned to them, that is to say—

'bodily sample' means a sample of bodily fluid or bodily tissue taken for the purpose of scientific tests;

'excluded' means excluded subject to the occurrence of mutation, to section 27 of the Family Law Reform Act 1987, to sections 27 to 29 of the Human Fertilisation and Embryology Act 1990 and to sections 33 to 47 of the Human Fertilisation and Embryology Act 2008;

'scientific tests' means scientific tests carried out under this Part of this Act and made with the object of ascertaining the inheritable characteristics of bodily fluids or bodily tissue.

PART IV MISCELLANEOUS AND GENERAL

26   Rebuttal of presumption as to legitimacy and illegitimacy

Any presumption of law as to the legitimacy or illegitimacy of any person may in any civil proceedings be rebutted by evidence which shows that it is more probable than not that that person is illegitimate or legitimate, as the case may be, and it shall not be necessary to prove that fact beyond reasonable doubt in order to rebut the presumption.

...

Law Reform (Miscellaneous Provisions) Act 1970

(1970 c. 33)

Legal consequences of termination of contract to marry

1   Engagements to marry not enforceable at law

(1) An agreement between two persons to marry one another shall not under the law of England and Wales have effect as a contract giving rise to legal rights and no action shall lie in England and Wales for breach of such an agreement, whatever the law applicable to the agreement.

(2) This section shall have effect in relation to agreements entered into before it comes into force, except that it shall not affect any action commenced before it comes into force.

2   Property of engaged couples

(1) Where an agreement to marry is terminated, any rule of law relating to the rights of husbands and wives in relation to property in which either or both has or have a beneficial interest, including any such rule as explained by section 37 of the Matrimonial Proceedings and Property Act 1970, shall apply, in relation to any property in which either or both of the parties to the agreement had a beneficial interest while the agreement was in force, as it applies in relation to property in which a husband or wife has a beneficial interest.

(2) Where an agreement to marry is terminated, section 17 of the Married Women's Property Act 1882 and section 7 of the Matrimonial Causes (Property and Maintenance) Act 1958 (which sections confer power on a judge of the High Court or the family court to settle disputes between husband and wife about property) shall apply, as if the parties were married, to any dispute between, or claim by, one of them in relation to property in which either or both had a beneficial interest while the agreement was in force; but an application made by virtue of this section to the judge under the said section 17, as originally enacted or as extended by the said section 7, shall be made within three years of the termination of the agreement.

3   Gifts between engaged couples

(1) A party to an agreement to marry who makes a gift of property to the other party to the agreement on the condition (express or implied) that it shall be returned if the agreement is terminated shall not be prevented from recovering the property by reason only of his having terminated the agreement.

(2) The gift of an engagement ring shall be presumed to be an absolute gift; this presumption may be rebutted by proving that the ring was given on the condition, express or implied, that it should be returned if the marriage did not take place for any reason.

...

Enticement of spouse, etc.

5   Abolition of actions for enticement, seduction and harbouring of spouse or child

No person shall be liable in tort under the law of England and Wales—

  (a) to any other person on the ground only of his having induced the wife or husband of that other person to leave or remain apart from the other spouse;

  (b) to a parent (or person standing in the place of a parent) on the ground only of his having deprived the parent (or other person) of the services of his or her child by raping, seducing or enticing that child; or

  (c) to any other person for harbouring the wife or child of that other person, except in the case of action accruing before this Act comes into force if an action in respect thereof has been begun before this Act comes into force.

Marriage (Registrar General's Licence) Act 1970

(1970 c. 34)

1   Marriages which may be solemnised by Registrar General's licence

(1) Subject to the provisions of subsection (2) below, any marriage which may be solemnised on the authority of certificates of a superintendent registrar may be solemnised on the authority of the Registrar General's licence elsewhere than at a registered building, the office of a superintendent registrar, or approved premises.

Provided that any such marriage shall not be solemnised according to the rites of the Church of England or the Church in Wales.

(2) The Registrar General shall not issue any licence for the solemnisation of a marriage as is mentioned in subsection (1) above unless he is satisfied that one of the persons to be married is seriously ill and is not expected to recover and cannot be moved to a place at which under the provisions of the Marriage Act 1949 (hereinafter called the 'principal Act') the marriage could be solemnised (disregarding for this purpose the provisions of that Act relating to marriages in pursuance of section 26(1)(dd) or 26B(6) of that Act).

(3) A marriage of a same sex couple according to religious rites or usages may not be solemnized in accordance with this Act unless the relevant governing authority has given written consent to marriages of same sex couples according to those religious rites or usages.

(4) For that purpose—

'relevant governing authority' means the person or persons recognised by the members of the relevant religious organisation as competent for the purpose of giving consent for the purposes of this section;

'relevant religious organisation' means the religious organisation according to whose rites or usages the marriage is to be solemnized.

2 Notice of marriage

(1) Where a marriage is intended to be solemnised on the authority of the Registrar General's licence, notice shall be given in the prescribed form by either of the persons to be married to the superintendent registrar of the registration district in which it is intended that the marriage shall be solemnised, and the notice shall state by or before whom it is intended that the marriage shall be solemnised.

(2) The provisions of section 27(4) of the principal Act (which relate to entries in the marriage notice book) shall apply to notices of marriage on the authority of the Registrar General's licence.

(3) The provisions of section 28 of the principal Act (declaration to accompany notice of marriage) shall apply to the giving of notice under this Act with the exception of paragraph (b) of subsection (1) of that section and with the modification that in section 28(2) references to the registrar of births and deaths or of marriages and deputy registrar shall be omitted.

(4) Sections 27D and 28A(1A) and (2) of the principal Act apply (with the appropriate modifications) to a marriage intended to be solemnized in pursuance of this Act as they apply to a marriage intended to be solemnized in pursuance of 26B(2), (4) or (6) of that Act.

3 Evidence of capacity, consent etc., to be produced

The person giving notice to the superintendent registrar under the provisions of the foregoing section shall produce to the superintendent registrar such evidence as the Registrar General may require to satisfy him—

(a) that there is no lawful impediment to the marriage;

(b) that the consent of any person whose consent to the marriage is required under section 3 of the principal Act has been duly given; and

(c) that there is sufficient reason why a licence should be granted;

(d) that the conditions contained in section 1(2) of this Act are satisfied and that the person in respect of whom such conditions are satisfied is able to and does understand the nature and purport of the marriage ceremony;

Provided that the certificate of a registered medical practitioner shall be sufficient evidence of any or all of the matters in subsection (1)(d) of this section referred to.

4 Application to be reported to Registrar General

Upon receipt of any notice and evidence as mentioned in sections 2 and 3 above respectively the superintendent registrar shall inform the Registrar General and shall comply with any directions he may give for verifying the evidence given.

5   Caveat against issue of Registrar General's licence

The provisions of section 29 of the principal Act (caveat against issue of certificate) shall apply to the issue of a licence by the Registrar General with the modification that a caveat may be entered with either the superintendent registrar or the Registrar General and in either case it shall be for the Registrar General to examine into the matter of the caveat and to decide whether or not the licence should be granted and his decision shall be final, and with a further modification that the references to the superintendent registrar in that section shall refer to the superintendent registrar of the registration district in which the marriage is intended to be solemnised.

6   Marriage of persons under eighteen

The provisions of section 3 of the principal Act (marriage of persons under 18) shall apply for the purposes of this Act to a marriage intended to be solemnised by Registrar General's licence as they apply to a marriage intended to be solemnised on the authority of certificates of a superintendent registrar under Part III of the principal Act with the modification that if the consent of any person whose consent is required under that Act cannot be obtained by reason of absence or inaccessibility or by reason of his being under any disability, the superintendent registrar shall not be required to dispense with the necessity for the consent of that person and the Registrar General may dispense with the necessity of obtaining the consent of that person, whether or not there is any other person whose consent is also required.

7   Issue of licence by Registrar General

Where the marriage is intended to be solemnised on the authority of the Registrar General and he is satisfied that sufficient grounds exist why a licence should be granted he shall issue in the prescribed form unless—

(a)   any lawful impediment to the issue of the licence has been shown to his satisfaction to exist; or

(b)   the issue of the licence has been forbidden under section 30 of the principal Act.

8   Period of validity of licence

(1)   A marriage may be solemnised on the authority of the Registrar General's licence at any time within one month from the day on which the notice of marriage was entered in the marriage notice book.

(2)   If the marriage is not solemnised within the said period of one month, the notice of marriage and the licence shall be void, and no person shall solemnise the marriage on the authority thereof.

9   Place of solemnisation

A marriage on the authority of the Registrar General's licence shall be solemnised in the place stated in the notice of marriage.

10   Manner of solemnisation

(1)   Any marriage to be solemnised on the authority of the Registrar General's licence shall be solemnised at the wish of the persons to be married either—

(a)   according to such form or ceremony, not being the rites or ceremonies of the Church of England or the Church in Wales, as the persons to be married shall see fit to adopt, or

(b)   by civil ceremony.

(2)   Except where the marriage is solemnised according to the usages of the Society of Friends or is a marriage between two persons professing the Jewish religion according to the usages of the Jews, it shall be solemnised in the presence of a registrar:

Provided that where the marriage is to be by civil ceremony it shall be solemnised in the presence of the superintendent registrar as well as the registrar.

(3)   Except where the marriage is solemnised according to the usages of the Society of Friends or is a marriage between two persons professing the Jewish religion according to the usages of the Jews, the persons to be married shall in some part of the ceremony in the presence of two or more

witnesses and the registrar and, where appropriate, the superintendent registrar, make the declaration and say to one another the words prescribed by section 44(3) or (3A) of the principal Act.

(4) No person who is a clergyman within the meaning of section 78 of the principal Act shall solemnise any marriage which is solemnised on the authority of the Registrar General.

11   Civil marriage followed by religious ceremony

(1) If the parties to a marriage solemnised on the authority of the Registrar General's licence before a superintendent registrar desire to add the religious ceremony ordained or used by the church or persuasion of which they are members and have given notice of their desire so to do a clergyman or minister of that church or persuasion upon the production of a certificate of their marriage before the superintendent registrar and upon the payment of the customary fees (if any), may, if he sees fit, read or celebrate in the presence of the parties to the marriage the marriage service of the church or persuasion to which he belongs or nominate some other minister to do so.

(2) The provisions of section 46(2) and (3) of the principal Act shall apply to such a reading or celebration as they apply to the reading or celebration of a marriage service following a marriage solemnised in the office of a superintendent registrar.

12   Proof of certain matters not necessary to validity of marriages

The provisions of section 48 of the principal Act (proof of certain matters not necessary to validity of marriages) shall apply with the appropriate modifications to a marriage solemnised under the authority of the Registrar General's licence as they apply to a marriage solemnised under the authority of a certificate of a superintendent registrar.

13   Void marriages

The provisions of section 49 of the principal Act (void marriages) shall apply to a marriage under the authority of the Registrar General's licence:—

(a) with the substitution in paragraph (b) for the words from 'certificates for marriage' onwards of the words 'a Registrar General's licence';

(c) with the substitution for paragraph (d) of the words 'on the authority of a licence which is void by virtue of section 8(2) of the Marriage (Registrar General's Licence) Act 1970';

(d) with the substitution for paragraph (e) of the words 'in any place other than the place specified in the notice of marriage and the Registrar General's licence';

(e) with the substitution for paragraphs (f) and (g) of the words 'in the absence of a registrar or, where the marriage is by civil ceremony, of a superintendent registrar, except where the marriage is solemnised according to the usages of the Society of Friends or is a marriage between two persons professing the Jewish religion according to the usages of the Jews.'

13A   Void marriages: additional provision about same sex couples

(1) If a same sex couple knowingly and wilfully intermarries under the provisions of this Act in the absence of the required consent, the marriage shall be void.

(2) In this section 'required consent' means consent under section 1(3).

14   Documentary authority for marriage

Where a marriage is to be solemnised on the authority of the Registrar General's licence a document issued by the superintendent registrar stating that the Registrar General's licence has been granted and that authority for the marriage to be solemnised has been given shall be delivered before the marriage to the following person, that is to say—

(a) if the marriage is to be solemnised according to the usages of the Society of Friends, the registering officer of that Society for the place where the marriage is to be solemnised;

(b) if the marriage is to be solemnised according to the usages of persons professing the Jewish religion, the officer of the synagogue by whom the marriage is required to be registered under Part IV of the principal Act;

(c) in any other case, the registrar in whose presence the marriage is to be solemnised.

15   Registration of marriages

A marriage solemnised on the authority of the Registrar General's licence shall be registered in accordance with the provisions of the principal Act which apply to the registration of marriages solemnised in the presence of a registrar or according to the usages of the Society of Friends or of persons professing the Jewish religion.

16   Offences

(1) It shall be an offence knowingly and wilfully—

  (a) to solemnise a marriage by Registrar General's licence in any place other than the place specified in the licence;

  (b) to solemnise a marriage by Registrar General's licence without the presence of a registrar except in the case of a marriage according to the usages of the Society of Friends or a marriage between two persons professing the Jewish religion according to the usages of the Jews;

  (c) to solemnise a marriage by Registrar General's licence after the expiration of one month from the date of entry of the notice of marriage in the marriage notice book;

  (d) to give false information by way of evidence as required by section 3 of this Act;

  (e) to give a false certificate as provided for in section 3 (1) (d) of this Act; and any person found guilty of any of the above-mentioned offences shall be liable on summary conviction to a fine not exceeding the prescribed sum or on indictment to a fine or to imprisonment not exceeding three years or to both such fine and such imprisonment.

(2) A superintendent registrar who knowingly and wilfully solemnises or permits to be solemnised in his presence, or a registrar who knowingly and wilfully registers a marriage by Registrar General's licence which is void by virtue of Part III of the principal Act as amended by this Act shall be guilty of an offence and shall be liable on summary conviction to a fine not exceeding the prescribed sum or on indictment to a fine or to imprisonment not exceeding three years or to both such fine and such imprisonment.

(3) No prosecution under this section shall be commenced after the expiration of three years from the commission of the offence.

(4) The provisions of section 75(2)(a) of the principal Act shall not apply to a marriage solemnised on the authority of the Registrar General's licence.

Matrimonial Proceedings and Property Act 1970

(1970 c. 45)

Provisions relating to property of married persons

37   Contributions by spouse in money or money's worth to the improvement of property

It is hereby declared that where a husband or wife contributes in money or money's worth to the improvement of real or personal property in which or in the proceeds of sale of which either or both of them has or have a beneficial interest, the husband or wife so contributing shall, if the contribution is of a substantial nature and subject to any agreement between them to the contrary express or implied, be treated as having then acquired by virtue of his or her contribution a share or an enlarged share, as the case may be, in that beneficial interest of such an extent as may have been then agreed or, in default of such agreement, as may seem in all the circumstances just to any court before which the question of the existence or extent of the beneficial interest of the husband or wife arises (whether in proceedings between them or in other proceedings).

39   Extension of section 17 of Married Women's Property Act 1882

An application may be made to the High Court or the family court under section 17 of the Married Women's Property Act 1882 (powers of the court in disputes between husband and wife about property) (including that section as extended by section 7 of the Matrimonial Causes (Property and Maintenance) Act 1958) by either of the parties to a marriage notwithstanding that their marriage has been dissolved or annulled so long as the application is made within the period of three years beginning with the date on which the marriage was dissolved or annulled; and references in the said section 17 and the said section 7 to a husband or a wife shall be construed accordingly.

…

Land Charges Act 1972

(1972 c. 61)

2   The register of land charges

(1) If a charge on or obligation affecting land falls into one of the classes described in this section, it may be registered in the register of land charges as a land charge of that class.

…

(7) A Class F land charge is a charge affecting any land by virtue of Part IV of the Family Law Act 1996.

Matrimonial Causes Act 1973

(1973 c. 18)

PART I DIVORCE, NULLITY AND OTHER MATRIMONIAL SUITS

Divorce

1   Divorce on breakdown of marriage

(1) Subject to section 3 below, a petition for divorce may be presented to the court by either party to a marriage on the ground that the marriage has broken down irretrievably.

(2) The court hearing a petition for divorce shall not hold the marriage to have broken down irretrievably unless the petitioner satisfies the court of one or more of the following facts, that is to say—

(a) that the respondent has committed adultery and the petitioner finds it intolerable to live with the respondent;

(b) that the respondent has behaved in such a way that the petitioner cannot reasonably be expected to live with the respondent;

(c) that the respondent has deserted the petitioner for a continuous period of at least two years immediately preceding the presentation of the petition;

(d) that the parties to the marriage have lived apart for a continuous period of at least two years immediately preceding the presentation of the petition (hereafter in this Act referred to as 'two years' separation') and the respondent consents to a decree being granted;

(e) that the parties to the marriage have lived apart for a continuous period of at least five years immediately preceding the presentation of the petition (hereafter in this Act referred to as 'five years' separation').

(3) On a petition for divorce it shall be the duty of the court to enquire, so far as it reasonably can, into the facts alleged by the petitioner and into any facts alleged by the respondent.

(4) If the court is satisfied on the evidence of any such fact as is mentioned in subsection (2) above, then, unless it is satisfied on all the evidence that the marriage has not broken down irretrievably, it shall, subject to section 5 below, grant a decree of divorce.

(5) Every decree of divorce shall in the first instance be a decree nisi and shall not be made absolute before the expiration of six months from its grant unless the High Court by general order from time to time fixes a shorter period, or unless in any particular case the court in which the proceedings are for the time being pending from time to time by special order fixes a shorter period than the period otherwise applicable for the time being by virtue of this subsection.

(6) Only conduct between the respondent and a person of the opposite sex may constitute adultery for the purposes of this section.

2 Supplemental provision as to facts raising presumption of breakdown

(1) One party to a marriage shall not be entitled to rely for the purposes of section 1(2)(a) above on adultery committed by the other if, after it became known to him that the other had committed that adultery, the parties have lived with each other for a period exceeding, or periods together exceeding, six months.

(2) Where the parties to a marriage have lived with each other after it became known to one party that the other had committed adultery, but subsection (1) above does not apply, in any proceedings for divorce in which the petitioner relies on that adultery the fact that the parties have lived with each other after that time shall be disregarded in determining for the purposes of section 1(2)(a) above whether the petitioner finds it intolerable to live with the respondent.

(3) Where in any proceedings for divorce the petitioner alleges that the respondent has behaved in such a way that the petitioner cannot reasonably be expected to live with him, but the parties to the marriage have lived with each other for a period or periods after the date of the occurrence of the final incident relied on by the petitioner and held by the court to support his allegation, that fact shall be disregarded in determining for the purposes of section 1(2)(b) above whether the petitioner cannot reasonably be expected to live with the respondent if the length of that period or of those periods together was six months or less.

(4) For the purposes of section 1(2)(c) above the court may treat a period of desertion as having continued at a time when the deserting party was incapable of continuing the necessary intention if the evidence before the court is such that, had that party not been so incapable, the court would have inferred that his desertion continued at that time.

(5) In considering for the purposes of section 1(2) above whether the period for which the respondent has deserted the petitioner or the period for which the parties to a marriage have lived apart has been continuous, no account shall be taken of any one period (not exceeding six months) or of any two or more periods (not exceeding six months in all) during which the parties resumed living with each other, but no period during which the parties lived with each other shall count as part of the period of desertion, or of the period for which the parties to the marriage lived apart, as the case may be.

(6) For the purposes of section 1(2)(d) and (e) above and this section a husband and wife shall be treated as living apart unless they are living with each other in the same household, and references in this section to the parties to a marriage living with each other shall be construed as references to their living with each other in the same household.

(7) Provision shall be made by rules of court for the purpose of ensuring that where in pursuance of section 1(2)(d) above the petitioner alleges that the respondent consents to a decree being granted the respondent has been given such information as will enable him to understand the consequences to him of his consenting to a decree being granted and the steps which he must take to indicate that he consents to the grant of a decree.

3   Bar on petitions for divorce within one year of marriage

(1)   No petition for divorce shall be presented to the court before the expiration of the period of one year from the date of the marriage.

(2)   Nothing in this section shall prohibit the presentation of a petition based on matters which occurred before the expiration of that period.

4   Divorce not precluded by previous judicial separation

(1)   A person shall not be prevented from presenting a petition for divorce, or the court from granting a decree of divorce, by reason only that the petitioner or respondent has at any time, on the same facts or substantially the same facts as those proved in support of the petition, been granted a decree of judicial separation or an order under, or having effect as if made under, the Matrimonial Proceedings (Magistrates' Courts) Act 1960 or Part I of the Domestic Proceedings and Magistrates' Courts Act 1978 or any corresponding enactments in force in Northern Ireland, the Isle of Man or any of the Channel Islands.

(2)   On a petition for divorce in such a case as is mentioned in subsection (1) above, the court may treat the decree or order as sufficient proof of any adultery, desertion or other fact by reference to which it was granted, but shall not grant a decree of divorce without receiving evidence from the petitioner.

(3)   Where a petition for divorce in such a case follows a decree of judicial separation or (subject to subsection (5) below) an order containing a provision exempting one party to the marriage from the obligation to cohabit with the other, for the purposes of that petition a period of desertion immediately preceding the institution of the proceedings for the decree or order shall, if the parties have not resumed cohabitation and the decree or order has been continuously in force since it was granted, be deemed immediately to precede the presentation of the petition.

(4)   For the purposes of section 1(2)(c) above the court may treat as a period during which the respondent has deserted the petitioner any of the following periods, that is to say—

  (a)   any period during which there is in force an injunction granted by the High Court, the family court or the county court which excludes the respondent from the matrimonial home;

  (b)   any period during which there is in force an order made by the High Court or a county court under section 1 or 9 of the Matrimonial Homes Act 1983 which prohibits the exercise by the respondent of the right to occupy a dwelling-house in which the applicant and the respondent have or at any time have had a matrimonial home;

  (c)   any period during which there is in force an order made by a magistrates' court under section 16(3) of the Domestic Proceedings and Magistrates' Courts Act 1978 which requires the respondent to leave the matrimonial home or prohibits the respondent from entering the matrimonial home.

(5)   Where—

  (a)   a petition for divorce is presented after the date on which Part I of the Domestic Proceedings and Magistrates' Courts Act 1978 comes into force, and

  (b)   an order made under the Matrimonial Proceedings (Magistrates' Courts) Act 1960 containing a provision exempting the petitioner from the obligation to cohabit with the respondent is in force on that date,

then, for the purposes of section 1(2)(c) above, the court may treat a period during which such a provision was included in that order (whether before or after that date) as a period during which the respondent has deserted the petitioner.

5   Refusal of decree in five year separation cases on ground of grave hardship to respondent

(1)   The respondent to a petition for divorce in which the petitioner alleges five years' separation may oppose the grant of a decree on the ground that the dissolution of the marriage will result in grave financial or other hardship to him and that it would in all the circumstances be wrong to dissolve the marriage.

(2) Where the grant of a decree is opposed by virtue of this section, then—

    (a) if the court finds that the petitioner is entitled to rely in support of his petition on the fact of five years' separation and makes no such finding as to any other fact mentioned in section 1(2) above, and

    (b) if apart from this section the court would grant a decree on the petition, the court shall consider all the circumstances, including the conduct of the parties to the marriage and the interests of those parties and of any children or other persons concerned, and if of opinion that the dissolution of the marriage will result in grave financial or other hardship to the respondent and that it would in all the circumstances be wrong to dissolve the marriage it shall dismiss the petition.

(3) For the purposes of this section hardship shall include the loss of the chance of acquiring any benefit which the respondent might acquire if the marriage were not dissolved.

6 Attempts at reconciliation of parties to marriage

(1) Provision shall be made by rules of court for requiring the legal representative acting for a petitioner for divorce to certify whether he has discussed with the petitioner the possibility of a reconciliation and given him the names and addresses of persons qualified to help effect a reconciliation between parties to a marriage who have become estranged.

(2) If at any stage of proceedings for divorce it appears to the court that there is a reasonable possibility of a reconciliation between the parties to the marriage, the court may adjourn the proceedings for such period as it thinks fit to enable attempts to be made to effect such a reconciliation.

The power conferred by the foregoing provision is additional to any other power of the court to adjourn proceedings.

7 Consideration by the court of certain agreements or arrangements

Provision may be made by rules of court for enabling the parties to a marriage, or either of them, in application made either before or after the presentation of a petition for divorce, to refer to the court any agreement or arrangement made or proposed to be made between them, being an agreement or arrangement which relates to, arises out of, or is connected with, the proceedings for divorce which are contemplated or, as the case may be, have begun, for enabling the court to express an opinion, should it think it desirable to do so, as to the reasonableness of the agreement or arrangement and to give such directions, if any, in the matter as it thinks fit.

8 Intervention of Queen's Proctor

(1) In the case of a petition for divorce—

    (a) the court may, if it thinks fit, direct all necessary papers in the matter to be sent to the Queen's Proctor, who shall under the directions of the Attorney-General instruct counsel to argue before the court any question in relation to the matter which the court considers it necessary or expedient to have fully argued;

    (b) any person may at any time during the progress of the proceedings or before the decree nisi is made absolute give information to the Queen's Proctor on any matter material to the due decision of the case, and the Queen's Proctor may thereupon take such steps as the Attorney General considers necessary or expedient.

(2) Where the Queen's Proctor intervenes or shows cause against a decree nisi in any proceedings for divorce, the court may make such order as may be just as to the payment by other parties to the proceedings of the costs incurred by any of those parties by reason of his so doing.

(3) The Queen's Proctor shall be entitled to charge as part of the expenses of his office—

    (a) the costs of any proceedings under subsection (1)(a) above;

    (b) where his reasonable costs of intervening or showing cause as mentioned in subsection (2) above are not fully satisfied by any order under that subsection, the amount of the difference;

    (c) if the Treasury so directs, any cost which he pays to any parties under an order made under subsection (2).

9   Proceedings after decree nisi: general powers of court

(1) Where a decree of divorce has been granted but not made absolute, then, without prejudice to section 8 above, any person (excluding a party to the proceedings other than the Queen's Proctor) may show cause why the decree should not be made absolute by reason of material facts not having been brought before the court; and in such a case the court may—

    (a) notwithstanding anything in section 1(5) above (but subject to section 10(2) to (4) below) make the decree absolute; or

    (b) rescind the decree; or

    (c) require further inquiry; or

    (d) otherwise deal with the case as it thinks fit.

(2) Where a decree of divorce has been granted and no application for it to be made absolute has been made by the party to whom it was granted, then, at any time after the expiration of three months from the earliest date on which that party could have made such an application, the party against whom it was granted may make an application to the court, and on that application the court may exercise any of the powers mentioned in paragraphs (a) to (d) of subsection (1) above.

10   Proceedings after decree nisi: special protection for respondent in separation cases

(1) Where in any case the court has granted a decree of divorce on the basis of a finding that the petitioner was entitled to rely in support of his petition on the fact of two years' separation coupled with the respondent's consent to a decree being granted and has made no such finding as to any other fact mentioned in section 1(2) above, the court may, on an application made by the respondent at any time before the decree is made absolute, rescind the decree if it is satisfied that the petitioner misled the respondent (whether intentionally or unintentionally) about any matter which the respondent took into account in deciding to give his consent.

(2) The following provisions of this section apply where—

    (a) the respondent to a petition for divorce in which the petitioner alleged two years' or five years' separation coupled, in the former case, with the respondent's consent to a decree being granted, has applied to the court for consideration under subsection (3) below of his financial position after the divorce; and

    (b) the court has granted a decree on the petition on the basis of a finding that the petitioner was entitled to rely in support of his petition on the fact of two years' or five years' separation (as the case may be) and has made no such finding as to any other fact mentioned in section 1(2) above.

(3) The court hearing an application by the respondent under subsection (2) above shall consider all the circumstances including the age, health, conduct, earning capacity, financial resources, and financial obligations of each of the parties, and the financial position of the respondent as, having regard to the divorce, it is likely to be after the death of the petitioner should the petitioner die first; and, subject to subsection (4) below, the court shall not make the decree absolute unless it is satisfied—

    (a) that the petitioner should not be required to make any financial provision for the respondent, or

    (b) that the financial provision made by the petitioner for the respondent is reasonable and fair or the best that can be made in the circumstances.

(4) The court may if it thinks fit make the decree absolute notwithstanding the requirements of subsection (3) above if—

    (a) it appears that there are circumstances making it desirable that the decree should be made absolute without delay, and

    (b) the court has obtained a satisfactory undertaking from the petitioner that he will make such financial provision for the respondent as the court may approve.

10A Proceedings after decree nisi: religious marriage

(1) This section applies if a decree of divorce has been granted but not made absolute and the parties to the marriage concerned—

(a) were married in accordance with—

(i)   the usages of the Jews, or

(ii) any other prescribed religious usages; and

(b) must co-operate if the marriage is to be dissolved in accordance with those usages.

(2) On the application of either party, the court may order that a decree of divorce is not to be made absolute until a declaration made by both parties that they have taken such steps as are required to dissolve the marriage in accordance with those usages is produced to the court.

(3) An order under subsection (2)—

(a) may be made only if the court is satisfied that in all the circumstances of the case it is just and reasonable to do so; and

(b) may be revoked at any time.

(4) A declaration of a kind mentioned in subsection (2)—

(a) must be in a specified form;

(b) must, in specified cases, be accompanied by such documents as may be specified; and

(c) must, in specified cases, satisfy such other requirements as may be specified.

(5) The validity of a decree of divorce made by reference to such a declaration is not to be affected by any inaccuracy in that declaration.

(6) 'Prescribed' means prescribed in an order made by the Lord Chancellor after consulting the Lord Chief Justice and such an order—

(a) must be made by statutory instrument;

(b) shall be subject to annulment in pursuance of a resolution of either House of Parliament.

(7) 'Specified' means specified in rules of court.

(8) The Lord Chief Justice may nominate a judicial office holder (as defined in section 109(4) of the Constitutional Reform Act 2005) to exercise his functions under this section.

Nullity

11 Grounds on which a marriage is void

A marriage celebrated after 31st July 1971 shall be void on the following grounds only, that is to say—

(a) that it is not a valid marriage under the provisions of the Marriages Acts 1949 to 1986 (that is to say where—

(i)   the parties are within the prohibited degrees of relationship;

(ii) either party is under the age of sixteen; or

(iii) the parties have intermarried in disregard of certain requirements as to the formation of marriage);

(b) that at the time of the marriage either party was already lawfully married or a civil partner;

…

(d) in the case of a polygamous marriage entered into outside England and Wales, that either party was at the time of the marriage domiciled in England and Wales.

For the purposes of paragraph (d) of this subsection a marriage is not polygamous if at its inception neither party has any spouse additional to the other.

12 Grounds on which a marriage is voidable

(1) A marriage celebrated after 31st July 1971 shall be voidable on the following grounds only, that is to say—

(a) that the marriage has not been consummated owing to the incapacity of either party to consummate it;

(b) that the marriage has not been consummated owing to the wilful refusal of the respondent to consummate it;

(c) that either party to the marriage did not validly consent to it, whether in consequence of duress, mistake, unsoundness of mind or otherwise;

(d) that at the time of the marriage either party, though capable of giving a valid consent, was suffering (whether continuously or intermittently) from mental disorder within the meaning of the Mental Health Act 1983 of such a kind or to such an extent as to be unfitted for marriage;

(e) that at the time of the marriage the respondent was suffering from venereal disease in a communicable form;

(f) that at the time of the marriage the respondent was pregnant by some person other than the petitioner.

(g) that an interim gender recognition certificate under the Gender Recognition Act 2004 has, after the time of the marriage, been issued to either party to the marriage;

(h) that the respondent is a person whose gender at the time of the marriage had become the acquired gender under the Gender Recognition Act 2004.

(2) Paragraphs (a) and (b) of subsection (1) do not apply to the marriage of a same sex couple.

13   Bars to relief where marriage is voidable

(1) The court shall not, in proceedings instituted after 31st July 1971, grant a decree of nullity on the ground that a marriage is voidable if the respondent satisfies the court—

(a) that the petitioner, with knowledge that it was open to him to have the marriage avoided, so conducted himself in relation to the respondent as to lead the respondent reasonably to believe that he would not seek to do so; and

(b) that it would be unjust to the respondent to grant the decree.

(2) Without prejudice to subsection (1) above, the court shall not grant a decree of nullity by virtue of section 12 above on the grounds mentioned in paragraph (c), (d), (e), (f) or (h) of that section unless—

(a) it is satisfied that proceedings were instituted within the period of three years from the date of the marriage, or

(b) leave for the institution of proceedings after the expiration of that period has been granted under subsection (4) below.

(2A) Without prejudice to subsection (1) above, the court shall not grant a decree of nullity by virtue of section 12 above on the ground mentioned in paragraph (g) of that section unless it is satisfied that proceedings were instituted within the period of six months from the date of issue of the interim gender recognition certificate.

(3) Without prejudice to subsections (1) and (2) above, the court shall not grant a decree of nullity by virtue of section 12 above on the grounds mentioned in paragraph (e), (f) or (h) of that section unless it is satisfied that the petitioner was at the time of the marriage ignorant of the facts alleged.

(4) In the case of proceedings for the grant of a decree of nullity by virtue of section 12 above on the grounds mentioned in paragraph (c), (d), (e), (f) or (h) of that section, a judge of the court may, on an application made to him, grant leave for the institution of proceedings after the expiration of the period of three years from the date of the marriage if—

(a) he is satisfied that the petitioner has at some time during that period suffered from mental disorder within the meaning of the Mental Health Act 1983, and

(b) he considers that in all the circumstances of the case it would be just to grant leave for the institution of proceedings.

(5) An application for leave under subsection (4) above may be made after the expiration of the period of three years from the date of the marriage.

14 Marriages governed by foreign law or celebrated abroad under English law

(1) Subject to subsection (3) where, apart from this Act, any matter affecting the validity of a marriage would fall to be determined (in accordance with the rules of private international law) by reference to the law of a country outside England and Wales, nothing in section 11, 12 or 13(1) above shall—

(a) preclude the determination of that matter as aforesaid; or

(b) require the application to the marriage of the grounds or bar there mentioned except so far as applicable in accordance with those rules.

(2) In the case of a marriage which purports to have been celebrated under the Foreign Marriage Acts 1892 to 1947 or has taken place outside England and Wales and purports to be a marriage under common law, section 11 above is without prejudice to any ground on which the marriage may be void under those Acts or, as the case may be, by virtue of the rules governing the celebration of marriages outside England and Wales under common law.

(3) No marriage is to be treated as valid by virtue of subsection (1) if, at the time when it purports to have been celebrated, either party was already a civil partner.

15 Application of sections 1(5), 8 and 9 to nullity proceedings

Sections 1(5), 8 and 9 as above shall apply in relation to proceedings for nullity of marriage as if for any reference in those provisions to divorce there were substituted a reference to nullity of marriage.

16 Effect of decree of nullity in case of voidable marriage

A decree of nullity granted after 31st July 1971 in respect of a voidable marriage shall operate to annul the marriage only as respects any time after the decree has been made absolute, and the marriage shall, notwithstanding the decree, be treated as if it had existed up to that time.

Other matrimonial suits

17 Judicial separation

(1) A petition for judicial separation may be presented to the court by either party to a marriage on the ground that any such fact as is mentioned in section 1(2) above exists, and the provisions of section 2 above shall apply accordingly for the purposes of a petition for judicial separation alleging any such fact, as they apply in relation to a petition for divorce alleging that fact.

(2) On a petition for judicial separation it shall be the duty of the court to inquire, so far as it reasonably can, into the facts alleged by the petitioner and into any facts alleged by the respondent, but the court shall not be concerned to consider whether the marriage has broken down irretrievably, and if it is satisfied on the evidence of any such fact as is mentioned in section 1(2) above it shall grant a decree of judicial separation.

(3) Sections 6 and 7 above shall apply for the purpose of encouraging the reconciliation of parties to proceedings for judicial separation and of enabling the parties to a marriage to refer to the court for its opinion an agreement or arrangement relevant to actual or contemplated proceedings for judicial separation, as they apply in relation to proceedings for divorce.

18 Effects of judicial separation

(1) Where the court grants a decree of judicial separation it shall no longer be obligatory for the petitioner to cohabit with the respondent.

(2) If while a decree of judicial separation is in force and the separation is continuing either of the parties to the marriage dies intestate as respects all or any of his or her real or personal property, the property as respects which he or she died intestate shall devolve as if the other party to the marriage had then been dead.

(3) Notwithstanding anything in section 2(1)(a) of the Matrimonial Proceedings (Magistrates' Courts) Act 1960, a provision in force under an order made, or having effect as if made, under that section exempting one party to a marriage from the obligation to cohabit with the other shall not have effect as a decree of judicial separation for the purposes of subsection (2) above.

...

General

20   Relief for respondent in divorce proceedings

If in any proceedings for divorce the respondent alleges and proves any such fact as is mentioned in subsection (2) of section 1 above (treating the respondent as the petitioner and the petitioner as the respondent for the purposes of that subsection) the court may give to the respondent the relief to which he would have been entitled if he had presented a petition seeking that relief.

PART II FINANCIAL RELIEF FOR PARTIES TO MARRIAGE AND CHILDREN OF FAMILY

Financial provision and property adjustment orders

21   Financial provision and property adjustment orders

(1) The financial provision orders for the purposes of this Act are the orders for periodical or lump sum provision available (subject to the provisions of this Act) under section 23 below for the purpose of adjusting the financial position of the parties to a marriage and any children of the family in connection with proceedings for divorce, nullity of marriage or judicial separation and under section 27(6) below on proof of neglect by one party to a marriage to provide, or to make a proper contribution towards, reasonable maintenance for the other or a child of the family, that is to say—

    (a) any order for periodical payments in favour of a party to a marriage under section 23(1)(a) or 27(6)(a) or in favour of a child of the family under section 23(1)(d), (2) or (4) or 27(6)(d);

    (b) any order for secured periodical payments in favour of a party to a marriage under section 23(1)(b) or 27(6)(b) or in favour of a child of the family under section 23(1)(e), (2) or (4) or 27(6)(e); and

    (c) any order for lump sum provision in favour of a party to a marriage under section 23(1)(c) or 27(6)(c) or in favour of a child of the family under section 23(1)(f), (2) or (4) or 27(6)(f);

and references in this Act (except in paragraphs 17(1) and 23 of Schedule 1 below) to periodical payments orders, secured periodical payments orders, and orders for the payment of a lump sum are references to all or some of the financial provision orders requiring the sort of financial provision in question according as the context of each reference may require.

(2) The property adjustment orders for the purposes of this Act are the orders dealing with property rights available (subject to the provisions of this Act) under section 24 below for the purpose of adjusting the financial position of the parties to a marriage and any children of the family on or after the grant of a decree of divorce, nullity of marriage or judicial separation, that is to say—

    (a) any order under subsection (1)(a) of that section for a transfer of property;

    (b) any order under subsection (1)(b) of that section for a settlement of property; and

    (c) any order under subsection (1)(c) or (d) of that section for a variation of settlement.

21A   Pension sharing orders

(1) For the purposes of this Act, a pension sharing order is an order which—

    (a) provides that one party's—

        (i)   shareable rights under a specified pension arrangement, or

        (ii) shareable state scheme rights, be subject to pension sharing for the benefit of the other party, and

    (b) specifies the percentage value to be transferred.

(2) In subsection (1) above—

    (a) the reference to shareable rights under a pension arrangement is to rights in relation to which pension sharing is available under Chapter I of Part IV of the Welfare Reform and Pensions Act 1999, or under corresponding Northern Ireland legislation,

(b) the reference to shareable state scheme rights is to rights in relation to which pension sharing is available under Chapter II of Part IV of the Welfare Reform and Pensions Act 1999, or under corresponding Northern Ireland legislation, and

(c) 'party' means a party to a marriage.

21B Pension compensation sharing orders

(1) For the purposes of this Act, a pension compensation sharing order is an order which—

(a) provides that one party's shareable rights to PPF compensation that derive from rights under a specified pension scheme are to be subject to pension compensation sharing for the benefit of the other party, and

(b) specifies the percentage value to be transferred.

(2) In subsection (1)—

(a) the reference to shareable rights to PPF compensation is to rights in relation to which pension compensation sharing is available under Chapter 1 of Part 3 of the Pensions Act 2008 …;

(b) 'party' means a party to a marriage;

(c) 'specified' means specified in the order.

21C Pension compensation: interpretation

In this Part—

'PPF compensation' means compensation payable under the pension compensation provisions;

'the pension compensation provisions' means—

(a) Chapter 3 of Part 2 of the Pensions Act 2004 (pension protection) and any regulations or order made under it,

(b) Chapter 1 of Part 3 of the Pensions Act 2008 (pension compensation on divorce etc) and any regulations or order made under it, and

(c) …

Ancillary relief in connection with divorce proceedings, etc.

22 Maintenance pending suit

(1) On a petition for divorce, nullity of marriage or judicial separation, the court may make an order for maintenance pending suit, that is to say, an order requiring either party to the marriage to make to the other such periodical payments for his or her maintenance and for such term, being a term beginning not earlier than the date of the presentation of the petition and ending with the date of the determination of the suit, as the court thinks reasonable.

(2) An order under this section may not require a party to a marriage to pay to the other party any amount in respect of legal services for the purposes of the proceedings.

(3) In subsection (2) 'legal services' has the same meaning as in section 22ZA.

22ZA Orders for payment in respect of legal services

(1) In proceedings for divorce, nullity of marriage or judicial separation, the court may make an order or orders requiring one party to the marriage to pay to the other ('the applicant') an amount for the purpose of enabling the applicant to obtain legal services for the purposes of the proceedings.

(2) The court may also make such an order or orders in proceedings under this Part for financial relief in connection with proceedings for divorce, nullity of marriage or judicial separation.

(3) The court must not make an order under this section unless it is satisfied that, without the amount, the applicant would not reasonably be able to obtain appropriate legal services for the purposes of the proceedings or any part of the proceedings.

(4) For the purposes of subsection (3), the court must be satisfied, in particular, that—

    (a) the applicant is not reasonably able to secure a loan to pay for the services, and

    (b) the applicant is unlikely to be able to obtain the services by granting a charge over any assets recovered in the proceedings.

(5) An order under this section may be made for the purpose of enabling the applicant to obtain legal services of a specified description, including legal services provided in a specified period or for the purposes of a specified part of the proceedings.

(6) An order under this section may—

    (a) provide for the payment of all or part of the amount by instalments of specified amounts, and

    (b) require the instalments to be secured to the satisfaction of the court.

(7) An order under this section may direct that payment of all or part of the amount is to be deferred.

(8) The court may at any time in the proceedings vary an order made under this section if it considers that there has been a material change of circumstances since the order was made.

(9) For the purposes of the assessment of costs in the proceedings, the applicant's costs are to be treated as reduced by any amount paid to the applicant pursuant to an order under this section for the purposes of those proceedings.

(10) In this section 'legal services', in relation to proceedings, means the following types of services—

    (a) providing advice as to how the law applies in the particular circumstances,

    (b) providing advice and assistance in relation to the proceedings,

    (c) providing other advice and assistance in relation to the settlement or other resolution of the dispute that is the subject of the proceedings, and

    (d) providing advice and assistance in relation to the enforcement of decisions in the proceedings or as part of the settlement or resolution of the dispute,

and they include, in particular, advice and assistance in the form of representation and any form of dispute resolution, including mediation.

(11) In subsections (5) and (6) 'specified' means specified in the order concerned.

22ZB Matters to which court is to have regard in deciding how to exercise power under section 22ZA

(1) When considering whether to make or vary an order under section 22ZA, the court must have regard to—

    (a) the income, earning capacity, property and other financial resources which each of the applicant and the paying party has or is likely to have in the foreseeable future,

    (b) the financial needs, obligations and responsibilities which each of the applicant and the paying party has or is likely to have in the foreseeable future,

    (c) the subject matter of the proceedings, including the matters in issue in them,

    (d) whether the paying party is legally represented in the proceedings,

    (e) any steps taken by the applicant to avoid all or part of the proceedings, whether by proposing or considering mediation or otherwise,

    (f) the applicant's conduct in relation to the proceedings,

    (g) any amount owed by the applicant to the paying party in respect of costs in the proceedings or other proceedings to which both the applicant and the paying party are or were party, and

    (h) the effect of the order or variation on the paying party.

(2) In subsection (1)(a) 'earning capacity', in relation to the applicant or the paying party, includes any increase in earning capacity which, in the opinion of the court, it would be reasonable to expect the applicant or the paying party to take steps to acquire.

(3) For the purposes of subsection (1)(h), the court must have regard, in particular, to whether the making or variation of the order is likely to—

    (a) cause undue hardship to the paying party, or

    (b) prevent the paying party from obtaining legal services for the purposes of the proceedings.

(4) The Lord Chancellor may by order amend this section by adding to, omitting or varying the matters mentioned in subsections (1) to (3).

(5) An order under subsection (4) must be made by statutory instrument.

(6) A statutory instrument containing an order under subsection (4) may not be made unless a draft of the instrument has been laid before, and approved by a resolution of, each House of Parliament.

(7) In this section 'legal services' has the same meaning as in section 22ZA.

23 Financial provision orders in connection with divorce proceedings, etc.

(1) On granting a decree of divorce, a decree of nullity of marriage or a decree of judicial separation or at any time thereafter (whether, in the case of a decree of divorce or of nullity of marriage, before or after the decree is made absolute), the court may make any one or more of the following orders, that is to say—

    (a) an order that either party to the marriage shall make to the other such periodical payments, for such term, as may be specified in the order;

    (b) an order that either party to the marriage shall secure to the other to the satisfaction of the court such periodical payments, for such term, as may be so specified;

    (c) an order that either party to the marriage shall pay to the other such lump sum or sums as may be so specified;

    (d) an order that a party to the marriage shall make to such person as may be specified in the order for the benefit of a child of the family, or to such a child, such periodical payments, for such term, as may be so specified;

    (e) an order that a party to the marriage shall secure to such person as may be so specified for the benefit of such a child, or to such a child, to the satisfaction of the court, such periodical payments, for such term, as may be so specified;

    (f) an order that a party to the marriage shall pay to such person as may be so specified for the benefit of such a child, or to such a child, such lump sum as may be so specified;

subject however, in the case of an order under paragraph (d), (e) or (f) above, to the restrictions imposed by section 29(1) and (3) below on the making of financial provision orders in favour of children who have attained the age of eighteen.

(2) The court may also, subject to those restrictions, make any one or more of the orders mentioned in subsection (1)(d), (e) and (f) above—

    (a) in any proceedings for divorce, nullity of marriage or judicial separation, before granting a decree; and

    (b) where any such proceedings are dismissed after the beginning of the trial, either forthwith or within a reasonable period after the dismissal.

(3) Without prejudice to the generality of subsection (1)(c) or (f) above—

    (a) an order under this section that a party to a marriage shall pay a lump sum to the other party may be made for the purpose of enabling that other party to meet any liabilities or expenses reasonably incurred by him or her in maintaining himself or herself or any child of the family before making an application for an order under this section in his or her favour;

    (b) an order under this section for the payment of a lump sum to or for the benefit of a child of the family may be made for the purpose of enabling any liabilities or expenses reasonably incurred by or for the benefit of that child before the making of an application for an order under this section in his favour to be met; and

(c) an order under this section for the payment of a lump sum may provide for the payment of that sum by instalments of such amount as may be specified in the order and may require the payment of the instalments to be secured to the satisfaction of the court.

(4) The power of the court under subsection (1) or (2)(a) above to make an order in favour of a child of the family shall be exercisable from time to time; and where the court makes an order in favour of a child under subsection (2)(b) above, it may from time to time, subject to the restrictions mentioned in subsection (1) above, make a further order in his favour of any of the kinds mentioned in subsection (1)(d), (e) or (f) above.

(5) Without prejudice to the power to give a direction under section 30 below for the settlement of an instrument by conveyancing counsel, where an order is made under subsection (1) (a), (b) or (c) above on or after granting a decree of divorce or nullity of marriage, neither the order nor any settlement made in pursuance of the order shall take effect unless the decree has been made absolute.

(6) Where the court—
    (a) makes an order under this section for the payment of a lump sum; and
    (b) directs—
        (i)   that payment of that sum or any part of it shall be deferred; or
        (ii) that that sum or any part of it shall be paid by instalments,
the court may order that the amount deferred or the instalments shall carry interest at such rate as may be specified by the order from such date, not earlier than the date of the order, as may be so specified, until the date when payment of it is due.

24   Property adjustment orders in connection with divorce proceedings, etc.

(1) On granting a decree of divorce, a decree of nullity of marriage or a decree of judicial separation or at any time thereafter (whether, in the case of a decree of divorce, or of nullity of marriage, before or after the decree is made absolute), the court may make any one or more of the following orders, that is to say—

    (a) an order that a party to the marriage shall transfer to the other party, to any child of the family or to such person as may be specified in the order for the benefit of such a child such property as may be so specified, being property to which the first-mentioned party is entitled, either in possession or reversion;

    (b) an order that a settlement of such property as may be so specified, being property to which a party to the marriage is so entitled, be made to the satisfaction of the court for the benefit of the other party to the marriage and of the children of the family or either or any of them;

    (c) an order varying for the benefit of the parties to the marriage and of the children of the family or either or any of them any ante-nuptial or post-nuptial settlement (including such a settlement made by will or codicil) made on the parties to the marriage, other than one in the form of a pension arrangement (within the meaning of section 25D below);

    (d) an order extinguishing or reducing the interest of either of the parties to the marriage under any such settlement, other than one in the form of a pension arrangement (within the meaning of section 25D below);

subject, however, in the case of an order under paragraph (a) above, to the restrictions imposed by section 29(1) and (3) below on the making of orders for a transfer of property in favour of children who have attained the age of eighteen.

(2) The court may make an order under subsection (1)(c) above notwithstanding that there are no children of the family.

(3) Without prejudice to the power to give a direction under section 30 below for the settlement of an instrument by conveyancing counsel, where an order is made under this section on or after granting a decree of divorce or nullity of marriage, neither the order nor any settlement made in pursuance of the order shall take effect unless the decree has been made absolute.

24A Orders for sale of property

(1) Where the court makes an order under section 22ZA or makes under section 23 or 24 of this Act a secured periodical payments order, an order for the payment of a lump sum or a property adjustment order, then, on making that order or at any time thereafter, the court may make a further order for the sale of such property as may be specified in the order, being property in which or in the proceeds of sale of which either or both of the parties to the marriage has or have a beneficial interest, either in possession or reversion.

(2) Any order made under subsection (1) above may contain such consequential or supplementary provisions as the court thinks fit and, without prejudice to the generality of the foregoing provision, may include—

(a) provision requiring the making of a payment out of the proceeds of sale of the property to which the order relates, and

(b) provision requiring any such property to be offered for sale to a person, or class of persons, specified in the order.

(3) Where an order is made under subsection (1) above on or after the grant of a decree of divorce or nullity of marriage, the order shall not take effect unless the decree has been made absolute.

(4) Where an order is made under subsection (1) above, the court may direct that the order, or such provision thereof as the court may specify, shall not take effect until the occurrence of an event specified by the court or the expiration of a period so specified.

(5) Where an order under subsection (1) above contains a provision requiring the proceeds of sale of the property to which the order relates to be used to secure periodical payments to a party to the marriage, the order shall cease to have effect on the death or re-marriage of, or formation of a civil partnership by, that person.

(6) Where a party to a marriage has a beneficial interest in any property, or in the proceeds of sale thereof, and some other person who is not a party to the marriage also has a beneficial interest in that property or in the proceeds of sale thereof, then, before deciding whether to make an order under this section in relation to that property, it shall be the duty of the court to give that other person an opportunity to make representations with respect to the order; and any representations made by that other person shall be included among the circumstances to which the court is required to have regard under section 25(1) below.

24B Pension sharing orders in connection with divorce proceedings, etc.

(1) On granting a decree of divorce or a decree of nullity of marriage or at any time thereafter (whether before or after the decree is made absolute), the court may, on an application made under this section, make one or more pension sharing orders in relation to the marriage.

(2) A pension sharing order under this section is not to take effect unless the decree on or after which it is made has been made absolute.

(3) A pension sharing order under this section may not be made in relation to a pension arrangement which—

(a) is the subject of a pension sharing order in relation to the marriage, or

(b) has been the subject of pension sharing between the parties to the marriage.

(4) A pension sharing order under this section may not be made in relation to shareable state scheme rights if—

(a) such rights are the subject of a pension sharing order in relation to the marriage, or

(b) such rights have been the subject of pension sharing between the parties to the marriage.

(5) A pension sharing order under this section may not be made in relation to the rights of a person under a pension arrangement if there is in force a requirement imposed by virtue of section 25B or 25C below which relates to benefits or future benefits to which he is entitled under the pension arrangement.

24C   Pension sharing orders: duty to stay

(1) No pension sharing order may be made so as to take effect before the end of such period after the making of the order as may be prescribed by regulations made by the Lord Chancellor.

(2) The power to make regulations under this section shall be exercisable by statutory instrument which shall be subject to annulment in pursuance of a resolution of either House of Parliament.

24D   Pension sharing orders: apportionment of charges

If a pension sharing order relates to rights under a pension arrangement, the court may include in the order provision about the apportionment between the parties of any charge under section 41 of the Welfare Reform and Pensions Act 1999 (charges in respect of pension sharing costs), or under corresponding Northern Ireland legislation.

24E   Pension compensation sharing orders in connection with divorce proceedings

(1) On granting a decree of divorce or a decree of nullity of marriage or at any time thereafter (whether before or after the decree is made absolute), the court may, on an application made under this section, make a pension compensation sharing order in relation to the marriage.

(2) A pension compensation sharing order under this section is not to take effect unless the decree on or after which it is made has been made absolute.

(3) A pension compensation sharing order under this section may not be made in relation to rights to PPF compensation that—

    (a) are the subject of pension attachment,

    (b) derive from rights under a pension scheme that were the subject of pension sharing between the parties to the marriage,

    (c) are the subject of pension compensation attachment, or

    (d) are or have been the subject of pension compensation sharing between the parties to the marriage.

(4) For the purposes of subsection (3)(a), rights to PPF compensation 'are the subject of pension attachment' if any of the following three conditions is met.

(5) The first condition is that—

    (a) the rights derive from rights under a pension scheme in relation to which an order was made under section 23 imposing a requirement by virtue of section 25B(4), and

    (b) that order, as modified under section 25E(3), remains in force.

(6) The second condition is that—

    (a) the rights derive from rights under a pension scheme in relation to which an order was made under section 23 imposing a requirement by virtue of section 25B(7), and

    (b) that order—

        (i)   has been complied with, or

        (ii) has not been complied with and, as modified under section 25E(5), remains in force.

(7) The third condition is that—

    (a) the rights derive from rights under a pension scheme in relation to which an order was made under section 23 imposing a requirement by virtue of section 25C, and

    (b) that order remains in force.

(8) For the purposes of subsection (3)(b), rights under a pension scheme 'were the subject of pension sharing between the parties to the marriage' if the rights were at any time the subject of a pension sharing order in relation to the marriage or a previous marriage between the same parties.

(9) For the purposes of subsection (3)(c), rights to PPF compensation 'are the subject of pension compensation attachment' if there is in force a requirement imposed by virtue of section 25F relating to them.

(10) For the purposes of subsection (3)(d), rights to PPF compensation 'are or have been the subject of pension compensation sharing between the parties to the marriage' if they are or have

ever been the subject of a pension compensation sharing order in relation to the marriage or a previous marriage between the same parties.

24F　Pension compensation sharing orders: duty to stay

(1)　No pension compensation sharing order may be made so as to take effect before the end of such period after the making of the order as may be prescribed by regulations made by the Lord Chancellor.

(2)　The power to make regulations under this section shall be exercisable by statutory instrument which shall be subject to annulment in pursuance of a resolution of either House of Parliament.

24G　Pension compensation sharing orders: apportionment of charges

The court may include in a pension compensation sharing order provision about the apportionment between the parties of any charge under section 117 of the Pensions Act 2008 (charges in respect of pension compensation sharing costs) ...

25　Matters to which court is to have regard in deciding how to exercise its powers under sections 23, 24, 24A, 24B and 24E

(1)　It shall be the duty of the court in deciding whether to exercise its powers under sections 23, 24, 24A, 24B or 24E above and, if so, in what manner, to have regard to all the circumstances of the case, first consideration being given to the welfare while a minor of any child of the family who has not attained the age of eighteen.

(2)　As regards the exercise of the powers of the court under section 23(1)(a), (b) or (c), 24, 24A, 24B or 24E above in relation to a party to the marriage, the court shall in particular have regard to the following matters—

   (a)　the income, earning capacity, property and other financial resources which each of the parties to the marriage has or is likely to have in the foreseeable future, including in the case of earning capacity any increase in that capacity which it would in the opinion of the court be reasonable to expect a party to the marriage to take steps to acquire;
   (b)　the financial needs, obligations and responsibilities which each of the parties to the marriage has or is likely to have in the foreseeable future;
   (c)　the standard of living enjoyed by the family before the breakdown of the marriage;
   (d)　the age of each party to the marriage and the duration of the marriage;
   (e)　any physical or mental disability of either of the parties to the marriage;
   (f)　the contributions which each of the parties has made or is likely in the foreseeable future to make to the welfare of the family, including any contribution by looking after the home or caring for the family;
   (g)　the conduct of each of the parties, if that conduct is such that it would in the opinion of the court be inequitable to disregard it;
   (h)　in the case of proceedings for divorce or nullity of marriage, the value to each of the parties to the marriage of any benefit which, by reason of the dissolution or annulment of the marriage, that party will lose the chance of acquiring.

(3)　As regards the exercise of the powers of the court under section 23(1)(d), (e) or (f), (2) or (4), 24 or 24A above in relation to a child of the family, the court shall in particular have regard to the following matters—

   (a)　the financial needs of the child;
   (b)　the income, earning capacity (if any), property and other financial resources of the child;
   (c)　any physical or mental disability of the child;
   (d)　the manner in which he was being and in which the parties to the marriage expected him to be educated or trained;
   (e)　the considerations mentioned in relation to the parties to the marriage in paragraphs (a), (b), (c) and (e) of subsection (2) above.

(4) As regards the exercise of the powers of the court under section 23(1)(d), (e) or (f), (2) or (4), 24 or 24A above against a party to a marriage in favour of a child of the family who is not the child of that party, the court shall also have regard—

    (a) to whether that party assumed any responsibility for the child's maintenance, and, if so, to the extent to which, and the basis upon which, that party assumed such responsibility and to the length of time for which that party discharged such responsibility;

    (b) to whether in assuming and discharging such responsibility that party did so knowing that the child was not his or her own;

    (c) to the liability of any other person to maintain the child.

25A Exercise of court's powers in favour of party to marriage on decree of divorce or nullity of marriage

(1) Where on or after the grant of a degree of divorce or nullity of marriage the court decides to exercise its powers under section 23(1)(a), (b) or (c), 24, 24A, 24B or 24E above in favour of a party to the marriage, it shall be the duty of the court to consider whether it would be appropriate so to exercise those powers that the financial obligations of each party towards the other will be terminated as soon after the grant of the decree as the court considers just and reasonable.

(2) Where the court decides in such a case to make a periodical payments or secured periodical payments order in favour of a party to the marriage, the court shall in particular consider whether it would be appropriate to require those payments to be made or secured only for such term as would in the opinion of the court be sufficient to enable the party in whose favour the order is made to adjust without undue hardship to the termination of his or her financial dependence on the other party.

(3) Where on or after the grant of a decree of divorce or nullity of marriage an application is made by a party to the marriage for a periodical payments order in his or her favour, then, if the court considers that no continuing obligation should be imposed on either party to make or secure periodical payments in favour of the other, the court may dismiss the application with a direction that the applicant shall not be entitled to make any further application in relation to that marriage for an order under section 23(1)(a) or (b) above.

25B Pensions

(1) The matters to which the court is to have regard under section 25(2) above include—

    (a) in the case of paragraph (a), any benefits under a pension arrangement which a party to the marriage has or is likely to have, and

    (b) in the case of paragraph (h), any benefits under a pension arrangement which, by reason of the dissolution or annulment of the marriage, a party to the marriage will lose the chance of acquiring,

and, accordingly, in relation to benefits under a pension arrangement, section 25(2)(a) above shall have effect as if 'in the foreseeable future' were omitted.

(3) The following provisions apply where, having regard to any benefits under a pension arrangement, the court determines to make an order under section 23 above.

(4) To the extent to which the order is made having regard to any benefits under a pension arrangement, the order may require the person responsible for the pension arrangement in question, if at any time any payment in respect of any benefits under the arrangement becomes due to the party with pension rights, to make a payment for the benefit of the other party.

(5) The order must express the amount of any payment required to be made by virtue of subsection (4) above as a percentage of the payment which becomes due to the party with pension rights.

(6) Any such payment by the person responsible for the arrangement—

    (a) shall discharge so much of his liability to the party with pension rights as corresponds to the amount of the payment, and

    (b) shall be treated for all purposes as a payment made by the party with pension rights in or towards the discharge of his liability under the order.

(7) Where the party with pension rights has a right of commutation under the arrangement, the order may require him to exercise it to any extent; and this section applies to any payment due in consequence of commutation in pursuance of the order as it applies to other payments in respect of benefits under the arrangement.

(7A) The power conferred by subsection (7) above may not be exercised for the purpose of commuting a benefit payable to the party with pension rights to a benefit payable to the other party.

(7B) The power conferred by subsection (4) or (7) above may not be exercised in relation to a pension arrangement which—

(a) is the subject of a pension sharing order in relation to the marriage, or

(b) has been the subject of pension sharing between the parties to the marriage.

(7C) In subsection (1) above, references to benefits under a pension arrangement include any benefits by way of pension, whether under a pension arrangement or not.

25C Pensions: lump sums

(1) The power of the court under section 23 above to order a party to a marriage to pay a lump sum to the other party includes, where the benefits which the party with pension rights has or is likely to have under a pension arrangement include any lump sum payable in respect of his death, power to make any of the following provision by the order.

(2) The court may—

(a) if the person responsible for the pension arrangement in question has power to deter-mine the person to whom the sum, or any part of it, is to be paid, require him to pay the whole or part of that sum, when it becomes due, to the other party,

(b) if the party with pension rights has power to nominate the person to whom the sum, or any part of it, is to be paid, require the party with pension rights to nominate the other party in respect of the whole or part of that sum,

(c) in any other case, require the person responsible for the pension arrangement in ques-tion to pay the whole or part of that sum, when it becomes due, for the benefit of the other party instead of to the person to whom, apart from the order, it would be paid.

(3) Any payment by the person responsible for the arrangement under an order made under section 23 above by virtue of this section shall discharge so much of his liability in respect of the party with pension rights as corresponds to the amount of the payment.

(4) The powers conferred by this section may not be exercised in relation to a pension arrange-ment which—

(a) is the subject of a pension sharing order in relation to the marriage, or

(b) has been the subject of pension sharing between the parties to the marriage.

25D Pensions: supplementary

(1) Where—

(a) an order made under section 23 above by virtue of section 25B or 25C above imposes any requirement on the person responsible for a pension arrangement ('the first arrange-ment') and the party with pension rights acquires rights under another pension arrange-ment ('the new arrangement') which are derived (directly or indirectly) from the whole of his rights under the first arrangement, and

(b) the person responsible for the new arrangement has been given notice in accordance with regulations made by the Lord Chancellor,

the order shall have effect as if it had been made instead in respect of the person responsible for the new arrangement.

(2) The Lord Chancellor may by regulations—

(a) in relation to any provision of sections 25B or 25C above which authorises the court making an order under section 23 above to require the person responsible for a pension arrangement to make a payment for the benefit of the other party, make provision as to the person to whom, and the terms on which, the payment is to be made, (ab) make, in relation to payment under a mistaken belief as to the continuation in force of a provision included by virtue of section 25B or 25C above in an order under section 23 above, provision about the rights or liabilities of the payer, the payee or the person to whom the payment was due,

(b) require notices to be given in respect of changes of circumstances relevant to such orders which include provision made by virtue of sections 25B and 25C above,

(ba) make provision for the person responsible for a pension arrangement to be discharged in prescribed circumstances from a requirement imposed by virtue of section 25B or 25C above,

(e) make provision about calculation and verification in relation to the valuation of—

(i) benefits under a pension arrangement, or

(ii) shareable state scheme rights,

for the purposes of the court's functions in connection with the exercise of any of its powers under this Part of this Act.

(2A) Regulations under subsection (2)(e) above may include—

(a) provision for calculation or verification in accordance with guidance from time to time prepared by a prescribed person, and

(b) provision by reference to regulations under section 30 or 49(4) of the Welfare Reform and Pensions Act 1999.

(2B) Regulations under subsection (2) above may make different provision for different cases.

(2C) Power to make regulations under this section shall be exercisable by statutory instrument which shall be subject to annulment in pursuance of a resolution of either House of Parliament.

(3) In this section and sections 25B and 25C above—

'occupational pension scheme' has the same meaning as in the Pension Schemes Act 1993;

'the party with pension rights' means the party to the marriage who has or is likely to have benefits under a pension arrangement and 'the other party' means the other party to the marriage;

'pension arrangement' means—

(a) an occupational pension scheme,

(b) a personal pension scheme,

(c) a retirement annuity contract,

(d) an annuity or insurance policy purchased, or transferred, for the purpose of giving effect to rights under an occupational pension scheme or a personal pension scheme, and

(e) an annuity purchased, or entered into, for the purpose of discharging liability in respect of a pension credit under section 29(1)(b) of the Welfare Reform and Pensions Act 1999 or under corresponding Northern Ireland legislation;

'personal pension scheme' has the same meaning as in the Pension Schemes Act 1993;

'prescribed' means prescribed by regulations;

'retirement annuity contract' means a contract or scheme approved under Chapter III of Part XIV of the Income and Corporation Taxes Act 1988;

'shareable state scheme rights' has the same meaning as in section 21A(1) above; and

'trustees or managers', in relation to an occupational pension scheme or a personal pension scheme, means—

(a) in the case of a scheme established under a trust, the trustees of the scheme, and

(b) in any other case, the managers of the scheme.

(4) In this section and sections 25B and 25C above, references to the person responsible for a pension arrangement are—

(a) in the case of an occupational pension scheme or a personal pension scheme, to the trustees or managers of the scheme,

(b) in the case of a retirement annuity contract or an annuity falling within paragraph (d) or (e) of the definition of 'pension arrangement' above, the provider of the annuity, and

(c) in the case of an insurance policy falling within paragraph (d) of the definition of that expression, the insurer.

25E   The Pension Protection Fund

(1) The matters to which the court is to have regard under section 25(2) include—

    (a) in the case of paragraph (a), any PPF compensation to which a party to the marriage is or is likely to be entitled, and

    (b) in the case of paragraph (h), any PPF compensation which, by reason of the dissolution or annulment of the marriage, a party to the marriage will lose the chance of acquiring entitlement to,

and, accordingly, in relation to PPF compensation, section 25(2)(a) shall have effect as if 'in the foreseeable future' were omitted.

(2) Subsection (3) applies in relation to an order under section 23 so far as it includes provision made by virtue of section 25B(4) which—

    (a) imposed requirements on the trustees or managers of an occupational pension scheme for which the Board has assumed responsibility in accordance with Chapter 3 of Part 2 of the Pensions Act 2004 (pension protection) or any provision in force in Northern Ireland corresponding to that Chapter, and

    (b) was made before the trustees or managers of the scheme received the transfer notice in relation to the scheme.

(3) The order is to have effect from the time when the trustees or managers of the scheme receive the transfer notice—

    (a) as if, except in prescribed descriptions of case—

        (i)   references in the order to the trustees or managers of the scheme were references to the Board, and

        (ii) references in the order to any pension or lump sum to which the party with pension rights is or may become entitled under the scheme were references to any PPF compensation to which that person is or may become entitled in respect of the pension or lump sum, and

    (b) subject to such other modifications as may be prescribed.

(4) Subsection (5) applies to an order under section 23 if—

    (a) it includes provision made by virtue of section 25B(7) which requires the party with pension rights to exercise his right of commutation under an occupational pension scheme to any extent, and

    (b) before the requirement is complied with the Board has assumed responsibility for the scheme as mentioned in subsection (2)(a).

(5) From the time the trustees or managers of the scheme receive the transfer notice, the order is to have effect with such modifications as may be prescribed.

(6) Regulations may modify section 25C as it applies in relation to an occupational pension scheme at any time when there is an assessment period in relation to the scheme.

(7) Where the court makes a pension sharing order in respect of a person's shareable rights under an occupational pension scheme, or an order which includes provision made by virtue of section 25B(4) or (7) in relation to such a scheme, the Board subsequently assuming responsibility for the scheme as mentioned in subsection (2)(a) does not affect—

    (a) the powers of the court under section 31 to vary or discharge the order or to suspend or revive any provision of it, or

    (b) on an appeal, the powers of the appeal court to affirm, reinstate, set aside or vary the order.

...

(9) In this section—

'assessment period' means an assessment period within the meaning of Part 2 of the Pensions Act 2004 (pension protection) (see sections 132 and 159 of that Act) . . .;

'the Board' means the Board of the Pension Protection Fund;

'occupational pension scheme' has the same meaning as in the Pension Schemes Act 1993;

'prescribed' means prescribed by regulations;

'regulations' means regulations made by the Lord Chancellor;

'shareable rights' are rights in relation to which pension sharing is available under Chapter 1 of Part 4 of the Welfare Reform and Pensions Act 1999...;

'transfer notice' has the same meaning as in section 160 of the Pensions Act 2004...

25F Attachment of pension compensation

(1) This section applies where, having regard to any PPF compensation to which a party to the marriage is or is likely to be entitled, the court determines to make an order under section 23.

(2) To the extent to which the order is made having regard to such compensation, the order may require the Board of the Pension Protection Fund, if at any time any payment in respect of PPF compensation becomes due to the party with compensation rights, to make a payment for the benefit of the other party.

(3) The order must express the amount of any payment required to be made by virtue of subsection (2) as a percentage of the payment which becomes due to the party with compensation rights.

(4) Any such payment by the Board of the Pension Protection Fund—

    (a) shall discharge so much of its liability to the party with compensation rights as corresponds to the amount of the payment, and

    (b) shall be treated for all purposes as a payment made by the party with compensation rights in or towards the discharge of that party's liability under the order.

(5) Where the party with compensation rights has a right to commute any PPF compensation, the order may require that party to exercise it to any extent; and this section applies to any payment due in consequence of commutation in pursuance of the order as it applies to other payments in respect of PPF compensation.

(6) The power conferred by subsection (5) may not be exercised for the purpose of commuting compensation payable to the party with compensation rights to compensation payable to the other party.

(7) The power conferred by subsection (2) or (5) may not be exercised in relation to rights to PPF compensation that—

    (a) derive from rights under a pension scheme that were at any time the subject of a pension sharing order in relation to the marriage, or a previous marriage between the same parties, or

    (b) are or have ever been the subject of a pension compensation sharing order in relation to the marriage or a previous marriage between the same parties.

25G Pension compensation: supplementary

(1) The Lord Chancellor may by regulations—

    (a) make provision, in relation to any provision of section 25F which authorises the court making an order under section 23 to require the Board of the Pension Protection Fund to make a payment for the benefit of the other party, as to the person to whom, and the terms on which, the payment is to be made;

    (b) make provision, in relation to payment under a mistaken belief as to the continuation in force of a provision included by virtue of section 25F in an order under section 23, about the rights or liabilities of the payer, the payee or the person to whom the payment was due;

    (c) require notices to be given in respect of changes of circumstances relevant to orders under section 23 which include provision made by virtue of section 25F;

    (d) make provision for the Board of the Pension Protection Fund to be discharged in prescribed circumstances from a requirement imposed by virtue of section 25F;

    (e) make provision about calculation and verification in relation to the valuation of PPF compensation for the purposes of the court's functions in connection with the exercise of any of its powers under this Part.

(2) Regulations under subsection (1)(e) may include—

    (a) provision for calculation or verification in accordance with guidance from time to time prepared by a prescribed person;

    (b) provision by reference to regulations under section 112 of the Pensions Act 2008.

(3) Regulations under subsection (1) may make different provision for different cases.

(4) The power to make regulations under subsection (1) is exercisable by statutory instrument which shall be subject to annulment in pursuance of a resolution of either House of Parliament.

(5) In this section and section 25F—

'the party with compensation rights' means the party to the marriage who is or is likely to be entitled to PPF compensation, and 'the other party' means the other party to the marriage;

'prescribed' means prescribed by regulations.

…

26 Commencement of proceedings for ancillary relief etc.

(1) Where a petition for divorce, nullity of marriage or judicial separation has been presented, then, subject to subsection (2) below, proceedings for maintenance pending suit under section 22 above, for a financial provision order under section 23 above, or for a property adjustment order may be begun, subject to and in accordance with rules of court, at any time after the presentation of the petition.

(2) Rules of court may provide, in such cases as may be prescribed by the rules—

    (a) that applications for any such relief as is mentioned in subsection (1) above shall be made in the petition or answer; and

    (b) that applications for any such relief which are not so made, or are not made until after the expiration of such period following the presentation of the petition or filing of the answer as may be so prescribed, shall be made only with the leave of the court.

Financial provision in case of neglect to maintain

27 Financial provision orders etc., in case of neglect by party to marriage to maintain other party or child of the family

(1) Either party to a marriage may apply to the court for an order under this section on the ground that the other party to the marriage (in this section referred to as the respondent)—

    (a) has failed to provide reasonable maintenance for the applicant, or

    (b) has failed to provide, or to make a proper contribution towards, reasonable maintenance for any child of the family.

(2) The court may not entertain an application under this section unless it has jurisdiction to do so by virtue of the Maintenance Regulation and Schedule 6 to the Civil Jurisdiction and Judgments (Maintenance) Regulations 2011.

(3) Where an application under this section is made on the ground mentioned in subsection (1)(a) above, then, in deciding—

    (a) whether the respondent has failed to provide reasonable maintenance for the applicant, and

    (b) what order, if any, to make under this section in favour of the applicant,

the court shall have regard to all the circumstances of the case including the matters mentioned in section 25(2) above, and where an application is also made under this section in respect of a child of the family who has not attained the age of eighteen, first consideration shall be given to the welfare of the child while a minor.

(3A) Where an application under this section is made on the ground mentioned in subsection (1)(b) above then, in deciding—

    (a) whether the respondent has failed to provide, or to make a proper contribution towards, reasonable maintenance for the child of the family to whom the application relates, and

    (b) what order, if any, to make under this section in favour of the child, the court shall have regard to all the circumstances of the case including the matters mentioned in section 25(3)(a) to (e) above, and where the child of the family to whom the application relates is not the child of the respondent, including also the matters mentioned in section 25(4) above.

(3B) In relation to an application under this section on the ground mentioned in subsection (1)(a) above, section 25(2)(c) above shall have effect as if for the reference therein to the breakdown of the marriage there were substituted a reference to the failure to provide reasonable maintenance for the applicant, and in relation to an application under this section on the ground mentioned in subsection (1)(b) above, section 25(2)(c) above (as it applies by virtue of section 25 (3)(e) above) shall have effect as if for the reference therein to the breakdown of the marriage there were substituted a reference to the failure to provide, or to make a proper contribution towards, reasonable maintenance for the child of the family to whom the application relates.

(5) Where on an application under this section it appears to the court that the applicant or any child of the family to whom the application relates is in immediate need of financial assistance, but it is not yet possible to determine what order, if any, should be made on the application, the court may make an interim order for maintenance, that is to say, an order requiring the respondent to make to the applicant until the determination of the application such periodical payments as the court thinks reasonable.

(6) Where on an application under this section the applicant satisfies the court of any ground mentioned in subsection (1) above, the court may make any one or more of the following orders, that is to say—

(a) an order that the respondent shall make to the applicant such periodical payments, for such term, as may be specified in the order;

(b) an order that the respondent shall secure to the applicant, to the satisfaction of the court, such periodical payments, for such term, as may be so specified;

(c) an order that the respondent shall pay to the applicant such lump sum as may be so specified;

(d) an order that the respondent shall make to such person as may be specified in the order for the benefit of the child to whom the application relates, or to that child, such periodical payments, for such term, as may be so specified;

(e) an order that the respondent shall secure to such person as may be so specified for the benefit of that child, or to that child, to the satisfaction of the court, such periodical payments, for such term, as may be so specified;

(f) an order that the respondent shall pay to such person as may be so specified for the benefit of that child, or to that child, such lump sum as may be so specified;

subject, however, in the case of an order under paragraph (d), (e) or (f) above, to the restrictions imposed by section 29(1) and (3) below on the making of financial provision orders in favour of children who have attained the age of eighteen.

(6A) An application for the variation under section 31 of this Act of a periodical payments order or secured periodical payments order made under this section in favour of a child may, if the child has attained the age of sixteen, be made by the child himself.

(6B) Where a periodical payments order made in favour of a child under this section ceases to have effect on the date on which the child attains the age of sixteen or at any time after that date but before or on the date on which he attains the age of eighteen, then if, on an application made to the court for an order under this subsection, it appears to the court that—

(a) the child is, will be or (if an order were made under this subsection) would be receiving instruction at an educational establishment or undergoing training for a trade, profession or vocation, whether or not he also is, will be or would be in gainful employment; or

(b) there are special circumstances which justify the making of an order under this subsection,

the court shall have power by order to revive the first mentioned order from such date as the court may specify, not being earlier than the date of the making of the application, and to exercise its power under section 31 of this Act in relation to any order so revived.

(7) Without prejudice to the generality of subsection (6)(c) or (f) above, an order under this section for the payment of a lump sum—

    (a) may be made for the purpose of enabling any liabilities or expenses reasonably incurred in maintaining the applicant or any child of the family to whom the application relates before the making of the application to be met;

    (b) may provide for the payment of that sum by instalments of such amount as may be specified in the order and may require the payment of the instalments to be secured to the satisfaction of the court.

Additional provisions with respect to financial provision and property adjustment orders

28　Duration of continuing financial provision orders in favour of party to marriage, and effect of remarriage or formation of a civil partnership

(1) Subject in the case of an order made on or after the grant of a decree of divorce or nullity of marriage to the provisions of sections 25A(2) above and 31(7) below, the term to be specified in a periodical payments or secured periodical payments order in favour of a party to a marriage shall be such term as the court thinks fit, except that the term shall not begin before or extend beyond the following limits, that is to say—

    (a) in the case of a periodical payments order, the term shall begin not earlier than the date of the making of an application for the order, and shall be so defined as not to extend beyond the death of either of the parties to the marriage or, where the order is made on or after the grant of a decree of divorce or nullity of marriage, the remarriage of, or formation of a civil partnership by, the party in whose favour the order is made; and

    (b) in the case of a secured periodical payments order, the term shall begin not earlier than the date of the making of an application for the order, and shall be so defined as not to extend beyond the death or, where the order is made on or after the grant of such a decree, the remarriage of, or formation of a civil partnership by, the party in whose favour the order is made.

(1A) Where a periodical payments or secured periodical payments order in favour of a party to a marriage is made on or after the grant of a decree of divorce or nullity of marriage, the court may direct that that party shall not be entitled to apply under section 31 below for the extension of the term specified in the order.

(2) Where a periodical payments or secured periodical payments order in favour of a party to a marriage is made otherwise than on or after the grant of a decree of divorce or nullity of marriage, and the marriage in question is subsequently dissolved or annulled but the order continues in force, the order shall, notwithstanding anything in it, cease to have effect on the remarriage of, or formation of a civil partnership by, that party, except in relation to any arrears due under or on the date of the remarriage or formation of the civil partnership.

(3) If after the grant of a decree dissolving or annulling a marriage either party to that marriage remarries, whether at any time before or after the commencement of this Act or forms a civil partnership, that party shall not be entitled to apply, by reference to the grant of that decree, for a financial provision order in his or her favour, or for a property adjustment order, against the other party to that marriage.

29　Duration of continuing financial provision orders in favour of children, and age limit on making certain orders in their favour

(1) Subject to subsection (3) below, no financial provision order and no order for a transfer of property under section 24(1)(a) above shall be made in favour of a child who has attained the age of eighteen.

(2) The term to be specified in a periodical payments or secured periodical payments order in favour of a child may begin with the date of the making of an application for the order in question or any later date or a date ascertained in accordance with subsection (5) or (6) below but—

(a) shall not in the first instance extend beyond the date of the birthday of the child next following his attaining the upper limit of the compulsory school age (construed in accordance with section 8 of the Education Act 1996) unless the court considers that in the circumstances of the case the welfare of the child requires that it should extend to a later date; and

(b) shall not in any event, subject to subsection (3) below, extend beyond the date of the child's eighteenth birthday.

(3) Subsection (1) above, and paragraph (b) of subsection (2), shall not apply in the case of a child, if it appears to the court that—

(a) the child is, or will be, or if an order were made without complying with either or both of those provisions would be, receiving instruction at an educational establishment or undergoing training for a trade, profession or vocation, whether or not he is also or will also be, in gainful employment; or

(b) there are special circumstances which justify the making of an order without complying with either or both of those provisions.

(4) Any periodical payments order in favour of a child shall, notwithstanding anything in the order, cease to have effect on the death of the person liable to make payments under the order, except in relation to any arrears due under the order on the date of the death.

(5) Where—

(a) a maintenance calculation ('the current calculation') is in force with respect to a child; and

(b) an application is made under Part II of this Act for a periodical payments or secured periodical payments order in favour of that child—

(i) in accordance with section 8 of the Child Support Act 1991; and

(ii) before the end of the period of 6 months beginning with the making of the current calculation,

the term to be specified in any such order made on that application may be expressed to begin on, or at any time after, the earliest permitted date.

(6) For the purposes of subsection (5) above, 'the earliest permitted date' is whichever is the later of—

(a) the date 6 months before the application is made; or

(b) the date on which the current calculation took effect or, where successive maintenance calculations have been continuously in force with respect to a child, on which the first of those calculations took effect.

(7) Where—

(a) a maintenance calculation ceases to have effect by or under a provision of the Child Support Act 1991; and

(b) an application is made before the end of the period of 6 months beginning with the relevant date, for a periodical payments or secured periodical payments order in favour of a child with respect to whom that maintenance calculation was in force immediately before it ceased to have effect,

the term to be specified in any such order made on that application may begin with the date on which that maintenance calculation ceased to have effect, or any later date.

(8) In subsection (7)(b) above—

(a) where the maintenance calculation ceased to have effect, the relevant date is the date on which it so ceased;

30   Direction for settlement of instrument for securing payments or effecting property adjustment

Where the court decides to make a financial provision order requiring any payments to be secured or a property adjustment order—

(a) it may direct that the matter be referred to one of the conveyancing counsel of the court for him to settle a proper instrument to be executed by all necessary parties; and

(b) where the order is to be made in proceedings for divorce, nullity of marriage or judicial separation it may, if it thinks fit, defer the grant of the decree in question until the instrument has been duly executed.

Variation, discharge and enforcement of certain orders etc.

31   Variation, discharge etc., of certain orders for financial relief

(1) Where the court has made an order to which this section applies, then, subject to the provisions of this section and of section 28(1A) above, the court shall have power to vary or discharge the order or to suspend any provision thereof temporarily and to revive the operation of any provision so suspended.

(2) This section applies to the following orders, that is to say—

(a) any order for maintenance pending suit and any interim order for maintenance;

(b) any periodical payments order;

(c) any secured periodical payments order;

(d) any order made by virtue of section 23(3)(c) or 27(7)(b) above (provision for payment of a lump sum by instalments);

(dd) any deferred order made by virtue of section 23(1)(c) (lump sums) which includes provision made by virtue of—

(i) section 25B(4)

(ii) section 25C, or

(iii) section 25F(2),

(provision in respect of pension rights or pension compensation rights);

(e) any order for a settlement of property under section 24(1)(b) or for a variation of settlement under section 24(1)(c) or (d) above, being an order made on or after the grant of a decree of judicial separation;

(f) any order made under section 24A(1) above for the sale of property;

(g) a pension sharing order under section 24B above, or a pension compensation sharing order under section 24E above, which is made at a time before the decree has been made absolute;

(2A) Where the court has made an order referred to in subsection (2)(a), (b) or (c) above, then, subject to the provisions of this section, the court shall have power to remit the payment of any arrears due under the order or of any part thereof.

(2B) Where the court has made an order referred to in subsection (2)(dd)(ii) above, this section shall cease to apply to the order on the death of either of the parties to the marriage.

(3) The powers exercisable by the court under this section in relation to an order shall be exercisable also in relation to any instrument executed in pursuance of the order.

(4) The court shall not exercise the powers conferred by this section in relation to an order for a settlement under section 24(1)(b) or for a variation of settlement under section 24(1)(c) or (d) above except on an application made in proceedings—

(a) for the rescission of the decree of judicial separation by reference to which the order was made, or

(b) for the dissolution of the marriage in question.

(4A) In relation to an order which falls within paragraph (g) of subsection (2) above ('the subsection (2) order')—

(a) the powers conferred by this section may be exercised—

(i) only on an application made before the subsection (2) order has or, but for paragraph (b) below, would have taken effect; and

        (ii) only if, at the time when the application is made, the decree has not been made absolute; and

    (b) an application made in accordance with paragraph (a) above prevents the subsection (2) order from taking effect before the application has been dealt with.

(4B) No variation of a pension sharing order, or a pension compensation sharing order, shall be made so as to take effect before the decree is made absolute.

(4C) The variation of a pension sharing order, or a pension compensation sharing order, prevents the order taking effect before the end of such period after the making of the variation as may be prescribed by regulations made by the Lord Chancellor.

(5) Subject to subsections (7A) to (7G) below and without prejudice to any power exercisable by virtue of subsection (2)(d), (dd), (e) or (g) above or otherwise than by virtue of this section, no property adjustment order or pension sharing order or pension compensation sharing order shall be made on an application for the variation of a periodical payments or secured periodical payments order made (whether in favour of a party to a marriage or in favour of a child of the family) under section 23 above, and no order for the payment of a lump sum shall be made on an application for the variation of a periodical payments or secured periodical payments order in favour of a party to a marriage (whether made under section 23 or under section 27 above).

(6) Where the person liable to make payments under a secured periodical payments order has died, an application under this section relating to that order (and to any order made under section 24A(1) above which requires the proceeds of sale of property to be used for securing those payments) may be made by the person entitled to payments under the periodical payments order or by the personal representatives of the deceased person, but no such application shall, except with the permission of the court, be made after the end of the period of six months from the date on which representation in regard to the estate of that person is first taken out.

(7) In exercising the powers conferred by this section the court shall have regard to all the circumstances of the case, first consideration being given to the welfare while a minor of any child of the family who has not attained the age of eighteen, and the circumstances of the case shall include any change in any of the matters to which the court was required to have regard when making the order to which the application relates, and—

    (a) in the case of a periodical payments or secured periodical payments order made on or after the grant of a decree of divorce or nullity of marriage, the court shall consider whether in all the circumstances and after having regard to any such change it would be appropriate to vary the order so that payments under the order are required to be made or secured only for such further period as will in the opinion of the court be sufficient (in the light of any proposed exercise by the court, where the marriage has been dissolved of its powers under subsection (7B) below) to enable the party in whose favour the order was made to adjust without undue hardship to the termination of those payments;

    (b) in a case where the party against whom the order was made has died, the circumstances of the case shall also include the changed circumstances resulting from his or her death.

(7A) Subsection (7B) below applies where, after the dissolution of a marriage, the court—

    (a) discharges a periodical payments order or secured periodical payments order made in favour of a party to the marriage; or

    (b) varies such an order so that payments under the order are required to be made or secured only for such further period as is determined by the court.

(7B) The court has power, in addition to any power it has apart from this subsection, to make supplemental provision consisting of any of—

    (a) an order for the payment of a lump sum in favour of a party to the marriage;

    (b) one or more property adjustment orders in favour of a party to the marriage;

  (ba) one or more pension sharing orders;

(bb) a pension compensation sharing order;

(c) a direction that the party in whose favour the original order discharged or varied was made is not entitled to make any further application for—

(i) a periodical payments or secured periodical payments order, or

(ii) an extension of the period to which the original order is limited by any variation made by the court.

(7C) An order for the payment of a lump sum made under subsection (7B) above may—

(a) provide for the payment of that sum by instalments of such amount as may be specified in the order; and

(b) require the payment of the instalments to be secured to the satisfaction of the court.

(7D) Section 23(6) above applies where the court makes an order for the payment of a lump sum under subsection (7B) above as it applies where it makes such an order under section 23 above.

(7E) If under subsection (7B) above the court makes more than one property adjustment order in favour of the same party to the marriage, each of those orders must fall within a different paragraph of section 21(2) above.

(7F) Sections 24A and 30 above apply where the court makes a property adjustment order under subsection (7B) above as they apply where it makes such an order under section 24 above.

(7G) Subsections (3) to (5) of section 24B above apply in relation to a pension sharing order under subsection (7B) above as they apply in relation to a pension sharing order under that section.

(7H) Subsections (3) to (10) of section 24E above apply in relation to a pension compensation sharing order under subsection (7B) above as they apply in relation to a pension compensation sharing order under that section.

(8) The personal representatives of a deceased person against whom a secured periodical payments order was made shall not be liable for having distributed any part of the estate of the deceased after the expiration of the period of six months referred to in subsection (6) above on the ground that they ought to have taken into account the possibility that the court might permit an application under this section to be made after that period by the person entitled to payments under the order; but this subsection shall not prejudice any power to recover any part of the estate so distributed arising by virtue of the making of an order in pursuance of this section.

(9) The following are to be left out of account when considering for the purposes of subsection (6) above when representation was first taken out—

(a) a grant limited to settled land or to trust property,

(b) any other grant that does not permit any of the estate to be distributed,

(c) a grant limited to real estate or to personal estate, unless a grant limited to the remainder of the estate has previously been made or is made at the same time,

(d) a grant, or its equivalent, made outside the United Kingdom (but see subsection (9A) below).

...

(10) Where the court, in exercise of its powers under this section, decides to vary or discharge a periodical payments or secured periodical payments order, then, subject to section 28(1) and (2) above, the court shall have power to direct that the variation or discharge shall not take effect until the expiration of such period as may be specified in the order.

(11) Where—

(a) a periodical payments or secured periodical payments order in favour of more than one child ('the order') is in force;

(b) the order requires payments specified in it to be made to or for the benefit of more than one child without apportioning those payments between them;

(c) a maintenance calculation ('the calculation') is made with respect to one or more, but not all, of the children with respect to whom those payments are to be made; and

(d) an application is made, before the end of the period of 6 months beginning with the date on which the assessment was made, for the variation or discharge of the order, the court may, in exercise of its powers under this section to vary or discharge the order, direct that the variation or discharge shall take effect from the date on which the assessment took effect or any later date.

(12) Where—

(a) an order ('the child order') of a kind prescribed for the purposes of section 10(1) of the Child Support Act 1991 is affected by a maintenance calculation;

(b) on the date on which the child order became so affected there was in force a periodical payments or secured periodical payments order ('the spousal order') in favour of a party to a marriage having the care of the child in whose favour the child order was made; and

(c) an application is made, before the end of the period of 6 months beginning with the date on which the maintenance calculation was made, for the spousal order to be varied or discharged,

the court may, in exercise of its powers under this section to vary or discharge the spousal order, direct that the variation or discharge shall take effect from the date on which the child order became so affected or any later date.

(13) For the purposes of subsection (12) above, an order is affected if it ceases to have effect or is modified by or under section 10 of the Child Support Act 1991.

(14) Subsections (11) and (12) above are without prejudice to any other power of the court to direct that the variation or discharge of an order under this section shall take effect from a date earlier than that on which the order for variation or discharge was made.

(15) The power to make regulations under subsection (4C) above shall be exercisable by statutory instrument which shall be subject to annulment in pursuance of a resolution of either House of Parliament.

32   Payment of certain arrears unenforceable without the leave of the court

(1) A person shall not be entitled to enforce through the High Court or the family court the payment of any arrears due under an order for maintenance pending suit, an interim order for maintenance or any financial provision order without the leave of that court if those arrears became due more than twelve months before proceedings to enforce the payment of them are begun.

(2) The court hearing an application for the grant of leave under this section may refuse leave, or may grant leave subject to such restrictions and conditions (including conditions as to the allowing of time for payment or the making of payments by instalments) as that court thinks proper, or may remit the payment of the arrears or any part thereof.

(3) An application for the grant of leave under this section shall be made in such manner as may be prescribed by rules of court.

33   Orders for repayment in certain cases of sums paid under certain orders

(1) Where on an application made under this section in relation to an order to which this section applies it appears to the court that by reason of—

(a) a change in the circumstances of the person entitled to, or liable to make, payments under the order since the order was made, or

(b) the changed circumstances resulting from the death of the person so liable,

the amount received by the person entitled to payments under the order in respect of a period after those circumstances changed or after the death of the person liable to make payments under the order, as the case may be, exceeds the amount which the person so liable or his or her personal representatives should have been required to pay, the court may order the respondent to the application to pay to the applicant such sum, not exceeding the amount of the excess, as the court thinks just.

(2) This section applies to the following orders, that is to say—

(a) any order for maintenance pending suit and any interim order for maintenance;

(b) any periodical payments order; and

(c) any secured periodical payments order.

(3) An application under this section may be made by the person liable to make payments under an order to which this section applies or his or her personal representatives and may be made against the person entitled to payments under the order or her or his personal representatives.

(4) An application under this section may be made in proceedings in the High Court or the family court for—

(a) the variation or discharge of the order to which this section applies, or

(b) leave to enforce, or the enforcement of, the payment of arrears under that order;

but when not made in such proceedings shall be made to a county court, and accordingly references in this section to the court are references to the High Court or a county court, as the circumstances require.

. . .

(6) An order under this section for the payment of any sum may provide for the payment of that sum by instalments of such amount as may be specified in the order.

Consent orders

33A   Consent orders for financial provision or property adjustment

(1) Notwithstanding anything in the preceding provisions of this Part of this Act, on an application for a consent order for financial relief the court may, unless it has reason to think that there are other circumstances into which it ought to inquire, make an order in the terms agreed on the basis only of the prescribed information furnished with the application.

(2) Subsection (1) above applies to an application for a consent order varying or discharging an order for financial relief as it applies to an application for an order for financial relief.

(3) In this section—

'consent order,' in relation to an application for an order, means an order in the terms applied for to which the respondent agrees;

'order for financial relief' means an order under any of sections 23, 24, 24A, 24B or 27 above; and

'prescribed' means prescribed by rules of court.

Maintenance agreements

34   Validity of maintenance agreements

(1) If a maintenance agreement includes a provision purporting to restrict any right to apply to a court for an order containing financial arrangements, then—

(a) that provision shall be void; but

(b) any other financial arrangements contained in the agreement shall not thereby be rendered void or unenforceable and shall, unless they are void or unenforceable for any other reason (and subject to sections 35 and 36 below), be binding on the parties to the agreement.

(2) In this section and in section 35 below—

'maintenance agreement' means any agreement in writing made, whether before or after the commencement of this Act, between the parties to a marriage, being—

(a) an agreement containing financial arrangements, whether made during the continuance or after the dissolution or annulment of the marriage; or

(b) a separation agreement which contains no financial arrangements in a case where no other agreement in writing between the same parties contains such arrangements;

'financial arrangements' means provisions governing the rights and liabilities towards one another when living separately of the parties to a marriage (including a marriage which has been dissolved or annulled) in respect of the making or securing of payments or the disposition or use of any property, including such rights and liabilities with respect to the maintenance or education of any child, whether or not a child of the family.

35   Alteration of agreements by court during lives of parties

(1) Where a maintenance agreement is for the time being subsisting and each of the parties to the agreement is for the time being either domiciled or resident in England and Wales, then, subject to subsections (1A) and (3) below, either party may apply to the court for an order under this section.

(1A) ...

(2) If the court is satisfied either—

(a) that by reason of a change in the circumstances in the light of which any financial arrangements contained in the agreement were made or, as the case may be, financial arrangements were omitted from it (including a change foreseen by the parties when making the agreement), the agreement should be altered so as to make different, or, as the case may be, so as to contain, financial arrangements, or

(b) that the agreement does not contain proper financial arrangements with respect to any child of the family,

then subject to subsections (4) and (5) below, the court may by order make such alterations in the agreement—

(i) by varying or revoking any financial arrangements contained in it, or

(ii) by inserting in it financial arrangements for the benefit of one of the parties to the agreement or of a child of the family,

as may appear to the court to be just having regard to all the circumstances, including, if relevant, the matters mentioned in section 25(4) above; and the agreement shall have effect thereafter as if any alteration made by the order had been made by agreement between the parties and for valuable consideration.

...

(4) Where the court decides to alter, by order under this section, an agreement by inserting provision for the making or securing by one of the parties to the agreement of periodical payments for the maintenance of the other party or by increasing the rate of the periodical payments which the agreement provides shall be made by one of the parties for the maintenance of the other, the term for which the payments or, as the case may be, the additional payments attributable to the increase are to be made under the agreement as altered by the order shall be such term as the court may specify, subject to the following limits, that is to say—

(a) where the payments will not be secured, the term shall be so defined as not to extend beyond the death of either of the parties to the agreement or the remarriage of, or formation of a civil partnership by, the party to whom the payments are to be made;

(b) where the payments will be secured, the term shall be so defined as not to extend beyond the death or remarriage of, or formation of a civil partnership by, that party.

(5) Where the court decides to alter, by order under this section, an agreement by inserting provision for the making or securing by one of the parties to the agreement of periodical payments for the maintenance of a child of the family or by increasing the rate of the periodical payments which the agreement provides shall be made or secured by one of the parties for the maintenance of such a child, then, in deciding the term for which under the agreement as altered by the order the payments, or as the case may be, the additional payments attributable to the increase are to be made or secured for the benefit of the child, the court shall apply the provisions of section 29(2) and (3) above as to age limits as if the order in question were a periodical payments or secured periodical payments order in favour of the child.

(6) For the avoidance of doubt it is hereby declared that nothing in this section or in section 34 above affects any power of a court before which any proceedings between the parties to a maintenance agreement are brought under any other enactment (including a provision of this Act) to make an order containing financial arrangements or any right of either party to apply for such an order in such proceedings.

36   Alteration of agreements by court after death of one party

(1) Where a maintenance agreement within the meaning of section 34 above provides for the continuation of payment under the agreement after the death of one of the parties and that party dies domiciled in England and Wales, the surviving party or the personal representatives of the deceased party may, subject to subsections (2) and (3) below, apply to the court for an order under section 35 above.

(2) An application under this section shall not, except with the permission of the court, be made after the end of the period of six months from the date on which representation in regard to the estate of the deceased is first taken out.

...

(4) If a maintenance agreement is altered by the court on an application made in pursuance of subsection (1) above, the like consequences shall ensue as if the alteration had been made immediately before the death by agreement between the parties and for valuable consideration.

(5) The provisions of this section shall not render the personal representatives of the deceased liable for having distributed any part of the estate of the deceased after the expiration of the period of six months referred to in subsection (2) above on the ground that they ought to have taken into account the possibility that the court might permit an application by virtue of this section to be made by the surviving party after that period, but this subsection shall not prejudice any power to recover any part of the estate so distributed arising by virtue of the making of an order in pursuance of this section.

(6) Section 31(9) above shall apply for the purposes of subsection (2) above as it applies for the purposes of subsection (6) of section 31.

Miscellaneous and supplemental

37 Avoidance of transactions intended to prevent or reduce financial relief

(1) For the purposes of this section 'financial relief' means relief under any of the provisions of sections 22, 23, 24, 24B, 27, 31 (except subsection (6)) and 35 above, and any reference in this section to defeating a person's claim for financial relief is a reference to preventing financial relief from being granted to that person, or to that person for the benefit of a child of the family, or reducing the amount of any financial relief which might be so granted, or frustrating or impeding the enforcement of any order which might be or has been made at his instance under any of those provisions.

(2) Where proceedings for financial relief are brought by one person against another, the court may, on the application of the first-mentioned person—

    (a) if it is satisfied that the other party to the proceedings is, with the intention of defeating the claim for financial relief, about to make any disposition or to transfer out of the jurisdiction or otherwise deal with any property, make such order as it thinks fit for restraining the other party from so doing or otherwise for protecting the claim;

    (b) if it is satisfied that the other party has, with that intention, made a reviewable disposition and that if the disposition were set aside financial relief or different financial relief would be granted to the applicant, make an order setting aside the disposition;

    (c) if it is satisfied, in a case where an order has been obtained under any of the provisions mentioned in subsection (1) above by the applicant against the other party, that the other party has, with that intention, made a reviewable disposition, make an order setting aside the disposition;

and an application for the purposes of paragraph (b) above shall be made in the proceedings for the financial relief in question.

(3) Where the court makes an order under subsection (2)(b) or (c) above setting aside a disposition it shall give such consequential directions as it thinks fit for giving effect to the order (including directions requiring the making of any payments or the disposal of any property).

(4) Any disposition made by the other party to the proceedings for financial relief in question (whether before or after the commencement of those proceedings) is a reviewable disposition for the purposes of subsection (2)(b) and (c) above unless it was made for valuable consideration (other than marriage) to a person who, at the time of the disposition, acted in relation to it in good faith and without notice of any intention on the part of the other party to defeat the applicant's claim for financial relief.

(5) Where an application is made under this section with respect to a disposition which took place less than three years before the date of the application or with respect to a disposition or other dealing with property which is about to take place and the court is satisfied—

(a) in a case falling within subsection (2)(a) or (b) above, that the disposition or other dealing would (apart from this section) have the consequence, or

(b) in a case falling within subsection (2)(c) above, that the disposition has had the consequence,

of defeating the applicant's claim for financial relief, it shall be presumed, unless the contrary is shown, that the person who disposed of or is about to dispose of or deal with the property did so or, as the case may be, is about to do so, with the intention of defeating the applicant's claim for financial relief.

(6) In this section 'disposition' does not include any provision contained in a will or codicil but, with that exception, includes any conveyance, assurance or gift of property of any description, whether made by an instrument or otherwise.

(7) This section does not apply to a disposition made before 1st January 1968.

38   Order for repayment in certain cases of sums paid after cessation of order by reason of remarriage or formation of civil partnership

(1) Where—

(a) a periodical payments or secured periodical payments order in favour of a party to a marriage (hereafter in this section referred to as 'a payments order') has ceased to have effect by reason of the remarriage of, or formation of a civil partnership by, that party, and

(b) the person liable to make payments under the order or his or her personal representatives made payments in accordance with it in respect of a period after the date of the remarriage or formation of the civil partnership in the mistaken belief that the order was still subsisting,

the person so liable or his or her personal representatives shall not be entitled to bring proceedings in respect of a cause of action arising out of the circumstances mentioned in paragraphs (a) and (b) above against the person entitled to payments under the order or her or his personal representatives, but may instead make an application against that person or her or his personal representatives under this section.

(2) On an application under this section the court to which the application is made may order the respondent to pay to the applicant a sum equal to the amount of the payments made in respect of the period mentioned in subsection (1)(b) above or, if it appears to the court that it would be unjust to make that order, it may either order the respondent to pay to the applicant such lesser sum as it thinks fit or dismiss the application.

(3) An application under this section may be made in proceedings in the High Court or the family court for leave to enforce, or the enforcement of, payment of arrears under the order in question, but when not made in such proceedings shall be made to the family court; and accordingly references in this section to the court are references to the High Court or the family court, as the circumstances require.

. . .

(5) An order under this section for the payment of any sum may provide for the payment of that sum by instalments of such amount as may be specified in the order.

(6) An officer of the family court and the collecting officer under an attachment of earnings order made to secure payments under a payments order, shall not be liable—

(a) in the case of an officer of the family court, for any act done by him, in pursuance of a payments order requiring payments to be made to the court or an officer of the court, after the date on which that order ceased to have effect by reason of the remarriage of, or formation of a civil partnership by, the person entitled to payments under it, and

(b) in the case of the collecting officer, for any act done by him after that date in accordance with any enactment or rule of court specifying how payments made to him in compliance with the attachment of earnings order are to be dealt with, if, but only if, the act was one which he would have been under a duty to do had the payments order not so ceased to have effect and the act was done before notice in writing of the fact that the person so entitled had remarried or formed civil partnership was given to him by or on behalf of that person, the person liable to make payments under the payments order or the personal representatives of either of those persons.

(7) In this section 'collecting officer,' in relation to an attachment of earnings order, means the officer of the High Court, or the officer of the family court, to whom a person makes payments in compliance with the order.

39 Settlement, etc., made in compliance with a property adjustment order may be avoided on bankruptcy of settlor

The fact that a settlement or transfer of property had to be made in order to comply with a property adjustment order shall not prevent that settlement or transfer from being a transaction in respect of which an order may be made under section 339 or 340 of the Insolvency Act 1986 (transactions at an undervalue and preferences).

40 Payments etc., under order made in favour of person suffering from mental disorder

(1) Where the court makes an order under this Part of this Act requiring payments (including a lump sum payment) to be made, or property to be transferred, to a party to a marriage and the court is satisfied that the person in whose favour the order is made ('P') lacks capacity (within the meaning of the Mental Capacity Act 2005) in relation to the provisions of the order then, subject to any order, direction or authority made or given in relation to P under that Act, the court may order the payments to be made, or as the case may be, the property to be transferred, to such person ('D') as it may direct.

(2) In carrying out any functions of his in relation to an order made under subsection (1), D must act in P's best interests (within the meaning of that Act).

40A Appeals relating to pension sharing orders which have taken effect

(1) Subsections (2) and (3) below apply where an appeal against a pension sharing order is begun on or after the day on which the order takes effect.

(2) If the pension sharing order relates to a person's rights under a pension arrangement, the appeal court may not set aside or vary the order if the person responsible for the pension arrangement has acted to his detriment in reliance on the taking effect of the order.

(3) If the pension sharing order relates to a person's shareable state scheme rights, the appeal court may not set aside or vary the order if the Secretary of State has acted to his detriment in reliance on the taking effect of the order.

(4) In determining for the purposes of subsection (2) or (3) above whether a person has acted to his detriment in reliance on the taking effect of the order, the appeal court may disregard any detriment which in its opinion is insignificant.

(5) Where subsection (2) or (3) above applies, the appeal court may make such further orders (including one or more pension sharing orders) as it thinks fit for the purpose of putting the parties in the position it considers appropriate.

(6) Section 24C above only applies to a pension sharing order under this section if the decision of the appeal court can itself be the subject of an appeal.

(7) In subsection (2) above, the reference to the person responsible for the pension arrangement is to be read in accordance with section 25D(4) above.

40B Appeals relating to pension compensation sharing orders which have taken effect

(1) This section applies where an appeal against a pension compensation sharing order is begun on or after the day on which the order takes effect.

(2) If the Board of the Pension Protection Fund has acted to its detriment in reliance on the taking effect of the order the appeal court—

(a) may not set aside or vary the order;

(b) may make such further orders (including a pension compensation sharing order) as it thinks fit for the purpose of putting the parties in the position it considers appropriate.

(3) In determining for the purposes of subsection (2) whether the Board has acted to its detriment the appeal court may disregard any detriment which in the court's opinion is insignificant.

(4) Section 24F (duty to stay) only applies to a pension compensation sharing order under this section if the decision of the appeal court can itself be the subject of an appeal.

PART IV MISCELLANEOUS AND SUPPLEMENTAL

...

48 Evidence

(1) The evidence of a husband or wife shall be admissible in any proceedings to prove that marital intercourse did or did not take place between them during any period.

(2) In any proceedings for nullity of marriage, evidence on the question of sexual capacity shall be heard in camera unless in any case the court is satisfied that in the interests of justice any such evidence ought to be heard in open court.

49 Parties to proceedings under this Act

(1) Where in a petition for divorce or judicial separation, or in any other pleading praying for either form of relief, one party to a marriage alleges that the other has committed adultery, he or she shall make the person alleged to have committed adultery with the other party to the marriage a party to the proceedings unless excused by the court on special grounds from doing so.

(2) Rules of court may, either generally or in such case as may be prescribed by the rules, exclude the application of subsection (1) above where the person alleged to have committed adultery with the other party to the marriage is not named in the petition or other pleading.

(3) Where in pursuance of subsection (1) above a person is made a party to proceedings for divorce or judicial separation, the court may, if after the close of the evidence on the part of the person making the allegation of adultery it is of opinion that there is not sufficient evidence against the person so made a party, dismiss him or her from the suit.

(4) Rules of court may make provision, in cases not failing within subsection (1) above, with respect to the joinder as parties to proceedings under this Act of persons involved in allegations of adultery or other improper conduct made in those proceedings, and with respect to the dismissal from such proceedings of any parties so joined, and rules of court made by virtue of this subsection may make different provision for different cases.

(5) In every case in which adultery with any party to a suit is alleged against any person not made a party to the suit or in which the court considers, in the interest of any person not already a party to the suit, that that person should be made a party to the suit, the court may if it thinks fit allow that person to intervene upon such terms, if any, as the court thinks just.

52 Interpretation

(1) In this Act—

'child', in relation to one or both of the parties to a marriage, includes an illegitimate child of that party or, as the case may be, of both parties;

'child of the family,' in relation to the parties to a marriage, means—

(a) a child of both of those parties; and

(b) any other child, not being a child who is placed with those parties as foster parents by a local authority or voluntary organisation, who has been treated by both of those parties as a child of their family;

'the court' (except where the context otherwise requires) means the High Court or the family court;

'education' includes training;

'maintenance calculation' has the same meaning as it has in the Child Support Act 1991 by virtue of section 54 of that Act as read with any regulations in force under that section;

...

(2) In this Act—

(a) references to financial provision orders, periodical payments and secured periodical payments orders and orders for the payment of a lump sum, and references to property adjustment orders, shall be construed in accordance with section 21 above;

(aa) references to pension sharing orders shall be construed in accordance with section 21A above; and

(b) references to orders for maintenance pending suit and to interim orders for maintenance shall be construed respectively in accordance with section 22 and section 27(5) above.

(3) For the avoidance of doubt it is hereby declared that references in this Act to remarriage include references to a marriage which is by law void or voidable.

(3A) References in this Act to the formation of a civil partnership by a person include references to a civil partnership which is by law void or voidable.

(4) Except where the contrary intention is indicated, references in this Act to any enactment include references to that enactment as amended, extended or applied by or under any subsequent enactment, including this Act.

...

Domicile and Matrimonial Proceedings Act 1973

(1973 c. 45)

PART I DOMICILE

Husband and wife

1 Abolition of wife's dependent domicile

(1) Subject to subsection (2) below, the domicile of a married woman as at any time after the coming into force of this section shall, instead of being the same as her husband's by virtue only of marriage, be ascertained by reference to the same factors as in the case of any other individual capable of having an independent domicile.

(2) Where immediately before this section came into force a woman was married and then had her husband's domicile by dependence, she is to be treated as retaining that domicile (as a domicile of choice, if it is not also her domicile of origin) unless and until it is changed by acquisition or revival of another domicile either on or after the coming into force of this section.

(3) This section extends to England and Wales, Scotland and Northern Ireland.

Minors and pupils

3 Age at which independent domicile can be acquired

(1) The time at which a person first becomes capable of having an independent domicile shall be when he attains the age of sixteen or marries under that age; and in the case of a person who immediately before 1 January 1974 was incapable of having an independent domicile, but had then attained the age of sixteen or been married, it shall be that date.

(2) This section extends to England and Wales and Northern Ireland (but not to Scotland).

4 Dependent domicile of child not living with his father

(1) Subsection (2) of this section shall have effect with respect to the dependent domicile of a child as at any time after the coming into force of this section when his father and mother are alive but living apart.

(2) The child's domicile as at that time shall be that of his mother if—
  (a) he then has his home with her and has no home with his father; or
  (b) he has at any time had her domicile by virtue of paragraph (a) above and has not since had a home with his father.

(3) As at any time after the coming into force of this section, the domicile of a child whose mother is dead shall be that which she last had before she died if at her death he had her domicile by virtue of subsection (2) above and he has not since had a home with his father.

(4) Nothing in this section prejudices any existing rule of law as to cases in which a child's domicile is regarded as being, by dependence, that of his mother.

(5) In this section, 'child' means a person incapable of having an independent domicile.

(6) This section extends to England and Wales, Scotland and Northern Ireland.

...

Inheritance (Provision for Family and Dependants) Act 1975

(1975 c. 63)

1 Application for financial provision from deceased's estate

(1) Where after the commencement of this Act a person dies domiciled in England and Wales and is survived by any of the following persons:—
  (a) the spouse or civil partner of the deceased;
  (b) a former spouse or former civil partner of the deceased, but not one who has formed a subsequent marriage or civil partnership;
  (ba) any person (not being a person included in paragraph (a) or (b) above) to whom subsection (1A) or (1B) below applies;
  (c) a child of the deceased;
  (d) any person (not being a child of the deceased) who in relation to any marriage or civil partnership to which the deceased was at any time a party, or otherwise in relation to any family in which the deceased at any time stood in the role of a parent, was treated by the deceased as a child of the family;
  (e) any person (not being a person included in the foregoing paragraphs of this subsection) who immediately before the death of the deceased was being maintained, either wholly or partly, by the deceased;
that person may apply to the court for an order under section 2 of this Act on the ground that the disposition of the deceased's estate effected by his will or the law relating to intestacy, or the combination of his will and that law, is not such as to make reasonable financial provision for the applicant.

(1A) This subsection applies to a person if the deceased died on or after 1st January 1996 and, during the whole of the period of two years ending immediately before the date when the deceased died, the person was living—
  (a) in the same household as the deceased, and
  (b) as the husband or wife of the deceased.

(1B) This subsection applies to a person if for the whole of the period of two years ending immediately before the date when the deceased died the person was living—
  (a) in the same household as the deceased, and
  (b) as the civil partner of the deceased.

(2) In this Act 'reasonable financial —
  (a) in the case of an application made by virtue of subsection (1)(a) above by the husband or wife of the deceased (except where the marriage with the deceased was the subject of a decree of judicial separation and at the date of death the decree was in force and the

separation was continuing), means such financial provision as it would be reasonable in all the circumstances of the case for a husband or wife to receive, whether or not that provision is required for his or her maintenance;

(aa) in the case of an application made by virtue of subsection (1)(a) above by the civil partner of the deceased (except where, at the date of death, a separation order under Chapter 2 of Part 2 of the Civil Partnership Act 2004 was in force in relation to the civil partnership and the separation was continuing), means such financial provision as it would be reasonable in all the circumstances of the case for a civil partner to receive, whether or not that provision is required for his or her maintenance;

(b) in the case of any other application made by virtue of subsection (1) above, means such financial provision as it would be reasonable in all the circumstances of the case for the applicant to receive for his maintenance.

(2A) The reference in subsection (1)(d) above to a family in which the deceased stood in the role of a parent includes a family of which the deceased was the only member (apart from the applicant).

(3) For the purposes of subsection (1)(e) above, a person is to be treated as being maintained by the deceased (either wholly or partly, as the case may be) only if the deceased was making a substantial contribution in money or money's worth towards the reasonable needs of that person, other than a contribution made for full valuable consideration pursuant to an arrangement of a commercial nature.

2 Powers of court to make orders

(1) Subject to the provisions of this Act, where an application is made for an order under this section, the court may, if it is satisfied that the disposition of the deceased's estate effected by his will or the law relating to intestacy, or the combination of his will and that law, is not such as to make reasonable financial provision for the applicant, make any one or more of the following orders:—

(a) an order for the making to the applicant out of the net estate of the deceased of such periodical payments and for such term as may be specified in the order;

(b) an order for the payment to the applicant out of that estate of a lump sum of such amount as may be so specified;

(c) an order for the transfer to the applicant of such property comprised in that estate as may be so specified;

(d) an order for the settlement for the benefit of the applicant of such property comprised in that estate as may be so specified;

(e) an order for the acquisition out of property comprised in that estate of such property as may be so specified and for the transfer of the property so acquired to the applicant or for the settlement thereof for his benefit;

(f) an order varying any ante-nuptial or post-nuptial settlement (including such a settlement made by will) made on the parties to a marriage to which the deceased was one of the parties, the variation being for the benefit of the surviving party to that marriage, or any child of that marriage, or any person who was treated by the deceased as a child of the family in relation to that marriage.

(g) an order varying any settlement made—
(i) during the subsistence of a civil partnership formed by the deceased, or
(ii) in anticipation of the formation of a civil partnership by the deceased,
on the civil partners (including such a settlement made by will), the variation being for the benefit of the surviving civil partner, or any child of both the civil partners, or any person who was treated by the deceased as a child of the family in relation to that civil partnership.

(h) an order varying for the applicant's benefit the trusts on which the deceased's estate is held (whether arising under the will, or the law relating to intestacy, or both).

(2) An order under subsection (1)(a) above providing for the making out of the net estate of the deceased of periodical payments may provide for—

  (a) payments of such amount as may be specified in the order,

  (b) payments equal to the whole of the income of the net estate or of such portion thereof as may be so specified,

  (c) payments equal to the whole of the income of such part of the net estate as the court may direct to be set aside or appropriated for the making out of the income thereof of payments under this section,

or may provide for the amount of the payments or any of them to be determined in any other way the court thinks fit.

(3) Where an order under subsection (1)(a) above provides for the making of payments of an amount specified in the order, the order may direct that such part of the net estate as may be so specified shall be set aside or appropriated for the making out of the income thereof of those payments; but no larger part of the net estate shall be so set aside or appropriated than is sufficient, at the date of the order, to produce by the income thereof the amount required for the making of those payments.

(3A) In assessing for the purposes of an order under this section the extent (if any) to which the net estate is reduced by any debts or liabilities (including any inheritance tax paid or payable out of the estate), the court may assume that the order has already been made.

(4) An order under this section may contain such consequential and supplemental provisions as the court thinks necessary or expedient for the purpose of giving effect to the order or for the purpose of securing that the order operates fairly as between one beneficiary of the estate of the deceased and another and may, in particular, but without prejudice to the generality of this subsection—

  (a) order any person who holds any property which forms part of the net estate of the deceased to make such payment or transfer such property as may be specified in the order;

  (b) vary the disposition of the deceased's estate effected by the will or the law relating to intestacy, or by both the will and the law relating to intestacy, in such manner as the court thinks fair and reasonable having regard to the provisions of the order and all the circumstances of the case;

  (c) confer on the trustees of any property which is the subject of an order under this section such powers as appear to the court to be necessary or expedient.

3   Matters to which court is to have regard in exercising powers under section 2

(1) Where an application is made for an order under section 2 of this Act, the court shall, in determining whether the disposition of the deceased's estate effected by his will or the law relating to intestacy, or the combination of his will and that law, is such as to make reasonable financial provision for the applicant and, if the court considers that reasonable financial provision has not been made, in determining whether and in what manner it shall exercise its powers under that section, have regard to the following matters, that is to say—

  (a) the financial resources and financial needs which the applicant has or is likely to have in the foreseeable future;

  (b) the financial resources and financial needs which any other applicant for an order under section 2 of this Act has or is likely to have in the foreseeable future;

  (c) the financial resources and financial needs which any beneficiary of the estate of the deceased has or is likely to have in the foreseeable future;

  (d) any obligations and responsibilities which the deceased had towards any applicant for an order under the said section 2 or towards any beneficiary of the estate of the deceased;

  (e) the size and nature of the net estate of the deceased;

  (f) any physical or mental disability of any applicant for an order under the said section 2 or any beneficiary of the estate of the deceased;

  (g) any other matter, including the conduct of the applicant or any other person, which in the circumstances of the case the court may consider relevant.

(2) This subsection applies, without prejudice to the generality of paragraph (g) of subsection (1) above, where an application for an order under section 2 of the Act is made by virtue of section 1(1)(a) or (b) of this Act.

The court shall, in addition to the matters specifically mentioned in paragraphs (a) to (f) of that subsection, have regard to—

(a) the age of the applicant and the duration of the marriage or civil partnership;

(b) the contribution made by the applicant to the welfare of the family of the deceased, including any contribution made by looking after the home or caring for the family.

In the case of an application by the wife or husband of the deceased, the court shall also, unless at the date of death a decree of judicial separation was in force and the separation was continuing, have regard to the provision which the applicant might reasonably have expected to receive if on the day on which the deceased died the marriage, instead of being terminated by the death, had been terminated by a decree of divorce; but nothing requires the court to treat such provision as setting an upper or lower limit on the provision which may be made by an order under section 2.

In the case of an application by the civil partner of the deceased, the court shall also, unless at the date of the death a separation order under Chapter 2 of Part 2 of the Civil Partnership Act 2004 was in force and the separation was continuing, have regard to the provision which the applicant might reasonably have expected to receive if on the day on which the deceased died the civil partnership, instead of being terminated by death, had been terminated by a dissolution order; but nothing requires the court to treat such provision as setting an upper or lower limit on the provision which may be made by an order under section 2.

(2A) Without prejudice to the generality of paragraph (g) of subsection (1) above, where an application for an order under section 2 of this Act is made by virtue of section 1(1)(ba) of this Act, the court shall, in addition to the matters specifically mentioned in paragraphs (a) to (f) of that subsection, have regard to—

(a) the age of the applicant and the length of the period during which the applicant lived as the husband or wife or civil partner of the deceased and in the same household as the deceased;

(b) the contribution made by the applicant to the welfare of the family of the deceased, including any contribution made by looking after the home or caring for the family.

(3) Without prejudice to the generality of paragraph (g) of subsection (1) above, where an application for an order under section 2 of this Act is made by virtue of section 1(1)(c) or 1(1)(d) of this Act, the court shall, in addition to the matters specifically mentioned in paragraphs (a) to (f) of that subsection, have regard to the manner in which the applicant was being or in which he might be expected to be educated or trained, and where the application is made by virtue of section 1(1)(d) the court shall also have regard—

(a) to whether the deceased maintained the applicant and, if so, to the length of time for which and basis on which the deceased did so, and to the extent of the contribution made by way of maintenance;

(aa) to whether and, if so, to what extent the deceased assumed responsibility for the maintenance of the applicant;

(b) to whether in maintaining or assuming responsibility for maintaining the applicant the deceased did so knowing that the applicant was not his own child;

(c) to the liability of any other person to maintain the applicant.

(4) Without prejudice to the generality of paragraph (g) of subsection (1) above, where an application for an order under section 2 of this Act is made by virtue of section 1(1)(e) of this Act, the court shall, in addition to the matters specifically mentioned in paragraphs (a) to (f) of that subsection, have regard—

(a) to the length of time for which and basis on which the deceased maintained the applicant, and to the extent of the contribution made by way of maintenance;

(b) to whether and, if so, to what extent the deceased assumed responsibility for the maintenance of the applicant.

(5) In considering the matters to which the court is required to have regard under this section, the court shall take into account the facts as known to the court at the date of the hearing.

4 Time-limit for applications

An application for an order under section 2 of this Act shall not, except with the permission of the court, be made after the end of the period of six months from the date on which representation with respect to the estate of the deceased is first taken out (but nothing prevents the making of an application before such representation is first taken out).

5 Interim orders

(1) Where on an application for an order under section 2 of this Act it appears to the court—

    (a) that the applicant is in immediate need of financial assistance, but it is not yet possible to determine what order (if any) should be made under that section; and

    (b) that property forming part of the net estate of the deceased is or can be made available to meet the need of the applicant;

the court may order that, subject to such conditions or restrictions, if any, as the court may impose and to any further order of the court, there shall be paid to the applicant out of the net estate of the deceased such sum or sums and (if more than one) at such intervals as the court thinks reasonable; and the court may order that, subject to the provisions of this Act, such payments are to be made until such date as the court may specify, not being later than the date on which the court either makes an order under the said section 2 or decides not to exercise its powers under that section.

(2) Subsections (2), (3) and (4) of section 2 of this Act shall apply in relation to an order under this section as they apply in relation to an order under that section.

(3) In determining what order, if any, should be made under this section the court shall, so far as the urgency of the case admits, have regard to the same matters as those to which the court is required to have regard under section 3 of this Act.

(4) An order made under section 2 of this Act may provide that any sum paid to the applicant by virtue of this section shall be treated to such an extent and in such manner as may be provided by that order as having been paid on account of any payment provided for by that order.

(5) In considering the matters to which the court is required to have regard under this section, the court shall take into account the facts as known to the court at the date of the hearing.

(6) In considering the financial resources of any person for the purposes of this section the court shall take into account his earning capacity and in considering the financial needs of any person for the purposes of this section the court shall take into account his financial obligations and responsibilities.

6 Variation, discharge etc. of orders for periodical payments

(1) Subject to the provisions of this Act, where the court has made an order under section 2(1)(a) of this Act (in this section referred to as 'the original order') for the making of periodical payments to any person (in this section referred to as 'the original recipient'), the court, on an application under this section, shall have power by order to vary or discharge the original order or to suspend any provision of it temporarily and to revive the operation of any provision so suspended.

(2) Without prejudice to the generality of subsection (1) above, an order made on an application for the variation of the original order may—

    (a) provide for the making out of any relevant property of such periodical payments and for such term as may be specified in the order to any person who has applied, or would but for section 4 of this Act be entitled to apply, for an order under section 2 of this Act (whether or not, in the case of an application, an order was made in favour of the applicant);

    (b) provide for the payment out of any relevant property of a lump sum of such amount as may be so specified to the original recipient or to any such person as is mentioned in paragraph above;

    (c) provide for the transfer of the relevant property, or such part thereof as may be so specified, to the original recipient or to any such person as is so mentioned.

(3) Where the original order provides that any periodical payments payable thereunder to the original recipient are to cease on the occurrence of an event specified in the order (other than the formation of a subsequent marriage or civil partnership by a former spouse or former civil partner) or on the expiration of a period so specified, then, if, before the end of the period of six months from the date of the occurrence of that event or of the expiration of that period, an application is made for an order under this section, the court shall have power to make any order which it would have had power to make if the application had been made before that date (whether in favour of the original recipient or any such person as is mentioned in subsection (2)(a) above and whether having effect from that date or from such later date as the court may specify).

(4) Any reference in this section to the original order shall include a reference to an order made under this section and any reference in this section to the original recipient shall include a reference to any person to whom periodical payments are required to be made by virtue of an order under this section.

(5) An application under this section may be made by any of the following persons, that is to say—

    (a) any person who by virtue of section 1(1) of this Act has applied, or would but for section 4 of this Act be entitled to apply, for an order under section 2 of this Act,

    (b) the personal representatives of the deceased,

    (c) the trustees of any relevant property, and

    (d) any beneficiary of the estate of the deceased.

(6) An order under this section may only affect—

    (a) property the income of which is at the date of the order applicable wholly or in part for the making of periodical payments to any person who has applied for an order under this Act, or

    (b) in the case of an application under subsection (3) above in respect of payments which have ceased to be payable on the occurrence of an event or the expiration of a period, property the income of which was so applicable immediately before the occurrence of that event or the expiration of that period, as the case may be, and any such property as is mentioned in paragraph (a) or (b) above is in subsections (2) and (5) above referred to as 'relevant property'.

(7) In exercising the powers conferred by this section the court shall have regard to all the circumstances of the case, including any change in any of the matters to which the court was required to have regard when making the order to which the application relates.

(8) Where the court makes an order under this section, it may give such consequential directions as it thinks necessary or expedient having regard to the provisions of the order.

(9) No such order as is mentioned in sections 2(1)(d), (e) or (f), 9, 10 or 11 of this Act shall be made on an application under this section.

(10) For the avoidance of doubt it is hereby declared that, in relation to an order which provides for the making of periodical payments which are to cease on the occurrence of an event specified in the order (other than the formation of a subsequent marriage or civil partnership by a former spouse or former civil partner) or on the expiration of a period so specified, the power to vary an order includes powers to provide for the making of periodical payments after the expiration of that period or the occurrence of that event.

7 Payment of lump sums by instalments

(1) An order under section 2(1)(b) or 6(2)(b) of this Act for the payment of a lump sum may provide for the payment of that sum by instalments of such amount as may be specified in the order.

(2) Where an order is made by virtue of subsection (1) above the court shall have power, on an application made by the person to whom the lump sum is payable, by the personal representatives of the deceased or by the trustees of the property out of which the lump sum is payable, to vary that order by varying the number of instalments payable, the amount of any instalment and the date on which any instalment becomes payable.

Property available for financial provision

8   Property treated as part of 'net estate'

(1) Where a deceased person has in accordance with the provisions of any enactment nominated any person to receive any sum of money or other property on his death and that nomination is in force at the time of his death, that sum of money, after deducting therefrom any capital transfer tax payable in respect thereof, or that other property, to the extent of the value thereof at the date of the death of the deceased after deducting therefrom any capital transfer tax so payable, shall be treated for the purposes of this Act as part of the net estate of the deceased; but this subsection shall not render any person liable for having paid that sum or transferred that other property to the person named in the nomination in accordance with the directions given in the nomination.

(2) Where any sum of money or other property is received by any person as a donatio mortis causa made by a deceased person, that sum of money, after deducting therefrom any capital transfer tax payable thereon, or that other property, to the extent of the value thereof at the date of the death of the deceased after deducting therefrom any capital transfer tax so payable, shall be treated for the purposes of this Act as part of the net estate of the deceased; but this subsection shall not render any person liable for having paid that sum or transferred that other property in order to give effect to that donatio mortis causa.

(3) The amount of capital transfer tax to be deducted for the purposes of this section shall not exceed the amount of that tax which has been borne by the person nominated by the deceased or, as the case may be, the person who has received a sum of money or other property as a donatio mortis causa.

9   Property held on a joint tenancy

(1) Where a deceased person was immediately before his death beneficially entitled to a joint tenancy of any property, then, if an application is made for an order under section 2 of this Act the court for the purpose of facilitating the making of financial provisions for the applicant under this Act may order that the deceased's severable share of that property shall, to such extent as appears to the court to be just in all the circumstances of the case, be treated for the purposes of this Act as part of the net estate of the deceased.

(1A) Where an order is made under subsection (1) the value of the deceased's severable share of the property concerned is taken for the purposes of this Act to be the value that the share would have had at the date of the hearing of the application for an order under section 2 had the share been severed immediately before the deceased's death, unless the court orders that the share is to be valued at a different date.

(2) In determining the extent to which any severable share is to be treated as part of the net estate of the deceased by virtue of an order under subsection (1) above, the court shall have regard to any capital transfer tax payable in respect of that severable share.

(3) Where an order is made under subsection (1) above, the provisions of this section shall not render any person liable for anything done by him before the order was made.

(4) For the avoidance of doubt it is hereby declared that for the purposes of this section there may be a joint tenancy of a chose in action.

Powers of court in relation to transactions intended to defeat
applications for financial provision

10   Dispositions intended to defeat applications for financial provision

(1) Where an application is made to the court for an order under section 2 of this Act, the applicant may, in the proceedings on that application, apply to the court for an order under subsection (2) below.

(2) Where on an application under subsection (1) above the court is satisfied—

    (a) that, less than six years before the date of the death of the deceased, the deceased with the intention of defeating an application for financial provision under this Act made a disposition, and

(b) that full valuable consideration for the disposition was not given by the person to whom or for the benefit of whom the disposition was made (in this section referred to as 'the donee') or by any other person, and

(c) that the exercise of the powers conferred by this section would facilitate the making of financial provision for the applicant under this Act,

then, subject to the provisions of this section and of sections 12 and 13 of this Act, the court may order the donee (whether or not at the date of the order he holds any interest in the property disposed of to him or for his benefit by the deceased) to provide, for the purpose of the making of that financial provision, such sum of money or other property as may be specified in the order.

(3) Where an order is made under subsection (2) above as respects any disposition made by the deceased which consisted of the payment of money to or for the benefit of the donee, the amount of any sum of money or the value of any property ordered to be provided under that subsection shall not exceed the amount of the payment made by the deceased after deducting therefrom any capital transfer tax borne by the donee in respect of that payment.

(4) Where an order is made under subsection (2) above as respects any disposition made by the deceased which consisted of the transfer of property (other than a sum of money) to or for the benefit of the donee, the amount of any sum of money or the value of any property ordered to be provided under that subsection shall not exceed the value at the date of the death of the deceased of the property disposed of by him to or for the benefit of the donee (or if that property has been disposed of by the person to whom it was transferred by the deceased, the value at the date of that disposal thereof) after deducting therefrom any capital transfer tax borne by the donee in respect of the transfer of that property by the deceased.

(5) Where an application (in this subsection referred to as 'the original application') is made for an order under subsection (2) above in relation to any disposition then, if, on an application under this subsection by the donee or by any applicant for an order under section 2 of this Act the court is satisfied—

(a) that, less than six years before the date of the death of the deceased, the deceased with the intention of defeating an application for financial provision under this Act made a disposition other than the disposition which is the subject of the original application, and

(b) that full valuable consideration for that other disposition was not given by the person to whom or for the benefit of whom that other disposition was made or by any other person,

the court may exercise in relation to the person to whom or for the benefit of whom that other disposition was made the powers which the court would have had under subsection (2) above if the original application had been made in respect of that other disposition and the court had been satisfied as to the matters set out in paragraphs (a), (b) and (c) of that subsection; and where any application is made under this subsection, any reference in this section (except in subsection (2)(b)) to the donee shall include a reference to the person to whom or for the benefit of whom that other disposition was made.

(6) In determining whether and in what manner to exercise its powers under this section, the court shall have regard to the circumstances in which any disposition was made and any valuable consideration which was given therefor, the relationship, if any, of the donee to the deceased, the conduct and financial resources of the donee and all the other circumstances of the case.

(7) In this section 'disposition' does not include—

(a) any provision in a will, any such nomination as is mentioned in section 8 (1) of this Act or any donatio mortis causa, or

(b) any appointment of property made, otherwise than by will, in the exercise of a special power of appointment,

but, subject to these exceptions, includes any payment of money (including the payment of a premium under a policy of assurance) and any conveyance, assurance, appointment or gift of property of any description, whether made by an instrument or otherwise.

(8) The provisions of this section do not apply to any disposition made before the commencement of this Act.

11   Contracts to leave property by will

(1) Where an application is made to a court for an order under section 2 of this Act, the applicant may, in the proceedings on that application, apply to the court for an order under this section.

(2) Where on an application under subsection (1) above the court is satisfied—

(a) that the deceased made a contract by which he agreed to leave by his will a sum of money or other property to any person or by which he agreed that a sum of money or other property would be paid or transferred to any person out of his estate, and

(b) that the deceased made that contract with the intention of defeating an application for financial provision under this Act, and

(c) that when the contract was made full valuable consideration for that contract was not given or promised by the person with whom or for the benefit of whom the contract was made (in this section referred to as 'the donee') or by any other person, and

(d) that the exercise of the powers conferred by this section would facilitate the making of financial provision for the applicant under this Act,

then, subject to the provisions of this section and of sections 12 and 13 of this Act, the court may make any one or more of the following orders, that is to say—

(i) if any money has been paid or any other property has been transferred to or for the benefit of the donee in accordance with the contract, an order directing the donee to provide, for the purpose of the making of that financial provision, such sum of money or other property as may be specified in the order;

(ii) if the money or all the money has not been paid or the property or all the property has not been transferred in accordance with the contract, an order directing the personal representatives not to make any payment or transfer any property, or not to make any further payment or transfer any further property, as the case may be, in accordance therewith or directing the personal representatives only to make such payment or transfer such property as may be specified in the order.

(3) Notwithstanding anything in subsection (2) above, the court may exercise its powers thereunder in relation to any contract made by the deceased only to the extent that the court considers that the amount of any sum of money paid or to be paid or the value of any property transferred or to be transferred in accordance with the contract exceeds the value of any valuable consideration given or to be given for that contract, and for this purpose the court shall have regard to the value of property at the date of the hearing.

(4) In determining whether and in what manner to exercise its powers under this section, the court shall have regard to the circumstances in which the contract was made, the relationship, if any, of the donee to the deceased, the conduct and financial resources of the donee and all the other circumstances of the case.

(5) Where an order has been made under subsection (2) above in relation to any contract, the rights of any person to enforce that contract or to recover damages or to obtain other relief for the breach thereof shall be subject to any adjustment made by the court under section 12 (3) of this Act and shall survive to such extent only as is consistent with giving effect to the terms of that order.

(6) The provisions of this section do not apply to a contract made before the commencement of this Act.

12   Provisions supplementary to sections 10 and 11

(1) Where the exercise of any of the powers conferred by section 10 or 11 of this Act is conditional on the court being satisfied that a disposition or contract was made by a deceased person with the intention of defeating an application for financial provision under this Act, that condition shall be fulfilled if the court is of the opinion that, on a balance of probabilities, the intention of the deceased (though not necessarily his sole intention) in making the disposition or contract was to

prevent an order for financial provision being made under this Act or to reduce the amount of the provision which might otherwise be granted by an order thereunder.

(2) Where an application is made under section 11 of this Act with respect to any contract made by the deceased and no valuable consideration was given or promised by any person for that contract then, notwithstanding anything in subsection (1) above, it shall be presumed, unless the contrary is shown, that the deceased made that contract with the intention of defeating an application for financial provision under this Act.

(3) Where the court makes an order under section 10 or 11 of this Act it may give such consequential directions as it thinks fit (including directions requiring the making of any payment or the transfer of any property) for giving effect to the order or for securing a fair adjustment of the rights of the persons affected thereby.

(4) Any power conferred on the court by the said section 10 or 11 to order the donee, in relation to any disposition or contract, to provide any sum of money or other property shall be exercisable in like manner in relation to the personal representatives of the donee, and—

(a) any reference in section 10(4) to the disposal of property by the donee shall include a reference to the disposal by the personal representative of the donee, and

(b) any reference in section 10(5) to an application by the donee under that subsection shall include a reference to an application by the personal representative of the donee;

but the court shall not have the power under the said section 10 or 11 to make an order in respect of any property forming part of the estate of the donee which has been distributed by the personal representative; and the personal representative shall not be liable for having distributed any such property before he has notice of the making of an application under the said section 10 or 11 on the ground that he ought to have taken into account the possibility that such an application would be made.

13   Provisions as to trustees in relation to sections 10 and 11

(1) Where an application is made for—

(a) an order under section 10 of this Act in respect of a disposition made by the deceased to any person as a trustee, or

(b) an order under section 11 of this Act in respect of any payment made or property transferred, in accordance with a contract made by the deceased, to any person as a trustee,

the powers of the court under the said section 10 or 11 to order that trustee to provide a sum of money or other property shall be subject to the following limitation (in addition, in a case of an application under section 10, to any provision regarding the deduction of capital transfer tax) namely, that the amount of any sum of money or the value of any property ordered to be provided—

(i) in the case of an application in respect of a disposition which consisted of the payment of money or an application in respect of the payment of money in accordance with a contract, shall not exceed the aggregate of so much of that money as is at the date of the order in the hands of the trustee and the value at that date of any property which represents that money or is derived therefrom and is at that date in the hands of the trustee;

(ii) in the case of an application in respect of a disposition which consisted of the transfer of property (other than a sum of money) or an application in respect of the transfer of property (other than a sum of money) in accordance with a contract, shall not exceed the aggregate of the value at the date of the order of so much of that property as is at that date in the hands of the trustee and the value at that date of any property which represents the first-mentioned property or is derived therefrom and is at that date in the hands of the trustee.

(2) Where any such application is made in respect of a disposition made to any person as a trustee or in respect of any payment made or property transferred in pursuance of a contract to any person as trustee, the trustee shall not be liable for having distributed any money or other property on the ground that he ought to have taken into account the possibility that such an application would be made.

(3) Where any such application is made in respect of a disposition made to any person as a trustee or in respect of any payment made or property transferred in accordance with a contract to any person as a trustee, any reference in the said section 10 or 11 to the donee shall be construed as including a reference to the trustee or trustees for the time being of the trust in question and any reference in subsection (1) or (2) above to a trustee shall be construed in the same way.

Special provisions relating to cases of divorce, separation etc.

14   Provision as to cases where no financial relief was granted in divorce proceedings etc.

(1) Where, within twelve months from the date on which a decree of divorce or nullity of marriage has been made absolute or a decree of judicial separation has been granted, a party to the marriage dies and—

  (a) an application for a financial provision order under section 23 of the Matrimonial Causes Act 1973 or a property adjustment order under section 24 of that Act has not been made by the other party to that marriage, or

  (b) such an application has been made but the proceedings thereon have not been determined at the time of the death of the deceased,

then, if an application for an order under section 2 of this Act is made by that other party, the court shall, notwithstanding anything in section 1 or section 3 of this Act, have power, if it thinks it just to do so, to treat that party for the purposes of that application as if the decree of divorce or nullity of marriage had not been made absolute or the decree of judicial separation had not been granted, as the case may be.

(2) This section shall not apply in relation to a decree of judicial separation unless at the date of the death of the deceased the decree was in force and the separation was continuing.

14A   Provision as to cases where no financial relief was granted in proceedings for the dissolution etc. of a civil partnership

(1) Subsection (2) below applies where—

  (a) a dissolution order, nullity order, separation order or presumption of death order has been made under Chapter 2 of Part 2 of the Civil Partnership Act 2004 in relation to a civil partnership,

  (b) one of the civil partners dies within twelve months from the date on which the order is made, and

  (c) either—

     (i) an application for a financial provision order under Part 1 of Schedule 5 to that Act or a property adjustment order under Part 2 of that Schedule has not been made by the other civil partner, or

     (ii) such an application has been made but the proceedings on the application have not been determined at the time of the death of the deceased.

(2) If an application for an order under section 2 of this Act is made by the surviving civil partner, the court shall, notwithstanding anything in section 1 or section 3 of this Act, have power, if it thinks it just to do so, to treat the surviving civil partner as if the order mentioned in subsection (1)(a) above had not been made.

(3) This section shall not apply in relation to a separation order unless at the date of the death of the deceased the separation order was in force and the separation was continuing.

15   Restriction imposed in divorce proceedings etc. on application under this Act

(1) On the grant of a decree of divorce, a decree of nullity of marriage or a decree of judicial separation or at any time thereafter the court, if it considers it just to do so, may, on the application of either party to the marriage, order that the other party to the marriage shall not on the death of the applicant be entitled to apply for an order under section 2 of this Act.

In this subsection 'the court' means the High Court or the family court.

(2) In the case of a decree of divorce or nullity of marriage an order may be made under subsection (1) above before or after the decree is made absolute, but if it is made before the decree is made absolute it shall not take effect unless the decree is made absolute.

(3) Where an order made under subsection (1) above on the grant of a decree of divorce or nullity of marriage has come into force with respect to a party to a marriage, then, on the death of the other party to that marriage, the court shall not entertain any application for an order under section 2 of this Act made by the first-mentioned party.

(4) Where an order made under subsection (1) above on the grant of a decree of judicial separation has come into force with respect to any party to a marriage, then, if, the other party to that marriage dies while the decree is in force and the separation is continuing, the court does not entertain any application for an order under section 2 of this Act made by the first-mentioned party.

15ZA   Restriction imposed in proceedings for the dissolution etc. of a civil partnership on application under this Act

(1) On making a dissolution order, nullity order, separation order or presumption of death order under Chapter 2 of Part 2 of the Civil Partnership Act 2004, or at any time after making such an order, the court, if it considers it just to do so, may, on the application of either of the civil partners, order that the other civil partner shall not on the death of the applicant be entitled to apply for an order under section 2 of this Act.

(2) In subsection (1) above 'the court' means the High Court or the family court.

(3) In the case of a dissolution order, nullity order or presumption of death order ('the main order') an order may be made under subsection (1) above before (as well as after) the main order is made final, but if made before the main order is made final it shall not take effect unless the main order is made final.

(4) Where an order under subsection (1) above made in connection with a dissolution order, nullity order or presumption of death order has come into force with respect to a civil partner, then, on the death of the other civil partner, the court shall not entertain any application for an order under section 2 of this Act made by the surviving civil partner.

(5) Where an order under subsection (1) above made in connection with a separation order has come into force with respect to a civil partner, then, if the other civil partner dies while the separation order is in force and the separation is continuing, the court shall not entertain any application for an order under section 2 of this Act made by the surviving civil partner.

15A   Restriction imposed in proceedings under Matrimonial and Family Proceedings Act 1984 on application under this Act

(1) On making an order under section 17 of the Matrimonial and Family Proceedings Act 1984 (orders for financial provision and property adjustment following overseas divorces, etc.) the court, if it considers it just to do so, may, on the application of either party to the marriage, order that the other party to the marriage shall not on the death of the applicant be entitled to apply for an order under section 2 of this Act.

In this subsection 'the court' means the High Court or the family court.

(2) Where an order under subsection (1) above has been made with respect to a party to a marriage which has been dissolved or annulled, then, on the death of the other party to that marriage, the court shall not entertain an application under section 2 of this Act made by the first-mentioned party.

(3) Where an order under subsection (1) above has been made with respect to a party to a marriage the parties to which have been legally separated, then, if the other party to the marriage dies while the legal separation is in force, the court shall not entertain an application under section 2 of this Act made by the first-mentioned party.

15B   Restriction imposed in proceedings under Schedule 7 to the Civil Partnership Act 2004 on application under this Act

(1) On making an order under paragraph 9 of Schedule 7 to the Civil Partnership Act 2004 (orders for financial provision, property adjustment and pension-sharing following overseas dissolution etc. of civil partnership) the court, if it considers it just to do so, may, on the application of either of the civil partners, order that the other civil partner shall not on the death of the applicant be entitled to apply for an order under section 2 of this Act.

(2) In subsection (1) above 'the court' means the High Court or the family court.

(3) Where an order under subsection (1) above has been made with respect to one of the civil partners in a case where a civil partnership has been dissolved or annulled, then, on the death of the other civil partner, the court shall not entertain an application under section 2 of this Act made by the surviving civil partner.

(4) Where an order under subsection (1) above has been made with respect to one of the civil partners in a case where civil partners have been legally separated, then, if the other civil partner dies while the legal separation is in force, the court shall not entertain an application under section 2 of this Act made by the surviving civil partner.

16   Variation and discharge of secured periodical payments orders made under Matrimonial Causes Act 1973

(1) Where an application for an order under section 2 of this Act is made to the court by any person who was at the time of the death of the deceased entitled to payments from the deceased under a secured periodical payments order made under the Matrimonial Causes Act 1973 or Schedule 5 to the Civil Partnership Act 2004, then, in the proceedings on that application, the court shall have power, if an application is made under this section by that person or by the personal representative of the deceased, to vary or discharge that periodical payments order or to revive the operation of any provision thereof which has been suspended under section 31 of that Act of 1973 or Part 11 of that Schedule.

(2) In exercising the powers conferred by this section the court shall have regard to all the circumstances of the case, including any order which the court proposes to make under section 2 or section 5 of this Act and any change (whether resulting from the death of the deceased or otherwise) in any of the matters to which the court was required to have regard when making the secured periodical payments order.

(3) The powers exercisable by the court under this section in relation to an order shall be exercisable also in relation to any instrument executed in pursuance of the order.

17   Variation and revocation of maintenance agreements

(1) Where an application for an order under section 2 of this Act is made to the court by any person who was at the time of the death of the deceased entitled to payments from the deceased under a maintenance agreement which provided for the continuation of payments under the agreement after the death of the deceased, then, in the proceedings on that application, the court shall have power, if an application is made under this section by that person or by the personal representative of the deceased, to vary or revoke that agreement.

(2) In exercising the powers conferred by this section the court shall have regard to all the circumstances of the case, including any order which the court proposes to make under section 2 or section 5 of this Act and any change (whether resulting from the death of the deceased or otherwise) in any of the circumstances in the light of which the agreement was made.

(3) If a maintenance agreement is varied by the court under this section the like consequences shall ensue as if the variation had been made immediately before the death of the deceased by agreement between the parties and for valuable consideration.

(4) In this section 'maintenance agreement', in relation to a deceased person, means any agreement made, whether in writing or not and whether before or after the commencement of this Act, by the deceased with any person with whom he formed a marriage or civil partnership, being an agreement which contained provisions governing the rights and liabilities towards one another when

living separately of the parties to that marriage or of the civil partners (whether or not the marriage or civil partnership has been dissolved or annulled) in respect of the making or securing of payments or the disposition or use of any property, including such rights and liabilities with respect to the maintenance or education of any child, whether or not a child of the deceased or a person who was treated by the deceased as a child of the family in relation to that marriage or civil partnership.

18   Availability of court's powers under this Act in applications under sections 31 and 36 of the Matrimonial Causes Act 1973

(1) Where—

(a) a person against whom a secured periodical payments order was made under the Matrimonial Causes Act 1973 has died and an application is made under section 31(6) of that Act for the variation or discharge of that order or for the revival of the operation of any provision thereof which has been suspended, or

(b) a party to a maintenance agreement within the meaning of section 34 of that Act has died, the agreement being one which provides for the continuation of payments thereunder after the death of one of the parties, and an application is made under section 36(1) of that Act, for the alteration of the agreement under section 35 thereof,

the court shall have power to direct that the application made under the said section 31(6) or 36(1) shall be deemed to have been accompanied by an application for an order under section 2 of this Act.

(2) Where the court gives a direction under subsection (1) above it shall have power, in the proceedings on the application under the said section 31(6) or 36(1), to make any order which the court would have had power to make under the provisions of this Act if the application under the said section 31(6) or 36(1), as the case may be, had been made jointly with an application for an order under the said section 2; and the court shall have power to give such consequential directions as may be necessary for enabling the court to exercise any of the powers available to the court under this Act in the case of an application for an order under section 2.

(3) Where an order made under section 15(1) of this Act is in force with respect to a party to a marriage, the court shall not give a direction under subsection (1) above with respect to any application made under the said section 31(6) or 36(1) by that party on the death of the other party.

18A   Availability of court's powers under this Act in applications under paragraphs 60 and 73 of Schedule 5 to the Civil Partnership Act 2004

(1) Where—

(a) a person against whom a secured periodical payments order was made under Schedule 5 to the Civil Partnership Act 2004 has died and an application is made under paragraph 60 of that Schedule for the variation or discharge of that order or for the revival of the operation of any suspended provision of the order, or

(b) a party to a maintenance agreement within the meaning of Part 13 of that Schedule has died, the agreement being one which provides for the continuation of payments under the agreement after the death of one of the parties, and an application is made under paragraph 73 of that Schedule for the alteration of the agreement under paragraph 69 of that Schedule,

the court shall have power to direct that the application made under paragraph 60 or 73 of that Schedule shall be deemed to have been accompanied by an application for an order under section 2 of this Act.

(2) Where the court gives a direction under subsection (1) above it shall have power, in the proceedings on the application under paragraph 60 or 73 of that Schedule, to make any order which the court would have had power to make under the provisions of this Act if the application under that paragraph had been made jointly with an application for an order under section 2 of this Act; and the court shall have power to give such consequential directions as may be necessary for enabling the court to exercise any of the powers available to the court under this Act in the case of an application for an order under section 2.

(3) Where an order made under section 15ZA(1) of this Act is in force with respect to a civil partner, the court shall not give a direction under subsection (1) above with respect to any application made under paragraph 60 or 73 of that Schedule by that civil partner on the death of the other civil partner.

Miscellaneous and supplementary provisions

19 Effect, duration and form of orders

(1) Where an order is made under section 2 of this Act then for all purposes, including the purposes of the enactments relating to capital transfer tax, the will or the law relating to intestacy, or both the will and the law relating to intestacy, as the case may be, shall have effect and be deemed to have had effect as from the deceased's death subject to the provisions of the order.

(2) Any order made under section 2 or 5 of this Act in favour of—

(a) an applicant who was the former spouse or former civil partner of the deceased; or

(b) an applicant who was the husband or wife of the deceased in a case where the marriage with the deceased was the subject of a decree of judicial separation and at the date of death the decree was in force and the separation was continuing, or

(c) an applicant who was the civil partner of the deceased in a case where, at the date of death, a separation order under Chapter 2 of Part 2 of the Civil Partnership Act 2004 was in force in relation to their civil partnership and the separation was continuing,

shall, in so far as it provides for the making of periodical payments, cease to have effect on the formation by the applicant of a subsequent marriage or civil partnership, except in relation to any arrears due under the order on the date of the formation of the subsequent marriage or civil partnership.

(3) A copy of every order made under this Act other than an order made under section 15(1) or 15ZA(1) of this Act shall be sent to the principal registry of the Family Division for entry and filing, and a memorandum of the order shall be endorsed on, or permanently annexed to, the probate or letters of administration under which the estate is being administered.

20 Provisions as to personal representatives

(1) The provisions of this Act shall not render the personal representative of a deceased person liable for having distributed any part of the estate of the deceased, after the end of the period of six months from the date on which the representation with respect to the estate of the deceased is first taken out, on the ground that he ought to have taken into account the possibility—

(a) that the court might permit the making of an application for an order under section 2 of this Act after the end of that period, or

(b) that, where an order has been made under the said section 2, the court might exercise in relation thereto the powers conferred on it by section 6 of this Act, but this subsection shall not prejudice any power to recover, by reason of the making of an order under this Act, any part of the estate so distributed.

(2) Where the personal representative of a deceased person pays any sum directed by an order under section 5 of this Act to be paid out of the deceased's net estate, he shall not be under any liability by reason of that estate not being sufficient to make the payment, unless at the time of making the payment he has reasonable cause to believe that the estate is not sufficient.

(3) Where a deceased person entered into a contract by which he agreed to leave by his will any sum of money or other property to any person or by which he agreed that a sum of money or other property would be paid or transferred to any person out of his estate, then, if the personal representative of the deceased has reason to believe that the deceased entered into the contract with the intention of defeating an application for financial provision under this Act, he may, notwithstanding anything in that contract, postpone the payment of that sum of money or the transfer of that property until the expiration of the period of six months from the date on which representation with respect to the estate of the deceased is first taken out or, if during that period an application is made for an order under section 2 of this Act, until the determination of the proceedings on that application.

...

23 Determination of date on which representation was first taken out

(1) The following are to be left out of account when considering for the purposes of this Act when representation with respect to the estate of a deceased person was first taken out—

    (a) a grant limited to settled land or to trust property,

    (b) any other grant that does not permit any of the estate to be distributed,

    (c) a grant limited to real estate or to personal estate, unless a grant limited to the remainder of the estate has previously been made or is made at the same time,

    (d) a grant, or its equivalent, made outside the United Kingdom (but see subsection (2) below).

(2) A grant sealed under section 2 of the Colonial Probates Act 1892 counts as a grant made in the United Kingdom for the purposes of this section, but is to be taken as dated on the date of sealing.

24 Effect of this Act on section 46(1)(vi) of Administration of Estates Act 1925

Section 46(1)(vi) of the Administration of Estates Act 1925, in so far as it provides for the devolution of property on the Crown, the Duchy of Lancaster or the Duke of Cornwall as bona vacantia, shall have effect subject to the provisions of this Act.

25 Interpretation

(1) In this Act—

'beneficiary' in relation to the estate of a deceased person, means—

    (a) a person who under the will of the deceased or under the law relating to intestacy is beneficially interested in the estate or would be so interested if an order had not been made under this Act, and

    (b) a person who has received any sum of money or other property which by virtue of section 8(1) or 8(2) of this Act is treated as part of the net estate of the deceased or would have received that sum or other property if an order had not been made under this Act;

'child' includes an illegitimate child and a child en ventre sa mère at the death of the deceased;

'the court', unless the context otherwise requires, means the High Court, or where the county court has jurisdiction by virtue of section 25 of the County Courts Act 1984, the county court;

'former civil partner' means a person whose civil partnership with the deceased was during the lifetime of the deceased either—

    (a) dissolved or annulled by an order made under the law of any part of the British Islands, or

...

'former spouse' means a person whose marriage with the deceased was during the lifetime of the deceased either—

    (a) dissolved or annulled by a decree of divorce or a decree of nullity of marriage granted under the law of any part of the British Islands, or

...

'net estate' in relation to a deceased person, means:—

    (a) all property of which the deceased had power to dispose by his will (otherwise than by virtue of a special power of appointment) less the amount of his funeral, testamentary and administration expenses, debts and liabilities, including any capital transfer tax payable out of his estate on his death;

    (b) any property in respect of which the deceased held a general power of appointment (not being a power exercisable by will) which has not been exercised;

    (c) any sum of money or other property which is treated for the purposes of this Act as part of the net estate of the deceased by virtue of section 8(1) or (2) of this Act;

    (d) any property which is treated for the purposes of this Act as part of the net estate of the deceased by virtue of an order made under section 9 of the Act;

    (e) any sum of money or other property which is, by reason of a disposition or contract made by the deceased, ordered under section 10 or 11 of this Act to be provided for the purpose of the making of financial provision under this Act;

'property' includes any chose in action;

'reasonable financial provision' has the meaning assigned to it by section 1 of this Act;

'valuable consideration' does not include marriage or a promise of marriage;

'will' includes codicil.

(2) For the purposes of paragraph (a) of the definition of 'net estate' in subsection (1) above a person who is not of full age and capacity shall be treated as having power to dispose by will of all property of which he would have had power to dispose by will if he had been of full age and capacity.

(3) Any reference in this Act to provision out of the net estate of a deceased person includes a reference to provision extending to the whole of that estate.

(4) For the purpose of this Act any reference to a spouse, wife or husband shall be treated as including a reference to a person who in good faith entered into a void marriage with the deceased person unless either—

(a) the marriage of the deceased and that person was dissolved or annulled during the lifetime of the deceased and the dissolution or annulment is recognised by the law of England and Wales, or

(b) that person has during the lifetime of the deceased formed a subsequent marriage or civil partnership.

(4A) For the purposes of this Act any reference to a civil partner shall be treated as including a reference to a person who in good faith formed a void civil partnership with the deceased unless either—

(a) the civil partnership between the deceased and that person was dissolved or annulled during the lifetime of the deceased and the dissolution or annulment is recognised by the law of England and Wales, or

(b) that person has during the lifetime of the deceased formed a subsequent civil partnership or marriage.

(5) Any reference in this Act to the formation of, or to a person who has formed, a subsequent marriage or civil partnership includes (as the case may be) a reference to the formation of, or to a person who has formed, a marriage or civil partnership which is by law void or voidable.

(5A) The formation of a marriage or civil partnership shall be treated for the purposes of this Act as the formation of a subsequent marriage or civil partnership, in relation to either of the spouses or civil partners, notwithstanding that the previous marriage or civil partnership of that spouse or civil partner was void or voidable.

(6) Any reference in this Act to an order or decree made under the Matrimonial Causes Act 1973 or under any section of that Act shall be construed as including a reference to an order or decree which is deemed to have been made under that Act or under that section thereof, as the case may be.

(6A) Any reference in this Act to an order made under, or under any provision of, the Civil Partnership Act 2004 shall be construed as including a reference to anything which is deemed to be an order made (as the case may be) under that Act or provision.

(7) Any reference in this Act to any enactment is a reference to that enactment as amended by or under any subsequent enactment.

Legitimacy Act 1976

(1976 c. 31)

1 Legitimacy of children of certain void marriages

(1) The child of a void marriage, whenever born, shall, subject to subsection (2) below and Schedule 1 to this Act, be treated as the legitimate child of his parents if at the time of the insemination resulting in the birth, or where there was no such insemination, the child's conception (or at the time of the celebration of the marriage if later) both or either of the parties reasonably believed that the marriage was valid.

(2) This section applies where the father of the child was domiciled in England and Wales at the time of the birth or, if he died before the birth, was so domiciled immediately before his death.

(3) It is hereby declared for the avoidance of doubt that subsection (1) above applies notwithstanding that the belief that the marriage was valid was due to a mistake as to law.

(4) In relation to a child born after the coming into force of section 28 of the Family Law Reform Act 1987, it shall be presumed for the purposes of subsection (1) above, unless the contrary is shown, that one of the parties to the void marriage reasonably believed at the time of the insemination resulting in the birth or, where there was no such insemination, the child's conception (or at the time of the celebration of the marriage if later) that the marriage was valid.

2 Legitimation by subsequent marriage of parents

Subject to the following provisions of this Act, where the parents of an illegitimate person marry one another, the marriage shall, if the father of the illegitimate person is at the date of marriage domiciled in England and Wales, render that person, if living, legitimate from the date of the marriage.

2A Legitimation by subsequent civil partnership of parents

Subject to the following provisions of this Act, where—

(a) a person ('the child') has a parent ('the female parent') by virtue of section 43 of the Human Fertilisation and Embryology Act 2008 (treatment provided to woman who agrees that second woman to be parent),

(b) at the time of the child's birth, the female parent and the child's mother are not civil partners of each other,

(c) the female parent and the child's mother subsequently enter into a civil partnership, and

(d) the female parent is at the date of the formation of the civil partnership domiciled in England and Wales,

the civil partnership shall render the child, if living, legitimate from the date of the formation of the civil partnership.

3 Legitimation by extraneous law

(1) Subject to the following provisions of this Act, where the parents of an illegitimate person marry one another and the father of the illegitimate person is not at the time of the marriage domiciled in England and Wales but is domiciled in a country by the law of which the illegitimate person became legitimated by virtue of such subsequent marriage, that person, if living, shall in England and Wales be recognised as having been so legitimated from the date of the marriage notwithstanding that, at the time of his birth, his father was domiciled in a country the law of which did not permit legitimation by subsequent marriage.

(2) Subject to the following provisions of this Act, where—

(a) a person ('the child') has a parent ('the female parent') by virtue of section 43 of the Human Fertilisation and Embryology Act 2008 (treatment provided to woman who agrees that second woman to be parent),

(b) at the time of the child's birth, the female parent and the child's mother are not civil partners of each other,

(c) the female parent and the child's mother subsequently enter into a civil partnership, and

(d) the female parent is not at the time of the formation of the civil partnership domiciled in England and Wales but is domiciled in a country by the law of which the child became legitimated by virtue of the civil partnership,

the child, if living, shall in England and Wales be recognised as having been so legitimated from the date of the formation of the civil partnership notwithstanding that, at the time of the child's birth, the female parent was domiciled in a country the law of which did not permit legitimation by subsequent civil partnership.

4 Legitimation of adopted child

(1) Section 39 of the Adoption Act 1976 or section 67 of the Adoption and Children Act 2002 does not prevent an adopted child being legitimated under section 2 or 3 above if either natural parent is the sole adoptive parent.

(2) Where an adopted child (with a sole adoptive parent) is legitimated—

    (a) subsection (2) of the said section 39 or subsection (3)(b) of the said section 67 shall not apply after the legitimation to the natural relationship with the other natural parent, and

    (b) revocation of the adoption order in consequence of the legitimation shall not affect section 39, 41 or 42 of the Adoption Act 1976 or section 67, 68 or 69 of the Adoption and Children Act 2002 as it applies to any instrument made before the date of legitimation.

5   Rights of legitimated persons and others to take interests in property

(1) Subject to any contrary indication, the rules of construction contained in this section apply to any instrument other than an existing instrument, so far as the instrument contains a disposition of property.

(2) For the purposes of this section, provisions of the law of intestate succession applicable to the estate of a deceased person shall be treated as if contained in an instrument executed by him (while of full capacity) immediately before his death.

(3) A legitimated person, and any other person, shall be entitled to take any interest as if the legitimated person had been born legitimate.

(4) A disposition which depends on the date of birth of a child or children of the parent or parents shall be construed as if—

    (a) a legitimated child had been born on the date of legitimation,

    (b) two or more legitimated children legitimated on the same date had been born on that date in the order of their actual births,

but this does not affect any reference to the age of a child.

(5) Examples of phrases in wills on which subsection (4) above can operate are—

    1. Children of A 'living at my death or born afterwards.'

    2. Children of A 'living at my death or born afterwards before any one of such children for the time being in existence attains a vested interest, and who attain the age of 21 years.'

    3. As in example 1 or 2, but referring to grandchildren of A, instead of children of A.

    4. A for life 'until he has a child' and then to his child or children.

Note. Subsection (4) above will not affect the reference to the age of 21 years in example 2.

(6) If an illegitimate person or a person adopted by one of his natural parents dies, or has died before the commencement of this Act, and—

    (a) after his death his parents marry or have married; and

    (b) the deceased would, if living at the time of the marriage, have become a legitimated person,

this section shall apply for the construction of the instrument so far as it relates to the taking of interests by, or in succession to, his spouse, children and remoter issue as if he had been legitimated by virtue of the marriage.

(7) In this section 'instrument' includes a private Act settling property, but not any other enactment.

6   Dispositions depending on date of birth

(1) Where a disposition depends on the date of birth of a child who was born illegitimate and who is legitimated (or, if deceased, is treated as legitimated), section 5(4) above does not affect entitlement under Part II of the Family Law Reform Act 1969 (illegitimate children).

(2) Where a disposition depends on the date of birth of an adopted child who is legitimated (or, if deceased, is treated as legitimated) section 5(4) above does not affect entitlement by virtue of section 42(2) of the Adoption Act 1976 or section 69(2) of the Adoption and Children Act 2002.

(3) This section applies for example where—

    (a) a testator dies in 1976 bequeathing a legacy to his eldest grandchild living at a specified time,

    (b) his daughter has an illegitimate child in 1977 who is the first grandchild,

    (c) his married son has a child in 1978,

    (d) subsequently the illegitimate child is legitimated,

and in all those cases the daughter's child remains the eldest grandchild of the testator throughout.

7   Protection of trustees and personal representatives

(1) A trustee or personal representative is not under a duty, by virtue of the law relating to trusts or the administration of estates, to enquire, before conveying or distributing any property, whether any person is illegitimate or has been adopted by one of his natural parents, and could be legitimated (or if deceased be treated as legitimated), if the fact could affect entitlement to the property.

(2) A trustee or personal representative shall not be liable to any person by reason of a conveyance or distribution of the property made without regard to any such fact if he has not received notice of the fact before the conveyance or distribution.

(3) This section does not prejudice the right of a person to follow the property, or any property representing it, into the hands of another person, other than a purchaser, who has received it.

8   Personal rights and obligations

A legitimated person shall have the same rights, and shall be under the same obligations in respect of the maintenance and support of himself or of any other person as if he had been born legitimate, and, subject to the provisions of this Act, the provisions of any Act relating to claims for damages, compensation, allowance, benefit or otherwise by or in respect of a legitimate child shall apply in like manner in the case of a legitimated person.

9   Re-registration of birth of legitimated person

(1) It shall be the duty of the parents of a legitimated person or, in cases where re-registration can be effected on information furnished by one parent and one of the parents is dead, of the surviving parent to furnish to the Registrar General information with a view to obtaining the re-registration of the birth of that person within three months after the date of the marriage or of the formation of the civil partnership by virtue of which he was legitimated.

(2) The failure of the parents or either of them to furnish information as required by subsection (1) above in respect of any legitimated person shall not affect the legitimation of that person.

(3) This section does not apply in relation to a person who was legitimated otherwise than by virtue of the subsequent marriage or civil partnership of his parents.

(4) Any parent who fails to give information as required by this section shall be liable on summary conviction to a fine not exceeding level 1 on the standard scale.

10   Interpretation

(1) In this Act, except where the context otherwise requires—

'disposition' includes the conferring of a power of appointment and any other disposition of an interest in or right over property;

'existing', in relation to an instrument, means one made before 1st January 1976;

'legitimated person' means a person legitimated or recognised as legitimated—

(a) under section 2, 2A or 3 above; or

(b) under section 1 or 8 of the Legitimacy Act 1926; or

(c) except in section 8, by a legitimation (whether or not by virtue of the subsequent marriage of his parents) recognised by the law of England and Wales and effected under the law of any other country;

and cognate expressions shall be construed accordingly;

'power of appointment' includes any discretionary power to transfer a beneficial interest in property without the furnishing of valuable consideration;

'void marriage' means a marriage not being voidable only, in respect of which the High Court has or had jurisdiction to grant a decree of nullity, or would have or would have had such jurisdiction if the parties were domiciled in England and Wales.

(2) For the purposes of this Act 'legitimated person' includes, where the context admits, a person legitimated, or recognised as legitimated, before the passing of the Children Act 1975.

(3) For the purposes of this Act, except where the context otherwise requires—

(a) the death of the testator is the date at which a will or codicil is to be regarded as made;

(b) an oral disposition of property shall be deemed to be contained in an instrument made when the disposition was made.

Adoption Act 1976

(1976 c. 36)

PART IV STATUS OF ADOPTED CHILDREN

38   Meaning of 'adoption' in Part IV

(1) In this Part 'adoption' means adoption—

    (a) by an adoption order;

    (b) by an order made under the Children Act 1975, the Adoption Act 1958, the Adoption Act 1950 or any enactment repealed by the Adoption Act 1950;

    (c) by an order made in Scotland, Northern Ireland, the Isle of Man or in any of the Channel Islands;

    (cc) which is a Convention adoption;

    (d) which is an overseas adoption; or

    (e) which is an adoption recognised by the law of England and Wales and effected under the law of any other country,

and cognate expressions shall be construed accordingly.

(2) The definition of adoption includes, where the context admits, an adoption effected before the passing of the Children Act 1975 but does not include an adoption of a kind mentioned in paragraphs (c) to (e) of subsection (1) effected on or after the day which is the appointed day for the purposes of Chapter 4 of Part 1 of the Adoption and Children Act 2002, and the date of an adoption effected by an order is the date of the making of the order.

39   Status conferred by adoption

(1) An adopted child shall be treated in law—

    (a) where the adopters are a married couple, as if he had been born as a child of the marriage (whether or not he was in fact born after the marriage was solemnized);

    (b) in any other case, as if he had been born to the adopter in wedlock (but not as a child of any actual marriage of the adopter).

(2) An adopted child shall, subject to subsections (3) and (3A), be treated in law as if he were not the child of any person other than the adopters or adopter.

(3) In the case of a child adopted by one of its natural parents as sole adoptive parent, subsection (2) has no effect as respects entitlement to property depending on relationship to that parent, or as respects anything else depending on that relationship.

...

(4) It is hereby declared that this section prevents an adopted child from being illegitimate.

(5) This section has effect—

    (a) in the case of an adoption before 1st January 1976, from that date, and

    (b) in the case of any other adoption, from the date of the adoption.

(6) Subject to the provisions of this Part, this section—

    (a) applies to the construction of enactments or instruments passed or made before the adoption or later, and so applies subject to any contrary indication; and

    (b) has effect as respects things done, or events occurring, after the adoption, or after 31st December 1975, whichever is the later.

41   Adoptive relatives

A relationship existing by virtue of section 39 may be referred to as an adoptive relationship, and—

    (a) a male adopter may be referred to as the adoptive father;

    (b) a female adopter may be referred to as the adoptive mother;

    (c) any other relative of any degree under an adoptive relationship may be referred to as an adoptive relative of that degree, but this section does not prevent the term 'parent,' or any other term not qualified by the word 'adoptive' being treated as including an adoptive relative.

42   Rules of construction for instruments concerning property

(1)   Subject to any contrary indication, the rules of construction contained in this section apply to any instrument, other than an existing instrument, so far as it contains a disposition of property.

(2)   In applying section 39(1) to a disposition which depends on the date of birth of a child or children of the adoptive parent or parents, the disposition shall be construed as if—

    (a)   the adopted child had been born on the date of adoption,

    (b)   two or more children adopted on the same date had been born on that date in the order of their actual births,

but this does not affect any reference to the age of a child.

(3)   Examples of phrases in wills on which subsection (2) can operate are—

    1.   Children of A 'living at my death or born afterwards.'

    2.   Children of A 'living at my death or born afterwards before any one of such children for the time being in existence attains a vested interest and who attain the age of 21 years.'

    3.   As in example 1 or 2, but referring to grandchildren of A instead of children of A.

    4.   A for life 'until he has a child,' and then to his child or children.

Note. Subsection (2) will not affect the reference to the age of 21 years in example 2.

(4)   Section 39(2) does not prejudice any interest vested in possession in the adopted child before the adoption, or any interest expectant (whether immediately or not) upon an interest so vested.

(5)   Where it is necessary to determine for the purposes of a disposition of property effected by an instrument whether a woman can have a child, it shall be presumed that once a woman has attained the age of 55 years she will not adopt a child after execution of the instrument, and, notwithstanding section 39, if she does so that child shall not be treated as her child or as the child of her spouse (if any) for the purposes of the instrument.

(6)   In this section, 'instrument' includes a private Act settling property, but not any other enactment.

43   Dispositions depending on date of birth

(1)   Where a disposition depends on the date of birth of a child who was born illegitimate and who is adopted by one of the natural parents as sole adoptive parent, section 42(2) does not affect entitlement under Part II of the Family Law Reform Act 1969 (illegitimate children).

(2)   Subsection (1) applies for example where—

    (a)   a testator dies in 1976 bequeathing a legacy to his eldest grandchild living at a specified time,

    (b)   his daughter has an illegitimate child in 1977 who is the first grandchild,

    (c)   his married son has a child in 1978,

    (d)   subsequently the illegitimate child is adopted by the mother as sole adoptive parent,

and in all those cases the daughter's child remains the eldest grandchild of the testator throughout.

44   Property devolving with peerages etc.

(1)   An adoption does not affect the descent of any peerage or dignity or title of honour.

(2)   An adoption shall not affect the devolution of any property limited (expressly or not) to devolve (as nearly as the law permits) along with any peerage or dignity or title of honour.

(3)   Subsection (2) applies only if and so far as a contrary intention is not expressed in the instrument, and shall have effect subject to the terms of the instrument.

45   Protection of trustees and personal representatives

(1)   A trustee or personal representative is not under a duty, by virtue of the law relating to trusts or the administration of estates, to enquire, before conveying or distributing any property, whether any adoption has been effected or revoked if that fact could affect entitlement to the property.

(2) A trustee or personal representative shall not be liable to any person by reason of a conveyance or distribution of the property made without regard to any such fact if he has not received notice of the fact before the conveyance or distribution.

(3) This section does not prejudice the right of a person to follow the property, or any property representing it, into the hands of another person, other than a purchaser, who has received it.

46   Meaning of 'disposition'

(1) In this Part, unless the context otherwise requires,—

'disposition' includes the conferring of a power of appointment and any other disposition of an interest in or right over property;

'power of appointment' includes any discretionary power to transfer a beneficial interest in property without the furnishing of valuable consideration.

(2) This Part applies to an oral disposition as if contained in an instrument made when the disposition was made.

(3) For the purposes of this Part, the death of the testator is the date at which a will or codicil is to be regarded as made.

(4) For the purposes of this Part, provisions of the law of intestate succession applicable to the estate of a deceased person shall be treated as if contained in an instrument executed by him (while of full capacity) immediately before his death.

47   Miscellaneous enactments

(1) Section 39 does not apply for the purposes of section 1 of and Schedule 1 to the Marriage Act 1949 or Schedule 1 to the Civil Partnership Act 2004 (prohibited degrees of kindred and affinity), or sections 64 and 65 of the Sexual Offences Act 2003 (sex with an adult relative).

(2) Section 39 does not apply for the purposes of any provision of—

    (a) the British Nationality Act 1981,

    (b) the Immigration Act 1971,

    (c) any instrument having effect under an enactment within paragraph (a) or (b), or

    (d) any other provision of the law for the time being in force which determines British citizenship, British overseas territory citizenship, the status of a British National (Overseas) or British Overseas citizenship.

...

Rent Act 1977

(1977 c. 42)

PART I   PRELIMINARY

Protected and statutory tenancies

1   Protected tenants and tenancies

Subject to this Part of this Act, a tenancy under which a dwelling-house (which may be a house or part of a house) is let as a separate dwelling is a protected tenancy for the purposes of this Act.

Any reference in this Act to a protected tenant shall be construed accordingly.

2   Statutory tenants and tenancies

(1) Subject to this Part of this Act—

    (a) after the termination of a protected tenancy of a dwelling-house the person who, immediately before that termination, was the protected tenant of the dwelling-house shall, if and so long as he occupies the dwelling-house as his residence, be the statutory tenant of it; and

(b) Part I of Schedule 1 to this Act shall have effect for determining what person (if any) is the statutory tenant of a dwelling-house or, as the case may be, is entitled to an assured tenancy of a dwelling-house by succession at any time after the death of a person who, immediately before his death, was either a protected tenant of the dwelling-house or the statutory tenant of it by virtue of paragraph (a) above.

...

3 Terms and conditions of statutory tenancies

(1) So long as he retains possession, a statutory tenant shall observe and be entitled to the benefit of all the terms and conditions of the original contract of tenancy, so far as they are consistent with the provisions of this Act.

(2) It shall be a condition of a statutory tenancy of a dwelling-house that the statutory tenant shall afford to the landlord access to the dwelling-house and all reasonable facilities for executing therein any repairs which the landlord is entitled to execute.

...

SCHEDULE 1 STATUTORY TENANCIES

PART I STATUTORY TENANTS BY SUCCESSION

1.—Paragraph 2 below shall have effect, subject to section 2(3) of this Act, for the purpose of determining who is the statutory tenant of a dwelling-house by succession after the death of the person (in this Part of this Schedule referred to as 'the original tenant') who, immediately before his death, was a protected tenant of the dwelling-house or the statutory tenant of it by virtue of his previous protected tenancy.

2.—The surviving spouse or surviving civil partner, (if any) of the original tenant, if residing in the dwelling-house immediately before the death of the original tenant, shall after the death be the statutory tenant if and so long as he or she occupies the dwelling-house as his or her residence.

(2) For the purposes of this paragraph—
   (a) a person who was living with the original tenant as his or her wife or husband shall be treated as the spouse of the original tenant, and
   (b) a person who was living with the original tenant as if they were civil partners shall be treated as the civil partner of the original tenant.

(3) If, immediately after the death of the original tenant, there is, by virtue of sub-paragraph (2) above, more than one person who fulfils the conditions in sub-paragraph (1) above, such one of them as may be decided by agreement or, in default of agreement, by the county court shall for the purposes of this paragraph be treated (according to whether that one of them is of the opposite sex to, or of the same sex as, the original tenant) as the surviving spouse or the surviving civil partner.

3.—(1) Where paragraph 2 above does not apply, but a person who was a member of the original tenant's family was residing with him in the dwelling-house at the time of and for the period of 2 years immediately before his death, then, after his death, that person or if there is more than one such person such one of them as may be decided by agreement, or in default of agreement by the county court, shall be entitled to an assured tenancy of the dwelling-house by succession.

(2) If the original tenant died within the period of 18 months beginning on the operative date, then, for the purposes of this paragraph, a person who was residing in the dwelling-house with the original tenant at the time of his death and for the period which began 6 months before the operative date and ended at the time of his death shall be taken to have been residing with the original tenant for the period of 2 years immediately before his death.

4.—A person who becomes the statutory tenant of a dwelling-house by virtue of paragraph 2 above is in this Part of this Schedule referred to as 'the first successor'.

5.—If, immediately before his death, the first successor was still a statutory tenant, paragraph 6 below shall have effect, for the purpose of determining who is entitled to an assured tenancy of the dwelling-house by succession.

6.—(1) Where a person who—

    (a) was a member of the original tenant's family immediately before that tenant's death, and

    (b) was a member of the first successor's family immediately before the first successor's death,

was residing in the dwelling-house with the first successor at the time of, and for the period of 2 years immediately before, the first successor's death, that person or, if there is more than one such person, such one of them as may be decided by agreement or, in default of agreement, by the county court shall be entitled to an assured tenancy of the dwelling-house by succession.

(2) If the first successor died within the period of 18 months beginning on the operative date, then, for the purposes of this paragraph, a person who was residing in the dwelling-house with the first successor at the time of his death and for the period which began 6 months before the operative date and ended at the time of his death shall be taken to have been residing with the first successor for the period of 2 years immediately before his death.

...

10.—(1) Where after a succession the successor becomes the tenant of the dwelling-house by the grant to him of another tenancy, 'the original tenant' and 'the first successor' in this Part of this Schedule shall, in relation to that other tenancy, mean the persons who were respectively the original tenant and the first successor at the time of the succession, and accordingly—

    (a) if the successor was the first successor, and, immediately before his death he was still the tenant (whether protected or statutory), paragraph 6 above shall apply on his death,

    (b) if the successor was not the first successor, no person shall become a statutory tenant on his death by virtue of this Part of this Schedule.

(2) Sub-paragraph (1) above applies—

    (a) even if a successor enters into more than one other tenancy of the dwelling-house, and

    (b) even if both the first successor and the successor on his death enter into other tenancies of the dwelling-house.

(3) In this paragraph 'succession' means the occasion on which a person becomes the statutory tenant of a dwelling-house by virtue of this Part of this Schedule and 'successor' shall be construed accordingly.

(4) This paragraph shall apply as respects a succession which took place before 27th August 1972 if, and only if, the tenancy granted after the succession, or the first of those tenancies, was granted on or after that date, and where it does not apply as respects a succession, no account should be taken of that succession in applying this paragraph as respects any later succession.

Domestic Proceedings and Magistrates' Courts Act 1978

(1978 c. 22)

PART I MATRIMONIAL PROCEEDINGS IN MAGISTRATES' COURTS

Powers of court to make orders for financial provision for parties to a marriage and children of the family

1 Grounds of application for financial provision

Either party to a marriage may apply to the family court for an order under section 2 of this Act on the ground that the other party to the marriage—

    (a) has failed to provide reasonable maintenance for the applicant; or

(b) has failed to provide, or to make a proper contribution towards, reasonable maintenance for any child of the family; or

(c) has behaved in such a way that the applicant cannot reasonably be expected to live with the respondent; or

(d) has deserted the applicant.[1]

2   Powers of court to make orders for financial provision

(1) Where on an application for an order under this section the applicant satisfies the court of any ground mentioned in section 1 of this Act, the court may, subject to the provisions of this Part of this Act, make any one or more of the following orders, that is to say—

(a) an order that the respondent shall make to the applicant such periodical payments, and for such term, as may be specified in the order;

(b) an order that the respondent shall pay to the applicant such lump sum as may be so specified;

(c) an order that the respondent shall make to the applicant for the benefit of a child of the family to whom the application relates, or to such a child, such periodical payments, and for such term, as may be so specified;

(d) an order that the respondent shall pay to the applicant for the benefit of a child of the family to whom the application relates, or to such a child, such lump sum as may be so specified.

(2) Without prejudice to the generality of subsection (1)(b) or (d) above, an order under this section for the payment of a lump sum may be made for the purpose of enabling any liability or expenses reasonably incurred in maintaining the applicant, or any child of the family to whom the application relates, before the making of the order to be met.

(3) The amount of any lump sum required to be paid by such an order under this section shall not exceed [£1,000] or such larger amount as the Lord Chancellor may from time to time by order fix for the purposes of this subsection.

(4) An order made by the Lord Chancellor under this section—

(a) shall be made only after consultation with the Lord Chief Justice;

(b) shall be made by statutory instrument and be subject to annulment in pursuance of a resolution of either House of Parliament.

(5) The Lord Chief Justice may nominate a judicial office holder (as defined in section 109(4) of the Constitutional Reform Act 2005) to exercise his functions under this section.

3   Matters to which court is to have regard in exercising its powers under section 2

(1) Where an application is made for an order under section 2 of this Act, it shall be the duty of the court, in deciding whether to exercise its powers under that section and, if so, in what manner, to have regard to all the circumstances of the case, first consideration being given to the welfare while a minor of any child of the family who has not attained the age of eighteen.

(2) As regards the exercise of its powers under subsection (1)(a) or (b) of section 2, the court shall in particular have regard to the following matters—

(a) the income, earning capacity, property and other financial resources which each of the parties to the marriage has or is likely to have in the foreseeable future, including in the case of earning capacity any increase in that capacity which it would in the opinion of the court be reasonable to expect a party to the marriage to take steps to acquire;

(b) the financial needs, obligations and responsibilities which each of the parties to the marriage has or is likely to have in the foreseeable future;

(c) the standard of living enjoyed by the parties to the marriage before the occurrence of the conduct which is alleged as the ground of the application;

(d) the age of each party to the marriage and the duration of the marriage;

---

[1] Paras (c) and (d) are repealed by the Family Law Act 1996, ss. 18(1), 66(3), Sch 10, as from a day to be appointed.

(e) any physical or mental disability of either of the parties to the marriage;

(f) the contributions which each of the parties has made or is likely in the foreseeable future to make to the welfare of the family, including any contribution by looking after the home or caring for the family;

(g) the conduct of each of the parties, if that conduct is such that it would in the opinion of the court be inequitable to disregard it.

(3) As regards the exercise of its powers under subsection (1)(c) or (d) of section 2, the court shall in particular have regard to the following matters—

(a) the financial needs of the child;

(b) the income, earning capacity (if any), property and other financial resources of the child;

(c) any physical or mental disability of the child;

(d) the standard of living enjoyed by the family before the occurrence of the conduct which is alleged as the ground of the application;

(e) the manner in which the child was being and in which the parties to the marriage expected him to be educated or trained;

(f) the matters mentioned in relation to the parties to the marriage in paragraphs (a) and (b) of subsection (2) above.

(4) As regards the exercise of its powers under section 2 in favour of a child of the family who is not the child of the respondent, the court shall also have regard—

(a) to whether the respondent has assumed any responsibility for the child's maintenance and, if he did, to the extent to which, and the basis on which, he assumed that responsibility and to the length of time during which he discharged that responsibility;

(b) to whether in assuming and discharging that responsibility the respondent did so knowing that the child was not his own child;

(c) to the liability of any other person to maintain the child.

4   Duration of orders for financial provision for a party to a marriage

(1) The term to be specified in any order made under section 2(1)(a) of this Act shall be such term as the court thinks fit except that the term shall not begin earlier than the date of the making of the application for the order and shall not extend beyond the death of either of the parties to the marriage.

(2) Where an order is made under the said section 2(1)(a) and the marriage of the parties affected by the order is subsequently dissolved or annulled but the order continues in force, the order shall, notwithstanding anything in it, cease to have effect on the remarriage of, or formation of a civil partnership by, the party in whose favour it was made, except in relation to any arrears due under the order on the date of the remarriage or formation of the civil partnership.

5   Age limit on making orders for financial provision for children and duration of such orders

(1) Subject to subsection (3) below, no order shall be made under section 2(1)(c) or (d) of this Act in favour of a child who has attained the age of eighteen.

(2) The term to be specified in an order made under section 2(1)(c) of this Act in favour of a child may begin with the date of the making of an application for the order in question or any later date or a date ascertained in accordance with subsection (5) or (6) below but—

(a) shall not in the first instance extend beyond the date of the birthday of the child next following his attaining the upper limit of the compulsory school age (construed in accordance with section 8 of the Education Act 1996) unless the court considers that in the circumstances of the case the welfare of the child requires that it should extend to a later date; and

(b) shall not in any event, subject to subsection (3) below, extend beyond the date of the child's eighteenth birthday.

(3) The court—

(a) may make an order under section 2(1)(c) or (d) of this Act in favour of a child who has attained the age of eighteen, and

   (b) may include in an order made under section 2(1)(c) of this Act in relation to a child who has not attained that age a provision for extending beyond the date when the child will attain that age the term for which by virtue of the order any payments are to be made to or for the benefit of that child,

if it appears to the court—

    (i) that the child is, or will be, or if such an order or provision were made would be, receiving instruction at an educational establishment or undergoing training for a trade, profession or vocation, whether or not he is also, or will also be, in gainful employment; or

   (ii) that there are special circumstances which justify the making of the order or provision.

  (4) Any order made under section 2(1)(c) of this Act in favour of a child shall, notwithstanding anything in the order, cease to have effect on the death of the person liable to make payments under the order.

  (5) Where—

   (a) a maintenance calculation ('the current calculation') is in force with respect to a child; and

   (b) an application is made for an order under section 2(1)(c) of this Act—

    (i) in accordance with section 8 of the Child Support Act 1991; and

   (ii) before the end of the period of 6 months beginning with the making of the current calculation,

the term to be specified in any such order made on that application may be expressed to begin on, or at any time after, the earliest permitted date.

  (6) For the purposes of subsection (5) above, 'the earliest permitted date' is whichever is the later of—

   (a) the date 6 months before the application is made; or

   (b) the date on which the current calculation took effect or, where successive maintenance calculations have been continuously in force with respect to a child, on which the first of those calculations took effect.

  (7) Where—

   (a) a maintenance calculation ceases to have effect by or under any provision of the Child Support Act 1991; and

   (b) an application is made, before the end of the period of 6 months beginning with the relevant date, for an order under section 2(1)(c) of this Act in relation to a child with respect to whom that maintenance calculation was in force immediately before it ceased to have effect,

the term to be specified in any such order, or in any interim order under section 19 of this Act, made on that application, may begin with the date on which that maintenance calculation ceased to have effect, or any later date.

  (8) In subsection (7)(b) above—

   (a) where the maintenance calculation ceased to have effect, the relevant date is the date on which it so ceased.

6 Orders for payments which have been agreed by the parties

  (1) Either party to a marriage may apply to the family court for an order under this section on the ground that either the party making the application or the other party to the marriage has agreed to make such financial provision as may be specified in the application and, subject to subsection (3) below, the court on such an application may, if—

   (a) it is satisfied that the applicant or the respondent, as the case may be, has agreed to make that provision, and

   (b) it has no reason to think that it would be contrary to the interests of justice to exercise its powers hereunder,

order that the applicant or the respondent, as the case may be, shall make the financial provision specified in the application.

(2) In this section 'financial provision' means the provision mentioned in any one or more of the following paragraphs, that is to say—

(a) the making of periodical payments by one party to the other,

(b) the payment of a lump sum by one party to the other,

(c) the making of periodical payments by one party to a child of the family or to the other party for the benefit of such a child,

(d) the payment by one party of a lump sum to a child of the family or to the other party for the benefit of such a child,

and any reference in this section to the financial provision specified in an application made under subsection (1) above or specified by the court under subsection (5) below is a reference to the type of provision specified in the application or by the court, as the case may be, to the amount so specified as the amount of any payment to be made thereunder and, in the case of periodical payments, to the term so specified as the term for which the payments are to be made.

(3) Where the financial provision specified in an application under subsection (1) above includes or consists of provision in respect of a child of the family, the court shall not make an order under that subsection unless it considers that the provision which the applicant or the respondent, as the case may be, has agreed to make in respect of that child provides for, or makes a proper contribution towards, the financial needs of the child.

(4) A party to a marriage who has applied for an order under section 2 of this Act shall not be precluded at any time before the determination of that application from applying for an order under this section; but if an order is made under this section on the application of either party and either of them has also made an application for an order under section 2 of this Act, the application made for the order under section 2 shall be treated as if it had been withdrawn.

(5) Where on an application under subsection (1) above the court decides—

(a) that it would be contrary to the interests of justice to make an order for the making of the financial provision specified in the application, or

(b) that any financial provision which the applicant or the respondent, as the case may be, has agreed to make in respect of a child of the family does not provide for, or make a proper contribution towards, the financial needs of that child,

but is of the opinion—

(i) that it would not be contrary to the interests of justice to make an order for the making of some other financial provision specified by the court, and

(ii) that, in so far as that other financial provision contains any provision for a child of the family, it provides for, or makes a proper contribution towards, the financial needs of that child,

then if both the parties agree, the court may order that the applicant or the respondent, as the case may be, shall make that other financial provision.

(6) Subject to subsection (8) below, the provisions of section 4 of this Act shall apply in relation to an order under this section which requires periodical payments to be made to a party to a marriage for his own benefit as they apply in relation to an order under section 2(1)(a) of this Act.

(7) Subject to subsection (8) below, the provisions of section 5 of this Act shall apply in relation to an order under this section for the making of financial provision in respect of a child of the family as they apply in relation to an order under section 2(1)(c) or (d) of this Act.

(8) Where the court makes an order under this section which contains provision for the making of periodical payments and, by virtue of subsection (4) above, an application for an order under section 2 of this Act is treated as if it had been withdrawn, then the term which may be specified as the term for which the payments are to be made may begin with the date of the making of the application for the order under section 2 or any later date.

(9) Where the respondent is not present or represented by counsel or solicitor at the hearing of an application for an order under subsection (1) above, the court shall not make an order under this section unless there is produced to the court such evidence as may be prescribed by rules of court of—

(a) the consent of the respondent to the making of the order,

(b) the financial resources of the respondent, and

(c) in a case where the financial provision specified in the application includes or consists of provision in respect of a child of the family to be made by the applicant to the respondent for the benefit of the child or to the child, the financial resources of the child.

7 Powers of court where parties are living apart by agreement

(1) Where the parties to a marriage have been living apart for a continuous period exceeding three months, neither party having deserted the other, and one of the parties has been making periodical payments for the benefit of the other party or of a child of the family, that other party may apply to the family court for an order under this section, and any application made under this subsection shall specify the aggregate amount of the payments so made during the period of three months immediately preceding the date of the making of the application.

(2) Where on an application for an order under this section the court is satisfied that the respondent has made the payments specified in the application, the court may, subject to the provisions of this Part of this Act, make one or both of the following orders, that is to say—

(a) an order that the respondent shall make to the applicant such periodical payments, and for such term, as may be specified in the order;

(b) an order that the respondent shall make to the applicant for the benefit of a child of the family to whom the application relates, or to such a child, such periodical payments, and for such term, as may be so specified.

(3) The court in the exercise of its powers under this section—

(a) shall not require the respondent to make payments which exceed in aggregate during any period of three months the aggregate amount paid by him for the benefit of the applicant or a child of the family during the period of three months immediately preceding the date of the making of the application;

(b) shall not require the respondent to make payments to or for the benefit of any person which exceed in amount the payments which the court considers that it would have required the respondent to make to or for the benefit of that person on an application under section 1 of this Act;

(c) shall not require payments to be made to or for the benefit of a child of the family who is not a child of the respondent unless the court considers that it would have made an order in favour of that child on an application under section 1 of this Act.

(4) Where on an application under this section the court considers that the orders which it has the power to make under this section—

(a) would not provide reasonable maintenance for the applicant, or

(b) if the application relates to a child of the family, would not provide, or make a proper contribution towards reasonable maintenance for that child,

the court shall refuse to make an order under this section, but the court may treat the application as if it were an application for an order under section 2 of this Act.

(5) The provisions of section 3 of this Act shall apply in relation to an application for an order under this section as they apply in relation to an application for an order under section 2 of this Act subject to the modification that for the reference in subsection 2(c) of the said section 3 to the occurrence of the conduct which is alleged as the ground of the application there shall be substituted a reference to the living apart of the parties to the marriage.

(6) The provisions of section 4 of this Act shall apply in relation to an order under this section which requires periodical payments to be made to the applicant for his own benefit as they apply in relation to an order made under section 2(1)(a) of this Act.

(7) The provisions of section 5 of this Act shall apply in relation to an order under this section for the making of periodical payments in respect of a child of the family as they apply in relation to an order under section 2(1)(c) of this Act.

Powers of court as to the custody etc. of children

8   Restrictions on making of orders under this Act: welfare of children

Where an application is made by a party to a marriage for an order under section 2, 6 or 7 of this Act, then, if there is a child of the family who is under the age of eighteen, the court shall not dismiss or make a final order on the application until it has decided whether to exercise any of its powers under the Children Act 1989 with respect to the child.

Interim orders

19   Interim orders

(1) Where an application is made for an order under section 2, 6 or 7 of this Act—

    (a) the family court at any time before making a final order on, or dismissing, the application, shall, subject to the provisions of this Part of this Act, have the

        (i) power to make an order (in this Part of this Act referred to as an 'interim maintenance order') which requires the respondent to make to the applicant or to any child of the family who is under the age of eighteen, or to the applicant for the benefit of such a child, such periodical payments as the court thinks reasonable.

(3) An interim maintenance order may provide for payments to be made from such date as the court may specify, except that, subject to section 5(5) and (6) of this Act, the date shall not be earlier than the date of the making of the application for an order under section 2, 6 or 7 of this Act.

(3A) Where an application is made for an order under section 6 of this Act by the party to the marriage who has agreed to make the financial provision specified in the application—

    (a) subsection (1) shall apply as if the reference in paragraph (i) to the respondent were a reference to the applicant and the references to the applicant were references to the respondent; and

    (b) subsection (3) shall apply accordingly.

(5) Subject to subsection (6) below, an interim order made on an application for an order under section 2, 6 or 7 of this Act shall cease to have effect on whichever of the following dates occurs first, that is to say—

    (a) the date, if any, specified for the purpose of the interim order;

    (b) the date of the expiration of the period of three months beginning with the date of the making of the interim order;

    (c) the date on which the family court either makes a final order on or dismisses the application.

(6) Where an interim order made under subsection (1) above would, but for this subsection, cease to have effect by virtue of subsection (5)(a) or (b) above, the family court shall have power by order to provide that the interim order shall continue in force for a further period, and any order continued in force under this subsection shall cease to have effect on whichever of the following dates occurs first, that is to say—

    (a) the date, if any, specified for the purpose in the order made under this subsection;

    (b) the date of the expiration of the period of three months beginning with the date of the making of the order under this subsection or, if more than one order has been made under this subsection with respect to the application, beginning with the date of the making of the first of those orders;

    (c) the date on which the court either makes a final order on, or dismisses, the application.

(7) Not more than one interim maintenance order may be made with respect to any application for an order under section 2, 6 or 7 of this Act, but without prejudice to the powers of a court under this section on any further such application.

(8) No appeal shall lie from the making of or refusal to make, the variation of or refusal to vary, or the revocation of or refusal to revoke, an interim maintenance order.

Variation, revocation and cessation of orders etc.

20   Variation, revival and revocation of orders for periodical payments

(1) Where the family court has made an order under section 2(1)(a) or (c) of this Act for the making of periodical payments, the court shall have power, on an application made under this section, to vary or revoke that order and also to make an order under section 2(1)(b) or (d) of this Act.

(2) Where the family court has made an order under section 6 of this Act for the making of periodical payments by a party to a marriage the court shall have power, on an application made under this section, to vary or revoke that order and also to make an order for the payment of a lump sum by that party either—

    (a) to the other party to the marriage, or

    (b) to a child of the family or to that other party for the benefit of that child.

(3) Where the family court has made an order under section 7 of this Act for the making of periodical payments, the court shall have power, on an application made under this section, to vary or revoke that order.

(5) Where the family court has made an interim maintenance order under section 19 of this Act, the court, on an application made under this section, shall have power to vary or revoke that order, except that the court shall not by virtue of this subsection extend the period for which the order is in force.

(6) The power of the court under this section to vary an order for the making of periodical payments shall include power to suspend any provision thereof temporarily and to revive any provision so suspended.

(7) Where the court has power by virtue of this section to make an order for the payment of a lump sum, the amount of the lump sum shall not exceed the maximum amount that may at that time be required to be paid under section 2(3) of this Act, but the court may make an order for the payment of a lump sum not exceeding that amount notwithstanding that the person required to pay the lump sum was required to pay a lump sum by a previous order under this Part of this Act.

(8) Where the court has power by virtue of subsection (2) above to make an order for the payment of a lump sum and the respondent or the applicant as the case may be has agreed to pay a lump sum of an amount exceeding the maximum amount that may at that time be required to be paid under section 2(3) of this Act, the court may, notwithstanding anything in subsection (7) above, make an order for the payment of a lump sum of that amount.

(9) An order by virtue of this section which varies an order for the making of periodical payments may provide that the payments as so varied shall be made from such date as the court may specify, except that, subject to subsections (9A) and (9B) below, the date shall not be earlier than the date of the making of the application under this section.

(9A) Where—

    (a) there is in force an order ('the order')—

        (i)   under section 2(1)(c) of this Act,

        (ii) under section 6(1) of this Act making provision of a kind mentioned in paragraph (c) of section 6(2) of this Act (regardless of whether it makes provision of any other kind mentioned in that paragraph),

        (iii) under section 7(2)(b) of this Act, or

        (iv) which is an interim maintenance order under which the payments are to be made to a child or to the applicant for the benefit of a child;

    (b) the order requires payments specified in it to be made to or for the benefit of more than one child without apportioning those payments between them;

    (c) a maintenance calculation ('the calculation') is made with respect to one or more, but not all, of the children with respect to whom those payments are to be made; and

    (d) an application is made, before the end of the period of 6 months beginning with the
        date on which the calculation was made, for the variation or revocation of the order,
the court may, in exercise of its powers under this section to vary or revoke the order, direct that the
variation or revocation shall take effect from the date on which the calculation took effect or any
later date.

    (9B) Where—

      (a) an order ('the child order') of a kind prescribed for the purposes of section 10(1) of the
          Child Support Act 1991 is affected by a maintenance calculation;

      (b) on the date on which the child order became so affected there was in force an order ('the
          spousal order')—

          (i)   under section 2(1)(a) of this Act,

          (ii) under section 6(1) of this Act making provision of a kind mentioned in section
              6(2)(a) of this Act (regardless of whether it makes provision of any other kind men-
              tioned in that paragraph),

          (iii) under section 7(2)(a) of this Act, or

          (iv) which is an interim maintenance order under which the payments are to be made to
              the applicant (otherwise than for the benefit of a child); and

      (c) an application is made, before the end of the period of 6 months beginning with the date
          on which the maintenance calculation was made, for the spousal order to be varied or
          revoked,

the court may, in exercise of its powers under this section to vary or revoke the spousal order, direct
that the variation or revocation shall take effect from the date on which the child order became so
affected or any later date.

    (9C) For the purposes of subsection (9B) above, an order is affected if it ceases to have effect or
is modified by or under section 10 of the Child Support Act 1991.

    (11) In exercising the powers conferred by this section, the court shall, so far as it appears to
the court just to do so, give effect to any agreement which has been reached between the parties in
relation to the application and, if there is no such agreement or if the court decides not to give effect
to the agreement, the court shall have regard to all the circumstances of the case, first consideration
being given to the welfare while a minor of any child of the family who has not attained the age of
eighteen, and the circumstances of the case shall include any change in any of the matters to which
the court was required to have regard when making the order to which the application relates or, in
the case of an application for the variation or revocation of an order made under section 6 of this Act
or on an appeal under section 29 of this Act, to which the court would have been required to have
regard if that order had been made under section 2 of this Act.

    (12) An application under this section may be made—

      (a) where it is for the variation or revocation of an order under section 2, 6, 7 or 19 of this Act
          for periodical payments, by either party to the marriage in question; and

      (b) where it is for the variation of an order under section 2(1)(c), 6 or 7 of this Act for periodi-
          cal payments to or in respect of a child, also by the child himself, if he has attained the
          age of sixteen.

20ZA   Variation of orders for periodical payments: further provisions

    (1) Subject to subsections (7) and (8) below, the power of the court under section 20 of this Act
to vary an order for the making of periodical payments shall include power, if the court is satisfied
that payment has not been made in accordance with the order, to exercise one of its powers under
section 1(4) and (4A) of the Maintenance Enforcement Act 1991.

. . .

    (6) Subsection (6) of section 1 of the Maintenance Enforcement Act 1991 (power of court to
order that account be opened) shall apply for the purposes of subsection (1) above as it applies for
the purposes of that section.

(7) Before varying the order by exercising one of its powers under section 1(4) and (4A) of the Maintenance Enforcement Act 1991, the court shall have regard to any representations made by the parties to the application.

...

(10) None of the powers of the court, conferred by this section shall be exercisable in relation to an order under this Part of this Act for the making of periodical payments unless, at the time when the order was made, the person required to make the payments was ordinarily resident in England and Wales.

20A Revival of orders for periodical payments

(1) Where an order made by the family court under this Part of this Act for the making of periodical payments to or in respect of a child (other than an interim maintenance order) ceases to have effect—

    (a) on the date on which the child attains the age of sixteen, or

    (b) at any time after that date but before or on the date on which he attains the age of eighteen,

the child may apply to the court for an order for its revival.

(2) If on such an application it appears to the court that—

    (a) the child is, will be or (if an order were made under this subsection) would be receiving instruction at an educational establishment or undergoing training for a trade, profession or vocation, whether or not while in gainful employment, or

    (b) there are special circumstances which justify the making of an order under this subsection,

the court shall have power by order to revive the order from such date as the court may specify, not being earlier than the date of the making of the application.

(3) Any order revived under this section may be varied or revoked under section 20 in the same way as it could have been varied or revoked had it continued in being.

...

25 Effect on certain orders of parties living together

(1) Where—

    (a) periodical payments are required to be made to one of the parties to a marriage (whether for his own benefit or for the benefit of a child of the family) by an order made under section 2 or 6 of this Act or by an interim maintenance order made under section 19 of this Act (otherwise than on an application under section 7 of this Act),

the order shall be enforceable notwithstanding that the parties to the marriage are living with each other at the date of the making of the order or that, although they are not living with each other at that date, they subsequently resume living with each other; but the order shall cease to have effect if after that date the parties continue to live with each other, or resume living with each other, for a continuous period exceeding six months.

(2) Where any of the following orders is made under this Part of this Act, that is to say—

    (a) an order under section 2 or 6 of this Act which requires periodical payments to be made to a child of the family, or

    (b) an interim maintenance order under section 19 of this Act (otherwise than on an application under section 7 of this Act) which requires periodical payments to be made to a child of the family,

then, unless the court otherwise directs, the order shall continue to have effect and be enforceable notwithstanding that the parties to the marriage in question are living with each other at the date of the making of the order or that, although they are not living with each other at that date, they subsequently resume living with each other.

(3) Any order made under section 7 of this Act, and any interim maintenance order made on an application for an order under that section, shall cease to have effect if the parties to the marriage resume living with each other.

(4) Where an order made under this Part of this Act ceases to have effect by virtue of subsection (1) or (3) above or by virtue of a direction given under subsection (2) above, the family court may, on an application made by either party to the marriage, make an order declaring that the first mentioned order ceased to have effect from such date as the court may specify.

Reconciliation

26   Reconciliation

(1) Where an application is made for an order under section 2 of this Act the court, before deciding whether to exercise its powers under that section, shall consider whether there is any possibility of reconciliation between the parties to the marriage in question: and if at any stage of the proceedings on that application it appears to the court that there is a reasonable possibility of such a reconciliation, the court may adjourn the proceedings for such period as it thinks fit to enable attempts to be made to effect a reconciliation.

(2) Where the court adjourns any proceedings under subsection (1) above, it may request an officer of the Service (within the meaning of the Criminal Justice and Court Services Act 2000), a Welsh family proceedings officer (within the meaning given by section 35 of the Children Act 2004) or any other person to attempt to effect a reconciliation between the parties to the marriage, and where any such request is made, that officer or other person shall report in writing to the court whether the attempt has been successful or not, but shall not include in that report any other information.

Provisions relating to High Court and county court

...

28   Powers of High Court and county court in relation to certain orders under Part I

(1) Where after the making by the family court of an order under this Part of this Act proceedings between, and relating to the marriage of, the parties to the proceedings in which that order was made have been commenced in the High Court or the family court, then, except in the case of an order for the payment of a lump sum, the court in which the proceedings or any application made therein are or is pending may, if it thinks fit, direct that the order under this Part shall cease to have effect on such date as may be specified in the direction.

...

Provisions relating to procedure, jurisdiction and enforcement

30   Provisions as to jurisdiction and procedure

...

(5) It is hereby declared that any jurisdiction conferred on the family court by this Part of this Act is exercisable notwithstanding that any party to the proceedings is not domiciled in England.

...

32   Enforcement etc. of orders for payment of money

...

(2) The family court when making an order under this Part of this Act for the making of a periodical payment by one person to another may direct that it shall be made to some third party on that other person's behalf instead of directly to that other person.

(3) Any person for the time being under an obligation to make payments in pursuance of any order for the payment of money made under this Part of this Act shall give notice of any change of address to such person, if any, as may be specified in the order; and any person who without reasonable excuse fails to give such a notice shall be liable on summary conviction to a fine not exceeding level 2 on the standard scale.

(4) A person shall not be entitled to enforce through the family court the payment of any arrears due under an order made by virtue of this Part of this Act without the leave of that court if

those arrears became due more than twelve months before proceedings to enforce the payment of them are begun.

(5) The court hearing an application for the grant of leave under subsection (4) above may refuse to leave, or may grant leave subject to such restrictions and conditions (including conditions as to the allowing of time for payment or the making of payment by instalments) as that court thinks proper, or may remit the payment of such arrears or any part thereof.

(6) An application for the grant of leave under subsection (4) above shall be made in such manner as may be prescribed by rules of court.

35 Orders for repayment in certain cases of sums paid after cessation of order by reason of remarriage or formation of civil partnership

(1) Where—

(a) an order made under section 2(1)(a), 6 or 7 of this Act has, by virtue of section 4(2) of this Act, ceased to have effect by reason of the remarriage of, or formation of a civil partnership by, the party in whose favour it was made, and

(b) the person liable to make payments under the order made payments in accordance with it in respect of a period after the date of that remarriage or the formation of that civil partnership in the mistaken belief that the order was still subsisting,

no proceedings in respect of a cause of action arising out of the circumstances mentioned in paragraphs (a) and (b) above shall be maintainable by the person so liable or his personal representatives against the person so entitled or his personal representatives, but on an application made under this section the family court may exercise the powers conferred on it by subsection (2) below.

(2) The family court may order the respondent to an application made under this section to pay to the applicant a sum equal to the amount of the payments made in respect of the period mentioned in subsection (1)(b) above or, if it appears to the court that it would be unjust to make that order, it may either order the respondent to pay to the applicant such lesser sum as it thinks fit or dismiss the application.

…

PART V SUPPLEMENTARY PROVISIONS

88 Interpretation

(1) In this Act—

'child,' in relation to one or both of the parties to a marriage, includes a child whose father and mother were not married to each other at the time of his birth;

'child of the family,' in relation to the parties to a marriage, means—

(a) a child of both of those parties; and

(b) any other child, not being a child who is placed with those parties as foster parents by a local authority or voluntary organisation, who has been treated by both of those parties as a child of their family;

'local authority' means the council of a county (other than a metropolitan county), of a metropolitan district or of a London borough, or the Common Council of the City of London;

'maintenance calculation' has the same meaning as it has in the Child Support Act 1991 by virtue of section 54 of that Act as read with any regulations in force under that section;

(2) References in this Act to the parties to a marriage living with each other shall be construed as references to their living with each other in the same household.

(3) For the avoidance of doubt it is hereby declared that references in this Act to remarriage include references to a marriage which is by law void or voidable.

…

Magistrates' Courts Act 1980

(1980 c. 43)

PART II ORDERS FOR PERIODICAL PAYMENT

59   Orders for periodical payment: means of payment

(1) In any case where a magistrates' court orders money to be paid periodically by one person (in this section referred to as 'the debtor') to another (in this section referred to as 'the creditor'), the court shall at the same time exercise one of its powers under paragraphs (a) and (b) of subsection (3) below.

. . .

(3) The powers of the court are—
   (a) the power to order that payments under the order be made directly by the debtor to the creditor;
   (b) the power to order that payments under the order be made to the designated officer for the court or for any other magistrates' court; . . .

(4) In any case where—
   (a) the court proposes to exercise its power under paragraph (c) of subsection (3) above, and
   (b) having given the debtor an opportunity of opening an account from which payments under the order may be made in accordance with the method of payment proposed to be ordered under that paragraph, the court is satisfied that the debtor has failed, without reasonable excuse, to open such an account,

the court in exercising its power under that paragraph may order that the debtor open such an account.

. . .

(6) The methods of payment referred to in subsection (3)(c) above are the following, that is to say—
   (a) payment by standing order; or
   (b) payment by any other method which requires one person to give his authority for payments of a specific amount to be made from an account of his to an account of another's on specific dates during the period for which the authority is in force and without the need for any further authority from him.

. . .

59A   Orders for periodical payment: proceedings by designated officer

(1) Where payments under an order made by a magistrates' court are required to be made periodically—
   (a) to or through the designated officer for a magistrates' court, or
   (b) by any method of payment falling within section 59(6) above,

and any sums payable under the order are in arrear, the relevant designated officer shall, if the person for whose benefit the payments are required to be made so requests in writing, and unless it appears to that designated officer that it is unreasonable in the circumstances to do so, proceed in his own name for the recovery of those sums.

(2) Where payments under an order made by a magistrates' court are required to be made periodically to or through the designated officer for a magistrates' court, the person for whose benefit the payments are required to be made may, at any time during the period in which the payments are required to be so made, give authority in writing to the relevant designated officer for him to proceed as mentioned in subsection (3) below.

(3) Where authority under subsection (2) above is given to the relevant designated officer, he shall, unless it appears to him that it is unreasonable in the circumstances to do so, proceed in his

own name for the recovery of any sums payable to or through him under the orders in question which, on or after the date of the giving of the authority, fall into arrear.

(4) In any case where—

(a) authority under subsection (2) above has been given to the relevant designated officer, and

(b) the person for whose benefit the payments are required to be made gives notice in writing to the relevant delegated officer cancelling the authority,

the authority shall cease to have effect and, accordingly, the relevant designated officer shall not continue any proceedings already commenced by virtue of the authority.

(5) The person for whose benefit the payments are required to be made shall have the same liability for all the costs properly incurred in or about proceedings taken under subsection (1) above at his request or under subsection (3) above by virtue of his authority (including any costs incurred as a result of any proceedings commenced not being continued) as if the proceedings had been taken by him.

(6) Nothing in subsection (1) or (3) above shall affect any right of a person to proceed in his own name for the recovery of sums payable on his behalf under an order of any court.

(7) In this section—

'the relevant designated officer', in relation to an order, means—

(a) in a case where payments under the order are required to be made to or through the designated officer for a magistrates' court, the designated officer for that magistrates' court; and

(b) in a case where such payments are required to be made by any method of payment falling within section 59(6) and the order was made by a magistrates' court, the designated officer for that magistrates' court;

…

60   Revocation, variation etc., of orders for periodical payment

(1) Where a magistrates' court has made an order for money to be paid periodically by one person to another, the court may, by order on complaint, revoke, revive or vary the order.

(2) The power under subsection (1) above to vary an order shall include power to suspend the operation of any provision of the order temporarily and to revive the operation of any provision so suspended.

…

(11) For the purposes of this section—

(a) 'creditor' and 'debtor' have the same meaning as they have in section 59 above;

…

Payments to children

62   Provisions as to payments required to be made to a child etc.

(1) Where—

(a) periodical payments are required to be made, or a lump sum is required to be paid, to a child under an order made by a magistrates' court, …

any sum required under the order to be paid to the child may be paid to the person with whom the child has his home, and that person—

(i) may proceed in his own name for the variation, revival or revocation of the order, and

(ii) may either proceed in his own name for the recovery of any sum required to be paid under the order or request or authorise the designated officer for the magistrates' court under subsection (1) or subsection (2) respectively of section 59A above, to proceed for the recovery of that sum.

(2) Where a child has a right under any enactment to apply for the revival of an order made by a magistrates' court which provided for the making of periodical payments to or for the benefit of

the child, the person with whom the child has his home may proceed in his own name for the revival of that order.

(3) Where any person by whom periodical payments are required to be paid to a child under an order made by a magistrates' court makes a complaint for the variation or revocation of that order, the person with whom the child has his home may answer the complaint in his own name.

(4) Nothing in subsections (1) and (2) above shall affect any right of a child to proceed in his own name for the variation, revival or revocation of an order or for the recovery of any sum payable thereunder.

(5) In this section references to the person with whom a child has his home—

    (a) in the case of any child who is being looked after by a local authority (within the meaning of section 22 of the Children Act 1989), are references to that local authority; and

    (b) in any other case, are references to the person who, disregarding any absence of the child at a hospital or boarding school and any other temporary absence, has care of the child.

...

(7) In this section 'child' means a person who has not attained the age of 18.

Orders other than for payment of money

63 Orders other than for payment of money

(1) Where under any Act passed after 31 December 1879 a magistrates' court has power to require the doing of anything other than payment of money, or to prohibit the doing of anything, any order of the court for the purpose of exercising that power may contain such provisions for the manner in which anything is to be done, for the time within which anything is to be done, or during which anything is not to be done, and generally for giving effect to the order, as the court thinks fit.

(2) The court may by order made on complaint suspend or rescind any such order as aforesaid.

(3) Where any person disobeys an order of a magistrates' court made under an Act passed after 31 December 1879 to do anything other than the payment of money or to abstain from doing anything the court may—

    (a) order him to pay a sum not exceeding £50 for every day during which he is in default or a sum not exceeding £5,000; or

    (b) commit him to custody until he has remedied his default or for a period not exceeding 2 months;

but a person who is ordered to pay a sum for every day during which he is in default or who is committed to custody until he has remedied his default shall not by virtue of this section be ordered to pay more than £1,000 or be committed for more than 2 months in all for doing or abstaining from doing the same thing contrary to the order (without prejudice to the operation of this section in relation to any subsequent default).

(4) Any sum ordered to be paid under subsection (3) above shall for the purposes of this Act be treated as adjudged to be paid by a conviction of a magistrates' court.

(5) The preceding provisions of this section shall not apply to any order for the enforcement of which provision is made by any other enactment.

...

PART III SATISFACTION AND ENFORCEMENT

General provisions

75 Power to dispense with immediate payment

(1) A magistrates' court by whose conviction or order a sum is adjudged to be paid may, instead of requiring immediate payment, allow time for payment, or order payment by instalments.

(2) Where a magistrates' court has allowed time for payment, the court may, on application by or on behalf of the person liable to make the payment, allow further time or order payment by instalments.

(3) Where a court has ordered payment by instalments and default is made in the payment of any one instalment, proceedings may be taken as if the default has been made in the payment of all the instalments then unpaid.

76 Enforcement of sums adjudged to be paid

(1) Subject to the following provisions of this Part of this Act, and to section 132 below, where default is made in paying a sum adjudged to be paid by a conviction or order of a magistrates' court, the court may issue a warrant of control for the purpose of recovering the sum or issue a warrant committing the defaulter to prison.

(2) A warrant of commitment may be issued as aforesaid either—

(a) where it appears on the return to a warrant of control that the money and goods of the defaulter are insufficient to pay the amount outstanding, as defined by paragraph 50(3) of Schedule 12 to the Tribunals, Courts and Enforcement Act 2007; or

(b) instead of a warrant of control.

(3) The period for which a person may be committed to prison under such a warrant as aforesaid shall not, subject to the provisions of any enactment passed after 31 December 1879, exceed the period applicable to the case under Schedule 4 to this Act.

...

Senior Courts Act 1981

(1981 c. 54)

PART II JURISDICTION: THE HIGH COURT

Powers

41 Wards of court

(1) Subject to the provisions of this section, no minor shall be made a ward of court except by virtue of an order to that effect made by the High Court.

(2) Where an application is made for such an order in respect of a minor, the minor shall become a ward of court on the making of the application, but shall cease to be a ward of court at the end of such period as may be prescribed unless within that period an order has been made in accordance with the application.

(2A) Subsection (2) does not apply with respect to a child who is the subject of a care order (as defined by section 105 of the Children Act 1989).

(3) The High Court may, either upon an application in that behalf or without such an application, order that any minor who is for the time being a ward of court shall cease to be a ward of court.

PART III PRACTICE AND PROCEDURE: THE HIGH COURT

Distribution of business

61 Distribution of business among Divisions

(1) Subject to any provision made by or under this or any other Act (and in particular to any rules of court made in pursuance of subsection (2) and any order under subsection (3)), business in

the High Court of any description mentioned in Schedule 1, as for the time being in force, shall be distributed among the Divisions in accordance with that Schedule.

...

SCHEDULES

SCHEDULE 1

DISTRIBUTION OF BUSINESS IN HIGH COURT

Family Division

3. To the Family Division are assigned—

  (a) all matrimonial causes and matters (whether at first instance or on appeal);

  (b) all causes and matters (whether at first instance or on appeal) relating to—

    (i) legitimacy;

    (ii) the exercise of the inherent jurisdiction of the High Court with respect to minors, the maintenance of minors and any proceedings under the Children Act 1989, except proceedings solely for the appointment of a guardian of a minor's estate;

    (iii) adoption;

    (iv) non-contentious or common form probate business;

  (c) applications for consent to the marriage of a minor or for a declaration under section 27B(5) of the Marriage Act 1949;

  (d) proceedings on appeal under section 13 of the Administration of Justice Act 1960 from an order or decision made under section 63(3) of the Magistrates' Courts Act 1980 to enforce an order of a magistrates' court made in matrimonial proceedings or proceedings under Part IV of the Family Law Act 1996 or with respect to the guardianship of a minor;

  (e) applications under Part III of the Family Law Act 1986;

  (e) proceedings under the Children Act 1989;

  (ea) proceedings under section 79 of the Childcare Act 2006;

  (f) all proceedings under—

    (i) Part IV or 4A of the Family Law Act 1996;

    (ii) the Child Abduction and Custody Act 1985;

    (iii) the Family Law Act 1986;

    (iv) section 54 of the Human Fertilisation and Embryology Act 2008;

    ...

  (fa) all proceedings relating to a debit or credit under section 29(1) or 49(1) of the Welfare Reform and Pensions Act 1999;

  (g) all proceedings for the purpose of enforcing an order made in any proceedings of a type described in this paragraph;

  (h) all proceedings under the Child Support Act 1991;

  (i) all proceedings under sections 6 and 8 of the Gender Recognition Act 2004;

  (j) all civil partnership causes and matters (whether at first instance or on appeal);

  (k) applications for consent to the formation of a civil partnership by a minor or for a declaration under paragraph 7 of Schedule 1 to the Civil Partnership Act 2004;

  (l) applications under section 58 of that Act (declarations relating to civil partnerships).

...

Administration of Justice Act 1982

(1982 c. 53)

2   Abolition of actions for loss of services etc

No person shall be liable in tort under the law of England and Wales or the law of Northern Ireland—

(a) to a husband on the ground only of his having deprived him of the services or society of his wife;

(b) to a parent (or person standing in the place of a parent) on the ground only of his having deprived him of the services of a child; or

(c) on the ground only—

(i)   of having deprived another of his menial servant;

(ii) of having deprived another of the services of his female servant by raping or seducing her; or

(iii) of enticement of a servant or harbouring a servant.

Marriage Act 1983

(1983 c. 32)

Marriages in England and Wales

1   Marriages of house-bound and detained persons in England and Wales

(1) Subject to the provisions of this Act and the Marriage Act 1949, the marriage of a person who is house-bound or is a detained person may be solemnized in England and Wales, on the authority of certificates of a superintendent registrar issued under Part III of the Marriage Act 1949, at the place where that person usually resides.

(2) For the purposes of this section a person is house-bound if—

(a) each notice of his or her marriage given in accordance with section 27 of the Marriage Act 1949 is accompanied by a statement, made in a form prescribed under that Act by a registered medical practitioner not more than 14 days before that notice is given, that, in his opinion—

(i)   by reason of illness or disability, he or she ought not to move or be moved from his or her home or the other place where he or she is at that time, and

(ii) it is likely that it will be the case for at least the three months following the date on which the statement is made that by reason of the illness or disability he or she ought not to move or be moved from that place; and

(b) he or she is not a detained person.

(3) For the purposes of this section, a person is a detained person if he or she is for the time being detained—

(a) otherwise than by virtue of section 2, 4, 5, 35, 36 or 136 of the Mental Health Act 1983 (short term detentions), as a patient in a hospital; or

(b) in a prison or other place to which the Prison Act 1952 applies.

Child Abduction Act 1984

(1984 c. 37)

PART I OFFENCES UNDER LAW OF ENGLAND AND WALES

1   Offence of abduction of child by parent etc.

(1) Subject to subsections (5) and (8) below, a person connected with a child under the age of sixteen commits an offence if he takes or sends the child out of the United Kingdom without the appropriate consent.

(2) A person is connected with a child for the purposes of this section if—

    (a)   he is a parent of the child; or

    (b)   in the case of a child whose parents were not married to each other at the time of his birth, there are reasonable grounds for believing that he is the father of the child; or

    (c)   he is a guardian of the child; or

    (ca) he is a special guardian of the child; or

    (d)   he is a person named in a child arrangements order as a person with whom the child is to live; or

    (e)   he has custody of the child.

(3) In this section 'the appropriate consent', in relation to a child, means—

    (a)   the consent of each of the following—

        (i)   the child's mother;

        (ii)   the child's father, if he has parental responsibility for him;

        (iii) any guardian of the child;

        (iiia) any special guardian of the child;

        (iv) any person named in a child arrangements order as a person with whom the child is to live;

        (v)   any person who has custody of the child; or (b) the leave of the court granted under or by virtue of any provision of Part II of the Children Act 1989; or

    (c)   if any person has custody of the child, the leave of the court which awarded custody to him.

(4) A person does not commit an offence under this section by taking or sending a child out of the United Kingdom without obtaining the appropriate consent if—

    (a)   he is a person named in a child arrangements order as a person with whom the child is to live, and he takes or sends the child out of the United Kingdom for a period of less than one month; or

    (b)   he is a special guardian of the child and he takes or sends the child out of the United Kingdom for a period of less than three months.

(4A) Subsection (4) above does not apply if the person taking or sending the child out of the United Kingdom does so in breach of an order under Part II of the Children Act 1989.

(5) A person does not commit an offence under this section by doing anything without the consent of another person whose consent is required under the foregoing provisions if—

    (a)   he does it in the belief that the other person—

        (i)   has consented; or

        (ii) would consent if he was aware of all the relevant circumstances; or

    (b)   he has taken all reasonable steps to communicate with the other person but has been unable to communicate with him; or

    (c)   the other person has unreasonably refused to consent.

(5A) Subsection (5)(c) above does not apply if—

    (a)   the person who refused to consent is a person—

        (i)   named in a child arrangements order as a person with whom the child is to live;

        (ia) who is a special guardian of the child; or

        (ii) who has custody of the child; or

    (b)   the person taking or sending the child out of the United Kingdom is, by so acting, in breach of an order made by a court in the United Kingdom.

(6) Where, in proceedings for an offence under this section, there is sufficient evidence to raise an issue as to the application of subsection (5) above, it shall be for the prosecution to prove that that subsection does not apply.

(7) For the purposes of this section—

    (a)   'guardian of a child', 'special guardian', 'child arrangements order' and 'parental responsibility' have the same meaning as in the Children Act 1989; and

(b) a person shall be treated as having custody of a child if there is in force an order of a court in the United Kingdom awarding him (whether solely or jointly with another person) custody, legal custody or care and control of the child.

(8) This section shall have effect subject to the provisions of the Schedule to this Act in relation to a child who is in the care of a local authority, detained in a place of safety, remanded otherwise than on bail or the subject of proceedings or an order relating to adoption.

2 Offence of abduction of child by other persons

(1) Subject to subsection (3) below, a person, other than one mentioned in subsection (2) below commits an offence if, without lawful authority or reasonable excuse, he takes or detains a child under the age of sixteen—

(a) so as to remove him from the lawful control of any person having lawful control of the child; or

(b) so as to keep him out of the lawful control of any person entitled to lawful control of the child.

(2) The persons are—

(a) where the father and mother of the child in question were married to each other at the time of his birth, the child's father and mother;

(b) where the father and mother of the child in question were not married to each other at the time of his birth, the child's mother; and

(c) any other person mentioned in section 1(2)(c) to (e) above.

(3) In proceedings against any person for an offence under this section, it shall be a defence for that person to prove—

(a) where the father and mother of the child in question were not married to each other at the time of his birth—

(i) that he is the child's father; or

(ii) that, at the time of the alleged offence, he believed, on reasonable grounds, that he was the child's father; or

(b) that, at the time of the alleged offence, he believed that the child had attained the age of sixteen.

3 Construction of references to taking, sending and detaining

For the purposes of this Part of this Act—

(a) a person shall be regarded as taking a child if he causes or induces the child to accompany him or any other person or causes the child to be taken;

(b) a person shall be regarded as sending a child if he causes the child to be sent;

(c) a person shall be regarded as detaining a child if he causes the child to be detained or induces the child to remain with him or any other person; and

(d) references to a child's parents and to a child whose parents were (or were not) married to each other at the time of his birth shall be construed in accordance with section 1 of the Family Law Reform Act 1987 (which extends their meaning).

SCHEDULE

MODIFICATIONS OF SECTION 1 FOR CHILDREN IN CERTAIN CASES

Children in care of local authorities and voluntary organisations

1.—(1) This paragraph applies in the case of a child who is in the care of a local authority within the meaning of the Children Act 1989 in England or Wales.

(2) Where this paragraph applies, section 1 of this Act shall have effect as if—

    (a) the reference in subsection (1) to the appropriate consent were a reference to the consent of the local authority in whose care the child is; and

    (b) subsections (3) to (6) were omitted.

Children in places of safety

2.—(1) This paragraph applies in the case of a child who is—

    (a) detained in a place of safety under paragraph 4(1)(a) of Schedule 1 or paragraph 6(4)
        (a) of Schedule 8 to the Powers of Criminal Courts (Sentencing) Act 2000 or paragraph
        21(2) of Schedule 2 to the Criminal Justice and Immigration Act 2008; or

    (aa) detained in a place of safety under paragraph 9(3) of the Schedule to the Street Offences Act 1959; or

    (b) remanded to local authority accommodation under section 23 of the Children and Young Persons Act 1969, paragraph 4 of Schedule 1 or paragraph 6 of Schedule 8 to the Powers of Criminal Courts (Sentencing) Act 2000 or paragraph 21 of Schedule 2 to the Criminal Justice and Immigration Act 2008; or

    (ba) remanded to local authority accommodation under paragraph 10 of the Schedule to the Street Offences Act 1959; or

    (bb) remanded to local authority accommodation or youth detention accommodation under section 91 of the Legal Aid, Sentencing and Punishment of Offenders Act 2012.

(2) Where this paragraph applies, section 1 of this Act shall have effect as if—

    (a) the reference in subsection (1) to the appropriate consent were a reference to the leave of any magistrates' court acting for the area in which the place of safety, local authority accommodation or youth detention accommodation is; and

    (b) subsections (3) to (6) were omitted.

Adoption and custodianship

3.—(1) This paragraph applies where—

    (a) a child is placed for adoption by an adoption agency under section 19 of the Adoption and Children Act 2002, or an adoption agency is authorised to place the child for adoption under that section; or

    (b) a placement order is in force in respect of the child; or

    (c) an application for such an order has been made in respect of the child and has not been disposed of; or

    (d) an application for an adoption order has been made in respect of the child and has not been disposed of; or

    (e) an order under section 84 of the Adoption and Children Act 2002 (giving parental responsibility prior to adoption abroad) has been made in respect of the child, or an application for such an order in respect of him has been made and has not been disposed of.

(2) Where this paragraph applies, section 1 of this Act shall have effect as if—

    (a) the reference in subsection (1) to the appropriate consent were—

        (i)   in a case within sub-paragraph (1)(a) above, a reference to the consent of each person who has parental responsibility for the child or to the leave of the High Court;

        (ii) in a case within sub-paragraph (1)(b) above, a reference to the leave of the court which made the placement order;

        (iii) in a case within sub-paragraph (1)(c) or (d) above, a reference to the leave of the court to which the application was made;

        (iv) in a case within sub-paragraph (1)(e) above, a reference to the leave of the court which made the order or, as the case may be, to which the application was made;

    (b) subsection (3) were omitted;

(c) in subsection (4), in paragraph (a), for the words from 'in whose favour' to the first mention of 'child' there were substituted 'who provides the child's home in a case falling within sub-paragraph (1)(a) or (b) of paragraph 3 of the Schedule to this Act'; and

(d) subsection (4A), (5), (5A) and (6) were omitted.

(3) Sub-paragraph (2) above shall be construed as if the references to the court included, in any case where the court is a magistrates' court, a reference to any magistrates' court acting for the same area as that court.

Cases within paragraphs 1 and 3

4. In the case of a child falling within both paragraph 1 and paragraph 3 above, the provisions of paragraph 3 shall apply to the exclusion of those in paragraph 1.

Interpretation

5. In this Schedule—

(a) 'adoption agency', 'adoption order', 'placed for adoption by an adoption agency' and 'placement order' have the same meaning as in the Adoption and Children Act 2002; and

(b) 'area', in relation to a magistrates' court, means the petty sessions area for which the court is appointed.

Matrimonial and Family Proceedings Act 1984

(1984 c. 42)

...

PART 4A THE FAMILY COURT

31A Establishment of the family court

(1) There is to be a court in England and Wales, called the family court, for the purpose of exercising the jurisdiction and powers conferred on it—

(a) by or under this or any other Act, or

(b) by or under any Act, or Measure, of the National Assembly for Wales.

(2) The family court is to be a court of record and have a seal.

31B Sittings

(1) Sittings of the family court may be held, and any other business of the family court may be conducted, at any place in England and Wales.

(2) Sittings of the family court at any place may be continuous or intermittent or occasional.

(3) Sittings of the family court may be held simultaneously to take any number of different cases in the same place or different places, and the court may adjourn cases from place to place at any time.

(4) The places at which the family court sits, and the days and times at which it sits in any place, are to be determined in accordance with directions given by the Lord Chancellor after consulting the Lord Chief Justice.

(5) The Lord Chief Justice may nominate a judicial office holder (as defined in section 109(4) of the Constitutional Reform Act 2005) to exercise functions of the Lord Chief Justice under this section.

31C Judges

(1) A person is a judge of the family court if the person—

(a) is the Lord Chief Justice,

(b) is the Master of the Rolls,

(c) is the President of the Queen's Bench Division,

(d) is the President of the Family Division,

(e) is the Chancellor of the High Court,

(f) is an ordinary judge of the Court of Appeal (including the vice-president, if any, of either division of that court),

(g) is the Senior President of Tribunals,

(h) is a puisne judge of the High Court,

(i) is a deputy judge of the High Court,

(j) is a Circuit judge,

(k) is the Judge Advocate General,

(l) is a Recorder,

(m) holds an office listed—

    (i) in the first column of the table in section 89(3C) of the Senior Courts Act 1981 (senior High Court Masters etc), or

    (ii) in column 1 of Part 2 of Schedule 2 to that Act (High Court Masters etc),

(n) is a district judge (which, by virtue of section 8(1C) of the County Courts Act 1984, here includes a deputy district judge appointed under section 8 of that Act),

(o) is a deputy district judge appointed under section 102 of the Senior Courts Act 1981,

(p) is a Chamber President, or a Deputy Chamber President, of a chamber of the Upper Tribunal or of a chamber of the First-tier Tribunal,

(q) is a judge of the Upper Tribunal by virtue of appointment under paragraph 1(1) of Schedule 3 to the Tribunals, Courts and Enforcement Act 2007,

(r) is a transferred-in judge of the Upper Tribunal (see section 31(2) of that Act),

(s) is a deputy judge of the Upper Tribunal (whether under paragraph 7 of Schedule 3 to, or section 31(2) of, that Act),

(t) is a judge of the First-tier Tribunal by virtue of appointment under paragraph 1(1) of Schedule 2 to that Act,

(u) is a transferred-in judge of the First-tier Tribunal (see section 31(2) of that Act),

(v) is a member of a panel of Employment Judges established for England and Wales or for Scotland,

(w) is a person appointed under section 30(1)(a) or (b) of the Courts-Martial (Appeals) Act 1951 (assistants to the Judge Advocate General),

(x) is a District Judge (Magistrates' Courts), or

(y) is a justice of the peace who is not a District Judge (Magistrates' Courts),

but see also section 9 of the Senior Courts Act 1981 (certain ex-judges may act as judges of the family court).

(2) A decision of the family court, if made by or by persons who include—

    (a) a judge within subsection (1)(a) to (i),

    (b) a person who has been a judge of the Court of Appeal, or

    (c) a person who has been a puisne judge of the High Court,

is (so far as relevant) to be followed by a judge within subsection (1)(j) to (y), and by a justices' clerk or an assistant to a justices' clerk, when carrying out functions of the family court unless doing so with a person within paragraphs (a) to (c) of this subsection.

(3) A fee-paid, or unsalaried, part-time judge of the family court may not act as a judge of the court in relation to any proceedings in the court in which the judge, or a partner or employer of the judge, or a body of which the judge is a member or officer, or a body of whose governing body the judge is a member, is directly or indirectly engaged as legal representative or agent for any party.

(4) In this section 'legal representative' means a person who, for the purposes of the Legal Services Act 2007, is an authorised person in relation to an activity which constitutes the exercise of a right of audience or the conduct of litigation (within the meaning of that Act).

31D   Composition of the court and distribution of its business

(1)   Rules may be made in accordance with Part 1 of Schedule 1 to the Constitutional Reform Act 2005 (process for making designated rules) about—

(a)   the composition of the family court, and

(b)   the distribution of business of the family court among judges of the court.

(2)   Rules about the composition of the family court may in particular—

(a)   provide for the court to be constituted differently for the purpose of deciding different matters;

(b)   make provision about who is to preside where the court is composed of more than one judge.

(3)   Rules about the distribution of business of the family court may in particular—

(a)   prohibit specified judges from conducting specified business;

(b)   prohibit judges from conducting specified business unless authorised to do so by a specified judicial office holder;

(c)   prohibit specified judges from conducting business, or specified business, unless authorised to do so by a specified judicial office holder;

(d)   prohibit specified judges from exercising specified powers of the court.

(4)   In subsection (3)—

'judge' does not include a judge within section 31C(1)(a) to (i);

'specified' means specified in, or of a description specified in, rules under this section.

(5)   Rules under this section—

(a)   may confer powers on the Lord Chief Justice or on a judicial office holder;

(b)   may be made only after consultation with the Family Procedure Rule Committee.

(6)   Family Procedure Rules are subject to rules under this section.

(7)   The Lord Chief Justice's power under paragraph 2(2)(b) of Schedule 1 to the Constitutional Reform Act 2005 to nominate a judicial office holder to make rules under this section includes power to nominate different judicial office holders to make rules under this section for different purposes.

(8)   Paragraph 5 of that Schedule (duty to make rules to achieve purpose specified by Lord Chancellor) does not apply in relation to rules under this section.

(9)   In this section 'judicial office holder' has the meaning given by section 109(4) of that Act.

(10)   No proceedings in the family court are to be with a jury.

31E   Family court has High Court and county court powers

(1)   In any proceedings in the family court, the court may make any order—

(a)   which could be made by the High Court if the proceedings were in the High Court, or

(b)   which could be made by the county court if the proceedings were in the county court.

(2)   In its application to a power of the High Court to issue a writ directed to an enforcement officer, subsection (1)(a) gives the family court power to issue a warrant, directed to an officer of the family court, containing provision corresponding to any that might be contained in the writ.

(3)   Subsection (1) is subject to section 38(3) of the County Courts Act 1984.

(4)   Subsection (1) is without prejudice to, and not limited by, any other powers of the family court.

(5)   The Lord Chancellor may by regulations make provision, about or in connection with the effect or execution of warrants issued by the family court for enforcing any order or judgment enforceable by the court, that corresponds to any provision applying in relation to the effect or execution of writs issued by the High Court, or warrants issued by the county court, for the purpose of enforcing any order or judgment enforceable by that court.

31F   Proceedings and decisions

(1)   The family court may adjourn a hearing, and may do so at any time including a time before the hearing has begun.

(2)   Any order made by the family court—

(a)   may be absolute or conditional;

(b)   may be final or interim;

(c)   may, subject to rules of court, be made without taking evidence.

(3)   Every judgment and order of the family court is, except as provided by this or any other Act or by rules of court, final and conclusive between the parties.

(4)   Where the family court has power to require the doing of anything other than the payment of money, or to prohibit the doing of anything, an order of the court made in exercising the power may contain provision—

(a)   as to the manner in which anything is to be done,

(b)   as to the time within which anything is to be done,

(c)   as to the time during which anything is not to be done, and

(d)   generally for giving effect to the order.

(5)   Where the family court has power to require the payment of money, an order of the court made in exercising the power may allow time for payment or order payment by instalments; and where the court has ordered payment by instalments and default is made in the payment of any one instalment, proceedings may be taken as if the default had been made in the payment of all the instalments then unpaid.

(6)   The family court has power to vary, suspend, rescind or revive any order made by it, including—

(a)   power to rescind an order and re-list the application on which it was made,

(b)   power to replace an order which for any reason appears to be invalid by another which the court has power to make, and

(c)   power to vary an order with effect from when it was originally made.

(7)   Subject to rules of court, the family court may proceed in the absence of one, some or all of the parties.

(8)   The family court has the same power to enforce an undertaking given by a solicitor in relation to any proceedings in that court as the High Court has to enforce an undertaking given by a solicitor in relation to any proceedings in the High Court.

(9)   In any case not expressly provided for by or in pursuance of this or any other Act, the general principles of practice in the High Court may be adopted and applied to proceedings in the family court.

31G   Witnesses and evidence

(1)   Subsection (2) applies where the family court is satisfied that a person in England and Wales is likely to be able to give material evidence, or produce any document or thing likely to be material evidence, in proceedings in the court.

(2)   The court may, if it is satisfied that it is in the interests of justice to do so, issue a summons—

(a)   requiring the person to attend before the court, at the time and place specified in the summons, to give evidence,

(b)   requiring the person to attend before the court, at the time and place specified in the summons, to produce the document or thing, or

(c)   requiring the person to produce the document or thing to the court.

(3)   Subsection (4) applies where without just excuse—

(a)   a person fails to attend before the court in answer to a summons under subsection (2)(a) or (b),

(b)   a person fails to produce a document or thing in answer to a summons under subsection (2)(b) or (c), or

(c)   a person attending before the court, whether or not in answer to a summons under subsection (2), refuses to be sworn or give evidence.

(4)   The court may—

(a)   commit the person to custody until the expiry of a period not exceeding one month specified by the court or until the person sooner gives evidence or produces the document or thing, or

(b) impose on the person a fine not exceeding £2,500, or

(c) both.

(5) A fine imposed under subsection (4) is deemed, for the purposes of any enactment, to be a sum adjudged to be paid by a conviction of a magistrates' court.

(6) Where in any proceedings in the family court it appears to the court that any party to the proceedings who is not legally represented is unable to examine or cross-examine a witness effectively, the court is to—

(a) ascertain from that party the matters about which the witness may be able to depose or on which the witness ought to be cross-examined, and

(b) put, or cause to be put, to the witness such questions in the interests of that party as may appear to the court to be proper.

(7) Subject to the provisions of any Act or instrument made under an Act or rule of law authorising the reception of unsworn evidence, evidence given before the family court is to be given on oath.

(8) An affidavit to be used in the family court may be sworn before—

(a) a judge of the court, or

(b) an officer of the court appointed by a judge of the court for the purpose,

as well as before a commissioner for oaths or any other person authorised to take affidavits under the Commissioners for Oaths Acts 1889 and 1891.

(9) An affidavit sworn before any such judge or officer may be sworn without the payment of any fee.

31H Contempt of court: power to limit court's powers

(1) The Lord Chancellor may by regulations made after consulting the Lord Chief Justice make provision limiting or removing, in circumstances specified in the regulations, any of the powers exercisable by the family court when dealing with a person for contempt of court.

(2) The Lord Chief Justice may nominate a judicial office holder (as defined in section 109(4) of the Constitutional Reform Act 2005) to exercise functions of the Lord Chief Justice under this section.

31I Powers of the High Court in respect of family court proceedings

(1) If the High Court, at any stage in proceedings in the family court, thinks it desirable that the proceedings, or any part of them, should be transferred to the High Court, it may order the transfer to the High Court of the proceedings or part.

(2) The power given by subsection (1) is without prejudice to section 29 of the Senior Courts Act 1981, and is to be exercised—

(a) in accordance with any directions given as to the distribution or transfer of proceedings, and

(b) subject to any provision made under section 1 of the Courts and Legal Services Act 1990 or made by or under any other enactment.

31J Overview of certain powers of the court under other Acts

The powers of the family court include its powers under—

(a) section 33 of the Senior Courts Act 1981 (powers exercisable before commencement of action);

(b) section 34 of that Act (power to order disclosure or inspection of documents or property of non-party);

(c) section 37 of that Act (power to grant injunction or appoint receiver);

(d) section 39 of that Act (power to order documents to be executed or indorsed by nominated person);

(e) section 70(1) and (2) of that Act (assessors);

(f) section 57 of the County Courts Act 1984 (evidence of prisoners);

(g) section 71 of that Act (powers as to payment of costs).

31K Appeals

(1) Subject to any order made under section 56(1) of the Access to Justice Act 1999 (power to provide for appeals to be made instead to the High Court or county court, or to the family court itself), if any party to any proceedings in the family court is dissatisfied with the decision of the court, that party may appeal from it to the Court of Appeal in such manner and subject to such conditions as may be provided by Family Procedure Rules.

(2) Subsection (1) does not—

    (a) confer any right of appeal from any decision where a right of appeal is conferred by some other enactment, or

    (b) take away any right of appeal from any decision where a right of appeal is so conferred,

and has effect subject to any enactment other than this Part; and in this subsection 'enactment' means an enactment whenever passed.

(3) The Lord Chancellor may, after consulting the Lord Chief Justice, by order make provision as to the circumstances in which appeals may be made against decisions taken by courts or judges on questions arising in connection with the transfer, or proposed transfer, of proceedings from or to the family court.

(4) Except to the extent provided for in any order made under subsection (3), no appeal may be made against any decision of a kind mentioned in that subsection.

(5) At the hearing of any proceedings in the family court in which there is a right of appeal or from which an appeal may be brought with permission, the judge, if requested to do so by any party, is to make a note—

    (a) of any question of law raised at the hearing,

    (b) of the facts in evidence in relation to any such question, and

    (c) of the court's decision on any such question and of the court's determination of the proceedings.

(6) Where such a note is made, and whether or not an appeal has been made, the court—

    (a) on the application of any party to the proceedings, and

    (b) on payment of the fee (if any) prescribed under section 92 of the Courts Act 2003,

is to provide that party with a copy of the note signed by the judge, and the copy so signed is to be used at the hearing of any appeal.

(7) Section 81 of the County Courts Act 1984 (powers of Court of Appeal on appeal from county court) applies to appeals from the family court to the Court of Appeal as it applies to appeals from the county court to the Court of Appeal.

(8) The Lord Chief Justice may nominate a judicial office holder (as defined in section 109(4) of the Constitutional Reform Act 2005) to exercise functions of the Lord Chief Justice under subsection (3).

31L Enforcement

(1) Payment of a fine or penalty imposed by the family court may be enforced upon the order of the court in like manner as a judgment of the court for the payment of money.

(2) Rules of court may, in relation to cases where under two or more orders made by or registered in the family court the same person is required to make periodical payments to the same recipient, make provision—

    (a) for recovery of payments under more than one of the orders to be dealt with in the same proceedings;

    (b) for apportioning, between some or all of the orders, payments made by the person required to make payments under the orders.

(3) Subsection (4) applies where—

    (a) periodical payments are required to be made, or a lump sum is required to be paid, to a child under an order made by the family court, or

    (b) periodical payments are required to be made to a child under an order registered in the family court.

(4) Any sum required under the order to be paid to the child may be paid to the person who looks after the child, and that person may proceed in that person's own name for—

(a) the variation, revival or revocation of the order, or

(b) the recovery of any sum required to be paid under the order.

(5) Where a child has a right under any Act or instrument made under an Act to apply for the revival of an order made by the family court which provided for the making of periodical payments to or for the benefit of the child, the person who looks after the child may proceed in the person's own name for the revival of the order.

(6) Where any person by whom periodical payments are required to be paid to a child under an order made by or registered in the family court applies for the variation or revocation of the order, the person who looks after the child may answer the application in the person's own name.

(7) Nothing in subsections (4) and (5) affects any right of a child to proceed in the child's own name for the variation, revival or revocation of an order or for the recovery of a sum payable under an order.

(8) In this section—

(a) a reference to the person who looks after a child is—

(i) in the case of a child who is being looked after by a local authority (within the meaning of section 22 of the Children Act 1989), a reference to that local authority, and

(ii) in any other case, a reference to the person who, disregarding any absence of the child at a hospital or boarding school and any other temporary absence, has care of the child;

(b) 'child' means a person under the age of 18;

(c) a reference to an order registered in the family court is a reference to an order registered in the court under the Maintenance Orders (Facilities for Enforcement) Act 1920, Part 2 of the Maintenance Orders Act 1950, Part 1 of the Maintenance Orders Act 1958, the Maintenance Orders (Reciprocal Enforcement) Act 1972 or Part 1 of the Civil Jurisdiction and Judgments Act 1982.

...

PART V FAMILY BUSINESS: DISTRIBUTION AND TRANSFER

Preliminary

32 What is family business

In this Part of this Act—

'family business' means business of any description which in the High Court is for the time being assigned to the Family Division and to no other Division by or under section 61 of (and Schedule 1 to) the Senior Courts Act 1981;

'family proceedings' means proceedings which are family business;

'matrimonial cause' means an action for divorce, nullity of marriage, or judicial separation.

Distribution and transfer of family business and proceedings

37 Directions as to distribution and transfer of family business and proceedings

The President of the Family Division may, with the concurrence of the Lord Chancellor, give directions with respect to the distribution and transfer between the High Court and the family court of family business and family proceedings.

38   Transfer of family proceedings from High Court

(1) At any stage in any family proceedings in the High Court the High Court may, if the proceedings are transferable under this section, either of its own motion or on the application of any party to the proceedings, order the transfer of the whole or any part of the proceedings to the family court.

(2) The following family proceedings are transferable to the family court under this section, namely—

  (a) all family proceedings commenced in the High Court which are within the jurisdiction of the family court;

  (b) wardship proceedings, except applications for an order that a minor be made, or cease to be, a ward of court, or any other proceedings which relate to the exercise of the inherent jurisdiction of the High Court with respect to minors; and

  (c) all family proceedings transferred to the High Court under section 39 below or section 41 of the County Courts Act 1984 (transfer to High Court by order of High Court); and

  (d) all matrimonial causes and matters transferred from a county court otherwise than as mentioned in paragraph (c) above.

...

(4) The transfer shall not affect any right of appeal from the order directing the transfer, or the right to enforce in the High Court any judgment signed, or order made, in that Court before the transfer.

(5) Where proceedings are transferred to the family court under this section, the family court—

  (a) if it has no jurisdiction apart from this paragraph, shall have jurisdiction to hear and determine those proceedings;

  (b) shall have jurisdiction to award any relief which could have been awarded by the High Court.

39   Transfer of family proceedings to High Court

(1) At any stage in any family proceedings in the family court, the family court may, if the proceedings are transferable under this section, either of its own motion or on the application of any party to the proceedings, order the transfer of the whole or any part of the proceedings to the High Court.

(2) The following family proceedings are transferable to the High Court under this section, namely—

  (a) all family proceedings commenced in the family court which are within the jurisdiction of the High Court, and

  (b) all family proceedings transferred from the High Court under section 38 above.

...

Police and Criminal Evidence Act 1984

(1984 c. 60)

80   Compellability of accused's spouse or civil partner

(2) In any proceedings the spouse or civil partner of a person charged in the proceedings shall, subject to subsection (4) below, be compellable to give evidence on behalf of that person.

(2A) In any proceedings the spouse or civil partner of a person charged in the proceedings shall, subject to subsection (4) below, be compellable—

  (a) to give evidence on behalf of any other person charged in the proceedings but only in respect of any specified offence with which that other person is charged; or

  (b) to give evidence for the prosecution but only in respect of any specified offence with which any person is charged in the proceedings.

(3) In relation to the spouse or civil partner of a person charged in any proceedings, an offence is a specified offence for the purposes of subsection (2A) above if—

    (a) it involves an assault on, or injury or a threat of injury to, the spouse or civil partner or a person who was at the material time under the age of 16;

    (b) it is a sexual offence alleged to have been committed in respect of a person who was at the material time under that age; or

    (c) it consists of attempting or conspiring to commit, or of aiding, abetting, counselling, procuring or inciting the commission of, an offence falling within paragraph (a) or (b) above.

(4) No person who is charged in any proceedings shall be compellable by virtue of subsection (2) or (2A) above to give evidence in the proceedings.

(4A) References in this section to a person charged in any proceedings do not include a person who is not, or is no longer, liable to be convicted of any offence in the proceedings (whether as a result of pleading guilty or for any other reason).

(5) In any proceedings a person who has been but is no longer married to the accused shall be compellable to give evidence as if that person and the accused had never been married.

(5A) In any proceedings a person who has been but is no longer the civil partner of the accused shall be compellable to give evidence as if that person and the accused had never been civil partners.

(6) Where in any proceedings the age of any person at any time is material for the purposes of subsection (3) above, his age at the material time shall for the purposes of that provision be deemed to be or to have been that which appears to the court to be or to have been his age at that time.

(7) In subsection (3)(b) above 'sexual offence' means an offence under the Protection of Children Act 1978 or Part I of the Sexual Offences Act 2003.

80A   Rule where accused's spouse or civil partner not compellable

The failure of the spouse or civil partner of a person charged in any proceedings to give evidence in the proceedings shall not be made the subject of any comment by the prosecution.

...

Surrogacy Arrangements Act 1985

(1985 c. 49)

1   Meaning of 'surrogate mother,' 'surrogacy arrangement' and other terms

(1) The following provisions shall have effect for the interpretation of this Act.

(2) 'Surrogate mother' means a woman who carries a child in pursuance of an arrangement—

    (a) made before she began to carry the child, and

    (b) made with a view to any child carried in pursuance of it being handed over to, and parental responsibility being met (so far as practicable) by, another person or other persons.

(3) An arrangement is a surrogacy arrangement if, were a woman to whom the arrangement relates to carry a child in pursuance of it, she would be a surrogate mother.

(4) In determining whether an arrangement is made with such a view as is mentioned in subsection (2) above regard may be had to the circumstances as a whole (and, in particular, where there is a promise or understanding that any payment will or may be made to the woman or for her benefit in respect of the carrying of any child in pursuance of the arrangement, to that promise or understanding).

(5) An arrangement may be regarded as made with such a view though subject to conditions relating to the handing over of any child.

(6) A woman who carries a child is to be treated for the purposes of subsection (2)(a) above as beginning to carry it at the time of the insemination or of the placing in her of an embryo, of an egg

in the process of fertilisation or of sperm and eggs, as the case may be, that results in her carrying the child.

(7) 'Body of persons' means a body of persons corporate or unincorporate.

(7A) 'Non-profit making body' means a body of persons whose activities are not carried on for profit.

(8) 'Payment' means payment in money or money's worth.

(9) This Act applies to arrangements whether or not they are lawful.

1A   Surrogacy arrangements unenforceable

No surrogacy arrangement is enforceable by or against any of the persons making it.

2   Negotiating surrogacy arrangements on a commercial basis, etc.

(1) No person shall on a commercial basis do any of the following acts in the United Kingdom, that is—

(a) initiate any negotiations with a view to the making of a surrogacy arrangement,

(aa) take part in any negotiations with a view to the making of a surrogacy arrangement,

(b) offer or agree to negotiate the making of a surrogacy arrangement, or

(c) compile any information with a view to its use in making, or negotiating the making of, surrogacy arrangements;

and no person shall in the United Kingdom knowingly cause another to do any of those acts on a commercial basis.

(2) A person who contravenes subsection (1) above is guilty of an offence; but it is not a contravention of that subsection—

(a) for a woman, with a view to becoming a surrogate mother herself, to do any act mentioned in that subsection or to cause such an act to be done, or

(b) for any person, with a view to a surrogate mother carrying a child for him, to do such an act or to cause such an act to be done.

(2A) A non-profit making body does not contravene subsection (1) merely because—

(a) the body does an act falling within subsection (1)(a) or (c) in respect of which any reasonable payment is at any time received by it or another, or

(b) it does an act falling within subsection (1)(a) or (c) with a view to any reasonable payment being received by it or another in respect of facilitating the making of any surrogacy arrangement.

(2B) A person who knowingly causes a non-profit making body to do an act falling within subsection (1)(a) or (c) does not contravene subsection (1) merely because—

(a) any reasonable payment is at any time received by the body or another in respect of the body doing the act, or

(b) the body does the act with a view to any reasonable payment being received by it or another person in respect of the body facilitating the making of any surrogacy arrangement.

(2C) Any reference in subsection (2A) or (2B) to a reasonable payment in respect of the doing of an act by a non-profit making body is a reference to a payment not exceeding the body's costs reasonably attributable to the doing of the act.

(3) For the purposes of this section, a person does an act on a commercial basis (subject to subsection (4) below) if—

(a) any payment is at any time received by himself or another in respect of it, or

(b) he does it with a view to any payment being received by himself or another in respect of making, or negotiating or facilitating the making of, any surrogacy arrangement.

In this subsection 'payment' does not include payment to or for the benefit of a surrogate mother or prospective surrogate mother.

(4) In proceedings against a person for an offence under subsection (1) above, he is not to be treated as doing an act on a commercial basis by reason of any payment received by another in respect of that act if it is proved that—

   (a) in a case where the payment was received before he did the act, he did not do the act knowing or having reasonable cause to suspect that any payment had been received in respect of the act; and

   (b) in any other case, he did not do the act with a view to any payment being received in respect of it.

(5) Where—

   (a) a person acting on behalf of a body of persons takes any part in negotiating or facilitating the making of a surrogacy arrangement in the United Kingdom, and

   (b) negotiating or facilitating the making of surrogacy arrangements is an activity of the body,

then, if the body at any time receives any payment made by or on behalf of—

   (i)   a woman who carries a child in pursuance of the arrangement,

   (ii) the person or persons for whom she carries it, or

   (iii) any person connected with the woman or with that person or those persons,

the body is guilty of an offence.

   For the purposes of this subsection, a payment received by a person connected with a body is to be treated as received by the body.

(5A) A non-profit making body is not guilty of an offence under subsection (5), in respect of the receipt of any payment described in that subsection, merely because a person acting on behalf of the body takes part in facilitating the making of a surrogacy arrangement.

(6) In proceedings against a body for an offence under subsection (5) above, it is a defence to prove that the payment concerned was not made in respect of the arrangement mentioned in para-graph (a) of that subsection.

(7) A person who in the United Kingdom takes part in the management or control—

   (a) of any body of persons, or

   (b) of any of the activities of any body of persons,

is guilty of an offence if the activity described in subsection (8) below is an activity of the body concerned.

(8) The activity referred to in subsection (7) above is negotiating or facilitating the making of surrogacy arrangements in the United Kingdom, being—

   (a) arrangements the making of which is negotiated or facilitated on a commercial basis, or

   (b) arrangements in the case of which payments are received (or treated for the purposes of subsection (5) above as received) by the body concerned in contravention of subsection (5) above.

(8A) A person is not guilty of an offence under subsection (7) if—

   (a) the body of persons referred to in that subsection is a non-profit making body, and

   (b) the only activity of that body which falls within subsection (8) is facilitating the making of surrogacy arrangements in the United Kingdom.

(8B) In subsection (8A)(b) 'facilitating the making of surrogacy arrangements' is to be con-strued in accordance with subsection (8).

(9) In proceedings against a person for an offence under subsection (7) above, it is a defence to prove that he neither knew nor had reasonable cause to suspect that the activity described in sub-section (8) above was an activity of the body concerned; and for the purposes of such proceedings any arrangement falling within subsection (8)(b) above shall be disregarded if it is proved that the payment concerned was not made in respect of the arrangement.

3 Advertisements about surrogacy

(1) This section applies to any advertisement containing an indication (however expressed)—

  (a) that any person is or may be willing to enter into a surrogacy arrangement or to negotiate or facilitate the making of a surrogacy arrangement, or

  (b) that any person is looking for a woman willing to become a surrogate mother or for persons wanting a woman to carry a child as a surrogate mother.

(1A) This section does not apply to any advertisement placed by, or on behalf of, a non-profit making body if the advertisement relates only to the doing by the body of acts that would not contravene section 2(1) even if done on a commercial basis (within the meaning of section 2).

(2) Where a newspaper or periodical containing an advertisement to which this section applies is published in the United Kingdom, any proprietor, editor or publisher of the newspaper or periodical is guilty of an offence.

(3) Where an advertisement to which this section applies is conveyed by means of an electronic communications network so as to be seen or heard (or both) in the United Kingdom, any person who in the United Kingdom causes it to be so conveyed knowing it to contain such an indication as is mentioned in subsection (1) above is guilty of an offence.

(4) A person who publishes or causes to be published in the United Kingdom an advertisement to which this section applies (not being an advertisement contained in a newspaper or periodical or conveyed by means of an electronic communications network) is guilty of an offence.

(5) A person who distributes or causes to be distributed in the United Kingdom an advertisement to which this section applies (not being an advertisement contained in a newspaper or periodical published outside the United Kingdom or an advertisement conveyed by means of an electronic communications network) knowing it to contain such an indication as is mentioned in subsection (1) above is guilty of an offence.

4 Offences

(1) A person guilty of an offence under this Act shall be liable on summary conviction—

  (b) to a fine not exceeding level 5 on the standard scale.

(2) No proceedings for an offence under this Act shall be instituted—

  (a) in England and Wales, except by or with the consent of the Director of Public Prosecutions; and

  (b) in Northern Ireland, except by or with the consent of the Director of Public Prosecutions for Northern Ireland.

(3) Where an offence under this Act committed by a body corporate is proved to have been committed with the consent or connivance of, or to be attributable to any neglect on the part of, any director, manager, secretary or other similar officer of the body corporate or any person who was purporting to act in any such capacity, he as well as the body corporate is guilty of the offence and is liable to be proceeded against and punished accordingly.

(4) Where the affairs of a body corporate are managed by its members, subsection (3) above shall apply in relation to the acts and defaults of a member in connection with his functions of management as if he were a director of the body corporate.

(5) In any proceedings for an offence under section 2 of this Act, proof of things done or of words written, spoken or published (whether or not in the presence of any party to the proceedings) by any person taking part in the management or control of a body of persons or of any of the activities of the body, or by any person doing any of the acts mentioned in subsection (1)(a) to (c) of that section on behalf of the body, shall be admissible as evidence of the activities of the body.

(6) In relation to an offence under this Act, section 127(1) of the Magistrates' Courts Act 1980 (information must be laid within six months of commission of offence), . . . shall have effect as if for the reference to six months there were substituted a reference to two years.

Housing Act 1985

(1985 c. 68)

PART IV SECURE TENANCIES AND RIGHTS OF SECURE TENANTS

Succession on death of tenant

86A Persons qualified to succeed tenant: England

(1) A person ('P') is qualified to succeed the tenant under a secure tenancy of a dwelling-house in England if—

    (a) P occupies the dwelling-house as P's only or principal home at the time of the tenant's death, and

    (b) P is the tenant's spouse or civil partner.

(2) A person ('P') is qualified to succeed the tenant under a secure tenancy of a dwelling-house in England if—

    (a) at the time of the tenant's death the dwelling-house is not occupied by a spouse or civil partner of the tenant as his or her only or principal home,

    (b) an express term of the tenancy makes provision for a person other than such a spouse or civil partner of the tenant to succeed to the tenancy, and

    (c) P's succession is in accordance with that term.

(3) Subsection (1) or (2) does not apply if the tenant was a successor as defined in section 88.

(4) In such a case, a person ('P') is qualified to succeed the tenant if—

    (a) an express term of the tenancy makes provision for a person to succeed a successor to the tenancy, and

    (b) P's succession is in accordance with that term.

(5) For the purposes of this section—

    (a) a person who was living with the tenant as the tenant's wife or husband is to be treated as the tenant's spouse, and

    (b) a person who was living with the tenant as if they were civil partners is to be treated as the tenant's civil partner.

(6) Subsection (7) applies if, on the death of the tenant, there is by virtue of subsection (5) more than one person who fulfils the condition in subsection (1)(b).

(7) Such one of those persons as may be agreed between them or as may, where there is no such agreement, be selected by the landlord is for the purpose of this section to be treated (according to whether that one of them is of the opposite sex to, or of the same sex as, the tenant) as the tenant's spouse or civil partner.

87 Persons qualified to succeed tenant: Wales

A person is qualified to succeed the tenant under a secure tenancy of a dwelling house in Wales if he occupies the dwelling-house as his only or principal home at the time of the tenant's death and either—

    (a) he is the tenant's spouse or civil partner, or

    (b) he is another member of the tenant's family and has resided with the tenant throughout the period of twelve months ending with the tenant's death;

unless, in either case, the tenant was himself a successor, as defined in section 88.

...

113 Members of a person's family

(1) A person is a member of another's family within the meaning of this Part if—

    (a) he is the spouse or civil partner of that person, or he and that person live together as husband and wife or as if they were civil partners, or

(b) he is that person's parent, grandparent, child, grandchild, brother, sister, uncle, aunt, nephew or niece.

(2) For the purpose of subsection (1)(b)—

(a) a relationship by marriage or civil partnership shall be treated as a relationship by blood,

(b) a relationship of the half-blood shall be treated as a relationship of the whole blood,

(c) the stepchild of a person shall be treated as his child, and

(d) an illegitimate child shall be treated as the legitimate child of his mother and reputed father.

Marriage (Prohibited Degrees of Relationship) Act 1986

(1986 c. 16)

1   Marriage between certain persons related by affinity not to be void

(1) A marriage solemnized after the commencement of this Act between a man and a woman who is the daughter or granddaughter of a former spouse of his (whether the former spouse is living or not) or who is the former spouse of his father or grandfather (whether his father or grandfather is living or not) shall not be void by reason only of that relationship if both the parties have attained the age of twenty-one at the time of the marriage and the younger party has not at any time before attaining the age of eighteen been a child of the family in relation to the other party.

(2) A marriage solemnized after the commencement of this Act between a man and a woman who is the grandmother of a former spouse of his (whether the former spouse is living or not) or is a former spouse of his grandson (whether his grandson is living or not) shall not be void by reason only of that relationship.

...

(5) In this section 'child of the family' in relation to any person, means a child who has lived in the same household as that person and been treated by that person as a child of his family.

(6) The Marriage Act 1949 shall have effect subject to the amendments specified in the Schedule to this Act, being amendments consequential on the preceding provisions of this section.

(7) Where, apart from this Act, any matter affecting the validity of a marriage would fall to be determined (in accordance with the rules of private international law) by reference to the law of a country outside England and Wales nothing in this Act shall preclude the determination of that matter in accordance with that law.

(8) Nothing in this section shall affect any marriage solemnized before the commencement of this Act.

Insolvency Act 1986

(1986 c. 45)

Chapter IV Administration by trustee

Preliminary

305   General functions of trustee

(1) This Chapter applies in relation to any bankruptcy where either—

(a) the appointment of a person as trustee of a bankrupt's estate takes effect, or

(b) the official receiver becomes trustee of a bankrupt's estate.

(2)   The function of the trustee is to get in, realise and distribute the bankrupt's estate in accordance with the following provisions of this Chapter; and in the carrying out of that function and in the management of the bankrupt's estate the trustee is entitled, subject to those provisions, to use his own discretion.

...

Acquisition, control and realisation of bankrupt's estate

306   Vesting of bankrupt's estate in trustee

(1)   The bankrupt's estate shall vest in the trustee immediately on his appointment taking effect or, in the case of the official receiver, on his becoming trustee.

(2)   Where any property which is, or is to be, comprised in the bankrupt's estate vests in the trustee (whether under this section or under any other provision of this Part), it shall so vest without any conveyance, assignment or transfer.

...

Chapter V   Effect of bankruptcy on certain rights, transactions, etc.

Rights under trusts of land

335A   Rights under trusts of land

(1)   Any application by a trustee of a bankrupt's estate under section 14 of the Trusts of Land and Appointment of Trustees Act 1996 (powers of court in relation to trusts of land) for an order under that section for the sale of land shall be made to the court having jurisdiction in relation to the bankruptcy.

(2)   On such an application the court shall make such order as it thinks just and reasonable having regard to—

(a)   the interests of the bankrupt's creditors;

(b)   where the application is made in respect of land which includes a dwelling house which is or has been the home of the bankrupt or the bankrupt's spouse or civil partner or former spouse or former civil partner—

   (i)   the conduct of the spouse, civil partner, former spouse or former civil partner, so far as contributing to the bankruptcy,

   (ii)   the needs and financial resources of the spouse, civil partner, former spouse or former civil partner, and

   (iii)   the needs of any children; and

(c)   all the circumstances of the case other than the needs of the bankrupt.

(3)   Where such an application is made after the end of the period of one year beginning with the first vesting under Chapter IV of this Part of the bankrupt's estate in a trustee, the court shall assume, unless the circumstances of the case are exceptional, that the interests of the bankrupt's creditors outweigh all other considerations.

(4)   The powers conferred on the court by this section are exercisable on an application whether it is made before or after the commencement of this section.

Rights of occupation

336   Rights of occupation etc. of bankrupt's spouse or civil partner

(1)   Nothing occurring in the initial period of the bankruptcy (that is to say, the period beginning with the day of the making of the bankruptcy application or (as the case may be) the presentation of the bankruptcy petition and ending with the vesting of the bankrupt's estate in a trustee) is to be taken as having given rise to any home rights under Part IV of the Family Law Act 1996 in relation to a dwelling house comprised in the bankrupt's estate.

(2) Where a spouse's or civil partner's home rights under the Act of 1996 are a charge on the estate or interest of the other spouse or civil partner, or of trustees for the other spouse or civil partner, and the other spouse or civil partner is made bankrupt—

(a) the charge continues to subsist notwithstanding the bankruptcy and, subject to the provisions of that Act, binds the trustee of the bankrupt's estate and persons deriving title under that trustee, and

(b) any application for an order under section 33 of that Act shall be made to the court having jurisdiction in relation to the bankruptcy.

(4) On such an application as is mentioned in subsection (2) the court shall make such order under section 33 of the Act of 1996 as it thinks just and reasonable having regard to—

(a) the interests of the bankrupt's creditors,

(b) the conduct of the spouse or former spouse or civil partner or former civil partner, so far as contributing to the bankruptcy,

(c) the needs and financial resources of the spouse or former spouse or civil partner or former civil partner,

(d) the needs of any children, and

(e) all the circumstances of the case other than the needs of the bankrupt.

(5) Where such an application is made after the end of the period of one year beginning with the first vesting under Chapter IV of this Part of the bankrupt's estate in a trustee, the court shall assume, unless the circumstances of the case are exceptional, that the interests of the bankrupt's creditors outweigh all other considerations.

337 Rights of occupation of bankrupt

(1) This section applies where—

(a) a person who is entitled to occupy a dwelling house by virtue of a beneficial estate or interest is made bankrupt, and

(b) any persons under the age of 18 with whom that person had at some time occupied that dwelling house had their home with that person at the time when the bankruptcy application was made or (as the case may be) the bankruptcy petition was presented and at the commencement of the bankruptcy.

(2) Whether or not the bankrupt's spouse or civil partner (if any) has home rights under Part IV of the Family Law Act 1996—

(a) the bankrupt has the following rights as against the trustee of his estate—

(i)   if in occupation, a right not to be evicted or excluded from the dwelling house or any part of it, except with the leave of the court,

(ii) if not in occupation, a right with the leave of the court to enter into and occupy the dwelling house, and

(b) the bankrupt's rights are a charge, having the like priority as an equitable interest created immediately before the commencement of the bankruptcy, on so much of his estate or interest in the dwelling house as vests in the trustee.

(3) The Act of 1996 has effect, with the necessary modifications, as if—

(a) the rights conferred by paragraph (a) of subsection (2) were home rights under that Act,

(b) any application for such leave as is mentioned in that paragraph were an application for an order under section 33 of that Act, and

(c) any charge under paragraph (b) of that subsection on the estate or interest of the trustee were a charge under that Act on the estate or interest of a spouse or civil partner.

(4) Any application for leave such as is mentioned in subsection (2)(a) or otherwise by virtue of this section for an order under section 33 of the Act of 1996 shall be made to the court having jurisdiction in relation to the bankruptcy.

(5) On such an application the court shall make such order under section 33 of the Act of 1996 as it thinks just and reasonable having regard to the interests of the creditors, to the bankrupt's

financial resources, to the needs of the children and to all the circumstances of the case other than the needs of the bankrupt.

(6) Where such an application is made after the end of the period of one year beginning with the first vesting (under Chapter IV of this Part) of the bankrupt's estate in a trustee, the court shall assume, unless the circumstances of the case are exceptional, that the interests of the bankrupt's creditors outweigh all other considerations.

Adjustment of prior transactions, etc.

339 Transactions at an undervalue

(1) Subject as follows in this section and sections 341 and 342, where an individual is made bankrupt and he has at a relevant time (defined in section 341) entered into a transaction with any person at an undervalue, the trustee of the bankrupt's estate may apply to the court for an order under this section.

(2) The court shall, on such an application, make such order as it thinks fit for restoring the position to what it would have been if that individual had not entered into that transaction.

(3) For the purposes of this section and sections 341 and 342, an individual enters into a transaction with a person at an undervalue if—

   (a) he makes a gift to that person or he otherwise enters into a transaction with that person on terms that provide for him to receive no consideration,

   (b) he enters into a transaction with that person in consideration of marriage or the formation of a civil partnership, or

   (c) he enters into a transaction with that person for a consideration the value of which, in money or money's worth, is significantly less than the value, in money or money's worth, of the consideration provided by the individual.

Family Law Act 1986

(1986 c. 55)

PART II RECOGNITION OF DIVORCES, ANNULMENTS AND LEGAL SEPARATIONS

Overseas divorces, annulments and legal separations

44 Recognition in United Kingdom of divorces, annulments and judicial separations granted in the British Islands

(1) Subject to section 52(4) and (5)(a) of this Act, no divorce or annulment obtained in any part of the British Islands shall be regarded as effective in any part of the United Kingdom unless granted by a court of civil jurisdiction.

(2) Subject to section 51 of this Act, the validity of any divorce, annulment or judicial separation granted by a court of civil jurisdiction in any part of the British Islands shall be recognised throughout the United Kingdom.

45 Recognition in the United Kingdom of overseas divorces, annulments and legal separations

(1) Subject to subsection (2) of this section and to sections 51 and 52 of this Act, the validity of a divorce, annulment or legal separation obtained in a country outside the British Islands (in this Part referred to as an overseas divorce, annulment or legal separation) shall be recognised in the United Kingdom if, and only if, it is entitled to recognition—

   (a) by virtue of sections 46 to 49 of this Act, or

   (b) by virtue of any enactment other than this Part.

(2) Subsection (1) and the following provisions of this Part do not apply to an overseas divorce, annulment or legal separation as regards which provision as to recognition is made by Articles 21 to 27, 41(1) and 42(1) of the Council Regulation.

46 Grounds for recognition

(1) The validity of an overseas divorce, annulment or legal separation obtained by means of proceedings shall be recognised if—

(a) the divorce, annulment or legal separation is effective under the law of the country in which it was obtained; and

(b) at the relevant date either party to the marriage—

(i)   was habitually resident in the country in which the divorce, annulment or legal separation was obtained; or

(ii) was domiciled in that country; or

(iii) was a national of that country.

(2) The validity of an overseas divorce, annulment or legal separation obtained otherwise than by means of proceedings shall be recognised if—

(a) the divorce, annulment or legal separation is effective under the law of the country in which it was obtained;

(b) at the relevant date—

(i)   each party to the marriage was domiciled in that country; or

(ii) either party to the marriage was domiciled in that country and the other party was domiciled in a country under whose law the divorce, annulment or legal separation is recognised as valid; and

(c) neither party to the marriage was habitually resident in the United Kingdom throughout the period of one year immediately preceding that date.

(3) In this section 'the relevant date' means—

(a) in the case of an overseas divorce, annulment or legal separation obtained by means of proceedings, the date of the commencement of the proceedings;

(b) in the case of an overseas divorce, annulment or legal separation obtained otherwise than by means of proceedings, the date on which it was obtained.

(4) Where in the case of an overseas annulment, the relevant date fell after the death of either party to the marriage, any reference in subsection (1) or (2) above to that date shall be construed in relation to that party as a reference to the date of death.

(5) For the purpose of this section, a party to a marriage shall be treated as domiciled in a country if he was domiciled in that country either according to the law of that country in family matters or according to the law of the part of the United Kingdom in which the question of recognition arises.

…

Supplemental

51 Refusal of recognition

(1) Subject to section 52 of this Act, recognition of the validity of—

(a) a divorce, annulment or judicial separation granted by a court of civil jurisdiction in any part of the British Islands, or

(b) an overseas divorce, annulment or legal separation,

may be refused in any part of the United Kingdom if the divorce, annulment or separation was granted or obtained at a time when it was irreconcilable with a decision determining the question of the subsistence or validity of the marriage of the parties previously given (whether before or after the commencement of this Part) by a court of civil jurisdiction in that part of the United Kingdom or by a court elsewhere and recognised or entitled to be recognised in that part of the United Kingdom.

(2) Subject to section 52 of this Act, recognition of the validity of—

(a) a divorce or judicial separation granted by a court of civil jurisdiction in any part of the British Islands, or

(b) an overseas divorce or legal separation,

may be refused in any part of the United Kingdom if the divorce or separation was granted or obtained at a time when, according to the law of that part of the United Kingdom (including its rules of private international law and the provisions of this Part), there was no subsisting marriage between the parties.

(3) Subject to section 52 of this Act, recognition by virtue of section 45 of this Act of the validity of an overseas divorce, annulment or legal separation may be refused if—

(a) in the case of a divorce, annulment or legal separation obtained by means of proceedings, it was obtained—

(i) without such steps having been taken for giving notice of the proceedings to a party to the marriage as, having regard to the nature of the proceedings and all the circumstances, should reasonably have been taken; or

(ii) without a party to the marriage having been given (for any reason other than lack of notice) such opportunity to take part in the proceedings as, having regard to those matters, he should reasonably have been given; or

(b) in the case of a divorce, annulment or legal separation obtained otherwise than by means of proceedings—

(i) there is no official document certifying that the divorce, annulment or legal separation is effective under the law of the country in which it was obtained; or

(ii) where either party to the marriage was domiciled in another country at the relevant date, there is no official document certifying that the divorce, annulment or legal separation is recognised as valid under the law of that other country; or

(c) in either case, recognition of the divorce, annulment or legal separation would be manifestly contrary to public policy.

(4) In this section—

'official', in relation to a document certifying that a divorce, annulment or legal separation is effective, or is recognised as valid, under the law of any country, means issued by a person or body appointed or recognised for the purpose under that law;

'the relevant date' has the same meaning as in section 46 of this Act;

'judicial separation' includes a separation order under the Family Law Act 1996;

and subsection (5) of that section shall apply for the purposes of this section as it applies for the purposes of that section.

(5) Nothing in this Part shall be construed as requiring the recognition of any finding of fault made in any proceedings for divorce, annulment or separation or of any maintenance, custody or other ancillary order made in any such proceedings.

PART III DECLARATIONS OF STATUS

55 Declarations as to marital status

(1) Subject to the following provisions of this section, any person may apply to the High Court or the family court for one or more of the following declarations in relation to a marriage specified in the application, that is to say—

(a) a declaration that the marriage was at its inception a valid marriage;

(b) a declaration that the marriage subsisted on a date specified in the application;

(c) a declaration that the marriage did not subsist on a date so specified;

(d) a declaration that the validity of a divorce, annulment or legal separation obtained in any country outside England and Wales in respect of the marriage is entitled to recognition in England and Wales;

(e) a declaration that the validity of a divorce, annulment or legal separation so obtained in respect of the marriage is not entitled to recognition in England and Wales.

(2) A court shall have jurisdiction to entertain an application under subsection (1) above if, and only if, either of the parties to the marriage to which the application relates—

(a) is domiciled in England and Wales on the date of the application, or

(b) has been habitually resident in England and Wales throughout the period of one year ending with that date, or

(c) died before that date and either—

(i) was at death domiciled in England and Wales, or

(ii) had been habitually resident in England and Wales throughout the period of one year ending with the date of death.

(3) Where an application under subsection (1) above is made to a court by any person other than a party to the marriage to which the application relates, the court shall refuse to hear the application if it considers that the applicant does not have a sufficient interest in the determination of that application.

55A Declarations of parentage

(1) Subject to the following provisions of this section, any person may apply to the High Court or the family court for a declaration as to whether or not a person named in the application is or was the parent of another person so named.

(2) A court shall have jurisdiction to entertain an application under subsection (1) above if, and only if, either of the persons named in it for the purposes of that subsection—

(a) is domiciled in England and Wales on the date of the application, or

(b) has been habitually resident in England and Wales throughout the period of one year ending with that date, or

(c) died before that date and either—

(i) was at death domiciled in England and Wales, or

(ii) had been habitually resident in England and Wales throughout the period of one year ending with the date of death.

(3) Except in a case falling within subsection (4) below, the court shall refuse to hear an application under subsection (1) above unless it considers that the applicant has a sufficient personal interest in the determination of the application (but this is subject to section 27 of the Child Support Act 1991).

(4) The excepted cases are where the declaration sought is as to whether or not—

(a) the applicant is the parent of a named person;

(b) a named person is the parent of the applicant; or

(c) a named person is the other parent of a named child of the applicant.

(5) Where an application under subsection (1) above is made and one of the persons named in it for the purposes of that subsection is a child, the court may refuse to hear the application if it considers that the determination of the application would not be in the best interests of the child.

(6) Where a court refuses to hear an application under subsection (1) above it may order that the applicant may not apply again for the same declaration without leave of the court.

(7) Where a declaration is made by a court on an application under subsection (1) above, the prescribed officer of the court shall notify the Registrar General, in such a manner and within such period as may be prescribed, of the making of that declaration.

56 Declarations of parentage, legitimacy or legitimation

(1) Any person may apply to the High Court or the family court for a declaration—

(b) that he is the legitimate child of his parents.

(2) Any person may apply to the High Court or the family court for one (or for one or, in the alternative, the other) of the following declarations, that is to say—

(a) a declaration that he has become a legitimated person;

(b) a declaration that he has not become a legitimated person.

(3) A court shall have jurisdiction to entertain an application under this section if, and only if, the applicant—

    (a) is domiciled in England and Wales on the date of the application; or

    (b) has been habitually resident in England and Wales throughout the period of one year ending with that date.

(4) Where a declaration is made by a court on an application under subsection (1) above, the prescribed officer of the court shall notify the Registrar General, in such manner and within such period as may be prescribed, of the making of that declaration.

(5) In this section 'legitimated person' means a person legitimated or recognised as legitimated—

    (a) under section 2, 2A or 3 of the Legitimacy Act 1976;

    (b) under section 1 or 8 of the Legitimacy Act 1926; or

    (c) by a legitimation (whether or not by virtue of the subsequent marriage of his parents) recognised by the law of England and Wales and effected under the law of another country.

...

58   General provisions as to the making and effect of declarations

(1) Where on an application to a court for a declaration under this Part the truth of the proposition to be declared is proved to the satisfaction of the court, the court shall make that declaration unless to do so would manifestly be contrary to public policy.

(2) Any declaration made under this Part shall be binding on Her Majesty and all other persons.

(3) A court, on the dismissal of an application for a declaration under this Part, shall not have power to make any declaration for which the application has not been made.

(4) No declaration which may be applied for under this Part may be made otherwise than under this Part by any court.

(5) No declaration may be made by any court, whether under this Part or otherwise—

    (a) that a marriage was at its inception void.

(6) Nothing in this section shall affect the powers of any court to grant a decree of nullity of marriage.

...

61   Abolition of right to petition for jactitation of marriage

No person shall after the commencement of this Part be entitled to petition the High Court or a county court for jactitation of marriage.

...

Family Law Reform Act 1987

(1987 c. 42)

PART I GENERAL PRINCIPLE

1   General principle

(1) In this Act and enactments passed and instruments made after the coming into force of this section, references (however expressed) to any relationship between two persons shall, unless the contrary intention appears, be construed without regard to whether or not the father and mother of either of them, or the father and mother of any person through whom the relationship is deduced, have or had been married to each other at any time.

(2) In this Act and enactments passed after the coming into force of this section, unless the contrary intention appears—

    (a) references to a person whose father and mother were married to each other at the time of his birth include; and

    (b) references to a person whose father and mother were not married to each other at the time of his birth do not include,

references to any person to whom subsection (3) below applies, and cognate references shall be construed accordingly.

(3) This subsection applies to any person who—

    (a) is treated as legitimate by virtue of section 1 of the Legitimacy Act 1976;

    (b) is a legitimated person within the meaning of section 10 of that Act;

    (ba) has a parent by virtue of section 42 of the Human Fertilisation and Embryology Act 2008 (which relates to treatment provided to a woman who is at the time of treatment a party to a civil partnership or, in certain circumstances, a void civil partnership);

    (bb) has a parent by virtue of section 43 of that Act (which relates to treatment provided to woman who agrees that second woman to be parent) who—

        (i) is the civil partner of the child's mother at the time of the child's birth, or

        (ii) was the civil partner of the child's mother at any time during the period beginning with the time mentioned in section 43(b) of that Act and ending with the child's birth;

    (c) is an adopted person within the meaning of Chapter 4 of Part I of the Adoption and Children Act 2002; or

    (d) is otherwise treated in law as legitimate.

(4) For the purpose of construing references falling within subsection (2) above, the time of a person's birth shall be taken to include any time during the period beginning with—

    (a) the insemination resulting in his birth; or

    (b) where there was no such insemination, his conception,

and (in either case) ending with his birth.

(5) A child whose parents are parties to a void civil partnership shall, subject to subsection (6), be treated as falling within subsection (3)(bb) if at the time when the parties registered as civil partners of each other both or either of the parties reasonably believed that the civil partnership was valid.

(6) Subsection (5) applies only where the woman who is a parent by virtue of section 43 was domiciled in England and Wales at the time of the birth or, if she died before the birth, was so domiciled immediately before her death.

(7) Subsection (5) applies even though the belief that the civil partnership was valid was due to a mistake as to law.

(8) It shall be presumed for the purposes of subsection (5), unless the contrary is shown, that one of the parties to a void civil partnership reasonably believed at the time of the formation of the civil partnership that the civil partnership was valid.

PART II RIGHTS AND DUTIES OF PARENTS ETC.

Parental rights and duties: general

2 Construction of enactments relating to parental rights and duties

(1) In the following enactments, namely—

    ...

    (b) section 6 of the Family Law Reform Act 1969;

    (c) the Guardianship of Minors Act 1971 (in this Act referred to as 'the 1971 Act');

    (d) Part I of the Guardianship Act 1973 (in this Act referred to as 'the 1973 Act');

    (e) Part II of the Children Act 1975;

(f) the Child Care Act 1980 except Part I and sections 13, 24, 64 and 65;

references (however expressed) to any relationship between two persons shall be construed in accordance with section 1 above.

PART III PROPERTY RIGHTS

18 Succession on intestacy

(1) In Part IV of the Administration of Estates Act 1925 (which deals with the distribution of the estate of an intestate), references (however expressed) to any relationship between two persons shall be construed in accordance with section 1 above.

(2) For the purposes of subsection (1) above and that Part of that Act, a person whose father and mother were not married to each other at the time of his birth shall be presumed not to have been survived by his father, or by any person related to him only through his father, unless the contrary is shown.

(2ZA) Subsection (2) does not apply if a person is recorded as the intestate's father, or as a parent (other than the mother) of the intestate—

(a) in a register of births kept (or having effect as if kept) under the Births and Deaths Registration Act 1953, or

(b) in a record of a birth included in an index kept under section 30(1) of that Act (indexes relating to certain other registers etc).

(2A) In the case of a person who has a parent by virtue of section 43 of the Human Fertilisation and Embryology Act 2008 (treatment provided to woman who agrees that second woman to be parent), the second and third references in subsection (2) to the person's father are to be read as references to the woman who is a parent of the person by virtue of that section.

(3) In section 50(1) of the Administration of Estates Act 1925 (which relates to the construction of documents), the reference to Part IV of that Act, or to the foregoing provisions of that Part, shall in relation to an instrument inter vivos made, or a will or codicil coming into operation, after the coming into force of this section (but not in relation to instruments inter vivos made or wills or codicils coming into operation earlier) be construed as including references to this section.

(4) This section does not affect any rights under the intestacy of a person dying before the coming into force of this section.

19 Dispositions of property

(1) In the following dispositions, namely—

(a) dispositions inter vivos made on or after the date on which this section comes into force; and

(b) dispositions by will or codicil where the will or codicil is made on or after that date;

references (whether express or implied) to any relationship between two persons shall be construed in accordance with section 1 above.

(2) It is hereby declared that the use, without more, of the word 'heir' or 'heirs' or any expression purporting to create an entailed interest in real or personal property does not show a contrary intention for the purposes of section 1 as applied by subsection (1) above.

(3) In relation to the dispositions mentioned in subsection (1) above, section 33 of the Trustee Act 1925 (which specifies the trust implied by a direction that income is to be held on protective trusts for the benefit of any person) shall have effect as if any reference (however expressed) to any relationship between two persons were construed in accordance with section 1 above.

(4) Where under any disposition of real or personal property, any interest in such property is limited (whether subject to any preceding limitation or charge or not) in such a way that it would, apart from this section, devolve (as nearly as the law permits) along with a dignity or title of honour, then—

(a) whether or not the disposition contains an express reference to the dignity or title of honour; and

(b)   whether or not the property or some interest in the property may in some event become severed from it,

nothing in this section shall operate to sever the property or any interest in it from the dignity or title, but the property or interest shall devolve in all respects as if this section had not been enacted.

(5)   This section is without prejudice to section 42 of the Adoption Act 1976 or section 69 of the Adoption and Children Act 2002 (construction of dispositions in cases of adoption).

(6)   In this section 'disposition' means a disposition, including an oral disposition, of real or personal property whether inter vivos or by will or codicil.

(7)   Notwithstanding any rule of law, a disposition made by will or codicil executed before the date on which this section comes into force shall not be treated for the purposes of this section as made on or after that date by reason only that the will or codicil is confirmed by a codicil executed on or after that date.

...

21   Entitlement to grant of probate etc.

(1)   For the purpose of determining the person or persons who would in accordance with probate rules be entitled to a grant of probate or administration in respect of the estate of a deceased person, the deceased shall be presumed, unless the contrary is shown, not to have been survived—

(a)   by any person related to him whose father and mother were not married to each other at the time of his birth; or

(b)   by any person whose relationship with him is deduced through such a person as is mentioned in paragraph (a) above.

(2)   In this section 'probate rules' means rules of court made under section 127 of the Supreme Court Act 1981.

(3)   This section does not apply in relation to the estate of a person dying before the coming into force of this section.

...

PART VI MISCELLANEOUS AND SUPPLEMENTAL

Miscellaneous

27   Artificial insemination

(1)   Where after the coming into force of this section a child is born in England and Wales as the result of the artificial insemination of a woman who—

(a)   was at the time of the insemination a party to a marriage (being a marriage which had not at that time been dissolved or annulled); and

(b)   was artificially inseminated with the semen of some person other than the other party to that marriage,

then, unless it is proved to the satisfaction of any court by which the matter has to be determined that the other party to that marriage did not consent to the insemination, the child shall be treated in law as the child of the parties to that marriage and shall not be treated as the child of any person other than the parties to that marriage.

(2)   Any reference in this section to a marriage includes a reference to a void marriage if at the time of the insemination resulting in the birth of the child both or either of the parties reasonably believed that the marriage was valid; and for the purposes of this section it shall be presumed, unless the contrary is shown, that one of the parties so believed at that time that the marriage was valid.

(3)   Nothing in this section shall affect the succession to any dignity or title of honour or render any person capable of succeeding to or transmitting a right to succeed to any such dignity or title.

...

Supplemental

30   Orders applying section 1 to other enactments

(1) The Lord Chancellor may by order make provision for the construction in accordance with section 1 above of such enactments passed before the coming into force of that section as may be specified in the order.

...

Housing Act 1988

(1988 c. 50)

PART I RENTED ACCOMMODATION

Chapter I Assured tenancies

Miscellaneous

17   Succession to assured tenancy by spouse or civil partner

(1) Subject to subsection (1D), in any case where—

    (a) the sole tenant under an assured periodic tenancy dies, and

    (b) immediately before the death, the tenant's spouse or civil partner was occupying the dwelling-house as his or her only or principal home

then, on the death, the tenancy vests by virtue of this section in the spouse or civil partner (and, accordingly, does not devolve under the tenant's will or intestacy).

(1A) Subject to subsection (1D), in any case where—

    (a) there is an assured periodic tenancy of a dwelling-house in England under which—

        (i) the landlord is a private registered provider of social housing, and

        (ii) the tenant is a sole tenant,

    (b) the tenant under the tenancy dies,

    (c) immediately before the death, the dwelling-house was not occupied by a spouse or civil partner of the tenant as his or her only or principal home,

    (d) an express term of the tenancy makes provision for a person other than such a spouse or civil partner of the tenant to succeed to the tenancy, and

    (e) there is a person whose succession is in accordance with that term,

then, on the death, the tenancy vests by virtue of this section in that person (and, accordingly, does not devolve under the tenant's will or intestacy).

(1B) Subject to subsection (1D), in any case where—

    (a) there is an assured tenancy of a dwelling-house in England for a fixed term of not less than two years under which—

        (i) the landlord is a private registered provider of social housing, and

        (ii) the tenant is a sole tenant,

    (b) the tenant under the tenancy dies, and

    (c) immediately before the death, the tenant's spouse or civil partner was occupying the dwelling-house as his or her only or principal home,

then, on the death, the tenancy vests by virtue of this section in the spouse or civil partner (and, accordingly, does not devolve under the tenant's will or intestacy).

(1C) Subject to subsection (1D), in any case where—
- (a) there is an assured tenancy of a dwelling-house in England for a fixed term of not less than two years under which—
  - (i) the landlord is a private registered provider of social housing, and
  - (ii) the tenant is a sole tenant,
- (b) the tenant under the tenancy dies,
- (c) immediately before the death, the dwelling-house was not occupied by a spouse or civil partner of the tenant as his or her only or principal home,
- (d) an express term of the tenancy makes provision for a person other than such a spouse or civil partner of the tenant to succeed to the tenancy, and
- (e) there is a person whose succession is in accordance with that term,

then, on the death, the tenancy vests by virtue of this section in that person (and accordingly does not devolve under the tenant's will or intestacy).

(1D) Subsection (1), (1A), (1B) or (1C) does not apply if the tenant was himself a successor as defined in subsection (2) or subsection (3).

(1E) In such a case, on the death, the tenancy vests by virtue of this section in a person ('P') (and, accordingly, does not devolve under the tenant's will or intestacy) if, and only if—
- (a) (in a case within subsection (1)) the tenancy is of a dwelling-house in England under which the landlord is a private registered provider of social housing,
- (b) an express term of the tenancy makes provision for a person to succeed a successor to the tenancy, and
- (c) P's succession is in accordance with that term.

(2) For the purposes of this section, a tenant is a successor in relation to a tenancy if—
- (a) the tenancy became vested in him either by virtue of this section or under the will or intestacy of a previous tenant; or
- (b) at some time before the tenant's death the tenancy was a joint tenancy held by himself and one or more other persons and, prior to his death, he became the sole tenant by survivorship; or
- (c) he became entitled to the tenancy as mentioned in section 39(5) below.

(3) For the purposes of this section, a tenant is also a successor in relation to a tenancy (in this subsection referred to as 'the new tenancy') which was granted to him (alone or jointly with others) if—
- (a) at some time before the grant of the new tenancy, he was, by virtue of subsection (2) above, a successor in relation to an earlier tenancy of the same or substantially the same dwelling-house as is let under the new tenancy; and
- (b) at all times since he became such a successor he has been a tenant (alone or jointly with others) of the dwelling-house which is let under the new tenancy or of a dwelling-house which is substantially the same as that dwelling-house.

(4) For the purposes of this section—
- (a) a person who was living with the tenant as his or her wife or husband shall be treated as the tenant's spouse, and
- (b) a person who was living with the tenant as if they were civil partners shall be treated as the tenant's civil partner.

(5) If, on the death of the tenant, there is, by virtue of subsection (4) above, more than one person who fulfils the condition in subsection (1)(b) or (1B)(c) above, such one of them as may be decided by agreement or, in default of agreement, by the county court shall for the purposes of this section be treated (according to whether that one of them is of the opposite sex to, or of the same sex as, the tenant) as the tenant's spouse or the tenant's civil partner.

(6) If, on the death of the tenant, there is more than one person in whom the tenancy would otherwise vest by virtue of subsection (1A), (1C) or (1E), the tenancy vests in such one of them as may be agreed between them or, in default of agreement, as is determined by the county court.

(7) This section does not apply to a fixed term assured tenancy that is a lease of a dwelling-house—

    (a) granted on payment of a premium calculated by reference to a percentage of the value of the dwelling-house or of the cost of providing it, or

    (b) under which the lessee (or the lessee's personal representatives) will or may be entitled to a sum calculated by reference, directly or indirectly, to the value of the dwelling-house.

Children Act 1989

(1989 c. 41)

PART I INTRODUCTORY

1 Welfare of the child

(1) When a court determines any question with respect to—

    (a) the upbringing of a child; or

    (b) the administration of a child's property or the application of any income arising from it,

the child's welfare shall be the court's paramount consideration.

(2) In any proceedings in which any question with respect to the upbringing of a child arises, the court shall have regard to the general principle that any delay in determining the question is likely to prejudice the welfare of the child.

(2A) A court, in the circumstances mentioned in subsection (4)(a) or (7), is as respects each parent within subsection (6)(a) to presume, unless the contrary is shown, that involvement of that parent in the life of the child concerned will further the child's welfare.

(2B) In subsection (2A) 'involvement' means involvement of some kind, either direct or indirect, but not any particular division of a child's time.

(3) In the circumstances mentioned in subsection (4), a court shall have regard in particular to—

    (a) the ascertainable wishes and feelings of the child concerned (considered in the light of his age and understanding);

    (b) his physical, emotional and educational needs;

    (c) the likely effect on him of any change in his circumstances;

    (d) his age, sex, background and any characteristics of his which the court considers relevant;

    (e) any harm which he has suffered or is at risk of suffering;

    (f) how capable each of his parents, and any other person in relation to whom the court considers the question to be relevant, is of meeting his needs;

    (g) the range of powers available to the court under this Act in the proceedings in question.

(4) The circumstances are that—

    (a) the court is considering whether to make, vary or discharge a section 8 order, and the making, variation or discharge of the order is opposed by any party to the proceedings; or

    (b) the court is considering whether to make, vary or discharge a special guardianship order or an order under Part IV.

(5) Where a court is considering whether or not to make one or more orders under this Act with respect to a child, it shall not make the order or any of the orders unless it considers that doing so would be better for the child than making no order at all.

(6) In subsection (2A) 'parent' means parent of the child concerned; and, for the purposes of that subsection, a parent of the child concerned—

    (a) is within this paragraph if that parent can be involved in the child's life in a way that does not put the child at risk of suffering harm; and

(b) is to be treated as being within paragraph (a) unless there is some evidence before the court in the particular proceedings to suggest that involvement of that parent in the child's life would put the child at risk of suffering harm whatever the form of the involvement.

(7) The circumstances referred to are that the court is considering whether to make an order under section 4(1)(c) or (2A) or 4ZA(1)(c) or (5) (parental responsibility of parent other than mother).

2   Parental responsibility for children

(1) Where a child's father and mother were married to each other at the time of his birth, they shall each have parental responsibility for the child.

(1A) Where a child—

(a) has a parent by virtue of section 42 of the Human Fertilisation and Embryology Act 2008; or

(b) has a parent by virtue of section 43 of that Act and is a person to whom section 1(3) of the Family Law Reform Act 1987 applies,

the child's mother and the other parent shall each have parental responsibility for the child.

(2) Where a child's father and mother were not married to each other at the time of his birth—

(a) the mother shall have parental responsibility for the child;

(b) the father shall have parental responsibility for the child if he has acquired it (and has not ceased to have it) in accordance with the provisions of this Act.

(2A) Where a child has a parent by virtue of section 43 of the Human Fertilisation and Embryology Act 2008 and is not a person to whom section 1(3) of the Family Law Reform Act 1987 applies—

(a) the mother shall have parental responsibility for the child;

(b) the other parent shall have parental responsibility for the child if she has acquired it (and has not ceased to have it) in accordance with the provisions of this Act.

(3) References in this Act to a child whose father and mother were, or (as the case may be) were not, married to each other at the time of his birth must be read with section 1 of the Family Law Reform Act 1987 (which extends their meaning).

(4) The rule of law that a father is the natural guardian of his legitimate child is abolished.

(5) More than one person may have parental responsibility for the same child at the same time.

(6) A person who has parental responsibility for a child at any time shall not cease to have that responsibility solely because some other person subsequently acquires parental responsibility for the child.

(7) Where more than one person has parental responsibility for a child, each of them may act alone and without the other (or others) in meeting that responsibility; but nothing in this Part shall be taken to affect the operation of any enactment which requires the consent of more than one person in a matter affecting the child.

(8) The fact that a person has parental responsibility for a child shall not entitle him to act in any way which would be incompatible with any order made with respect to the child under this Act.

(9) A person who has parental responsibility for a child may not surrender or transfer any part of that responsibility to another but may arrange for some or all of it to be met by one or more persons acting on his behalf.

(10) The person with whom any such arrangement is made may himself be a person who already has parental responsibility for the child concerned.

(11) The making of any such arrangement shall not affect any liability of the person making it which may arise from any failure to meet any part of his parental responsibility for the child concerned.

3   Meaning of 'parental responsibility'

(1) In this Act 'parental responsibility' means all the rights, duties, powers, responsibilities and authority which by law a parent of a child has in relation to the child and his property.

(2) It also includes the rights, powers and duties which a guardian of the child's estate (appointed, before the commencement of section 5, to act generally) would have had in relation to the child and his property.

(3) The rights referred to in subsection (2) include, in particular, the right of the guardian to receive or recover in his own name, for the benefit of the child, property of whatever description and wherever situated which the child is entitled to receive or recover.

(4) The fact that a person has, or does not have, parental responsibility for a child shall not affect—

(a) any obligation which he may have in relation to the child (such as a statutory duty to maintain the child); or

(b) any rights which, in the event of the child's death, he (or any other person) may have in relation to the child's property.

(5) A person who—

(a) does not have parental responsibility for a particular child; but

(b) has care of the child,

may (subject to the provisions of this Act) do what is reasonable in all the circumstances of the case for the purpose of safeguarding or promoting the child's welfare.

4 Acquisition of parental responsibility by father

(1) Where a child's father and mother were not married to each other at the time of his birth, the father shall acquire parental responsibility for the child if—

(a) except where subsection (1C) applies, he becomes registered as the child's father under any of the enactments specified in subsection (1A);

(b) he and the child's mother make an agreement (a 'parental responsibility agreement') providing for him to have parental responsibility for the child; or

(c) the court, on his application, orders that he shall have parental responsibility for the child.

(1A) The enactments referred to in subsection (1)(a) are—

(a) paragraphs (a), (b) and (c) of section 10(1) and of section 10A(1) of the Births and Deaths Registration Act 1953;

(aa) regulations under section 2C, 2D, 2E, 10B or 10C of the Births and Deaths Registration Act 1953;

...

(1B) The Secretary of State may by order amend subsection (1A) so as to add further enactments to the list in that subsection.

(1C) The father of a child does not acquire parental responsibility by virtue of subsection (1)(a) if, before he became registered as the child's father under the enactment in question—

(a) the court considered an application by him for an order under subsection (1)(c) in relation to the child but did not make such an order, or

(b) in a case where he had previously acquired parental responsibility for the child, the court ordered that he was to cease to have that responsibility.

(2) No parental responsibility agreement shall have effect for the purposes of this Act unless—

(a) it is made in the form prescribed by regulations made by the Lord Chancellor; and

(b) where regulations are made by the Lord Chancellor prescribing the manner in which such agreements must be recorded, it is recorded in the prescribed manner.

(2A) A person who has acquired parental responsibility under subsection (1) shall cease to have that responsibility only if the court so orders.

(3) The court may make an order under subsection (2A) on the application—

(a) of any person who has parental responsibility for the child; or

(b) with the leave of the court, of the child himself,

subject, in the case of parental responsibility acquired under subsection (1)(c), to section 12(4).

(4) The court may only grant leave under subsection (3)(b) if it is satisfied that the child has sufficient understanding to make the proposed application.

4ZA   Acquisition of parental responsibility by second female parent

(1) Where a child has a parent by virtue of section 43 of the Human Fertilisation and Embryology Act 2008 and is not a person to whom section 1(3) of the Family Law Reform Act 1987 applies, that parent shall acquire parental responsibility for the child if—

(a) except where subsection (3A) applies, she becomes registered as a parent of the child under any of the enactments specified in subsection (2);

(b) she and the child's mother make an agreement providing for her to have parental responsibility for the child; or

(c) the court, on her application, orders that she shall have parental responsibility for the child.

(2) The enactments referred to in subsection (1)(a) are—

(a) paragraphs (a), (b) and (c) of section 10(1B) and of section 10A(1B) of the Births and Deaths Registration Act 1953;

(aa) regulations under section 2C, 2D, 10B or 10C of the Births and Deaths Registration Act 1953;

(b) paragraphs (a), (b) and (d) of section 18B(1) and sections 18B(3)(a) and 20(1)(a) of the Registration of Births, Deaths and Marriages (Scotland) Act 1965; and

(c) sub-paragraphs (a), (b) and (c) of Article 14ZA(3) of the Births and Deaths Registration (Northern Ireland) Order 1976.

(3) The Secretary of State may by order amend subsection (2) so as to add further enactments to the list in that subsection.

(3A) A person who is a parent of a child by virtue of section 43 of the Human Fertilisation and Embryology Act 2008 does not acquire parental responsibility by virtue of subsection (1)(a) if, before she became registered as a parent of the child under the enactment in question—

(a) the court considered an application by her for an order under subsection (1)(c) in relation to the child but did not make such an order, or

(b) in a case where she had previously acquired parental responsibility for the child, the court ordered that she was to cease to have that responsibility.

(4) An agreement under subsection (1)(b) is also a 'parental responsibility agreement', and section 4(2) applies in relation to such an agreement as it applies in relation to parental responsibility agreements under section 4.

(5) A person who has acquired parental responsibility under subsection (1) shall cease to have that responsibility only if the court so orders.

(6) The court may make an order under subsection (5) on the application—

(a) of any person who has parental responsibility for the child; or

(b) with the leave of the court, of the child himself,

subject, in the case of parental responsibility acquired under subsection (1)(c), to section 12(4).

(7) The court may only grant leave under subsection (6)(b) if it is satisfied that the child has sufficient understanding to make the proposed application.

4A   Acquisition of parental responsibility by step-parent

(1) Where a child's parent ('parent A') who has parental responsibility for the child is married to, or a civil partner of, a person who is not the child's parent ('the step-parent')—

(a) parent A or, if the other parent of the child also has parental responsibility for the child, both parents may by agreement with the step-parent provide for the step-parent to have parental responsibility for the child; or

(b) the court may, on the application of the step-parent, order that the step-parent shall have parental responsibility for the child.

(2) An agreement under subsection (1)(a) is also a 'parental responsibility agreement', and section 4(2) applies in relation to such agreements as it applies in relation to parental responsibility agreements under section 4.

(3) A parental responsibility agreement under subsection (1)(a), or an order under subsection (1)(b), may only be brought to an end by an order of the court made on the application—

>   (a) of any person who has parental responsibility for the child; or
>   (b) with the leave of the court, of the child himself.

(4) The court may only grant leave under subsection (3)(b) if it is satisfied that the child has sufficient understanding to make the proposed application.

5 Appointment of guardians

(1) Where an application with respect to a child is made to the court by any individual, the court may by order appoint that individual to be the child's guardian if—

>   (a) the child has no parent with parental responsibility for him; or
>   (b) a parent, guardian or special guardian of the child's was named in a child arrangements order as a person with whom the child was to live and has died while the order was in force; or
>   (c) paragraph (b) does not apply, and the child's only or last surviving special guardian dies.

(2) The power conferred by subsection (1) may also be exercised in any family proceedings if the court considers that the order should be made even though no application has been made for it.

(3) A parent who has parental responsibility for his child may appoint another individual to be the child's guardian in the event of his death.

(4) A guardian of a child may appoint another individual to take his place as the child's guardian in the event of his death; and a special guardian of a child may appoint another individual to be the child's guardian in the event of his death.

(5) An appointment under subsection (3) or (4) shall not have effect unless it is made in writing, is dated and is signed by the person making the appointment or—

>   (a) in the case of an appointment made by a will which is not signed by the testator, is signed at the direction of the testator in accordance with the requirements of section 9 of the Wills Act 1837; or
>   (b) in any other case, is signed at the direction of the person making the appointment, in his presence and in the presence of two witnesses who each attest the signature.

(6) A person appointed as a child's guardian under this section shall have parental responsibility for the child concerned.

(7) Where—

>   (a) on the death of any person making an appointment under subsection (3) or (4), the child concerned has no parent with parental responsibility for him; or
>   (b) immediately before the death of any person making such an appointment, a child arrangements order was in force in which the person was named as a person with whom the child was to live or the person was the child's only (or last surviving) special guardian,

the appointment shall take effect on the death of that person.

(8) Where, on the death of any person making an appointment under subsection (3) or (4)—

>   (a) the child concerned has a parent with parental responsibility for him; and
>   (b) subsection (7)(b) does not apply,

the appointment shall take effect when the child no longer has a parent who has parental responsibility for him.

(9) Subsections (1) and (7) do not apply if the child arrangements order referred to in paragraph (b) of those subsections also named a surviving parent of the child as a person with whom the child was to live.

(10) Nothing in this section shall be taken to prevent an appointment under subsection (3) or (4) being made by two or more persons acting jointly.

(11) Subject to any provision made by rules of court, no court shall exercise the High Court's inherent jurisdiction to appoint a guardian of the estate of any child.

(12) Where rules of court are made under subsection (11) they may prescribe the circumstances in which, and conditions subject to which, an appointment of such a guardian may be made.

(13) A guardian of a child may only be appointed in accordance with the provisions of this section.

6 Guardians: revocation and disclaimer

(1) An appointment under section 5(3) or (4) revokes an earlier such appointment (including one made in an unrevoked will or codicil) made by the same person in respect of the same child, unless it is clear (whether as the result of an express provision in the later appointment or by any necessary implication) that the purpose of the later appointment is to appoint an additional guardian.

(2) An appointment under section 5(3) or (4) (including one made in an unrevoked will or codicil) is revoked if the person who made the appointment revokes it by a written and dated instrument which is signed—

(a) by him; or

(b) at his direction, in his presence and in the presence of two witnesses who each attest the signature.

(3) An appointment under section 5(3) or (4) (other than one made in a will or codicil) is revoked if, with the intention of revoking the appointment, the person who made it—

(a) destroys the instrument by which it was made; or

(b) has some other person destroy that instrument in his presence.

(3A) An appointment under section 5(3) or (4) (including one made in an unrevoked will or codicil) is revoked if the person appointed is the spouse of the person who made the appointment and either—

(a) a decree of a court of civil jurisdiction in England and Wales dissolves or annuls the marriage, or

(b) the marriage is dissolved or annulled and the divorce or annulment is entitled to recognition in England and Wales by virtue of Part II of the Family Law Act 1986, unless a contrary intention appears by the appointment.

(3B) An appointment under section 5(3) or (4) (including one made in an unrevoked will or codicil) is revoked if the person appointed is the civil partner of the person who made the appointment and either—

(a) an order of a court of civil jurisdiction in England and Wales dissolves or annuls the civil partnership, or

(b) the civil partnership is dissolved or annulled and the dissolution or annulment is entitled to recognition in England and Wales by virtue of Chapter 3 of Part 5 of the Civil Partnership Act 2004,

unless a contrary intention appears by the appointment.

(4) For the avoidance of doubt, an appointment under section 5(3) or (4) made in a will or codicil is revoked if the will or codicil is revoked.

(5) A person who is appointed as a guardian under section 5(3) or (4) may disclaim his appointment by an instrument in writing signed by him and made within a reasonable time of his first knowing that the appointment has taken effect.

(6) Where regulations are made by the Lord Chancellor prescribing the manner in which such disclaimers must be recorded, no such disclaimer shall have effect unless it is recorded in the prescribed manner.

(7) Any appointment of a guardian under section 5 may be brought to an end at any time by order of the court—

(a) on the application of any person who has parental responsibility for the child;

(b) on the application of the child concerned, with leave of the court; or

(c) in any family proceedings, if the court considers that it should be brought to an end even though no application has been made.

7 Welfare reports

(1) A court considering any question with respect to a child under this Act may—

(a) ask an officer of the Service or a Welsh family proceedings officer; or

(b) ask a local authority to arrange for—

    (i) an officer of the authority; or

    (ii) such other person (other than an officer of the Service or a Welsh family proceedings officer) as the authority considers appropriate,

to report to the court on such matters relating to the welfare of that child as are required to be dealt with in the report.

(2) The Lord Chancellor, after consulting the Lord Chief Justice, may make regulations specifying matters which, unless the court orders otherwise, must be dealt with in any report under this section.

(3) The report may be made in writing, or orally, as the court requires.

(4) Regardless of any enactment or rule of law which would otherwise prevent it from doing so, the court may take account of—

(a) any statement contained in the report; and

(b) any evidence given in respect of the matters referred to in the report,

in so far as the statement or evidence is, in the opinion of the court, relevant to the question which it is considering.

(5) It shall be the duty of the authority or officer of the Service or a Welsh family proceedings officer to comply with any request for a report under this section.

(6) The Lord Chief Justice may nominate a judicial office holder (as defined in section 109(4) of the Constitutional Reform Act 2005) to exercise his functions under subsection (2).

PART II ORDERS WITH RESPECT TO CHILDREN IN FAMILY PROCEEDINGS

General

8 Child arrangements orders and other orders with respect to children

(1) In this Act—

'child arrangements order' means an order regulating arrangements relating to any of the following—

(a) with whom a child is to live, spend time or otherwise have contact, and

(b) when a child is to live, spend time or otherwise have contact with any person;

'a prohibited steps order' means an order that no step which could be taken by a parent in meeting his parental responsibility for a child, and which is of a kind specified in the order, shall be taken by any person without the consent of the court; and

'a specific issue order' means an order giving directions for the purpose of determining a specific question which has arisen, or which may arise, in connection with any aspect of parental responsibility for a child.

(2) In this Act 'a section 8 order' means any of the orders mentioned in subsection (1) and any order varying or discharging such an order.

(3) For the purposes of this Act 'family proceedings' means any proceedings—

(a) under the inherent jurisdiction of the High Court in relation to children; and

(b) under the enactments mentioned in subsection (4), but does not include proceedings on an application for leave under section 100(3).

(4) The enactments are—

(a) Parts I, II and IV of this Act;

    (b)   the Matrimonial Causes Act 1973;

    (ba) Schedule 5 to the Civil Partnership Act 2004;

    (c)   ...

    (d)   the Adoption and Children Act 2002;

    (e)   the Domestic Proceedings and Magistrates' Courts Act 1978;

    (ea) Schedule 6 to the Civil Partnership Act 2004;

    (f)   ...

    (g)   Part III of the Matrimonial and Family Proceedings Act 1984;

    (h)   the Family Law Act 1996;

    (i)   sections 11 and 12 of the Crime and Disorder Act 1998.

9   Restrictions on making section 8 orders

(1) No court shall make any section 8 order, other than a child arrangements order to which subsection (6B) applies, with respect to a child who is in the care of a local authority.

(2) No application may be made by a local authority for a child arrangements order and no court shall make such an order in favour of a local authority.

(3) A person who is, or was at any time within the last six months, a local authority foster parent of a child may not apply for leave to apply for a section 8 order with respect to the child unless—

    (a) he has the consent of the authority;

    (b) he is a relative of the child; or

    (c) the child has lived with him for at least one year preceding the application.

(5) No court shall exercise its powers to make a specific issue order or prohibited steps order—

    (a) with a view to achieving a result which could be achieved by making a child arrangements order or an order under section 51A of the Adoption and Children Act 2002 (post-adoption contact); or

    (b) in any way which is denied to the High Court (by section 100(2)) in the exercise of its inherent jurisdiction with respect to children.

(6) No court shall make a section 8 order which is to have effect for a period which will end after the child has reached the age of sixteen unless it is satisfied that the circumstances of the case are exceptional.

(6A) Subsection (6) does not apply to a child arrangements order to which subsection (6B) applies.

(6B) This subsection applies to a child arrangements order if the arrangements regulated by the order relate only to either or both of the following—

    (a) with whom the child concerned is to live, and

    (b) when the child is to live with any person.

(7) No court shall make any section 8 order, other than one varying or discharging such an order, with respect to a child who has reached the age of sixteen unless it is satisfied that the circumstances of the case are exceptional.

10   Power of court to make section 8 orders

(1) In any family proceedings in which a question arises with respect to the welfare of any child, the court may make a section 8 order with respect to the child if—

    (a) an application for the order has been made by a person who—

        (i)   is entitled to apply for a section 8 order with respect to the child; or

        (ii) has obtained the leave of the court to make the application; or

    (b) the court considers that the order should be made even though no such application has been made.

(2) The court may also make a section 8 order with respect to any child on the application of a person who—

    (a) is entitled to apply for a section 8 order with respect to the child; or

    (b) has obtained the leave of the court to make the application.

(3) This section is subject to the restrictions imposed by section 9.

(4) The following persons are entitled to apply to the court for any section 8 order with respect to a child—

    (a)   any parent, guardian or special guardian of the child;

    (aa) any person who by virtue of section 4A has parental responsibility for the child;

    (b)   any person who is named, in a child arrangements order that is in force with respect to the child, as a person with whom the child is to live.

(5) The following persons are entitled to apply for a child arrangements order with respect to a child—

    (a)   any party to a marriage (whether or not subsisting) in relation to whom the child is a child of the family;

    (aa) any civil partner in a civil partnership (whether or not subsisting) in relation to whom the child is a child of the family;

    (b)   any person with whom the child has lived for a period of at least three years;

    (c)   any person who—

        (i)   in any case where a child arrangements order in force with respect to the child regulates arrangements relating to with whom the child is to live or when the child is to live with any person, has the consent of each of the persons named in the order as a person with whom the child is to live;

        (ii) in any case where the child is in the care of a local authority, has the consent of that authority; or

        (iii) in any other case, has the consent of each of those (if any) who have parental responsibility for the child.

    (d)   any person who has parental responsibility for the child by virtue of provision made under section 12(2A).

(5A) A local authority foster parent is entitled to apply for a child arrangements order to which subsection (5C) applies with respect to a child if the child has lived with him for a period of at least one year immediately preceding the application.

(5B) A relative of a child is entitled to apply for a child arrangements order to which subsection (5C) applies with respect to the child if the child has lived with the relative for a period of at least one year immediately preceding the application.

(5C) This subsection applies to a child arrangements order if the arrangements regulated by the order relate only to either or both of the following—

    (a) with whom the child concerned is to live, and

    (b) when the child is to live with any person.

(6) A person who would not otherwise be entitled (under the previous provisions of this section) to apply for the variation or discharge of a section 8 order shall be entitled to do so if—

    (a) the order was made on his application; or

    (b) in the case of a child arrangements order, he is named in provisions of the order regulating arrangements relating to—

        (i)   with whom the child concerned is to spend time or otherwise have contact, or

        (ii) when the child is to spend time or otherwise have contact with any person.

(7) Any person who falls within a category of person prescribed by rules of court is entitled to apply for any such section 8 order as may be prescribed in relation to that category of person.

(7A) If a special guardianship order is in force with respect to a child, an application for a child arrangements order to which subsection (7B) applies may only be made with respect to him, if apart from this subsection the leave of the court is not required, with such leave.

(7B) This subsection applies to a child arrangements order if the arrangements regulated by the order consist of, or include, arrangements which relate to either or both of the following—

    (a) with whom the child concerned is to live, and

    (b) when the child is to live with any person.

(8) Where the person applying for leave to make an application for a section 8 order is the child concerned, the court may only grant leave if it is satisfied that he has sufficient understanding to make the proposed application for the section 8 order.

(9) Where the person applying for leave to make an application for a section 8 order is not the child concerned, the court shall, in deciding whether or not to grant leave, have particular regard to—

(a) the nature of the proposed application for the section 8 order;

(b) the applicant's connection with the child;

(c) any risk there might be of that proposed application disrupting the child's life to such an extent that he would be harmed by it; and

(d) where the child is being looked after by a local authority—

(i)   the authority's plans for the child's future; and

(ii) the wishes and feelings of the child's parents.

(10) The period of three years mentioned in subsection (5)(b) need not be continuous but must not have begun more than five years before, or ended more than three months before, the making of the application.

11   General principles and supplementary provisions

(1) In proceedings in which any question of making a section 8 order, or any other question with respect to such an order arises, the court shall (in the light of any provision in rules of court that is of the kind mentioned in subsection (2)(a) or (b))—

(a) draw up a timetable with a view to determining the question without delay; and

(b) give such directions as it considers appropriate for the purpose of ensuring, so far as is reasonably practicable, that that timetable is adhered to.

(2) Rules of court may—

(a) specify periods within which specified steps must be taken in relation to proceedings in which such questions arise; and

(b) make other provision with respect to such proceedings for the purpose of ensuring, so far as is reasonably practicable, that such questions are determined without delay.

(3) Where a court has power to make a section 8 order, it may do so at any time during the course of the proceedings in question even though it is not in a position to dispose finally of those proceedings.

...

(5) Where—

(a) a child arrangements order has been made with respect to a child; and

(b) the child has two parents who each have parental responsibility for him,

the order, so far as it has the result that there are times when the child lives or is to live with one of the parents, shall cease to have effect if the parents live together for a continuous period of more than six months.

(6) A child arrangements order made with respect to a child, so far as it provides for the child to spend time or otherwise have contact with one of the child's parents at times when the child is living with the child's other parent, shall cease to have effect if the parents live together for a continuous period of more than six months.

(7) A section 8 order may—

(a) contain directions about how it is to be carried into effect;

(b) impose conditions which must be complied with by any person—

(i)   who is named in the order as a person with whom the child concerned is to live, spend time or otherwise have contact;

(ii) who is a parent of the child;

(iii) who is not a parent of his but who has parental responsibility for him; or

(iv) with whom the child is living,

and to whom the conditions are expressed to apply;

(c) be made to have effect for a specified period, or contain provisions which are to have effect for a specified period;

(d) make such incidental, supplemental or consequential provision as the court thinks fit.

11A Activity directions

(1) Subsection (2) applies in proceedings in which the court is considering whether to make provision about one or more of the matters mentioned in subsection (1A) by making—

(a) a child arrangements order with respect to the child concerned, or

(b) an order varying or discharging a child arrangements order with respect to the child concerned.

(1A) The matters mentioned in this subsection are—

(a) with whom a child is to live,

(b) when a child is to live with any person,

(c) with whom a child is to spend time or otherwise have contact, and

(d) when a child is to spend time or otherwise have contact with any person.

(2) The court may make an activity direction in connection with the provision that the court is considering whether to make.

(2A) Subsection (2B) applies in proceedings in which subsection (2) does not apply and in which the court is considering—

(a) whether a person has failed to comply with a provision of a child arrangements order, or

(b) what steps to take in consequence of a person's failure to comply with a provision of a child arrangements order.

(2B) The court may make an activity direction in connection with that provision of the child arrangements order.

(3) An activity direction is a direction requiring an individual who is a party to the proceedings concerned to take part in an activity that would, in the court's opinion, help to establish, maintain or improve the involvement in the life of the child concerned of—

(a) that individual, or

(b) another individual who is a party to the proceedings.

(4) The direction is to specify the activity and the person providing the activity.

(5) The activities that may be so required include, in particular—

(a) programmes, classes and counselling or guidance sessions of a kind that—

(i) may assist a person as regards establishing, maintaining or improving involvement in a child's life;

(ii) may, by addressing a person's violent behaviour, enable or facilitate involvement in a child's life;

(b) sessions in which information or advice is given as regards making or operating arrangements for involvement in a child's life, including making arrangements by means of mediation.

(6) No individual may be required by an activity direction—

(a) to undergo medical or psychiatric examination, assessment or treatment;

(b) to take part in mediation.

(7) A court may not on the same occasion—

(a) make an activity direction under subsection (2), and

(b) dispose finally of the proceedings as they relate to the matters mentioned in subsection (1A) in connection with which the activity direction is made.

(7A) A court may not on the same occasion—

(a) make an activity direction under subsection (2B), and

(b) dispose finally of the proceedings as they relate to failure to comply with the provision in connection with which the activity direction is made.

(8) Each of subsections (2) and (2B) has effect subject to the restrictions in sections 11B and 11E.

(9) In considering whether to make an activity direction, the welfare of the child concerned is to be the court's paramount consideration.

11B Activity directions: further provision

(1) A court may not make an activity direction under section 11A(2) in connection with any matter mentioned in section 11A(1A) unless there is a dispute as regards the provision about that matter that the court is considering whether to make in the proceedings.

(2) A court may not make an activity direction requiring an individual who is a child to take part in an activity unless the individual is a parent of the child in relation to whom the court is considering provision about a matter mentioned in section 11A(1A).

(3) A court may not make an activity direction in connection with the making, variation or discharge of a child arrangements order, if the child arrangements order is, or would if made be, an excepted order.

(4) A child arrangements order with respect to a child is an excepted order if—
    (a) it is made in proceedings that include proceedings on an application for a relevant adoption order in respect of the child; or
    (b) it makes provision as regards contact between the child and a person who would be a parent or relative of the child but for the child's adoption by an order falling within subsection (5).

(5) An order falls within this subsection if it is—
    (a) a relevant adoption order;
    (b) an adoption order, within the meaning of section 72(1) of the Adoption Act 1976, other than an order made by virtue of section 14 of that Act on the application of a married couple one of whom is the mother or the father of the child;
    (c) ...

(6) A relevant adoption order is an adoption order, within the meaning of section 46(1) of the Adoption and Children Act 2002, other than an order made—
    (a) on an application under section 50 of that Act by a couple (within the meaning of that Act) one of whom is the mother or the father of the person to be adopted, or
    (b) on an application under section 51(2) of that Act.

(7) A court may not make an activity direction in relation to an individual unless the individual is habitually resident in England and Wales; and a direction ceases to have effect if the individual subject to the direction ceases to be habitually resident in England and Wales.

11C Activity conditions

(1) This section applies if in any family proceedings the court makes—
    (a) a child arrangements order containing—
        (i) provision for a child to live with different persons at different times,
        (ii) provision regulating arrangements relating to with whom a child is to spend time or otherwise have contact, or
        (iii) provision regulating arrangements relating to when a child is to spend time or otherwise have contact with any person; or
    (b) an order varying a child arrangements order so as to add, vary or omit provision of a kind mentioned in paragraph (a)(i), (ii) or (iii).

(2) The child arrangements order may impose, or the child arrangements order may be varied so as to impose, a condition (an 'activity condition') requiring an individual falling within subsection (3) to take part in an activity that would, in the court's opinion, help to establish, maintain or improve the involvement in the life of the child concerned of—
    (a) that individual, or
    (b) another individual who is a party to the proceedings.

(3) An individual falls within this subsection if he is—
    (a) for the purposes of the child arrangements order so made or varied, a person with whom the child concerned lives or is to live;

(b) a person whose contact with the child concerned is provided for in that order; or

(c) a person upon whom that order imposes a condition under section 11(7)(b).

(4) The condition is to specify the activity and the person providing the activity.

(5) Subsections (5) and (6) of section 11A have effect as regards the activities that may be required by an activity condition as they have effect as regards the activities that may be required by an activity direction.

(6) Subsection (2) has effect subject to the restrictions in sections 11D and 11E.

11D   Activity conditions: further provision

(1) A child arrangements order may not impose an activity condition on an individual who is a child unless the individual is a parent of the child concerned.

(2) If a child arrangements order is an excepted order (within the meaning given by section 11B(4)), it may not impose (and it may not be varied so as to impose) an activity condition.

(3) A child arrangements order may not impose an activity condition on an individual unless the individual is habitually resident in England and Wales; and a condition ceases to have effect if the individual subject to the condition ceases to be habitually resident in England and Wales.

11E   Activity directions and conditions: making

(1) Before making an activity direction (or imposing an activity condition by means of a child arrangements order), the court must satisfy itself as to the matters falling within subsections (2) to (4).

(2) The first matter is that the activity proposed to be specified is appropriate in the circumstances of the case.

(3) The second matter is that the person proposed to be specified as the provider of the activity is suitable to provide the activity.

(4) The third matter is that the activity proposed to be specified is provided in a place to which the individual who would be subject to the direction (or the condition) can reasonably be expected to travel.

(5) Before making such a direction (or such an order), the court must obtain and consider information about the individual who would be subject to the direction (or the condition) and the likely effect of the direction (or the condition) on him.

(6) Information about the likely effect of the direction (or the condition) may, in particular, include information as to—

(a) any conflict with the individual's religious beliefs;

(b) any interference with the times (if any) at which he normally works or attends an educational establishment.

(7) The court may ask an officer of the Service or a Welsh family proceedings officer to provide the court with information as to the matters in subsections (2) to (5); and it shall be the duty of the officer of the Service or Welsh family proceedings officer to comply with any such request.

(8) In this section 'specified' means specified in an activity direction (or in an activity condition).

11F   Activity directions and conditions: financial assistance

(1) The Secretary of State may by regulations make provision authorising him to make payments to assist individuals falling within subsection (2) in paying relevant charges or fees.

(2) An individual falls within this subsection if he is required by an activity direction or condition to take part in an activity that is expected to help to establish, maintain or improve the involvement of that or another individual in the life of a child, not being a child ordinarily resident in Wales.

(3) The National Assembly for Wales may by regulations make provision authorising it to make payments to assist individuals falling within subsection (4) in paying relevant charges or fees.

(4) An individual falls within this subsection if he is required by an activity direction or condition to take part in an activity that is expected to help to establish, maintain or improve the involvement of that or another individual in the life of a child who is ordinarily resident in Wales.

(5) A relevant charge or fee, in relation to an activity required by an activity direction or condition, is a charge or fee in respect of the activity payable to the person providing the activity.

(6) Regulations under this section may provide that no assistance is available to an individual unless—

(a) the individual satisfies such conditions as regards his financial resources as may be set out in the regulations;

(b) the activity in which the individual is required by an activity direction or condition to take part is provided to him in England or Wales;

(c) where the activity in which the individual is required to take Part is provided to him in England, it is provided by a person who is for the time being approved by the Secretary of State as a provider of activities required by an activity direction or condition;

(d) where the activity in which the individual is required to take Part is provided to him in Wales, it is provided by a person who is for the time being approved by the National Assembly for Wales as a provider of activities required by an activity direction or condition.

(7) Regulations under this section may make provision—

(a) as to the maximum amount of assistance that may be paid to or in respect of an individual as regards an activity in which he is required by an activity direction or condition to take part;

(b) where the amount may vary according to an individual's financial resources, as to the method by which the amount is to be determined;

(c) authorising payments by way of assistance to be made directly to persons providing activities required by an activity direction or condition.

11G   Activity directions and conditions: monitoring

(1) This section applies if in any family proceedings the court—

(a) makes an activity direction in relation to an individual, or

(b) makes a child arrangements order that imposes, or varies a child arrangements order so as to impose, an activity condition on an individual.

(2) The court may on making the direction (or imposing the condition by means of a child arrangements order) ask an officer of the Service or a Welsh family proceedings officer—

(a) to monitor, or arrange for the monitoring of, the individual's compliance with the direction (or the condition);

(b) to report to the court on any failure by the individual to comply with the direction (or the condition).

(3) It shall be the duty of the officer of the Service or Welsh family proceedings officer to comply with any request under subsection (2).

11H   Monitoring contact and shared residence

(1) This section applies if in any family proceedings the court makes—

(a) a child arrangements order containing provision of a kind mentioned in section 11C(1)(a)(i), (ii) or (iii), or

(b) an order varying a child arrangements order so as to add, vary or omit provision of any of those kinds.

(2) The court may ask an officer of the Service or a Welsh family proceedings officer—

(a) to monitor whether an individual falling within subsection (3) complies with each provision of any of those kinds that is contained in the child arrangements order (or in the child arrangements order as varied);

(b) to report to the court on such matters relating to the individual's compliance as the court may specify in the request.

(3) An individual falls within this subsection if the child arrangements order so made (or the contact order as so varied)—

(za) provides for the child concerned to live with different persons at different times and names the individual as one of those persons;

(a) imposes requirements on the individual with regard to the child concerned spending time or otherwise having contact with some other person;

(b) names the individual as a person with whom the child concerned is to spend time or otherwise have contact; or

(c) imposes a condition under section 11(7)(b) on the individual.

(4) If the child arrangements order (or the child arrangements order as varied) includes an activity condition, a request under subsection (2) is to be treated as relating to the provisions of the order other than the activity condition.

(5) The court may make a request under subsection (2)—

(a) on making the child arrangements order (or the order varying the child arrangements order), or

(b) at any time during the subsequent course of the proceedings as they relate to contact with the child concerned or to the child's living arrangements.

(6) In making a request under subsection (2), the court is to specify the period for which the officer of the Service or Welsh family proceedings officer is to monitor compliance with the order; and the period specified may not exceed twelve months.

(7) It shall be the duty of the officer of the Service or Welsh family proceedings officer to comply with any request under subsection (2).

(8) The court may order any individual falling within subsection (3) to take such steps as may be specified in the order with a view to enabling the officer of the Service or Welsh family proceedings officer to comply with the court's request under subsection (2).

(9) But the court may not make an order under subsection (8) with respect to an individual who is a child unless he is a parent of the child with respect to whom the order falling within subsection (1) was made.

(10) A court may not make a request under subsection (2) in relation to a child arrangements order that is an excepted order (within the meaning given by section 11B(4)).

11I   Child arrangements orders: warning notices

Where the court makes (or varies) a child arrangements order, it is to attach to the child arrangements order (or the order varying the child arrangements order) a notice warning of the consequences of failing to comply with the child arrangements order.

11J   Enforcement orders

(1) This section applies if a child arrangements order with respect to a child has been made.

(2) If the court is satisfied beyond reasonable doubt that a person has failed to comply with a provision of the child arrangements order, it may make an order (an 'enforcement order') imposing on the person an unpaid work requirement.

(3) But the court may not make an enforcement order if it is satisfied that the person had a reasonable excuse for failing to comply with the provision.

(4) The burden of proof as to the matter mentioned in subsection (3) lies on the person claiming to have had a reasonable excuse, and the standard of proof is the balance of probabilities.

(5) The court may make an enforcement order in relation to the child arrangements order only on the application of—

(a) a person who is, for the purposes of the child arrangements order, a person with whom the child concerned lives or is to live;

(b) a person whose contact with the child concerned is provided for in the child arrangements order;

(c) any individual subject to a condition under section 11(7)(b) or activity condition imposed by the child arrangements order; or

(d) the child concerned.

(6) Where the person proposing to apply for an enforcement order in relation to a child arrangements order is the child concerned, the child must obtain the leave of the court before making such an application.

(7) The court may grant leave to the child concerned only if it is satisfied that he has sufficient understanding to make the proposed application.

(8) Subsection (2) has effect subject to the restrictions in sections 11K and 11L.

(9) The court may suspend an enforcement order for such period as it thinks fit.

(10) Nothing in this section prevents a court from making more than one enforcement order in relation to the same person on the same occasion.

(11) Proceedings in which any question of making an enforcement order, or any other question with respect to such an order, arises are to be regarded for the purposes of section 11(1) and (2) as proceedings in which a question arises with respect to a section 8 order.

(12) In Schedule A1—

   (a) Part 1 makes provision as regards an unpaid work requirement;

   (b) Part 2 makes provision in relation to the revocation and amendment of enforcement orders and failure to comply with such orders.

11K Enforcement orders: further provision

(1) A court may not make an enforcement order against a person in respect of a failure to comply with a provision of a child arrangements order unless it is satisfied that before the failure occurred the person had been given (in accordance with rules of court) a copy of, or otherwise informed of the terms of—

   (a) in the case of a failure to comply with a provision of a child arrangements order where the order was varied before the failure occurred, a notice under section 11I relating to the order varying the child arrangements order or, where more than one such order has been made, the last order preceding the failure in question;

   (b) in any other case, a notice under section 11I relating to the child arrangements order.

(2) A court may not make an enforcement order against a person in respect of any failure to comply with a provision of a child arrangements order occurring before the person attained the age of 18.

(3) A court may not make an enforcement order against a person in respect of a failure to comply with a provision of a child arrangements order where the child arrangements order is an excepted order (within the meaning given by section 11B (4)).

(4) A court may not make an enforcement order against a person unless the person is habitually resident in England and Wales; and an enforcement order ceases to have effect if the person subject to the order ceases to be habitually resident in England and Wales.

11L Enforcement orders: making

(1) Before making an enforcement order as regards a person in breach of a provision of a child arrangements order, the court must be satisfied that—

   (a) making the enforcement order proposed is necessary to secure the person's compliance with the child arrangements order or any child arrangements order that has effect in its place;

   (b) the likely effect on the person of the enforcement order proposed to be made is proportionate to the seriousness of the breach.

(2) Before making an enforcement order, the court must satisfy itself that provision for the person to work under an unpaid work requirement imposed by an enforcement order can be made in the local justice area in which the person in breach resides or will reside.

(3) Before making an enforcement order as regards a person in breach of a provision of a child arrangements order, the court must obtain and consider information about the person and the likely effect of the enforcement order on him.

(4) Information about the likely effect of the enforcement order may, in particular, include information as to—

   (a) any conflict with the person's religious beliefs;

   (b) any interference with the times (if any) at which he normally works or attends an educational establishment.

(5) A court that proposes to make an enforcement order may ask an officer of the Service or a Welsh family proceedings officer to provide the court with information as to the matters in subsections (2) and (3).

(6) It shall be the duty of the officer of the Service or Welsh family proceedings officer to comply with any request under this section.

(7) In making an enforcement order in relation to a child arrangements order, a court must take into account the welfare of the child who is the subject of the child arrangements order.

11M Enforcement orders: monitoring

(1) On making an enforcement order in relation to a person, the court is to ask an officer of the Service or a Welsh family proceedings officer

    (a) to monitor, or arrange for the monitoring of, the person's compliance with the unpaid work requirement imposed by the order;

    (b) to report to the court if a report under paragraph 8 of Schedule A1 is made in relation to the person;

    (c) to report to the court on such other matters relating to the person's compliance as may be specified in the request;

    (d) to report to the court if the person is, or becomes, unsuitable to perform work under the requirement.

(2) It shall be the duty of the officer of the Service or Welsh family proceedings officer to comply with any request under this section.

11N Enforcement orders: warning notices

Where the court makes an enforcement order, it is to attach to the order a notice warning of the consequences of failing to comply with the order.

11O Compensation for financial loss

(1) This section applies if a child arrangements order with respect to a child has been made.

(2) If the court is satisfied that—

    (a) an individual has failed to comply with a provision of the child arrangements order, and

    (b) a person falling within subsection (6) has suffered financial loss by reason of the breach,

it may make an order requiring the individual in breach to pay the person compensation in respect of his financial loss.

(3) But the court may not make an order under subsection (2) if it is satisfied that the individual in breach had a reasonable excuse for failing to comply with the particular provision of the child arrangements order.

(4) The burden of proof as to the matter mentioned in subsection (3) lies on the individual claiming to have had a reasonable excuse.

(5) An order under subsection (2) may be made only on an application by the person who claims to have suffered financial loss.

(6) A person falls within this subsection if he is—

    (a) a person who is, for the purposes of the child arrangements order, a person with whom the child concerned lives or is to live;

    (b) a person whose contact with the child concerned is provided for in the child arrangements order;

    (c) an individual subject to a condition under section 11(7)(b) or an activity condition imposed by the child arrangements order; or

    (d) the child concerned.

(7) Where the person proposing to apply for an order under subsection (2) is the child concerned, the child must obtain the leave of the court before making such an application.

(8) The court may grant leave to the child concerned only if it is satisfied that he has sufficient understanding to make the proposed application.

(9) The amount of compensation is to be determined by the court, but may not exceed the amount of the applicant's financial loss.

(10) In determining the amount of compensation payable by the individual in breach, the court must take into account the individual's financial circumstances.

(11) An amount ordered to be paid as compensation may be recovered by the applicant as a civil debt due to him.

(12) Subsection (2) has effect subject to the restrictions in section 11P.

(13) Proceedings in which any question of making an order under subsection (2) arises are to be regarded for the purposes of section 11(1) and (2) as proceedings in which a question arises with respect to a section 8 order.

(14) In exercising its powers under this section, a court is to take into account the welfare of the child concerned.

11P   Orders under section 11O(2): further provision

(1) A court may not make an order under section 11O(2) requiring an individual to pay compensation in respect of a failure by him to comply with a provision of a child arrangements order unless it is satisfied that before the failure occurred the individual had been given (in accordance with rules of court) a copy of, or otherwise informed of the terms of—

    (a) in the case of a failure to comply with a provision of a child arrangements order where the order was varied before the failure occurred, a notice under section 11I relating to the order varying the child arrangements order or, where more than one such order has been made, the last order preceding the failure in question;

    (b) in any other case, a notice under section 11I relating to the child arrangements order.

(2) A court may not make an order under section 11O(2) requiring an individual to pay compensation in respect of a failure by him to comply with a provision of a child arrangements order where the failure occurred before the individual attained the age of 18.

(3) A court may not make an order under section 11O(2) requiring an individual to pay compensation in respect of a failure by him to comply with a provision of a child arrangements order where the child arrangements order is an excepted order (within the meaning given by section 11B(4)).

12   Child arrangements orders and parental responsibility

(1) Where—

    (a) the court makes a child arrangements order with respect to a child,

    (b) the father of the child, or a woman who is a parent of the child by virtue of section 43 of the Human Fertilisation and Embryology Act 2008, is named in the order as a person with whom the child is to live, and

    (c) the father, or the woman, would not otherwise have parental responsibility for the child,

the court must also make an order under section 4 giving the father, or under section 4ZA giving the woman, that responsibility.

(1A) Where—

    (a) the court makes a child arrangements order with respect to a child,

    (b) the father of the child, or a woman who is a parent of the child by virtue of section 43 of the Human Fertilisation and Embryology Act 2008, is named in the order as a person with whom the child is to spend time or otherwise have contact but is not named in the order as a person with whom the child is to live, and

    (c) the father, or the woman, would not otherwise have parental responsibility for the child,

the court must decide whether it would be appropriate, in view of the provision made in the order with respect to the father or the woman, for him or her to have parental responsibility for the child and, if it decides that it would be appropriate for the father or the woman to have that responsibility, must also make an order under section 4 giving him, or under section 4ZA giving her, that responsibility.

(2) Where the court makes a child arrangements order and a person who is not a parent or guardian of the child concerned is named in the order as a person with whom the child is to live,

that person shall have parental responsibility for the child, while the order remains in force so far as providing for the child to live with that person.

(2A) Where the court makes a child arrangements order and—

    (a) a person who is not the parent or guardian of the child concerned is named in the order as a person with whom the child is to spend time or otherwise have contact, but

    (b) the person is not named in the order as a person with whom the child is to live,

the court may provide in the order for the person to have parental responsibility for the child while paragraphs (a) and (b) continue to be met in the person's case.

(3) Where a person has parental responsibility for a child as a result of subsection (2) or (2A), he shall not have the right—

    (b) to agree, or refuse to agree, to the making of an adoption order, or an order under section 84 of the Adoption and Children Act 2002 with respect to the child; or

    (c) to appoint a guardian for the child.

(4) Where subsection (1) requires the court to make an order under section 4 or 4ZA in respect of a parent of a child, the court shall not bring that order to an end at any time while the child arrangements order concerned remains in force so far as providing for the child to live with that parent.

13   Change of child's name or removal from jurisdiction

(1) Where a child arrangements order to which subsection (4) applies is in force with respect to a child, no person may—

    (a) cause the child to be known by a new surname; or

    (b) remove him from the United Kingdom;

without either the written consent of every person who has parental responsibility for the child or the leave of the court.

(2) Subsection (1)(b) does not prevent the removal of a child, for a period of less than one month, by a person named in the child arrangements order as a person with whom the child is to live.

(3) In making a child arrangements order to which subsection (4) applies, the court may grant the leave required by subsection (1)(b), either generally or for specified purposes.

(4) This subsection applies to a child arrangements order if the arrangements regulated by the order consist of, or include, arrangements which relate to either or both of the following—

    (a) with whom the child concerned is to live, and

    (b) when the child is to live with any person.

…

Special guardianship

14A   Special guardianship orders

(1) A 'special guardianship order' is an order appointing one or more individuals to be a child's 'special guardian' (or special guardians).

(2) A special guardian—

    (a) must be aged eighteen or over; and

    (b) must not be a parent of the child in question,

and subsections (3) to (6) are to be read in that light.

(3) The court may make a special guardianship order with respect to any child on the application of an individual who—

    (a) is entitled to make such an application with respect to the child; or

    (b) has obtained the leave of the court to make the application,

or on the joint application of more than one such individual.

(4) Section 9(3) applies in relation to an application for leave to apply for a special guardianship order as it applies in relation to an application for leave to apply for a section 8 order.

(5) The individuals who are entitled to apply for a special guardianship order with respect to a child are—

    (a) any guardian of the child;

    (b) any individual who is named in a child arrangements order as a person with whom the child is to live;

    (c) any individual listed in subsection (5)(b) or (c) of section 10 (as read with subsection (10) of that section);

    (d) a local authority foster parent with whom the child has lived for a period of at least one year immediately preceding the application;

    (e) a relative with whom the child has lived for a period of at least one year immediately preceding the application.

(6) The court may also make a special guardianship order with respect to a child in any family proceedings in which a question arises with respect to the welfare of the child if—

    (a) an application for the order has been made by an individual who falls within subsection (3)(a) or (b) (or more than one such individual jointly); or

    (b) the court considers that a special guardianship order should be made even though no such application has been made.

(7) No individual may make an application under subsection (3) or (6)(a) unless, before the beginning of the period of three months ending with the date of the application, he has given written notice of his intention to make the application—

    (a) if the child in question is being looked after by a local authority, to that local authority, or

    (b) otherwise, to the local authority in whose area the individual is ordinarily resident.

(8) On receipt of such a notice, the local authority must investigate the matter and prepare a report for the court dealing with—

    (a) the suitability of the applicant to be a special guardian;

    (b) such matters (if any) as may be prescribed by the Secretary of State; and

    (c) any other matter which the local authority consider to be relevant.

(9) The court may itself ask a local authority to conduct such an investigation and prepare such a report, and the local authority must do so.

(10) The local authority may make such arrangements as they see fit for any person to act on their behalf in connection with conducting an investigation or preparing a report referred to in subsection (8) or (9).

(11) The court may not make a special guardianship order unless it has received a report dealing with the matters referred to in subsection (8).

(12) Subsections (8) and (9) of section 10 apply in relation to special guardianship orders as they apply in relation to section 8 orders.

(13) This section is subject to section 29(5) and (6) of the Adoption and Children Act 2002.

14B Special guardianship orders: making

(1) Before making a special guardianship order, the court must consider whether, if the order were made—

    (a) a child arrangements order containing contact provision should also be made with respect to the child,

    (b) any section 8 order in force with respect to the child should be varied or discharged,

    (c) where provision contained in a child arrangements order made with respect to the child is not discharged, any enforcement order relating to that provision should be revoked, and

    (d) where an activity direction has been made—

        (i) in proceedings for the making, variation or discharge of a child arrangements order with respect to the child, or

        (ii) in other proceedings that relate to such an order,

        that direction should be discharged.

(1A) In subsection (1) 'contact provision' means provision which regulates arrangements relating to—

    (a) with whom a child is to spend time or otherwise have contact, or

    (b) when a child is to spend time or otherwise have contact with any person;

but in paragraphs (a) and (b) a reference to spending time or otherwise having contact with a person is to doing that otherwise than as a result of living with the person.

(2) On making a special guardianship order, the court may also—

    (a) give leave for the child to be known by a new surname;

    (b) grant the leave required by section 14C(3)(b), either generally or for specified purposes.

14C Special guardianship orders: effect

(1) The effect of a special guardianship order is that while the order remains in force—

    (a) a special guardian appointed by the order has parental responsibility for the child in respect of whom it is made; and

    (b) subject to any other order in force with respect to the child under this Act, a special guardian is entitled to exercise parental responsibility to the exclusion of any other person with parental responsibility for the child (apart from another special guardian).

(2) Subsection (1) does not affect—

    (a) the operation of any enactment or rule of law which requires the consent of more than one person with parental responsibility in a matter affecting the child; or

    (b) any rights which a parent of the child has in relation to the child's adoption or placement for adoption.

(3) While a special guardianship order is in force with respect to a child, no person may—

    (a) cause the child to be known by a new surname; or

    (b) remove him from the United Kingdom,

without either the written consent of every person who has parental responsibility for the child or the leave of the court.

(4) Subsection (3)(b) does not prevent the removal of a child, for a period of less than three months, by a special guardian of his.

(5) If the child with respect to whom a special guardianship order is in force dies, his special guardian must take reasonable steps to give notice of that fact to—

    (a) each parent of the child with parental responsibility; and

    (b) each guardian of the child,

but if the child has more than one special guardian, and one of them has taken such steps in relation to a particular parent or guardian, any other special guardian need not do so as respects that parent or guardian.

(6) This section is subject to section 29(7) of the Adoption and Children Act 2002.

14D Special guardianship orders: variation and discharge

(1) The court may vary or discharge a special guardianship order on the application of—

    (a) the special guardian (or any of them, if there are more than one);

    (b) any parent or guardian of the child concerned;

    (c) any individual who is named in a child arrangements order as a person with whom the child is to live;

    (d) any individual not falling within any of paragraphs (a) to (c) who has, or immediately before the making of the special guardianship order had, parental responsibility for the child;

    (e) the child himself; or

    (f) a local authority designated in a care order with respect to the child.

(2) In any family proceedings in which a question arises with respect to the welfare of a child with respect to whom a special guardianship order is in force, the court may also vary or discharge the special guardianship order if it considers that the order should be varied or discharged, even though no application has been made under subsection (1).

(3) The following must obtain the leave of the court before making an application under subsection (1)—

    (a) the child;

    (b) any parent or guardian of his;

    (c) any step-parent of his who has acquired, and has not lost, parental responsibility for him by virtue of section 4A;

    (d) any individual falling within subsection (1)(d) who immediately before the making of the special guardianship order had, but no longer has, parental responsibility for him.

(4) Where the person applying for leave to make an application under subsection (1) is the child, the court may only grant leave if it is satisfied that he has sufficient understanding to make the proposed application under subsection (1).

(5) The court may not grant leave to a person falling within subsection (3)(b)(c) or (d) unless it is satisfied that there has been a significant change in circumstances since the making of the special guardianship order.

14E   Special guardianship orders: supplementary

(1) In proceedings in which any question of making, varying or discharging a special guardianship order arises, the court shall (in the light of any provision in rules of court that is of the kind mentioned in section 11(2)(a) or (b))—

    (a) draw up a timetable with a view to determining the question without delay; and

    (b) give such directions as it considers appropriate for the purpose of ensuring, so far as is reasonably practicable, that the timetable is adhered to.

(2) Subsection (1) applies also in relation to proceedings in which any other question with respect to a special guardianship order arises.

(3) The power to make rules in subsection (2) of section 11 applies for the purposes of this section as it applies for the purposes of that.

(4) A special guardianship order, or an order varying one, may contain provisions which are to have effect for a specified period.

(5) Section 11(7) (apart from paragraph (c)) applies in relation to special guardianship orders and orders varying them as it applies in relation to section 8 orders.

14F   Special guardianship support services

(1) Each local authority must make arrangements for the provision within their area of special guardianship support services, which means—

    (a) counselling, advice and information; and

    (b) such other services as are prescribed,

in relation to special guardianship.

(2) The power to make regulations under subsection (1)(b) is to be exercised so as to secure that local authorities provide financial support.

(3) At the request of any of the following persons—

    (a) a child with respect to whom a special guardianship order is in force;

    (b) a special guardian;

    (c) a parent;

    (d) any other person who falls within a prescribed description,

a local authority may carry out an assessment of that person's needs for special guardianship support services (but, if the Secretary of State so provides in regulations, they must do so if he is a person of a prescribed description, or if his case falls within a prescribed description, or if both he and his case fall within prescribed descriptions).

(4) A local authority may, at the request of any other person, carry out an assessment of that person's needs for special guardianship support services.

(5) Where, as a result of an assessment, a local authority decide that a person has needs for special guardianship support services, they must then decide whether to provide any such services to that person.

(6) If—

    (a) a local authority decide to provide any special guardianship support services to a person, and

    (b) the circumstances fall within a prescribed description,

the local authority must prepare a plan in accordance with which special guardianship support services are to be provided to him, and keep the plan under review.

(7) The Secretary of State may by regulations make provision about assessments, preparing and reviewing plans, the provision of special guardianship support services in accordance with plans and reviewing the provision of special guardianship support services.

(8) The regulations may in particular make provision—

    (a) about the type of assessment which is to be carried out, or the way in which an assessment is to be carried out;

    (b) about the way in which a plan is to be prepared;

    (c) about the way in which, and the time at which, a plan or the provision of special guardianship support services is to be reviewed;

    (d) about the considerations to which a local authority are to have regard in carrying out an assessment or review or preparing a plan;

    (e) as to the circumstances in which a local authority may provide special guardianship support services subject to conditions (including conditions as to payment for the support or the repayment of financial support);

    (f) as to the consequences of conditions imposed by virtue of paragraph (e) not being met (including the recovery of any financial support provided);

    (g) as to the circumstances in which this section may apply to a local authority in respect of persons who are outside that local authority's area;

    (h) as to the circumstances in which a local authority may recover from another local authority the expenses of providing special guardianship support services to any person.

(9) A local authority may provide special guardianship support services (or any part of them) by securing their provision by—

    (a) another local authority; or

    (b) a person within a description prescribed in regulations of persons who may provide special guardianship support services,

and may also arrange with any such authority or person for that other authority or that person to carry out the local authority's functions in relation to assessments under this section.

(10) A local authority may carry out an assessment of the needs of any person for the purposes of this section at the same time as an assessment of his needs is made under any other provision of this Act or under any other enactment.

(11) Section 27 (co-operation between authorities) applies in relation to the exercise of functions of a local authority under this section as it applies in relation to the exercise of functions of a local authority under Part 3.

Financial relief

15 Orders for financial relief with respect to children

(1) Schedule 1 (which consists primarily of the re-enactment, with consequential amendments and minor modifications, of provisions of section 6 of the Family Law Reform Act 1969, the Guardianship of Minors Acts 1971 and 1973, the Children Act 1975 and of sections 15 and 16 of the Family Law Reform Act 1987) makes provision in relation to financial relief for children.

Family assistance orders

16 Family assistance orders

(1) Where, in any family proceedings, the court has power to make an order under this Part with respect to any child, it may (whether or not it makes such an order) make an order requiring—

    (a) an officer of the Service or a Welsh family proceedings officer to be made available; or

(b) a local authority to make an officer of the authority available,

to advise, assist and (where appropriate) befriend any person named in the order.

(2) The persons who may be named in an order under this section ('a family assistance order') are—

    (a) any parent, guardian or special guardian of the child;

    (b) any person with whom the child is living or who is named in a child arrangements order as a person with whom the child is to live, spend time or otherwise have contact;

    (c) the child himself.

(3) No court may make a family assistance order unless—

    (b) it has obtained the consent of every person to be named in the order other than the child.

(4) A family assistance order may direct—

    (a) the person named in the order; or

    (b) such of the persons named in the order as may be specified in the order,

to take such steps as may be so specified with a view to enabling the officer concerned to be kept informed of the address of any person named in the order and to be allowed to visit any such person.

(4A) If the court makes a family assistance order with respect to a child and the order is to be in force at the same time as contact provision contained in a child arrangements order made with respect to the child, the family assistance order may direct the officer concerned to give advice and assistance as regards establishing, improving and maintaining contact to such of the persons named in the order as may be specified in the order.

(4B) In subsection (4A) 'contact provision' means provision which regulates arrangements relating to—

    (a) with whom a child is to spend time or otherwise have contact, or

    (b) when a child is to spend time or otherwise have contact with any person.

(5) Unless it specifies a shorter period, a family assistance order shall have effect for a period of twelve months beginning with the day on which it is made.

(6) If the court makes a family assistance order with respect to a child and the order is to be in force at the same time as a section 8 order made with respect to the child, the family assistance order may direct the officer concerned to report to the court on such matters relating to the section 8 order as the court may require (including the question whether the section 8 order ought to be varied or discharged).

(7) A family assistance order shall not be made so as to require a local authority to make an officer of theirs available unless—

    (a) the authority agree; or

    (b) the child concerned lives or will live within their area.

16A Risk assessments

(1) This section applies to the following functions of officers of the Service or Welsh family proceedings officers—

    (a) any function in connection with family proceedings in which the court has power to make an order under this Part with respect to a child or in which a question with respect to such an order arises;

    (b) any function in connection with an order made by the court in such proceedings.

(2) If, in carrying out any function to which this section applies, an officer of the Service or a Welsh family proceedings officer is given cause to suspect that the child concerned is at risk of harm, he must—

    (a) make a risk assessment in relation to the child, and

    (b) provide the risk assessment to the court.

(3) A risk assessment, in relation to a child who is at risk of suffering harm of a particular sort, is an assessment of the risk of that harm being suffered by the child.

PART III LOCAL AUTHORITY SUPPORT FOR CHILDREN AND FAMILIES

Provision of services for children and their families

17 Provision of services for children in need, their families and others

(1) It shall be the general duty of every local authority (in addition to the other duties imposed on them by this Part)—

    (a) to safeguard and promote the welfare of children within their area who are in need; and

    (b) so far as is consistent with that duty, to promote the upbringing of such children by their families,

by providing a range and level of services appropriate to those children's needs.

(2) For the purpose principally of facilitating the discharge of their general duty under this section, every local authority shall have the specific duties and powers set out in Part 1 of Schedule 2.

(3) Any service provided by an authority in the exercise of functions conferred on them by this section may be provided for the family of a particular child in need or for any member of his family, if it is provided with a view to safeguarding or promoting the child's welfare.

(4) The appropriate national authority may by order amend any provision of Part I of Schedule 2 or add any further duty or power to those for the time being mentioned there.

(4A) Before determining what (if any) services to provide for a particular child in need in the exercise of functions conferred on them by this section, a local authority shall, so far as is reasonably practicable and consistent with the child's welfare—

    (a) ascertain the child's wishes and feelings regarding the provision of those services; and

    (b) give due consideration (having regard to his age and understanding) to such wishes and feelings of the child as they have been able to ascertain.

(5) Every local authority—

    (a) shall facilitate the provision by others (including in particular voluntary organisations) of services which it is a function of the authority to provide by virtue of this section, or section 18, 20, 22A to 22C, 23B to 23D, 24A or 24B; and

    (b) may make such arrangements as they see fit for any person to act on their behalf in the provision of any such service.

(6) The services provided by a local authority in the exercise of functions conferred on them by this section may include providing accommodation and giving assistance in kind or in cash.

(7) Assistance may be unconditional or subject to conditions as to the repayment of the assistance or of its value (in whole or in part).

(8) Before giving any assistance or imposing any conditions, a local authority shall have regard to the means of the child concerned and of each of his parents.

(9) No person shall be liable to make any repayment of assistance or of its value at any time when he is in receipt of universal credit (except in such circumstances as may be prescribed).

(10) For the purposes of this Part a child shall be taken to be in need if—

    (a) he is unlikely to achieve or maintain, or to have the opportunity of achieving or maintaining, a reasonable standard of health or development without the provision for him of services by a local authority under this Part;

    (b) his health or development is likely to be significantly impaired, or further impaired, without the provision for him of such services; or

    (c) he is disabled,

and 'family', in relation to such a child, includes any person who has parental responsibility for the child and any other person with whom he has been living.

(11) For the purposes of this Part, a child is disabled if he is blind, deaf or dumb or suffers from mental disorder of any kind or is substantially and permanently handicapped by illness, injury or congenital deformity or such other disability as may be prescribed; and in this Part—

'development' means physical, intellectual, emotional, social or behavioural development; and 'health' means physical or mental health.

17ZA Young carers' needs assessments: England

(1) A local authority in England must assess whether a young carer within their area has needs for support and, if so, what those needs are, if—

(a) it appears to the authority that the young carer may have needs for support, or

(b) the authority receive a request from the young carer or a parent of the young carer to assess the young carer's needs for support.

(2) An assessment under subsection (1) is referred to in this Part as a 'young carer's needs assessment'.

(3) In this Part 'young carer' means a person under 18 who provides or intends to provide care for another person (but this is qualified by section 17ZB(3)).

(4) Subsection (1) does not apply in relation to a young carer if the local authority have previously carried out a care-related assessment of the young carer in relation to the same person cared for.

(5) But subsection (1) does apply (and so a young carer's needs assessment must be carried out) if it appears to the authority that the needs or circumstances of the young carer or the person cared for have changed since the last care-related assessment.

(6) 'Care-related assessment' means—

(a) a young carer's needs assessment;

(b) an assessment under any of the following—

(i) section 1 of the Carers (Recognition and Services) Act 1995;

(ii) section 1 of the Carers and Disabled Children Act 2000;

(iii) section 4(3) of the Community Care (Delayed Discharges) Act 2003.

(7) A young carer's needs assessment must include an assessment of whether it is appropriate for the young carer to provide, or continue to provide, care for the person in question, in the light of the young carer's needs for support, other needs and wishes.

(8) A local authority, in carrying out a young carer's needs assessment, must have regard to—

(a) the extent to which the young carer is participating in or wishes to participate in education, training or recreation, and

(b) the extent to which the young carer works or wishes to work.

(9) A local authority, in carrying out a young carer's needs assessment, must involve—

(a) the young carer,

(b) the young carer's parents, and

(c) any person who the young carer or a parent of the young carer requests the authority to involve.

(10) A local authority that have carried out a young carer's needs assessment must give a written record of the assessment to—

(a) the young carer,

(b) the young carer's parents, and

(c) any person to whom the young carer or a parent of the young carer requests the authority to give a copy.

(11) Where the person cared for is under 18, the written record must state whether the local authority consider him or her to be a child in need.

(12) A local authority in England must take reasonable steps to identify the extent to which there are young carers within their area who have needs for support.

17ZB Young carers' needs assessments: supplementary

(1) This section applies for the purposes of section 17ZA.

(2) 'Parent', in relation to a young carer, includes—

(a) a parent of the young carer who does not have parental responsibility for the young carer, and

(b) a person who is not a parent of the young carer but who has parental responsibility for the young carer.

(3) A person is not a young carer if the person provides or intends to provide care—

(a) under or by virtue of a contract, or

(b) as voluntary work.

(4) But in a case where the local authority consider that the relationship between the person cared for and the person under 18 providing or intending to provide care is such that it would be appropriate for the person under 18 to be regarded as a young carer, that person is to be regarded as such (and subsection (3) is therefore to be ignored in that case).

(5) The references in section 17ZA and this section to providing care include a reference to providing practical or emotional support.

(6) Where a local authority—

(a) are required to carry out a young carer's needs assessment, and

(b) are required or have decided to carry out some other assessment of the young carer or of the person cared for;

the local authority may, subject to subsection (7), combine the assessments.

(7) A young carer's needs assessment may be combined with an assessment of the person cared for only if the young carer and the person cared for agree.

(8) The Secretary of State may by regulations make further provision about carrying out a young carer's needs assessment; the regulations may, in particular—

(a) specify matters to which a local authority is to have regard in carrying out a young carer's needs assessment;

(b) specify matters which a local authority is to determine in carrying out a young carer's needs assessment;

(c) make provision about the manner in which a young carer's needs assessment is to be carried out;

(d) make provision about the form a young carer's needs assessment is to take.

(9) The Secretary of State may by regulations amend the list in section 17ZA(6)(b) so as to—

(a) add an entry,

(b) remove an entry, or

(c) vary an entry.

17ZC Consideration of young carers' needs assessments

A local authority that carry out a young carer's needs assessment must consider the assessment and decide—

(a) whether the young carer has needs for support in relation to the care which he or she provides or intends to provide;

(b) if so, whether those needs could be satisfied (wholly or partly) by services which the authority may provide under section 17; and

(c) if they could be so satisfied, whether or not to provide any such services in relation to the young carer.

...

17A Direct payments

(1) The appropriate national authority may by regulations make provision for and in connection with requiring or authorising the responsible authority in the case of a person of a prescribed description who falls within subsection (2) to make, with that person's consent, such payments to him as they may determine in accordance with the regulations in respect of his securing the provision of the service mentioned in that subsection.

(2) A person falls within this subsection if he is—

(a) a person with parental responsibility for a disabled child,

(b) a disabled person with parental responsibility for a child, or

(c) a disabled child aged 16 or 17,

and a local authority ('the responsible authority') have decided for the purposes of section 17 that the child's needs (or, if he is such a disabled child, his needs) call for the provision by them of a service in exercise of functions conferred on them under that section.

(3) Subsections (3) to (5) and (7) of section 57 of the 2001 Act shall apply, with any necessary modifications, in relation to regulations under this section as they apply in relation to regulations under that section.

(3A) The modifications mentioned in subsection (3) include, in particular, the omission of the provisions inserted into section 57 of the 2001 Act by the Health and Social Care Act 2008.

(4) Regulations under this section shall provide that, where payments are made under the regulations to a person falling within subsection (5)—

(a) the payments shall be made at the rate mentioned in subsection (4)(a) of section 57 of the 2001 Act (as applied by subsection (3)); and

(b) subsection (4)(b) of that section shall not apply.

(5) A person falls within this subsection if he is—

(a) a person falling within subsection (2)(a) or (b) and the child in question is aged 16 or 17, or

(b) a person who is in receipt of universal credit (except in such circumstances as may be prescribed).

(6) In this section—

'the 2001 Act' means the Health and Social Care Act 2001;

'disabled' in relation to an adult has the same meaning as that given by section 17(11) in relation to a child;

'prescribed' means specified in or determined in accordance with regulations under this section (and has the same meaning in the provisions of the 2001 Act mentioned in subsection (3) as they apply by virtue of that subsection).

17B Vouchers for persons with parental responsibility for disabled children

(1) The appropriate national authority may by regulations make provision for the issue by a local authority of vouchers to a person with parental responsibility for a disabled child.

(2) 'Voucher' means a document whereby, if the local authority agrees with the person with parental responsibility that it would help him care for the child if the person with parental responsibility had a break from caring, that person may secure the temporary provision of services for the child under section 17.

(3) The regulations may, in particular, provide—

(a) for the value of a voucher to be expressed in terms of money, or of the delivery of a service for a period of time, or both;

(b) for the person who supplies a service against a voucher, or for the arrangement under which it is supplied, to be approved by the local authority;

(c) for a maximum period during which a service (or a service of a prescribed description) can be provided against a voucher.

18 Day care for pre-school and other children

(1) Every local authority shall provide such day care for children in need within their area who are—

(a) aged five or under; and

(b) not yet attending schools, as is appropriate.

(2) A local authority in Wales may provide day care for children within their area who satisfy the conditions mentioned in subsection (1)(a) and (b) even though they are not in need.

(3) A local authority may provide facilities (including training, advice, guidance and counselling) for those—

(a) caring for children in day care; or

(b) who at any time accompany such children while they are in day care.

(4) In this section 'day care' means any form of care or supervised activity provided for children during the day (whether or not it is provided on a regular basis).

(5) Every local authority shall provide for children in need within their area who are attending any school such care or supervised activities as is appropriate—

(a) outside school hours; or

(b) during school holidays.

(6) A local authority in Wales may provide such care or supervised activities for children within their area who are attending any school even though those children are not in need.

(7) In this section 'supervised activity' means an activity supervised by a responsible person.

...

Provision of accommodation for children

20 Provision of accommodation for children: general

(1) Every local authority shall provide accommodation for any child in need within their area who appears to them to require accommodation as a result of—

(a) there being no person who has parental responsibility for him;

(b) his being lost or having been abandoned; or

(c) the person who has been caring for him being prevented (whether or not permanently, and for whatever reason) from providing him with suitable accommodation or care.

(2) Where a local authority provide accommodation under subsection (1) for a child who is ordinarily resident in the area of another local authority, that other local authority may take over the provision of accommodation for the child within—

(a) three months of being notified in writing that the child is being provided with accommodation; or

(b) such other longer period as may be prescribed.

(3) Every local authority shall provide accommodation for any child in need within their area who has reached the age of sixteen and whose welfare the authority consider is likely to be seriously prejudiced if they do not provide him with accommodation.

(4) A local authority may provide accommodation for any child within their area (even though a person who has parental responsibility for him is able to provide him with accommodation) if they consider that to do so would safeguard or promote the child's welfare.

(5) A local authority may provide accommodation for any person who has reached the age of sixteen but is under twenty-one in any community home which takes children who have reached the age of sixteen if they consider that to do so would safeguard or promote his welfare.

(6) Before providing accommodation under this section, a local authority shall, so far as is reasonably practicable and consistent with the child's welfare—

(a) ascertain the child's wishes and feelings regarding the provision of accommodation; and

(b) give due consideration (having regard to his age and understanding) to such wishes and feelings of the child as they have been able to ascertain.

(7) A local authority may not provide accommodation under this section for any child if any person who—

(a) has parental responsibility for him;

(b) is willing and able to—

(i) provide accommodation for him; or

(ii) arrange for accommodation to be provided for him, objects.

(8) Any person who has parental responsibility for a child may at any time remove the child from accommodation provided by or on behalf of the local authority under this section.

(9) Subsections (7) and (8) do not apply while any person—

(a) who is named in a child arrangements order as a person with whom the child is to live;

(aa) who is a special guardian of the child; or

(b) who has care of the child by virtue of an order made in the exercise of the High Court's inherent jurisdiction with respect to children, agrees to the child being looked after in accommodation provided by or on behalf of the local authority.

(10) Where there is more than one such person as is mentioned in subsection (9), all of them must agree.

(11) Subsections (7) and (8) do not apply where a child who has reached the age of sixteen agrees to being provided with accommodation under this section.

21   Provision of accommodation for children in police protection or detention or on remand, etc.

(1) Every local authority shall make provision for the reception and accommodation of children who are removed or kept away from home under Part V.

(2) Every local authority shall receive, and provide accommodation for, children—

   (a) in police protection whom they are requested to receive under section 46(3)(f);

   (b) whom they are requested to receive under section 38(6) of the Police and Criminal Evidence Act 1984...

(2A) In subsection (2)(c)(iii), the following terms have the same meanings as in Part 1 of the Criminal Justice and Immigration Act 2008 (see section 7 of that Act)—

'local authority residence requirement';

'youth rehabilitation order';

'youth rehabilitation order with fostering'.

(3) Where a child has been—

   (a) removed under Part V; or

   (b) detained under section 38 of the Police and Criminal Evidence Act 1984,

and he is not being provided with accommodation by a local authority or in a hospital vested in the Secretary of State or the Welsh Ministers or otherwise made available pursuant to arrangements made by the Secretary of State, the National Health Service Commissioning Board or a clinical commissioning group under the National Health Service Act 2006 or a Local Health Board, any reasonable expenses of accommodating him shall be recoverable from the local authority in whose area he is ordinarily resident.

Duties of local authorities in relation to children looked after by them

22   General duty of local authority in relation to children looked after by them

(1) In this Act, any reference to a child who is looked after by a local authority is a reference to a child who is—

   (a) in their care; or

   (b) provided with accommodation by the authority in the exercise of any functions (in particular those under this Act) which are social services functions within the meaning of the Local Authority Social Services Act 1970, apart from functions under sections 17, 23B and 24B.

(2) In subsection (1) 'accommodation' means accommodation which is provided for a continuous period of more than 24 hours.

(3) It shall be the duty of a local authority looking after any child—

   (a) to safeguard and promote his welfare; and

   (b) to make such use of services available for children cared for by their own parents as appears to the authority reasonable in his case.

(3A) The duty of a local authority under subsection (3)(a) to safeguard and promote the welfare of a child looked after by them includes in particular a duty to promote the child's educational achievement.

(3B) A local authority in England must appoint at least one person for the purpose of discharging the duty imposed by virtue of subsection (3A).

(3C) A person appointed by a local authority under subsection (3B) must be an officer employed by that authority or another local authority in England.

(4) Before making any decision with respect to a child whom they are looking after, or proposing to look after, a local authority shall, so far as is reasonably practicable, ascertain the wishes and feelings of—

(a) the child;

(b) his parents;

(c) any person who is not a parent of his but who has parental responsibility for him; and

(d) any other person whose wishes and feelings the authority consider to be relevant, regarding the matter to be decided.

(5) In making any such decision a local authority shall give due consideration—

(a) having regard to his age and understanding, to such wishes and feelings of the child as they have been able to ascertain;

(b) to such wishes and feelings of any person mentioned in subsection (4)(b) to (d) as they have been able to ascertain; and

(c) to the child's religious persuasion, racial origin and cultural and linguistic background.

(6) If it appears to a local authority that it is necessary, for the purpose of protecting members of the public from serious injury, to exercise their powers with respect to a child whom they are looking after in a manner which may not be consistent with their duties under this section, they may do so.

(7) If the appropriate national authority considers it necessary, for the purpose of protecting members of the public from serious injury, to give directions to a local authority with respect to the exercise of their powers with respect to a child whom they are looking after, the appropriate national authority may give such directions to the local authority.

(8) Where any such directions are given to an authority they shall comply with them even though doing so is inconsistent with their duties under this section.

22A Provision of accommodation for children in care

When a child is in the care of a local authority, it is their duty to provide the child with accommodation.

22B Maintenance of looked after children

It is the duty of a local authority to maintain a child they are looking after in other respects apart from the provision of accommodation.

22C Ways in which looked after children are to be accommodated and maintained

(1) This section applies where a local authority are looking after a child ('C').

(2) The local authority must make arrangements for C to live with a person who falls within subsection (3) (but subject to subsection (4)).

(3) A person ('P') falls within this subsection if—

(a) P is a parent of C;

(b) P is not a parent of C but has parental responsibility for C; or

(c) in a case where C is in the care of the local authority and there was a child arrangements order in force with respect to C immediately before the care order was made, P was a person named in the child arrangements order as a person with whom C was to live.

(4) Subsection (2) does not require the local authority to make arrangements of the kind mentioned in that subsection if doing so—

(a) would not be consistent with C's welfare; or

(b) would not be reasonably practicable.

(5) If the local authority are unable to make arrangements under subsection (2), they must place C in the placement which is, in their opinion, the most appropriate placement available.

(6) In subsection (5) 'placement' means—

(a) placement with an individual who is a relative, friend or other person connected with C and who is also a local authority foster parent;

(b) placement with a local authority foster parent who does not fall within paragraph (a);

(c) placement in a children's home in respect of which a person is registered under Part 2 of the Care Standards Act 2000; or

(d) subject to section 22D, placement in accordance with other arrangements which comply with any regulations made for the purposes of this section.

(7) In determining the most appropriate placement for C, the local authority must, subject to subsection (9B) and the other provisions of this Part (in particular, to their duties under section 22)—

(a) give preference to a placement falling within paragraph (a) of subsection (6) over placements falling within the other paragraphs of that subsection;

(b) comply, so far as is reasonably practicable in all the circumstances of C's case, with the requirements of subsection (8); and

(c) comply with subsection (9) unless that is not reasonably practicable.

(8) The local authority must ensure that the placement is such that—

(a) it allows C to live near C's home;

(b) it does not disrupt C's education or training;

(c) if C has a sibling for whom the local authority are also providing accommodation, it enables C and the sibling to live together;

(d) if C is disabled, the accommodation provided is suitable to C's particular needs.

(9) The placement must be such that C is provided with accommodation within the local authority's area.

(9A) Subsection (9B) applies (subject to subsection (9C)) where the local authority are a local authority in England and—

(a) are considering adoption for C, or

(b) are satisfied that C ought to be placed for adoption but are not authorised under section 19 of the Adoption and Children Act 2002 (placement with parental consent) or by virtue of section 21 of that Act (placement orders) to place C for adoption.

(9B) Where this subsection applies—

(a) subsections (7) to (9) do not apply to the local authority,

(b) the local authority must consider placing C with an individual within subsection (6)(a), and

(c) where the local authority decide that a placement with such an individual is not the most appropriate placement for C, the local authority must consider placing C with a local authority foster parent who has been approved as a prospective adopter.

(9C) Subsection (9B) does not apply where the local authority have applied for a placement order under section 21 of the Adoption and Children Act 2002 in respect of C and the application has been refused.

(10) The local authority may determine—

(a) the terms of any arrangements they make under subsection (2) in relation to C (including terms as to payment); and

(b) the terms on which they place C with a local authority foster parent (including terms as to payment but subject to any order made under section 49 of the Children Act 2004).

(11) The appropriate national authority may make regulations for, and in connection with, the purposes of this section.

(12) In this Act 'local authority foster parent' means a person who is approved as a local authority foster parent in accordance with regulations made by virtue of paragraph 12F of Schedule 2.

22D   Review of child's case before making alternative arrangements for accommodation

(1) Where a local authority are providing accommodation for a child ('C') other than by arrangements under section 22C(6)(d), they must not make such arrangements for C unless they

have decided to do so in consequence of a review of C's case carried out in accordance with regulations made under section 26.

(2) But subsection (1) does not prevent a local authority making arrangements for C under section 22C(6)(d) if they are satisfied that in order to safeguard C's welfare it is necessary—

(a) to make such arrangements; and

(b) to do so as a matter of urgency.

22E Children's homes provided by appropriate national authority

Where a local authority place a child they are looking after in a children's home provided, equipped and maintained by an appropriate national authority under section 82(5), they must do so on such terms as that national authority may from time to time determine.

22F Regulations as to children looked after by local authorities

Part 2 of Schedule 2 has effect for the purposes of making further provision as to children looked after by local authorities and in particular as to the regulations which may be made under section 22C(11).

22G General duty of local authority to secure sufficient accommodation for looked after children

(1) It is the general duty of a local authority to take steps that secure, so far as reasonably practicable, the outcome in subsection (2).

(2) The outcome is that the local authority are able to provide the children mentioned in subsection (3) with accommodation that—

(a) is within the authority's area; and

(b) meets the needs of those children.

(3) The children referred to in subsection (2) are those—

(a) that the local authority are looking after,

(b) in respect of whom the authority are unable to make arrangements under section 22C(2), and

(c) whose circumstances are such that it would be consistent with their welfare for them to be provided with accommodation that is in the authority's area.

(4) In taking steps to secure the outcome in subsection (2), the local authority must have regard to the benefit of having—

(a) a number of accommodation providers in their area that is, in their opinion, sufficient to secure that outcome; and

(b) a range of accommodation in their area capable of meeting different needs that is, in their opinion, sufficient to secure that outcome.

(5) In this section 'accommodation providers' means—

local authority foster parents; and children's homes in respect of which a person is registered under Part 2 of the Care Standards Act 2000.

Visiting

23ZA Duty of local authority to ensure visits to, and contact with, looked after children and others

(1) This section applies to—

(a) a child looked after by a local authority;

(b) a child who was looked after by a local authority but who has ceased to be looked after by them as a result of prescribed circumstances.

(2) It is the duty of the local authority—

(a) to ensure that a person to whom this section applies is visited by a representative of the authority ('a representative');

(b) to arrange for appropriate advice, support and assistance to be available to a person to whom this section applies who seeks it from them.

(3) The duties imposed by subsection (2)—

(a) are to be discharged in accordance with any regulations made for the purposes of this section by the appropriate national authority;

(b) are subject to any requirement imposed by or under an enactment applicable to the place in which the person to whom this section applies is accommodated.

(4) Regulations under this section for the purposes of subsection (3)(a) may make provision about—

(a) the frequency of visits;

(b) circumstances in which a person to whom this section applies must be visited by a representative; and

(c) the functions of a representative.

(5) In choosing a representative a local authority must satisfy themselves that the person chosen has the necessary skills and experience to perform the functions of a representative.

23ZB Independent visitors for children looked after by a local authority

(1) A local authority looking after a child must appoint an independent person to be the child's visitor if—

(a) the child falls within a description prescribed in regulations made by the appropriate national authority; or

(b) in any other case, it appears to them that it would be in the child's interests to do so.

(2) A person appointed under this section must visit, befriend and advise the child.

(3) A person appointed under this section is entitled to recover from the appointing authority any reasonable expenses incurred by that person for the purposes of that person's functions under this section.

(4) A person's appointment as a visitor in pursuance of this section comes to an end if—

(a) the child ceases to be looked after by the local authority;

(b) the person resigns the appointment by giving notice in writing to the appointing authority; or

(c) the authority give him notice in writing that they have terminated it.

(5) The ending of such an appointment does not affect any duty under this section to make a further appointment.

(6) Where a local authority propose to appoint a visitor for a child under this section, the appointment shall not be made if—

(a) the child objects to it; and

(b) the authority are satisfied that the child has sufficient understanding to make an informed decision.

(7) Where a visitor has been appointed for a child under this section, the local authority shall terminate the appointment if—

(a) the child objects to its continuing; and

(b) the authority are satisfied that the child has sufficient understanding to make an informed decision.

(8) If the local authority give effect to a child's objection under subsection (6) or (7) and the objection is to having anyone as the child's visitor, the authority does not have to propose to appoint another person under subsection (1) until the objection is withdrawn.

(9) The appropriate national authority may make regulations as to the circumstances in which a person is to be regarded for the purposes of this section as independent of the appointing authority.

Advice and assistance for certain children and young persons

23A The responsible authority and relevant children

(1) The responsible local authority shall have the functions set out in section 23B in respect of a relevant child.

(2) In subsection (1) 'relevant child' means (subject to subsection (3)) a child who—

    (a) is not being looked after by any local authority;

    (b) was, before last ceasing to be looked after, an eligible child for the purposes of paragraph 19B of Schedule 2; and

    (c) is aged sixteen or seventeen.

(3) The appropriate national authority may prescribe—

    (a) additional categories of relevant children; and

    (b) categories of children who are not to be relevant children despite falling within subsection (2).

(4) In subsection (1) the 'responsible local authority' is the one which last looked after the child.

(5) If under subsection (3)(a) the appropriate national authority prescribes a category of relevant children which includes children who do not fall within subsection (2)(b) (for example, because they were being looked after by a local authority in Scotland), the appropriate national authority may in the regulations also provide for which local authority is to be the responsible local authority for those children.

23B Additional functions of the responsible authority in respect of relevant children

(1) It is the duty of each local authority to take reasonable steps to keep in touch with a relevant child for whom they are the responsible authority, whether he is within their area or not.

(2) It is the duty of each local authority to appoint a personal adviser for each relevant child (if they have not already done so under paragraph 19C of Schedule 2).

(3) It is the duty of each local authority, in relation to any relevant child who does not already have a pathway plan prepared for the purposes of paragraph 19B of Schedule 2—

    (a) to carry out an assessment of his needs with a view to determining what advice, assistance and support it would be appropriate for them to provide him under this Part; and

    (b) to prepare a pathway plan for him.

    ...

(8) The responsible local authority shall safeguard and promote the child's welfare and, unless they are satisfied that his welfare does not require it, support him by—

    (a) maintaining him;

    (b) providing him with or maintaining him in suitable accommodation; and

    (c) providing support of such other descriptions as may be prescribed.

(9) Support under subsection (8) may be in cash.

(10) The appropriate national authority may by regulations make provision about the meaning of 'suitable accommodation' and in particular about the suitability of landlords or other providers of accommodation.

(11) If the local authority have lost touch with a relevant child, despite taking reasonable steps to keep in touch, they must without delay—

    (a) consider how to re-establish contact; and

    (b) take reasonable steps to do so,

and while the child is still a relevant child must continue to take such steps until they succeed.

(12) Subsections (7) to (9) of section 17 apply in relation to support given under this section as they apply in relation to assistance given under that section.

(13) Subsections (4) and (5) of section 22 apply in relation to any decision by a local authority for the purposes of this section as they apply in relation to the decisions referred to in that section.

23C Continuing functions in respect of former relevant children

(1) Each local authority shall have the duties provided for in this section towards—

    (a) a person who has been a relevant child for the purposes of section 23A (and would be one if he were under eighteen), and in relation to whom they were the last responsible authority; and

    (b) a person who was being looked after by them when he attained the age of eighteen, and immediately before ceasing to be looked after was an eligible child, and in this section such a person is referred to as a 'former relevant child'.

  (2) It is the duty of the local authority to take reasonable steps—

    (a) to keep in touch with a former relevant child whether he is within their area or not; and

    (b) if they lose touch with him, to re-establish contact.

  (3) It is the duty of the local authority—

    (a) to continue the appointment of a personal adviser for a former relevant child; and

    (b) to continue to keep his pathway plan under regular review.

  (4) It is the duty of the local authority to give a former relevant child—

    (a) assistance of the kind referred to in section 24B(1), to the extent that his welfare requires it;

    (b) assistance of the kind referred to in section 24B(2), to the extent that his welfare and his educational or training needs require it;

    (c) other assistance, to the extent that his welfare requires it.

  (5) The assistance given under subsection (4)(c) may be in kind or, in exceptional circumstances, in cash.

  (5A) It is the duty of the local authority to pay the relevant amount to a former relevant child who pursues higher education in accordance with a pathway plan prepared for that person.

  (5B) The appropriate national authority may by regulations—

    (a) prescribe the relevant amount for the purposes of subsection (5A);

    (b) prescribe the meaning of 'higher education' for those purposes;

    (c) make provision as to the payment of the relevant amount;

    (d) make provision as to the circumstances in which the relevant amount (or any part of it) may be recovered by the local authority from a former relevant child to whom a payment has been made.

  (5C) The duty set out in subsection (5A) is without prejudice to that set out in subsection (4)(b).

  (6) Subject to subsection (7), the duties set out in subsections (2), (3) and (4) subsist until the former relevant child reaches the age of twenty-one.

  (7) If the former relevant child's pathway plan sets out a programme of education or training which extends beyond his twenty-first birthday—

    (a) the duty set out in subsection (4)(b) continues to subsist for so long as the former relevant child continues to pursue that programme; and

    (b) the duties set out in subsections (2) and (3) continue to subsist concurrently with that duty.

  (8) For the purposes of subsection (7)(a) there shall be disregarded any interruption in a former relevant child's pursuance of a programme of education or training if the local authority are satisfied that he will resume it as soon as is reasonably practicable.

  (9) Section 24B(5) applies in relation to a person being given assistance under subsection (4)(b) or who is in receipt of a payment under subsection (5A) as it applies in relation to a person to whom section 24B(3) applies.

  (10) Subsections (7) to (9) of section 17 apply in relation to assistance given under this section as they apply in relation to assistance given under that section.

23CZA Arrangements for certain former relevant children to continue to live with former foster parents

  (1) Each local authority in England have the duties provided for in subsection (3) in relation to a staying put arrangement.

  (2) A 'staying put arrangement' is an arrangement under which—

    (a) a person who is a former relevant child by virtue of section 23C(1)(b), and

    (b) a person (a 'former foster parent') who was the former relevant child's local authority foster parent immediately before the former relevant child ceased to be looked after by the local authority,

continue to live together after the former relevant child has ceased to be looked after.

(3) It is the duty of the local authority (in discharging the duties in section 23C(3) and by other means)—

    (a) to monitor the staying put arrangement, and

    (b) to provide advice, assistance and support to the former relevant child and the former foster parent with a view to maintaining the staying put arrangement.

(4) Support provided to the former foster parent under subsection (3)(b) must include financial support.

(5) Subsection (3)(b) does not apply if the local authority consider that the staying put arrangement is not consistent with the welfare of the former relevant child.

(6) The duties set out in subsection (3) subsist until the former relevant child reaches the age of 21.

23CA   Further assistance to pursue education or training

(1) This section applies to a person if—

    (a) he is under the age of twenty-five or of such lesser age as may be prescribed by the appropriate national authority;

    (b) he is a former relevant child (within the meaning of section 23C) towards whom the duties imposed by subsections (2), (3) and (4) of that section no longer subsist; and

    (c) he has informed the responsible local authority that he is pursuing, or wishes to pursue, a programme of education or training.

(2) It is the duty of the responsible local authority to appoint a personal adviser for a person to whom this section applies.

(3) It is the duty of the responsible local authority—

    (a) to carry out an assessment of the needs of a person to whom this section applies with a view to determining what assistance (if any) it would be appropriate for them to provide to him under this section; and

    (b) to prepare a pathway plan for him.

(4) It is the duty of the responsible local authority to give assistance of a kind referred to subsection (5) to a person to whom this section applies to the extent that his educational or training needs require it.

(5) The kinds of assistance are—

    (a) contributing to expenses incurred by him in living near the place where he is, or will be, receiving education or training; or

    (b) making a grant to enable him to meet expenses connected with his education and training.

(6) If a person to whom this section applies pursues a programme of education or training in accordance with the pathway plan prepared for him, the duties of the local authority under this section (and under any provision applicable to the pathway plan prepared under this section for that person) subsist for as long as he continues to pursue that programme.

(7) For the purposes of subsection (6), the local authority may disregard any interruption in the person's pursuance of a programme of education or training if they are satisfied that he will resume it as soon as is reasonably practicable.

(8) Subsections (7) to (9) of section 17 apply to assistance given to a person under this section as they apply to assistance given to or in respect of a child under that section, but with the omission in subsection (8) of the words 'and of each of his parents'.

(9) Subsection (5) of section 24B applies to a person to whom this section applies as it applies to a person to whom subsection (3) of that section applies.

(10) Nothing in this section affects the duty imposed by subsection (5A) of section 23C to the extent that it subsists in relation to a person to whom this section applies; but the duty to make a payment under that subsection may be taken into account in the assessment of the person's needs under subsection (3)(a).

(11) In this section 'the responsible local authority' means, in relation to a person to whom this section applies, the local authority which had the duties provided for in section 23C towards him.

Personal advisers and pathway plans

23D Personal advisers

(1) The appropriate national authority may by regulations require local authorities to appoint a personal adviser for children or young persons of a prescribed description who have reached the age of sixteen but not the age of twenty-five who are not—

(a) children who are relevant children for the purposes of section 23A;

(b) the young persons referred to in section 23C; or

(c) the children referred to in paragraph 19C of Schedule 2; or

(d) persons to whom section 23CA applies.

(2) Personal advisers appointed under or by virtue of this Part shall (in addition to any other functions) have such functions as the appropriate national authority prescribes.

23E Pathway plans

(1) In this Part, a reference to a 'pathway plan' is to a plan setting out—

(a) in the case of a plan prepared under paragraph 19B of Schedule 2—

(i) the advice, assistance and support which the local authority intend to provide a child under this Part, both while they are looking after him and later; and

(ii) when they might cease to look after him; and

(b) in the case of a plan prepared under section 23B or 23CA, the advice, assistance and support which the local authority intend to provide under this Part,

and dealing with such other matters (if any) as may be prescribed.

(1A) A local authority may carry out an assessment under section 23B(3) or 23CA(3) of a person's needs at the same time as any assessment of his needs is made under—

(a) the Chronically Sick and Disabled Persons Act 1970;

(b) Part 4 of the Education Act 1996 or Part 3 of the Children and Families Act 2014 (in the case of an assessment under section 23B(3));

(c) the Disabled Persons (Services, Consultation and Representation) Act 1986; or

(d) any other enactment.

(1B) The appropriate national authority may by regulations make provision as to assessments for the purposes of section 23B(3) or 23CA.

(1C) Regulations under subsection (1B) may in particular make provision about—

(a) who is to be consulted in relation to an assessment;

(b) the way in which an assessment is to be carried out, by whom and when;

(c) the recording of the results of an assessment;

(d) the considerations to which a local authority are to have regard in carrying out an assessment.

(1D) A local authority shall keep each pathway plan prepared by them under section 23B or 23CA under review.

(2) The appropriate national authority may by regulations make provision about pathway plans and their review.

24 Persons qualifying for advice and assistance

(1) In this Part 'a person qualifying for advice and assistance' means a person to whom subsection (1A) or (1B) applies.

(1A) This subsection applies to a person—

(a) who has reached the age of sixteen but not the age of twenty-one;

(b) with respect to whom a special guardianship order is in force (or, if he has reached the age of eighteen, was in force when he reached that age); and

(c) who was, immediately before the making of that order, looked after by a local authority.

(1B) This subsection applies to a person to whom subsection (1A) does not apply, and who—

(a) is under twenty-one; and

(b) at any time after reaching the age of sixteen but while still a child was, but is no longer, looked after, accommodated or fostered.

(2) In subsection (1B)(b), 'looked after, accommodated or fostered' means—

(a) looked after by a local authority;

(b) accommodated by or on behalf of a voluntary organisation;

(c) accommodated in a private children's home;

(d) accommodated for a consecutive period of at least three months—

(i) by any Local Health Board, Special Health Authority or by a local authority in the exercise of education functions, or

(ii) in any care home or independent hospital or in any accommodation provided pursuant to arrangements made by the Secretary of State, the National Health Service Commissioning Board or a clinical commissioning group under the National Health Service Act 2006 or by a National Health Service trust or an NHS foundation trust; or

(e) privately fostered.

(3) Subsection (2)(d) applies even if the period of three months mentioned there began before the child reached the age of sixteen.

(4) In the case of a person qualifying for advice and assistance by virtue of subsection (2)(a), it is the duty of the local authority which last looked after him to take such steps as they think appropriate to contact him at such times as they think appropriate with a view to discharging their functions under sections 24A and 24B.

(5) In each of sections 24A and 24B, the local authority under the duty or having the power mentioned there ('the relevant authority') is—

(za) in the case of a person to whom subsection (1A) applies, a local authority determined in accordance with regulations made by the appropriate national authority;

(a) in the case of a person qualifying for advice and assistance by virtue of subsection (2)(a), the local authority which last looked after him; or

(b) in the case of any other person qualifying for advice and assistance, the local authority within whose area the person is (if he has asked for help of a kind which can be given under section 24A or 24B).

24A Advice and assistance

(1) The relevant authority shall consider whether the conditions in subsection (2) are satisfied in relation to a person qualifying for advice and assistance.

(2) The conditions are that—

(a) he needs help of a kind which they can give under this section or section 24B; and

(b) in the case of a person to whom section 24(1A) applies, or to whom section 24(1B) applies and who was not being looked after by any local authority, they are satisfied that the person by whom he was being looked after does not have the necessary facilities for advising or befriending him.

(3) If the conditions are satisfied—

(a) they shall advise and befriend him if he is a person to whom section 24(1A) applies, or he is a person to whom section 24(1B) applies and he was being looked after by a local authority or was accommodated by or on behalf of a voluntary organisation; and

(b) in any other case they may do so.

(4) Where as a result of this section a local authority are under a duty, or are empowered, to advise and befriend a person, they may also give him assistance.

(5) The assistance may be in kind and, in exceptional circumstances, assistance may be given—

(a) by providing accommodation, if in the circumstances assistance may not be given in respect of the accommodation under section 24B, or

(b) in cash.

(6) Subsections (7) to (9) of section 17 apply in relation to assistance given under this section or section 24B as they apply in relation to assistance given under that section.

24B   Employment, education and training

(1) The relevant local authority may give assistance to any person who qualifies for advice and assistance by virtue of section 24(1A) or section 24(2)(a) by contributing to expenses incurred by him in living near the place where he is, or will be, employed or seeking employment.

(2) The relevant local authority may give assistance to a person to whom subsection (3) applies by—

    (a) contributing to expenses incurred by the person in question in living near the place where he is, or will be, receiving education or training; or

    (b) making a grant to enable him to meet expenses connected with his education or training.

(3) This subsection applies to any person who—

    (a) is under twenty-five; and

    (b) qualifies for advice and assistance by virtue of section 24(1A) or section 24(2)(a), or would have done so if he were under twenty-one.

(4) Where a local authority are assisting a person under subsection (2) they may disregard any interruption in his attendance on the course if he resumes it as soon as is reasonably practicable.

(5) Where the local authority are satisfied that a person to whom subsection (3) applies who is in full-time further or higher education needs accommodation during a vacation because his term-time accommodation is not available to him then, they shall give him assistance by—

    (a) providing him with suitable accommodation during the vacation; or

    (b) paying him enough to enable him to secure such accommodation himself.

(6) The appropriate national authority may prescribe the meaning of 'full-time', 'further education', 'higher education' and 'vacation' for the purposes of subsection (5).

24C   Information

(1) Where it appears to a local authority that a person—

    (a) with whom they are under a duty to keep in touch under section 23B, 23C or 24; or

    (b) whom they have been advising and befriending under section 24A; or

    (c) to whom they have been giving assistance under section 24B, proposes to live, or is living, in the area of another local authority, they must inform that other authority.

(2) Where a child who is accommodated—

    (a) by a voluntary organisation or in a private children's home;

    (b) by any Local Health Board or Special Health Authority by a local authority in the exercise of education functions; or

    (c) in any care home or independent hospital or any accommodation provided pursuant to arrangements made by the Secretary of State, the National Health Service Commissioning Board or a clinical commissioning group under the National Health Service Act 2006 or by a National Health Service trust or an NHS foundation trust,

ceases to be so accommodated, after reaching the age of sixteen, the organisation, authority or (as the case may be) person carrying on the home shall inform the local authority within whose area the child proposes to live.

(3) Subsection (2) only applies, by virtue of paragraph (b) or (c), if the accommodation has been provided for a consecutive period of at least three months.

(4) In a case where a child was accommodated by a local authority in the exercise of education functions, subsection (2) applies only if the local authority who accommodated the child are different from the local authority within whose area the child proposes to live.

24D   Representations: sections 23A to 24B

(1) Every local authority shall establish a procedure for considering representations (including complaints) made to them by—

    (a) a relevant child for the purposes of section 23A or a young person falling within section 23C;

(b) a person qualifying for advice and assistance; or

(c) a person falling within section 24B(2),

about the discharge of their functions under this Part in relation to him.

(1A) Regulations may be made by the appropriate national authority imposing time limits on the making of representations under subsection (1).

(2) In considering representations under subsection (1), a local authority shall comply with regulations (if any) made by the appropriate national authority for the purposes of this subsection.

Secure accommodation

25   Use of accommodation for restricting liberty

(1) Subject to the following provisions of this section, a child who is being looked after by a local authority may not be placed, and, if placed, may not be kept, in accommodation provided for the purpose of restricting liberty ('secure accommodation') unless it appears—

    (a) that—

        (i)   he has a history of absconding and is likely to abscond from any other description of accommodation; and

        (ii) if he absconds, he is likely to suffer significant harm; or

    (b) that if he is kept in any other description of accommodation he is likely to injure himself or other persons.

(2) The appropriate national authority may by regulations—

    (a) specify a maximum period—

        (i)   beyond which a child may not be kept in secure accommodation without the authority of the court; and

        (ii) for which the court may authorise a child to be kept in secure accommodation;

    (b) empower the court from time to time to authorise a child to be kept in secure accommodation for such further period as the regulations may specify; and

    (c) provide that applications to the court under this section shall be made only by local authorities.

(3) It shall be the duty of a court hearing an application under this section to determine whether any relevant criteria for keeping a child in secure accommodation are satisfied in his case.

(4) If a court determines that any such criteria are satisfied, it shall make an order authorising the child to be kept in secure accommodation and specifying the maximum period for which he may be so kept.

(5) On any adjournment of the hearing of an application under this section, a court may make an interim order permitting the child to be kept during the period of the adjournment in secure accommodation.

(6) No court shall exercise the powers conferred by this section in respect of a child who is not legally represented in that court unless, having been informed of his right to apply for the provision of representation under Part 1 of the Legal Aid, Sentencing and Punishment of Offenders Act 2012 and having had the opportunity to do so, he refused or failed to apply.

(7) The appropriate national authority may by regulations provide that—

    (a) this section shall or shall not apply to any description of children specified in the regulations;

    (b) this section shall have effect in relation to children of a description specified in the regulations subject to such modifications as may be so specified;

    (c) such other provisions as may be so specified shall have effect for the purpose of determining whether a child of a description specified in the regulations may be placed or kept in secure accommodation.

(8) The giving of an authorisation under this section shall not prejudice any power of any court in England and Wales or Scotland to give directions relating to the child to whom the authorisation relates.

(9) This section is subject to section 20(8).

Independent reviewing officers

25A Appointment of independent reviewing officer

(1) If a local authority are looking after a child, they must appoint an individual as the independent reviewing officer for that child's case.

(2) The initial appointment under subsection (1) must be made before the child's case is first reviewed in accordance with regulations made under section 26.

(3) If a vacancy arises in respect of a child's case, the local authority must make another appointment under subsection (1) as soon as is practicable.

(4) An appointee must be of a description prescribed in regulations made by the appropriate national authority.

25B Functions of the independent reviewing officer

(1) The independent reviewing officer must—

(a) monitor the performance by the local authority of their functions in relation to the child's case;

(b) participate, in accordance with regulations made by the appropriate national authority, in any review of the child's case;

(c) ensure that any ascertained wishes and feelings of the child concerning the case are given due consideration by the local authority;

(d) perform any other function which is prescribed in regulations made by the appropriate national authority.

(2) An independent reviewing officer's functions must be performed—

(a) in such manner (if any) as may be prescribed in regulations made by the appropriate national authority; and

(b) having regard to such guidance as that authority may issue in relation to the discharge of those functions.

(3) If the independent reviewing officer considers it appropriate to do so, the child's case may be referred by that officer to—

(a) an officer of the Children and Family Court Advisory and Support Service; or

(b) a Welsh family proceedings officer.

(4) If the independent reviewing officer is not an officer of the local authority, it is the duty of the authority—

(a) to co-operate with that individual; and

(b) to take all such reasonable steps as that individual may require of them to enable that individual's functions under this section to be performed satisfactorily.

25C Referred cases

(1) In relation to children whose cases are referred to officers under section 25B(3), the Lord Chancellor may by regulations—

(a) extend any functions of the officers in respect of family proceedings (within the meaning of section 12 of the Criminal Justice and Court Services Act 2000) to other proceedings;

(b) require any functions of the officers to be performed in the manner prescribed by the regulations.

(2) The power to make regulations in this section is exercisable in relation to functions of Welsh family proceedings officers only with the consent of the Welsh Ministers.

Supplemental

26 Review of cases and inquiries into representations

(1) The appropriate national authority may make regulations requiring the case of each child who is being looked after by a local authority to be reviewed in accordance with the provisions of the regulations.

(2) The regulations may, in particular, make provision—

    (a) as to the manner in which each case is to be reviewed;

    (b) as to the considerations to which the local authority are to have regard in reviewing each case;

    (c) as to the time when each case is first to be reviewed and the frequency of subsequent reviews;

    (d) requiring the authority, before conducting any review, to seek the views of—

        (i) the child;

        (ii) his parents;

        (iii) any person who is not a parent of his but who has parental responsibility for him; and

        (iv) any other person whose views the authority consider to be relevant, including, in particular, the views of those persons in relation to any particular matter which is to be considered in the course of the review;

    (e) requiring the authority, in the case of a child who is in their care—

        (i) to keep the section 31A plan for the child under review and, if they are of the opinion that some change is required, to revise the plan, or make a new plan, accordingly,

        (ii) to consider whether an application should be made to discharge the care order;

    (f) requiring the authority, in the case of a child in accommodation provided by the authority,

        (i) if there is no plan for the future care of the child, to prepare one,

        (ii) if there is such a plan for the child, to keep it under review and, if they are of the opinion that some change is required, to revise the plan or make a new plan, accordingly,

        (iii) to consider whether the accommodation accords with the requirements of this Part;

    (g) requiring the authority to inform the child so far as is reasonably practicable of any steps he may take under this Act;

    (h) requiring the authority to make arrangements, including arrangements with such other bodies providing services as it considers appropriate, to implement any decision which they propose to make in the course, or as a result, of the review;

    (i) requiring the authority to notify details of the result of the review and of any decision taken by them in consequence of the review to—

        (i) the child;

        (ii) his parents;

        (iii) any person who is not a parent of his but who has parental responsibility for him; and

        (iv) any other person whom they consider ought to be notified;

    (j) requiring the authority to monitor the arrangements which they have made with a view to ensuring that they comply with the regulations;

(3) Every local authority shall establish a procedure for considering any representations (including any complaint) made to them by—

    (a) any child who is being looked after by them or who is not being looked after by them but is in need;

    (b) a parent of his;

    (c) any person who is not a parent of his but who has parental responsibility for him;

    (d) any local authority foster parent;

    (e) such other person as the authority consider has a sufficient interest in the child's welfare to warrant his representations being considered by them,

about the discharge by the authority of any of their qualifying functions in relation to the child.

(3A) The following are qualifying functions for the purposes of subsection (3)—

    (a) functions under this Part,

(b) such functions under Part 4 or 5 as are specified by the appropriate national authority in regulations.

(3B) The duty under subsection (3) extends to representations (including complaints) made to the authority by—

(a) any person mentioned in section 3(1) of the Adoption and Children Act 2002 (persons for whose needs provision is made by the Adoption Service) and any other person to whom arrangements for the provision of adoption support services (within the meaning of that Act) extend,

(b) such other person as the authority consider has sufficient interest in a child who is or may be adopted to warrant his representations being considered by them,

about the discharge by the authority of such functions under the Adoption and Children Act 2002 as are specified by the appropriate national authority in regulations.

(3C) The duty under subsection (3) extends to any representations (including complaints) which are made to the authority by—

(a) a child with respect to whom a special guardianship order is in force,

(b) a special guardian or a parent of such a child,

(c) any other person the authority consider has a sufficient interest in the welfare of such a child to warrant his representations being considered by them, or

(d) any person who has applied for an assessment under section 14F(3) or (4),

about the discharge by the authority of such functions under section 14F as may be specified by the appropriate national authority in regulations.

(4) The procedure shall ensure that at least one person who is not a member or officer of the authority takes part in—

(a) the consideration; and

(b) any discussions which are held by the authority about the action (if any) to be taken in relation to the child in the light of the consideration,

but this subsection is subject to subsection (5A).

(4A) Regulations may be made by the appropriate national authority imposing time limits on the making of representations under this section.

(5) In carrying out any consideration of representations under this section a local authority shall comply with any regulations made by the appropriate national authority for the purpose of regulating the procedure to be followed.

(5A) Regulations under subsection (5) may provide that subsection (4) does not apply in relation to any consideration or discussion which takes place as part of a procedure for which provision is made by the regulations for the purpose of resolving informally the matters raised in the representations.

(6) The appropriate national authority may make regulations requiring local authorities to monitor the arrangements that they have made with a view to ensuring that they comply with any regulations made for the purposes of subsection (5).

(7) Where any representation has been considered under the procedure established by a local authority under this section, the authority shall—

(a) have due regard to the findings of those considering the representation; and

(b) take such steps as are reasonably practicable to notify (in writing)—

(i) the person making the representation;

(ii) the child (if the authority consider that he has sufficient understanding); and

(iii) such other persons (if any) as appear to the authority to be likely to be affected, of the authority's decision in the matter and their reasons for taking that decision and of any action which they have taken, or propose to take.

(8) Every local authority shall give such publicity to their procedure for considering representations under this section as they consider appropriate.

...

26A   Advocacy services

(1) Every local authority shall make arrangements for the provision of assistance to—

(a) persons who make or intend to make representations under section 24D; and

(b) children who make or intend to make representations under section 26.

(2) The assistance provided under the arrangements shall include assistance by way of representation.

...

(3) The arrangements—

(a) shall secure that a person may not provide assistance if he is a person who is prevented from doing so by regulations made by the appropriate national authority; and

(b) shall comply with any other provision made by the regulations in relation to the arrangements.

(4) The appropriate national authority may make regulations requiring local authorities to monitor the steps that they have taken with a view to ensuring that they comply with regulations made for the purposes of subsection (3).

(5) Every local authority shall give such publicity to their arrangements for the provision of assistance under this section as they consider appropriate.

27   Co-operation between authorities

(1) Where it appears to a local authority that any authority mentioned in subsection (3) could, by taking any specified action, help in the exercise of any of their functions under this Part, they may request the help of that other authority, specifying the action in question.

(2) An authority whose help is so requested shall comply with the request if it is compatible with their own statutory or other duties and obligations and does not unduly prejudice the discharge of any of their functions.

(3) The authorities are—

(a) any local authority;

...

(c) any local housing authority;

(ca) the National Health Service Commissioning Board;

(d) any clinical commissioning group, Local Health Board, Special Health Authority, National Health Service trust or NHS foundation trust, and

(e) any person authorised by the appropriate national authority for the purposes of this section.

29   Recoupment of cost of providing services etc.

(1) Where a local authority provide any service under section 17 or 18, other than advice, guidance or counselling, they may recover from a person specified in subsection (4) such charge for the service as they consider reasonable.

(2) Where the authority are satisfied that that person's means are insufficient for it to be reasonably practicable for him to pay the charge, they shall not require him to pay more than he can reasonably be expected to pay.

(3) No person shall be liable to pay any charge under subsection (1) for a service provided under section 17 or section 18(1) or (5) at any time when he is in receipt of universal credit (except in such circumstances as may be prescribed).

(3A) No person shall be liable to pay any charge under subsection (1) for a service provided under section 18(2) or (6) at any time when he is in receipt of universal credit (except in such circumstances as may be prescribed).

(3B) No person shall be liable to pay any charge under subsection (1) for a service provided under section 18(2) or (6) at any time when—

(a) he is in receipt of guarantee state pension credit under section 1(3)(a) of the State Pension Credit Act 2002, or

(b) he is a member of a couple (within the meaning of that Act) the other member of which is in receipt of guarantee state pension credit.

(4) The persons are—

    (a) where the service is provided for a child under sixteen, each of his parents;

    (b) where it is provided for a child who has reached the age of sixteen, the child himself; and

    (c) where it is provided for a member of the child's family, that member.

(5) Any charge under subsection (1) may, without prejudice to any other method of recovery, be recovered summarily as a civil debt.

(6) Part III of Schedule 2 makes provision in connection with contributions towards the maintenance of children who are being looked after by local authorities and consists of the re-enactment with modifications of provisions in Part V of the Child Care Act 1980.

(7) Where a local authority provide any accommodation under section 20(1) for a child who was (immediately before they began to look after him) ordinarily resident within the area of another local authority, they may recover from that other authority any reasonable expenses incurred by them in providing the accommodation and maintaining him.

(8) Where a local authority provide accommodation under section 21(1) or (2)(a) or (b) for a child who is ordinarily resident within the area of another local authority and they are not maintaining him in—

    (a) a community home provided by them;

    (b) a controlled community home; or

    (c) a hospital vested in the Secretary of State or the Welsh Ministers, or any other hospital made available pursuant to arrangements made by the Secretary of State, the National Health Service Commissioning Board or a clinical commissioning group under the National Health Service Act 2006 or by a Local Health Board;

they may recover from that other authority any reasonable expenses incurred by them in providing the accommodation and maintaining him.

(9) Except where subsection (10) applies, where a local authority comply with any request under section 27(2) in relation to a child or other person who is not ordinarily resident within their area, they may recover from the local authority in whose area the child or person is ordinarily resident any reasonable expenses incurred by them in respect of that person.

(10) Where a local authority ('authority A') comply with any request under section 27 (2) from another local authority ('authority B') in relation to a child or other person—

    (a) whose responsible authority is authority B for the purposes of section 23B or 23C; or

    (b) whom authority B are advising or befriending or to whom they are giving assistance by virtue of section 24(5)(a),

authority A may recover from authority B any reasonable expenses incurred by them in respect of that person.

30 Miscellaneous

(1) Nothing in this Part shall affect any duty imposed on a local authority by or under any other enactment.

(2) Any question arising under section 20(2), 21(3) or 29(7) to (9) as to the ordinary residence of a child shall be determined by agreement between the local authorities concerned or, in default of agreement, by the determining authority.

(2A) For the purposes of subsection (2) 'the determining authority' is—

    (a) in a case where all the local authorities concerned are in Wales, the Welsh Ministers;

    (b) in any other case, the Secretary of State.

(2B) In a case where—

    (a) the determining authority is the Secretary of State, and

    (b) one or more of the local authorities concerned are in Wales,

the Secretary of State must consult the Welsh Ministers before making a determination for the purposes of subsection (2).

    ...

(4) The appropriate national authority may make regulations for determining, as respects any education functions specified in the regulations, whether a child who is being looked after by a local authority is to be treated, for purposes so specified, as a child of parents of sufficient resources or as a child of parents without resources.

30A Meaning of appropriate national authority
In this Part 'the appropriate national authority' means—
    (a) in relation to England, the Secretary of State; and
    (b) in relation to Wales, the Welsh Ministers.

PART IV CARE AND SUPERVISION

General

31 Care and supervision orders
(1) On the application of any local authority or authorised person, the court may make an order—
    (a) placing the child with respect to whom the application is made in the care of a designated local authority; or
    (b) putting him under the supervision of a designated local authority.
(2) A court may only make a care order or supervision order if it is satisfied—
    (a) that the child concerned is suffering, or is likely to suffer, significant harm; and
    (b) that the harm, or likelihood of harm, is attributable to—
        (i) the care given to the child, or likely to be given to him if the order were not made, not being what it would be reasonable to expect a parent to give to him; or
        (ii) the child's being beyond parental control.
(3) No care order or supervision order may be made with respect to a child who has reached the age of seventeen (or sixteen, in the case of a child who is married).
(3A) A court deciding whether to make a care order—
    (a) is required to consider the permanence provisions of the section 31A plan for the child concerned, but
    (b) is not required to consider the remainder of the section 31A plan, subject to section 34(11).
(3B) For the purposes of subsection (3A), the permanence provisions of a section 31A plan are such of the plan's provisions setting out the long-term plan for the upbringing of the child concerned as provide for any of the following—
    (a) the child to live with any parent of the child's or with any other member of, or any friend of, the child's family;
    (b) adoption;
    (c) long-term care not within paragraph (a) or (b).
(3C) The Secretary of State may by regulations amend this section for the purpose of altering what for the purposes of subsection (3A) are the permanence provisions of a section 31A plan.
(4) An application under this section may be made on its own or in any other family proceedings.
(5) The court may—
    (a) on an application for a care order, make a supervision order;
    (b) on an application for a supervision order, make a care order.
(6) Where an authorised person proposes to make an application under this section he shall—
    (a) if it is reasonably practicable to do so; and
    (b) before making the application,
consult the local authority appearing to him to be the authority in whose area the child concerned is ordinarily resident.

(7) An application made by an authorised person shall not be entertained by the court if, at the time when it is made, the child concerned is—

    (a) the subject of an earlier application for a care order, or supervision order, which has not been disposed of; or

    (b) subject to—

        (i) a care order or supervision order;

        (ii) a youth rehabilitation order within the meaning of Part 1 of the Criminal Justice and Immigration Act 2008; or . . .

(8) The local authority designated in a care order must be—

    (a) the authority within whose area the child is ordinarily resident; or

    (b) where the child does not reside in the area of a local authority, the authority within whose area any circumstances arose in consequence of which the order is being made.

(9) In this section—

'authorised person' means—

    (a) the National Society for the Prevention of Cruelty to Children and any of its officers; and

    (b) any person authorised by order of the Secretary of State to bring proceedings under this section and any officer of a body which is so authorised.

'harm' means ill-treatment or the impairment of health or development including, for example, impairment suffered from seeing or hearing the ill-treatment of another;

'development' means physical, intellectual, emotional, social or behavioural development;

'health' means physical or mental health; and

'ill-treatment' includes sexual abuse and forms of ill-treatment which are not physical.

(10) Where the question of whether harm suffered by a child is significant turns on the child's health or development, his health or development shall be compared with that which could reasonably be expected of a similar child.

(11) In this Act—

'a care order' means (subject to section 105(1)) an order under subsection (1)(a) and (except where express provision to the contrary is made) includes an interim care order made under section 38; and

'a supervision order' means an order under subsection (1)(b) and (except where express provision to the contrary is made) includes an interim supervision order made under section 38.

31A Care orders: care plans

(1) Where an application is made on which a care order might be made with respect to a child, the appropriate local authority must, within such time as may be prescribed, prepare a plan ('a care plan') for the future care of the child.

(2) While the application is pending, the authority must keep any care plan prepared by them under review and, if they are of the opinion some change is required, revise the plan, or make a new plan, accordingly.

(3) A care plan must give any prescribed information and do so in the prescribed manner.

(4) For the purposes of this section, the appropriate local authority, in relation to a child in respect of whom a care order might be made, is the local authority proposed to be designated in the order.

(4A) In this section 'prescribed'—

    (a) in relation to a care plan whose preparation is the responsibility of a local authority for an area in England, means prescribed by the Secretary of State; and

    (b) in relation to a care plan whose preparation is the responsibility of a local authority in Wales, means prescribed by the Welsh Ministers.

(5) In section 31(3A) and this section, references to a care order do not include an interim care order.

(6) A plan prepared, or treated as prepared, under this section is referred to in this Act as a 'section 31A plan'.

32   Period within which application for order under this Part must be disposed of

(1) A court in which an application for an order under this Part is proceeding shall (in the light of any provision in rules of court that is of the kind mentioned in subsection (2)(a) or (b))—

(a) draw up a timetable with a view to disposing of the application—

(i)   without delay, and

(ii) in any event within twenty-six weeks beginning with the day on which the application was issued; and

(b) give such directions as it considers appropriate for the purpose of ensuring, so far as is reasonably practicable, that that timetable is adhered to.

(2) Rules of court may—

(a) specify periods within which specified steps must be taken in relation to such proceedings; and

(b) make other provision with respect to such proceedings for the purpose of ensuring, so far as is reasonably practicable, that they are disposed of without delay.

(3) A court, when drawing up a timetable under subsection (1)(a), must in particular have regard to—

(a) the impact which the timetable would have on the welfare of the child to whom the application relates; and

(b) the impact which the timetable would have on the conduct of the proceedings.

(4) A court, when revising a timetable drawn up under subsection (1)(a) or when making any decision which may give rise to a need to revise such a timetable (which does not include a decision under subsection (5)), must in particular have regard to—

(a) the impact which any revision would have on the welfare of the child to whom the application relates; and

(b) the impact which any revision would have on the duration and conduct of the proceedings.

(5) A court in which an application under this Part is proceeding may extend the period that is for the time being allowed under subsection (1)(a)(ii) in the case of the application, but may do so only if the court considers that the extension is necessary to enable the court to resolve the proceedings justly.

(6) When deciding whether to grant an extension under subsection (5), a court must in particular have regard to—

(a) the impact which any ensuing timetable revision would have on the welfare of the child to whom the application relates, and

(b) the impact which any ensuing timetable revision would have on the duration and conduct of the proceedings;

and here 'ensuing timetable revision' means any revision, of the timetable under subsection (1)(a) for the proceedings, which the court considers may ensue from the extension.

(7) When deciding whether to grant an extension under subsection (5), a court is to take account of the following guidance: extensions are not to be granted routinely and are to be seen as requiring specific justification.

(8) Each separate extension under subsection (5) is to end no more than eight weeks after the later of—

(a) the end of the period being extended; and

(b) the end of the day on which the extension is granted.

(9) The Lord Chancellor may by regulations amend subsection (1)(a)(ii), or the opening words of subsection (8), for the purpose of varying the period for the time being specified in that provision.

(10) Rules of court may provide that a court—

(a) when deciding whether to exercise the power under subsection (5), or

(b) when deciding how to exercise that power,

must, or may or may not, have regard to matters specified in the rules, or must take account of any guidance set out in the rules.

Care orders

33 Effect of care order

(1) Where a care order is made with respect to a child it shall be the duty of the local authority designated by the order to receive the child into their care and to keep him in their care while the order remains in force.

(2) Where—

(a) a care order has been made with respect to a child on the application of an authorised person; but

(b) the local authority designated by the order was not informed that that person proposed to make the application,

the child may be kept in the care of that person until received into the care of the authority.

(3) While a care order is in force with respect to a child, the local authority designated by the order shall—

(a) have parental responsibility for the child; and

(b) have the power (subject to the following provisions of this section) to determine the extent to which—

(i) a parent, guardian or special guardian of the child; or

(ii) a person who by virtue of section 4A has parental responsibility for the child,

may meet his parental responsibility for him.

(4) The authority may not exercise the power in subsection (3)(b) unless they are satisfied that it is necessary to do so in order to safeguard or promote the child's welfare.

(5) Nothing in subsection (3)(b) shall prevent a person mentioned in that provision who has care of the child from doing what is reasonable in all the circumstances of the case for the purpose of safeguarding or promoting his welfare.

(6) While a care order is in force with respect to a child, the local authority designated by the order shall not—

(a) cause the child to be brought up in any religious persuasion other than that in which he would have been brought up if the order had not been made; or

(b) have the right—

(i) ...

(ii) to agree or refuse to agree to the making of an adoption order, or an order under section 84 of the Adoption and Children Act 2002 with respect to the child; or

(iii) to appoint a guardian for the child.

(7) While a care order is in force with respect to a child, no person may—

(a) cause the child to be known by a new surname; or

(b) remove him from the United Kingdom,

without either the written consent of every person who has parental responsibility for the child or the leave of the court.

(8) Subsection (7)(b) does not—

(a) prevent the removal of such a child, for a period of less than one month, by the authority in whose care he is; or

(b) apply to arrangements for such a child to live outside England and Wales (which are governed by paragraph 19 of Schedule 2).

(9) The power in subsection (3)(b) is subject (in addition to being subject to the provisions of this section) to any right, duty, power, responsibility or authority which a person mentioned in that provision has in relation to the child and his property by virtue of any other enactment.

34 Parental contact etc. with children in care

(1) Where a child is in the care of a local authority, the authority shall (subject to the provisions of this section and their duty under section 22(3)(a)) allow the child reasonable contact with—

(a) his parents;

(b) any guardian or special guardian of his;

(ba) any person who by virtue of section 4A has parental responsibility for him;

(c) where there was a child arrangements order in force with respect to the child immediately before the care order was made, any person named in the child arrangements order as a person with whom the child was to live; and

(d) where, immediately before the care order was made, a person had care of the child by virtue of an order made in the exercise of the High Court's inherent jurisdiction with respect to children, that person.

(2) On the application made by the authority or the child, the court may make such order as it considers appropriate with respect to the contact which is to be allowed between the child and any named person.

(3) On an application made by—

(a) any person mentioned in paragraphs (a) to (d) of subsection (1); or

(b) any person who has obtained the leave of the court to make the application,

the court may make such order as it considers appropriate with respect to the contact which is to be allowed between the child and that person.

(4) On an application made by the authority or the child, the court may make an order authorising the authority to refuse to allow contact between the child and any person who is mentioned in paragraphs (a) to (d) of subsection (1) and named in the order.

(5) When making a care order with respect to a child, or in any family proceedings in connection with a child who is in the care of a local authority, the court may make an order under this section, even though no application for such an order has been made with respect to the child, if it considers that the order should be made.

(6) An authority may refuse to allow the contact that would otherwise be required by virtue of subsection (1) or an order under this section if—

(a) they are satisfied that it is necessary to do so in order to safeguard or promote the child's welfare; and

(b) the refusal—

(I) is decided upon as a matter of urgency; and

(ii) does not last for more than seven days.

(6A) Where (by virtue of an order under this section, or because subsection (6) applies) a local authority in England are authorised to refuse to allow contact between the child and a person mentioned in any of paragraphs (a) to (c) of paragraph 15(1) of Schedule 2, paragraph 15(1) of that Schedule does not require the authority to endeavour to promote contact between the child and that person.

(7) An order under this section may impose such conditions as the court considers appropriate.

(8) The Secretary of State may by regulations make provision as to—

(za) what a local authority in England must have regard to in considering whether contact between a child and a person mentioned in any of paragraphs (a) to (d) of subsection (1) is consistent with safeguarding and promoting the child's welfare;

(a) the steps to be taken by a local authority who have exercised their powers under subsection (6);

(b) the circumstances in which, and conditions subject to which, the terms of any order made under this section may be departed from by agreement between the local authority and the person in relation to whom this order is made;

(c) notification by a local authority of any variation or suspension of arrangements made (otherwise than under an order under this section) with a view to affording any person contact with a child to whom this section applies.

(9) The court may vary or discharge any order made under this section on the application of the authority, the child concerned or the person named in the order.

(10) An order under this section may be made either at the same time as the care order itself or later.

(11) Before making, varying or discharging an order under this section or making a care order with respect to any child the court shall—

(a) consider the arrangements which the authority have made, or propose to make, for affording any person contact with a child to whom this section applies; and

(b) invite the parties to the proceedings to comment on those arrangements.

Supervision orders

35   Supervision orders

(1) While a supervision order is in force it shall be the duty of the supervisor—

(a) to advise, assist and befriend the supervised child;

(b) to take such steps as are reasonably necessary to give effect to the order; and

(c) where—

(i) the order is not wholly complied with; or

(ii) the supervisor considers that the order may no longer be necessary,

to consider whether or not to apply to the court for its variation or discharge.

(2) Parts I and II of Schedule 3 make further provision with respect to supervision orders.

36   Education supervision orders

(1) On the application of any local authority, the court may make an order putting the child with respect to whom the application is made under the supervision of a designated local authority.

(2) In this Act 'an education supervision order' means an order under subsection (1).

(3) A court may only make an education supervision order if it is satisfied that the child concerned is of compulsory school age and is not being properly educated.

(4) For the purposes of this section, a child is being properly educated only if he is receiving efficient full-time education suitable to his age, ability and aptitude and any special educational needs he may have.

(5) Where a child is—

(a) the subject of a school attendance order which is in force under section 437 of the Education Act 1996 and which has not been complied with; or

(b) is not attending regularly within the meaning of section 444 of that Act—

(i) a school at which he is a registered pupil,

(ii) any place at which education is provided for him in the circumstances mentioned in subsection (1) or (1A) of section 444ZA of that Act, or

(iii) any place which he is required to attend in the circumstances mentioned in subsection (1B) or (2) of that section,

then, unless it is proved that he is being properly educated, it shall be assumed that he is not.

(6) An education supervision order may not be made with respect to a child who is in the care of a local authority.

(7) The local authority designated in an education supervision order must be—

(a) the authority within whose area the child concerned is living or will live; or

(b) where—

(i) the child is a registered pupil at a school; and

(ii) the authority mentioned in paragraph (a) and the authority within whose area the school is situated agree,

the latter authority.

(8) Where a local authority propose to make an application for an education supervision order they shall, before making the application, consult the appropriate local authority if different.

(9) The appropriate local authority is—

  (a) in the case of a child who is being provided with accommodation by, or on behalf of, a local authority, that authority; and

  (b) in any other case, the local authority within whose area the child concerned lives, or will live.

(10) Part III of Schedule 3 makes further provision with respect to education supervision orders.

Powers of court

37 Powers of court in certain family proceedings

(1) Where, in any family proceedings in which a question arises with respect to the welfare of any child, it appears to the court that it may be appropriate for a care or supervision order to be made with respect to him, the court may direct the appropriate authority to undertake an investigation of the child's circumstances.

(2) Where the court gives a direction under this section the local authority concerned shall, when undertaking the investigation, consider whether they should—

  (a) apply for a care order or for a supervision order with respect to the child;

  (b) provide services or assistance for the child or his family; or

  (c) take any other action with respect to the child.

(3) Where a local authority undertake an investigation under this section, and decide not to apply for a care order or supervision order with respect to the child concerned, they shall inform the court of—

  (a) their reasons for so deciding;

  (b) any service or assistance which they have provided, or intend to provide, for the child and his family; and

  (c) any other action which they have taken, or propose to take, with respect to the child.

(4) The information shall be given to the court before the end of the period of eight weeks beginning with the date of the direction, unless the court otherwise directs.

(5) The local authority named in a direction under subsection (1) must be—

  (a) the authority in whose area the child is ordinarily resident; or

  (b) where the child is not ordinarily resident in the area of a local authority, the authority within whose area any circumstances arose in consequence of which the direction is being given.

(6) If, on the conclusion of any investigation or review under this section, the authority decide not to apply for a care order or supervision order with respect to the child—

  (a) they shall consider whether it would be appropriate to review the case at a later date; and

  (b) if they decide that it would be, they shall determine the date on which that review is to begin.

38 Interim orders

(1) Where—

  (a) in any proceedings on an application for a care order or supervision order, the proceedings are adjourned; or

  (b) the court gives a direction under section 37(1),

the court may make an interim care order or an interim supervision order with respect to the child concerned.

(2) A court shall not make an interim care order or interim supervision order under this section unless it is satisfied that there are reasonable grounds for believing that the circumstances with respect to the child are as mentioned in section 31(2).

(3) Where, in any proceedings on an application for a care order or supervision order, a court makes a child arrangements order with respect to the living arrangements of the child concerned,

it shall also make an interim supervision order with respect to him unless satisfied that his welfare will be satisfactorily safeguarded without an interim order being made.

(3A) For the purposes of subsection (3), a child arrangements order is one made with respect to the living arrangements of the child concerned if the arrangements regulated by the order consist of, or include, arrangements which relate to either or both of the following—

    (a) with whom the child is to live, and

    (b) when the child is to live with any person.

(4) An interim order made under or by virtue of this section shall have effect for such period as may be specified in the order, but shall in any event cease to have effect on whichever of the following events first occurs—

    ...

    (c) in a case which falls within subsection (1)(a), the disposal of the application;

    (d) in a case which falls within subsection (1)(b), the disposal of an application for a care order or supervision order made by the authority with respect to the child;

    (da) in a case which falls within subsection (1)(b) and in which—

        (i)   no direction has been given under section 37(4), and

        (ii) no application for a care order or supervision order has been made with respect to the child,

    the expiry of the period of eight weeks beginning with the date on which the order is made;

    (e) in a case which falls within subsection (1)(b) and in which—

        (i)   the court has given a direction under section 37(4), but

        (ii) no application for a care order or supervision order has been made with respect to the child,

    the expiry of the period fixed by that direction.

    ...

(6) Where the court makes an interim care order, or interim supervision order, it may give such directions (if any) as it considers appropriate with regard to the medical or psychiatric examination or other assessment of the child; but if the child is of sufficient understanding to make an informed decision he may refuse to submit to the examination or other assessment.

(7) A direction under subsection (6) may be to the effect that there is to be—

    (a) no such examination or assessment; or

    (b) no such examination or assessment unless the court directs otherwise.

(8) A direction under subsection (6) may be—

    (a) given when the interim order is made or at any time while it is in force; and

    (b) varied at any time on the application of any person falling within any class of person prescribed by rules of court for the purposes of this subsection.

(9) Paragraphs 4 and 5 of Schedule 3 shall not apply in relation to an interim supervision order.

(10) Where a court makes an order under or by virtue of this section it shall, in determining the period for which the order is to be in force, consider whether any party who was, or might have been, opposed to the making of the order was in a position to argue his case against the order in full.

38A   Power to include exclusion requirement in interim care order

(1) Where—

    (a) on being satisfied that there are reasonable grounds for believing that the circumstances with respect to a child are as mentioned in section 31(2)(a) and (b)(i), the court makes an interim care order with respect to a child, and

    (b) the conditions mentioned in subsection (2) are satisfied, the court may include an exclusion requirement in the interim care order.

(2) The conditions are—

    (a) that there is reasonable cause to believe that, if a person ('the relevant person') is excluded from a dwelling-house in which the child lives, the child will cease to suffer, or cease to be likely to suffer, significant harm, and

(b) that another person living in the dwelling-house (whether a parent of the child or some other person)—

  (i) is able and willing to give to the child the care which it would be reasonable to expect a parent to give him, and

  (ii) consents to the inclusion of the exclusion requirement.

(3) For the purposes of this section an exclusion requirement is any one or more of the following—

  (a) a provision requiring the relevant person to leave a dwelling-house in which he is living with the child,

  (b) a provision prohibiting the relevant person from entering a dwelling-house in which the child lives, and

  (c) a provision excluding the relevant person from a defined area in which a dwelling-house in which the child lives is situated.

(4) The court may provide that the exclusion requirement is to have effect for a shorter period than the other provisions of the interim care order.

(5) Where the court makes an interim care order containing an exclusion requirement, the court may attach a power of arrest to the exclusion requirement.

(6) Where the court attaches a power of arrest to an exclusion requirement of an interim care order, it may provide that the power of arrest is to have effect for a shorter period than the exclusion requirement.

(7) Any period specified for the purposes of subsection (4) or (6) may be extended by the court (on one or more occasions) on an application to vary or discharge the interim care order.

(8) Where a power of arrest is attached to an exclusion requirement of an interim care order by virtue of subsection (5), a constable may arrest without warrant any person whom he has reasonable cause to believe to be in breach of the requirement.

(9) Sections 47(7), (11) and (12) and 48 of, and Schedule 5 to, the Family Law Act 1996 shall have effect in relation to a person arrested under subsection (8) of this section as they have effect in relation to a person arrested under section 47(6) of that Act.

(10) If, while an interim care order containing an exclusion requirement is in force, the local authority have removed the child from the dwelling-house from which the relevant person is excluded to other accommodation for a continuous period of more than 24 hours, the interim care order shall cease to have effect in so far as it imposes the exclusion requirement.

38B Undertakings relating to interim care orders

(1) In any case where the court has power to include an exclusion requirement in an interim care order, the court may accept an undertaking from the relevant person.

(2) No power of arrest may be attached to any undertaking given under subsection (1).

(3) An undertaking given to a court under subsection (1)—

  (a) shall be enforceable as if it were an order of the court, and

  (b) shall cease to have effect if, while it is in force, the local authority have removed the child from the dwelling-house from which the relevant person is excluded to other accommodation for a continuous period of more than 24 hours.

(4) This section has effect without prejudice to the powers of the High Court and family court apart from this section.

(5) In this section 'exclusion requirement' and 'relevant person' have the same meaning as in section 38A.

39 Discharge and variation etc. of care orders and supervision orders

(1) A care order may be discharged by the court on the application of—

  (a) any person who has parental responsibility for the child;

  (b) the child himself; or

  (c) the local authority designated by the order.

(2) A supervision order may be varied or discharged by the court on the application of—

(a) any person who has parental responsibility for the child;

(b) the child himself; or

(c) the supervisor.

(3) On the application of a person who is not entitled to apply for the order to be discharged, but who is a person with whom the child is living, a supervision order may be varied by the court in so far as it imposes a requirement which affects that person.

(3A) On the application of a person who is not entitled to apply for the order to be discharged, but who is a person to whom an exclusion requirement contained in the order applies, an interim care order may be varied or discharged by the court in so far as it imposes the exclusion requirement.

(3B) Where a power of arrest has been attached to an exclusion requirement of an interim care order, the court may, on the application of any person entitled to apply for the discharge of the order so far as it imposes the exclusion requirement, vary or discharge the order in so far as it confers a power of arrest (whether or not any application has been made to vary or discharge any other provision of the order).

(4) Where a care order is in force with respect to a child the court may, on the application of any person entitled to apply for the order to be discharged, substitute a supervision order for the care order.

(5) When a court is considering whether to substitute one order for another under subsection (4) any provision of this Act which would otherwise require section 31(2) to be satisfied at the time when the proposed order is substituted or made shall be disregarded.

40   Orders pending appeals in cases about care or supervision orders

(1) Where—

(a) a court dismisses an application for a care order; and

(b) at the time when the court dismisses the application, the child concerned is the subject of an interim care order,

the court may make a care order with respect to the child to have effect subject to such directions (if any) as the court may see fit to include in the order.

(2) Where—

(a) a court dismisses an application for a care order, or an application for a supervision order; and

(b) at the time when the court dismisses the application, the child concerned is the subject of an interim supervision order,

the court may make a supervision order with respect to the child to have effect subject to such directions (if any) as the court may see fit to include in the order.

(3) Where a court grants an application to discharge a care order or supervision order, it may order that—

(a) its decision is not to have effect; or

(b) the care order, or supervision order, is to continue to have effect but subject to such directions as the court sees fit to include in the order.

(4) An order made under this section shall only have effect for such period, not exceeding the appeal period, as may be specified in the order.

(5) Where—

(a) an appeal is made against any decision of a court under this section; or

(b) any application is made to the appellate court in connection with a proposed appeal against that decision,

the appellate court may extend the period for which the order in question is to have effect, but not so as to extend it beyond the end of the appeal period.

(6) In this section 'the appeal period' means—

(a) where an appeal is made against the decision in question, the period between the making of that decision and the determination of the appeal; and

(b) otherwise, the period during which an appeal may be made against the decision.

Representation of child

41 Representation of child and of his interests in certain proceedings

(1) For the purpose of any specified proceedings, the court shall appoint an officer of the Service or a Welsh family proceedings officer for the child concerned unless satisfied that it is not necessary to do so in order to safeguard his interests.

(2) The officer of the Service or Welsh family proceedings officer shall—

(a) be appointed in accordance with rules of court; and

(b) be under a duty to safeguard the interests of the child in the manner prescribed by such rules.

(3) Where—

(a) the child concerned is not represented by a solicitor; and

(b) any of the conditions mentioned in subsection (4) is satisfied,

the court may appoint a solicitor to represent him.

(4) The conditions are that—

(a) no officer of the Service or Welsh family proceedings officer has been appointed for the child;

(b) the child has sufficient understanding to instruct a solicitor and wishes to do so;

(c) it appears to the court that it would be in the child's best interests for him to be represented by a solicitor.

(5) Any solicitor appointed under or by virtue of this section shall be appointed, and shall represent the child, in accordance with rules of court.

(6) In this section 'specified proceedings' means any proceedings—

(a) on an application for a care order or supervision order;

(b) in which the court has given a direction under section 37(1) and has made, or is considering whether to make, an interim care order;

(c) on an application for the discharge of a care order or the variation or discharge of a supervision order;

(d) on an application under section 39(4);

(e) in which the court is considering whether to make a child arrangements order with respect to the living arrangements of a child who is the subject of a care order;

(f) with respect to contact between a child who is the subject of a care order and any other person;

(g) under Part V;

(h) on an appeal against—

(i) the making of, or refusal to make, a care order, supervision order or any order under section 34;

(ii) the making of, or refusal to make, a child arrangements order with respect to the living arrangements of a child who is the subject of a care order; or

(iii) the variation or discharge, or refusal of an application to vary or discharge, an order of a kind mentioned in subparagraph (i) or (ii);

(iv) the refusal of an application under section 39(4); or

(v) the making of, or refusal to make, an order under Part V;

(hh) on an application for the making or revocation of a placement order (within the meaning of section 21 of the Adoption and Children Act 2002); or

(i) which are specified for the time being, for the purposes of this section, by rules of court.

(6A) The proceedings which may be specified under subsection (6)(i) include (for example) proceedings for the making, varying or discharging of a section 8 order.

(6B) For the purposes of subsection (6), a child arrangements order is one made with respect to the living arrangements of a child if the arrangements regulated by the order consist of, or include, arrangements which relate to either or both of the following—

(a) with whom the child is to live, and

(b) when the child is to live with any person.

...

(11) Regardless of any enactment or rule of law which would otherwise prevent it from doing so, the court may take account of—

    (a) any statement contained in a report made by an officer of the Service or a Welsh family proceedings officer who is appointed under this section for the purpose of the proceedings in question; and

    (b) any evidence given in respect of the matters referred to in the report,

in so far as the statement or evidence is, in the opinion of the court, relevant to the question which the court is considering.

…

42　Right of officer of the Service to have access to local authority records

(1) Where an officer of the Service or Welsh family proceedings officer has been appointed under section 41 he shall have the right at all reasonable times to examine and take copies of—

    (a) any records of, or held by, a local authority or an authorised person which were compiled in connection with the making, or proposed making, by any person of any application under this Act with respect to the child concerned;

    (b) any records of, or held by, a local authority which were compiled in connection with any functions which are social services functions within the meaning of the Local Authority Social Services Act 1970, so far as those records relate to that child; or

    (c) any records of, or held by, an authorised person which were compiled in connection with the activities of that person, so far as those records relate to that child.

(2) Where an officer of the Service or Welsh family proceedings officer takes a copy of any record which he is entitled to examine under this section, that copy or any part of it shall be admissible as evidence of any matter referred to in any—

    (a) report which he makes to the court in the proceedings in question; or

    (b) evidence which he gives in those proceedings.

(3) Subsection (2) has effect regardless of any enactment or rule of law which would otherwise prevent the record in question being admissible in evidence.

(4) In this section 'authorised person' has the same meaning as in section 31.

PART V PROTECTION OF CHILDREN

43　Child assessment orders

(1) On the application of a local authority or authorised person for an order to be made under this section with respect to a child, the court may make the order if, but only if, it is satisfied that—

    (a) the applicant has reasonable cause to suspect that the child is suffering, or is likely to suffer, significant harm;

    (b) an assessment of the state of the child's health or development, or of the way in which he has been treated, is required to enable the applicant to determine whether or not the child is suffering, or is likely to suffer, significant harm; and

    (c) it is unlikely that such an assessment will be made, or be satisfactory, in the absence of an order under this section.

(2) In this Act 'a child assessment order' means an order under this section.

(3) A court may treat an application under this section as an application for an emergency protection order.

(4) No court shall make a child assessment order if it is satisfied—

    (a) that there are grounds for making an emergency protection order with respect to the child; and

    (b) that it ought to make such an order rather than a child assessment order.

(5) A child assessment order shall—

    (a) specify the date by which the assessment is to begin; and

(b) have effect for such period, not exceeding 7 days beginning with that date, as may be specified in the order.

(6) Where a child assessment order is in force with respect to a child it shall be the duty of any person who is in a position to produce the child—

(a) to produce him to such person as may be named in the order; and

(b) to comply with such directions relating to the assessment of the child as the court thinks fit to specify in the order.

(7) A child assessment order authorises any person carrying out the assessment, or any part of the assessment, to do so in accordance with the terms of the order.

(8) Regardless of subsection (7), if the child is of sufficient understanding to make an informed decision he may refuse to submit to a medical or psychiatric examination or other assessment.

(9) The child may only be kept away from home—

(a) in accordance with directions specified in the order;

(b) if it is necessary for the purposes of the assessment; and

(c) for such period or periods as may be specified in the order.

(10) Where the child is to be kept away from home, the order shall contain such directions as the court thinks fit with regard to the contact that he must be allowed to have with other persons while away from home.

(11) Any person making an application for a child assessment order shall take such steps as are reasonably practicable to ensure that notice of the application is given to—

(a) the child's parents;

(b) any person who is not a parent of his but who has parental responsibility for him;

(c) any other person caring for the child;

(d) any person named in a child arrangements order as a person with whom the child is to spend time or otherwise have contact;

(e) any person who is allowed to have contact with the child by virtue of an order under section 34; and

(f) the child,

before the hearing of the application.

(12) Rules of court may make provision as to the circumstances in which—

(a) any of the persons mentioned in subsection (11); or

(b) such other person as may be specified in the rules,

may apply to the court for a child assessment order to be varied or discharged.

(13) In this section 'authorised person' means a person who is an authorised person for the purposes of section 31.

44   Orders for emergency protection of children

(1) Where any person ('the applicant') applies to the court for an order to be made under this section with respect to a child, the court may make the order if, but only if, it is satisfied that—

(a) there is reasonable cause to believe that the child is likely to suffer significant harm if—

(i) he is not removed to accommodation provided by or on behalf of the applicant; or

(ii) he does not remain in the place in which he is then being accommodated;

(b) in the case of an application made by a local authority—

(i) enquiries are being made with respect to the child under section 47 (1)(b); and

(ii) those enquiries are being frustrated by access to the child being unreasonably refused to a person authorised to seek access and that the applicant has reasonable cause to believe that access to the child is required as a matter of urgency; or

(c) in the case of an application made by an authorised person—

(i) the applicant has reasonable cause to suspect that a child is suffering, or is likely to suffer, significant harm;

(ii) the applicant is making enquiries with respect to the child's welfare; and

       (iii) those enquiries are being frustrated by access to the child being unreasonably refused to a person authorised to seek access and the applicant has reasonable cause to believe that access to the child is required as a matter of urgency.

(2) In this section—

    (a) 'authorised person' means a person who is an authorised person for the purposes of section 31; and

    (b) 'a person authorised to seek access' means—

       (i) in the case of an application by a local authority, an officer of the local authority or a person authorised by the authority to act on their behalf in connection with the enquiries; or

       (ii) in the case of an application by an authorised person, that person.

(3) Any person—

    (a) seeking access to a child in connection with enquiries of a kind mentioned in subsection (1); and

    (b) purporting to be a person authorised to do so,

shall, on being asked to do so, produce some duly authenticated document as evidence that he is such a person.

(4) While an order under this section ('an emergency protection order') is in force it—

    (a) operates as a direction to any person who is in a position to do so to comply with any request to produce the child to the applicant;

    (b) authorises—

       (i) the removal of the child at any time to accommodation provided by or on behalf of the applicant and his being kept there; or

       (ii) the prevention of the child's removal from any hospital, or other place, in which he was being accommodated immediately before the making of the order; and

    (c) gives the applicant parental responsibility for the child.

(5) Where an emergency protection order is in force with respect to a child, the applicant—

    (a) shall only exercise the power given by virtue of subsection (4)(b) in order to safeguard the welfare of the child;

    (b) shall take, and shall only take, such action in meeting his parental responsibility for the child as is reasonably required to safeguard or promote the welfare of the child (having regard in particular to the duration of the order); and

    (c) shall comply with the requirements of any regulations made by the Secretary of State for the purposes of this subsection.

(6) Where the court makes an emergency protection order, it may give such directions (if any) as it considers appropriate with respect to—

    (a) the contact which is, or is not, to be allowed between the child and any named person;

    (b) the medical or psychiatric examination or other assessment of the child.

(7) Where any direction is given under subsection (6)(b), the child may, if he is of sufficient understanding to make an informed decision, refuse to submit to the examination or other assessment.

(8) A direction under subsection (6)(a) may impose conditions and one under subsection (6)(b) may be to the effect that there is to be—

    (a) no such examination or other assessment; or

    (b) no such examination or assessment unless the court directs otherwise.

(9) A direction under subsection (6) may be—

    (a) given when the emergency protection order is made or at any time while it is in force; and

    (b) varied at any time on the application of any person falling within any class of person prescribed by rules of court for the purposes of this subsection.

(10) Where an emergency protection order is in force with respect to a child and—

    (a) the applicant has exercised the power given by subsection (4)(b)(i) but it appears to him that it is safe for the child to be returned; or

(b) the applicant has exercised the power given by subsection (4)(b)(ii) but it appears to him that it is safe for the child to be allowed to be removed from the place in question,

he shall return the child or (as the case may be) allow him to be removed.

(11) Where he is required by subsection (10) to return the child the applicant shall—

(a) return him to the care of the person from whose care he was removed; or

(b) if that is not reasonably practicable, return him to the care of—

(i) a parent of his;

(ii) any person who is not a parent of his but who has parental responsibility for him; or

(iii) such other person as the applicant (with the agreement of the court) considers appropriate.

(12) Where the applicant has been required by subsection (10) to return the child, or to allow him to be removed, he may again exercise his powers with respect to the child (at any time while the emergency protection order remains in force) if it appears to him that a change in the circumstances of the case makes it necessary for him to do so.

(13) Where an emergency protection order has been made with respect to a child, the applicant shall, subject to any direction given under subsection (6), allow the child reasonable contact with—

(a) his parents;

(b) any person who is not a parent of his but who has parental responsibility for

(c) any person with whom he was living immediately before the making of the order;

(d) any person named in a child arrangements order as a person with whom the child is to spend time or otherwise have contact;

(e) any person who is allowed to have contact with the child by virtue of an order under section 34; and

(f) any person acting on behalf of any of those persons.

(14) Wherever it is reasonably practicable to do so, an emergency protection order shall name the child; and where it does not name him it shall describe him as clearly as possible.

(15) A person shall be guilty of an offence if he intentionally obstructs any person exercising the power under subsection (4)(b) to remove, or prevent the removal of, a child.

(16) A person guilty of an offence under subsection (15) shall be liable on summary conviction to a fine not exceeding level 3 on the standard scale.

44A   Power to include exclusion requirement in emergency protection order

(1) Where—

(a) on being satisfied as mentioned in section 44(1)(a), (b) or (c), the court makes an emergency protection order with respect to a child, and

(b) the conditions mentioned in subsection (2) are satisfied,

the court may include an exclusion requirement in the emergency protection order.

(2) The conditions are—

(a) that there is reasonable cause to believe that, if a person ('the relevant person') is excluded from a dwelling-house in which the child lives, then—

(i) in the case of an order made on the ground mentioned in section 44 (1)(a), the child will not be likely to suffer significant harm, even though the child is not removed as mentioned in section 44(1)(a)(i) or does not remain as mentioned in section 44(1)(a)(ii), or

(ii) in the case of an order made on the ground mentioned in paragraph (b) or (c) of section 44(1), the enquiries referred to in that paragraph will cease to be frustrated, and

(b) that another person living in the dwelling-house (whether a parent of the child or some other person)—

(i) is able and willing to give to the child the care which it would be reasonable to expect a parent to give him, and

(ii) consents to the inclusion of the exclusion requirement.

(3) For the purposes of this section an exclusion requirement is any one or more of the following—

    (a) a provision requiring the relevant person to leave a dwelling-house in which he is living with the child,

    (b) a provision prohibiting the relevant person from entering a dwelling-house in which the child lives, and

    (c) a provision excluding the relevant person from a defined area in which a dwelling-house in which the child lives is situated.

(4) The court may provide that the exclusion requirement is to have effect for a shorter period than the other provisions of the order.

(5) Where the court makes an emergency protection order containing an exclusion requirement, the court may attach a power of arrest to the exclusion requirement.

(6) Where the court attaches a power of arrest to an exclusion requirement of an emergency protection order, it may provide that the power of arrest is to have effect for a shorter period than the exclusion requirement.

(7) Any period specified for the purposes of subsection (4) or (6) may be extended by the court (on one or more occasions) on an application to vary or discharge the emergency protection order.

(8) Where a power of arrest is attached to an exclusion requirement of an emergency protection order by virtue of subsection (5), a constable may arrest without warrant any person whom he has reasonable cause to believe to be in breach of the requirement.

(9) Sections 47(7), (11) and (12) and 48 of, and Schedule 5 to, the Family Law Act 1996 shall have effect in relation to a person arrested under subsection (8) of this section as they have effect in relation to a person arrested under section 47(6) of that Act.

(10) If, while an emergency protection order containing an exclusion requirement is in force, the applicant has removed the child from the dwelling-house from which the relevant person is excluded to other accommodation for a continuous period of more than 24 hours, the order shall cease to have effect in so far as it imposes the exclusion requirement.

44B Undertakings relating to emergency protection orders

(1) In any case where the court has power to include an exclusion requirement in an emergency protection order, the court may accept an undertaking from the relevant person.

(2) No power of arrest may be attached to any undertaking given under subsection (1).

(3) An undertaking given to a court under subsection (1)—

    (a) shall be enforceable as if it were an order of the court, and

    (b) shall cease to have effect if, while it is in force, the applicant has removed the child from the dwelling-house from which the relevant person is excluded to other accommodation for a continuous period of more than 24 hours.

(4) This section has effect without prejudice to the powers of the High Court and family court apart from this section.

(5) In this section 'exclusion requirement' and 'relevant person' have the same meaning as in section 44A.

45 Duration of emergency protection orders and other supplemental provisions

(1) An emergency protection order shall have effect for such period, not exceeding eight days, as may be specified in the order.

(2) Where—

    (a) the court making an emergency protection order would, but for this subsection, specify a period of eight days as the period for which the order is to have effect; but

    (b) the last of those eight days is a public holiday (that is to say, Christmas Day, Good Friday, a bank holiday or a Sunday),

the court may specify a period which ends at noon on the first later day which is not such a holiday.

(3) Where an emergency protection order is made on an application under section 46 (7), the period of eight days mentioned in subsection (1) shall begin with the first day on which the child was taken into police protection under section 46.

(4) Any person who—

(a) has parental responsibility for a child as the result of an emergency protection order; and

(b) is entitled to apply for a care order with respect to the child,

may apply to the court for the period during which the emergency protection order is to have effect to be extended.

(5) On an application under subsection (4) the court may extend the period during which the order is to have effect by such period, not exceeding seven days, as it thinks fit, but may do so only if it has reasonable cause to believe that the child concerned is likely to suffer significant harm if the order is not extended.

(6) An emergency protection order may only be extended once.

(7) Regardless of any enactment or rule of law which would otherwise prevent it from doing so, a court hearing an application for, or with respect to, an emergency protection order may take account of—

(a) any statement contained in any report made to the court in the course of, or in connection with, the hearing; or

(b) any evidence given during the hearing,

which is, in the opinion of the court, relevant to the application.

(8) Any of the following may apply to the court for an emergency protection order to be discharged—

(a) the child;

(b) a parent of his;

(c) any person who is not a parent of his but who has parental responsibility for him; or

(d) any person with whom he was living immediately before the making of the order.

(8A) On the application of a person who is not entitled to apply for the order to be discharged, but who is a person to whom an exclusion requirement contained in the order applies, an emergency protection order may be varied or discharged by the court in so far as it imposes the exclusion requirement.

(8B) Where a power of arrest has been attached to an exclusion requirement of an emergency protection order, the court may, on the application of any person entitled to apply for the discharge of the order so far as it imposes the exclusion requirement, vary or discharge the order in so far as it confers a power of arrest (whether or not any application has been made to vary or discharge any other provision of the order).

. . .

(10) No appeal may be made against—

(a) the making of, or refusal to make, an emergency protection order;

(b) the extension of, or refusal to extend, the period during which such an order is to have effect;

(c) the discharge of, or refusal to discharge, such an order; or

(d) the giving of, or refusal to give, any direction in connection with such an order.

(11) Subsection (8) does not apply—

(a) where the person who would otherwise be entitled to apply for the emergency protection order to be discharged—

(i) was given notice (in accordance with rules of court) of the hearing at which the order was made; and

(ii) was present at that hearing; or

(b) to any emergency protection order the effective period of which has been extended under subsection (5).

(12) A court making an emergency protection order may direct that the applicant may, in exercising any powers which he has by virtue of the order, be accompanied by a registered medical practitioner, registered nurse or registered midwife, if he so chooses.

...

46   Removal and accommodation of children by police in cases of emergency

(1) Where a constable has reasonable cause to believe that a child would otherwise be likely to suffer significant harm, he may—

  (a) remove the child to suitable accommodation and keep him there; or

  (b) take such steps as are reasonable to ensure that the child's removal from any hospital, or other place, in which he is then being accommodated is prevented.

(2) For the purposes of this Act, a child with respect to whom a constable has exercised his powers under this section is referred to as having been taken into police protection.

(3) As soon as is reasonably practicable after taking a child into police protection, the constable concerned shall—

  (a) inform the local authority within whose area the child was found of the steps that have been, and are proposed to be, taken with respect to the child under this section and the reasons for taking them;

  (b) give details to the authority within whose area the child is ordinarily resident ('the appropriate authority') of the place at which the child is being accommodated;

  (c) inform the child (if he appears capable of understanding)—

      (i)   of the steps that have been taken with respect to him under this section and of the reasons for taking them; and

      (ii) of the further steps that may be taken with respect to him under this section;

  (d) take such steps as are reasonably practicable to discover the wishes and feelings of the child;

  (e) secure that the case is inquired into by an officer designated for the purposes of this section by the chief officer of the police area concerned; and

  (f) where the child was taken into police protection by being removed to accommodation which is not provided—

      (i)   by or on behalf of a local authority; or

      (ii) as a refuge, in compliance with the requirements of section 51,

      secure that he is moved to accommodation which is so provided.

(4) As soon as is reasonably practicable after taking a child into police protection, the constable concerned shall take such steps as are reasonably practicable to inform—

  (a) the child's parents;

  (b) every person who is not a parent of his but who has parental responsibility for him; and

  (c) any other person with whom the child was living immediately before being taken into police protection,

of the steps that he has taken under this section with respect to the child, the reasons for taking them and the further steps that may be taken with respect to him under this section.

(5) On completing any inquiry under subsection (3)(e), the officer conducting it shall release the child from police protection unless he considers that there is still reasonable cause for believing that the child would be likely to suffer significant harm if released.

(6) No child may be kept in police protection for more than 72 hours.

(7) While a child is being kept in police protection, the designated officer may apply on behalf of the appropriate authority for an emergency protection order to be made under section 44 with respect to the child.

(8) An application may be made under subsection (7) whether or not the authority know of it or agree to its being made.

(9) While a child is being kept in police protection—

    (a) neither the constable concerned nor the designated officer shall have parental responsibility for him; but

    (b) the designated officer shall do what is reasonable in all the circumstances of the case for the purpose of safeguarding or promoting the child's welfare (having regard in particular to the length of the period during which the child will be so protected).

(10) Where a child has been taken into police protection, the designated officer shall allow—

    (a) the child's parents;

    (b) any person who is not a parent of the child but who has parental responsibility for him;

    (c) any person with whom the child was living immediately before he was taken into police protection;

    (d) any person named in a child arrangements order as a person with whom the child is to spend time or otherwise have contact;

    (e) any person who is allowed to have contact with the child by virtue of an order under section 34; and

    (f) any person acting on behalf of any of those persons,

to have such contact (if any) with the child as, in the opinion of the designated officer, is both reasonable and in the child's best interests.

(11) Where a child who has been taken into police protection is in accommodation provided by, or on behalf of, the appropriate authority, subsection (10) shall have effect as if it referred to the authority rather than to the designated officer.

47   Local authority's duty to investigate

(1) Where a local authority—

    (a) are informed that a child who lives, or is found, in their area—

        (i)   is the subject of an emergency protection order; or

        (ii) is in police protection;

    (b) have reasonable cause to suspect that a child who lives, or is found, in their area is suffering, or is likely to suffer, significant harm,

the authority shall make, or cause to be made, such enquiries as they consider necessary to enable them to decide whether they should take any action to safeguard or promote the child's welfare.

(2) Where a local authority have obtained an emergency protection order with respect to a child, they shall make, or cause to be made, such enquiries as they consider necessary to enable them to decide what action they should take to safeguard or promote the child's welfare.

(3) The enquiries shall, in particular, be directed towards establishing—

    (a) whether the authority should make any application to the court, or exercise any of their other powers under this Act or section 11 of the Crime and Disorder Act 1998 (child safety orders), with respect to the child;

    (b) whether, in the case of a child—

        (i)   with respect to whom an emergency protection order has been made; and

        (ii) who is not in accommodation provided by or on behalf of the authority, it would be in the child's best interests (while an emergency protection order remains in force) for him to be in such accommodation; and

    (c) whether, in the case of a child who has been taken into police protection, it would be in the child's best interests for the authority to ask for an application to be made under section 46(7).

(4) Where enquiries are being made under subsection (1) with respect to a child, the local authority concerned shall (with a view to enabling them to determine what action, if any, to take with respect to him) take such steps as are reasonably practicable—

    (a) to obtain access to him; or

    (b) to ensure that access to him is obtained, on their behalf, by a person authorised by them for the purpose,

unless they are satisfied that they already have sufficient information with respect to him.

(5) Where, as a result of any such enquiries, it appears to the authority that there are matters connected with the child's education which should be investigated, they shall consult the local authority (as defined in section 579(1) of the Education Act 1996), if different, specified in subsection (5ZA).

(5ZA) The local authority referred to in subsection (5) is—

    (a) the local authority who—

        (i)   maintain any school at which the child is a pupil, or

        (ii) make arrangements for the provision of education for the child otherwise than at school pursuant to section 19 of the Education Act 1996, or

    (b) in a case where the child is a pupil at a school which is not maintained by a local authority, the local authority in whose area the school is situated.

(5A) For the purposes of making a determination under this section as to the action to be taken with respect to a child, a local authority shall, so far as is reasonably practicable and consistent with the child's welfare—

    (a) ascertain the child's wishes and feelings regarding the action to be taken with respect to him; and

    (b) give due consideration (having regard to his age and understanding) to such wishes and feelings of the child as they have been able to ascertain.

(6) Where, in the course of enquiries made under this section—

    (a) any officer of the local authority concerned; or

    (b) any person authorised by the authority to act on their behalf in connection with those enquiries—

        (i)   is refused access to the child concerned; or

        (ii) is denied information as to his whereabouts,

the authority shall apply for an emergency protection order, a child assessment order, a care order or a supervision order with respect to the child unless they are satisfied that his welfare can be satisfactorily safeguarded without their doing so.

(7) If, on the conclusion of any enquiries or review made under this section, the authority decide not to apply for an emergency protection order, a child assessment order, a care order or a supervision order they shall—

    (a) consider whether it would be appropriate to review the case at a later date; and

    (b) if they decide that it would be, determine the date on which that review is to begin.

(8) Where, as a result of complying with this section, a local authority conclude that they should take action to safeguard or promote the child's welfare they shall take that action (so far as it is both within their power and reasonably practicable for them to do so).

(9) Where a local authority are conducting enquiries under this section, it shall be the duty of any person mentioned in subsection (11) to assist them with those enquiries (in particular by providing relevant information and advice) if called upon by the authority to do so.

(10) Subsection (9) does not oblige any person to assist a local authority where doing so would be unreasonable in all the circumstances of the case.

(11) The persons are—

    (a)   any local authority;

    (c)   any local housing authority;

    (ca) the National Health Service Commissioning Board;

    (d)   any clinical commissioning group, Local Health Board, Special Health Authority, National Health Service trust or NHS foundation trust; and

    (e)   any person authorised by the Secretary of State for the purposes of this section.

(12) Where a local authority are making enquiries under this section with respect to a child who appears to them to be ordinarily resident within the area of another authority, they shall consult that other authority, who may undertake the necessary enquiries in their place.

48   Powers to assist in discovery of children who may be in need of emergency protection

(1) Where it appears to a court making an emergency protection order that adequate information as to the child's whereabouts—

(a) is not available to the applicant for the order; but

(b) is available to another person,

it may include in the order a provision requiring that other person to disclose, if asked to do so by the applicant, any information that he may have as to the child's whereabouts.

(2) No person shall be excused from complying with such a requirement on the ground that complying might incriminate him or his spouse or civil partner of an offence; but a statement or admission made in complying shall not be admissible in evidence against either of them in proceedings for any offence other than perjury.

(3) An emergency protection order may authorise the applicant to enter premises specified by the order and search for the child with respect to whom the order is made.

(4) Where the court is satisfied that there is reasonable cause to believe that there may be another child on those premises with respect to whom an emergency protection order ought to be made, it may make an order authorising the applicant to search for that other child on those premises.

(5) Where—

(a) an order has been made under subsection (4);

(b) the child concerned has been found on the premises; and

(c) the applicant is satisfied that the grounds for making an emergency protection order exist with respect to him,

the order shall have effect as if it were an emergency protection order.

(6) Where an order has been made under subsection (4), the applicant shall notify the court of its effect.

(7) A person shall be guilty of an offence if he intentionally obstructs any person exercising the power of entry and search under subsection (3) or (4).

(8) A person guilty of an offence under subsection (7) shall be liable on summary conviction to a fine not exceeding level 3 on the standard scale.

(9) Where, on an application made by any person for a warrant under this section, it appears to the court—

(a) that a person attempting to exercise powers under an emergency protection order has been prevented from doing so by being refused entry to the premises concerned or access to the child concerned; or

(b) that any such person is likely to be so prevented from exercising any such powers,

it may issue a warrant authorising any constable to assist the person mentioned in paragraph (a) or (b) in the exercise of those powers using reasonable force if necessary.

(10) Every warrant issued under this section shall be addressed to, and executed by, a constable who shall be accompanied by the person applying for the warrant if—

(a) that person so desires; and

(b) the court by whom the warrant is issued does not direct otherwise.

(11) A court granting an application for a warrant under this section may direct that the constable concerned may, in executing the warrant, be accompanied by a registered medical practitioner, registered nurse or registered midwife if he so chooses.

...

(12) An application for a warrant under this section shall be made in the manner and form prescribed by rules of court.

(13) Wherever it is reasonably practicable to do so, an order under subsection (4), an application for a warrant under this section and any such warrant shall name the child; and where it does not name him it shall describe him as clearly as possible.

49   Abduction of children in care etc.

(1) A person shall be guilty of an offence if, knowingly and without lawful authority or reasonable excuse, he—

(a) takes a child to whom this section applies away from the responsible person;

(b) keeps such a child away from the responsible person; or

(c) induces, assists or incites such a child to run away or stay away from the responsible person.

(2) This section applies in relation to a child who is—

(a) in care;

(b) the subject of an emergency protection order; or

(c) in police protection,

and in this section 'the responsible person' means any person who for the time being has care of him by virtue of the care order, the emergency protection order, or section 46, as the case may be.

(3) A person guilty of an offence under this section shall be liable on summary conviction to imprisonment for a term not exceeding six months, or to a fine not exceeding level 5 on the standard scale, or to both.

50   Recovery of abducted children etc.

(1) Where it appears to the court that there is reason to believe that a child to whom this section applies—

(a) has been unlawfully taken away or is being unlawfully kept away from the responsible person;

(b) has run away or is staying away from the responsible person; or

(c) is missing,

the court may make an order under this section ('a recovery order').

(2) This section applies to the same children to whom section 49 applies and in this section 'the responsible person' has the same meaning as in section 49.

(3) A recovery order—

(a) operates as a direction to any person who is in a position to do so to produce the child on request to any authorised person;

(b) authorises the removal of the child by any authorised person;

(c) requires any person who has information as to the child's whereabouts to disclose that information, if asked to do so, to a constable or an officer of the court;

(d) authorises a constable to enter any premises specified in the order and search for the child, using reasonable force if necessary.

(4) The court may make a recovery order only on the application of—

(a) any person who has parental responsibility for the child by virtue of a care order or emergency protection order; or

(b) where the child is in police protection, the designated officer.

(5) A recovery order shall name the child and—

(a) any person who has parental responsibility for the child by virtue of a care order or emergency protection order; or

(b) where the child is in police protection, the designated officer.

(6) Premises may only be specified under subsection (3)(d) if it appears to the court that there are reasonable grounds for believing the child to be on them.

(7) In this section—

'an authorised person' means—

(a) any person specified by the court;

(b) any constable;

(c) any person who is authorised—

(i)   after the recovery order is made; and

(ii) by a person who has parental responsibility for the child by virtue of a care order or an emergency protection order,

to exercise any power under a recovery order; and

'the designated officer' means the officer designated for the purposes of section 46.

(8) Where a person is authorised as mentioned in subsection (7)(c)—

(a) the authorisation shall identify the recovery order; and

(b) any person claiming to be so authorised shall, if asked to do so, produce some duly authenticated document showing that he is so authorised.

(9) A person shall be guilty of an offence if he intentionally obstructs an authorised person exercising the power under subsection (3)(b) to remove a child.

(10) A person guilty of an offence under this section shall be liable on summary conviction to a fine not exceeding level 3 on the standard scale.

(11) No person shall be excused from complying with any request made under subsection (3)(c) on the ground that complying with it might incriminate him or his spouse or civil partner of an offence; but a statement or admission made in complying shall not be admissible in evidence against either of them in proceedings for an offence other than perjury.

(12) Where a child is made the subject of a recovery order whilst being looked after by a local authority, any reasonable expenses incurred by an authorised person in giving effect to the order shall be recoverable from the authority.

...

51   Refuges for children at risk

(1) Where it is proposed to use a voluntary home or private children's home to provide a refuge for children who appear to be at risk of harm, the Secretary of State may issue a certificate under this section with respect to that home.

(2) Where a local authority or voluntary organisation arrange for a foster parent to provide such a refuge, the Secretary of State may issue a certificate under this section with respect to that foster parent.

(3) In subsection (2) 'foster parent' means a person who is, or who from time to time is, a local authority foster parent or a foster parent with whom children are placed by a voluntary organisation.

(4) The Secretary of State may by regulations—

(a) make provision as to the manner in which certificates may be issued;

(b) impose requirements which must be complied with while any certificate is in force; and

(c) provide for the withdrawal of certificates in prescribed circumstances.

(5) Where a certificate is in force with respect to a home, none of the provisions mentioned in subsection (7) shall apply in relation to any person providing a refuge for any child in that home.

(6) Where a certificate is in force with respect to a foster parent, none of those provisions shall apply in relation to the provision by him of a refuge for any child in accordance with arrangements made by the local authority or voluntary organisation.

(7) The provisions are—

(a) section 49;

(b) sections 82 (recovery of certain fugitive children) and 83 (harbouring) of the Children (Scotland) Act 1995, so far as they apply in relation to anything done in England and Wales;

(c) section 32(3) of the Children and Young Persons Act 1969 (compelling, persuading, inciting or assisting any person to be absent from detention, etc.), so far as it applies in relation to anything done in England and Wales;

(d) section 2 of the Child Abduction Act 1984.

52   Rules and regulations

(1) Without prejudice to section 93 or any other power to make such rules, rules of court may be made with respect to the procedure to be followed in connection with proceedings under this Part.

(2) The rules may, in particular make provision—

(a) as to the form in which any application is to be made or direction is to be given;

(b) prescribing the persons who are to be notified of—

(i)   the making, or extension, of an emergency protection order; or

(ii)   the making of an application under section 45(4) or (8) or 46(7); and

(c) as to the content of any such notification and the manner in which, and person by whom, it is to be given.

(3) The Secretary of State may by regulations provide that, where—

(a) an emergency protection order has been made with respect to a child;

(b) the applicant for the order was not the local authority within whose area the child is ordinarily resident; and

(c) that local authority are of the opinion that it would be in the child's best interests for the applicant's responsibilities under the order to be transferred to them,

that authority shall (subject to their having complied with any requirements imposed by the regulations) be treated, for the purposes of this Act, as though they and not the original applicant had applied for, and been granted, the order.

(4) Regulations made under subsection (3) may, in particular, make provision as to—

(a) the considerations to which the local authority shall have regard in forming an opinion as mentioned in subsection (3)(c); and

(b) the time at which responsibility under any emergency protection order is to be treated as having been transferred to a local authority.

PART VI COMMUNITY HOMES

53 Provision of community homes by local authorities

(1) Every local authority shall make such arrangements as they consider appropriate for securing that homes ('community homes') are available—

(a) for the care and accommodation of children looked after by them; and

(b) for purposes connected with the welfare of children (whether or not looked after by them),

and may do so jointly with one or more other local authorities.

(2) In making such arrangements, a local authority shall have regard to the need for ensuring the availability of accommodation—

(a) of different descriptions; and

(b) which is suitable for different purposes and the requirements of different descriptions of children.

(3) A community home may be a home—

(a) provided, equipped, maintained and (subject to subsection (3A)) managed by a local authority; or

(b) provided by a voluntary organisation but in respect of which a local authority and the organisation—

(i)   propose that, in accordance with an instrument of management, the equipment, maintenance and (subject to subsection (3B)) management of the home shall be the responsibility of the local authority; or

(ii)   so propose that the management, equipment and maintenance of the home shall be the responsibility of the voluntary organisation.

(3A) A local authority may make arrangements for the management by another person of accommodation provided by the local authority for the purpose of restricting the liberty of children.

(3B) Where a local authority are to be responsible for the management of a community home provided by a voluntary organisation, the local authority may, with the consent of the body of managers constituted by the instrument of management for the home, make arrangements for the management by another person of accommodation provided for the purpose of restricting the liberty of children.

(4) Where a local authority are to be responsible for the management of a community home provided by a voluntary organisation, the authority shall designate the home as a controlled community home.

(5) Where a voluntary organisation are to be responsible for the management of a community home provided by the organisation, the local authority shall designate the home as an assisted community home.

(6) Schedule 4 shall have effect for the purpose of supplementing the provisions of this Part.

...

PART VII VOLUNTARY HOMES AND VOLUNTARY ORGANISATIONS

59 Provision of accommodation by voluntary organisations

(1) Where a voluntary organisation provide accommodation for a child, they shall do so by—

    (a)   placing him (subject to subsection (2)) with—

       (i)   a family;

       (ii) a relative of his; or

       (iii) any other suitable person,

       on such terms as to payment by the organisation and otherwise as the organisation may determine (subject to section 49 of the Children Act 2004);

    (aa) maintaining him in a children's home in respect of which a person is registered under Part 2 of the Care Standards Act 2000; or

    (f)   making such other arrangements (subject to subsection (3)) as seem appropriate to them.

(1A) Where under subsection (1)(aa) a voluntary organisation maintains a child in a home provided, equipped and maintained by an appropriate national authority under section 82(5), it shall do so on such terms as that national authority may from time to time determine.

(2) The appropriate national authority may make regulations as to the placing of children with foster parents by voluntary organisations.

(3) The appropriate national authority may make regulations as to the arrangements which may be made under subsection (1)(f).

(3A) Regulations under subsection (2) or (3) may in particular make provision which (with any necessary modifications) is similar to that which may be made under section 22C by virtue of any of paragraphs 12B, 12E and 12F of Schedule 2.

(4) The appropriate national authority may make regulations requiring any voluntary organisation who are providing accommodation for a child—

    (a) to review his case; and

    (b) to consider any representations (including any complaint) made to them by any person falling within a prescribed class of person,

in accordance with the provisions of the regulations.

(5A) Regulations under subsection (4) may, in particular—

    (a) apply with modifications any provision of section 25A or 25B;

    (b) make provision which (with any necessary modifications) is similar to any provision which may be made under section 25A, 25B or 26.

(6) Regulations under subsections (2) to (4) may provide that any person who, without reasonable excuse, contravenes or fails to comply with a regulation shall be guilty of an offence and liable on summary conviction to a fine not exceeding level 4 on the standard scale.

(7) In this Part 'appropriate national authority' means—

    (a) in relation to England, the Secretary of State; and

    (b) in relation to Wales, the Welsh Ministers.

60   Voluntary homes

(3) In this Act 'voluntary home' means a children's home which is carried on by a voluntary organisation but does not include a community home.

(4) Schedule 5 shall have effect for the purpose of supplementing the provisions of this Part.

61   Duties of voluntary organisations

(1) Where a child is accommodated by or on behalf of a voluntary organisation, it shall be the duty of the organisation—

    (a) to safeguard and promote his welfare;

    (b) to make such use of the services and facilities available for children cared for by their own parents as appears to the organisation reasonable in his case; and

    (c) to advise, assist and befriend him with a view to promoting his welfare when he ceases to be so accommodated.

(2) Before making any decision with respect to any such child the organisation shall, so far as is reasonably practicable, ascertain the wishes and feelings of—

    (a) the child;

    (b) his parents;

    (c) any person who is not a parent of his but who has parental responsibility for him; and

    (d) any other person whose wishes and feelings the organisation consider to be relevant,

regarding the matter to be decided.

(3) In making any such decision the organisation shall give due consideration—

    (a) having regard to the child's age and understanding, to such wishes and feelings of his as they have been able to ascertain;

    (b) to such other wishes and feelings mentioned in subsection (2) as they have been able to ascertain; and

    (c) to the child's religious persuasion, racial origin and cultural and linguistic background.

62   Duties of local authorities

(1) Every local authority shall satisfy themselves that any voluntary organisation providing accommodation—

    (a) within the authority's area for any child; or

    (b) outside that area for any child on behalf of the authority,

are satisfactorily safeguarding and promoting the welfare of the children so provided with accommodation.

(2) Every local authority shall arrange for children who are accommodated within their area by or on behalf of voluntary organisations to be visited, from time to time, in the interests of their welfare.

(3) The appropriate national authority may make regulations—

    (a) requiring every child who is accommodated within a local authority's area, by or on behalf of a voluntary organisation, to be visited by an officer of the authority—

        (i)   in prescribed circumstances; and

        (ii) on specified occasions or within specified periods; and

    (b) imposing requirements which must be met by any local authority, or officer of a local authority, carrying out functions under this section.

(4) Subsection (2) does not apply in relation to community homes.

(5) Where a local authority are not satisfied that the welfare of any child who is accommodated by or on behalf of a voluntary organisation is being satisfactorily safeguarded or promoted they shall—

    (a) unless they consider that it would not be in the best interests of the child, take such steps as are reasonably practicable to secure that the care and accommodation of the child is undertaken by—

        (i)   a parent of his;

        (ii) any person who is not a parent of his but who has parental responsibility for him; or

        (iii) a relative of his; and

(b) consider the extent to which (if at all) they should exercise any of their functions with respect to the child.

...

PART VIII REGISTERED CHILDREN'S HOMES

63   Private children's homes etc.

(11) Schedule 6 shall have effect with respect to private children's homes.

(12) Schedule 7 shall have effect for the purpose of setting out the circumstances in which a person may foster more than three children without being treated, for the purposes of this Act and the Care Standards Act 2000, as carrying on a children's home.

64   Welfare of children in children's homes

(1) Where a child is accommodated in a private children's home, it shall be the duty of the person carrying on the home to—

(a) safeguard and promote the child's welfare;

(b) make such use of the services and facilities available for children cared for by their own parents as appears to that person reasonable in the case of the child; and

(c) advise, assist and befriend him with a view to promoting his welfare when he ceases to be so accommodated.

(2) Before making any decision with respect to any such child the person carrying on the home shall, so far as is reasonably practicable, ascertain the wishes and feelings of—

(a) the child;

(b) his parents;

(c) any other person who is not a parent of his but who has parental responsibility for him; and

(d) any person whose wishes and feelings the person carrying on the home considers to be relevant,

regarding the matter to be decided.

(3) In making any such decision the person concerned shall give due consideration—

(a) having regard to the child's age and understanding, to such wishes and feelings of his as he has been able to ascertain;

(b) to such other wishes and feelings mentioned in subsection (2) as he has been able to ascertain; and

(c) to the child's religious persuasion, racial origin and cultural and linguistic background.

(4) Section 62, except subsection (4), shall apply in relation to any person who is carrying on a private children's home as it applies in relation to any voluntary organisation.

...

PART IX PRIVATE ARRANGEMENTS FOR FOSTERING CHILDREN

66   Privately fostered children

(1) In this Part—

(a) 'a privately fostered child' means a child who is under the age of sixteen and who is cared for, and provided with accommodation in their own home by, someone other than—

(i) a parent of his;

(ii) a person who is not a parent of his but who has parental responsibility for him; or

(iii) a relative of his; and

(b) 'to foster privately' means to look after the child in circumstances in which he is a privately fostered child as defined by this section.

(2) A child is not a privately fostered child if the person caring for and accommodating him—

(a) has done so for a period of less than 28 days; and

(b) does not intend to do so for any longer period.

(3) Subsection (1) is subject to—

(a) the provisions of section 63; and

(b) the exceptions made by paragraphs 1 to 5 of Schedule 8.

(4) In the case of a child who is disabled, subsection (1)(a) shall have effect as if for 'sixteen' there were substituted 'eighteen'.

(4A) The Secretary of State may by regulations make provision as to the circumstances in which a person who provides accommodation to a child is, or is not, to be treated as providing him with accommodation in the person's own home.

(5) Schedule 8 shall have effect for the purposes of supplementing the provision made by this Part.

67   Welfare of privately fostered children

(1) It shall be the duty of every local authority to satisfy themselves that the welfare of children who are or are proposed to be privately fostered within their area is being or will be satisfactorily safeguarded and promoted and to secure that such advice is given to those concerned with them as appears to the authority to be needed.

(2) The Secretary of State may make regulations—

(a) requiring every child who is privately fostered within a local authority's area to be visited by an officer of the authority—

(i)   in prescribed circumstances; and

(ii)   on specified occasions or within specified periods; and

(b) imposing requirements which are to be met by any local authority, or officer of a local authority, in carrying out functions under this section.

(2A) Regulations under subsection (2)(b) may impose requirements as to the action to be taken by a local authority for the purposes of discharging their duty under subsection (1) where they have received notification of a proposal that a child be privately fostered.

(3) Where any person who is authorised by a local authority for the purpose has reasonable cause to believe that—

(a) any privately fostered child is being accommodated in premises within the authority's area; or

(b) it is proposed to accommodate any such child in any such premises,

he may at any reasonable time inspect those premises and any children there.

(4) Any person exercising the power under subsection (3) shall, if so required, produce some duly authenticated document showing his authority to do so.

(5) Where a local authority are not satisfied that the welfare of any child who is or is proposed to be privately fostered within their area is being or will be satisfactorily safeguarded or promoted they shall—

(a) unless they consider that it would not be in the best interests of the child, take such steps as are reasonably practicable to secure that the care and accommodation of the child is undertaken by—

(i)   a parent of his;

(ii)   any person who is not a parent of his but who has parental responsibility for him; or

(iii) a relative of his; and

(b) consider the extent to which (if at all) they should exercise any of their functions under this Act with respect to the child.

(6) The Secretary of State may make regulations requiring a local authority to monitor the way in which the authority discharge their functions under this Part (and the regulations may in particular require the authority to appoint an officer for that purpose).

68   Persons disqualified from being private foster parents

(1) Unless he has disclosed the fact to the appropriate local authority and obtained their written consent, a person shall not foster a child privately if he is disqualified from doing so by regulations made by the Secretary of State for the purposes of this section.

(2) The regulations may, in particular, provide for a person to be so disqualified where—

  (a) an order of a kind specified in the regulations has been made at any time with respect to him;

  (b) an order of a kind so specified has been made at any time with respect to any child who has been in his care;

  (c) a requirement of a kind so specified has been imposed at any time with respect to any such child, under or by virtue of any enactment;

  (d) he has been convicted of any offence of a kind so specified, or discharged absolutely or conditionally for any such offence;

  (e) a prohibition has been imposed on him at any time under section 69 or under any other specified enactment;

  (f) his rights and powers with respect to a child have at any time been vested in a specified authority under a specified enactment.

(2A) A conviction in respect of which a probation order was made before 1st October 1992 (which would not otherwise be treated as a conviction) is to be treated as a conviction for the purposes of subsection (2)(d).

(3) Unless he has disclosed the fact to the appropriate local authority and obtained their written consent, a person shall not foster a child privately if—

  (a) he lives in the same household as a person who is himself prevented from fostering a child by subsection (1); or

  (b) he lives in a household at which any such person is employed.

(3A) A person shall not foster a child privately if—

  (a) he is barred from regulated activity relating to children (within the meaning of section 3(2) of the Safeguarding Vulnerable Groups Act 2006); or

  (b) he lives in the same household as a person who is barred from such activity.

(4) Where an authority refuse to give their consent under this section, they shall inform the applicant by a written notice which states—

  (a) the reason for the refusal;

  (b) the applicant's right under paragraph 8 of Schedule 8 to appeal against the refusal; and

  (c) the time within which he may do so.

(5) In this section—

'the appropriate authority' means the local authority within whose area it is proposed to foster the child in question; and

'enactment' means any enactment having effect, at any time, in any part of the United Kingdom.

69   Power to prohibit private fostering

(1) This section applies where a person—

  (a) proposes to foster a child privately; or

  (b) is fostering a child privately.

(2) Where the local authority for the area within which the child is proposed to be, or is being, fostered are of the opinion that—

  (a) he is not a suitable person to foster a child;

  (b) the premises in which the child will be, or is being, accommodated are not suitable; or

(c) it would be prejudicial to the welfare of the child for him to be, or continue to be, accommodated by that person in those premises,

the authority may impose a prohibition on him under subsection (3).

(3) A prohibition imposed on any person under this subsection may prohibit him from fostering privately—

(a) any child in any premises within the area of the local authority; or

(b) any child in premises specified in the prohibition;

(c) a child identified in the prohibition, in premises specified in the prohibition.

(4) A local authority who have imposed a prohibition on any person under subsection (3) may, if they think fit, cancel the prohibition—

(a) of their own motion; or

(b) on an application made by that person,

if they are satisfied that the prohibition is no longer justified.

(5) Where a local authority impose a requirement on any person under paragraph 6 of Schedule 8, they may also impose a prohibition on him under subsection (3).

(6) Any prohibition imposed by virtue of subsection (5) shall not have effect unless—

(a) the time specified for compliance with the requirement has expired; and

(b) the requirement has not been complied with.

(7) A prohibition imposed under this section shall be imposed by notice in writing addressed to the person on whom it is imposed and informing him of—

(a) the reason for imposing the prohibition;

(b) his right under paragraph 8 of Schedule 8 to appeal against the prohibition; and

(c) the time within which he may do so.

70   Offences

(1) A person shall be guilty of an offence if—

(a) being required, under any provision made by or under this Part, to give any notice or information—

(i) he fails without reasonable excuse to give the notice within the time specified in that provision; or

(ii) he fails without reasonable excuse to give the information within a reasonable time; or

(iii) he makes, or causes or procures another person to make, any statement in the notice or information which he knows to be false or misleading in a material particular;

(b) he refuses to allow a privately fostered child to be visited by a duly authorised officer of a local authority;

(c) he intentionally obstructs another in the exercise of the power conferred by section 67(3);

(d) he contravenes section 68;

(e) he fails without reasonable excuse to comply with any requirement imposed by a local authority under this Part;

(f) he accommodates a privately fostered child in any premises in contravention of a prohibition imposed by a local authority under this Part;

(g) he knowingly causes to be published, or publishes, an advertisement which he knows contravenes paragraph 10 of Schedule 8.

(2) Where a person contravenes section 68(3), he shall not be guilty of an offence under this section if he proves that he did not know, and had no reasonable ground for believing, that any person to whom section 68(1) applied was living or employed in the premises in question.

(3) A person guilty of an offence under subsection (1)(a) shall be liable on summary conviction to a fine not exceeding level 5 on the standard scale.

(4) A person guilty of an offence under subsection (1)(b), (c) or (g) shall be liable on summary conviction to a fine not exceeding level 3 on the standard scale.

(5) A person guilty of a offence under subsection 1(d) or (f) shall be liable on summary conviction to imprisonment for a term not exceeding six months, or to a fine not exceeding level 5 on the standard scale, or to both.

(6) A person guilty of an offence under subsection (1)(e) shall be liable on summary conviction to a fine not exceeding level 4 on the standard scale.

(7) If any person who is required, under any provision of this Part, to give a notice fails to give the notice within the time specified in that provision, proceedings for the offence may be brought at any time within six months from the date when evidence of the offence came to the knowledge of the local authority.

(8) Subsection (7) is not affected by anything in section 127(1) of the Magistrates' Courts Act 1980 (time limit for proceedings).

...

PART XII MISCELLANEOUS AND GENERAL

Notification of children accommodated in certain establishments

85 Children accommodated by health authorities and local education authorities

(1) Where a child is provided with accommodation by any Local Health Board, Special Health Authority, National Health Service trust or NHS foundation trust or by a local authority in the exercise of education functions ('the accommodating authority')—

  (a) for a consecutive period of at least three months; or

  (b) with the intention, on the part of that authority, of accommodating him for such a period,

the accommodating authority shall notify the appropriate officer of the responsible authority.

(2) Where subsection (1) applies with respect to a child, the accommodating authority shall also notify the appropriate officer of the responsible authority when they cease to accommodate the child.

(2A) In a case where the child is provided with accommodation by a local authority in the exercise of education functions, subsections (1) and (2) apply only if the local authority providing the accommodation is different from the responsible authority.

(2ZA) Where a child is provided with accommodation—

  (a) by a body which is not mentioned in subsection (1), and

  (b) pursuant to arrangements made by the Secretary of State, the National Health Service Commissioning Board or a clinical commissioning group under the National Health Service Act 2006,

subsections (1) and (2) apply in relation to the Secretary of State, the Board or (as the case may be) the clinical commissioning group as if it were the accommodating authority.

(3) In this section 'the responsible authority' means—

  (a) the local authority appearing to the accommodating authority to be the authority within whose area the child was ordinarily resident immediately before being accommodated; or

  (b) where it appears to the accommodating authority that a child was not ordinarily resident within the area of any local authority, the local authority within whose area the accommodation is situated.

(3A) In this section and sections 86 and 86A 'the appropriate officer' means—

  (a) in relation to a local authority in England, their director of children's services; and

  (b) in relation to a local authority in Wales, their lead director for children and young people's services.

(4) Where the appropriate officer of a local authority has been notified under this section, the local authority shall—

  (a) take such steps as are reasonably practicable to enable them to determine whether the child's welfare is adequately safeguarded and promoted while he is accommodated by the accommodating authority; and

(b) consider the extent to which (if at all) they should exercise any of their functions under this Act with respect to the child.

(5) For the purposes of subsection (4)(b), if the child is not in the area of the local authority, they must treat him as if he were in that area.

...

86A Visitors for children notified to local authority under section 85 or 86

(1) This section applies if the appropriate officer of a local authority—

    (a) has been notified with respect to a child under section 85(1) or 86(1); and

    (b) has not been notified with respect to that child under section 85(2) or, as the case may be, 86(2).

(2) The local authority must, in accordance with regulations made under this section, make arrangements for the child to be visited by a representative of the authority ('a representative').

(3) It is the function of a representative to provide advice and assistance to the local authority on the performance of their duties under section 85(4) or, as the case may be, 86(3).

(4) Regulations under this section may make provision about—

    (a) the frequency of visits under visiting arrangements;

    (b) circumstances in which visiting arrangements must require a child to be visited; and

    (c) additional functions of a representative.

(5) Regulations under this section are to be made by the Secretary of State and the Welsh Ministers acting jointly.

(6) In choosing a representative a local authority must satisfy themselves that the person chosen has the necessary skills and experience to perform the functions of a representative.

(7) In this section 'visiting arrangements' means arrangements made under subsection (2).

...

Effect and duration of orders etc.

91 Effect and duration of orders etc.

(1) The making of a child arrangements order with respect to the living arrangements of a child who is the subject of a care order discharges the care order.

(1A) For the purposes of subsection (1), a child arrangements order is one made with respect to the living arrangements of a child if the arrangements regulated by the order consist of, or include, arrangements which relate to either or both of the following—

    (a) with whom the child is to live, and

    (b) when the child is to live with any person.

(2) The making of a care order with respect to a child who is the subject of any section 8 order discharges that order.

(2A) Where an activity direction has been made with respect to a child, the making of a care order with respect to the child discharges the direction.

(3) The making of a care order with respect to a child who is the subject of a supervision order discharges that other order.

(4) The making of a care order with respect to a child who is a ward of court brings that wardship to an end.

(5) The making of a care order with respect to a child who is the subject of a school attendance order made under section 437 of the Education Act 1996 discharges the school attendance order.

(5A) The making of a special guardianship order with respect to a child who is the subject of—

    (a) a care order; or

    (b) an order under section 34,

discharges that order.

(6) Where an emergency protection order is made with respect to a child who is in care, the care order shall have effect subject to the emergency protection order.

(7) Any order made under section 4(1), 4ZA(1), 4A(1) or 5(1) shall continue in force until the child reaches the age of eighteen, unless it is brought to an end earlier.

(8) Any—

(a) agreement under section 4, 4ZA or 4A; or

(b) appointment under section 5(3) or (4),

shall continue in force until the child reaches the age of eighteen, unless it is brought to an end earlier.

(9) An order under Schedule 1 has effect as specified in that Schedule.

(10) A section 8 order shall, if it would otherwise still be in force, cease to have effect when the child reaches the age of sixteen, unless it is to have effect beyond that age by virtue of section 9(6).

(10A) Subsection (10) does not apply to provision in a child arrangements order which regulates arrangements relating to—

(a) with whom a child is to live, or

(b) when a child is to live with any person.

(11) Where a section 8 order has effect with respect to a child who has reached the age of sixteen, it shall, if it would otherwise still be in force, cease to have effect when he reaches the age of eighteen.

(12) Any care order, other than an interim care order, shall continue in force until the child reaches the age of eighteen, unless it is brought to an end earlier.

(13) Any order made under any other provision of this Act in relation to a child shall, if it would otherwise still be in force, cease to have effect when he reaches the age of eighteen.

(14) On disposing of any application for an order under this Act, the court may (whether or not it makes any other order in response to the application) order that no application for an order under this Act of any specified kind may be made with respect to the child concerned by any person named in the order without leave of the court.

(15) Where an application ('the previous application') has been made for—

(a) the discharge of a care order;

(b) the discharge of a supervision order;

(c) the discharge of an education supervision order;

(d) the substitution of a supervision order for a care order; or

(e) a child assessment order,

no further application of a kind mentioned in paragraphs (a) to (e) may be made with respect to the child concerned, without leave of the court, unless the period between the disposal of the previous application and the making of the further application exceeds six months.

(16) Subsection (15) does not apply to applications made in relation to interim orders.

(17) Where—

(a) a person has made an application for an order under section 34;

(b) the application has been refused; and

(c) a period of less than six months has elapsed since the refusal,

that person may not make a further application for such an order with respect to the same child, unless he has obtained the leave of the court.

Jurisdiction and procedure etc.

92 Jurisdiction of courts

...

(7) For the purposes of this Act 'the court' means the High Court or the family court.

(8) Subsection (7) is subject to any express provision as to the jurisdiction of any court made by any other provision of this Act.

...

(11) Part II of Schedule 11 makes amendments consequential on this section.

...

95   Attendance of child at hearing under Part IV or V

(1) In any proceedings in which a court is hearing an application for an order under Part IV or V, or is considering whether to make any such order, the court may order the child concerned to attend such stage or stages of the proceedings as may be specified in the order.

(2) The power conferred by subsection (1) shall be exercised in accordance with rules of court.

(3) Subsections (4) to (6) apply where—

    (a) an order under subsection (1) has not been complied with; or

    (b) the court has reasonable cause to believe that it will not be complied with.

(4) The court may make an order authorising a constable, or such person as may be specified in the order—

    (a) to take charge of the child and to bring him to the court; and

    (b) to enter and search any premises specified in the order if he has reasonable cause to believe that the child may be found on the premises.

(5) The court may order any person who is in a position to do so to bring the child to the court.

(6) Where the court has reason to believe that a person has information about the whereabouts of the child it may order him to disclose it to the court.

96   Evidence given by, or with respect to, children

(1) Subsection (2) applies where a child who is called as a witness in any civil proceedings does not, in the opinion of the court, understand the nature of an oath.

(2) The child's evidence may be heard by the court if, in its opinion—

    (a) he understands that it is his duty to speak the truth; and

    (b) he has sufficient understanding to justify his evidence being heard.

(3) The Lord Chancellor may, with the concurrence of the Lord Chief Justice, by order make provision for the admissibility of evidence which would otherwise be inadmissible under any rule of law relating to hearsay.

(4) An order under subsection (3) may only be made with respect to—

    (a) civil proceedings in general or such civil proceedings, or class of civil proceedings, as may be prescribed; and

    (b) evidence in connection with the upbringing, maintenance or welfare of a child.

(5) An order under subsection (3)—

    (a) may, in particular, provide for the admissibility of statements which are made orally or in a prescribed form or which are recorded by any prescribed method of recording;

    (b) may make different provision for different purposes and in relation to different descriptions of court; and

    (c) may make such amendments and repeals in any enactment relating to evidence (other than in this Act) as the Lord Chancellor considers necessary or expedient in consequence of the provision made by the order.

(6) Subsection (5)(b) is without prejudice to section 104(4).

(7) In this section—

'civil proceedings' means civil proceedings, before any tribunal, in relation to which the strict rules of evidence apply, whether as a matter of law or by agreement of the parties, and references to 'the court' shall be construed accordingly; and

'prescribed' means prescribed by an order under subsection (3).

. . .

98   Self-incrimination

(1) In any proceedings in which a court is hearing an application for an order under Part IV or V, no person shall be excused from—

    (a) giving evidence on any matter; or

    (b) answering any question put to him in the course of his giving evidence, on the ground that doing so might incriminate him or his spouse or civil partner of an offence.

(2) A statement or admission made in such proceedings shall not be admissible in evidence against the person making it or his spouse or civil partner in proceedings for an offence other than perjury.

100 Restrictions on use of wardship jurisdiction

(1) Section 7 of the Family Law Reform Act 1969 (which gives the High Court power to place a ward of court in the care, or under the supervision, of a local authority) shall cease to have effect.

(2) No court shall exercise the High Court's inherent jurisdiction with respect to children—

   (a) so as to require a child to be placed in the care, or put under the supervision, of a local authority;

   (b) so as to require a child to be accommodated by or on behalf of a local authority; or

   (c) so as to make a child who is the subject of a care order a ward of court; or

   (d) for the purpose of conferring on any local authority power to determine any question which has arisen, or which may arise, in connection with any aspect of parental responsibility for a child.

(3) No application for any exercise of the court's inherent jurisdiction with respect to children may be made by a local authority unless the authority have obtained the leave of the court.

(4) The court may only grant leave if it is satisfied that—

   (a) the result which the authority wish to achieve could not be achieved through the making of any order of a kind to which subsection (5) applies; and

   (b) there is reasonable cause to believe that if the court's inherent jurisdiction is not exercised with respect to the child he is likely to suffer significant harm.

(5) This subsection applies to any order—

   (a) made otherwise than in the exercise of the court's inherent jurisdiction; and

   (b) which the local authority is entitled to apply for (assuming, in the case of any application which may only be made with leave, that leave is granted).

...

Search warrants

102 Power of constable to assist in exercise of certain powers to search for children or inspect premises

(1) Where, on an application made by any person for a warrant under this section, it appears to the court—

   (a) that a person attempting to exercise powers under any enactment mentioned in subsection (6) has been prevented from doing so by being refused entry to the premises concerned or refused access to the child concerned; or

   (b) that any such person is likely to be so prevented from exercising any such powers,

it may issue a warrant authorising any constable to assist that person in the exercise of those powers, using reasonable force if necessary.

(2) Every warrant issued under this section shall be addressed to, and executed by, a constable who shall be accompanied by the person applying for the warrant if—

   (a) that person so desires; and

   (b) the court by whom the warrant is issued does not direct otherwise.

(3) A court granting an application for a warrant under this section may direct that the constable concerned may, in executing the warrant, be accompanied by a registered medical practitioner, registered nurse or registered midwife if he so chooses.

...

(4) An application for a warrant under this section shall be made in the manner and form prescribed by rules of court.

(5) Where—

   (a) an application for a warrant under this section relates to a particular child; and

   (b) it is reasonably practicable to do so,

the application and any warrant granted on the application shall name the child; and where it does not name him it shall describe him as clearly as possible.

> (6) The enactments are—
>> (a) sections 62, 64, 67, 76, 79U, 80, 86 and 87;
>> (b) paragraph 8(1)(b) and (2)(b) of Schedule 3;
>
> ...

General

105 Interpretation

> (1) In this Act—

'activity condition' has the meaning given by section 11C;

'activity direction' has the meaning given by section 11A;

'adoption agency' means a body which may be referred to as an adoption agency by virtue of section 2 of the Adoption and Children Act 2002;

'bank holiday' means a day which is a bank holiday under the Banking and Financial Dealings Act 1971;

'care home' has the same meaning as in the Care Standards Act 2000;

'care order' has the meaning given by section 31(11) and also includes any order which by or under any enactment has the effect of, or is deemed to be, a care order for the purposes of this Act; and any reference to a child who is in the care of an authority is a reference to a child who is in their care by virtue of a care order;

'child' means, subject to paragraph 16 of Schedule 1, a person under the age of eighteen;

'child arrangements order' has the meaning given by section 8(1);

'child assessment order' has the meaning given by section 43(2);

'child of the family', in relation to parties to a marriage, or to two people who are civil partners of each other, means—

> (a) a child of both of them, and
> (b) any other child, other than a child placed with them as foster parents by a local authority or voluntary organisation, who has been treated by both of them as a child of their family.

'children's home' has the same meaning as it has for the purposes of the Care Standards Act 2000 (see section 1 of that Act);

'clinical commissioning group' means a body established under section 14D of the National Health Service Act 2006;

'community home' has the meaning given by section 53;

'day care' has the same meaning given by section 18;

'disabled', in relation to a child, has the same meaning as in section 17(11);

'domestic premises' has the meaning given by section 71(12);

'dwelling-house' includes—

> (a) any building or part of a building which is occupied as a dwelling;
> (b) any caravan, house-boat or structure which is occupied as a dwelling;

and any yard, garden, garage or outhouse belonging to it and occupied with it;

'education functions' has the meaning given by section 579(1) of the Education Act 1996;

'education supervision order' has the meaning given in section 36;

'emergency protection order' means an order under section 44;'

enforcement order' has the meaning given by section 11J;

'family assistance order' has the meaning given in section 16(2);

'family proceedings' has the meaning given by section 8(3);

'functions' includes powers and duties;

'guardian of a child' means a guardian (other than a guardian of the estate of a child) appointed in accordance with the provisions of section 5;

'harm' has the same meaning as in section 31(9) and the question of whether harm is significant shall be determined in accordance with section 31(10);

'health service hospital' means a health service hospital within the meaning given by the National Health Service Act 2006 or the National Health Service (Wales) Act 2006;

'hospital' has the same meaning as in the Mental Health Act 1983, except that it does not include a hospital at which high security psychiatric services within the meaning of that Act are provided;

'ill-treatment' has the same meaning as in section 31(9);

'independent hospital'—

    (a) in relation to England, means a hospital as defined by section 275 of the National Health Service Act 2006 that is not a health service hospital as defined by that section; and

    (b) in relation to Wales, has the same meaning as in the Care Standards Act 2000;

'independent school' has the same meaning as in the Education Act 1996;

'local authority' means, in relation to England, the council of a county, a metropolitan district, a London Borough or the Common Council of the City of London, in relation to Wales, the council of a county or a county borough and, in relation to Scotland, a local authority within the meaning of section 1(2) of the Social Work (Scotland) Act 1968;

'local authority foster parent' has the meaning given in section 22C(12);

'Local Health Board' means a Local Health Board established under section 11 of the National Health Service (Wales) Act 2006;

'local housing authority' has the same meaning as in the Housing Act 1985;

'officer of the Service' has the same meaning as in the Criminal Justice and Court Services Act 2000;

'parental responsibility' has the meaning given in section 3;

'parental responsibility agreement' has the meaning given in sections 4(1), 4ZA(4) and 4A(2);

'prescribed' means prescribed by regulations made under this Act;

'private children's home' means a children's home in respect of which a person is registered under Part II of the Care Standards Act 2000 which is not a community home or a voluntary home;

'privately fostered child' and 'to foster a child privately' have the same meaning as in section 66;

'prohibited steps order' has the meaning given by section 8(1);

'registered pupil' has the same meaning as in the Education Act 1996;

'relative', in relation to a child, means a grandparent, brother, sister, uncle or aunt (whether of the full blood or half blood or by marriage or civil partnership) or step-parent;

'responsible person', in relation to a child who is the subject of a supervision order, has the meaning given in paragraph 1 of Schedule 3;

'school' has the same meaning as in the Education Act 1996...;

'section 31A plan' has the meaning given by section 31A(6);

'service', in relation to any provision, made under Part III, includes any facility;

'signed', in relation to any person, includes the making by that person of his mark;

'special educational needs' has the same meaning as in the Education Act 1996;

'special guardian' and 'special guardianship order' have the meaning given by section 14A;

'Special Health Authority' means a Special Health Authority established under section 28 of the National Health Service Act 2006 or section 22 of the National Health Service (Wales) Act 2006;

'specific issue order' has the meaning given by section 8(1);

'supervision order' has the meaning given by section 31(11);

'supervised child' and 'supervisor', in relation to a supervision order or an education supervision order, mean respectively the child who is (or is to be) under supervision and the person under whose supervision he is (or is to be) by virtue of the order;

'upbringing', in relation to any child, includes the care of the child but not his maintenance;

'voluntary home' has the meaning given by section 60;

'voluntary organisation' means a body (other than a public or local authority) whose activities are not carried on for profit.

'Welsh family proceedings officer' has the meaning given by section 35 of the Children Act 2004.

    (2) References in this Act to a child whose father and mother were, or (as the case may be) were not, married to each other at the time of his birth must be read with section 1 of the Family Law Reform Act 1987 (which extends the meaning of such references).

    ...

(4) References in this Act to a child who is looked after by a local authority have the same meaning as they have (by virtue of section 22) in Part III.

(5) References in this Act to accommodation provided by or on behalf of a local authority are references to accommodation so provided in the exercise of functions of that or any other local authority which are social services functions within the meaning of the Local Authority Social Services Act 1970.

...

(6) In determining the 'ordinary residence' of a child for any purpose of this Act, there shall be disregarded any period in which he lives in any place—
(a) which is a school or other institution;
(b) in accordance with the requirements of a supervision order under this Act;
(ba) in accordance with the requirements of a youth rehabilitation order under Part 1 of the Criminal Justice and Immigration Act 2008; or
(c) while he is being provided with accommodation by or on behalf of a local authority.

...

(7) References in this Act to children who are in need shall be construed in accordance with section 17.

(7A) References in this Act to a hospital or accommodation made available or provided pursuant to arrangements made by the Secretary of State under the National Health Service Act 2006 are references to a hospital or accommodation made available or provided pursuant to arrangements so made in the exercise of the public health functions of the Secretary of State (within the meaning of that Act).

(7B) References in this Act to arrangements made by the National Health Service Commissioning Board or a clinical commissioning group under the National Health Service Act 2006 include references to arrangements so made by virtue of section 7A of that Act.

(8) Any notice or other document required under this Act to be served on any person may be served on him by being delivered personally to him, or being sent by post to him in a registered letter or by the recorded delivery service at his proper address.

(9) Any such notice or other document required to be served on a body corporate or a firm shall be duly served if it is served on the secretary or clerk of that body or a partner of that firm.

(10) For the purposes of this section, and of section 7 of the Interpretation Act 1978 in its application to this section, the proper address of a person—
(a) in the case of a secretary or clerk of a body corporate, shall be that of the registered or principal office of that body;
(b) in the case of a partner of a firm, shall be that of the principal office of the firm; and
(c) in any other case, shall be last known address of the person to be served.

SCHEDULES

SCHEDULE A1

ENFORCEMENT ORDERS

PART 1 UNPAID WORK REQUIREMENT

General

1.—Subject to the modifications in paragraphs 2 and 3,[1] Chapter 4 of Part 12 of the Criminal Justice Act 2003 has effect in relation to an enforcement order as it has effect in relation to a community order (within the meaning of Part 12 of that Act).

[1] The modifications referred to here are incorporated into the Criminal Justice Act 2003 as reproduced in this volume.

References to an offender

2.—Subject to paragraph 3, references in Chapter 4 of Part 12 of the Criminal Justice Act 2003 to an offender are to be treated as including references to a person subject to an enforcement order.

Specific modifications

3.—(1) The power of the Secretary of State by order under section 197(3) to amend the definition of 'responsible officer' and to make consequential amendments includes power to make any amendments of this Part (including further modifications of Chapter 4 of Part 12 of the Criminal Justice Act 2003) that appear to the Secretary of State to be necessary or expedient in consequence of any amendment made by virtue of section 197(3)(a) or (b).

...

PART 2 REVOCATION, AMENDMENT OR BREACH OF ENFORCEMENT ORDER

Power to revoke

4.—(1) This paragraph applies where a court has made an enforcement order in respect of a person's failure to comply with a provision of a child arrangements order and the enforcement order is in force.

(2) The court may revoke the enforcement order if it appears to the court that—

(a) in all the circumstances no enforcement order should have been made,

(b) having regard to circumstances which have arisen since the enforcement order was made, it would be appropriate for the enforcement order to be revoked, or

(c) having regard to the person's satisfactory compliance with the child arrangements order or any contact order that has effect in its place, it would be appropriate for the enforcement order to be revoked.

(3) The enforcement order may be revoked by the court under sub-paragraph (2) of its own motion or on an application by the person subject to the enforcement order.

(4) In deciding whether to revoke the enforcement order under sub-paragraph (2)(b), the court is to take into account—

(a) the extent to which the person subject to the enforcement order has complied with it, and

(b) the likelihood that the person will comply with the child arrangements order or any child arrangements order that has effect in its place in the absence of an enforcement order.

(5) In deciding whether to revoke the enforcement order under sub-paragraph (2)(c), the court is to take into account the likelihood that the person will comply with the child arrangements order or any child arrangements order that has effect in its place in the absence of an enforcement order.

Amendment by reason of change of residence

5.—(1) This paragraph applies where a court has made an enforcement order in respect of a person's failure to comply with a provision of a child arrangements order and the enforcement order is in force.

(2) If the court is satisfied that the person has changed, or proposes to change, his residence from the local justice area specified in the order to another local justice area, the court may amend the order by substituting the other area for the area specified.

(3) The enforcement order may be amended by the court under subparagraph (2) of its own motion or on an application by the person subject to the enforcement order.

Amendment of hours specified under unpaid work requirement

6.—(1) This paragraph applies where a court has made an enforcement order in respect of a person's failure to comply with a provision of a child arrangements order and the enforcement order is in force.

(2) If it appears to the court that, having regard to circumstances that have arisen since the enforcement order was made, it would be appropriate to do so, the court may reduce the number of hours specified in the order (but not below the minimum specified in section 199(2)(a) of the Criminal Justice Act 2003).

(3) In amending the enforcement order under sub-paragraph (2), the court must be satisfied that the effect on the person of the enforcement order as proposed to be amended is no more than is required to secure his compliance with the child arrangements order or any child arrangements order that has effect in its place.

(4) The enforcement order may be amended by the court under subparagraph (2) of its own motion or on an application by the person subject to the enforcement order.

Amendment to extend unpaid work requirement

7.—(1) This paragraph applies where a court has made an enforcement order in respect of a person's failure to comply with a provision of a child arrangements order and the enforcement order is in force.

(2) If it appears to the court that, having regard to circumstances that have arisen since the enforcement order was made, it would be appropriate to do so, the court may, in relation to the order, extend the period of twelve months specified in section 200(2) of the Criminal Justice Act 2003 (as substituted by paragraph 3).

(3) The period may be extended by the court under sub-paragraph (2) of its own motion or on an application by the person subject to the enforcement order.

Warning and report following breach

8.—(1) This paragraph applies where a court has made an enforcement order in respect of a person's failure to comply with a provision of a child arrangements order.

(2) If the responsible officer is of the opinion that the person has failed without reasonable excuse to comply with the unpaid work requirement imposed by the enforcement order, the officer must give the person a warning under this paragraph unless—

(a) the person has within the previous twelve months been given a warning under this paragraph in relation to a failure to comply with the unpaid work requirement, or

(b) the responsible officer reports the failure to the appropriate person.

(3) A warning under this paragraph must—

(a) describe the circumstances of the failure,

(b) state that the failure is unacceptable, and

(c) inform the person that, if within the next twelve months he again fails to comply with the unpaid work requirement, the warning and the subsequent failure will be reported to the appropriate person.

(4) The responsible officer must, as soon as practicable after the warning has been given, record that fact.

(5) If—

(a) the responsible officer has given a warning under this paragraph to a person subject to an enforcement order, and

(b) at any time within the twelve months beginning with the date on which the warning was given, the responsible officer is of the opinion that the person has since that date failed without reasonable excuse to comply with the unpaid work requirement imposed by the enforcement order,

the officer must report the failure to the appropriate person.

(6) A report under sub-paragraph (5) must include a report of the warning given to the person subject to the enforcement order.

(7) The appropriate person, in relation to an enforcement order, is the officer of the Service or the Welsh family proceedings officer who is required under section 11M to report on matters relating to the enforcement order.

(8) 'Responsible officer', in relation to a person subject to an enforcement order, has the same meaning as in section 197 of the Criminal Justice Act 2003 (as modified by paragraph 2).

Breach of an enforcement order

9.—(1) This paragraph applies where a court has made an enforcement order ('the first order') in respect of a person's failure to comply with a provision of a child arrangements order.

(2) If the court is satisfied beyond reasonable doubt that the person has failed to comply with the unpaid work requirement imposed by the first order, the court may—

(a) amend the first order so as to make the requirement more onerous, or

(b) make an enforcement order ('the second order') in relation to the person and (if the first order is still in force) provide for the second order to have effect either in addition to or in substitution for the first order.

(3) But the court may not exercise its powers under sub-paragraph (2) if it is satisfied that the person had a reasonable excuse for failing to comply with the unpaid work requirement imposed by the first order.

(4) The burden of proof as to the matter mentioned in sub-paragraph (3) lies on the person claiming to have had a reasonable excuse, and the standard of proof is the balance of probabilities.

(5) The court may exercise its powers under sub-paragraph (2) in relation to the first order only on the application of a person who would be able to apply under section 11J for an enforcement order if the failure to comply with the first order were a failure to comply with a provision of the child arrangements order to which the first order relates.

(6) Where the person proposing to apply to the court is the child with respect to whom the child arrangements order was made, subsections (6) and (7) of section 11J have effect in relation to the application as they have effect in relation to an application for an enforcement order.

(7) An application to the court to exercise its powers under sub-paragraph (2) may only be made while the first order is in force.

(8) The court may not exercise its powers under sub-paragraph (2) in respect of a failure by the person to comply with the unpaid work requirement imposed by the first order unless it is satisfied that before the failure occurred the person had been given (in accordance with rules of court) a copy of, or otherwise informed of the terms of, a notice under section 11N relating to the first order.

(9) In dealing with the person under sub-paragraph (2)(a), the court may—

(a) increase the number of hours specified in the first order (but not above the maximum specified in section 199(2)(b) of the Criminal Justice Act 2003, as substituted by paragraph 3);

(b) in relation to the order, extend the period of twelve months specified in section 200(2) of the Criminal Justice Act 2003 (as substituted by paragraph 3).

(10) In exercising its powers under sub-paragraph (2), the court must be satisfied that, taking into account the extent to which the person has complied with the unpaid work requirement imposed by the first order, the effect on the person of the proposed exercise of those powers—

(a) is no more than is required to secure his compliance with the child arrangements order or any contact order that has effect in its place, and

(b) is no more than is proportionate to the seriousness of his failures to comply with the provisions of the child arrangements order and with the first order.

(11) Where the court exercises its powers under sub-paragraph (2) by making an enforcement order in relation to a person who has failed to comply with another enforcement order—

(a) sections 11K(4), 11L(2) to (7), 11M and 11N have effect as regards the making of the order in relation to the person as they have effect as regards the making of an enforcement order in relation to a person who has failed to comply with a provision of a child arrangements order;

(b) this Part of this Schedule has effect in relation to the order so made as if it were an enforcement order made in respect of the failure for which the other order was made.

(12) Sub-paragraph (2) is without prejudice to section 63(3) of the Magistrates' Courts Act 1980 as it applies in relation to enforcement orders.

Provision relating to amendment of enforcement orders

10. Sections 11L(2) to (7) and 11M have effect in relation to the making of an order under paragraph 6(2), 7(2) or 9(2)(a) amending an enforcement order as they have effect in relation to the making of an enforcement order; and references in sections 11L(2) to (7) and 11M to an enforcement order are to be read accordingly.

Section 15(1)

SCHEDULE 1

FINANCIAL PROVISION FOR CHILDREN

Orders for financial relief against parents

1.—(1) On an application made by a parent, guardian or special guardian of a child, or by any person who is named in a child arrangements order as a person with whom a child is to live, the court may make one or more of the orders mentioned in sub-paragraph (2).

(2) The orders referred to in sub-paragraph (1) are—

(a) an order requiring either or both parents of a child—
   (i)   to make to the applicant for the benefit of the child; or
   (ii) to make to the child himself,
   such periodical payments, for such term, as may be specified in the order;

(b) an order requiring either or both parents of a child—
   (i)   to secure to the applicant for the benefit of the child; or
   (ii) to secure to the child himself,
   such periodical payments, for such term, as may be so specified;

(c) an order requiring either or both parents of a child—
   (i)   to pay to the applicant for the benefit of the child; or
   (ii) to pay to the child himself,
   such lump sum as may be so specified;

(d) an order requiring a settlement to be made for the benefit of the child, and to the satisfaction of the court, of property—
   (i)   to which either parent is entitled (either in possession or in reversion); and
   (ii) which is specified in the order;

(e) an order requiring either or both parents of a child—
   (i)   to transfer to the applicant, for the benefit of the child; or
   (ii) to transfer to the child himself,
   such property to which the parent is, or the parents are, entitled (either in possession or in reversion) as may be specified in the order.

(3) The powers conferred by this paragraph may be exercised at any time.

(4) An order under sub-paragraph (2)(a) or (b) may be varied or discharged by a subsequent order made on the application of any person by or to whom payments were required to be made under the previous order.

(5) Where a court makes an order under this paragraph—

(a) it may at any time make a further such order under sub-paragraph (2)(a), (b) or (c) with respect to the child concerned if he has not reached the age of eighteen;

(b) it may not make more than one order under sub-paragraph (2)(d) or (e) against the same person in respect of the same child.

(6) On making, varying or discharging a special guardianship order, or on making, varying or discharging provision in a child arrangements order with respect to the living arrangements of a

child, the court may exercise any of its powers under this Schedule even though no application has been made to it under this Schedule.

(6A) For the purposes of sub-paragraph (6) provision in a child arrangements order is with respect to the living arrangements of a child if it regulates arrangements relating to—

    (a) with whom the child is to live, or

    (b) when the child is to live with any person.

(7) Where a child is a ward of court, the court may exercise any of its powers under this Schedule even though no application has been made to it.

Orders for financial relief for persons over eighteen

2.—(1) If, on an application by a person who has reached the age of eighteen, it appears to the court—

    (a) that the applicant is, will be or (if an order were made under this paragraph) would be receiving instruction at an educational establishment or undergoing training for a trade, profession or vocation, whether or not while in gainful employment; or

    (b) that there are special circumstances which justify the making of an order under this paragraph,

the court may make one or both of the orders mentioned in sub-paragraph (2).

(2) The orders are—

    (a) an order requiring either or both of the applicant's parents to pay to the applicant such periodical payments, for such term, as may be specified in the order;

    (b) an order requiring either or both of the applicant's parents to pay to the applicant such lump sum as may be so specified.

(3) An application may not be made under this paragraph by any person if, immediately before he reached the age of sixteen, a periodical payments order was in force with respect to him.

(4) No order shall be made under this paragraph at a time when the parents of the applicant are living with each other in the same household.

(5) An order under sub-paragraph (2)(a) may be varied or discharged by a subsequent order made on the application of any person by or to whom payments were required to be made under the previous order.

(6) In sub-paragraph (3) 'periodical payments order' means an order made under—

    (a) this Schedule;

    (b) ...

    (c) section 23 or 27 of the Matrimonial Causes Act 1973;

    (d) Part I of the Domestic Proceedings and Magistrates' Courts Act 1978,

    (e) Part 1 or 9 of Schedule 5 to the Civil Partnership Act 2004 (financial relief in the High Court or a county court etc.)

    (f) Schedule 6 to the 2004 Act (financial relief in the magistrates' courts etc.), for the making or securing of periodical payments.

(7) The powers conferred by this paragraph shall be exercisable at any time.

(8) Where the court makes an order under this paragraph it may from time to time while that order remains in force make a further such order.

Duration of orders for financial relief

3.—(1) The term to be specified in an order for periodical payments made under paragraph 1(2)(a) or (b) in favour of a child may begin with the date of the making of an application for the order in question or any later date or a date ascertained in accordance with sub-paragraph (5) or (6) but—

    (a) shall not in the first instance extend beyond the child's seventeenth birthday unless the court thinks it right in the circumstances of the case to specify a later date; and

    (b) shall not in any event extend beyond the child's eighteenth birthday.

(2) Paragraph (b) of sub-paragraph (1) shall not apply in the case of a child if it appears to the court that—

    (a) the child is, or will be or (if an order were made without complying with that paragraph) would be receiving instruction at an educational establishment or undergoing training for a trade, profession or vocation, whether or not while in gainful employment; or

    (b) there are special circumstances which justify the making of an order without complying with that paragraph.

(3) An order for periodical payments made under paragraph 1(2)(a) or 2(2)(a) shall, notwith-standing anything in the order, cease to have effect on the death of the person liable to make payments under the order.

(4) Where an order is made under paragraph 1(2)(a) or (b) requiring periodical payments to be made or secured to the parent of a child, the order shall cease to have effect if—

    (a) any parent making or securing the payments; and

    (b) any parent to whom the payments are made or secured,

live together for a period of more than six months.

(5) Where—

    (a) a maintenance calculation ('the current calculation') is in force with respect to a child; and

    (b) an application is made for an order under paragraph 1(2)(a) or (b) of this Schedule for periodical payments in favour of that child—

        (i) in accordance with section 8 of the Child Support Act 1991; and

        (ii) before the end of the period of 6 months beginning with the making of the current calculation,

the term to be specified in any such order made on that application may be expressed to begin on, or at any time after, the earliest permitted date.

(6) For the purposes of subsection (5) above, 'the earliest permitted date' is whichever is the later of—

    (a) the date 6 months before the application is made; or

    (b) the date on which the current calculation took effect or, where successive maintenance calculations have been continuously in force with respect to a child, on which the first of those calculations took effect.

(7) Where—

    (a) a maintenance calculation ceases to have effect by or under any provision of the Child Support Act 1991, and

    (b) an application is made, before the end of the period of 6 months beginning with the rel-evant date, for an order for periodical payments under paragraph 1(2)(a) or (b) in favour of a child with respect to whom that maintenance calculation was in force immediately before it ceased to have effect,

the term to be specified in any such order, or in any interim order under paragraph 9, made on that application may begin with the date on which that maintenance calculation ceased to have effect, or any later date.

(8) In sub-paragraph (7)(b)—

    (a) where the maintenance calculation ceased to have effect, the relevant date is the date on which it so ceased.

Matters to which court is to have regard in making orders for financial relief

4.—(1) In deciding whether to exercise its powers under paragraph 1 or 2, and if so in what manner, the court shall have regard to all the circumstances including—

    (a) the income, earning capacity, property and other financial resources which each person mentioned in sub-paragraph (4) has or is likely to have in the foreseeable future;

    (b) the financial needs, obligations and responsibilities which each person mentioned in sub-paragraph (4) has or is likely to have in the foreseeable future;

(c) the financial needs of the child;

(d) the income, earning capacity (if any), property and other financial resources of the child;

(e) any physical or mental disability of the child;

(f) the manner in which the child was being, or was expected to be, educated or trained.

(2) In deciding whether to exercise its powers under paragraph 1 against a person who is not the mother or father of the child, and if so in what manner, the court shall in addition have regard to—

(a) whether that person had assumed responsibility for the maintenance of the child and, if so, the extent to which and basis on which he assumed that responsibility and the length of the period during which he met that responsibility;

(b) whether he did so knowing that the child was not his child;

(c) the liability of any other person to maintain the child.

(3) Where the court makes an order under paragraph 1 against a person who is not the father of the child, it shall record in the order that the order is made on the basis that the person against whom the order is made is not the child's father.

(4) The persons mentioned in sub-paragraph (1) are—

(a) in relation to a decision whether to exercise its powers under paragraph 1, any parent of the child;

(b) in relation to a decision whether to exercise its powers under paragraph 2, the mother and father of the child;

(c) the applicant for the order;

(d) any other person in whose favour the court proposes to make the order.

(5) In the case of a child who has a parent by virtue of section 42 or 43 of the Human Fertilisation and Embryology Act 2008, any reference in sub-paragraph (2), (3) or (4) to the child's father is a reference to the woman who is a parent of the child by virtue of that section.

Provisions relating to lump sums

5.—(1) Without prejudice to the generality of paragraph 1, an order under that paragraph for the payment of a lump sum may be made for the purpose of enabling any liabilities or expenses—

(a) incurred in connection with the birth of the child or in maintaining the child; and

(b) reasonably incurred before the making of the order,
to be met.

...

(3) The power of the court under paragraph 1 or 2 to vary or discharge an order for the making or securing of periodical payments by a parent shall include power to make an order under that provision for the payment of a lump sum by that parent.

...

(5) An order made under paragraph 1 or 2 for the payment of a lump sum may provide for the payment of that sum by instalments.

(6) Where the court provides for the payment of a lump sum by instalments the court, on an application made either by the person liable to pay or the person entitled to receive that sum, shall have power to vary that order by varying—

(a) the number of instalments payable;

(b) the amount of any instalment payable;

(c) the date on which any instalment becomes payable.

(7) The Lord Chief Justice may nominate a judicial office holder (as defined in section 109(4) of the Constitutional Reform Act 2005) to exercise his functions under this paragraph.

Variation etc. of orders for periodical payments

6.—(1) In exercising its powers under paragraph 1 or 2 to vary or discharge an order for the making or securing of periodical payments the court shall have regard to all the circumstances of the case, including any change in any of the matters to which the court was required to have regard when making the order.

(2) The power of the court under paragraph 1 or 2 to vary an order for the making or securing of periodical payments shall include power to suspend any provision of the order temporarily and to revive any provision so suspended.

(3) Where on an application under paragraph 1 or 2 for the variation or discharge of an order for the making or securing of periodical payments the court varies the payments required to be made under that order, the court may provide that the payments as so varied shall be made from such date as the court may specify, except that, subject to sub-paragraph (9), the date shall not be earlier than the date of the making of the application.

(4) An application for the variation of an order made under paragraph 1 for the making or securing of periodical payments to or for the benefit of a child may, if the child has reached the age of sixteen, be made by the child himself.

(5) Where an order for the making or securing of periodical payments made under paragraph 1 ceases to have effect on the date on which the child reaches the age of sixteen, or at any time after that date but before or on the date on which he reaches the age of eighteen, the child may apply to the court which made the order for an order for its revival.

(6) If on such an application it appears to the court that—

(a) the child is, will be or (if an order were made under this sub-paragraph) would be receiving instruction at an educational establishment or undergoing training for a trade, profession or vocation, whether or not while in gainful employment; or

(b) there are special circumstances which justify the making of an order under this paragraph,

the court shall have power by order to revive the order from such date as the court may specify, not being earlier than the date of the making of the application.

(7) Any order which is revived by an order under sub-paragraph (5) may be varied or discharged under that provision, on the application of any person by whom or to whom payments are required to be made under the revived order.

(8) An order for the making or securing of periodical payments made under paragraph 1 or 2 may be varied or discharged, after the death of either parent, on the application of a guardian or special guardian of the child concerned.

(9) Where—

(a) an order under paragraph 1(2)(a) or (b) for the making or securing of periodical payments in favour of more than one child ('the order') is in force;

(b) the order requires payments specified in it to be made to or for the benefit of more than one child without apportioning those payments between them;

(c) a maintenance calculation ('the calculation') is made with respect to one or more, but not all, of the children with respect to whom those payments are to be made; and

(d) an application is made, before the end of the period of 6 months beginning with the date on which the calculation was made, for the variation or discharge of the order,

the court may, in exercise of its powers under paragraph 1 to vary or discharge the order, direct that the variation or discharge shall take effect from the date on which the calculation took effect or any later date.

Variation of orders for periodical payments etc. made by magistrates' courts

6A.—(1) Subject to sub-paragraph (7), the power of the family court—

(a) under paragraph 1 or 2 to vary an order for the making of periodical payments, or

(b) under paragraph 5(6) to vary an order for the payment of a lump sum by instalments,

shall include power, if the court is satisfied that payment has not been made in accordance with the order, to exercise one of its powers under section 1(4) and (4A) of the Maintenance Enforcement Act 1991.

...

(6)　Subsection (6) of section 1 of the Maintenance Enforcement Act 1991 (power of court to order that account be opened) shall apply for the purposes of sub-paragraph (1) as it applies for the purposes of that section.

(7)　Before varying the order by exercising one of its powers under section 1(4) and (4A) of the Maintenance Enforcement Act 1991, the court shall have regard to any representations made by the parties to the application.

...

(9)　None of the powers of the court conferred by this paragraph shall be exercisable in relation to an order under this Schedule for the making of periodical payments, or for the payment of a lump sum by instalments, unless at the time when the order was made the person required to make the payments was ordinarily resident in England and Wales.

Variation of orders for secured periodical payments after death of parent

7.—(1)　Where the parent liable to make payments under a secured periodical payments order has died, the persons who may apply for the variation or discharge of the order shall include the personal representatives of the deceased parent.

(2)　No application for the variation of the order shall, except with the permission of the court, be made after the end of the period of six months from the date on which representation in regard to the estate of that parent is first taken out.

(3)　The personal representatives of a deceased person against whom a secured periodical payments order was made shall not be liable for having distributed any part of the estate of the deceased after the end of the period of six months referred to in sub-paragraph (2) on the ground that they ought to have taken into account the possibility that the court might permit an application for variation to be made after that period by the person entitled to payments under the order.

(4)　Sub-paragraph (3) shall not prejudice any power to recover any part of the estate so distributed arising by virtue of the variation of an order in accordance with this paragraph.

(5)　Where an application to vary a secured periodical payments order is made after the death of the parent liable to make payments under the order, the circumstances to which the court is required to have regard under paragraph 6(1) shall include the changed circumstances resulting from the death of the parent.

(6)　The following are to be left out of account when considering for the purposes of sub-paragraph (2) when representation was first taken out—

    (a)　a grant limited to settled land or to trust property,

    (b)　any other grant that does not permit any of the estate to be distributed,

    (c)　a grant limited to real estate or to personal estate, unless a grant limited to the remainder of the estate has previously been made or is made at the same time,

    (d)　a grant, or its equivalent, made outside the United Kingdom (but see sub-paragraph (6A)).

(6A)　A grant sealed under section 2 of the Colonial Probates Act 1892 counts as a grant made in the United Kingdom for the purposes of sub-paragraph (6), but is to be taken as dated on the date of sealing.

(7)　In this paragraph 'secured periodical payments order' means an order for secured periodical payments under paragraph 1(2)(b).

Financial relief under other enactments

8.—(1)　This paragraph applies where a child arrangements order to which sub-paragraph (1A) applies or a special guardianship order is made with respect to a child at a time when there is in force an order ('the financial relief order') made under any enactment other than this Act and requiring a person to contribute to the child's maintenance.

(1A)　This sub-paragraph applies to a child arrangements order if the arrangements regulated by the order consist of, or include, arrangements which relate to either or both of the following—

    (a)　with whom the child concerned is to live, and

    (b)　when the child is to live with any person.

(2) Where this paragraph applies, the court may, on the application of—

    (a) any person required by the financial relief order to contribute to the child's maintenance; or

    (b) any person who is named in a child arrangements order as a person with whom the child is to live or in whose favour a special guardianship order with respect to the child is in force,

make an order revoking the financial relief order, or varying it by altering the amount of any sum payable under that order or by substituting the applicant for the person to whom any such sum is otherwise payable under that order.

Interim orders

9.—(1) Where an application is made under paragraph 1 or 2 the court may, at any time before it disposes of the application, make an interim order—

    (a) requiring either or both parents to make such periodical payments, at such times and for such term as the court thinks fit; and

    (b) giving any direction which the court thinks fit.

(2) An interim order made under this paragraph may provide for payments to be made from such date as the court may specify, except that, subject to paragraph 3(5) and (6), the date shall not be earlier than the date of the making of the application under paragraph 1 or 2.

(3) An interim order made under this paragraph shall cease to have effect when the application is disposed of or, if earlier, on the date specified for the purposes of this paragraph in the interim order.

(4) An interim order in which a date has been specified for the purposes of sub-paragraph (3) may be varied by substituting a later date.

Alteration of maintenance agreements

10.—(1) In this paragraph and in paragraph 11 'maintenance agreement' means any agreement in writing made with respect to a child, whether before or after the commencement of this paragraph, which—

    (a) is or was made between the father and mother of the child; and

    (b) contains provision with respect to the making or securing of payments, or the disposition or use of any property, for the maintenance or education of the child,

and any such provisions are in this paragraph, and paragraph 11, referred to as 'financial arrangements'.

(2) Subject to sub-paragraph (2A), where a maintenance agreement is for the time being subsisting and each of the parties to the agreement is for the time being either domiciled or resident in England and Wales, then, either party may apply to the court for an order under this paragraph.

(2A) If an application or part of an application relates to a matter where jurisdiction falls to be determined by reference to the jurisdictional requirements of the Maintenance Regulation and Schedule 6 to the Civil Jurisdiction and Judgments (Maintenance) Regulations 2011—

    (a) the requirement as to domicile or residence in sub-paragraph (2) does not apply to the application or that part of it, but

    (b) the court may not entertain the application or that part of it unless it has jurisdiction to do so by virtue of that Regulation and that Schedule.

(2B) In sub-paragraph (2A), 'the Maintenance Regulation' means Council Regulation (EC) No 4/2009 including as applied in relation to Denmark by virtue of the Agreement made on 19th October 2005 between the European Community and the Kingdom of Denmark.

(3) If the court to which the application is made is satisfied either—

    (a) that, by reason of a change in the circumstances in the light of which any financial arrangements contained in the agreement were made (including a change foreseen by the parties when making the agreement), the agreement should be altered so as to make different financial arrangements; or

(b) that the agreement does not contain proper financial arrangements with respect to the child,

then that court may by order make such alterations in the agreement by varying or revoking any financial arrangements contained in it as may appear to it to be just having regard to all the circumstances.

(4) If the maintenance agreement is altered by an order under this paragraph, the agreement shall have effect thereafter as if the alteration had been made by agreement between the parties and for valuable consideration.

(5) Where a court decides to make an order under this paragraph altering the maintenance agreement—

(a) by inserting provision for the making or securing by one of the parties to the agreement of periodical payments for the maintenance of the child; or

(b) by increasing the rate of periodical payments required to be made or secured by one of the parties for the maintenance of the child,

then, in deciding the term for which under the agreement as altered by the order the payments or (as the case may be) the additional payments attributable to the increase are to be made or secured for the benefit of the child, the court shall apply the provisions of sub-paragraphs (1) and (2) of paragraph 3 as if the order were an order under paragraph 1(2)(a) or (b).

...

(7) For the avoidance of doubt it is hereby declared that nothing in this paragraph affects any power of a court before which any proceedings between the parties to a maintenance agreement are brought under any other enactment to make an order containing financial arrangements or any right of either party to apply for such an order in such proceedings.

(8) In the case of a child who has a parent by virtue of section 42 or 43 of the Human Fertilisation and Embryology Act 2008, the reference in sub-paragraph (1)(a) to the child's father is a reference to the woman who is a parent of the child by virtue of that section.

11.—(1) Where a maintenance agreement provides for the continuation, after the death of one of the parties, of payments for the maintenance of a child and that party dies domiciled in England and Wales, the surviving party or the personal representatives of the deceased party may apply to the High Court or the family court for an order under paragraph 10.

(2) If a maintenance agreement is altered by a court on an application under this paragraph, the agreement shall have effect thereafter as if the alteration had been made, immediately before the death, by agreement between the parties and for valuable consideration.

(3) An application under this paragraph shall not, except with leave of the High Court or the family court, be made after the end of the period of six months beginning with the day on which representation in regard to the estate of the deceased is first taken out.

(4) The following are to be left out of account when considering for the purposes of sub-paragraph (3) when representation was first taken out—

(a) a grant limited to settled land or to trust property,

(b) any other grant that does not permit any of the estate to be distributed,

(c) a grant limited to real estate or to personal estate, unless a grant limited to the remainder of the estate has previously been made or is made at the same time,

(d) a grant, or its equivalent, made outside the United Kingdom (but see sub-paragraph (4A)).

...

(6) The provisions of this paragraph shall not render the personal representatives of the deceased liable for having distributed any part of the estate of the deceased after the expiry of the period of six months referred to in sub-paragraph (3) on the ground that they ought to have taken into account the possibility that a court might grant leave for an application by virtue of this paragraph to be made by the surviving party after that period.

(7) Sub-paragraph (6) shall not prejudice any power to recover any part of the estate so distributed arising by virtue of the making of an order in pursuance of this paragraph.

Enforcement of orders for maintenance

12.—(1) Any person for the time being under an obligation to make payments in pursuance of any order for the payment of money made by the family court under this Act shall give notice of any change of address to such person (if any) as may be specified in the order.

(2) Any person failing without reasonable excuse to give such a notice shall be guilty of an offence and liable on summary conviction to a fine not exceeding level 2 on the standard scale.

Direction for settlement of instrument by conveyancing counsel

13.—Where the High Court or the family court decides to make an order under this Act for the securing of periodical payments or for the transfer or settlement of property, it may direct that the matter be referred to one of the conveyancing counsel of the court to settle a proper instrument to be executed by all necessary parties.

Jurisdiction in relation to matters relating to maintenance

14.—(1) If an application under paragraph 1 or 2, or part of such an application, relates to a matter where jurisdiction falls to be determined by reference to the jurisdictional requirements of the Maintenance Regulation and Schedule 6 to the Civil Jurisdiction and Judgments (Maintenance) Regulations 2011, the court may not entertain the application or that part of it unless it has jurisdiction to do so by virtue of that Regulation and that Schedule.

(2) In sub-paragraph (1), 'the Maintenance Regulation' means Council Regulation (EC) No 4/2009 including as applied in relation to Denmark by virtue of the Agreement made on 19th October 2005 between the European Community and the Kingdom of Denmark.

Local authority contribution to child's maintenance

15.—(1) Where a child lives, or is to live, with a person as the result of a child arrangements order, a local authority may make contributions to that person towards the cost of the accommodation and maintenance of the child.

(2) Sub-paragraph (1) does not apply where the person with whom the child lives, or is to live, is a parent of the child or the husband or wife or civil partner of a parent of the child.

Interpretation

16.—(1) In this Schedule 'child' includes, in any case where an application is made under paragraph 2 or 6 in relation to a person who has reached the age of eighteen, that person.

(2) In this Schedule, except paragraphs 2 and 15, 'parent' includes—

    (a) any party to a marriage (whether or not subsisting) in relation to whom the child concerned is a child of the family, and

    (b) any civil partner in a civil partnership (whether or not subsisting) in relation to whom the child concerned is a child of the family;

and for this purpose any reference to either parent or both parents shall be read as a reference to any parent of his and to all of his parents.

(3) In this Schedule, 'maintenance calculation' has the same meaning as it has in the Child Support Act 1991 by virtue of section 54 of that Act as read with any regulations in force under that section.

Sections 17, 23 and 29   # SCHEDULE 2

LOCAL AUTHORITY SUPPORT FOR CHILDREN AND FAMILIES

PART I PROVISION OF SERVICES FOR FAMILIES

Identification of children in need and provision of information

1.—(1) Every local authority shall take reasonable steps to identify the extent to which there are children in need within their area.

(2) Every local authority shall—
   (a) publish information—
      (i) about services provided by them under sections 17, 18, 20, 23B to 23D, 24A and 24B; and
      (ii) where they consider it appropriate, about the provision by others (including, in particular, voluntary organisations) of services which the authority have power to provide under those sections; and
   (b) take such steps as are reasonably practicable to ensure that those who might benefit from the services receive the information relevant to them.

Maintenance of a register of disabled children

2.—(1) Every local authority shall open and maintain a register of disabled children within their area.

(2) The register may be kept by means of a computer.

Assessment of children's needs

3.—Where it appears to a local authority that a child within their area is in need, the authority may assess his needs for the purposes of this Act at the same time as any assessment of his needs is made under—
   (a) the Chronically Sick and Disabled Persons Act 1970;
   (b) Part IV of the Education Act 1996;
   (ba) Part 3 of the Children and Families Act 2014;
   (c) the Disabled Persons (Services, Consultation and Representation) Act 1986; or
   (d) any other enactment.

Prevention of neglect and abuse

4.—(1) Every local authority shall take reasonable steps, through the provision of services under Part III of this Act, to prevent children within their area suffering ill-treatment or neglect.

(2) Where a local authority believe that a child who is at any time within their area—
   (a) is likely to suffer harm; but
   (b) lives or proposes to live in the area of another local authority
they shall inform that other local authority.

(3) When informing that other local authority they shall specify—
   (a) the harm that they believe he is likely to suffer; and
   (b) (if they can) where the child lives or proposes to live.

Provision of accommodation in order to protect child

5.—(1) Where—
   (a) it appears to a local authority that a child who is living on particular premises is suffering, or is likely to suffer, ill treatment at the hands of another person who is living on those premises; and
   (b) that other person proposes to move from the premises,
the authority may assist that other person to obtain alternative accommodation.

(2) Assistance given under this paragraph may be in cash.

(3) Subsections (7) to (9) of section 17 shall apply in relation to assistance given under this paragraph as they apply in relation to assistance given under that section.

Provision for disabled children

6.—(1) Every local authority shall provide services designed—
   (a) to minimise the effect on disabled children within their area of their disabilities;
   (b) to give such children the opportunity to lead lives which are as normal as possible; and
   (c) to assist individuals who provide care for such children to continue to do so, or to do so more effectively, by giving them breaks from caring.

(2) The duty imposed by sub-paragraph (1)(c) shall be performed in accordance with regulations made by the appropriate national authority.

Provision to reduce need for care proceedings etc.

7.—Every local authority shall take reasonable steps designed—

    (a) to reduce the need to bring—

        (i) proceedings for care or supervision orders with respect to children within their area;

        (ii) criminal proceedings against such children;

        (iii) any family or other proceedings with respect to such children which might lead to them being placed in the authority's care; or

        (iv) proceedings under the inherent jurisdiction of the High Court with respect to children;

    (b) to encourage children within their area not to commit criminal offences; and

    (c) to avoid the need for children within their area to be placed in secure accommodation.

Provision for children living with their families

8.—Every local authority shall make such provision as they consider appropriate for the following services to be available with respect to children in need within their area while they are living with their families—

    (a) advice, guidance and counselling;

    (b) occupational, social, cultural or recreational activities;

    (c) home help (which may include laundry facilities);

    (d) facilities for, or assistance with, travelling to and from home for the purpose of taking advantage of any other service provided under this Act or of any similar service;

    (e) assistance to enable the child concerned and his family to have a holiday.

Provision for accommodated children

8A.—(1) Every local authority shall make provision for such services as they consider appropriate to be available with respect to accommodated children.

(2) 'Accommodated children' are those children in respect of whose accommodation the local authority have been notified under section 85 or 86.

(3) The services shall be provided with a view to promoting contact between each accommodated child and that child's family.

(4) The services may, in particular, include—

    (a) advice, guidance and counselling;

    (b) services necessary to enable the child to visit, or to be visited by, members of the family;

    (c) assistance to enable the child and members of the family to have a holiday together.

(5) Nothing in this paragraph affects the duty imposed by paragraph 10.

Family centres

9.—(1) Every local authority shall provide such family centres as they consider appropriate in relation to children within their area.

(2) 'Family centre' means a centre at which any of the persons mentioned in sub-paragraph (3) may—

    (a) attend for occupational, social, cultural or recreational activities;

    (b) attend for advice, guidance and counselling; or

    (c) be provided with accommodation while he is receiving advice, guidance or counselling.

(3) The persons are—

    (a) a child;

    (b) his parents;

    (c) any person who is not a parent of his but who has parental responsibility for him;

    (d) any other person who is looking after him.

Maintenance of the family home

10.—Every local authority shall take such steps as are reasonably practicable, where any child within their area who is in need and whom they are not looking after is living apart from his family—

(a) to enable him to live with his family; or

(b) to promote contact between him and his family, if,

in their opinion, it is necessary to do so in order to safeguard or promote his welfare.

Duty to consider racial groups to which children in need belong

11.—Every local authority shall, in making any arrangements—

(a) for the provision of day care within their area; or

(b) designed to encourage persons to act as local authority foster parents, have regard to the different racial groups to which children within their area who are in need belong.

PART II CHILDREN LOOKED AFTER BY LOCAL AUTHORITIES

Regulations as to conditions under which child in care is allowed to live with parent, etc.

12A.—Regulations under section 22C may, in particular, impose requirements on a local authority as to—

(a) the making of any decision by a local authority to allow a child in their care to live with any person falling within section 22C(3) (including requirements as to those who must be consulted before the decision is made and those who must be notified when it has been made);

(b) the supervision or medical examination of the child concerned;

(c) the removal of the child, in such circumstances as may be prescribed, from the care of the person with whom the child has been allowed to live;

(d) the records to be kept by local authorities.

Regulations as to placements of a kind specified in section 22C(6)(d)

12B.—Regulations under section 22C as to placements of the kind specified in section 22C(6)(d) may, in particular, make provision as to

(a) the persons to be notified of any proposed arrangements;

(b) the opportunities such persons are to have to make representations in relation to the arrangements proposed;

(c) the persons to be notified of any proposed changes in arrangements;

(d) the records to be kept by local authorities;

(e) the supervision by local authorities of any arrangements made.

Placements out of area

12C.—Regulations under section 22C may, in particular, impose requirements which a local authority must comply with—

(a) before a child looked after by them is provided with accommodation at a place outside the area of the authority; or

(b) if the child's welfare requires the immediate provision of such accommodation, within such period of the accommodation being provided as may be prescribed.

Avoidance of disruption in education

12D.—(1) Regulations under section 22C may, in particular, impose requirements which a local authority must comply with before making any decision concerning a child's placement if he is in the fourth key stage.

(2) A child is 'in the fourth key stage' if he is a pupil in the fourth key stage for the purposes of Part 6 or 7 of the Education Act 2002 (see section 82 and 103 of that Act).

Regulations as to placing of children with local authority foster parents

12E.—Regulations under section 22C may, in particular, make provision—

(a) with regard to the welfare of children placed with local authority foster parents;

(b) as to the arrangements to be made by local authorities in connection with the health and education of such children;

(c) as to the records to be kept by local authorities;

(d) for securing that where possible the local authority foster parent with whom a child is to be placed is—

(i) of the same religious persuasion as the child; or

(ii) gives an undertaking that the child will be brought up in that religious persuasion;

(e) for securing the children placed with local authority foster parents, and the premises in which they are accommodated, will be supervised and inspected by a local authority and that the children will be removed from those premises if their welfare appears to require it.

12F.—(1) Regulations under section 22C may, in particular, also make provision—

(a) for securing that a child is not placed with a local authority foster parent unless that person is for the time being approved as a local authority foster parent by such local authority as may be prescribed;

(b) establishing a procedure under which any person in respect of whom a qualifying determination has been made may apply to the appropriate national authority for a review of that determination by a panel constituted by that national authority.

(2) A determination is a qualifying determination if—

(a) it relates to the issue of whether a person should be approved, or should continue to be approved, as a local authority foster parent; and

(b) it is of a prescribed description.

(3) Regulations made by virtue of sub-paragraph (1)(b) may include provision as to—

(a) the duties and powers of a panel;

(b) the administration and procedures of a panel;

(c) the appointment of members of a panel (including the number, or any limit on the number, of members who may be appointed and any conditions for appointment);

(d) the payment of fees to members of a panel;

(e) the duties of any person in connection with a review conducted under the regulations;

(f) the monitoring of any such reviews.

(4) Regulations made by virtue of sub-paragraph (3)(e) may impose a duty to pay to the appropriate national authority such sum as that national authority may determine; but such a duty may not be imposed upon a person who has applied for a review of a qualifying determination.

(5) The appropriate national authority must secure that, taking one financial year with another, the aggregate of the sums which become payable to it under regulations made by virtue of sub-paragraph (4) does not exceed the cost to it of performing its independent review functions.

(6) The appropriate national authority may make an arrangement with an organisation under which independent review functions are performed by the organisation on the national authority's behalf.

(7) If the appropriate national authority makes such an arrangement with an organisation, the organisation is to perform its functions under the arrangement in accordance with any general or special directions given by that national authority.

(8) The arrangement may include provision for payments to be made to the organisation by the appropriate national authority.

(9) Payments made by the appropriate national authority in accordance with such provision shall be taken into account in determining (for the purpose of sub-paragraph (5)) the cost to that national authority of performing its independent review functions.

(10) Where the Welsh Ministers are the appropriate national authority, sub-paragraphs (6) and (8) also apply as if references to an organisation included references to the Secretary of State.

(11) In this paragraph—

'financial year' means a period of twelve months ending with 31st March;

'independent review function' means a function conferred or imposed on a national authority by regulations made by virtue of sub-paragraph (1)(b);

'organisation' includes a public body and a private or voluntary organisation.

12G.—Regulations under section 22C may, in particular, also make provision as to the circumstances in which local authorities may make arrangements for duties imposed on them by the regulations to be discharged on their behalf.

…

Promotion and maintenance of contact between child and family

15.—(1) Where a child is being looked after by a local authority, the authority shall, unless it is not reasonably practicable or consistent with his welfare, endeavour to promote contact between the child and—

(a) his parents;

(b) any person who is not a parent of his but who has parental responsibility for him; and

(c) any relative, friend or other person connected with him.

(2) Where a child is being looked after by a local authority—

(a) the authority shall take such steps as are reasonably practicable to secure that—

(i) his parents; and

(ii) any person who is not a parent of his but who has parental responsibility for him, are kept informed of where he is being accommodated; and

(b) every such person shall secure that the authority are kept informed of his or her address.

(3) Where a local authority ('the receiving authority') take over the provision of accommodation for a child from another local authority ('the transferring authority') under section 20(2)—

(a) the receiving authority shall (where reasonably practicable) inform—

(i) the child's parents; and

(ii) any person who is not a parent of his but who has parental responsibility for him;

(b) sub-paragraph (2)(a) shall apply to the transferring authority, as well as the receiving authority, until at least one such person has been informed of the change; and

(c) sub-paragraph (2)(b) shall not require any person to inform the receiving authority of his address until he has been so informed.

(4) Nothing in this paragraph requires a local authority to inform any person of the whereabouts of a child if—

(a) the child is in the care of the authority; and

(b) the authority has reasonable cause to believe that informing the person would prejudice the child's welfare.

(5) Any person who fails (without reasonable excuse) to comply with sub-paragraph (2)(b) shall be guilty of an offence and liable on summary conviction to a fine not exceeding level 2 on the standard scale.

(6) It shall be a defence in any proceedings under sub-paragraph (5) to prove that the defendant was residing at the same address as another person who was the child's parent or had parental responsibility for the child and had reasonable cause to believe that the other person had informed the appropriate authority that both of them were residing at that address.

Visits to or by children: expenses

16.—(1) This paragraph applies where—

(a) a child is being looked after by a local authority; and

(b) the conditions mentioned in sub-paragraph (3) are satisfied.

(2) The authority may—

(a) make payments to—

(i) a parent of the child;

    (ii) any person who is not a parent of his but who has parental responsibility for him; or

    (iii) any relative, friend or other person connected with him, in respect of travelling, subsistence or other expenses incurred by that person in visiting the child; or

  (b) make payments to the child, or to any person on his behalf, in respect of travelling, subsistence or other expenses incurred by or on behalf of the child in his visiting—

    (i) a parent of his;

    (ii) any person who is not a parent of his but who has parental responsibility for him; or

    (iii) any relative, friend or other person connected with him.

 (3) The conditions are that—

  (a) it appears to the authority that the visit in question could not otherwise be made without undue financial hardship; and

  (b) the circumstances warrant the making of the payments.

...

Arrangements to assist children to live abroad

 19.—(1) A local authority may only arrange for, or assist in arranging for, any child in their care to live outside England and Wales with the approval of the court.

 (2) A local authority may, with the approval of every person who has parental responsibility for the child arrange for, or assist in arranging for, any other child looked after by them to live outside England and Wales.

 (3) The court shall not give its approval under sub-paragraph (1) unless it is satisfied that—

  (a) living outside England and Wales would be in the child's best interests;

  (b) suitable arrangements have been, or will be, made for his reception and welfare in the country in which he will live;

  (c) the child has consented to living in that country; and

  (d) every person who has parental responsibility for the child has consented to his living in that country.

 (4) Where the court is satisfied that the child does not have sufficient understanding to give or withhold his consent, it may disregard sub-paragraph (3)(c) and give its approval if the child is to live in the country concerned with a parent, guardian, special guardian, or other suitable person.

 (5) Where a person whose consent is required by sub-paragraph (3)(d) fails to give his consent, the court may disregard that provision and give its approval if it is satisfied that that person—

  (a) cannot be found;

  (b) is incapable of consenting; or

  (c) is withholding his consent unreasonably.

 (6) Section 85 of the Adoption and Children Act 2002 (which imposes restrictions on taking children out of the United Kingdom) shall not apply in the case of any child who is to live outside England and Wales with the approval of the court given under this paragraph.

 (7) Where a court decides to give its approval under this paragraph it may order that its decision is not to have effect during the appeal period.

 (8) In sub-paragraph (7) 'the appeal period' means—

  (a) where an appeal is made against the decision, the period between the making of the decision and the determination of the appeal; and

  (b) otherwise, the period during which an appeal may be made against the decision.

 (9) This paragraph does not apply to a local authority placing a child for adoption with prospective adopters.

Preparation for ceasing to be looked after

 19A.—It is the duty of the local authority looking after a child to advise, assist and befriend him with a view to promoting his welfare when they have ceased to look after him.

 19B.—(1) A local authority shall have the following additional functions in relation to an eligible child whom they are looking after.

(2) In sub-paragraph (1) 'eligible child' means, subject to sub-paragraph (3), a child who—

(a) is aged sixteen or seventeen; and

(b) has been looked after by a local authority for a prescribed period, or periods amounting in all to a prescribed period, which began after he reached a prescribed age and ended after he reached the age of sixteen.

(3) The appropriate national authority may prescribe—

(a) additional categories of eligible children; and

(b) categories of children who are not to be eligible children despite falling within sub-paragraph (2).

(4) For each eligible child, the local authority shall carry out an assessment of his needs with a view to determining what advice, assistance and support it would be appropriate for them to provide him under this Act—

(a) while they are still looking after him; and

(b) after they cease to look after him,

and shall then prepare a pathway plan for him.

(5) The local authority shall keep the pathway plan under regular review.

(6) Any such review may be carried out at the same time as a review of the child's case carried out by virtue of section 26.

(7) The appropriate national authority may by regulations make provision as to assessments for the purposes of sub-paragraph (4).

(8) The regulations may in particular provide for the matters set out in section 23B(6).

Preparation for ceasing to be looked after: staying put arrangements

19BA.—(1) This paragraph applies in relation to an eligible child (within the meaning of paragraph 19B) who has been placed by a local authority in England with a local authority foster parent.

(2) When carrying out the assessment of the child's needs in accordance with paragraph 19B(4), the local authority must determine whether it would be appropriate to provide advice, assistance and support under this Act in order to facilitate a staying put arrangement, and with a view to maintaining such an arrangement, after the local authority cease to look after him or her.

(3) The local authority must provide advice, assistance and support under this Act in order to facilitate a staying put arrangement if—

(a) the local authority determine under sub-paragraph (2) that it would be appropriate to do so, and

(b) the eligible child and the local authority foster parent wish to make a staying put arrangement.

(4) In this paragraph, 'staying put arrangement' has the meaning given by section 23CZA.

Personal advisers

19C.—A local authority shall arrange for each child whom they are looking after who is an eligible child for the purposes of paragraph 19B to have a personal adviser.

Death of children being looked after by local authorities

20.—(1) If a child who is being looked after by a local authority dies, the authority—

(a) shall notify the appropriate national authority and (in the case of a local authority in England) Her Majesty's Chief Inspector of Education, Children's Services and Skills;

(b) shall, so far as is reasonably practicable, notify the child's parents and every person who is not a parent of his but who has parental responsibility for him;

(c) may, with the consent (so far as it is reasonably practicable to obtain it) of every person who has parental responsibility for the child, arrange for the child's body to be buried or cremated; and

(d) may, if the conditions mentioned in sub-paragraph (2) are satisfied, make payments to any person who has parental responsibility for the child, or any relative, friend or other person connected with the child, in respect of travelling, subsistence or other expenses incurred by that person in attending the child's funeral.

(2) The conditions are that—

(a) it appears to the authority that the person concerned could not otherwise attend the child's funeral without undue financial hardship; and

(b) that the circumstances warrant the making of the payments.

(3) Sub-paragraph (1) does not authorise cremation where it does not accord with the practice of the child's religious persuasion.

(4) Where a local authority have exercised their power under sub-paragraph (1)(c) with respect to a child who was under sixteen when he died, they may recover from any parent of the child any expenses incurred by them.

(5) Any sums so recoverable shall, without prejudice to any other method of recovery, be recoverable summarily as a civil debt.

(6) Nothing in this paragraph affects any enactment regulating or authorising the burial, cremation or anatomical examination of the body of a deceased person.

PART III CONTRIBUTIONS TOWARDS MAINTENANCE OF CHILDREN LOOKED AFTER BY LOCAL AUTHORITIES

Liability to contribute

21.—(1) Where a local authority are looking after a child (other than in the cases mentioned in sub-paragraph (7)) they shall consider whether they should recover contributions towards the child's maintenance from any person liable to contribute ('a contributor').

(2) An authority may only recover contributions from a contributor if they consider it reasonable to do so.

(3) The persons liable to contribute are—

(a) where the child is under sixteen, each of his parents;

(b) where he has reached the age of sixteen, the child himself.

(4) A parent is not liable to contribute during any period when he is in receipt of universal credit (except in such circumstances as may be prescribed).

(5) A person is not liable to contribute towards the maintenance of a child in the care of a local authority in respect of any period during which the child is living with, under arrangements made by the authority in accordance with section 22C, a parent of his.

(6) A contributor is not obliged to make any contribution towards a child's maintenance except as agreed or determined in accordance with this Part of this Schedule.

(7) The cases are where the child is looked after by a local authority under—

(a) section 21;

(b) an interim care order;

(c) section 92 of the Powers of Criminal Courts (Sentencing) Act 2000.

Agreed contributions

22.—(1) Contributions towards a child's maintenance may only be recovered if the local authority have served a notice ('a contribution notice') on the contributor specifying—

(a) the weekly sum which they consider that he should contribute; and

(b) arrangements for payment.

(2) The contribution notice must be in writing and dated.

(3) Arrangements for payment shall, in particular, include—

(a) the date on which liability to contribute begins (which must not be earlier than the date of the notice);

(b) the date on which liability under the notice will end (if the child has not before that date ceased to be looked after by the authority); and

(c) the date on which the first payment is to be made.

(4) The authority may specify in a contribution notice a weekly sum which is a standard contribution determined by them for all children looked after by them.

(5) The authority may not specify in a contribution notice a weekly sum greater than that which they consider—

    (a) they would normally be prepared to pay if they had placed a similar child with local authority foster parents; and

    (b) it is reasonably practicable for the contributor to pay (having regard to his means).

(6) An authority may at any time withdraw a contribution notice (without prejudice to their power to serve another).

(7) Where the authority and the contributor agree—

    (a) the sum which the contributor is to contribute; and

    (b) arrangements for payment,

(whether as specified in the contribution notice or otherwise) and the contributor notifies the authority in writing that he so agrees, the authority may recover summarily as a civil debt any contribution which is overdue and unpaid.

(8) A contributor may, by serving a notice in writing on the authority, withdraw his agreement in relation to any period of liability falling after the date of service of the notice.

(9) Sub-paragraph (7) is without prejudice to any other method of recovery.

Contribution orders

23.—(1) Where a contributor has been served with a contribution notice and has—

    (a) failed to reach any agreement with the local authority as mentioned in paragraph 22(7) within the period of one month beginning with the day on which the contribution notice was served; or

    (b) served a notice under paragraph 22(8) withdrawing his agreement,

the authority may apply to the court for an order under this paragraph.

(2) On such an application the court may make an order ('a contribution order') requiring the contributor to contribute a weekly sum towards the child's maintenance in accordance with arrangements for payment specified by the court.

(3) A contribution order—

    (a) shall not specify a weekly sum greater than that specified in the contribution notice; and

    (b) shall be made with due regard to the contributor's means.

(4) A contribution order shall not—

    (a) take effect before the date specified in the contribution notice; or

    (b) have effect while the contributor is not liable to contribute (by virtue of paragraph 21); or

    (c) remain in force after the child has ceased to be looked after by the authority who obtained the order.

(5) An authority may not apply to the court under sub-paragraph (1) in relation to a contribution notice which they have withdrawn.

(6) Where—

    (a) a contribution order is in force;

    (b) the authority serve another contribution notice; and

    (c) the contributor and the authority reach an agreement under paragraph 22(7) in respect of that other contribution notice,

the effect of the agreement shall be to discharge the order from the date on which it is agreed that the agreement shall take effect.

(7) Where an agreement is reached under sub-paragraph (6) the authority shall notify the court—

    (a) of the agreement; and

    (b) of the date on which it took effect.

(8) A contribution order may be varied or revoked on the application of the contributor or the authority.

(9) In proceedings for the variation of a contribution order, the authority shall specify—

(a) the weekly sum which, having regard to paragraph 22, they propose that the contributor should contribute under the order as varied; and

(b) the proposed arrangements for payment.

(10) Where a contribution order is varied, the order—

(a) shall not specify a weekly sum greater than that specified by the authority in the proceedings for variation; and

(b) shall be made with due regard to the contributor's means.

(11) An appeal shall lie in accordance with rules of court from any order made under this paragraph.

Enforcement of contribution orders etc.

24.—...

(2) Where a contributor has agreed, or has been ordered, to make contributions to a local authority, any other local authority within whose area the contributor is for the time being living may—

(a) at the request of the local authority who served the contribution notice; and

(b) subject to agreement as to any sum to be deducted in respect of services rendered,

collect from the contributor any contributions due on behalf of the authority who served the notice.

...

(4) The power to collect sums under sub-paragraph (2) includes the power to—

(a) receive and give a discharge for any contributions due; and

(b) (if necessary) enforce payment of any contributions,

even though those contributions may have fallen due at a time when the contributor was living elsewhere.

(5) Any contribution collected under sub-paragraph (2) shall be paid (subject to any agreed deduction) to the local authority who served the contribution notice.

(6) In any proceedings under this paragraph, a document which purports to be—

(a) a copy of an order made by a court under or by virtue of paragraph 23; and

(b) certified as a true copy by designated officer for the court,

shall be evidence of the order.

(7) In any proceedings under this paragraph, a certificate which—

(a) purports to be signed by the clerk or some other duly authorised officer of the local authority who obtained the contribution order; and

(b) states that any sum due to the authority under the order is overdue and unpaid,

shall be evidence that the sum is overdue and unpaid.

Regulations

25.—The appropriate national authority may make regulations—

(a) as to the considerations which a local authority must take into account in deciding—

(i) whether it is reasonable to recover contributions; and

(ii) what the arrangements for payment should be;

(b) as to the procedures a local authority must follow in reaching agreements with—

(i) contributors (under paragraphs 22 and 23); and

(ii) any other local authority (under paragraph 23).

SCHEDULE 3

SUPERVISION ORDERS

PART I GENERAL

Meaning of 'responsible person'

1.—In this Schedule, 'the responsible person', in relation to a supervised child, means—

    (a) any person who has parental responsibility for the child; and

    (b) any other person with whom the child is living.

Power of supervisor to give directions to supervised child

2.—(1) A supervision order may require the supervised child to comply with any directions given from time to time by the supervisor which require him to do all or any of the following things—

    (a) to live at a place or places specified in the directions for a period or periods so specified;

    (b) to present himself to a person or persons specified in the directions at a place or places and on a day or days so specified;

    (c) to participate in activities specified in the directions on a day or days so specified.

(2) It shall be for the supervisor to decide whether, and to what extent, he exercises his power to give directions and to decide the form of any directions which he gives.

(3) Sub-paragraph (1) does not confer on a supervisor power to give directions in respect of any medical or psychiatric examination or treatment (which are matters dealt with in paragraphs 4 and 5).

Imposition of obligations on responsible person

3.—(1) With the consent of any responsible person, a supervision order may include a requirement—

    (a) that he take all reasonable steps to ensure that the supervised child complies with any direction given by the supervisor under paragraph 2;

    (b) that he take all reasonable steps to ensure that the supervised child complies with any requirement included in the order under paragraph 4 or 5;

    (c) that he comply with any directions given by the supervisor requiring him to attend at a place specified in the directions for the purpose of taking part in activities so specified.

(2) A direction given under sub-paragraph (1)(c) may specify the time at which the responsible person is to attend and whether or not the supervised child is required to attend with him.

(3) A supervision order may require any person who is a responsible person in relation to the supervised child to keep the supervisor informed of his address, if it differs from the child's.

Psychiatric and medical examinations

4.—(1) A supervision order may require the supervised child—

    (a) to submit to a medical or psychiatric examination; or

    (b) to submit to any such examination from time to time as directed by the supervisor.

(2) Any such examination shall be required to be conducted—

    (a) by, or under the direction of, such registered medical practitioner as may be specified in the order;

    (b) at a place specified in the order and at which the supervised child is to attend as a non-resident patient; or

    (c) at—

        (i) a health service hospital; or

        (ii) in the case of a psychiatric examination, a hospital, independent hospital or care home,

    at which the supervised child is, or is to attend as, a resident patient.

(3) A requirement of a kind mentioned in sub-paragraph (2)(c) shall not be included unless the court is satisfied, on the evidence of a registered medical practitioner, that—

    (a) the child may be suffering from a physical or mental condition that requires, and may be susceptible to, treatment; and

    (b) a period as a resident patient is necessary if the examination is to be carried out properly.

(4) No court shall include a requirement under this paragraph in a supervision order unless it is satisfied that—

    (a) where the child has sufficient understanding to make an informed decision, he consents to its inclusion; and

    (b) satisfactory arrangements have been, or can be, made for the examination.

Psychiatric and medical treatment

5.—(1) Where a court which proposes to make or vary a supervision order is satisfied, on the evidence of a registered medical practitioner approved for the purposes of section 12 of the Mental Health Act 1983, that the mental condition of the supervised child—

    (a) is such as requires, and may be susceptible to, treatment; but

    (b) is not such as to warrant his detention in pursuance of a hospital order under Part III of that Act,

the court may include in the order a requirement that the supervised child shall, for a period specified in the order, submit to such treatment as is so specified.

(2) The treatment specified in accordance with sub-paragraph (1) must be—

    (a) by, or under the direction of, such registered medical practitioner as may be specified in the order;

    (b) as a non-resident patient at such a place as may be so specified; or

    (c) as a resident patient in a hospital, independent hospital or care home.

(3) Where a court which proposes to make or vary a supervision order is satisfied, on the evidence of a registered medical practitioner, that the physical condition of the supervised child is such as requires, and may be susceptible to, treatment, the court may include in the order a requirement that the supervised child shall, for a period specified in the order, submit to such treatment as is so specified.

(4) The treatment specified in accordance with sub-paragraph (3) must be—

    (a) by, or under the direction of, such registered medical practitioner as may be specified in the order;

    (b) as a non-resident patient at such place as may be so specified; or

    (c) as a resident patient in a health service hospital.

(5) No court shall include a requirement under this paragraph in a supervision order unless it is satisfied—

    (a) where the child has sufficient understanding to make an informed decision, that he consents to its inclusion; and

    (b) that satisfactory arrangements have been, or can be, made for the treatment.

(6) If a medical practitioner by whom or under whose direction a supervised person is being treated in pursuance of a requirement included in a supervision order by virtue of this paragraph is unwilling to continue to treat or direct the treatment of the supervised child or is of the opinion that—

    (a) the treatment should be continued beyond the period specified in the order;

    (b) the supervised child needs different treatment;

    (c) he is not susceptible to treatment; or

    (d) he does not require further treatment,

the practitioner shall make a report in writing to that effect to the supervisor.

PART II MISCELLANEOUS

Life of supervision order

6.—(1) Subject to sub-paragraph (2) and section 91, a supervision order shall cease to have effect at the end of the period of one year beginning with the date on which it was made.

(2) A supervision order shall also cease to have effect if an event mentioned in section 25(1)(a) or (b) of the Child Abduction and Custody Act 1985 (termination of existing orders) occurs with respect to the child.

(3) Where the supervisor applies to the court to extend, or further extend, a supervision order the court may extend the order for such period as it may specify.

(4) A supervision order may not be extended so as to run beyond the end of the period of three years beginning with the date on which it was made.

Information to be given to supervisor etc.

8.—(1) A supervision order may require the supervised child—
  (a) to keep the supervisor informed of any change in his address; and
  (b) to allow the supervisor to visit him at the place where he is living.

(2) The responsible person in relation to any child with respect to whom a supervision order is made shall—
  (a) if asked by the supervisor, inform him of the child's address (if it is known to him); and
  (b) if he is living with the child, allow the supervisor reasonable contact with the child.

Selection of supervisor

9.—(1) A supervision order shall not designate a local authority as the supervisor unless—
  (a) the authority agree; or
  (b) the supervised child lives or will live within their area.

Effect of supervision order on earlier orders

10.—The making of a supervision order with respect to any child brings to an end any earlier care or supervision order which—
  (a) was made with respect to that child; and
  (b) would otherwise continue in force.

Local authority functions and expenditure

11.—(1) The Secretary of State may make regulations with respect to the exercise by a local authority of their functions where a child has been placed under their supervision by a supervision order.

(2) Where a supervision order requires compliance with directions given by virtue of this section, any expenditure incurred by the supervisor for the purposes of the directions shall be defrayed by the local authority designated in the order.

PART III EDUCATION SUPERVISION ORDERS

Effect of orders

12.—(1) Where an education supervision order is in force with respect to a child, it shall be the duty of the supervisor—
  (a) to advise, assist and befriend, and give directions to—
    (i)   the supervised child; and
    (ii) his parents,
    in such a way as will, in the opinion of the supervisor, secure that he is properly educated;

(b) where any such directions given to—
    (i)   the supervised child; or
    (ii)   a parent of his,
    have not been complied with, to consider what further steps to take in the exercise of the supervisor's powers under this Act.

(2) Before giving any directions under sub-paragraph (1) the supervisor shall, so far as is reasonably practicable, ascertain the wishes and feelings of—
    (a) the child; and
    (b) his parents,
    including, in particular, their wishes as to the place at which the child should be educated.

(3) When settling the terms of any such directions, the supervisor shall give due consideration—
    (a) having regard to the child's age and understanding, to such wishes and feelings of his as the supervisor has been able to ascertain; and
    (b) to such wishes and feelings of the child's parents as he has been able to ascertain.

(4) Directions may be given under this paragraph at any time while the education supervision order is in force.

13.—(1) Where an education supervision order is in force with respect to a child, the duties of the child's parents under sections 7 and 444 of the Education Act 1996 (duties to secure education of children and to secure regular attendance of registered pupils) shall be superseded by their duty to comply with any directions in force under the education supervision order.

(2) Where an education supervision order is made with respect to a child—
    (a) any school attendance order—
        (i)   made under section 437 of the Education Act 1996 with respect to the child; and
        (ii)   in force immediately before the making of the education supervision order,
        shall cease to have effect; and
    (b) while the education supervision order remains in force, the following provisions shall not apply with respect to the child—
        (i)   section 437 of that Act (school attendance orders);
        (ii)   section 9 of that Act (pupils to be educated in accordance with wishes of their parents);
        (iii) sections 411 and 423 of that Act (parental preference and appeals against admission decisions);
    (c) a youth rehabilitation order made under Part 1 of the Criminal Justice and Immigration Act 2008 with respect to the child, while the education supervision order is in force, may not include an education requirement (within the meaning of that Part);
    (d) any education requirement of a kind mentioned in paragraph (c), which was in force with respect to the child immediately before the making of the education supervision order, shall cease to have effect.

Effect where child also subject to supervision order

14.—(1) This paragraph applies where an education supervision order and a supervision order, or youth rehabilitation order (within the meaning of Part 1 of the Criminal Justice and Immigration Act 2008), are in force at the same time with respect to the same child.

(2) Any failure to comply with a direction given by the supervisor under the education supervision order shall be disregarded if it would not have been reasonably practicable to comply with it without failing to comply with a direction or instruction given under the other order.

Duration of orders

15.—(1) An education supervision order shall have effect for a period of one year, beginning with the date on which it is made.

(2) An education supervision order shall not expire if, before it would otherwise have expired, the court has (on the application of the authority in whose favour the order was made) extended the period during which it is in force.

(3) Such an application may not be made earlier than three months before the date on which the order would otherwise expire.

(4) The period during which an education supervision order is in force may be extended under sub-paragraph (2) on more than one occasion.

(5) No one extension may be for a period of more than three years.

(6) An education supervision order shall cease to have effect on—

    (a) the child's ceasing to be of compulsory school age; or

    (b) the making of a care order with respect to the child;

and sub-paragraphs (1) to (4) are subject to this sub-paragraph.

Information to be given to supervisor etc.

16.—(1) An education supervision order may require the child—

    (a) to keep the supervisor informed of any change in his address; and

    (b) to allow the supervisor to visit him at the place where he is living.

(2) A person who is the parent of a child with respect to whom an education supervision order has been made shall—

    (a) if asked by the supervisor, inform him of the child's address (if it is known to him); and

    (b) if he is living with the child, allow the supervisor reasonable contact with the child.

Discharge of orders

17.—(1) The court may discharge any education supervision order on the application of—

    (a) the child concerned;

    (b) a parent of his; or

    (c) the local authority designated in the order.

(2) On discharging an education supervision order, the court may direct the local authority within whose area the child lives, or will live, to investigate the circumstances of the child.

Offences

18.—(1) If a parent of a child with respect to whom an education supervision order is in force persistently fails to comply with a direction given under the order he shall be guilty of an offence.

(2) It shall be a defence for any person charged with such an offence to prove that—

    (a) he took all reasonable steps to ensure that the direction was complied with:

    (b) the direction was unreasonable; or

    (c) he had complied with—

        (i) a requirement included in a supervision order made with respect to the child; or

        (ii) directions given under such a requirement,

        and that it was not reasonably practicable to comply both with the direction and with the requirement or directions mentioned in this paragraph.

(3) A person guilty of an offence under this paragraph shall be liable on summary conviction to a fine not exceeding level 3 on the standard scale.

Persistent failure of child to comply with directions

19.—(1) Where a child with respect to whom an education supervision order is in force persistently fails to comply with any direction given under the order, the local authority designated in the order shall notify the appropriate local authority, if different.

(2) Where a local authority have been notified under sub-paragraph (1) they shall investigate the circumstances of the child.

(3) In this paragraph 'the appropriate local authority' has the same meaning as in section 36.

Miscellaneous

20.—The Secretary of State may by regulations make provision modifying, or displacing, the provisions of any enactment about education in relation to any child with respect to whom an education supervision order is in force to such extent as appears to the Secretary of State to be necessary or expedient in consequence of the provision made by this Act with respect to such orders.

Interpretation

21.—In this Part of this Schedule 'parent' has the same meaning as in the Education Act 1996.

...

Section 63(12)

SCHEDULE 7

FOSTER PARENTS: LIMITS ON NUMBER OF FOSTER CHILDREN

Interpretation

1.—For the purposes of this Schedule, a person fosters a child if—
   (a) he is a local authority foster parent in relation to the child;
   (b) he is a foster parent with whom the child has been placed by a voluntary organisation; or
   (c) he fosters the child privately.

The usual fostering limit

2.—Subject to what follows, a person may not foster more than three children ('the usual fostering limit').

Siblings

3.—A person may exceed the usual fostering limit if the children concerned are all siblings with respect to each other.

Exemption by local authority

4.—(1) A person may exceed the usual fostering limit if he is exempted from it by the local authority within whose area he lives.

(2) In considering whether to exempt a person, a local authority shall have regard, in particular, to—
   (a) the number of children whom the person proposes to foster;
   (b) the arrangements which the person proposes for the care and accommodation of the fostered children;
   (c) the intended and likely relationship between the person and the fostered children;
   (d) the period of time for which he proposes to foster the children; and
   (e) whether the welfare of the fostered children (and of any other children who are or will be living in the accommodation) will be safeguarded and promoted.

(3) Where a local authority exempt a person, they shall inform him by notice in writing—
   (a) that he is so exempted;
   (b) of the children, described by name, whom he may foster; and
   (c) of any condition to which the exemption is subject.

(4) A local authority may at any time by notice in writing—
   (a) vary or cancel an exemption; or
   (b) impose, vary or cancel a condition to which the exemption is subject,

and, in considering whether to do so, they shall have regard in particular to the considerations mentioned in sub-paragraph (2).

(5) The Secretary of State may make regulations amplifying or modifying the provisions of this paragraph in order to provide for cases where children need to be placed with foster parents as a matter of urgency.

Effect of exceeding fostering limit

5.—(1) A person shall cease to be treated as fostering and shall be treated, for the purposes of this Act and the Care Standards Act 2000, as carrying on a children's home if—

    (a) he exceeds the usual fostering limit; or

    (b) where he is exempted under paragraph 4,—

        (i) he fosters any child not named in the exemption; and

        (ii) in so doing, he exceeds the usual fostering limit.

(2) Sub-paragraph (1) does not apply if the children concerned are all siblings in respect of each other.

Complaints etc.

6.—(1) Every local authority shall establish a procedure for considering any representations (including any complaint) made to them about the discharge of their functions under paragraph 4 by a person exempted or seeking to be exempted under that paragraph.

(2) In carrying out any consideration of representations under subparagraph (1), a local authority shall comply with any regulations made by the Secretary of State for the purposes of this paragraph.

Section 66(5)

SCHEDULE 8

PRIVATELY FOSTERED CHILDREN

Exemptions

1.—A child is not a privately fostered child while he is being looked after by a local authority.

2.—(1) A child is not a privately fostered child while he is in the care of any person—

    (a) in premises in which any—

        (i) parent of his;

        (ii) person who is not a parent of his but who has parental responsibility for him; or

        (iii) person who is a relative of his and who has assumed responsibility for his care,

        is for the time being living;

    (b) ...

    (c) in accommodation provided by or on behalf of any voluntary organisation;

    (d) in any school in which he is receiving full-time education;

    (e) in any health service hospital;

    (f) in any care home or independent hospital; or

    (g) in any home or institution not specified in this paragraph but provided, equipped and maintained by the Secretary of State.

(2) Sub-paragraph (1)(c) to (g) does not apply where the person caring for the child is doing so in his personal capacity and not in the course of carrying out his duties in relation to the establishment mentioned in the paragraph in question.

3.—A child is not a privately fostered child while he is in the care of any person in compliance with—

    (a) a youth rehabilitation order made under section 1 of the Criminal Justice and Immigration Act 2008; or

    ...

4.—A child is not a privately fostered child while he is liable to be detained, or subject to guardianship, under the Mental Health Act 1983.

5.—A child is not a privately fostered child while he is placed in the care of a person who proposes to adopt him under arrangements made by an adoption agency within the meaning of—

    (a) section 2 of the Adoption and Children Act 2002;

    ...

Power of local authority to impose requirements

6.—(1) Where a person is fostering any child privately, or proposes to foster any child privately, the appropriate local authority may impose on him requirements as to—

    (a) the number, age and sex of the children who may be privately fostered by him;

    (b) the standard of the accommodation and equipment to be provided for them;

    (c) the arrangements to be made with respect to their health and safety; and

    (d) particular arrangements which must be made with respect to the provision of care for them,

and it shall be his duty to comply with any such requirement before the end of such period as the authority may specify unless, in the case of a proposal, the proposal is not carried out.

(2) A requirement may be limited to a particular child, or class of child.

(3) A requirement (other than one imposed under sub-paragraph (1)(a)) may be limited by the authority so as to apply only when the number of children fostered by the person exceeds a specified number.

(4) A requirement shall be imposed by notice in writing addressed to the person on whom it is imposed and informing him of—

    (a) the reason for imposing the requirement;

    (b) his right under paragraph 8 to appeal against it; and

    (c) the time within which he may do so.

(5) A local authority may at any time vary any requirement, impose any additional requirement or remove any requirement.

(6) In this Schedule—

    (a) 'the appropriate local authority' means—

        (i)   the local authority within whose area the child is being fostered; or

        (ii)   in the case of a proposal to foster a child, the local authority within whose area it is proposed that he will be fostered; and

    (b) 'requirement', in relation to any person, means a requirement imposed on him under this paragraph.

Regulations requiring notification of fostering etc.

7.—(1) The Secretary of State may by regulations make provision as to—

    (a) the circumstances in which notification is required to be given in connection with children who are, have been or are proposed to be fostered privately; and

    (b) the manner and form in which such notification is to be given.

(2) The regulations may, in particular—

    (a) require any person who is, or proposes to be, involved (whether or not directly) in arranging for a child to be fostered privately to notify the appropriate authority;

    (b) require any person who is—

        (i)   a parent of a child; or

        (ii)   a person who is not a parent of his but who has parental responsibility for a child, and who knows that it is proposed that the child should be fostered privately, to notify the appropriate authority;

    (c) require any parent of a privately fostered child, or person who is not a parent of such a child but who has parental responsibility for him, to notify the appropriate authority of any change in his address;

    (d) require any person who proposes to foster a child privately, to notify the appropriate authority of his proposal;

    (e) require any person who is fostering a child privately, or proposes to do so, to notify the appropriate authority of—

        (i)   any offence of which he has been convicted;

        (ii)   any disqualification imposed on him under section 68; or

        (iii) any prohibition imposed on him under section 69;

(f) require any person who is fostering a child privately, to notify the appropriate authority of any change in his address;

(g) require any person who is fostering a child privately to notify the appropriate authority in writing of any person who begins, or ceases, to be part of his household;

(h) require any person who has been fostering a child privately, but has ceased to do so, to notify the appropriate authority (indicating, where the child has died, that this is the reason).

7A. Every local authority must promote public awareness in their area of requirements as to notification for which provision is made under paragraph 7.

Appeals

8.—(1) A person aggrieved by—

(a) a requirement imposed under paragraph 6;

(b) a refusal of consent under section 68;

(c) a prohibition imposed under section 69;

(d) a refusal to cancel such a prohibition;

(e) a refusal to make an exemption under paragraph 4 of Schedule 7;

(f) a condition imposed in such an exemption; or

(g) a variation or cancellation of such an exemption,

may appeal to the court.

(2) The appeal must be made within fourteen days from the date on which the person appealing is notified of the requirement, refusal, prohibition, condition, variation or cancellation.

(3) Where the appeal is against—

(a) a requirement imposed under paragraph 6;

(b) a condition of an exemption imposed under paragraph 4 of Schedule 7; or

(c) a variation or cancellation of such an exemption,

the requirement, condition, variation or cancellation shall not have effect while the appeal is pending.

(4) Where it allows an appeal against a requirement or prohibition, the court may, instead of cancelling the requirement or prohibition—

(a) vary the requirement, or allow more time for compliance with it; or

(b) if an absolute prohibition has been imposed, substitute for it a prohibition on using the premises after such time as the court may specify unless such specified requirements as the local authority had power to impose under paragraph 6 are complied with.

(5) Any requirement or prohibition specified or substituted by a court under this paragraph shall be deemed for the purposes of Part IX (other than this paragraph) to have been imposed by the local authority under paragraph 6 or (as the case may be) section 69.

(6) Where it allows an appeal against a refusal to make an exemption, a condition imposed in such an exemption or a variation or cancellation of such an exemption, the court may—

(a) make an exemption;

(b) impose a condition; or

(c) vary the exemption.

(7) Any exemption made or varied under sub-paragraph (6), or any condition imposed under that sub-paragraph, shall be deemed for the purposes of Schedule 7 (but not for the purposes of this paragraph) to have been made, varied or imposed under that Schedule.

(8) Nothing in sub-paragraph (1)(e) to (g) confers any right of appeal on—

(a) a person who is, or would be if exempted under Schedule 7, a local authority foster parent; or

(b) a person who is, or would be if so exempted, a person with whom a child is placed by a voluntary organisation.

Extension of Part IX to certain school children during holidays

9.—(1) Where a child under sixteen who is a pupil at a school lives at the school during school holidays for a period of more than two weeks, Part IX shall apply in relation to the child as if—

(a) while living at the school, he were a privately fostered child; and

(b) paragraphs 2(1)(c) and (d) and 6 were omitted.

But this sub-paragraph does not apply to a school which is a children's home in respect of which a person is registered under Part 2 of the Care Standards Act 2000.

(2) Sub-paragraph (3) applies to any person who proposes to care for and accommodate one or more children at a school in circumstances in which some or all of them will be treated as private foster children by virtue of this paragraph.

(3) That person shall, not less than two weeks before the first of those children is treated as a private foster child by virtue of this paragraph during the holiday in question, give written notice of his proposal to the local authority within whose area the child is ordinarily resident ('the appropriate authority'), stating the estimated number of the children.

(4) A local authority may exempt any person from the duty of giving notice under sub-paragraph (3).

(5) Any such exemption may be granted for a special period or indefinitely and may be revoked at any time by notice in writing given to the person exempted.

(6) Where a child who is treated as a private foster child by virtue of this paragraph dies, the person caring for him at the school shall, not later than 48 hours after his death, give written notice of it—

(a) to the appropriate authority; and

(b) where reasonably practicable, to each parent of the child and to every person who is not a parent of his but who has parental responsibility for him.

(7) Where a child who is treated as a foster child by virtue of this paragraph ceases for any other reason to be such a child, the person caring for him at the school shall give written notice of the fact to the appropriate local authority.

Prohibition of advertisements relating to fostering

10.—No advertisement indicating that a person will undertake, or will arrange for, a child to be privately fostered shall be published, unless it states that person's name and address.

Avoidance of insurances on lives of privately fostered children

11.—A person who fosters a child privately and for reward shall be deemed for the purposes of the Life Assurance Act 1774 to have no interest in the life of the child.

...

Human Fertilisation and Embryology Act 1990

(1990 c. 37)

Principal terms used

1 Meaning of 'embryo', 'gamete' and associated expressions

(1) In this Act (except in section 4A or in the term 'human admixed embryo')—

(a) embryo means a live human embryo and does not include a human admixed embryo (as defined by section 4A(6)), and

(b) references to an embryo include an egg that is in the process of fertilisation or is undergoing any other process capable of resulting in an embryo.

(2) This Act, so far as it governs bringing about the creation of an embryo, applies only to bringing about the creation of an embryo outside the human body; and in this Act—

(a) references to embryos the creation of which was brought about *in vitro* (in their application to those where fertilisation or any other process by which an embryo is created is complete) are to those where fertilisation or any other process by which the embryo was created began outside the human body whether or not it was completed there, and

(b) references to embryos taken from a woman do not include embryos whose creation was brought about *in vitro*.

(3) This Act, so far as it governs the keeping or use of an embryo, applies only to keeping or using an embryo outside the human body.

(4) In this Act (except in section 4A)—

(a) references to eggs are to live human eggs, including cells of the female germ line at any stage of maturity, but (except in subsection (1)(b)) not including eggs that are in the process of fertilisation or are undergoing any other process capable of resulting in an embryo,

(b) references to sperm are to live human sperm, including cells of the male germ line at any stage of maturity, and

(c) references to gametes are to be read accordingly.

(5) For the purposes of this Act, sperm is to be treated as partner-donated sperm if the donor of the sperm and the recipient of the sperm declare that they have an intimate physical relationship.

(6) If it appears to the Secretary of State necessary or desirable to do so in the light of developments in science or medicine, regulations may provide that in this Act (except in section 4A) 'embryo', 'eggs', 'sperm' or 'gametes' includes things specified in the regulations which would not otherwise fall within the definition.

(7) Regulations made by virtue of subsection (6) may not provide for anything containing any nuclear or mitochondrial DNA that is not human to be treated as an embryo or as eggs, sperm or gametes.

...

2   Other terms

(1) In this Act—

'the Authority' means the Human Fertilisation and Embryology Authority established under section 5 of this Act,

'basic partner treatment services' means treatment services that are provided for a woman and a man together without using—

(a) the gametes of any other person, or

(b) embryos created outside the woman's body,

...

'directions' means directions under section 23 of this Act,

...

'licence' means a licence under Schedule 2 to this Act and, in relation to a licence, 'the person responsible' has the meaning given by section 17 of this Act, and

'non-medical fertility services' means any services that are provided, in the course of a business, for the purpose of assisting women to carry children, but are not medical, surgical or obstetric services,

'nuclear DNA', in relation to an embryo, includes DNA in the pronucleus of the embryo,

...

'treatment services' means medical, surgical or obstetric services provided to the public or a section of the public for the purpose of assisting women to carry children.

...

(3) For the purposes of this Act, a woman is not to be treated as carrying a child until the embryo has become implanted.

...

Licence conditions

...

13   Conditions of licences for treatment

...

(5) A woman shall not be provided with treatment services unless account has been taken of the welfare of any child who may be born as a result of the treatment (including the need of that child for supportive parenting), and of any other child who may be affected by the birth.

(6) A woman shall not be provided with treatment services of a kind specified in Part 1 of Schedule 3ZA unless she and any man or woman who is to be treated together with her have been given a suitable opportunity to receive proper counselling about the implications of her being provided with treatment services of that kind, and have been provided with such relevant information as is proper.

(6A) A woman shall not be provided with treatment services after the happening of any event falling within any paragraph of Part 2 of Schedule 3ZA unless (before or after the event) she and the intended second parent have been given a suitable opportunity to receive proper counselling about the implications of the woman being provided with treatment services after the happening of that event, and have been provided with such relevant information as is proper.

(6B) The reference in subsection (6A) to the intended second parent is a reference to—

(a) any man as respects whom the agreed fatherhood conditions in section 37 of the Human Fertilisation and Embryology Act 2008 ('the 2008 Act') are for the time being satisfied in relation to treatment provided to the woman mentioned in subsection (6A), and

(b) any woman as respects whom the agreed female parenthood conditions in section 44 of the 2008 Act are for the time being satisfied in relation to treatment provided to the woman mentioned in subsection (6A).

(6C) In the case of treatment services falling within paragraph 1 of Schedule 3ZA (use of gametes of a person not receiving those services) or paragraph 3 of that Schedule (use of embryo taken from a woman not receiving those services), the information provided by virtue of subsection (6) or (6A) must include such information as is proper about—

(a) the importance of informing any resulting child at an early age that the child results from the gametes of a person who is not a parent of the child, and

(b) suitable methods of informing such a child of that fact.

(6D) Where the person responsible receives from a person ('X') notice under section 37(1)(c) or 44(1)(c) of the 2008 Act of X's withdrawal of consent to X being treated as the parent of any child resulting from the provision of treatment services to a woman ('W'), the person responsible—

(a) must notify W in writing of the receipt of the notice from X, and

(b) no person to whom the licence applies may place an embryo or sperm and eggs in W, or artificially inseminate W, until W has been so notified.

(6E) Where the person responsible receives from a woman ('W') who has previously given notice under section 37(1)(b) or 44(1)(b) of the 2008 Act that she consents to another person ('X') being treated as a parent of any child resulting from the provision of treatment services to W—

(a) notice under section 37(1)(c) or 44(1)(c) of the 2008 Act of the withdrawal of W's consent, or

(b) a notice under section 37(1)(b) or 44(1)(b) of the 2008 Act in respect of a person other than X,

the person responsible must take reasonable steps to notify X in writing of the receipt of the notice mentioned in paragraph (a) or (b).

...

(8) Subsections (9) and (10) apply in determining any of the following—

(a) the persons who are to provide gametes for use in pursuance of the licence in a case where consent is required under paragraph 5 of Schedule 3 for the use in question;

(b) the woman from whom an embryo is to be taken for use in pursuance of the licence, in a case where her consent is required under paragraph 7 of Schedule 3 for the use of the embryo;

(c) which of two or more embryos to place in a woman.

(9) Persons or embryos that are known to have a gene, chromosome or mitochondrion abnormality involving a significant risk that a person with the abnormality will have or develop—

(a) a serious physical or mental disability,

(b) a serious illness, or

(c) any other serious medical condition,

must not be preferred to those that are not known to have such an abnormality.

(10) Embryos that are known to be of a particular sex and to carry a particular risk, compared with embryos of that sex in general, that any resulting child will have or develop—

    (a) a gender-related serious physical or mental disability,

    (b) a gender-related serious illness, or

    (c) any other gender-related serious medical condition,

must not be preferred to those that are not known to carry such a risk.

(11) For the purposes of subsection (10), a physical or mental disability, illness or other medical condition is gender-related if—

    (a) it affects only one sex, or

    (b) it affects one sex significantly more than the other.

(12) No embryo appropriated for the purpose mentioned in paragraph 1(1)(ca) of Schedule 2 (training in embryological techniques) shall be kept or used for the provision of treatment services.

(13) The person responsible shall comply with any requirement imposed on that person by section 31ZD.

...

Information

31 Register of information

(1) The Authority shall keep a register which is to contain any information which falls within subsection (2) and which—

    (a) immediately before the coming into force of section 24 of the Human Fertilisation and Embryology Act 2008, was contained in the register kept under this section by the Authority, or

    (b) is obtained by the Authority.

(2) Subject to subsection (3), information falls within this subsection if it relates to—

    (a) the provision for any identifiable individual of treatment services other than basic partner treatment services,

    (b) the procurement or distribution of any sperm, other than sperm which is partner-donated sperm and has not been stored, in the course of providing non-medical fertility services for any identifiable individual,

    (c) the keeping of the gametes of any identifiable individual or of an embryo taken from any identifiable woman,

    (d) the use of the gametes of any identifiable individual other than their use for the purpose of basic partner treatment services, or

    (e) the use of an embryo taken from any identifiable woman,

or if it shows that any identifiable individual is a relevant individual.

(3) Information does not fall within subsection (2) if it is provided to the Authority for the purposes of any voluntary contact register as defined by section 31ZF(1).

(4) In this section 'relevant individual' means an individual who was or may have been born in consequence of—

    (a) treatment services, other than basic partner treatment services, or

    (b) the procurement or distribution of any sperm (other than partner-donated sperm which has not been stored) in the course of providing non-medical fertility services.

31ZA Request for information as to genetic parentage etc.

(1) A person who has attained the age of 16 ('the applicant') may by notice to the Authority require the Authority to comply with a request under subsection (2).

(2) The applicant may request the Authority to give the applicant notice stating whether or not the information contained in the register shows that a person ('the donor') other than a parent of the applicant would or might, but for the relevant statutory provisions, be the parent of the applicant, and if it does show that—

    (a) giving the applicant so much of that information as relates to the donor as the Authority is required by regulations to give (but no other information), or

   (b) stating whether or not that information shows that there are other persons of whom the donor is not the parent but would or might, but for the relevant statutory provisions, be the parent and if so—
      (i)   the number of those other persons,
      (ii) the sex of each of them, and
      (iii) the year of birth of each of them.

(3) The Authority shall comply with a request under subsection (2) if—
   (a) the information contained in the register shows that the applicant is a relevant individual, and
   (b) the applicant has been given a suitable opportunity to receive proper counselling about the implications of compliance with the request.

(4) Where a request is made under subsection (2)(a) and the applicant has not attained the age of 18 when the applicant gives notice to the Authority under subsection (1), regulations cannot require the Authority to give the applicant any information which identifies the donor.

(5) Regulations cannot require the Authority to give any information as to the identity of a person whose gametes have been used or from whom an embryo has been taken if a person to whom a licence applied was provided with the information at a time when the Authority could not have been required to give information of the kind in question.

(6) The Authority need not comply with a request made under subsection (2)(b) by any applicant if it considers that special circumstances exist which increase the likelihood that compliance with the request would enable the applicant—
   (a) to identify the donor, in a case where the Authority is not required by regulations under subsection (2)(a) to give the applicant information which identifies the donor, or
   (b) to identify any person about whom information is given under subsection (2)(b).

(7) In this section—
'relevant individual' has the same meaning as in section 31;
'the relevant statutory provisions' means sections 27 to 29 of this Act and sections 33 to 47 of the Human Fertilisation and Embryology Act 2008.

31ZB   Request for information as to intended spouse etc.

(1) Subject to subsection (4), a person ('the applicant') may by notice to the Authority require the Authority to comply with a request under subsection (2).

(2) The applicant may request the Authority to give the applicant notice stating whether or not information contained in the register shows that, but for the relevant statutory provisions, the applicant would or might be related to a person specified in the request ('the specified person') as—
   (a) a person whom the applicant proposes to marry,
   (b) a person with whom the applicant proposes to enter into a civil partnership, or
   (c) a person with whom the applicant is in an intimate physical relationship or with whom the applicant proposes to enter into an intimate physical relationship.

(3) Subject to subsection (5), the Authority shall comply with a request under subsection (2) if—
   (a) the information contained in the register shows that the applicant is a relevant individual,
   (b) the Authority receives notice in writing from the specified person consenting to the request being made and that notice has not been withdrawn, and
   (c) the applicant and the specified person have each been given a suitable opportunity to receive proper counselling about the implications of compliance with the request.

(4) A request may not be made under subsection (2)(c) by a person who has not attained the age of 16.

(5) Where a request is made under subsection (2)(c) and the specified person has not attained the age of 16 when the applicant gives notice to the Authority under subsection (1), the Authority must not comply with the request.

(6) Where the Authority is required under subsection (3) to comply with a request under subsection (2), the Authority must take all reasonable steps to give the applicant and the specified

person notice stating whether or not the information contained in the register shows that, but for the relevant statutory provisions, the applicant and the specified person would or might be related.

(7) In this section—

'relevant individual' has the same meaning as in section 31;

'the relevant statutory provisions' has the same meaning as in section 31ZA.

31ZC   Power of Authority to inform donor of request for information

(1) Where—

    (a) the Authority has received from a person ('the applicant') a notice containing a request under subsection (2)(a) of section 31ZA, and

    (b) compliance by the Authority with its duty under that section has involved or will involve giving the applicant information relating to a person other than the parent of the applicant who would or might, but for the relevant statutory provisions, be a parent of the applicant ('the donor'),

the Authority may notify the donor that a request under section 31ZA(2)(a) has been made, but may not disclose the identity of the applicant or any information relating to the applicant.

(2) In this section 'the relevant statutory provisions' has the same meaning as in section 31ZA.

31ZD   Provision to donor of information about resulting children

(1) This section applies where a person ('the donor') has consented under Schedule 3 (whether before or after the coming into force of this section) to—

    (a) the use of the donor's gametes, or an embryo the creation of which was brought about using the donor's gametes, for the purposes of treatment services provided under a licence, or

    (b) the use of the donor's gametes for the purposes of non-medical fertility services provided under a licence.

(2) In subsection (1)—

    (a) 'treatment services' do not include treatment services provided to the donor, or to the donor and another person together, and

    (b) 'non-medical fertility services' do not include any services involving partner-donated sperm.

(3) The donor may by notice request the appropriate person to give the donor notice stating—

    (a) the number of persons of whom the donor is not a parent but would or might, but for the relevant statutory provisions, be a parent by virtue of the use of the gametes or embryos to which the consent relates,

    (b) the sex of each of those persons, and

    (c) the year of birth of each of those persons.

(4) Subject to subsections (5) to (7), the appropriate person shall notify the donor whether the appropriate person holds the information mentioned in subsection (3) and, if the appropriate person does so, shall comply with the request.

(5) The appropriate person need not comply with a request under subsection (3) if the appropriate person considers that special circumstances exist which increase the likelihood that compliance with the request would enable the donor to identify any of the persons falling within paragraphs (a) to (c) of subsection (3).

(6) In the case of a donor who consented as described in subsection (1)(a), the Authority need not comply with a request made to it under subsection (3) where the person who held the licence referred to in subsection (1)(a) continues to hold a licence under paragraph 1 of Schedule 2, unless the donor has previously made a request under subsection (3) to the person responsible and the person responsible—

    (a) has notified the donor that the information concerned is not held, or

    (b) has failed to comply with the request within a reasonable period.

(7) In the case of a donor who consented as described in subsection (1)(b), the Authority need not comply with a request made to it under subsection (3) where the person who held the licence

referred to in subsection (1)(b) continues to hold a licence under paragraph 1A of Schedule 2, unless the donor has previously made a request under subsection (3) to the person responsible and the person responsible—

    (a) has notified the donor that the information concerned is not held, or

    (b) has failed to comply with the request within a reasonable period.

  (8) In this section 'the appropriate person' means—

    (a) in the case of a donor who consented as described in paragraph (a) of subsection (1)—

      (i) where the person who held the licence referred to in that paragraph continues to hold a licence under paragraph 1 of Schedule 2, the person responsible, or

      (ii) the Authority, and

    (b) in the case of a donor who consented as described in paragraph (b) of subsection (1)—

      (i) where the person who held the licence referred to in that paragraph continues to hold a licence under paragraph 1A of Schedule 2, the person responsible, or

      (ii) the Authority.

  (9) In this section 'the relevant statutory provisions' has the same meaning as in section 31ZA.

31ZE　Provision of information about donor-conceived genetic siblings

  (1) For the purposes of this section two relevant individuals are donor-conceived genetic siblings of each other if a person ('the donor') who is not the parent of either of them would or might, but for the relevant statutory provisions, be the parent of both of them.

  (2) Where—

    (a) the information on the register shows that a relevant individual ('A') is the donor-conceived genetic sibling of another relevant individual ('B'),

    (b) A has provided information to the Authority ('the agreed information') which consists of or includes information which enables A to be identified with the request that it should be disclosed to—

      (i) any donor-conceived genetic sibling of A, or

      (ii) such siblings of A of a specified description which includes B, and

    (c) the conditions in subsection (3) are satisfied,

then, subject to subsection (4), the Authority shall disclose the agreed information to B.

  (3) The conditions referred to in subsection (2)(c) are—

    (a) that each of A and B has attained the age of 18,

    (b) that B has requested the disclosure to B of information about any donor-conceived genetic sibling of B, and

    (c) that each of A and B has been given a suitable opportunity to receive proper counselling about the implications of disclosure under subsection (2).

  (4) The Authority need not disclose any information under subsection (2) if it considers that the disclosure of information will lead to A or B identifying the donor unless—

    (a) the donor has consented to the donor's identity being disclosed to A or B, or

    (b) were A or B to make a request under section 31ZA(2)(a), the Authority would be required by regulations under that provision to give A or B information which would identify the donor.

  (5) In this section—

'relevant individual' has the same meaning as in section 31;

'the relevant statutory provisions' has the same meaning as in section 31ZA.

31ZF　Power of Authority to keep voluntary contact register

  (1) In this section and section 31ZG, a 'voluntary contact register' means a register of persons who have expressed their wish to receive information about any person to whom they are genetically related as a consequence of the provision to any person of treatment services in the United Kingdom before 1 August 1991.

  (2) The Authority may—

    (a) set up a voluntary contact register in such manner as it thinks fit,

(b) keep a voluntary contact register in such manner as it thinks fit,

(c) determine criteria for eligibility for inclusion on the register and the particulars that may be included,

(d) charge a fee to persons who wish their particulars to be entered on the register,

(e) arrange for samples of the DNA of such persons to be analysed at their request,

(f) make such arrangements as it thinks fit for the disclosure of information on the register between persons who appear to the Authority to be genetically related, and

(g) impose such conditions as it thinks fit to prevent a person ('A') from disclosing information to a person to whom A is genetically related ('B') where that information would identify any person who is genetically related to both A and B.

(3) The Authority may make arrangements with any person by whom a voluntary contact register is kept before the commencement of this section for the supply by that person to the Authority of the information contained in the register maintained by that person.

31ZG   Financial assistance for person setting up or keeping voluntary contact register

(1) The Authority may, instead of keeping a voluntary contact register, give financial assistance to any person who sets up or keeps a voluntary contact register.

(2) Financial assistance under subsection (1) may be given in any form, and in particular, may be given by way of—

(a) grants,

(b) loans,

(c) guarantees, or

(d) incurring expenditure for the person assisted.

(3) Financial assistance under subsection (1) may be given on such terms and conditions as the Authority considers appropriate.

(4) A person receiving assistance under subsection (1) must comply with the terms and conditions on which it is given, and compliance may be enforced by the Authority.

...

32   Information to be provided to Registrar General

(1) This section applies where a claim is made before the Registrar General that a person is or is not the parent of a child and it is necessary or desirable for the purpose of any function of the Registrar General to determine whether the claim is or may be well-founded.

(2) The Authority shall comply with any request made by the Registrar General by notice to the Authority to disclose whether any information on the register kept in pursuance of section 31 of this Act tends to show that that the person may be a parent of the child by virtue of any of the relevant statutory provisions and, if it does, disclose that information.

(2A) In subsection (2) 'the relevant statutory provisions' means—

(a) section 28 of this Act, and

(b) sections 35 to 47 of the Human Fertilisation and Embryology Act 2008.

...

33A   Disclosure of information

(1) No person shall disclose any information falling within section 31(2) which the person obtained (whether before or after the coming into force of section 24 of the Human Fertilisation and Embryology Act 2008) in the person's capacity as—

(a) a member or employee of the Authority,

(b) any person exercising functions of the Authority by virtue of section 8B or 8C of this Act (including a person exercising such functions by virtue of either of those sections as a member of staff or as an employee),

(c) any person engaged by the Authority to provide services to the Authority,

    (d) any person employed by, or engaged to provide services to, a person mentioned in paragraph (c),

    (e) a person to whom a licence applies,

    (f) a person to whom a third party agreement applies, or

    (g) a person to whom directions have been given.

(2) Subsection (1) does not apply where—

    (a) the disclosure is made to a person as a member or employee of the Authority or as a person exercising functions of the Authority as mentioned in subsection (1)(b),

    (b) the disclosure is made to or by a person falling within subsection (1)(c) for the purpose of the provision of services which that person is engaged to provide to the Authority,

    (c) the disclosure is made by a person mentioned in subsection (1)(d) for the purpose of enabling a person falling within subsection (1)(c) to provide services which that person is engaged to provide to the Authority,

    (d) the disclosure is made to a person to whom a licence applies for the purpose of that person's functions as such,

    (e) the disclosure is made to a person to whom a third party agreement applies for the purpose of that person's functions under that agreement,

    (f) the disclosure is made in pursuance of directions given by virtue of section 24,

    (g) the disclosure is made so that no individual can be identified from the information,

    (h) the disclosure is of information other than identifying donor information and is made with the consent required by section 33B,

    (i) the disclosure—

        (i) is made by a person who is satisfied that it is necessary to make the disclosure to avert an imminent danger to the health of an individual ('P'),

        (ii) is of information falling within section 31(2)(a) which could be disclosed by virtue of paragraph (h) with P's consent or could be disclosed to P by virtue of subsection (5), and

        (iii) is made in circumstances where it is not reasonably practicable to obtain P's consent,

    (j) the disclosure is of information which has been lawfully made available to the public before the disclosure is made,

    (k) the disclosure is made in accordance with sections 31ZA to 31ZE,

    (l) the disclosure is required or authorised to be made—

        (i) under regulations made under section 33D, or

        (ii) in relation to any time before the coming into force of the first regulations under that section, under regulations made under section 251 of the National Health Service Act 2006,

    (m) the disclosure is made by a person acting in the capacity mentioned in subsection (1)(a) or (b) for the purpose of carrying out the Authority's duties under section 8A,

    (n) the disclosure is made by a person acting in the capacity mentioned in subsection (1)(a) or (b) in pursuance of an order of a court under section 34 or 35,

    (o) the disclosure is made by a person acting in the capacity mentioned in subsection (1)(a) or (b) to the Registrar General in pursuance of a request under section 32,

    (p) the disclosure is made by a person acting in the capacity mentioned in subsection (1)(a) or (b) to any body or person discharging a regulatory function for the purpose of assisting that body or person to carry out that function,

    (q) the disclosure is made for the purpose of establishing in any proceedings relating to an application for an order under subsection (1) of section 54 of the Human Fertilisation and Embryology Act 2008 whether the condition specified in paragraph (a) or (b) of that subsection is met,

    (r) the disclosure is made under section 3 of the Access to Health Records Act 1990,

    (s) ...

    (t) the disclosure is made necessarily for—

     (i)   the purpose of the investigation of any offence (or suspected offence), or

    (ii)   any purpose preliminary to proceedings, or for the purposes of, or in connection with, any proceedings.

(3) Subsection (1) does not apply to the disclosure of information in so far as—

    (a) the information identifies a person who, but for sections 27 to 29 of this Act or sections 33 to 47 of the Human Fertilisation and Embryology Act 2008, would or might be a parent of a person who instituted proceedings under section 1A of the Congenital Disabilities (Civil Liability) Act 1976, and

    (b) the disclosure is made for the purpose of defending such proceedings, or instituting connected proceedings for compensation against that parent.

(4) Paragraph (t) of subsection (2), so far as relating to disclosure for the purpose of the investigation of an offence or suspected offence, or for any purpose preliminary to, or in connection with proceedings, does not apply—

    (a) to disclosure of identifying donor information, or

    (b) to disclosure, in circumstances in which subsection (1) of section 34 of this Act applies, of information relevant to the determination of the question mentioned in that subsection, made by any person acting in a capacity mentioned in any of paragraphs (c) to (g) of subsection (1).

(5) Subsection (1) does not apply to the disclosure to any individual of information which—

    (a) falls within subsection (2) of section 31 of this Act by virtue of any of paragraphs (a) to (e) of that subsection, and

    (b) relates only to that individual or, in the case of an individual who is treated together with, or gives a notice under section 37 or 44 of the Human Fertilisation and Embryology Act 2008 in respect of, another, only to that individual and that other.

(6) In subsection (2)—

    (a) in paragraph (p) 'regulatory function' has the same meaning as in section 32 of the Legislative and Regulatory Reform Act 2006, and

    (b) in paragraph (t) references to 'proceedings' include any formal procedure for dealing with a complaint.

(7) In this section 'identifying donor information' means information enabling a person to be identified as a person whose gametes were used in accordance with consent given under paragraph 5 of Schedule 3 for the purposes of treatment services or non-medical fertility services in consequence of which an identifiable individual was, or may have been, born.

33B   Consent required to authorise certain disclosures

(1) This section has effect for the purposes of section 33A(2)(h).

(2) Subject to subsection (5), the consent required by this section is the consent of each individual who can be identified from the information.

(3) Consent in respect of a person who has not attained the age of 18 years ('C') may be given—

    (a) by C, in a case where C is competent to deal with the issue of consent, or

    (b) by a person having parental responsibility for C, in any other case.

(4) Consent to disclosure given at the request of another shall be disregarded unless, before it is given, the person requesting it takes reasonable steps to explain to the individual from whom it is requested the implications of compliance with the request.

(5) In the case of information which shows that any identifiable individual ('A') was, or may have been, born in consequence of treatment services, the consent required by this section does not include A's consent if the disclosure is necessarily incidental to the disclosure of information falling within section 31(2)(a).

(6) The reference in subsection (3) to parental responsibility is—

    (a) in relation to England and Wales, to be read in accordance with the Children Act 1989;

    ...

33C   Power to provide for additional exceptions from section 33A(1)

(1) Regulations may provide for additional exceptions from section 33A(1).

(2) No exception may be made under this section for—

    (a) disclosure of a kind mentioned in paragraph (a) or (b) of subsection (4) of section 33A, or

    (b) disclosure in circumstances in which section 32 of this Act applies of information having the tendency mentioned in subsection (2) of that section, made by any person acting in a capacity mentioned in any of paragraphs (c) to (g) of subsection (1) of section 33A.

...

34   Disclosure in interests of justice

(1) Where in any proceedings before a court the question whether a person is or is not the parent of a child by virtue of sections 27 to 29 of this Act or sections 33 to 47 of the Human Fertilisation and Embryology Act 2008 falls to be determined, the court may on the application of any party to the proceedings make an order requiring the Authority—

    (a) to disclose whether or not any information relevant to that question is contained in the register kept in pursuance of section 31 of this Act, and

    (b) if it is, to disclose so much of it as is specified in the order, but such an order may not require the Authority to disclose any information falling within section 31(2)(c) to (e) of this Act.

(2) The court must not make an order under subsection (1) above unless it is satisfied that the interests of justice require it to do so, taking into account—

    (a) any representations made by any individual who may be affected by the disclosure, and

    (b) the welfare of the child, if under 18 years old, and of any other person under that age who may be affected by the disclosure.

(3) If the proceedings before the court are civil proceedings, it—

    (a) may direct that the whole or any part of the proceedings on the application for an order under subsection (2) above shall be heard in camera, and

    (b) if it makes such an order, may then or later direct that the whole or any part of any later stage of the proceedings shall be heard in camera.

(4) An application for a direction under subsection (3) above shall be heard in camera unless the court otherwise directs.

...

Offences

41   Offences

...

(5) A person who discloses any information in contravention of section 33A of this Act is guilty of an offence and liable—

    (a) on conviction on indictment, to imprisonment for a term not exceeding two years or a fine or both, and

    (b) on summary conviction, to imprisonment for a term not exceeding six months or a fine not exceeding the statutory maximum or both.

    ...

(11) It is a defence for a person charged with an offence under this Act to prove—

    (a) that at the material time he was a person to whom a licence applied or to whom directions had been given, and

    (b) that he took all such steps as were reasonable and exercised all due diligence to avoid committing the offence.

42   Consent to prosecution

No proceedings for an offence under this Act shall be instituted—

    (a) in England and Wales, except by or with the consent of the Director of Public Prosecutions,

...

Miscellaneous and General

...

49   Short title, commencement etc.

...

(4) Section 27 of the Family Law Reform Act 1987 (artificial insemination) does not have effect in relation to children carried by women as the result of their artificial insemination after the commencement of sections 27 to 29 of this Act.

...

Section 12

SCHEDULE 3

CONSENTS TO USE OR STORAGE OF GAMETES, EMBRYOS OR HUMAN ADMIXED EMBRYOS ETC

Consent

1.—(1) A consent under this Schedule, and any notice under paragraph 4 varying or withdrawing a consent under this Schedule, must be in writing and, subject to sub-paragraph (2), must be signed by the person giving it.

(2) A consent under this Schedule by a person who is unable to sign because of illness, injury or physical disability (a 'person unable to sign'), and any notice under paragraph 4 by a person unable to sign varying or withdrawing a consent under this Schedule, is to be taken to comply with the requirement of sub-paragraph (1) as to signature if it is signed at the direction of the person unable to sign, in the presence of the person unable to sign and in the presence of at least one witness who attests the signature.

(3) In this Schedule 'effective consent' means a consent under this Schedule which has not been withdrawn.

2.—(1) A consent to the use of any embryo must specify one or more of the following purposes—
   (a)   use in providing treatment services to the person giving consent, or that person and another specified person together,
   (b)   use in providing treatment services to persons not including the person giving consent,
   (ba) use for the purpose of training persons in embryo biopsy, embryo storage or other embryological techniques, or
   (c)   use for the purposes of any project of research,
and may specify conditions subject to which the embryo may be so used.

...

(2) A consent to the storage of any gametes, any embryo or any human admixed embryo must—
   (a)   specify the maximum period of storage (if less than the statutory storage period),
   (b)   except in a case falling within paragraph (c), state what is to be done with the gametes, embryo or human admixed embryo if the person who gave the consent dies or is unable, because the person lacks capacity to do so, to vary the terms of the consent or to withdraw it, and
   (c)   where the consent is given by virtue of paragraph 8(2A) or 13(2), state what is to be done with the embryo or human admixed embryo if the person to whom the consent relates dies,
and may (in any case) specify conditions subject to which the gametes, embryo or human admixed embryo may remain in storage.

(2A) A consent to the use of a person's human cells to bring about the creation *in vitro* of an embryo or human admixed embryo is to be taken unless otherwise stated to include consent to the use of the cells after the person's death.

...

(3) A consent under this Schedule must provide for such other matters as the Authority may specify in directions.

...

Procedure for giving consent

3.—(1) Before a person gives consent under this Schedule—

(a) he must be given a suitable opportunity to receive proper counselling about the implications of taking the proposed steps, and

(b) he must be provided with such relevant information as is proper.

(2) Before a person gives consent under this Schedule he must be informed of the effect of paragraph 4 and, if relevant, paragraph 4A below.

Variation and withdrawal of consent

4.—(1) The terms of any consent under this Schedule may from time to time be varied, and the consent may be withdrawn, by notice given by the person who gave the consent to the person keeping the gametes, human cells, embryo or human admixed embryo to which the consent is relevant.

(2) Subject to sub-paragraph (3), the terms of any consent to the use of any embryo cannot be varied, and such consent cannot be withdrawn, once the embryo has been used—

(a) in providing treatment services,

(aa) in training persons in embryo biopsy, embryo storage or other embryological techniques, or

(b) for the purposes of any project of research.

(3) Where the terms of any consent to the use of an embryo ('embryo A') include consent to the use of an embryo or human admixed embryo whose creation may be brought about *in vitro* using embryo A, that consent to the use of that subsequent embryo or human admixed embryo cannot be varied or withdrawn once embryo A has been used for one or more of the purposes mentioned in sub-paragraph (2)(a) or (b).

...

4A.—(1) This paragraph applies where—

(a) a permitted embryo, the creation of which was brought about *in vitro*, is in storage,

(b) it was created for use in providing treatment services,

(c) before it is used in providing treatment services, one of the persons whose gametes were used to bring about its creation ('P') gives the person keeping the embryo notice withdrawing P's consent to the storage of the embryo, and

(d) the embryo was not to be used in providing treatment services to P alone.

(2) The person keeping the embryo must as soon as possible take all reasonable steps to notify each interested person in relation to the embryo of P's withdrawal of consent.

(3) For the purposes of sub-paragraph (2), a person is an interested person in relation to an embryo if the embryo was to be used in providing treatment services to that person.

(4) Storage of the embryo remains lawful until—

(a) the end of the period of 12 months beginning with the day on which the notice mentioned in sub-paragraph (1) was received from P, or

(b) if, before the end of that period, the person keeping the embryo receives a notice from each person notified of P's withdrawal under sub-paragraph (2) stating that the person consents to the destruction of the embryo, the time at which the last of those notices is received.

(5) The reference in sub-paragraph (1)(a) to a permitted embryo is to be read in accordance with section 3ZA.

Use of gametes for treatment of others

5.—(1) A person's gametes must not be used for the purposes of treatment services or non-medical fertility services unless there is an effective consent by that person to their being so used and they are used in accordance with the terms of the consent.

(2) A person's gametes must not be received for use for those purposes unless there is an effective consent by that person to their being so used.

(3) This paragraph does not apply to the use of a person's gametes for the purpose of that person, or that person and another together, receiving treatment services.

In vitro fertilisation and subsequent use of embryo

6.—(1) A person's gametes or human cells must not be used to bring about the creation of any embryo *in vitro* unless there is an effective consent by that person to any embryo, the creation of which may be brought about with the use of those gametes or human cells being used for one or more of the purposes mentioned in paragraph 2(1)(a), (b) and (c) above.

(2) An embryo the creation of which was brought about *in vitro* must not be received by any person unless there is an effective consent by each relevant person in relation to the embryo to the use for one or more of the purposes mentioned in paragraph 2(1)(a), (b), (ba) and (c) above of the embryo.

(3) An embryo the creation of which was brought about *in vitro* must not be used for any purpose unless there is an effective consent by each relevant person in relation to the embryo to the use for that purpose of the embryo and the embryo is used in accordance with those consents.

(3A) If the Authority is satisfied that the parental consent conditions in paragraph 15 are met in relation to the proposed use under a licence of the human cells of a person who has not attained the age of 18 years ('C'), the Authority may in the licence authorise the application of sub-paragraph (3B) in relation to C.

(3B) Where the licence authorises the application of this sub-paragraph, the effective consent of a person having parental responsibility for C—

>   (a) to the use of C's human cells to bring about the creation of an embryo *in vitro* for use for the purposes of a project of research, or
>   (b) to the use for those purposes of an embryo in relation to which C is a relevant person by reason only of the use of C's human cells,

is to be treated for the purposes of sub-paragraphs (1) to (3) as the effective consent of C.

(3C) If C attains the age of 18 years or the condition in paragraph 15(3) ceases to be met in relation to C, paragraph 4 has effect in relation to C as if any effective consent previously given under sub-paragraphs (1) to (3) by a person having parental responsibility for C had been given by C but, subject to that, sub-paragraph (3B) ceases to apply in relation to C.

(3D) Sub-paragraphs (1) to (3) have effect subject to paragraphs 16 and 20.

(3E) For the purposes of sub-paragraphs (2), (3) and (3B), each of the following is a relevant person in relation to an embryo the creation of which was brought about *in vitro* ('embryo A')—

>   (a) each person whose gametes or human cells were used to bring about the creation of embryo A,
>   (b) each person whose gametes or human cells were used to bring about the creation of any other embryo, the creation of which was brought about *in vitro*, which was used to bring about the creation of embryo A, and
>   (c) each person whose gametes or human cells were used to bring about the creation of any human admixed embryo, the creation of which was brought about *in vitro*, which was used to bring about the creation of embryo A.

(4) Any consent required by this paragraph is in addition to any consent that may be required by paragraph 5 above.

Embryos obtained by lavage, etc.

7.—(1) An embryo taken from a woman must not be used for any purpose unless there is an effective consent by her to the use of the embryo for that purpose and it is used in accordance with the consent.

(2) An embryo taken from a woman must not be received by any person for use for any purpose unless there is an effective consent by her to the use of the embryo for that purpose.

(3) Sub-paragraphs (1) and (2) do not apply to the use, for the purpose of providing a woman with treatment services, of an embryo taken from her.

(4) An embryo taken from a woman must not be used to bring about the creation of any embryo *in vitro* or any human admixed embryo in vitro.

Storage of gametes and embryos

8.—(1) A person's gametes must not be kept in storage unless there is an effective consent by that person to their storage and they are stored in accordance with the consent.

(2) An embryo the creation of which was brought about *in vitro* must not be kept in storage unless there is an effective consent, by each relevant person in relation to the embryo, to the storage of the embryo and the embryo is stored in accordance with those consents.

(2A) Where a licence authorises the application of paragraph 6(3B) in relation to a person who has not attained the age of 18 years ('C'), the effective consent of a person having parental responsibility for C to the storage of an embryo in relation to which C is a relevant person by reason only of the use of C's human cells is to be treated for the purposes of sub-paragraph (2) as the effective consent of C.

(2B) If C attains the age of 18 years or the condition in paragraph 15(3) ceases to be met in relation to C, paragraph 4 has effect in relation to C as if any effective consent previously given under sub-paragraph (2) by a person having parental responsibility for C had been given by C but, subject to sub-paragraph (2A) ceases to apply in relation to C.

(2C) For the purposes of sub-paragraphs (2) and (2A), each of the following is a relevant person in relation to an embryo the creation of which was brought about *in vitro* ('embryo A')—

(a) each person whose gametes or human cells were used to bring about the creation of embryo A,

(b) each person whose gametes or human cells were used to bring about the creation of any other embryo, the creation of which was brought about *in vitro*, which was used to bring about the creation of embryo A, and

(c) each person whose gametes or human cells were used to bring about the creation of any human admixed embryo, the creation of which was brought about *in vitro*, which was used to bring about the creation of embryo A.

(3) An embryo taken from a woman must not be kept in storage unless there is an effective consent by her to its storage and it is stored in accordance with the consent.

(4) Sub-paragraph (1) has effect subject to paragraphs 9 and 10; and sub-paragraph (2) has effect subject to paragraphs 4A(4), 16 and 20.

Cases where consent not required for storage

9.—(1) The gametes of a person ('C') may be kept in storage without C's consent if the following conditions are met.

(2) Condition A is that the gametes are lawfully taken from or provided by C before C attains the age of 18 years.

(3) Condition B is that, before the gametes are first stored, a registered medical practitioner certifies in writing that C is expected to undergo medical treatment and that in the opinion of the registered medical practitioner—

(a) the treatment is likely to cause a significant impairment of C's fertility, and

(b) the storage of the gametes is in C's best interests.

(4) Condition C is that, at the time when the gametes are first stored, either—

(a) C has not attained the age of 16 years and is not competent to deal with the issue of consent to the storage of the gametes, or

(b) C has attained that age but, although not lacking capacity to consent to the storage of the gametes, is not competent to deal with the issue of consent to their storage.

(5) Condition D is that C has not, since becoming competent to deal with the issue of consent to the storage of the gametes—

    (a) given consent under this Schedule to the storage of the gametes, or

    (b) given written notice to the person keeping the gametes that C does not wish them to continue to be stored.

...

10.—(1) The gametes of a person ('P') may be kept in storage without P's consent if the following conditions are met.

(2) Condition A is that the gametes are lawfully taken from or provided by P after P has attained the age of 16 years.

(3) Condition B is that, before the gametes are first stored, a registered medical practitioner certifies in writing that P is expected to undergo medical treatment and that in the opinion of the registered medical practitioner—

    (a) the treatment is likely to cause a significant impairment of P's fertility,

    (b) P lacks capacity to consent to the storage of the gametes,

    (c) P is likely at some time to have that capacity, and

    (d) the storage of the gametes is in P's best interests.

(4) Condition C is that, at the time when the gametes are first stored, P lacks capacity to consent to their storage.

(5) Condition D is that P has not subsequently, at a time when P has capacity to give a consent under this Schedule—

    (a) given consent to the storage of the gametes, or

    (b) given written notice to the person keeping the gametes that P does not wish them to continue to be stored.

...

11.— A person's gametes must not be kept in storage by virtue of paragraph 9 or 10 after the person's death.

...

SCHEDULE 3ZA

CIRCUMSTANCES IN WHICH OFFER OF COUNSELLING REQUIRED AS CONDITION OF LICENCE FOR TREATMENT

PART 1 KINDS OF TREATMENT IN RELATION TO WHICH COUNSELLING MUST BE OFFERED

1.—The treatment services involve the use of the gametes of any person and that person's consent is required under paragraph 5 of Schedule 3 for the use in question.

2.—The treatment services involve the use of any embryo the creation of which was brought about *in vitro*.

3.—The treatment services involve the use of an embryo taken from a woman and the consent of the woman from whom the embryo was taken was required under paragraph 7 of Schedule 3 for the use in question.

PART 2 EVENTS IN CONNECTION WITH WHICH COUNSELLING MUST BE OFFERED

4.—A man gives the person responsible a notice under paragraph (a) of subsection (1) of section 37 of the Human Fertilisation and Embryology Act 2008 (agreed fatherhood conditions) in a case where the woman for whom the treatment services are provided has previously given a notice under paragraph (b) of that subsection referring to the man.

5.—The woman for whom the treatment services are provided gives the person responsible a notice under paragraph (b) of that subsection in a case where the man to whom the notice relates has previously given a notice under paragraph (a) of that subsection.

6.—A woman gives the person responsible notice under paragraph (a) of subsection (1) of section 44 of that Act (agreed female parenthood conditions) in a case where the woman for whom the treatment services are provided has previously given a notice under paragraph (b) of that subsection referring to her.

7.—The woman for whom the treatment services are provided gives the person responsible a notice under paragraph (b) of that subsection in a case where the other woman to whom the notice relates has previously given a notice under paragraph (a) of that subsection.

...

Courts and Legal Services Act 1990

(1990 c. 41)

...

Miscellaneous

58 Conditional fee agreements

(1) A conditional fee agreement which satisfies all of the conditions applicable to it by virtue of this section shall not be unenforceable by reason only of its being a conditional fee agreement; but (subject to subsection (5)) any other conditional fee agreement shall be unenforceable.

(2) For the purposes of this section and section 58A—

   (a) a conditional fee agreement is an agreement with a person providing advocacy or litigation services which provides for his fees and expenses, or any part of them, to be payable only in specified circumstances;

   (b) a conditional fee agreement provides for a success fee if it provides for the amount of any fees to which it applies to be increased, in specified circumstances, above the amount which would be payable if it were not payable only in specified circumstances and

   (c) references to a success fee, in relation to a conditional fee agreement, are to the amount of the increase.

(3) The following conditions are applicable to every conditional fee agreement—

   (a) it must be in writing;

   (b) it must not relate to proceedings which cannot be the subject of an enforceable conditional fee agreement; and

   (c) it must comply with such requirements (if any) as may be prescribed by the Lord Chancellor.

(4) The following further conditions are applicable to a conditional fee agreement which provides for a success fee—

   (a) it must relate to proceedings of a description specified by order made by the Lord Chancellor;

   (b) it must state the percentage by which the amount of the fees which would be payable if it were not a conditional fee agreement is to be increased; and

   (c) that percentage must not exceed the percentage specified in relation to the description of proceedings to which the agreement relates by order made by the Lord Chancellor.

(4A) The additional conditions are applicable to a conditional fee agreement which—

   (a) provides for a success fee, and

   (b) relates to proceedings of a description specified by order made by the Lord Chancellor for the purposes of this subsection.

(4B) The additional conditions are that—

    (a) the agreement must provide that the success fee is subject to a maximum limit,

    (b) the maximum limit must be expressed as a percentage of the descriptions of damages awarded in the proceedings that are specified in the agreement,

    (c) that percentage must not exceed the percentage specified by order made by the Lord Chancellor in relation to the proceedings or calculated in a manner so specified, and

    (d) those descriptions of damages may only include descriptions of damages specified by order made by the Lord Chancellor in relation to the proceedings.

(5) If a conditional fee agreement is an agreement to which section 57 of the Solicitors Act 1974 (non-contentious business agreements between solicitor and client) applies, subsection (1) shall not make it unenforceable.

58A Conditional fee agreements: supplementary

(1) The proceedings which cannot be the subject of an enforceable conditional fee agreement are—

    (a) criminal proceedings, apart from proceedings under section 82 of the Environmental Protection Act 1990; and

    (b) family proceedings.

(2) In subsection (1) 'family proceedings' means proceedings under any one or more of the following—

    (a) the Matrimonial Causes Act 1973;

    (b) the Adoption and Children Act 2002;

    (c) the Domestic Proceedings and Magistrates' Courts Act 1978;

    (d) Part III of the Matrimonial and Family Proceedings Act 1984;

    (e) Parts I, II and IV of the Children Act 1989;

    (f) Parts 4 and 4A of the Family Law Act 1996;

    (fa) Chapter 2 of Part 2 of the Civil Partnership Act 2004 (proceedings for dissolution etc. of civil partnership);

    (fb) Schedule 5 to the 2004 Act (financial relief in the High Court or a county court etc.);

    (fc) Schedule 6 to the 2004 Act (financial relief in magistrates' courts etc.);

    (fd) ...; and

    (g) the inherent jurisdiction of the High Court in relation to children.

    ...

(4) In section 58 and this section (and in the definitions of 'advocacy services' and 'litigation services' as they apply for their purposes) 'proceedings' includes any sort of proceedings for resolving disputes (and not just proceedings in a court), whether commenced or contemplated.

    ...

58B Litigation funding agreements

(1) A litigation funding agreement which satisfies all of the conditions applicable to it by virtue of this section shall not be unenforceable by reason only of its being a litigation funding agreement.

(2) For the purposes of this section a litigation funding agreement is an agreement under which—

    (a) a person ('the funder') agrees to fund (in whole or in part) the provision of advocacy or litigation services (by someone other than the funder) to another person ('the litigant'); and

    (b) the litigant agrees to pay a sum to the funder in specified circumstances.

(3) The following conditions are applicable to a litigation funding agreement—

    (a) the funder must be a person, or person of a description, prescribed by the Lord Chancellor;

    (b) the agreement must be in writing;

    (c) the agreement must not relate to proceedings which by virtue of section 58A(1) and (2) cannot be the subject of an enforceable conditional fee agreement or to proceedings of any such description as may be prescribed by the Lord Chancellor;

    ...

Maintenance Enforcement Act 1991

(1991 c. 17)

The High Court and family court

1   Maintenance orders in the High Court and family court: means of payment, attachment of earnings and revocation, variation, etc.

(1)   Where the High Court or the family court makes a qualifying periodical maintenance order, it may at the same time exercise either of its powers under subsection (4) below in relation to the order, whether of its own motion or on an application made under this subsection by an interested party.

(1A)   Where the family court makes a qualifying periodical maintenance order, it may at the same time exercise any of its powers under subsection (4A) below in relation to the order, whether of its own motion or on an application made under this subsection by an interested party.

(2)   For the purposes of this section, a periodical maintenance order is an order—

    (a)   which requires money to be paid periodically by one person ('the debtor') to another ('the creditor'); and

    (b)   which is a maintenance order;

and such an order is a 'qualifying periodical maintenance order' if, at the time it is made, the debtor is ordinarily resident in England and Wales.

(3)   Where the High Court or the family court has made a qualifying periodical maintenance order, it may at any later time—

    (a)   on an application made under this subsection by an interested party, or

    (b)   of its own motion, in the course of any proceedings concerning the order,

exercise either of its powers under subsection (4) below in relation to the order.

(3A)   Where the family court has made a qualifying periodical maintenance order, it may at any later time—

    (a)   on an application made under this subsection by an interested party, or

    (b)   of its own motion, in the course of any proceedings concerning the order,

exercise any of its powers under subsection (4A) below in relation to the order.

(4)   The powers mentioned in subsections (1) and (3) above are—

    (a)   the power to order that payments required to be made by the debtor to the creditor under the qualifying periodical maintenance order in question shall be so made by such a method of payment falling within subsection (5) below as the court may specify in the particular case; or

    (b)   the power, by virtue of this section, to make an attachment of earnings order under the Attachment of Earnings Act 1971 to secure payments under the qualifying periodical maintenance order in question.

(4A)   The powers mentioned in subsections (1A) and (3A) above are—

    (a)   the power to order that payments under the qualifying periodical maintenance order in question be made to the court;

    (b)   the power to order that payments under the qualifying periodical maintenance order in question required to be made to the court are to be so made by such method of payment falling within subsection (5) below as the court may specify in the particular case; or

    (c)   the power to order that payments under the qualifying periodical maintenance order in question be made in accordance with arrangements for their collection made by the Secretary of State under section 30 of the Child Support Act 1991 and regulations made under that section.

(5)   The methods of payment mentioned in subsection (4)(a) above are—

    (a)   payment by standing order; or

    (b)   payment by any other method which requires the debtor to give his authority for payments of a specific amount to be made from an account of his to an account of the creditor's on specific dates during the period for which the authority is in force and without the need for any further authority from the debtor; or

(c) any method of payment specified in regulations made by the Lord Chancellor.

(6) In any case where—

(a) the court proposes to exercise its power under paragraph (a) of subsection (4) above or under paragraph (b) of subsection (4A) above, and

(b) having given the debtor an opportunity of opening an account from which payments under the order may be made in accordance with the method of payment proposed to be ordered under that paragraph, the court is satisfied that the debtor has failed, without reasonable excuse, to open such an account,

the court in exercising its power under that paragraph may order that the debtor open such an account.

(7) Where in the exercise of its powers under subsection (1), (1A), (3) or (3A) above, the High Court or the family court has made in relation to a qualifying periodical maintenance order such an order as is mentioned in subsection (4)(a) or (4A) above (a 'means of payment order'), it may at any later time—

(a) on an application made under this subsection by an interested party, or

(b) of its own motion, in the course of any proceedings concerning the qualifying periodical maintenance order,

revoke, suspend, revive or vary the means of payment order.

(8) In deciding whether to exercise any of its powers under this section the court in question having (if practicable) given every interested party an opportunity to make representations shall have regard to any representations made by any such party.

(8A) No order made by the family court under subsection (4) or (4A)(a) or (b) above has effect at any time when the Secretary of State is, under section 30 of the Child Support Act 1991 and regulations made under that section, arranging for the collection of payments under the qualifying periodical maintenance order in question.

(9) Nothing in this section shall be taken to prejudice—

(a) any power under the Attachment of Earnings Act 1971 which would, apart from this section, be exercisable by the High Court or the family court; or

(b) any right of any person to make any application under that Act; and subsection (7) above is without prejudice to any other power of the High Court or the family court to revoke, suspend, revive or vary an order.

(10) For the purposes of this section—

'debtor' and 'creditor' shall be construed in accordance with subsection (2) above;

'interested party' means any of the following, that is to say—

(a) the debtor;

(b) the creditor; and

(c) in a case where the person who applied for the qualifying periodical maintenance order in question is a person other than the creditor, that other person;

'maintenance order' means any order specified in Schedule 8 to the Administration of Justice Act 1970 and includes any such order which has been discharged, if any arrears are recoverable under it;

'qualifying periodical maintenance order' shall be construed in accordance with subsection (2) above, and the references to such an order in subsections (3) and (7) above are references to any such order, whether made before or after the coming into force of this section;

and the reference in subsection (2) above to an order requiring money to be paid periodically by one person to another includes a reference to an order requiring a lump sum to be paid by instalments by one person to another.

...

Child Support Act 1991

(1991 c. 48)

The basic principles

1   The duty to maintain

(1) For the purposes of this Act, each parent of a qualifying child is responsible for maintaining him.

(2) For the purposes of this Act, a non-resident parent shall be taken to have met his responsibility to maintain any qualifying child of his by making periodical payments of maintenance with respect to the child of such amount, and at such intervals, as may be determined in accordance with the provisions of this Act.

(3) Where a maintenance calculation made under this Act requires the making of periodical payments, it shall be the duty of the non-resident parent with respect to whom the calculation was made to make those payments.

2   Welfare of children: the general principle

Where, in any case which falls to be dealt with under this Act, the Secretary of State is considering the exercise of any discretionary power conferred by this Act, the Secretary of State shall have regard to the welfare of any child likely to be affected by the decision.

3   Meaning of certain terms used in this Act

(1) A child is a 'qualifying child' if—

(a) one of his parents is, in relation to him, a non-resident parent; or

(b) both of his parents are, in relation to him, non-resident parents.

(2) The parent of any child is a 'non-resident parent', in relation to him, if—

(a) that parent is not living in the same household with the child; and

(b) the child has his home with a person who is, in relation to him, a person with care.

(3) A person is a 'person with care', in relation to any child, if he is a person—

(a) with whom the child has his home;

(b) who usually provides day to day care for the child (whether exclusively or in conjunction with any other person); and

(c) who does not fall within a prescribed category of person.

(4) The Secretary of State shall not, under subsection (3)(c), prescribe as a category—

(a) parents;

(b) guardians;

(c) persons named, in a child arrangements order under section 8 of the Children Act 1989, as persons with whom a child is to live;

…

(5) For the purposes of this Act there may be more than one person with care in relation to the same qualifying child.

(6) Periodical payments which are required to be paid in accordance with a maintenance calculation are referred to in this Act as 'child support maintenance'.

(7) Expressions are defined in this section only for the purposes of this Act.

4   Child support maintenance

(1) A person who is, in relation to any qualifying child or any qualifying children, either the person with care or the non-resident parent may apply to the Secretary of State for a maintenance calculation to be made under this Act with respect to that child, or any of those children.

(2) Where a maintenance calculation has been made in response to an application under this section the Secretary of State may, if the person with care applies to the Secretary of State under this subsection, arrange for—

(a) the collection of the child support maintenance payable in accordance with the calculation;

(b) the enforcement of the obligation to pay child support maintenance in accordance with the calculation.

(2A) The Secretary of State may only make arrangements under subsection (2)(a) if—

(a) the non-resident parent agrees to the arrangements, or

(b) the Secretary of State is satisfied that without the arrangements child support maintenance is unlikely to be paid in accordance with the calculation.

(3) Where an application under subsection (2) for the enforcement of the obligation mentioned in subsection (2)(b) authorises the Secretary of State to take steps to enforce that obligation whenever the Secretary of State considers it necessary to do so, the Secretary of State may act accordingly.

(4) A person who applies to the Secretary of State under this section shall, so far as that person reasonably can, comply with such regulations as may be made by the Secretary of State with a view to the Secretary of State being provided with the information which is required to enable—

(a) the non-resident parent to be identified or traced (where that is necessary);

(b) the amount of child support maintenance payable by the non-resident parent to be calculated; and

(c) that amount to be recovered from the non-resident parent.

(5) Any person who has applied to the Secretary of State under this section may at any time request the Secretary of State to cease acting under this section.

(6) It shall be the duty of the Secretary of State to comply with any request made under subsection (5) (but subject to any regulations made under subsection (8)).

(7) The obligation to provide information which is imposed by subsection (4)—

(a) shall not apply in such circumstances as may be prescribed; and

(b) may, in such circumstances as may be prescribed, be waived by the Secretary of State.

(8) The Secretary of State may by regulations make such incidental, supplemental or transitional provision as he thinks appropriate with respect to cases in which he is requested to cease to act under this section.

(10) No application may be made at any time under this section with respect to a qualifying child or any qualifying children if—

(a) there is in force a written maintenance agreement made before 5th April 1993, or a maintenance order made before a prescribed date, in respect of that child or those children and the person who is, at that time, the non-resident parent; or

(aa) a maintenance order made on or after the date prescribed for the purposes of paragraph (a) is in force in respect of them, but has been so for less than the period of one year beginning with the date on which it was made;

    ...

5 Child support maintenance: supplemental provisions

(1) Where—

(a) there is more than one person with care of a qualifying child; and

(b) one or more, but not all, of them have parental responsibility for the child;

no application may be made for a maintenance calculation with respect to the child by any of those persons who do not have parental responsibility for the child.

(2) Where more than one application for a maintenance calculation is made with respect to the child concerned, only one of them may be proceeded with.

(3) The Secretary of State may by regulations make provision as to which of two or more applications for a maintenance calculation with respect to the same child is to be proceeded with.

    ...

8 Role of the courts with respect to maintenance for children

(1) This subsection applies in any case where the Secretary of State would have jurisdiction to make a maintenance calculation with respect to a qualifying child and a non-resident parent of his on an application duly made by a person entitled to apply for such a calculation with respect to that child.

(2) Subsection (1) applies even though the circumstances of the case are such that the Secretary of State would not make a calculation if it were applied for.

(3) Except as provided in subsection (3A), in any case where subsection (1) applies, no court shall exercise any power which it would otherwise have to make, vary or revive any maintenance order in relation to the child and non-resident parent concerned.

(3A) Unless a maintenance calculation has been made with respect to the child concerned, subsection (3) does not prevent a court from varying a maintenance order in relation to that child and the non-resident parent concerned—

    (a) if the maintenance order was made on or after the date prescribed for the purposes of section 4(10)(a) or 7(10)(a); or

    (b) where the order was made before then, in any case in which section 4(10) or 7(10) prevents the making of an application for a maintenance calculation with respect to or by that child.

(4) Subsection (3) does not prevent a court from revoking a maintenance order.

(5) The Lord Chancellor . . . may by order provide that, in such circumstances as may be specified by the order, this section shall not prevent a court from exercising any power which it has to make a maintenance order in relation to a child if—

    (a) a written agreement (whether or not enforceable) provides for the making, or securing, by a non-resident parent of the child of periodical payments to or for the benefit of the child; and

    (b) the maintenance order which the court makes is, in all material respects, in the same terms as that agreement.

(5A) The Lord Chancellor may make an order under subsection (5) only with the concurrence of the Lord Chief Justice.

(6) This section shall not prevent a court from exercising any power which it has to make a maintenance order in relation to a child if—

    (a) a maintenance calculation is in force with respect to the child;

    (b) the non-resident parent's gross weekly income exceeds the figure referred to in paragraph 10(3) of Schedule 1 (as it has effect from time to time pursuant to regulations made under paragraph 10A(1)(b)); and

    (c) the court is satisfied that the circumstances of the case make it appropriate for the non-resident parent to make or secure the making of periodical payments under a maintenance order in addition to the child support maintenance payable by him in accordance with the maintenance calculation.

(7) This section shall not prevent a court from exercising any power which it has to make a maintenance order in relation to a child if—

    (a) the child is, will be or (if the order were to be made) would be receiving instruction at an educational establishment or undergoing training for a trade, profession or vocation (whether or not while in gainful employment); and

    (b) the order is made solely for the purposes of requiring the person making or securing the making of periodical payments fixed by the order to meet some or all of the expenses incurred in connection with the provision of the instruction or training.

(8) This section shall not prevent a court from exercising any power which it has to make a maintenance order in relation to a child if—

    (a) an allowance under Part 4 of the Welfare Reform Act 2012 (personal independence payment) is paid to or in respect of him; or

    (b) no such allowance is paid but he is disabled,

and the order is made solely for the purpose of requiring the person making or securing the making of periodical payments fixed by the order to meet some or all of any expenses attributable to the child's disability.

(9) For the purposes of subsection (8), a child is disabled if he is blind, deaf or dumb or is substantially and permanently handicapped by illness, injury, mental disorder or congenital deformity or such other disability as may be prescribed.

(10) This section shall not prevent a court from exercising any power which it has to make a maintenance order in relation to a child if the order is made against a person with care of the child.

(11) In this Act 'maintenance order', in relation to any child, means an order which requires the making or securing of periodical payments to or for the benefit of the child and which is made under—

    (a) Part II of the Matrimonial Causes Act 1973;

    (b) the Domestic Proceedings and Magistrates' Courts Act 1978;

    (c) Part III of the Matrimonial and Family Proceedings Act 1984;

    ...

    (e) Schedule 1 to the Children Act 1989;

    (ea) Schedule 5, 6 or 7 to the Civil Partnership Act 2004; or

    (f) any other prescribed enactment, and includes any order varying or reviving such an order.

(12) The Lord Chief Justice may nominate a judicial office holder (as defined in section 109(4) of the Constitutional Reform Act 2005) to exercise his functions under this section.

9 Agreements about maintenance

(1) In this section 'maintenance agreement' means any agreement for the making, or for securing the making, of periodical payments by way of maintenance, or in Scotland aliment, to or for the benefit of any child.

(2) Nothing in this Act shall be taken to prevent any person from entering into a maintenance agreement.

(2A) The Secretary of State may, with a view to reducing the need for applications under sections 4 and 7—

    (a) take such steps as the Secretary of State considers appropriate to encourage the making and keeping of maintenance agreements, and

    (b) in particular, before accepting an application under those sections, invite the applicant to consider with the Secretary of State whether it is possible to make such an agreement.

(3) Subject to section 4(10)(a) and (ab) and section 7(10), the existence of a maintenance agreement shall not prevent any party to the agreement, or any other person, from applying for a maintenance calculation with respect to any child to or for whose benefit periodical payments are to be made or secured under the agreement.

(4) Where any agreement contains a provision which purports to restrict the right of any person to apply for a maintenance calculation, that provision shall be void.

(5) Where section 8 would prevent any court from making a maintenance order in relation to a child and a non-resident parent of his, no court shall exercise any power that it has to vary any agreement so as—

    (a) to insert a provision requiring that non-resident parent to make or secure the making of periodical payments by way of maintenance, or in Scotland aliment, to or for the benefit of that child; or

    (b) to increase the amount payable under such a provision.

(6) In any case in which section 4(10) or 7(10) prevents the making of an application for a maintenance calculation, ... subsection (5) shall have effect with the omission of paragraph (b).

9A Maintenance agreements: indicative calculations

(1) A person with care or non-resident parent in relation to any qualifying child or qualifying children may apply to the Secretary of State for an indicative calculation with respect to that child or any of those children.

(2) ...

(3) An indicative calculation is a calculation of the amount of child support maintenance which the Secretary of State considers would in accordance with section 11 be fixed by a maintenance calculation if such a calculation were made with respect to the child or children in question.

(4) An indicative calculation does not create any liability on any person to pay child support maintenance.

(5) The Secretary of State may limit the number of applications the Secretary of State will accept under this section in any particular case in such manner as the Secretary of State thinks fit.

(6) Where a person who is alleged to be the parent of a child with respect to whom an application for an indicative calculation has been made denies being one of the child's parents, the Secretary of State shall not make the indicative calculation on the assumption that the person is one of the child's parents unless the case falls within paragraph (b) of Case A3 in section 26(2).

10   Relationship between maintenance calculations and certain court orders and related matters

(1) Where an order of a kind prescribed for the purposes of this subsection is in force with respect to any qualifying child with respect to whom a maintenance calculation is made, the order—

  (a) shall, so far as it relates to the making or securing of periodical payments, cease to have effect to such extent as may be determined in accordance with regulations made by the Secretary of State; or

  (b) where the regulations so provide, shall, so far as it so relates, have effect subject to such modifications as may be so determined.

(2) Where an agreement of a kind prescribed for the purposes of this subsection is in force with respect to any qualifying child with respect to whom a maintenance calculation is made, the agreement—

  (a) shall, so far as it relates to the making or securing of periodical payments, be unenforceable to such extent as may be determined in accordance with regulations made by the Secretary of State; or

  (b) where the regulations so provide, shall, so far as it so relates, have effect subject to such modifications as may be so determined.

(3) Any regulations under this section may, in particular, make such provision with respect to—

  (a) any case where any person with respect to whom an order or agreement of a kind prescribed for the purposes of subsection (1) or (2) has effect applies to the prescribed court, before the end of the prescribed period, for the order or agreement to be varied in the light of the maintenance calculation and of the provisions of this Act;

  (b) the recovery of any arrears under the order or agreement which fell due before the coming into force of the maintenance calculation,

as the Secretary of State considers appropriate and may provide that, in prescribed circumstances, an application to any court which is made with respect to an order of a prescribed kind relating to the making or securing of periodical payments to or for the benefit of a child shall be treated by the court as an application for the order to be revoked.

(4) The Secretary of State may by regulations make provision for—

  (a) notification to be given by the Secretary of State to the prescribed person in any case where the Secretary of State considers that the making of a maintenance calculation has affected, or is likely to affect, any order of a kind prescribed for the purposes of this subsection;

  (b) notification to be given by the prescribed person to the Secretary of State in any case where a court makes an order which it considers has affected, or is likely to affect, a maintenance calculation.

(5) Rules of court may require any person who, in prescribed circumstances, makes an application to the family court for a maintenance order to furnish the court with a statement in a prescribed form, and signed by an officer of the Secretary of State, as to whether or not, at the time when the

statement is made, there is a maintenance calculation in force with respect to that person or the child concerned.

In this subsection—

'maintenance order' means an order of a prescribed kind for the making or securing of periodical payments to or for the benefit of a child; and

'prescribed' means prescribed by the rules.

Maintenance calculations

11   Maintenance calculations

(1) An application for a maintenance calculation made to the Secretary of State shall be dealt with by the Secretary of State in accordance with the provision made by or under this Act.

(2) The Secretary of State shall (unless the Secretary of State decides not to make a maintenance calculation in response to the application, or makes a decision under section 12) determine the application by making a decision under this section about whether any child support maintenance is payable and, if so, how much.

. . .

(6) The amount of child support maintenance to be fixed by a maintenance calculation shall be determined in accordance with Part I of Schedule I unless an application for a variation has been made and agreed.

(7) If the Secretary of State has agreed to a variation, the amount of child support maintenance to be fixed shall be determined on the basis determined under section 28F(4).

(8) Part II of Schedule I makes further provision with respect to maintenance calculations.

12   Default and interim maintenance decisions

(1) Where the Secretary of State—

(a) is required to make a maintenance calculation; or

(b) is proposing to make a decision under section 16 or 17,

and it appears to the Secretary of State that the Secretary of State does not have sufficient information to enable such a decision to be made, the Secretary of State may make a default maintenance decision.

(2) Where an application for a variation has been made under section 28A(1) in connection with an application for a maintenance calculation . . ., the Secretary of State may make an interim maintenance decision.

(3) The amount of child support maintenance fixed by an interim maintenance decision shall be determined in accordance with Part I of Schedule 1.

(4) The Secretary of State may by regulations make provision as to default and interim maintenance decisions.

(5) The regulations may, in particular, make provision as to—

(a) the procedure to be followed in making a default or an interim maintenance decision; and

(b) a default rate of child support maintenance to apply where a default maintenance decision is made.

Information

14   Information required by Secretary of State

(1) The Secretary of State may make regulations requiring any information or evidence needed for the determination of any application made . . . under this Act, or any question arising in connection with such an application . . ., or needed for the making of any decision or in connection with the imposition of any condition or requirement under this Act, or needed in connection with the collection or enforcement of child support or other maintenance under this Act, to be furnished—

(a) by such persons as may be determined in accordance with regulations made by the Secretary of State; and

(b) in accordance with the regulations.

(1A) Regulations under subsection (1) may make provision for notifying any person who is required to furnish any information or evidence under the regulations of the possible consequences of failing to do so.

(3) The Secretary of State may by regulations make provision authorising the disclosure by the Secretary of State, in such circumstances as may be prescribed, of such information held by the Secretary of State for purposes of this Act as may be prescribed.

(4) The provisions of Schedule 2 (which relate to information which is held for purposes other than those of this Act but which is required by the Secretary of State) shall have effect.

14A   Information—offences

(1) This section applies to—

    (a) persons who are required to comply with regulations under section 4(4) or 7(5); and

    (b) persons specified in regulations under section 14(1)(a).

(2) Such a person is guilty of an offence if, pursuant to a request for information under or by virtue of those regulations—

    (a) he makes a statement or representation which he knows to be false; or

    (b) he provides, or knowingly causes or knowingly allows to be provided, a document or other information which he knows to be false in a material particular.

(3) Such a person is guilty of an offence if, following such a request, he fails to comply with it.

(3A) In the case of regulations under section 14 which require a person liable to make payments of child support maintenance to notify—

    (a) a change of address, or

    (b) any other change of circumstances,

a person who fails to comply with the requirement is guilty of an offence.

(4) It is a defence for a person charged with an offence under subsection (3) or (3A) to prove that he had a reasonable excuse for failing to comply.

(5) A person guilty of an offence under this section is liable on summary conviction to a fine not exceeding level 3 on the standard scale.

(6) In England and Wales, an information relating to an offence under subsection (2) may be tried by a magistrates' court if it is laid within the period of 12 months beginning with the commission of the offence.

    ...

15   Powers of inspectors

(1) The Secretary of State may appoint, on such terms as the Secretary of State thinks fit, persons to act as inspectors under this section.

(2) The function of inspectors is to acquire information which the Secretary of State needs for any of the purposes of this Act.

(3) Every inspector is to be given a certificate of his appointment.

(4) An inspector has power, at any reasonable time and either alone or accompanied by such other persons as he thinks fit, to enter any premises which—

    (a) are liable to inspection under this section; and

    (b) are premises to which it is reasonable for him to require entry in order that he may exercise his functions under this section,

and may there make such examination and inquiry as he considers appropriate.

(4A) Premises liable to inspection under this section are those which are not used wholly as a dwelling house and which the inspector has reasonable grounds for suspecting are—

    (a) premises at which a non-resident parent is or has been employed;

    (b) premises at which a non-resident parent carries out, or has carried out, a trade, profession, vocation or business;

    (c) premises at which there is information held by a person ('A') whom the inspector has reasonable grounds for suspecting has information about a non-resident parent acquired in the course of A's own trade, profession, vocation or business.

(5) An inspector exercising his powers may question any person aged 18 or over whom he finds on the premises.

(6) If required to do so by an inspector exercising his powers, any such person shall furnish to the inspector all such information and documents as the inspector may reasonably require.

(7) No person shall be required under this section to answer any question or to give any evidence tending to incriminate himself or, in the case of a person who is married or is a civil partner, his or her spouse or civil partner.

(8) On applying for admission to any premises in the exercise of his powers, an inspector shall, if so required, produce his certificate.

(9) If any person—

    (a) intentionally delays or obstructs any inspector exercising his powers; or

    (b) without reasonable excuse, refuses or neglects to answer any question or furnish any information or to produce any document when required to do so under this section,

he shall be guilty of an offence and liable on summary conviction to a fine not exceeding level 3 on the standard scale.

(10) In this section—

'certificate' means a certificate of appointment issued under this section;

'inspector' means an inspector appointed under this section;

'powers' means powers conferred by this section.

(11) In this section, 'premises' includes—

    (a) moveable structures and vehicles, vessels, aircraft and hovercraft;

    (b) installations that are offshore installations for the purposes of the Mineral Workings (Offshore Installations) Act 1971; and

    (c) places of all other descriptions whether or not occupied as land or otherwise,

and references in this section to the occupier of premises are to be construed, in relation to premises that are not occupied as land, as references to any person for the time being present at the place in question.

Reviews and appeals

16 Revision of decisions

(1) Any decision to which subsection (1A) applies may be revised by the Secretary of State—

    (a) either within the prescribed period or in prescribed cases or circumstances; and

    (b) either on an application made for the purpose or on the Secretary of State's own initiative; and regulations may prescribe the procedure by which a decision of the Secretary of State may be so revised.

(1A) This subsection applies to—

    (a) a decision of the Secretary of State under section 11, 12 or 17;

    ...

    (c) a decision of the First-tier Tribunal on a referral under section 28D(1)(b).

(1B) Where the Secretary of State revises a decision under section 12(1)—

    (a) the Secretary of State may (if appropriate) do so as if revising a decision under section 11; and

    (b) if the Secretary of State does that, the decision as revised is to be treated as one under section 11 instead of section 12(1) (and, in particular, is to be so treated for the purposes of an appeal against it under section 20).

(2) In making a decision under subsection (1), the Secretary of State need not consider any issue that is not raised by the application or, as the case may be, did not cause the Secretary of State to act on the Secretary of State's own initiative.

(3) Subject to subsections (4) and (5) and section 28ZC, a revision under this section shall take effect as from the date on which the original decision took (or was to take) effect.

(4) Regulations may provide that, in prescribed cases or circumstances, a revision under this section shall take effect as from such other date as may be prescribed.

(5) Where a decision is revised under this section, for the purpose of any rule as to the time allowed for bringing an appeal, the decision shall be regarded as made on the date on which it is so revised.

(6) Except in prescribed circumstances, an appeal against a decision of the Secretary of State shall lapse if the decision is revised under this section before the appeal is determined.

17 Decisions superseding earlier decisions

(1) Subject to subsection (2), the following, namely—

    (a) any decision of the Secretary of State under section 11 or 12 or this section, whether as originally made or as revised under section 16;

    (b) any decision of an appeal tribunal or the First-tier Tribunal under section 20;

    ...

    (d) any decision of an appeal tribunal or the First-tier Tribunal on a referral under section 28D(1)(b);

    (e) any decision of a Child Support Commissioner or the Upper Tribunal on an appeal from such a decision as is mentioned in paragraph (b) or (d);

may be superseded by a decision made by the Secretary of State, either on an application made for the purpose or on the Secretary of State's own initiative.

(2) The Secretary of State may by regulations make provision with respect to the exercise of the power under subsection (1).

(3) Regulations under subsection (2) may, in particular—

    (a) make provision about the cases and circumstances in which the power under subsection (1) is exercisable, including provision restricting the exercise of that power by virtue of change of circumstance;

    (b) make provision with respect to the consideration by the Secretary of State, when acting under subsection (1), of any issue which has not led to the Secretary of State's so acting;

    (c) make provision with respect to procedure in relation to the exercise of the power under subsection (1).

(4) Subject to subsection (5) and section 28ZC, a decision under this section shall take effect as from the beginning of the maintenance period in which it is made or, where applicable, the beginning of the maintenance period in which the application was made.

(4A) In subsection (4), a 'maintenance period' is (except where a different meaning is prescribed for prescribed cases) a period of seven days, the first one beginning on the effective date of the first decision made by the Secretary of State under section 11 or (if earlier) the Secretary of State's first default or interim maintenance decision (under section 12) in relation to the non-resident parent in question, and each subsequent one beginning on the day after the last day of the previous one.

(5) Regulations may provide that, in prescribed cases or circumstances, a decision under this section shall take effect as from such other date as may be prescribed.

(6) In this section—

'appeal tribunal' means an appeal tribunal constituted under Chapter 1 of Part 1 of the Social Security Act 1998 (the functions of which have been transferred to the First-tier Tribunal);

'Child Support Commissioner' means a person appointed as such under section 22 (the functions of whom have been transferred to the Upper Tribunal).

20 Appeals to First-tier Tribunal

(1) A qualifying person has a right of appeal to the First-tier Tribunal against—

    (a) a decision of the Secretary of State under section 11, 12 or 17 (whether as originally made or as revised under section 16);

    (b) a decision of the Secretary of State not to make a maintenance calculation under section 11 or not to supersede a decision under section 17;

    (ba) a decision of the Secretary of State to make a liability order under section 32M;

    ...

    (d) the imposition (by virtue of section 41A) of a requirement to make penalty payments, or their amount;

(2) In subsection (1), 'qualifying person' means—

    (a) in relation to paragraphs (a) and (b)—

        (i) the person with care, or non-resident parent, with respect to whom the Secretary of State made the decision, or

        (ii) in a case relating to a maintenance calculation which was applied for under section 7, either of those persons or the child concerned;

    (aa) in relation to paragraph (ba), the person against whom the order is made;

    (c) in relation to paragraph (d), the parent who has been required to make penalty payments; and

    (d) in relation to paragraph (e), the person required to pay fees.

(2A) Regulations may provide that, in such cases or circumstances as may be prescribed, there is a right of appeal against a decision mentioned in subsection (1)(a) or (b) only if the Secretary of State has considered whether to revise the decision under section 16.

(2B) The regulations may in particular provide that that condition is met only where—

    (a) the consideration by the Secretary of State was on an application,

    (b) the Secretary of State considered issues of a specified description, or

    (c) the consideration by the Secretary of State satisfied any other condition specified in the regulations.

(3) A person with a right of appeal under this section shall be given such notice as may be prescribed of—

    (a) that right; and

    (b) the relevant decision, or the imposition of the requirement.

(4) Regulations may make—

    (a) provision as to the manner in which, and the time within which, appeals are to be brought;

    ...

    (c) provision that, where in accordance with regulations under subsection (2A) there is no right of appeal against a decision, any purported appeal may be treated as an application for revision under section 16.

(5) The regulations may in particular make any provision of a kind mentioned in Schedule 5 to the Social Security Act 1998.

(5A) An appeal lies by virtue of subsection (1)(ba) only on the following grounds—

    (a) that the person has not failed to pay an amount of child support maintenance;

    (b) that the amount in respect of which the liability order is made exceeds the amount of child support maintenance which the person has failed to pay.

(7) In deciding an appeal under this section, the First-tier Tribunal—

    (a) need not consider any issue that is not raised by the appeal; and

    (b) shall not take into account any circumstances not obtaining at the time when the Secretary of State made the decision or imposed the requirement.

(7A) In deciding an appeal against a decision of the Secretary of State to make a liability order, the First-tier Tribunal shall not question the maintenance calculation by reference to which the liability order was made.

(8) If an appeal under this section is allowed, the First-tier Tribunal may—

    (a) itself make such decision as it considers appropriate; or

    (b) remit the case to the Secretary of State, together with such directions (if any) as it considers appropriate.

...

23A   Redetermination of appeals

(1) This section applies where an application is made to the First-tier Tribunal for permission to appeal to the Upper Tribunal from any decision of the First-tier Tribunal under section 20.

    ...

(3) If each of the principal parties to the case expresses the view that the decision was errone-ous in point of law, the First-tier Tribunal shall set aside the decision and refer the case for determi-nation by a differently constituted First-tier Tribunal.

(4) The 'principal parties' are—

  (a) the Secretary of State; and
  (b) those who are qualifying persons for the purposes of section 20(2) in relation to the deci-sion in question.

24   Appeals to Upper Tribunal

(1) Each of the following may appeal to the Upper Tribunal under section 11 of the Tribunals, Courts and Enforcement Act 2007 from any decision of the First-tier Tribunal under section 20 of this Act—

      ...

  (b) the Secretary of State, and
  (c) any person who is aggrieved by the decision of an appeal tribunal.

(2) Where a question which would otherwise fall to be determined by the Secretary of State under this Act first arises in the course of an appeal to the Upper Tribunal, that tribunal may, if it thinks fit, determine the question even though it has not been considered by the Secretary of State.

26   Disputes about parentage

(1) Where a person who is alleged to be a parent of the child with respect to whom an applica-tion for a maintenance calculation has been made ... ('the alleged parent') denies that he is one of the child's parents, the Secretary of State shall not make a maintenance calculation on the assump-tion that the alleged parent is one of the child's parents unless the case falls within one of those set out in subsection (2).

(2) The Cases are—

Case A1
Where—

  (a) the child is habitually resident in England and Wales;
  (b) the Secretary of State is satisfied that the alleged parent was married to the child's mother at some time in the period beginning with the conception and ending with the birth of the child; and
  (c) the child has not been adopted.

Case A2
Where—

  (a) the child is habitually resident in England and Wales;
  (b) the alleged parent has been registered as father of the child under section 10 or 10A of, or regulations made under section 2C, 2D, 2E, 10B or 10C of, the Births and Deaths Registration Act 1953, or in any register kept under section 13 (register of births and still-births) or section 44 (Register of Corrections Etc) of the Registration of Births, Deaths and Marriages (Scotland) Act 1965, or under Article 14 or 18(1)(b)(ii) of the Births and Deaths Registration (Northern Ireland) Order 1976; and
  (c) the child has not subsequently been adopted.

Case A3
Where the result of a scientific test (within the meaning of section 27A) taken by the alleged parent would be relevant to determining the child's parentage, and the alleged parent—

  (a) refuses to take such a test; or
  (b) has submitted to such a test, and it shows that there is no reasonable doubt that the alleged parent is a parent of the child.

Case A
Where the alleged parent is a parent of the child in question by virtue of having adopted him.

Case B

Where the alleged parent is a parent of the child in question by virtue of an order under section 30 of the Human Fertilisation and Embryology Act 1990 or section 54 of the Human Fertilisation and Embryology Act 2008 (parental orders).

Case B1

Where the Secretary of State is satisfied that the alleged parent is a parent of the child in question by virtue of section 27 or 28 of the Human Fertilisation and Embryology Act 1990 or any of sections 33 to 46 of the Human Fertilisation and Embryology Act 2008 (which relate to children resulting from assisted reproduction).

Case C

Where—
- (a) either—
  - (i) a declaration that the alleged parent is a parent of the child in question (or a declaration which has that effect) is in force under section 55A or 56 of the Family Law Act 1986...; or
  ...and
  - (b) the child has not subsequently been adopted.

...

Case F

Where—
- (a) the alleged parent has been found, or adjudged, to be the father of the child in question—
  - (i) in proceedings before any court in England and Wales which are relevant proceedings for the purposes of section 12 of the Civil Evidence Act 1968...; or
  - (ii) in affiliation proceedings before any court in the United Kingdom, (whether or not he offered any defence to the allegation of paternity) and that finding or adjudication still subsists; and
- (b) the child has not subsequently been adopted.
- (3) In this section—
'adopted' means adopted within the meaning of Part IV of the Adoption Act 1976 or Chapter 4 of Part 1 of the Adoption and Children Act 2002;
...

27 Applications for declaration of parentage under Family Law Act 1986

(1) This section applies where—
- (a) an application for a maintenance calculation has been made..., or a maintenance calculation is in force, with respect to a person ('the alleged parent') who denies that he is a parent of a child with respect to whom the application or calculation was made...;
- (b) the Secretary of State is not satisfied that the case falls within one of those set out in section 26(2); and
- (c) the Secretary of State or the person with care makes an application for a declaration under section 55A of the Family Law Act 1986 as to whether or not the alleged parent is one of the child's parents.

(2) Where this section applies—
- (a) if it is the person with care who makes the application, she shall be treated as having a sufficient personal interest for the purposes of subsection (3) of that section; and
- (b) if it is the Secretary of State who makes the application, that subsection shall not apply.

27A Recovery of fees for scientific tests

(1) This section applies in any case where—
- (a) an application for a maintenance calculation has been made or a maintenance calculation is in force;

(b) scientific tests have been carried out (otherwise than under a direction or in response to a request) in relation to bodily samples obtained from a person who is alleged to be a parent of a child with respect to whom the application or calculation is made …;

(c) the results of the tests do not exclude the alleged parent from being one of the child's parents; and

(d) one of the conditions set out in subsection (2) is satisfied.

(2) The conditions are that—

(a) the alleged parent does not deny that he is one of the child's parents;

(b) in proceedings under section 55A of the Family Law Act 1986, a court has made a declaration that the alleged parent is a parent of the child in question; or

…

(3) In any case to which this section applies, any fee paid by the Secretary of State in connection with scientific tests may be recovered by it from the alleged parent as a debt due to the Crown.

(4) In this section—

'bodily sample' means a sample of bodily fluid or bodily tissue taken for the purpose of scientific tests;

'direction' means a direction given by a court under section 20 of the Family Law Reform Act 1969 (tests to determine paternity);

'request' means a request made by a court under section 70 of the Law Reform (Miscellaneous Provisions) (Scotland) Act 1990 (blood and other samples in civil proceedings); and

'scientific tests' means scientific tests made with the object of ascertaining the inheritable characteristics of bodily fluids or bodily tissue.

(5) Any sum recovered by the Secretary of State under this section shall be paid by it into the Consolidated Fund.

…

Decisions and appeals dependent on other cases

28ZA   Decisions involving issues that arise on appeal in other cases

(1) This section applies where—

(a) a decision by the Secretary of State falls to be made under section 11, 12, 16 or 17…; and

(b) an appeal is pending against a decision given in relation to a different matter by the Upper Tribunal or a court.

(2) If the Secretary of State considers it possible that the result of the appeal will be such that, if it were already determined, it would affect the decision in some way—

(a) the Secretary of State need not, except in such cases or circumstances as may be prescribed, make the decision while the appeal is pending;

(b) the Secretary of State may, in such cases or circumstances as may be prescribed, make the decision on such basis as may be prescribed.

(3) Where the Secretary of State acts in accordance with subsection (2)(b), following the determination of the appeal the Secretary of State shall if appropriate revise the decision (under section 16) in accordance with that determination.

(4) For the purposes of this section, an appeal against a decision is pending if—

(a) an appeal against the decision has been brought but not determined;

(b) an application for leave to appeal against the decision has been made but not determined; or

(c) in such circumstances as may be prescribed, an appeal against the decision has not been brought (or, as the case may be, an application for leave to appeal against the decision has not been made) but the time for doing so has not yet expired.

(5) In paragraphs (a), (b) and (c) of subsection (4), any reference to an appeal, or an application for leave to appeal, against a decision includes a reference to—

(a) an application for, or for leave to apply for, judicial review of the decision under section 31 of the Supreme Court Act 1981;

…

28ZB   Appeals involving issues that arise on appeal in other cases

(1) This section applies where—

    (a) an appeal ('appeal A') in relation to a decision or the imposition of a requirement falling within section 20(1) is made to the First-tier Tribunal, or from the First-tier Tribunal to the Upper Tribunal; and

    (b) an appeal ('appeal B') is pending against a decision given in a different case by the Upper Tribunal or a court.

(2) If the Secretary of State considers it possible that the result of appeal B will be such that, if it were already determined, it would affect the determination of appeal A, the Secretary of State may serve notice requiring the First-tier Tribunal or Upper Tribunal—

    (a) not to determine appeal A but to refer it to the Secretary of State; or

    (b) to deal with the appeal in accordance with subsection (4).

(3) Where appeal A is referred to the Secretary of State under subsection (2)(a), following the determination of appeal B and in accordance with that determination, the Secretary of State shall if appropriate—

    (a) in a case where appeal A has not been determined by the First-tier Tribunal, revise (under section 16) the decision which gave rise to that appeal; or

    (b) in a case where appeal A has been determined by the First-tier Tribunal, make a decision (under section 17) superseding the tribunal's decision.

(4) Where appeal A is to be dealt with in accordance with this subsection, the First-tier Tribunal or Upper Tribunal shall either—

    (a) stay appeal A until appeal B is determined; or

    (b) if the First-tier Tribunal or Upper Tribunal considers it to be in the interests of the appellant to do so, determine appeal A as if—

        (i) appeal B had already been determined; and

        (ii) the issues arising on appeal B had been decided in the way that was most unfavourable to the appellant.

In this subsection 'the appellant' means the person who appealed or, as the case may be, first appealed against the decision or the imposition of the requirement mentioned in subsection (1)(a).

(5) Where the First-tier Tribunal or Upper Tribunal acts in accordance with subsection (4)(b), following the determination of appeal B the Secretary of State shall, if appropriate, make a decision (under section 17) superseding the decision of the First-tier Tribunal or Upper Tribunal in accordance with that determination.

(6) For the purposes of this section, an appeal against a decision is pending if—

    (a) an appeal against the decision has been brought but not determined;

    (b) an application for leave to appeal against the decision has been made but not determined; or

    (c) in such circumstances as may be prescribed, an appeal against the decision has not been brought (or, as the case may be, an application for leave to appeal against the decision has not been made) but the time for doing so has not yet expired.

(7) In this section—

    (a) the reference in subsection (1)(a) to an appeal to the Upper Tribunal includes a reference to an application for leave to appeal to the Upper Tribunal; and

    (b) any reference in paragraph (a), (b) or (c) of subsection (6) to an appeal, or to an application for leave to appeal, against a decision includes a reference to—

        (i) an application for, or for leave to apply for, judicial review of the decision under section 31 of the Supreme Court Act 1981; or

        (ii) ...

(8) Regulations may make provision supplementing that made by this section.

Cases of error

28ZC   Restrictions on liability in certain cases of error

(1) Subject to subsection (2), this section applies where—

    (a) the effect of the determination, whenever made, of an appeal to the Upper Tribunal or the court ('the relevant determination') is that the adjudicating authority's decision out of which the appeal arose was erroneous in point of law; and

    (b) after the date of the relevant determination a decision falls to be made by the Secretary of State in accordance with that determination (or would, apart from this section, fall to be so made)—

        (i) with respect to an application for a maintenance calculation (made after the commencement date) . . .;

        (ii) as to whether to revise, under section 16, any decision (made after the commencement date) referred to in section 16(1A); or

        (iii) on an application under section 17 (made after the commencement date) for any decision (made after the commencement date) referred to in section 17(1).

(2) This section does not apply where the decision of the Secretary of State mentioned in subsection (1)(b)—

    (a) is one which, but for section 28ZA(2)(a), would have been made before the date of the relevant determination; or

    (b) is one made in pursuance of section 28ZB(3) or (5).

(3) In so far as the decision relates to a person's liability . . . in respect of a period before the date of the relevant determination, it shall be made as if the adjudicating authority's decision had been found by the Upper Tribunal or court not to have been erroneous in point of law.

(4) Subsection (1)(a) shall be read as including a case where—

    (a) the effect of the relevant determination is that part or all of a purported regulation or order is invalid; and

    (b) the error of law made by the adjudicating authority was to act on the basis that the purported regulation or order (or the part held to be invalid) was valid.

(5) It is immaterial for the purposes of subsection (1)—

    (a) where such a decision as is mentioned in paragraph (b)(i) falls to be made; or

    (b) where such a decision as is mentioned in paragraph (b)(ii) or (iii) falls to be made on an application under section 16 or (as the case may be) section 17,

whether the application was made before or after the date of the relevant determination.

(6) In this section—

'adjudicating authority' means the Secretary of State, or a child support officer or, in the case of a decision made on a referral under section 28D(1)(b), the First-tier Tribunal;

'the commencement date' means the date of the coming into force of section 44 of the Social Security Act 1998; and

'the court' means the High Court, the Court of Appeal, the Court of Session, the High Court or Court of Appeal in Northern Ireland, the Supreme Court or the Court of Justice of the European Union.

(7) The date of the relevant determination shall, in prescribed cases, be determined for the purposes of this section in accordance with any regulations made for that purpose.

(8) Regulations made under subsection (7) may include provision—

    (a) for a determination of a higher court to be treated as if it had been made on the date of a determination of a lower court or the Upper Tribunal; or

    (b) for a determination of a lower court or the Upper Tribunal to be treated as if it had been made on the date of a determination of a higher court.

28ZD   Correction of errors and setting aside of decisions

(1) Regulations may make provision with respect to—

    (a) the correction of accidental errors in any decision of the Secretary of State or record of a decision of the Secretary of State given under this Act;

    …

(2) Nothing in subsection (1) shall be construed as derogating from any power to correct errors which is exercisable apart from regulations made by virtue of that subsection.

Variations

28A   Application for variation of usual rules for calculating maintenance

(1) Where an application for a maintenance calculation is made under section 4 or 7, … the person with care or the non-resident parent or (in the case of an application under section 7) either of them or the child concerned may apply to the Secretary of State for the rules by which the calculation is made to be varied in accordance with this Act.

(2) Such an application is referred to in this Act as an 'application for a variation'.

(3) An application for a variation may be made at any time before the Secretary of State has reached a decision (under section 11 or 12(1)) on the application for a maintenance calculation …

(4) A person who applies for a variation—

    (a) need not make the application in writing unless the Secretary of State directs in any case that he must; and

    (b) must say upon what grounds the application is made.

(5) In other respects an application for a variation is to be made in such manner as may be prescribed.

(6) Schedule 4A has effect in relation to applications for a variation.

28B   Preliminary consideration of applications

(1) Where an application for a variation has been duly made to the Secretary of State, it may give it a preliminary consideration.

(2) The Secretary of State may on completing such a preliminary consideration, reject the application (and proceed to make a decision on the application for a maintenance calculation without any variation) if it appears to the Secretary of State—

    (a) that there are no grounds on which a variation could be agreed to;

    (b) that the Secretary of State has insufficient information to make a decision on the application for the maintenance calculation under section 11 (apart from any information needed in relation to the application for a variation), and therefore that the Secretary of State's decision would be made under section 12(1); or

    (c) that other prescribed circumstances apply.

28C   Imposition of regular payments condition

(1) Where—

    (a) an application for a variation is made by the non-resident parent; and

    (b) the Secretary of State makes an interim maintenance decision,

the Secretary of State may also, if the Secretary of State has completed a preliminary consideration (under section 28B) of the application for a variation and has not rejected it under that section, impose on the non-resident parent one of the conditions mentioned in subsection (2) (a 'regular payments condition').

(2) The conditions are that—

    (a) the non-resident parent must make the payments of child support maintenance specified in the interim maintenance decision;

    (b) the non-resident parent must make such lesser payments of child support maintenance as may be determined in accordance with regulations made by the Secretary of State.

(3) Where the Secretary of State imposes a regular payments condition, the Secretary of State shall give written notice of the imposition of the condition and of the effect of failure to comply with it to—

    (a) the non-resident parent;

    (b) all the persons with care concerned; and

    (c) if the application for the maintenance calculation was made under section 7, the child who made the application.

(4) A regular payments condition shall cease to have effect—

    (a) when the Secretary of State has made a decision on the application for a maintenance calculation under section 11 (whether the Secretary of State agrees to a variation or not);

    (b) on the withdrawal of the application for a variation.

(5) Where a non-resident parent has failed to comply with a regular payments condition, the Secretary of State may in prescribed circumstances refuse to consider the application for a variation, and instead reach a decision under section 11 as if no such application had been made.

(6) The question whether a non-resident parent has failed to comply with a regular payments condition is to be determined by the Secretary of State.

(7) Where the Secretary of State determines that a non-resident parent has failed to comply with a regular payments condition the Secretary of State shall give written notice of the determination to—

    (a) that parent;

    (b) all the persons with care concerned; and

    (c) if the application for the maintenance calculation was made under section 7, the child who made the application.

28D   Determination of applications

(1) Where an application for a variation has not failed, the Secretary of State shall, in accordance with the relevant provisions of, or made under, this Act—

    (a) either agree or not to a variation, and make a decision under section 11 or 12(1); or

    (b) refer the application to the First-tier Tribunal for the tribunal to determine what variation, if any, is to be made.

(2) For the purposes of subsection (1), an application for a variation has failed if—

    (a) it has been withdrawn; or

    (b) the Secretary of State has rejected it on completing a preliminary consideration under section 28B; or

    (c) the Secretary of State has refused to consider it under section 28C(5).

(2A) Subsection (2B) applies if—

    (a) the application for a variation is made by the person with care or (in the case of an application for a maintenance calculation under section 7) the person with care or the child concerned, and

    (b) it appears to the Secretary of State that consideration of further information or evidence may affect the decision under subsection (1)(a) whether or not to agree to a variation.

(2B) Before making the decision under subsection (1)(a) the Secretary of State must—

    (a) consider any such further information or evidence that is available to the Secretary of State, and

    (b) where necessary, take such steps as the Secretary of State considers appropriate to obtain any such further information or evidence.

(3) In dealing with an application for a variation which has been referred to it under subsection (1)(b), the First-tier Tribunal shall have the same powers, and be subject to the same duties, apart from the duty under subsection (2B), as would the Secretary of State in dealing with the application.

28E   Matters to be taken into account

(1) In determining whether to agree to a variation, the Secretary of State shall have regard both to the general principles set out in subsection (2) and to such other considerations as may be prescribed.

(2) The general principles are that—

(a) parents should be responsible for maintaining their children whenever they can afford to do so;

(b) where a parent has more than one child, his obligation to maintain any one of them should be no less of an obligation than his obligation to maintain any other of them.

(3) In determining whether to agree to a variation, the Secretary of State shall take into account any representations made to the Secretary of State—

(a) by the person with care or non-resident parent concerned; or

(b) where the application for the current calculation was made under section 7, by either of them or the child concerned.

(4) In determining whether to agree to a variation, no account shall be taken of the fact that—

(a) any part of the income of the person with care concerned is, or would be if the Secretary of State agreed to a variation, derived from any benefit; or

(b) some or all of any child support maintenance might be taken into account in any manner in relation to any entitlement to benefit.

(5) In this section 'benefit' has such meaning as may be prescribed.

28F   Agreement to a variation

(1) The Secretary of State may agree to a variation if—

(a) the Secretary of State is satisfied that the case is one which falls within one or more of the cases set out in Part I of Schedule 4B or in regulations made under that Part; and

(b) it is the Secretary of State's opinion that, in all the circumstances of the case, it would be just and equitable to agree to a variation.

(2) In considering whether it would be just and equitable in any case to agree to a variation, the Secretary of State—

(a) must have regard, in particular, to the welfare of any child likely to be affected if the Secretary of State did agree to a variation; and

(b) must, or as the case may be must not, take any prescribed factors into account, or must take them into account (or not) in prescribed circumstances.

(3) The Secretary of State shall not agree to a variation (and shall proceed to make a decision on the application for a maintenance calculation without any variation) if satisfied that—

(a) the Secretary of State has insufficient information to make a decision on the application for the maintenance calculation under section 11, and therefore that the decision would be made under section 12(1); or

(b) other prescribed circumstances apply.

(4) Where the Secretary of State agrees to a variation, the Secretary of State shall—

(a) determine the basis on which the amount of child support maintenance is to be calculated in response to the application for a maintenance calculation . . .; and

(b) make a decision under section 11 on that basis.

(5) If the Secretary of State has made an interim maintenance decision, it is to be treated as having been replaced by the Secretary of State's decision under section 11, and except in prescribed circumstances any appeal connected with it (under section 20) shall lapse.

(6) In determining whether or not to agree to a variation, the Secretary of State shall comply with regulations made under Part II of Schedule 4B.

28G   Variations: revision and supersession

(1) An application for a variation may also be made when a maintenance calculation is in force.

(2) The Secretary of State may by regulations provide for—

(a) sections 16, 17 and 20; and

(b) sections 28A to 28F and Schedules 4A and 4B,

to apply with prescribed modifications in relation to such applications.

(3) The Secretary of State may by regulations provide that, in prescribed cases (or except in prescribed cases), a decision under section 17 made otherwise than pursuant to an application for a variation may be made on the basis of a variation agreed to for the purposes of an earlier decision without a new application for a variation having to be made.
...

Voluntary payments

28J Voluntary payments

(1) This section applies where—
  (a) a person has applied for a maintenance calculation under section 4(1) or 7 (1), ...
  (b) the Secretary of State has neither made a decision under section 11 or 12 on the application, nor decided not to make a maintenance calculation; and
  (c) the non-resident parent makes a voluntary payment.

(2) A 'voluntary payment' is a payment—
  (a) on account of child support maintenance which the non-resident parent expects to become liable to pay following the determination of the application (whether or not the amount of the payment is based on any estimate of his potential liability which the Secretary of State has agreed to give); and
  (b) made before the maintenance calculation has been notified to the non-resident parent or (as the case may be) before the Secretary of State has notified the non-resident parent that the Secretary of State has decided not to make a maintenance calculation.

(3) In such circumstances and to such extent as may be prescribed—
  (a) the voluntary payment may be set off against arrears of child support maintenance which accrued by virtue of the maintenance calculation taking effect on a date earlier than that on which it was notified to the non-resident parent;
  (b) the amount payable under a maintenance calculation may be adjusted to take account of the voluntary payment.

(4) A voluntary payment shall be made to the Secretary of State unless the Secretary of State agrees, on such conditions as the Secretary of State may specify, that it may be made to the person with care, or to or through another person.

(5) The Secretary of State may by regulations make provision as to voluntary payments, and the regulations may in particular—
  (a) prescribe what payments or descriptions of payment are, or are not, to count as 'voluntary payments';
  (b) prescribe the extent to which and circumstances in which a payment, or a payment of a prescribed description, counts.

Collection and enforcement

29 Collection of child support maintenance

(1) The Secretary of State may (subject to section 4(2A) and 7(3A)) arrange for the collection of any child support maintenance payable in accordance with a maintenance calculation where—
  ...
  (b) an application has been made to the Secretary of State under section 4(2) or 7(3) for the Secretary of State to arrange for its collection.

(2) Where a maintenance calculation is made under this Act, payments of child support maintenance under the calculation shall be made in accordance with regulations made by the Secretary of State.

(3) The regulations may, in particular, make provision—
  (a) for payments of child support maintenance to be made—
    (i) to the person caring for the child or children in question;
    (ii) to, or through, the Secretary of State; or

     (iii) to, or through, such other person as the Secretary of State may, from time to time, specify;

(b) as to the method by which payments of child support maintenance are to be made;

(c) for determining, on the basis of prescribed assumptions, the total amount of the payments of child support maintenance payable in a reference period (including provision for adjustments to such an amount);

(ca) requiring payments of child support maintenance to be made—
     (i) by reference to such an amount and a reference period; and
     (ii) at prescribed intervals falling in a reference period;

(d) as to the method and timing of the transmission of payments which are made, to or through the Secretary of State or any other person, in accordance with the regulations;

(e) empowering the Secretary of State to direct any person liable to make payments in accordance with the calculation—
     (i) to make them by standing order or by any other method which requires one person to give his authority for payments to be made from an account of his to an account of another's on specific dates during the period for which the authority is in force and without the need for any further authority from him;
     (ii) to open an account from which payments under the calculation may be made in accordance with the method of payment which that person is obliged to adopt;

(f) providing for the making of representations with respect to matters with which the regulations are concerned.

(3A) In subsection (3)(c) and (ca) 'a reference period' means—
(a) a period of 52 weeks beginning with a prescribed date; or
(b) in prescribed circumstances, a prescribed period.

(4) If the regulations include provision for payment by means of deduction in accordance with an order under section 31, they must make provision—
(a) for that method of payment not to be used in any case where there is good reason not to use it; and
(b) for the person against whom the order under section 31 would be made to have a right of appeal to a magistrates' court (or, in Scotland, to the sheriff) against a decision that the exclusion required by paragraph (a) does not apply.

(5) On an appeal under regulations made under subsection (4)(b) the court or (as the case may be) the sheriff shall not question the maintenance calculation by reference to which the order under section 31 would be made.

(6) Regulations under subsection (4)(b) may include—
(a) provision with respect to the period within which a right of appeal under the regulations may be exercised;
(b) provision with respect to the powers of a magistrates' court (or, in Scotland, of the sheriff) in relation to an appeal under the regulations.

(7) If the regulations include provision for payment by means of deduction in accordance with an order under section 31, they may make provision—
(a) prescribing matters which are, or are not, to be taken into account in determining whether there is good reason not to use that method of payment;
(b) prescribing circumstances in which good reason not to use that method of payment is, or is not, to be regarded as existing.

30 Collection and enforcement of other forms of maintenance

(1) Where the Secretary of State is arranging for the collection of any payments under section 29 or subsection (2), the Secretary of State may also arrange for the collection of any periodical payments, or secured periodical payments, of a prescribed kind which are payable to or for the benefit of any person who falls within a prescribed category.

(2) The Secretary of State may, except in prescribed cases, arrange for the collection of any periodical payments, or secured periodical payments, of a prescribed kind which are payable for the benefit of a child even though the Secretary of State is not arranging for the collection of child support maintenance with respect to that child.

(3) Where—

(a) the Secretary of State is arranging, under this Act, for the collection of different payments ('the payments') from the same non-resident parent;

(b) an amount is collected by the Secretary of State from the non-resident parent which is less than the total amount due in respect of the payments; and

(c) the non-resident parent has not stipulated how that amount is to be allocated by the Secretary of State as between the payments,

the Secretary of State may allocate that amount as the Secretary of State sees fit.

(4) In relation to England and Wales, the Secretary of State may by regulations make provision for sections 29 and 31 to 40 to apply, with such modifications (if any) as he considers necessary or expedient, for the purpose of enabling the Secretary of State to enforce any obligation to pay any amount for the collection of which the Secretary of State is authorised under this section to make arrangements.

...

31   Deduction from earnings orders

(1) This section applies where any person ('the liable person') is liable to make payments of child support maintenance.

(2) The Secretary of State may make an order ('a deduction from earnings order') against a liable person to secure the payment of any amount due under the maintenance calculation in question.

(3) A deduction from earnings order may be made so as to secure the payment of—

(a) arrears of child support maintenance payable under the calculation;

(b) amounts of child support maintenance which will become due under the calculation; or

(c) both such arrears and such future amounts.

(4) A deduction from earnings order—

(a) shall be expressed to be directed at a person ('the employer') who has the liable person in his employment; and

(b) shall have effect from such date as may be specified in the order.

(5) A deduction from earnings order shall operate as an instruction to the employer to—

(a) make deductions from the liable person's earnings; and

(b) pay the amounts deducted to the Secretary of State.

(6) The Secretary of State shall serve a copy of any deduction from earnings order made under this section on—

(a) the person who appears to the Secretary of State to have the liable person in question in his employment; and

(b) the liable person.

(7) Where—

(a) a deduction from earnings order has been made; and

(b) a copy of the order has been served on the liable person's employer,

it shall be the duty of that employer to comply with the order; but he shall not be under any liability for non-compliance before the end of the period of 7 days beginning with the date on which the copy was served on him.

(8) In this section and section 32 'earnings' means (subject to such exceptions as may be prescribed) any sums payable to a person which fall within one or more of the following paragraphs—

(a) sums payable by way of wages or salary (including any fees, bonus, commission, overtime pay or other emoluments payable in addition to wages or salary or payable under a contract of service);

    (b) periodical payments by way of pension (including an annuity payable for the purpose of providing a pension), whether or not in respect of past services;

    (c) periodical payments by way of compensation for the loss, abolition or relinquishment, or diminution in the emoluments, of any office or employment;

    (d) sums payable by way of statutory sick pay.

(9) For the purposes of this section and section 32 any person who (as a principal and not as a servant or agent) pays to the liable person any earnings is to be treated as having the liable person in his employment; and the following are to be read accordingly—

    (a) in this section and section 32, references to the liable person's employer; and

    (b) in section 32(3), 'employment', 'employed' and 're-employed'.

32 Regulations about deduction from earnings orders

(1) The Secretary of State may by regulations make provision with respect to deduction from earnings orders.

(2) The regulations may, in particular, make provision—

    (b) requiring any deduction from earnings under an order to be made in the prescribed manner;

    (bb) for the amount or amounts which are to be deducted from the liable person's earnings not to exceed a prescribed proportion of his earnings (as determined by the employer);

    (c) requiring an order to specify the amount or amounts to which the order relates and the amount or amounts which are to be deducted from the liable person's earnings in order to meet his liabilities under the maintenance calculation in question;

    (d) requiring the intervals between deductions to be made under an order to be specified in the order;

    (e) as to the payment of sums deducted under an order to the Secretary of State;

    (f) allowing the person who deducts and pays any amount under an order to deduct from the liable person's earnings a prescribed sum towards his administrative costs;

    (g) with respect to the notification to be given to the liable person of amounts deducted, and amounts paid, under the order;

    (h) requiring any person on whom a copy of an order is served to notify the Secretary of State in the prescribed manner and within a prescribed period if he does not have the liable person in his employment or if the liable person ceases to be in his employment;

    (i) as to the operation of an order where any earnings are paid to the liable person by or on behalf of the Crown;

    (j) for the variation of orders;

    (k) similar to that made by section 31(7), in relation to any variation of an order;

    (l) for an order to lapse when the employer concerned ceases to have the liable person in his employment;

    (m) as to the revival of an order in such circumstances as may be prescribed;

    (n) allowing or requiring an order to be discharged;

    (o) as to the giving of notice by the Secretary of State to the employer concerned that an order has lapsed or has ceased to have effect.

(3) The regulations may include provision that while a deduction from earnings order is in force—

    (a) the liable person shall from time to time notify the Secretary of State, in the prescribed manner and within a prescribed period, of each occasion on which he leaves any employment or becomes employed, or re-employed, and shall include in such a notification a statement of his earnings and expected earnings from the employment concerned and of such other matters as may be prescribed;

    (b) any person who becomes the liable person's employer and knows that the order is in force shall notify the Secretary of State, in the prescribed manner and within a prescribed period, that he is the liable person's employer, and shall include in such a notification a statement of the liable person's earnings and expected earnings from the employment concerned and of such other matters as may be prescribed.

(4) The regulations may include provision with respect to the priority as between a deduction from earnings order and—

    (a) any other deduction from earnings order;

    (b) any order under any other enactment relating to England and Wales which provides for deductions from the liable person's earnings;

    (c) any diligence against earnings.

(5) The regulations may include a provision that a liable person may appeal to a magistrates' court if he is aggrieved by the making of a deduction from earnings order against him, or by the terms of any such order, or there is a dispute as to whether payments constitute earnings or as to any other prescribed matter relating to the order.

(6) On an appeal under subsection (5) the court or (as the case may be) the sheriff shall not question the maintenance calculation by reference to which the deduction from earnings order was made.

(7) Regulations made by virtue of subsection (5) may include—

    (a) provision with respect to the period within which a right of appeal under the regulations may be exercised;

    (b) provision as to the powers of a magistrates' court, . . . in relation to an appeal (which may include provision as to the quashing of a deduction from earnings order or the variation of the terms of such an order).

(8) If any person fails to comply with the requirements of a deduction from earnings order, or with any regulation under this section which is designated for the purposes of this subsection, he shall be guilty of an offence.

(9) In subsection (8) 'designated' means designated by the regulations.

(10) It shall be a defence for a person charged with an offence under subsection (8) to prove that he took all reasonable steps to comply with the requirements in question.

(11) Any person guilty of an offence under subsection (8) shall be liable on summary conviction to a fine not exceeding level two on the standard scale.

32A   Orders for regular deductions from accounts

(1) If in relation to any person it appears to the Secretary of State—

    (a) that the person has failed to pay an amount of child support maintenance; and

    (b) that the person holds an account with a deposit-taker;

the Secretary of State may make an order against that person to secure the payment of any amount due under the maintenance calculation in question by means of regular deductions from the account.

(2) An order under this section may be made so as to secure the payment of—

    (a) arrears of child support maintenance payable under the calculation;

    (b) amounts of child support maintenance which will become payable under the calculation; or

    (c) both such arrears and such future amounts.

(3) An order under this section may be made in respect of amounts due under a maintenance calculation which is the subject of an appeal only if it appears to the Secretary of State—

    (a) that liability for the amounts would not be affected were the appeal to succeed; or

    (b) where paragraph (a) does not apply, that the making of an order under this section in respect of the amounts would nonetheless be fair in all the circumstances.

(4) An order under this section—

    (a) may not be made in respect of an account of a prescribed description; and

    (b) may be made in respect of a joint account which is held by the person against whom the order is made and one or more other persons, and which is not of a description prescribed under paragraph (a), if (but only if) regulations made by the Secretary of State so provide.

(5) An order under this section—

    (a) shall specify the account in respect of which it is made;

    (b) shall be expressed to be directed at the deposit-taker with which the account is held; and

    (c) shall have effect from such date as may be specified in the order.

(6) An order under this section shall operate as an instruction to the deposit-taker at which it is directed to—

    (a) make deductions from the amount (if any) standing to the credit of the account specified in the order; and

    (b) pay the amount deducted to the Secretary of State.

(7) The Secretary of State shall serve a copy of any order made under this section on—

    (a) the deposit-taker at which it is directed;

    (b) the person against whom it is made; and

    (c) if the order is made in respect of a joint account, the other account-holders.

(8) Where—

    (a) an order under this section has been made; and

    (b) a copy of the order has been served on the deposit-taker at which it is directed,

it shall be the duty of that deposit-taker to comply with the order; but the deposit-taker shall not be under any liability for non-compliance before the end of the period of 7 days beginning with the day on which the copy was served on the deposit-taker.

(9) Where regulations have been made under section 29(3)(a), a person liable to pay an amount of child support maintenance is to be taken for the purposes of this section to have failed to pay an amount of child support maintenance unless it is paid to or through the person specified in, or by virtue of, the regulations for the case in question.

32B   Orders under section 32A: joint accounts

(1) Before making an order under section 32A in respect of a joint account the Secretary of State shall offer each of the account-holders an opportunity to make representations about—

    (a) the proposal to make the order; and

    (b) the amounts to be deducted under the order, if it is made.

(2) The amounts to be deducted from a joint account under such an order shall not exceed the amounts that appear to the Secretary of State to be fair in all the circumstances.

(3) In determining those amounts the Secretary of State shall have particular regard to—

    (a) any representations made in accordance with subsection (1)(b);

    (b) the amount contributed to the account by each of the account-holders; and

    (c) such other matters as may be prescribed.

32C   Regulations about orders under section 32A

(1) The Secretary of State may by regulations make provision with respect to orders under section 32A.

(2) Regulations under subsection (1) may, in particular, make provision—

    (a) requiring an order to specify the amount or amounts in respect of which it is made;

    (b) requiring an order to specify the amounts which are to be deducted under it in order to meet liabilities under the maintenance calculation in question;

    (c) requiring an order to specify the dates on which deductions are to be made under it;

    (d) for the rate of deduction under an order not to exceed such rate as may be specified in, or determined in accordance with, the regulations;

    (e) as to circumstances in which amounts standing to the credit of an account are to be disregarded for the purposes of section 32A;

    (f) as to the payment of sums deducted under an order to the Secretary of State;

(g) allowing the deposit-taker at which an order is directed to deduct from the amount standing to the credit of the account specified in the order a prescribed amount towards its administrative costs before making any deduction required by section 32A(6)(a);

(h) with respect to notifications to be given to the person against whom an order is made (and, in the case of an order made in respect of a joint account, to the other account-holders) of amounts deducted, and amounts paid, under the order;

(i) requiring the deposit-taker at which an order is directed to notify the Secretary of State in the prescribed manner and within a prescribed period—

    (i) if the account specified in the order does not exist at the time at which the order is served on the deposit-taker;

    (ii) of any other accounts held with the deposit-taker at that time by the person against whom the order is made;

(j) requiring the deposit-taker at which an order is directed to notify the Secretary of State in the prescribed manner and within a prescribed period if, after the time at which the order is served on the deposit-taker—

    (i) the account specified in the order is closed;

    (ii) a new account of any description is opened with the deposit-taker by the person against whom the order is made;

(k) as to circumstances in which the deposit-taker at which an order is directed, the person against whom the order is made and (in the case of an order made in respect of a joint account) the other account-holders may apply to the Secretary of State for the Secretary of State to review the order and as to such a review;

(l) for the variation of orders;

(m) similar to that made by section 32A(8), in relation to any variation of an order;

(n) for an order to lapse in such circumstances as may be prescribed;

(o) as to the revival of an order in such circumstances as may be prescribed;

(p) allowing or requiring an order to be discharged;

(q) as to the giving of notice by the Secretary of State to the deposit-taker that an order has lapsed or ceased to have effect.

(3) The Secretary of State may by regulations make provision with respect to priority as between an order under section 32A and—

(a) any other order under that section;

(b) any order under any other enactment relating to England and Wales which provides for deductions from the same account;

(c) any diligence done in Scotland against the same account.

(4) The Secretary of State shall by regulations make provision for any person affected to have a right to appeal to a court—

(a) against the making of an order under section 32A;

(b) against any decision made by the Secretary of State on an application under regulations made under subsection (2)(k).

(5) On an appeal under regulations made under subsection (4)(a), the court shall not question the maintenance calculation by reference to which the order was made.

(6) Regulations under subsection (4) may include—

(a) provision with respect to the period within which a right of appeal under the regulations may be exercised;

(b) provision with respect to the powers of the court to which the appeal under the regulations lies.

32D Orders under section 32A: offences

(1) A person who fails to comply with the requirements of—

(a) an order under section 32A, or

(b) any regulation under section 32C which is designated by the regulations for the purposes of this paragraph,

commits an offence.

(2) It shall be a defence for a person charged with an offence under subsection (1) to prove that the person took all reasonable steps to comply with the requirements in question.

(3) A person guilty of an offence under subsection (1) shall be liable on summary conviction to a fine not exceeding level two on the standard scale.

32E Lump sum deductions: interim orders

(1) The Secretary of State may make an order under this section if it appears to the Secretary of State that a person (referred to in this section and sections 32F to 32J as 'the liable person') has failed to pay an amount of child support maintenance and—

(a) an amount stands to the credit of an account held by the liable person with a deposit-taker; or

(b) an amount not within paragraph (a) that is of a prescribed description is due or accruing to the liable person from another person (referred to in this section and sections 32F to 32J as the 'third party').

(2) An order under this section—

(a) may not be made by virtue of subsection (1)(a) in respect of an account of a prescribed description; and

(b) may be made by virtue of subsection (1)(a) in respect of a joint account which is held by the liable person and one or more other persons, and which is not of a description prescribed under paragraph (a) of this subsection, if (but only if) regulations made by the Secretary of State so provide.

(3) The Secretary of State may by regulations make provision as to conditions that are to be disregarded in determining whether an amount is due or accruing to the liable person for the purposes of subsection (1)(b).

(4) An order under this section—

(a) shall be expressed to be directed at the deposit-taker or third party in question;

(b) if made by virtue of subsection (1)(a), shall specify the account in respect of which it is made; and

(c) shall specify the amount of arrears of child support maintenance in respect of which the Secretary of State proposes to make an order under section 32F.

(5) An order under this section may specify an amount of arrears due under a maintenance calculation which is the subject of an appeal only if it appears to the Secretary of State—

(a) that liability for the amount would not be affected were the appeal to succeed; or

(b) where paragraph (a) does not apply, that the making of an order under section 32F in respect of the amount would nonetheless be fair in all the circumstances.

(6) The Secretary of State shall serve a copy of any order made under this section on—

(a) the deposit-taker or third party at which it is directed;

(b) the liable person; and

(c) if the order is made in respect of a joint account, the other account-holders.

(7) An order under this section shall come into force at the time at which it is served on the deposit-taker or third party at which it is directed.

(8) An order under this section shall cease to be in force at the earliest of the following—

(a) the time at which the prescribed period ends;

(b) the time at which the order under this section lapses or is discharged; and

(c) the time at which an order under section 32F made in pursuance of the proposal specified in the order under this section is served on the deposit-taker or third party at which that order is directed.

(9) Where regulations have been made under section 29(3)(a), a person liable to pay an amount of child support maintenance is to be taken for the purposes of this section to have failed to pay the

amount unless it is paid to or through the person specified in, or by virtue of, the regulations for the case in question.

32F   Lump sum deductions: final orders

(1) The Secretary of State may make an order under this section in pursuance of a proposal specified in an order under section 32E if—

    (a) the order in which the proposal was specified ('the interim order') is in force;

    (b) the period prescribed for the making of representations to the Secretary of State in respect of the proposal specified in the interim order has expired; and

    (c) the Secretary of State has considered any representations made to the Secretary of State during that period.

(2) An order under this section—

    (a) shall be expressed to be directed at the deposit-taker or third party at which the interim order was directed;

    (b) if the interim order was made by virtue of section 32E(1)(a), shall specify the account specified in the interim order; and

    (c) shall specify the amount of arrears of child support maintenance in respect of which it is made.

(3) The amount so specified—

    (a) shall not exceed the amount of arrears specified in the interim order which remain unpaid at the time at which the order under this section is made; and

    (b) if the order is made in respect of a joint account, shall not exceed the amount that appears to the Secretary of State to be fair in all the circumstances.

(4) In determining the amount to be specified in an order made in respect of a joint account the Secretary of State shall have particular regard—

    (a) to the amount contributed to the account by each of the account-holders; and

    (b) to such other matters as may be prescribed.

(5) An order under this section may specify an amount of arrears due under a maintenance calculation which is the subject of an appeal only if it appears to the Secretary of State—

    (a) that liability for the amount would not be affected were the appeal to succeed; or

    (b) where paragraph (a) does not apply, that the making of an order under this section in respect of the amount would nonetheless be fair in all the circumstances.

(6) The Secretary of State shall serve a copy of any order made under this section on—

    (a) the deposit-taker or third party at which it is directed;

    (b) the liable person; and

    (c) if the order is made in respect of a joint account, the other account-holders.

32G   Orders under sections 32E and 32F: freezing of accounts etc.

(1) During the relevant period, an order under section 32E or 32F which specifies an account held with a deposit-taker shall operate as an instruction to the deposit-taker not to do anything that would reduce the amount standing to the credit of the account below the amount specified in the order (or, if already below that amount, that would further reduce it).

(2) During the relevant period, any other order under section 32E or 32F shall operate as an instruction to the third party at which it is directed not to do anything that would reduce the amount due to the liable person below the amount specified in the order (or, if already below that amount, that would further reduce it).

(3) Subsections (1) and (2) have effect subject to regulations made under section 32I(1).

(4) In this section 'the relevant period', in relation to an order under section 32E, means the period during which the order is in force.

(5) In this section and section 32H 'the relevant period', in relation to an order under section 32F, means the period which—

    (a) begins with the service of the order on the deposit-taker or third party at which it is directed; and

(b) (subject to subsection (6)) ends with the end of the period during which an appeal can be brought against the order by virtue of regulations under section 32J(5).

(6) If an appeal is brought by virtue of the regulations, the relevant period ends at the time at which—

(a) proceedings on the appeal (including any proceedings on a further appeal) have been concluded; and

(b) any period during which a further appeal may ordinarily be brought has ended.

(7) References in this section and sections 32H and 32J to the amount due to the liable person are to be read as references to the total of any amounts within section 32E(1)(b) that are due or accruing to the liable person from the third party in question.

32H   Orders under section 32F: deductions and payments

(1) Once the relevant period has ended, an order under section 32F which specifies an account held with a deposit-taker shall operate as an instruction to the deposit-taker—

(a) If the amount standing to the credit of the account is less than the remaining amount, to pay to the Secretary of State the amount standing to the credit of the account; and

(b) otherwise, to deduct from the account and pay to the Secretary of State the remaining amount.

(2) If an amount of arrears specified in the order remains unpaid after any payment required by subsection (1) has been made, the order shall operate until the relevant time as an instruction to the deposit-taker—

(a) to pay to the Secretary of State any amount (not exceeding the remaining amount) standing to the credit of the account specified in the order; and

(b) not to do anything else that would reduce the amount standing to the credit of the account.

(3) Once the relevant period has ended, any other order under section 32F shall operate as an instruction to the third party at which it is directed—

(a) if the amount due to the liable person is less than the remaining amount, to pay to the Secretary of State the amount due to the liable person; and

(b) otherwise, to deduct from the amount due to the liable person and pay to the Secretary of State the remaining amount.

(4) If an amount of arrears specified in the order remains unpaid after any payment required by subsection (3) has been made, the order shall operate until the relevant time as an instruction to the third party—

(a) to pay to the Secretary of State any amount (not exceeding the remaining amount) due to the liable person; and

(b) not to do anything else that would reduce any amount due to the liable person.

(5) This section has effect subject to regulations made under sections 32I(1) and 32J(2)(c).

(6) In this section—

'the relevant time' means the earliest of the following—

(a) the time at which the remaining amount is paid;

(b) the time at which the order lapses or is discharged; and

(c) the time at which a prescribed event occurs or prescribed circumstances arise;

'the remaining amount', in relation to any time, means the amount of arrears specified in the order under section 32F which remains unpaid at that time.

32I   Power to disapply sections 32G(1) and (2) and 32H(2)(b) and (4)(b)

(1) The Secretary of State may by regulations make provision as to circumstances in which things that would otherwise be in breach of sections 32G(1) and (2) and 32H(2)(b) and (4)(b) may be done.

(2) Regulations under subsection (1) may require the Secretary of State's consent to be obtained in prescribed circumstances.

(3) Regulations under subsection (1) which require the Secretary of State's consent to be obtained may provide for an application for that consent to be made—

(a) by the deposit-taker or third party at which the order under section 32E or 32F is directed;

(b) by the liable person; and

(c) if the order is made in respect of a joint account, by any of the other account-holders.

(4) If regulations under subsection (1) require the Secretary of State's consent to be obtained, the Secretary of State shall by regulations provide for a person of a prescribed description to have a right of appeal to a court against the withholding of that consent.

(5) Regulations under subsection (4) may include—

(a) provision with respect to the period within which a right of appeal under the regulations may be exercised;

(b) provision with respect to the powers of the court to which the appeal under the regulations lies.

32J Regulations about orders under section 32E or 32F

(1) The Secretary of State may by regulations make provision with respect to orders under section 32E or 32F.

(2) The regulations may, in particular, make provision—

(a) as to circumstances in which amounts standing to the credit of an account are to be disregarded for the purposes of sections 32E, 32G and 32H;

(b) as to the payment to the Secretary of State of sums deducted under an order under section 32F;

(c) allowing a deposit-taker or third party at which an order under section 32F is directed to deduct from the amount standing to the credit of the account specified in the order, or due to the liable person, a prescribed amount towards its administrative costs before making any payment to the Secretary of State required by section 32H;

(d) with respect to notifications to be given to the liable person (and, in the case of an order made in respect of a joint account, to the other account-holders) as to amounts deducted, and amounts paid, under an order under section 32F;

(e) requiring a deposit-taker or third party at which an order under section 32E or 32F is directed to supply information of a prescribed description to the Secretary of State, or to notify the Secretary of State if a prescribed event occurs or prescribed circumstances arise;

(f) for the variation of an order under section 32E or 32F;

(g) for an order under section 32E or 32F to lapse in such circumstances as may be prescribed;

(h) as to the revival of an order under section 32E or 32F in such circumstances as may be prescribed;

(i) allowing or requiring an order under section 32E or 32F to be discharged.

(3) Where regulations under subsection (1) make provision for the variation of an order under section 32E or 32F, the power to vary the order shall not be exercised so as to increase the amount of arrears of child support maintenance specified in the order.

(4) The Secretary of State may by regulations make provision with respect to priority as between an order under section 32F and—

(a) any other order under that section;

(b) any order under any other enactment relating to England and Wales which provides for payments to be made from amounts to which the order under section 32F relates;

(c) any diligence done in Scotland against amounts to which the order under section 32F relates.

(5) The Secretary of State shall by regulations make provision for any person affected by an order under section 32F to have a right to appeal to a court against the making of the order.

(6) On an appeal under regulations under subsection (5), the court shall not question the maintenance calculation by reference to which the order under section 32F was made.

(7) Regulations under subsection (5) may include—

    (a) provision with respect to the period within which a right of appeal under the regulations may be exercised;

    (b) provision with respect to the powers of the court to which the appeal under the regulations lies.

32K   Lump sum deduction orders: offences

(1) A person who fails to comply with the requirements of—

    (a) an order under section 32E or 32F; or

    (b) any regulation under section 32J which is designated by the regulations for the purposes of this paragraph,

commits an offence.

(2) It shall be a defence for a person charged with an offence under subsection (1) to prove that the person took all reasonable steps to comply with the requirements in question.

(3) A person guilty of an offence under subsection (1) shall be liable on summary conviction to a fine not exceeding level two on the standard scale.

32L   Orders preventing avoidance

(1) The Secretary of State may apply to the court, on the grounds that a person—

    (a) has failed to pay an amount of child support maintenance, and

    (b) with the intention of avoiding payment of child support maintenance, is about to make a disposition or to transfer out of the jurisdiction or otherwise deal with any property,

for an order restraining or, in Scotland, interdicting the person from doing so.

(2) The Secretary of State may apply to the court, on the grounds that a person—

    (a) has failed to pay an amount of child support maintenance, and

    (b) with the intention of avoiding payment of child support maintenance, has at any time made a reviewable disposition,

for an order setting aside or, in Scotland, reducing the disposition.

(3) If the court is satisfied of the grounds mentioned in subsection (1) or (2) it may make an order under that subsection.

(4) Where the court makes an order under subsection (1) or (2) it may make such consequential provision by order or directions as it thinks fit for giving effect to the order (including provision requiring the making of any payments or the disposal of any property).

(5) Any disposition is a reviewable disposition for the purposes of subsection (2), unless it was made for valuable or, in Scotland, adequate consideration (other than marriage) to a person who, at the time of the disposition, acted in relation to it in good faith and without notice of an intention to avoid payment of child support maintenance.

(6) Subsection (7) applies where an application is made under this section with respect to—

    (a) a disposition or other dealing with property which is about to take place, or

    (b) a disposition which took place after the making of the application on which the maintenance calculation concerned was made.

(7) If the court is satisfied—

    (a) in a case falling within subsection (1), that the disposition or other dealing would (apart from this section) have the consequence of making ineffective a step that has been or may be taken to recover the amount outstanding, or

    (b) in a case falling within subsection (2), that the disposition has had that consequence,

it is to be presumed, unless the contrary is shown, that the person who disposed of or is about to dispose of or deal with the property did so or, as the case may be, is about to do so, with the intention of avoiding payment of child support maintenance.

(8) In this section 'disposition' does not include any provision contained in a will or codicil but, with that exception, includes any conveyance, assurance or gift of property of any description, whether made by an instrument or otherwise.

(9) This section does not apply to a disposition made before the coming into force of section 24 of the Child Maintenance and Other Payments Act 2008.

(10) In this section 'the court' means—

(a) in relation to England and Wales, the High Court or the family court;

(b) ...

32M Liability orders

(1) If it appears to the Secretary of State that a person has failed to pay an amount of child support maintenance, it may make an order against the person in respect of that amount.

(2) An order under subsection (1) (a 'liability order') may be made in respect of an amount due under a maintenance calculation which is the subject of an appeal only if it appears to the Secretary of State—

(a) that liability for the amount would not be affected were the appeal to succeed, or

(b) where paragraph (a) does not apply, that the making of a liability order in respect of the amount would nonetheless be fair in all the circumstances.

(3) A liability order shall not come into force before—

(a) the end of the period during which an appeal can be brought under section 20 against the making of the order, and

(b) if an appeal is brought under section 20, the time at which proceedings on the appeal (including any proceedings on a further appeal) have been concluded and any period during which a further appeal may ordinarily be brought has ended.

(4) Where regulations have been made under section 29(3)(a), a person liable to pay an amount of child support maintenance is to be taken for the purposes of this section to have failed to pay the amount, unless it is paid to or through the person specified in, or by virtue of, the regulations for the case in question.

32N Regulations about liability orders

(1) The Secretary of State may by regulations make provision with respect to liability orders.

(2) Regulations under subsection (1) may, in particular—

(a) make provision about the form and content of a liability order;

(b) make provision for a liability order not to come into force if, before it does so, the whole of the amount in respect of which it is made is paid;

(c) make provision for the discharge of a liability order;

(d) make provision for the revival of a liability order in prescribed circumstances.

...

35 Enforcement of liability orders by taking control of goods

(1) Where a liability order has been made against a person ('the liable person'), the Secretary of State may use the procedure in Schedule 12 to the Tribunals, Courts and Enforcement Act 2007 (taking control of goods) to recover the amount in respect of which the order was made, to the extent that it remains unpaid.

...

36 Enforcement in county courts

(1) Where a liability order has been made against a person, the amount in respect of which the order was made, to the extent that it remains unpaid, shall be recoverable by means of a third party debt order or a charging order, as if it were payable under a county court order.

...

39B Disqualification for holding or obtaining driving licence or United Kingdom passport

(1) The Secretary of State may make an order under this section (referred to in this section and sections 39C to 39F as a 'disqualification order') against a person where—

(a) the Secretary of State has sought to recover an amount from the person by means of taking enforcement action by virtue of section 35 or 38, or by means of a third party debt order or a charging order by virtue of section 36;

(b) the whole or any part of the amount remains unpaid; and

(c) the Secretary of State is of the opinion that there has been wilful refusal or culpable neglect on the part of the person.

(2) For the purposes of subsection (1)(a), the Secretary of State is to be taken to have sought to recover an amount by means of a charging order if an interim charging order has been made, whether or not any further steps have been taken to recover the amount.

(3) A disqualification order shall provide that the person against whom it is made is disqualified for holding or obtaining—

(a) a driving licence,

(b) a United Kingdom passport, or

(c) both a driving licence and a United Kingdom passport,

while the order has effect.

(4) Before making a disqualification order against a person, the Secretary of State shall consider whether the person needs the relevant document in order to earn a living.

(5) A disqualification order shall specify the amount in respect of which it is made.

(6) That amount shall be the aggregate of—

(a) the amount sought to be recovered as mentioned in subsection (1)(a), or so much of it as remains unpaid; and

(b) the amount which the person against whom the order is made is required to pay by the order under section 39DA(1).

(7) The Secretary of State shall serve a copy of the disqualification order (together with a copy of the order under section 39DA(1)) on the person against whom it is made.

(8) In this section—

'driving licence' means a licence to drive a motor vehicle granted under Part 3 of the Road Traffic Act 1988;

'relevant document', in relation to a disqualification order made against a person, means the document (or documents) for the holding or obtaining of which the person is disqualified by the order;

'United Kingdom passport' has the same meaning as in the Immigration Act 1971 (see section 33(1)).

39C Period for which disqualification orders are to have effect

(1) A disqualification order shall specify the period for which it is to have effect.

(1A) That period shall not exceed 12 months (subject to any extension under section 39CA or 39CB).

(1B) That period shall begin to run with—

(a) the first day after the end of the period within which an appeal may be brought against the order under section 39CB(1); or

(b) if the running of the period is suspended at that time, the first day when its running is no longer suspended.

(2) On making a disqualification order, the Secretary of State may include in the order provision suspending the running of the period for which the order is to have effect until such day and on such conditions (if any) as the Secretary of State thinks just.

(3) After making a disqualification order, the Secretary of State may by order suspend the running of the period for which it has effect until such day and on such conditions (if any) as the Secretary of State thinks just.

(4) The powers conferred by subsections (2) and (3) may be exercised by the Secretary of State only—

(a) if the person against whom the disqualification order is made agrees to pay the amount specified in the order; or

(b) if the Secretary of State is satisfied that the suspension in question is justified by exceptional circumstances.

(5) The Secretary of State may make a further disqualification order if the amount specified in a previous disqualification order has not been paid in full by the end of the period for which the order has effect.

39CA   Surrender of relevant documents

(1) A person against whom a disqualification order is made who holds any relevant document shall surrender it in the prescribed manner to the prescribed person within the required period.

(2) For this purpose 'the required period' means the period of 7 days beginning with the start of the period for which the order has effect or has effect again following a period of suspension.

(3) But, if immediately before the end of the required period the person has a good reason for not surrendering any relevant document, the person shall instead surrender it as soon as practicable after the end of that period.

(4) The Secretary of State may by regulations make provision prescribing circumstances in which a person is, or is not, to be regarded for the purposes of subsection (3) as having a good reason for not surrendering any relevant document.

(5) The requirements imposed by subsections (1) and (3) cease to have effect if the period for which the disqualification order has effect is suspended or ends.

(6) A person who fails to comply with a requirement imposed by subsection (1) or (3) commits an offence.

(7) A person guilty of an offence under subsection (6) shall be liable on summary conviction to a fine not exceeding level 3 on the standard scale.

(8) On sentencing a person for an offence under that subsection the court may by order extend the period for which the disqualification order is to have effect by such period as may be specified in the order under this subsection.

(9) But the power conferred by subsection (8) may not be exercised so as to provide for the disqualification order to have effect for a period exceeding 2 years in total.

(10) In this section 'relevant document' has the same meaning as in section 39.

(11) Where this section applies in relation to a driving licence at any time before the commencement of Schedule 3 to the Road Safety Act 2006, any reference in this section to any relevant document includes the licence's counterpart (within the meaning of section 108(1) of the Road Traffic Act 1988).

39CB   Appeals against disqualification orders

(1) A person against whom a disqualification order is made may appeal to the court against the order within a prescribed period (which must begin with the first day on which that person had actual notice of the order).

(2) Where an appeal is brought under subsection (1), the running of the period for which the order has effect shall be suspended until the time at which the appeal is determined, withdrawn or discontinued.

(3) If—

(a) the person against whom a disqualification order is made does not bring an appeal within the period specified in subsection (1), and

(b) prescribed conditions are satisfied,

the court may grant leave for an appeal to be brought after the end of that period.

(4) On granting leave under subsection (3) the court may suspend the running of the period for which the order has effect until such time and on such conditions (if any) as it thinks just.

(5) On an appeal under this section the court—

(a) shall reconsider the exercise by the Secretary of State of the powers under section 39B; and

(b) may by order affirm, vary or revoke the disqualification order.

(6) On an appeal under this section the court shall not question—

    (a) the liability order by reference to which the Secretary of State acted as mentioned in section 39B(1)(a);

    (b) any liability order made against the same person after the disqualification order was made; or

    (c) the maintenance calculation by reference to which any liability order within paragraph (a) or (b) was made.

(7) The power under subsection (5) to vary a disqualification order includes power to extend the period for which it has effect; but that power may not be exercised so as to provide for it to have effect for a period exceeding 2 years in total.

(8) If, on appeal under this section, the court affirms or varies a disqualification order, the court shall substitute for the amount specified under section 39B(5) the aggregate of—

    (a) the amount sought to be recovered as mentioned in section 39B(1)(a), or so much of it as remains unpaid;

    (b) the amount which the person against whom the order was made is required to pay by the order under section 39DA(1), so far as remaining unpaid;

    (c) the amount which that person is required to pay by the order under section 39DA(2); and

    (d) if a liability order has been made against that person since the disqualification order was made, the amount in respect of which the liability order was made, so far as remaining unpaid.

(9) On the affirmation or variation of the disqualification order by the court, any existing suspension of the running of the period for which the order is to have effect shall cease.

(10) But the court may suspend the running of that period until such time and on such conditions (if any) as it thinks fit if—

    (a) the person against whom the disqualification order was made agrees to pay the amount specified in the order; or

    (b) the court is of the opinion that the suspension in question is justified by exceptional circumstances.

(11) If, on an appeal under this section, the court revokes a disqualification order, the court shall also revoke the order made under section 39DA(1).

(12) But subsection (11) does not apply if the court is of the opinion that, having regard to all the circumstances, it is reasonable to require the person against whom the disqualification order was made to pay the costs mentioned in section 39DA(1).

(13) In this section 'the court' means—

    (a) in relation to England and Wales, a magistrates' court;

    (b) …

39D Power to order search

(1) On an appeal under section 39CB the court may order the person against whom the disqualification order was made to be searched.

(2) Any money found on such a search shall, unless the court otherwise directs, be applied towards payment of any amount that would otherwise, on the affirmation or variation of the order, be substituted under section 39CB(8) for the amount specified under section 39B(5); and the balance (if any) shall be returned to the person searched.

(3) The court shall not allow the application under subsection (2) of money found on a search under subsection (1) if it is satisfied that the money does not belong to the person searched.

39DA Recovery of Secretary of State's costs

(1) On making a disqualification order against any person the Secretary of State shall also make an order requiring that person to pay an amount in respect of the costs incurred by the Secretary of State in exercising functions under section 39B.

(2) If on an appeal under section 39CB the court affirms or varies a disqualification order made against any person, the court shall also make an order requiring that person to pay an amount in

respect of the costs incurred by the Secretary of State in connection with the appeal ('the Secretary of State's appeal costs').

(3) If—

    (a) on an appeal under that section the court revokes a disqualification order made against any person, and

    (b) the court is satisfied that, having regard to all the circumstances, it is reasonable to require that person to pay an amount in respect of the Secretary of State's appeal costs,

the court shall also make an order requiring that person to pay an amount in respect of those costs.

(4) Any amount payable by virtue of an order made under this section shall be—

    (a) specified in the order; and

    (b) determined in accordance with regulations made by the Secretary of State.

(5) The provisions of this Act with respect to—

    (a) the collection of child support maintenance, and

    (b) the enforcement of an obligation to pay child support maintenance,

apply equally (with any necessary modifications) to amounts which a person is required to pay under this section.

39E Variation and revocation of orders following payment

(1) If part of the amount specified in a disqualification order is paid to any person authorised to receive it, the Secretary of State may, on an application made by the person against whom the order is made, by order—

    (a) reduce the period for which the disqualification order is to have effect; or

    (b) revoke the disqualification order.

(1A) The power conferred by subsection (1) shall be exercisable by the court instead of by the Secretary of State at any time when an appeal brought under section 39CB against the order has not been determined, withdrawn or discontinued.

(2) If the whole of the amount specified in a disqualification order is paid to any person authorised to receive it, the Secretary of State shall, on an application made by the person against whom the order is made, by order revoke the disqualification order.

39F Power to make supplementary provision

(1) The Secretary of State may by regulations make provision with respect to—

    (a) disqualification orders;

    (b) appeals against disqualification orders; and

    (c) orders under section 39DA.

(2) The regulations may, in particular, make provision—

    (a) as to the form and content of a disqualification order;

    (b) as to the surrender of documents under section 39CA and their return when the period for which a disqualification order has effect is suspended or has ended;

    (c) that a statement in writing to the effect that wages of any amount have been paid to a person during any period, purporting to be signed by or on behalf of the person's employer, shall be evidence (or, in Scotland, sufficient evidence) of the facts stated for the purposes of an appeal under section 39CB;

    (d) permitting or requiring the court to dismiss an appeal brought under that section where the person who brought it fails to appear at the hearing;

    (e) requiring the court to send notice to the Secretary of State of any order made on an appeal under that section;

    (f) as to the exercise by the Secretary of State and the court of the power conferred by section 39E(1);

    (g) as to the revival of a disqualification order in such circumstances as may be prescribed;

    (h) for sections 39C to 39E to have effect with prescribed modifications in cases where a person against whom a disqualification order has effect is outside the United Kingdom.

...

39H   Applications for curfew orders

(1)   The Secretary of State may apply to the court for an order requiring a person to remain, for periods specified in the order, at a place so specified (a 'curfew order') where—

    (a)   the Secretary of State has sought to recover an amount from the person by means of taking enforcement action by virtue of section 35 or 38, or by means of a third party debt order or a charging order by virtue of section 36;

    (b)   the whole or any part of the amount remains unpaid; and

    (c)   the Secretary of State is of the opinion that there has been wilful refusal or culpable neglect on the part of the person.

(2)   For the purposes of subsection (1)(a), the Secretary of State is to be taken to have sought to recover an amount by means of a charging order if an interim charging order has been made, whether or not any further steps have been taken to recover the amount.

(3)   On an application for a curfew order the court shall (in the presence of the person from whom the Secretary of State has sought to recover the amount) inquire as to—

    (a)   the person's means; and

    (b)   whether there has been wilful refusal or culpable neglect on the part of the person.

(4)   On an application for a curfew order the court shall not question—

    (a)   the liability order by reference to which the Secretary of State acted as mentioned in subsection (1)(a); or

    (b)   the maintenance calculation by reference to which that liability order was made.

(5)   If, but only if, the court is of the opinion that there has been wilful refusal or culpable neglect on the part of the person from whom the Secretary of State has sought to recover the amount, it may make a curfew order against the person.

(6)   The court may not make a curfew order against a person who is under the age of 18.

(7)   In this section and sections 39I to 39O 'the court' means—

    (a)   in England and Wales, a magistrates' court;

    (b)   …

39I   Curfew orders: duration etc.

(1)   The periods and places specified as mentioned in section 39H(1) may include different periods and different places for different days, but shall not include periods which amount to less than 2 hours or more than 12 hours in any one day.

(2)   A curfew order shall specify the period for which the requirements imposed by the order shall have effect.

(3)   The period so specified—

    (a)   shall not exceed 6 months; and

    (b)   shall begin to run with the day on which the order is made unless the order provides (subject to such conditions, if any, as may be specified in the order) for it to begin to run with a later day.

(4)   The court shall (so far as practicable) ensure that any requirement imposed by a curfew order is such as to avoid—

    (a)   any conflict with the religious beliefs of the person against whom the order is made; and

    (b)   any interference with the times (if any) at which that person normally works or attends any educational establishment.

(5)   On making a curfew order—

    (a)   a magistrates' court may not specify in the order any place outside England and Wales; and

    (b)   the sheriff may not specify in the order any place outside Scotland.

39J   Recovery of costs relating to curfew orders

(1)   On making a curfew order the court shall also make an order requiring the person against whom the curfew order is made to pay an amount (determined in accordance with regulations made by the Secretary of State) specified in the order in respect of—

(a) the costs of the application for the curfew order; and

(b) the costs of monitoring compliance with the requirements imposed by the curfew order.

(2) The provisions of this Act with respect to—

(a) the collection of child support maintenance; and

(b) the enforcement of an obligation to pay child support maintenance,

apply equally (with any necessary modifications) to amounts which a person is required to pay by an order under this section.

39K   Curfew orders: the amount due

(1) A curfew order shall specify the amount in respect of which it is made, which shall be the aggregate of—

(a) the amount sought to be recovered as mentioned in section 39H(1)(a), or so much of it as remains unpaid; and

(b) the amount which the person against whom the curfew order is made is required to pay by the order under section 39J.

(2) If part of the amount in respect of which a curfew order was made is paid to any person authorised to receive it, the court may, on an application by the Secretary of State or the person against whom the curfew order was made, by order—

(a) reduce the period for which the requirements imposed by the curfew order have effect;

(b) provide for that period to begin to run with a day later than that with which it would otherwise have begun to run;

(c) suspend the running of that period, or provide for any existing such suspension to be extended, until a day specified in the order; or

(d) revoke the curfew order.

(3) An order under subsection (2)(b) or (c) may include provision for its effect to be subject to specified conditions.

(4) On the hearing of an application made under subsection (2) the Secretary of State may make representations to the court as to which of the powers conferred by that subsection it would be appropriate for the court to exercise, and the person against whom the curfew order was made may reply to those representations.

(5) If the whole of the amount in respect of which a curfew order was made is paid to any person authorised to receive it, the court shall, on an application by the Secretary of State or the person against whom the order was made, by order revoke the curfew order.

(6) The Secretary of State may make a further application under section 39H if the amount in respect of which a curfew order was made has not been paid in full when the requirements imposed by the order cease to have effect.

39L   Power to order search

(1) On making a curfew order, the court may order the person against whom the order is made to be searched.

(2) Any money found on such a search shall, unless the court otherwise directs, be applied towards payment of the amount in respect of which the curfew order is made; and the balance (if any) shall be returned to the person searched.

(3) The court shall not allow the application under subsection (2) of money found on a search under this section if it is satisfied that the money does not belong to the person searched.

(4) The court may exercise the powers conferred on it by section 39K(2) and (5) without the need for an application where money found on a search under this section is applied towards payment of the amount in respect of which a curfew order is made.

39M   Monitoring of curfew orders

(1) A curfew order shall—

(a) provide for a person's compliance with the requirements imposed by the order to be monitored; and

(b) make a person specified in the order responsible for that monitoring.

(2) The court may not make a curfew order unless—

  (a) it has been notified by the Secretary of State that arrangements for monitoring compliance with the requirements imposed by such orders are available in the area in which the place proposed to be specified in the order is situated and the notice has not been withdrawn;

  (b) it is satisfied that the necessary provision can be made under those arrangements; and

  (c) it has the consent of any person (other than the person against whom the order is to be made) whose co-operation is necessary to secure the monitoring of compliance with the requirements imposed by the order.

(3) If a curfew order cannot be made because of the absence of any consent required by subsection (2)(c), the court may treat the application for the order as an application under section 40 (or, in the case of an application made to the sheriff, as an application under section 40A).

(4) The Secretary of State may by regulations make provision as to—

  (a) the cases or circumstances in which the person responsible for monitoring a person's compliance with the requirements imposed by a curfew order may allow that person to be absent from the place specified in the curfew order during a period so specified; and

  (b) the requirements which may be imposed in connection with such an absence.

39N Breaches of curfew orders

(1) The person responsible for monitoring a person's compliance with the requirements imposed by a curfew order, or the Secretary of State, may apply to the court where it appears that the person subject to the requirements in question has failed to comply with—

  (a) any of those requirements; or

  (b) any requirements imposed by virtue of section 39M(4).

(2) On any such application the court shall (in the presence of the person subject to the requirements in question) inquire as to whether the person has failed without reasonable excuse to comply with any of those requirements.

(3) If the court is of the opinion that the person has failed without reasonable excuse to comply with any of those requirements, it may—

  (a) issue a warrant of commitment against that person; or

  (b) by order provide for the requirements imposed by the curfew order to have effect for a specified further period.

(4) A warrant issued under subsection (3)(a) shall order the person against whom it is issued—

  (a) to be imprisoned for a period specified in the warrant; but

  (b) to be released (unless in custody for some other reason) on payment of the amount in respect of which the curfew order in question was made.

(5) A warrant issued under subsection (3)(a) may be directed to such person or persons as the court issuing it thinks fit.

(6) The power conferred by subsection (3)(b) may not be exercised so as to provide for the requirements imposed by the curfew order to have effect for a period exceeding 6 months after the making of the order under that subsection.

(7) Where, following the issue of a warrant under subsection (3)(a), part of the amount specified in the curfew order is paid to any person authorised to receive it, the court may, on an application by the Secretary of State or the person against whom the warrant was issued—

  (a) reduce the period specified in the warrant; or

  (b) order the release of the person against whom the warrant was issued.

(8) On the hearing of an application made under subsection (7) the Secretary of State may make representations to the court as to which of the powers conferred by that subsection it would be appropriate for the court to exercise, and the person against whom the warrant was issued may reply to those representations.

39O   Effect of custody on curfew orders and power to make curfew orders

(1) The court may not make a curfew order against a person at any time when the person is in custody for any reason.

(2) The running of the period during which the requirements imposed by a curfew order have effect shall be suspended for the whole of any day during any part of which the person against whom the order is made is in custody for any reason.

(3) If the period during which the requirements imposed by a curfew order have effect would have begun to run but for its being suspended by virtue of this section, that period shall instead begin to run with the first day when its running is no longer suspended.

39P   Power to make supplementary provision about curfew orders: England and Wales

(1) The Secretary of State may by regulations make provision for England and Wales with respect to curfew orders.

(2) The regulations may, in particular, make provision—

   (a) as to the form and content of a curfew order;
   (b) allowing an application for a curfew order to be renewed where no curfew order is made;
   (c) that a statement in writing to the effect that wages of any amount have been paid during any period to a person, purporting to be signed by or on behalf of that person's employer, shall be evidence of the facts stated;
   (d) that a justice of the peace may issue a summons to a person to appear before a magistrates' court and (if that person does not appear) may issue a warrant for that person's arrest;
   (e) that, for the purpose of securing a person's presence before a magistrates' court, a justice of the peace may issue a warrant for that person's arrest without issuing a summons;
   (f) as to the execution of a warrant for arrest;
   (g) for the amendment or revocation of requirements imposed by a curfew order, on an application made to a magistrates' court by the Secretary of State or the person against whom the order was made;
   (h) similar to that made by sections 39J, 39L and 39M(2) and (3), in relation to any amendment of a curfew order;
   (i) as to the exercise by a magistrates' court of the powers conferred by sections 39K(2) and (3) and 39N(7).

...

40   Commitment to prison

(2A) The Secretary of State may apply to a magistrates' court for the issue of a warrant committing a person to prison where—

   (a) the Secretary of State has sought to recover an amount from the person by means of taking enforcement action by virtue of section 35 or 38, or by means of a third party debt order or a charging order by virtue of section 36;
   (b) the whole or any part of the amount remains unpaid; and
   (c) the Secretary of State is of the opinion that there has been wilful refusal or culpable neglect on the part of the person from whom the Secretary of State has sought to recover the amount ('the liable person').

(2B) For the purposes of subsection (2A)(a), the Secretary of State is to be taken to have sought to recover an amount by means of a charging order if an interim charging order has been made, whether or not any further steps have been taken to recover the amount.

(2C) On an application under subsection (2A) the court shall (in the presence of the liable person) inquire as to—

   (a) the liable person's means; and
   (b) whether there has been wilful refusal or culpable neglect on the part of the liable person.

(2D) On an application under subsection (2A) the court shall not question—

    (a) the liability order by reference to which the Secretary of State acted as mentioned in paragraph (a) of that subsection; or

    (b) the maintenance calculation by reference to which that liability order was made.

(3) If, but only if, the court is of the opinion that there has been wilful refusal or culpable neglect on the part of the liable person it may—

    (a) issue a warrant of commitment against him; or

    (b) fix a term of imprisonment and postpone the issue of the warrant until such time and on such conditions (if any) as it thinks just.

(4) Any such warrant—

    (a) shall be made in respect of an amount equal to the aggregate of—

        (i) the amount sought to be recovered as mentioned in subsection (2A)(a), or so much of it as remains outstanding; and

        (ii) an amount (determined in accordance with regulations made by the Secretary of State) in respect of the costs of commitment; and

    (b) shall state that amount.

(5) No warrant may be issued under this section against a person who is under the age of 18.

(6) A warrant issued under this section shall order the liable person—

    (a) to be imprisoned for a specified period; but

    (b) to be released (unless he is in custody for some other reason) on payment of the amount stated in the warrant.

(7) The maximum period of imprisonment which may be imposed by virtue of subsection (6) shall be calculated in accordance with Schedule 4 to the Magistrates' Courts Act 1980 (maximum periods of imprisonment in default of payment) but shall not exceed six weeks.

(8) The Secretary of State may by regulations make provision for the period of imprisonment specified in any warrant issued under this section to be reduced where there is part payment of the amount in respect of which the warrant was issued.

(9) A warrant issued under this section may be directed to such person or persons as the court issuing it thinks fit.

(10) On acting as mentioned in subsection (3), the court may order the liable person to be searched.

(10A) Any money found on such a search shall, unless the court otherwise directs, be applied towards payment of the relevant amount; and the balance (if any) shall be returned to the person searched.

(10B) The reference in subsection (10A) to the relevant amount is—

    (a) where the order under subsection (10) is made by virtue of the court acting under subsection (3)(a), to the amount mentioned in subsection (4)(a);

    (b) where the order under subsection (10) is made by virtue of the court acting under subsection (3)(b), to the amount mentioned in subsection (4)(a)(i).

(10C) The court shall not allow the application under subsection (10A) of money found on a search under subsection (10) if it is satisfied that the money does not belong to the person searched.

(11) The Secretary of State may by regulations make provision—

    (a) as to the form of any warrant issued under this section;

    (b) allowing an application under this section to be renewed where no warrant is issued or term of imprisonment is fixed;

    (c) that a statement in writing to the effect that wages of any amount have been paid to the liable person during any period, purporting to be signed by or on behalf of his employer, shall be evidence of the facts stated;

    (d) that, for the purposes of enabling an inquiry to be made as to the liable person's conduct and means, a justice of the peace may issue a summons to him to appear before a magistrates' court and (if he does not obey) may issue a warrant for his arrest;

(e) that for the purpose of enabling such an inquiry, a justice of the peace may issue a warrant for the liable person's arrest without issuing a summons;

(f) as to the execution of a warrant for arrest.

...

41   Arrears of child support maintenance

(1) This section applies where—

(a) the Secretary of State is authorised under section 4 or 7 to recover child support maintenance payable by a non-resident parent in accordance with a maintenance calculation; and

(b) the non-resident parent has failed to make one or more payments of child support maintenance due from him in accordance with that calculation.

(2) Where the Secretary of State recovers any such arrears the Secretary of State may, in such circumstances as may be prescribed and to such extent as may be prescribed, retain them if the Secretary of State is satisfied that the amount of any benefit paid to or in respect of the person with care of the child or children in question would have been less had the non-resident parent made the payment or payments of child support maintenance in question.

(2A) In determining for the purposes of subsection (2) whether the amount of any benefit paid would have been less at any time than the amount which was paid at that time, in a case where the maintenance calculation had effect from a date earlier than that on which it was made, the calculation shall be taken to have been in force at that time.

(6) Any sums retained by the Secretary of State by virtue of this section shall be paid by it into the Consolidated Fund.

41A   Penalty payments

(1) The Secretary of State may by regulations make provision for the payment to the Secretary of State by non-resident parents who are in arrears with payments of child support maintenance of penalty payments determined in accordance with the regulations.

(2) The amount of a penalty payment in respect of any week may not exceed 25% of the amount of child support maintenance payable for that week, but otherwise is to be determined by the Secretary of State.

(3) The liability of a non-resident parent to make a penalty payment does not affect his liability to pay the arrears of child support maintenance concerned.

(4) Regulations under subsection (1) may, in particular, make provision—

(a) as to the time at which a penalty payment is to be payable;

(b) for the Secretary of State to waive a penalty payment, or part of it.

(5) The provisions of this Act with respect to—

(a) the collection of child support maintenance;

(b) the enforcement of an obligation to pay child support maintenance,

apply equally (with any necessary modifications) to penalty payments payable by virtue of regulations under this section.

(6) The Secretary of State shall pay penalty payments received by the Secretary of State into the Consolidated Fund.

41B   Repayment of overpaid child support maintenance

(1) This section applies where it appears to the Secretary of State that a non-resident parent has made a payment by way of child support maintenance which amounts to an overpayment by him of that maintenance and that—

(a) it would not be possible for the non-resident parent to recover the amount of the overpayment by way of an adjustment of the amount payable under a maintenance calculation; or

(b) it would be inappropriate to rely on an adjustment of the amount payable under a maintenance calculation as the means of enabling the non-resident parent to recover the amount of overpayment.

(1A) This section also applies where the non-resident parent has made a voluntary payment and it appears to the Secretary of State—

    (a) that he is not liable to pay child support maintenance; or

    (b) that he is liable, but some or all of the payment amounts to an overpayment,

and, in a case falling within paragraph (b), it also appears to it that subsection (1)(a) or (b) applies.

(2) The Secretary of State may make such payment to the non-resident parent by way of reimbursement, or partial reimbursement, of the overpayment as the Secretary of State considers appropriate.

(3) Where the Secretary of State has made a payment under this section the Secretary of State may, in such circumstances as may be prescribed, require the relevant person to pay to the Secretary of State the whole, or a specified proportion, of the amount of that payment.

(4) Any such requirement shall be imposed by giving the relevant person a written demand for the amount which the Secretary of State wishes to recover from him.

(5) Any sum which a person is required to pay to the Secretary of State under this section shall be recoverable from him by the Secretary of State as a debt due to the Crown.

(6) The Secretary of State may by regulations make provision in relation to any case in which—

    (a) one or more overpayments of child support maintenance are being reimbursed to the Secretary of State by the relevant person; and

    (b) child support maintenance has continued to be payable by the non-resident parent concerned to the person with care concerned, or again becomes so payable.

(7) For the purposes of this section—

    (a) a payment made by a person under a maintenance calculation which was not validly made; and

    (b) a voluntary payment made in the circumstances set out in subsection (1A)(a),

shall be treated as an overpayment of child support maintenance made by a non-resident parent.

(8) In this section 'relevant person', in relation to an overpayment, means the person with care to whom the overpayment was made.

(9) Any sum recovered by the Secretary of State under this section shall be paid by the Secretary of State into the Consolidated Fund.

41C Power to treat liability as satisfied

(1) The Secretary of State may by regulations—

    (a) make provision enabling the Secretary of State in prescribed circumstances to set off liabilities to pay child support maintenance to which this section applies;

    (b) make provision enabling the Secretary of State in prescribed circumstances to set off against a person's liability to pay child support maintenance to which this section applies a payment made by the person which is of a prescribed description.

(2) Liability to pay child support maintenance shall be treated as satisfied to the extent that it is the subject of setting off under regulations under subsection (1).

(3) In subsection (1), the references to child support maintenance to which this section applies are to child support maintenance for the collection of which the Secretary of State is authorised to make arrangements.

41D Power to accept part payment of arrears in full and final satisfaction

(1) The Secretary of State may, in relation to any arrears of child support maintenance, accept payment of part in satisfaction of liability for the whole.

(2) The Secretary of State must by regulations make provision with respect to the exercise of the power under subsection (1).

(3) The regulations must provide that unless one of the conditions in subsection (4) is satisfied the Secretary of State may not exercise the power under subsection (1) without the appropriate consent.

(4) The conditions are—

(a) that the Secretary of State would be entitled to retain the whole of the arrears under section 41(2) if the Secretary of State recovered them;

(b) that the Secretary of State would be entitled to retain part of the arrears under section 41(2) if the Secretary of State recovered them, and the part of the arrears that the Secretary of State would not be entitled to retain is equal to or less than the payment accepted under subsection (1).

(5) Unless the maintenance calculation was made under section 7, the appropriate consent is the written consent of the person with care with respect to whom the maintenance calculation was made.

(6) If the maintenance calculation was made under section 7, the appropriate consent is—

(a) the written consent of the child who made the application under section 7(1), and

(b) if subsection (7) applies, the written consent of the person with care of that child.

(7) This subsection applies if—

(a) the maintenance calculation was made under section 7(2), or

(b) the Secretary of State has made arrangements under section 7(3) on the application of the person with care.

41E   Power to write off arrears

(1) The Secretary of State may extinguish liability in respect of arrears of child support maintenance if it appears to the Secretary of State—

(a) that the circumstances of the case are of a description specified in regulations made by the Secretary of State, and

(b) that it would be unfair or otherwise inappropriate to enforce liability in respect of the arrears.

(2) The Secretary of State may by regulations make provision with respect to the exercise of the power under subsection (1).

Special cases

42   Special cases

(1) The Secretary of State may by regulations provide that in prescribed circumstances a case is to be treated as a special case for the purposes of this Act.

(2) Those regulations may, for example, provide for the following to be special cases—

(a) each parent of a child is a non-resident parent in relation to the child;

(b) there is more than one person who is a person with care in relation to the same child;

(c) there is more than one qualifying child in relation to the same non-resident parent but the person who is the person with care in relation to one of those children is not the person who is the person with care in relation to all of them;

(d) a person is a non-resident parent in relation to more than one child and the other parent of each of those children is not the same person;

(e) the person with care has care of more than one qualifying child and there is more than one non-resident parent in relation to those children;

(f) a qualifying child has his home in two or more separate households;

(g) the same persons are the parents of two or more children and each parent is—

(i)   a non-resident parent in relation to one or more of the children, and

(ii) a person with care in relation to one or more of the children.

(3) The Secretary of State may by regulations make provision with respect to special cases.

(4) Regulations made under subsection (3) may, in particular—

(a) modify any provision made by or under this Act, in its application to any special case or any special case falling within a prescribed category;

(b) make new provision for any such case; or

(c) provide for any prescribed provision made by or under this Act not to apply to any such case.

43   Recovery of child support maintenance by deduction from benefit

(1) The power of the Secretary of State to make regulations under section 5 of the Social Security Administration Act 1992 by virtue of subsection (1)(p) of that section may be exercised with a view to securing the making of payments in respect of child support maintenance by a non-resident parent.

(2) The reference in subsection (1) to the making of payments in respect of child support maintenance includes the recovery of—

(a) arrears of child support maintenance, and

(b) fees payable under section 6 of the Child Maintenance and Other Payments Act 2008.

(3) For the purposes of this section, the benefits to which section 5 of the 1992 Act applies are to be taken as including war disablement pensions and war widows' pensions (within the meaning of section 150 of the Social Security Contributions and Benefits Act 1992 (interpretation)).

43A   Recovery of arrears from deceased's estate

(1) The Secretary of State may by regulations make provision for the recovery from the estate of a deceased person of arrears of child support maintenance for which the deceased person was liable immediately before death.

(2) Regulations under subsection (1) may, in particular—

(a) make provision for arrears of child support maintenance for which a deceased person was so liable to be a debt payable by the deceased's executor or administrator out of the deceased's estate to the Secretary of State;

(b) make provision for establishing the amount of any such arrears;

(c) make provision about procedure in relation to claims under the regulations.

(3) Regulations under subsection (1) may include provision for proceedings (whether by appeal or otherwise) to be instituted, continued or withdrawn by the deceased's executor or administrator.

Jurisdiction

44   Jurisdiction

(1) The Secretary of State shall have jurisdiction to make a maintenance calculation with respect to a person who is—

(a) a person with care;

(b) a non-resident parent; or

(c) a qualifying child,

only if that person is habitually resident in the United Kingdom, except in the case of a non-resident parent who falls within subsection (2A).

(2) Where the person with care is not an individual, subsection (1) shall have effect as if paragraph (a) were omitted.

(2A) A non-resident parent falls within this subsection if he is not habitually resident in the United Kingdom, but is—

(a) employed in the civil service of the Crown, including Her Majesty's Diplomatic Service and Her Majesty's Overseas Civil Service;

(b) a member of the naval, military or air forces of the Crown, including any person employed by an association established for the purposes of Part XI of the Reserve Forces Act 1996;

(c) employed by a company of a prescribed description registered under the Companies Act 1985 in England and Wales or in Scotland, or under the Companies (Northern Ireland) Order 1986; or

(d) employed by a body of a prescribed description.

(4) The Secretary of State does not have jurisdiction under this section if the exercise of jurisdiction would be contrary to the jurisdictional requirements of the Maintenance Regulation.

(5) In subsection (4) 'the Maintenance Regulation' means Council Regulation (EC) No 4/2009 including as applied in relation to Denmark by virtue of the Agreement made on 19th October 2005 between the European Community and the Kingdom of Denmark.

45 Jurisdiction of courts in certain proceedings under this Act

(1) The Lord Chancellor... may by order make such provision as he considers necessary to secure that appeals, or such class of appeals as may be specified in the order—

(a) shall be made to a court instead of being made to the First-tier Tribunal; or

(b) shall be so made in such circumstances as may be so specified.

...

Miscellaneous and supplemental

46A Finality of decisions

(1) Subject to the provisions of this Act and to any provision made by or under Chapter 2 of Part 1 of the Tribunals, Courts and Enforcement Act 2007, any decision of the Secretary of State or the First-tier Tribunal made in accordance with the foregoing provisions of this Act shall be final.

(2) If and to the extent that regulations so provide, any finding of fact or other determination embodied in or necessary to such a decision, or on which such a decision is based, shall be conclusive for the purposes of—

(a) further such decisions;

(b) decisions made in accordance with sections 8 to 16 of the Social Security Act 1998, or with regulations under section 11 of that Act; and

(c) decisions made under the Vaccine Damage Payments Act 1979.

46B Matters arising as respects decisions

(1) Regulations may make provision as respects matters arising pending—

(a) any decision of the Secretary of State under section 11, 12 or 17;

(b) any decision of the First-tier Tribunal under section 20; or

(c) any decision of the Upper Tribunal in relation to a decision of the First-tier Tribunal under this Act.

(2) Regulations may also make provision as respects matters arising out of the revision under section 16, or on appeal, of any such decision as is mentioned in subsection (1).

...

49A Transfer of arrears

(1) The Secretary of State may by regulations make provision enabling the Secretary of State in prescribed circumstances to enter into arrangements ('transfer arrangements') under which liability in respect of arrears of child support maintenance becomes debt due to the person with whom the arrangements are entered into ('the transferee').

(2) Liability which is the subject of transfer arrangements—

(a) ceases to be liability in relation to which the Secretary of State's functions with respect to collection and enforcement are exercisable, and

(b) becomes debt in which only the transferee has an interest.

(3) Regulations under subsection (1) must provide that unless one of the conditions in subsection (4) is satisfied the Secretary of State may not enter into transfer arrangements in relation to arrears of child support maintenance without the appropriate consent.

(4) The conditions are—

(a) that the Secretary of State would be entitled to retain the whole of the arrears under section 41(2) if the Secretary of State recovered them;

(b) that the Secretary of State would be entitled to retain part of the arrears under section 41(2) if the Secretary of State recovered them, and the part of the arrears that the Secretary of State would not be entitled to retain is equal to or less than the transfer payment.

(5) In subsection (4)(b), 'transfer payment' means—
    (a) the payment that the Secretary of State would receive from the transferee on the arrangements taking effect, and
    (b) such other payments under the transfer arrangements as may be prescribed.

(6) Unless the maintenance calculation was made under section 7, the appropriate consent is the written consent of the person with care with respect to whom the maintenance calculation was made.

(7) If the maintenance calculation was made under section 7, the appropriate consent is—
    (a) the written consent of the child who made the application under section 7(1), and
    (b) if subsection (8) applies, the written consent of the person with care of that child.

(8) This subsection applies if—
    (a) the maintenance calculation was made under section 7(2), or
    (b) the Secretary of State has made arrangements under section 7(3) on the application of the person with care.

(9) Regulations under subsection (1) may, in particular—
    (a) specify when arrears of child support maintenance may be the subject of transfer arrangements;
    (b) specify the descriptions of person with whom transfer arrangements may be entered into;
    (c) specify terms and conditions which transfer arrangements must include;
    (d) provide that a payment made to the Secretary of State under transfer arrangements may be treated for prescribed purposes as if it were a payment of child support maintenance.

(10) Regulations under subsection (1) may include—
    (a) provision with respect to the recovery of debt to which a person is entitled by virtue of transfer arrangements;
    (b) provision enabling the Secretary of State in prescribed circumstances to prevent a person entitled to debt by virtue of transfer arrangements from taking steps to recover it;
    (c) provision enabling the Secretary of State to supply information of a prescribed description to a person entitled to debt by virtue of transfer arrangements for the purpose of enabling the debt to be recovered.

49B   Disclosure of information relating to family proceedings

(1) Where this section applies, a disclosure of information relating to family proceedings made to the Secretary of State for the purposes of the Secretary of State's functions relating to child support, or to a person providing services to the Secretary of State for those purposes, by a party to the proceedings is not (if it would otherwise be) a contempt of court or punishable as a contempt of court.

(2) This section applies if—
    (a) the party is a person with care or non-resident parent in relation to a child,
    (b) child support maintenance is payable, or an application for a maintenance calculation has been made, in respect of the child, and
    (c) the party reasonably considers that the information is relevant to the exercise of the Secretary of State's functions relating to child support in relation to the child.

(3) This section also applies if—
    (a) an application for a maintenance calculation has been made under section 7(1) by the party, or child support maintenance is payable in accordance with a maintenance calculation made on an application made under section 7(1) by the party, and
    (b) the party reasonably considers that the information is relevant to the exercise of the Secretary of State's functions relating to child support in relation to the party.

(4) A disclosure by a party's representative is to be treated for the purposes of this section as a disclosure by the party, if the representative is instructed by the party to make the disclosure.

(5) In this section, 'representative' means—

   (a) in England and Wales—
     (i) a barrister or a solicitor, solicitor's employee or other authorised litigator (as defined in the Courts and Legal Services Act 1990) who has been instructed to act for a party in relation to the proceedings,
     (ii) a non-professional person who gives lay advice on behalf of an organisation in the lay advice sector, or
     (iii) any person permitted by the court to sit beside an unrepresented litigant in court to assist that litigant by prompting, taking notes and giving advice to the litigant;
   (b) ...
  (6) This section does not apply if the court dealing with the proceedings so directs.

49C Meaning of 'family proceedings'

  (1) In section 49B, 'family proceedings' means any of the following proceedings commenced on or after the day on which that section comes into force—
   (a) proceedings for ancillary relief (within the meaning of subsection (2));
   (b) proceedings under section 17 of the Married Women's Property Act 1882 (questions between husband and wife as to property);
   (c) proceedings under any of the following provisions of the 1973 Act—
     (i) section 27 (financial provision in cases of neglect to maintain);
     (ii) section 35 (alteration of maintenance agreements);
   (d) proceedings under Part 1 of the Domestic Proceedings and Magistrates' Courts Act 1978 (powers of court to make orders for financial provision);
   (e) proceedings relating to orders for financial provision within the meaning of section 8 of the Family Law (Scotland) Act 1984;
   (f) proceedings relating to an action for aliment within the meaning of section 2 of that Act;
   (g) proceedings under Part 3 of the Matrimonial and Family Proceedings Act 1984 (financial relief in England and Wales after overseas divorce etc.);
   (h) proceedings under Schedule 1 to the Children Act 1989 (financial provision for children);
   (i) proceedings under sections 33 to 40 of the Family Law Act 1996 (occupation orders);
   (j) proceedings under any of the following provisions of the 2004 Act—
     (i) section 66 (disputes between civil partners about property);
     (ii) paragraph 41 of Schedule 5 (orders where failure to maintain);
     (iii) paragraph 69 of Schedule 5 (alteration of maintenance agreements by the court);
     (iv) Schedule 6 (financial relief in magistrates' courts etc.);
     (v) Schedule 7 (financial relief in England and Wales after overseas dissolution etc. of a civil partnership).
  (2) In subsection (1), 'ancillary relief' means any of the following—
   (a) an order under section 37(2)(b) or (c) of the 1973 Act or paragraph 74(3) or (4) of Schedule 5 to the 2004 Act (avoidance of disposition orders);
   (b) any of the orders mentioned in section 21(1) of the 1973 Act (except an order under section 27(6) of that Act) or any of the orders mentioned in paragraph 2(1) of Schedule 5 to the 2004 Act (financial provision orders) made under Part 1 of that Schedule;
   (c) an order under section 22 of the 1973 Act (orders for maintenance pending suit);
   (d) an order under paragraph 38 of Schedule 5 to the 2004 Act (orders for maintenance pending outcome of proceedings);
   (e) any of the orders mentioned in section 21(2) of the 1973 Act or any of the orders mentioned in paragraph 7(1) of Schedule 5 to the 2004 Act (property adjustment orders);
   (f) an order under section 31 of the 1973 Act or an order under Part 11 of Schedule 5 to the 2004 Act (variation orders);
   (g) an order under section 24B of the 1973 Act or an order under paragraph 15 of Schedule 5 to the 2004 Act (pension sharing orders).

(3) The Secretary of State may by order amend this section so as to provide that 'family proceedings' in section 49B includes proceedings of a description specified in the order, other than proceedings commenced before the day on which the order comes into force.

(4) An order under subsection (3) may be made only with the consent of the Lord Chancellor.

(5) In this section—

'the 1973 Act' means the Matrimonial Causes Act 1973;

'the 2004 Act' means the Civil Partnership Act 2004.

49D Disclosure of information to credit reference agencies

(1) Subject to subsection (3), the Secretary of State may supply qualifying information to a credit reference agency for use for the purpose of furnishing information relevant to the financial standing of individuals.

(2) The reference in subsection (1) to qualifying information is to information which—

(a) is held by the Secretary of State for the purposes of this Act,

(b) relates to a person who is liable to pay child support maintenance, and

(c) is of a prescribed description.

(3) Information may not be supplied under subsection (1) without the consent of the person to whom it relates, unless a liability order against that person is in force.

(4) No provision may be made under section 14(3) authorising the supply of information by the Secretary of State to credit reference agencies.

(5) In this section, 'credit reference agency' has the same meaning as in the Consumer Credit Act 1974.

50 Unauthorised disclosure of information

(1) Any person who is, or has been, employed in employment to which this subsection applies is guilty of an offence if, without lawful authority, he discloses any information which—

(a) was acquired by him in the course of that employment; and

(b) relates to a particular person.

...

(2) It is not an offence under this section—

(a) to disclose information in the form of a summary or collection of information so framed as not to enable information relating to any particular person to be ascertained from it; or

(b) to disclose information which has previously been disclosed to the public with lawful authority.

(3) It is a defence for a person charged with an offence under this section to prove that at the time of the alleged offence—

(a) he believed that he was making the disclosure in question with lawful authority and had no reasonable cause to believe otherwise; or

(b) he believed that the information in question had previously been disclosed to the public with lawful authority and had no reasonable cause to believe otherwise.

(4) A person guilty of an offence under this section shall be liable—

(a) on conviction on indictment, to imprisonment for a term not exceeding two years or a fine or both; or

(b) on summary conviction, to imprisonment for a term not exceeding six months or a fine not exceeding the statutory maximum or both.

...

50A Use of computers

Any decision falling to be made under or by virtue of this Act by the Secretary of State may be made, not only by a person authorised to exercise the Secretary of State's decision-making function, but also by a computer for whose operation such a person is responsible.

...

51A   Pilot schemes

(1) Any regulations made under this Act may be made so as to have effect for a specified period not exceeding 24 months.

(2) Regulations which, by virtue of subsection (1), are to have effect for a limited period are referred to in this section as a 'pilot scheme'.

(3) A pilot scheme may provide that its provisions are to apply only in relation to—

(a) one or more specified areas or localities;

(b) one or more specified classes of person;

(c) persons selected by reference to prescribed criteria, or on a sampling basis.

(4) A pilot scheme may make consequential or transitional provision with respect to the cessation of the scheme on the expiry of the specified period.

(5) A pilot scheme may be replaced by a further pilot scheme making the same or similar provision.

(6) This section does not apply to regulations under—

(a) subsection (2A) of section 20 as substituted by section 10 of the Child Support, Pensions and Social Security Act 2000;

(b) subsection (3A) of section 20 as it has effect apart from section 10 of the Child Support, Pensions and Social Security Act 2000.

...

54   Interpretation

(1) In this Act—

'non-resident parent' has the meaning given in section 3(2);

'application for a variation' means an application under section 28A or 28G;

'benefit Acts' means the Social Security Contributions and Benefits Act 1992 and the Social Security Administration Act 1992;

'charging order' has the same meaning as in section 1 of the Charging Orders Act 1979;

'child benefit' has the same meaning as in the Child Benefit Act 1975;

'child support maintenance' has the meaning given in section 3(6);

'curfew order' has the meaning given in section 39H(1);

'deduction from earnings order' has the meaning given in section 31(2);

'default maintenance decision' has the meaning given in section 12;

'deposit-taker' means a person who, in the course of a business, may lawfully accept deposits in the United Kingdom;

'disability living allowance' has the same meaning as in the benefit Acts;

'interim maintenance decision' has the meaning given in section 12;

'liability order' has the meaning given in section 32M(2);

'maintenance agreement' has the meaning given in section 9(1);

'maintenance calculation' means a calculation of maintenance made under this Act and, except in prescribed circumstances, includes a default maintenance decision and an interim maintenance decision.

'maintenance order' has the meaning given in section 8(11);

'parent', in relation to any child, means any person who is in law the mother or father of the child;

'parent with care' means a person who is, in relation to a child, both a parent and a person with care.

'parental responsibility', in the application of this Act—

(a) to England and Wales, has the same meaning as in the Children Act 1989;

...

'person with care' has the meaning given in section 3(3);

'prescribed' means prescribed by regulations made by the Secretary of State;

'qualifying child' has the meaning given in section 3(1).

'voluntary payment' has the meaning given in section 28J.

(2) The definition of 'deposit-taker' in subsection (1) is to be read with—

(a) section 22 of the Financial Services and Markets Act 2000;

(b) any relevant order under that section; and

(c) Schedule 2 to that Act.

55 Meaning of 'child'

(1) In this Act, 'child' means (subject to subsection (2)) a person who—

(a) has not attained the age of 16, or

(b) has not attained the age of 20 and satisfies such conditions as may be prescribed.

(2) A person who is or has been party to a marriage or civil partnership is not a child for the purposes of this Act.

(3) For the purposes of subsection (2), 'marriage' and 'civil partnership' include a void marriage and a void civil partnership respectively.

...

SCHEDULES

Section 11   # SCHEDULE 1

MAINTENANCE CALCULATIONS

PART I CALCULATION OF WEEKLY AMOUNT OF CHILD SUPPORT MAINTENANCE

General rule

1.—(1) Subject to paragraph 5A, the weekly rate of child support maintenance is the basic rate unless a reduced rate, a flat rate or the nil rate applies.

(2) Unless the nil rate applies, the amount payable weekly to a person with care is—

(a) the applicable rate, if paragraph 6 does not apply; or

(b) if paragraph 6 does apply, that rate as apportioned between the persons with care in accordance with paragraph 6,

as adjusted, in either case, by applying the rules about shared care in paragraph 7 or 8.

Basic rate

2.—(1) Subject to sub-paragraph (2), the basic rate is the following percentage of the non-resident parent's gross weekly income—

12% where the non-resident parent has one qualifying child;

16% where the non-resident parent has two qualifying children;

19% where the non-resident parent has three or more qualifying children.

(2) If the gross weekly income of the non-resident parent exceeds £800, the basic rate is the aggregate of the amount found by applying sub-paragraph (1) in relation to the first £800 of that income and the following percentage of the remainder—

9% where the non-resident parent has one qualifying child;

12% where the non-resident parent has two qualifying children;

15% where the non-resident parent has three or more qualifying children.

(3) If the non-resident parent also has one or more relevant other children, gross weekly income shall be treated for the purposes of sub-paragraphs (1) and (2) as reduced by the following percentage—

11% where the non-resident parent has one relevant other child;

14% where the non-resident parent has two relevant other children;

16% where the non-resident parent has three or more relevant other children.

Reduced rate

3.—(1) A reduced rate is payable if—

    (a) neither a flat rate nor the nil rate applies; and

    (b) the non-resident parent's gross weekly income is less than £200 but more than £100.

(2) The reduced rate payable shall be prescribed in, or determined in accordance with, regulations.

(3) The regulations may not prescribe, or result in, a rate of less than £7.

Flat rate

4.—(1) Except in a case falling within sub-paragraph (2), a flat rate of £7 is payable if the nil rate does not apply and—

    (a) the non-resident parent's gross weekly income is £100 or less; or

    (b) he receives any benefit, pension or allowance prescribed for the purposes of this paragraph of this sub-paragraph; or

    (c) he or his partner (if any) receives any benefit prescribed for the purposes of this paragraph of this sub-paragraph.

(2) A flat rate of a prescribed amount is payable if the nil rate does not apply and—

    (a) the non-resident parent has a partner who is also a non-resident parent;

    (b) the partner is a person with respect to whom a maintenance calculation is in force; and

    (c) the non-resident parent or his partner receives any benefit prescribed under subparagraph (1)(c).

(3) The benefits, pensions and allowances which may be prescribed for the purposes of sub-paragraph (1)(b) include ones paid to the non-resident parent under the law of a place outside the United Kingdom.

Nil rate

5.—The rate payable is nil if the non-resident parent—

    (a) is of a prescribed description; or

    (b) has a gross weekly income of below £7.

Non-resident parent party to other maintenance arrangement

5A.—(1) This paragraph applies where—

    (a) the non-resident parent is a party to a qualifying maintenance arrangement with respect to a child of his who is not a qualifying child, and

    (b) the weekly rate of child support maintenance apart from this paragraph would be the basic rate or a reduced rate or calculated following agreement to a variation where the rate would otherwise be a flat rate or the nil rate.

(2) The weekly rate of child support maintenance is the greater of £7 and the amount found as follows.

(3) First, calculate the amount which would be payable if the non-resident parent's qualifying children also included every child with respect to whom the non-resident parent is a party to a qualifying maintenance arrangement.

(4) Second, divide the amount so calculated by the number of children taken into account for the purposes of the calculation.

(5) Third, multiply the amount so found by the number of children who, for purposes other than the calculation under sub-paragraph (3), are qualifying children of the non-resident parent.

(6) For the purposes of this paragraph, the non-resident parent is a party to a qualifying maintenance arrangement with respect to a child if the non-resident parent is—

    (a) liable to pay maintenance or aliment for the child under a maintenance order, or

    (b) a party to an agreement of a prescribed description which provides for the non-resident parent to make payments for the benefit of the child,

and the child is habitually resident in the United Kingdom.

Apportionment

6.—(1) If the non-resident parent has more than one qualifying child and in relation to them there is more than one person with care, the amount of child support maintenance payable is (subject to paragraph 7 or 8) to be determined by apportioning the rate between the persons with care.

(2) The rate of maintenance liability is to be divided by the number of qualifying children, and shared among the persons with care according to the number of qualifying children in relation to whom each is a person with care.

Shared care—basic and reduced rate

7.—(1) This paragraph applies where the rate of child support maintenance payable is the basic rate or a reduced rate or is determined under paragraph 5A.

(2) If the care of a qualifying child is, or is to be, shared between the non-resident parent and the person with care, so that the non-resident parent from time to time has care of the child overnight, the amount of child support maintenance which he would otherwise have been liable to pay the person with care, as calculated in accordance with the preceding paragraphs of this Part of this Schedule, is to be decreased in accordance with this paragraph.

(3) First, there is to be a decrease according to the number of such nights which the Secretary of State determines there to have been, or expects there to be, or both during a prescribed twelve-month period.

(4) The amount of that decrease for one child is set out in the following Table—

Number of nights	Fraction to subtract
52 to 103	One-seventh
104 to 155	Two-sevenths
156 to 174	Three-sevenths
175 or more	One-half

(5) If the person with care is caring for more than one qualifying child of the non-resident parent, the applicable decrease is the sum of the appropriate fractions in the Table divided by the number of such qualifying children.

(6) If the applicable fraction is one-half in relation to any qualifying child in the care of the person with care, the total amount payable to the person with care is then to be further decreased by £7 for each such child.

(7) If the application of the preceding provisions of this paragraph would decrease the weekly amount of child support maintenance (or the aggregate of all such amounts) payable by the non-resident parent to the person with care (or all of them) to less than £7, he is instead liable to pay child support maintenance at the rate of £7 a week, apportioned (if appropriate) in accordance with paragraph 6.

Shared care—flat rate

8.—(1) This paragraph applies only if—

(a) the rate of child support maintenance payable is a flat rate; and

(b) that rate applies because the non-resident parent falls within paragraph 4(1)(b) or (c) or 4(2).

(2) If the care of a qualifying child is, or is to be, shared as mentioned in paragraph 7(2) for at least 52 nights during a prescribed 12-month period, the amount of child support maintenance payable by the non-resident parent to the person with care of that child is nil.

Regulations about shared care

9.—(1) The Secretary of State may by regulations provide—

(za) for how it is to be determined whether the care of a qualifying child is to be shared as mentioned in paragraph 7(2);

(a) for which nights are to count for the purposes of shared care under paragraphs 7 and 8;

(b) for what counts, or does not count, as 'care' for those purposes; and

(ba) for how it is to be determined how many nights count for those purposes;

(2) Regulations under sub-paragraph (1)(ba) may include provision enabling the Secretary of State to proceed for a prescribed period on the basis of a prescribed assumption.

Gross weekly income

10.—(1) For the purposes of this Schedule, gross weekly income is to be determined in such manner as is provided for in regulations.

(2) The regulations may, in particular—

(a) provide for determination in prescribed circumstances by reference to income of a prescribed description in a prescribed past period;

(b) provide for the Secretary of State to estimate any income or make an assumption as to any fact where, in the Secretary of State's view, the information at the Secretary of State's disposal is unreliable or insufficient, or relates to an atypical period in the life of the non-resident parent.

(3) Any amount of gross weekly income (calculated as above) over £3,000 is to be ignored for the purposes of this Schedule.

Regulations about rates, figures, etc.

10A.—(1) The Secretary of State may by regulations provide that—

(a) paragraph 2 is to have effect as if different percentages were substituted for those set out there;

(b) paragraph 2(2), 3(1) or (3), 4(1), 5, 5A(2), 7(7) or 10(3) is to have effect as if different amounts were substituted for those set out there.

(2) The Secretary of State may by regulations provide that—

(a) the Table in paragraph 7(4) is to have effect as if different numbers of nights were set out in the first column and different fractions were substituted for those set out in the second column;

(b) paragraph 7(6) is to have effect as if a different amount were substituted for that mentioned there, or as if the amount were an aggregate amount and not an amount for each qualifying child, or both.

Regulations about income

10B.—The Secretary of State may by regulations provide that, in such circumstances and to such extent as may be prescribed—

(a) where the Secretary of State is satisfied that a person has intentionally deprived himself of a source of income with a view to reducing the amount of his gross weekly income, his gross weekly income shall be taken to include income from that source of an amount estimated by the Secretary of State;

(b) a person is to be treated as possessing income which he does not possess;

(c) income which a person does possess is to be disregarded.

References to various terms

10C.—(1) References in this Part of this Schedule to 'qualifying children' are to those qualifying children with respect to whom the maintenance calculation falls to be made or with respect to whom a maintenance calculation in respect of the non-resident parent has effect.

(2) References in this Part of this Schedule to 'relevant other children' are to—

(a) children other than qualifying children in respect of whom the non-resident parent or his partner receives child benefit under Part IX of the Social Security Contributions and Benefits Act 1992; and

(b) such other description of children as may be prescribed.

(3) In this Part of this Schedule, a person 'receives' a benefit, pension, or allowance for any week if it is paid or due to be paid to him in respect of that week.

(4) In this Part of this Schedule, a person's 'partner' is—

(a) if they are a couple, the other member of that couple;

(b) if the person is a husband or wife by virtue of a marriage entered into under a law which permits polygamy, another party to the marriage who is of the opposite sex and is a member of the same household.

(5) In sub-paragraph (4)(a), 'couple' means—

(a) a man and a woman who are married to each other and are members of the same household,

(b) a man and a woman who are not married to each other but are living together as husband and wife,

(c) two people of the same sex who are civil partners of each other and are members of the same household, or

(d) two people of the same sex who are not civil partners of each other but are living together as if they were civil partners.

(6) For the purposes of this paragraph, two people of the same sex are to be regarded as living together as if they were civil partners if, but only if, they would be regarded as living together as husband and wife were they instead two people of the opposite sex.

PART II GENERAL PROVISIONS ABOUT MAINTENANCE CALCULATIONS

Effective date of calculation

11.—(1) A maintenance calculation shall take effect on such date as may be determined in accordance with regulations made by the Secretary of State.

(2) That date may be earlier than the date on which the calculation is made.

Form of calculation

12.—Every maintenance calculation shall be made in such form and contain such information as the Secretary of State may direct.

...

Consolidated applications and calculations

14.—The Secretary of State may by regulations provide—

(a) for two or more applications for maintenance calculations to be treated, in prescribed circumstances, as a single application; and

(b) for the replacement, in prescribed circumstances, of a maintenance calculation made on the application of one person by a later maintenance calculation made on the application of that or any other person.

Separate calculations for different periods

15.—Where the Secretary of State is satisfied that the circumstances of a case require different amounts of child support maintenance to be calculated in respect of different periods, the Secretary of State may make separate maintenance calculations each expressed to have effect in relation to a different specified period.

Termination of calculations

16.—(1) A maintenance calculation shall cease to have effect—

    (a) on the death of the non-resident parent, or of the person with care, with respect to whom it was made;

    (b) on there no longer being any qualifying child with respect to whom it would have effect;

    (c) on the non-resident parent with respect to whom it was made ceasing to be a parent of—

        (i) the qualifying child with respect to whom it was made; or

        (ii) where it was made with respect to more than one qualifying child, all of the qualifying children with respect to whom it was made;

    ...

(10) A person with care with respect to whom a maintenance calculation is in force shall provide the Secretary of State with such information, in such circumstances, as may be prescribed, with a view to assisting the Secretary of State in determining whether the calculation has ceased to have effect.

(11) The Secretary of State may by regulations make such supplemental, incidental or transitional provision as he thinks necessary or expedient in consequence of the provisions of this paragraph.

...

SCHEDULE 4A   APPLICATIONS FOR A VARIATION

Interpretation

1.—In this Schedule, 'regulations' means regulations made by the Secretary of State.

Applications for a variation

2.—Regulations may make provision—

    (a) as to the procedure to be followed in considering an application for a variation;

    ...

Completion of preliminary consideration

3.—Regulations may provide for determining when the preliminary consideration of an application for a variation is to be taken to have been completed.

Information

4.—If any information which is required (by regulations under this Act) to be furnished to the Secretary of State in connection with an application for a variation has not been furnished within such period as may be prescribed, the Secretary of State may nevertheless proceed to consider the application.

Joint consideration of applications for a variation and appeals

5.—(1) Regulations may provide for two or more applications for a variation with respect to the same application for a maintenance calculation to be considered together.

    ...

SCHEDULE 4B   APPLICATIONS FOR A VARIATION: THE CASES AND CONTROLS

PART I THE CASES

General

1.—(1) The cases in which a variation may be agreed are those set out in this Part of this Schedule or in regulations made under this Part.

(2) In this Schedule 'applicant' means the person whose application for a variation is being considered.

Special expenses

2.—(1) A variation applied for by a non-resident parent may be agreed with respect to his special expenses.

(2) In this paragraph 'special expenses' means the whole, or any amount above a prescribed amount, or any prescribed part, of expenses which fall within a prescribed description of expenses.

(3) In prescribing descriptions of expenses for the purposes of this paragraph, the Secretary of State may, in particular, make provision with respect to—

    (a) costs incurred by a non-resident parent in maintaining contact with the child, or with any of the children, with respect to whom the application for a maintenance calculation has been made;

    (b) costs attributable to a long-term illness or disability of a relevant other child (within the meaning of paragraph 10C(2) of Schedule 1);

    (c) debts of a prescribed description incurred, before the non-resident parent became a non-resident parent in relation to a child with respect to whom the maintenance calculation has been applied for—

        (i)   for the joint benefit of both parents;

        (ii) for the benefit of any such child; or

        (iii) for the benefit of any other child falling within a prescribed category;

    (d) boarding school fees for a child in relation to whom the application for a maintenance calculation has been made;

    (e) the cost to the non-resident parent of making payments in relation to a mortgage on the home he and the person with care shared, if he no longer has an interest in it, and she and a child in relation to whom the application for a maintenance calculation has been made still live there.

(4) For the purposes of sub-paragraph (3)(b)—

    (a) 'disability' and 'illness' have such meaning as may be prescribed; and

    (b) the question whether an illness or disability is long-term shall be determined in accordance with regulations made by the Secretary of State.

(5) For the purposes of sub-paragraph (3)(d), the Secretary of State may prescribe—

    (a) the meaning of 'boarding school fees'; and

    (b) components of such fees (whether or not itemised as such) which are, or are not, to be taken into account,

and may provide for estimating any such component.

Property or capital transfers

3.—(1) A variation may be agreed in the circumstances set out in sub-paragraph (2) if before 5th April 1993—

    (a) a court order of a prescribed kind was in force with respect to the non-resident parent and either the person with care with respect to the application for the maintenance calculation or the child, or any of the children, with respect to whom that application was made; or

(b) an agreement of a prescribed kind between the non-resident parent and any of those persons was in force.

(2) The circumstances are that in consequence of one or more transfers of property of a prescribed kind and exceeding (singly or in aggregate) a prescribed minimum value—

(a) the amount payable by the non-resident parent by way of maintenance was less than would have been the case had that transfer or those transfers not been made; or

(b) no amount was payable by the non-resident parent by way of maintenance.

(3) For the purposes of sub-paragraph (2), 'maintenance' means periodical payments of maintenance made (otherwise than under this Act) with respect to the child, or any of the children, with respect to whom the application for a maintenance calculation has been made.

Additional cases

4.—(1) The Secretary of State may by regulations prescribe other cases in which a variation may be agreed.

(2) Regulations under this paragraph may, for example, make provision with respect to cases where—

(a) the non-resident parent has assets which exceed a prescribed value;

(b) a person's lifestyle is inconsistent with his income for the purposes of a calculation made under Part I of Schedule 1;

(c) a person has income which is not taken into account in such a calculation;

(d) a person has unreasonably reduced the income which is taken into account in such a calculation.

PART II REGULATORY CONTROLS

5.—(1) The Secretary of State may by regulations make provision with respect to the variations from the usual rules for calculating maintenance which may be allowed when a variation is agreed.

(2) No variations may be made other than those which are permitted by the regulations.

(3) Regulations under this paragraph may, in particular, make provision for a variation to result in—

(a) a person's being treated as having more, or less, income than would be taken into account without the variation in a calculation under Part I of Schedule 1;

(b) a person's being treated as liable to pay a higher, or a lower, amount of child support maintenance than would result without the variation from a calculation under that Part.

(4) Regulations may provide for the amount of any special expenses to be taken into account in a case falling within paragraph 2, for the purposes of a variation, not to exceed such amount as may be prescribed or as may be determined in accordance with the regulations.

(5) Any regulations under this paragraph may in particular make different provision with respect to different levels of income.

(6) The Secretary of State may by regulations provide for the application, in connection with child support maintenance payable following a variation, of paragraph 7(2) to (7) of Schedule 1 (subject to any prescribed modifications).

Social Security Administration Act 1992

(1992 c. 5)

PART III OVERPAYMENTS AND ADJUSTMENTS OF BENEFIT

74A Payment of benefit where maintenance payments collected by Secretary of State

(1) This section applies where—

(a) a person ('the claimant') is entitled to a benefit to which this section applies;

(b) the Secretary of State is collecting periodical payments of child or spousal maintenance made in respect of the claimant or a member of the claimant's family; and

(c) the inclusion of any such periodical payment in the claimant's relevant income would, apart from this section, have the effect of reducing the amount of the benefit to which the claimant is entitled.

(2) The Secretary of State may, to such extent as he considers appropriate, treat any such periodical payment as not being relevant income for the purposes of calculating the amount of benefit to which the claimant is entitled.

(3) The Secretary of State may, to the extent that any periodical payment collected by him is treated as not being relevant income for those purposes, retain the whole or any part of that payment.

(4) Any sum retained by the Secretary of State under subsection (3) shall be paid by him into the Consolidated Fund.

(5) In this section—

'child' means a person under the age of 16;

'child maintenance', 'spousal maintenance' and 'relevant income' have such meaning as may be prescribed;

'couple' has the meaning given by section 137(1) of the Contributions and Benefits Act;

'family' means—

(a) a couple;

(b) a couple and a member of the same household for whom one of them is, or both are, responsible and who is a child or a person of a prescribed description;

(c) except in prescribed circumstances, a person who is not a member of a couple and a member of the same household for whom that person is responsible and who is a child or a person of a prescribed description;

(6) For the purposes of this section, the Secretary of State may by regulations make provision as to the circumstances in which—

(a) persons are to be treated as being or not being members of the same household;

(b) one person is to be treated as responsible or not responsible for another.

(7) The benefits to which this section applies are universal credit, and support allowance and such other benefits (if any) as may be prescribed.

...

PART V THE DUTY TO MAINTAIN

105 Failure to maintain—general

(1) If—

(a) any person persistently refuses or neglects to maintain himself or any person whom he is liable to maintain; and

(b) in consequence of his refusal or neglect, universal credit is paid to or in respect of him or such a person, he shall be guilty of an offence and liable on summary conviction to a fine of an amount not exceeding level 4 on the standard scale.

...

(3) Subject to subsection (4), for the purposes of this Part, a person shall be liable to maintain another person if that other person is—

(a) his or her spouse or civil partner.

(4) For the purposes of this section, in its application to an income-based jobseeker's allowance or an income-related employment and support allowance, subsection (3)(b) shall not apply.

Pensions Act 1995

(1995 c. 26)

PART IV MISCELLANEOUS AND GENERAL

Pensions on divorce etc.

166 Pensions on divorce etc.

(4) Nothing in the provisions mentioned in subsection (5) applies to a court exercising its powers under section 23 of the Matrimonial Causes Act 1973 (financial provision in connection with divorce proceedings, etc.) in respect of any benefits under a pension arrangement (within the meaning of section 25B(1) of the Matrimonial Causes Act 1973) which a party to the marriage has or is likely to have.

(4A) Nothing in the provisions mentioned in subsection (5) applies to a court exercising its powers under Part 6 of Schedule 5 to the Civil Partnership Act 2004 (making Part 1 orders having regard to pension benefits).

(5) The provisions referred to in subsection (4) and (4A) are—

(a) section 203(1) and (2) of the Army Act 1955, 203(1) and (2) of the Air Force Act 1955, 128G(1) and (2) of the Naval Discipline Act 1957 or 159(4) and (4A) of the Pension Schemes Act 1993 (which prevent assignment, or orders being made restraining a person from receiving anything which he is prevented from assigning),

(b) section 91 of this Act,

(c) any provision of any enactment (whether passed or made before or after this Act is passed) corresponding to any of the enactments mentioned in paragraphs (a) and (b), and

(d) any provision of the arrangement in question corresponding to any of those enactments.

(6) Subsections (3) to (7) of section 25B, and section 25C of the Matrimonial Causes Act 1973, as inserted by this section, do not affect the powers of the court under section 31 of that Act (variation, discharge, etc.) in relation to any order made before the commencement of this section.

Child Support Act 1995

(1995 c. 34)

Miscellaneous

18 Deferral of right to apply for maintenance assessment

(6) Neither section 4(10) nor section 7(10) of the 1991 Act shall apply in relation to a maintenance order made in the circumstances mentioned in subsection (7) or (8) of section 8 of the 1991 Act.

(7) The Secretary of State may by regulations make provision for section 4(10), or section 7(10), of the 1991 Act not to apply in relation to such other cases as may be prescribed.

...

Supplemental

26　Regulations and orders

(1) Any power under this Act to make regulations or orders shall be exercisable by statutory instrument.

(2) Any such power may be exercised to make different provision for different cases, including different provision for different areas.

(3) Any such power includes power—

>   (a) to make such incidental, supplemental, consequential or transitional provision as appears to the Secretary of State to be expedient; and
>
>   (b) to provide for a person to exercise a discretion in dealing with any matter.

...

27　Interpretation

(1) In this Act 'the 1991 Act' means the Child Support Act 1991.

(2) Expressions in this Act which are used in the 1991 Act have the same meaning in this Act as they have in that Act.

28　Financial provisions

There shall be paid out of money provided by Parliament—

>   (a) any expenditure incurred by the Secretary of State under or by virtue of this Act;
>
>   (b) any increase attributable to this Act in the sums payable out of money so provided under or by virtue of any other enactment.

Civil Evidence Act 1995

(1995 c. 38)

Supplementary provisions as to hearsay evidence

...

7　Evidence formerly admissible at common law

...

(3) The common law rules effectively preserved by section 9(3) and (4) of the Civil Evidence Act 1968, that is, any rule of law whereby in civil proceedings—

>   (a) evidence of a person's reputation is admissible for the purpose of proving his good or bad character, or
>
>   (b) evidence of reputation or family tradition is admissible—
>
>>   (i)　for the purpose of proving or disproving pedigree or the existence of a marriage, or
>>
>>   (ii)　for the purpose of proving or disproving the existence of any public or general right or of identifying any person or thing,

shall continue to have effect in so far as they authorise the court to treat such evidence as proving or disproving that matter.

Where any such rule applies, reputation or family tradition shall be treated for the purposes of this Act as a fact and not as a statement or multiplicity of statements about the matter in question.

(4) The words in which a rule of law mentioned in this section is described are intended only to identify the rule and shall not be construed as altering it in any way.

Family Law Act 1996

(1996 c. 27)

PART I PRINCIPLES OF PARTS II AND III

1   The general principles underlying section 22

The court and any person, in exercising functions under or in consequence of section 22, shall have regard to the following general principles—

(a) that the institution of marriage is to be supported;

(b) that the parties to a marriage which may have broken down are to be encouraged to take all practicable steps, whether by marriage counselling or otherwise, to save the marriage;

...

PART II DIVORCE AND SEPARATION

Marriage support services

22   Funding for marriage support services

(1) The Secretary of State may, with the approval of the Treasury, make grants in connection with—

(a) the provision of marriage support services;

(b) research into the causes of marital breakdown;

(c) research into ways of preventing marital breakdown.

(2) Any grant under this section may be made subject to such conditions as the Secretary of State considers appropriate.

(3) In exercising his power to make grants in connection with the provision of marriage support services, the Secretary of State is to have regard, in particular, to the desirability of services of that kind being available when they are first needed.

PART IV FAMILY HOMES AND DOMESTIC VIOLENCE

Rights to occupy matrimonial or civil partnership home

30   Rights concerning home where one spouse or civil partner has no estate, etc.

(1) This section applies if—

(a) one spouse or civil partner ('A') is entitled to occupy a dwelling-house by virtue of—

(i)   a beneficial estate or interest or contract; or

(ii) any enactment giving A the right to remain in occupation; and

(b) the other spouse or civil partner ('B') is not so entitled.

(2) Subject to the provisions of this Part, B has the following rights ('home rights')—

(a) if in occupation, a right not to be evicted or excluded from the dwelling-house or any part of it by A except with the leave of the court given by an order under section 33;

(b) if not in occupation, a right with the leave of the court so given to enter into and occupy the dwelling-house.

(3) If B is entitled under this section to occupy a dwelling-house or any part of a dwelling-house, any payment or tender made or other thing done by B in or towards satisfaction of any liability of A in respect of rent, mortgage payments or other outgoings affecting the dwelling-house is, whether or not it is made or done in pursuance of an order under section 40, as good as if made or done by A.

(4) B's occupation by virtue of this section—

    (a) is to be treated, for the purposes of the Rent (Agriculture) Act 1976 and the Rent Act 1977 (other than Part V and sections 103 to 106 of that Act), as occupation by A as A's residence, and

    (b) if B occupies the dwelling-house as B's only or principal home, is to be treated, for the purposes of the Housing Act 1985, Part I of the Housing Act 1988, Chapter 1 of Part 5 of the Housing Act 1996 and the Prevention of Social Housing Fraud Act 2013, as occupation by A as A's only or principal home.

(5) If B—

    (a) is entitled under this section to occupy a dwelling-house or any part of a dwelling-house, and

    (b) makes any payment in or towards satisfaction of any liability of A in respect of mortgage payments affecting the dwelling-house,

the person to whom the payment is made may treat it as having been made by A, but the fact that that person has treated any such payment as having been so made does not affect any claim of B against A to an interest in the dwelling-house by virtue of the payment.

(6) If B is entitled under this section to occupy a dwelling-house or part of a dwelling-house by reason of an interest of A under a trust, all the provisions of subsections (3) to (5) apply in relation to the trustees as they apply in relation to A.

(7) This section does not apply to a dwelling-house which—

    (a) in the case of spouses, has at no time been, and was at no time intended by them to be, a matrimonial home of theirs; and

    (b) in the case of civil partners, has at no time been, and was at no time intended by them to be, a civil partnership home of theirs.

(8) B's home rights continue—

    (a) only so long as the marriage or civil partnership subsists, except to the extent that an order under section 33(5) otherwise provides; and

    (b) only so long as A is entitled as mentioned in subsection (1) to occupy the dwelling-house, except where provision is made by section 31 for those rights to be a charge on an estate or interest in the dwelling-house.

(9) It is hereby declared that a person—

    (a) who has an equitable interest in a dwelling-house or in its proceeds of sale, but

    (b) is not a person in whom there is vested (whether solely or as joint tenant) a legal estate in fee simple or a legal term of years absolute in the dwelling-house,

is to be treated, only for the purpose of determining whether he has home rights, as not being entitled to occupy the dwelling-house by virtue of that interest.

31 Effect of home rights as charge on dwelling-house

(1) Subsections (2) and (3) apply if, at any time during a marriage or civil partnership, A is entitled to occupy a dwelling-house by virtue of a beneficial estate or interest.

(2) B's home rights are a charge on the estate or interest.

(3) The charge created by subsection (2) has the same priority as if it were an equitable interest created at whichever is the latest of the following dates—

    (a) the date on which A acquires the estate or interest;

    (b) the date of the marriage or of the formation of the civil partnership; and

    (c) 1st January 1968 (the commencement date of the Matrimonial Homes Act 1967).

(4) Subsections (5) and (6) apply if, at any time when B's home rights are a charge on an interest of A under a trust, there are, apart from A or B, no persons, living or unborn, who are or could become beneficiaries under the trust.

(5) The rights are a charge also on the estate or interest of the trustees for A.

(6) The charge created by subsection (5) has the same priority as if it were an equitable interest created (under powers overriding the trusts) on the date when it arises.

(7) In determining for the purposes of subsection (4) whether there are any persons who are not, but could become, beneficiaries under the trust, there is to be disregarded any potential exercise of a general power of appointment exercisable by either or both of A and B alone (whether or not the exercise of it requires the consent of another person).

(8) Even though B's home rights are a charge on an estate or interest in the dwelling-house, those rights are brought to an end by—

    (a) the death of A, or

    (b) the termination (otherwise than by death) of the marriage or civil partnership, unless the court directs otherwise by an order made under section 33(5).

(9) If—

    (a) B's home rights are a charge on an estate or interest in the dwelling-house, and

    (b) that estate or interest is surrendered to merge in some other estate or interest expectant on it in such circumstances that, but for the merger, the person taking the estate or interest would be bound by the charge,

the surrender has effect subject to the charge and the persons thereafter entitled to the other estate or interest are, for so long as the estate or interest surrendered would have endured if not so surrendered, to be treated for all purposes of this Part as deriving title to the other estate or interest under A or, as the case may be, under the trustees for A, by virtue of the surrender.

(10) If the title to the legal estate by virtue of which A is entitled to occupy a dwelling-house (including any legal estate held by trustees for A) is registered under the Land Registration Act 2002 or any enactment replaced by that Act—

    (a) registration of a land charge affecting the dwelling-house by virtue of this Part is to be effected by registering a notice under that Act; and

    (b) B's home rights are not to be capable of falling within paragraph 2 of Schedule 1 or 3 to that Act.

(12) If—

    (a) B's home rights are a charge on the estate of A or of trustees of A, and

    (b) that estate is the subject of a mortgage,

then if, after the date of the creation of the mortgage ('the first mortgage'), the charge is registered under section 2 of the Land Charges Act 1972, the charge is, for the purposes of section 94 of the Law of Property Act 1925 (which regulates the rights of mortgagees to make further advances ranking in priority to subsequent mortgages), to be deemed to be a mortgage subsequent in date to the first mortgage.

(13) It is hereby declared that a charge under subsection (2) or (5) is not registrable under subsection (10) or under section 2 of the Land Charges Act 1972 unless it is a charge on a legal estate.

32   Further provisions relating to home rights

Schedule 4 (provisions supplementary to sections 30 and 31) has effect.

Occupation orders

33   Occupation orders where applicant has estate or interest etc. or has home rights

(1) If—

    (a) a person ('the person entitled')—

        (i) is entitled to occupy a dwelling-house by virtue of a beneficial estate or interest or contract or by virtue of any enactment giving him the right to remain in occupation, or

        (ii) has home rights in relation to a dwelling-house, and

    (b) the dwelling-house—

        (i) is or at any time has been the home of the person entitled and of another person with whom he is associated, or

        (ii) was at any time intended by the person entitled and any such other person to be their home, the person entitled may apply to the court for an order containing any of the provisions specified in subsections (3), (4) and (5).

(2) If an agreement to marry is terminated, no application under this section may be made by virtue of section 62(3)(e) by reference to that agreement after the end of the period of three years beginning with the day on which it is terminated.

(2A) If a civil partnership agreement (as defined by section 73 of the Civil Partnership Act 2004) is terminated, no application under this section may be made by virtue of section 62(3) (eza) by reference to that agreement after the end of the period of three years beginning with the day on which it is terminated.

(3) An order under this section may—

    (a) enforce the applicant's entitlement to remain in occupation as against the other person ('the respondent');

    (b) require the respondent to permit the applicant to enter and remain in the dwelling-house or part of the dwelling-house;

    (c) regulate the occupation of the dwelling-house by either or both parties;

    (d) if the respondent is entitled as mentioned in subsection (1)(a)(i), prohibit, suspend or restrict the exercise by him of his right to occupy the dwelling-house;

    (e) if the respondent has home rights in relation to the dwelling-house and the applicant is the other spouse or civil partner, restrict or terminate those rights;

    (f) require the respondent to leave the dwelling-house or part of the dwelling-house; or

    (g) exclude the respondent from a defined area in which the dwelling-house is included.

(4) An order under this section may declare that the applicant is entitled as mentioned in subsection (1)(a)(i) or has home rights.

(5) If the applicant has home rights and the respondent is the other spouse or civil partner, an order under this section made during the marriage or civil partnership may provide that those rights are not brought to an end by—

    (a) the death of the other spouse or civil partner; or

    (b) the termination (otherwise than by death) of the marriage or civil partnership.

(6) In deciding whether to exercise its powers under subsection (3) and (if so) in what manner, the court shall have regard to all the circumstances including—

    (a) the housing needs and housing resources of each of the parties and of any relevant child;

    (b) the financial resources of each of the parties;

    (c) the likely effect of any order, or of any decision by the court not to exercise its powers under subsection (3), on the health, safety or well-being of the parties and of any relevant child; and

    (d) the conduct of the parties in relation to each other and otherwise.

(7) If it appears to the court that the applicant or any relevant child is likely to suffer significant harm attributable to conduct of the respondent if an order under this section containing one or more of the provisions mentioned in subsection (3) is not made, the court shall make the order unless it appears to it that—

    (a) the respondent or any relevant child is likely to suffer significant harm if the order is made; and

    (b) the harm likely to be suffered by the respondent or child in that event is as great as, or greater than, the harm attributable to conduct of the respondent which is likely to be suffered by the applicant or child if the order is not made.

(8) The court may exercise its powers under subsection (5) in any case where it considers that in all the circumstances it is just and reasonable to do so.

(9) An order under this section—

    (a) may not be made after the death of either of the parties mentioned in subsection (1); and

    (b) except in the case of an order made by virtue of subsection (5)(a), ceases to have effect on the death of either party.

(10) An order under this section may, in so far as it has continuing effect, be made for a specified period, until the occurrence of a specified event or until further order.

34   Effect of order under section 33 where rights are charge on dwelling-house

(1) If B's home rights are a charge on the estate or interest of A or of trustees for A—

    (a) an order under section 33 against A has, except so far as a contrary intention appears, the same effect against persons deriving title under A or under the trustees and affected by the charge, and

    (b) sections 33(1), (3), (4) and (10) and 30(3) to (6) apply in relation to any person deriving title under A or under the trustees and affected by the charge as they apply in relation to A.

(2) The court may make an order under section 33 by virtue of subsection (1)(b) if it considers that in all the circumstances it is just and reasonable to do so.

35   One former spouse or former civil partner with no existing right to occupy

(1) This section applies if—

    (a) one former spouse or former civil partner is entitled to occupy a dwelling-house by virtue of a beneficial estate or interest or contract, or by virtue of any enactment giving him the right to remain in occupation;

    (b) the other former spouse or former civil partner is not so entitled; and

    (c) the dwelling-house—

        (i) in the case of former spouses, was at any time their matrimonial home or was at any time intended by them to be their matrimonial home, or

        (ii) in the case of former civil partners, was at any time their civil partnership home or was at any time intended by them to be their civil partnership home.

(2) The former spouse or former civil partner not so entitled may apply to the court for an order under this section against the other former spouse or former civil partner ('the respondent').

(3) If the applicant is in occupation, an order under this section must contain provision—

    (a) giving the applicant the right not to be evicted or excluded from the dwelling-house or any part of it by the respondent for the period specified in the order; and

    (b) prohibiting the respondent from evicting or excluding the applicant during that period.

(4) If the applicant is not in occupation, an order under this section must contain provision—

    (a) giving the applicant the right to enter into and occupy the dwelling-house for the period specified in the order; and

    (b) requiring the respondent to permit the exercise of that right.

(5) An order under this section may also—

    (a) regulate the occupation of the dwelling-house by either or both of the parties;

    (b) prohibit, suspend or restrict the exercise by the respondent of his right to occupy the dwelling-house;

    (c) require the respondent to leave the dwelling-house or part of the dwelling-house; or

    (d) exclude the respondent from a defined area in which the dwelling-house is included.

(6) In deciding whether to make an order under this section containing provision of the kind mentioned in subsection (3) or (4) and (if so) in what manner, the court shall have regard to all the circumstances including—

    (a) the housing needs and housing resources of each of the parties and of any relevant child;

    (b) the financial resources of each of the parties;

    (c) the likely effect of any order, or of any decision by the court not to exercise its powers under subsection (3) or (4), on the health, safety or well-being of the parties and of any relevant child;

    (d) the conduct of the parties in relation to each other and otherwise;

    (e) the length of time that has elapsed since the parties ceased to live together;

(f) the length of time that has elapsed since the marriage or civil partnership was dissolved or annulled; and

(g) the existence of any pending proceedings between the parties—

    (i) for an order under section 23A or 24 of the Matrimonial Causes Act 1973 (property adjustment orders in connection with divorce proceedings etc.);

    (ia) for a property adjustment order under Part 2 of Schedule 5 to the Civil Partnership Act 2004;

    (ii) for an order under paragraph 1(2)(d) or (e) of Schedule 1 to the Children Act 1989 (orders for financial relief against parents); or

    (iii) relating to the legal or beneficial ownership of the dwelling-house.

(7) In deciding whether to exercise its power to include one or more of the provisions referred to in subsection (5) ('a subsection (5) provision') and (if so) in what manner, the court shall have regard to all the circumstances including the matters mentioned in subsection (6)(a) to (e).

(8) If the court decides to make an order under this section and it appears to it that, if the order does not include a subsection (5) provision, the applicant or any relevant child is likely to suffer significant harm attributable to conduct of the respondent, the court shall include the subsection (5) provision in the order unless it appears to the court that—

(a) the respondent or any relevant child is likely to suffer significant harm if the provision is included in the order; and

(b) the harm likely to be suffered by the respondent or child in that event is as great as or greater than the harm attributable to conduct of the respondent which is likely to be suffered by the applicant or child if the provision is not included.

(9) An order under this section—

(a) may not be made after the death of either of the former spouses or former civil partners; and

(b) ceases to have effect on the death of either of them.

(10) An order under this section must be limited so as to have effect for a specified period not exceeding six months, but may be extended on one or more occasions for a further specified period not exceeding six months.

(11) A former spouse or former civil partner who has an equitable interest in the dwelling-house or in the proceeds of sale of the dwelling-house but in whom there is not vested (whether solely or as joint tenant) a legal estate in fee simple or a legal term of years absolute in the dwelling-house is to be treated (but only for the purpose of determining whether he is eligible to apply under this section) as not being entitled to occupy the dwelling-house by virtue of that interest.

(12) Subsection (11) does not prejudice any right of such a former spouse or former civil partner to apply for an order under section 33.

(13) So long as an order under this section remains in force, subsections (3) to (6) of section 30 apply in relation to the applicant—

(a) as if he were B (the person entitled to occupy the dwelling-house by virtue of that section); and

(b) as if the respondent were A (the person entitled as mentioned in subsection (1)(a) of that section).

36 One cohabitant or former cohabitant with no existing right to occupy

(1) This section applies if—

(a) one cohabitant or former cohabitant is entitled to occupy a dwelling-house by virtue of a beneficial estate or interest or contract or by virtue of any enactment giving him the right to remain in occupation;

(b) the other cohabitant or former cohabitant is not so entitled; and

(c) that dwelling-house is the home in which they cohabit or a home in which they at any time cohabited or intended to cohabit.

(2) The cohabitant or former cohabitant not so entitled may apply to the court for an order under this section against the other cohabitant or former cohabitant ('the respondent').

(3) If the applicant is in occupation, an order under this section must contain provision—

(a) giving the applicant the right not to be evicted or excluded from the dwelling-house or any part of it by the respondent for the period specified in the order; and

(b) prohibiting the respondent from evicting or excluding the applicant during that period.

(4) If the applicant is not in occupation, an order under this section must contain provision—

(a) giving the applicant the right to enter into and occupy the dwelling-house for the period specified in the order; and

(b) requiring the respondent to permit the exercise of that right.

(5) An order under this section may also—

(a) regulate the occupation of the dwelling-house by either or both of the parties;

(b) prohibit, suspend or restrict the exercise by the respondent of his right to occupy the dwelling-house;

(c) require the respondent to leave the dwelling-house or part of the dwelling-house; or

(d) exclude the respondent from a defined area in which the dwelling-house is included.

(6) In deciding whether to make an order under this section containing provision of the kind mentioned in subsection (3) or (4) and (if so) in what manner, the court shall have regard to all the circumstances including—

(a) the housing needs and housing resources of each of the parties and of any relevant child;

(b) the financial resources of each of the parties;

(c) the likely effect of any order, or of any decision by the court not to exercise its powers under subsection (3) or (4), on the health, safety or well-being of the parties and of any relevant child;

(d) the conduct of the parties in relation to each other and otherwise;

(e) the nature of the parties' relationship and in particular the level of commitment involved in it;

(f) the length of time during which they have cohabited;

(g) whether there are or have been any children who are children of both parties or for whom both parties have or have had parental responsibility;

(h) the length of time that has elapsed since the parties ceased to live together; and

(i) the existence of any pending proceedings between the parties—

(i)   for an order under paragraph 1(2)(d) or (e) of Schedule 1 to the Children Act 1989 (orders for financial relief against parents); or

(ii) relating to the legal or beneficial ownership of the dwelling-house.

(7) In deciding whether to exercise its powers to include one or more of the provisions referred to in subsection (5) ('a subsection (5) provision') and (if so) in what manner, the court shall have regard to all the circumstances including—

(a) the matters mentioned in subsection (6)(a) to (d); and

(b) the questions mentioned in subsection (8).

(8) The questions are—

(a) whether the applicant or any relevant child is likely to suffer significant harm attributable to conduct of the respondent if the subsection (5) provision is not included in the order; and

(b) whether the harm likely to be suffered by the respondent or child if the provision is included is as great as or greater than the harm attributable to conduct of the respondent which is likely to be suffered by the applicant or child if the provision is not included.

(9) An order under this section—

(a) may not be made after the death of either of the parties; and

(b) ceases to have effect on the death of either of them.

(10) An order under this section must be limited so as to have effect for a specified period not exceeding six months, but may be extended on one occasion for a further specified period not exceeding six months.

(11) A person who has an equitable interest in the dwelling-house or in the proceeds of sale of the dwelling-house but in whom there is not vested (whether solely or as joint tenant) a legal estate in fee simple or a legal term of years absolute in the dwelling-house is to be treated (but only for the purpose of determining whether he is eligible to apply under this section) as not being entitled to occupy the dwelling-house by virtue of that interest.

(12) Subsection (11) does not prejudice any right of such a person to apply for an order under section 33.

(13) So long as the order remains in force, subsections (3) to (6) of section 30 apply in relation to the applicant—

  (a) as if he were B (the person entitled to occupy the dwelling-house by virtue of that section); and

  (b) as if the respondent were A (the person entitled as mentioned in subsection (1)(a) of that section).

37   Neither spouse or civil partner entitled to occupy

(1) This section applies if—

  (a) one spouse or former spouse and the other spouse or former spouse occupy a dwelling-house which is or was the matrimonial home; but

  (b) neither of them is entitled to remain in occupation—

    (i)   by virtue of a beneficial estate or interest or contract; or

    (ii) by virtue of any enactment giving him the right to remain in occupation.

(1A) This section also applies if—

  (a) one civil partner or former civil partner and the other civil partner or former civil partner occupy a dwelling-house which is or was the civil partnership home; but

  (b) neither of them is entitled to remain in occupation—

    (i)   by virtue of a beneficial estate or interest or contract; or

    (ii) by virtue of any enactment giving him the right to remain in occupation.

(2) Either of the parties may apply to the court for an order against the other under this section.

(3) An order under this section may—

  (a) require the respondent to permit the applicant to enter and remain in the dwelling-house or part of the dwelling-house;

  (b) regulate the occupation of the dwelling-house by either or both of the parties;

  (c) require the respondent to leave the dwelling-house or part of the dwelling-house; or

  (d) exclude the respondent from a defined area in which the dwelling-house is included.

(4) Subsections (6) and (7) of section 33 apply to the exercise by the court of its powers under this section as they apply to the exercise by the court of its powers under subsection (3) of that section.

(5) An order under this section must be limited so as to have effect for a specified period not exceeding six months, but may be extended on one or more occasions for a further specified period not exceeding six months.

38   Neither cohabitant or former cohabitant entitled to occupy

(1) This section applies if—

  (a) one cohabitant or former cohabitant and the other cohabitant or former cohabitant occupy a dwelling-house which is the home in which they cohabit or cohabited; but

  (b) neither of them is entitled to remain in occupation—

    (i)   by virtue of a beneficial estate or interest or contract; or

    (ii) by virtue of any enactment giving him the right to remain in occupation.

(2) Either of the parties may apply to the court for an order against the other under this section.

(3) An order under this section may—

(a) require the respondent to permit the applicant to enter and remain in the dwelling-house or part of the dwelling-house;

(b) regulate the occupation of the dwelling-house by either or both of the parties;

(c) require the respondent to leave the dwelling-house or part of the dwelling-house; or

(d) exclude the respondent from a defined area in which the dwelling-house is included.

(4) In deciding whether to exercise its powers to include one or more of the provisions referred to in subsection (3) ('a subsection (3) provision') and (if so) in what manner, the court shall have regard to all the circumstances including—

(a) the housing needs and housing resources of each of the parties and of any relevant child;

(b) the financial resources of each of the parties;

(c) the likely effect of any order, or of any decision by the court not to exercise its powers under subsection (3), on the health, safety or well-being of the parties and of any relevant child;

(d) the conduct of the parties in relation to each other and otherwise; and

(e) the questions mentioned in subsection (5).

(5) The questions are—

(a) whether the applicant or any relevant child is likely to suffer significant harm attributable to conduct of the respondent if the subsection (3) provision is not included in the order; and

(b) whether the harm likely to be suffered by the respondent or child if the provision is included is as great as or greater than the harm attributable to conduct of the respondent which is likely to be suffered by the applicant or child if the provision is not included.

(6) An order under this section shall be limited so as to have effect for a specified period not exceeding six months, but may be extended on one occasion for a further specified period not exceeding six months.

39 Supplementary provisions

(1) In this Part an 'occupation order' means an order under section 33, 35, 36, 37 or 38.

(2) An application for an occupation order may be made in other family proceedings or without any other family proceedings being instituted.

(3) If—

(a) an application for an occupation order is made under section 33, 35, 36, 37 or 38, and

(b) the court considers that it has no power to make the order under the section concerned, but that it has power to make an order under one of the other sections,

the court may make an order under that other section.

(4) The fact that a person has applied for an occupation order under sections 35 to 38, or that an occupation order has been made, does not affect the right of any person to claim a legal or equitable interest in any property in any subsequent proceedings (including subsequent proceedings under this Part).

40 Additional provisions that may be included in certain occupation orders

(1) The court may on, or at any time after, making an occupation order under section 33, 35 or 36—

(a) impose on either party obligations as to—

(i) the repair and maintenance of the dwelling-house; or

(ii) the discharge of rent, mortgage payments or other outgoings affecting the dwelling-house;

(b) order a party occupying the dwelling-house or any part of it (including a party who is entitled to do so by virtue of a beneficial estate or interest or contract or by virtue of any enactment giving him the right to remain in occupation) to make periodical payments to the other party in respect of the accommodation, if the other party would (but for the order) be entitled to occupy the dwelling-house by virtue of a beneficial estate or interest or contract or by virtue of any such enactment;

    (c) grant either party possession or use of furniture or other contents of the dwelling-house;

    (d) order either party to take reasonable care of any furniture or other contents of the dwelling-house;

    (e) order either party to take reasonable steps to keep the dwelling-house and any furniture or other contents secure.

  (2) In deciding whether and, if so, how to exercise its powers under this section, the court shall have regard to all the circumstances of the case including—

    (a) the financial needs and financial resources of the parties; and

    (b) the financial obligations which they have, or are likely to have in the foreseeable future, including financial obligations to each other and to any relevant child.

  (3) An order under this section ceases to have effect when the occupation order to which it relates ceases to have effect.

Non-molestation orders

42 Non-molestation orders

  (1) In this Part a 'non-molestation order' means an order containing either or both of the following provisions—

    (a) provision prohibiting a person ('the respondent') from molesting another person who is associated with the respondent;

    (b) provision prohibiting the respondent from molesting a relevant child.

  (2) The court may make a non-molestation order—

    (a) if an application for the order has been made (whether in other family proceedings or without any other family proceedings being instituted) by a person who is associated with the respondent; or

    (b) if in any family proceedings to which the respondent is a party the court considers that the order should be made for the benefit of any other party to the proceedings or any relevant child even though no such application has been made.

  (3) In subsection (2) 'family proceedings' includes proceedings in which the court has made an emergency protection order under section 44 of the Children Act 1989 which includes an exclusion requirement (as defined in section 44A(3) of that Act).

  (4) Where an agreement to marry is terminated, no application under subsection (2) (a) may be made by virtue of section 62(3)(e) by reference to that agreement after the end of the period of three years beginning with the day on which it is terminated.

  (4ZA) If a civil partnership agreement (as defined by section 73 of the Civil Partnership Act 2004) is terminated, no application under this section may be made by virtue of section 62 (3)(eza) by reference to that agreement after the end of the period of three years beginning with the day on which it is terminated.

  (4A) A court considering whether to make an occupation order shall also consider whether to exercise the power conferred by subsection (2)(b).

  (4B) In this Part 'the applicant', in relation to a non-molestation order, includes (where the context permits) the person for whose benefit such an order would be or is made in exercise of the power conferred by subsection (2)(b).

  (5) In deciding whether to exercise its powers under this section and, if so, in what manner, the court shall have regard to all the circumstances including the need to secure the health, safety and well-being—

    (a) of the applicant; and

    (b) of any relevant child.

  (6) A non-molestation order may be expressed so as to refer to molestation in general, to particular acts of molestation, or to both.

(7) A non-molestation order may be made for a specified period or until further order.

(8) A non-molestation order which is made in other family proceedings ceases to have effect if those proceedings are withdrawn or dismissed.

42A   Offence of breaching non-molestation order

(1) A person who without reasonable excuse does anything that he is prohibited from doing by a non-molestation order is guilty of an offence.

(2) In the case of a non-molestation order made by virtue of section 45(1), a person can be guilty of an offence under this section only in respect of conduct engaged in at a time when he was aware of the existence of the order.

(3) Where a person is convicted of an offence under this section in respect of any conduct, that conduct is not punishable as a contempt of court.

(4) A person cannot be convicted of an offence under this section in respect of any conduct which has been punished as a contempt of court.

(5) A person guilty of an offence under this section is liable—
   (a) on conviction on indictment, to imprisonment for a term not exceeding five years, or a fine, or both;
   (b) on summary conviction, to imprisonment for a term not exceeding 12 months, or a fine not exceeding the statutory maximum, or both.

(6) A reference in any enactment to proceedings under this Part, or to an order under this Part, does not include a reference to proceedings for an offence under this section or to an order made in such proceedings.

'Enactment' includes an enactment contained in subordinate legislation within the meaning of the Interpretation Act 1978.

Further provisions relating to occupation and non-molestation orders

43   Leave of court required for applications by children under sixteen

(1) A child under the age of sixteen may not apply for an occupation order or a non-molestation order except with the leave of the court.

(2) The court may grant leave for the purposes of subsection (1) only if it is satisfied that the child has sufficient understanding to make the proposed application for the occupation order or non-molestation order.

44   Evidence of agreement to marry or form a civil partnership

(1) Subject to subsection (2), the court shall not make an order under section 33 or 42 by virtue of section 62(3)(e) unless there is produced to it evidence in writing of the existence of the agreement to marry.

(2) Subsection (1) does not apply if the court is satisfied that the agreement to marry was evidenced by—
   (a) the gift of an engagement ring by one party to the agreement to the other in contemplation of their marriage, or
   (b) a ceremony entered into by the parties in the presence of one or more other persons assembled for the purpose of witnessing the ceremony.

(3) Subject to subsection (4), the court shall not make an order under section 33 or 42 by virtue of section 62(3)(eza) unless there is produced to it evidence in writing of the existence of the civil partnership agreement (as defined by section 73 of the Civil Partnership Act 2004).

(4) Subsection (3) does not apply if the court is satisfied that the civil partnership agreement was evidenced by—
   (a) a gift by one party to the agreement to the other as a token of the agreement, or
   (b) a ceremony entered into by the parties in the presence of one or more other persons assembled for the purpose of witnessing the ceremony.

45 Ex parte orders

(1) The court may, in any case where it considers that it is just and convenient to do so, make an occupation order or a non-molestation order even though the respondent has not been given such notice of the proceedings as would otherwise be required by rules of court.

(2) In determining whether to exercise its powers under subsection (1), the court shall have regard to all the circumstances including—

(a) any risk of significant harm to the applicant or a relevant child, attributable to conduct of the respondent, if the order is not made immediately;

(b) whether it is likely that the applicant will be deterred or prevented from pursuing the application if an order is not made immediately; and

(c) whether there is reason to believe that the respondent is aware of the proceedings but is deliberately evading service and that the applicant or a relevant child will be seriously prejudiced by the delay involved.

(3) If the court makes an order by virtue of subsection (1) it must afford the respondent an opportunity to make representations relating to the order as soon as just and convenient at a full hearing.

(4) If, at a full hearing, the court makes an occupation order ('the full order'), then—

(a) for the purposes of calculating the maximum period for which the full order may be made to have effect, the relevant section is to apply as if the period for which the full order will have effect began on the date on which the initial order first had effect; and

(b) the provisions of section 36(10) or 38(6) as to the extension of orders are to apply as if the full order and the initial order were a single order.

(5) In this section—

'full hearing' means a hearing of which notice has been given to all the parties in accordance with rules of court;

'initial order' means an occupation order made by virtue of subsection (1); and

'relevant section' means section 33(10), 35(10), 36(10), 37(5) or 38(6).

46 Undertakings

(1) In any case where the court has power to make an occupation order or non-molestation order, the court may accept an undertaking from any party to the proceedings.

(2) No power of arrest may be attached to any undertaking given under subsection (1).

(3) The court shall not accept an undertaking under subsection (1) instead of making an occupation order in any case where apart from this section a power of arrest would be attached to the order.

(3A) The court shall not accept an undertaking under subsection (1) instead of making a non-molestation order in any case where it appears to the court that—

(a) the respondent has used or threatened violence against the applicant or a relevant child; and

(b) for the protection of the applicant or child it is necessary to make a non-molestation order so that any breach may be punishable under section 42A.

(4) An undertaking given to a court under subsection (1) is enforceable as if the court had made an occupation order or a non-molestation order in terms corresponding to those of the undertaking.

(5) This section has effect without prejudice to the powers of the High Court and the family court apart from this section.

47 Arrest for breach of order

(2) If—

(a) the court makes an occupation order; and

(b) it appears to the court that the respondent has used or threatened violence against the applicant or a relevant child,

it shall attach a power of arrest to one or more provisions of the order unless satisfied that in all the circumstances of the case the applicant or child will be adequately protected without such a power of arrest.

(3) Subsection (2) does not apply in any case where the occupation order is made by virtue of section 45(1), but in such a case the court may attach a power of arrest to one or more provisions of the order if it appears to it—

    (a) that the respondent has used or threatened violence against the applicant or a relevant child; and

    (b) that there is a risk of significant harm to the applicant or child, attributable to conduct of the respondent, if the power of arrest is not attached to those provisions immediately.

(4) If, by virtue of subsection (3), the court attaches a power of arrest to any provisions of an occupation order, it may provide that the power of arrest is to have effect for a shorter period than the other provisions of the order.

(5) Any period specified for the purposes of subsection (4) may be extended by the court (on one or more occasions) on an application to vary or discharge the occupation order.

(6) If, by virtue of subsection (2) or (3), a power of arrest is attached to certain provisions of an order, a constable may arrest without warrant a person whom he has reasonable cause for suspecting to be in breach of any such provision.

(7) If a power of arrest is attached under subsection (2) or (3) to certain provisions of the order and the respondent is arrested under subsection (6)—

    (a) he must be brought before the relevant judicial authority within the period of 24 hours beginning at the time of his arrest; and

    (b) if the matter is not then disposed of forthwith, the relevant judicial authority before whom he is brought may remand him.

In reckoning for the purposes of this subsection any period of 24 hours, no account is to be taken of Christmas Day, Good Friday or any Sunday.

(8) If the court—

    (a) has made a non-molestation order, or

    (b) has made an occupation order but has not attached a power of arrest under subsection (2) or (3) to any provision of the order, or has attached that power only to certain provisions of the order,

then, if at any time the applicant considers that the respondent has failed to comply with the order, he may apply to the relevant judicial authority for the issue of a warrant for the arrest of the respondent.

(9) The relevant judicial authority shall not issue a warrant on an application under subsection (8) unless—

    (a) the application is substantiated on oath; and

    (b) the relevant judicial authority has reasonable grounds for believing that the respondent has failed to comply with the order.

(10) If a person is brought before a court by virtue of a warrant issued under subsection (9) and the court does not dispose of the matter forthwith, the court may remand him.

(11) Schedule 5 (which makes provision corresponding to that applying in magistrates' courts in civil cases under sections 128 and 129 of the Magistrates' Courts Act 1980) has effect in relation to the powers of the High Court and the family court to remand a person by virtue of this section.

(12) If a person remanded under this section is granted bail, he may be required by the relevant judicial authority to comply, before release on bail or later, with such requirements as appear to that authority to be necessary to secure that he does not interfere with witnesses or otherwise obstruct the course of justice.

48   Remand for medical examination and report

(1) If the relevant judicial authority has reason to consider that a medical report will be required, any power to remand a person under section 47(7)(b) or (10) may be exercised for the purpose of enabling a medical examination and report to be made.

(2) If such a power is so exercised, the adjournment must not be for more than 4 weeks at a time unless the relevant judicial authority remands the accused in custody.

(3) If the relevant judicial authority so remands the accused, the adjournment must not be for more than 3 weeks at a time.

(4) If there is reason to suspect that a person who has been arrested—

(a) under section 47(6), or

(b) under a warrant issued on an application made under section 47(8),

is suffering from mental disorder within the meaning of the Mental Health Act 1983, the relevant judicial authority has the same power to make an order under section 35 of that Act (remand for report on accused's mental condition) as the Crown Court has under that section in the case of an accused person within the meaning of that section.

49 Variation and discharge of orders

(1) An occupation order or non-molestation order may be varied or discharged by the court on an application by—

(a) the respondent, or

(b) the person on whose application the order was made.

(2) In the case of a non-molestation order made by virtue of section 42(2)(b), the order may be varied or discharged by the court even though no such application has been made.

(3) If B's home rights are, under section 31, a charge on the estate or interest of A or of trustees for A, an order under section 33 against A may also be varied or discharged by the court on an application by any person deriving title under A or under the trustees and affected by the charge.

(4) If, by virtue of section 47(3), a power of arrest has been attached to certain provisions of an occupation order, the court may vary or discharge the order under subsection (1) in so far as it confers a power of arrest (whether or not any application has been made to vary or discharge any other provision of the order).

...

Transfer of tenancies

53 Transfer of certain tenancies

Schedule 7 makes provision in relation to the transfer of certain tenancies on divorce etc. or on separation of cohabitants.

Dwelling-house subject to mortgage

54 Dwelling-house subject to mortgage

(1) In determining for the purposes of this Part whether a person is entitled to occupy a dwelling-house by virtue of an estate or interest, any right to possession of the dwelling-house conferred on a mortgagee of the dwelling-house under or by virtue of his mortgage is to be disregarded.

(2) Subsection (1) applies whether or not the mortgagee is in possession.

(3) Where a person ('A') is entitled to occupy a dwelling-house by virtue of an estate or interest, a connected person does not by virtue of—

(a) any home rights conferred by section 30, or

(b) any rights conferred by an order under section 35 or 36,

have any larger right against the mortgagee to occupy the dwelling-house than A has by virtue of his estate or interest and of any contract with the mortgagee.

(4) Subsection (3) does not apply, in the case of home rights, if under section 31 those rights are a charge, affecting the mortgagee, on the estate or interest mortgaged.

(5) In this section 'connected person', in relation to any person, means that person's spouse, former spouse, civil partner, former civil partner, cohabitant or former cohabitant.

55 Actions by mortgagees: joining connected persons as parties

(1) This section applies if a mortgagee of land which consists of or includes a dwelling-house brings an action in any court for the enforcement of his security.

(2) A connected person who is not already a party to the action is entitled to be made a party in the circumstances mentioned in subsection (3).

(3) The circumstances are that—

(a) the connected person is enabled by section 30(3) or (6) (or by section 30 (3) or (6) as applied by section 35(13) or 36(13)), to meet the mortgagor's liabilities under the mortgage;

(b) he has applied to the court before the action is finally disposed of in that court; and

(c) the court sees no special reason against his being made a party to the action and is satisfied—

(i) that he may be expected to make such payments or do such other things in or towards satisfaction of the mortgagor's liabilities or obligations as might affect the outcome of the proceedings; or

(ii) that the expectation of it should be considered under section 36 of the Administration of Justice Act 1970.

(4) In this section 'connected person' has the same meaning as in section 54.

56   Actions by mortgagees: service of notice on certain persons

(1) This section applies if a mortgagee of land which consists, or substantially consists, of a dwelling-house brings an action for the enforcement of his security, and at the relevant time there is—

(a) in the case of unregistered land, a land charge of Class F registered against the person who is the estate owner at the relevant time or any person who, where the estate owner is a trustee, preceded him as trustee during the subsistence of the mortgage; or

(b) in the case of registered land, a subsisting registration of—

(i) a notice under section 31(10);

(ii) a notice under section 2(8) of the Matrimonial Homes Act 1983; or

(iii) a notice or caution under section 2(7) of the Matrimonial Homes Act 1967.

(2) If the person on whose behalf—

(a) the land charge is registered, or

(b) the notice or caution is entered,

is not a party to the action, the mortgagee must serve notice of the action on him.

(3) If—

(a) an official search has been made on behalf of the mortgagee which would disclose any land charge of Class F, notice or caution within subsection (1)(a) or (b),

(b) a certificate of the result of the search has been issued, and

(c) the action is commenced within the priority period,

the relevant time is the date of the certificate.

(4) In any other case the relevant time is the time when the action is commenced.

(5) The priority period is, for both registered and unregistered land, the period for which, in accordance with section 11(5) and (6) of the Land Charges Act 1972, a certificate on an official search operates in favour of a purchaser.

Jurisdiction and procedure etc.

57   Jurisdiction of courts

(1) For the purposes of this Part 'the court' means the High Court or the family court.

...

58   Contempt proceedings

The powers of the court in relation to contempt of court arising out of a person's failure to comply with an order under this Part may be exercised by the relevant judicial authority.

...

60   Provision for third parties to act on behalf of victims of domestic violence

(1) Rules of court may provide for a prescribed person, or any person in a prescribed category, ('a representative') to act on behalf of another in relation to proceedings to which this Part applies.

(2) Rules made under this section may, in particular, authorise a representative to apply for an occupation order or for a non-molestation order for which the person on whose behalf the representative is acting could have applied.

(3) Rules made under this section may prescribe—

(a) conditions to be satisfied before a representative may make an application to the court on behalf of another; and

(b) considerations to be taken into account by the court in determining whether, and if so how, to exercise any of its powers under this Part when a representative is acting on behalf of another.

(4) Any rules made under this section may be made so as to have effect for a specified period and may make consequential or transitional provision with respect to the expiry of the specified period.

(5) Any such rules may be replaced by further rules made under this section.

...

General

62   Meaning of 'cohabitants', 'relevant child' and 'associated persons'

(1) For the purposes of this Part—

(a) 'cohabitants' are two persons who are neither married to each other nor civil partners of each other but are living together as husband and wife or as if they were civil partners; and

(b) 'cohabit' and 'former cohabitants' are to be read accordingly, but the latter expression does not include cohabitants who have subsequently married each other or become civil partners of each other.

(2) In this Part, 'relevant child', in relation to any proceedings under this Part, means—

(a) any child who is living with or might reasonably be expected to live with either party to the proceedings;

(b) any child in relation to whom an order under the Adoption Act 1976, the Adoption and Children Act 2002 or the Children Act 1989 is in question in the proceedings; and

(c) any other child whose interests the court considers relevant.

(3) For the purposes of this Part, a person is associated with another person if—

(a)   they are or have been married to each other;

(aa) they are or have been civil partners of each other;

(b)   they are cohabitants or former cohabitants;

(c)   they live or have lived in the same household, otherwise than merely by reason of one of them being the other's employee, tenant, lodger or boarder;

(d)   they are relatives;

(e)   they have agreed to marry one another (whether or not that agreement has been terminated);

(eza) they have entered into a civil partnership agreement (as defined by section 73 of the Civil Partnership Act 2004) (whether or not that agreement has been terminated);

(ea) they have or have had an intimate personal relationship with each other which is or was of significant duration;

(f)   in relation to any child, they are both persons falling within subsection (4); or

(g)   they are parties to the same family proceedings (other than proceedings under this Part).

(4) A person falls within this subsection in relation to a child if—

(a) he is a parent of the child; or

(b) he has or has had parental responsibility for the child.

(5) If a child has been adopted or falls within subsection (7), two persons are also associated with each other for the purposes of this Part if—

(a) one is a natural parent of the child or a parent of such a natural parent; and

(b) the other is the child or any person—

(i) who has become a parent of the child by virtue of an adoption order or has applied for an adoption order, or

(ii) with whom the child has at any time been placed for adoption.

(6) A body corporate and another person are not, by virtue of subsection (3)(f) or (g), to be regarded for the purposes of this Part as associated with each other.

(7) A child falls within this subsection if—

(a) an adoption agency, within the meaning of section 2 of the Adoption and Children Act 2002, has power to place him for adoption under section 19 of that Act (placing children with parental consent) or he has become the subject of an order under section 21 of that Act (placement orders), or

(b) he is freed for adoption by virtue of an order made—

(i) in England and Wales, under section 18 of the Adoption Act 1976,

...

63   Interpretation of Part IV

(1) In this Part—

'adoption order' means an adoption order within the meaning of section 72(1) of the Adoption Act 1976 or section 46(1) of the Adoption and Children Act 2002;

'associated', in relation to a person, is to be read with section 62(3) to (6);

'child' means a person under the age of eighteen years;

'cohabit', 'cohabitant' and 'former cohabitant' have the meaning given by section 62(1);

'the court' is to be read with section 57;

'development' means physical, intellectual, emotional, social or behavioural development;

'dwelling-house' includes (subject to subsection (4))—

(a) any building or part of a building which is occupied as a dwelling,

(b) any caravan, house-boat or structure which is occupied as a dwelling,

and any yard, garden, garage or outhouse belonging to it and occupied with it;

'family proceedings' means any proceedings—

(a) under the inherent jurisdiction of the High Court in relation to children; or

(b) under the enactments mentioned in subsection (2);

'harm'—

(a) in relation to a person who has reached the age of eighteen years, means ill-treatment or the impairment of health; and

(b) in relation to a child, means ill-treatment or the impairment of health or development;

'health' includes physical or mental health;

'home rights' has the meaning given by section 30;

'ill-treatment' includes forms of ill-treatment which are not physical and, in relation to a child, includes sexual abuse;

'mortgage', 'mortgagor' and 'mortgagee' have the same meaning as in the Law of Property Act 1925;

'mortgage payments' includes any payments which, under the terms of the mortgage, the mortgagor is required to make to any person;

'non-molestation order' has the meaning given by section 42(1);

'occupation order' has the meaning given by section 39;

'parental responsibility' has the same meaning as in the Children Act 1989;

'relative', in relation to a person, means—

(a) the father, mother, stepfather, stepmother, son, daughter, stepson, stepdaughter, grand-mother, grandfather, grandson or granddaughter of that person or of that person's spouse, former spouse, civil partner or former civil partner, or

(b) the brother, sister, uncle, aunt, niece, nephew or first cousin (whether of the full blood or of the half blood or by marriage or civil partnership) of that person or of that person's spouse, former spouse, civil partner or former civil partner,

and includes, in relation to a person who is cohabiting or has cohabited with another person, any person who would fall within paragraph (a) or (b) if the parties were married to each other or were civil partners of each other;

'relevant child', in relation to any proceedings under this Part, has the meaning given by section 62(2);

'the relevant judicial authority', in relation to any order under this Part, means—

(a) where the order was made by the High Court, a judge of that court;

(aa) where the order was made by the family court, a judge of that court.

(2) The enactments referred to in the definition of 'family proceedings' are—

...

(b) this Part;

(ba) Part 4A;

(c) the Matrimonial Causes Act 1973;

(d) the Adoption Act 1976;

(e) the Domestic Proceedings and Magistrates' Courts Act 1978;

(f) Part III of the Matrimonial and Family Proceedings Act 1984;

(g) Parts I, II and IV of the Children Act 1989;

(h) section 54 of the Human Fertilisation and Embryology Act 2008;

(i) the Adoption and Children Act 2002.

(j) Schedules 5 to 7 to the Civil Partnership Act 2004.

(3) Where the question of whether harm suffered by a child is significant turns on the child's health or development, his health or development shall be compared with that which could reasonably be expected of a similar child.

(4) For the purposes of sections 31, 32, 53 and 54 and such other provisions of this Part (if any) as may be prescribed, this Part is to have effect as if paragraph (b) of the definition of 'dwelling-house' were omitted.

(5) It is hereby declared that this Part applies as between the parties to a marriage even though either of them is, or has at any time during the marriage been, married to more than one person.

PART 4A FORCED MARRIAGE

Forced marriage protection orders

63A Forced marriage protection orders

(1) The court may make an order for the purposes of protecting—

(a) a person from being forced into a marriage or from any attempt to be forced into a marriage; or

(b) a person who has been forced into a marriage.

(2) In deciding whether to exercise its powers under this section and, if so, in what manner, the court must have regard to all the circumstances including the need to secure the health, safety and well-being of the person to be protected.

(3) In ascertaining that person's well-being, the court must, in particular, have such regard to the person's wishes and feelings (so far as they are reasonably ascertainable) as the court considers appropriate in the light of the person's age and understanding.

(4) For the purposes of this Part a person ('A') is forced into a marriage if another person ('B') forces A to enter into a marriage (whether with B or another person) without A's free and full consent.

(5) For the purposes of subsection (4) it does not matter whether the conduct of B which forces A to enter into a marriage is directed against A, B or another person.

(6) In this Part—

'force' includes coerce by threats or other psychological means (and related expressions are to be read accordingly); and

'forced marriage protection order' means an order under this section.

63B   Contents of orders

(1) A forced marriage protection order may contain—

    (a) such prohibitions, restrictions or requirements; and

    (b) such other terms;

as the court considers appropriate for the purposes of the order.

(2) The terms of such orders may, in particular, relate to—

    (a) conduct outside England and Wales as well as (or instead of) conduct within England and Wales;

    (b) respondents who are, or may become, involved in other respects as well as (or instead of) respondents who force or attempt to force, or may force or attempt to force, a person to enter into a marriage;

    (c) other persons who are, or may become, involved in other respects as well as respondents of any kind.

(3) For the purposes of subsection (2) examples of involvement in other respects are—

    (a) aiding, abetting, counselling, procuring, encouraging or assisting another person to force, or to attempt to force, a person to enter into a marriage; or

    (b) conspiring to force, or to attempt to force, a person to enter into a marriage.

63C   Applications and other occasions for making orders

(1) The court may make a forced marriage protection order—

    (a) on an application being made to it; or

    (b) without an application being made to it but in the circumstances mentioned in subsection (6).

(2) An application may be made by—

    (a) the person who is to be protected by the order; or

    (b) a relevant third party.

(3) An application may be made by any other person with the leave of the court.

(4) In deciding whether to grant leave, the court must have regard to all the circumstances including—

    (a) the applicant's connection with the person to be protected;

    (b) the applicant's knowledge of the circumstances of the person to be protected; and

    (c) the wishes and feelings of the person to be protected so far as they are reasonably ascertainable and so far as the court considers it appropriate, in the light of the person's age and understanding, to have regard to them.

(5) An application under this section may be made in other family proceedings or without any other family proceedings being instituted.

(6) The circumstances in which the court may make an order without an application being made are where—

    (a) any other family proceedings are before the court ('the current proceedings');

    (b) the court considers that a forced marriage protection order should be made to protect a person (whether or not a party to the current proceedings); and

    (c) a person who would be a respondent to any such proceedings for a forced marriage protection order is a party to the current proceedings.

(7) In this section—

'family proceedings' has the same meaning as in Part 4 (see section 63(1) and (2)) but also includes—

> (a) proceedings under the inherent jurisdiction of the High Court in relation to adults;
>
> (b) proceedings in which the court has made an emergency protection order under section 44 of the Children Act 1989 (c. 41) which includes an exclusion requirement (as defined in section 44A(3) of that Act); and
>
> (c) proceedings in which the court has made an order under section 50 of the Act of 1989 (recovery of abducted children etc.); and

'relevant third party' means a person specified, or falling within a description of persons specified, by order of the Lord Chancellor.

(8) An order of the Lord Chancellor under subsection (7) may, in particular, specify the Secretary of State.

63CA Offence of breaching order

(1) A person who without reasonable excuse does anything that the person is prohibited from doing by a forced marriage protection order is guilty of an offence.

(2) In the case of a forced marriage protection order made by virtue of section 63D(1), a person can be guilty of an offence under this section only in respect of conduct engaged in at a time when the person was aware of the existence of the order.

(3) Where a person is convicted of an offence under this section in respect of any conduct, that conduct is not punishable as a contempt of court.

(4) A person cannot be convicted of an offence under this section in respect of any conduct which has been punished as a contempt of court.

(5) A person guilty of an offence under this section is liable—

> (a) on conviction on indictment, to imprisonment for a term not exceeding five years, or a fine, or both;
>
> (b) on summary conviction, to imprisonment for a term not exceeding 12 months, or a fine, or both.

(6) A reference in any enactment to proceedings under this Part, or to an order under this Part, does not include a reference to proceedings for an offence under this section or to an order made in proceedings for such an offence.

(7) 'Enactment' includes an enactment contained in subordinate legislation within the meaning of the Interpretation Act 1978.

Further provision about orders

63D Ex parte orders: Part 4A

(1) The court may, in any case where it considers that it is just and convenient to do so, make a forced marriage protection order even though the respondent has not been given such notice of the proceedings as would otherwise be required by rules of court.

(2) In deciding whether to exercise its powers under subsection (1), the court must have regard to all the circumstances including—

> (a) any risk of significant harm to the person to be protected or another person if the order is not made immediately;
>
> (b) whether it is likely that an applicant will be deterred or prevented from pursuing an application if an order is not made immediately; and
>
> (c) whether there is reason to believe that—
>
>> (i) the respondent is aware of the proceedings but is deliberately evading service; and
>>
>> (ii) the delay involved in effecting substituted service will cause serious prejudice to the person to be protected or (if a different person) an applicant.

(3) The court must give the respondent an opportunity to make representations about any order made by virtue of subsection (1).

(4) The opportunity must be—

    (a) as soon as just and convenient; and

    (b) at a hearing of which notice has been given to all the parties in accordance with rules of court.

63E   Undertakings instead of orders

(1) In any case where the court has power to make a forced marriage protection order, the court may accept an undertaking from the respondent instead of making the order.

(2) But a court may not accept an undertaking under subsection (1) if it appears to the court—

    (a) that the respondent has used or threatened violence against the person to be protected, and

    (b) that, for the person's protection, it is necessary to make a forced marriage protection order so that any breach of it by the respondent may be punishable under section 63CA.

    ...

(4) An undertaking given to the court under subsection (1) is enforceable as if the court had made the order in terms corresponding to those of the undertaking.

(5) This section is without prejudice to the powers of the court apart from this section.

63F   Duration of orders

A forced marriage protection order may be made for a specified period or until varied or discharged.

63G   Variation of orders and their discharge

(1) The court may vary or discharge a forced marriage protection order on an application by—

    (a) any party to the proceedings for the order;

    (b) the person being protected by the order (if not a party to the proceedings for the order); or

    (c) any person affected by the order.

(2) In addition, the court may vary or discharge a forced marriage protection order made by virtue of section 63C(1)(b) even though no application under subsection (1) above has been made to the court.

(3) Section 63D applies to a variation of a forced marriage protection order as it applies to the making of such an order.

(4) Section 63E applies to proceedings for a variation of a forced marriage protection order as it applies to proceedings for the making of such an order.

(5) Accordingly, references in sections 63D and 63E to making a forced marriage protection order are to be read for the purposes of subsections (3) and (4) above as references to varying such an order.

    ...

Arrest for breach of orders

63J   Arrest under warrant

    ...

(2) An interested party may apply to the relevant judge for the issue of a warrant for the arrest of a person if the interested party considers that the person has failed to comply with a forced marriage protection order or is otherwise in contempt of court in relation to the order.

(3) The relevant judge must not issue a warrant on an application under subsection (2) unless—

    (a) the application is substantiated on oath; and

    (b) the relevant judge has reasonable grounds for believing that the person to be arrested has failed to comply with the order or is otherwise in contempt of court in relation to the order.

(4) In this section 'interested party', in relation to a forced marriage protection order, means—

    (a) the person being protected by the order;

    (b) (if a different person) the person who applied for the order; or

    (c) any other person;

but no application may be made under subsection (2) by a person falling within paragraph (c) without the leave of the relevant judge.

63K   Remand: general

(1) The court before which an arrested person is brought by virtue of a warrant issued under section 63J may, if the matter is not then disposed of immediately, remand the person concerned.

(2) Schedule 5 has effect in relation to the powers of the court to remand a person by virtue of this section but as if the following modifications were made to the Schedule.

(3) The modifications are that—

(a) in paragraph 2(1) of Schedule 5, the reference to section 47 is to be read as a reference to this section; and

(b) in paragraph 2(5)(b) of the Schedule, the reference to section 48(1) is to be read as a reference to section 63L(1).

(4) Subsection (5) applies if a person remanded under this section is granted bail under Schedule 5 as modified above.

(5) The person may be required by the relevant judge to comply, before release on bail or later, with such requirements as appear to the relevant judge to be necessary to secure that the person does not interfere with witnesses or otherwise obstruct the course of justice.

63L   Remand: medical examination and report

(1) Any power to remand a person under section 63K(1) may be exercised for the purpose of enabling a medical examination and report to be made if the relevant judge has reason to consider that a medical report will be required.

(2) If such a power is so exercised, the adjournment must not be for more than 4 weeks at a time unless the relevant judge remands the accused in custody.

(3) If the relevant judge remands the accused in custody, the adjournment must not be for more than 3 weeks at a time.

(4) Subsection (5) applies if there is reason to suspect that a person who has been arrested—

...

(b) under a warrant issued on an application made under section 63J(2);

is suffering from mental disorder within the meaning of the Mental Health Act 1983

(5) The relevant judge has the same power to make an order under section 35 of the Mental Health Act 1983 (c. 20) (remand for report on accused's mental condition) as the Crown Court has under section 35 of that Act in the case of an accused person within the meaning of that section.

Jurisdiction and procedure

63M   Jurisdiction of courts: Part 4A

(1) For the purposes of this Part 'the court' means the High Court or the family court.

...

63O   Contempt proceedings: Part 4A

The powers of the court in relation to contempt of court arising out of a person's failure to comply with a forced marriage protection order or otherwise in connection with such an order may be exercised by the relevant judge.

...

Supplementary

63Q   Guidance

(1) The Secretary of State may from time to time prepare and publish guidance to such descriptions of persons as the Secretary of State considers appropriate about—

(a) the effect of this Part or any provision of this Part; or

(b) other matters relating to forced marriages.

(2) A person exercising public functions to whom guidance is given under this section must have regard to it in the exercise of those functions.

(3) Nothing in this section permits the Secretary of State to give guidance to any court or tribunal.

63R   Other protection or assistance against forced marriage

(1) This Part does not affect any other protection or assistance available to a person who—

    (a) is being, or may be, forced into a marriage or subjected to an attempt to be forced into a marriage; or

    (b) has been forced into a marriage.

(2) In particular, it does not affect—

    (a) the inherent jurisdiction of the High Court;

    (b) any criminal liability;

    (c) any civil remedies under the Protection from Harassment Act 1997 (c. 40);

    (d) any right to an occupation order or a non-molestation order under Part 4 of this Act;

    (e) any protection or assistance under the Children Act 1989 (c. 41);

    (f) any claim in tort; or

    (g) the law of marriage.

63S   Interpretation of Part 4A

In this Part—

'the court' is to be read with section 63M;

'force' (and related expressions), in relation to a marriage, are to be read in accordance with section 63A(4) to (6);

'forced marriage protection order' has the meaning given by section 63A(6);

'marriage' means any religious or civil ceremony of marriage (whether or not legally binding); and

'the relevant judge', in relation to any order under this Part, means—

    (a) where the order was made by the High Court, a judge of that court; and

    (b) where the order was made by the family court, a judge of that court.

PART V SUPPLEMENTAL

64   Provision for separate representation for children

(1) The Lord Chancellor may by regulations provide for the separate representation of children in proceedings in England and Wales which relate to any matter in respect of which a question has arisen, or may arise, under—

    ...

    (b) Part IV;

    (c) the 1973 Act;

    (d) the Domestic Proceedings and Magistrates' Courts Act 1978; or

    (e) Schedule 5 or 6 to the Civil Partnership Act 2004.

(2) The regulations may provide for such representation only in specified circumstances.

...

Section 32   **SCHEDULE 4**

PROVISIONS SUPPLEMENTARY
TO SECTIONS 30 AND 31

Interpretation

1.— In this Schedule 'legal representative' means a person who, for the purposes of the Legal Services Act 2007, is an authorised person in relation to an activity which constitutes a reserved instrument activity (within the meaning of that Act).

Restriction on registration where spouse or civil partner entitled to more than one charge

2.—Where one spouse or civil partner is entitled by virtue of section 31 to a registrable charge in respect of each of two or more dwelling-houses, only one of the charges to which that spouse or civil partner is so entitled shall be registered under section 31(10) or under section 2 of the Land Charges Act 1972 at any one time, and if any of those charges is registered under either of those provisions the Chief Land Registrar, on being satisfied that any other of them is so registered, shall cancel the registration of the charge first registered.

Contract for sale of house affected by registered charge to include term requiring cancellation of registration before completion

3.—(1) Where one spouse or civil partner is entitled by virtue of section 31 to a charge on an estate in a dwelling-house and the charge is registered under section 31(10) or section 2 of the Land Charges Act 1972, it shall be a term of any contract for the sale of that estate whereby the vendor agrees to give vacant possession of the dwelling-house on completion of the contract that the vendor will before such completion procure the cancellation of the registration of the charge at his expense.

(2) Sub-paragraph (1) shall not apply to any such contract made by a vendor who is entitled to sell the estate in the dwelling-house freed from any such charge.

(3) If, on the completion of such a contract as is referred to in sub-paragraph (1), there is delivered to the purchaser or his legal representative an application by the spouse or civil partner entitled to the charge for the cancellation of the registration of that charge, the term of the contract for which sub-paragraph (1) provides shall be deemed to have been performed.

(4) This paragraph applies only if and so far as a contrary intention is not expressed in the contract.

(5) This paragraph shall apply to a contract for exchange as it applies to a contract for sale.

(6) This paragraph shall, with the necessary modifications, apply to a contract for the grant of a lease or underlease of a dwelling-house as it applies to a contract for the sale of an estate in a dwelling-house.

Cancellation of registration after termination of marriage or civil partnership, etc.

4.—(1) Where a spouse's or civil partner's home rights are a charge on an estate in the dwelling-house and the charge is registered under section 31(10) or under section 2 of the Land Charges Act 1972, the Chief Land Registrar shall, subject to sub-paragraph (2), cancel the registration of the charge if he is satisfied—

    (a) in the case of a marriage—

        (i) by the production of a certificate or other sufficient evidence, that either spouse is dead,

        (ii) by the production of an official copy of a decree or order of a court, that the marriage has been terminated otherwise than by death, or

    (iii) by the production of an order of the court, that the spouse's home rights constitut-
ing the charge have been terminated by the order, and

  (b) in the case of a civil partnership—

    (i) by the production of a certificate or other sufficient evidence, that either civil part-
ner is dead,

    (ii) by the production of an official copy of an order or decree of a court, that the civil
partnership has been terminated otherwise than by death, or

    (iii) by the production of an order of the court, that the civil partner's home rights con-
stituting the charge have been terminated by the order.

(2) Where—

  (a) the marriage or civil partnership in question has been terminated by the death of the
spouse or civil partner entitled to an estate in the dwelling-house or otherwise than by
death, and

  (b) an order affecting the charge of the spouse or civil partner not so entitled had been made
under section 33(5),

then if, after the making of the order, registration of the charge was renewed or the charge registered in pursuance of sub-paragraph (3), the Chief Land Registrar shall not cancel the registration of
the charge in accordance with sub-paragraph (1) unless he is also satisfied that the order has ceased
to have effect.

(3) Where such an order has been made, then, for the purposes of sub-paragraph (2), the spouse
or civil partner entitled to the charge affected by the order may—

  (a) if before the date of the order the charge was registered under section 31 (10) or under
section 2 of the Land Charges Act 1972, renew the registration of the charge, and

  (b) if before the said date the charge was not so registered, register the charge under section
31(10) or under section 2 of the Land Charges Act 1972.

(4) Renewal of the registration of a charge in pursuance of sub-paragraph (3) shall be effected
in such manner as may be prescribed, and an application for such renewal or for registration of a
charge in pursuance of that sub-paragraph shall contain such particulars of any order affecting the
charge made under section 33(5) as may be prescribed.

(5) The renewal in pursuance of sub-paragraph (3) of the registration of a charge shall not
affect the priority of the charge.

(6) In this paragraph 'prescribed' means prescribed by rules made under section 16 of the Land
Charges Act 1972 or by land registration rules under the Land Registration Act 2002, as the circumstances of the case require.

Release of home rights

5.—(1) A spouse or civil partner entitled to home rights may by a release in writing release
those rights or release them as respects part only of the dwelling-house affected by them.

(2) Where a contract is made for the sale of an estate or interest in a dwelling-house, or for the
grant of a lease or underlease of a dwelling-house, being (in either case) a dwelling-house affected
by a charge registered under section 31(10) or under section 2 of the Land Charges Act 1972, then,
without prejudice to sub-paragraph (1), the home rights constituting the charge shall be deemed to
have been released on the happening of whichever of the following events first occurs—

  (a) the delivery to the purchaser or lessee, as the case may be, or his legal representative on
completion of the contract of an application by the spouse or civil partner entitled to the
charge for the cancellation of the registration of the charge; or

  (b) the lodging of such an application at Her Majesty's Land Registry.

Postponement of priority of charge

6.—A spouse or civil partner entitled by virtue of section 31 to a charge on an estate or interest may agree in writing that any other charge on, or interest in, that estate or interest shall rank in priority to the charge to which that spouse or civil partner is so entitled.

SCHEDULE 5 POWERS OF HIGH COURT AND COUNTY COURT TO REMAND

Interpretation

1.—In this Schedule 'the court' means the High Court or the family court and includes—
- (a) in relation to the High Court, a judge of that court, and
- (b) in relation to the family court, a judge of that court.

Remand in custody or on bail

2.—(1) Where a court has power to remand a person under section 47, the court may—
- (a) remand him in custody, that is to say, commit him to custody to be brought before the court at the end of the period of remand or at such earlier time as the court may require, or
- (b) remand him on bail—
    - (i) by taking from him a recognizance (with or without sureties) conditioned as provided in sub-paragraph (3), or
    - (ii) by fixing the amount of the recognizances with a view to their being taken subsequently in accordance with paragraph 4 and in the meantime committing the person to custody in accordance with paragraph (a).

(2) Where a person is brought before the court after remand, the court may further remand him.

(3) Where a person is remanded on bail under sub-paragraph (1), the court may direct that his recognizance be conditioned for his appearance—
- (a) before that court at the end of the period of remand, or
- (b) at every time and place to which during the course of the proceedings the hearing may from time to time be adjourned.

(4) Where a recognizance is conditioned for a person's appearance in accordance with sub-paragraph (1)(b), the fixing of any time for him next to appear shall be deemed to be a remand; but nothing in this sub-paragraph or sub-paragraph (3) shall deprive the court of power at any subsequent hearing to remand him afresh.

(5) Subject to paragraph 3, the court shall not remand a person under this paragraph for a period exceeding 8 clear days, except that—
- (a) if the court remands him on bail, it may remand him for a longer period if he and the other party consent, and
- (b) if the court adjourns a case under section 48(1), the court may remand him for the period of the adjournment.

(6) Where the court has power under this paragraph to remand a person in custody it may, if the remand is for a period not exceeding 3 clear days, commit him to the custody of a constable.

Further remand

3.—(1) If the court is satisfied that any person who has been remanded under paragraph 2 is unable by reason of illness or accident to appear or be brought before the court at the expiration of the period for which he was remanded, the court may, in his absence, remand him for a further time; and paragraph 2(5) shall not apply.

(2) Notwithstanding anything in paragraph 2(1), the power of the court under sub-paragraph (1) to remand a person on bail for a further time may be exercised by enlarging his recognizance and those of any sureties for him to a later time.

(3) Where a person remanded on bail under paragraph 2 is bound to appear before the court at any time and the court has no power to remand him under sub-paragraph (1), the court may in his absence enlarge his recognizance and those of any sureties for him to a later time; and the enlargement of his recognizance shall be deemed to be a further remand.

Postponement of taking of recognizance

4.—Where under paragraph 2(1)(b)(ii) the court fixes the amount in which the principal and his sureties, if any, are to be bound, the recognizance may thereafter be taken by such person as may be prescribed by rules of court, and the same consequences shall follow as if it had been entered into before the court.

SCHEDULE 7 TRANSFER OF CERTAIN TENANCIES ON DIVORCE ETC. OR ON SEPARATION OF COHABITANTS

PART I GENERAL

Interpretation

1.—In this Schedule—
'civil partner', except in paragraph 2, includes (where the context requires) former civil partner;
'cohabitant', except in paragraph 3, includes (where the context requires) former cohabitant;
'the court' means the High Court or the family court,
'landlord' includes—
  (a) any person from time to time deriving title under the original landlord; and
  (b) in relation to any dwelling-house, any person other than the tenant who is, or (but for Part VII of the Rent Act 1977 or Part II of the Rent (Agriculture) Act 1976) would be, entitled to possession of the dwelling-house;
'Part II order' means an order under Part II of this Schedule;
'a relevant tenancy' means—
  (a) a protected tenancy or statutory tenancy within the meaning of the Rent Act 1977;
  (b) a statutory tenancy within the meaning of the Rent (Agriculture) Act 1976;
  (c) a secure tenancy within the meaning of section 79 of the Housing Act 1985;
  (d) an assured tenancy or assured agricultural occupancy within the meaning of Part I of the Housing Act 1988; or
  (e) an introductory tenancy within the meaning of Chapter I of Part V of the Housing Act 1996;
'spouse', except in paragraph 2, includes (where the context requires) former spouse; and
'tenancy' includes sub-tenancy.

Cases in which the court may make an order

2.—(1) This paragraph applies if one spouse or civil partner is entitled, either in his own right or jointly with the other spouse or civil partner, to occupy a dwelling-house by virtue of a relevant tenancy.
  (2) The court may make a Part II order—
  (a) on granting a decree of divorce, a decree of nullity of marriage or a decree of judicial separation or at any time thereafter (whether, in the case of a decree of divorce or nullity of marriage, before or after the decree is made absolute), or
  (b) at any time when it has power to make a property adjustment order under Part 2 of Schedule 5 to the Civil Partnership Act 2004 with respect to the civil partnership.

3.—(1) This paragraph applies if one cohabitant is entitled, either in his own right or jointly with the other cohabitant, to occupy a dwelling-house by virtue of a relevant tenancy.

(3) If the cohabitants cease to cohabit, the court may make a Part II order.

4.—The court shall not make a Part II order unless the dwelling-house is or was—

(a) in the case of spouses, a matrimonial home;

(aa) in the case of civil partners, a civil partnership home; or

(b) in the case of cohabitants, a home in which they cohabited.

Matters to which the court must have regard

5.—In determining whether to exercise its powers under Part II of this Schedule and, if so, in what manner, the court shall have regard to all the circumstances of the case including—

(a) the circumstances in which the tenancy was granted to either or both of the spouses, civil partners or cohabitants or, as the case requires, the circumstances in which either or both of them became tenant under the tenancy;

(b) the matters mentioned in section 33(6)(a), (b) and (c) and, where the parties are cohabitants and only one of them is entitled to occupy the dwelling-house by virtue of the relevant tenancy, the further matters mentioned in section 36(6)(e), (f), (g) and (h); and

(c) the suitability of the parties as tenants.

PART II ORDERS THAT MAY BE MADE

References to entitlement to occupy

6.—References in this Part of this Schedule to a spouse, a civil partner or a cohabitant being entitled to occupy a dwelling-house by virtue of a relevant tenancy apply whether that entitlement is in his own right or jointly with the other spouse, civil partner or cohabitant.

Protected, secure or assured tenancy or assured agricultural occupancy

7.—(1) If a spouse, civil partner or cohabitant is entitled to occupy the dwelling-house by virtue of a protected tenancy within the meaning of the Rent Act 1977, a secure tenancy within the meaning of the Housing Act 1985, an assured tenancy or assured agricultural occupancy within the meaning of Part I of the Housing Act 1988 or an introductory tenancy within the meaning of Chapter I of Part V of the Housing Act 1996, the court may by order direct that, as from such date as may be specified in the order, there shall, by virtue of the order and without further assurance, be transferred to, and vested in, the other spouse, civil partner or cohabitant—

(a) the estate or interest which the spouse, civil partner or cohabitant so entitled had in the dwelling-house immediately before that date by virtue of the lease or agreement creating the tenancy and any assignment of that lease or agreement, with all rights, privileges and appurtenances attaching to that estate or interest but subject to all covenants, obligations, liabilities and incumbrances to which it is subject; and

(b) where the spouse, civil partner or cohabitant so entitled is an assignee of such lease or agreement, the liability of that spouse, civil partner or cohabitant under any covenant of indemnity by the assignee express or implied in the assignment of the lease or agreement to that spouse, civil partner or cohabitant.

(2) If an order is made under this paragraph, any liability or obligation to which the spouse, civil partner or cohabitant so entitled is subject under any covenant having reference to the dwelling-house in the lease or agreement, being a liability or obligation falling due to be discharged or performed on or after the date so specified, shall not be enforceable against that spouse, civil partner or cohabitant.

(3) If the spouse, civil partner or cohabitant so entitled is a successor within the meaning of Part 4 of the Housing Act 1985—

(a) his former spouse (or, in the case of judicial separation, his spouse),

(b) his former civil partner (or, if a separation order is in force, his civil partner), or

(c) his former cohabitant,

is to be deemed also to be a successor within the meaning of that Part.

(3A) If the spouse, civil partner or cohabitant so entitled is a successor within the meaning of section 132 of the Housing Act 1996—

    (a) his former spouse (or, in the case of judicial separation, his spouse),

    (b) his former civil partner (or, if a separation order is in force, his civil partner), or

    (c) his former cohabitant,

is to be deemed also to be a successor within the meaning of that section.

(4) If the spouse, civil partner or cohabitant so entitled is for the purposes of section 17 of the Housing Act 1988 a successor in relation to the tenancy or occupancy—

    (a) his former spouse (or, in the case of judicial separation, his spouse),

    (b) his former civil partner (or, if a separation order is in force, his civil partner), or

    (c) his former cohabitant,

is to be deemed to be a successor in relation to the tenancy or occupancy for the purposes of that section.

(5) If the transfer under sub-paragraph (1) is of an assured agricultural occupancy, then, for the purposes of Chapter III of Part I of the Housing Act 1988—

    (a) the agricultural worker condition is fulfilled with respect to the dwelling-house while the spouse, civil partner or cohabitant to whom the assured agricultural occupancy is transferred continues to be the occupier under that occupancy, and

    (b) that condition is to be treated as so fulfilled by virtue of the same paragraph of Schedule 3 to the Housing Act 1988 as was applicable before the transfer.

Statutory tenancy within the meaning of the Rent Act 1977

8.—(1) This paragraph applies if the spouse, civil partner or cohabitant is entitled to occupy the dwelling-house by virtue of a statutory tenancy within the meaning of the Rent Act 1977.

(2) The court may by order direct that, as from the date specified in the order—

    (a) that spouse, civil partner or cohabitant is to cease to be entitled to occupy the dwelling-house; and

    (b) the other spouse, civil partner or cohabitant is to be deemed to be the tenant or, as the case may be, the sole tenant under that statutory tenancy.

(3) The question whether the provisions of paragraphs 1 to 3, or (as the case may be) paragraphs 5 to 7 of Schedule 1 to the Rent Act 1977, as to the succession by the surviving spouse or surviving civil partner of a deceased tenant, or by a member of the deceased tenant's family, to the right to retain possession are capable of having effect in the event of the death of the person deemed by an order under this paragraph to be the tenant or sole tenant under the statutory tenancy is to be determined according as those provisions have or have not already had effect in relation to the statutory tenancy.

Statutory tenancy within the meaning of the Rent (Agriculture) Act 1976

9.—(1) This paragraph applies if the spouse, civil partner or cohabitant is entitled to occupy the dwelling-house by virtue of a statutory tenancy within the meaning of the Rent (Agriculture) Act 1976.

(2) The court may by order direct that, as from such date as may be specified in the order—

    (a) that spouse, civil partner or cohabitant is to cease to be entitled to occupy the dwelling-house; and

    (b) the other spouse, civil partner or cohabitant is to be deemed to be the tenant or, as the case may be, the sole tenant under that statutory tenancy.

(3) A spouse, civil partner or cohabitant who is deemed under this paragraph to be the tenant under a statutory tenancy is (within the meaning of that Act) a statutory tenant in his own right, or a statutory tenant by succession, according as the other spouse, civil partner or cohabitant was a statutory tenant in his own right or a statutory tenant by succession.

PART III SUPPLEMENTARY PROVISIONS

Compensation

10.—(1) If the court makes a Part II order, it may by the order direct the making of a payment by the spouse, civil partner or cohabitant to whom the tenancy is transferred ('the transferee') to the other spouse, civil partner or cohabitant ('the transferor').

(2) Without prejudice to that, the court may, on making an order by virtue of sub-paragraph (1) for the payment of a sum—

    (a) direct that payment of that sum or any part of it is to be deferred until a specified date or until the occurrence of a specified event, or

    (b) direct that that sum or any part of it is to be paid by instalments.

(3) Where an order has been made by virtue of sub-paragraph (1), the court may, on the application of the transferee or the transferor—

    (a) exercise its powers under sub-paragraph (2), or

    (b) vary any direction previously given under that sub-paragraph,

at any time before the sum whose payment is required by the order is paid in full.

(4) In deciding whether to exercise its powers under this paragraph and, if so, in what manner, the court shall have regard to all the circumstances including—

    (a) the financial loss that would otherwise be suffered by the transferor as a result of the order;

    (b) the financial needs and financial resources of the parties; and

    (c) the financial obligations which the parties have, or are likely to have in the foreseeable future, including financial obligations to each other and to any relevant child.

(5) The court shall not give any direction under sub-paragraph (2) unless it appears to it that immediate payment of the sum required by the order would cause the transferee financial hardship which is greater than any financial hardship that would be caused to the transferor if the direction were given.

Liabilities and obligations in respect of the dwelling-house

11.—(1) If the court makes a Part II order, it may by the order direct that both spouses, civil partners or cohabitants are to be jointly and severally liable to discharge or perform any or all of the liabilities and obligations in respect of the dwelling-house (whether arising under the tenancy or otherwise) which—

    (a) have at the date of the order fallen due to be discharged or performed by one only of them; or

    (b) but for the direction, would before the date specified as the date on which the order is to take effect fall due to be discharged or performed by one only of them.

(2) If the court gives such a direction, it may further direct that either spouse, civil partner or cohabitant is to be liable to indemnify the other in whole or in part against any payment made or expenses incurred by the other in discharging or performing any such liability or obligation.

Date when order made between spouses or civil partners takes effect

12.—The date specified in a Part II order as the date on which the order is to take effect must not be earlier than—

    (a) in the case of a marriage in respect of which a decree of divorce or nullity has been granted, the date on which the decree is made absolute;

    (b) in the case of a civil partnership in respect of which a dissolution or nullity order has been made, the date on which the order is made final.

Effect of remarriage or subsequent civil partnership

13.—(1) If after the grant of a decree dissolving or annulling a marriage either spouse remarries or forms a civil partnership, that spouse is not entitled to apply, by reference to the grant of that decree, for a Part II order.

(2) If after the making of a dissolution or nullity order either civil partner forms a subsequent civil partnership or marries, that civil partner is not entitled to apply, by reference to the making of that order, for a Part II order.

(3) In sub-paragraphs (1) and (2)—

   (a) the references to remarrying and marrying include references to cases where the marriage is by law void or voidable, and

   (b) the references to forming a civil partnership include references to cases where the civil partnership is by law void or voidable.

Rules of court

14.—(1) Rules of court shall be made requiring the court, before it makes an order under this Schedule, to give the landlord of the dwelling-house to which the order will relate an opportunity of being heard.

(2) Rules of court may provide that an application for a Part II order by reference to an order or decree may not, without the leave of the court by which that order was made or decree was granted, be made after the expiration of such period from the order or grant as may be prescribed by the rules.

Saving for other provisions of Act

15.—(1) If a spouse or civil partner is entitled to occupy a dwelling-house by virtue of a tenancy, this Schedule does not affect the operation of sections 30 and 31 in relation to the other spouse's or civil partner's home rights.

(2) If a spouse, civil partner or cohabitant is entitled to occupy a dwelling-house by virtue of a tenancy, the court's powers to make orders under this Schedule are additional to those conferred by sections 33, 35 and 36.

Trusts of Land and Appointment of Trustees Act 1996

(1996 c. 47)

PART I TRUSTS OF LAND

Introductory

1 Meaning of 'trust of land'

   (1) In this Act—

   (a) 'trust of land' means (subject to subsection (3)) any trust of property which consists of or includes land, and

   (b) 'trustees of land' means trustees of a trust of land.

   (2) The reference in subsection (1)(a) to a trust—

   (a) is to any description of trust (whether express, implied, resulting or constructive), including a trust for sale and a bare trust, and

   (b) includes a trust created, or arising, before the commencement of this Act.

...

Settlements and trusts for sale as trusts of land

2   Trusts in place of settlements

(1) No settlement created after the commencement of this Act is a settlement for the purposes of the Settled Land Act 1925; and no settlement shall be deemed to be made under that Act after that commencement.

(2) Subsection (1) does not apply to a settlement created on the occasion of an alteration in any interest in, or of a person becoming entitled under, a settlement which—

(a) is in existence at the commencement of this Act, or

(b) derives from a settlement within paragraph (a) or this paragraph.

(3) But a settlement created as mentioned in subsection (2) is not a settlement for the purposes of the Settled Land Act 1925 if provision to the effect that it is not is made in the instrument, or any of the instruments by which it is created.

(4) Where at any time after the commencement of this Act there is in the case of any settlement which is a settlement for the purposes of the Settled Land Act 1925 no relevant property which is, or is deemed to be, subject to the settlement, the settlement permanently ceases at that time to be a settlement for the purposes of that Act.

In this subsection 'relevant property' means land and personal chattels to which section 67(1) of the Settled Land Act 1925 (heirlooms) applies.

(5) No land held on charitable, ecclesiastical or public trusts shall be or be deemed to be settled land after the commencement of this Act, even if it was or was deemed to be settled land before that commencement.

(6) Schedule 1 has effect to make provision consequential on this section (including provision to impose a trust in circumstances in which apart from this section, there would be a settlement for the purposes of the Settled Land Act 1925 (and there would not otherwise be a trust)).

3   Abolition of doctrine of conversion

(1) Where land is held by trustees subject to a trust for sale, the land is not to be regarded as personal property; and where personal property is subject to a trust for sale in order that the trustees may acquire land, the personal property is not to be regarded as land.

(2) Subsection (1) does not apply to a trust created by a will if the testator died before the commencement of this Act.

(3) Subject to that, subsection (1) applies to a trust whether it is created, or arises, before or after that commencement.

4   Express trusts for sale as trusts of land

(1) In the case of every trust for sale of land created by a disposition there is to be implied, despite any provision to the contrary made by the disposition, a power for the trustees to postpone sale of the land; and the trustees are not liable in any way for postponing sale of the land, in the exercise of their discretion, for an indefinite period.

(2) Subsection (1) applies to a trust whether it is created, or arises, before or after the commencement of this Act.

(3) Subsection (1) does not affect any liability incurred by trustees before that commencement.

5   Implied trusts for sale as trusts of land

(1) Schedule 2 has effect in relation to statutory provisions which impose a trust for sale of land in certain circumstances so that in those circumstances there is instead a trust of the land (without a duty to sell).

(2) Section 1 of the Settled Land Act 1925 does not apply to land held on any trust arising by virtue of that Schedule (so that any such land is subject to a trust of land).

Functions of trustees of land

6   General powers of trustees

(1) For the purpose of exercising their functions as trustees, the trustees of land have in relation to the land subject to the trust all the powers of an absolute owner.

(2) Where in the case of any land subject to a trust of land each of the beneficiaries interested in the land is a person of full age and capacity who is absolutely entitled to the land, the powers conferred on the trustees by subsection (1) include the power to convey the land to the beneficiaries even though they have not required the trustees to do so; and where land is conveyed by virtue of this subsection—

      (a) the beneficiaries shall do whatever is necessary to secure that it vests in them, and

      (b) if they fail to do so, the court may make an order requiring them to do so.

(3) The trustees of land have power to acquire land under the power conferred by section 8 of the Trustee Act 2000.

(5) In exercising the powers conferred by this section trustees shall have regard to the rights of the beneficiaries.

(6) The powers conferred by this section shall not be exercised in contravention of, or of any order made in pursuance of, any other enactment or any rule of law or equity.

(7) The reference in subsection (6) to an order includes an order of any court or of the Charity Commission.

(8) Where any enactment other than this section confers on trustees authority to act subject to any restriction, limitation or condition, trustees of land may not exercise the powers conferred by this section to do any act which they are prevented from doing under the other enactment by reason of the restriction, limitation or condition.

(9) The duty of care under section 1 of the Trustee Act 2000 applies to trustees of land when exercising the powers conferred by this section.

7   Partition by trustees

(1) The trustees of land may, where beneficiaries of full age are absolutely entitled in undivided shares to land subject to the trust, partition the land, or any part of it, and provide (by way of mortgage or otherwise) for the payment of any equality money.

(2) The trustees shall give effect to any such partition by conveying the partitioned land in severalty (whether or not subject to any legal mortgage created for raising equality money), either absolutely or in trust, in accordance with the rights of those beneficiaries.

(3) Before exercising their powers under subsection (2) the trustees shall obtain the consent of each of those beneficiaries.

(4) Where a share in the land is affected by an incumbrance, the trustees may either give effect to it or provide for its discharge from the property allotted to that share as they think fit.

(5) If a share in the land is absolutely vested in a minor, subsections (1) to (4) apply as if he were of full age, except that the trustees may act on his behalf and retain land or other property representing his share in trust for him.

(6) Subsection (1) is subject to sections 21 (part-unit: interests) and 22 (part-unit: charging) of the Commonhold and Leasehold Reform Act 2002.

8   Exclusion and restriction of powers

(1) Sections 6 and 7 do not apply in the case of a trust of land created by a disposition in so far as provision to the effect that they do not apply is made by the disposition.

(2) If the disposition creating such a trust makes provision requiring any consent to be obtained to the exercise of any power conferred by section 6 or 7, the power may not be exercised without that consent.

(3) Subsection (1) does not apply in the case of charitable, ecclesiastical or public trusts.

(4) Subsections (1) and (2) have effect subject to any enactment which prohibits or restricts the effect of provision of the description mentioned in them.

9   Delegation by trustees

(1) The trustees of land may, by power of attorney, delegate to any beneficiary or beneficiaries of full age and beneficially entitled to an interest in possession in land subject to the trust any of their functions as trustees which relate to the land.

(2) Where trustees purport to delegate to a person by a power of attorney under subsection (1) functions relating to any land and another person in good faith deals with him in relation to the land, he shall be presumed in favour of that other person to have been a person to whom the functions could be delegated unless that other person has knowledge at the time of the transaction that he was not such a person.

And it shall be conclusively presumed in favour of any purchaser whose interest depends on the validity of that transaction that that other person dealt in good faith and did not have such knowledge if that other person makes a statutory declaration to that effect before or within three months after the completion of the purchase.

(3) A power of attorney under subsection (1) shall be given by all the trustees jointly and (unless expressed to be irrevocable and to be given by way of security) may be revoked by any one or more of them; and such a power is revoked by the appointment as a trustee of a person other than those by whom it is given (though not by any of those persons dying or otherwise ceasing to be a trustee).

(4) Where a beneficiary to whom functions are delegated by a power of attorney under subsection (1) ceases to be a person beneficially entitled to an interest in possession in land subject to the trust—

(a) if the functions are delegated to him alone, the power is revoked,

(b) if the functions are delegated to him and to other beneficiaries to be exercised by them jointly (but not separately), the power is revoked if each of the other beneficiaries ceases to be so entitled (but otherwise functions exercisable in accordance with the power are so exercisable by the remaining beneficiary or beneficiaries), and

(c) if the functions are delegated to him and to other beneficiaries to be exercised by them separately (or either separately or jointly), the power is revoked in so far as it relates to him.

(5) A delegation under subsection (1) may be for any period or indefinite.

(6) A power of attorney under subsection (1) cannot be an enduring power of attorney or lasting power of attorney within the meaning of the Mental Capacity Act 2005.

(7) Beneficiaries to whom functions have been delegated under subsection (1) are, in relation to the exercise of the functions, in the same position as trustees (with the same duties and liabilities); but such beneficiaries shall not be regarded as trustees for any other purposes (including, in particular, the purposes of any enactment permitting the delegation of functions by trustees or imposing requirements relating to the payment of capital money).

(9) Neither this section nor the repeal by this Act of section 29 of the Law of Property Act 1925 (which is superseded by this section) affects the operation after the commencement of this Act of any delegation effected before that commencement.

9A   Duties of trustees in connection with delegation etc.

(1) The duty of care under section 1 of the Trustee Act 2000 applies to trustees of land in deciding whether to delegate any of their functions under section 9.

(2) Subsection (3) applies if the trustees of land—

(a) delegate any of their functions under section 9, and

(b) the delegation is not irrevocable.

(3) While the delegation continues, the trustees—

(a) must keep the delegation under review,

(b) if circumstances make it appropriate to do so, must consider whether there is a need to exercise any power of intervention that they have, and

(c) if they consider that there is a need to exercise such a power, must do so.

(4) 'Power of intervention' includes—

    (a) a power to give directions to the beneficiary;

    (b) a power to revoke the delegation.

(5) The duty of care under section 1 of the 2000 Act applies to trustees in carrying out any duty under subsection (3).

(6) A trustee of land is not liable for any act or default of the beneficiary, or beneficiaries, unless the trustee fails to comply with the duty of care in deciding to delegate any of the trustees' functions under section 9 or in carrying out any duty under subsection (3).

(7) Neither this section nor the repeal of section 9(8) by the Trustee Act 2000 affects the operation after the commencement of this section of any delegation effected before that commencement.

Consents and consultation

10   Consents

(1) If a disposition creating a trust of land requires the consent of more than two persons to the exercise by the trustees of any function relating to the land, the consent of any two of them to the exercise of the function is sufficient in favour of a purchaser.

(2) Subsection (1) does not apply to the exercise of a function by trustees of land held on charitable, ecclesiastical or public trusts.

(3) Where at any time a person whose consent is expressed by a disposition creating a trust of land to be required to the exercise by the trustees of any function relating to the land is not of full age—

    (a) his consent is not, in favour of a purchaser, required to the exercise of the function, but

    (b) the trustees shall obtain the consent of a parent who has parental responsibility for him (within the meaning of the Children Act 1989) or of a guardian of his.

11   Consultation with beneficiaries

(1) The trustees of land shall in the exercise of any function relating to land subject to the trust—

    (a) so far as practicable, consult the beneficiaries of full age and beneficially entitled to an interest in possession in the land, and

    (b) so far as consistent with the general interest of the trust, give effect to the wishes of those beneficiaries, or (in case of dispute) of the majority (according to the value of their combined interests).

(2) Subsection (1) does not apply—

    (a) in relation to a trust created by a disposition in so far as provision that it does not apply is made by the disposition,

    (b) in relation to a trust created or arising under a will made before the commencement of this Act, or

    (c) in relation to the exercise of the power mentioned in section 6(2).

(3) Subsection (1) does not apply to a trust created before the commencement of this Act by a disposition, or a trust created after that commencement by reference to such a trust, unless provision to the effect that it is to apply is made by a deed executed—

    (a) in a case in which the trust was created by one person and he is of full capacity, by that person, or

    (b) in a case in which the trust was created by more than one person, by such of the persons who created the trust as are alive and of full capacity.

(4) A deed executed for the purposes of subsection (3) is irrevocable.

Right of beneficiaries to occupy trust land

12   The right to occupy

(1) A beneficiary who is beneficially entitled to an interest in possession in land subject to a trust of land is entitled by reason of his interest to occupy the land at any time if at that time—

(a) the purposes of the trust include making the land available for his occupation (or for the occupation of beneficiaries of a class of which he is a member or of beneficiaries in general), or

(b) the land is held by the trustees so as to be so available.

(2) Subsection (1) does not confer on a beneficiary a right to occupy land if it is either unavailable or unsuitable for occupation by him.

(3) This section is subject to section 13.

13　Exclusion and restriction of right to occupy

(1) Where two or more beneficiaries are (or apart from this subsection would be) entitled under section 12 to occupy land, the trustees of land may exclude or restrict the entitlement of any one or more (but not all) of them.

(2) Trustees may not under subsection (1)—

(a) unreasonably exclude any beneficiary's entitlement to occupy land, or

(b) restrict any such entitlement to an unreasonable extent.

(3) The trustees of land may from time to time impose reasonable conditions on any beneficiary in relation to his occupation of land by reason of his entitlement under section 12.

(4) The matters to which trustees are to have regard in exercising the powers conferred by this section include—

(a) the intentions of the person or persons (if any) who created the trust,

(b) the purposes for which the land is held, and

(c) the circumstances and wishes of each of the beneficiaries who is (or apart from any previous exercise by the trustees of those powers would be) entitled to occupy the land under section 12.

(5) The conditions which may be imposed on a beneficiary under subsection (3) include, in particular, conditions requiring him—

(a) to pay any outgoings or expenses in respect of the land, or

(b) to assume any other obligation in relation to the land or to any activity which is or is proposed to be conducted there.

(6) Where the entitlement of any beneficiary to occupy land under section 12 has been excluded or restricted, the conditions which may be imposed on any other beneficiary under subsection (3) include, in particular, conditions requiring him to—

(a) make payments by way of compensation to the beneficiary whose entitlement has been excluded or restricted, or

(b) forgo any payment or other benefit to which he would otherwise be entitled under the trust so as to benefit that beneficiary.

(7) The powers conferred on trustees by this section may not be exercised—

(a) so as prevent any person who is in occupation of land (whether or not by reason of an entitlement under section 12) from continuing to occupy the land, or

(b) in a manner likely to result in any such person ceasing to occupy the land,

unless he consents or the court has given approval.

(8) The matters to which the court is to have regard in determining whether to give approval under subsection (7) include the matters mentioned in subsection (4)(a) to (c).

Powers of court

14　Applications for order

(1) Any person who is a trustee of land or has an interest in property subject to a trust of land may make an application to the court for an order under this section.

(2) On an application for an order under this section the court may make any such order—

(a) relating to the exercise by the trustees of any of their functions (including an order relieving them of any obligation to obtain the consent of, or to consult, any person in connection with the exercise of any of their functions), or

(b) declaring the nature or extent of a person's interest in property subject to the trust, as the court thinks fit.

(3) The court may not under this section make any order as to the appointment or removal of trustees.

(4) The powers conferred on the court by this section are exercisable on an application whether it is made before or after the commencement of this Act.

15   Matters relevant in determining applications

(1) The matters to which the court is to have regard in determining an application for an order under section 14 include—

    (a) the intentions of the person or persons (if any) who created the trust,

    (b) the purposes for which the property subject to the trust is held,

    (c) the welfare of any minor who occupies or might reasonably be expected to occupy any land subject to the trust as his home, and

    (d) the interests of any secured creditor of any beneficiary.

(2) In the case of an application relating to the exercise in relation to any land of the powers conferred on the trustees by section 13, the matters to which the court is to have regard also include the circumstances and wishes of each of the beneficiaries who is (or apart from any previous exercise by the trustees of those powers would be) entitled to occupy the land under section 12.

(3) In the case of any other application, other than one relating to the exercise of the power mentioned in section 6(2), the matters to which the court is to have regard also include the circumstances and wishes of any beneficiaries of full age and entitled to an interest in possession in property subject to the trust or (in case of dispute) of the majority (according to the value of their combined interests).

(4) This section does not apply to an application if section 335A of the Insolvency Act 1986 (which is inserted by Schedule 3 and relates to applications by a trustee of a bankrupt) applies to it.

Purchaser protection

16   Protection of purchasers

(1) A purchaser of land which is or has been subject to a trust need not be concerned to see that any requirement imposed on the trustees by section 6(5), 7(3) or 11(1) has been complied with.

(2) Where—

    (a) trustees of land who convey land which (immediately before it is conveyed) is subject to the trust contravene section 6(6) or (8), but

    (b) the purchaser of the land from the trustees has no actual notice of the contravention,

the contravention does not invalidate the conveyance.

(3) Where the powers of trustees of land are limited by virtue of section 8—

    (a) the trustees shall take all reasonable steps to bring the limitation to the notice of any purchaser of the land from them, but

    (b) the limitation does not invalidate any conveyance by the trustees to a purchaser who has no actual notice of the limitation.

(4) Where trustees of land convey land which (immediately before it is conveyed) is subject to the trust to persons believed by them to be beneficiaries absolutely entitled to the land under the trust and of full age and capacity—

    (a) the trustees shall execute a deed declaring that they are discharged from the trust in relation to that land, and

    (b) if they fail to do so, the court may make an order requiring them to do so.

(5) A purchaser of land to which a deed under subsection (4) relates is entitled to assume that, as from the date of the deed, the land is not subject to the trust unless he has actual notice that the trustees were mistaken in their belief that the land was conveyed to beneficiaries absolutely entitled to the land under the trust and of full age and capacity.

(6) Subsections (2) and (3) do not apply to land held on charitable, ecclesiastical or public trusts.

(7) This section does not apply to registered land.

Supplementary

17   Application of provisions to trusts of proceeds of sale

(2)   Section 14 applies in relation to a trust of proceeds of sale of land and trustees of such a trust as in relation to a trust of land and trustees of land.

(3)   In this section 'trust of proceeds of sale of land' means (subject to subsection (5)) any trust of property (other than a trust of land) which consists of or includes—

(a)   any proceeds of a disposition of land held in trust (including settled land), or

(b)   any property representing any such proceeds.

(4)   The references in subsection (3) to a trust—

(a)   are to any description of trust (whether express, implied, resulting or constructive), including a trust for sale and a bare trust, and

(b)   include a trust created, or arising, before the commencement of this Act.

(5)   A trust which (despite section 2) is a settlement for the purposes of the Settled Land Act 1925 cannot be a trust of proceeds of sale of land.

(6)   In subsection (3)—

(a)   'disposition' includes any disposition made, or coming into operation, before the commencement of this Act, and

(b)   the reference to settled land includes personal chattels to which section 67(1) of the Settled Land Act 1925 (heirlooms) applies.

18   Application of Part to personal representatives

(1)   The provisions of this Part relating to trustees, other than sections 10, 11 and 14, apply to personal representatives, but with appropriate modifications and without prejudice to the functions of personal representatives for the purposes of administration.

(2)   The appropriate modifications include—

(a)   the substitution of references to persons interested in the due administration of the estate for references to beneficiaries, and

(b)   the substitution of references to the will for references to the disposition creating the trust.

(3)   Section 3(1) does not apply to personal representatives if the death occurs before the commencement of this Act.

PART II APPOINTMENT AND RETIREMENT
OF TRUSTEES

19   Appointment and retirement of trustee at instance of beneficiaries

(1)   This section applies in the case of a trust where—

(a)   there is no person nominated for the purpose of appointing new trustees by the instrument, if any, creating the trust, and

(b)   the beneficiaries under the trust are of full age and capacity and (taken together) are absolutely entitled to the property subject to the trust.

(2)   The beneficiaries may give a direction or directions of either or both of the following descriptions—

(a)   a written direction to a trustee or trustees to retire from the trust, and

(b)   a written direction to the trustees or trustee for the time being (or, if there are none, to the personal representative of the last person who was a trustee) to appoint by writing to be a trustee or trustees the person or persons specified in the direction.

(3)   Where—

(a)   a trustee has been given a direction under subsection (2)(a),

(b)   reasonable arrangements have been made for the protection of any rights of his in connection with the trust,

(c) after he has retired there will be either a trust corporation or at least two persons to act as trustees to perform the trust, and

(d) either another person is to be appointed to be a new trustee on his retirement (whether in compliance with a direction under subsection (2)(b) or otherwise) or the continuing trustees by deed consent to his retirement,

he shall make a deed declaring his retirement and shall be deemed to have retired and be discharged from the trust.

(4) Where a trustee retires under subsection (3) he and the continuing trustees (together with any new trustee) shall (subject to any arrangements for the protection of his rights) do anything necessary to vest the trust property in the continuing trustees (or the continuing and new trustees).

(5) This section has effect subject to the restrictions imposed by the Trustee Act 1925 on the number of trustees.

...

21   Supplementary

(1) For the purposes of section 19 or 20 a direction is given by beneficiaries if—

(a) a single direction is jointly given by all of them, or

(b) (subject to subsection (2)) a direction is given by each of them (whether solely or jointly with one or more, but not all, of the others),

and none of them by writing withdraws the direction given by him before it has been complied with.

(2) Where more than one direction is given each must specify for appointment or retirement the same person or persons.

(3) Subsection (7) of section 36 of the Trustee Act 1925 (powers of trustees appointed under that section) applies to a trustee appointed under section 19 or 20 as if he were appointed under that section.

(4) A direction under section 19 or 20 must not specify a person or persons for appointment if the appointment of that person or those persons would be in contravention of section 35(1) of the Trustee Act 1925 or section 24(1) of the Law of Property Act 1925 (requirements as to identity of trustees).

(5) Sections 19 and 20 do not apply in relation to a trust created by a disposition in so far as provision that they do not apply is made by the disposition.

(6) Sections 19 and 20 do not apply in relation to a trust created before the commencement of this Act by a disposition in so far as provision to the effect that they do not apply is made by a deed executed—

(a) in a case in which the trust was created by one person and he is of full capacity, by that person, or

(b) in a case in which the trust was created by more than one person, by such of the persons who created the trust as are alive and of full capacity.

(7) A deed executed for the purposes of subsection (6) is irrevocable.

(8) Where a deed is executed for the purposes of subsection (6)—

(a) it does not affect anything done before its execution to comply with a direction under section 19 or 20, but

(b) a direction under section 19 or 20 which has been given but not complied with before its execution shall cease to have effect.

PART III SUPPLEMENTARY

22   Meaning of 'beneficiary'

(1) In this Act 'beneficiary', in relation to a trust, means any person who under the trust has an interest in property subject to the trust (including a person who has such an interest as a trustee or a personal representative).

(2) In this Act references to a beneficiary who is beneficially entitled do not include a beneficiary who has an interest in property subject to the trust only by reason of being a trustee or personal representative.

(3) For the purposes of this Act a person who is a beneficiary only by reason of being an annuitant is not to be regarded as entitled to an interest in possession in land subject to the trust.

23 Other interpretation provisions

(1) In this Act 'purchaser' has the same meaning as in Part I of the Law of Property Act 1925.

(2) Subject to that, where an expression used in this Act is given a meaning by the Law of Property Act 1925 it has the same meaning as in that Act unless the context otherwise requires.

(3) In this Act 'the court' means—
  (a) the High Court, or
  (b) the county court.

SCHEDULES

Section 2

SCHEDULE 1

PROVISIONS CONSEQUENTIAL ON SECTION 2

Minors

1.—(1) Where after the commencement of this Act a person purports to convey a legal estate in land to a minor, or two or more minors, alone, the conveyance—
  (a) is not effective to pass the legal estate, but
  (b) operates as a declaration that the land is held in trust for the minor or minors (or if he purports to convey it to the minor or minors in trust for any persons, for those persons).

(2) Where after the commencement of this Act a person purports to convey a legal estate in land to—
  (a) a minor or two or more minors, and
  (b) another person who is, or other persons who are, of full age,

the conveyance operates to vest the land in the other person or persons in trust for the minor or minors and the other person or persons (or if he purports to convey it to them in trust for any persons, for those persons).

(3) Where immediately before the commencement of this Act a conveyance is operating (by virtue of section 27 of the Settled Land Act 1925) as an agreement to execute a settlement in favour of a minor or minors—
  (a) the agreement ceases to have effect on the commencement of this Act, and
  (b) the conveyance subsequently operates instead as a declaration that the land is held in trust for the minor or minors.

2.—Where after the commencement of this Act a legal estate in land would, by reason of intestacy or in any other circumstances not dealt with in paragraph 1, vest in a person who is a minor if he were a person of full age, the land is held in trust for the minor.

Family charges

3.—Where, by virtue of an instrument coming into operation after the commencement of this Act, land becomes charged voluntarily (or in consideration of marriage or the formation of a civil partnership) or by way of family arrangement, whether immediately or after an interval, with the payment of—
  (a) a rentcharge for the life of a person or a shorter period, or
  (b) capital, annual or periodical sums for the benefit of a person,

the instrument operates as a declaration that the land is held in trust for giving effect to the charge.
...

Housing Act 1996

(1996 c. 52)

...

PART VII HOMELESSNESS

Homelessness and threatened homelessness

175   Homelessness and threatened homelessness

(1) A person is homeless if he has no accommodation available for his occupation, in the United Kingdom or elsewhere, which he—

    (a) is entitled to occupy by virtue of an interest in it or by virtue of an order of a court,

    (b) has an express or implied licence to occupy, or

    (c) occupies as a residence by virtue of any enactment or rule of law giving him the right to remain in occupation or restricting the right of another person to recover possession.

(2) A person is also homeless if he has accommodation but—

    (a) he cannot secure entry to it, or

    (b) it consists of a moveable structure, vehicle or vessel designed or adapted for human habitation and there is no place where he is entitled or permitted both to place it and to reside in it.

(3) A person shall not be treated as having accommodation unless it is accommodation which it would be reasonable for him to continue to occupy.

(4) A person is threatened with homelessness if it is likely that he will become homeless within 28 days.

176   Meaning of accommodation available for occupation

Accommodation shall be regarded as available for a person's occupation only if it is available for occupation by him together with—

    (a) any other person who normally resides with him as a member of his family, or

    (b) any other person who might reasonably be expected to reside with him.

References in this Part to securing that accommodation is available for a person's occupation shall be construed accordingly.

177   Whether it is reasonable to continue to occupy accommodation

(1) It is not reasonable for a person to continue to occupy accommodation if it is probable that this will lead to domestic violence or other violence against him, or against—

    (a) a person who normally resides with him as a member of his family, or

    (b) any other person who might reasonably be expected to reside with him.

(1A) For this purpose 'violence' means—

    (a) violence from another person; or

    (b) threats of violence from another person which are likely to be carried out;

and violence is 'domestic violence' if it is from a person who is associated with the victim.

(2) In determining whether it would be, or would have been, reasonable for a person to continue to occupy accommodation, regard may be had to the general circumstances prevailing in relation to housing in the district of the local housing authority to whom he has applied for accommodation or for assistance in obtaining accommodation.

(3) The Secretary of State may by order specify—

    (a) other circumstances in which it is to be regarded as reasonable or not reasonable for a person to continue to occupy accommodation, and

    (b) other matters to be taken into account or disregarded in determining whether it would be, or would have been, reasonable for a person to continue to occupy accommodation.

178   Meaning of associated person

(1) For the purposes of this Part, a person is associated with another person if—

(a)   they are or have been married to each other;

(aa) they are or have been civil partners of each other;

(b)   they are cohabitants or former cohabitants;

(c)   they live or have lived in the same household;

(d)   they are relatives;

(e)   they have agreed to marry one another (whether or not that agreement has been terminated);

(ea) they have entered into a civil partnership agreement between them (whether or not that agreement has been terminated);

(f)   in relation to a child, each of them is a parent of the child or has, or has had, parental responsibility for the child.

(2) If a child has been adopted or falls within subsection (2A), two persons are also associated with each other for the purposes of this Part if—

(a)   one is a natural parent of the child or a parent of such a natural parent, and

(b)   the other is the child or a person—

(i)   who has become a parent of the child by virtue of an adoption order or who has applied for an adoption order, or

(ii)   with whom the child has at any time been placed for adoption.

(2A) A child falls within this subsection if—

(a)   an adoption agency, within the meaning of section 2 of the Adoption and Children Act 2002, is authorised to place him for adoption under section 19 of that Act (placing children with parental consent) or he has become the subject of an order under section 21 of that Act (placement orders), or

(b)   he is freed for adoption by virtue of an order made—

(i)   in England and Wales, under section 18 of the Adoption Act 1976,

...

(3) In this section—

'adoption order' means an adoption order within the meaning of section 72(1) of the Adoption Act 1976 or section 46(1) of the Adoption and Children Act 2002;

'child' means a person under the age of 18 years;

'civil partnership agreement' has the meaning given by section 73 of the Civil Partnership Act 2004;

'cohabitants' means—

(a)   a man and a woman who, although not married to each other, are living together as husband and wife, or

(b)   two people of the same sex who, although not civil partners of each other, are living together as if they were civil partners;

and 'former cohabitants' shall be construed accordingly;

'parental responsibility' has the same meaning as in the Children Act 1989; and

'relative', in relation to a person, means—

(a)   the father, mother, stepfather, stepmother, son, daughter, stepson, stepdaughter, grandmother, grandfather, grandson or granddaughter of that person or of that person's spouse, civil partner, former spouse or former civil partner, or

(b)   the brother, sister, uncle, aunt, niece or nephew (whether of the full blood or of the half blood or by marriage or civil partnership) of that person or of that person's spouse, civil partner, former spouse or former civil partner,

and includes, in relation to a person who is living or has lived with another person as husband and wife, a person who would fall within paragraph (a) or (b) if the parties were married to each other.

...

Interim duty to accommodate

188   Interim duty to accommodate in case of apparent priority need

(1) If the local housing authority have reason to believe that an applicant may be homeless, eligible for assistance and have a priority need, they shall secure that accommodation is available for his occupation pending a decision as to the duty (if any) owed to him under the following provisions of this Part.

(1A) But if the local housing authority have reason to believe that the duty under section 193(2) may apply in relation to an applicant in the circumstances referred to in section 195A(1), they shall secure that accommodation is available for the applicant's occupation pending a decision of the kind referred to in subsection (1) regardless of whether the applicant has a priority need.

(2) The duty under this section arises irrespective of any possibility of the referral of the applicant's case to another local housing authority (see sections 198 to 200).

(3) The duty ceases when the authority's decision is notified to the applicant, even if the applicant requests a review of the decision (see section 202).

The authority may secure that accommodation is available for the applicant's occupation pending a decision on a review.

189   Priority need for accommodation

(1) The following have a priority need for accommodation—
   (a) a pregnant woman or a person with whom she resides or might reasonably be expected to reside;
   (b) a person with whom dependent children reside or might reasonably be expected to reside;
   (c) a person who is vulnerable as a result of old age, mental illness or handicap or physical disability or other special reason, or with whom such a person resides or might reasonably be expected to reside;
   (d) a person who is homeless or threatened with homelessness as a result of an emergency such as flood, fire or other disaster.

...

Duties to persons found to be homeless or threatened with homelessness

190   Duties to persons becoming homeless intentionally

(1) This section applies where the local housing authority are satisfied that an applicant is homeless and is eligible for assistance but are also satisfied that he became homeless intentionally.

(2) If the authority are satisfied that the applicant has a priority need, they shall—
   (a) secure that accommodation is available for his occupation for such period as they consider will give him a reasonable opportunity of securing accommodation for his occupation, and
   (b) provide him with (or secure that he is provided with) advice and assistance in any attempts he may make to secure that accommodation becomes available for his occupation.

(3) If they are not satisfied that he has a priority need, they shall provide him with (or secure that he is provided with) advice and assistance in any attempts he may make to secure that accommodation becomes available for his occupation.

(4) The applicant's housing needs shall be assessed before advice and assistance is provided under subsection (2)(b) or (3).

(5) The advice and assistance provided under subsection (2)(b) or (3) must include information about the likely availability in the authority's district of types of accommodation appropriate to the applicant's housing needs (including, in particular, the location and sources of such types of accommodation).

191   Becoming homeless intentionally

(1) A person becomes homeless intentionally if he deliberately does or fails to do anything in consequence of which he ceases to occupy accommodation which is available for his occupation and which it would have been reasonable for him to continue to occupy.

(2) For the purposes of subsection (1) an act or omission in good faith on the part of a person who was unaware of any relevant fact shall not be treated as deliberate.

(3) A person shall be treated as becoming homeless intentionally if—

(a) he enters into an arrangement under which he is required to cease to occupy accommodation which it would have been reasonable for him to continue to occupy, and

(b) the purpose of the arrangement is to enable him to become entitled to assistance under this Part,

and there is no other good reason why he is homeless.

192   Duty to persons not in priority need who are not homeless intentionally

(1) This section applies where the local housing authority—

(a) are satisfied that an applicant is homeless and eligible for assistance, and

(b) are not satisfied that he became homeless intentionally,

but are not satisfied that he has a priority need.

(2) The authority shall provide the applicant with (or secure that he is provided with) advice and assistance in any attempts he may make to secure that accommodation becomes available for his occupation.

(3) The authority may secure that accommodation is available for occupation by the applicant.

(4) The applicant's housing needs shall be assessed before advice and assistance is provided under subsection (2).

(5) The advice and assistance provided under subsection (2) must include information about the likely availability in the authority's district of types of accommodation appropriate to the applicant's housing needs (including, in particular, the location and sources of such types of accommodation).

193   Duty to persons with priority need who are not homeless intentionally

(1) This section applies where the local housing authority are satisfied that an applicant is homeless, eligible for assistance and has a priority need, and are not satisfied that he became homeless intentionally.

(2) Unless the authority refer the application to another local housing authority (see section 198), they shall secure that accommodation is available for occupation by the applicant.
...

195   Duties in case of threatened homelessness

(1) This section applies where the local housing authority are satisfied that an applicant is threatened with homelessness and is eligible for assistance.

(2) If the authority—

(a) are satisfied that he has a priority need, and

(b) are not satisfied that he became threatened with homelessness intentionally,

they shall take reasonable steps to secure that accommodation does not cease to be available for his occupation.

(3) Subsection (2) does not affect any right of the authority, whether by virtue of a contract, enactment or rule of law, to secure vacant possession of any accommodation.

(4) Where, in a case which is not a restricted threatened homelessness case, in pursuance of the duty under subsection (2) the authority secure that accommodation other than that occupied by the applicant when he made his application is available for occupation by him, the provisions of section 193(3) to (9) (period for which duty owed) apply, with any necessary modifications, in relation to the duty under this section as they apply in relation to the duty under section 193 in a case which is not a restricted case (within the meaning of that section).

(4A) Where, in a restricted threatened homelessness case, in pursuance of the duty under subsection (2) the authority secure that accommodation other than that occupied by the applicant when he made his application is available for occupation by him, the provisions of section 193(3) to (9) (period for which duty owed) apply, with any necessary modifications, in relation to the duty under this section as they apply in relation to the duty under section 193 in a restricted case (within the meaning of that section).

(4B) In subsections (4) and (4A) 'a restricted threatened homelessness case' means a case where the local housing authority would not be satisfied as mentioned in subsection (1) without having had regard to a restricted person.

(5) If the authority—

(a) are not satisfied that the applicant has a priority need, or

(b) are satisfied that he has a priority need but are also satisfied that he became threatened with homelessness intentionally,

they shall provide him with (or secure that he is provided with) advice and assistance in any attempts he may make to secure that accommodation does not cease to be available for his occupation.

(6) The applicant's housing needs shall be assessed before advice and assistance is provided under subsection (5).

(7) The advice and assistance provided under subsection (5) must include information about the likely availability in the authority's district of types of accommodation appropriate to the applicant's housing needs (including, in particular, the location and sources of such types of accommodation).

(8) If the authority decide that they owe the applicant the duty under subsection (5) by virtue of paragraph (b) of that subsection, they may, pending a decision on a review of that decision—

(a) secure that accommodation does not cease to be available for his occupation; and

(b) if he becomes homeless, secure that accommodation is so available.

(9) If the authority—

(a) are not satisfied that the applicant has a priority need; and

(b) are not satisfied that he became threatened with homelessness intentionally,

the authority may take reasonable steps to secure that accommodation does not cease to be available for the applicant's occupation.

...

196 Becoming threatened with homelessness intentionally

(1) A person becomes threatened with homelessness intentionally if he deliberately does or fails to do anything the likely result of which is that he will be forced to leave accommodation which is available for his occupation and which it would have been reasonable for him to continue to occupy.

(2) For the purposes of subsection (1) an act or omission in good faith on the part of a person who was unaware of any relevant fact shall not be treated as deliberate.

(3) A person shall be treated as becoming threatened with homelessness intentionally if—

(a) he enters into an arrangement under which he is required to cease to occupy accommodation which it would have been reasonable for him to continue to occupy, and

(b) the purpose of the arrangement is to enable him to become entitled to assistance under this Part,

and there is no other good reason why he is threatened with homelessness.

...

Supplementary provisions

213A Co-operation in certain cases involving children

(1) This section applies where a local housing authority have reason to believe that an applicant with whom a person under the age of 18 normally resides, or might reasonably be expected to reside—

(a) may be ineligible for assistance;

(b) may be homeless and may have become so intentionally; or

(c) may be threatened with homelessness intentionally.

(2) A local housing authority shall make arrangements for ensuring that, where this section applies—

    (a) the applicant is invited to consent to the referral of the essential facts of his case to the social services authority for the district of the housing authority (where that is a different authority); and

    (b) if the applicant has given that consent, the social services authority are made aware of those facts and of the subsequent decision of the housing authority in respect of his case.

(3) Where the local housing authority and the social services authority for a district are the same authority (a 'unitary authority'); that authority shall make arrangements for ensuring that, where this section applies—

    (a) the applicant is invited to consent to the referral to the social services department of the essential facts of his case; and

    (b) if the applicant has given that consent, the social services department is made aware of those facts and of the subsequent decision of the authority in respect of his case.

(4) Nothing in subsection (2) or (3) affects any power apart from this section to disclose information relating to the applicant's case to the social services authority or to the social services department (as the case may be) without the consent of the applicant.

(5) Where a social services authority—

    (a) are aware of a decision of a local housing authority that the applicant is ineligible for assistance, became homeless intentionally or became threatened with homelessness intentionally, and

    (b) request the local housing authority to provide them with advice and assistance in the exercise of their social services functions under Part 3 of the Children Act 1989,

the local housing authority shall provide them with such advice and assistance as is reasonable in the circumstances.

(6) A unitary authority shall make arrangements for ensuring that, where they make a decision of a kind mentioned in subsection (5)(a), the housing department provide the social services department with such advice and assistance as the social services department may reasonably request.

(7) In this section, in relation to a unitary authority—

'the housing department' means those persons responsible for the exercise of their housing functions; and

'the social services department' means those persons responsible for the exercise of their social services functions under Part 3 of the Children Act 1989.

Education Act 1996

(1996 c. 56)

PART I GENERAL

Chapter I The statutory system of education

Compulsory education

7 Duty of parents to secure education of children of compulsory school age

The parent of every child of compulsory school age shall cause him to receive efficient full-time education suitable—

    (a) to his age, ability and aptitude, and

    (b) to any special educational needs he may have,

either by regular attendance at school or otherwise.

8 Compulsory school age

(1) Subsections (2) and (3) apply to determine for the purposes of any enactment whether a person is of compulsory school age.

(2) A person begins to be of compulsory school age—

    (a) when he attains the age of five, if he attains that age on a prescribed day, and

    (b) otherwise at the beginning of the prescribed day next following his attaining that age.

(3) A person ceases to be of compulsory school age at the end of the day which is the school leaving date for any calendar year—

    (a) if he attains the age of 16 after that day but before the beginning of the school year next following,

    (b) if he attains that age on that day, or

    (c) (unless paragraph (a) applies) if that day is the school leaving date next following his attaining that age.

(4) The Secretary of State may by order—

    (a) provide that such days in the year as are specified in the order shall be, for each calendar year, prescribed days for the purposes of subsection (2);

    (b) determine the day in any calendar year which is to be the school leaving date for that year.

Education in accordance with parental wishes

9 Pupils to be educated in accordance with parents' wishes

In exercising or performing all their respective powers and duties under the Education Acts, the Secretary of State and local authorities shall have regard to the general principle that pupils are to be educated in accordance with the wishes of their parents, so far as that is compatible with the provision of efficient instruction and training and the avoidance of unreasonable public expenditure.

...

PART V THE CURRICULUM

...

Chapter IV Miscellaneous and supplementary provisions

Sex education

...

405 Exemption from sex education

If the parent of any pupil in attendance at a maintained school requests that he may be wholly or partly excused from receiving sex education at the school, the pupil shall, except so far as such education is comprised in the National Curriculum, be so excused accordingly until the request is withdrawn.

...

PART VI SCHOOL ADMISSIONS, ATTENDANCE AND CHARGES

...

Chapter II School attendance

School attendance orders

437 School attendance orders

(1) If it appears to a local authority that a child of compulsory school age in their area is not receiving suitable education, either by regular attendance at school or otherwise, they shall serve a

notice in writing on the parent requiring him to satisfy them within the period specified in the notice that the child is receiving such education.

(2) That period shall not be less than 15 days beginning with the day on which the notice is served.

(3) If—

    (a) a parent on whom a notice has been served under subsection (1) fails to satisfy the local authority, within the period specified in the notice, that the child is receiving suitable education, and

    (b) in the opinion of the authority it is expedient that the child should attend school,

the authority shall serve on the parent an order (referred to in this Act as a 'school attendance order'), in such form as may be prescribed, requiring him to cause the child to become a registered pupil at a school named in the order.

(4) A school attendance order shall (subject to any amendment made by the local authority) continue in force for so long as the child is of compulsory school age, unless—

    (a) it is revoked by the authority, or

    (b) a direction is made in respect of it under section 443(2) or 447(5).

(5) Where a maintained school is named in a school attendance order, the local authority shall inform the governing body and the head teacher.

(6) Where a maintained school is named in a school attendance order, the governing body (and, in the case of a maintained school, the local authority) shall admit the child to the school.

(7) Subsection (6) does not affect any power to exclude from a school a pupil who is already a registered pupil there.

...

442   Revocation of order at request of parent

(1) This section applies where a school attendance order is in force in respect of a child.

(2) If at any time the parent applies to the local authority requesting that the order be revoked on the ground that arrangements have been made for the child to receive suitable education otherwise than at school, the authority shall comply with the request, unless they are of the opinion that no satisfactory arrangements have been made for the education of the child otherwise than at school.

(3) If a parent is aggrieved by a refusal of the local authority to comply with a request under subsection (2), he may refer the question to the Secretary of State.

(4) Where a question is referred to the Secretary of State under subsection (3), he shall give such direction determining the question as he thinks fit.

...

School attendance: offences and education supervision orders

443   Offence: failure to comply with school attendance order

(1) If a parent on whom a school attendance order is served fails to comply with the requirements of the order, he is guilty of an offence, unless he proves that he is causing the child to receive suitable education otherwise than at school.

(2) If, in proceedings for an offence under this section, the parent is acquitted, the court may direct that the school attendance order shall cease to be in force.

(3) A direction under subsection (2) does not affect the duty of the local authority to take further action under section 437 if at any time the authority are of the opinion that, having regard to any change of circumstances, it is expedient to do so.

(4) A person guilty of an offence under this section is liable on summary conviction to a fine not exceeding level 3 on the standard scale.

444   Offence: failure to secure regular attendance at school of registered pupil

(1) If a child of compulsory school age who is a registered pupil at a school fails to attend regularly at the school, his parent is guilty of an offence.

(1A) If in the circumstances mentioned in subsection (1) the parent knows that his child is failing to attend regularly at the school and fails to cause him to do so, he is guilty of an offence.

(1B) It is a defence for a person charged with an offence under subsection (1A) to prove that he had a reasonable justification for his failure to cause the child to attend regularly at the school.

(2) Subsections (2A) to (6) below apply in proceedings for an offence under this section in respect of a child who is not a boarder at the school at which he is a registered pupil.

(2A) The child shall not be taken to have failed to attend regularly at the school by reason of his absence from the school at any time if the parent proves that at that time the child was prevented from attending by reason of sickness or any unavoidable cause.

(3) The child shall not be taken to have failed to attend regularly at the school by reason of his absence from the school—

    (a) with leave, . . . or

    (c) on any day exclusively set apart for religious observance by the religious body to which his parent belongs.

. . .

(8) A person guilty of an offence under subsection (1) is liable on summary conviction to a fine not exceeding level 3 on the standard scale.

(8A) A person guilty of an offence under subsection (1A) is liable on summary conviction—

    (a) to a fine not exceeding level 4 on the standard scale, or

    (b) to imprisonment for a term not exceeding 51 weeks,

or both.

(8B) If, on the trial of an offence under subsection (1A), the court finds the defendant not guilty of that offence but is satisfied that he is guilty of an offence under subsection (1), the court may find him guilty of that offence.

(9) In this section 'leave', in relation to a school, means leave granted by any person authorised to do so by the governing body or proprietor of the school.

. . .

447 Education supervision orders

(1) Before instituting proceedings for an offence under section 443 or 444, a local authority shall consider whether it would be appropriate (instead of or as well as instituting the proceedings) to apply for an education supervision order with respect to the child.

(2) The court—

    (a) by which a person is convicted of an offence under section 443, or

    (b) before which a person is charged with an offence under section 444,

may direct the local authority instituting the proceedings to apply for an education supervision order with respect to the child unless the authority, decide that the child's welfare will be satisfactorily safeguarded even though no education supervision order is made.

(2A) A local authority may not make a decision as mentioned in subsection (2) unless—

    (a) they are the appropriate authority, or

    (b) they have consulted that authority.

(3) Where, following a direction under subsection (2), a local authority decide not to apply for an education supervision order, they shall inform the court of the reasons for their decision.

(4) Unless the court has directed otherwise, the information required under subsection (3) shall be given to the court before the end of the period of eight weeks beginning with the date on which the direction was given.

(5) Where—

    (a) a local authority apply for an education supervision order with respect to a child who is the subject of a school attendance order, and

    (b) the court decides that section 36(3) of the Children Act 1989 (education supervision orders) prevents it from making the order,

the court may direct that the school attendance order shall cease to be in force.

(6) In this section—

'the appropriate local authority' has the same meaning as in section 36(9) of the Children Act 1989, and

'education supervision order' means an education supervision order under that Act.

...

PART X MISCELLANEOUS AND GENERAL

Chapter II Punishment and restraint of pupils

Corporal punishment

548 No right to give corporal punishment

(1) Corporal punishment given by, or on the authority of, a member of staff to a child—

    (a) for whom education is provided at any relevant educational institution, or

    (b) for whom education is provided, otherwise than at a relevant educational institution, under any arrangements made by a local authority, or

    (c) for whom specified early years education is provided otherwise than at a relevant educational institution

cannot be justified in any proceedings on the ground that it was given in pursuance of a right exercisable by the member of staff by virtue of his position as such.

(2) Subsection (1) applies to corporal punishment so given to a child at any time, whether at the relevant educational institution or other place at which education is provided for the child, or elsewhere.

(3) The following provisions have effect for the purposes of this section.

(4) Any reference to giving corporal punishment to a child is to doing anything for the purpose of punishing that child (whether or not there are other reasons for doing it) which, apart from any justification, would constitute battery.

(5) However, corporal punishment shall not be taken to be given to a child by virtue of any thing done for reasons that include averting—

    (a) an immediate danger of personal injury to, or

    (b) an immediate danger to the property of,

any person (including the child himself).

(6) 'Member of staff', in relation to the child concerned, means—

    (a) any person who works as a teacher at the relevant educational institution or other place at which education is provided for the child, or

    (b) any other person who (whether in connection with the provision of education for the child or otherwise)—

        (i) works at that institution or place, or

        (ii) otherwise provides his services there (whether or not for payment),

and has lawful control or charge of the child.

(7) 'Child' (except in subsection (8)) means a person under the age of 18.

(7A) 'Relevant educational institution' means—

    (a) a school, or

    (b) an independent educational institution in England other than a school.

(7B) In subsection (7A)(b) 'independent educational institution' has the same meaning as in Chapter 1 of Part 4 of the Education and Skills Act 2008 (see section 92 of that Act).

(8) 'Specified early years education' means—

    (a) in relation to England, early years provision as defined by section 20 of the Childcare Act 2006 which is provided under arrangements made by a local authority in England in pursuance of the duty imposed by section 7 of that Act (whether or not the local authority provides the early years provision);

(b) in relation to Wales, full-time or part-time education suitable for children who have not attained compulsory school age which is provided—

(i)   by a local authority in Wales, or

(ii) by any other person who is in receipt of financial assistance given by such an authority under arrangements made by them in pursuance of the duty imposed by section 118 of the School Standards and Framework Act 1998.

...

Protection from Harassment Act 1997

(1997 c. 40)

England and Wales

1   Prohibition of harassment

(1) A person must not pursue a course of conduct—

(a) which amounts to harassment of another, and

(b) which he knows or ought to know amounts to harassment of the other.

(1A) A person must not pursue a course of conduct—

(a) which involves harassment of two or more persons, and

(b) which he knows or ought to know involves harassment of those persons, and

(c) by which he intends to persuade any person (whether or not one of those mentioned above)—

(i)   not to do something that he is entitled or required to do, or

(ii)   to do something that he is not under any obligation to do.

(2) For the purposes of this section or section 2A(2)(c), the person whose course of conduct is in question ought to know that it amounts to or involves harassment of another if a reasonable person in possession of the same information would think the course of conduct amounted to or involved harassment of the other.

(3) Subsection (1) or (1A) does not apply to a course of conduct if the person who pursued it shows—

(a) that it was pursued for the purpose of preventing or detecting crime,

(b) that it was pursued under any enactment or rule of law or to comply with any condition or requirement imposed by any person under any enactment, or

(c) that in the particular circumstances the pursuit of the course of conduct was reasonable.

2   Offence of harassment

(1) A person who pursues a course of conduct in breach of section 1(1) or (1A) is guilty of an offence.

(2) A person guilty of an offence under this section is liable on summary conviction to imprisonment for a term not exceeding six months, or a fine not exceeding level 5 on the standard scale, or both.

2A   Offence of stalking

(1) A person is guilty of an offence if—

(a) the person pursues a course of conduct in breach of section 1(1), and

(b) the course of conduct amounts to stalking.

(2) For the purposes of subsection (1)(b) (and section 4A(1)(a)) a person's course of conduct amounts to stalking of another person if—

(a) it amounts to harassment of that person,

(b) the acts or omissions involved are ones associated with stalking, and

(c) the person whose course of conduct it is knows or ought to know that the course of conduct amounts to harassment of the other person.

(3) The following are examples of acts or omissions which, in particular circumstances, are ones associated with stalking—

(a) following a person,

(b) contacting, or attempting to contact, a person by any means,

(c) publishing any statement or other material—

    (i) relating or purporting to relate to a person, or

    (ii) purporting to originate from a person,

(d) monitoring the use by a person of the internet, email or any other form of electronic communication,

(e) loitering in any place (whether public or private),

(f) interfering with any property in the possession of a person,

(g) watching or spying on a person.

(4) A person guilty of an offence under this section is liable on summary conviction to imprisonment for a term not exceeding 51 weeks, or a fine not exceeding level 5 on the standard scale, or both.

(5) In relation to an offence committed before the commencement of section 281(5) of the Criminal Justice Act 2003, the reference in subsection (4) to 51 weeks is to be read as a reference to six months.

(6) This section is without prejudice to the generality of section 2.

...

3 Civil remedy

(1) An actual or apprehended breach of section 1(1) may be the subject of a claim in civil proceedings by the person who is or may be the victim of the course of conduct in question.

(2) On such a claim, damages may be awarded for (among other things) any anxiety caused by the harassment and any financial loss resulting from the harassment.

(3) Where—

(a) in such proceedings the High Court or the county court grants an injunction for the purpose of restraining the defendant from pursuing any conduct which amounts to harassment, and

(b) the plaintiff considers that the defendant has done anything which he is prohibited from doing by the injunction,

the plaintiff may apply for the issue of a warrant for the arrest of the defendant.

(4) An application under subsection (3) may be made—

(a) where the injunction was granted by the High Court, to a judge of that court, and

(b) where the injunction was granted by the county court, to a judge of that court.

(5) The judge to whom an application under subsection (3) is made may only issue a warrant if—

(a) the application is substantiated on oath, and

(b) the judge has reasonable grounds for believing that the defendant has done anything which he is prohibited from doing by the injunction.

(6) Where—

(a) the High Court or the county court grants an injunction for the purpose mentioned in subsection (3)(a), and

(b) without reasonable excuse the defendant does anything which he is prohibited from doing by the injunction,

he is guilty of an offence.

(7) Where a person is convicted of an offence under subsection (6) in respect of any conduct, that conduct is not punishable as a contempt of court.

(8) A person cannot be convicted of an offence under subsection (6) in respect of any conduct which has been punished as a contempt of court.

(9) A person guilty of an offence under subsection (6) is liable—

    (a) on conviction on indictment, to imprisonment for a term not exceeding five years, or a fine, or both, or

    (b) on summary conviction, to imprisonment for a term not exceeding six months, or a fine not exceeding the statutory maximum, or both.

3A   Injunctions to protect persons from harassment within section 1 (1A)

(1) This section applies where there is an actual or apprehended breach of section 1 (1A) by any person ('the relevant person').

(2) In such a case—

    (a) any person who is or may be a victim of the course of conduct in question, or

    (b) any person who is or may be a person falling within section 1(1A)(c),

may apply to the High Court or the county court for an injunction restraining the relevant person from pursuing any conduct which amounts to harassment in relation to any person or persons mentioned or described in the injunction.

(3) Section 3(3) to (9) apply in relation to an injunction granted under subsection (2) above as they apply in relation to an injunction granted as mentioned in section 3(3)(a).

4   Putting people in fear of violence

(1) A person whose course of conduct causes another to fear, on at least two occasions, that violence will be used against him is guilty of an offence if he knows or ought to know that his course of conduct will cause the other so to fear on each of those occasions.

(2) For the purposes of this section, the person whose course of conduct is in question ought to know that it will cause another to fear that violence will be used against him on any occasion if a reasonable person in possession of the same information would think the course of conduct would cause the other so to fear on that occasion.

(3) It is a defence for a person charged with an offence under this section to show that—

    (a) his course of conduct was pursued for the purpose of preventing or detecting crime,

    (b) his course of conduct was pursued under any enactment or rule of law or to comply with any condition or requirement imposed by any person under any enactment, or

    (c) the pursuit of his course of conduct was reasonable for the protection of himself or another or for the protection of his or another's property.

(4) A person guilty of an offence under this section is liable—

    (a) on conviction on indictment, to imprisonment for a term not exceeding five years, or a fine, or both, or

    (b) on summary conviction, to imprisonment for a term not exceeding six months, or a fine not exceeding the statutory maximum, or both.

(5) If on the trial on indictment of a person charged with an offence under this section the jury find him not guilty of the offence charged, they may find him guilty of an offence under section 2 or 2A.

(6) The Crown Court has the same powers and duties in relation to a person who is by virtue of subsection (5) convicted before it of an offence under section 2 or 2A as a magistrates' court would have on convicting him of the offence.

4A   Stalking involving fear of violence or serious alarm or distress

(1) A person ('A') whose course of conduct—

    (a) amounts to stalking, and

    (b) either—

        (i) causes another ('B') to fear, on at least two occasions, that violence will be used against B, or

        (ii) causes B serious alarm or distress which has a substantial adverse effect on B's usual day-to-day activities, is guilty of an offence if A knows or ought to know that A's course of conduct will cause B so to fear on each of those occasions or (as the case may be) will cause such alarm or distress.

(2) For the purposes of this section A ought to know that A's course of conduct will cause B to fear that violence will be used against B on any occasion if a reasonable person in possession of the same information would think the course of conduct would cause B so to fear on that occasion.

(3) For the purposes of this section A ought to know that A's course of conduct will cause B serious alarm or distress which has a substantial adverse effect on B's usual day-to-day activities if a reasonable person in possession of the same information would think the course of conduct would cause B such alarm or distress.

(4) It is a defence for A to show that—

    (a) A's course of conduct was pursued for the purpose of preventing or detecting crime,

    (b) A's course of conduct was pursued under any enactment or rule of law or to comply with any condition or requirement imposed by any person under any enactment, or

    (c) the pursuit of A's course of conduct was reasonable for the protection of A or another or for the protection of A's or another's property.

(5) A person guilty of an offence under this section is liable—

    (a) on conviction on indictment, to imprisonment for a term not exceeding five years, or a fine, or both, or

    (b) on summary conviction, to imprisonment for a term not exceeding twelve months, or a fine not exceeding the statutory maximum, or both.

(6) In relation to an offence committed before the commencement of section 154(1) of the Criminal Justice Act 2003, the reference in subsection (5)(b) to twelve months is to be read as a reference to six months.

(7) If on the trial on indictment of a person charged with an offence under this section the jury find the person not guilty of the offence charged, they may find the person guilty of an offence under section 2 or 2A.

(8) The Crown Court has the same powers and duties in relation to a person who is by virtue of subsection (7) convicted before it of an offence under section 2 or 2A as a magistrates' court would have on convicting the person of the offence.

(9) This section is without prejudice to the generality of section 4.

5 Restraining orders on conviction

(1) A court sentencing or otherwise dealing with a person ('the defendant') convicted of an offence may (as well as sentencing him or dealing with him in any other way) make an order under this section.

(2) The order may, for the purpose of protecting the victim or victims of the offence, or any other person mentioned in the order, from conduct which—

    (a) amounts to harassment, or

    (b) will cause a fear of violence,

prohibit the defendant from doing anything described in the order.

(3) The order may have effect for a specified period or until further order.

(3A) In proceedings under this section both the prosecution and the defence may lead, as further evidence, any evidence that would be admissible in proceedings for an injunction under section 3.

(4) The prosecutor, the defendant or any other person mentioned in the order may apply to the court which made the order for it to be varied or discharged by a further order.

(4A) Any person mentioned in the order is entitled to be heard on the hearing of an application under subsection (4).

(5) If without reasonable excuse the defendant does anything which he is prohibited from doing by an order under this section, he is guilty of an offence.

(6) A person guilty of an offence under this section is liable—

    (a) on conviction on indictment, to imprisonment for a term not exceeding five years, or a fine, or both, or

    (b) on summary conviction, to imprisonment for a term not exceeding six months, or a fine not exceeding the statutory maximum, or both.

(7) A court dealing with a person for an offence under this section may vary or discharge the order in question by a further order.

5A Restraining orders on acquittal

(1) A court before which a person ('the defendant') is acquitted of an offence may, if it considers it necessary to do so to protect a person from harassment by the defendant, make an order prohibiting the defendant from doing anything described in the order.

(2) Subsections (3) to (7) of section 5 apply to an order under this section as they apply to an order under that one.

(3) Where the Court of Appeal allow an appeal against conviction they may remit the case to the Crown Court to consider whether to proceed under this section.

(4) Where—

    (a) the Crown Court allows an appeal against conviction, or

    (b) a case is remitted to the Crown Court under subsection (3),

the reference in subsection (1) to a court before which a person is acquitted of an offence is to be read as referring to that court.

(5) A person made subject to an order under this section has the same right of appeal against the order as if—

    (a) he had been convicted of the offence in question before the court which made the order, and

    (b) the order had been made under section 5.

7 Interpretation of this group of sections

(1) This section applies for the interpretation of sections 1 to 5A.

(2) References to harassing a person include alarming the person or causing the person distress.

(3) A 'course of conduct' must involve—

    (a) in the case of conduct in relation to a single person (see section 1(1)), conduct on at least two occasions in relation to that person, or

    (b) in the case of conduct in relation to two or more persons (see section 1(1A)), conduct on at least one occasion in relation to each of those persons.

(3A) A person's conduct on any occasion shall be taken, if aided, abetted, counselled or procured by another—

    (a) to be conduct on that occasion of the other (as well as conduct of the person whose conduct it is); and

    (b) to be conduct in relation to which the other's knowledge and purpose, and what he ought to have known, are the same as they were in relation to what was contemplated or reasonably foreseeable at the time of the aiding, abetting, counselling or procuring.

(4) 'Conduct' includes speech.

(5) References to a person, in the context of the harassment of a person, are references to a person who is an individual.

Crime and Disorder Act 1998

(1998 c. 37)

PART I PREVENTION OF CRIME AND DISORDER

Chapter I England and Wales

Youth crime and disorder

8   Parenting orders

(1) This section applies where, in any court proceedings—

(a) a child safety order is made in respect of a child or the court determines on an application under section 12(6) below that a child has failed to comply with any requirement included in such an order;

(aa) a parental compensation order is made in relation to a child's behaviour;

(b) an injunction is granted under section 1 of the Anti-social Behaviour, Crime and Policing Act 2014, an order is made under section 22 of that Act or a sexual harm prevention order is made in respect of a child or young person;

(c) a child or young person is convicted of an offence; or

(d) a person is convicted of an offence under section 443 (failure to comply with school attendance order) or section 444 (failure to secure regular attendance at school of registered pupil) of the Education Act 1996.

(2) Subject to subsection (3) and section 9(1) below, if in the proceedings the court is satisfied that the relevant condition is fulfilled, it may make a parenting order in respect of a person who is a parent or guardian of the child or young person or, as the case may be, the person convicted of the offence under section 443 or 444 ('the parent').

(3) A court shall not make a parenting order unless it has been notified by the Secretary of State that arrangements for implementing such orders are available in the area in which it appears to the court that the parent resides or will reside and the notice has not been withdrawn.

(4) A parenting order is an order which requires the parent—

(a) to comply, for a period not exceeding twelve months, with such requirements as are specified in the order, and

(b) subject to subsection (5) below, to attend, for a concurrent period not exceeding three months, such counselling or guidance programme as may be specified in directions given by the responsible officer.

(5) A parenting order may, but need not, include such a requirement as is mentioned in subsection (4)(b) above in any case where a parenting order under this section or any other enactment has been made in respect of the parent on a previous occasion.

(6) The relevant condition is that the parenting order would be desirable in the interests of preventing—

(a) in a case falling within paragraph (a), (aa), or (b) of subsection (1) above, any repetition of the kind of behaviour which led to the order being made or the injunction granted;

(b) in a case falling within paragraph (c) of that subsection, the commission of any further offence by the child or young person;

(c) in a case falling within paragraph (d) of that subsection, the commission of any further offence under section 443 or 444 of the Education Act 1996.

(7) The requirements that may be specified under subsection (4)(a) above are those which the court considers desirable in the interests of preventing any such repetition or, as the case may be, the commission of any such further offence.

(7A) A counselling or guidance programme which a parent is required to attend by virtue of subsection (4)(b) above may be or include a residential course but only if the court is satisfied—

    (a) that the attendance of the parent at a residential course is likely to be more effective than his attendance at a non-residential course in preventing any such repetition or, as the case may be, the commission of any such further offence, and

    (b) that any interference with family life which is likely to result from the attendance of the parent at a residential course is proportionate in all the circumstances.

(8) In this section and section 9 below 'responsible officer', in relation to a parenting order, means one of the following who is specified in the order, namely—

    (a)   an officer of a local probation board or an officer of a provider of probation services;

    (b)   a social worker of a local authority; and

    (bb) a person nominated by a person appointed as director of children's services under section 18 of the Children Act 2004 or by a person appointed as chief education officer under section 532 of the Education Act 1996;

    (c)   a member of a youth offending team.

(9) In this section 'sexual harm prevention order' means an order under section 103A of the Sexual Offences Act 2003 (sexual harm prevention orders).

9   Parenting orders: supplemental

(1) Where a person under the age of 16 is convicted of an offence the court by or before which he is so convicted—

    (a) if it is satisfied that the relevant condition is fulfilled, shall make a parenting order; and

    (b) if it is not so satisfied, shall state in open court that it is not and why it is not.

(1A) The requirements of subsection (1) do not apply where the court makes a referral order in respect of the offence.

(1B) If an injunction under section 1 of the Anti-social Behaviour, Crime and Policing Act 2014 is granted or an order is made under section 22 of that Act is made in respect of a person under the age of 16 the court which grants the injunction or makes the order—

    (a) must make a parenting order if it is satisfied that the relevant condition is fulfilled;

    (b) if it is not so satisfied, must state in open court that it is not and why it is not.

(2) Before making a parenting order—

    (a) in a case falling within paragraph (a) of subsection (1) of section 8 above;

    (b) in a case falling within paragraph (b) or (c) of that subsection, where the person concerned is under the age of 16;

    (c) in a case falling within paragraph (d) of that subsection, where the person to whom the offence related is under that age;

a court shall obtain and consider information about the person's family circumstances and the likely effect of the order on those circumstances.

(2A) In a case where a court proposes to make both a referral order in respect of a child or young person convicted of an offence and a parenting order, before making the parenting order the court shall obtain and consider a report by an appropriate officer—

    (a) indicating the requirements proposed by that officer to be included in the parenting order;

    (b) indicating the reasons why he considers those requirements would be desirable in the interests of preventing the commission of any further offence by the child or young person; and

    (c) if the child or young person is aged under 16, containing the information required by subsection (2) above.

(2B) In subsection (2A) above 'an appropriate officer' means—

    (a) an officer of a local probation board or an officer of a provider of probation services;

    (b) a social worker of a local authority; or

    (c) a member of a youth offending team.

(3) Before making a parenting order, a court shall explain to the parent in ordinary language—

(a) the effect of the order and of the requirements proposed to be included in it;

(b) the consequences which may follow (under subsection (7) below) if he fails to comply with any of those requirements; and

(c) that the court has power (under subsection (5) below) to review the order on the application either of the parent or of the responsible officer.

(4) Requirements specified in, and directions given under, a parenting order shall, as far as practicable, be such as to avoid—

(a) any conflict with the parent's religious beliefs; and

(b) any interference with the times, if any, at which he normally works or attends an educational establishment.

(5) If while a parenting order is in force it appears to the court which made it, on the application of the responsible officer or the parent, that it is appropriate to make an order under this subsection, the court may make an order discharging the parenting order or varying it—

(a) by cancelling any provision included in it; or

(b) by inserting in it (either in addition to or in substitution for any of its provisions) any provision that could have been included in the order if the court had then had power to make it and were exercising the power.

(6) Where an application under subsection (5) above for the discharge of a parenting order is dismissed, no further application for its discharge shall be made under that subsection by any person except with the consent of the court which made the order.

(7) If while a parenting order is in force the parent without reasonable excuse fails to comply with any requirement included in the order, or specified in directions given by the responsible officer, he shall be liable on summary conviction to a fine not exceeding level 3 on the standard scale.

(7A) In this section 'referral order' means an order under section 16(2) or (3) of the Powers of Criminal Courts (Sentencing) Act 2000 (referral of offender to youth offender panel).

10 Appeals against parenting orders

(1) An appeal shall lie—

(a) to the county court against the making of a parenting order by virtue of paragraph (a) of subsection (1) of section 8 above; and

(b) to the Crown Court against the making of a parenting order by virtue of paragraph (b) of that subsection.

(2) On an appeal under subsection (1) above the county court or the Crown Court—

(a) may make such orders as may be necessary to give effect to its determination of the appeal; and

(b) may also make such incidental or consequential orders as appear to it to be just.

(3) Any order of the county court or the Crown Court made on an appeal under subsection (1) above (other than one directing that an application be reheard by a magistrates' court) shall, for the purposes of subsections (5) to (7) of section 9 above, be treated as if it were an order of the court from which the appeal was brought and not an order of the county court or the Crown Court.

(4) A person in respect of whom a parenting order is made by virtue of section 8(1)(c) or 8A above shall have the same right of appeal against the making of the order as if—

(a) the offence that led to the making of the order were an offence committed by him; and

(b) the order were a sentence passed on him for the offence.

(5) A person in respect of whom a parenting order is made by virtue of section 8(1)(d) above shall have the same right of appeal against the making of the order as if the order were a sentence passed on him for the offence that led to the making of the order.

...

11 Child safety orders

(1) Subject to subsection (2) below, if the family court, on the application of a local authority, is satisfied that one or more of the conditions specified in subsection (3) below are fulfilled with respect to a child under the age of 10, it may make an order (a 'child safety order') which—

   (a) places the child, for a period (not exceeding the permitted maximum) specified in the order, under the supervision of the responsible officer; and
   (b) requires the child to comply with such requirements as are so specified.

(2) A court shall not make a child safety order unless it has been notified by the Secretary of State that arrangements for implementing such orders are available in the area in which it appears that the child resides or will reside and the notice has not been withdrawn.

(3) The conditions are—

   (a) that the child has committed an act which, if he had been aged 10 or over, would have constituted an offence;
   (b) that a child safety order is necessary for the purpose of preventing the commission by the child of such an act as is mentioned in paragraph (a) above;
        … and
   (d) that the child has acted in a manner that caused or was likely to cause harassment, alarm or distress to one or more persons not of the same household as himself.

(4) The maximum period permitted for the purposes of subsection (1)(a) above is twelve months.

(5) The requirements that may be specified under subsection (1)(b) above are those which the court considers desirable in the interests of—

   (a) securing that the child receives appropriate care, protection and support and is subject to proper control; or
   (b) preventing any repetition of the kind of behaviour which led to the child safety order being made.

(6) Proceedings under this section or section 12 below shall be family proceedings for the purposes of the 1989 Act; and the standard of proof applicable to such proceedings shall be that applicable to civil proceedings.

(7) In this section 'local authority' has the same meaning as in the 1989 Act.

(8) In this section and section 12 below, 'responsible officer', in relation to a child safety order, means one of the following who is specified in the order, namely—

   (a) a social worker of a local authority; and
   (b) a member of a youth offending team.

12 Child safety orders: supplemental

(1) Before making a child safety order, the family court shall obtain and consider information about the child's family circumstances and the likely effect of the order on those circumstances.

(2) Before making a child safety order, the family court shall explain to the parent or guardian of the child in ordinary language—

   (a) the effect of the order and of the requirements proposed to be included in it;
   (b) the consequences which may follow (under subsection (6) below) if the child fails to comply with any of those requirements; and
   (c) that the court has power (under subsection (4) below) to review the order on the application either of the parent or guardian or of the responsible officer.

(3) Requirements included in a child safety order shall, as far as practicable, be such as to avoid—

   (a) any conflict with the parent's religious beliefs; and
   (b) any interference with the times, if any, at which the child normally attends school.

(4) If while a child safety order is in force in respect of a child it appears to the court which made it, on the application of the responsible officer or a parent or guardian of the child, that it is

appropriate to make an order under this subsection, the court may make an order discharging the child safety order or varying it—

    (a) by cancelling any provision included in it; or

    (b) by inserting in it (either in addition to or in substitution for any of its provisions) any provision that could have been included in the order if the court had then had power to make it and were exercising the power.

(5) Where an application under subsection (4) above for the discharge of a child safety order is dismissed, no further application for its discharge shall be made under that subsection by any person except with the consent of the court which made the order.

(6) Where a child safety order is in force and it is proved to the satisfaction of the court which made it, on the application of the responsible officer, that the child has failed to comply with any requirement included in the order, the court—

    ...

    (b) may make an order varying the order—

        (i) by cancelling any provision included in it; or

        (ii) by inserting in it (either in addition to or in substitution for any of its provisions) any provision that could have been included in the order if the court had then had power to make it and were exercising the power.

...

13A　Parental compensation orders

(1) A magistrates' court may make an order under this section (a 'parental compensation order') if on the application of a local authority it is satisfied, on the civil standard of proof—

    (a) that the condition mentioned in subsection (2) below is fulfilled with respect to a child under the age of 10; and

    (b) that it would be desirable to make the order in the interests of preventing a repetition of the behaviour in question.

(2) The condition is that the child has taken, or caused loss of or damage to, property in the course of—

    (a) committing an act which, if he had been aged 10 or over, would have constituted an offence; or

    (b) acting in a manner that caused or was likely to cause harassment, alarm or distress to one or more persons not of the same household as himself.

(3) A parental compensation order is an order which requires any person specified in the order who is a parent or guardian of the child (other than a local authority) to pay compensation of an amount specified in the order to any person or persons specified in the order who is, or are, affected by the taking of the property or its loss or damage.

(4) The amount of compensation specified may not exceed £5,000 in all.

...

13B　Parental compensation orders: the compensation

(1) When specifying the amount of compensation for the purposes of section 13A(3) above, the magistrates' court shall take into account—

    (a) the value of the property taken or damaged, or whose loss was caused, by the child;

    (b) any further loss which flowed from the taking of or damage to the property, or from its loss;

    (c) whether the child, or any parent or guardian of his, has already paid any compensation for the property (and if so, how much);

    (d) whether the child, or any parent or guardian of his, has already made any reparation (and if so, what it consisted of);

    (e) the means of those to be specified in the order as liable to pay the compensation, so far as the court can ascertain them;

(f) whether there was any lack of care on the part of the person affected by the taking of the property or its loss or damage which made it easier for the child to take or damage the property or to cause its loss.

...

13C Parental compensation orders: supplemental

(1) Before deciding whether or not to make a parental compensation order in favour of any person, the magistrates' court shall take into account the views of that person about whether a parental compensation order should be made in his favour.

(2) Before making a parental compensation order, the magistrates' court shall obtain and consider information about the child's family circumstances and the likely effect of the order on those circumstances.

...

Human Rights Act 1998

(1998 c. 42)

Introduction

1   The Convention Rights

(1) In this Act 'the Convention rights' means the rights and fundamental freedoms set out in—

(a) Articles 2 to 12 and 14 of the Convention,

(b) Articles 1 to 3 of the First Protocol, and

(c) Article 1 of the Thirteenth Protocol,

as read with Articles 16 to 18 of the Convention.

(2) Those Articles are to have effect for the purposes of this Act subject to any designated derogation or reservation (as to which see sections 14 and 15).

(3) The Articles are set out in Schedule 1.

(4) The Secretary of State may by order make such amendments to this Act as he considers appropriate to reflect the effect, in relation to the United Kingdom, of a protocol.

(5) In subsection (4) 'protocol' means a protocol to the Convention—

(a) which the United Kingdom has ratified; or

(b) which the United Kingdom has signed with a view to ratification.

(6) No amendment may be made by an order under subsection (4) so as to come into force before the protocol concerned is in force in relation to the United Kingdom.

2   Interpretation of Convention rights

(1) A court or tribunal determining a question which has arisen in connection with a Convention right must take into account any—

(a) judgment, decision, declaration or advisory opinion of the European Court of Human Rights,

(b) opinion of the Commission given in a report adopted under Article 31 of the Convention,

(c) decision of the Commission in connection with Article 26 or 27(2) of the Convention, or

(d) decision of the Committee of Ministers taken under Article 46 of the Convention,

whenever made or given, so far as, in the opinion of the court or tribunal, it is relevant to the proceedings in which that question has arisen.

(2) Evidence of any judgment, decision, declaration or opinion of which account may have to be taken under this section is to be given in proceedings before any court or tribunal in such manner as may be provided by rules.

(3) In this section 'rules' means rules of court or, in the case of proceedings before a tribunal, rules made for the purposes of this section—

    (a) by the Lord Chancellor or the Secretary of State...

Legislation

3   Interpretation of legislation

(1) So far as it is possible to do so, primary legislation and subordinate legislation must be read and given effect in a way which is compatible with the Convention rights.

(2) This section—

    (a) applies to primary legislation and subordinate legislation whenever enacted;

    (b) does not affect the validity, continuing operation or enforcement of any incompatible primary legislation; and

    (c) does not affect the validity, continuing operation or enforcement of any incompatible subordinate legislation if (disregarding any possibility of revocation) primary legislation prevents removal of the incompatibility.

4   Declaration of incompatibility

(1) Subsection (2) applies in any proceedings in which a court determines whether a provision of primary legislation is compatible with a Convention right.

(2) If the court is satisfied that the provision is incompatible with a Convention right, it may make a declaration of that incompatibility.

(3) Subsection (4) applies in any proceedings in which a court determines whether a provision of subordinate legislation, made in the exercise of a power conferred by primary legislation, is compatible with a Convention right.

(4) If the court is satisfied—

    (a) that the provision is incompatible with a Convention right, and

    (b) that (disregarding any possibility of revocation) the primary legislation concerned prevents removal of the incompatibility,

it may make a declaration of that incompatibility.

(5) In this section 'court' means—

    (a) the Supreme Court;

    (b) the Judicial Committee of the Privy Council;

    ...

    (e) in England and Wales or Northern Ireland, the High Court or the Court of Appeal;

    (f) the Court of Protection, in any matter being dealt with by the President of the Family Division, the Chancellor of the High Court or a puisne judge of the High Court.

(6) A declaration under this section ('a declaration of incompatibility')—

    (a) does not affect the validity, continuing operation or enforcement of the provision in respect of which it is given; and

    (b) is not binding on the parties to the proceedings in which it is made.

...

Public authorities

6   Acts of public authorities

(1) It is unlawful for a public authority to act in a way which is incompatible with a Convention right.

(2) Subsection (1) does not apply to an act if—

    (a) as the result of one or more provisions of primary legislation, the authority could not have acted differently; or

    (b) in the case of one or more provisions of, or made under, primary legislation which cannot be read or given effect in a way which is compatible with the Convention rights, the authority was acting so as to give effect to or enforce those provisions.

(3) In this section 'public authority' includes—

    (a) a court or tribunal, and

    (b) any person certain of whose functions are functions of a public nature,

but does not include either House of Parliament or a person exercising functions in connection with proceedings in Parliament.

(4) …

(5) In relation to a particular act, a person is not a public authority by virtue only of subsection (3)(b) if the nature of the act is private.

(6) 'An act' includes a failure to act but does not include a failure to—

    (a) introduce in, or lay before, Parliament a proposal for legislation; or

    (b) make any primary legislation or remedial order.

7 Proceedings

(1) A person who claims that a public authority has acted (or proposes to act) in a way which is made unlawful by section 6(1) may—

    (a) bring proceedings against the authority under this Act in the appropriate court or tribunal, or

    (b) rely on the Convention right or rights concerned in any legal proceedings,

but only if he is (or would be) a victim of the unlawful act.

(2) In subsection (1)(a) 'appropriate court or tribunal' means such court or tribunal as may be determined in accordance with rules; and proceedings against an authority include a counterclaim or similar proceeding.

(3) If the proceedings are brought on an application for judicial review, the applicant is to be taken to have a sufficient interest in relation to the unlawful act only if he is, or would be, a victim of that act.

    …

(5) Proceedings under subsection (1)(a) must be brought before the end of—

    (a) the period of one year beginning with the date on which the act complained of took place; or

    (b) such longer period as the court or tribunal considers equitable having regard to all the circumstances,

but that is subject to any rule imposing a stricter time limit in relation to the procedure in question.

(6) In subsection (1)(b) 'legal proceedings' includes—

    (a) proceedings brought by or at the instigation of a public authority; and

    (b) an appeal against the decision of a court or tribunal.

(7) For the purposes of this section, a person is a victim of an unlawful act only if he would be a victim for the purposes of Article 34 of the Convention if proceedings were brought in the European Court of Human Rights in respect of that act.

(8) Nothing in this Act creates a criminal offence.

(9) In this section 'rules' means—

    (a) in relation to proceedings before a court or tribunal outside Scotland, rules made by the Lord Chancellor or the Secretary of State for the purposes of this section or rules of court,

    …

and includes provision made by order under section 1 of the Courts and Legal Services Act 1990.

(10) In making rules, regard must be had to section 9.

(11) The Minister who has power to make rules in relation to a particular tribunal may, to the extent he considers it necessary to ensure that the tribunal can provide an appropriate remedy in relation to an act (or proposed act) of a public authority which is (or would be) unlawful as a result of section 6(1), by order add to—

    (a) the relief or remedies which the tribunal may grant; or

    (b) the grounds on which it may grant any of them.

(12) An order made under subsection (11) may contain such incidental, supplemental, consequential or transitional provision as the Minister making it considers appropriate.

...

8 Judicial remedies

(1) In relation to any act (or proposed act) of a public authority which the court finds is (or would be) unlawful, it may grant such relief or remedy, or make such order, within its powers as it considers just and appropriate.

(2) But damages may be awarded only by a court which has power to award damages, or to order the payment of compensation, in civil proceedings.

(3) No award of damages is to be made unless, taking account of all the circumstances of the case, including—

  (a) any other relief or remedy granted, or order made, in relation to the act in question (by that or any other court), and

  (b) the consequences of any decision (of that or any other court) in respect of that act,

the court is satisfied that the award is necessary to afford just satisfaction to the person in whose favour it is made.

(4) In determining—

  (a) whether to award damages, or

  (b) the amount of an award,

the court must take into account the principles applied by the European Court of Human Rights in relation to the award of compensation under Article 41 of the Convention.

(5) A public authority against which damages are awarded is to be treated—

  (a) ...

  (b) for the purposes of the Civil Liability (Contribution) Act 1978 as liable in respect of damage suffered by the person to whom the award is made.

(6) In this section—

'court' includes a tribunal;

'damages' means damages for an unlawful act of a public authority; and

'unlawful' means unlawful under section 6(1).

...

Section 1(3)

SCHEDULE 1

THE ARTICLES

PART I THE CONVENTION RIGHTS AND FREEDOMS

Article 2   Right to life

1 Everyone's right to life shall be protected by law. No one shall be deprived of his life intentionally save in the execution of a sentence of a court following his conviction of a crime for which this penalty is provided by law.

2 Deprivation of life shall not be regarded as inflicted in contravention of this Article when it results from the use of force which is no more than absolutely necessary:

  (a) in defence of any person from unlawful violence;

  (b) in order to effect a lawful arrest or to prevent the escape of a person lawfully detained;

  (c) in action lawfully taken for the purpose of quelling a riot or insurrection.

Article 3   Prohibition of torture

No one shall be subjected to torture or to inhuman or degrading treatment or punishment.

...

Article 5   Right to liberty and security

1 Everyone has the right to liberty and security of person. No one shall be deprived of his liberty save in the following cases and in accordance with a procedure prescribed by law:

    (a) the lawful detention of a person after conviction by a competent court;

    (b) the lawful arrest or detention of a person for non-compliance with the lawful order of a court or in order to secure the fulfilment of any obligation prescribed by law;

    (c) the lawful arrest or detention of a person effected for the purpose of bringing him before the competent legal authority on reasonable suspicion of having committed an offence or when it is reasonably considered necessary to prevent his committing an offence or fleeing after having done so;

    (d) the detention of a minor by lawful order for the purpose of educational supervision or his lawful detention for the purpose of bringing him before the competent legal authority;

    (e) the lawful detention of persons for the prevention of the spreading of infectious diseases, of persons of unsound mind, alcoholics or drug addicts or vagrants;

    (f) the lawful arrest or detention of a person to prevent his effecting an unauthorised entry into the country or of a person against whom action is being taken with a view to deportation or extradition.

2 Everyone who is arrested shall be informed promptly, in a language which he understands, of the reasons for his arrest and of any charge against him.

3 Everyone arrested or detained in accordance with the provisions of paragraph 1(c) of this Article shall be brought promptly before a judge or other officer authorised by law to exercise judicial power and shall be entitled to trial within a reasonable time or to release pending trial. Release may be conditioned by guarantees to appear for trial.

4 Everyone who is deprived of his liberty by arrest or detention shall be entitled to take proceedings by which the lawfulness of his detention shall be decided speedily by a court and his release ordered if the detention is not lawful.

5 Everyone who has been the victim of arrest or detention in contravention of the provisions of this Article shall have an enforceable right to compensation.

Article 6   Right to a fair trial

1 In the determination of his civil rights and obligations or of any criminal charge against him, everyone is entitled to a fair and public hearing within a reasonable time by an independent and impartial tribunal established by law. Judgment shall be pronounced publicly but the press and public may be excluded from all or part of the trial in the interest of morals, public order or national security in a democratic society, where the interests of juveniles or the protection of the private life of the parties so require, or to the extent strictly necessary in the opinion of the court in special circumstances where publicity would prejudice the interests of justice.

2 Everyone charged with a criminal offence shall be presumed innocent until proved guilty according to law.

3 Everyone charged with a criminal offence has the following minimum rights:

    (a) to be informed promptly, in a language which he understands and in detail, of the nature and cause of the accusation against him;

    (b) to have adequate time and facilities for the preparation of his defence;

    (c) to defend himself in person or through legal assistance of his own choosing or, if he has not sufficient means to pay for legal assistance, to be given it free when the interests of justice so require;

    (d) to examine or have examined witnesses against him and to obtain the attendance and examination of witnesses on his behalf under the same conditions as witnesses against him;

    (e) to have the free assistance of an interpreter if he cannot understand or speak the language used in court.

Article 7   No punishment without law

1 No one shall be held guilty of any criminal offence on account of any act or omission which did not constitute a criminal offence under national or international law at the time when it was

committed. Nor shall a heavier penalty be imposed than the one that was applicable at the time the criminal offence was committed.

2 This Article shall not prejudice the trial and punishment of any person for any act or omission which, at the time when it was committed, was criminal according to the general principles of law recognised by civilised nations.

Article 8   Right to respect for private and family life

1 Everyone has the right to respect for his private and family life, his home and his correspondence.

2 There shall be no interference by a public authority with the exercise of this right except such as is in accordance with the law and is necessary in a democratic society in the interests of national security, public safety or the economic well-being of the country, for the prevention of disorder or crime, for the protection of health or morals, or for the protection of the rights and freedoms of others.

Article 9   Freedom of thought, conscience and religion

1 Everyone has the right to freedom of thought, conscience and religion; this right includes freedom to change his religion or belief and freedom, either alone or in community with others and in public or private, to manifest his religion or belief, in worship, teaching, practice and observance.

2 Freedom to manifest one's religion or beliefs shall be subject only to such limitations as are prescribed by law and are necessary in a democratic society in the interests of public safety, for the protection of public order, health or morals, or for the protection of the rights and freedoms of others. …

Article 12   Right to marry

Men and women of marriageable age have the right to marry and to found a family, according to the national laws governing the exercise of this right.

Article 14   Prohibition of discrimination

The enjoyment of the rights and freedoms set forth in this Convention shall be secured without discrimination on any ground such as sex, race, colour, language, religion, political or other opinion, national or social origin, association with a national minority, property, birth or other status.

Article 17   Prohibition of abuse of rights

Nothing in this Convention may be interpreted as implying for any State, group or person any right to engage in any activity or perform any act aimed at the destruction of any of the rights and freedoms set forth herein or at their limitation to a greater extent than is provided for in the Convention.

Article 18   Limitation on use of restrictions on rights

The restrictions permitted under this Convention to the said rights and freedoms shall not be applied for any purpose other than those for which they have been prescribed.

PART II THE FIRST PROTOCOL

Article 1   Protection of property

Every natural or legal person is entitled to the peaceful enjoyment of his possessions. No one shall be deprived of his possessions except in the public interest and subject to the conditions provided for by law and by the general principles of international law.

The preceding provisions shall not, however, in any way impair the right of a State to enforce such laws as it deems necessary to control the use of property in accordance with the general interest or to secure the payment of taxes or other contributions or penalties.

Article 2   Right to education

No person shall be denied the right to education. In the exercise of any functions which it assumes in relation to education and to teaching, the State shall respect the right of parents to ensure such education and teaching in conformity with their own religious and philosophical convictions.

Powers of Criminal Courts (Sentencing) Act 2000

(2000 c. 6)

…

PART VI FINANCIAL PENALTIES AND ORDERS

…

Young offenders

137 Power to order parent or guardian to pay fine, costs, compensation or surcharge

(1) Where—

(a) a child or young person (that is to say, any person aged under 18) is convicted of any offence for the commission of which a fine or costs may be imposed or a compensation order may be made, and

(b) the court is of the opinion that the case would best be met by the imposition of a fine or costs or the making of such an order, whether with or without any other punishment, the court shall order that the fine, compensation or costs awarded be paid by the parent or guardian of the child or young person instead of by the child or young person himself, unless the court is satisfied—

(i) that the parent or guardian cannot be found; or

(ii) that it would be unreasonable to make an order for payment, having regard to the circumstances of the case.

(1A) Where but for this subsection a court would order a child or young person to pay a surcharge under section 161A of the Criminal Justice Act 2003, the court shall order that the surcharge be paid by the parent or guardian of the child or young person instead of by the child or young person himself, unless the court is satisfied—

(a) that the parent or guardian cannot be found; or

(b) that it would be unreasonable to make an order for payment, having regard to the circumstances of the case.

…

(3) In the case of a young person aged 16 or over, subsections (1) to (2) above shall have effect as if, instead of imposing a duty, they conferred a power to make such an order as is mentioned in those subsections.

(4) Subject to subsection (5) below, no order shall be made under this section without giving the parent or guardian an opportunity of being heard.

(5) An order under this section may be made against a parent or guardian who, having been required to attend, has failed to do so.

(6) A parent or guardian may appeal to the Crown Court against an order under this section made by a magistrates' court.

(7) A parent or guardian may appeal to the Court of Appeal against an order under this section made by the Crown Court, as if he had been convicted on indictment and the order were a sentence passed on his conviction.

(8) In relation to a child or young person for whom a local authority have parental responsibility and who—

(a) is in their care, or

(b) is provided with accommodation by them in the exercise of any functions (in particular those under the Children Act 1989) which are social services functions within the meaning of the Local Authority Social Services Act 1970,

references in this section to his parent or guardian shall be construed as references to that authority.

(9) In subsection (8) above 'local authority' and 'parental responsibility' have the same meanings as in the Children Act 1989.

138 Fixing of fine, compensation or surcharge to be paid by parent or guardian

(1) For the purposes of any order under section 137 above made against the parent or guardian of a child or young person—

(za) Subsection (3) of section 161A of the Criminal Justice Act 2003 (surcharges) and subsection (4A) of section 164 of that Act (fixing of fines) shall have effect as if any reference in those subsections to the offender's means were a reference to those of the parent or guardian;

(a) section 164 of the Criminal Justice Act 2003 (fixing of fines) shall have effect as if any reference in subsections (1) to (4) to the financial circumstances of the offender were a reference to the financial circumstances of the parent or guardian, and as if subsection (5) were omitted;

(b) section 130(11) above (determination of compensation order) shall have effect as if any reference to the means of the person against whom the compensation order is made were a reference to the financial circumstances of the parent or guardian; and

(c) section 130(12) above (preference to be given to compensation if insufficient means to pay both compensation and a fine) shall have effect as if the reference to the offender were a reference to the parent or guardian;

but in relation to an order under section 137 made against a local authority this subsection has effect subject to subsection (2) below.

(2) For the purposes of any order under section 137 above made against a local authority, section 164(1) of the Criminal Justice Act 2003 and section 130(11) above shall not apply.

(3) For the purposes of any order under section 137 above, where the parent or guardian of an offender who is a child or young person—

(a) has failed to comply with an order under section 136 above, or

(b) has otherwise failed to co-operate with the court in its inquiry into his financial circumstances,

and the court considers that it has insufficient information to make a proper determination of the parent's or guardian's financial circumstances, it may make such determination as it thinks fit.

(4) Where a court has, in fixing the amount of a fine, determined the financial circumstances of a parent or guardian under subsection (3) above, subsections (2) to (4) of section 165 of the Criminal Justice Act 2003 (remission of fines) shall (so far as applicable) have effect as they have effect in the case mentioned in section 165(1), but as if the reference in section 165(2) to the offender's financial circumstances were a reference to the financial circumstances of the parent or guardian.

(5) In this section 'local authority' has the same meaning as in the Children Act 1989.

...

PART VII FURTHER POWERS OF COURTS

Young offenders

150 Binding over of parent or guardian

(1) Where a child or young person (that is to say, any person aged under 18) is convicted of an offence, the powers conferred by this section shall be exercisable by the court by which he is sentenced for that offence, and where the offender is aged under 16 when sentenced it shall be the duty of that court—

(a) to exercise those powers if it is satisfied, having regard to the circumstances of the case, that their exercise would be desirable in the interests of preventing the commission by him of further offences; and

(b) if it does not exercise them, to state in open court that it is not satisfied as mentioned in paragraph (a) above and why it is not so satisfied;

but this subsection has effect subject to section 19(5) above and paragraph 13(5) of Schedule 1 to this Act (cases where referral orders made or extended).

(2) The powers conferred by this section are as follows—

    (a) with the consent of the offender's parent or guardian, to order the parent or guardian to enter into a recognizance to take proper care of him and exercise proper control over him; and

    (b) if the parent or guardian refuses consent and the court considers the refusal unreasonable, to order the parent or guardian to pay a fine not exceeding £1,000;

and where the court has passed on the offender a sentence which consists of or includes a youth rehabilitation order, it may include in the recognizance a provision that the offender's parent or guardian ensure that the offender complies with the requirements of that sentence.

(3) An order under this section shall not require the parent or guardian to enter into a recognizance for an amount exceeding £1,000.

(4) An order under this section shall not require the parent or guardian to enter into a recognizance—

    (a) for a period exceeding three years; or

    (b) where the offender will attain the age of 18 in a period shorter than three years, for a period exceeding that shorter period.

. . .

(8) A parent or guardian may appeal to the Crown Court against an order under this section made by a magistrates' court.

(9) A parent or guardian may appeal to the Court of Appeal against an order under this section made by the Crown Court, as if he had been convicted on indictment and the order were a sentence passed on his conviction.

(10) A court may vary or revoke an order made by it under this section if, on the application of the parent or guardian, it appears to the court, having regard to any change in the circumstances since the order was made, to be in the interests of justice to do so.

(11) For the purposes of this section, taking 'care' of a person includes giving him protection and guidance and 'control' includes discipline.

. . .

Care Standards Act 2000

(2000 c. 14)

PART I INTRODUCTORY

Preliminary

1 Children's homes

(1) Subsections (2) to (6) have effect for the purposes of this Act.

(2) An establishment is a children's home (subject to the following provisions of this section) if it provides care and accommodation wholly or mainly for children.

(3) An establishment is not a children's home merely because a child is cared for and accommodated there by a parent or relative of his or by a foster parent.

(4) An establishment in Wales is not a children's home if it is—

    (a) a health service hospital;

    (b) an independent hospital or an independent clinic; or

    (c) a residential family centre,

or if it is of a description excepted by regulations.

(4A) An establishment in England is not a children's home if it is—

    (a) a hospital (within the meaning of the National Health Service Act 2006); or

    (b) a residential family centre,

or if it is of a description excepted by regulations.

(5) Subject to subsection (6), an establishment is not a children's home if it is a school.

(6) A school is a children's home at any time if at that time accommodation is provided for children at the school and either—

    (a) in each year that fell within the period of two years ending at that time, accommodation was provided for children, either at the school or under arrangements made by the proprietor of the school, for more than 295 days; or

    (b) it is intended to provide accommodation for children, either at the school or under arrangements made by the proprietor of the school, for more than 295 days in any year;

and in this subsection 'year' means a period of twelve months.

But accommodation shall not for the purposes of paragraph (a) be regarded as provided to children for a number of days unless there is at least one child to whom it is provided for that number of days; and paragraph (b) shall be construed accordingly.

(7) For the purposes of this section a person is a foster parent in relation to a child if—

    (a) he is a local authority foster parent in relation to the child;

    (b) he is a foster parent with whom a child has been placed by a voluntary organisation under section 59(1)(a) of the 1989 Act; or

    (c) he fosters the child privately.

…

4 Other basic definitions

(1) This section has effect for the purposes of this Act.

…

(4) 'Fostering agency' means, subject to subsection (6)—

    (a) an undertaking which consists of or includes discharging functions of local authorities in connection with the placing of children with foster parents; or

    (b) a voluntary organisation which places children with foster parents under section 59 (1) of the 1989 Act.

…

(6) The definitions in subsections (2) to (5) do not include any description of establishment, undertaking or organisation excepted from those definitions by regulations.

(7) 'Voluntary adoption agency' means an adoption society within the meaning of the Adoption and Children Act 2002 which is a voluntary organisation within the meaning of that Act.

(7A) 'Adoption support agency' has the meaning given by section 8 of the Adoption and Children Act 2002.

(8) Below in this Act—

    (a) any reference to a description of establishment is a reference to—

        (i) a children's home,

        (ii) a children's home providing accommodation for the purpose of restricting liberty,

        (iii) an independent hospital in Wales,

        (iv) an independent hospital in Wales in which treatment or nursing (or both) are provided for persons liable to be detained under the Mental Health Act 1983,

        (v) an independent clinic in Wales,

        (vi) a care home in Wales, or

        (vii) a residential family centre;

    (b) a reference to any establishment is a reference to an establishment of any of those descriptions.

(9) Below in this Act—

(a) any reference to a description of agency is a reference to—

    (i) an independent medical agency in Wales or, where the activities of an independent medical agency are carried on from two or more branches, a branch in Wales of an independent medical agency,

    (ii) a domiciliary care agency in Wales or, where the activities of a domiciliary care agency are carried on from two or more branches, a branch in Wales of a domiciliary care agency,

    (iii) a nurses agency in Wales or, where the activities of a nurses agency are carried on from two or more branches, a branch in Wales of a nurses agency,

    (iv) a fostering agency or, where the activities of a fostering agency are carried on from two or more branches, a branch of a fostering agency,

    (v) a voluntary adoption agency, or

    (vi) an adoption support agency or, where the activities of an adoption support agency are carried on from two or more branches, a branch of an adoption support agency;

(b) a reference to any agency is a reference to an agency or branch of any of those descriptions.

(10) This Act applies to a provider of social work services as it applies to an agency, except in so far as the undertaking of that provider consists of or includes the carrying on of an establishment; and 'provider of social work services' has the same meaning as in Part 1 of the Children and Young Persons Act 2008.

PART II ESTABLISHMENTS AND AGENCIES

Registration

11   Requirement to register

(1) Any person who carries on or manages an establishment or agency of any description without being registered under this Part in respect of it (as an establishment or, as the case may be, agency of that description) shall be guilty of an offence.

(3) The references in subsection (1) to an agency do not include a reference to a voluntary adoption agency.

…

PART III LOCAL AUTHORITY SERVICES

43   Introductory

(1) This section has effect for the purposes of this Part.

(2) 'Relevant functions', in relation to a local authority, means relevant adoption functions and relevant fostering functions.

(3) In relation to a local authority—

(a) 'relevant adoption functions' means functions under the Adoption and Children Act 2002 of making or participating in arrangements for the adoption of children or the provision of adoption support services (as defined in section 2(6) of the Adoption and Children Act 2002); and

(b) 'relevant fostering functions' means functions under section 22C of the 1989 Act in connection with placements with local authority foster parents or regulations under paragraph 12E(a), (b), (d) or (e) or 12F.

…

48   Regulation of the exercise of relevant fostering functions

(1) Regulations may make provision about the exercise by local authorities of relevant fostering functions, and may in particular make provision—

    (a) as to the persons who are fit to work for local authorities in connection with the exercise of such functions;

    (b) as to the fitness of premises to be used by local authorities in their exercise of such functions;

    (c) as to the management and control of the operations of local authorities in their exercise of such functions;

    (d) as to the numbers of persons, or persons of any particular type, working for local authorities in connection with the exercise of such functions;

    (e) as to the management and training of such persons;

    (f) as to the fees or expenses which may be paid to persons assisting local authorities in making decisions in the exercise of such functions.

(2) Regulations under subsection (1)(a) may, in particular, make provision for prohibiting persons from working for local authorities in such positions as may be prescribed unless they are registered in, or in a particular part of, one of the registers maintained under section 56(1).

49   National minimum standards

(1) Subsections (1), (2) and (3) of section 23 shall apply to local authorities in their exercise of relevant functions as they apply to establishments and agencies.

…

PART V THE CHILDREN'S COMMISSIONER FOR WALES

72   Children's Commissioner for Wales

(1) There shall be an office of the Children's Commissioner for Wales or Comisiynydd Plant Cymru.

…

72A   Principal aim of the Commissioner

The principal aim of the Commissioner in exercising his functions is to safeguard and promote the rights and welfare of children to whom this Part applies.

…

73   Review and monitoring of arrangements

(1) The Commissioner may review, and monitor the operation of, arrangements falling within subsection (2), (2A), (2B), (2C), (3) or (4) for the purpose of ascertaining whether, and to what extent, the arrangements are effective in safeguarding and promoting the rights and welfare of children—

    (a) to or in respect of whom services are provided in Wales by, or on behalf of or under arrangements with, a person mentioned in Schedule 2B; or

    (b) to or in respect of whom regulated children's services in Wales are provided.

(1A) The Commissioner may also assess the effect on such children of the failure of any person to make such arrangements.

…

74   Examination of cases

(1) Regulations may, in connection with the Commissioner's functions under this Part, make provision for the examination by the Commissioner of the cases of particular children to whom this Part applies.

    …

(2) The regulations may include provision about—

    (a) the types of case which may be examined;

(b) the circumstances in which an examination may be made;

(c) the procedure for conducting an examination, including provision about the representation of parties;

(d) the publication of reports following an examination.

(3) The regulations may make provision for—

(a) requiring persons to provide the Commissioner with information; or

(b) requiring persons who hold or are accountable for information to provide the Commissioner with explanations or other assistance,

for the purposes of an examination or for the purposes of determining whether any recommendation made in a report following an examination has been complied with.

(4) For the purposes mentioned in subsection (3), the Commissioner shall have the same powers as the High Court in respect of—

(a) the attendance and examination of witnesses (including the administration of oaths and affirmations and the examination of witnesses abroad); and

(b) the provision of information.

(5) No person shall be compelled for the purposes mentioned in subsection (3) to give any evidence or provide any information which he could not be compelled to give or provide in civil proceedings before the High Court.

(6) The regulations may make provision for the payment by the Commissioner of sums in respect of expenses or allowances to persons who attend or provide information for the purposes mentioned in subsection (3).

...

76   Further functions

(1) Regulations may confer power on the Commissioner to assist a child to whom this Part applies—

(a)   in making a complaint or representation to or in respect of a provider of regulated children's services in Wales;

(aa)   in making a complaint or representation to or in respect of a person mentioned in Schedule 2B or section 73(2B); or

(b)   in any prescribed proceedings,

and in this subsection 'proceedings' includes a procedure of any kind and any prospective proceedings.

...

(2) For the purposes of subsection (1), assistance includes—

(a) financial assistance; and

(b) arranging for representation, or the giving of advice or assistance, by any person,

and the regulations may provide for assistance to be given on conditions, including (in the case of financial assistance) conditions requiring repayment in circumstances specified in the regulations.

(3) The Commissioner may, in connection with his functions under this Part, give advice and information to any person.

(4) Regulations may, in connection with the Commissioner's functions under this Part, confer further functions on him.

(5) The regulations may, in particular,

(a) include provision about the making of reports on any matter connected with any of his functions;

(b) provide that the Commissioner may make a joint report with the Commissioner for Older People in Wales where they have discharged their respective functions under this Act and the Commissioner for Older People (Wales) Act 2006 in relation to the same matters.

...

(6) Apart from identifying any person investigated, a report by the Commissioner shall not—

(a) mention the name of any person; or

(b) include any particulars which, in the opinion of the Commissioner, are likely to identify any person and can be omitted without impairing the effectiveness of the report, unless, after taking account of the public interest (as well as the interests of any person who made a complaint and other persons), the Commissioner considers it necessary for the report to mention his name or include such particulars.

(7) For the purposes of the law of defamation, the publication of any matter by the Commissioner in a report is absolutely privileged.

(8) The Commissioner or a person authorised by him may for the purposes of any function of the Commissioner under section 72B or 73 or subsection (4) of this section at any reasonable time—

(a) enter any premises, other than a private dwelling, for the purposes of interviewing any child accommodated or cared for there; and

(b) if the child consents, interview the child in private.

77 Restrictions

(1) This Part does not authorise the Commissioner to enquire into or report on any matter so far as it is the subject of legal proceedings before, or has been determined by, a court or tribunal.

(2) This Part does not authorise the Commissioner to exercise any function which by virtue of an enactment is also exercisable by a prescribed person.

Criminal Justice and Court Services Act 2000

(2000 c. 43)

PART I THE NEW SERVICES

...

Chapter II Children and Family Court Advisory and Support Service

11 Establishment of the Service

(1) There shall be a body corporate to be known as the Children and Family Court Advisory and Support Service (referred to in this Part as the Service) which is to exercise the functions conferred on it by virtue of this Act and any other enactment.

(2) Schedule 2 (which makes provision about the constitution of the Service, its powers and other matters relating to it) is to have effect.

(3) References in this Act or any other enactment to an officer of the Service are references to—

(a) any member of the staff of the Service appointed under paragraph 5(1)(a) of that Schedule, and

(b) any other individual exercising functions of an officer of the Service by virtue of section 13(2) or (4).

12 Principal functions of the Service

(1) In respect of family proceedings in which the welfare of children other than children ordinarily resident in Wales is or may be in question, it is a function of the Service to—

(a) safeguard and promote the welfare of the children,

(b) give advice to any court about any application made to it in such proceedings,

(c) make provision for the children to be represented in such proceedings,

(d) provide information, advice and other support for the children and their families.

(2) The Service must also make provision for the performance of any functions conferred on officers of the Service by virtue of this Act or any other enactment (whether or not they are exercisable for the purposes of the functions conferred on the Service by subsection (1)).

(3) Regulations may provide for grants to be paid by the Service to any person for the purpose of furthering the performance of any of the Service's functions.

(4) The regulations may provide for the grants to be paid on conditions, including conditions—

    (a) regulating the purposes for which the grant or any part of it may be used,

    (b) requiring repayment to the Service in specified circumstances.

(5) In this section, 'family proceedings' has the same meaning as in the Matrimonial and Family Proceedings Act 1984 and also includes any other proceedings which are family proceedings for the purposes of the Children Act 1989, but—

    (a) references to family proceedings include (where the context allows) family proceedings which are proposed or have been concluded.

...

13 Other powers of the Service

(1) The Service may make arrangements with organisations under which the organisations perform functions of the Service on its behalf.

(2) Arrangements under subsection (1) may provide for the organisations to designate individuals who may perform functions of officers of the Service.

...

15 Right to conduct litigation and right of audience

(1) The Service may authorise an officer of the Service of a prescribed description—

    (a) to conduct litigation in relation to any proceedings in any court,

    (b) to exercise a right of audience in any proceedings before any court, in the exercise of his functions.

...

SCHEDULE 2 CHILDREN AND FAMILY COURT ADVISORY AND SUPPORT SERVICE

Constitution

1. The Service is to consist of a chairman, and not less than nine other members, appointed by the Secretary of State.

2.—(1) Regulations may provide—

    (a) for the appointment of the chairman and other members and for the co-option by the Service for particular purposes of additional members (including the number, or limits on the number, of persons who may be appointed or co-opted and any conditions to be fulfilled for appointment or co-option),

    (b) for the tenure of office of the chairman and other members and any co-opted members (including the circumstances in which they cease to hold office or may be removed or suspended from office).

(2) References below in this Schedule to members of the Service do not include co-opted members.

...

Delegation

7. The Service may arrange for the chairman or any other member to discharge functions of the Service on its behalf.

...

Supervision

9.—(1) Functions and other powers of the Service, and functions of any officer of the Service, must be performed in accordance with any directions given by the Secretary of State.

(2) In particular, the directions may make provision for the purpose of ensuring that the services provided are of appropriate quality and meet appropriate standards.

...

Complaints

15. The Service must make and publicise a scheme for dealing with complaints made by or on behalf of prescribed persons in relation to the performance by the Service and its officers of their functions.

…

Criminal Justice and Police Act 2001

(2001 c. 16)

PART 1   PROVISIONS FOR COMBATTING CRIME AND DISORDER

Chapter 3   Other provisions for combatting crime and disorder

Further provision about intimidation etc.

42A   Offence of harassment etc. of a person in his home

(1) A person commits an offence if—

   (a) that person is present outside or in the vicinity of any premises that are used by any individual ('the resident') as his dwelling;

   (b) that person is present there for the purpose (by his presence or otherwise) of representing to the resident or another individual (whether or not one who uses the premises as his dwelling), or of persuading the resident or such another individual—

     (i) that he should not do something that he is entitled or required to do; or

     (ii) that he should do something that he is not under any obligation to do;

   (c) that person—

     (i) intends his presence to amount to the harassment of, or to cause alarm or distress to, the resident; or

     (ii) knows or ought to know that his presence is likely to result in the harassment of, or to cause alarm or distress to, the resident; and

   (d) the presence of that person—

     (i) amounts to the harassment of, or causes alarm or distress to, any person falling within subsection (2); or

     (ii) is likely to result in the harassment of, or to cause alarm or distress to, any such person.

(2) A person falls within this subsection if he is—

   (a) the resident,

   (b) a person in the resident's dwelling, or

   (c) a person in another dwelling in the vicinity of the resident's dwelling.

(3) The references in subsection (1)(c) and (d) to a person's presence are references to his presence either alone or together with that of any other persons who are also present.

(4) For the purposes of this section a person (A) ought to know that his presence is likely to result in the harassment of, or to cause alarm or distress to, a resident if a reasonable person in possession of the same information would think that A's presence was likely to have that effect.

(5) A person guilty of an offence under this section shall be liable, on summary conviction, to imprisonment for a term not exceeding 51 weeks or to a fine not exceeding level 4 on the standard scale, or to both.

(6) In relation to an offence committed before the commencement of section 281(5) of the Criminal Justice Act 2003 (alteration of penalties for summary offences), the reference in subsection (5) to 51 weeks is to be read as a reference to 6 months.

(7) In this section 'dwelling' has the same meaning as in Part 1 of the Public Order Act 1986.

Land Registration Act 2002

(2002 c. 9)

PART 3 DISPOSITIONS OF REGISTERED LAND

…

26 Protection of disponees

(1) Subject to subsection (2), a person's right to exercise owner's powers in relation to a registered estate or charge is to be taken to be free from any limitation affecting the validity of a disposition.

(2) Subsection (1) does not apply to a limitation—

(a) reflected by an entry in the register, or

(b) imposed by, or under, this Act.

(3) This section has effect only for the purpose of preventing the title of a disponee being questioned (and so does not affect the lawfulness of a disposition).

…

PART 4 NOTICES AND RESTRICTIONS

Notices

…

33 Excluded interests

No notice may be entered in the register in respect of any of the following—

(a) an interest under—

(i) a trust of land, or

(ii) a settlement under the Settled Land Act 1925 (c. 18),

…

Restrictions

40 Nature

(1) A restriction is an entry in the register regulating the circumstances in which a disposition of a registered estate or charge may be the subject of an entry in the register.

(2) A restriction may, in particular—

(a) prohibit the making of an entry in respect of any disposition, or a disposition of a kind specified in the restriction;

(b) prohibit the making of an entry—

(i) indefinitely,

(ii) for a period specified in the restriction, or

(iii) until the occurrence of an event so specified.

(3) Without prejudice to the generality of subsection (2)(b)(iii), the events which may be specified include—

(a) the giving of notice,

(b) the obtaining of consent, and

(c) the making of an order by the court or registrar.

(4) The entry of a restriction is to be made in relation to the registered estate or charge to which it relates.

41 Effect

(1) Where a restriction is entered in the register, no entry in respect of a disposition to which the restriction applies may be made in the register otherwise than in accordance with the terms of the restriction, subject to any order under subsection (2).

(2) The registrar may by order—

    (a) disapply a restriction in relation to a disposition specified in the order or dispositions of a kind so specified, or

    (b) provide that a restriction has effect, in relation to a disposition specified in the order or dispositions of a kind so specified, with modifications so specified.

(3) The power under subsection (2) is exercisable only on the application of a person who appears to the registrar to have a sufficient interest in the restriction.

42 Power of registrar to enter

(1) The registrar may enter a restriction in the register if it appears to him that it is necessary or desirable to do so for the purpose of—

    (a) preventing invalidity or unlawfulness in relation to dispositions of a registered estate or charge,

    (b) securing that interests which are capable of being overreached on a disposition of a registered estate or charge are overreached, or

    (c) protecting a right or claim in relation to a registered estate or charge.

(2) No restriction may be entered under subsection (1)(c) for the purpose of protecting the priority of an interest which is, or could be, the subject of a notice.

(3) The registrar must give notice of any entry made under this section to the proprietor of the registered estate or charge concerned, except where the entry is made in pursuance of an application under section 43.

(4) For the purposes of subsection (1)(c), a person entitled to the benefit of a charging order relating to an interest under a trust shall be treated as having a right or claim in relation to the trust property.

43 Applications

(1) A person may apply to the registrar for the entry of a restriction under section 42 (1) if—

    (a) he is the relevant registered proprietor, or a person entitled to be registered as such proprietor,

    (b) the relevant registered proprietor, or a person entitled to be registered as such proprietor, consents to the application, or

    (c) he otherwise has a sufficient interest in the making of the entry.

...

46 Power of court to order entry

(1) If it appears to the court that it is necessary or desirable to do so for the purpose of protecting a right or claim in relation to a registered estate or charge, it may make an order requiring the registrar to enter a restriction in the register.

(2) No order under this section may be made for the purpose of protecting the priority of an interest which is, or could be, the subject of a notice.

(3) The court may include in an order under this section a direction that an entry made in pursuance of the order is to have overriding priority.

(4) If an order under this section includes a direction under subsection (3), the registrar must make such entry in the register as rules may provide.

(5) The court may make the exercise of its power under subsection (3) subject to such terms and conditions as it thinks fit.

...

PART 6 REGISTRATION: GENERAL

...

Applications

71   Duty to disclose unregistered interests

Where rules so provide—

(a) a person applying for registration under Chapter 1 of Part 2 must provide to the registrar such information as the rules may provide about any interest affecting the estate to which the application relates which—

(i) falls within any of the paragraphs of Schedule 1, and

(ii) is of a description specified by the rules;

(b) a person applying to register a registrable disposition of a registered estate must provide to the registrar such information as the rules may provide about any unregistered interest affecting the estate which—

(i) falls within any of the paragraphs of Schedule 3, and

(ii) is of description specified by the rules.

...

Miscellaneous

77   Duty to act reasonably

(1) A person must not exercise any of the following rights without reasonable cause—

(a) the right to lodge a caution under section 15,

(b) the right to apply for the entry of a notice or restriction, and

(c) the right to object to an application to the registrar.

(2) The duty under this section is owed to any person who suffers damage in consequence of its breach.

...

PART 12 MISCELLANEOUS AND GENERAL

Miscellaneous

...

116   Proprietary estoppel and mere equities

It is hereby declared for the avoidance of doubt that, in relation to registered land, each of the following—

(a) an equity by estoppel, and

(b) a mere equity,

has effect from the time the equity arises as an interest capable of binding successors in title (subject to the rules about the effect of dispositions on priority).

...

Sections 11 and 12   SCHEDULE 1

UNREGISTERED INTERESTS WHICH OVERRIDE
FIRST REGISTRATION

...

Interests of persons in actual occupation

2.—An interest belonging to a person in actual occupation, so far as relating to land of which he is in actual occupation, except for an interest under a settlement under the Settled Land Act 1925 (c. 18).

...

Sections 29 and 30   **SCHEDULE 3**

UNREGISTERED INTERESTS WHICH OVERRIDE REGISTERED DISPOSITIONS

...

Interests of persons in actual occupation

2.—An interest belonging at the time of the disposition to a person in actual occupation, so far as relating to land of which he is in actual occupation, except for—

(a) an interest under a settlement under the Settled Land Act 1925 (c. 18);

(b) an interest of a person of whom inquiry was made before the disposition and who failed to disclose the right when he could reasonably have been expected to do so;

(c) an interest—

(i) which belongs to a person whose occupation would not have been obvious on a reasonably careful inspection of the land at the time of the disposition, and

(ii) of which the person to whom the disposition is made does not have actual knowledge at that time;

(d) a leasehold estate in land granted to take effect in possession after the end of the period of three months beginning with the date of the grant and which has not taken effect in possession at the time of the disposition.

...

Adoption and Children Act 2002

(2002 c. 38)

PART 1 ADOPTION

Chapter 1 Introductory

1 Considerations applying to the exercise of powers

(1) Subsections (2) to (4) apply whenever a court or adoption agency is coming to a decision relating to the adoption of a child.

(2) The paramount consideration of the court or adoption agency must be the child's welfare, throughout his life.

(3) The court or adoption agency must at all times bear in mind that, in general, any delay in coming to the decision is likely to prejudice the child's welfare.

(4) The court or adoption agency must have regard to the following matters (among others)—

(a) the child's ascertainable wishes and feelings regarding the decision (considered in the light of the child's age and understanding),

(b) the child's particular needs,

(c) the likely effect on the child (throughout his life) of having ceased to be a member of the original family and become an adopted person,

(d) the child's age, sex, background and any of the child's characteristics which the court or agency considers relevant,

(e) any harm (within the meaning of the Children Act 1989 (c. 41)) which the child has suffered or is at risk of suffering,

(f) the relationship which the child has with relatives, and with any other person in relation to whom the court or agency considers the relationship to be relevant, including—

(i) the likelihood of any such relationship continuing and the value to the child of its doing so,

(ii) the ability and willingness of any of the child's relatives, or of any such person, to provide the child with a secure environment in which the child can develop, and otherwise to meet the child's needs,

(iii) the wishes and feelings of any of the child's relatives, or of any such person, regarding the child.

(5) In placing a child for adoption, an adoption agency in Wales must give due consideration to the child's religious persuasion, racial origin and cultural and linguistic background.

(6) In coming to a decision relating to the adoption of a child, a court or adoption agency must always consider the whole range of powers available to it in the child's case (whether under this Act or the Children Act 1989); and the court must not make any order under this Act unless it considers that making the order would be better for the child than not doing so.

(7) In this section, 'coming to a decision relating to the adoption of a child', in relation to a court, includes—

(a) coming to a decision in any proceedings where the orders that might be made by the court include an adoption order (or the revocation of such an order), a placement order (or the revocation of such an order) or an order under section 26 or 51A (or the revocation or variation of such an order),

(b) coming to a decision about granting leave in respect of any action (other than the initiation of proceedings in any court) which may be taken by an adoption agency or individual under this Act,

but does not include coming to a decision about granting leave in any other circumstances.

(8) For the purposes of this section—

(a) references to relationships are not confined to legal relationships,

(b) references to a relative, in relation to a child, include the child's mother and father.

(9) In this section 'adoption agency in Wales' means an adoption agency that is—

(a) a local authority in Wales, or

(b) a registered adoption society whose principal office is in Wales.

Chapter 2 The Adoption Service

The Adoption Service

2 **Basic definitions**

(1) The services maintained by local authorities under section 3(1) may be collectively referred to as 'the Adoption Service', and a local authority or registered adoption society may be referred to as an adoption agency.

(2) In this Act, 'registered adoption society' means a voluntary organisation which is an adoption society registered under Part 2 of the Care Standards Act 2000 (c. 14); but in relation to the provision of any facility of the Adoption Service, references to a registered adoption society or to an adoption agency do not include an adoption society which is not registered in respect of that facility.

(3) A registered adoption society is to be treated as registered in respect of any facility of the Adoption Service unless it is a condition of its registration that it does not provide that facility.

(4) No application for registration under Part 2 of the Care Standards Act 2000 may be made in respect of an adoption society which is an unincorporated body.

(5) In this Act—

'the 1989 Act' means the Children Act 1989 (c. 41),

'adoption society' means a body whose functions consist of or include making arrangements for the adoption of children,

'voluntary organisation' means a body other than a public or local authority the activities of which are not carried on for profit.

(6) In this Act, 'adoption support services' means—

(a) counselling, advice and information, and

(b) any other services prescribed by regulations,

in relation to adoption.

(7) The power to make regulations under subsection (6)(b) is to be exercised so as to secure that local authorities provide financial support.

(8) In this Chapter, references to adoption are to the adoption of persons, wherever they may be habitually resident, effected under the law of any country or territory, whether within or outside the British Islands.

3 Maintenance of adoption service

(1) Each local authority must continue to maintain within their area a service designed to meet the needs, in relation to adoption, of—

- (a) children who may be adopted, their parents and guardians,
- (b) persons wishing to adopt a child, and
- (c) adopted persons, their parents, natural parents and former guardians;

and for that purpose must provide the requisite facilities.

(2) Those facilities must include making, and participating in, arrangements—

- (a) for the adoption of children, and
- (b) for the provision of adoption support services.

(3) As part of the service, the arrangements made for the purposes of subsection (2) (b)—

- (a) must extend to the provision of adoption support services to persons who are within a description prescribed by regulations,
- (b) may extend to the provision of those services to other persons.

(4) A local authority may provide any of the requisite facilities by securing their provision by—

- (a) registered adoption societies, or
- (b) other persons who are within a description prescribed by regulations of persons who may provide the facilities in question.

(5) The facilities of the service must be provided in conjunction with the local authority's other social services and with registered adoption societies in their area, so that help may be given in a coordinated manner without duplication, omission or avoidable delay.

(6) The social services referred to in subsection (5) are the functions of a local authority which are social services functions within the meaning of the Local Authority Social Services Act 1970 (c. 42) (which include, in particular, those functions in so far as they relate to children).

3A Recruitment, assessment and approval of prospective adopters

(1) The Secretary of State may give directions requiring one or more named local authorities in England, or one or more descriptions of local authority in England, to make arrangements for all or any of their functions within subsection (3) to be carried out on their behalf by one or more other adoption agencies.

(2) The Secretary of State may by order require all local authorities in England to make arrangements for all or any of their functions within subsection (3) to be carried out on their behalf by one or more other adoption agencies.

(3) The functions are their functions in relation to—

- (a) the recruitment of persons as prospective adopters;
- (b) the assessment of prospective adopters' suitability to adopt a child;
- (c) the approval of prospective adopters as suitable to adopt a child.

4 Assessments etc. for adoption support services

(1) A local authority must at the request of—

- (a) any of the persons mentioned in paragraphs (a) to (c) of section 3(1), or
- (b) any other person who falls within a description prescribed by regulations (subject to subsection (7)(a)),

carry out an assessment of that person's needs for adoption support services.

(2) A local authority may, at the request of any person, carry out an assessment of that person's needs for adoption support services.

(3) A local authority may request the help of the persons mentioned in paragraph (a) or of section 3(4) in carrying out an assessment.

(4) Where, as a result of an assessment, a local authority decide that a person has needs for adoption support services, they must then decide whether to provide any such services to that person.

(5) If—

(a) a local authority decide to provide any adoption support services to a person, and

(b) the circumstances fall within a description prescribed by regulations,

the local authority must prepare a plan in accordance with which adoption support services are to be provided to the person and keep the plan under review.

(6) Regulations may make provision about assessments, preparing and reviewing plans, the provision of adoption support services in accordance with plans and reviewing the provision of adoption support services.

(7) The regulations may in particular make provision—

(a) as to the circumstances in which a person mentioned in paragraph (b) of subsection (1) is to have a right to request an assessment of his needs in accordance with that subsection,

(b) about the type of assessment which, or the way in which an assessment, is to be carried out,

(c) about the way in which a plan is to be prepared,

(d) about the way in which, and time at which, a plan or the provision of adoption support services is to be reviewed,

(e) about the considerations to which a local authority are to have regard in carrying out an assessment or review or preparing a plan,

(f) as to the circumstances in which a local authority may provide adoption support services subject to conditions,

(g) as to the consequences of conditions imposed by virtue of paragraph (f) not being met (including the recovery of any financial support provided by a local authority),

(h) as to the circumstances in which this section may apply to a local authority in respect of persons who are outside that local authority's area,

(i) as to the circumstances in which a local authority may recover from another local authority the expenses of providing adoption support services to any person.

(8) A local authority may carry out an assessment of the needs of any person under this section at the same time as an assessment of his needs is made under any other enactment.

(9) If at any time during the assessment of the needs of any person under this section, it appears to a local authority that—

(za) there may be a need for the provision to that person of services that may be provided pursuant to arrangements made by a clinical commissioning group under the National Health Service Act 2006 (including by virtue of section 7A of that Act),

(a) there may be a need for the provision of services to that person by (in Wales, a Health Authority or Local Health Board), or

(b) there may be a need for the provision to him of any services which fall within the education functions (as defined in section 579(1) of the Education Act 1996) of another local authority (as defined in section 579(1) of that Act),

the local authority must notify that clinical commissioning group, Health Authority, Local Health Board or other local authority.

(10) Where it appears to a local authority that another local authority could, by taking any specified action, help in the exercise of any of their functions under this section, they may request the help of that other local authority, specifying the action in question.

(11) A local authority whose help is so requested must comply with the request if it is consistent with the exercise of their functions.

4A   Adoption support services: personal budgets

(1) This section applies where—

(a) after carrying out an assessment under section 4, a local authority in England decide to provide any adoption support services to a person ('the recipient'), and

(b) the recipient is an adopted person or the parent of an adopted person.

(2) The local authority must prepare a personal budget for the recipient if asked to do so by the recipient or (in prescribed circumstances) a person of a prescribed description.

(3) The authority prepare a 'personal budget' for the recipient if they identify an amount as available to secure the adoption support services that they have decided to provide, with a view to the recipient being involved in securing those services.

(4) Regulations may make provision about personal budgets, in particular—

(a) about requests for personal budgets;

(b) about the amount of a personal budget;

(c) about the sources of the funds making up a personal budget;

(d) for payments ('direct payments') representing all or part of a personal budget to be made to the recipient, or (in prescribed circumstances) a person of a prescribed description, in order to secure any adoption support services to which the budget relates;

(e) about the description of adoption support services to which personal budgets and direct payments may (and may not) relate;

(f) for a personal budget or direct payment to cover the agreed cost of the adoption support services to which the budget or payment relates;

(g) about when, how, to whom and on what conditions direct payments may (and may not) be made;

(h) about when direct payments may be required to be repaid and the recovery of unpaid sums;

(i) about conditions with which a person or body making direct payments must comply before, after or at the time of making a direct payment;

(j) about arrangements for providing information, advice or support in connection with personal budgets and direct payments.

(5) If the regulations include provision authorising direct payments, they must—

(a) require the consent of the recipient, or (in prescribed circumstances) a person of a prescribed description, to be obtained before direct payments are made;

(b) require the authority to stop making direct payments where the required consent is withdrawn.

(6) Any adoption support services secured by means of direct payments made by a local authority are to be treated as adoption support services provided by the authority for all purposes, subject to any prescribed conditions or exceptions.

(7) On the occasion of the first exercise of the power to make regulations under this section—

(a) the statutory instrument containing the regulations is not to be made unless a draft of the instrument has been laid before, and approved by a resolution of, each House of Parliament, and

(b) accordingly section 140(2) does not apply to the instrument.

(8) In this section 'prescribed' means prescribed by regulations

4B   Adoption support services: duty to provide information

(1) Except in circumstances prescribed by regulations, a local authority in England must provide the information specified in subsection (2) to—

(a) any person who has contacted the authority to request information about adopting a child,

(b) any person who has informed the authority that he or she wishes to adopt a child,

(c) any person within the authority's area who the authority are aware is a parent of an adopted child, and

(d) any person within the authority's area who is a parent of an adopted child and has contacted the authority to request any of the information specified in subsection (2).

(2) The information is—

(a) information about the adoption support services available to people in the authority's area;

(b) information about the right to request an assessment under section 4 (assessments etc for adoption support services), and the authority's duties under that section and regulations made under it;

(c) information about the authority's duties under section 4A (adoption support services: personal budgets) and regulations made under it;

(d) any other information prescribed by regulations.

...

8   Adoption support agencies

(1) In this Act, 'adoption support agency' means an undertaking the purpose of which, or one of the purposes of which, is the provision of adoption support services; but an undertaking is not an adoption support agency—

(a) merely because it provides information in connection with adoption other than for the purpose mentioned in section 98(1), or

(b) if it is excepted by virtue of subsection (2).

'Undertaking' has the same meaning as in the Care Standards Act 2000 (c. 14).

(2) The following are excepted—

(a)   a registered adoption society, whether or not the society is registered in respect of the provision of adoption support services,

(b)   a local authority,...

(ca) the National Health Service Commissioning Board,

(d)   a Special Health Authority, clinical commissioning group (in Wales, a Health Authority or Local Health Board), NHS trust or NHS foundation trust,

(e)   the Registrar General,

(f)   any person, or description of persons, excepted by regulations.

...

(4) In this section 'local authority' includes any body that is a local authority as defined in section 579(1) of the Education Act 1996 (in addition to the bodies mentioned in the definition in section 144(1)).

Supplemental

13   Information concerning adoption

(1) Each adoption agency must give to the appropriate Minister any statistical or other general information he requires about—

(a) its performance of all or any of its functions relating to adoption,

(b) the children and other persons in relation to whom it has exercised those functions.

(2) The following persons—

(aa) the relevant officer of the family court, and

(c)   the relevant officer of the High Court,

must give to the appropriate Minister any statistical or other general information he requires about the proceedings under this Act of the court in question.

(3) In subsection (2), 'relevant officer', in relation to the family court or the High Court, means the officer of that court who is designated to act for the purposes of that subsection by a direction given by the Lord Chancellor.

(4) The information required to be given to the appropriate Minister under this section must be given at the times, and in the form, directed by him.

(5) The appropriate Minister may publish from time to time abstracts of the information given to him under this section.

...

15   Inspection of premises etc.

(1) The appropriate Minister may arrange for any premises in which—

(a) a child is living with a person with whom the child has been placed by an adoption agency, or

(b) a child in respect of whom a notice of intention to adopt has been given under section 44

is, or will be, living,

to be inspected from time to time.

(2) The appropriate Minister may require an adoption agency—

(a) to give him any information, or

(b) to allow him to inspect any records (in whatever form they are held),

relating to the discharge of any of its functions in relation to adoption which the appropriate Minister specifies.

(3) An inspection under this section must be conducted by a person authorised by the appropriate Minister.

(4) An officer of a local authority may only be so authorised with the consent of the authority.

(5) A person inspecting any premises under subsection (1) may—

(a) visit the child there,

(b) make any examination into the state of the premises and the treatment of the child there which he thinks fit.

(6) A person authorised to inspect any records under this section may at any reasonable time have access to, and inspect and check the operation of, any computer (and associated apparatus) which is being or has been used in connection with the records in question.

(7) A person authorised to inspect any premises or records under this section may—

(a) enter the premises for that purpose at any reasonable time,

(b) require any person to give him any reasonable assistance he may require.

(8) A person exercising a power under this section must, if required to do so, produce a duly authenticated document showing his authority.

(9) Any person who intentionally obstructs another in the exercise of a power under this section is guilty of an offence and liable on summary conviction to a fine not exceeding level 3 on the standard scale.

...

Chapter 3 Placement for adoption and adoption orders

Placement of children by adoption agency for adoption

18 Placement for adoption by agencies

(1) An adoption agency may—

(a) place a child for adoption with prospective adopters, or

(b) where it has placed a child with any persons (whether under this Part or not), leave the child with them as prospective adopters,

but, except in the case of a child who is less than six weeks old, may only do so under section 19 or a placement order.

(2) An adoption agency may only place a child for adoption with prospective adopters if the agency is satisfied that the child ought to be placed for adoption.

(3) A child who is placed or authorised to be placed for adoption with prospective adopters by a local authority is looked after by the authority.

(4) If an application for an adoption order has been made by any persons in respect of a child and has not been disposed of—

(a) an adoption agency which placed the child with those persons may leave the child with them until the application is disposed of, but

(b) apart from that, the child may not be placed for adoption with any prospective adopters.

'Adoption order' includes a Scottish or Northern Irish adoption order.

(5) References in this Act (apart from this section) to an adoption agency placing a child for adoption—

(a) are to its placing a child for adoption with prospective adopters, and

(b) include, where it has placed a child with any persons (whether under this Act or not), leaving the child with them as prospective adopters;

and references in this Act (apart from this section) to a child who is placed for adoption by an adoption agency are to be interpreted accordingly.

(6) References in this Chapter to an adoption agency being, or not being, authorised to place a child for adoption are to the agency being or (as the case may be) not being authorised to do so under section 19 or a placement order.

(7) This section is subject to sections 30 to 35 (removal of children placed by adoption agencies).

19 Placing children with parental consent

(1) Where an adoption agency is satisfied that each parent or guardian of a child has consented to the child—

(a) being placed for adoption with prospective adopters identified in the consent, or

(b) being placed for adoption with any prospective adopters who may be chosen by the agency,

and has not withdrawn the consent, the agency is authorised to place the child for adoption accordingly.

(2) Consent to a child being placed for adoption with prospective adopters identified in the consent may be combined with consent to the child subsequently being placed for adoption with any prospective adopters who may be chosen by the agency in circumstances where the child is removed from or returned by the identified prospective adopters.

(3) Subsection (1) does not apply where—

(a) an application has been made on which a care order might be made and the application has not been disposed of, or

(b) a care order or placement order has been made after the consent was given.

(4) References in this Act to a child placed for adoption under this section include a child who was placed under this section with prospective adopters and continues to be placed with them, whether or not consent to the placement has been withdrawn.

(5) This section is subject to section 52 (parental etc. consent).

20 Advance consent to adoption

(1) A parent or guardian of a child who consents to the child being placed for adoption by an adoption agency under section 19 may, at the same or any subsequent time, consent to the making of a future adoption order.

(2) Consent under this section—

(a) where the parent or guardian has consented to the child being placed for adoption with prospective adopters identified in the consent, may be consent to adoption by them, or

(b) may be consent to adoption by any prospective adopters who may be chosen by the agency.

(3) A person may withdraw any consent given under this section.

(4) A person who gives consent under this section may, at the same or any subsequent time, by notice given to the adoption agency—

(a) state that he does not wish to be informed of any application for an adoption order, or

(b) withdraw such a statement.

(5) A notice under subsection (4) has effect from the time when it is received by the adoption agency but has no effect if the person concerned has withdrawn his consent.

(6) This section is subject to section 52 (parental etc. consent).

21 Placement orders

(1) A placement order is an order made by the court authorising a local authority to place a child for adoption with any prospective adopters who may be chosen by the authority.

(2) The court may not make a placement order in respect of a child unless—

(a) the child is subject to a care order,

(b) the court is satisfied that the conditions in section 31(2) of the 1989 Act (conditions for making a care order) are met, or

(c) the child has no parent or guardian.

(3) The court may only make a placement order if, in the case of each parent or guardian of the child, the court is satisfied—

(a) that the parent or guardian has consented to the child being placed for adoption with any prospective adopters who may be chosen by the local authority and has not withdrawn the consent, or

(b) that the parent's or guardian's consent should be dispensed with.

This subsection is subject to section 52 (parental etc. consent).

(4) A placement order continues in force until—

(a) it is revoked under section 24,

(b) an adoption order is made in respect of the child, or

(c) the child marries, forms a civil partnership or attains the age of 18 years.

'Adoption order' includes a Scottish or Northern Irish adoption order.

22 Applications for placement orders

(1) A local authority must apply to the court for a placement order in respect of a child if—

(a) the child is placed for adoption by them or is being provided with accommodation by them,

(b) no adoption agency is authorised to place the child for adoption,

(c) the child has no parent or guardian or the authority consider that the conditions in section 31(2) of the 1989 Act are met, and

(d) the authority are satisfied that the child ought to be placed for adoption.

(2) If—

(a) an application has been made (and has not been disposed of) on which a care order might be made in respect of a child, or

(b) a child is subject to a care order and the appropriate local authority are not authorised to place the child for adoption,

the appropriate local authority must apply to the court for a placement order if they are satisfied that the child ought to be placed for adoption.

(3) If—

(a) a child is subject to a care order, and

(b) the appropriate local authority are authorised to place the child for adoption under section 19,

the authority may apply to the court for a placement order.

(4) If a local authority—

(a) are under a duty to apply to the court for a placement order in respect of a child, or

(b) have applied for a placement order in respect of a child and the application has not been disposed of,

the child is looked after by the authority.

(5) Subsections (1) to (3) do not apply in respect of a child—

(a) if any persons have given notice of intention to adopt, unless the period of four months beginning with the giving of the notice has expired without them applying for an adoption order or their application for such an order has been withdrawn or refused, or

(b) if an application for an adoption order has been made and has not been disposed of.

'Adoption order' includes a Scottish or Northern Irish adoption order.

(6) Where—

(a) an application for a placement order in respect of a child has been made and has not been disposed of, and

(b) no interim care order is in force,

the court may give any directions it considers appropriate for the medical or psychiatric examination or other assessment of the child; but a child who is of sufficient understanding to make an informed decision may refuse to submit to the examination or other assessment.

(7) The appropriate local authority—

   (a) in relation to a care order, is the local authority in whose care the child is placed by the order, and

   (b) in relation to an application on which a care order might be made, is the local authority which makes the application.

23   Varying placement orders

(1) The court may vary a placement order so as to substitute another local authority for the local authority authorised by the order to place the child for adoption.

(2) The variation may only be made on the joint application of both authorities.

24   Revoking placement orders

(1) The court may revoke a placement order on the application of any person.

(2) But an application may not be made by a person other than the child or the local authority authorised by the order to place the child for adoption unless—

   (a) the court has given leave to apply, and

   (b) the child is not placed for adoption by the authority.

(3) The court cannot give leave under subsection (2)(a) unless satisfied that there has been a change in circumstances since the order was made.

(4) If the court determines, on an application for an adoption order, not to make the order, it may revoke any placement order in respect of the child.

(5) Where—

   (a) an application for the revocation of a placement order has been made and has not been disposed of, and

   (b) the child is not placed for adoption by the authority,

the child may not without the court's leave be placed for adoption under the order.

25   Parental responsibility

(1) This section applies while—

   (a) a child is placed for adoption under section 19 or an adoption agency is authorised to place a child for adoption under that section, or

   (b) a placement order is in force in respect of a child.

(2) Parental responsibility for the child is given to the agency concerned.

(3) While the child is placed with prospective adopters, parental responsibility is given to them.

(4) The agency may determine that the parental responsibility of any parent or guardian, or of prospective adopters, is to be restricted to the extent specified in the determination.

26   Contact

(1) On an adoption agency being authorised to place a child for adoption, or placing a child for adoption who is less than six weeks old—

   (a) any contact provision in a child arrangements order under section 8 of the 1989 Act ceases to have effect,

   (b) any order under section 34 of that Act (parental etc contact with children in care) ceases to have effect, and

   (c) any activity direction made in proceedings for the making, variation or discharge of a child arrangements order with respect to the child, or made in other proceedings that relate to such an order, is discharged.

(2) While an adoption agency is so authorised or a child is placed for adoption—

   (a) no application may be made for—

      (i)   a child arrangements order under section 8 of the 1989 Act containing contact provision, or

      (ii) an order under section 34 of that Act, but

(b) the court may make an order under this section requiring the person with whom the child lives, or is to live, to allow the child to visit or stay with the person named in the order, or for the person named in the order and the child otherwise to have contact with each other.

(3) An application for an order under this section may be made by—

(a) the child or the agency,

(b) any parent, guardian or relative,

(c) any person in whose favour there was provision which ceased to have effect by virtue of subsection (1)(a) or an order which ceased to have effect by virtue of subsection (1)(b),

(d) if a child arrangements order was in force immediately before the adoption agency was authorised to place the child for adoption or (as the case may be) placed the child for adoption at a time when he was less than six weeks old, any person named in the order as a person with whom the child was to live,

(e) if a person had care of the child immediately before that time by virtue of an order made in the exercise of the High Court's inherent jurisdiction with respect to children, that person,

(f) any person who has obtained the court's leave to make the application.

(4) When making a placement order, the court may on its own initiative make an order under this section.

...

(5A) In this section 'contact provision' means provision which regulates arrangements relating to—

(a) with whom a child is to spend time or otherwise have contact, or

(b) when a child is to spend time or otherwise have contact with any person;

but in paragraphs (a) and (b) a reference to spending time or otherwise having contact with a person is to doing that otherwise than as a result of living with the person.

(6) In this section 'activity direction' has the meaning given by section 11A of the 1989 Act.

27 Contact: supplementary

(1) An order under section 26—

(a) has effect while the adoption agency is authorised to place the child for adoption or the child is placed for adoption, but

(b) may be varied or revoked by the court on an application by the child, the agency or a person named in the order.

(2) The agency may refuse to allow the contact that would otherwise be required by virtue of an order under that section if—

(a) it is satisfied that it is necessary to do so in order to safeguard or promote the child's welfare, and

(b) the refusal is decided upon as a matter of urgency and does not last for more than seven days.

(3) Regulations may make provision as to—

(a) the steps to be taken by an agency which has exercised its power under subsection (2),

(b) the circumstances in which, and conditions subject to which, the terms of any order under section 26 may be departed from by agreement between the agency and any person for whose contact with the child the order provides,

(c) notification by an agency of any variation or suspension of arrangements made (otherwise than under an order under that section) with a view to allowing any person contact with the child.

(4) Before making a placement order the court must—

(a) consider the arrangements which the adoption agency has made, or proposes to make, for allowing any person contact with the child, and

(b) invite the parties to the proceedings to comment on those arrangements.

(5) An order under section 26 may provide for contact on any conditions the court considers appropriate.

28   Further consequences of placement

(1) Where a child is placed for adoption under section 19 or an adoption agency is authorised to place a child for adoption under that section—

(a) a parent or guardian of the child may not apply for a child arrangements order regulating the child's living arrangements unless an application for an adoption order has been made and the parent or guardian has obtained the court's leave under subsection (3) or (5) of section 47,

(b) if an application has been made for an adoption order, a guardian of the child may not apply for a special guardianship order unless he has obtained the court's leave under subsection (3) or (5) of that section.

(2) Where—

(a) a child is placed for adoption under section 19 or an adoption agency is authorised to place a child for adoption under that section, or

(b) a placement order is in force in respect of a child,then (whether or not the child is in England and Wales) a person may not do either of the following things, unless the court gives leave or each parent or guardian of the child gives written consent.

(3) Those things are—

(a) causing the child to be known by a new surname, or

(b) removing the child from the United Kingdom.

(4) Subsection (3) does not prevent the removal of a child from the United Kingdom for a period of less than one month by a person who provides the child's home.

(5) For the purposes of subsection (1)(a), a child arrangements order regulates a child's living arrangements if the arrangements regulated by the order consist of, or include, arrangements which relate to either or both of the following—

(a) with whom the child is to live, and

(b) when the child is to live with any person.

29   Further consequences of placement orders

(1) Where a placement order is made in respect of a child and either—

(a) the child is subject to a care order, or

(b) the court at the same time makes a care order in respect of the child,

the care order does not have effect at any time when the placement order is in force.

(2) On the making of a placement order in respect of a child, any order mentioned in section 8(1) of the 1989 Act, and any supervision order in respect of the child, ceases to have effect.

(3) Where a placement order is in force—

(a) no prohibited steps order or specific issue order, and

(b) no supervision order or child assessment order,

may be made in respect of the child.

(4) Where a placement order is in force, a child arrangements order may be made with respect to the child's living arrangements only if—

(a) an application for an adoption order has been made in respect of the child, and

(b) the child arrangements order is applied for by a parent or guardian who has obtained the court's leave under subsection (3) or (5) of section 47 or by any other person who has obtained the court's leave under this subsection.

(4A) For the purposes of subsection (4), a child arrangements order is one made with respect to a child's living arrangements if the arrangements regulated by the order consist of, or include, arrangements which relate to either or both of the following—

(a) with whom the child is to live, and

(b) when the child is to live with any person.

(5) Where a placement order is in force, no special guardianship order may be made in respect of the child unless—

(a) an application has been made for an adoption order, and

(b) the person applying for the special guardianship order has obtained the court's leave under this subsection or, if he is a guardian of the child, has obtained the court's leave under section 47(5).

(6) Section 14A(7) of the 1989 Act applies in respect of an application for a special guardianship order for which leave has been given as mentioned in subsection (5)(b) with the omission of the words 'the beginning of the period of three months ending with'.

(7) Where a placement order is in force—

(a) section 14C(1)(b) of the 1989 Act (special guardianship: parental responsibility) has effect subject to any determination under section 25(4) of this Act,

(b) section 14C(3) and (4) of the 1989 Act (special guardianship: removal of child from UK etc.) does not apply.

Removal of children who are or may be placed by adoption agencies

30 General prohibitions on removal

(1) Where—

(a) a child is placed for adoption by an adoption agency under section 19, or

(b) a child is placed for adoption by an adoption agency and either the child is less than six weeks old or the agency has at no time been authorised to place the child for adoption,

a person (other than the agency) must not remove the child from the prospective adopters.

(2) Where—

(a) a child who is not for the time being placed for adoption is being provided with accommodation by a local authority, and

(b) the authority have applied to the court for a placement order and the application has not been disposed of,

only a person who has the court's leave (or the authority) may remove the child from the accommodation.

(3) Where subsection (2) does not apply, but—

(a) a child who is not for the time being placed for adoption is being provided with accommodation by an adoption agency, and

(b) the agency is authorised to place the child for adoption under section 19 or would be so authorised if any consent to placement under that section had not been withdrawn,

a person (other than the agency) must not remove the child from the accommodation.

(4) This section is subject to sections 31 to 33 but those sections do not apply if the child is subject to a care order.

(5) This group of sections (that is, this section and those sections) apply whether or not the child in question is in England and Wales.

(6) This group of sections does not affect the exercise by any local authority or other person of any power conferred by any enactment, other than section 20(8) of the 1989 Act (removal of children from local authority accommodation).

(7) This group of sections does not prevent the removal of a child who is arrested.

(8) A person who removes a child in contravention of this section is guilty of an offence and liable on summary conviction to imprisonment for a term not exceeding three months, or a fine not exceeding level 5 on the standard scale, or both.

31 Recovery by parent etc. where child not placed or is a baby

(1) Subsection (2) applies where—

(a) a child who is not for the time being placed for adoption is being provided with accommodation by an adoption agency, and

(b) the agency would be authorised to place the child for adoption under section 19 if consent to placement under that section had not been withdrawn.

(2) If any parent or guardian of the child informs the agency that he wishes the child to be returned to him, the agency must return the child to him within the period of seven days beginning

with the request unless an application is, or has been, made for a placement order and the application has not been disposed of.

(3) Subsection (4) applies where—

    (a) a child is placed for adoption by an adoption agency and either the child is less than six weeks old or the agency has at no time been authorised to place the child for adoption, and

    (b) any parent or guardian of the child informs the agency that he wishes the child to be returned to him,

unless an application is, or has been, made for a placement order and the application has not been disposed of.

(4) The agency must give notice of the parent's or guardian's wish to the prospective adopters who must return the child to the agency within the period of seven days beginning with the day on which the notice is given.

(5) A prospective adopter who fails to comply with subsection (4) is guilty of an offence and liable on summary conviction to imprisonment for a term not exceeding three months, or a fine not exceeding level 5 on the standard scale, or both.

(6) As soon as a child is returned to an adoption agency under subsection (4), the agency must return the child to the parent or guardian in question.

32   Recovery by parent etc. where child placed and consent withdrawn

(1) This section applies where—

    (a) a child is placed for adoption by an adoption agency under section 19, and

    (b) consent to placement under that section has been withdrawn,

unless an application is, or has been, made for a placement order and the application has not been disposed of.

(2) If a parent or guardian of the child informs the agency that he wishes the child to be returned to him—

    (a) the agency must give notice of the parent's or guardian's wish to the prospective adopters, and

    (b) the prospective adopters must return the child to the agency within the period of 14 days beginning with the day on which the notice is given.

(3) A prospective adopter who fails to comply with subsection (2)(b) is guilty of an offence and liable on summary conviction to imprisonment for a term not exceeding three months, or a fine not exceeding level 5 on the standard scale, or both.

(4) As soon as a child is returned to an adoption agency under this section, the agency must return the child to the parent or guardian in question.

(5) Where a notice under subsection (2) is given, but—

    (a) before the notice was given, an application—

        (i)   for an adoption order (including a Scottish or Northern Irish adoption order),

        (ii)   for a special guardianship order,

        (iii)   for a child arrangements order to which subsection (6) applies, or

        (iv)   for permission to apply for an order within sub-paragraph (ii) or (iii),

        was made in respect of the child, and

    (b) the application (and, in a case where permission is given on an application to apply for an order within paragraph (a)(ii) or (iii), the application for the order) has not been disposed of,

the prospective adopters are not required by virtue of the notice to return the child to the agency unless the court so orders.

(6) A child arrangements order is one to which this subsection applies if it is an order regulating arrangements that consist of, or include, arrangements which relate to either or both of the following—

    (a) with whom a child is to live, and

    (b) when the child is to live with any person.

33   Recovery by parent etc. where child placed and placement order refused

(1) This section applies where—

    (a) a child is placed for adoption by a local authority under section 19,

    (b) the authority have applied for a placement order and the application has been refused, and

    (c) any parent or guardian of the child informs the authority that he wishes the child to be returned to him.

(2) The prospective adopters must return the child to the authority on a date determined by the court.

(3) A prospective adopter who fails to comply with subsection (2) is guilty of an offence and liable on summary conviction to imprisonment for a term not exceeding three months, or a fine not exceeding level 5 on the standard scale, or both.

(4) As soon as a child is returned to the authority, they must return the child to the parent or guardian in question.

34   Placement orders: prohibition on removal

(1) Where a placement order in respect of a child—

    (a) is in force, or

    (b) has been revoked, but the child has not been returned by the prospective adopters or remains in any accommodation provided by the local authority,

a person (other than the local authority) may not remove the child from the prospective adopters or from accommodation provided by the authority.

(2) A person who removes a child in contravention of subsection (1) is guilty of an offence.

(3) Where a court revoking a placement order in respect of a child determines that the child is not to remain with any former prospective adopters with whom the child is placed, they must return the child to the local authority within the period determined by the court for the purpose; and a person who fails to do so is guilty of an offence.

(4) Where a court revoking a placement order in respect of a child determines that the child is to be returned to a parent or guardian, the local authority must return the child to the parent or guardian as soon as the child is returned to the authority or, where the child is in accommodation provided by the authority, at once.

(5) A person guilty of an offence under this section is liable on summary conviction to imprisonment for a term not exceeding three months, or a fine not exceeding level 5 on the standard scale, or both.

(6) This section does not affect the exercise by any local authority or other person of a power conferred by any enactment, other than section 20(8) of the 1989 Act.

(7) This section does not prevent the removal of a child who is arrested.

(8) This section applies whether or not the child in question is in England and Wales.

35   Return of child in other cases

(1) Where a child is placed for adoption by an adoption agency and the prospective adopters give notice to the agency of their wish to return the child, the agency must—

    (a) receive the child from the prospective adopters before the end of the period of seven days beginning with the giving of the notice, and

    (b) give notice to any parent or guardian of the child of the prospective adopters' wish to return the child.

(2) Where a child is placed for adoption by an adoption agency, and the agency—

    (a) is of the opinion that the child should not remain with the prospective adopters, and

    (b) gives notice to them of its opinion,

the prospective adopters must, not later than the end of the period of seven days beginning with the giving of the notice, return the child to the agency.

(3) If the agency gives notice under subsection (2)(b), it must give notice to any parent or guardian of the child of the obligation to return the child to the agency.

(4) A prospective adopter who fails to comply with subsection (2) is guilty of an offence and liable on summary conviction to imprisonment for a term not exceeding three months, or a fine not exceeding level 5 on the standard scale, or both.

(5) Where—
- (a) an adoption agency gives notice under subsection (2) in respect of a child,
- (b) before the notice was given, an application—
    - (i)   for an adoption order (including a Scottish or Northern Irish adoption order),
    - (ii)   for a special guardianship order,
    - (iii) for a child arrangements order to which subsection (5A) applies, or
    - (iv) for permission to apply for an order within sub-paragraph (ii) or (iii),
      was made in respect of the child, and
- (c) the application (and, in a case where permission is given on an application to apply for an order within paragraph (b)(ii) or (iii), the application for the order) has not been disposed of,

prospective adopters are not required by virtue of the notice to return the child to the agency unless the court so orders.

(5A) A child arrangements order is one to which this subsection applies if it is an order regulating arrangements that consist of, or include, arrangements which relate to either or both of the following—
- (a) with whom a child is to live, and
- (b) when a child is to live with any person.

(6) This section applies whether or not the child in question is in England and Wales.

Removal of children in non-agency cases

36   Restrictions on removal

(1) At any time when a child's home is with any persons ('the people concerned') with whom the child is not placed by an adoption agency, but the people concerned—
- (a) have applied for an adoption order in respect of the child and the application has not been disposed of,
- (b) have given notice of intention to adopt, or
- (c) have applied for leave to apply for an adoption order under section 42(6) and the application has not been disposed of,

a person may remove the child only in accordance with the provisions of this group of sections (that is, this section and sections 37 to 40).

The reference to a child placed by an adoption agency includes a child placed by a Scottish or Northern Irish adoption agency.

(2) For the purposes of this group of sections, a notice of intention to adopt is to be disregarded if—
- (a) the period of four months beginning with the giving of the notice has expired without the people concerned applying for an adoption order, or
- (b) the notice is a second or subsequent notice of intention to adopt and was given during the period of five months beginning with the giving of the preceding notice.

(3) For the purposes of this group of sections, if the people concerned apply for leave to apply for an adoption order under section 42(6) and the leave is granted, the application for leave is not to be treated as disposed of until the period of three days beginning with the granting of the leave has expired.

(4) This section does not prevent the removal of a child who is arrested.

(5) Where a parent or guardian may remove a child from the people concerned in accordance with the provisions of this group of sections, the people concerned must at the request of the parent or guardian return the child to the parent or guardian at once.

(6) A person who—
- (a) fails to comply with subsection (5), or
- (b) removes a child in contravention of this section,

is guilty of an offence and liable on summary conviction to imprisonment for a term not exceeding three months, or a fine not exceeding level 5 on the standard scale, or both.

(7) This group of sections applies whether or not the child in question is in England and Wales.

37   Applicants for adoption

If section 36(1)(a) applies, the following persons may remove the child—

(a) a person who has the court's leave,

(b) a local authority or other person in the exercise of a power conferred by any enactment, other than section 20(8) of the 1989 Act.

38   Local authority foster parents

(1) This section applies if the child's home is with local authority foster parents.

(2) If—

(a) the child has had his home with the foster parents at all times during the period of five years ending with the removal and the foster parents have given notice of intention to adopt, or

(b) an application has been made for leave under section 42(6) and has not been disposed of, the following persons may remove the child.

(3) They are—

(a) a person who has the court's leave,

(b) a local authority or other person in the exercise of a power conferred by any enactment, other than section 20(8) of the 1989 Act.

(4) If subsection (2) does not apply but—

(a) the child has had his home with the foster parents at all times during the period of one year ending with the removal, and

(b) the foster parents have given notice of intention to adopt, the following persons may remove the child.

(5) They are—

(a) a person with parental responsibility for the child who is exercising the power in section 20(8) of the 1989 Act,

(b) a person who has the court's leave,

(c) a local authority or other person in the exercise of a power conferred by any enactment, other than section 20(8) of the 1989 Act.

39   Partners of parents

(1) This section applies if a child's home is with a partner of a parent and the partner has given notice of intention to adopt.

(2) If the child's home has been with the partner for not less than three years (whether continuous or not) during the period of five years ending with the removal, the following persons may remove the child—

(a) a person who has the court's leave,

(b) a local authority or other person in the exercise of a power conferred by any enactment, other than section 20(8) of the 1989 Act.

(3) If subsection (2) does not apply, the following persons may remove the child—

(a) a parent or guardian,

(b) a person who has the court's leave,

(c) a local authority or other person in the exercise of a power conferred by any enactment, other than section 20(8) of the 1989 Act.

40   Other non-agency cases

(1) In any case where sections 37 to 39 do not apply but—

(a) the people concerned have given notice of intention to adopt, or

(b) the people concerned have applied for leave under section 42(6) and the application has not been disposed of, the following persons may remove the child.

(2) They are—
    (a) a person who has the court's leave,
    (b) a local authority or other person in the exercise of a power conferred by any enactment, other than section 20(8) of the 1989 Act.

Breach of restrictions on removal

41   Recovery orders

(1) This section applies where it appears to the court—
    (a) that a child has been removed in contravention of any of the preceding provisions of this Chapter or that there are reasonable grounds for believing that a person intends to remove a child in contravention of those provisions, or
    (b) that a person has failed to comply with section 31(4), 32(2), 33(2), 34(3) or 35(2).

(2) The court may, on the application of any person, by an order—
    (a) direct any person who is in a position to do so to produce the child on request to any person mentioned in subsection (4),
    (b) authorise the removal of the child by any person mentioned in that subsection,
    (c) require any person who has information as to the child's whereabouts to disclose that information on request to any constable or officer of the court,
    (d) authorise a constable to enter any premises specified in the order and search for the child, using reasonable force if necessary.

(3) Premises may only be specified under subsection (2)(d) if it appears to the court that there are reasonable grounds for believing the child to be on them.

(4) The persons referred to in subsection (2) are—
    (a) any person named by the court,
    (b) any constable,
    (c) any person who, after the order is made under that subsection, is authorised to exercise any power under the order by an adoption agency which is authorised to place the child for adoption.

(5) A person who intentionally obstructs a person exercising a power of removal conferred by the order is guilty of an offence and liable on summary conviction to a fine not exceeding level 3 on the standard scale.

(6) A person must comply with a request to disclose information as required by the order even if the information sought might constitute evidence that he had committed an offence.

(7) But in criminal proceedings in which the person is charged with an offence (other than one mentioned in subsection (8))—
    (a) no evidence relating to the information provided may be adduced, and
    (b) no question relating to the information may be asked,
by or on behalf of the prosecution, unless evidence relating to it is adduced, or a question relating to it is asked, in the proceedings by or on behalf of the person.

(8) The offences excluded from subsection (7) are—
    (a) an offence under section 2 or 5 of the Perjury Act 1911 (c. 6) (false statements made on oath otherwise than in judicial proceedings or made otherwise than on oath),

...

Preliminaries to adoption

42   Child to live with adopters before application

(1) An application for an adoption order may not be made unless—
    (a) if subsection (2) applies, the condition in that subsection is met,
    (b) if that subsection does not apply, the condition in whichever is applicable of subsections (3) to (5) applies.

(2) If—

    (a) the child was placed for adoption with the applicant or applicants by an adoption agency or in pursuance of an order of the High Court, or

    (b) the applicant is a parent of the child,

        the condition is that the child must have had his home with the applicant or, in the case of an application by a couple, with one or both of them at all times during the period of ten weeks preceding the application.

(3) If the applicant or one of the applicants is the partner of a parent of the child, the condition is that the child must have had his home with the applicant or, as the case may be, applicants at all times during the period of six months preceding the application.

(4) If the applicants are local authority foster parents, the condition is that the child must have had his home with the applicants at all times during the period of one year preceding the application.

(5) In any other case, the condition is that the child must have had his home with the applicant or, in the case of an application by a couple, with one or both of them for not less than three years (whether continuous or not) during the period of five years preceding the application.

(6) But subsections (4) and (5) do not prevent an application being made if the court gives leave to make it.

(7) An adoption order may not be made unless the court is satisfied that sufficient opportunities to see the child with the applicant or, in the case of an application by a couple, both of them together in the home environment have been given—

    (a) where the child was placed for adoption with the applicant or applicants by an adoption agency, to that agency,

    (b) in any other case, to the local authority within whose area the home is.

. . .

43   Reports where child placed by agency

Where an application for an adoption order relates to a child placed for adoption by an adoption agency, the agency must—

    (a) submit to the court a report on the suitability of the applicants and on any other matters relevant to the operation of section 1, and

    (b) assist the court in any manner the court directs.

44   Notice of intention to adopt

(1) This section applies where persons (referred to in this section as 'proposed adopters') wish to adopt a child who is not placed for adoption with them by an adoption agency.

(2) An adoption order may not be made in respect of the child unless the proposed adopters have given notice to the appropriate local authority of their intention to apply for the adoption order (referred to in this Act as a 'notice of intention to adopt').

(3) The notice must be given not more than two years, or less than three months, before the date on which the application for the adoption order is made.

(4) Where—

    (a) if a person were seeking to apply for an adoption order, subsection (4) or (5) of section 42 would apply, but

    (b) the condition in the subsection in question is not met,

the person may not give notice of intention to adopt unless he has the court's leave to apply for an adoption order.

(5) On receipt of a notice of intention to adopt, the local authority must arrange for the investigation of the matter and submit to the court a report of the investigation.

(6) In particular, the investigation must, so far as practicable, include the suitability of the proposed adopters and any other matters relevant to the operation of section 1 in relation to the application.

(7) If a local authority receive a notice of intention to adopt in respect of a child whom they know was (immediately before the notice was given) looked after by another local authority, they must, not more than seven days after the receipt of the notice, inform the other local authority in writing that they have received the notice.

(8) Where—

    (a) a local authority have placed a child with any persons otherwise than as prospective adopters, and

    (b) the persons give notice of intention to adopt,

the authority are not to be treated as leaving the child with them as prospective adopters for the purposes of section 18(1)(b).

(9) In this section, references to the appropriate local authority, in relation to any proposed adopters, are—

    (a) in prescribed cases, references to the prescribed local authority,

    (b) in any other case, references to the local authority for the area in which, at the time of giving the notice of intention to adopt, they have their home,

and 'prescribed' means prescribed by regulations.

45 Suitability of adopters

(1) Regulations under section 9 may make provision as to the matters to be taken into account by an adoption agency in determining, or making any report in respect of, the suitability of any persons to adopt a child.

(2) In particular, the regulations may make provision for the purpose of securing that, in determining the suitability of a couple to adopt a child, proper regard is had to the need for stability and permanence in their relationship.

46 Adoption orders

(1) An adoption order is an order made by the court on an application under section 50 or 51 giving parental responsibility for a child to the adopters or adopter.

(2) The making of an adoption order operates to extinguish—

    (a) the parental responsibility which any person other than the adopters or adopter has for the adopted child immediately before the making of the order,

    (b) any order under the 1989 Act or the Children (Northern Ireland) Order 1995 (S.I. 1995/755 (N.I. 2)),

    (c) any order under the Children (Scotland) Act 1995 (c. 36) other than an excepted order, and

    ...

    (d) any duty arising by virtue of an agreement or an order of a court to make payments, so far as the payments are in respect of the adopted child's maintenance or upbringing for any period after the making of the adoption order.

'Excepted order' means an order under section 9, 11(1)(d) or 13 of the Children (Scotland) Act 1995 or an exclusion order within the meaning of section 76(1) of that Act.

(3) An adoption order—

    (a) does not affect parental responsibility so far as it relates to any period before the making of the order, and

    (b) in the case of an order made on an application under section 51(2) by the partner of a parent of the adopted child, does not affect the parental responsibility of that parent or any duties of that parent within subsection (2)(d).

(4) Subsection (2)(d) does not apply to a duty arising by virtue of an agreement—

    (a) which constitutes a trust, or

    (b) which expressly provides that the duty is not to be extinguished by the making of an adoption order.

(5) An adoption order may be made even if the child to be adopted is already an adopted child.

(6) Before making an adoption order, the court must consider whether there should be arrangements for allowing any person contact with the child; and for that purpose the court must consider any existing or proposed arrangements and obtain any views of the parties to the proceedings.

47 Conditions for making adoption orders

(1) An adoption order may not be made if the child has a parent or guardian unless one of the following three conditions is met; but this section is subject to section 52 (parental etc. consent).

(2) The first condition is that, in the case of each parent or guardian of the child, the court is satisfied—

  (a) that the parent or guardian consents to the making of the adoption order,

  (b) that the parent or guardian has consented under section 20 (and has not withdrawn the consent) and does not oppose the making of the adoption order, or

  (c) that the parent's or guardian's consent should be dispensed with.

(3) A parent or guardian may not oppose the making of an adoption order under subsection (2)(b) without the court's leave.

(4) The second condition is that—

  (a) the child has been placed for adoption by an adoption agency with the prospective adopters in whose favour the order is proposed to be made,

  (b) either—

    (i)   the child was placed for adoption with the consent of each parent or guardian and the consent of the mother was given when the child was at least six weeks old, or

    (ii) the child was placed for adoption under a placement order, and

  (c) no parent or guardian oppose the making of the adoption order.

(5) A parent or guardian may not oppose the making of an adoption order under the second condition without the court's leave.

(6) The third condition is that the child

  (a) is the subject of a Scottish permanence order which includes provision granting authority for the child to be adopted, or

  (b) is free for adoption by virtue of an order made under Article 17(1) or 18(1) of the Adoption (Northern Ireland) Order 1987 (S.I. 1987/2203 (N.I. 22)).

(7) The court cannot give leave under subsection (3) or (5) unless satisfied that there has been a change in circumstances since the consent of the parent or guardian was given or, as the case may be, the placement order was made.

(8) An adoption order may not be made in relation to a person who is or has been married.

(8A) An adoption order may not be made in relation to a person who is or has been a civil partner.

(9) An adoption order may not be made in relation to a person who has attained the age of 19 years.

...

48 Restrictions on making adoption orders

(1) The court may not hear an application for an adoption order in relation to a child, where a previous application to which subsection (2) applies made in relation to the child by the same persons was refused by any court, unless it appears to the court that, because of a change in circumstances or for any other reason, it is proper to hear the application.

(2) This subsection applies to any application—

  (a) for an adoption order or a Scottish or Northern Irish adoption order, or

  (b) for an order for adoption made in the Isle of Man or any of the Channel Islands.

49 Applications for adoption

(1) An application for an adoption order may be made by—

  (a) a couple, or

  (b) one person,

but only if it is made under section 50 or 51 and one of the following conditions is met.

(2) The first condition is that at least one of the couple (in the case of an application under section 50) or the applicant (in the case of an application under section 51) is domiciled in a part of the British Islands.

(3) The second condition is that both of the couple (in the case of an application under section 50) or the applicant (in the case of an application under section 51) have been habitually resident in a part of the British Islands for a period of not less than one year ending with the date of the application.

(4) An application for an adoption order may only be made if the person to be adopted has not attained the age of 18 years on the date of the application.

(5) References in this Act to a child, in connection with any proceedings (whether or not concluded) for adoption, (such as 'child to be adopted' or 'adopted child') include a person who has attained the age of 18 years before the proceedings are concluded.

50   Adoption by couple

(1) An adoption order may be made on the application of a couple where both of them have attained the age of 21 years.

(2) An adoption order may be made on the application of a couple where—

    (a) one of the couple is the mother or the father of the person to be adopted and has attained the age of 18 years, and

    (b) the other has attained the age of 21 years.

51   Adoption by one person

(1) An adoption order may be made on the application of one person who has attained the age of 21 years and is not married or a civil partner.

(2) An adoption order may be made on the application of one person who has attained the age of 21 years if the court is satisfied that the person is the partner of a parent of the person to be adopted.

(3) An adoption order may be made on the application of one person who has attained the age of 21 years and is married if the court is satisfied that—

    (a) the person's spouse cannot be found,

    (b) the spouses have separated and are living apart, and the separation is likely to be permanent, or

    (c) the person's spouse is by reason of ill-health, whether physical or mental, incapable of making an application for an adoption order.

(3A) An adoption order may be made on the application of one person who has attained the age of 21 years and is a civil partner if the court is satisfied that—

    (a) the person's civil partner cannot be found,

    (b) the civil partners have separated and are living apart, and the separation is likely to be permanent, or

    (c) the person's civil partner is by reason of ill-health, whether physical or mental, incapable of making an application for an adoption order.

(4) An adoption order may not be made on an application under this section by the mother or the father of the person to be adopted unless the court is satisfied that—

    (a) the other natural parent is dead or cannot be found,

    (b) by virtue of the provisions specified in subsection (5), there is no other parent, or

    (c) there is some other reason justifying the child's being adopted by the applicant alone,

and, where the court makes an adoption order on such an application, the court must record that it is satisfied as to the fact mentioned in paragraph (a) or (b) or, in the case of paragraph (c), record the reason.

(5) The provisions referred to in subsection (4)(b) are—

    (a) section 28 of the Human Fertilisation and Embryology Act 1990 (disregarding subsections (5A) to (5I) of that section), or

    (b) sections 34 to 47 of the Human Fertilisation and Embryology Act 2008 (disregarding sections 39, 40 and 46 of that Act).

Post-adoption contact

51A Post-adoption contact

(1) This section applies where—

(a) an adoption agency has placed or was authorised to place a child for adoption, and

(b) the court is making or has made an adoption order in respect of the child.

(2) When making the adoption order or at any time afterwards, the court may make an order under this section—

(a) requiring the person in whose favour the adoption order is or has been made to allow the child to visit or stay with the person named in the order under this section, or for the person named in that order and the child otherwise to have contact with each other, or

(b) prohibiting the person named in the order under this section from having contact with the child.

(3) The following people may be named in an order under this section—

(a) any person who (but for the child's adoption) would be related to the child by blood (including half-blood), marriage or civil partnership;

(b) any former guardian of the child;

(c) any person who had parental responsibility for the child immediately before the making of the adoption order;

(d) any person who was entitled to make an application for an order under section 26 in respect of the child (contact with children placed or to be placed for adoption) by virtue of subsection (3)(c), (d) or (e) of that section;

(e) any person with whom the child has lived for a period of at least one year.

(4) An application for an order under this section may be made by—

(a) a person who has applied for the adoption order or in whose favour the adoption order is or has been made,

(b) the child, or

(c) any person who has obtained the court's leave to make the application.

(5) In deciding whether to grant leave under subsection (4)(c), the court must consider—

(a) any risk there might be of the proposed application disrupting the child's life to such an extent that he or she would be harmed by it (within the meaning of the 1989 Act),

(b) the applicant's connection with the child, and

(c) any representations made to the court by—

(i)   the child, or

(ii) a person who has applied for the adoption order or in whose favour the adoption order is or has been made.

(6) When making an adoption order, the court may on its own initiative make an order of the type mentioned in subsection (2)(b).

(7) The period of one year mentioned in subsection (3)(e) need not be continuous but must not have begun more than five years before the making of the application.

(8) Where this section applies, an order under section 8 of the 1989 Act may not make provision about contact between the child and any person who may be named in an order under this section.

51B Orders under section 51A: supplementary

(1) An order under section 51A—

(a) may contain directions about how it is to be carried into effect,

(b) may be made subject to any conditions the court thinks appropriate,

(c) may be varied or revoked by the court on an application by the child, a person in whose favour the adoption order was made or a person named in the order, and

(d) has effect until the child's 18th birthday, unless revoked.

(2) Subsection (3) applies to proceedings—
   (a) on an application for an adoption order in which—
        (i)   an application is made for an order under section 51A, or
        (ii)   the court indicates that it is considering making such an order on its own initiative;
   (b) on an application for an order under section 51A;
   (c) on an application for such an order to be varied or revoked.
(3) The court must (in the light of any rules made by virtue of subsection (4))—
   (a) draw up a timetable with a view to determining without delay whether to make, (or as the case may be) vary or revoke an order under section 51A, and
   (b) give directions for the purpose of ensuring, so far as is reasonably practicable, that that timetable is adhered to.
(4) Rules of court may—
   (a) specify periods within which specified steps must be taken in relation to proceedings to which subsection (3) applies, and
   (b) make other provision with respect to such proceedings for the purpose of ensuring, so far as is reasonably practicable, that the court makes determinations about orders under section 51A without delay.

Placement and adoption: general

52   Parental etc. consent

(1) The court cannot dispense with the consent of any parent or guardian of a child to the child being placed for adoption or to the making of an adoption order in respect of the child unless the court is satisfied that—
   (a) the parent or guardian cannot be found or lacks capacity (within the meaning of the Mental Capacity Act 2005) to give consent, or
   (b) the welfare of the child requires the consent to be dispensed with.
(2) The following provisions apply to references in this Chapter to any parent or guardian of a child giving or withdrawing—
   (a) consent to the placement of a child for adoption, or
   (b) consent to the making of an adoption order (including a future adoption order).
(3) Any consent given by the mother to the making of an adoption order is ineffective if it is given less than six weeks after the child's birth.
(4) The withdrawal of any consent to the placement of a child for adoption, or of any consent given under section 20, is ineffective if it is given after an application for an adoption order is made.
(5) 'Consent' means consent given unconditionally and with full understanding of what is involved; but a person may consent to adoption without knowing the identity of the persons in whose favour the order will be made.
(6) 'Parent' (except in subsections (9) and (10) below) means a parent having parental responsibility.
(7) Consent under section 19 or 20 must be given in the form prescribed by rules, and the rules may prescribe forms in which a person giving consent under any other provision of this Part may do so (if he wishes).
(8) Consent given under section 19 or 20 must be withdrawn—
   (a) in the form prescribed by rules, or
   (b) by notice given to the agency.
(9) Subsection (10) applies if—
   (a) an agency has placed a child for adoption under section 19 in pursuance of consent given by a parent of the child, and
   (b) at a later time, the other parent of the child acquires parental responsibility for the child.
(10) The other parent is to be treated as having at that time given consent in accordance with this section in the same terms as those in which the first parent gave consent.

53   Modification of 1989 Act in relation to adoption

    (1) Where—

        (a) a local authority are authorised to place a child for adoption, or

        (b) a child who has been placed for adoption by a local authority is less than six weeks old,

regulations may provide for the following provisions of the 1989 Act to apply with modifications, or not to apply, in relation to the child.

    (2) The provisions are—

        (a) section 22(4)(b), (c) and (d) and (5)(b) (duty to ascertain wishes and feelings of certain persons),

        (b) paragraphs 15 and 21 of Schedule 2 (promoting contact with parents and parents' obligation to contribute towards maintenance).

    (3) Where a registered adoption society is authorised to place a child for adoption or a child who has been placed for adoption by a registered adoption society is less than six weeks old, regulations may provide—

        (a) for section 61 of that Act to have effect in relation to the child whether or not he is accommodated by or on behalf of the society,

        (b) for subsections (2)(b) to (d) and (3)(b) of that section (duty to ascertain wishes and feelings of certain persons) to apply with modifications, or not to apply, in relation to the child.

    (4) Where a child's home is with persons who have given notice of intention to adopt, no contribution is payable (whether under a contribution order or otherwise) under Part 3 of Schedule 2 to that Act (contributions towards maintenance of children looked after by local authorities) in respect of the period referred to in subsection (5).

    (5) That period begins when the notice of intention to adopt is given and ends if—

        (a) the period of four months beginning with the giving of the notice expires without the prospective adopters applying for an adoption order, or

        (b) an application for such an order is withdrawn or refused.

    ...

54   Disclosing information during adoption process

Regulations under section 9 may require adoption agencies in prescribed circumstances to disclose in accordance with the regulations prescribed information to prospective adopters.

55   Revocation of adoptions on legitimation

    (1) Where any child adopted by one natural parent as sole adoptive parent subsequently becomes a legitimated person on the marriage of the natural parents, the court by which the adoption order was made may, on the application of any of the parties concerned, revoke the order.

Disclosure of information in relation to a person's adoption

56   Information to be kept about a person's adoption

    (1) In relation to an adopted person, regulations may prescribe—

        (a) the information which an adoption agency must keep in relation to his adoption,

        (b) the form and manner in which it must keep that information.

    (2) Below in this group of sections (that is, this section and sections 57 to 65), any information kept by an adoption agency by virtue of subsection (1)(a) is referred to as section 56 information.

    (3) Regulations may provide for the transfer in prescribed circumstances of information held, or previously held, by an adoption agency to another adoption agency.

57   Restrictions on disclosure of protected etc. information

    (1) Any section 56 information kept by an adoption agency which—

        (a) is about an adopted person or any other person, and

        (b) is or includes identifying information about the person in question, may only be disclosed by the agency to a person (other than the person the information is about) in pursuance of this group of sections.

(2) Any information kept by an adoption agency—

(a) which the agency has obtained from the Registrar General on an application under section 79(5) and any other information which would enable the adopted person to obtain a certified copy of the record of his birth, or

(b) which is information about an entry relating to the adopted person in the Adoption Contact Register,

may only be disclosed to a person by the agency in pursuance of this group of sections.

(3) In this group of sections, information the disclosure of which to a person is restricted by virtue of subsection (1) or (2) is referred to (in relation to him) as protected information.

(4) Identifying information about a person means information which, whether taken on its own or together with other information disclosed by an adoption agency, identifies the person or enables the person to be identified.

(5) This section does not prevent the disclosure of protected information in pursuance of a prescribed agreement to which the adoption agency is a party.

(6) Regulations may authorise or require an adoption agency to disclose protected information to a person who is not an adopted person.

58   Disclosure of other information

(1) This section applies to any section 56 information other than protected information.

(2) An adoption agency may for the purposes of its functions disclose to any person in accordance with prescribed arrangements any information to which this section applies.

(3) An adoption agency must, in prescribed circumstances, disclose prescribed information to a prescribed person.

59   Offence

Regulations may provide that a registered adoption society which discloses any information in contravention of section 57 is to be guilty of an offence and liable on summary conviction to a fine not exceeding level 5 on the standard scale.

60   Disclosing information to adopted adult

(1) This section applies to an adopted person who has attained the age of 18 years.

(2) The adopted person has the right, at his request, to receive from the appropriate adoption agency—

(a) any information which would enable him to obtain a certified copy of the record of his birth, unless the High Court or family court orders otherwise,

(b) any prescribed information disclosed to the adopters by the agency by virtue of section 54.

(3) The High Court or family court may make an order under subsection (2)(a), on an application by the appropriate adoption agency, if satisfied that the circumstances are exceptional.

(4) The adopted person also has the right, at his request, to receive from the court which made the adoption order a copy of any prescribed document or prescribed order relating to the adoption.

(5) Subsection (4) does not apply to a document or order so far as it contains information which is protected information.

61   Disclosing protected information about adults

(1) This section applies where—

(a) a person applies to the appropriate adoption agency for protected information to be disclosed to him, and

(b) none of the information is about a person who is a child at the time of the application.

(2) The agency is not required to proceed with the application unless it considers it appropriate to do so.

(3) If the agency does proceed with the application it must take all reasonable steps to obtain the views of any person the information is about as to the disclosure of the information about him.

(4) The agency may then disclose the information if it considers it appropriate to do so.

(5) In deciding whether it is appropriate to proceed with the application or disclose the information, the agency must consider—

    (a) the welfare of the adopted person,

    (b) any views obtained under subsection (3),

    (c) any prescribed matters,

and all the other circumstances of the case.

(6) This section does not apply to a request for information under section 60(2) or to a request for information which the agency is authorised or required to disclose in pursuance of regulations made by virtue of section 57(6).

62 Disclosing protected information about children

(1) This section applies where—

    (a) a person applies to the appropriate adoption agency for protected information to be disclosed to him, and

    (b) any of the information is about a person who is a child at the time of the application.

(2) The agency is not required to proceed with the application unless it considers it appropriate to do so.

(3) If the agency does proceed with the application, then, so far as the information is about a person who is at the time a child, the agency must take all reasonable steps to obtain—

    (a) the views of any parent or guardian of the child, and

    (b) the views of the child, if the agency considers it appropriate to do so having regard to his age and understanding and to all the other circumstances of the case, as to the disclosure of the information.

(4) And, so far as the information is about a person who has at the time attained the age of 18 years, the agency must take all reasonable steps to obtain his views as to the disclosure of the information.

(5) The agency may then disclose the information if it considers it appropriate to do so.

(6) In deciding whether it is appropriate to proceed with the application, or disclose the information, where any of the information is about a person who is at the time a child—

    (a) if the child is an adopted child, the child's welfare must be the paramount consideration,

    (b) in the case of any other child, the agency must have particular regard to the child's welfare.

(7) And, in deciding whether it is appropriate to proceed with the application or disclose the information, the agency must consider—

    (a) the welfare of the adopted person (where subsection (6)(a) does not apply),

    (b) any views obtained under subsection (3) or (4),

    (c) any prescribed matters,

and all the other circumstances of the case.

(8) This section does not apply to a request for information under section 60(2) or to a request for information which the agency is authorised or required to disclose in pursuance of regulations made by virtue of section 57(6).

63 Counselling

(1) Regulations may require adoption agencies to give information about the availability of counselling to persons—

    (a) seeking information from them in pursuance of this group of sections,

    (b) considering objecting or consenting to the disclosure of information by the agency in pursuance of this group of sections, or

    (c) considering entering with the agency into an agreement prescribed for the purposes of section 57(5).

(2) Regulations may require adoption agencies to make arrangements to secure the provision of counselling for persons seeking information from them in prescribed circumstances in pursuance of this group of sections.

(3) The regulations may authorise adoption agencies—

(a) to disclose information which is required for the purposes of such counselling to the persons providing the counselling,

(b) where the person providing the counselling is outside the United Kingdom, to require a prescribed fee to be paid.

(4) The regulations may require any of the following persons to provide counselling for the purposes of arrangements under subsection (2)—

(a) a local authority...

(b) a registered adoption society...

(c) an adoption support agency in respect of which a person is registered under Part 2 of the Care Standards Act 2000 (c. 14).

...

64   Other provision to be made by regulations

(1) Regulations may make provision for the purposes of this group of sections, including provision as to—

(a) the performance by adoption agencies of their functions,

(b) the manner in which information may be received, and

(c) the matters mentioned below in this section.

(2) Regulations may prescribe—

(a) the manner in which agreements made by virtue of section 57(5) are to be recorded,

(b) the information to be provided by any person on an application for the disclosure of information under this group of sections.

(3) Regulations may require adoption agencies—

(a) to give to prescribed persons prescribed information about the rights or opportunities to obtain information, or to give their views as to its disclosure, given by this group of sections,

(b) to seek prescribed information from, or give prescribed information to, the Registrar General in prescribed circumstances.

(4) Regulations may require the Registrar General—

(a) to disclose to any person (including an adopted person) at his request any information which the person requires to assist him to make contact with the adoption agency which is the appropriate adoption agency in the case of an adopted person specified in the request (or, as the case may be, in the applicant's case),

(b) to disclose to the appropriate adoption agency any information which the agency requires about any entry relating to the adopted person on the Adoption Contact Register.

(5) Regulations may provide for the payment of a prescribed fee in respect of the disclosure in prescribed circumstances of any information in pursuance of section 60, 61 or 62; but an adopted person may not be required to pay any fee in respect of any information disclosed to him in relation to any person who (but for his adoption) would be related to him by blood (including half-blood), marriage or civil partnership.

(6) Regulations may provide for the payment of a prescribed fee by an adoption agency obtaining information under subsection (4)(b).

65   Sections 56 to 65: interpretation

(1) In this group of sections—

'appropriate adoption agency', in relation to an adopted person or to information relating to his adoption, means—

(a) if the person was placed for adoption by an adoption agency, that agency or (if different) the agency which keeps the information in relation to his adoption,

(b) in any other case, the local authority to which notice of intention to adopt was given,

'prescribed' means prescribed by subordinate legislation,

'regulations' means regulations under section 9,

'subordinate legislation' means regulations or, in relation to information to be given by a court, rules.

...

Chapter 4 Status of adopted children

66 Meaning of adoption in Chapter 4

(1) In this Chapter 'adoption' means—

   (a) adoption by an adoption order or a Scottish or Northern Irish adoption order,

   (b) adoption by an order made in the Isle of Man or any of the Channel Islands,

   (c) an adoption effected under the law of a Convention country outside the British Islands, and certified in pursuance of Article 23(1) of the Convention (referred to in this Act as a 'Convention adoption'),

   (d) an overseas adoption, or

   (e) an adoption recognised by the law of England and Wales and effected under the law of any other country;

and related expressions are to be interpreted accordingly.

(2) But references in this Chapter to adoption do not include an adoption effected before the day on which this Chapter comes into force (referred to in this Chapter as 'the appointed day').

(3) Any reference in an enactment to an adopted person within the meaning of this Chapter includes a reference to an adopted child within the meaning of Part 4 of the Adoption Act 1976 (c. 36).

67 Status conferred by adoption

(1) An adopted person is to be treated in law as if born as the child of the adopters or adopter.

(2) An adopted person is the legitimate child of the adopters or adopter and, if adopted by—

   (a) a couple, or

   (b) one of a couple under section 51(2),

is to be treated as the child of the relationship of the couple in question.

(3) An adopted person—

   (a) if adopted by one of a couple under section 51(2), is to be treated in law as not being the child of any person other than the adopter and the other one of the couple, and

   (b) in any other case, is to be treated in law, subject to subsection (4), as not being the child of any person other than the adopters or adopter;

but this subsection does not affect any reference in this Act to a person's natural parent or to any other natural relationship.

(4) In the case of a person adopted by one of the person's natural parents as sole adoptive parent, subsection (3)(b) has no effect as respects entitlement to property depending on relationship to that parent, or as respects anything else depending on that relationship.

(5) This section has effect from the date of the adoption.

(6) Subject to the provisions of this Chapter and Schedule 4, this section—

   (a) applies for the interpretation of enactments or instruments passed or made before as well as after the adoption, and so applies subject to any contrary indication, and

   (b) has effect as respects things done, or events occurring, on or after the adoption.

68 Adoptive relatives

(1) A relationship existing by virtue of section 67 may be referred to as an adoptive relationship, and—

   (a) an adopter may be referred to as an adoptive parent or (as the case may be) as an adoptive father or adoptive mother,

   (b) any other relative of any degree under an adoptive relationship may be referred to as an adoptive relative of that degree.

(2) Subsection (1) does not affect the interpretation of any reference, not qualified by the word 'adoptive', to a relationship.

(3) A reference (however expressed) to the adoptive mother and father of a child adopted by—

(a) a couple of the same sex, or

(b) a partner of the child's parent, where the couple are of the same sex,

is to be read as a reference to the child's adoptive parents.

69 Rules of interpretation for instruments concerning property

(1) The rules of interpretation contained in this section apply (subject to any contrary indication and to Schedule 4) to any instrument so far as it contains a disposition of property.

(2) In applying section 67(1) and (2) to a disposition which depends on the date of birth of a child or children of the adoptive parent or parents, the disposition is to be interpreted as if—

(a) the adopted person had been born on the date of adoption,

(b) two or more people adopted on the same date had been born on that date in the order of their actual births;

but this does not affect any reference to a person's age.

(3) Examples of phrases in wills on which subsection (2) can operate are—

1. Children of A 'living at my death or born afterwards'.

2. Children of A 'living at my death or born afterwards before any one of such children for the time being in existence attains a vested interest and who attain the age of 21 years'.

3. As in example 1 or 2, but referring to grandchildren of A instead of children of A.

4. A for life 'until he has a child', and then to his child or children.

Note. Subsection (2) will not affect the reference to the age of 21 years in example 2.

(4) Section 67(3) does not prejudice—

(a) any qualifying interest,

(b) any interest expectant (whether immediately or not) upon a qualifying interest, or

(c) any contingent interest (other than a contingent interest in remainder) which the adopted person has immediately before the adoption in the estate of a deceased parent, whether testate or intestate.

'Qualifying interest' means an interest vested in possession in the adopted person before the adoption.

(5) Where it is necessary to determine for the purposes of a disposition of property effected by an instrument whether a woman can have a child—

(a) it must be presumed that once a woman has attained the age of 55 years she will not adopt a person after execution of the instrument, and

(b) if she does so, then (in spite of section 67) that person is not to be treated as her child or (if she does so as one of a couple) as the child of the other one of the couple for the purposes of the instrument.

(6) In this section, 'instrument' includes a private Act settling property, but not any other enactment.

70 Dispositions depending on date of birth

(1) Where a disposition depends on the date of birth of a person who was born illegitimate and who is adopted by one of the natural parents as sole adoptive parent, section 69(2) does not affect entitlement by virtue of Part 3 of the Family Law Reform Act 1987 (c. 42) (dispositions of property).

(2) Subsection (1) applies for example where—

(a) a testator dies in 2001 bequeathing a legacy to his eldest grandchild living at a specified time,

(b) his unmarried daughter has a child in 2002 who is the first grandchild,

(c) his married son has a child in 2003,

(d) subsequently his unmarried daughter adopts her child as sole adoptive parent.

In that example the status of the daughter's child as the eldest grandchild of the testator is not affected by the events described in paragraphs (c) and (d).

71 Property devolving with peerages etc.

(1) An adoption does not affect the descent of any peerage or dignity or title of honour.

(2) An adoption does not affect the devolution of any property limited (expressly or not) to devolve (as nearly as the law permits) along with any peerage or dignity or title of honour.

(3) Subsection (2) applies only if and so far as a contrary intention is not expressed in the instrument, and has effect subject to the terms of the instrument.

72 Protection of trustees and personal representatives

(1) A trustee or personal representative is not under a duty, by virtue of the law relating to trusts or the administration of estates, to enquire, before conveying or distributing any property, whether any adoption has been effected or revoked if that fact could affect entitlement to the property.

(2) A trustee or personal representative is not liable to any person by reason of a conveyance or distribution of the property made without regard to any such fact if he has not received notice of the fact before the conveyance or distribution.

(3) This section does not prejudice the right of a person to follow the property, or any property representing it, into the hands of another person, other than a purchaser, who has received it.

73 Meaning of disposition

(1) This section applies for the purposes of this Chapter.

(2) A disposition includes the conferring of a power of appointment and any other disposition of an interest in or right over property; and in this subsection a power of appointment includes any discretionary power to transfer a beneficial interest in property without the furnishing of valuable consideration.

(3) This Chapter applies to an oral disposition as if contained in an instrument made when the disposition was made.

(4) The date of death of a testator is the date at which a will or codicil is to be regarded as made.

(5) The provisions of the law of intestate succession applicable to the estate of a deceased person are to be treated as if contained in an instrument executed by him (while of full capacity) immediately before his death.

74 Miscellaneous enactments

(1) Section 67 does not apply for the purposes of—

    (a) section 1 of and Schedule 1 to the Marriage Act 1949 or Schedule 1 to the Civil Partnership Act 2004 (prohibited degrees of kindred and affinity), or

    (b) sections 64 and 65 of the Sexual Offences Act 2003 (sex with an adult relative).

(2) Section 67 does not apply for the purposes of any provision of—

    (a) the British Nationality Act 1981 (c. 61),

    (b) the Immigration Act 1971 (c. 77),

    (c) any instrument having effect under an enactment within paragraph (a) or (b), or

    (d) any other provision of the law for the time being in force which determines British citizenship, British overseas territories citizenship, the status of a British National (Overseas) or British Overseas citizenship.

75 Pensions

Section 67(3) does not affect entitlement to a pension which is payable to or for the benefit of a person and is in payment at the time of the person's adoption.

76 Insurance

(1) Where a child is adopted whose natural parent has effected an insurance with a friendly society or a collecting society or an industrial insurance company for the payment on the death of the child of money for funeral expenses, then—

    (a) the rights and liabilities under the policy are by virtue of the adoption transferred to the adoptive parents, and

    (b) for the purposes of the enactments relating to such societies and companies, the adoptive parents are to be treated as the person who took out the policy.

(2) Where the adoption is effected by an order made by virtue of section 51(2), the references in subsection (1) to the adoptive parents are to be read as references to the adopter and the other one of the couple.

Chapter 5   The registers

Adopted Children Register etc.

77   Adopted Children Register

(1) The Registrar General must continue to maintain in the General Register Office a register, to be called the Adopted Children Register.

(2) The Adopted Children Register is not to be open to public inspection or search.

(3) No entries may be made in the Adopted Children Register other than entries—

(a) directed to be made in it by adoption orders, or

(b) required to be made under Schedule 1.

(4) A certified copy of an entry in the Adopted Children Register, if purporting to be sealed or stamped with the seal of the General Register Office, is to be received as evidence of the adoption to which it relates without further or other proof.

(5) Where an entry in the Adopted Children Register contains a record—

(a) of the date of birth of the adopted person, or

(b) of the country, or the district and sub-district, of the birth of the adopted person,

a certified copy of the entry is also to be received, without further or other proof, as evidence of that date, or country or district and sub-district, (as the case may be) in all respects as if the copy were a certified copy of an entry in the registers of live-births.

(6) Schedule 1 (registration of adoptions and the amendment of adoption orders) is to have effect.

78   Searches and copies

(1) The Registrar General must continue to maintain at the General Register Office an index of the Adopted Children Register.

(2) Any person may—

(a) search the index,

(b) have a certified copy of any entry in the Adopted Children Register.

(3) But a person is not entitled to have a certified copy of an entry in the Adopted Children Register relating to an adopted person who has not attained the age of 18 years unless the applicant has provided the Registrar General with the prescribed particulars.

'Prescribed' means prescribed by regulations made by the Registrar General with the approval of the Secretary of State.

(4) The terms, conditions and regulations as to payment of fees, and otherwise, applicable under the Births and Deaths Registration Act 1953 (c. 20), and the Registration Service Act 1953 (c. 37), in respect of—

(a) searches in the index kept in the General Register Office of certified copies of entries in the registers of live-births,

(b) the supply from that office of certified copies of entries in those certified copies,

also apply in respect of searches, and supplies of certified copies, under subsection (2).

79   Connections between the register and birth records

(1) The Registrar General must make traceable the connection between any entry in the registers of live-births or other records which has been marked 'Adopted' and any corresponding entry in the Adopted Children Register.

(2) Information kept by the Registrar General for the purposes of subsection (1) is not to be open to public inspection or search.

(3) Any such information, and any other information which would enable an adopted person to obtain a certified copy of the record of his birth, may only be disclosed by the Registrar General in accordance with this section.

(4) In relation to a person adopted before the appointed day the court may, in exceptional circumstances, order the Registrar General to give any information mentioned in subsection (3) to a person.

(5) On an application made in the prescribed manner by the appropriate adoption agency in respect of an adopted person a record of whose birth is kept by the Registrar General, the Registrar General must give the agency any information relating to the adopted person which is mentioned in subsection (3).

'Appropriate adoption agency' has the same meaning as in section 65.

(6) In relation to a person adopted before the appointed day, Schedule 2 applies instead of subsection (5).

(7) On an application made in the prescribed manner by an adopted person a record of whose birth is kept by the Registrar General and who—

(a) is under the age of 18 years, and

(b) intends to be married or form a civil partnership,

the Registrar General must inform the applicant whether or not it appears from information contained in the registers of live-births or other records that the applicant and the intended spouse or civil partner may be within the prohibited degrees of relationship for the purposes of the Marriage Act 1949 (c. 76) or for the purposes of the Civil Partnership Act 2004 (c. 33).

(8) Before the Registrar General gives any information by virtue of this section, any prescribed fee which he has demanded must be paid.

(9) In this section—

'appointed day' means the day appointed for the commencement of sections 56 to 65,

'prescribed' means prescribed by regulations made by the Registrar General with the approval of the Secretary of State.

80 Adoption Contact Register

(1) The Registrar General must continue to maintain at the General Register Office in accordance with regulations a register in two Parts to be called the Adoption Contact Register.

(2) Part 1 of the register is to contain the prescribed information about adopted persons who have given the prescribed notice expressing their wishes as to making contact with their relatives.

(3) The Registrar General may only make an entry in Part 1 of the register for an adopted person—

(a) a record of whose birth is kept by the Registrar General,

(b) who has attained the age of 18 years, and

(c) who the Registrar General is satisfied has such information as is necessary to enable him to obtain a certified copy of the record of his birth.

(4) Part 2 of the register is to contain the prescribed information about persons who have given the prescribed notice expressing their wishes, as relatives of adopted persons, as to making contact with those persons.

(5) The Registrar General may only make an entry in Part 2 of the register for a person—

(a) who has attained the age of 18 years, and

(b) who the Registrar General is satisfied is a relative of an adopted person and has such information as is necessary to enable him to obtain a certified copy of the record of the adopted person's birth.

(6) Regulations may provide for—

(a) the disclosure of information contained in one Part of the register to persons for whom there is an entry in the other Part,

(b) the payment of prescribed fees in respect of the making or alteration of entries in the register and the disclosure of information contained in the register.

81   Adoption Contact Register: supplementary

(1) The Adoption Contact Register is not to be open to public inspection or search.

(2) In section 80, 'relative', in relation to an adopted person, means any person who (but for his adoption) would be related to him by blood (including half-blood), marriage or civil partnership.

(3) The Registrar General must not give any information entered in the register to any person except in accordance with subsection (6)(a) of that section or regulations made by virtue of section 64(4)(b).

(4) In section 80, 'regulations' means regulations made by the Registrar General with the approval of the Secretary of State, and 'prescribed' means prescribed by such regulations.

General

82   Interpretation

(1) In this Chapter—

'records' includes certified copies kept by the Registrar General of entries in any register of births,

'registers of live-births' means the registers of live-births made under the Births and Deaths Registration Act 1953 (c. 20).

(2) Any register, record or index maintained under this Chapter may be maintained in any form the Registrar General considers appropriate; and references (however expressed) to entries in such a register, or to their amendment, marking or cancellation, are to be read accordingly.

…

Chapter 7 Miscellaneous

Restrictions

92   Restriction on arranging adoptions etc.

(1) A person who is neither an adoption agency nor acting in pursuance of an order of the High Court or the family court must not take any of the steps mentioned in subsection (2).

(2) The steps are—

(a) asking a person other than an adoption agency to provide a child for adoption,

(b) asking a person other than an adoption agency to provide prospective adopters for a child,

(c) offering to find a child for adoption,

(d) offering a child for adoption to a person other than an adoption agency,

(e) handing over a child to any person other than an adoption agency with a view to the child's adoption by that or another person,

(f) receiving a child handed over to him in contravention of paragraph (e),

(g) entering into an agreement with any person for the adoption of a child, or for the purpose of facilitating the adoption of a child, where no adoption agency is acting on behalf of the child in the adoption,

(h) initiating or taking part in negotiations of which the purpose is the conclusion of an agreement within paragraph (g),

(i) causing another person to take any of the steps mentioned in paragraphs (a) to (h).

(3) Subsection (1) does not apply to a person taking any of the steps mentioned in paragraphs (d), (e), (g), (h) and (i) of subsection (2) if the following condition is met.

(4) The condition is that—

(a) the prospective adopters are parents, relatives or guardians of the child (or one of them is), or

(b) the prospective adopter is the partner of a parent of the child.

(5) References to an adoption agency in subsection (2) include a prescribed person outside the United Kingdom exercising functions corresponding to those of an adoption agency, if the functions are being exercised in prescribed circumstances in respect of the child in question.

(6) The Secretary of State may, after consultation with the Assembly, by order make any amendments of subsections (1) to (4), and any consequential amendments of this Act, which he considers necessary or expedient.

(7) In this section—
    (a) 'agreement' includes an arrangement (whether or not enforceable),
    (b) 'prescribed' means prescribed by regulations made by the Secretary of State after consultation with the Assembly.

93 Offence of breaching restrictions under section 92

(1) If a person contravenes section 92(1), he is guilty of an offence; and, if that person is an adoption society, the person who manages the society is also guilty of the offence.

(2) A person is not guilty of an offence under subsection (1) of taking the step mentioned in paragraph (f) of section 92(2) unless it is proved that he knew or had reason to suspect that the child was handed over to him in contravention of paragraph (e) of that subsection.

(3) A person is not guilty of an offence under subsection (1) of causing a person to take any of the steps mentioned in paragraphs (a) to (h) of section 92(2) unless it is proved that he knew or had reason to suspect that the step taken would contravene the paragraph in question.

(4) But subsections (2) and (3) only apply if sufficient evidence is adduced to raise an issue as to whether the person had the knowledge or reason mentioned.

(5) A person guilty of an offence under this section is liable on summary conviction to imprisonment for a term not exceeding six months, or a fine not exceeding £10,000, or both.

94 Restriction on reports

(1) A person who is not within a prescribed description may not, in any prescribed circumstances, prepare a report for any person about the suitability of a child for adoption or of a person to adopt a child or about the adoption, or placement for adoption, of a child.

'Prescribed' means prescribed by regulations made by the Secretary of State after consultation with the Assembly.

(2) If a person—
    (a) contravenes subsection (1), or
    (b) causes a person to prepare a report, or submits to any person a report which has been prepared, in contravention of that subsection,
he is guilty of an offence.

(3) If a person who works for an adoption society—
    (a) contravenes subsection (1), or
    (b) causes a person to prepare a report, or submits to any person a report which has been prepared, in contravention of that subsection,
the person who manages the society is also guilty of the offence.

(4) A person is not guilty of an offence under subsection (2)(b) unless it is proved that he knew or had reason to suspect that the report would be, or had been, prepared in contravention of subsection (1).

But this subsection only applies if sufficient evidence is adduced to raise an issue as to whether the person had the knowledge or reason mentioned.

(5) A person guilty of an offence under this section is liable on summary conviction to imprisonment for a term not exceeding six months, or a fine not exceeding level 5 on the standard scale, or both.

95 Prohibition of certain payments

(1) This section applies to any payment (other than an excepted payment) which is made for or in consideration of—
    (a) the adoption of a child,

(b) giving any consent required in connection with the adoption of a child,

(c) removing from the United Kingdom a child who is a Commonwealth citizen, or is habitually resident in the United Kingdom, to a place outside the British Islands for the purpose of adoption,

(d) a person (who is neither an adoption agency nor acting in pursuance of an order of the High Court or family court) taking any step mentioned in section 92(2),

(e) preparing, causing to be prepared or submitting a report the preparation of which contravenes section 94(1).

(2) In this section and section 96, removing a child from the United Kingdom has the same meaning as in section 85.

(3) Any person who—

(a) makes any payment to which this section applies,

(b) agrees or offers to make any such payment, or

(c) receives or agrees to receive or attempts to obtain any such payment,

is guilty of an offence.

(4) A person guilty of an offence under this section is liable on summary conviction to imprisonment for a term not exceeding six months, or a fine not exceeding £10,000, or both.

96   Excepted payments

(1) A payment is an excepted payment if it is made by virtue of, or in accordance with provision made by or under, this Act, the Adoption (Scotland) Act 1978 (c. 28), the Adoption and Children (Scotland) Act 2007 (asp 4) or the Adoption (Northern Ireland) Order 1987 (S.I. 1987/2203 (N.I.22)).

(2) A payment is an excepted payment if it is made to a registered adoption society by—

(a) a parent or guardian of a child, or

(b) a person who adopts or proposes to adopt a child,

in respect of expenses reasonably incurred by the society in connection with the adoption or proposed adoption of the child.

(3) A payment is an excepted payment if it is made in respect of any legal or medical expenses incurred or to be incurred by any person in connection with an application to a court which he has made or proposes to make for an adoption order, a placement order, or an order under section 26, 51A or 84.
…

97   Sections 92 to 96: interpretation

In sections 92 to 96—

(a) 'adoption agency' includes a Scottish or Northern Irish adoption agency,

(b) 'payment' includes reward,

(c) references to adoption are to the adoption of persons, wherever they may be habitually resident, effected under the law of any country or territory, whether within or outside the British Islands.
…

Proceedings

99   Proceedings for offences

Proceedings for an offence by virtue of section 9 or 59 may not, without the written consent of the Attorney General, be taken by any person other than Her Majesty's Chief Inspector of Education, Children's Services and Skills or the Assembly.
…

The Children and Family Court Advisory and Support Service

102   Officers of the Service

(1) For the purposes of—

(a) any relevant application,

(b) the signification by any person of any consent to placement or adoption, rules must provide for the appointment in prescribed cases of an officer of the Children and Family Court Advisory and Support Service ('the Service') or a Welsh family proceedings officer.

(2) The rules may provide for the appointment of such an officer in other circumstances in which it appears to the Lord Chancellor to be necessary or expedient to do so.

(3) The rules may provide for the officer—

(a) to act on behalf of the child upon the hearing of any relevant application, with the duty of safeguarding the interests of the child in the prescribed manner,

(b) where the court so requests, to prepare a report on matters relating to the welfare of the child in question,

(c) to witness documents which signify consent to placement or adoption,

(d) to perform prescribed functions.

(4) A report prepared in pursuance of the rules on matters relating to the welfare of a child must—

(a) deal with prescribed matters (unless the court orders otherwise), and

(b) be made in the manner required by the court.

(5) A person who—

(a) in the case of an application for the making, varying or revocation of a placement order, is employed by the local authority which made the application,

(b) in the case of an application for an adoption order in respect of a child who was placed for adoption, is employed by the adoption agency which placed him, or

(c) is within a prescribed description,

is not to be appointed under subsection (1) or (2).

(6) In this section, 'relevant application' means an application for—

(a) the making, varying or revocation of a placement order,

(b) the making of an order under section 26, or the varying or revocation of such an order,

(c) the making of an adoption order, or

(d) the making of an order under section 84.

(7) Rules may make provision as to the assistance which the court may require an officer of the Service or a Welsh family proceedings officer to give to it.

(8) In this section and section 103 'Welsh family proceedings officer' has the meaning given by section 35 of the Children Act 2004.

103 Right of officers of the Service to have access to adoption agency records

(1) Where an officer of the Service or a Welsh family proceedings officer has been appointed to act under section 102(1), he has the right at all reasonable times to examine and take copies of any records of, or held by, an adoption agency which were compiled in connection with the making, or proposed making, by any person of any application under this Part in respect of the child concerned.

(2) Where an officer of the Service or a Welsh family proceedings officer takes a copy of any record which he is entitled to examine under this section, that copy or any part of it is admissible as evidence of any matter referred to in any—

(a) report which he makes to the court in the proceedings in question, or

(b) evidence which he gives in those proceedings.

(3) Subsection (2) has effect regardless of any enactment or rule of law which would otherwise prevent the record in question being admissible in evidence.

Evidence

104 Evidence of consent

(1) If a document signifying any consent which is required by this Part to be given is witnessed in accordance with rules, it is to be admissible in evidence without further proof of the signature of the person by whom it was executed.

(2) A document signifying any such consent which purports to be witnessed in accordance with rules is to be presumed to be so witnessed, and to have been executed and witnessed on the date and at the place specified in the document, unless the contrary is proved.

...

PART 2 AMENDMENTS OF THE CHILDREN ACT 1989

111 Parental responsibility of unmarried father

...

(7) Paragraph (a) of section 4(1) of the 1989 Act, as substituted by subsection (2) of this section, does not confer parental responsibility on a man who was registered under an enactment referred to in paragraph (a), (b) or (c) of section 4(1A) of that Act, as inserted by subsection (3) of this section, before the commencement of subsection (3) in relation to that paragraph.

...

PART 3 MISCELLANEOUS AND FINAL PROVISIONS

Chapter 1 Miscellaneous

Advertisements in the United Kingdom

123 Restriction on advertisements etc.

(1) A person must not—

  (a) publish or distribute an advertisement or information to which this section applies, or

  (b) cause such an advertisement or information to be published or distributed.

(2) This section applies to an advertisement indicating that—

  (a) the parent or guardian of a child wants the child to be adopted,

  (b) a person wants to adopt a child,

  (c) a person other than an adoption agency is willing to take any step mentioned in paragraphs (a) to (e), (g) and (h) and (so far as relating to those paragraphs) (i) of section 92(2),

  (d) a person other than an adoption agency is willing to receive a child handed over to him with a view to the child's adoption by him or another, or

  (e) a person is willing to remove a child from the United Kingdom for the purposes of adoption.

(3) This section applies to—

  ...

  (b) information about a particular child as a child available for adoption.

(4) For the purposes of this section and section 124—

  (a) publishing or distributing an advertisement or information means publishing it or distributing it to the public and includes doing so by electronic means (for example, by means of the internet),

  (b) the public includes selected members of the public as well as the public generally or any section of the public.

(5) Subsection (1) does not apply to publication or distribution by or on behalf of an adoption agency.

(6) The Secretary of State may by order make any amendments of this section which he considers necessary or expedient in consequence of any developments in technology relating to publishing or distributing advertisements or other information by electronic or electromagnetic means.

...

124 Offence of breaching restriction under section 123

(1) A person who contravenes section 123(1) is guilty of an offence.

(2) A person is not guilty of an offence under this section unless it is proved that he knew or had reason to suspect that section 123 applied to the advertisement or information.

But this subsection only applies if sufficient evidence is adduced to raise an issue as to whether the person had the knowledge or reason mentioned.

(3) A person guilty of an offence under this section is liable on summary conviction to imprisonment for a term not exceeding three months, or a fine not exceeding level 5 on the standard scale, or both.

Adoption and Children Act Register

125   Adoption and Children Act Register

(1) The Secretary of State may establish and maintain a register, to be called the Adoption and Children Act Register, containing—

    (a) prescribed information about children who are suitable for adoption, children for whom a local authority in England are considering adoption and prospective adopters who are suitable to adopt a child,

    (b) prescribed information about persons included in the register in pursuance of paragraph (a) in respect of things occurring after their inclusion.

(1A) Regulations may provide that the register may contain—

    (a) prescribed information about children who a Welsh, Scottish or Northern Irish adoption agency is satisfied are suitable for adoption,

    (b) prescribed information about prospective adopters who a Welsh, Scottish or Northern Irish adoption agency is satisfied are suitable to adopt a child,

    (c) prescribed information about persons included in the register in pursuance of paragraph (a) or (b) in respect of things occurring after their inclusion.

(2) For the purpose of giving assistance in finding persons with whom children may be placed for purposes other than adoption, regulations may—

    (a) provide for the register to contain information about such persons and the children who may be placed with them, and

    (b) apply any of the other provisions of this group of sections (that is, this section and sections 126 to 131), with or without modifications.

(3) The register is not to be open to public inspection or search (subject to regulations under section 128A).

(4) Regulations may make provision about the retention of information in the register.

(5) Information is to be kept in the register in any form the Secretary of State considers appropriate.

126   Use of an organisation to establish the register

(1) The Secretary of State may make an arrangement with an organisation under which any function of his of establishing and maintaining the register, and disclosing information entered in, or compiled from information entered in, the register to any person is performed wholly or partly by the organisation on his behalf.

(2) The arrangement may include provision for payments to be made to the organisation by the Secretary of State.

(3) If the Secretary of State makes an arrangement under this section with an organisation, the organisation is to perform the functions exercisable by virtue of this section in accordance with any directions given by the Secretary of State and the directions may be of general application or be special directions.

…

(5) References in this group of sections to the registration organisation are to any organisation for the time being performing functions in respect of the register by virtue of arrangements under this section.

127   Use of an organisation as agency for payments

(1) Regulations may authorise an organisation with which an arrangement is made under section 126 to act as agent for the payment or receipt of sums payable by adoption agencies to other adoption agencies and may require adoption agencies to pay or receive such sums through the organisation.

(2) The organisation is to perform the functions exercisable by virtue of this section in accordance with any directions given by the Secretary of State; and the directions may be of general application or be special directions.

...

128 Supply of information for the register

(1) Regulations may require adoption agencies to give prescribed information to the Secretary of State or the registration organisation for entry in the register.

(2) Information is to be given to the Secretary of State or the registration organisation when required by regulations and in the prescribed form and manner.

(3) Regulations may require an agency giving information which is entered on the register to pay a prescribed fee to the Secretary of State or the registration organisation.

(4) But an adoption agency is not to disclose any information to the Secretary of State or the registration organisation—

  (a) about prospective adopters who are suitable to adopt a child, or persons who were included in the register as such prospective adopters, without their consent,

  (b) about children suitable for adoption or for whom a local authority in England are considering adoption, or persons who were included in the register as such children, without the consent of the prescribed person.

(5) Consent under subsection (4) is to be given in the prescribed form.

128A Search and inspection of the register by prospective adopters

(1) Regulations may make provision enabling prospective adopters who are suitable to adopt a child to search and inspect the register, for the purposes of assisting them to find a child for whom they would be appropriate adopters.

(2) Regulations under subsection (1) may make provision enabling prospective adopters to search and inspect only prescribed parts of the register, or prescribed content on the register.

(3) Access to the register for the purpose of searching and inspecting it may be granted on any prescribed terms and conditions.

(4) Regulations may prescribe the steps to be taken by prospective adopters in respect of information received by them as a result of searching or inspecting the register.

(5) Regulations may make provision requiring prospective adopters, in prescribed circumstances, to pay a prescribed fee to the Secretary of State or the registration organisation in respect of searching or inspecting the register.

(6) On the occasion of the first exercise of the power to make regulations under this section—

  (a) the statutory instrument containing the regulations is not to be made unless a draft of the instrument has been laid before, and approved by a resolution of, each House of Parliament, and

  (b) accordingly section 140(2) does not apply to the instrument.

129 Disclosure of information

(1) Information entered in the register, or compiled from information entered in the register, may only be disclosed under subsection (2), (2A) or (3) or section 128A.

(2) Prescribed information entered in the register may be disclosed by the Secretary of State or the registration organisation—

  (a) where an adoption agency is acting on behalf of a child who is suitable for adoption or for whom a local authority in England is considering adoption, to the agency to assist in finding prospective adopters with whom it would be appropriate for the child to be placed,

  (b) where an adoption agency is acting on behalf of prospective adopters who are suitable to adopt a child, to the agency to assist in finding a child appropriate for adoption by them.

(2A) Regulations may make provision permitting the disclosure of prescribed information entered in the register, or compiled from information entered in the register—

    (a) to an adoption agency or to a Welsh, Scottish or Northern Irish adoption agency for any prescribed purpose, or

    (b) for the purpose of enabling the information to be entered in a register which is maintained in respect of Wales, Scotland or Northern Ireland and which contains information about children who are suitable for adoption or prospective adopters who are suitable to adopt a child.

(3) Prescribed information entered in the register, or compiled from information entered in the register, may be disclosed by the Secretary of State or the registration organisation to any prescribed person for use for statistical or research purposes, or for other prescribed purposes.

(4) Regulations may prescribe the steps to be taken by adoption agencies in respect of information received by them by virtue of subsection (2) or (2A).

(5) Subsection (1) does not apply—

    (a) to a disclosure of information with the authority of the Secretary of State.

(6) Information disclosed to any person under subsection (2), (2A) or (3) may be given on any prescribed terms or conditions.

(7) Regulations may, in prescribed circumstances, require a prescribed fee to be paid to the Secretary of State or the registration organisation—

    (a) by a prescribed adoption agency in respect of information disclosed under subsection (2) or (2A),

    (aa) by a prescribed Welsh, Scottish or Northern Irish adoption agency in respect of information disclosed under subsection (2A), or

    (b) by a person in respect of information disclosed under subsection (2A) or (3).

(8) If any information entered in the register is disclosed to a person in contravention of subsection (1), the person disclosing it is guilty of an offence.

(9) A person guilty of an offence under subsection (8) is liable on summary conviction to imprisonment for a term not exceeding three months, or a fine not exceeding level 5 on the standard scale, or both.

...

131 Supplementary

(1) In this group of sections—

    (za) 'adoption agency' means—

        (i) a local authority in England,

        (ii) a registered adoption society whose principal office is in England,

    (a) 'organisation' includes a public body and a private or voluntary organisation,

    (b) 'prescribed' means prescribed by regulations,

    (c) 'the register' means the Adoption and Children Act Register,

    (ca) 'Welsh adoption agency' means—

        (i) a local authority in Wales,

        (ii) a registered adoption society whose principal office is in Wales.

    ...

(2) For the purposes of this group of sections (except sections 125(1A) and 129(2A))—

    (a) a child is suitable for adoption if an adoption agency is satisfied that the child ought to be placed for adoption,

    (b) prospective adopters are suitable to adopt a child if an adoption agency is satisfied that they are suitable to have a child placed with them for adoption.

(2A) For the purposes of sections 125(1A) and 129(2A)—

    (a) a child is suitable for adoption if a Welsh, Scottish or Northern Irish adoption agency is satisfied that the child ought to be placed for adoption,

    (b) prospective adopters are suitable to adopt a child if a Welsh, Scottish or Northern Irish adoption agency is satisfied that they are suitable to have a child placed with them for adoption.

(3) Nothing authorised or required to be done by virtue of this group of sections constitutes an offence under section 93, 94 or 95.

...

138 Proceedings in Great Britain

Proceedings for an offence by virtue of section 9, 59, 93, 94, 95 or 129—

    (a) may not be brought more than six years after the commission of the offence but, subject to that,

    (b) may be brought within a period of six months from the date on which evidence sufficient in the opinion of the prosecutor to warrant the proceedings came to his knowledge.

...

Chapter 2 Final provisions

...

144 General interpretation etc.

    (1) In this Act—

'appropriate Minister' means—

    (a) in relation to England, Scotland or Northern Ireland, the Secretary of State,

    (b) in relation to Wales, the Assembly,

and in relation to England and Wales means the Secretary of State and the Assembly acting jointly,

'the Assembly' means the National Assembly for Wales,

'body' includes an unincorporated body,

'by virtue of' includes 'by' and 'under',

'child', except where used to express a relationship, means a person who has not attained the age of 18 years,

'the Convention' means the Convention on Protection of Children and Co-operation in respect of Intercountry Adoption, concluded at the Hague on 29th May 1993,

'Convention adoption order' means an adoption order which, by virtue of regulations under section 1 of the Adoption (Intercountry Aspects) Act 1999 (c. 18) (regulations giving effect to the Convention), is made as a Convention adoption order,

'Convention country' means a country or territory in which the Convention is in force,

'court' means the High Court or the family court,

'enactment' includes an enactment comprised in subordinate legislation,

'fee' includes expenses,

'guardian' has the same meaning as in the 1989 Act and includes a special guardian within the meaning of that Act,

'information' means information recorded in any form,

'local authority' means any unitary authority, or any county council so far as they are not a unitary authority,

    ...

'notice' means a notice in writing,

'registration authority' (in Part 1) has the same meaning as in the Care Standards Act 2000 (c. 14),

'regulations' means regulations made by the appropriate Minister, unless they are required to be made by the Lord Chancellor, the Secretary of State or the Registrar General,

'relative', in relation to a child, means a grandparent, brother, sister, uncle or aunt, whether of the full blood or half-blood or by marriage or civil partnership,

'rules' means Family Procedure Rules made by virtue of section 141(1),

    ...

'subordinate legislation' has the same meaning as in the Interpretation Act 1978 (c. 30),

'unitary authority' means—

    (a) the council of any county so far as they are the council for an area for which there are no district councils,

(b) the council of any district comprised in an area for which there is no county council,

(c) the council of a county borough,

(d) the council of a London borough,

(e) the Common Council of the City of London.

...

(4) In this Act, a couple means—

(a)   a married couple, or

(aa)   two people who are civil partners of each other, or

(b)   two people (whether of different sexes or the same sex) living as partners in an enduring family relationship.

(5) Subsection (4)(b) does not include two people one of whom is the other's parent, grandparent, sister, brother, aunt or uncle.

(6) References to relationships in subsection (5)—

(a) are to relationships of the full blood or half blood or, in the case of an adopted person,
such of those relationships as would exist but for adoption, and

(b) include the relationship of a child with his adoptive, or former adoptive, parents,

but do not include any other adoptive relationships.

(7) For the purposes of this Act, a person is the partner of a child's parent if the person and the
parent are a couple but the person is not the child's parent.

...

SCHEDULES

SCHEDULE 1 REGISTRATION OF ADOPTIONS

Registration of adoption orders

1.—(1) Every adoption order must contain a direction to the Registrar General to make in the
Adopted Children Register an entry in the form prescribed by regulations made by the Registrar
General with the approval of the Secretary of State.

(2) Where, on an application to a court for an adoption order in respect of a child, the identity
of the child with a child to whom an entry in the registers of live-births or other records relates is
proved to the satisfaction of the court, any adoption order made in pursuance of the application
must contain a direction to the Registrar General to secure that the entry in the register or, as the
case may be, record in question is marked with the word 'Adopted'.

(3) Where an adoption order is made in respect of a child who has previously been the subject
of an adoption order made by a court in England or Wales under Part 1 of this Act or any other
enactment—

(a) sub-paragraph (2) does not apply, and

(b) the order must contain a direction to the Registrar General to mark the previous entry in
the Adopted Children Register with the word 'Re-adopted'.

(4) Where an adoption order is made, the prescribed officer of the court which made the order
must communicate the order to the Registrar General in the prescribed manner; and the Registrar
General must then comply with the directions contained in the order.

'Prescribed' means prescribed by rules.

...

Amendment of orders and rectification of Registers and other records

4.—(1) The court by which an adoption order has been made may, on the application of the
adopter or the adopted person, amend the order by the correction of any error in the particulars
contained in it.

(2) The court by which an adoption order has been made may, if satisfied on the application of the adopter or the adopted person that within the period of one year beginning with the date of the order any new name—

(a) has been given to the adopted person (whether in baptism or otherwise), or

(b) has been taken by the adopted person,

either in place of or in addition to a name specified in the particulars required to be entered in the Adopted Children Register in pursuance of the order, amend the order by substituting or, as the case may be, adding that name in those particulars.

(3) The court by which an adoption order has been made may, if satisfied on the application of any person concerned that a direction for the marking of an entry in the registers of live-births, the Adopted Children Register or other records included in the order in pursuance of paragraph 1(2) or (3) was wrongly so included, revoke that direction.

(4) Where an adoption order is amended or a direction revoked under sub-paragraphs (1) to (3), the prescribed officer of the court must communicate the amendment in the prescribed manner to the Registrar General.

'Prescribed' means prescribed by rules.

(5) The Registrar General must then—

(a) amend the entry in the Adopted Children Register accordingly, or

(b) secure that the marking of the entry in the registers of live-births, the Adopted Children Register or other records is cancelled,

as the case may be.

(6) Where an adoption order is quashed or an appeal against an adoption order allowed by any court, the court must give directions to the Registrar General to secure that—

(a) any entry in the Adopted Children Register, and

(b) any marking of an entry in that Register, the registers of live-births or other records as the case may be, which was effected in pursuance of the order,

is cancelled.

(7) Where an adoption order has been amended, any certified copy of the relevant entry in the Adopted Children Register which may be issued pursuant to section 78(2)(b) must be a copy of the entry as amended, without the reproduction of—

(a) any note or marking relating to the amendment, or

(b) any matter cancelled in pursuance of it.

(8) A copy or extract of an entry in any register or other record, being an entry the marking of which has been cancelled, is not to be treated as an accurate copy unless both the marking and the cancellation are omitted from it.

…

Marking of entries on re-registration of birth on legitimation

5.—(1) Without prejudice to paragraphs 2(4) and 4(5), where, after an entry in the registers of live-births or other records has been marked in accordance with paragraph 1 or 2, the birth is re-registered under section 14 of the Births and Deaths Registration Act 1953 (c. 20) (reregistration of births of legitimated persons), the entry made on the re-registration must be marked in the like manner.

(2) Without prejudice to paragraph 4(9), where an entry in the registers of live-births or other records is marked in pursuance of paragraph 3 and the birth in question is subsequently reregistered under section 14 of that Act, the entry made on re-registration must be marked in the like manner.

Cancellations in registers on legitimation

6.—(1) This paragraph applies where an adoption order is revoked under section 55(1).

(2) The prescribed officer of the court must communicate the revocation in the prescribed manner to the Registrar General who must then cancel or secure the cancellation of—

(a) the entry in the Adopted Children Register relating to the adopted person, and

(b) the marking with the word 'Adopted' of any entry relating to the adopted person in the registers of live-births or other records.

'Prescribed' means prescribed by rules.

(3) A copy or extract of an entry in any register or other record, being an entry the marking of which is cancelled under this paragraph, is not to be treated as an accurate copy unless both the marking and the cancellation are omitted from it.

Section 79(6)   **SCHEDULE 2**

DISCLOSURE OF BIRTH RECORDS BY REGISTRAR GENERAL

1. On an application made in the prescribed manner by an adopted person—
  (a) a record of whose birth is kept by the Registrar General, and
  (b) who has attained the age of 18 years,
the Registrar General must give the applicant any information necessary to enable the applicant to obtain a certified copy of the record of his birth.

'Prescribed' means prescribed by regulations made by the Registrar General with the approval of the Secretary of State.

2.—(1) Before giving any information to an applicant under paragraph 1, the Registrar General must inform the applicant that counselling services are available to the applicant—
  (a) from a registered adoption society, an organisation within section 144(3) (b) or an adoption society which is registered under Article 4 of the Adoption (Northern Ireland) Order 1987 (S.I. 1987/2203 (N.I. 22)),
  (b) if the applicant is in England and Wales, at the General Register Office or from any local authority or registered adoption support agency,

...

(2) In sub-paragraph (1)(b), 'registered adoption support agency' means an adoption support agency in respect of which a person is registered under Part 2 of the Care Standards Act 2000 (c. 14).

...

(4) If the applicant chooses to receive counselling from a person or body within sub-paragraph (1), the Registrar General must send to the person or body the information to which the applicant is entitled under paragraph 1.

...

4.—(1) Where a person—
  (a) was adopted before 12th November 1975, and
  (b) applies for information under paragraph 1,
the Registrar General must not give the information to the applicant unless the applicant has attended an interview with a counsellor arranged by a person or body from whom counselling services are available as mentioned in paragraph 2.

(2) Where the Registrar General is prevented by sub-paragraph (1) from giving information to a person who is not living in the United Kingdom, the Registrar General may give the information to any body which—
  (a) the Registrar General is satisfied is suitable to provide counselling to that person, and
  (b) has notified the Registrar General that it is prepared to provide such counselling.

...

Section 147   **SCHEDULE 6**

GLOSSARY

In this Act, the expressions listed in the left-hand column below have the meaning given by, or are to be interpreted in accordance with, the provisions of this Act or (where stated) of the 1989 Act listed in the right-hand column.

Expression	Provision
the 1989 Act	section 2(5)
Adopted Children Register	section 77
Adoption and Children Act Register	section 125
adoption (in relation to Chapter 4 of Part 1)	section 66
adoption agency	section 2(1)
adoption agency placing a child for adoption	section 18(5)
Adoption Contact Register	section 80
adoption order	section 46(1)
Adoption Service	section 2(1)
adoption society	section 2(5)
adoption support agency	section 8
adoption support services	section 2(6)
appointed day (in relation to Chapter 4 of Part 1)	section 66(2)
appropriate Minister	section 144
Assembly	section 144
Body	section 144
by virtue of	section 144
care order	section 105(1) of the 1989 Act
Child	sections 49(5) and 144
child arrangements order	section 8(1) of the 1989 Act
child assessment order	section 43(2) of the 1989 Act
child in the care of a local authority	section 105(1) of the 1989 Act
child looked after by a local authority	section 22 of the 1989 Act
child placed for adoption by an adoption agency	section 18(5)
child to be adopted, adopted child	section 49(5)
consent (in relation to making adoption orders or placing for adoption)	section 52
the Convention	section 144
Convention adoption	section 66(1)(c)
Convention adoption order	section 144
Convention country	section 144
Couple	section 144(4)
Court	section 144
disposition (in relation to Chapter 4 of Part 1)	section 73
Enactment	section 144
Fee	section 144
Guardian	section 144
information	section 144
interim care order	section 38 of the 1989 Act
local authority	section 144
local authority foster parent	section 22C(12) of the 1989 Act
Northern Irish adoption agency	section 144
Northern Irish adoption order	section 144

Expression	Provision
notice	section 144
notice of intention to adopt	section 44(2)
overseas adoption	section 87
parental responsibility	section 3 of the 1989 Act
partner, in relation to a parent of a child	section 144(7)
placement order	section 21
placing, or placed, for adoption	sections 18(5) and 19(4)
prohibited steps order	section 8(1) of the 1989 Act
records (in relation to Chapter 5 of Part 1)	section 82
registered adoption society	section 2(2)
registers of live-births (in relation to Chapter 5 of Part 1)	section 82
registration authority (in Part 1)	section 144
regulations	section 144
relative	section 144, read with section 1(8)
rules	section 144
Scottish adoption agency	section 144(3)
Scottish adoption order	section 144
specific issue order	section 8(1) of the 1989 Act
subordinate legislation	section 144
supervision order	section 31(11) of the 1989 Act
unitary authority	section 144
voluntary organisation	section 2(5)

Human Fertilisation and Embryology (Deceased Fathers) Act 2003

(2003 c. 24)

3 Retrospective, transitional and transitory provision

(1) This Act shall (in addition to any case where the sperm or embryo is used on or after the coming into force of section 1) apply to any case where the sperm of a man, or any embryo the creation of which was brought about with the sperm of a man, was used on or after 1st August 1991 and before the coming into force of that section.

(2) Where the child concerned was born before the coming into force of section 1 of this Act, section 28(5A) or (as the case may be) (5B) of the Human Fertilisation and Embryology Act 1990 (c. 37) shall have effect as if for paragraph (e) there were substituted—

      '(e) the woman has elected in writing not later than the end of the period of six months beginning with the coming into force of this subsection for the man to be treated for the purpose mentioned in subsection (5I) below as the father of the child,'.

(3) Where the child concerned was born before the coming into force of section 1 of this Act, section 28(5C) of the Act of 1990 shall have effect as if for paragraph (f) there were substituted—

      '(f) the woman has elected in writing not later than the end of the period of six months beginning with the coming into force of this subsection for the other party to the marriage to be treated for the purpose mentioned in subsection (5I) below as the father of the child,'.

(4) Where the child concerned was born before the coming into force of section 1 of this Act, section 28(5D) of the Act of 1990 shall have effect as if for paragraph (f) there were substituted—

> '(f) the woman has elected in writing not later than the end of the period of six months beginning with the coming into force of this subsection for the man to be treated for the purpose mentioned in subsection (5I) below as the father of the child,'.

(5) Where the child concerned was born before the coming into force of section 1 of this Act, section 28 of the Act of 1990 shall have effect as if—

- (a) subsection (5E) were omitted; and
- (b) in subsection (5F) for the words from '(which requires' to 'that day)' there were substituted '(which requires an election to be made not later than the end of a period of six months)'.

(6) Where the man who might be treated as the father of the child died before the passing of this Act—

- (a) subsections (5A) and (5B) of section 28 of the Act of 1990 shall have effect as if paragraph (d) of each subsection were omitted;
- (b) subsections (5C) and (5D) of that section of that Act shall have effect as if paragraph (e) of each subsection were omitted;

…

Anti-social Behaviour Act 2003

(2003 c. 38)

PART 3 PARENTAL RESPONSIBILITIES

Truancy and misbehaviour at school

19 Parenting contracts in cases of misbehaviour at school or truancy

(1) This section applies where a pupil has been excluded on disciplinary grounds from a relevant school for a fixed period or permanently.

(1A) This section also applies where a local authority or the governing body of a relevant school have reason to believe that a child who is a registered pupil at a relevant school has engaged in behaviour connected with the school which—

- (a) has caused, or is likely to cause—
    - (i) significant disruption to the education of other pupils, or
    - (ii) significant detriment to the welfare of the child himself or of other pupils or to the health or safety of any staff, or
- (b) forms part of a pattern of behaviour which (if continued) will give rise to a risk of future exclusion from the school on disciplinary grounds.

(1B) For the purposes of subsection (1A) the child's behaviour is connected with the school to the extent that it consists of—

- (a) conduct at the school, or
- (b) conduct elsewhere in circumstances in which it would be reasonable for the school to regulate his conduct.

(2) This section also applies where a child of compulsory school age has failed to attend regularly at

- (a) a relevant school at which he is a registered pupil,
- (b) any place at which education is provided for him in the circumstances mentioned in subsection (1) or (1A) of section 444ZA of the Education Act 1996, and
- (c) any place at which he is required to attend in the circumstances mentioned in subsection (1B) or (2) of that section.

(3) A local authority or the governing body of a relevant school may enter into a parenting contract with a parent of the pupil or child.

(4) A parenting contract is a document which contains—

(a) a statement by the parent that he agrees to comply with such requirements as may be specified in the document for such period as may be so specified, and

(b) a statement by the local authority or governing body that it agrees to provide support to the parent for the purpose of complying with those requirements.

(5) The requirements mentioned in subsection (4) may include (in particular) a requirement to attend a counselling or guidance programme.

(6) The purpose of the requirements mentioned in subsection (4)—

(a) in a case falling within subsection (1) or (1A), is to improve the behaviour of the pupil,

(b) in a case falling within subsection (2), is to ensure that the child attends regularly at the relevant school at which he is a registered pupil.

(7) A parenting contract must be signed by the parent and signed on behalf of the local authority or governing body.

(8) A parenting contract does not create any obligations in respect of whose breach any liability arises in contract or in tort.

(9) Local authorities and governing bodies of relevant schools must, in carrying out their functions in relation to parenting contracts, have regard to any guidance which is issued by the appropriate person from time to time for that purpose.

20 Parenting orders in cases of exclusion or potential exclusion from school

(1) Subsection (2) applies where—

(a) a pupil has been excluded on disciplinary grounds from a relevant school for a fixed period or permanently, and

(b) such conditions as may be prescribed in regulations made by the appropriate person are satisfied.

(2) A relevant body may apply to a magistrates' court for a parenting order in respect of a parent of the pupil.

(2A) A relevant body may also apply to a magistrates' court for a parenting order in respect of a pupil at a relevant school if—

(a) it appears to the body making the application that the pupil has engaged in behaviour which would warrant the exclusion of the pupil from the school on disciplinary grounds for a fixed period or permanently, and

(b) such conditions as may be prescribed in regulations made by the appropriate person are satisfied.

(2B) For the purposes of subsection (2A), there are to be disregarded—

(a) any practice restricting the use of exclusion at a particular school, or at schools of a particular description, and

(b) any grounds that might exist for not excluding the pupil, to the extent that those grounds relate to his education or welfare after exclusion.

(3) If an application is made under subsection (2) or (2A), the court may make a parenting order in respect of a pupil if it is satisfied—

(a) in the case of an application under subsection (2A), that the pupil has engaged in behaviour of the kind mentioned in that subsection, and

(b) in any case, that the making of the order would be desirable in the interests of improving the behaviour of the pupil.

(4) A parenting order is an order which requires the parent—

(a) to comply, for a period not exceeding twelve months, with such requirements as are specified in the order, and

(b) subject to subsection (5), to attend, for a concurrent period not exceeding three months, such counselling or guidance programme as may be specified in directions given by the responsible officer.

(5) A parenting order under this section may, but need not, include a requirement mentioned in subsection (4)(b) in any case where a parenting order under this section or any other enactment has been made in respect of the parent on a previous occasion.

(6) A counselling or guidance programme which a parent is required to attend by virtue of subsection (4)(b) may be or include a residential course but only if the court is satisfied that the following two conditions are fulfilled.

(7) The first condition is that the attendance of the parent at a residential course is likely to be more effective than his attendance at a non-residential course in improving the behaviour of the pupil.

(8) The second condition is that any interference with family life which is likely to result from the attendance of the parent at a residential course is proportionate in all the circumstances.

(9) In this section 'a relevant body' means—

(a) a local authority,

(b) the governing body of any relevant school in England at which the pupil to whom the application relates is a pupil or from which he has been excluded.

21   Parenting orders: supplemental

(1) In deciding whether to make a parenting order under section 20, a court must take into account (amongst other things)—

(a) any refusal by the parent to enter into a parenting contract under section 19 in respect of the pupil in a case falling within subsection (1) or (1A) of that section, or

(b) if the parent has entered into such a parenting contract, any failure by the parent to comply with the requirements specified in the contract.

(1A) In deciding whether to make a parenting order under section 20, a court must also take into account any failure by the parent without reasonable excuse to attend a reintegration interview under section 102 of the Education and Inspections Act 2006 (reintegration interview in case of fixed period exclusion) when requested to do so in accordance with regulations under that section.

(2) Before making a parenting order under section 20 in the case of a pupil under the age of 16, a court must obtain and consider information about the pupil's family circumstances and the likely effect of the order on those circumstances.

(3) Subsections (3) to (7) of section 9 of the Crime and Disorder Act 1998 (c. 37) (supplemental provisions about parenting orders) are to apply in relation to a parenting order under section 20 as they apply in relation to a parenting order under section 8 of that Act.

...

(5) Local authorities, governing bodies, head teachers and responsible officers must, in carrying out their functions in relation to parenting orders, have regard to any guidance which is issued by the appropriate person from time to time for that purpose.

22   Parenting orders: appeals

(1) An appeal lies to the Crown Court against the making of a parenting order under section 20.

(2) Subsections (2) and (3) of section 10 of the Crime and Disorder Act 1998 (appeals against parenting orders) are to apply in relation to an appeal under this section as they apply in relation to an appeal under subsection (1)(b) of that section.

...

Courts Act 2003

(2003 c. 39)

PART 7 PROCEDURE RULES AND PRACTICE DIRECTIONS

...

Family Procedure Rules and practice directions

75 Family Procedure Rules

(1) There are to be rules of court (to be called 'Family Procedure Rules') governing the practice and procedure to be followed in family proceedings.

(2) Family Procedure Rules are to be made by a committee known as the Family Procedure Rule Committee.

(3) 'Family proceedings' means—

    (a) proceedings in the family court, and

    (b) proceedings in the Family Division of the High Court which are business assigned, by or under section 61 of (and Schedule 1 to) the Senior Courts Act 1981, to that Division of the High Court and no other.

(4) The power to make Family Procedure Rules includes power to make different provision for different cases or different areas, including different provision—

    (a) for a specified court or description of courts, or

    (b) for specified descriptions of proceedings or a specified jurisdiction.

(5) Any power to make Family Procedure Rules is to be exercised with a view to securing that—

    (a) the family justice system is accessible, fair and efficient, and

    (b) the rules are both simple and simply expressed.

76 Further provision about scope of Family Procedure Rules

(1) Family Procedure Rules may not be made in respect of matters which may be dealt with in probate rules made under section 127 of the 1981 Act.

(2) Family Procedure Rules may—

    (a) modify or exclude the application of any provision of the County Courts Act 1984 (c. 28), and

    (aa) provide, subject to any provision that may be made in rules under section 31O(1) of the Matrimonial and Family Proceedings Act 1984, for any functions of a court in family proceedings to be carried out by officers or other staff of the court.

(2A) Family Procedure Rules may, for the purposes of the law relating to contempt of court, authorise the publication in such circumstances as may be specified of information relating to family proceedings held in private.

(2B) In subsection (2A) 'family proceedings held in private' means family proceedings at which the general public have no right to be present.

(3) Family Procedure Rules may modify the rules of evidence as they apply to family proceedings.

(4) Family Procedure Rules may apply any rules of court (including in particular Civil Procedure Rules) which relate to—

    (a) courts which are outside the scope of Family Procedure Rules, or

    (b) proceedings other than family proceedings.

(5) Any rules of court, not made by the Family Procedure Rule Committee, which apply to proceedings of a particular kind in a court within the scope of Family Procedure Rules may be applied by Family Procedure Rules to family proceedings in such a court.

(6) In subsections (4) and (5) 'rules of court' includes any provision governing the practice and procedure of a court which is made by or under an enactment.

(7) Where Family Procedure Rules may be made by applying other rules, the other rules may be applied—

    (a) to any extent,

    (b) with or without modification, and

    (c) as amended from time to time.

(8) Family Procedure Rules may, instead of providing for any matter, refer to provision made or to be made about that matter by directions.

…

81   Practice directions relating to family proceedings

(1) Directions may be given in accordance with Part 1 of Schedule 2 to the Constitutional Reform Act 2005 as to the practice and procedure of—

    (za) the civil division of the Court of Appeal in proceedings on appeal from the Family Division of the High Court or from the family court,

    (zb) the Family Division of the High Court in proceedings which are business assigned, by or under section 61 of (and Schedule 1 to) the Senior Courts Act 1981, to that Division of the High Court and no other, and

    (aa) the family court.

(2) Directions as to the practice and procedure mentioned in subsection (1) which are given otherwise than under subsection (1) may not be given without the approval of—

    (a) the Lord Chancellor, and

    (b) the Lord Chief Justice.

(2A) Directions as to the practice and procedure mentioned in subsection (1) (whether given under subsection (1) or otherwise) may provide for any matter which, by virtue of paragraph 3 of Schedule 1 to the Civil Procedure Act 1997, may be provided for by Civil Procedure Rules.

(3) The power to give directions under subsection (1) includes power—

    (a) to vary or revoke directions as to the practice and procedure mentioned in subsection (1), whether given under subsection (1) or otherwise,

    (b) to give directions containing different provision for different cases (including different areas), and

    (c) to give directions containing provision for a specific court, for specific proceedings or for a specific jurisdiction.

(4) Subsection (2)(a) does not apply to directions to the extent that they consist of guidance about any of the following—

    (a) the application or interpretation of the law;

    (b) the making of judicial decisions.

(5) Subsection (2)(a) does not apply to directions to the extent that they consist of criteria for determining which judges may be allocated to hear particular categories of case; but the directions may, to that extent, be given only—

    (a) after consulting the Lord Chancellor, and

    (b) with the approval of the Lord Chief Justice.

(5) In this section—

'Civil Procedure Rules' has the same meaning as in the Civil Procedure Act 1997;

…

PART 9   FINAL PROVISIONS

107   Interpretation

(1) In this Act—

'the 1933 Act' means the Children and Young Persons Act 1933 (c. 12);

'the 1968 Act' means the Criminal Appeal Act 1968 (c. 19);

…

'the 1980 Act' means the Magistrates' Courts Act 1980 (c. 43);

'the 1981 Act' means the Supreme Court Act 1981 (c. 54);

'the 1990 Act' means the Courts and Legal Services Act 1990 (c. 41);

'the 1997 Act' means the Civil Procedure Act 1997 (c. 12).

...

Section 97(1)

SCHEDULE 5

COLLECTION OF FINES AND OTHER SUMS IMPOSED ON CONVICTION

PART 1 INTRODUCTORY

Application of Schedule

1.—This Schedule applies if a person aged 18 or over ('P') is liable to pay a sum which is or is treated for the purposes of Part 3 of the 1980 Act as a sum adjudged to be paid by a conviction of a magistrates' court.

Meaning of 'the sum due'

2.—(1) In this Schedule 'the sum due' means the sum adjudged to be paid as mentioned in paragraph 1—

(2) For the purposes of this Schedule—

a 'fine' does not include any pecuniary forfeiture or pecuniary compensation payable on conviction; and

'a sum required to be paid by a compensation order' means any sum required to be paid by an order made under section 130(1) of the Powers of Criminal Courts (Sentencing) Act 2000.

Meaning of 'existing defaulter' etc.

3.—(1) For the purposes of this Schedule, P is an existing defaulter if it is shown that—

    (b)   the sum due or any other sum is registered for enforcement against him as a fine under—

        (i)   section 71 of the Road Traffic Offenders Act 1988,

        (ii)   section 9 of the Criminal Justice and Police Act 2001, or

        (iii) any other enactment specified in fines collection regulations,

    (c)   he is in default on a collection order in respect of another sum falling within paragraph 1, or

    (d)   he is in default in payment of another sum falling within paragraph 1 but in respect of which no collection order has been made.

(2) For the purposes of this Schedule, P's existing default can be disregarded only if he shows that there was an adequate reason for it.

(3) Sub-paragraph (2) is subject to sub-paragraph (4).

(4) Where a sum is registered for enforcement against P as mentioned in sub-paragraph (1)(b), P's existing default is not one which can be disregarded for the purposes of the following provisions of this Schedule.

(7) 'Collection order' means an order made under Part 4 of this Schedule.

...

PART 3 ATTACHMENT OF EARNINGS ORDERS AND APPLICATIONS FOR BENEFIT DEDUCTIONS

Application of Part

7. —(1) This Part does not apply where the court is leaving P's case following an appeal under paragraph 23, 32, 37(9) or 37A(4).

(2) In the following provisions of this Part, 'the relevant court' means—

(a) the court which is imposing the liability to pay the sum due, or

(b) the magistrates' court responsible for enforcing payment of the sum due.

(3) For the purposes of this Schedule—

(a) an attachment of earnings order, or

(b) an application for benefit deductions,

is an order or application to secure the payment of the whole of the sum due.

Attachment of earnings order or application for benefit deductions where P is liable to pay compensation

7A. —(1) This paragraph applies if the sum due consists of or includes a sum required to be paid by a compensation order.

(2) The relevant court must make an attachment of earnings order if it appears to the court—

(a) that P is in employment, and

(b) that it is not impracticable or inappropriate to make the order.

(3) The relevant court must make an application for benefit deductions if it appears to the court—

(a) that P is entitled to a relevant benefit, and

(b) that it is not impracticable or inappropriate to make the application.

(4) If it appears to the court that (apart from this sub-paragraph) both sub-paragraph (2) and sub-paragraph (3) would apply, the court must make either an attachment of earnings order or an application for benefit deductions.

Attachment of earnings order or application for benefit deductions without P's consent

8. —(1) This paragraph applies if—

(a) paragraph 7A does not apply, and

(b) the relevant court concludes that P is an existing defaulter and that his existing default (or defaults) cannot be disregarded.

(2) The court must make an attachment of earnings order if it appears to the court—

(a) that P is in employment, and

(b) that it is not impracticable or inappropriate to make the order.

(3) The court must make an application for benefit deductions if it appears to the court—

(a) that P is entitled to a relevant benefit, and

(b) that it is not impracticable or inappropriate to make the application.

(4) If it appears to the court that (apart from this sub-paragraph) both sub-paragraph (2) and sub-paragraph (3) would apply, the court must make either an attachment of earnings order or an application for benefit deductions.

Attachment of earnings order or application for benefit deductions with P's consent

9. —(1) This paragraph applies if—

(a) paragraph 7A does not apply, and

(b) the relevant court concludes that P is not an existing defaulter or, if he is, that his existing default (or defaults) can be disregarded.

(2) The court may make—

(a) an attachment of earnings order, or

(b) an application for benefit deductions,

if P consents.

…

Meaning of 'relevant benefit' and 'application for benefit deductions'

10. In this Schedule—
    (a) 'relevant benefit' means a benefit from which the Secretary of State may make deductions by virtue of section 24 of the Criminal Justice Act 1991 (recovery of fines etc. by deductions from income support etc.), and
    (b) 'application for benefit deductions', in relation to a relevant benefit, means an application to the Secretary of State asking him to deduct sums from any amounts payable to P by way of the benefit.

...

Criminal Justice Act 2003

(2003 c. 44)

* The provisions reproduced here are as modified for the purposes of enforcement of contact orders under the Children Act 1989, as amended by the Children and Adoption Act 2006.
...

PART 12 SENTENCING

...

Chapter 4 Further provisions about orders under Chapters 2 and 3

Introductory

196 Meaning of 'relevant order' etc

(1) In this Chapter 'relevant order' means—
    (a) a community order, or
    (c) a suspended sentence order.
(1A) In this Chapter 'suspended sentence order' means a suspended sentence order that imposes one or more community requirements.
...

197 Meaning of 'the responsible officer'

(1) For the purposes of this Part, 'the responsible officer', in relation to an offender to whom a relevant order relates, means—
    ...
    (c) in any other case, the qualifying officer who, as respects the offender, is for the time being responsible for discharging the functions conferred by this Part on the responsible officer.
(2) The following are qualifying officers for the purposes of subsection (1)(c)—
    (a) in a case where the offender is aged under 18 at the time when the relevant order is made, an officer of a local probation board appointed for or assigned to the local justice area for the time being specified in the order or a member of a youth offending team established by a local authority for the time being specified in the order;
    (b) in any other case, an officer of a local probation board appointed for or assigned to the local justice area for the time being specified in the order.
(3) The Secretary of State may by order—
    (a) amend subsections (1) and (2), and
    (b) make any other amendments of this Part that appear to him to be necessary or expedient in consequence of any amendment made by virtue of paragraph (a).

(4) An order under subsection (3) may, in particular, provide for the court to determine which of two or more descriptions of 'responsible officer' is to apply in relation to any relevant order.

198 Duties of responsible officer

(1) Where a relevant order has effect, it is the duty of the responsible officer—

  (a) to make any arrangements that are necessary in connection with the requirements imposed by the order, and

  (b) to promote the offender's compliance with those requirements.

(1A) Subsection (1B) applies where—

  (a) an enforcement order is in force, and

  (b) an officer of the Children and Family Court Advisory and Support Service or a Welsh family proceedings officer (as defined in section 35 of the Children Act 2004) is required under section 11M of the Children Act 1989 to report on matters relating to the order.

(1B) The officer of the Service or the Welsh family proceedings officer may request the responsible officer to report to him on such matters relating to the order as he may require for the purpose of making a report under section 11M(1)(c) or (d); and it shall be the duty of the responsible officer to comply with such a request.

(2) In this section 'responsible officer' does not include a person falling within section 197(1)(a).

Requirements available in case of all offenders

199 Unpaid work requirement

(1) In this Part 'unpaid work requirement', in relation to a relevant order, means a requirement that the offender must perform unpaid work in accordance with section 200.

(2) The number of hours which a person may be required to work under an unpaid work requirement must be specified in the relevant order and must be in the aggregate—

  (a) not less than 40, and

  (b) not more than 200.

…

(5) Where on the same occasion and in relation to the same person the court makes more than one enforcement order imposing an unpaid work requirement, the court may direct that the hours of work specified in any of those requirements is to be concurrent with or additional to those specified in any other of those orders, but so that the total number of hours which are not concurrent does not exceed the maximum specified in subsection (2)(b).

200 Obligations of person subject to unpaid work requirement

(1) An offender in respect of whom an unpaid work requirement of a relevant order is in force must perform for the number of hours specified in the order such work at such times as he may be instructed by the responsible officer.

(2) Subject to paragraphs 7 and 9 of Schedule A1 to the Children Act 1989, the work required to be performed under an unpaid work requirement imposed by an enforcement order must be performed during a period of twelve months.

(2A) But the period of twelve months is not to run while the enforcement order is suspended under section 11J(9) of the Children Act 1989.

(3) Unless revoked, a community order imposing an unpaid work requirement remains in force until the offender has worked under it for the number of hours specified in it.

(4) Where an unpaid work requirement is imposed by a suspended sentence order, the supervision period as defined by section 189(1A) continues until the offender has worked under the order for the number of hours specified in the order, but does not continue beyond the end of the operational period as defined by section 189(1)(a).

…

Gender Recognition Act 2004

(2004 c. 7)

Applications for gender recognition certificate

1 Applications

(1) A person of either gender who is aged at least 18 may make an application for a gender recognition certificate on the basis of—

(a) living in the other gender, or

(b) having changed gender under the law of a country or territory outside the United Kingdom.

(2) In this Act 'the acquired gender', in relation to a person by whom an application under subsection (1) is or has been made, means—

(a) in the case of an application under paragraph (a) of that subsection, the gender in which the person is living, or

(b) in the case of an application under paragraph (b) of that subsection, the gender to which the person has changed under the law of the country or territory concerned.

(3) An application under subsection (1) is to be determined by a Gender Recognition Panel.

(4) Schedule 1 (Gender Recognition Panels) has effect.

2 Determination of applications

(1) In the case of an application under section 1(1)(a), the Panel must grant the application if satisfied that the applicant—

(a) has or has had gender dysphoria,

(b) has lived in the acquired gender throughout the period of two years ending with the date on which the application is made,

(c) intends to continue to live in the acquired gender until death, and

(d) complies with the requirements imposed by and under section 3.

(2) In the case of an application under section 1(1)(b), the Panel must grant the application if satisfied—

(a) that the country or territory under the law of which the applicant has changed gender is an approved country or territory, and

(b) that the applicant complies with the requirements imposed by and under section 3.

(3) The Panel must reject an application under section 1(1) if not required by subsection (1) or (2) to grant it.

(3A) This section does not apply to an application under section 1(1)(a) which states that it is an application for a certificate to be granted in accordance with section 3A.

(4) In this Act 'approved country or territory' means a country or territory prescribed by order made by the Secretary of State after consulting the Scottish Ministers and the Department of Finance and Personnel in Northern Ireland.

3 Evidence

(1) An application under section 1(1)(a) must include either—

(a) a report made by a registered medical practitioner practising in the field of gender dysphoria and a report made by another registered medical practitioner (who may, but need not, practise in that field), or

(b) a report made by a registered psychologist practising in that field and a report made by a registered medical practitioner (who may, but need not, practise in that field).

(2) But subsection (1) is not complied with unless a report required by that subsection and made by—

(a) a registered medical practitioner, or

(b) a registered psychologist,

practising in the field of gender dysphoria includes details of the diagnosis of the applicant's gender dysphoria.

(3) And subsection (1) is not complied with in a case where—

(a) the applicant has undergone or is undergoing treatment for the purpose of modifying sexual characteristics, or

(b) treatment for that purpose has been prescribed or planned for the applicant, unless at least one of the reports required by that subsection includes details of it.

(4) An application under section 1(1)(a) must also include a statutory declaration by the applicant that the applicant meets the conditions in section 2(1)(b) and (c).

(5) An application under section 1(1)(b) must include evidence that the applicant has changed gender under the law of an approved country or territory.

(6) Any application under section 1(1) must include—

(a) a statutory declaration as to whether or not the applicant is married or a civil partner,

(b) any other information or evidence required by an order made by the Secretary of State, and

(c) any other information or evidence which the Panel which is to determine the application may require,

and may include any other information or evidence which the applicant wishes to include.

(6A) If the applicant is married, an application under section 1(1) must include a statutory declaration as to whether the marriage is a marriage under the law of England and Wales, of Scotland, of Northern Ireland, or of a country or territory outside the United Kingdom.

(6B) If the applicant is married, and the marriage is a protected marriage, an application under section 1(1) must also include—

(a) a statutory declaration by the applicant's spouse that the spouse consents to the marriage continuing after the issue of a full gender recognition certificate ('a statutory declaration of consent') (if the spouse has made such a declaration), or

(b) a statutory declaration by the applicant that the applicant's spouse has not made a statutory declaration of consent (if that is the case).

(6C) If an application includes a statutory declaration of consent by the applicant's spouse, the Gender Recognition Panel must give the spouse notice that the application has been made.

. . .

(8) If the Panel which is to determine the application requires information or evidence under subsection (6)(c) it must give reasons for doing so.

(9) This section does not apply to an application under section 1(1)(a) which states that it is an application for a certificate to be granted in accordance with section 3A.

3A   Alternative grounds for granting applications

(1) This section applies to an application under section 1(1)(a) which states that it is an application for a certificate to be granted in accordance with this section.

(2) The Panel must grant the application if satisfied that the applicant complies with the requirements imposed by and under section 3B and meets the conditions in subsections (3) to (6).

(3) The first condition is that the applicant was a party to a protected marriage or a protected civil partnership on or before the date the application was made.

(4) The second condition is that the applicant—

(a) was living in the acquired gender six years before the commencement of section 12 of the Marriage (Same Sex Couples) Act 2013,

(b) continued to live in the acquired gender until the date the application was made, and

(c) intends to continue to live in the acquired gender until death.

(5) The third condition is that the applicant—

(a) has or has had gender dysphoria, or

(b) has undergone surgical treatment for the purpose of modifying sexual characteristics.

(6) The fourth condition is that the applicant is ordinarily resident in England, Wales or Scotland.

(7) The Panel must reject the application if not required by subsection (2) to grant it.

3B Evidence for granting applications on alternative grounds

(1) This section applies to an application under section 1(1)(a) which states that it is an application for a certificate to be granted in accordance with section 3A.

(2) The application must include either—

    (a) a report made by a registered medical practitioner, or

    (b) a report made by a registered psychologist practising in the field of gender dysphoria.

(3) If the application is based on the applicant having or having had gender dysphoria—

    (a) the reference in subsection (2) to a registered medical practitioner is to one practising in the field of gender dysphoria, and

    (b) that subsection is not complied with unless the report includes details of the diagnosis of the applicant's gender dysphoria.

(4) Subsection (2) is not complied with in a case where—

    (a) the applicant has undergone or is undergoing treatment for the purpose of modifying sexual characteristics, or

    (b) treatment for that purpose has been prescribed or planned for the applicant,

unless the report required by that subsection includes details of it.

(5) The application must also include a statutory declaration by the applicant that the applicant meets the conditions in section 3A(3) and (4).

(6) The application must include—

    (a) a statutory declaration as to whether or not the applicant is married or a civil partner,

    (b) any other information or evidence required by an order made by the Secretary of State, and

    (c) any other information or evidence which the Panel which is to determine the application may require,

and may include any other information or evidence which the applicant wishes to include.

(7) If the applicant is married, the application must include a statutory declaration as to whether the marriage is a marriage under the law of England and Wales, of Scotland, of Northern Ireland, or of a country or territory outside the United Kingdom.

(8) If the applicant is married, and the marriage is a protected marriage, the application must also include—

    (a) a statutory declaration of consent by the applicant's spouse (if the spouse has made such a declaration), or

    (b) a statutory declaration by the applicant that the applicant's spouse has not made a statutory declaration of consent (if that is the case).

(9) If the application includes a statutory declaration of consent by the applicant's spouse, the Panel must give the spouse notice that the application has been made.

(10) If the Panel which is to determine the application requires information or evidence under subsection (6)(c) it must give reasons for doing so.

4 Successful applications

(1) If a Gender Recognition Panel grants an application under section 1(1) it must issue a gender recognition certificate to the applicant.

(2) The certificate is to be a full gender recognition certificate if—

    (a) the applicant is neither a civil partner nor married,

    (b) the applicant is a party to a protected marriage and the applicant's spouse consents to the marriage continuing after the issue of a full gender recognition certificate, or

    (c) the applicant is a party to a protected civil partnership and the Panel has decided to issue a full gender recognition certificate to the other party to the civil partnership.

(3) The certificate is to be an interim gender recognition certificate if—

    (a) the applicant is a party to a protected marriage and the applicant's spouse does not consent to the marriage continuing after the issue of a full gender recognition certificate,

    (b) the applicant is a party to a marriage that is not a protected marriage,

    (c) the applicant is a party to a protected civil partnership and the other party to the civil partnership has not made an application under section 1(1),

    (d) the applicant is a party to a protected civil partnership and the Panel has decided not to issue a full gender recognition certificate to the other party to the civil partnership, or

    (e) the applicant is a party to a civil partnership that is not a protected civil partnership.

(3A) If a Gender Recognition Panel issues a full gender recognition certificate under this section to an applicant who is a party to a protected marriage, the Panel must give the applicant's spouse notice of the issue of the certificate.

(3B) Subsection (2)(c) is subject to section 5B.

(4) Schedule 2 (annulment or dissolution of marriage after issue of interim gender recognition certificate) has effect.

...

Issue of full certificate after interim certificate: applicant married

4A Married person with interim certificate: issue of full certificate

(1) A Gender Recognition Panel must issue a full gender recognition certificate to a person in either of the following cases.

(2) Case A is where, on an application by the person, the Panel is satisfied that—

    (a) an interim gender recognition certificate has been issued to the person;

    (b) the person was a party to a protected marriage at the time when the interim gender recognition certificate was issued;

    (c) the person is a party to a protected marriage; and

    (d) the person's spouse now consents to the marriage continuing after the issue of the full gender recognition certificate.

(3) Case B is where, on an application by the person, the Panel is satisfied that—

    (a) an interim gender recognition certificate has been issued to the person;

    (b) the person was a party to a civil partnership at the time when the interim gender recognition certificate was issued;

    (c) a conversion application has been made within the period of six months beginning with the day on which that certificate was issued;

    (d) the conversion application has resulted in the civil partnership being converted into a marriage;

    (e) the person is a party to that marriage; and

    (f) the person's spouse consents to the marriage continuing after the issue of the full gender recognition certificate.

(4) If, on an application under subsection (2) or (3), the Panel is not satisfied as mentioned in that subsection, the Panel must reject the application.

(5) An application under subsection (2) must be made within the period of six months beginning with the day on which the interim gender recognition certificate is issued.

(6) An application under subsection (3) must be made within the period of six months beginning with the day on which the civil partnership is converted into a marriage.

(7) An application under subsection (2) or (3) must include a statutory declaration of consent made by the person's spouse.

(8) An application under subsection (3) must also include—

    (a) evidence of the date on which the conversion application was made, and

    (b) evidence of the conversion of the civil partnership into a marriage.

(9) If an application is made under this section, the Gender Recognition Panel must give the applicant's spouse—

(a) notice of the application; and

(b) if the Panel grants the application, notice of the issue of the full gender recognition certificate.

(10) In this section 'conversion application' means an application for the conversion of a civil partnership into a marriage under regulations under section 9 of the Marriage (Same Sex Couples) Act 2013.

4B   Application under section 4A: death of spouse

(1) In a case where an application is made under section 4A(2) or (3) and the applicant's spouse dies before the application is determined—

(a) the application is to be treated as an application, made under section 5(2) in a case where a spouse has died, for a full gender recognition certificate to be issued; and

(b) that application is to be treated as having been made at the time when the application under section 4A was made.

(2) The Gender Recognition Panel determining the application must specify the period within which the applicant is to produce the required evidence in support of the new application.

(3) In this section—

'new application' means the application under section 5(2) which the person is, by virtue of subsection (1), treated as having made;

'required evidence' means the evidence required by section 5(4).

Issue of full certificate after interim certificate: applicant no longer married or civil partner

5   Issue of full certificates where applicant has been married

(1) A court which—

(a) makes absolute a decree of nullity granted on the ground that an interim gender recognition certificate has been issued to a party to the marriage, or

(b) ...

must, on doing so, issue a full gender recognition certificate to that party and send a copy to the Secretary of State.

(2) If an interim gender recognition certificate has been issued to a person and either—

(a) the person's marriage is dissolved or annulled (otherwise than on the ground mentioned in subsection (1)) in proceedings instituted during the period of six months beginning with the day on which it was issued, or

(b) the person's spouse dies within that period,

the person may make an application for a full gender recognition certificate at any time within the period specified in subsection (3) (unless the person is again married or is a civil partner).

(3) That period is the period of six months beginning with the day on which the marriage is dissolved or annulled or the death occurs.

(4) An application under subsection (2) must include evidence of the dissolution or annulment of the marriage and the date on which proceedings for it were instituted, or of the death of the spouse and the date on which it occurred.

(5) An application under subsection (2) is to be determined by a Gender Recognition Panel.

(6) The Panel—

(a) must grant the application if satisfied that the applicant is neither married nor a civil partner, and

(b) otherwise must reject it.

(7) If the Panel grants the application it must issue a full gender recognition certificate to the applicant.

5A   Issue of full certificates where applicant has been a civil partner

(1) A court which—

(a) makes final a nullity order made on the ground that an interim gender recognition certificate has been issued to a civil partner, or

(b) (in Scotland) grants a decree of dissolution on that ground,

must, on doing so, issue a full gender recognition certificate to that civil partner and send a copy to the Secretary of State.

(2) If an interim gender recognition certificate has been issued to a person and either—

(a) the person's civil partnership is dissolved or annulled (otherwise than on the ground mentioned in subsection (1)) in proceedings instituted during the period of six months beginning with the day on which it was issued, or

(b) the person's civil partner dies within that period,

the person may make an application for a full gender recognition certificate at any time within the period specified in subsection (3) (unless the person is again a civil partner or is married).

(3) That period is the period of six months beginning with the day on which the civil partnership is dissolved or annulled or the death occurs.

(4) An application under subsection (2) must include evidence of the dissolution or annulment of the civil partnership and the date on which proceedings for it were instituted, or of the death of the civil partner and the date on which it occurred.

(5) An application under subsection (2) is to be determined by a Gender Recognition Panel.

(6) The Panel—

(a) must grant the application if satisfied that the applicant is neither a civil partner nor married, and

(b) otherwise must reject it.

(7) If the Panel grants the application it must issue a full gender recognition certificate to the applicant.

Other provision about applications and certificates

5B   Applications by both civil partners

(1) This section applies where the Panel decides to issue a full gender recognition certificate to a party to a protected civil partnership.

(2) The Panel must not issue the full gender recognition certificate to that person unless the Panel issues a full gender recognition certificate to the other party to the protected civil partnership.

(3) In such a case, the Panel must issue both certificates on the same day.

(4) Those certificates take effect at the beginning of the day on which they are issued.

6   Errors

(1) Where a gender recognition certificate has been issued to a person, the person or the Secretary of State may make an application for—

(a) an interim gender recognition certificate, on the ground that a full gender recognition certificate has incorrectly been issued instead of an interim certificate;

(b) a full gender recognition certificate, on the ground that an interim gender recognition certificate has incorrectly been issued instead of a full certificate; or

(c) a corrected certificate, on the ground that the certificate which has been issued contains an error.

(2) If the certificate was issued by a court the application is to be determined by the court but in any other case it is to be determined by a Gender Recognition Panel.

(3) The court or Panel—

(a) must grant the application if satisfied that the ground on which the application is made is correct, and

(b) otherwise must reject it.

(4) If the court or Panel grants the application it must issue a correct, or a corrected, gender recognition certificate to the applicant.

...

8   Appeals etc.

(1) An applicant to a Gender Recognition Panel under section 1(1), 4A, 5(2), 5A(2) or 6(1) may appeal to the High Court, family court...on a point of law against a decision by the Panel to reject the application.

(2) An appeal under subsection (1) must be heard in private if the applicant so requests.

(3) On such an appeal the court must—

    (a) allow the appeal and issue the certificate applied for,

    (b) allow the appeal and refer the matter to the same or another Panel for re-consideration, or

    (c) dismiss the appeal.

(4) If an application under section 1(1) is rejected, the applicant may not make another application before the end of the period of six months beginning with the date on which it is rejected.

(5) If an application under section 1(1), 4A, 5(2), 5A(2) or 6(1) is granted but the Secretary of State considers that its grant was secured by fraud, the Secretary of State may refer the case to the High Court, family court...

(5A) If an application under section 1(1), 4A, 5(2), 5A(2) or 6(1) is granted, the applicant's spouse may apply to the High Court or Court of Session to quash the decision to grant the application on the grounds that its grant was secured by fraud.

(6) On a reference under subsection (5) or an application under subsection (5A) the court—

    (a) must either quash or confirm the decision to grant the application, and

    (b) if it quashes it, must revoke the gender recognition certificate issued on the grant of the application and may make any order which it considers appropriate in consequence of, or otherwise in connection with, doing so.

Consequences of issue of gender recognition certificate etc.

9   General

(1) Where a full gender recognition certificate is issued to a person, the person's gender becomes for all purposes the acquired gender (so that, if the acquired gender is the male gender, the person's sex becomes that of a man and, if it is the female gender, the person's sex becomes that of a woman).

(2) Subsection (1) does not affect things done, or events occurring, before the certificate is issued; but it does operate for the interpretation of enactments passed, and instruments and other documents made, before the certificate is issued (as well as those passed or made afterwards).

(3) Subsection (1) is subject to provision made by this Act or any other enactment or any subordinate legislation.

10   Registration

(1) Where there is a UK birth register entry in relation to a person to whom a full gender recognition certificate is issued, the Secretary of State must send a copy of the certificate to the appropriate Registrar General.

(1A) Where a full gender recognition certificate is issued to a person who is a party to—

    (a) a marriage under the law of England and Wales, or

    (b) a civil partnership under that law,

the Secretary of State must send a copy of the certificate to the Registrar General for England and Wales.

(2) In this Act 'UK birth register entry', in relation to a person to whom a full gender recognition certificate is issued, means—

    (a) an entry of which a certified copy is kept by a Registrar General, or

    (b) an entry in a register so kept,

containing a record of the person's birth or adoption (or, if there would otherwise be more than one, the most recent).

...

11A   Change in gender of party to marriage

(1) This section applies in relation to a protected marriage if (by virtue of section 4(2)(b) or 4A) a full gender recognition certificate is issued to a party to the marriage.

(2) The continuity of the protected marriage is not affected by the relevant change in gender.

(3) If the protected marriage is a foreign marriage—

(a) the continuity of the marriage continues by virtue of subsection (2) notwithstanding any impediment under the proper law of the marriage;

(b) the proper law of the marriage is not affected by its continuation by virtue of subsection (2).

(4) In this section—

'foreign marriage' means a marriage under the law of a country or territory outside the United Kingdom;

'impediment' means anything which affects the continuation of a marriage merely by virtue of the relevant change in gender;

'proper law', in relation to a protected marriage, means the law of the country or territory under which the marriage was entered into;

'relevant change in gender' means the change or changes of gender occurring by virtue of the issue of the full gender recognition certificate or certificates.

11B   Change in gender of civil partners

The continuity of a civil partnership is not affected by the issuing of full gender recognition certificates (by virtue of section 4(2)(c)) to both civil partners.

12   Parenthood

The fact that a person's gender has become the acquired gender under this Act does not affect the status of the person as the father or mother of a child.

13   Social security benefits and pensions

Schedule 5 (entitlement to benefits and pensions) has effect.

...

15   Succession etc.

The fact that a person's gender has become the acquired gender under this Act does not affect the disposal or devolution of property under a will or other instrument made before the appointed day.

16   Peerages etc.

The fact that a person's gender has become the acquired gender under this Act—

(a) does not affect the descent of any peerage or dignity or title of honour, and

(b) does not affect the devolution of any property limited (expressly or not) by a will or other instrument to devolve (as nearly as the law permits) along with any peerage or dignity or title of honour unless an intention that it should do so is expressed in the will or other instrument.

17   Trustees and personal representatives

(1) A trustee or personal representative is not under a duty, by virtue of the law relating to trusts or the administration of estates, to enquire, before conveying or distributing any property, whether a full gender recognition certificate has been issued to any person or revoked (if that fact could affect entitlement to the property).

(2) A trustee or personal representative is not liable to any person by reason of a conveyance or distribution of the property made without regard to whether a full gender recognition certificate has been issued to any person or revoked if the trustee or personal representative has not received notice of the fact before the conveyance or distribution.

(3) This section does not prejudice the right of a person to follow the property, or any property representing it, into the hands of another person who has received it unless that person has purchased it for value in good faith and without notice.

18 Orders where expectations defeated

(1) This section applies where the disposition or devolution of any property under a will or other instrument (made on or after the appointed day) is different from what it would be but for the fact that a person's gender has become the acquired gender under this Act.

(2) A person may apply to the High Court . . . for an order on the ground of being adversely affected by the different disposition or devolution of the property.

(3) The court may, if it is satisfied that it is just to do so, make in relation to any person benefiting from the different disposition or devolution of the property such order as it considers appropriate.

(4) An order may, in particular, make provision for—

(a) the payment of a lump sum to the applicant,

(b) the transfer of property to the applicant,

(c) the settlement of property for the benefit of the applicant,

(d) the acquisition of property and either its transfer to the applicant or its settlement for the benefit of the applicant.

(5) An order may contain consequential or supplementary provisions for giving effect to the order or for ensuring that it operates fairly as between the applicant and the other person or persons affected by it; and an order may, in particular, confer powers on trustees.

. . .

20 Gender-specific offences

(1) Where (apart from this subsection) a relevant gender-specific offence could be committed or attempted only if the gender of a person to whom a full gender recognition certificate has been issued were not the acquired gender, the fact that the person's gender has become the acquired gender does not prevent the offence being committed or attempted.

(2) An offence is a 'relevant gender-specific offence' if—

(a) either or both of the conditions in subsection (3) are satisfied, and

(b) the commission of the offence involves the accused engaging in sexual activity.

(3) The conditions are—

(a) that the offence may be committed only by a person of a particular gender, and

(b) that the offence may be committed only on, or in relation to, a person of a particular gender,

and the references to a particular gender include a gender identified by reference to the gender of the other person involved.

. . .

Supplementary

22 Prohibition on disclosure of information

(1) It is an offence for a person who has acquired protected information in an official capacity to disclose the information to any other person.

(2) 'Protected information' means information which relates to a person who has made an application under section 1(1) and which—

(a) concerns that application or any application by the person under section 4A, 5(2), 5A(2) or 6(1), or

(b) if the application under section 1(1) is granted, otherwise concerns the person's gender before it becomes the acquired gender.

(3) A person acquires protected information in an official capacity if the person acquires it—

(a) in connection with the person's functions as a member of the civil service, a constable or the holder of any other public office or in connection with the functions of a local or public authority or of a voluntary organisation,

(b) as an employer, or prospective employer, of the person to whom the information relates or as a person employed by such an employer or prospective employer, or

(c) in the course of, or otherwise in connection with, the conduct of business or the supply of professional services.

(4) But it is not an offence under this section to disclose protected information relating to a person if—

(a) the information does not enable that person to be identified,

(b) that person has agreed to the disclosure of the information,

(c) the information is protected information by virtue of subsection (2)(b) and the person by whom the disclosure is made does not know or believe that a full gender recognition certificate has been issued,

(d) the disclosure is in accordance with an order of a court or tribunal,

(e) the disclosure is for the purpose of instituting, or otherwise for the purposes of, proceedings before a court or tribunal,

(f) the disclosure is for the purpose of preventing or investigating crime,

(g) the disclosure is made to the Registrar General for England and Wales...

(h) the disclosure is made for the purposes of the social security system or a pension scheme,

(i) the disclosure is in accordance with provision made by an order under subsection (5), or

(j) the disclosure is in accordance with any provision of, or made by virtue of, an enactment other than this section.

...

(8) A person guilty of an offence under this section is liable on summary conviction to a fine not exceeding level 5 on the standard scale.

...

25 Interpretation

In this Act—

'the acquired gender' is to be construed in accordance with section 1(2),

'approved country or territory' has the meaning given by section 2(4),

'the appointed day' means the day appointed by order under section 26,

...

'full gender recognition certificate' and 'interim gender recognition certificate' mean the certificates issued as such under section 4, 5 or 5A and 'gender recognition certificate' means either of those sorts of certificate,

'gender dysphoria' means the disorder variously referred to as gender dysphoria, gender identity disorder and transsexualism,

'Gender Recognition Panel' (and 'Panel') is to be construed in accordance with Schedule 1,

'protected civil partnership' means a civil partnership under the law of England and Wales;

'protected marriage' means—

(a) a marriage under the law of England and Wales, or

(b) a marriage under the law of a country or territory outside the United Kingdom,

'registered psychologist' means a person registered in the part of the register maintained under the Health and Social Work Professions Order 2001 which relates to practitioner psychologists,

'statutory declaration of consent' has the meaning given by section 3(6B)(a),

'subordinate legislation' means an Order in Council, an order, rules, regulations, a scheme, a warrant, bye-laws or any other instrument made under an enactment, and

'UK birth register entry' has the meaning given by section 10(2).

...

SCHEDULE 1

GENDER RECOGNITION PANELS

List of persons eligible to sit

1.—(1) Subject to sub-paragraph (1A), the Lord Chancellor must . . . make appointments to a list of persons eligible to sit as members of Gender Recognition Panels.

(1A) The Lord Chancellor may appoint a person under sub-paragraph (1) only with the concurrence of all of the following—

(a) the Lord Chief Justice of England and Wales;

(b) the Lord President of the Court of Session;

(c) the Lord Chief Justice of Northern Ireland.

(2) The only persons who may be appointed to the list are persons who—

(a) have a relevant legal qualification ('legal members'), or

(b) are registered medical practitioners or registered psychologists ('medical members').

(3) The following have a relevant legal qualification—

(a) a person who has a 7 year general qualification within the meaning of section 71 of the Courts and Legal Services Act 1990 (c. 41),

(b) . . .

President

2.—(1) Subject to sub-paragraph (1A), the Lord Chancellor must . . . —

(a) appoint one of the legal members to be the President of Gender Recognition Panels ('the President'), and

(b) appoint another of the legal members to be the Deputy President of Gender Recognition Panels ('the Deputy President').

(1A) The Lord Chancellor may appoint a person under sub-paragraph (1) only with the concurrence of all of the following—

(a) the Lord Chief Justice of England and Wales;

(b) the Lord President of the Court of Session;

(c) the Lord Chief Justice of Northern Ireland.

. . .

Membership of panels

4.—(1) The President must make arrangements for determining the membership of Panels.

(2) The arrangements must ensure that a Panel determining an application under section 1(1)(a) includes—

(a) at least one legal member, and

(b) at least one medical member.

(3) But a Panel need not include a medical member when determining an application under section 1(1)(a) for a certificate to be granted in accordance with section 3A.

5.—The arrangements must ensure that a Panel determining an application under section 1(1)(b), 5(2), 5A(2) or 6(1) includes at least one legal member.

Procedure

6.—(1) Where a Panel consists of more than one member, either the President or Deputy President or another legal member nominated by the President must preside.

(2) Decisions of a Panel consisting of more than one member may be taken by majority vote (and, if its members are evenly split, the member presiding has a casting vote).

(3) Panels are to determine applications in private.

(4) A Panel must determine an application without a hearing unless the Panel considers that a hearing is necessary.

(5) The President may give directions about the practice and procedure of Panels.

(6) Panels must give reasons for their decisions.

(7) Where a Panel has determined an application, the Secretary of State must communicate to the applicant the Panel's decision and its reasons for making its decision.

...

SCHEDULE 3 REGISTRATION

PART 1 ENGLAND AND WALES

Introductory

1.—In this Part—

'the Registrar General' means the Registrar General for England and Wales, and

'the 1953 Act' means the Births and Deaths Registration Act 1953 (c. 20).

Gender Recognition Register

2.—(1) The Registrar General must maintain, in the General Register Office, a register to be called the Gender Recognition Register.

(2) In this Part 'the Gender Recognition Register' means the register maintained under sub-paragraph (1).

(3) The form in which the Gender Recognition Register is maintained is to be determined by the Registrar General.

(4) The Gender Recognition Register is not to be open to public inspection or search.

Entries in Gender Recognition Register and marking of existing birth register entries

3.—(1) If the Registrar General receives under section 10(1) a copy of a full gender recognition certificate issued to a person, the Registrar General must—

  (a) make an entry in the Gender Recognition Register containing such particulars as may be prescribed in relation to the person's birth and any other prescribed matter,

  (b) secure that the UK birth register entry is marked in such manner as may be prescribed, and

  (c) make traceable the connection between the entry in the Gender Recognition Register and the UK birth register entry.

(2) Sub-paragraph (1) does not apply if the certificate was issued after an application under section 6(1) and that sub-paragraph has already been complied with in relation to the person.

(3) No certified copy of the UK birth register entry and no short certificate of birth compiled from that entry is to include anything marked by virtue of sub-paragraph (1)(b).

(4) Information kept by the Registrar General for the purposes of sub-paragraph (1) (c) is not to be open to public inspection or search.

(5) 'Prescribed' means prescribed by regulations made by the Registrar General with the approval of the Secretary of State.

Indexing of entries in Gender Recognition Register

4.—(1) The Registrar General must make arrangements for each entry made in the Gender Recognition Register to be included in the relevant index kept in the General Register Office.

(2) Any right to search the relevant index includes the right to search entries included in it by virtue of sub-paragraph (1).

(3) Where by virtue of sub-paragraph (1) an index includes entries in the Gender Recognition Register, the index must not disclose that fact.

(4) 'The relevant index', in relation to an entry made in the Gender Recognition Register in relation to a person, means the index of the certified copies of entries in registers, or of entries in registers, which includes the person's UK birth register entry.

Certified copies of entries in Gender Recognition Register

5.—(1) Anyone who may have a certified copy of the UK birth register entry of a person issued with a full gender recognition certificate may have a certified copy of the entry made in relation to the person in the Gender Recognition Register.

(2) Any fee which would be payable for a certified copy of the person's UK birth register entry is payable for a certified copy of the entry made in relation to the person in the Gender Recognition Register.

(3) If the person's UK birth register entry is an entry in the Gender Recognition Register, sub-paragraph (1) applies as if the person's UK birth register entry were the most recent entry within section 10(2)(a) or (b) containing a record of the person's birth or adoption which is not an entry in the Gender Recognition Register.

(4) A certified copy of an entry in the Gender Recognition Register must not disclose the fact that the entry is contained in the Gender Recognition Register.

(5) A certified copy of an entry in the Gender Recognition Register must be sealed or stamped with the seal of the General Register Office.

Short certificates of birth compiled from Gender Recognition Register

6.—Where a short certificate of birth under section 33 of the 1953 Act is compiled from the Gender Recognition Register, the certificate must not disclose that fact.

Gender recognition register: re-registration

7.—(1) Section 10A of the 1953 Act (re-registration where parents not married) applies where an entry relating to a person's birth has been made in the Gender Recognition Register as where the birth of a child has been registered under that Act.

(2) In its application by virtue of sub-paragraph (1) section 10A has effect—

(a) as if the reference to the registrar in subsection (1) were to the Registrar General, and

(b) with the omission of subsection (2).

(3) Sections 14 and 14A of the 1953 Act (re-registration in cases of legitimation and after declaration of parentage) apply where an entry relating to a person's birth has been made in the Gender Recognition Register as if the references in those sections to the Registrar General authorising re-registration of the person's birth were to the Registrar General's re-registering it.

Correction etc. of Gender Recognition Register

8.—(1) Any power or duty of the Registrar General or any other person to correct, alter, amend, mark or cancel the marking of a person's UK birth register entry is exercisable, or falls to be performed, by the Registrar General in relation to an entry in the Gender Recognition Register which—

(a) relates to that person, and

(b) under paragraph 4(1) is included in the index which includes the person's UK birth register entry.

(2) If the person's UK birth register entry is an entry in the Gender Recognition Register, the references in sub-paragraph (1) to the person's UK birth register entry are to the most recent entry within section 10(2)(a) or (b) containing a record of the person's birth or adoption which is not an entry in the Gender Recognition Register.

(3) The Registrar General may correct the Gender Recognition Register by entry in the margin (without any alteration of the original entry) in consequence of the issue of a full gender recognition certificate after an application under section 6(1).

Revocation of gender recognition certificate etc.

9.—(1) This paragraph applies if, after an entry has been made in the Gender Recognition Register in relation to a person, the High Court ... makes an order under section 8(6) quashing the decision to grant the person's application under section 1(1), 5(2) or 5A(2).

(2) The High Court ... must inform the Registrar General.

(3) Subject to any appeal, the Registrar General must—

(a) cancel the entry in the Gender Recognition Register, and

(b) cancel, or secure the cancellation, of any marking of an entry relating to the person made by virtue of paragraph 3(1)(b).

Evidence

10.—(1) Section 34(5) of the 1953 Act (certified copy of entry in register under that Act deemed to be true copy) applies in relation to the Gender Recognition Register as if it were a register under that Act.

(2) A certified copy of an entry made in the Gender Recognition Register in relation to a person is to be received, without further or other proof, as evidence—

(a) if the relevant index is the index of the Adopted Children Register, of the matters of which a certified copy of an entry in that Register is evidence,

(b) if the relevant index is the index of the Parental Order Register, of the matters of which a certified copy of an entry in that Register is evidence, and

(c) otherwise, of the person's birth.

Registration of marriages and civil partnerships

11A.—(1) The Registrar General may make regulations about—

(a) the registration of qualifying marriages, and

(b) the registration of qualifying civil partnerships.

(2) The regulations may, in particular, provide for the maintenance of—

(a) a separate register in relation to qualifying marriages, and

(b) a separate register in relation to qualifying civil partnerships.

(3) In this paragraph—

'qualifying civil partnership' means a civil partnership under the law of England and Wales in a case where a full gender recognition certificate has been issued to each of the civil partners;

'qualifying marriage' means a marriage under the law of England and Wales in a case where a full gender recognition certificate has been issued to one, or each, of the spouses.

...

SCHEDULE 5 BENEFITS AND PENSIONS

PART 1 INTRODUCTORY

1.—This Schedule applies where a full gender recognition certificate is issued to a person.

PART 2 STATE BENEFITS

Introductory

2.—(1) In this Part of this Schedule 'the 1992 Act' means—

(a) in England and Wales and Scotland, the Social Security Contributions and Benefits Act 1992 (c. 4), ...

(2) In this Part of this Schedule 'the Administration Act' means—

(a) in England and Wales and Scotland, the Social Security Administration Act 1992 (c. 5), ...

(3) Expressions used in this Part of this Schedule and in Part 2 of the 1992 Act have the same meaning in this Part of this Schedule as in Part 2 of the 1992 Act.

Widowed mother's allowance

3.—(1) If (immediately before the certificate is issued) the person is, or but for section 1 of the Administration Act would be, entitled to a widowed mother's allowance under section 37 of the 1992 Act (allowance for woman whose husband died before 9th April 2001)—

(a) the person is not entitled to that allowance afterwards, but

(b) (instead) subsections (2) to (5) of section 39A of the 1992 Act (widowed parent's allowance) apply in relation to the person.

(2) If (immediately before the certificate is issued) the person is (actually) entitled to a widowed mother's allowance, the entitlement to widowed parent's allowance conferred by sub-paragraph (1) is not subject to section 1 of the Administration Act.

Widow's pension

4.—If (immediately before the certificate is issued) the person is entitled to a widow's pension under section 38 of the 1992 Act (pension for woman whose husband died before 9th April 2001), the person is not entitled to that pension afterwards.

Widowed parent's allowance

5.—If (immediately before the certificate is issued) the person is, or but for section 1 of the Administration Act would be, entitled to a widowed parent's allowance by virtue of subsection (1)(b) of section 39A of the 1992 Act (allowance for man whose wife died before 9th April 2001), subsections (2) to (5) of that section continue to apply in relation to the person afterwards.

Long-term incapacity benefit etc.

6.—If (immediately before the certificate is issued) the person is entitled to incapacity benefit, or a Category A retirement pension, under—

(a) section 40 of the 1992 Act (long-term incapacity benefit etc. for woman whose husband died before 9th April 2001), or

(b) section 41 of the 1992 Act (long-term incapacity benefit etc. for man whose wife died before that date),

the person is not so entitled afterwards.

Category A retirement pension

7.—(1) Any question—

(a) whether the person is entitled to a Category A retirement pension (under section 44 of the 1992 Act) for any period after the certificate is issued, and

(b) (if so) the rate at which the person is so entitled for the period,

is to be decided as if the person's gender had always been the acquired gender.

(2) Accordingly, if (immediately before the certificate is issued) the person—

(a) is a woman entitled to a Category A retirement pension, but

(b) has not attained the age of 65,

the person ceases to be so entitled when it is issued.

(3) And, conversely, if (immediately before the certificate is issued) the person—

(a) is a man who has attained the age at which a woman of the same age attains pensionable age, but

(b) has not attained the age of 65,

the person is to be treated for the purposes of section 44 of the 1992 Act as attaining pensionable age when it is issued.

(4) But sub-paragraph (1) does not apply if and to the extent that the decision of any question to which it refers is affected by—

(a) the payment or crediting of contributions, or the crediting of earnings, in respect of a period ending before the certificate is issued, or

(b) preclusion from regular employment by responsibilities at home for such a period.

(5) Paragraph 10 makes provision about deferment of Category A retirement pensions.

Category B retirement pension etc.

8.—(1) Any question whether the person is entitled to—

(a) a Category B retirement pension (under section 48A, 48B, 48BB or 51 of the 1992 Act), or

      (b) an increase in a Category A retirement pension under section 51A or 52 of the 1992 Act (increase in Category A retirement pension by reference to amount of Category B retirement pension),

for any period after the certificate is issued is (in accordance with section 9(1)) to be decided as if the person's gender were the acquired gender (but subject to sub-paragraph (4)).

    (2) Accordingly, if (immediately before the certificate is issued) the person is a woman entitled to—

      (a) a Category B retirement pension, or

      (b) an increase in a Category A retirement pension under section 51A or 52 of the 1992 Act, the person may cease to be so entitled when it is issued.

    (3) And, conversely, if (immediately before the certificate is issued) the person—

      (a) is a man who has attained the age at which a woman of the same age attains pensionable age, but

      (b) has not attained the age of 65,

the person is to be treated for the purposes of sections 48A, 48B and 48BB of the 1992 Act as attaining pensionable age when it is issued.

    (4) But a person who is a man (immediately before the certificate is issued) is not entitled to a Category B retirement pension under section 48B of the 1992 Act for any period after it is issued if the person—

      (a) attains (or has attained) the age of 65 before 6th April 2010, and

      (b) would not have been entitled to a Category B retirement pension under section 51 of the 1992 Act for that period if still a man.

    (5) Paragraph 10 makes provision about deferment of Category B retirement pensions.

Shared additional pension

9.—(1) Any question—

      (a) whether the person is entitled to a shared additional pension (under section 55A of the 1992 Act) for any period after the certificate is issued, and

      (b) (if so) the rate at which the person is so entitled for the period,

is to be decided on the basis of the person attaining pensionable age on the same date as someone of the acquired gender (and the same age).

    (2) Accordingly, if (immediately before the certificate is issued) the person—

      (a) is a woman entitled to a shared additional pension, but

      (b) has not attained the age of 65,

the person ceases to be so entitled when it is issued.

    (3) And, conversely, if (immediately before the certificate is issued) the person—

      (a) is a man who has attained the age at which a woman of the same age attains pensionable age, but

      (b) has not attained the age of 65,

the person is to be treated for the purposes of section 55A of the 1992 Act as attaining pensionable age when it is issued.

    (4) Paragraph 10 makes provision about deferment of shared additional pensions.

Deferment of pensions

10.—(1) The person's entitlement to—

      (a) a Category A retirement pension,

      (b) a Category B retirement pension, or

      (c) a shared additional pension,

is not to be taken to have been deferred for any period ending before the certificate is issued unless the condition in sub-paragraph (2) is satisfied.

    (2) The condition is that the entitlement both—

      (a) was actually deferred during the period, and

(b) would have been capable of being so deferred had the person's gender been the acquired gender.

Category C retirement pension for widows

11.—If (immediately before the certificate is issued) the person is entitled to a Category C retirement pension under section 78(2) of the 1992 Act, the person is not entitled to that pension afterwards.

Graduated retirement benefit: Great Britain

12.—(1) The provision that may be made by regulations under paragraph 15 of Schedule 3 to the Social Security (Consequential Provisions) Act 1992 (c. 6) (power to retain provisions repealed by Social Security Act 1973 (c. 38), with or without modification, for transitional purposes) includes provision modifying the preserved graduated retirement benefit provisions in consequence of this Act.

(2) 'The preserved graduated retirement benefit provisions' are the provisions of the National Insurance Act 1965 (c. 51) relating to graduated retirement benefit continued in force, with or without modification, by regulations having effect as if made under that paragraph.

...

PART 3 OCCUPATIONAL PENSION SCHEMES

Guaranteed minimum pensions etc.: Great Britain

14.—(1) In this paragraph 'the 1993 Act' means the Pension Schemes Act 1993 (c. 48); and expressions used in this paragraph and in that Act have the same meaning in this paragraph as in that Act.

(2) The fact that the person's gender has become the acquired gender does not affect the operation of section 14 of the 1993 Act (guaranteed minimum) in relation to the person, except to the extent that its operation depends on section 16 of the 1993 Act (revaluation); and sub-paragraphs (3) and (5) have effect subject to that.

(3) If (immediately before the certificate is issued) the person is a woman who is entitled to a guaranteed minimum pension but has not attained the age of 65—

(a) the person is for the purposes of section 13 of the 1993 Act and the guaranteed minimum pension provisions to be treated after it is issued as not having attained pensionable age (so that the entitlement ceases) but as attaining pensionable age on subsequently attaining the age of 65, and

(b) in a case where the person's guaranteed minimum pension has commenced before the certificate is issued, it is to be treated for the purposes of Chapter 3 of Part 4 of the 1993 Act (anti-franking) as if it had not.

(4) But sub-paragraph (3)(a) does not—

(a) affect any pension previously paid to the person, or

(b) prevent section 15 of the 1993 Act (increase of guaranteed minimum where commencement of guaranteed minimum pension postponed) operating to increase the person's guaranteed minimum by reason of a postponement of the commencement of the person's guaranteed minimum pension for a period ending before the certificate is issued.

(5) If (immediately before the certificate is issued) the person is a man who—

(a) has attained the age of 60, but

(b) has not attained the age of 65,

the person is to be treated for the purposes of section 13 of the 1993 Act and the guaranteed minimum pension provisions as attaining pensionable age when it is issued.

(6) If at that time the person has attained the age of 65, the fact that the person's gender has become the acquired gender does not affect the person's pensionable age for those purposes.

(7) The fact that the person's gender has become the acquired gender does not affect any guaranteed minimum pension to which the person is entitled as a widow or widower immediately before the certificate is issued (except in consequence of the operation of the previous provisions of this Schedule).

(8) If a transaction to which section 19 of the 1993 Act applies which is carried out before the certificate is issued discharges a liability to provide a guaranteed minimum pension for or in respect of the person, it continues to do so afterwards.

(9) 'The guaranteed minimum pension provision' means so much of the 1993 Act (apart from section 13) and of any other enactment as relates to guaranteed minimum pensions.

...

Domestic Violence, Crime and Victims Act 2004

(2004 c. 28)

PART 1 DOMESTIC VIOLENCE ETC

...

Causing or allowing a child or vulnerable adult to die or suffer serious physical harm

5 The offence

(1) A person ('D') is guilty of an offence if—
- (a) a child or vulnerable adult ('V') dies or suffers serious physical harm as a result of the unlawful act of a person who—
  - (i) was a member of the same household as V, and
  - (ii) had frequent contact with him,
- (b) D was such a person at the time of that act,
- (c) at that time there was a significant risk of serious physical harm being caused to V by the unlawful act of such a person, and
- (d) either D was the person whose act caused the death or serious physical harm or—
  - (i) D was, or ought to have been, aware of the risk mentioned in paragraph (c),
  - (ii) D failed to take such steps as he could reasonably have been expected to take to protect V from the risk, and
  - (iii) the act occurred in circumstances of the kind that D foresaw or ought to have foreseen.

(2) The prosecution does not have to prove whether it is the first alternative in subsection (1)(d) or the second (sub-paragraphs (i) to (iii)) that applies.

(3) If D was not the mother or father of V—
- (a) D may not be charged with an offence under this section if he was under the age of 16 at the time of the act that caused the death or serious physical harm;
- (b) for the purposes of subsection (1)(d)(ii) D could not have been expected to take any such step as is referred to there before attaining that age.

(4) For the purposes of this section—
- (a) a person is to be regarded as a 'member' of a particular household, even if he does not live in that household, if he visits it so often and for such periods of time that it is reasonable to regard him as a member of it;
- (b) where V lived in different households at different times, 'the same household as V' refers to the household in which V was living at the time of the act that caused the death or serious physical harm.

(5) For the purposes of this section an 'unlawful' act is one that—

(a) constitutes an offence, or

(b) would constitute an offence but for being the act of—

(i) a person under the age of ten, or

(ii) a person entitled to rely on a defence of insanity.

Paragraph (b) does not apply to an act of D.

(6) In this section—

'act' includes a course of conduct and also includes omission;

'child' means a person under the age of 16;

'serious' harm means harm that amounts to grievous bodily harm for the purposes of the Offences against the Person Act 1861 (c. 100);

'vulnerable adult' means a person aged 16 or over whose ability to protect himself from violence, abuse or neglect is significantly impaired through physical or mental disability or illness, through old age or otherwise.

(7) A person guilty of an offence under this section of causing or allowing a person's death is liable on conviction on indictment to imprisonment for a term not exceeding 14 years or to a fine, or to both.

(8) A person guilty of an offence under this section of causing or allowing a person to suffer serious physical harm is liable on conviction on indictment to imprisonment for a term not exceeding 10 years or to a fine, or to both.

…

PART 3 VICTIMS ETC

Chapter 1 The Victims' Code

32 Code of practice for victims

(1) The Secretary of State for Justice must issue a code of practice as to the services to be provided to a victim of criminal conduct by persons appearing to him to have functions relating to—

(a) victims of criminal conduct, or

(b) any aspect of the criminal justice system.

(2) The code may restrict the application of its provisions to

(a) specified descriptions of victims;

(b) victims of specified offences or descriptions of conduct;

(c) specified persons or descriptions of persons appearing to the Secretary of State for Justice to have functions of the kind mentioned in subsection (1).

(3) The code may include provision requiring or permitting the services which are to be provided to a victim to be provided to one or more others—

(a) instead of the victim (for example where the victim has died);

(b) as well as the victim.

(4) The code may make different provision for different purposes, including different provision for—

(a) different descriptions of victims;

(b) persons who have different functions or descriptions of functions;

(c) different areas.

(5) The code may not require anything to be done by—

(a) a person acting in a judicial capacity;

(b) a person acting in the discharge of a function of a member of the Crown Prosecution Service which involves the exercise of a discretion.

(6) In determining whether a person is a victim of criminal conduct for the purposes of this section, it is immaterial that no person has been charged with or convicted of an offence in respect of the conduct.

(7) In this section—

'criminal conduct' means conduct constituting an offence;

'specified' means specified in the code.

...

34   Effect of non-compliance

(1) If a person fails to perform a duty imposed on him by a code issued under section 32, the failure does not of itself make him liable to criminal or civil proceedings.

(2) But the code is admissible in evidence in criminal or civil proceedings and a court may take into account a failure to comply with the code in determining a question in the proceedings.

Chapter 2 Representations and information

Imprisonment or detention

35   Victims' rights to make representations and receive information

(1) This section applies if—

(a) a court convicts a person ('the offender') of a sexual or violent offence, and

(b) a relevant sentence is imposed on him in respect of the offence.

(2) But section 39 applies (instead of this section) if a hospital direction and a limitation direction are given in relation to the offender.

(3) The local probation board for the area in which the sentence is imposed, or the provider of probation services operating in the local justice area in which the sentence is imposed, must take all reasonable steps to ascertain whether a person who appears to the board to be the victim of the offence or to act for the victim of the offence wishes—

(a) to make representations about the matters specified in subsection (4);

(b) to receive the information specified in subsection (5).

(3A) The provider of probation services mentioned in subsection (3) is the provider of probation services identified as such by arrangements under section 3 of the Offender Management Act 2007.

(4) The matters are—

(a) whether the offender should be subject to any licence conditions or supervision requirements in the event of his release;

(b) if so, what licence conditions or supervision requirements.

(5) The information is information about any licence conditions or supervision requirements to which the offender is to be subject in the event of his release.

(6) If a person whose wishes have been ascertained under subsection (3) makes representations to the local probation board or provider of probation services mentioned in that subsection or the relevant probation body about a matter specified in subsection (4), the relevant probation body must forward those representations to the persons responsible for determining the matter.

(7) If a local probation board or a provider of probation services has ascertained under subsection (3) that a person wishes to receive the information specified in subsection (5), the relevant probation body must take all reasonable steps—

(a) to inform the person whether or not the offender is to be subject to any licence conditions or supervision requirements in the event of his release,

(b) if he is, to provide the person with details of any licence conditions or supervision requirements which relate to contact with the victim or his family, and

(c) to provide the person with such other information as the relevant probation body considers appropriate in all the circumstances of the case.

(8) In this section 'the relevant probation body' is—

    (a) in a case where the offender is to be supervised on release by an officer of a local proba-tion board, or an officer of a provider of probation services, that local probation board or that provider of probation services (as the case may be);

...

Chapter 3 Other matters relating to victims etc

...

Commissioner for victims and witnesses

48   Commissioner for Victims and Witnesses

(1) The Secretary of State for Justice must appoint a Commissioner for Victims and Witnesses (referred to in this Part as the Commissioner).

(2) Before appointing the Commissioner the Secretary of State for Justice must consult the Attorney General and the Secretary of State for the Home Department as to the person to be appointed.

...

49   General functions of Commissioner

(1) The Commissioner must—

    (a) promote the interests of victims and witnesses;

    (b) take such steps as he considers appropriate with a view to encouraging good practice in the treatment of victims and witnesses;

    (c) keep under review the operation of the code of practice issued under section 32.

(2) The Commissioner may, for any purpose connected with the performance of his duties under subsection (1)—

    (a) make proposals to the Secretary of State for Justice for amending the code (at the request of the Secretary of State for Justice or on his own initiative);

    (b) make a report to the Secretary of State for Justice;

    (c) make recommendations to an authority within his remit;

    (e) consult any person he thinks appropriate.

(3) If the Commissioner makes a report to the Secretary of State for Justice under subsection (2)(b)—

    (a) the Commissioner must send a copy of the report to the Attorney General and the Secretary of State for the Home Department; ...

(4) The Commissioner must prepare in respect of each calendar year a report on the carrying out of the functions of the Commissioner during the year.

(5) The Commissioner must send a copy of each report prepared under subsection (4) to—

    (a) the Secretary of State for Justice,

    (b) the Attorney General, and

    (c) the Secretary of State for the Home Department.

(6) Reports under subsection (2)(b) or (4) must be published by the Commissioner.

...

50   Advice

(1) If he is required to do so by a Minister of the Crown, the Commissioner must give advice to the Minister of the Crown in connection with any matter which—

    (a) is specified by the Minister, and

    (b) relates to victims or witnesses.

...

(3) In this section 'Minister of the Crown' includes the Treasury.

51   Restrictions on exercise of functions

The Commissioner must not exercise any of his functions in relation to—

(a) a particular victim or witness;

(b) the bringing or conduct of particular proceedings;

(c) anything done or omitted to be done by a person acting in a judicial capacity or on the instructions of or on behalf of such a person.

52   'Victims' and 'Witnesses'

(1) This section applies for the purposes of sections 48 to 51.

(2) 'Victim' means—

(a) a victim of an offence, or

(b) a victim of anti-social behaviour.

(3) It is immaterial for the purposes of subsection (2)(a) that—

(a) no complaint has been made about the offence;

(b) no person has been charged with or convicted of the offence.

(4) 'Witness' means a person (other than a defendant)—

(a) who has witnessed conduct in relation to which he may be or has been called to give evidence in relevant proceedings;

(b) who is able to provide or has provided anything which might be used or has been used as evidence in relevant proceedings; or

(c) who is able to provide or has provided anything mentioned in subsection (5) (whether or not admissible in evidence in relevant proceedings).

(5) The things referred to in subsection (4)(c) are—

(a) anything which might tend to confirm, has tended to confirm or might have tended to confirm evidence which may be, has been or could have been admitted in relevant proceedings;

(b) anything which might be, has been or might have been referred to in evidence given in relevant proceedings by another person;

(c) anything which might be, has been or might have been used as the basis for any cross examination in the course of relevant proceedings.

(6) For the purposes of subsection (4)—

(a) a person is a defendant in relation to any criminal proceedings if he might be, has been or might have been charged with or convicted of an offence in the proceedings;

(b) a person is a defendant in relation to any other relevant proceedings if he might be, has been or might have been the subject of an order made in those proceedings.

(7) In subsections (4) to (6) 'relevant proceedings' means—

(a) criminal proceedings;

(b) proceedings of any other kind in respect of anti-social behaviour.

(8) For the purposes of this section—

(a) 'anti-social behaviour' means behaviour by a person which causes or is likely to cause harassment, alarm or distress to one or more persons not of the same household as the person;

(b) a person is a victim of anti-social behaviour if the behaviour has caused him harassment, alarm or distress and he is not of the same household as the person who engages in the behaviour.

…

Grants

56   Grants for assisting victims, witnesses etc

(1) The Secretary of State may pay such grants to such persons as he considers appropriate in connection with measures which appear to him to be intended to assist victims, witnesses or other persons affected by offences.

(2) The Secretary of State may make a grant under this section subject to such conditions as he considers appropriate.

...

Children Act 2004

(2004 c. 31)

PART 1 CHILDREN'S COMMISSIONER

1 Establishment

(1) There is to be an office of Children's Commissioner.

(2) Schedule 1 has effect with respect to the Children's Commissioner.

2 Primary function: children's rights, views and interests

(1) The Children's Commissioner's primary function is promoting and protecting the rights of children in England.

(2) The primary function includes promoting awareness of the views and interests of children in England.

(3) In the discharge of the primary function the Children's Commissioner may, in particular—

(a) advise persons exercising functions or engaged in activities affecting children on how to act compatibly with the rights of children;

(b) encourage such persons to take account of the views and interests of children;

(c) advise the Secretary of State on the rights, views and interests of children;

(d) consider the potential effect on the rights of children of government policy proposals and government proposals for legislation;

(e) bring any matter to the attention of either House of Parliament;

(f) investigate the availability and effectiveness of complaints procedures so far as relating to children;

(g) investigate the availability and effectiveness of advocacy services for children;

(h) investigate any other matter relating to the rights or interests of children;

(i) monitor the implementation in England of the United Nations Convention on the Rights of the Child;

(j) publish a report on any matter considered or investigated under this section.

(4) In the discharge of the primary function, the Children's Commissioner must have particular regard to the rights of children who are within section 8A (children living away from home or receiving social care) and other groups of children who the Commissioner considers to be at particular risk of having their rights infringed.

(5) The Children's Commissioner may not conduct an investigation of the case of an individual child in the discharge of the primary function.

2A United Nations Convention on the Rights of the Child

(1) The Children's Commissioner must, in particular, have regard to the United Nations Convention on the Rights of the Child in considering for the purposes of the primary function what constitute the rights and interests of children (generally or so far as relating to a particular matter).

(2) The references in section 2(3)(i) and this section to the United Nations Convention on the Rights of the Child are to the Convention on the Rights of the Child adopted by the General Assembly of the United Nations on 20th November 1989 (including any Protocols to that Convention which are in force in relation to the United Kingdom), subject to any reservations, objections or interpretative declarations by the United Kingdom for the time being in force.

2B   Involving children in the discharge of the primary function

(1) The Children's Commissioner must take reasonable steps to involve children in the discharge of the primary function.

(2) The Commissioner must in particular take reasonable steps to—

    (a) ensure that children are aware of the Commissioner's primary function and how they may communicate with him or her, and

    (b) consult children, and organisations working with children, on the matters the Commissioner proposes to consider or investigate in the discharge of the primary function.

(3) The Children's Commissioner must for the purposes of this section have particular regard to children who are within section 8A (children living away from home or receiving social care) and other groups of children who the Commissioner considers do not have adequate means by which they can make their views known.

2C   Primary function: reports

(1) This section applies where the Children's Commissioner publishes a report in the discharge of the primary function.

(2) The Commissioner must, if and to the extent he or she considers it appropriate, also publish the report in a version which is suitable for children (or, if the report relates to a particular group of children, for those children).

(3) Where the report contains recommendations about the exercise by a person of functions of a public nature, the Commissioner may require that person to state in writing, within such period as the Commissioner may reasonably require, what action the person has taken or proposes to take in response to the recommendations.

2D   Provision of advice and assistance to certain children in England

(1) The Children's Commissioner may provide advice and assistance to any child who is within section 8A (children living away from home or receiving social care).

(2) The Children's Commissioner may in particular under this section make representations on behalf of a child who is within section 8A to a person in England who is—

    (a) providing the child with accommodation or services, or

    (b) otherwise exercising functions in relation to the child.

…

3   Inquiries initiated by Commissioner

(1) Where the Children's Commissioner considers that the case of an individual child in England raises issues of public policy of relevance to other children, he may hold an inquiry into that case for the purpose of investigating and making recommendations about those issues.

(2) The Children's Commissioner may only conduct an inquiry under this section if he is satisfied that the inquiry would not duplicate work that is the function of another person (having consulted such persons as he considers appropriate).

    …

(4) The Children's Commissioner may, if he thinks fit, hold an inquiry under this section, or any part of it, in private.

(5) As soon as possible after completing an inquiry under this section the Children's Commissioner must—

    (a) publish a report containing his recommendations; and

    (b) send a copy to the Secretary of State.

(6) The report need not identify any individual child if the Children's Commissioner considers that it would be undesirable for the identity of the child to be made public.

(7) Where the Children's Commissioner has published a report under this section containing recommendations in respect of any person exercising functions of a public nature, he may require

that person to state in writing, within such period as the Children's Commissioner may reasonably require, what action the person has taken or proposes to take in response to the recommendations.

(8) Subsections (2) and (3) of section 250 of the Local Government Act 1972 (c. 70) apply for the purposes of an inquiry held under this section with the substitution for references to the person appointed to hold the inquiry of references to the Children's Commissioner.

...

5 Functions of Commissioner in Wales

(1) The Children's Commissioner has the function of promoting and protecting the rights of children in Wales, except in so far as relating to any matter falling within the remit of the Children's Commissioner for Wales under section 72B, 73 or 74 of the Care Standards Act 2000 (c. 14).

(1A) The function under subsection (1) includes promoting awareness of the views and interests of children in Wales.

(2) Subsections (3) to (5) of section 2 and sections 2A to 2C, 2E and 2F apply in relation to the Children's Commissioner's function under subsection (1) as in relation to the Commissioner's primary function.

(2A) For the purposes of subsection (2)—

    (a) section 2(3)(i) has effect as if for 'in England' there were substituted 'in Wales, except in so far as relating to any matter falling within the remit of the Children's Commissioner for Wales under section 72B, 73 or 74 of the Care Standards Act 2000,',

    (b) sections 2(4) and 2B(3) have effect as if for 'children who are within section 8A (children living away from home or receiving social care) and other groups of children' there were substituted 'groups of children',

    (c) section 2E(1) has effect as if 'and the function under section 2D' were omitted, and

    (d) section 2F(1) has effect as if 'or the function under section 2D' were omitted.

(3) In discharging his function under subsection (1) above the Children's Commissioner must take account of the views of, and any work undertaken by, the Children's Commissioner for Wales.

(4) Where the Children's Commissioner considers that the case of an individual child in Wales raises issues of public policy of relevance to other children, other than issues relating to a matter referred to in subsection (1) above, he may hold an inquiry into that case for the purpose of investigating and making recommendations about those issues.

(5) Subsections (2) to (8) of section 3 apply in relation to an inquiry under subsection (4) above.

...

8 Annual reports

(1) As soon as possible after the end of each financial year the Children's Commissioner must make a report on—

    (a) the way in which he has discharged his functions under this Part; and

    (b) what he has found in the course of exercising those functions during the year.

...

(5) If the Children's Commissioner does not consider a report made under this section to be suitable for children, the Commissioner must publish a version of the report which is suitable for children.

...

8A Children in England living away from home or receiving social care

(1) For the purposes of this Part, a child is within this section if he or she is within any of subsections (2) to (5).

(2) A child is within this subsection if he or she is provided with accommodation by a school or college in England to which section 87(1) of the Children Act 1989 applies.

(3) A child is within this subsection if he or she is accommodated in an establishment (within the meaning of the Care Standards Act 2000) in respect of which Her Majesty's Chief Inspector of Education, Children's Services and Skills is the registration authority under section 5 of that Act.

(4) A child is within this subsection if functions are being exercised in relation to him or her by an agency (within the meaning of the Care Standards Act 2000) in respect of which Her Majesty's Chief Inspector of Education, Children's Services and Skills is the registration authority under section 5 of that Act.

(5) A child is within this subsection if a local authority in England exercises social services functions (within the meaning of the Local Authority Social Services Act 1970) in relation to him or her.

(6) For the purposes of this Part, a person who is not a child is to be treated as a child who is within this section if—

    (a) he or she is aged 18 or over and under 25, and

    (b) a local authority in England has provided services to him or her under any of sections 23C to 24D of the Children Act 1989 at any time after he or she reached the age of 16.

9   Commissioner's functions in relation to certain young people

(1) This section applies for the purposes of this Part, other than sections 2A and 8A (and references in this Part to a child who is within section 8A).

(2) For the purposes of the Children's Commissioner's functions in respect of children in England, a reference to a child includes, in addition to a person under the age of 18—

    (a) a person aged 18 or over for whom an EHC plan is maintained by a local authority,

    (b) a person aged 18 or over and under 25 to whom a local authority in England has provided services under any of sections 23C to 24D of the Children Act 1989 at any time after reaching the age of 16, or

    (c) a person aged 18 or over and under 25 who has been looked after by a local authority (in Wales, Scotland or Northern Ireland) at any time after reaching the age of 16.

(3) For the purposes of the Children's Commissioner's functions in respect of children in Wales, Scotland and Northern Ireland, a reference to a child includes, in addition to a person under the age of 18, a person aged 18 or over and under 25—

    (a) who has a learning disability,

    (b) who has been looked after by a local authority (in Wales, Scotland or Northern Ireland) at any time after reaching the age of 16, or

    (c) to whom a local authority in England has provided services under any of sections 23C to 24D of the Children Act 1989 at any time after reaching the age of 16.

(4) For the purposes of this section—

'EHC plan' means a plan within section 37(2) of the Children and Families Act 2014 (education, health and care plans);

'learning disability' means a state of arrested or incomplete development of mind which induces significant impairment of intelligence and social functioning;

a person is 'looked after by a local authority' if—

    (a) for the purposes of the Children Act 1989, he or she is looked after by a local authority in Wales;

    ...

PART 2 CHILDREN'S SERVICES IN ENGLAND

General

9A   Targets for safeguarding and promoting the welfare of children

(1) The Secretary of State may, in accordance with regulations, set safeguarding targets for a local authority in England.

(2) The regulations may, in particular—

    (a) make provision about matters by reference to which safeguarding targets may, or must, be set;

    (b) make provision about periods to which safeguarding targets may, or must, relate;

(c) make provision about the procedure for setting safeguarding targets;

(d) specify requirements with which a local authority in England must comply in connection with the setting of safeguarding targets.

(3) In exercising their functions, a local authority in England must act in the manner best calculated to secure that any safeguarding targets set under this section (so far as relating to the area of the authority) are met.

(4) 'Safeguarding targets', in relation to a local authority in England, are targets for safeguarding and promoting the welfare of children in the authority's area.

10   Co-operation to improve well-being

(1) Each local authority in England must make arrangements to promote co-operation between—

(a) the authority;

(b) each of the authority's relevant partners; and

(c) such other persons or bodies as the authority consider appropriate, being persons or bodies of any nature who exercise functions or are engaged in activities in relation to children in the authority's area.

(2) The arrangements are to be made with a view to improving the well-being of children in the authority's area so far as relating to—

(a) physical and mental health and emotional well-being;

(b) protection from harm and neglect;

(c) education, training and recreation;

(d) the contribution made by them to society;

(e) social and economic well-being.

(3) In making arrangements under this section a local authority in England must have regard to the importance of parents and other persons caring for children in improving the well-being of children.

(4) For the purposes of this section each of the following is a relevant partner of a local authority in England—

(a) where the authority is a county council for an area for which there is also a district council, the district council;

(b) the local policing body and the chief officer of police for a police area any part of which falls within the area of the children's services authority;

(c) a local probation board for an area any part of which falls within the area of the authority;

(ca) the Secretary of State in relation to his functions under sections 2 and 3 of the Offender Management Act 2007, so far as they are exercisable in relation to England;

(cb) any provider of probation services that is required by arrangements under section 3(2) of the Offender Management Act 2007 to act as a relevant partner of the authority;

(d) a youth offending team for an area any part of which falls within the area of the authority;

(da) the National Health Service Commissioning Board;

(db) any clinical commissioning group for an area any part of which falls within the area of the authority;

(f) a person providing services in pursuance of section 68 of the Education and Skills Act 2008 in any part of the area of the authority;

(fa) the governing body of a maintained school that is maintained by the authority;

(fb) the proprietor of a school approved by the Secretary of State under section 342 of the Education Act 1996 and situated in the authority's area;

(fc) the proprietor of a city technology college, city college for the technology of the arts or Academy situated in the authority's area;

(fd) the governing body of an institution within the further education sector the main site of which is situated in the authority's area;

(fe) the Secretary of State, in relation to the Secretary of State's functions under section 2 of the Employment and Training Act 1973.

(5) The relevant partners of a local authority in England must co-operate with the authority in the making of arrangements under this section.

(5A) For the purposes of arrangements under this section a relevant person or body may—

(a) provide staff, goods, services, accommodation or other resources to another relevant person or body;

(b) make contributions to a fund out of which relevant payments may be made.

(8) A local authority in England and each of their relevant partners must in exercising their functions under this section have regard to any guidance given to them for the purpose by the Secretary of State.

(9) Arrangements under this section may include arrangements relating to—

(a) persons aged 18 and 19;

(b) persons over the age of 19 who are receiving services under sections 23C to 24D of the Children Act 1989 (c. 41);

(c) persons over the age of 19 but under the age of 25—

(i) for whom an EHC plan is maintained, or

(ii) who have a learning difficulty or disability, within the meaning of section 15ZA(6) and (7) of the Education Act 1996, and are receiving services under section 15ZA of the Education Act 1996 or section 66, 86 or 87 of the Apprenticeships, Skills, Children and Learning Act 2009.

(10) In deciding for the purposes of subsection (4)(fd) whether the main site of an institution within the further education sector is situated within the area of a children's services authority, the authority and the governing body of the institution must have regard to any guidance given to them by the Secretary of State.

(11) In this section—

'governing body', in relation to an institution within the further education sector, has the meaning given by section 90 of the Further and Higher Education Act 1992;

'institution within the further education sector' has the meaning given by section 4(3) of the Education Act 1996;

'maintained school' has the meaning given by section 39(1) of the Education Act 2002;

'proprietor', in relation to a city technology college, city college for the technology of the arts, Academy or other school, means the person or body of persons responsible for its management;

'relevant payment', in relation to a fund, means a payment in respect of expenditure incurred, by a relevant person or body contributing to the fund, in the exercise of its functions;

'relevant person or body' means—

(a) a children's services authority in England;

(b) a relevant partner of a children's services authority in England.

11   Arrangements to safeguard and promote welfare

(1) This section applies to each of the following—

(a) a local authority in England;

(b) a district council which is not such an authority;

(ba) the National Health Service Commissioning Board;

(bb) a clinical commissioning group;

(d) a Special Health Authority, so far as exercising functions in relation to England, designated by order made by the Secretary of State for the purposes of this section;

(g) an NHS foundation trust;

(h) the local policing body and chief officer of police for a police area in England;

(i) the British Transport Police Authority, so far as exercising functions in relation to England;

(ia) the National Crime Agency;

(j) a local probation board for an area in England;

(ja) the Secretary of State in relation to his functions under sections 2 and 3 of the Offender Management Act 2007, so far as they are exercisable in relation to England;

(k) a youth offending team for an area in England;

(l) the governor of a prison or secure training centre in England (or, in the case of a contracted out prison or secure training centre, its director);

(m) any person to the extent that he is providing services in pursuance of section 74 of the Education and Skills Act 2008.

(2) Each person and body to whom this section applies must make arrangements for ensuring that—

(a) their functions are discharged having regard to the need to safeguard and promote the welfare of children; and

(b) any services provided by another person pursuant to arrangements made by the person or body in the discharge of their functions are provided having regard to that need.

(3) In the case of a local authority in England, the reference in subsection (2) to functions of the authority does not include functions to which section 175 of the Education Act 2002 (c. 32) applies.

(4) Each person and body to whom this section applies must in discharging their duty under this section have regard to any guidance given to them for the purpose by the Secretary of State.

12 Information databases

(1) The Secretary of State may for the purpose of arrangements under section 10 or 11 above or under section 175 of the Education Act 2002—

(a) by regulations require local authorities in England to establish and operate databases containing information in respect of persons to whom such arrangements relate;

(b) himself establish and operate, or make arrangements for the operation and establishment of, one or more databases containing such information.

(2) The Secretary of State may for the purposes of arrangements under subsection (1)(b) by regulations establish a body corporate to establish and operate one or more databases.

(3) A database under this section may only include information falling within subsection (4) in relation to a person to whom arrangements specified in subsection (1) relate.

(4) The information referred to in subsection (3) is information of the following descriptions in relation to a person—

(a) his name, address, gender and date of birth;

(b) a number identifying him;

(c) the name and contact details of any person with parental responsibility for him (within the meaning of section 3 of the Children Act 1989 (c. 41)) or who has care of him at any time;

(d) details of any education being received by him (including the name and contact details of any educational institution attended by him);

(e) the name and contact details of any person providing primary medical services in relation to him under Part 1 of the National Health Service Act 2006 (c. 41);

(f) the name and contact details of any person providing to him services of such description as the Secretary of State may by regulations specify;

(g) information as to the existence of any cause for concern in relation to him;

(h) information of such other description, not including medical records or other personal records, as the Secretary of State may by regulations specify.

(5) The Secretary of State may by regulations make provision in relation to the establishment and operation of any database or databases under this section.

(6) Regulations under subsection (5) may in particular make provision—
- (a) as to the information which must or may be contained in any database under this section (subject to subsection (3));
- (b) requiring a person or body specified in subsection (7) to disclose information for inclusion in the database;
- (c) permitting a person or body specified in subsection (8) to disclose information for inclusion in the database;
- (d) permitting or requiring the disclosure of information included in any such database;
- (e) permitting or requiring any person to be given access to any such database for the purpose of adding or reading information;
- (f) as to the conditions on which such access must or may be given;
- (g) as to the length of time for which information must or may be retained;
- (h) as to procedures for ensuring the accuracy of information included in any such database;
- (i) in a case where a database is established by virtue of subsection (1)(b), requiring local authorities in England to participate in the operation of the database.

(7) The persons and bodies referred to in subsection (6)(b) are—
- (a) the persons and bodies specified in section 11(1);
- (b) the Learning and Skills Council for England;
- (c) the governing body of a maintained school in England (within the meaning of section 175 of the Education Act 2002 (c. 32));
- (d) the governing body of an institution in England within the further education sector (within the meaning of that section);
- (e) the proprietor of an independent school in England (within the meaning of the Education Act 1996 (c. 56));
- (ea) the proprietor of an alternative provision Academy that is not an independent school (within the meaning of that Act);
- (f) a person or body of such other description as the Secretary of State may by regulations specify.

(8) The persons and bodies referred to in subsection (6)(c) are—
- (a) a person registered under Part 3 of the Childcare Act 2006 (regulation of provision of childcare in England);
- (b) a voluntary organisation exercising functions or engaged in activities in relation to persons to whom arrangements specified in subsection (1) relate;
- (c) the Commissioners for Her Majesty's Revenue and Customs;
- (ca) a private registered provider of social housing;
- (d) a registered social landlord;
- (e) a person or body of such other description as the Secretary of State may by regulations specify.

(9) The Secretary of State may provide information for inclusion in a database under this section.

(10) The provision which may be made under subsection (6)(e) includes provision for a person of a description specified in the regulations to determine what must or may be done under the regulations.

(11) Regulations under subsection (5) may also provide that anything which may be done under regulations under subsection (6)(c) to (e) or (9) may be done notwithstanding any rule of common law which prohibits or restricts the disclosure of information.

(12) Any person or body establishing or operating a database under this section must in the establishment or operation of the database have regard to any guidance, and comply with any direction, given to that person or body by the Secretary of State.

(13) Guidance or directions under subsection (12) may in particular relate to—
- (a) the management of a database under this section;
- (b) the technical specifications for any such database;

(c) the security of any such database;

(d) the transfer and comparison of information between databases under this section;

(e) the giving of advice in relation to rights under the Data Protection Act 1998 (c. 29).

...

Local Safeguarding Children Boards

13   Establishment of LSCBs

(1) Each local authority in England must establish a Local Safeguarding Children Board for their area.

(2) A Board established under this section must include such representative or representatives of—

(a) the authority by which it is established, and

(b) each Board partner of that authority,

as the Secretary of State may by regulations prescribe.

(3) For the purposes of this section each of the following is a Board partner of a local authority in England—

(a) where the authority is a county council for an area for which there is also a district council, the district council;

(b) the chief officer of police for a police area any part of which falls within the area of the authority;

(c) a local probation board for an area any part of which falls within the area of the authority;

(ca) the Secretary of State in relation to his functions under sections 2 and 3 of the Offender Management Act 2007, so far as they are exercisable in relation to England;

(cb) any provider of probation services that is required by arrangements under section 3(2) of the Offender Management Act 2007 to act as a Board partner of the authority;

(d) a youth offending team for an area any part of which falls within the area of the authority;

(da) the National Health Service Commissioning Board;

(db) any clinical commissioning group for an area any part of which falls within the area of the authority;

(f) an NHS foundation trust all or most of whose hospitals, establishments and facilities are situated in the area of the authority;

(g) a person providing services in pursuance of section 68 of the Education and Skills Act 2008 in any part of the area of the authority;

(h) the Children and Family Court Advisory and Support Service;

(i) the governor of any secure training centre in the area of the authority (or, in the case of a contracted out secure training centre, its director);

(j) the governor of any prison in the area of the authority which ordinarily detains children (or, in the case of a contracted out prison, its director).

(4) A local authority in England must take reasonable steps to ensure that the Local Safeguarding Children Board established by them includes representatives of relevant persons and bodies of such descriptions as may be prescribed by the Secretary of State in regulations.

(5) A Local Safeguarding Children Board established under this section may also include representatives of such other relevant persons or bodies as the authority by which it is established consider, after consulting their Board partners, should be represented on it.

(5A) A children's services authority in England must take reasonable steps to ensure that the Local Safeguarding Children Board established by them also includes two persons who appear to the authority to be representative of persons living in the authority's area.

(5B) An authority may pay remuneration, allowances and expenses to persons who are included by virtue of subsection (5A) in a Local Safeguarding Children Board established by them.

(6) For the purposes of subsections (4) and (5), relevant persons and bodies are persons and bodies of any nature exercising functions or engaged in activities relating to children in the area of the authority in question.

(7) In the establishment and operation of a Local Safeguarding Children Board under this section—

  (a) the authority establishing it must co-operate with each of their Board partners; and

  (b) each Board partner must co-operate with the authority.

(8) Two or more local authorities in England may discharge their respective duties under subsection (1) by establishing a Local Safeguarding Children Board for their combined area (and where they do so, any reference in this section or sections 14 to 16 to the authority establishing the Board shall be read as a reference to the authorities establishing it).

14   Functions and procedure of LSCBs

(1) The objective of a Local Safeguarding Children Board established under section 13 is—

  (a) to co-ordinate what is done by each person or body represented on the Board by virtue of section 13(2), (4) or (5) for the purposes of safeguarding and promoting the welfare of children in the area of the authority by which it is established; and

  (b) to ensure the effectiveness of what is done by each such person or body for those purposes.

(2) A Local Safeguarding Children Board established under section 13 is to have such functions in relation to its objective as the Secretary of State may by regulations prescribe (which may in particular include functions of review or investigation).

(3) The Secretary of State may by regulations make provision as to the procedures to be followed by a Local Safeguarding Children Board established under section 13.

...

Local authority administration

17   Children and young people's plans

(1) The Secretary of State may by regulations require a Children's Trust Board established by virtue of arrangements under section 10 from time to time to prepare and publish a children and young people's plan.

(2) A children and young people's plan is a plan setting out the strategy of the persons or bodies represented on the Board for co-operating with each other with a view to improving the well-being of children and relevant young persons in the area of the authority that established the Board.

(3) In subsection (2) 'well-being' means well-being so far as relating to the matters specified in section 10(2)(a) to (e).

(4) Regulations under this section may in particular make provision as to—

  (a) the matters to be dealt with in a children and young people's plan;

  (b) the period to which a children and young people's plan is to relate;

  (c) when and how a children and young people's plan must be published;

  (d) keeping a children and young people's plan under review;

  (e) revising a children and young people's plan;

  (f) consultation to be carried out during preparation or revision of a children and young people's plan;

  (g) other steps required or permitted to be taken in connection with the preparation or revision of a children and young people's plan.

(5) In this section 'relevant young persons' means persons, other than children, in relation to whom arrangements under section 10 may be made.

17A   Children and young people's plans: implementation

(1) This section applies where a Children's Trust Board prepares a children and young people's plan in accordance with regulations under section 17.

(2) The persons and bodies whose strategy for co-operation is set out in the plan must have regard to the plan in exercising their functions.

(3) The Board must—

    (a) monitor the extent to which the persons and bodies whose strategy for co-operation is set out in the plan are acting in accordance with the plan;

    (b) prepare and publish an annual report about the extent to which, during the year to which the report relates, those persons and bodies have acted in accordance with the plan.

18   Director of children's services

(1) A local authority in England may, and with effect from the appointed day must, appoint an officer for the purposes of—

    (a) the functions conferred on or exercisable by the authority which are specified in subsection (2); and

    (b) such other functions conferred on or exercisable by the authority as may be prescribed by the Secretary of State by regulations.

(2) The functions referred to in subsection (1)(a) are—

    (a) education functions conferred on or exercisable by the authority;

    (b) functions conferred on or exercisable by the authority which are social services functions (within the meaning of the Local Authority Social Services Act 1970 (c. 42)), so far as those functions relate to children;

    (c) the functions conferred on the authority under sections 23C to 24D of the Children Act 1989 (c. 41) (so far as not falling within paragraph (b));

    (d) the functions conferred on the authority under sections 10 to 12, 12C, 12D and 17A of this Act;

    (e) any functions exercisable by the authority under section 75 of the National Health Service Act 2006 or section 33 of the National Health Service (Wales) Act 2006 on behalf of an NHS body (within the meaning of those sections), so far as those functions relate to children; and

    (f) the functions conferred on the authority under Part 1 of the Childcare Act 2006.

(3) Subsection (2)(a) does not include—

    (a) functions under section 120(3) of the Education Reform Act 1988 (c. 40) (functions of LEAs with respect to higher and further education);

    (b) functions under section 85(2) and (3) of the Further and Higher Education Act 1992 (c. 13) (finance and government of locally funded further and higher education);

    (c) functions under section 15B of the Education Act 1996 (c. 56) (education for persons who have attained the age of 19);

    (d) functions under section 22 of the Teaching and Higher Education Act 1998 (c. 30) (financial support to students);

    (e) such other education functions conferred on or exercisable by a local authority in England as the Secretary of State may by regulations prescribe.

(4) An officer appointed by a local authority in England under this section is to be known as their 'director of children's services'.

(5) The director of children's services appointed by a local authority in England may also have responsibilities relating to such functions conferred on or exercisable by the authority, in addition to those specified in subsection (1), as the authority consider appropriate.

(6) The functions in relation to which a director of children's services may have responsibilities by virtue of subsection (5) include those referred to in subsection (3)(a) to (e).

(7) A local authority in England must have regard to any guidance given to them by the Secretary of State for the purposes of this section.

(8) Two or more local authorities in England may for the purposes of this section, if they consider that the same person can efficiently discharge, for both or all of them, the responsibilities of director of children's services, concur in the appointment of a person as director of children's services for both or all of them.

(9) The amendments in Schedule 2—

(a) have effect, in relation to any authority which appoint a director of children's services before the appointed day, from the day of his appointment; and

(b) on and after the appointed day have effect for all purposes.

(10) In this section—

'the appointed day' means such day as the Secretary of State may by order appoint;

'education functions' has the meaning given by section 579(1) of the Education Act 1996.

19 Lead member for children's services

(1) A local authority in England must, in making arrangements for the discharge of—

(a) the functions conferred on or exercisable by the authority specified in section 18(1)(a) and (b), and

(b) such other functions conferred on or exercisable by the authority as the authority consider appropriate,

designate one of their members as their 'lead member for children's services'.

(2) A local authority in England must have regard to any guidance given to them by the Secretary of State for the purposes of subsection (1).

...

PART 3 CHILDREN'S SERVICES IN WALES

General

25 Co-operation to improve well-being: Wales

(1) Each children's services authority in Wales must make arrangements to promote co-operation between—

(a) the authority;

(b) each of the authority's relevant partners; and

(c) such other persons or bodies as the authority consider appropriate, being persons or bodies of any nature who exercise functions or are engaged in activities in relation to children in the authority's area.

(2) The arrangements are to be made with a view to improving the well-being of children in the authority's area so far as relating to—

(a) physical and mental health and emotional well-being;

(b) protection from harm and neglect;

(c) education, training and recreation;

(d) the contribution made by them to society;

(e) social and economic well-being.

(3) In making arrangements under this section a local authority in Wales must have regard to the importance of parents and other persons caring for children in improving the well-being of children.

(4) For the purposes of this section each of the following is the relevant partner of a local authority in Wales—

(a) the local policing body and the chief officer of police for a police area any part of which falls within the area of the local authority;

(b) a local probation board for an area any part of which falls within the area of the authority;

(ba) the Secretary of State in relation to his functions under sections 2 and 3 of the Offender Management Act 2007, so far as they are exercisable in relation to Wales;

(bb) any provider of probation services that is required by arrangements under section 3(2) of the Offender Management Act 2007 to act as a relevant partner of the authority;

(c) a youth offending team for an area any part of which falls within the area of the authority;

(d) a Local Health Board for an area any part of which falls within the area of the authority;

(e) an NHS trust providing services in the area of the authority;

(f) the Assembly to the extent that it is discharging functions under Part 2 of the Learning and Skills Act 2000.

(5) The relevant partners of a local authority in Wales must co-operate with the authority in the making of arrangements under this section.

(6) A local authority in Wales and any of their relevant partners may for the purposes of arrangements under this section—

(a) provide staff, goods, services, accommodation or other resources;

(b) establish and maintain a pooled fund.

(7) For the purposes of subsection (6) a pooled fund is a fund—

(a) which is made up of contributions by the authority and the relevant partner or partners concerned; and

(b) out of which payments may be made towards expenditure incurred in the discharge of functions of the authority and functions of the relevant partner or partners.

(8) A local authority in Wales and each of their relevant partners must in exercising their functions under this section have regard to any guidance given to them for the purpose by the Assembly.

(9) The Assembly must obtain the consent of the Secretary of State before giving guidance under subsection (8) at any time after the coming into force of any of paragraphs (a) to (c) of subsection (4).

(10) Arrangements under this section may include arrangements relating to—

(a) persons aged 18 and 19;

(b) persons over the age of 19 who are receiving—

(i) services under sections 23C to 24D of the Children Act 1989 (c. 41); or

(ii) youth support services (within the meaning of section 123 of the Learning and Skills Act 2000 (c. 21)).

26 Children and young people's plans: Wales

(1A) A local authority in Wales must, in accordance with regulations made by the Welsh Ministers, prepare and publish a plan setting out the authority's strategy for discharging their functions in relation to children and relevant young persons.

(1B) A local authority in Wales must include in their plan—

(a) the arrangements made or to be made under section 25 by the authority;

(b) the local authority's strategy under section 2 of the Children and Families (Wales) Measure 2010 (strategies for contributing to the eradication of child poverty).

(c) the scheme for the authority's area under Part 1 of the Mental Health (Wales) Measure 2010.

(1C) A local authority in Wales may include in their plan—

(a) the strategy or proposals in relation to children and relevant young persons of any partner of the authority;

(b) the strategy under section 2 of the Children and Families (Wales) Measure 2010 (strategies for contributing to the eradication of child poverty) of any partner of the authority.

(1D) The powers of a local authority in subsection (1C) are subject to any duty imposed in regulations under subsection (2)(a).

(2) Regulations under this section may in particular make provision as to—

(a) the matters to be dealt with in a plan under this section;

(b) the period to which a plan under this section is to relate;

(c) when and how a plan under this section must be published;

(d) keeping a plan under this section under review;

(e) consultation to be carried out before a plan under this section is published;

(f) implementation of a plan under this section.

(3) The matters for which provision may be made under subsection (2)(a) include in particular—

   (a) the arrangements made or to be made under section 25 by a local authority in Wales;

   (b) the strategy or proposals in relation to children and relevant young persons of any partner.

(4) Regulations under this section may require a local authority in Wales to obtain the Assembly's approval before publishing a plan under this section; and may provide that the Assembly may modify a plan before approving it.

(5) A local authority in Wales must have regard to any guidance given to them by the Assembly in relation to how they are to discharge their functions under regulations under this section.

(6) In this section—

'partner' means any person or body with whom a local authority in Wales has made an arrangement under section 25;

'relevant young persons' means the persons, in addition to children, in relation to whom arrangements under section 25 may be made.

27   Responsibility for functions under sections 25 and 26

(1) A local authority in Wales must—

   (a) appoint an officer, to be known as the 'lead director for children and young people's services', for the purposes of co-ordinating and overseeing arrangements made under sections 25 and 26; and

   (b) designate one of their members, to be known as the 'lead member for children and young people's services', to have as his special care the discharge of the authority's functions under those sections.

(2) A Local Health Board must—

   (a) appoint an officer, to be known as the Board's 'lead officer for children and young people's services', for the purposes of the Board's functions under section 25; and

   (b) designate one of the Board's members who is not an officer as its 'lead member for children and young people's services' to have the discharge of those functions as his special care.

(3) An NHS trust to which section 25 applies must—

   (a) appoint an executive director, to be known as the trust's 'lead executive director for children and young people's services', for the purposes of the trust's functions under that section; and

   (b) designate one of the trust's non-executive directors as its 'lead non-executive director for children and young people's services' to have the discharge of those functions as his special care.

(4) Each local authority in Wales, Local Health Board and NHS trust to which section 25 applies must have regard to any guidance given to them by the Assembly in relation to—

   (a) their functions under this section;

   (b) the responsibilities of the persons appointed or designated by them under this section.

28   Arrangements to safeguard and promote welfare: Wales

(1) This section applies to each of the following—

   (a) a local authority in Wales;

   (b) a Local Health Board;

   (c) an NHS trust;

   (d) the local policing body and chief officer of police for a police area in Wales;

   (e) the British Transport Police Authority, so far as exercising functions in relation to Wales;

   (ea) the National Crime Agency;

   (f) a local probation board for an area in Wales;

  (fa) the Secretary of State in relation to his functions under sections 2 and 3 of the Offender Management Act 2007, so far as they are exercisable in relation to Wales;

  (g) a youth offending team for an area in Wales;

  (h) the governor of a prison or secure training centre in Wales (or, in the case of a contracted out prison or secure training centre, its director);

  (i) any person to the extent that he is providing services pursuant to arrangements made by a local authority in Wales under section 123(1)(b) of the Learning and Skills Act 2000 (c. 21) (youth support services).

  (2) Each person and body to whom this section applies must make arrangements for ensuring that—

  (a) their functions are discharged having regard to the need to safeguard and promote the welfare of children; and

  (b) any services provided by another person pursuant to arrangements made by the person or body in the discharge of their functions are provided having regard to that need.

  (3) In the case of a local authority in Wales, the reference in subsection (2) to functions of the authority does not include functions to which section 175 of the Education Act 2002 (c. 32) applies.

  (4) The persons and bodies referred to in subsection (1)(a) to (c) and (i) must in discharging their duty under this section have regard to any guidance given to them for the purpose by the Assembly.

  (5) The persons and bodies referred to in subsection (1)(d) to (h) must in discharging their duty under this section have regard to any guidance given to them for the purpose by the Secretary of State after consultation with the Assembly.

29 Information databases: Wales

  (1) The Assembly may for the purpose of arrangements under section 25 or 28 above or under section 175 of the Education Act 2002—

  (a) by regulations require local authorities in Wales to establish and operate databases containing information in respect of persons to whom such arrangements relate;

  (b) itself establish and operate, or make arrangements for the operation and establishment of, one or more databases containing such information.

  (2) The Assembly may for the purposes of arrangements under subsection (1)(b) by regulations establish a body corporate to establish and operate one or more databases.

  (3) A database under this section may only include information falling within subsection (4) in relation to a person to whom arrangements specified in subsection (1) relate.

  (4) The information referred to in subsection (3) is information of the following descriptions in relation to a person—

  (a) his name, address, gender and date of birth;

  (b) a number identifying him;

  (c) the name and contact details of any person with parental responsibility for him (within the meaning of section 3 of the Children Act 1989 (c. 41)) or who has care of him at any time;

  (d) details of any education being received by him (including the name and contact details of any educational institution attended by him);

  (e) the name and contact details of any person providing primary medical services in relation to him under the National Health Service (Wales) Act 2006;

  (f) the name and contact details of any person providing to him services of such description as the Assembly may by regulations specify;

  (g) information as to the existence of any cause for concern in relation to him;

  (h) information of such other description, not including medical records or other personal records, as the Assembly may by regulations specify.

  (5) The Assembly may by regulations make provision in relation to the establishment and operation of any database or databases under this section.

(6) Regulations under subsection (5) may in particular make provision—

    (a) as to the information which must or may be contained in any database under this section (subject to subsection (3));

    (b) requiring a person or body specified in subsection (7) to disclose information for inclusion in the database;

    (c) permitting a person or body specified in subsection (8) to disclose information for inclusion in the database;

    (d) permitting or requiring the disclosure of information included in any such database;

    (e) permitting or requiring any person to be given access to any such database for the purpose of adding or reading information;

    (f) as to the conditions on which such access must or may be given;

    (g) as to the length of time for which information must or may be retained;

    (h) as to procedures for ensuring the accuracy of information included in any such database;

    (i) in a case where a database is established by virtue of subsection (1)(b), requiring local authorities in Wales to participate in the operation of the database.

(7) The persons and bodies referred to in subsection (6)(b) are—

    (a) the persons and bodies specified in section 28(1);

    (b) the National Assembly for Wales to the extent that it is discharging its functions under Part 2 of the Learning and Skills Act 2000;

    (c) the governing body of a maintained school in Wales (within the meaning of section 175 of the Education Act 2002 (c. 32));

    (d) the governing body of an institution in Wales within the further education sector (within the meaning of that section);

    (e) the proprietor of an independent school in Wales (within the meaning of the Education Act 1996 (c. 56));

    (f) a person or body of such other description as the Assembly may by regulations specify.

(8) The persons and bodies referred to in subsection (6)(c) are—

    (a) a person registered in Wales for child minding or the provision of day care under Part 2 of the Children and Families (Wales) Measure 2010;

    (b) a voluntary organisation exercising functions or engaged in activities in relation to persons to whom arrangements specified in subsection (1) relate;

    (c) the Commissioners for Her Majesty's Revenue and Customs;

    (d) a registered social landlord or private registered provider of social housing;

    (e) a person or body of such other description as the Assembly may by regulations specify.

(9) The Assembly and the Secretary of State may provide information for inclusion in a database under this section.

(10) The provision which may be made under subsection (6)(e) includes provision for a person of a description specified in the regulations to determine what must or may be done under the regulations.

(11) Regulations under subsection (5) may also provide that anything which may be done under regulations under subsection (6)(c) to (e) or (9) may be done notwithstanding any rule of common law which prohibits or restricts the disclosure of information.

(12) Regulations under subsections (1)(a) and (5) may only be made with the consent of the Secretary of State.

(13) Any person or body establishing or operating a database under this section must in the establishment or operation of the database have regard to any guidance, and comply with any direction, given to that person by the Assembly.

(14) Guidance or directions under subsection (13) may in particular relate to—

    (a) the management of a database under this section;

    (b) the technical specifications for any such database;

    (c) the security of any such database;

(d) the transfer and comparison of information between databases under this section;

(e) the giving of advice in relation to rights under the Data Protection Act 1998 (c. 29).

...

Local Safeguarding Children Boards

31 Establishment of LSCBs in Wales

(1) Each local authority in Wales must establish a Local Safeguarding Children Board for their area.

(2) A Board established under this section must include such representative or representatives of—

(a) the authority by which it is established, and

(b) each Board partner of that authority,

as the Assembly may by regulations prescribe.

(3) For the purposes of this section each of the following is a Board partner of a local authority in Wales—

(a) the chief officer of police for a police area any part of which falls within the area of the authority;

(b) a local probation board for an area any part of which falls within the area of the authority;

(ba) the Secretary of State in relation to his functions under sections 2 and 3 of the Offender Management Act 2007, so far as they are exercisable in relation to Wales;

(bb) any provider of probation services that is required by arrangements under section 3(2) of the Offender Management Act 2007 to act as a Board partner of the authority;

(c) a youth offending team for an area any part of which falls within the area of the authority;

(d) a Local Health Board for an area any part of which falls within the area of the authority;

(e) an NHS trust providing services in the area of the authority;

(f) the governor of any secure training centre within the area of the authority (or, in the case of a contracted out secure training centre, its director);

(g) the governor of any prison in the area of the authority which ordinarily detains children (or, in the case of a contracted out prison, its director).

(4) Regulations under subsection (2) that make provision in relation to a Board partner referred to in subsection (3)(a) to (c), (f) or (g) may only be made with the consent of the Secretary of State.

(5) A local authority in Wales must take reasonable steps to ensure that the Local Safeguarding Children Board established by them includes representatives of relevant persons and bodies of such descriptions as may be prescribed by the Assembly in regulations.

(6) A Local Safeguarding Children Board established under this section may also include representatives of such other relevant persons or bodies as the authority by which it is established consider, after consulting their Board partners, should be represented on it.

(7) For the purposes of subsections (5) and (6), relevant persons and bodies are persons and bodies of any nature exercising functions or engaged in activities relating to children in the area of the authority in question.

(8) In the establishment and operation of a Local Safeguarding Children Board under this section—

(a) the authority establishing it must co-operate with each of their Board partners; and

(b) each Board partner must co-operate with the authority.

(9) Two or more local authorities in Wales may discharge their respective duties under subsection (1) by establishing a Local Safeguarding Children Board for their combined area (and where they do so, any reference in this section and sections 32 to 34 to the authority establishing the Board shall be read as a reference to the authorities establishing it).

32   Functions and procedure of LSCBs in Wales

(1) The objective of a Local Safeguarding Children Board established under section 31 is—

(a) to co-ordinate what is done by each person or body represented on the Board for the purposes of safeguarding and promoting the welfare of children in the area of the authority by which it is established; and

(b) to ensure the effectiveness of what is done by each such person or body for those purposes.

(2) A Local Safeguarding Children Board established under section 31 is to have such functions in relation to its objective as the Assembly may by regulations prescribe (which may in particular include functions of review or investigation).

(3) The Assembly may by regulations make provision as to the procedures to be followed by a Local Safeguarding Children Board established under section 31.

...

PART 4 ADVISORY AND SUPPORT SERVICES FOR FAMILY PROCEEDINGS

CAFCASS functions in Wales

35   Functions of the assembly relating to family proceedings

(1) In respect of family proceedings in which the welfare of children ordinarily resident in Wales is or may be in question, it is a function of the Assembly to—

(a) safeguard and promote the welfare of the children;

(b) give advice to any court about any application made to it in such proceedings;

(c) make provision for the children to be represented in such proceedings;

(d) provide information, advice and other support for the children and their families.

(2) The Assembly must also make provision for the performance of the functions conferred on Welsh family proceedings officers by virtue of any enactment (whether or not they are exercisable for the purposes of subsection (1)).

(3) In subsection (1), 'family proceedings' has the meaning given by section 12 of the Criminal Justice and Court Services Act 2000 (c. 43).

(4) In this Part, 'Welsh family proceedings officer' means—

(a) any member of the staff of the Assembly appointed to exercise the functions of a Welsh family proceedings officer; and

(b) any other individual exercising functions of a Welsh family proceedings officer by virtue of section 36(2) or (4).

36   Ancillary powers of the assembly

(1) The Assembly may make arrangements with organisations under which the organisations perform the functions of the Assembly under section 35 on its behalf.

(2) Arrangements under subsection (1) may provide for the organisations to designate individuals who may perform functions of Welsh family proceedings officers.

(3) The Assembly may only make an arrangement under subsection (1) if it is of the opinion—

(a) that the functions in question will be performed efficiently and to the required standard; and

(b) that the arrangement represents good value for money.

(4) The Assembly may make arrangements with individuals under which they may perform functions of Welsh family proceedings officers.

(5) The Assembly may make arrangements with an organisation or individual under which staff of the Assembly engaged in the exercise of its functions under section 35 may work for the organisation or individual.

(6) The Assembly may make arrangements with an organisation or individual under which any services provided by the Assembly's staff to the Assembly in the exercise of its functions under section 35 are also made available to the organisation or individual.

(7) The Assembly may charge for anything done under arrangements under subsection (5) and (6).

(8) In this section, references to organisations include public bodies and private or voluntary organisations.

37   Welsh family proceedings officers

(1) The Assembly may authorise a Welsh family proceedings officer of a description prescribed in regulations made by the Secretary of State—

> (a) to conduct litigation in relation to any proceedings in any court,
> (b) to exercise a right of audience in any proceedings in any court, in the exercise of his functions.

(2) A Welsh family proceedings officer exercising a right to conduct litigation by virtue of subsection (1)(a) who would otherwise have such a right by virtue of the fact that he is a person who, for the purposes of the Legal Services Act 2007, is an authorised person in relation to that activity is to be treated as having acquired that right solely by virtue of this section.

(3) A Welsh family proceedings officer exercising a right of audience by virtue of subsection (1)(b) who would otherwise have such a right by virtue of the fact that he is a person who, for the purposes of the Legal Services Act 2007, is an authorised person in relation to that activity is to be treated as having acquired that right solely by virtue of this section.

(4) A Welsh family proceedings officer may, subject to rules of court, be cross-examined in any proceedings to the same extent as any witness.

(5) But a Welsh family proceedings officer may not be cross-examined merely because he is exercising a right to conduct litigation or a right of audience granted in accordance with this section.

(6) In this section, 'right to conduct litigation' and 'right of audience' have the same meanings as in section 119 of the Courts and Legal Services Act 1990.

. . .

41   Sharing of information

(1) The Assembly and the Children and Family Court Advisory and Support Service may provide any information to each other for the purposes of their respective functions under this Part and Part 1 of the Criminal Justice and Court Services Act 2000 (c. 43).

(2) A Welsh family proceedings officer and an officer of the Service (within the meaning given by section 11(3) of that Act) may provide any information to each other for the purposes of any of their respective functions.

. . .

PART 5   MISCELLANEOUS

. . .

Local authority services

49   Payments to foster parents

(1) The appropriate person may by order make provision as to the payments to be made—

> (a) by a local authority in England or Wales or a person exercising functions on its behalf to a local authority foster parent with whom any child is placed by that authority or person under section 22C of the Children Act 1989;
> (b) by a voluntary organisation to any person with whom any child is placed by that organisation under section 59(1)(a) of that Act.

(2) In subsection (1)—

'appropriate person' means—

    (a) the Secretary of State, in relation to a local authority in England;

    (b) the Assembly, in relation to a children's services authority in Wales;

'local authority foster parent' and 'voluntary organisation' have the same meanings as in the Children Act 1989.

...

Other provisions

...

58 Reasonable punishment

(1) In relation to any offence specified in subsection (2), battery of a child cannot be justified on the ground that it constituted reasonable punishment.

(2) The offences referred to in subsection (1) are—

    (a) an offence under section 18 or 20 of the Offences against the Person Act 1861 (c. 100) (wounding and causing grievous bodily harm);

    (b) an offence under section 47 of that Act (assault occasioning actual bodily harm);

    (c) an offence under section 1 of the Children and Young Persons Act 1933 (c. 12) (cruelty to persons under 16).

(3) Battery of a child causing actual bodily harm to the child cannot be justified in any civil proceedings on the ground that it constituted reasonable punishment.

(4) For the purposes of subsection (3) 'actual bodily harm' has the same meaning as it has for the purposes of section 47 of the Offences against the Person Act 1861.

...

PART 6 GENERAL

...

65 Interpretation

(1) In this Act—

'the Assembly' means the National Assembly for Wales;

'child' means, subject to section 9, a person under the age of eighteen (and 'children' is to be construed accordingly);

'local authority' means—

    (a) a local authority in England;

    (b) a local authority in Wales;

'local authority in England' means—

    (a) a county council in England;

    (b) a metropolitan district council;

    (c) a non-metropolitan district council for an area for which there is no county council;

    (d) a London Borough council;

    (e) the Common Council of the City of London (in their capacity as a local authority);

    (f) the Council of the Isles of Scilly;

'local authority in Wales' means—

    (a) a county council in Wales;

    (b) a county borough council;

...

SCHEDULES

SCHEDULE 1   CHILDREN'S COMMISSIONER

Status

1.—(1) The Children's Commissioner is to be a corporation sole.

(2) The Children's Commissioner is not to be regarded as the servant or agent of the Crown or as enjoying any status, immunity or privilege of the Crown; and his property is not to be regarded as property of, or property held on behalf of, the Crown.

General powers

2.—(1) The Children's Commissioner may do anything which appears to him to be necessary or expedient for the purpose of, or in connection with, the exercise of his functions.

(2) In particular he may—

    (a) co-operate with other public authorities in the United Kingdom;

    (b) enter into contracts; and

    (c) acquire, hold and dispose of any property.

Appointment and tenure of office

3.—(1) The Children's Commissioner is to be appointed by the Secretary of State.

(2) The Secretary of State must take reasonable steps to involve children in the appointment of the Children's Commissioner.

(3) Subject to the provisions of this paragraph, a person shall hold and vacate office as the Children's Commissioner in accordance with the terms and conditions of his appointment as determined by the Secretary of State.

(4) An appointment as the Children's Commissioner shall be for a term not exceeding six years.

(5) A person who has held office as the Children's Commissioner is not eligible for reappointment.

(6) The Children's Commissioner may at any time resign by notice in writing to the Secretary of State.

(7) The Secretary of State may remove the Children's Commissioner from office if he is satisfied that he has—

    (a) become unfit or unable properly to discharge his functions; or

    (b) behaved in a way that is not compatible with his continuing in office.

...

Civil Partnership Act 2004

(2004 c. 33)

PART 1   INTRODUCTION

1   Civil partnership

(1) A civil partnership is a relationship between two people of the same sex ('civil partners')—

    (a) which is formed when they register as civil partners of each other—

        (i)   in England or Wales (under Part 2),

    ...

(2) Subsection (1) is subject to the provisions of this Act under or by virtue of which a civil partnership is void.

(3) A civil partnership ends only
  (a) on death, dissolution or annulment, or
  (b) in the case of a civil partnership formed as mentioned in subsection (1)(a)(i) or (iv), on the conversion of the civil partnership into a marriage under section 9 of the Marriage (Same Sex Couples) Act 2013.

(4) The references in subsection (3) to dissolution and annulment are to dissolution and annulment having effect under or recognised in accordance with this Act.

...

PART 2 CIVIL PARTNERSHIP: ENGLAND AND WALES

Chapter 1 Registration

Formation, eligibility and parental etc. consent

2 Formation of civil partnership by registration

(1) For the purposes of section 1, two people are to be regarded as having registered as civil partners of each other once each of them has signed the civil partnership document—
  (a) at the invitation of, and in the presence of, a civil partnership registrar, and
  (b) in the presence of each other and two witnesses.

(2) Subsection (1) applies regardless of whether subsections (3) and (4) are complied with.

(3) After the civil partnership document has been signed under subsection (1), it must also be signed, in the presence of the civil partners and each other, by—
  (a) each of the two witnesses, and
  (b) the civil partnership registrar.

(4) After the witnesses and the civil partnership registrar have signed the civil partnership document, the relevant registration authority must ensure that—
  (a) the fact that the two people have registered as civil partners of each other, and
  (b) any other information prescribed by regulations,
is recorded in the register as soon as is practicable.

(5) No religious service is to be used while the civil partnership registrar is officiating at the signing of a civil partnership document.

(6) 'The civil partnership document' has the meaning given by section 7(1).

(7) 'The relevant registration authority' means the registration authority in whose area the registration takes place.

3 Eligibility

(1) Two people are not eligible to register as civil partners of each other if—
  (a) they are not of the same sex,
  (b) either of them is already a civil partner or lawfully married,
  (c) either of them is under 16, or
  (d) they are within prohibited degrees of relationship.

(2) Part 1 of Schedule 1 contains provisions for determining when two people are within prohibited degrees of relationship.

4 Parental etc. consent where proposed civil partner under 18

(1) The consent of the appropriate persons is required before a child and another person may register as civil partners of each other.

(2) Part 1 of Schedule 2 contains provisions for determining who are the appropriate persons for the purposes of this section.

(3) The requirement of consent under subsection (1) does not apply if the child is a surviving civil partner or a widower or a widow.

(4) Nothing in this section affects any need to obtain the consent of the High Court before a ward of court and another person may register as civil partners of each other.

(5) In this Part 'child', except where used to express a relationship, means a person who is under 18.

Registration procedure: general

5 Types of pre-registration procedure

(1) Two people may register as civil partners of each other under—

(a) the standard procedure;

(b) the procedure for house-bound persons;

(c) the procedure for detained persons;

(d) the special procedure (which is for cases where a person is seriously ill and not expected to recover).

(2) The procedures referred to in subsection (1)(a) to (c) are subject to—

(a) section 20 (modified procedures for certain non-residents);

(b) Schedule 3 (former spouses one of whom has changed sex).

(3) The procedures referred to in subsection (1) (including the procedures as modified by section 20 and Schedule 3) are subject to—

(a) Part 2 of Schedule 1 (provisions applicable in connection with prohibited degrees of relationship), and

(b) Parts 2 and 3 of Schedule 2 (provisions applicable where proposed civil partner is under 18).

(4) This section is also subject to section 249 and Schedule 23 (immigration control and formation of civil partnerships).

6 Place of registration

(1) The place at which two people may register as civil partners of each other—

(a) must be in England or Wales,

(b) ... and

(c) must be specified in the notices, or notice, of proposed civil partnership required by this Chapter.

...

(3) Subsections (3A) and (3B) apply in the case of registration under the standard procedure (including that procedure modified as mentioned in section 5).

(3A) The place must be—

(a) on approved premises, or

(b) in a register office.

(3B) If it is in a register office, the place must be open to any person wishing to attend the registration.

(3C) In this Chapter 'register office' means a register office provided under section 10 of the Registration Service Act 1953.

6A Power to approve premises

(1) The Secretary of State may by regulations make provision for and in connection with the approval by registration authorities of premises for the purposes of section 6(3A)(a).

...

(2A) Regulations under this section may provide that premises approved for the registration of civil partnerships may differ from those premises approved for the registration of civil marriages.

...

(2C) The power conferred by section 258(2), in its application to the power conferred by this section, includes in particular—

(a) power to make provision in relation to religious premises that differs from provision in relation to other premises;

(b) power to make different provision for different kinds of religious premises.

...

(3A) For the avoidance of doubt, nothing in this Act places an obligation on religious organisations to host civil partnerships if they do not wish to do so.

(3B) 'Civil marriage' means marriage solemnised otherwise than according to the rites of the Church of England or any other religious usages.

(3C) 'Religious premises' means premises which—

(a) are used solely or mainly for religious purposes, or

(b) have been so used and have not subsequently been used solely or mainly for other purposes.

7   The civil partnership document

(1) In this Part 'the civil partnership document' means—

(a) in relation to the special procedure, a Registrar General's licence, and

(b) in relation to any other procedure, a civil partnership schedule.

(2) Before two people are entitled to register as civil partners of each other—

(a) the civil partnership document must be delivered to the civil partnership registrar, and

(b) the civil partnership registrar may then ask them for any information required (under section 2(4)) to be recorded in the register.

The standard procedure

8   Notice of proposed civil partnership and declaration

(1) For two people to register as civil partners of each other under the standard procedure a notice of proposed civil partnership must be given—

(a) if the proposed civil partners have resided in the area of the same registration authority for the period of 7 days immediately before the giving of the notice, by each of them to that registration authority;

(b) if the proposed civil partners have not resided in the area of the same registration authority for that period, by each of them to the registration authority in whose area he or she has resided for that period.

(2) A notice of proposed civil partnership must contain such information as may be prescribed by regulations.

(3) A notice of proposed civil partnership must also include the necessary declaration, made and signed by the person giving the notice—

(a) at the time when the notice is given, and

(b) in the presence of an authorised person;

and the authorised person must attest the declaration by adding his name, description and place of residence.

(4) The necessary declaration is a solemn declaration in writing—

(a) that the proposed civil partner believes that there is no impediment of kindred or affinity or other lawful hindrance to the formation of the civil partnership;

(b) that the proposed civil partners have for the period of 7 days immediately before the giving of the notice had their usual places of residence in the area of the registration authority, or in the areas of the registration authorities, to which notice is given.

(5) Where a notice of proposed civil partnership is given to a registration authority in accordance with this section, the registration authority must ensure that the following information is recorded in the register as soon as possible—

(a) the fact that the notice has been given and the information in it;

(b) the fact that the authorised person has attested the declaration.

(6) 'Authorised person' means an employee or officer or other person provided by a registration authority who is authorised by that authority to attest notices of proposed civil partnership.

(7) For the purposes of this Chapter, a notice of proposed civil partnership is recorded when subsection (5) is complied with.

9 Power to require evidence of name etc.

(1) The registration authority to which a notice of proposed civil partnership is given may require the person giving the notice to provide it with specified evidence—

(a) relating to that person, or

(b) if the registration authority considers that the circumstances are exceptional, relating not only to that person but also to that person's proposed civil partner.

(2) Such a requirement may be imposed at any time before the registration authority issues the civil partnership schedule under section 14.

(3) 'Specified evidence', in relation to a person, means such evidence as may be specified in guidance issued by the Registrar General—

(a) of the person's name and surname,

(b) of the person's age,

(c) as to whether the person has previously formed a civil partnership or a marriage and, if so, as to the ending of the civil partnership or marriage, and

(d) of the person's nationality.

10 Proposed civil partnership to be publicised

(1) Where a notice of proposed civil partnership has been given to a registration authority, the registration authority must keep the relevant information on public display during the waiting period.

(2) 'The relevant information' means—

(a) the name of the person giving the notice,

(b) the name of that person's proposed civil partner, and

(c) such other information included in the notice of proposed civil partnership as may be prescribed by regulations.

(3) All information that a registration authority is required for the time being to keep on public display under subsection (1) must be kept on display by it at one register office provided for a district within its area.

11 Meaning of 'the waiting period'

In this Chapter 'the waiting period', in relation to a notice of proposed civil partnership, means the period—

(a) beginning the day after the notice is recorded, and

(b) subject to section 12, ending at the end of the period of 15 days beginning with that day.

12 Power to shorten the waiting period

(1) If the Registrar General, on an application being made to him, is satisfied that there are compelling reasons because of the exceptional circumstances of the case for shortening the period of 15 days mentioned in section 11(b), he may shorten it to such period as he considers appropriate.

(2) Regulations may make provision with respect to the making, and granting, of applications under subsection (1).

(3) Regulations under subsection (2) may provide for—

(a) the power conferred by subsection (1) to be exercised by a registration authority on behalf of the Registrar General in such classes of case as are prescribed by the regulations;

(b) the making of an appeal to the Registrar General against a decision taken by a registration authority in accordance with regulations made by virtue of paragraph (a).

13 Objection to proposed civil partnership

(1) Any person may object to the issue of a civil partnership schedule under section 14 by giving any registration authority notice of his objection.

(2) A notice of objection must—

(a) state the objector's place of residence and the ground of objection, and

(b) be signed by or on behalf of the objector.

(3) If a notice of objection is given to a registration authority, it must ensure that the fact that it has been given and the information in it are recorded in the register as soon as possible.

14   Issue of civil partnership schedule

(1) As soon as the waiting period in relation to each notice of proposed civil partnership has expired, the registration authority in whose area it is proposed that the registration take place is under a duty, at the request of one or both of the proposed civil partners, to issue a document to be known as a 'civil partnership schedule'.

(2) Regulations may make provision as to the contents of a civil partnership schedule.

(3) The duty in subsection (1) does not apply if the registration authority is not satisfied that there is no lawful impediment to the formation of the civil partnership.

(4) If an objection to the issue of the civil partnership schedule has been recorded in the register, no civil partnership schedule is to be issued until—

(a) the relevant registration authority has investigated the objection and is satisfied that the objection ought not to obstruct the issue of the civil partnership schedule, or

(b) the objection has been withdrawn by the person who made it.

(5) 'The relevant registration authority' means the authority which first records that a notice of proposed civil partnership has been given by one of the proposed civil partners.

15   Appeal against refusal to issue civil partnership schedule

(1) If the registration authority refuses to issue a civil partnership schedule—

(a) because an objection to its issue has been made under section 13, or

(b) in reliance on section 14(3),

either of the proposed civil partners may appeal to the Registrar General.

(2) On an appeal under this section the Registrar General must either confirm the refusal or direct that a civil partnership schedule be issued.

16   Frivolous objections and representations: liability for costs etc.

(1) Subsection (3) applies if—

(a) a person objects to the issue of a civil partnership schedule, but

(b) the Registrar General declares that the grounds on which the objection is made are frivolous and ought not to obstruct the issue of the civil partnership schedule.

(2) Subsection (3) also applies if—

(a) in reliance on section 14(3), the registration authority refuses to issue a civil partnership schedule as a result of a representation made to it, and

(b) on an appeal under section 15 against the refusal, the Registrar General declares that the representation is frivolous and ought not to obstruct the issue of the civil partnership schedule.

(3) The person who made the objection or representation is liable for—

(a) the costs of the proceedings before the Registrar General, and

(b) damages recoverable by the proposed civil partner to whom the objection or representation relates.

(4) For the purpose of enabling any person to recover any such costs and damages, a copy of a declaration of the Registrar General purporting to be sealed with the seal of the General Register Office is evidence that the Registrar General has made the declaration.

17   Period during which registration may take place

(1) The proposed civil partners may not register as civil partners of each other on the production of the civil partnership schedule until the waiting period in relation to each notice of proposed civil partnership has expired.

(2) Subject to subsection (1), under the standard procedure, they may register as civil partners by signing the civil partnership schedule at any time during the applicable period.

(3) If they do not register as civil partners by signing the civil partnership schedule before the end of the applicable period—

(a) the notices of proposed civil partnership and the civil partnership schedule are void, and

(b) no civil partnership registrar may officiate at the signing of the civil partnership schedule by them.

(4) The applicable period, in relation to two people registering as civil partners of each other, is the period of 12 months beginning with—

(a) the day on which the notices of proposed civil partnership are recorded, or

(b) if the notices are not recorded on the same day, the earlier of those days.

The procedures for house-bound and detained persons

18   House-bound persons

(1) This section applies if two people wish to register as civil partners of each other at the place where one of them is house-bound.

(2) A person is house-bound at any place if, in relation to that person, a statement is made by a registered medical practitioner that, in his opinion—

(a) because of illness or disability, that person ought not to move or be moved from the place where he is at the time when the statement is made, and

(b) it is likely to be the case for at least the following 3 months that because of the illness or disability that person ought not to move or be moved from that place.

(3) The procedure under which the two people concerned may register as civil partners of each other is the same as the standard procedure, except that—

(a) each notice of proposed civil partnership must be accompanied by a statement under subsection (2) ('a medical statement'), which must have been made not more than 14 days before the day on which the notice is recorded,

(b) the fact that the registration authority to whom the notice is given has received the medical statement must be recorded in the register, and

(c) the applicable period (for the purposes of section 17) is the period of 3 months beginning with—

(i) the day on which the notices of proposed civil partnership are recorded, or

(ii) if the notices are not recorded on the same day, the earlier of those days.

(4) A medical statement must contain such information and must be made in such manner as may be prescribed by regulations.

(5) A medical statement may not be made in relation to a person who is detained as described in section 19(2).

(6) For the purposes of this Chapter, a person in relation to whom a medical statement is made is to be treated, if he would not otherwise be so treated, as resident and usually resident at the place where he is for the time being.

19   Detained persons

(1) This section applies if two people wish to register as civil partners of each other at the place where one of them is detained.

(2) 'Detained' means detained—

(a) as a patient in a hospital (but otherwise than by virtue of section 2, 4, 5, 35, 36 or 136 of the Mental Health Act 1983 (c. 20) (short term detentions)), or

(b) in a prison or other place to which the Prison Act 1952 (c. 52) applies.

(3) The procedure under which the two people concerned may register as civil partners of each other is the same as the standard procedure, except that—

(a) each notice of proposed civil partnership must be accompanied by a supporting statement, which must have been made not more than 21 days before the day on which the notice is recorded,

(b) the fact that the registration authority to whom the notice is given has received the supporting statement must be recorded in the register, and

(c) the applicable period (for the purposes of section 17) is the period of 3 months beginning with—

  (i) the day on which the notices of proposed civil partnership are recorded, or

  (ii) if the notices are not recorded on the same day, the earlier of those days.

(4) A supporting statement, in relation to a detained person, is a statement made by the responsible authority which—

(a) identifies the establishment where the person is detained, and

(b) states that the responsible authority has no objection to that establishment being specified in a notice of proposed civil partnership as the place at which the person is to register as a civil partner.

(5) A supporting statement must contain such information and must be made in such manner as may be prescribed by regulations.

(6) 'The responsible authority' means—

(a) if the person is detained in a hospital, the hospital's managers;

(b) if the person is detained in a prison or other place to which the 1952 Act applies, the governor or other officer for the time being in charge of that prison or other place.

(7) 'Patient' and 'hospital' have the same meaning as in Part 2 of the 1983 Act and 'managers', in relation to a hospital, has the same meaning as in section 145(1) of the 1983 Act.

(8) For the purposes of this Chapter, a detained person is to be treated, if he would not otherwise be so treated, as resident and usually resident at the place where he is for the time being.

...

The special procedure

21 Notice of proposed civil partnership

(1) For two people to register as civil partners of each other under the special procedure, one of them must—

(a) give a notice of proposed civil partnership to the registration authority for the area in which it is proposed that the registration take place, and

(b) comply with any requirement made under section 22.

(2) The notice must contain such information as may be prescribed by regulations.

(3) Subsections (3) to (6) of section 8 (necessary declaration etc.), apart from paragraph (b) of subsection (4), apply for the purposes of this section as they apply for the purposes of that section.

22 Evidence to be produced

(1) The person giving a notice of proposed civil partnership to a registration authority under the special procedure must produce to the authority such evidence as the Registrar General may require to satisfy him—

(a) that there is no lawful impediment to the formation of the civil partnership,

(b) that the conditions in subsection (2) are met, and

(c) that there is sufficient reason why a licence should be granted.

(2) The conditions are that one of the proposed civil partners—

(a) is seriously ill and not expected to recover,

(b) cannot be moved to a place where they could be registered as civil partners of each other under the standard procedure, and

(c) understands the nature and purport of signing a Registrar General's licence.

(3) The certificate of a registered medical practitioner is sufficient evidence of any or all of the matters referred to in subsection (2).

23 Application to be reported to Registrar General

On receiving a notice of proposed civil partnership under section 21 and any evidence under section 22, the registration authority must—

(a) inform the Registrar General, and

(b) comply with any directions the Registrar General may give for verifying the evidence given.

24   Objection to issue of registrar general's licence

(1) Any person may object to the Registrar General giving authority for the issue of his licence by giving the Registrar General or any registration authority notice of his objection.

(2) A notice of objection must—

(a) state the objector's place of residence and the ground of objection, and

(b) be signed by or on behalf of the objector.

(3) If a notice of objection is given to a registration authority, it must ensure that the fact that it has been given and the information in it are recorded in the register as soon as possible.

25   Issue of registrar general's licence

(1) This section applies where a notice of proposed civil partnership is given to a registration authority under section 21.

(2) The registration authority may issue a Registrar General's licence if, and only if, given authority to do so by the Registrar General.

(3) The Registrar General—

(a) may not give his authority unless he is satisfied that one of the proposed civil partners is seriously ill and not expected to recover, but

(b) if so satisfied, must give his authority unless a lawful impediment to the issue of his licence has been shown to his satisfaction to exist.

(4) A licence under this section must state that it is issued on the authority of the Registrar General.

(5) Regulations may (subject to subsection (4)) make provision as to the contents of a licence under this section.

(6) If an objection has been made to the Registrar General giving authority for the issue of his licence, he is not to give that authority until—

(a) he has investigated the objection and decided whether it ought to obstruct the issue of his licence, or

(b) the objection has been withdrawn by the person who made it.

(7) Any decision of the Registrar General under subsection (6)(a) is final.

26   Frivolous objections: liability for costs

(1) This section applies if—

(a) a person objects to the Registrar General giving authority for the issue of his licence, but

(b) the Registrar General declares that the grounds on which the objection is made are frivolous and ought not to obstruct the issue of his licence.

(2) The person who made the objection is liable for—

(a) the costs of the proceedings before the Registrar General, and

(b) damages recoverable by the proposed civil partner to whom the objection relates.

(3) For the purpose of enabling any person to recover any such costs and damages, a copy of a declaration of the Registrar General purporting to be sealed with the seal of the General Register Office is evidence that the Registrar General has made the declaration.

27   Period during which registration may take place

(1) If a Registrar General's licence has been issued under section 25, the proposed civil partners may register as civil partners by signing it at any time within 1 month from the day on which the notice of proposed civil partnership was given.

(2) If they do not register as civil partners by signing the licence within the 1 month period—

(a) the notice of proposed civil partnership and the licence are void, and

(b) no civil partnership registrar may officiate at the signing of the licence by them.

Supplementary

28   Registration authorities

In this Chapter 'registration authority' means—

(a) in relation to England, a county council, the council of any district comprised in an area for which there is no county council, a London borough council, the Common Council of the City of London or the Council of the Isles of Scilly;

(b) in relation to Wales, a county council or a county borough council.

29　Civil partnership registrars

(1) A civil partnership registrar is an individual who is designated by a registration authority as a civil partnership registrar for its area.

(2) It is the duty of each registration authority to ensure that there is a sufficient number of civil partnership registrars for its area to carry out in that area the functions of civil partnership registrars.

(3) Each registration authority must inform the Registrar General as soon as is practicable—

(a) of any designation it has made of a person as a civil partnership registrar, and

(b) of the ending of any such designation.

30　The Registrar general and the register

(1) In this Chapter 'the Registrar General' means the Registrar General for England and Wales.

(2) The Registrar General must provide a system for keeping any records that relate to civil partnerships and are required by this Chapter to be made.

(3) The system may, in particular, enable those records to be kept together with other records kept by the Registrar General.

(4) In this Chapter 'the register' means the system for keeping records provided under subsection (2).

31　Offences relating to civil partnership schedule

(1) A person commits an offence if he issues a civil partnership schedule knowing that he does so—

(a) before the waiting period in relation to each notice of proposed civil partnership has expired,

(b) after the end of the applicable period, or

(c) at a time when its issue has been forbidden under Schedule 2 by a person entitled to forbid its issue.

(2) A person commits an offence if, in his actual or purported capacity as a civil partnership registrar, he officiates at the signing of a civil partnership schedule by proposed civil partners knowing that he does so—

(a) at a place other than the place specified in the notices of proposed civil partnership and the civil partnership schedule,

(aa) on premises that are not approved premises although the signing is purportedly in accordance with section 6(3A)(a),…

(b) in the absence of a civil partnership registrar,

(c) before the waiting period in relation to each notice of proposed civil partnership has expired, or

(d) even though the civil partnership is void under section 49(b) or (c).

(3) A person guilty of an offence under subsection (1) or (2)(a), (aa), (b), (c) or (d) is liable on conviction on indictment to imprisonment for a term not exceeding 5 years or to a fine (or both).

(3A) A person guilty of an offence under subsection (2)(ab) is liable on conviction on indictment to imprisonment for a term not exceeding 14 years or to a fine or both.

(4) A prosecution under this section may not be commenced more than 3 years after the commission of the offence.

32　Offences relating to Registrar General's licence

(1) A person commits an offence if—

(a) he gives information by way of evidence in response to a requirement under section 22(1), knowing that the information is false;

(b) he gives a certificate as provided for by section 22(3), knowing that the certificate is false.

(2) A person commits an offence if, in his actual or purported capacity as a civil partnership registrar, he officiates at the signing of a Registrar General's licence by proposed civil partners knowing that he does so—

    (a) at a place other than the place specified in the licence,

    (b) in the absence of a civil partnership registrar,

    (c) after the end of 1 month from the day on which the notice of proposed civil partnership was given, or

    (d) even though the civil partnership is void under section 49(b) or (c).

(3) A person guilty of an offence under subsection (1) or (2) is liable—

    (a) on conviction on indictment, to imprisonment not exceeding 3 years or to a fine (or both);

    (b) on summary conviction, to a fine not exceeding the statutory maximum.

(4) A prosecution under this section may not be commenced more than 3 years after the commission of the offence.

33 Offences relating to the recording of civil partnerships

(1) A civil partnership registrar commits an offence if he refuses or fails to comply with the provisions of this Chapter or of any regulations made under section 36.

(2) A civil partnership registrar guilty of an offence under subsection (1) is liable—

    (a) on conviction on indictment, to imprisonment for a term not exceeding 2 years or to a fine (or both);

    (b) on summary conviction, to a fine not exceeding the statutory maximum;

and on conviction shall cease to be a civil partnership registrar.

(3) A person commits an offence if—

    (a) under arrangements made by a registration authority for the purposes of section 2(4), he is under a duty to record information required to be recorded under section 2(4), but

    (b) he refuses or without reasonable cause omits to do so.

(4) A person guilty of an offence under subsection (3) is liable on summary conviction to a fine not exceeding level 3 on the standard scale.

(5) A person commits an offence if he records in the register information relating to the formation of a civil partnership by the signing of a civil partnership schedule, knowing that the civil partnership is void under section 49(b) or (c).

(6) A person guilty of an offence under subsection (5) is liable on conviction on indictment, to imprisonment for a term not exceeding 5 years or to a fine (or both).

(7) A person commits an offence if he records in the register information relating to the formation of a civil partnership by the signing of a Registrar General's licence, knowing that the civil partnership is void under section 49(b) or (c).

(8) A person guilty of an offence under subsection (7) is liable—

    (a) on conviction on indictment, to imprisonment for a term not exceeding 3 years or to a fine (or both);

    (b) on summary conviction, to a fine not exceeding the statutory maximum.

(9) A prosecution under subsection (5) or (7) may not be commenced more than 3 years after the commission of the offence.

34 Fees

(1) The Secretary of State may by order provide for fees, of such amounts as may be specified in the order, to be payable to such persons as may be prescribed by the order in respect of—

    (a) the giving of a notice of proposed civil partnership and the attestation of the necessary declaration;

    (b) the making of an application under section 12(1) (application to reduce waiting period);

    (c) the issue of a Registrar General's licence;

(d) the attendance of the civil partnership registrar when two people sign the civil partnership document;

(e) such other services provided in connection with civil partnerships either by registration
authorities or by or on behalf of the Registrar General as may be prescribed by the order.

(2) The Registrar General may remit the fee for the issue of his licence in whole or in part in
any case where it appears to him that the payment of the fee would cause hardship to the proposed
civil partners.

(3) Where a civil partnership registrar for any area attends when two people sign the civil partnership schedule on approved premises, in accordance with section 6(3A)(a)—

(a) subsection (1)(d) does not apply, but

(b) the registration authority for that area is entitled from those people a fee of an amount
determined by the authority in accordance with regulations under section 6A.

35   Power to assimilate provisions relating to civil registration

(1) The Secretary of State may by order make—

(a) such amendments of this Act as appear to him appropriate for the purpose of assimi-
lating any provision connected with the formation or recording of civil partnerships in
England and Wales to any provision made in relation to civil marriage in England and
Wales, and

(b) such amendments of other enactments and of subordinate legislation as appear to him
appropriate in consequence of any amendments made under paragraph (a).

(2) 'Civil marriage' means marriage solemnised otherwise than according to the rites of the
Church of England or any other religious usages.

(3) 'Amendment' includes repeal or revocation.

(4) 'Subordinate legislation' has the same meaning as in the Interpretation Act 1978 (c. 30).

36   Regulations and orders

(1) Regulations may make provision supplementing the provisions of this Chapter.

(2) Regulations may in particular make provision—

(a) relating to the use of Welsh in documents and records relating to civil partnerships;

(b) with respect to the retention of documents relating to civil partnerships;

(c) prescribing the duties of civil partnership registrars;

(d) prescribing the duties of persons in whose presence any declaration is made for the purposes of this Chapter;

(e) for the issue by the Registrar General of guidance supplementing any provision made by
the regulations.

(f) for the issue by registration authorities or the Registrar General of certified copies of
entries in the register and for such copies to be received in evidence.

(3) In this Chapter, except in subsection 6A, 'regulations' means regulations made by the
Registrar General with the approval of the Secretary of State.

(4) Any power to make regulations or an order under this Chapter is exercisable by statutory
instrument.

(5) A statutory instrument containing regulations under section 6A or an order under section
34 is subject to annulment in pursuance of a resolution of either House of Parliament.

(6) No order may be made under section 35 unless a draft of the statutory instrument containing the order has been laid before, and approved by a resolution of, each House of Parliament.

Chapter 2 Dissolution, nullity and other proceedings

Introduction

37   Powers to make orders and effect of orders

(1) The court may, in accordance with this Chapter—

(a) make an order (a 'dissolution order') which dissolves a civil partnership on the ground
that it has broken down irretrievably;

    (b) make an order (a 'nullity order') which annuls a civil partnership which is void or voidable;

    (c) make an order (a 'presumption of death order') which dissolves a civil partnership on the ground that one of the civil partners is presumed to be dead;

    (d) make an order (a 'separation order') which provides for the separation of the civil partners.

(2) Every dissolution, nullity or presumption of death order—

    (a) is, in the first instance, a conditional order, and

    (b) may not be made final before the end of the prescribed period (see section 38); and any reference in this Chapter to a conditional order is to be read accordingly.

(3) A nullity order made where a civil partnership is voidable annuls the civil partnership only as respects any time after the order has been made final, and the civil partnership is to be treated (despite the order) as if it had existed up to that time.

(4) In this Chapter, other than in sections 58 to 61, 'the court' means—

    (a) the High Court, or

    (b) the family court.

(5) This Chapter is subject to sections 219 to 224 (jurisdiction of the court).

38 The period before conditional orders may be made final

(1) Subject to subsections (2) to (4), the prescribed period for the purposes of section 37(2)(b) is—

    (a) 6 weeks from the making of the conditional order, or

    (b) if the 6 week period would end on a day on which the office or registry of the court dealing with the case is closed, the period of 6 weeks extended to the end of the first day on which the office or registry is next open.

(2) The Lord Chancellor may by order amend this section so as to substitute a different definition of the prescribed period for the purposes of section 37(2)(b).

(3) But the Lord Chancellor may not under subsection (2) provide for a period longer than 6 months to be the prescribed period.

(4) In a particular case the court dealing with the case may by order shorten the prescribed period.

(5) The power to make an order under subsection (2) is exercisable by statutory instrument.

(6) An instrument containing such an order is subject to annulment in pursuance of a resolution of either House of Parliament.

39 Intervention of the Queen's Proctor

(1) This section applies if an application has been made for a dissolution, nullity or presumption of death order.

(2) The court may, if it thinks fit, direct that all necessary papers in the matter are to be sent to the Queen's Proctor who must under the directions of the Attorney General instruct counsel to argue before the court any question in relation to the matter which the court considers it necessary or expedient to have fully argued.

(3) If any person at any time—

    (a) during the progress of the proceedings, or

    (b) before the conditional order is made final,

gives information to the Queen's Proctor on any matter material to the due decision of the case, the Queen's Proctor may take such steps as the Attorney General considers necessary or expedient.

(4) If the Queen's Proctor intervenes or shows cause against the making of the conditional order in any proceedings relating to its making, the court may make such order as may be just as to—

    (a) the payment by other parties to the proceedings of the costs incurred by him in doing so, or

    (b) the payment by the Queen's Proctor of any costs incurred by any of those parties because of his doing so.

(5) The Queen's Proctor is entitled to charge as part of the expenses of his office—

    (a) the costs of any proceedings under subsection (2);

    (b) if his reasonable costs of intervening or showing cause as mentioned in subsection (4) are not fully satisfied by an order under subsection (4)(a), the amount of the difference;

    (c) if the Treasury so directs, any costs which he pays to any parties under an order made under subsection (4)(b).

40   Proceedings before order has been made final

(1) This section applies if—

    (a) a conditional order has been made, and

    (b) the Queen's Proctor, or any person who has not been a party to proceedings in which the order was made, shows cause why the order should not be made final on the ground that material facts have not been brought before the court.

(2) This section also applies if—

    (a) a conditional order has been made,

    (b) 3 months have elapsed since the earliest date on which an application could have been made for the order to be made final,

    (c) no such application has been made by the civil partner who applied for the conditional order, and

    (d) the other civil partner makes an application to the court under this subsection.

(3) The court may—

    (a) make the order final,

    (b) rescind the order,

    (c) require further inquiry, or

    (d) otherwise deal with the case as it thinks fit.

(4) Subsection (3)(a)—

    (a) applies despite section 37(2) (period before conditional orders may be made final), but

    (b) is subject to section 48(4) (protection for respondent in separation cases).

41   Time bar on applications for dissolution orders

(1) No application for a dissolution order may be made to the court before the end of the period of 1 year from the date of the formation of the civil partnership.

(2) Nothing in this section prevents the making of an application based on matters which occurred before the end of the 1 year period.

42   Attempts at reconciliation of civil partners

(1) This section applies in relation to cases where an application is made for a dissolution or separation order.

(2) Rules of court must make provision for requiring the legal representative acting for the applicant to certify whether he has—

    (a) discussed with the applicant the possibility of a reconciliation with the other civil partner, and

    (b) given the applicant the names and addresses of persons qualified to help effect a reconciliation between civil partners who have become estranged.

(3) If at any stage of proceedings for the order it appears to the court that there is a reasonable possibility of a reconciliation between the civil partners, the court may adjourn the proceedings for such period as it thinks fit to enable attempts to be made to effect a reconciliation between them.

(4) The power to adjourn under subsection (3) is additional to any other power of adjournment.

43   Consideration by the court of certain agreements or arrangements

(1) This section applies in relation to cases where—

    (a) proceedings for a dissolution or separation order are contemplated or have begun, and

    (b) an agreement or arrangement is made or proposed to be made between the civil partners which relates to, arises out of, or is connected with, the proceedings.

(2) Rules of court may make provision for enabling—

    (a) the civil partners, or either of them, to refer the agreement or arrangement to the court, and

    (b) the court—

        (i) to express an opinion, if it thinks it desirable to do so, as to the reasonableness of the agreement or arrangement, and

        (ii) to give such directions, if any, in the matter as it thinks fit.

Dissolution of civil partnership

44 Dissolution of civil partnership which has broken down irretrievably

(1) Subject to section 41, an application for a dissolution order may be made to the court by either civil partner on the ground that the civil partnership has broken down irretrievably.

(2) On an application for a dissolution order the court must inquire, so far as it reasonably can, into—

    (a) the facts alleged by the applicant, and

    (b) any facts alleged by the respondent.

(3) The court hearing an application for a dissolution order must not hold that the civil partnership has broken down irretrievably unless the applicant satisfies the court of one or more of the facts described in subsection (5)(a), (b), (c) or (d).

(4) But if the court is satisfied of any of those facts, it must make a dissolution order unless it is satisfied on all the evidence that the civil partnership has not broken down irretrievably.

(5) The facts referred to in subsections (3) and (4) are—

    (a) that the respondent has behaved in such a way that the applicant cannot reasonably be expected to live with the respondent;

    (b) that—

        (i) the applicant and the respondent have lived apart for a continuous period of at least 2 years immediately preceding the making of the application ('2 years' separation'), and

        (ii) the respondent consents to a dissolution order being made;

    (c) that the applicant and the respondent have lived apart for a continuous period of at least 5 years immediately preceding the making of the application ('5 years' separation');

    (d) that the respondent has deserted the applicant for a continuous period of at least 2 years immediately preceding the making of the application.

45 Supplemental provisions as to facts raising presumption of breakdown

(1) Subsection (2) applies if—

    (a) in any proceedings for a dissolution order the applicant alleges, in reliance on section 44(5)(a), that the respondent has behaved in such a way that the applicant cannot reasonably be expected to live with the respondent, but

    (b) after the date of the occurrence of the final incident relied on by the applicant and held by the court to support his allegation, the applicant and the respondent have lived together for a period (or periods) which does not, or which taken together do not, exceed 6 months.

(2) The fact that the applicant and respondent have lived together as mentioned in subsection (1)(b) must be disregarded in determining, for the purposes of section 44(5)(a), whether the applicant cannot reasonably be expected to live with the respondent.

(3) Subsection (4) applies in relation to cases where the applicant alleges, in reliance on section 44(5)(b), that the respondent consents to a dissolution order being made.

(4) Rules of court must make provision for the purpose of ensuring that the respondent has been given such information as will enable him to understand—

    (a) the consequences to him of consenting to the making of the order, and

    (b) the steps which he must take to indicate his consent.

(5) For the purposes of section 44(5)(d) the court may treat a period of desertion as having continued at a time when the deserting civil partner was incapable of continuing the necessary intention, if the evidence before the court is such that, had he not been so incapable, the court would have inferred that the desertion continued at that time.

(6) In considering for the purposes of section 44(5) whether the period for which the civil partners have lived apart or the period for which the respondent has deserted the applicant has been continuous, no account is to be taken of—

    (a) any one period not exceeding 6 months, or

    (b) any two or more periods not exceeding 6 months in all,

during which the civil partners resumed living with each other.

(7) But no period during which the civil partners have lived with each other counts as part of the period during which the civil partners have lived apart or as part of the period of desertion.

(8) For the purposes of section 44(5)(b) and (c) and this section civil partners are to be treated as living apart unless they are living with each other in the same household, and references in this section to civil partners living with each other are to be read as references to their living with each other in the same household.

46 Dissolution order not precluded by previous separation order etc.

(1) Subsections (2) and (3) apply if any of the following orders has been made in relation to a civil partnership—

    (a) a separation order;

    (b) an order under Schedule 6 (financial relief in magistrates' courts etc.);

    (c) an order under section 33 of the Family Law Act 1996 (c. 27) (occupation orders);

    (d) an order under section 37 of the 1996 Act (orders where neither civil partner entitled to occupy the home).

(2) Nothing prevents—

    (a) either civil partner from applying for a dissolution order, or

    (b) the court from making a dissolution order,

on the same facts, or substantially the same facts, as those proved in support of the making of the order referred to in subsection (1).

(3) On the application for the dissolution order, the court—

    (a) may treat the order referred to in subsection (1) as sufficient proof of any desertion or other fact by reference to which it was made, but

    (b) must not make the dissolution order without receiving evidence from the applicant.

(4) If—

    (a) the application for the dissolution order follows a separation order or any order requiring the civil partners to live apart,

    (b) there was a period of desertion immediately preceding the institution of the proceedings for the separation order, and

    (c) the civil partners have not resumed living together and the separation order has been continuously in force since it was made,

the period of desertion is to be treated for the purposes of the application for the dissolution order as if it had immediately preceded the making of the application.

(5) For the purposes of section 44(5)(d) the court may treat as a period during which the respondent has deserted the applicant any period during which there is in force—

    (a) an injunction granted by the High Court, the family court or the county court which excludes the respondent from the civil partnership home, or

    (b) an order under section 33 or 37 of the 1996 Act which prohibits the respondent from occupying a dwelling-house in which the applicant and the respondent have, or at any time have had, a civil partnership home.

47 Refusal of dissolution in 5 year separation cases on ground of grave hardship

(1) The respondent to an application for a dissolution order in which the applicant alleges 5 years' separation may oppose the making of an order on the ground that—

    (a) the dissolution of the civil partnership will result in grave financial or other hardship to him, and

    (b) it would in all the circumstances be wrong to dissolve the civil partnership.

(2) Subsection (3) applies if—

    (a) the making of a dissolution order is opposed under this section,

    (b) the court finds that the applicant is entitled to rely in support of his application on the fact of 5 years' separation and makes no such finding as to any other fact mentioned in section 44(5), and

    (c) apart from this section, the court would make a dissolution order.

(3) The court must—

    (a) consider all the circumstances, including the conduct of the civil partners and the interests of the civil partners and of any children or other persons concerned, and

    (b) if it is of the opinion that the ground mentioned in subsection (1) is made out, dismiss the application for the dissolution order.

(4) 'Hardship' includes the loss of the chance of acquiring any benefit which the respondent might acquire if the civil partnership were not dissolved.

48 Proceedings before order made final: protection for respondent in separation cases

(1) The court may, on an application made by the respondent, rescind a conditional dissolution order if—

    (a) it made the order on the basis of a finding that the applicant was entitled to rely on the fact of 2 years' separation coupled with the respondent's consent to a dissolution order being made,

    (b) it made no such finding as to any other fact mentioned in section 44(5), and

    (c) it is satisfied that the applicant misled the respondent (whether intentionally or unintentionally) about any matter which the respondent took into account in deciding to give his consent.

(2) Subsections (3) to (5) apply if—

    (a) the respondent to an application for a dissolution order in which the applicant alleged—

        (i) 2 years' separation coupled with the respondent's consent to a dissolution order being made, or

        (ii) 5 years' separation,

    has applied to the court for consideration under subsection (3) of his financial position after the dissolution of the civil partnership, and

    (b) the court—

        (i) has made a conditional dissolution order on the basis of a finding that the applicant was entitled to rely in support of his application on the fact of 2 years' or 5 years' separation, and

        (ii) has made no such finding as to any other fact mentioned in section 44(5).

(3) The court hearing an application by the respondent under subsection (2) must consider all the circumstances, including—

    (a) the age, health, conduct, earning capacity, financial resources and financial obligations of each of the parties, and

    (b) the financial position of the respondent as, having regard to the dissolution, it is likely to be after the death of the applicant should the applicant die first.

(4) Subject to subsection (5), the court must not make the order final unless it is satisfied that—

    (a) the applicant should not be required to make any financial provision for the respondent, or

(b) the financial provision made by the applicant for the respondent is—

    (i)   reasonable and fair, or

    (ii) the best that can be made in the circumstances.

(5) The court may if it thinks fit make the order final if—

(a) it appears that there are circumstances making it desirable that the order should be made final without delay, and

(b) it has obtained a satisfactory undertaking from the applicant that he will make such financial provision for the respondent as it may approve.

Nullity

49   Grounds on which civil partnership is void

Where two people register as civil partners of each other in England and Wales, the civil partnership is void if—

(a) at the time when they do so, they are not eligible to register as civil partners of each other under Chapter 1 (see section 3),

(b) at the time when they do so they both know—

    (i)   that due notice of proposed civil partnership has not been given,

    (ii)   that the civil partnership document has not been duly issued,

    (iii) that the civil partnership document is void under section 17(3) or 27(2) (registration after end of time allowed for registering),

    (iv) that the place of registration is a place other than that specified in the notices (or notice) of proposed civil partnership and the civil partnership document,

    (v)   that a civil partnership registrar is not present, or

    (vi) that the place of registration is on premises that are not approved premises although the registration is purportedly in accordance with section 6(3A)(a), or

(c) the civil partnership document is void under paragraph 6(5) of Schedule 2 (civil partnership between child and another person forbidden).

50   Grounds on which civil partnership is voidable

(1) Where two people register as civil partners of each other in England and Wales, the civil partnership is voidable if—

(a) either of them did not validly consent to its formation (whether as a result of duress, mistake, unsoundness of mind or otherwise);

(b) at the time of its formation either of them, though capable of giving a valid consent, was suffering (whether continuously or intermittently) from mental disorder of such a kind or to such an extent as to be unfitted for civil partnership;

(c) at the time of its formation, the respondent was pregnant by some person other than the applicant;

(d) an interim gender recognition certificate under the Gender Recognition Act 2004 (c. 7) has, after the time of its formation, been issued to either civil partner;

(e) the respondent is a person whose gender at the time of its formation had become the acquired gender under the 2004 Act.

(2) In this section and section 51 'mental disorder' has the same meaning as in the Mental Health Act 1983 (c. 20).

51   Bars to relief where civil partnership is voidable

(1) The court must not make a nullity order on the ground that a civil partnership is voidable if the respondent satisfies the court—

(a) that the applicant, with knowledge that it was open to him to obtain a nullity order, conducted himself in relation to the respondent in such a way as to lead the respondent reasonably to believe that he would not seek to do so, and

(b) that it would be unjust to the respondent to make the order.

(2) Without prejudice to subsection (1), the court must not make a nullity order by virtue of section 50(1)(a), (b), (c) or (e) unless—

    (a) it is satisfied that proceedings were instituted within 3 years from the date of the formation of the civil partnership, or

    (b) leave for the institution of proceedings after the end of that 3 year period has been granted under subsection (3).

(3) A judge of the court may, on an application made to him, grant leave for the institution of proceedings if he—

    (a) is satisfied that the applicant has at some time during the 3 year period suffered from mental disorder, and

    (b) considers that in all the circumstances of the case it would be just to grant leave for the institution of proceedings.

(4) An application for leave under subsection (3) may be made after the end of the 3 year period.

(5) Without prejudice to subsection (1), the court must not make a nullity order by virtue of section 50(1)(d) unless it is satisfied that proceedings were instituted within the period of 6 months from the date of issue of the interim gender recognition certificate.

(6) Without prejudice to subsections (1) and (2), the court must not make a nullity order by virtue of section 50(1)(c) or (e) unless it is satisfied that the applicant was at the time of the formation of the civil partnership ignorant of the facts alleged.

52 Proof of certain matters not necessary to validity of civil partnership

(1) Where two people have registered as civil partners of each other in England and Wales, it is not necessary in support of the civil partnership to give any proof—

    (a) that any person whose consent to the civil partnership was required by section 4 (parental etc. consent) had given his consent, or

    (aa) that before the registration either of the civil partners resided, or resided for any period, in the area stated in the notices of proposed civil partnership to be the area of that person's place of residence,

and no evidence is to be given to prove the contrary in any proceedings touching the validity of the civil partnership.

(2) Subsection (1)(a) is subject to section 49(c) (civil partnership void if forbidden).

53 Power to validate civil partnership

(1) Where two people have registered as civil partners of each other in England and Wales, the Lord Chancellor may by order validate the civil partnership if it appears to him that it is or may be void under section 49(b).

(2) An order under subsection (1) may include provisions for relieving a person from any liability under section 31(2), 32(2) or 33(5) or (7).

(3) The draft of an order under subsection (1) must be advertised, in such manner as the Lord Chancellor thinks fit, not less than one month before the order is made.

(4) The Lord Chancellor must—

    (a) consider all objections to the order sent to him in writing during that month, and

    (b) if it appears to him necessary, direct a local inquiry into the validity of any such objections.

(5) An order under subsection (1) is subject to special parliamentary procedure.

...

Presumption of death orders

55 Presumption of death orders

(1) The court may, on an application made by a civil partner, make a presumption of death order if it is satisfied that reasonable grounds exist for supposing that the other civil partner is dead.

(2) In any proceedings under this section the fact that—

    (a) for a period of 7 years or more the other civil partner has been continually absent from the applicant, and

(b) the applicant has no reason to believe that the other civil partner has been living within
        that time,

is evidence that the other civil partner is dead until the contrary is proved.

Separation orders

56   Separation orders

(1) An application for a separation order may be made to the court by either civil partner on the
ground that any such fact as is mentioned in section 44(5)(a), (b), (c) or (d) exists.

(2) On an application for a separation order the court must inquire, so far as it reasonably can,
into—

(a) the facts alleged by the applicant, and

(b) any facts alleged by the respondent,

but whether the civil partnership has broken down irretrievably is irrelevant.

(3) If the court is satisfied on the evidence of any such fact as is mentioned in section 44(5)(a),
(b), (c) or (d) it must make a separation order.

(4) Section 45 (supplemental provisions as to facts raising presumption of breakdown) applies
for the purposes of an application for a separation order alleging any such fact as it applies in relation
to an application for a dissolution order alleging that fact.

57   Effect of separation order

If either civil partner dies intestate as respects all or any of his or her real or personal property
while—

(a) a separation order is in force, and

(b) the separation is continuing,

the property as respects which he or she died intestate devolves as if the other civil partner had then
been dead.

Declarations

58   Declarations

(1) Any person may apply to the High Court or the family court for one or more of the following
declarations in relation to a civil partnership specified in the application—

(a) a declaration that the civil partnership was at its inception a valid civil partnership;

(b) a declaration that the civil partnership subsisted on a date specified in the application;

(c) a declaration that the civil partnership did not subsist on a date so specified;

...

(2) Where an application under subsection (1) is made to a court by a person other than a civil
partner in the civil partnership to which the application relates, the court must refuse to hear the
application if it considers that the applicant does not have a sufficient interest in the determination
of that application.

59   General provisions as to making and effect of declarations

(1) Where on an application for a declaration under section 58 the truth of the proposition to be
declared is proved to the satisfaction of the court, the court must make the declaration unless to do
so would be manifestly contrary to public policy.

(2) Any declaration under section 58 binds Her Majesty and all other persons.

(3) The court, on the dismissal of an application for a declaration under section 58, may not
make any declaration for which an application has not been made.

(4) No declaration which may be applied for under section 58 may be made otherwise than
under section 58 by any court.

(5) No declaration may be made by any court, whether under section 58 or otherwise, that a
civil partnership was at its inception void.

(6) Nothing in this section affects the powers of any court to make a nullity order in respect of a civil partnership.

60 The attorney general and proceedings for declarations

(1) On an application for a declaration under section 58 the court may at any stage of the proceedings, of its own motion or on the application of any party to the proceedings, direct that all necessary papers in the matter be sent to the Attorney General.

(2) The Attorney General, whether or not he is sent papers in relation to an application for a declaration under section 58, may—

(a) intervene in the proceedings on that application in such manner as he thinks necessary or expedient, and

(b) argue before the court dealing with the application any question in relation to the application which the court considers it necessary to have fully argued.

(3) Where any costs are incurred by the Attorney General in connection with any application for a declaration under section 58, the court may make such order as it considers just as to the payment of those costs by parties to the proceedings.

61 Supplementary provisions as to declarations

(1) Any declaration made under section 58, and any application for such a declaration, must be in the form prescribed by rules of court.

(2) Rules of court may make provision—

(a) as to the information required to be given by any applicant for a declaration under section 58;

(b) requiring notice of an application under section 58 to be served on the Attorney General and on persons who may be affected by any declaration applied for.

(3) No proceedings under section 58 affect any final judgment or order already pronounced or made by any court of competent jurisdiction.

(4) The court hearing an application under section 58 may direct that the whole or any part of the proceedings must be heard in private.

(5) An application for a direction under subsection (4) must be heard in private unless the court otherwise directs.

General provisions

62 Relief for respondent in dissolution proceedings

(1) If in any proceedings for a dissolution order the respondent alleges and proves any such fact as is mentioned in section 44(5)(a), (b), (c) or (d) the court may give to the respondent the relief to which he would have been entitled if he had made an application seeking that relief.

(2) When applying subsection (1), treat—

(a) the respondent as the applicant, and

(b) the applicant as the respondent,

for the purposes of section 44(5).

...

64 Parties to proceedings under this chapter

(1) Rules of court may make provision with respect to—

(a) the joinder as parties to proceedings under sections 37 to 56 of persons involved in allegations of improper conduct made in those proceedings,

(b) the dismissal from such proceedings of any parties so joined, and

(c) the persons who are to be parties to proceedings on an application under section 58.

(2) Rules of court made under this section may make different provision for different cases.

(3) In every case in which the court considers, in the interest of a person not already a party to the proceedings, that the person should be made a party, the court may if it thinks fit allow the person to intervene upon such terms, if any, as the court thinks just.

Chapter 3 Property and financial arrangements

65 Contribution by civil partner to property improvement

(1) This section applies if—

(a) a civil partner contributes in money or money's worth to the improvement of real or personal property in which or in the proceeds of sale of which either or both of the civil partners has or have a beneficial interest, and

(b) the contribution is of a substantial nature.

(2) The contributing partner is to be treated as having acquired by virtue of the contribution a share or an enlarged share (as the case may be) in the beneficial interest of such an extent—

(a) as may have been then agreed, or

(b) in default of such agreement, as may seem in all the circumstances just to any court before which the question of the existence or extent of the beneficial interest of either of the civil partners arises (whether in proceedings between them or in any other proceedings).

(3) Subsection (2) is subject to any agreement (express or implied) between the civil partners to the contrary.

66 Disputes between civil partners about property

(1) In any question between the civil partners in a civil partnership as to title to or possession of property, either civil partner may apply to—

(a) the High Court, or

(b) the family court.

(2) On such an application, the court may make such order with respect to the property as it thinks fit (including an order for the sale of the property).

67 Applications under section 66 where property not in possession etc.

(1) The right of a civil partner ('A') to make an application under section 66 includes the right to make such an application where A claims that the other civil partner ('B') has had in his possession or under his control—

(a) money to which, or to a share of which, A was beneficially entitled, or

(b) property (other than money) to which, or to an interest in which, A was beneficially entitled,

and that either the money or other property has ceased to be in B's possession or under B's control or that A does not know whether it is still in B's possession or under B's control.

(2) For the purposes of subsection (1)(a) it does not matter whether A is beneficially entitled to the money or share—

(a) because it represents the proceeds of property to which, or to an interest in which, A was beneficially entitled, or

(b) for any other reason.

(3) Subsections (4) and (5) apply if, on such an application being made, the court is satisfied that B—

(a) has had in his possession or under his control money or other property as mentioned in subsection (1)(a) or (b), and

(b) has not made to A, in respect of that money or other property, such payment or disposition as would have been appropriate in the circumstances.

(4) The power of the court to make orders under section 66 includes power to order B to pay to A—

(a) in a case falling within subsection (1)(a), such sum in respect of the money to which the application relates, or A's s share of it, as the court considers appropriate, or

(b) in a case falling within subsection (1)(b), such sum in respect of the value of the property to which the application relates, or A's interest in it, as the court considers appropriate.

(5) If it appears to the court that there is any property which—

(a) represents the whole or part of the money or property, and

(b) is property in respect of which an order could (apart from this section) have been made under section 66,

the court may (either instead of or as well as making an order in accordance with subsection (4)) make any order which it could (apart from this section) have made under section 66.

(6) Any power of the court which is exercisable on an application under section 66 is exercisable in relation to an application made under that section as extended by this section.

68   Applications under section 66 by former civil partners

(1) This section applies where a civil partnership has been dissolved or annulled.

(2) Subject to subsection (3), an application may be made under section 66 (including that section as extended by section 67) by either former civil partner despite the dissolution or annulment (and references in those sections to a civil partner are to be read accordingly).

(3) The application must be made within the period of 3 years beginning with the date of the dissolution or annulment.

69   Actions in tort between civil partners

(1) This section applies if an action in tort is brought by one civil partner against the other during the subsistence of the civil partnership.

(2) The court may stay the proceedings if it appears—

(a) that no substantial benefit would accrue to either civil partner from the continuation of the proceedings, or

(b) that the question or questions in issue could more conveniently be disposed of on an application under section 66.

(3) Without prejudice to subsection (2)(b), the court may in such an action—

(a) exercise any power which could be exercised on an application under section 66, or

(b) give such directions as it thinks fit for the disposal under that section of any question arising in the proceedings.

70   Assurance policy by civil partner for benefit of other civil partner etc.

Section 11 of the Married Women's Property Act 1882 (c. 75) (money payable under policy of assurance not to form part of the estate of the insured) applies in relation to a policy of assurance—

(a) effected by a civil partner on his own life, and

(b) expressed to be for the benefit of his civil partner, or of his children, or of his civil partner and children, or any of them,

as it applies in relation to a policy of assurance effected by a husband and expressed to be for the benefit of his wife, or of his children, or of his wife and children, or of any of them.

70A   Money and property derived from housekeeping allowance

Section 1 of the Matrimonial Property Act 1964 (money and property derived from housekeeping allowance to be treated as belonging to husband and wife in equal shares) applies in relation to—

(a) money derived from any allowance made by a civil partner for the expenses of the civil partnership home or for similar purposes, and

(b) any property acquired out of such money,

as it applies in relation to money derived from any allowance made by a husband or wife for the expenses of the matrimonial home or for similar purposes, and any property acquired out of such money.

71   Wills, administration of estates and family provision

Schedule 4 amends enactments relating to wills, administration of estates and family provision so that they apply in relation to civil partnerships as they apply in relation to marriage.

72   Financial relief for civil partners and children of family

(1) Schedule 5 makes provision for financial relief in connection with civil partnerships that corresponds to provision made for financial relief in connection with marriages by Part 2 of the Matrimonial Causes Act 1973 (c. 18).

(2) Any rule of law under which any provision of Part 2 of the 1973 Act is interpreted as applying to dissolution of a marriage on the ground of presumed death is to be treated as applying (with any necessary modifications) in relation to the corresponding provision of Schedule 5.

(3) Schedule 6 makes provision for financial relief in connection with civil partnerships that corresponds to provision made for financial relief in connection with marriages by the Domestic Proceedings and Magistrates' Courts Act 1978 (c. 22).

…

Chapter 4   Civil partnership agreements

73   Civil partnership agreements unenforceable

(1) A civil partnership agreement does not under the law of England and Wales have effect as a contract giving rise to legal rights.

(2) No action lies in England and Wales for breach of a civil partnership agreement, whatever the law applicable to the agreement.

(3) In this section and section 74 'civil partnership agreement' means an agreement between two people—

    (a) to register as civil partners of each other—

        (i)   in England and Wales (under this Part),

    …

(4) This section applies in relation to civil partnership agreements whether entered into before or after this section comes into force, but does not affect any action commenced before it comes into force.

74   Property where civil partnership agreement is terminated

(1) This section applies if a civil partnership agreement is terminated.

(2) Section 65 (contributions by civil partner to property improvement) applies, in relation to any property in which either or both of the parties to the agreement had a beneficial interest while the agreement was in force, as it applies in relation to property in which a civil partner has a beneficial interest.

(3) Sections 66 and 67 (disputes between civil partners about property) apply to any dispute between or claim by one of the parties in relation to property in which either or both had a beneficial interest while the agreement was in force, as if the parties were civil partners of each other.

(4) An application made under section 66 or 67 by virtue of subsection (3) must be made within 3 years of the termination of the agreement.

(5) A party to a civil partnership agreement who makes a gift of property to the other party on the condition (express or implied) that it is to be returned if the agreement is terminated is not prevented from recovering the property merely because of his having terminated the agreement.

Chapter 6   Miscellaneous

80   False statements etc. with reference to civil partnerships

(1) A person commits an offence if—

    (a) for the purpose of procuring the formation of a civil partnership, or a document mentioned in subsection (2), he—

        (i)   makes or signs a declaration required under this Part or Part 5, or

        (ii) gives a notice or certificate soc required,

    knowing that the declaration, notice or certificate is false,

(b) for the purpose of a record being made in any register relating to civil partnerships, he—

(i) makes a statement as to any information which is required to be registered under this Part or Part 5, or

(ii) causes such a statement to be made,

knowing that the statement is false,

(c) he forbids the issue of a document mentioned in subsection (2)(a) or (b) by representing himself to be a person whose consent to a civil partnership between a child and another person is required under this Part or Part 5, knowing the representation to be false, or

(d) with respect to a declaration made under paragraph 5(1) of Schedule 1 he makes a statement mentioned in paragraph 6 of that Schedule which he knows to be false in a material particular.

(2) The documents are—

(a) a civil partnership schedule or a Registrar General's licence under Chapter 1;

(b) a document required by an Order in Council under section 210 or 211 as an authority for two people to register as civil partners of each other;

(c) a certificate of no impediment under section 240.

(3) A person guilty of an offence under subsection (1) is liable—

(a) on conviction on indictment, to imprisonment for a term not exceeding 7 years or to a fine (or both);

(b) on summary conviction, to a fine not exceeding the statutory maximum.

(4) The Perjury Act 1911 (c. 6) has effect as if this section were contained in it.

…

84 Evidence

(1) Any enactment or rule of law relating to the giving of evidence by a spouse applies in relation to a civil partner as it applies in relation to the spouse.

(2) Subsection (1) is subject to any specific amendment made by or under this Act which relates to the giving of evidence by a civil partner.

(3) For the avoidance of doubt, in any such amendment, references to a person's civil partner do not include a former civil partner.

(4) References in subsections (1) and (2) to giving evidence are to giving evidence in any way (whether by supplying information, making discovery, producing documents or otherwise).

(5) Any rule of law—

(a) which is preserved by section 7(3) of the Civil Evidence Act 1995 (c. 38) or section 118(1) of the Criminal Justice Act 2003 (c. 44), and

(b) under which in any proceedings evidence of reputation or family tradition is admissible for the purpose of proving or disproving the existence of a marriage,

is to be treated as applying in an equivalent way for the purpose of proving or disproving the existence of a civil partnership.

…

PART 6 RELATIONSHIPS ARISING THROUGH CIVIL PARTNERSHIP

246 Interpretation of statutory references to stepchildren etc.

(1) In any provision to which this section applies, references to a stepchild or step-parent of a person (here, 'A'), and cognate expressions, are to be read as follows—

A's stepchild includes a person who is the child of A's civil partner (but is not A's child);

A's step-parent includes a person who is the civil partner of A's parent (but is not A's parent);

A's stepdaughter includes a person who is the daughter of A's civil partner (but is not A's daughter);

A's stepson includes a person who is the son of A's civil partner (but is not A's son);

A's stepfather includes a person who is the civil partner of A's father (but is not A's parent);

A's stepmother includes a person who is the civil partner of A's mother (but is not A's parent);

A's stepbrother includes a person who is the son of the civil partner of A's parent (but is not the son of either of A's parents);

A's stepsister includes a person who is the daughter of the civil partner of A's parent (but is not the daughter of either of A's parents).

(2) For the purposes of any provision to which this section applies—

'brother-in-law' includes civil partner's brother,

'daughter-in-law' includes daughter's civil partner,

'father-in-law' includes civil partner's father,

'mother-in-law' includes civil partner's mother,

'parent-in-law' includes civil partner's parent,

'sister-in-law' includes civil partner's sister, and

'son-in-law' includes son's civil partner.

247   Provisions to which section 246 applies: Acts of Parliament etc.

(1) Section 246 applies to—

    (a) any provision listed in Schedule 21 (references to stepchildren, in-laws etc. in existing Acts),

    (b) except in so far as otherwise provided, any provision made by a future Act, and

    (c) except in so far as otherwise provided, any provision made by future subordinate legislation.

(2) A Minister of the Crown may by order—

    (a) amend Schedule 21 by adding to it any provision of an existing Act;

    (b) provide for section 246 to apply to prescribed provisions of existing subordinate legislation.

...

SCHEDULES

Sections 3(2) and 1(3)   **SCHEDULE 1**

PROHIBITED DEGREES OF RELATIONSHIP: ENGLAND AND WALES

PART 1 THE PROHIBITIONS

Absolute prohibitions

1.—(1) Two people are within prohibited degrees of relationship if one falls within the list below in relation to the other.

Adoptive child	Grandchild
Adoptive parent	Parent
Child	Parent's sibling
Former adoptive child	Sibling
Former adoptive parent	Sibling's child
Grandparent	

(2) In the list 'sibling' means a brother, sister, half-brother or half-sister.

Qualified prohibitions

2.—(1) Two people are within prohibited degrees of relationship if one of them falls within the list below in relation to the other, unless—

(a) both of them have reached 21 at the time when they register as civil partners of each other, and

(b) the younger has not at any time before reaching 18 been a child of the family in relation to the other.

Child of former civil partner	Former spouse of grandparent
Child of former spouse	Former spouse of parent
Former civil partner of grandparent	Grandchild of former civil partner
Former civil partner of parent	Grandchild of former spouse

(2) 'Child of the family', in relation to another person, means a person who—

(a) has lived in the same household as that other person, and

(b) has been treated by that other person as a child of his family.

...

PART 2 SPECIAL PROVISIONS RELATING TO QUALIFIED PROHIBITIONS

Provisions relating to paragraph 2

4.—Paragraphs 5 to 7 apply where two people are subject to paragraph 2 but intend to register as civil partners of each other by signing a civil partnership schedule.

5.—(1) The fact that a notice of proposed civil partnership has been given must not be recorded in the register unless the registration authority—

(a) is satisfied by the production of evidence that both the proposed civil partners have reached 21, and

(b) has received a declaration made by each of the proposed civil partners—

(i)   specifying their affinal relationship, and

(ii) declaring that the younger of them has not at any time before reaching 18 been a child of the family in relation to the other.

(2) Sub-paragraph (1) does not apply if a declaration is obtained under paragraph 7.

(3) A declaration under sub-paragraph (1)(b) must contain such information and must be signed and attested in such manner as may be prescribed by regulations.

(4) The fact that a registration authority has received a declaration under sub-paragraph (1)(b) must be recorded in the register.

(5) A declaration under sub-paragraph (1)(b) must be filed and kept by the registration authority.

6.—(1) Sub-paragraph (2) applies if—

(a) a registration authority receives from a person who is not one of the proposed civil partners a written statement signed by that person which alleges that a declaration made under paragraph 5 is false in a material particular, and

(b) the register shows that such a statement has been received.

(2) The registration authority in whose area it is proposed that the registration take place must not issue a civil partnership schedule unless a declaration is obtained under paragraph 7.

7.—(1) Either of the proposed civil partners may apply to the High Court or the family court for a declaration that, given that—

(a) both of them have reached 21, and

(b) the younger of those persons has not at any time before reaching 18 been a child of the family in relation to the other,

there is no impediment of affinity to the formation of the civil partnership.

(3) Such an application may be made whether or not any statement has been received by the registration authority under paragraph 6.

8. Section 13 (objection to proposed civil partnership) does not apply in relation to a civil partnership to which paragraphs 5 to 7 apply, except so far as an objection to the issue of a civil partnership schedule is made under that section on a ground other than the affinity between the proposed civil partners.

...

Section 4(2) and 5(3)   SCHEDULE 2

CIVIL PARTNERSHIPS OF PERSONS UNDER 18: ENGLAND AND WALES

PART 1 APPROPRIATE PERSONS

1.—Column 2 of the table specifies the appropriate persons (or person) to give consent to a child whose circumstances fall within column 1 and who intends to register as the civil partner of another—

Case	Appropriate persons
1. The circumstances do not fall within any of items 2 to 8.	Each of the following— (a) any parent of the child who has parental responsibility for him, and (b) any guardian of the child.
2. A special guardianship order is in force with respect to the child and the circumstances do not fall within any of items 3 to 7.	Each of the child's special guardians.
3. A care order has effect with respect to the child and the circumstances do not fall within item 5.	Each of the following— (a) the local authority designated in the order, and (b) each parent, guardian or special guardian (in so far as their parental responsibility has not been restricted under section 33(3) of the 1989 Act).
4. A child arrangements order to which paragraph 2A applies has effect with respect to the child and the circumstances do not fall within item 5.	Each of the persons with whom the child lives, or is to live, as a result of the order.
5. An adoption agency is authorised to place the child for adoption under section 19 of the 2002 Act.	Either— (a) the adoption agency, or (b) if a care order has effect with respect to the child, the local authority designated in the order.
6. A placement order is in force with respect to the child.	The local authority authorised by the placement order to place the child for adoption.
7. The child has been placed for adoption with prospective adopters.	The prospective adopters (in so far as their parental responsibility has not been restricted under section 25(4) of the 2002 Act), in addition to any person specified in relation to item 5 or 6.
8. The circumstances do not fall within any of items 2 to 7, but a child arrangements order to which paragraph 2A applies was in force with respect to the child immediately before he reached 16.	The persons with whom the child lived, or was to live, as a result of the order.

2.—In the table—

'the 1989 Act' means the Children Act 1989 (c. 41) and 'guardian of a child', 'parental responsibility', 'child arrangements order', 'special guardian', 'special guardianship order' and 'care order' have the same meaning as in that Act;

'the 2002 Act' means the Adoption and Children Act 2002 (c. 38) and 'adoption agency', 'placed for adoption', 'placement order' and 'local authority' have the same meaning as in that Act;

'appropriate local authority' means the local authority authorised by the placement order to place the child for adoption.

2A.—A child arrangements order (as defined by section 8 of the Children Act 1989) is one to which this paragraph applies if the order regulates arrangements that consist of, or include, arrangements which relate to either or both of the following—

(a) with whom the child is to live, and

(b) when the child is to live with any person.

PART 2 OBTAINING CONSENT: GENERAL

Consent of appropriate person unobtainable

3.—(1) This paragraph applies if—

(a) a child and another person intend to register as civil partners of each other under any procedure other than the special procedure, and

(b) the registration authority to whom the child gives a notice of proposed civil partnership is satisfied that the consent of a person whose consent is required ('A') cannot be obtained because A is absent, inaccessible or under a disability.

(2) If there is any other person whose consent is also required, the registration authority must dispense with the need for A's consent.

(3) If no other person's consent is required—

(a) the Registrar General may dispense with the need for any consent, or

(b) the court may, on an application being made to it, consent to the child registering as the civil partner of the person mentioned in sub-paragraph (1)(a).

(4) The consent of the court under sub-paragraph (3)(b) has the same effect as if it had been given by A.

Consent of appropriate person refused

4.—(1) This paragraph applies if—

(a) a child and another person intend to register as civil partners of each other under any procedure other than the special procedure, and

(b) any person whose consent is required refuses his consent.

(2) The court may, on an application being made to it, consent to the child registering as the civil partner of the person mentioned in sub-paragraph (1)(a).

(3) The consent of the court under sub-paragraph (2) has the same effect as if it had been given by the person who has refused his consent.

Declaration

5.—If one of the proposed civil partners is a child and is not a surviving civil partner, the necessary declaration under section 8 must also—

(a) state in relation to each appropriate person—

(i)   that that person's consent has been obtained,

(ii) that the need to obtain that person's consent has been dispensed with under paragraph 3, or

(iii) that the court has given consent under paragraph 3 or 4, or

(b) state that no person exists whose consent is required to a civil partnership between the child and another person.

Forbidding proposed civil partnership

6.—(1) This paragraph applies if it has been recorded in the register that a notice of proposed civil partnership between a child and another person has been given.

(2) Any person whose consent is required to a child and another person registering as civil partners of each other may forbid the issue of a civil partnership schedule by giving any registration authority written notice that he forbids it.

(3) A notice under sub-paragraph (2) must specify—

(a) the name of the person giving it,

(b) his place of residence, and

(c) the capacity, in relation to either of the proposed civil partners, in which he forbids the issue of the civil partnership schedule.

(4) On receiving the notice, the registration authority must as soon as is practicable record in the register the fact that the issue of a civil partnership schedule has been forbidden.

(5) If the issue of a civil partnership schedule has been forbidden under this paragraph, the notice of proposed civil partnership and all proceedings on it are void.

(6) Sub-paragraphs (2) and (5) do not apply if the court has given its consent under paragraph 3 or 4.

Evidence

7.—(1) This paragraph applies if, for the purpose of obtaining a civil partnership schedule, a person declares that the consent of any person or persons whose consent is required under section 4 has been given.

(2) The registration authority may refuse to issue the civil partnership schedule unless satisfied by the production of written evidence that the consent of that person or those persons has in fact been given.

Issue of civil partnership schedule

8.—The duty in section 14(1) to issue a civil partnership schedule does not apply if its issue has been forbidden under paragraph 6.

9.—If a proposed civil partnership is between a child and another person, the civil partnership schedule must contain a statement that the issue of the civil partnership schedule has not been forbidden under paragraph 6.

PART 3 OBTAINING CONSENT: SPECIAL PROCEDURE

Consent of appropriate person unobtainable or refused

10.—(1) Sub-paragraph (2) applies if—

(a) a child and another person intend to register as civil partners of each other under the special procedure, and

(b) the Registrar General is satisfied that the consent of a person ('A') whose consent is required cannot be obtained because A is absent, inaccessible, or under a disability.

(2) If this sub-paragraph applies—

(a) the Registrar General may dispense with the need for A's consent (whether or not there is any other person whose consent is also required), or

(b) the court may, on application being made, consent to the child registering as the civil partner of the person mentioned in sub-paragraph (1)(a).

(3) The consent of the court under sub-paragraph (2)(b) has the same effect as if it had been given by A.

(4) Sub-paragraph (5) applies if—

(a) a child and another person intend to register as civil partners of each other under the special procedure, and

(b) any person whose consent is required refuses his consent.

(5) The court may, on application being made, consent to the child registering as the civil partner of the person mentioned in sub-paragraph (4)(a).

(6) The consent of the court under sub-paragraph (5) has the same effect as if it had been given by the person who has refused his consent.

Declaration

11.—If one of the proposed civil partners is a child and is not a surviving civil partner, the necessary declaration under section 8 must also—
- (a) state in relation to each appropriate person—
    - (i)   that that person's consent has been obtained,
    - (ii) that the need to obtain that person's consent has been dispensed with under paragraph 10(2), or
    - (iii) that the court has given consent under paragraph 10(2) or (5), or
- (b) state that no person exists whose consent is required to a civil partnership between the child and another person.

Forbidding proposed civil partnership

12.—Paragraph 6 applies in relation to the special procedure as if—
- (a) any reference to forbidding the issue of a civil partnership schedule were a reference to forbidding the Registrar General to give authority for the issue of his licence, and
- (b) sub-paragraph (6) referred to the court giving its consent under paragraph 10(2) or (5).

Evidence

13.—(1) This paragraph applies—
- (a) if a child and another person intend to register as civil partners of each other under the special procedure, and
- (b) the consent of any person ('A') is required to the child registering as the civil partner of that person.

(2) The person giving the notice (under section 21) of proposed civil partnership to the registration authority must produce to the authority such evidence as the Registrar General may require to satisfy him that A's consent has in fact been given.

(3) The power to require evidence under sub-paragraph (2) is in addition to the power to require evidence under section 22.

Issue of registrar general's licence

14.—The duty of the Registrar General under section 25(3)(b) to give authority for the issue of his licence does not apply if he has been forbidden to do so by virtue of paragraph 12.

PART 4 PROVISIONS RELATING TO THE COURT

15.—(1) For the purposes of Parts 2 and 3 of this Schedule, 'the court' means—
- (a) the High Court, or
- (c) the family court.

(2) Rules of court may be made for enabling applications under Part 2 or 3 of this Schedule—
- (a) if made to the High Court, to be heard in chambers;
- ...
- (c) if made to the family court, to be heard and determined otherwise than in open court.

(3) Rules of court must provide that, where an application is made in consequence of a refusal to give consent, notice of the application is to be served on the person who has refused consent.

Section 5(2)   **SCHEDULE 3**

REGISTRATION BY FORMER SPOUSES ONE OF WHOM HAS CHANGED SEX

Application of schedule

1.—This Schedule applies if—

   (a) a court—

     (i) makes absolute a decree of nullity granted on the ground that an interim gender recognition certificate has been issued to a party to the marriage, or

     ...

   and, on doing so, issues a full gender recognition certificate (under section 5(1) of the Gender Recognition Act 2004 (c. 7)) to that party, and

   (b) the parties wish to register in England or Wales as civil partners of each other without being delayed by the waiting period.

The relevant period

2.—For the purposes of this Schedule the relevant period is the period—

   (a) beginning with the issue of the full gender recognition certificate, and

   (b) ending at the end of 1 month from the day on which it is issued.

Modifications of standard procedure and procedures for house-bound and detained persons

3.—If—

   (a) each of the parties gives a notice of proposed civil partnership during the relevant period, and

   (b) on doing so, each makes an election under this paragraph,Chapter 1 of Part 2 applies with the modifications given in paragraphs 4 to 6.

4.—(1) Omit—

   (a) section 10 (proposed civil partnership to be publicised);

   (b) section 11 (meaning of 'the waiting period');

   (c) section 12 (power to shorten the waiting period).

(2) In section 14 (issue of civil partnership schedule), for subsection (1) substitute—

'(1) As soon as the notices of proposed civil partnership have been given, the registration authority in whose area it is proposed that the registration take place must, at the request of one or both of the proposed civil partners, issue a document to be known as a civil partnership schedule'.

(3) For section 17 (period during which registration may take place) substitute—

'17   Period during which registration may take place

(1) The proposed civil partners may register as civil partners by signing the civil partnership schedule at any time during the applicable period.

(2) If they do not register as civil partners by signing the civil partnership schedule before the end of the applicable period—

   (a) the notices of proposed civil partnership and the civil partnership schedule are void, and

   (b) no civil partnership registrar may officiate at the signing of the civil partnership schedule by them.

(3) The applicable period, in relation to two people registering as civil partners of each other, is the period of 1 month beginning with—

   (a) the day on which the notices of proposed civil partnership are given, or

   (b) if the notices are not given on the same day, the earlier of those days.'

5.—In section 18 (house-bound persons), in subsection (3)—

   (a) treat the reference to the standard procedure as a reference to the standard procedure as modified by this Schedule, and

   (b) omit paragraph (c) (which provides for a 3 month registration period).

6.—In section 19 (detained persons), in subsection (3)—

(a) treat the reference to the standard procedure as a reference to the standard procedure as modified by this Schedule, and

(b) omit paragraph (c) (which provides for a 3 month registration period).

...

Section 71   **SCHEDULE 4**

WILLS, ADMINISTRATION OF ESTATES AND FAMILY PROVISION

PART 1 WILLS

...

5.—Except where a contrary intention is shown, it is presumed that if a testator—

(a) devises or bequeaths property to his civil partner in terms which in themselves would give an absolute interest to the civil partner, but

(b) by the same instrument purports to give his issue an interest in the same property,the gift to the civil partner is absolute despite the purported gift to the issue.

...

Section 72(1)   **SCHEDULE 5**

FINANCIAL RELIEF: PROVISION CORRESPONDING TO PROVISION MADE BY PART 2 OF THE MATRIMONIAL CAUSES ACT 1973

PART 1 FINANCIAL PROVISION IN CONNECTION WITH DISSOLUTION, NULLITY OR SEPARATION

Circumstances in which orders under this Part may be made

1.—(1) The court may make any one or more of the orders set out in paragraph 2(1)—

(a) on making a dissolution, nullity or separation order, or

(b) at any time afterwards.

(2) The court may make any one or more of the orders set out in paragraph 2(1)(d), (e) and (f)—

(a) in proceedings for a dissolution, nullity or separation order, before making the order;

(b) if proceedings for a dissolution, nullity or separation order are dismissed after the beginning of the trial, either straightaway or within a reasonable period after the dismissal.

(3) The power of the court to make an order under sub-paragraph (1) or (2)(a) in favour of a child of the family is exercisable from time to time.

(4) If the court makes an order in favour of a child under sub-paragraph (2)(b), it may from time to time make a further order in the child's favour of any of the kinds set out in paragraph 2(1)(d), (e) or (f).

The orders: periodical and secured periodical payments and lump sums

2.—(1) The orders are—

(a) an order that either civil partner must make to the other such periodical payments for such term as may be specified;

(b) an order that either civil partner must secure to the other, to the satisfaction of the court, such periodical payments for such term as may be specified;

    (c) an order that either civil partner must pay to the other such lump sum or sums as may be specified;

    (d) an order that one of the civil partners must make—

        (i)   to such person as may be specified for the benefit of a child of the family, or

        (ii) to a child of the family,

        such periodical payments for such term as may be specified;

    (e) an order that one of the civil partners must secure—

        (i)   to such person as may be specified for the benefit of a child of the family, or

        (ii) to a child of the family,

        to the satisfaction of the court, such periodical payments for such term as may be specified;

    (f) an order that one of the civil partners must pay such lump sum as may be specified—

        (i)   to such person as may be specified for the benefit of a child of the family, or

        (ii) to a child of the family.

  (5) 'Specified' means specified in the order.

Particular provision that may be made by lump sum orders

3.—(1) An order under this Part requiring one civil partner to pay the other a lump sum may be made for the purpose of enabling the other civil partner to meet any liabilities or expenses reasonably incurred by the other in maintaining—

    (a) himself or herself, or

    (b) a child of the family,

before making an application for an order under this Part in his or her favour.

  (2) An order under this Part requiring a lump sum to be paid to or for the benefit of a child of the family may be made for the purpose of enabling any liabilities or expenses reasonably incurred by or for the benefit of the child before making an application for an order under this Part to be met.

  (3) An order under this Part for the payment of a lump sum may—

    (a) provide for its payment by instalments of such amount as may be specified, and

    (b) require the payment of the instalments to be secured to the satisfaction of the court.

  (4) Sub-paragraphs (1) to (3) do not restrict the powers to make the orders set out in paragraph 2(1)(c) and (f).

  (5) If the court—

    (a) makes an order under this Part for the payment of a lump sum, and

    (b) directs that—

        (i)   payment of the sum or any part of it is to be deferred, or

        (ii) the sum or any part of it is to be paid by instalments,

it may provide for the deferred amount or the instalments to carry interest at such rate as may be specified from such date as may be specified until the date when payment of it is due.

  (6) A date specified under sub-paragraph (5) must not be earlier than the date of the order.

  (7) 'Specified' means specified in the order.

When orders under this Part may take effect

4.—(1) If an order is made under paragraph 2(1)(a), (b) or (c) on or after making a dissolution or nullity order, neither the order nor any settlement made in pursuance of it takes effect unless the dissolution or nullity order has been made final.

  (2) This paragraph does not affect the power of the court to give a direction under paragraph 76 (settlement of instrument by conveyancing counsel).

Restrictions on making of orders under this part

5.—The power to make an order under paragraph 2(1)(d), (e) or (f) is subject to paragraph 49(1) and (5) (restrictions on orders in favour of children who have reached 18).

PART 2 PROPERTY ADJUSTMENT ON OR AFTER DISSOLUTION, NULLITY OR SEPARATION

Circumstances in which property adjustment orders may be made

6.—(1) The court may make one or more property adjustment orders—

(a) on making a dissolution, nullity or separation order, or

(b) at any time afterwards.

(2) In this Schedule 'property adjustment order' means a property adjustment order under this Part.

Property adjustment orders

7.—(1) The property adjustment orders are—

(a) an order that one of the civil partners must transfer such property as may be specified, being property to which he is entitled—

(i)   to the other civil partner,

(ii)   to a child of the family, or

(iii) to such person as may be specified for the benefit of a child of the family;

(b) an order that a settlement of such property as may be specified, being property to which one of the civil partners is entitled, be made to the satisfaction of the court for the benefit of—

(i)   the other civil partner and the children of the family, or

(ii)   either or any of them;

(c) an order varying for the benefit of—

(i)   the civil partners and the children of the family, or

(ii)   either or any of them,

a relevant settlement;

(d) an order extinguishing or reducing the interest of either of the civil partners under a relevant settlement.

(3) The court may make a property adjustment order under sub-paragraph (1)(c) even though there are no children of the family.

(4) In this paragraph—

'entitled' means entitled in possession or reversion,

'relevant settlement' means, in relation to a civil partnership, a settlement made, during its subsistence or in anticipation of its formation, on the civil partners including one made by will or codicil, but not including one in the form of a pension arrangement (within the meaning of Part 4), and

'specified' means specified in the order.

When property adjustment orders may take effect

8.—(1) If a property adjustment order is made on or after making a dissolution or nullity order, neither the property adjustment order nor any settlement made under it takes effect unless the dissolution or nullity order has been made final.

(2) This paragraph does not affect the power to give a direction under paragraph 76 (settlement of instrument by conveyancing counsel).

Restrictions on making property adjustment orders

9.—The power to make a property adjustment order under paragraph 7(1)(a) is subject to paragraph 49(1) and (5) (restrictions on making orders in favour of children who have reached 18).

PART 3 SALE OF PROPERTY ORDERS

Circumstances in which sale of property orders may be made

10.—(1) The court may make a sale of property order—
  (a) on making—
      (i)   under Part 1, a secured periodical payments order or an order for the payment of a lump sum,
      (ii) a property adjustment order, or
      (iii) an order under paragraph 38A for a payment in respect of legal services, or
  (b) at any time afterwards.

(3) In this Schedule 'sale of property order' means a sale of property order under this Part.

Sale of property orders

11.—(1) A sale of property order is an order for the sale of such property as may be specified, being property in which, or in the proceeds of sale of which, either or both of the civil partners has or have a beneficial interest, either in possession or reversion.

(2) A sale of property order may contain such consequential or supplementary provisions as the court thinks fit.

(3) A sale of property order may in particular include—
  (a) provision requiring the making of a payment out of the proceeds of sale of the property to which the order relates, and
  (b) provision requiring any property to which the order relates to be offered for sale to a specified person, or class of persons.

(4) 'Specified' means specified in the order.

When sale of property orders may take effect

12.—(1) If a sale of property order is made on or after the making of a dissolution or nullity order, it does not take effect unless the dissolution or nullity order has been made final.

(2) Where a sale of property order is made, the court may direct that—
  (a) the order, or
  (b) such provision of it as the court may specify,
is not to take effect until the occurrence of an event specified by the court or the end of a period so specified.

When sale of property orders cease to have effect

13.—If a sale of property order contains a provision requiring the proceeds of sale of the property to which the order relates to be used to secure periodical payments to a civil partner, the order ceases to have effect—
  (a) on the death of the civil partner, or
  (b) on the formation of a subsequent civil partnership or marriage by the civil partner.

Protection of third parties

14.—(1) Sub-paragraphs (2) and (3) apply if—
  (a) a civil partner has a beneficial interest in any property, or in the proceeds of sale of any property, and
  (b) another person ('A') who is not the other civil partner also has a beneficial interest in the property or the proceeds.

(2) Before deciding whether to make a sale of property order in relation to the property, the court must give A an opportunity to make representations with respect to the order.

(3) Any representations made by A are included among the circumstances to which the court is required to have regard under paragraph 20.

PART 4 PENSION SHARING ORDERS ON OR AFTER DISSOLUTION OR NULLITY ORDER

Circumstances in which pension sharing orders may be made

15.—(1) The court may make a pension sharing order—

(a) on making a dissolution or nullity order, or

(b) at any time afterwards.

(4) In this Schedule 'pension sharing order' means a pension sharing order under this Part.

Pension sharing orders

16.—(1) A pension sharing order is an order which—

(a) provides that one civil partner's—

(i) shareable rights under a specified pension arrangement, or

(ii) shareable state scheme rights,

are to be subject to pension sharing for the benefit of the other civil partner, and

(b) specifies the percentage value to be transferred.

(5) Shareable rights under a pension arrangement are rights in relation to which pension sharing is available under—

(a) Chapter 1 of Part 4 of the Welfare Reform and Pensions Act 1999 (c. 30), or

(b) corresponding Northern Ireland legislation.

(6) Shareable state scheme rights are rights in relation to which pension sharing is available under—

(a) Chapter 2 of Part 4 of the 1999 Act, or

(b) corresponding Northern Ireland legislation.

(7) In this Part 'pension arrangement' means—

(a) an occupational pension scheme,

(b) a personal pension scheme,

(c) a retirement annuity contract,

(d) an annuity or insurance policy purchased, or transferred, for the purpose of giving effect to rights under—

(i) an occupational pension scheme, or

(ii) a personal pension scheme, and

(e) an annuity purchased, or entered into, for the purpose of discharging liability in respect of a pension credit under—

(i) section 29(1)(b) of the 1999 Act, or

(ii) corresponding Northern Ireland legislation.

(8) In sub-paragraph (4)—

'occupational pension scheme' has the same meaning as in the Pension Schemes Act 1993 (c. 48);

'personal pension scheme' has the same meaning as in the 1993 Act;

'retirement annuity contract' means a contract or scheme approved under Chapter 3 of Part 14 of the Income and Corporation Taxes Act 1988 (c. 1).

Pension sharing orders: apportionment of charges

17.—If a pension sharing order relates to rights under a pension arrangement, the court may include in the order provision about the apportionment between the civil partners of any charge under—

(a) section 41 of the 1999 Act (charges in respect of pension sharing costs), or

(b) corresponding Northern Ireland legislation.

Restrictions on making of pension sharing orders

18.—(1) A pension sharing order may not be made in relation to a pension arrangement which—

(a) is the subject of a pension sharing order in relation to the civil partnership, or

(b) has been the subject of pension sharing between the civil partners.

(2) A pension sharing order may not be made in relation to shareable state scheme rights if—

(a) such rights are the subject of a pension sharing order in relation to the civil partnership, or

(b) such rights have been the subject of pension sharing between the civil partners.

(3) A pension sharing order may not be made in relation to the rights of a person under a pension arrangement if there is in force a requirement imposed by virtue of Part 6 which relates to benefits or future benefits to which that person is entitled under the pension arrangement.

When pension sharing orders may take effect

19.—(1) A pension sharing order is not to take effect unless the dissolution or nullity order on or after which it is made has been made final.

(2) No pension sharing order may be made so as to take effect before the end of such period after the making of the order as may be prescribed by regulations made by the Lord Chancellor.

(3) The power to make regulations under sub-paragraph (2) is exercisable by statutory instrument which is subject to annulment in pursuance of a resolution of either House of Parliament.

PART 4A PENSION COMPENSATION SHARING ORDERS ON OR AFTER DISSOLUTION OR NULLITY ORDER

Circumstances in which pension compensation sharing orders may be made

19A.—(1) The court may make a pension compensation sharing order—

(a) on making a dissolution or nullity order, or

(b) at any time afterwards.

(2) In this Schedule 'pension compensation sharing order' means a pension compensation sharing order under this Part.

Pension compensation sharing orders

19B.—(1) A pension compensation sharing order is an order which—

(a) provides that one civil partner's shareable rights to PPF compensation that derive from rights under a specified pension scheme are to be subject to pension compensation sharing for the benefit of the other civil partner, and

(b) specifies the percentage value to be transferred.

(2) Shareable rights to PPF compensation are rights in relation to which pension compensation sharing is available under—

(a) Chapter 1 of Part 3 of the Pensions Act 2008, or

(b) corresponding Northern Ireland legislation.

(3) In sub-paragraph (1) 'specified' means specified in the order.

Pension compensation sharing orders: apportionment of charges

19C.—The court may include in a pension compensation sharing order provision about the apportionment between the civil partners of any charge under—

(a) section 117 of the Pensions Act 2008 (charges in respect of pension compensation sharing costs), or

(b) corresponding Northern Ireland legislation.

Restrictions on making pension compensation sharing orders

19D.—(1) A pension compensation sharing order may not be made in relation to rights to PPF compensation that—

(a) are the subject of pension attachment,

(b) derive from rights under a pension scheme that were the subject of pension sharing between the civil partners,

(c) are the subject of pension compensation attachment, or

(d) are or have been the subject of pension compensation sharing between the civil partners.

(2) For the purposes of sub-paragraph (1)(a), rights to PPF compensation 'are the subject of pension attachment' if any of the following three conditions is met.

(3) The first condition is that—

(a) the rights derive from rights under a pension scheme in relation to which an order was made under Part 1 imposing a requirement by virtue of paragraph 25(2), and

(b) that order, as modified under paragraph 31, remains in force.

(4) The second condition is that—

(a) the rights derive from rights under a pension scheme in relation to which an order was made under Part 1 imposing a requirement by virtue of paragraph 25(5), and

(b) that order—

(i)   has been complied with, or

(ii) has not been complied with and, as modified under paragraph 32, remains in force.

(5) The third condition is that—

(a) the rights derive from rights under a pension scheme in relation to which an order was made under Part 1 imposing a requirement by virtue of paragraph 26, and

(b) that order remains in force.

(6) For the purposes of sub-paragraph (1)(b), rights under a pension scheme 'were the subject of pension sharing between the civil partners' if the rights were at any time the subject of a pension sharing order in relation to the civil partnership or a previous civil partnership between the same parties.

(7) For the purposes of sub-paragraph (1)(c), rights to PPF compensation 'are the subject of pension compensation attachment' if there is in force a requirement imposed by virtue of Part 6 relating to them.

(8) For the purposes of sub-paragraph (1)(d), rights to PPF compensation 'are or have been the subject of pension compensation sharing between the civil partners' if they are or have ever been the subject of a pension compensation sharing order in relation to the civil partnership or a previous civil partnership between the same parties.

When pension compensation sharing orders may take effect

19E.—(1) A pension compensation sharing order is not to take effect unless the dissolution or nullity order on or after which it is made has been made final.

(2) No pension compensation sharing order may be made so as to take effect before the end of such period after the making of the order as may be prescribed by regulations made by the Lord Chancellor.

(3) The power to make regulations under sub-paragraph (2) is exercisable by statutory instrument which is subject to annulment in pursuance of a resolution of either House of Parliament.

Interpretation

19F.—In this Schedule—

'PPF compensation' means compensation payable under the pension compensation provisions;

'the pension compensation provisions' means—

(a) Chapter 3 of Part 2 of the Pensions Act 2004 (pension protection) and any regulations or order made under it,

(b) Chapter 1 of Part 3 of the Pensions Act 2008 (pension compensation sharing) and any regulations or order made under it, and

(c) any provision corresponding to the provisions mentioned in paragraph (a) or (b) in force in Northern Ireland.

PART 5 MATTERS TO WHICH COURT IS TO HAVE REGARD UNDER PARTS 1 TO 4A

General

20.—The court in deciding—

(a) whether to exercise its powers under—

(i)   Part 1 (financial provision on dissolution etc.),

(ii) Part 2 (property adjustment orders),

(iii) Part 3 (sale of property orders),

(iv) any provision of Part 4 (pension sharing orders) other than paragraph 17 (apportionment of charges), or

(v) any provision of Part 4A (pension compensation sharing orders) other than paragraph 19C (apportionment of charges), and

(b) if so, in what way,

must have regard to all the circumstances of the case, giving first consideration to the welfare, while under 18, of any child of the family who has not reached 18.

Particular matters to be taken into account when exercising powers in relation to civil partners

21.—(1) This paragraph applies to the exercise by the court in relation to a civil partner of its powers under—

(a) Part 1 (financial provision on dissolution etc.) by virtue of paragraph 2(1) (a), (b) or (c),

(b) Part 2 (property adjustment orders),

(c) Part 3 (sale of property orders),

(d) Part 4 (pension sharing orders), or

(e) Part 4A (pension compensation sharing orders).

(2) The court must in particular have regard to—

(a) the income, earning capacity, property and other financial resources which each civil partner—

(i)   has, or

(ii) is likely to have in the foreseeable future,

including, in the case of earning capacity, any increase in that capacity which it would in the opinion of the court be reasonable to expect a civil partner in the civil partnership to take steps to acquire;

(b) the financial needs, obligations and responsibilities which each civil partner has or is likely to have in the foreseeable future;

(c) the standard of living enjoyed by the family before the breakdown of the civil partnership;

(d) the age of each civil partner and the duration of the civil partnership;

(e) any physical or mental disability of either of the civil partners;

(f) the contributions which each civil partner has made or is likely in the foreseeable future to make to the welfare of the family, including any contribution by looking after the home or caring for the family;

(g) the conduct of each civil partner, if that conduct is such that it would in the opinion of the court be inequitable to disregard it;

(h) in the case of proceedings for a dissolution or nullity order, the value to each civil partner of any benefit which, because of the dissolution or annulment of the civil partnership, that civil partner will lose the chance of acquiring.

Particular matters to be taken into account when exercising powers in relation to children

22.—(1) This paragraph applies to the exercise by the court in relation to a child of the family of its powers under—

(a) Part 1 (financial provision on dissolution etc.) by virtue of paragraph 2(1) (d), (e) or (f)),

(b) Part 2 (property adjustment orders), or

(c) Part 3 (sale of property orders).

(2) The court must in particular have regard to—

(a) the financial needs of the child;

(b) the income, earning capacity (if any), property and other financial resources of the child;

(c) any physical or mental disability of the child;

(d) the way in which the child was being and in which the civil partners expected the child to be educated or trained;

(e) the considerations mentioned in relation to the civil partners in paragraph 21(2)(a), (b), (c) and (e).

(3) In relation to the exercise of any of those powers against a civil partner ('A') in favour of a child of the family who is not A's child, the court must also have regard to—

(a) whether A has assumed any responsibility for the child's maintenance;

(b) if so, the extent to which, and the basis upon which, A assumed such responsibility and the length of time for which A discharged such responsibility;

(c) whether in assuming and discharging such responsibility A did so knowing that the child was not A's child;

(d) the liability of any other person to maintain the child.

Terminating financial obligations

23.—(1) Sub-paragraphs (2) and (3) apply if, on or after the making of a dissolution or nullity order, the court decides to exercise its powers under—

(a) Part 1 (financial provision on dissolution etc.) by virtue of paragraph 2(1) (a), (b) or (c),

(b) Part 2 (property adjustment orders),

(c) Part 3 (sale of property orders),

(d) Part 4 (pension sharing orders), or

(e) Part 4A (pension compensation sharing orders),

in favour of one of the civil partners.

(2) The court must consider whether it would be appropriate to exercise those powers in such a way that the financial obligations of each civil partner towards the other will be terminated as soon after the making of the dissolution or nullity order as the court considers just and reasonable.

(3) If the court decides to make—

(a) a periodical payments order, or

(b) a secured periodical payments order,

in favour of one of the civil partners ('A'), it must in particular consider whether it would be appropriate to require the payments to be made or secured only for such term as would in its opinion be sufficient to enable A to adjust without undue hardship to the termination of A's financial dependence on the other civil partner.

(4) If—

(a) on or after the making of a dissolution or nullity order, an application is made by one of the civil partners for a periodical payments or secured periodical payments order in that civil partner's favour, but

(b) the court considers that no continuing obligation should be imposed on either civil partner to make or secure periodical payments in favour of the other,

the court may dismiss the application with a direction that the applicant is not entitled to make any future application in relation to that civil partnership for an order under Part 1 by virtue of paragraph 2(1)(a) or (b).

PART 6 MAKING OF PART 1 ORDERS HAVING REGARD TO PENSION BENEFITS

Pension benefits to be included in matters to which court is to have regard

24.—(1) The matters to which the court is to have regard under paragraph 21(2)(a) include any pension benefits under a pension arrangement or by way of pension which a civil partner has or is likely to have; and, accordingly, in relation to any pension benefits paragraph 21 (2)(a)(ii) has effect as if 'in the foreseeable future' were omitted.

(2) The matters to which the court is to have regard under paragraph 21(2)(h) include any pension benefits which, because of the making of a dissolution or nullity order, a civil partner will lose the chance of acquiring.

(3) 'Pension benefits' means—

(a) benefits under a pension arrangement, or

(b) benefits by way of pension (whether under a pension arrangement or not).

Provisions applying where pension benefits taken into account in decision to make Part 1 order

25.—(1) This paragraph applies if, having regard to any benefits under a pension arrangement, the court decides to make an order under Part 1.

(2) To the extent to which the Part 1 order is made having regard to any benefits under a pension arrangement, it may require the person responsible for the pension arrangement, if at any time any payment in respect of any benefits under the arrangement becomes due to the civil partner with pension rights, to make a payment for the benefit of the other civil partner.

(3) The Part 1 order must express the amount of any payment required to be made by virtue of sub-paragraph (2) as a percentage of the payment which becomes due to the civil partner with pension rights.

(4) Any such payment by the person responsible for the arrangement—

(a) discharges so much of his liability to the civil partner with pension rights as corresponds to the amount of the payment, and

(b) is to be treated for all purposes as a payment made by the civil partner with pension rights in or towards the discharge of that civil partner's liability under the order.

(5) If the civil partner with pension rights has a right of commutation under the arrangement, the Part 1 order may require that civil partner to exercise it to any extent.

(6) This paragraph applies to any payment due in consequence of commutation in pursuance of the Part 1 order as it applies to other payments in respect of benefits under the arrangement.

(7) The power conferred by sub-paragraph (5) may not be exercised for the purpose of commuting a benefit payable to the civil partner with pension rights to a benefit payable to the other civil partner.

(8) The powers conferred by sub-paragraphs (2) and (5) may not be exercised in relation to a pension arrangement which—

(a) is the subject of a pension sharing order in relation to the civil partnership, or

(b) has been the subject of pension sharing between the civil partners.

Pensions: lump sums

26.—(1) This paragraph applies if the benefits which the civil partner with pension rights has or is likely to have under a pension arrangement include any lump sum payable in respect of that civil partner's death.

(2) The court's power under Part 1 to order a civil partner to pay a lump sum to the other civil partner includes the power to make by the order any provision in sub-paragraph (3) to (5).

(3) If the person responsible for the pension arrangement has power to determine the person to whom the sum, or any part of it, is to be paid, the court may require him to pay the whole or part of that sum, when it becomes due, to the other civil partner.

(4) If the civil partner with pension rights has power to nominate the person to whom the sum, or any part of it, is to be paid, the court may require the civil partner with pension rights to nominate the other civil partner in respect of the whole or part of that sum.

(5) In any other case, the court may require the person responsible for the pension arrangement in question to pay the whole or part of that sum, when it becomes due, for the benefit of the other civil partner instead of to the person to whom, apart from the order, it would be paid.

(6) Any payment by the person responsible for the arrangement under an order made under Part 1 made by virtue of this paragraph discharges so much of his liability in respect of the civil partner with pension rights as corresponds to the amount of the payment.

(7) The powers conferred by this paragraph may not be exercised in relation to a pension arrangement which—

  (a) is the subject of a pension sharing order in relation to the civil partnership, or
  (b) has been the subject of pension sharing between the civil partners.

Pensions: supplementary

27.—If—

  (a) a Part 1 order made by virtue of paragraph 25 or 26 imposes any requirement on the person responsible for a pension arrangement ('the first arrangement'),
  (b) the civil partner with pension rights acquires rights under another pension arrangement ('the new arrangement') which are derived (directly or indirectly) from the whole of that civil partner's rights under the first arrangement, and
  (c) the person responsible for the new arrangement has been given notice in accordance with regulations made by the Lord Chancellor,

the Part 1 order has effect as if it had been made instead in respect of the person responsible for the new arrangement.

Regulations

28.—(1) The Lord Chancellor may by regulations—

  (a) make provision, in relation to any provision of paragraph 25 or 26 which authorises the court making a Part 1 order to require the person responsible for a pension arrangement to make a payment for the benefit of the other civil partner, as to—
    (i)   the person to whom, and
    (ii) the terms on which,
    the payment is to be made;
  (b) make provision, in relation to payment under a mistaken belief as to the continuation in force of a provision included by virtue of paragraph 25 or 26 in a Part 1 order, about the rights or liabilities of the payer, the payee or the person to whom the payment was due;
  (c) require notices to be given in respect of changes of circumstances relevant to Part 1 orders which include provision made by virtue of paragraphs 25 and 26;
  (d) make provision for the person responsible for a pension arrangement to be discharged in prescribed circumstances from a requirement imposed by virtue of paragraph 25 or 26;
  (e) make provision about calculation and verification in relation to the valuation of—
    (i)   benefits under a pension arrangement, or
    (ii) shareable state scheme rights (within the meaning of paragraph 16(3)),
    for the purposes of the court's functions in connection with the exercise of any of its powers under this Schedule.

(2) Regulations under sub-paragraph (1)(e) may include—

  (a) provision for calculation or verification in accordance with guidance from time to time prepared by a prescribed person, and
  (b) provision by reference to regulations under section 30 or 49(4) of the 1999 Act.

(3) The power to make regulations under paragraph 27 or this paragraph is exercisable by statutory instrument which is subject to annulment in pursuance of a resolution of either House of Parliament.

(4) 'Prescribed' means prescribed by regulations.

Interpretation of provisions relating to pensions

29.—(1) In this Part 'the civil partner with pension rights' means the civil partner who has or is likely to have benefits under a pension arrangement.

(2) In this Part 'pension arrangement' has the same meaning as in Part 4.

(3) In this Part, references to the person responsible for a pension arrangement are to be read in accordance with section 26 of the Welfare Reform and Pensions Act 1999 (c. 30).

PART 7 PENSION PROTECTION FUND
COMPENSATION ETC.

PPF compensation to be included in matters to which court is to have regard

30.—(1) The matters to which a court is to have regard under paragraph 21(2)(a) include any PPF compensation to which a civil partner is or is likely to be entitled; and, accordingly, in relation to any PPF compensation paragraph 21(2)(a)(ii) has effect as if 'in the foreseeable future' were omitted.

(2) The matters to which a court is to have regard under paragraph 21(2)(h) include any PPF compensation which, because of the making of a dissolution or nullity order, a civil partner will lose the chance of acquiring entitlement to.

...

Assumption of responsibility by PPF Board in paragraph 25(2) cases

31.—(1) This paragraph applies to an order under Part 1 so far as it includes provision made by virtue of paragraph 25(2) which—

(a) imposed requirements on the trustees or managers of an occupational pension scheme for which the Board has assumed responsibility, and

(b) was made before the trustees or managers received the transfer notice.

(2) From the time the trustees or managers of the scheme receive the transfer notice, the order has effect—

(a) except in descriptions of case prescribed by regulations, with the modifications set out in sub-paragraph (3), and

(b) with such other modifications as may be prescribed by regulations.

(3) The modifications are that—

(a) references in the order to the trustees or managers of the scheme have effect as references to the Board, and

(b) references in the order to any pension or lump sum to which the civil partner with pension rights is or may become entitled under the scheme have effect as references to any PPF compensation to which that person is or may become entitled in respect of the pension or lump sum.

Assumption of responsibility by PPF Board in paragraph 25(5) cases

32.—(1) This paragraph applies to an order under Part 1 if—

(a) it includes provision made by virtue of paragraph 25(5) which requires the civil partner with pension rights to exercise his right of commutation under an occupational pension scheme to any extent, and

(b) before the requirement is complied with the Board has assumed responsibility for the scheme.

(2) From the time the trustees or managers of the scheme receive the transfer notice, the order has effect with such modifications as may be prescribed by regulations.

Lump sums: power to modify paragraph 26 in respect of assessment period

33.—Regulations may modify paragraph 26 in its application to an occupational pension scheme during an assessment period in relation to the scheme.

Assumption of responsibility by the board not to affect power of court to vary order etc.

34.—(1) This paragraph applies where the court makes, in relation to an occupational pension scheme—

(a) a pension sharing order, or

(b) an order including provision made by virtue of paragraph 25(2) or (5).

(2) If the Board subsequently assumes responsibility for the scheme, that does not affect—

(a) the powers of the court under paragraph 51 to vary or discharge the order or to suspend or revive any provision of it;

(b) on an appeal, the powers of the appeal court to affirm, reinstate, set aside or vary the order.

Attachment of PPF compensation

34A.—(1) This paragraph applies if, having regard to any PPF compensation to which a civil partner is or is likely to be entitled, the court decides to make an order under Part 1.

(2) To the extent to which the Part 1 order is made having regard to such compensation, it may require the Board, if at any time any payment in respect of PPF compensation becomes due to the civil partner with compensation rights, to make a payment for the benefit of the other civil partner.

(3) The Part 1 order must express the amount of any payment required to be made by virtue of sub-paragraph (2) as a percentage of the payment which becomes due to the civil partner with compensation rights.

(4) Any such payment by the Board—

(a) discharges so much of its liability to the civil partner with compensation rights as corresponds to the amount of the payment, and

(b) is to be treated for all purposes as a payment made by the civil partner with compensation rights in or towards the discharge of that civil partner's liability under the order.

(5) If the civil partner with compensation rights has a right to commute any PPF compensation, the Part 1 order may require that civil partner to exercise it to any extent.

(6) This paragraph applies to any payment due in consequence of commutation in pursuance of the Part 1 order as it applies to other payments in respect of PPF compensation.

(7) The power conferred by sub-paragraph (5) may not be exercised for the purpose of commuting a benefit payable to the civil partner with compensation rights to a benefit payable to the other civil partner.

(8) The powers conferred by sub-paragraphs (2) and (5) may not be exercised in relation to rights to PPF compensation that—

(a) derive from rights under a pension scheme that were at any time the subject of a pension sharing order in relation to the civil partnership or a previous civil partnership between the same parties, or

(b) are or have ever been the subject of a pension compensation sharing order in relation to the civil partnership or a previous civil partnership between the same parties.

Regulations

34B.—(1) Regulations may—

(a) make provision, in relation to any provision of paragraph 34A which authorises the court making a Part 1 order to require the Board to make a payment for the benefit of the other civil partner, as to the person to whom, and the terms on which, the payment is to be made;

(b) make provision, in relation to payment under a mistaken belief as to the continuation in force of a provision included by virtue of paragraph 34A in a Part 1 order, about the rights or liabilities of the payer, the payee or the person to whom the payment was due;

(c) require notices to be given in respect of changes of circumstances relevant to Part 1 orders which include provision made by virtue of paragraph 34A;

(d) make provision for the Board to be discharged in prescribed circumstances from a requirement imposed by virtue of paragraph 34A;

(e) make provision about calculation and verification in relation to the valuation of PPF compensation for the purposes of the court's functions in connection with the exercise of any of its powers under this Schedule.

(2) Regulations under sub-paragraph (1)(e) may include—

(a) provision for calculation or verification in accordance with guidance from time to time prepared by a prescribed person;

(b) provision by reference to regulations under section 112 of the Pensions Act 2008.

35.—Regulations may make such consequential modifications of any provision of, or made by virtue of, this Schedule as appear to the Lord Chancellor necessary or expedient to give effect to the provisions of this Part.

36.—(1) In this Part 'regulations' means regulations made by the Lord Chancellor.

(2) A power to make regulations under this Part is exercisable by statutory instrument which is subject to annulment in pursuance of a resolution of either House of Parliament.

Interpretation

37.—(1) In this Part—

'assessment period' means—

(a) an assessment period within the meaning of Part 2 of the Pensions Act 2004 (pension protection),

...

'the Board' means the Board of the Pension Protection Fund;

'the civil partner with compensation rights' means the civil partner who is or is likely to be entitled to PPF compensation;

'the civil partner with pension rights' has the meaning given by paragraph 29(1);

'occupational pension scheme' has the same meaning as in the Pension Schemes Act 1993 (c. 48);

'prescribed' means prescribed by regulations;

'transfer notice' has the same meaning as in—

(a) Chapter 3 of Part 2 of the 2004 Act,

...

(2) References in this Part to the Board assuming responsibility for a scheme are to the Board assuming responsibility for the scheme in accordance with—

(a) Chapter 3 of Part 2 of the 2004 Act (pension protection),

...

PART 8 MAINTENANCE AND OTHER PAYMENTS PENDING OUTCOME OF DISSOLUTION, NULLITY OR SEPARATION PROCEEDINGS

Maintenance orders

38.—(1) On an application for a dissolution, nullity or separation order, the court may make an order requiring either civil partner to make to the other for the other's maintenance such periodical payments for such term—

(a) beginning no earlier than the date on which the application was made, and

(b) ending with the date on which the proceedings are determined,as the court thinks reasonable.

(2) An order under this paragraph may not require one civil partner to pay to the other any amount in respect of legal services for the purposes of the proceedings.

(3) In sub-paragraph (2) 'legal services' has the same meaning as in paragraph 38A.

Orders in respect of legal services

38A.—(1) In proceedings for a dissolution, nullity or separation order, the court may make an order or orders requiring one civil partner to pay to the other ('the applicant') an amount for the purpose of enabling the applicant to obtain legal services for the purposes of the proceedings.

(2) The court may also make such an order or orders in proceedings under this Schedule for financial relief in connection with proceedings for a dissolution, nullity or separation order.

(3) The court must Not make an order under this paragraph unless it is satisfied that, without the amount, the applicant would not reasonably be able to obtain appropriate legal services for the purposes of the proceedings or any part of the proceedings.

(4) For the purposes of sub-paragraph (3), the court must be satisfied, in particular, that—

    (a) the applicant is not reasonably able to secure a loan to pay for the services, and

    (b) the applicant is unlikely to be able to obtain the services by granting a charge over any assets recovered in the proceedings.

(5) An order under this paragraph may be made for the purpose of enabling the applicant to obtain legal services of a specified description, including legal services provided in a specified period or for the purposes of a specified part of the proceedings.

(6) An order under this paragraph may—

    (a) provide for the payment of all or part of the amount by instalments of specified amounts, and

    (b) require the instalments to be secured to the satisfaction of the court.

(7) An order under this paragraph may direct that payment of all or part of the amount is to be deferred.

(8) The court may at any time in the proceedings vary an order made under this paragraph if it considers that there has been a material change of circumstances since the order was made.

(9) For the purposes of the assessment of costs in the proceedings, the applicant's costs are to be treated as reduced by any amount paid to the applicant pursuant to an order under this section for the purposes of those proceedings.

(10) In this paragraph 'legal services', in relation to proceedings, means the following types of services—

    (a) providing advice as to how the law applies in the particular circumstances,

    (b) providing advice and assistance in relation to the proceedings,

    (c) providing other advice and assistance in relation to the settlement or other resolution of the dispute that is the subject of the proceedings, and

    (d) providing advice and assistance in relation to the enforcement of decisions in the proceedings or as part of the settlement or resolution of the dispute,

and they include, in particular, advice and assistance in the form of representation and any form of dispute resolution, including mediation.

(11) In sub-paragraphs (5) and (6) 'specified' means specified in the order concerned.

38B.—(1) When considering whether to make or vary an order under paragraph 38A, the court must have regard to—

    (a) the income, earning capacity, property and other financial resources which each of the applicant and the paying party has or is likely to have in the foreseeable future,

    (b) the financial needs, obligations and responsibilities which each of the applicant and the paying party has or is likely to have in the foreseeable future,

    (c) the subject matter of the proceedings, including the matters in issue in them,

    (d) whether the paying party is legally represented in the proceedings,

    (e) any steps taken by the applicant to avoid all or part of the proceedings, whether by proposing or considering mediation or otherwise,

   (f) the applicant's conduct in relation to the proceedings,

   (g) any amount owed by the applicant to the paying party in respect of costs in the proceedings or other proceedings to which both the applicant and the paying party are or were party, and

   (h) the effect of the order or variation on the paying party.

(2) In sub-paragraph (1)(a) 'earning capacity', in relation to the applicant or the paying party, includes any increase in earning capacity which, in the opinion of the court, it would be reasonable to expect the applicant or the paying party to take steps to acquire.

(3) For the purposes of sub-paragraph (1)(h), the court must have regard, in particular, to whether the making or variation of the order is likely to—

   (a) cause undue hardship to the paying party, or

   (b) prevent the paying party from obtaining legal services for the purposes of the proceedings.

(4) The Lord Chancellor may by order amend this paragraph by adding to, omitting or varying the matters mentioned in sub-paragraphs (1) to (3).

(5) An order under sub-paragraph (4) must be made by statutory instrument.

(6) A statutory instrument containing an order under sub-paragraph (4) may not be made unless a draft of the instrument has been laid before, and approved by a resolution of, each House of Parliament.

(7) In this paragraph 'legal services' has the same meaning as in paragraph 38A.

PART 9 FAILURE TO MAINTAIN: FINANCIAL PROVISION (AND INTERIM ORDERS)

Circumstances in which orders under this Part may be made

39.—(1) Either civil partner in a subsisting civil partnership may apply to the court for an order under this Part on the ground that the other civil partner ('the respondent')—

   (a) has failed to provide reasonable maintenance for the applicant, or

   (b) has failed to provide, or to make a proper contribution towards, reasonable maintenance for any child of the family.

(2) The court must not entertain an application under this paragraph unless it has jurisdiction to do so by virtue of the Maintenance Regulation and Schedule 6 to the Civil Jurisdiction and Judgments (Maintenance) Regulations 2011.

(3) If, on an application under this paragraph, it appears to the court that—

   (a) the applicant or any child of the family to whom the application relates is in immediate need of financial assistance, but

   (b) it is not yet possible to determine what order, if any, should be made on the application, the court may make an interim order.

(4) If, on an application under this paragraph, the applicant satisfies the court of a ground mentioned in sub-paragraph (1), the court may make one or more of the orders set out in paragraph 41.
…

Interim orders

40.—An interim order is an order requiring the respondent to make to the applicant, until the determination of the application, such periodical payments as the court thinks reasonable.

Orders that may be made where failure to maintain established

41.—(1) The orders are—

   (a) an order that the respondent must make to the applicant such periodical payments for such term as may be specified;

(b) an order that the respondent must secure to the applicant, to the satisfaction of the court, such periodical payments for such term as may be specified;

(c) an order that the respondent must pay to the applicant such lump sum as may be specified;

(d) an order that the respondent must make such periodical payments for such term as may be specified—

  (i)   to such person as may be specified, for the benefit of the child to whom the application relates, or

  (ii) to the child to whom the application relates;

(e) an order that the respondent must secure—

  (i)   to such person as may be specified for the benefit of the child to whom the application relates, or

  (ii) to the child to whom the application relates,

  (iii) to the satisfaction of the court, such periodical payments for such term as may be specified;

(f) an order that the respondent must pay such lump sum as may be specified—

  (i)   to such person as may be specified for the benefit of the child to whom the application relates, or

  (ii) to the child to whom the application relates.

(5) In this Part 'specified' means specified in the order.

Particular provision that may be made by lump sum orders

42.—(1) An order under this Part for the payment of a lump sum may be made for the purpose of enabling any liabilities or expenses reasonably incurred in maintaining the applicant or any child of the family to whom the application relates before the making of the application to be met.

(2) An order under this Part for the payment of a lump sum may—

(a) provide for its payment by instalments of such amount as may be specified, and

(b) require the payment of the instalments to be secured to the satisfaction of the court.

(3) Sub-paragraphs (1) and (2) do not restrict the power to make an order by virtue of paragraph 41(1)(c) or (f).

Matters to which the court is to have regard on application under paragraph 39(1)(a)

43.—(1) This paragraph applies if an application under paragraph 39 is made on the ground mentioned in paragraph 39(1)(a).

(2) In deciding—

(a) whether the respondent has failed to provide reasonable maintenance for the applicant, and

(b) what order, if any, to make under this Part in favour of the applicant,

the court must have regard to all the circumstances of the case including the matters mentioned in paragraph 21(2).

(3) If an application is also made under paragraph 39 in respect of a child of the family who has not reached 18, the court must give first consideration to the welfare of the child while under 18.

(4) Paragraph 21(2)(c) has effect as if for the reference in it to the breakdown of the civil partnership there were substituted a reference to the failure to provide reasonable maintenance for the applicant.

Matters to which the court is to have regard on application under paragraph 39(1)(b)

44.—(1) This paragraph applies if an application under paragraph 39 is made on the ground mentioned in paragraph 39(1)(b).

(2) In deciding—

    (a) whether the respondent has failed to provide, or to make a proper contribution towards, reasonable maintenance for the child of the family to whom the application relates, and

    (b) what order, if any, to make under this Part in favour of the child,

the court must have regard to all the circumstances of the case.

(3) Those circumstances include—

    (a) the matters mentioned in paragraph 22(2)(a) to (e), and

    (b) if the child of the family to whom the application relates is not the child of the respondent, the matters mentioned in paragraph 22(3).

(4) Paragraph 21(2)(c) (as it applies by virtue of paragraph 22(2)(e)) has effect as if for the reference in it to the breakdown of the civil partnership there were substituted a reference to—

    (a) the failure to provide, or

    (b) the failure to make a proper contribution towards,

reasonable maintenance for the child of the family to whom the application relates.

Restrictions on making orders under this part

45.—The power to make an order under paragraph 41(1)(d), (e) or (f) is subject to paragraph 49(1) and (5) (restrictions on orders in favour of children who have reached 18).

PART 10 COMMENCEMENT OF CERTAIN PROCEEDINGS AND DURATION OF CERTAIN ORDERS

Commencement of proceedings for ancillary relief, etc.

46.—(1) Sub-paragraph (2) applies if an application for a dissolution, nullity or separation order has been made.

(2) Subject to sub-paragraph (3), proceedings for—

    (a) an order under Part 1 (financial provision on dissolution etc.),

    (b) a property adjustment order, or

    (c) an order under Part 8 (maintenance pending outcome of dissolution, nullity or separation proceedings),

may be begun (subject to and in accordance with rules of court) at any time after the presentation of the application.

(3) Rules of court may provide, in such cases as may be prescribed by the rules, that—

    (a) an application for any such relief as is mentioned in sub-paragraph (2) must be made in the application or response, and

    (b) an application for any such relief which—

        (i)   is not so made, or

        (ii) is not made until after the end of such period following the presentation of the application or filing of the response as may be so prescribed,

        may be made only with the leave of the court.

Duration of periodical and secured periodical payments orders for a civil partner

47.—(1) The court may specify in a periodical payments or secured periodical payments order in favour of a civil partner such term as it thinks fit, except that the term must not—

    (a) begin before the date of the making of an application for the order, or

    (b) extend beyond the limits given in sub-paragraphs (2) and (3).

(2) The limits in the case of a periodical payments order are—

    (a) the death of either civil partner;

    (b) where the order is made on or after the making of a dissolution or nullity order, the formation of a subsequent civil partnership or marriage by the civil partner in whose favour the order is made.

(3) The limits in the case of a secured periodical payments order are—

    (a) the death of the civil partner in whose favour the order is made;

    (b) where the order is made on or after the making of a dissolution or nullity order, the formation of a subsequent civil partnership or marriage by the civil partner in whose favour the order is made.

(4) In the case of an order made on or after the making of a dissolution or nullity order, sub-paragraphs (1) to (3) are subject to paragraphs 23(3) and 59(4).

(5) If a periodical payments or secured periodical payments order in favour of a civil partner is made on or after the making of a dissolution or nullity order, the court may direct that that civil partner is not entitled to apply under paragraph 51 for the extension of the term specified in the order.

(6) If—

    (a) a periodical payments or secured periodical payments order in favour of a civil partner is made otherwise than on or after the making of a dissolution or nullity order, and

    (b) the civil partnership is subsequently dissolved or annulled but the order continues in force,

the order ceases to have effect (regardless of anything in it) on the formation of a subsequent civil partnership or marriage by that civil partner, except in relation to any arrears due under it on the date of its formation.

Subsequent civil partnership or marriage

48.—If after the making of a dissolution or nullity order one of the civil partners forms a subsequent civil partnership or marriage, that civil partner is not entitled to apply, by reference to the dissolution or nullity order, for—

    (a) an order under Part 1 in that civil partner's favour, or

    (b) a property adjustment order,

against the other civil partner in the dissolved or annulled civil partnership.

Duration of continuing orders in favour of children, and age limit on making certain orders in their favour

49.—(1) Subject to sub-paragraph (5)—

    (a) no order under Part 1,

    (b) no property adjustment order made by virtue of paragraph 7(1)(a) (transfer of property), and

    (c) no order made under Part 9 (failure to maintain) by virtue of paragraph 41,

is to be made in favour of a child who has reached 18.

(2) The term to be specified in a periodical payments or secured periodical payments order in favour of a child may begin with—

    (a) the date of the making of an application for the order or a later date, or

    (b) a date ascertained in accordance with sub-paragraph (7) or (8).

(3) The term to be specified in such an order—

    (a) must not in the first instance extend beyond the date of the birthday of the child next following the child's reaching the upper limit of the compulsory school age unless the court considers that in the circumstances of the case the welfare of the child requires that it should extend to a later date, and

    (b) must not in any event, subject to sub-paragraph (5), extend beyond the date of the child's 18th birthday.

(4) Sub-paragraph (3)(a) must be read with section 8 of the Education Act 1996 (c. 56) (which applies to determine for the purposes of any enactment whether a person is of compulsory school age).

(5) Sub-paragraphs (1) and (3)(b) do not apply in the case of a child if it appears to the court that—

    (a) the child is, or will be, or, if an order were made without complying with either or both of those provisions, would be—

        (i) receiving instruction at an educational establishment, or

        (ii) undergoing training for a trade, profession or vocation,

    whether or not the child also is, will be or would be in gainful employment, or

    (b) there are special circumstances which justify the making of an order without complying with either or both of sub-paragraphs (1) and (3)(b).

(6) A periodical payments order in favour of a child, regardless of anything in the order, ceases to have effect on the death of the person liable to make payments under the order, except in relation to any arrears due under the order on the date of the death.

(7) If—

    (a) a maintenance calculation ('the current calculation') is in force with respect to a child, and

    (b) an application is made under this Schedule for a periodical payments or secured periodical payments order in favour of that child—

        (i) in accordance with section 8 of the Child Support Act 1991 (c. 48), and

        (ii) before the end of 6 months beginning with the making of the current calculation, the term to be specified in any such order made on that application may be expressed to begin on, or at any time after, the earliest permitted date.

(8) 'The earliest permitted date' is whichever is the later of—

    (a) the date 6 months before the application is made, or

    (b) the date on which the current calculation took effect or, where successive maintenance calculations have been continuously in force with respect to a child, on which the first of those calculations took effect.

(9) If—

    (a) a maintenance calculation ceases to have effect by or under any provision of the 1991 Act, and

    (b) an application is made, before the end of 6 months beginning with the relevant date, for a periodical payments or secured periodical payments order in favour of a child with respect to whom that maintenance calculation was in force immediately before it ceased to have effect,

the term to be specified in any such order made on that application may begin with the date on which that maintenance calculation ceased to have effect or any later date.

(10) 'The relevant date' means the date on which the maintenance calculation ceased to have effect.

(11) In this paragraph 'maintenance calculation' has the same meaning as it has in the 1991 Act by virtue of section 54 of the 1991 Act as read with any regulations in force under that section.

PART 11   VARIATION, DISCHARGE ETC. OF CERTAIN ORDERS FOR FINANCIAL RELIEF

Orders etc. to which this Part applies

50.—(1) This Part applies to the following orders—

    (a) a periodical payments order under Part 1 (financial provision on dissolution etc.) or Part 9 (failure to maintain);

    (b) a secured periodical payments order under Part 1 or 9;

(c) an order under Part 8 (maintenance pending outcome of dissolution proceedings etc.);

(d) an interim order under Part 9;

(e) an order made under Part 1 by virtue of paragraph 3(3) or under Part 9 by virtue of paragraph 42(2) (lump sum by instalments);

(f) a deferred order made under Part 1 by virtue of paragraph 2(1)(c) (lump sum for civil partner) which includes provision made by virtue of—

    (i) paragraph 25(2),

    (ii) paragraph 26, or

    (iii) paragraph 34A(2),

(provision in respect of pension rights or pension compensation rights);

(g) a property adjustment order made on or after the making of a separation order by virtue of paragraph 7(1)(b), (c) or (d) (order for settlement or variation of settlement);

(h) a sale of property order;

(i) a pension sharing order, or a pension compensation sharing order, made before the dissolution or nullity order has been made final.

(2) If the court has made an order referred to in sub-paragraph (1)(f)(ii), this Part ceases to apply to the order on the death of either of the civil partners.

(3) The powers exercisable by the court under this Part in relation to an order are also exercisable in relation to any instrument executed in pursuance of the order.

Powers to vary, discharge, suspend or revive order

51.—(1) If the court has made an order to which this Part applies, it may—

(a) vary or discharge the order,

(b) suspend any provision of it temporarily, or

(c) revive the operation of any provision so suspended.

(2) Sub-paragraph (1) is subject to the provisions of this Part and paragraph 47(5).

Power to remit arrears

52.—(1) If the court has made an order referred to in paragraph 50(1)(a), (b), (c) or (d), it may remit the payment of any arrears due under the order or under any part of the order.

(2) Sub-paragraph (1) is subject to the provisions of this Part.

Additional powers on discharging or varying a periodical or secured periodical payments order after dissolution of civil partnership

53.—(1) Sub-paragraph (2) applies if, after the dissolution of a civil partnership, the court—

(a) discharges a periodical payments order or secured periodical payments order made in favour of a civil partner, or

(b) varies such an order so that payments under the order are required to be made or secured only for such further period as is determined by the court.

(2) The court may make supplemental provision consisting of any of the following—

(a) an order for the payment of a lump sum in favour of one of the civil partners;

(b) one or more property adjustment orders in favour of one of the civil partners;

(c) one or more pension sharing orders;

(ca) a pension compensation sharing order;

(d) a direction that the civil partner in whose favour the original order discharged or varied was made is not entitled to make any further application for—

    (i) a periodical payments or secured periodical payments order, or

    (ii) an extension of the period to which the original order is limited by any variation made by the court.

(3) The power under sub-paragraph (2) is in addition to any power the court has apart from that sub-paragraph.

54.—(1) An order for the payment of a lump sum under paragraph 53 may—

(a) provide for the payment of it by instalments of such amount as may be specified, and

(b) require the payment of the instalments to be secured to the satisfaction of the court.

(2) Sub-paragraphs (5) and (6) of paragraph 3 (interest on deferred instalments) apply where the court makes an order for the payment of a lump sum under paragraph 53 as they apply where it makes such an order under Part 1.

(3) If under paragraph 53 the court makes more than one property adjustment order in favour of the same civil partner, each of those orders must fall within a different paragraph of paragraph 7(1) (types of property adjustment orders).

(4) Part 3 (orders for the sale of property) and paragraph 76 (direction for settlement of instrument) apply where the court makes a property adjustment order under paragraph 53 as they apply where it makes any other property adjustment order.

(5) Paragraph 18 (restrictions on making of pension sharing order) applies in relation to a pension sharing order under paragraph 53 as it applies in relation to any other pension sharing order.

(6) Paragraph 19D (restrictions on making pension compensation sharing orders) applies in relation to a pension compensation sharing order under paragraph 53 as it applies in relation to any other pension compensation sharing order.

Variation etc. of periodical or secured periodical payments orders made in cases of failure to maintain

55.—(1) An application for the variation under paragraph 51 of a periodical payments order or secured periodical payments order made under Part 9 in favour of a child may, if the child has reached 16, be made by the child himself.

(2) Sub-paragraph (3) applies if a periodical payments order made in favour of a child under Part 9 ceases to have effect—

(a) on the date on which the child reaches 16, or

(b) at any time after that date but before or on the date on which the child reaches 18.

(3) If, on an application made to the court for an order under this sub-paragraph, it appears to the court that—

(a) the child is, will be or, if an order were made under this sub-paragraph, would be—

(i) receiving instruction at an educational establishment, or

(ii) undergoing training for a trade, profession or vocation,

whether or not the child also is, will be or would be in gainful employment, or

(b) there are special circumstances which justify the making of an order under this sub-paragraph,

the court may by order revive the order mentioned in sub-paragraph (2) from such date as it may specify.

(4) A date specified under sub-paragraph (3) must not be earlier than the date of the application under that sub-paragraph.

(5) If under sub-paragraph (3) the court revives an order it may exercise its power under paragraph 51 in relation to the revived order.

Variation etc. of property adjustment, pension sharing and pension compensation sharing orders

56.—The court must not exercise the powers conferred by this Part in relation to a property adjustment order falling within paragraph 7(1)(b), (c) or (d) (order for settlement or for variation of settlement) except on an application made in proceedings—

(a) for the rescission of the separation order by reference to which the property adjustment order was made, or

(b) for a dissolution order in relation to the civil partnership.

57.—(1) In relation to a pension sharing order or pension compensation sharing order which is made at a time before the dissolution or nullity order has been made final—

    (a) the powers conferred by this Part (by virtue of paragraph 50(1)(i)) may be exercised—

        (i)   only on an application made before the pension sharing order or pension compensation sharing order has or, but for paragraph (b), would have taken effect, and

        (ii) only if, at the time when the application is made, the dissolution or nullity order has not been made final, and

    (b) an application made in accordance with paragraph (a) prevents the pension sharing order or pension compensation sharing order from taking effect before the application has been dealt with.

(2) No variation of a pension sharing order or pension compensation sharing order is to be made so as to take effect before the order is made final.

(3) The variation of a pension sharing order or pension compensation sharing order prevents the order taking effect before the end of such period after the making of the variation as may be prescribed by regulations made by the Lord Chancellor.

(4) The power to make regulations under sub-paragraph (3) is exercisable by statutory instrument which is subject to annulment in pursuance of a resolution of either House of Parliament.

58.—(1) Sub-paragraphs (2) and (3)—

    (a) are subject to paragraphs 53 and 54, and

    (b) do not affect any power exercisable by virtue of paragraph 50(e), (f), (g) or (i) or otherwise than by virtue of this Part.

(2) No property adjustment order, pension sharing order or pension compensation sharing order may be made on an application for the variation of a periodical payments or secured periodical payments order made (whether in favour of a civil partner or in favour of a child of the family) under Part 1.

(3) No order for the payment of a lump sum may be made on an application for the variation of a periodical payments or secured periodical payments order in favour of a civil partner (whether made under Part 1 or 9).

Matters to which court is to have regard in exercising powers under this Part

59.   (1) In exercising the powers conferred by this Part the court must have regard to all the circumstances of the case, giving first consideration to the welfare, while under 18, of any child of the family who has not reached 18.

(2) The circumstances of the case include, in particular, any change in any of the matters to which the court was required to have regard when making the order to which the application relates.

(3) Sub-paragraph (4) applies in the case of—

    (a) a periodical payments order, or

    (b) a secured periodical payments order,

made on or after the making of a dissolution or nullity order.

(4) The court must consider whether in all the circumstances, and after having regard to any such change, it would be appropriate to vary the order so that payments under the order are required—

    (a) to be made, or

    (b) to be secured,

only for such further period as will in the opinion of the court be sufficient to enable the civil partner in whose favour the order was made to adjust without undue hardship to the termination of those payments.

(5) In considering what further period will be sufficient, the court must, if the civil partnership has been dissolved, take into account any proposed exercise by it of its powers under paragraph 53.

(6) If the civil partner against whom the order was made has died, the circumstances of the case also include the changed circumstances resulting from that civil partner's death.

Variation of secured periodical payments order where person liable has died

60.—(1) This paragraph applies if the person liable to make payments under a secured periodical payments order has died.

(2) Subject to sub-paragraph (3), an application under this Part relating to the order (and to any sale of property order which requires the proceeds of sale of property to be used for securing those payments) may be made by—

    (a) the person entitled to payments under the periodical payments order, or

    (b) the personal representatives of the deceased person.

(3) No such application may be made without the leave of the court after the end of 6 months from the date on which representation in regard to the estate of that person is first taken out.

(4) The personal representatives of the person who has died are not liable for having distributed any part of the estate of the deceased after the end of the 6 month period on the ground that they ought to have taken into account the possibility that the court might allow an application under this paragraph to be made after that period by the person entitled to payments under the order.

(5) Sub-paragraph (4) does not affect any power to recover any part of the estate so distributed arising by virtue of the making of an order in pursuance of this paragraph.

(6) The following are to be left out of account when considering for the purposes of sub-paragraph (3) when representation was first taken out—

    (a) a grant limited to settled land or to trust property,

    (b) any other grant that does not permit any of the estate to be distributed,

    (c) a grant limited to real estate or to personal estate, unless a grant limited to the remainder of the estate has previously been made or is made at the same time,

    (d) a grant, or its equivalent, made outside the United Kingdom (but see sub-paragraph (7)).

. . .

Power to direct when variation etc. is to take effect

61.—(1) If the court, in exercise of its powers under this Part, decides—

    (a) to vary, or

    (b) to discharge,

a periodical payments or secured periodical payments order, it may direct that the variation or discharge is not to take effect until the end of such period as may be specified in the order.

(2) Sub-paragraph (1) is subject to paragraph 47(1) and (6).

62.—(1) If—

    (a) a periodical payments or secured periodical payments order in favour of more than one child ('the order') is in force,

    (b) the order requires payments specified in it to be made to or for the benefit of more than one child without apportioning those payments between them,

    (c) a maintenance calculation ('the calculation') is made with respect to one or more, but not all, of the children with respect to whom those payments are to be made, and

    (d) an application is made, before the end of the period of 6 months beginning with the date on which the calculation was made, for the variation or discharge of the order,

the court may, in exercise of its powers under this Part to vary or discharge the order, direct that the variation or discharge is to take effect from the date on which the calculation took effect or any later date.

(2) If—

    (a) an order ('the child order') of a kind prescribed for the purposes of section 10(1) of the Child Support Act 1991 (c. 48) is affected by a maintenance calculation,

    (b) on the date on which the child order became so affected there was in force a periodical payments or secured periodical payments order ('the civil partner's order') in favour of a civil partner having the care of the child in whose favour the child order was made, and

    (c) an application is made, before the end of the period of 6 months beginning with the date on which the maintenance calculation was made, for the civil partner's order to be varied or discharged,

the court may, in exercise of its powers under this Part to vary or discharge the civil partner's order, direct that the variation or discharge is to take effect from the date on which the child order became so affected or any later date.

(3) For the purposes of sub-paragraph (2), an order is affected if it ceases to have effect or is modified by or under section 10 of the 1991 Act.

(4) Sub-paragraphs (1) and (2) do not affect any other power of the court to direct that the variation of discharge of an order under this Part is to take effect from a date earlier than that on which the order for variation or discharge was made.

(5) In this paragraph 'maintenance calculation' has the same meaning as it has in the 1991 Act by virtue of section 54 of the 1991 Act as read with any regulations in force under that section.

PART 12 ARREARS AND REPAYMENTS

Payment of certain arrears unenforceable without the leave of the court

63.—(1) This paragraph applies if any arrears are due under—
    (a) an order under Part 1 (financial provision on dissolution etc.),
    (b) an order under Part 8 (maintenance pending outcome of dissolution, nullity or separation proceedings), or
    (c) an order under Part 9 (failure to maintain),

and the arrears became due more than 12 months before proceedings to enforce the payment of them are begun.

(2) A person is not entitled to enforce through the High Court or the family court the payment of the arrears without the leave of that court.

(3) The court hearing an application for the grant of leave under this paragraph may—
    (a) refuse leave,
    (b) grant leave subject to such restrictions and conditions (including conditions as to the allowing of time for payment or the making of payment by instalments) as that court thinks proper, or
    (c) remit the payment of the arrears or of any part of them.

(4) An application for the grant of leave under this paragraph must be made in such manner as may be prescribed by rules of court.

Orders for repayment in certain cases of sums paid under certain orders

64.—(1) This paragraph applies if—
    (a) a person ('R') is entitled to receive payments under an order listed in sub-paragraph (2), and
    (b) R's circumstances or the circumstances of the person ('P') liable to make payments under the order have changed since the order was made, or the circumstances have changed as a result of P's death.

(2) The orders are—
    (a) any order under Part 8 (maintenance pending outcome of dissolution, nullity or separation proceedings);
    (b) any interim order under Part 9;
    (c) any periodical payments order;
    (d) any secured periodical payments order.

(3) P or P's personal representatives may (subject to sub-paragraph (7)) apply for an order under this paragraph against R or R's personal representatives.

(4) If it appears to the court that, because of the changed circumstances or P's death, the amount received by R in respect of a relevant period exceeds the amount which P or P's personal representatives should have been required to pay, it may order the respondent to the application to pay to the applicant such sum, not exceeding the amount of the excess, as it thinks just.

(5) 'Relevant period' means a period after the circumstances changed or (as the case may be) after P's death.

(6) An order under this paragraph for the payment of any sum may provide for the payment of that sum by instalments of such amount as may be specified in the order.

(7) An application under this paragraph—

(a) may be made in proceedings in the High Court or the family court for—

(i)   the variation or discharge of the order listed in sub-paragraph (2), or

(ii) leave to enforce, or the enforcement of, the payment of arrears under that order, but

(b) if not made in such proceedings, must be made to the family court;

and accordingly references in this paragraph to the court are references to the High Court or the family court, as the circumstances require.

Orders for repayment after cessation of order because of subsequent civil partnership etc.

65.—(1) Sub-paragraphs (3) and (4) apply if—

(a) a periodical payments or secured periodical payments order in favour of a civil partner ('R') has ceased to have effect because of the formation of a subsequent civil partnership or marriage by R, and

(b) the person liable to make payments under the order ('P') (or P's personal representatives) has made payments in accordance with it in respect of a relevant period in the mistaken belief that the order was still subsisting.

(2) 'Relevant period' means a period after the date of the formation of the subsequent civil partnership or marriage.

(3) P (or P's personal representatives) is not entitled to bring proceedings in respect of a cause of action arising out of the circumstances mentioned in sub-paragraph (1)(a) and (b) against R (or R's personal representatives).

(4) But, on an application under this paragraph by P (or P's personal representatives) against R (or R's personal representatives), the court—

(a) may order the respondent to pay to the applicant a sum equal to the amount of the payments made in respect of the relevant period, or

(b) if it appears to the court that it would be unjust to make that order, may—

(i)   order the respondent to pay to the applicant such lesser sum as it thinks fit, or

(ii) dismiss the application.

(5) An order under this paragraph for the payment of any sum may provide for the payment of that sum by instalments of such amount as may be specified in the order.

(6) An application under this paragraph—

(a) may be made in proceedings in the High Court or the family court for leave to enforce, or the enforcement of, payment of arrears under the order in question, but

(b) if not made in such proceedings, must be made to the family court;

and accordingly references in this paragraph to the court are references to the High Court or the family court, as the circumstances require.

...

(8) Subject to sub-paragraph (9)—

(a) an officer of the family court is not liable for any act done by him, in pursuance of a payments order requiring payments to be made to the court or an officer of the court, after the date on which that order ceased to have effect because of the formation of a subsequent civil partnership or marriage by the person entitled to payments under it, and

(b) the collecting officer under an attachment of earnings order made to secure payments under a payments order is not liable for any act done by him after that date in accordance with any enactment or rule of court specifying how payments made to him in compliance with the attachment of earnings order are to be dealt with.

(9) Sub-paragraph (8) applies if (and only if) the act—

(a) was one which the officer would have been under a duty to do had the payments order not ceased to have effect, and

(b) was done before notice in writing of the formation of the subsequent civil partnership or marriage was given to him by or on behalf of—

(i)   the person entitled to payments under the payments order,

(ii)   the person liable to make payments under it, or

(iii) the personal representatives of either of them.

(10) In sub-paragraphs (8) and (9) 'payments order' means a periodical payments order or secured periodical payments order and 'collecting officer', in relation to an attachment of earnings order, means—

(a)   the officer of the High Court, or

(aa)   the officer of the family court,

to whom a person makes payments in compliance with the order.

PART 13 CONSENT ORDERS AND MAINTENANCE AGREEMENTS

Consent orders for financial relief

66.—(1) Regardless of anything in the preceding provisions of this Schedule, on an application for a consent order for financial relief, the court may, unless it has reason to think that there are other circumstances into which it ought to inquire, make an order in the terms agreed on the basis only of such information supplied with the application as is required by rules of court.

(2) Sub-paragraph (1) applies to an application for a consent order varying or discharging an order for financial relief as it applies to an application for an order for financial relief.

(3) In this paragraph—

'consent order', in relation to an application for an order, means an order in the terms applied for to which the respondent agrees;

'order for financial relief' means an order under any of Parts 1, 2, 3, 4 and 9.

Meaning of 'maintenance agreement' and 'financial arrangements'

67.—(1) In this Part 'maintenance agreement' means any agreement in writing between the civil partners in a civil partnership which—

(a) is made during the continuance or after the dissolution or annulment of the civil partnership and contains financial arrangements, or

(b) is a separation agreement which contains no financial arrangements but is made in a case where no other agreement in writing between the civil partners contains financial arrangements.

(2) In this Part 'financial arrangements' means provisions governing the rights and liabilities towards one another when living separately of the civil partners in a civil partnership (including a civil partnership which has been dissolved or annulled) in respect of—

(a) the making or securing of payments, or

(b) the disposition or use of any property,

including such rights and liabilities with respect to the maintenance or education of a child (whether or not a child of the family).

(3) 'Education' includes training.

Validity of maintenance agreements

68.—If a maintenance agreement includes a provision purporting to restrict any right to apply to a court for an order containing financial arrangements—

(a) that provision is void, but

(b) any other financial arrangements contained in the agreement—

    (i) are not void or unenforceable as a result, and

    (ii) unless void or unenforceable for any other reason, are (subject to paragraphs 69 and 73) binding on the parties to the agreement.

Alteration of agreements by court during lives of parties

69.—(1) Subject to sub-paragraph (1A), either party to a maintenance agreement may apply to the court for an order under this paragraph if—

(a) the maintenance agreement is for the time being subsisting, and

(b) each of the parties to the agreement is for the time being domiciled or resident in England and Wales.

(1A) ...

(2) The court may make an order under this paragraph if it is satisfied that—

(a) because of a change in the circumstances in the light of which—

    (i) any financial arrangements contained in the agreement were made, or

    (ii) financial arrangements were omitted from it,

    the agreement should be altered so as to make different financial arrangements or so as to contain financial arrangements, or

(b) that the agreement does not contain proper financial arrangements with respect to any child of the family.

(3) In sub-paragraph (2)(a) the reference to a change in the circumstances includes a change foreseen by the parties when making the agreement.

(4) An order under this paragraph may make such alterations in the agreement—

(a) by varying or revoking any financial arrangements contained in it, or

(b) by inserting in it financial arrangements for the benefit of one of the parties to the agreement or of a child of the family,

as appear to the court to be just having regard to all the circumstances, including, if relevant, the matters mentioned in paragraph 22(3).

(5) The effect of the order is that the agreement is to be treated as if any alteration made by the order had been made by agreement between the partners and for valuable consideration.

(6) The power to make an order under this paragraph is subject to paragraph 71.

...

Provisions relating to periodical and secured periodical payments: duration

71.—(1) If a court decides to make an order under paragraph 69 altering an agreement—

(a) by inserting provision for the making or securing by one of the parties to the agreement of periodical payments for the maintenance of the other party, or

(b) by increasing the rate of the periodical payments which the agreement provides shall be made by one of the parties for the maintenance of the other,

it may specify such term as it thinks fit as the term for which the payments or, as the case may be, the additional payments attributable to the increase are to be made under the altered agreement, except that the term must not extend beyond the limits in sub-paragraphs (2) and (3).

(2) The limits if the payments are not to be secured are—

(a) the death of either of the parties to the agreement, or

(b) the formation of a subsequent civil partnership or marriage by the party to whom the payments are to be made.

(3) The limits if the payments are to be secured are—

(a) the death of the party to whom the payments are to be made, or

   (b) the formation of a subsequent civil partnership or marriage by that party.

  (4) Sub-paragraph (5) applies if a court decides to make an order under paragraph 69 altering an agreement by—

   (a) inserting provision for the making or securing by one of the parties to the agreement of periodical payments for the maintenance of a child of the family, or

   (b) increasing the rate of the periodical payments which the agreement provides shall be made or secured by one of the parties for the maintenance of such a child.

  (5) The court, in deciding the term for which under the agreement as altered by the order—

   (a) the payments are to be made or secured for the benefit of the child, or

   (b) the additional payments attributable to the increase are to be made or secured for the benefit of the child,

must apply paragraph 49(2) to (5) (age limits) as if the order in question were a periodical payments or secured periodical payments order in favour of the child.

Saving

72.—Nothing in paragraphs 68 to 71 affects—

   (a) any power of a court before which any proceedings between the parties to a maintenance agreement are brought under any other enactment (including a provision of this Schedule) to make an order containing financial arrangements, or

   (b) any right of either party to apply for such an order in such proceedings.

Alteration of agreements by court after death of one party

73.—(1) This paragraph applies if—

   (a) a maintenance agreement provides for the continuation of payments under the agreement after the death of one of the parties, and

   (b) that party ('A') dies domiciled in England and Wales.

  (2) Subject to sub-paragraph (4), the surviving party or A's personal representatives may apply to the court for an order under paragraph 69.

  (3) If a maintenance agreement is altered by a court on an application made under sub-paragraph (2), the same consequences follow as if the alteration had been made immediately before the death by agreement between the parties and for valuable consideration.

  (4) An application under this paragraph may not, without the leave of the court, be made after the end of 6 months from the date on which representation in regard to A's estate is first taken out.

  (5) A's personal representatives are not liable for having distributed any part of A's estate after the end of the 6 month period on the ground that they ought to have taken into account the possibility that a court might allow an application by virtue of this paragraph to be made by the surviving party after that period.

  (6) Sub-paragraph (5) does not affect any power to recover any part of the estate so distributed arising by virtue of the making of an order in pursuance of this paragraph.

  (7) Paragraph 60(6) applies for the purposes of sub-paragraph (4) as it applies for the purposes of paragraph 60(3).

PART 14 MISCELLANEOUS AND SUPPLEMENTARY

Avoidance of transactions intended to prevent or reduce financial relief

74.—(1) This paragraph applies if proceedings for relief ('financial relief') are brought by one person ('A') against another ('B') under Part 1, 2, 4, 8, 9, or 11 (other than paragraph 60(2)), or paragraph 69.

  (2) If the court is satisfied, on an application by A, that B is, with the intention of defeating A's claim for financial relief, about to—

   (a) make any disposition, or

   (b) transfer out of the jurisdiction or otherwise deal with any property, it may make such order as it thinks fit for restraining B from doing so or otherwise for protecting the claim.

(3) If the court is satisfied, on an application by A, that—

    (a) B has, with the intention of defeating A's claim for financial relief, made a reviewable disposition, and

    (b) if the disposition were set aside, financial relief or different financial relief would be granted to A,

it make an order setting aside the disposition.

(4) If the court is satisfied, on an application by A in a case where an order has been obtained by A against B under any of the provisions mentioned in sub-paragraph (1), that B has, with the intention of defeating A's claim for financial relief, made a reviewable disposition, it may make an order setting aside the disposition.

(5) An application for the purposes of sub-paragraph (3) must be made in the proceedings for the financial relief in question.

(6) If the court makes an order under sub-paragraph (3) or (4) setting aside a disposition it must give such consequential directions as it thinks fit for giving effect to the order (including directions requiring the making of any payments or the disposal of any property).

75.—(1) Any reference in paragraph 74 to defeating A's claim for financial relief is to—

    (a) preventing financial relief from being granted to A, or to A for the benefit of a child of the family,

    (b) reducing the amount of any financial relief which might be so granted, or

    (c) frustrating or impeding the enforcement of any order which might be or has been made at A's instance under any of those provisions.

(2) In paragraph 74 and this paragraph 'disposition'—

    (a) does not include any provision contained in a will or codicil, but

    (b) subject to paragraph (a), includes any conveyance, assurance or gift of property of any description (whether made by an instrument or otherwise).

(3) Any disposition made by B (whether before or after the commencement of the proceedings for financial relief) is a reviewable disposition for the purposes of paragraphs 74(3) and (4) unless it was made—

    (a) for valuable consideration (other than formation of a civil partnership), and

    (b) to a person who, at the time of the disposition, acted in relation to it in good faith and without notice of any intention on B's part to defeat A's claim for financial relief.

(4) If an application is made under paragraph 74 with respect to a disposition which took place less than 3 years before the date of the application or with respect to a disposition or other dealing with property which is about to take place and the court is satisfied—

    (a) in a case falling within paragraph 74(2) or (3), that the disposition or other dealing would (apart from paragraph 74) have the consequence of defeating A's claim for financial relief, or

    (b) in a case falling within paragraph 74(4), that the disposition has had the consequence of defeating A's claim for financial relief,

it is presumed, unless the contrary is shown, that the person who disposed of or is about to dispose of or deal with the property did so or, as the case may be, is about to do so, with the intention of defeating A's claim for financial relief.

Direction for settlement of instrument for securing payments or effecting property adjustment

76.—(1) This paragraph applies if the court decides to make—

    (a) an order under Part 1 or 9 requiring any payments to be secured, or

    (b) a property adjustment order.

(2) The court may direct that the matter be referred to one of the conveyancing counsel of the court for him to settle a proper instrument to be executed by all necessary parties.

(3) If the order referred to in sub-paragraph (1) is to be made in proceedings for a dissolution, nullity or separation order, the court may, if it thinks fit, defer the making of the dissolution, nullity or separation order until the instrument has been duly executed.

Settlement, etc., made in compliance with a property adjustment order may be avoided on bankruptcy of settlor

77.—The fact that—
(a) a settlement, or
(b) a transfer of property,

had to be made in order to comply with a property adjustment order does not prevent the settlement or transfer from being a transaction in respect of which an order may be made under section 339 or 340 of the Insolvency Act 1986 (c. 45) (transfers at an undervalue and preferences).

Payments etc., under order made in favour of person suffering from mental disorder

78.—(1) This paragraph applies if—
(a) the court makes an order under this Schedule requiring—
(i)   payments (including a lump sum payment) to be made, or
(ii)   property to be transferred,
to a civil partner, and
(b) the court is satisfied that the person in whose favour the order is made is incapable, because of mental disorder, of managing and administering his or her property and affairs.

(2) 'Mental disorder' has the same meaning as in the Mental Health Act 1983 (c. 20).

(3) Subject to any order, direction or authority made or given in relation to that person under Part 8 of the 1983 Act, the court may order the payments to be made or, as the case may be, the property to be transferred to such persons having charge of that person as the court may direct.

Appeals relating to pension sharing orders which have taken effect

79.—(1) Sub-paragraphs (2) and (3) apply if an appeal against a pension sharing order is begun on or after the day on which the order takes effect.

(2) If the pension sharing order relates to a person's rights under a pension arrangement, the appeal court may not set aside or vary the order if the person responsible for the pension arrangement has acted to his detriment in reliance on the order taking effect.

(3) If the pension sharing order relates to a person's shareable state scheme rights, the appeal court may not set aside or vary the order if the Secretary of State has acted to his detriment in reliance on the taking effect of the order.

(4) In determining for the purposes of sub-paragraph (2) or (3) whether a person has acted to his detriment in reliance on the taking effect of the order, the appeal court may disregard any detriment which in its opinion is insignificant.

(5) Where sub-paragraph (2) or (3) applies, the appeal court may make such further orders (including one or more pension sharing orders) as it thinks fit for the purpose of putting the parties in the position it considers appropriate.

(6) Paragraph 19 only applies to a pension sharing order under this paragraph if the decision of the appeal court can itself be the subject of an appeal.

(7) In sub-paragraph (2), the reference to the person responsible for the pension arrangement is to be read in accordance with paragraph 29(3).

Appeals relating to pension compensation sharing orders which have taken effect

79A.—(1) This paragraph applies where an appeal against a pension compensation sharing order is begun on or after the day on which the order takes effect.

(2) If the Board of the Pension Protection Fund has acted to its detriment in reliance on the taking effect of the order the appeal court—

(a) may not set aside or vary the order;

(b) may make such further orders (including a pension compensation sharing order) as it thinks fit for the purpose of putting the parties in the position it considers appropriate.

(3) In determining for the purposes of subparagraph (2) whether the Board has acted to its detriment the appeal court may disregard any detriment which in the court's opinion is insignificant.

(4) Paragraph 19E only applies to a pension compensation sharing order under this paragraph if the decision of the appeal court can itself be the subject of an appeal.

Interpretation

80.—(1) References in this Schedule to—

(a) periodical payments orders,

(b) secured periodical payments orders, and

(c) orders for the payment of a lump sum, are references to such of the orders that may be made under Parts 1 and 9 (other than interim orders) as are relevant in the context of the reference in question.

(2) In this Schedule 'child of the family', in relation to two people who are civil partners of each other, means—

(a) a child of both of them, and

(b) any other child, other than a child placed with them as foster parents by a local authority or voluntary organisation, who has been treated by both the civil partners as a child of their family.

(3) In this Schedule 'the court' (except where the context otherwise requires) means—

(a) the High Court, or

(b) the family court.

(4) References in this Schedule to a subsequent civil partnership include a civil partnership which is by law void or voidable.

(5) References in this Schedule to a subsequent marriage include a marriage which is by law void or voidable.

Section 72(3)

SCHEDULE 6

FINANCIAL RELIEF: PROVISION CORRESPONDING TO PROVISION MADE BY THE DOMESTIC PROCEEDINGS AND MAGISTRATES' COURTS ACT 1978

PART 1 FAILURE TO MAINTAIN ETC.: FINANCIAL PROVISION

Circumstances in which orders under this Part may be made

1.—(1) On an application to it by one of the civil partners, the family court may make any one or more of the orders set out in paragraph 2 if it is satisfied that the other civil partner—

(a) has failed to provide reasonable maintenance for the applicant,

(b) has failed to provide, or to make a proper contribution towards, reasonable maintenance for any child of the family,

    (c) has behaved in such a way that the applicant cannot reasonably be expected to live with the respondent, or

    (d) has deserted the applicant.

(2) The power of the court under sub-paragraph (1) is subject to the following provisions of this Schedule.

The orders: periodical and secured periodical payments and lump sums

2.—(1) The orders are—

    (a) an order that the respondent must make to the applicant such periodical payments for such term as may be specified;

    (b) an order that the respondent must pay to the applicant such lump sum as may be specified;

    (c) an order that the respondent must make—

        (i) to the applicant for the benefit of a child of the family to whom the application relates, or

        (ii) to a child of the family to whom the application relates; such periodical payments for such term as may be specified;

    (d) an order that the respondent must pay such lump sum as may be specified—

        (i) to the applicant for the benefit of a child of the family to whom the application relates, or

        (ii) to such a child of the family to whom the application relates.

(2) The amount of a lump sum required to be paid under sub-paragraph (1)(b) or (d) must not exceed—

    (a) £1,000, or

    (b) such larger amount as the Lord Chancellor may from time to time by order fix for the purposes of this sub-paragraph.

(3) The power to make an order under sub-paragraph (2) is exercisable by statutory instrument which is subject to annulment in pursuance of a resolution of either House of Parliament.

(4) 'Specified' means specified in the order.

Particular provision that may be made by lump sum orders

3.—(1) An order under this Part for the payment of a lump sum may be made for the purpose of enabling any liability or expenses reasonably incurred in maintaining the applicant or any child of the family to whom the application relates before the making of the order to be met.

(2) Sub-paragraph (1) does not restrict the power to make the orders set out in paragraph 2(1)(b) and (d).

Matters to which court is to have regard in exercising its powers under this Part—general

4.—If an application is made for an order under this Part, the court, in deciding—

    (a) whether to exercise its powers under this Part, and

    (b) if so, in what way,

must have regard to all the circumstances of the case, giving first consideration to the welfare while under 18 of any child of the family who has not reached 18.

Particular matters to be taken into account when exercising powers in relation to civil partners

5.—(1) This paragraph applies in relation to the exercise by the court of its power to make an order by virtue of paragraph 2(1)(a) or (b).

(2) The court must in particular have regard to—

    (a) the income, earning capacity, property and other financial resources which each civil partner—

    (i)   has, or

    (ii) is likely to have in the foreseeable future,

including, in the case of earning capacity, any increase in that capacity which it would in the opinion of the court be reasonable to expect a civil partner in the civil partnership to take steps to acquire;

(b) the financial needs, obligations and responsibilities which each civil partner has or is likely to have in the foreseeable future;

(c) the standard of living enjoyed by the civil partners before the occurrence of the conduct which is alleged as the ground of the application;

(d) the age of each civil partner and the duration of the civil partnership;

(e) any physical or mental disability of either civil partner;

(f) the contributions which each civil partner has made or is likely in the foreseeable future to make to the welfare of the family, including any contribution by looking after the home or caring for the family;

(g) the conduct of each civil partner, if that conduct is such that it would in the opinion of the court be inequitable to disregard it.

Particular matters to be taken into account when exercising powers in relation to children

6.—(1) This paragraph applies in relation to the exercise by the court of its power to make an order by virtue of paragraph 2(1)(c) or (d).

(2) The court must in particular have regard to—

(a) the financial needs of the child;

(b) the income, earning capacity (if any), property and other financial resources of the child;

(c) any physical or mental disability of the child;

(d) the standard of living enjoyed by the family before the occurrence of the conduct which is alleged as the ground of the application;

(e) the way in which the child was being and in which the civil partners expected the child to be educated or trained;

(f) the considerations mentioned in relation to the civil partners in paragraph 5(2)(a) and (b).

(3) In relation to the exercise of its power to make an order in favour of a child of the family who is not the respondent's child, the court must also have regard to—

(a) whether the respondent has assumed any responsibility for the child's maintenance;

(b) if so, the extent to which, and the basis on which, the respondent assumed that responsibility and the length of time during which the respondent discharged that responsibility;

(c) whether in assuming and discharging that responsibility the respondent did so knowing that the child was not the respondent's child;

(d) the liability of any other person to maintain the child.

Reconciliation

7.—(1) If an application is made for an order under this Part—

(a) the court, before deciding whether to exercise its powers under this Part, must consider whether there is any possibility of reconciliation between the civil partners, and

(b) if at any stage of the proceedings on that application it appears to the court that there is a reasonable possibility of such a reconciliation, the court may adjourn the proceedings for such period as it thinks fit to enable attempts to be made to effect a reconciliation.

(2) If the court adjourns any proceedings under sub-paragraph (1), it may request—

(a) an officer of the Children and Family Court Advisory and Support Service, or

(b) any other person, to attempt to effect a reconciliation between the civil partners.

(3) If any such request is made, the officer or other person—

    (a) must report in writing to the court whether the attempt has been successful, but

    (b) must not include in the report any other information.

...

PART 2 ORDERS FOR AGREED FINANCIAL PROVISION

Orders for payments which have been agreed by the parties

9.—(1) Either civil partner may apply to the family court for an order under this Part on the ground that that civil partner or the other civil partner has agreed to make such financial provision as may be specified in the application.

(2) On such an application, the court may order that the applicant or the respondent (as the case may be) is to make the financial provision specified in the application, if—

    (a) it is satisfied that the applicant or the respondent (as the case may be) has agreed to make that provision, and

    (b) it has no reason to think that it would be contrary to the interests of justice to do so.

(3) Sub-paragraph (2) is subject to paragraph 12.

Meaning of 'financial provision' and of references to specified financial provision

10.—(1) In this Part 'financial provision' means any one or more of the following—

    (a) the making of periodical payments by one civil partner to the other;

    (b) the payment of a lump sum by one civil partner to the other;

    (c) the making of periodical payments by one civil partner to a child of the family or to the other civil partner for the benefit of such a child;

    (d) the payment by one party of a lump sum to a child of the family or to the other civil partner for the benefit of such a child.

(2) Any reference in this Part to the financial provision specified in an application or specified by the court is a reference—

    (a) to the type of provision specified in the application or by the court,

    (b) to the amount so specified as the amount of any payment to be made under the application or order, and

    (c) in the case of periodical payments, to the term so specified as the term for which the payments are to be made.

Evidence to be produced where respondent not present etc.

11.—(1) This paragraph applies if—

    (a) the respondent is not present, or

    (b) is not represented by counsel or a solicitor,

at the hearing of an application for an order under this Part.

(2) The court must not make an order under this Part unless there is produced to it such evidence as may be prescribed by rules of court of—

    (a) the consent of the respondent to the making of the order,

    (b) the financial resources of the respondent, and

    (c) if the financial provision specified in the application includes or consists of provision in respect of a child of the family to be made by the applicant to the respondent for the benefit of the child or to the child, the financial resources of the child.

Exercise of powers in relation to children

12.—(1) This paragraph applies if the financial provision specified in an application under this Part—

    (a) includes, or

    (b) consists of,

provision in respect of a child of the family.

(2) The court must not make an order under this Part unless it considers that the provision which the applicant or the respondent (as the case may be) has agreed to make in respect of the child provides for, or makes a proper contribution towards, the financial needs of the child.

Power to make alternative orders

13.—(1) This paragraph applies if on an application under this Part the court decides—
  (a) that it would be contrary to the interests of justice to make an order for the making of the financial provision specified in the application, or
  (b) that any financial provision which the applicant or the respondent (as the case may be) has agreed to make in respect of a child of the family does not provide for, or make a proper contribution towards, the financial needs of that child.

(2) If the court is of the opinion—
  (a) that it would not be contrary to the interests of justice to make an order for the making of some other financial provision specified by the court, and
  (b) that, in so far as that other financial provision contains any provision for a child of the family, it provides for, or makes a proper contribution towards, the financial needs of that child,

then, if both the civil partners agree, the court may order that the applicant or the respondent (as the case may be) is to make that other financial provision.

Relationship between this Part and Part 1

14.—(1) A civil partner who has applied for an order under Part 1 is not precluded at any time before the determination of the application from applying for an order under this Part.

(2) If—
  (a) an order is made under this Part on the application of either civil partner, and
  (b) either of them has also made an application for a Part 1 order, the application for the Part 1 order is to be treated as if it had been withdrawn.

PART 3 ORDERS OF COURT WHERE CIVIL PARTNERS LIVING APART BY AGREEMENT

Powers of court where civil partners are living apart by agreement

15.—(1) If—
  (a) the civil partners have been living apart for a continuous period exceeding 3 months, neither civil partner having deserted the other, and
  (b) one of the civil partners has been making periodical payments for the benefit of the other civil partner or of a child of the family,

the other civil partner may apply to the family court for an order under this Part.

(2) An application made under sub-paragraph (1) must specify the total amount of the payments made by the respondent during the period of 3 months immediately preceding the date of the making of the application.

(3) If on an application for an order under this Part the court is satisfied that the respondent has made the payments specified in the application, the court may make one or both of the orders set out in paragraph 16.

(4) Sub-paragraph (3) is subject to the provisions of this Schedule.

The orders that may be made under this Part

16.—(1) The orders are—
  (a) an order that the respondent is to make to the applicant such periodical payments for such term as may be specified;

(b) an order that the respondent is to make—

    (i) to the applicant for the benefit of a child of the family to whom the application relates, or

    (ii) to a child of the family to whom the application relates. such periodical payments for such term as may be specified.

(2) 'Specified' means specified in the order.

Restrictions on orders under this Part

17.—The court in the exercise of its powers under this Part must not require—

  (a) the respondent to make payments whose total amount during any period of 3 months exceeds the total amount paid by him for the benefit of—

    (i) the applicant, or

    (ii) a child of the family,

  during the period of 3 months immediately preceding the date of the making of the application;

  (b) the respondent to make payments to or for the benefit of any person which exceed in amount the payments which the court considers that it would have required the respondent to make to or for the benefit of that person on an application under Part 1;

  (c) payments to be made to or for the benefit of a child of the family who is not the respondent's child, unless the court considers that it would have made an order in favour of that child on an application under Part 1.

Relationship with powers under Part 1

18.—(1) Sub-paragraph (2) applies if on an application under this Part the court considers that the orders which it has the power to make under this Part—

  (a) would not provide reasonable maintenance for the applicant, or

  (b) if the application relates to a child of the family, would not provide, or make a proper contribution towards, reasonable maintenance for that child.

(2) The court—

  (a) must refuse to make an order under this Part, but

  (b) may treat the application as if it were an application for an order under Part 1.

Matters to be taken into consideration

19.—Paragraphs 4 to 6 apply in relation to an application for an order under this Part as they apply in relation to an application for an order under Part 1, subject to the modification that for the reference in paragraph 5(2)(c) to the occurrence of the conduct which is alleged as the ground of the application substitute a reference to the living apart of the civil partners.

PART 4 INTERIM ORDERS

Circumstances in which interim orders may be made

20.—(1) This paragraph applies if an application has been made for an order under Part 1, 2 or 3.

(2) The family court may make an interim order—

  (a) at any time before making a final order on, or dismissing, the application,

  …

(4) Not more than one interim order may be made with respect to an application for an order under Part 1, 2 or 3.

(5) Sub-paragraph (4) does not affect the power of a court to make an interim order on a further application under Part 1, 2 or 3.

Meaning of interim order

21.—(1) An interim order is an order requiring the respondent to make such periodical payments as the court thinks reasonable—

(a) to the applicant,

(b) to any child of the family who is under 18, or

(c) to the applicant for the benefit of such a child.

(2) In relation to an interim order in respect of an application for an order under Part 2 by the civil partner who has agreed to make the financial provision specified in the application, sub-paragraph (1) applies as if—

(a) the reference to the respondent were a reference to the applicant, and

(b) the references to the applicant were references to the respondent.

When interim order may start

22.—(1) An interim order may provide for payments to be made from such date as the court may specify, except that the date must not be earlier than the date of the making of the application for an order under Part 1, 2 or 3.

(2) Sub-paragraph (1) is subject to paragraph 27(7) and (8).

...

When interim order ceases to have effect

24.—(1) Subject to sub-paragraphs (2) and (3), an interim order made on an application for an order under Part 1, 2 or 3 ceases to have effect on the earliest of the following dates—

(a) the date, if any, specified for the purpose in the interim order;

(b) the date on which the period of 3 months beginning with the date of the making of the interim order ends;

(c) the date on which the family court either makes a final order on, or dismisses, the application.

(2) If an interim order made under this Part would, but for this sub-paragraph, cease to have effect under sub-paragraph (1)(a) or (b)—

(a) the family court,

...

may by order provide that the interim order is to continue in force for a further period.

(3) An order continued in force under sub-paragraph (2) ceases to have effect on the earliest of the following dates—

(a) the date, if any, specified for the purpose in the order continuing it;

(b) the date on which ends the period of 3 months beginning with—

(i)   the date of the making of the order continuing it, or

(ii) if more than one such order has been made with respect to the application, the date of the making of the first such order;

(c) the date on which the court either makes a final order on, or dismisses, the application.

...

PART 5 COMMENCEMENT AND DURATION OF ORDERS UNDER PARTS 1, 2 AND 3

Duration of periodical payments order for a civil partner

26.—(1) The court may specify in a periodical payments order made under paragraph 2 (1)(a) or Part 3 in favour of a civil partner such term as it thinks fit, except that the term must not—

(a) begin before the date of the making of the application for the order, or

(b) extend beyond the death of either of the civil partners.

(2) If—

    (a) a periodical payments order is made under paragraph 2(1)(a) or Part 3 in favour of one of the civil partners, and

    (b) the civil partnership is subsequently dissolved or annulled but the order continues in force,

the periodical payments order ceases to have effect (regardless of anything in it) on the formation of a subsequent civil partnership or marriage by that civil partner, except in relation to any arrears due under the order on the date of that event.

Age limit on making orders for financial provision for children and duration of such orders

27.—(1) Subject to sub-paragraph (5), no order is to be made under paragraph 2(1)(c) or (d) or Part 3 in favour of a child who has reached 18.

(2) The term to be specified in a periodical payments order made under paragraph 2 (1)(c) or Part 3 in favour of a child may begin with—

    (a) the date of the making of an application for the order or a later date, or

    (b) a date ascertained in accordance with sub-paragraph (7) or (8).

(3) The term to be specified in such an order—

    (a) must not in the first instance extend beyond the date of the birthday of the child next following his reaching the upper limit of the compulsory school age unless the court considers that in the circumstances of the case the welfare of the child requires that it should extend to a later date, and

    (b) must not in any event, subject to sub-paragraph (5), extend beyond the date of the child's 18th birthday.

(4) Sub-paragraph (3)(a) must be read with section 8 of the Education Act 1996 (c. 56) (which applies to determine for the purposes of any enactment whether a person is of compulsory school age).

(5) Sub-paragraphs (1) and (3)(b) do not apply in the case of a child if it appears to the court that—

    (a) the child is, or will be, or, if such an order were made without complying with either or both of those provisions, would be—

        (i) receiving instruction at an educational establishment, or

        (ii) undergoing training for a trade, profession or vocation,

    whether or not also the child is, will be or would be, in gainful employment, or

    (b) there are special circumstances which justify the making of the order without complying with either or both of sub-paragraphs (1) and (3)(b).

(6) Any order made under paragraph 2(1)(c) or Part 3 in favour of a child, regardless of anything in the order, ceases to have effect on the death of the person liable to make payments under the order.

(7) If—

    (a) a maintenance calculation ('current calculation') is in force with respect to a child, and

    (b) an application is made for an order under paragraph 2(1)(c) or Part 3—

        (i) in accordance with section 8 of the Child Support Act 1991 (c. 48), and

        (ii) before the end of 6 months beginning with the making of the current calculation,

    the term to be specified in any such order made on that application may be expressed to begin on, or at any time after, the earliest permitted date.

(8) 'The earliest permitted date' is whichever is the later of—

    (a) the date 6 months before the application is made, or

    (b) the date on which the current calculation took effect or, where successive maintenance calculations have been continuously in force with respect to a child, on which the first of those calculations took effect.

(9) If—

    (a) a maintenance calculation ceases to have effect by or under any provision of the 1991 Act, and

    (b) an application is made, before the end of 6 months beginning with the relevant date, for a periodical payments order under paragraph 2(1)(c) or Part 3 in favour of a child with respect to whom that maintenance calculation was in force immediately before it ceased to have effect,

the term to be specified in any such order, or in any interim order under Part 4, made on that application, may begin with the date on which that maintenance calculation ceased to have effect or any later date.

(10) 'The relevant date' means the date on which the maintenance calculation ceased to have effect.

(11) In this Schedule 'maintenance calculation' has the same meaning as it has in the 1991 Act by virtue of section 54 of the 1991 Act as read with any regulations in force under that section.

Application of paragraphs 26 and 27 to Part 2 orders

28.—(1) Subject to sub-paragraph (3), paragraph 26 applies in relation to an order under Part 2 which requires periodical payments to be made to a civil partner for his own benefit as it applies in relation to an order under paragraph 2(1)(a).

(2) Subject to sub-paragraph (3), paragraph 27 applies in relation to an order under Part 2 for the making of financial provision in respect of a child of the family as it applies in relation to an order under paragraph 2(1)(c) or (d).

(3) If—

    (a) the court makes an order under Part 2 which contains provision for the making of periodical payments, and

    (b) by virtue of paragraph 14, an application for an order under Part 1 is treated as if it had been withdrawn,

the term which may be specified under Part 2 as the term for which the payments are to be made may begin with the date of the making of the application for the order under Part 1 or any later date.

Effect on certain orders of parties living together

29.—(1) Sub-paragraph (2) applies if periodical payments are required to be made to a civil partner (whether for the civil partner's own benefit or for the benefit of a child of the family)—

    (a) by an order made under Part 1 or 2, or

    (b) by an interim order made under Part 4 (otherwise than on an application under Part 3).

(2) The order is enforceable even though—

    (a) the civil partners are living with each other at the date of the making of the order, or

    (b) if they are not living with each other at that date, they subsequently resume living with each other;

but the order ceases to have effect if after that date the parties continue to live with each other, or resume living with each other, for a continuous period exceeding 6 months.

(3) Sub-paragraph (4) applies if—

    (a) an order is made under Part 1 or 2 which requires periodical payments to be made to a child of the family, or

    (b) an interim order is made under Part 4 (otherwise than on an application under Part 3) which requires periodical payments to be made to a child of the family.

(4) Unless the court otherwise directs, the order continues to have effect and is enforceable even if—

    (a) the civil partners are living with each other at the date of the making of the order, or

    (b) if they are not living with each other at that date, they subsequently resume living with each other.

(5) An order made under Part 3, and any interim order made on an application for an order under that Part, ceases to have effect if the civil partners resume living with each other.

(6) If an order made under this Schedule ceases to have effect under—

(a) sub-paragraph (2) or (5), or

(b) a direction given under sub-paragraph (4),

the family court may, on an application made by either civil partner, make an order declaring that the order ceased to have effect from such date as the court may specify.

PART 6 VARIATION ETC. OF ORDERS

Power to vary, revoke, suspend or revive order

30.—(1) If the family court has made an order for the making of periodical payments under Part 1, 2 or 3, the court may, on an application made under this Part—

(a) vary or revoke the order,

(b) suspend any provision of it temporarily, or

(c) revive any provision so suspended.

(2) If the family court has made an interim order under Part 4, the court may, on an application made under this Part—

(a) vary or revoke the order,

(b) suspend any provision of it temporarily, or

(c) revive any provision so suspended,

except that it may not by virtue of this sub-paragraph extend the period for which the order is in force.

Powers to order lump sum on variation

31.—(1) If the family court has made an order under paragraph 2(1)(a) or (c) for the making of periodical payments, the court may, on an application made under this Part, make an order for the payment of a lump sum under paragraph 2(1)(b) or (d).

(2) If the family court has made an order under Part 2 for the making of periodical payments by a civil partner the court may, on an application made under this Part, make an order for the payment of a lump sum by that civil partner—

(a) to the other civil partner, or

(b) to a child of the family or to that other civil partner for the benefit of that child.

(3) Where the court has power by virtue of this paragraph to make an order for the payment of a lump sum—

(a) the amount of the lump sum must not exceed the maximum amount that may at that time be required to be paid under Part 1, but

(b) the court may make an order for the payment of a lump sum not exceeding that amount even if the person required to pay it was required to pay a lump sum by a previous order under this Schedule.

(4) Where—

(a) the court has power by virtue of this paragraph to make an order for the payment of a lump sum, and

(b) the respondent or the applicant (as the case may be) has agreed to pay a lump sum of an amount exceeding the maximum amount that may at that time be required to be paid under Part 1, the court may, regardless of sub-paragraph (3), make an order for the payment of a lump sum of that amount.

Power to specify when order as varied is to take effect

32.—An order made under this Part which varies an order for the making of periodical payments may provide that the payments as so varied are to be made from such date as the court may specify, except that, subject to paragraph 33, the date must not be earlier than the date of the making of the application under this Part.

    33.—(1) If—

      (a) there is in force an order ('the order')—
- (i) under paragraph 2(1)(c),
- (ii) under Part 2 making provision of a kind set out in paragraph 10(1)(c) (regardless of whether it makes provision of any other kind mentioned in paragraph 10(1)(c)),
- (iii) under paragraph 16(1)(b), or
- (iv) which is an interim order under Part 4 under which the payments are to be made to a child or to the applicant for the benefit of a child,

      (b) the order requires payments specified in it to be made to or for the benefit of more than one child without apportioning those payments between them,

      (c) a maintenance calculation ('the calculation') is made with respect to one or more, but not all, of the children with respect to whom those payments are to be made, and

      (d) an application is made, before the end of 6 months beginning with the date on which the calculation was made, for the variation or revocation of the order,

the court may, in exercise of its powers under this Part to vary or revoke the order, direct that the variation or revocation is to take effect from the date on which the calculation took effect or any later date.

    (2) If—

      (a) an order ('the child order') of a kind prescribed for the purposes of section 10(1) of the Child Support Act 1991 is affected by a maintenance calculation,

      (b) on the date on which the child order became so affected there was in force an order ('the civil partner's order')—
- (i) under paragraph 2(1)(a),
- (ii) under Part 2 making provision of a kind set out in paragraph 10(1)(a) (regardless of whether it makes provision of any other kind mentioned in paragraph 10(1)(a)),
- (iii) under paragraph 16(1)(a), or
- (iv) which is an interim order under Part 4 under which the payments are to be made to the applicant (otherwise than for the benefit of a child), and

      (c) an application is made, before the end of 6 months beginning with the date on which the maintenance calculation was made, for the civil partner's order to be varied or revoked,

the court may, in exercise of its powers under this Part to vary or revoke the civil partner's order, direct that the variation or revocation is to take effect from the date on which the child order became so affected or any later date.

    (3) For the purposes of sub-paragraph (2), an order is affected if it ceases to have effect or is modified by or under section 10 of the 1991 Act.

Matters to which court is to have regard in exercising powers under this Part

    34.—(1) In exercising the powers conferred by this Part the court must, so far as it appears to the court just to do so, give effect to any agreement which has been reached between the civil partners in relation to the application.

    (2) If—

      (a) there is no such agreement, or

      (b) if the court decides not to give effect to the agreement,

the court must have regard to all the circumstances of the case, giving first consideration to the welfare while under 18 of any child of the family who has not reached 18.

    (3) Those circumstances include any change in any of the matters—

      (a) to which the court was required to have regard when making the order to which the application relates, or

(b) in the case of an application for the variation or revocation of an order made under Part 2 or on an appeal made by virtue of paragraph 46, to which the court would have been required to have regard if that order had been made under Part 1.

Variation of orders for periodical payments: further provisions

35.—(1) The power of the court under paragraphs 30 to 34 to vary an order for the making of periodical payments includes power, if the court is satisfied that payment has not been made in accordance with the order, to exercise one of its powers under section 1(4) and (4A) of the Maintenance Enforcement Act 1991.

(2) Sub-paragraph (1) is subject to paragraph 37.

...

37.—(1) Before varying the order by exercising one of its powers under section 1(4) and (4A) of the 1991 Act, the court must have regard to any representations made by the parties to the application.

...

38.—(1) Section 1(6) of the 1991 Act (power of court to order that account be opened) applies for the purposes of paragraph 35 as it applies for the purposes of section 1 of the 1991 Act.

(2) None of the powers of the court conferred by paragraphs 35 to 37 and sub-paragraph (1) is exercisable in relation to an order under this Schedule for the making of periodical payments unless, at the time when the order was made, the person required to make the payments was ordinarily resident in England and Wales.

Persons who may apply under this Part

39.—An application under paragraph 30 or 31 may be made—
(a) if it is for the variation or revocation of an order under Part 1, 2, 3 or 4 for periodical payments, by either civil partner, and
(b) if it is for the variation of an order under paragraph 2(1)(c) or Part 2 or 3 for periodical payments to or in respect of a child, also by the child himself, if he has reached 16.

Revival of orders for periodical payments

40.—(1) If an order made by the family court under this Schedule for the making of periodical payments to or in respect of a child (other than an interim order) ceases to have effect—
(a) on the date on which the child reaches 16, or
(b) at any time after that date but before or on the date on which he reaches 18,
the child may apply to the court which made the order for an order for its revival.

(2) If on such an application it appears to the court that—
(a) the child is, will be or (if an order were made under this sub-paragraph) would be receiving instruction at an educational establishment or undergoing training for a trade, profession or vocation, whether or not while in gainful employment, or
(b) there are special circumstances which justify the making of an order under this sub-paragraph,
the court may by order revive the order from such date as the court may specify, not being earlier than the date of the making of the application.

(3) Any order revived under this paragraph may be varied or revoked under paragraphs 30 to 34 in the same way as it could have been varied or revoked had it continued in being.

...

PART 7 ARREARS AND REPAYMENTS

Enforcement etc. of orders for payment of money

43.—Section 32 of the Domestic Proceedings and Magistrates' Courts Act 1978 (c. 22) applies in relation to orders under this Schedule as it applies in relation to orders under Part 1 of that Act.

Orders for repayment after cessation of order because of subsequent
civil partnership etc.

44.—(1) Sub-paragraphs (3) and (4) apply if—

(a) an order made under paragraph 2(1)(a) or Part 2 or 3 has, under paragraph 26(2), ceased to have effect because of the formation of a subsequent civil partnership or marriage by the party ('R') in whose favour it was made, and

(b) the person liable to make payments under the order ('P') made payments in accordance with it in respect of a relevant period in the mistaken belief that the order was still subsisting.

(2) 'Relevant period' means a period after the date of the formation of the subsequent civil partnership or marriage.

(3) No proceedings in respect of a cause of action arising out of the circumstances mentioned in sub-paragraph (1)(a) and (b) is maintainable by P (or P's personal representatives) against R (or R's personal representatives).

(4) But on an application made under this paragraph by P (or P's personal representatives) against R (or R's personal representatives) the family court—

(a) may order the respondent to pay to the applicant a sum equal to the amount of the payments made in respect of the relevant period, or

(b) if it appears to the court that it would be unjust to make that order, may—

(i) order the respondent to pay to the applicant such lesser sum as it thinks fit, or

(ii) dismiss the application.

(5) An order under this paragraph for the payment of any sum may provide for the payment of that sum by instalments of such amount as may be specified in the order.

(6) An application under this paragraph—

(a) may (but need not) be made in proceedings for leave to enforce, or the enforcement of, the payment of arrears under an order made under paragraph 2 (1)(a) or Part 2 or 3,

...

(8) Subject to sub-paragraph (9)—

(a) an officer of the family court is not liable for any act done by him, in pursuance of an order under paragraph 2(1)(a), or Part 2 or 3, requiring payments to be made to the court or an officer of the court, after the date on which that order ceased to have effect because of the formation of a subsequent civil partnership or marriage by the person entitled to payments under it, and

(b) the collecting officer under an attachment of earnings order made to secure payments under an order under paragraph 2(1)(a), or Part 2 or 3, is not liable for any act done by him, after the date on which that order ceased to have effect because of the formation of a subsequent civil partnership or marriage by the person entitled to payments under it, in accordance with any enactment or rule of court specifying how payments made to him in compliance with the attachment of earnings order are to be dealt with.

(9) Sub-paragraph (8) applies if (but only if) the act—

(a) was one which he would have been under a duty to do had the order under paragraph 2(1)(a) or Part 2 or 3 not ceased to have effect, and

(b) was done before notice in writing of the formation of the subsequent civil partnership or marriage was given to him by or on behalf of—

(i) the person entitled to payments under the order,

(ii) the person liable to make payments under it, or

(iii) the personal representatives of either of them.

(10) In this paragraph 'collecting officer', in relation to an attachment of earnings order, means—

(a) the officer of the High Court, or

(b) the officer designated by the Lord Chancellor,

to whom a person makes payments in compliance with the order.

PART 8 SUPPLEMENTARY

Restrictions on making of orders under this Schedule: welfare of children

45.—If—

(a) an application is made by a civil partner for an order under Part 1, 2 or 3, and

(b) there is a child of the family who is under 18,

the court must not dismiss or make a final order on the application until it has decided whether to exercise any of its powers under the Children Act 1989 (c. 41) with respect to the child.

Constitution of courts, powers of High Court and county court in relation to orders and appeals

46.—The following provisions of the Domestic Proceedings and Magistrates' Courts Act 1978 (c. 22) apply in relation to an order under this Schedule relating to a civil partnership as they apply in relation to an order under Part 1 of that Act relating to a marriage—

(a) section 28 (powers of the High Court and the family court in relation to certain orders),

...

Provisions as to jurisdiction and procedure

47.—...

(2) Any jurisdiction conferred on the family court by this Schedule is exercisable even if any party to the proceedings is not domiciled in England and Wales.

...

Meaning of 'child of the family'

48.—In this Schedule 'child of the family', in relation to two people who are civil partners of each other, means—

(a) a child of both of them, and

(b) any other child, other than a child placed with them as foster parents by a local authority or voluntary organisation, who has been treated by both the civil partners as a child of their family.

...

Section 247

SCHEDULE 21

REFERENCES TO STEPCHILDREN ETC. IN EXISTING ACTS

...

24.—Section 113(2) of the Housing Act 1985 (c. 68) (members of a person's family).

...

33.—The definition of 'relative' in section 105(1) of the Children Act 1989 (c. 41) (interpretation).

...

43.—The definition of 'relative' in section 63(1) of the Family Law Act 1996 (c. 27) (interpretation of Part 4 of the 1996 Act).

...

45.—Section 140(2) of the Housing Act 1996 (c. 52) (members of a person's family: Chapter 1).

...

47.—The definition of 'relative' in section 178(3) of that Act (meaning of associated person).

...

Equality Act 2006

(2006 c. 3)

PART 1 THE COMMISSION FOR EQUALITY AND HUMAN RIGHTS

The Commission

1   Establishment

There shall be a body corporate known as the Commission for Equality and Human Rights.

...

3   General duty

The Commission shall exercise its functions under this Part with a view to encouraging and supporting the development of a society in which—

    (a) people's ability to achieve their potential is not limited by prejudice or discrimination,

    (b) there is respect for and protection of each individual's human rights,

    (c) there is respect for the dignity and worth of each individual,

    (d) each individual has an equal opportunity to participate in society, and

    (e) there is mutual respect between groups based on understanding and valuing of diversity and on shared respect for equality and human rights.

...

Duties

8   Equality and diversity

    (1) The Commission shall, by exercising the powers conferred by this Part—

        (a) promote understanding of the importance of equality and diversity,

        (b) encourage good practice in relation to equality and diversity,

        (c) promote equality of opportunity,

        (d) promote awareness and understanding of rights under the Equality Act 2010,

        (e) enforce that Act,

        (f) work towards the elimination of unlawful discrimination, and

        (g) work towards the elimination of unlawful harassment.

    (2) In subsection (1)—

'diversity' means the fact that individuals are different,

'equality' means equality between individuals, and

'unlawful' is to be construed in accordance with section 34.

    (3) In promoting equality of opportunity between disabled persons and others, the Commission may, in particular, promote the favourable treatment of disabled persons.

    (4) In this Part 'disabled person' means a person who—

        (a) is a disabled person within the meaning of the Equality Act 2010, or

        (b) has been a disabled person within that meaning (whether or not at a time when that Act had effect).

9   Human rights

    (1) The Commission shall, by exercising the powers conferred by this Part—

        (a) promote understanding of the importance of human rights,

        (b) encourage good practice in relation to human rights,

        (c) promote awareness, understanding and protection of human rights, and

        (d) encourage public authorities to comply with section 6 of the Human Rights Act 1998 (c. 42) (compliance with Convention rights).

(2) In this Part 'human rights' means—

    (a) the Convention rights within the meaning given by section 1 of the Human Rights Act 1998, and

    (b) other human rights.

(3) In determining what action to take in pursuance of this section the Commission shall have particular regard to the importance of exercising the powers conferred by this Part in relation to the Convention rights.

(4) In fulfilling a duty under section 8 the Commission shall take account of any relevant human rights.

(5) A reference in this Part (including this section) to human rights does not exclude any matter by reason only of its being a matter to which section 8 relates.

10 Groups

...

(2) In this Part 'group' means a group or class of persons who share a common attribute in respect of any of the following matters—

    (a) age,

    (b) disability,

    (c) gender,

    (d) gender reassignment (within the meaning of section 7 of the Equality Act 2010),

    (e) race,

    (f) religion or belief, and

    (g) sexual orientation.

(3) For the purposes of this Part a reference to a group (as defined in subsection (2)) includes a reference to a smaller group or smaller class, within a group, of persons who share a common attribute (in addition to the attribute by reference to which the group is defined) in respect of any of the matters specified in subsection (2)(a) to (g).

...

35 General

In this Part—

...

  'sexual orientation' has the same meaning as in section 12 of the Equality Act 2010.

...

Children and Adoption Act 2006

(2006 c. 20)

PART 1 ORDERS WITH RESPECT TO CHILDREN IN FAMILY PROCEEDINGS

...

Transitional provision

8 Transitional provision

(1) This section applies to any contact order under section 8 of the Children Act 1989 made before, and in force on, the relevant date.

(2) For so long as a contact order to which this section applies continues in force on and after the relevant date without being varied, the circumstances in which a notice under section 11I of the Children Act 1989 is to be attached to the contact order include—

(a) where an application for such a notice to be attached to the contact order is made by a person who, as regards the order, falls within any of paragraphs (a) to (d) of section 11J(5) of the Children Act 1989;

(b) where, in any family proceedings, a question arises with respect to the contact order.

(3) Where the person proposing to apply under subsection (2)(a) is the child with respect to whom the contact order was made, subsections (6) and (7) of section 11J have effect in relation to the application under subsection (2)(a) as they have effect in relation to an application under section 11J for an enforcement order.

(4) If a failure to comply with a contact order to which this section applies occurs while the contact order continues in force as described in subsection (2), each of sections 11K(1) and 11P(1) of the Children Act 1989 is to have effect, in relation to the failure, as if for paragraphs (a) and (b) there were substituted 'a notice under section 11I relating to the contact order'.

(5) In this section 'relevant date' means the day on which sections 3 to 5 come into force.

...

Child Maintenance and Other Payments Act 2008

(2008 c. 6)

PART 1 THE CHILD MAINTENANCE AND ENFORCEMENT COMMISSION

6 Fees

(1) The Secretary of State may by regulations make provision about the charging of fees by the Secretary of State in connection with the exercise of its functions.

(2) Regulations under subsection (1) may, in particular, make provision—

(a) about when a fee may be charged;

(b) about the amount which may be charged

(c) for the supply of information needed for the purpose of determining the amount which may be charged;

(d) about who is liable to pay any fee charged (including provision for the apportionment of fees and the matters to be taken into account in determining an apportionment);

(e) about when any fee charged is payable;

(f) about the recovery of fees charged;

(g) about reduction or repayment of fees.

(h) about waiver of fees (including the matters to be taken into account in determining a waiver).

(3) The power conferred by subsection (1) includes power to make provision for the charging of fees which are not related to costs.

(3A) The Secretary of State must review the effect of the first regulations made under subsection (1).

(3B) The review must take place before the end of the period of 30 months beginning with the day on which those regulations come into force.

(3C) After the review, the Secretary of State must make and publish a report containing—

(a) the conclusions of the review, and

(b) a statement as to what the Secretary of State proposes to do in view of those conclusions.

(3D) The report must be laid before Parliament by the Secretary of State.

(4) The Secretary of State may by regulations provide that the provisions of the Child Support Act 1991 (c. 48) with respect to—

(a) the collection of child support maintenance,

(b) the enforcement of any obligation to pay child support maintenance,

shall apply equally (with any necessary modifications) to fees payable by virtue of regulations under subsection (1).

(5) The Secretary of State may by regulations make provision for a person affected by a decision of the Secretary of State under regulations under subsection (1) to have a right of appeal against the decision to the First-tier Tribunal.

(6) Subsections (3) to (5), (7) and (8) of section 20 of the Child Support Act 1991 (appeals to First-tier Tribunal) apply to appeals under regulations under subsection (5) as they apply to appeals under that section.

(7) The Secretary of State shall pay into the Consolidated Fund any amount which the Secretary of State receives in respect of fees charged by it under regulations under this section.

…

8 Contracting out

(1) Any function of the Secretary of State relating to child support may be exercised by, or by employees of, such person (if any) as the Secretary of State may authorise for the purpose.

(2) An authorisation given by virtue of subsection (1) may authorise the exercise of the function concerned—

(a) either wholly or to such extent as may be specified in the authorisation,

(b) either generally or in such cases or areas as may be so specified, and

(c) either unconditionally or subject to the fulfilment of such conditions as may be so specified.

(3) An authorisation given by virtue of subsection (1)—

(a) may specify its duration,

(b) may be revoked at any time by the Secretary of State, and

(c) shall not prevent the Secretary of State or any other person from exercising the function to which the authorisation relates.

(4) Where a person is authorised to exercise any function by virtue of subsection (1), anything done or omitted to be done by or in relation to that person (or an employee of that person) in, or in connection with, the exercise or purported exercise of the function shall be treated for all purposes as done or omitted to be done by or in relation to the Secretary of State.

(5) Subsection (4) shall not apply—

(a) for the purposes of so much of any contract made between the authorised person and the Secretary of State as relates to the exercise of the function, or

(b) for the purposes of any criminal proceedings brought in respect of anything done or omitted to be done by the authorised person (or an employee of that person).

(6) Where—

(a) a person is authorised to exercise any function by virtue of subsection (1), and

(b) the authorisation is revoked at a time when a relevant contract is subsisting,

the authorised person shall be entitled to treat the relevant contract as repudiated by the Secretary of State (and not as frustrated by reason of the revocation).

(7) In subsection (6), the reference to a relevant contract is to so much of any contract made between the authorised person and the Secretary of State as relates to the exercise of the function.

…

PART 3 CHILD SUPPORT ETC.

...

Miscellaneous

43 Extinction of liability in respect of interest and fees

Any outstanding liability in respect of the following is extinguished—

    (a) interest under the Child Support (Arrears, Interest and Adjustment of Maintenance Assessments) Regulations 1992 (S.I. 1992/1816);

    (b) fees under the Child Support Fees Regulations 1992 (S.I. 1992/3094).

...

SCHEDULE 5 FINANCIAL RELIEF: PROVISION CORRESPONDING TO PROVISION MADE BY PART 2 OF THE MATRIMONIAL CAUSES ACT 1973

Power to require a decision about whether to stay in the statutory scheme

1.—(1) The Secretary of State may require the interested parties in relation to an existing case to choose whether or not to stay in the statutory scheme, so far as future accrual of liability is concerned.

    (2) The reference in sub-paragraph (1) to an existing case is to any of the following—

        (a) a maintenance assessment,

        (b) an application for a maintenance assessment,

        (c) a maintenance calculation made under existing rules, and

        (d) an application for a maintenance calculation which will fall to be made under existing rules.

    (3) For the purposes of this paragraph, a maintenance calculation is made (or will fall to be made) under existing rules if the amount of the periodical payments required to be paid in accordance with it is (or will be) determined otherwise than in accordance with Part 1 of Schedule 1 to the Child Support Act 1991 (c. 48) as amended by this Act.

...

Human Fertilisation and Embryology Act 2008

(2008 c. 22)

PART 2 PARENTHOOD IN CASES INVOLVING ASSISTED REPRODUCTION

Meaning of 'mother'

33 Meaning of 'mother'

    (1) The woman who is carrying or has carried a child as a result of the placing in her of an embryo or of sperm and eggs, and no other woman, is to be treated as the mother of the child.

    (2) Subsection (1) does not apply to any child to the extent that the child is treated by virtue of adoption as not being the woman's child.

    (3) Subsection (1) applies whether the woman was in the United Kingdom or elsewhere at the time of the placing in her of the embryo or the sperm and eggs.

Application of sections 35 to 47

34   Application of sections 35 to 47

(1) Sections 35 to 47 apply, in the case of a child who is being or has been carried by a woman (referred to in those sections as 'W') as a result of the placing in her of an embryo or of sperm and eggs or her artificial insemination, to determine who is to be treated as the other parent of the child.

(2) Subsection (1) has effect subject to the provisions of sections 39, 40 and 46 limiting the purposes for which a person is treated as the child's other parent by virtue of those sections.

Meaning of 'father'

35   Woman married to a man at time of treatment

(1) If—

(a) at the time of the placing in her of the embryo or of the sperm and eggs or of her artificial insemination, W was a party to a marriage with a man, and

(b) the creation of the embryo carried by her was not brought about with the sperm of the other party to the marriage,

then, subject to section 38(2) to (4), the other party to the marriage is to be treated as the father of the child unless it is shown that he did not consent to the placing in her of the embryo or the sperm and eggs or to her artificial insemination (as the case may be).

(2) This section applies whether W was in the United Kingdom or elsewhere at the time mentioned in subsection (1)(a).

36   Treatment provided to woman where agreed fatherhood conditions apply

If no man is treated by virtue of section 35 as the father of the child and no woman is treated by virtue of section 42 as a parent of the child but—

(a) the embryo or the sperm and eggs were placed in W, or W was artificially inseminated, in the course of treatment services provided in the United Kingdom by a person to whom a licence applies,

(b) at the time when the embryo or the sperm and eggs were placed in W, or W was artificially inseminated, the agreed fatherhood conditions (as set out in section 37) were satisfied in relation to a man, in relation to treatment provided to W under the licence,

(c) the man remained alive at that time, and

(d) the creation of the embryo carried by W was not brought about with the man's sperm, then, subject to section 38(2) to (4), the man is to be treated as the father of the child.

37   The agreed fatherhood conditions

(1) The agreed fatherhood conditions referred to in section 36(b) are met in relation to a man ('M') in relation to treatment provided to W under a licence if, but only if,—

(a) M has given the person responsible a notice stating that he consents to being treated as the father of any child resulting from treatment provided to W under the licence,

(b) W has given the person responsible a notice stating that she consents to M being so treated,

(c) neither M nor W has, since giving notice under paragraph (a) or (b), given the person responsible notice of the withdrawal of M's or W's consent to M being so treated,

(d) W has not, since the giving of the notice under paragraph (b), given the person responsible—

(i) a further notice under that paragraph stating that she consents to another man being treated as the father of any resulting child, or

(ii) a notice under section 44(1)(b) stating that she consents to a woman being treated as a parent of any resulting child, and

(e) W and M are not within prohibited degrees of relationship in relation to each other.

(2) A notice under subsection (1)(a), (b) or (c) must be in writing and must be signed by the person giving it.

(3) A notice under subsection (1)(a), (b) or (c) by a person ('S') who is unable to sign because of illness, injury or physical disability is to be taken to comply with the requirement of subsection (2) as to signature if it is signed at the direction of S, in the presence of S and in the presence of at least one witness who attests the signature.

38 Further provision relating to sections 35 and 36

(1) Where a person is to be treated as the father of the child by virtue of section 35 or 36, no other person is to be treated as the father of the child.

(2) In England and Wales and Northern Ireland, sections 35 and 36 do not affect any presumption, applying by virtue of the rules of common law, that a child is the legitimate child of the parties to a marriage.

(3) ...

(4) Sections 35 and 36 do not apply to any child to the extent that the child is treated by virtue of adoption as not being the man's child.

39 Use of sperm, or transfer of embryo, after death of man providing sperm

(1) If—

  (a) the child has been carried by W as a result of the placing in her of an embryo or of sperm and eggs or her artificial insemination,

  (b) the creation of the embryo carried by W was brought about by using the sperm of a man after his death, or the creation of the embryo was brought about using the sperm of a man before his death but the embryo was placed in W after his death,

  (c) the man consented in writing (and did not withdraw the consent)—

   (i)   to the use of his sperm after his death which brought about the creation of the embryo carried by W or (as the case may be) to the placing in W after his death of the embryo which was brought about using his sperm before his death, and

   (ii) to being treated for the purpose mentioned in subsection (3) as the father of any resulting child,

  (d) W has elected in writing not later than the end of the period of 42 days from the day on which the child was born for the man to be treated for the purpose mentioned in subsection (3) as the father of the child, and

  (e) no-one else is to be treated—

   (i)   as the father of the child by virtue of section 35 or 36 or by virtue of section 38(2) or (3), or

   (ii) as a parent of the child by virtue of section 42 or 43 or by virtue of adoption,

     then the man is to be treated for the purpose mentioned in subsection (3) as the father of the child.

(2) Subsection (1) applies whether W was in the United Kingdom or elsewhere at the time of the placing in her of the embryo or of the sperm and eggs or of her artificial insemination.

(3) The purpose referred to in subsection (1) is the purpose of enabling the man's particulars to be entered as the particulars of the child's father in a relevant register of births.

(4) ...

40 Embryo transferred after death of husband etc. who did not provide sperm

(1) If—

  (a) the child has been carried by W as a result of the placing in her of an embryo,

  (b) the embryo was created at a time when W was a party to a marriage with a man,

  (c) the creation of the embryo was not brought about with the sperm of the other party to the marriage,

  (d) the other party to the marriage died before the placing of the embryo in W,

  (e) the other party to the marriage consented in writing (and did not withdraw the consent)—

- (i) to the placing of the embryo in W after his death, and
- (ii) to being treated for the purpose mentioned in subsection (4) as the father of any resulting child,
- (f) W has elected in writing not later than the end of the period of 42 days from the day on which the child was born for the man to be treated for the purpose mentioned in subsection (4) as the father of the child, and
- (g) no-one else is to be treated—
  - (i) as the father of the child by virtue of section 35 or 36 or by virtue of section 38(2) or (3), or
  - (ii) as a parent of the child by virtue of section 42 or 43 or by virtue of adoption,

then the man is to be treated for the purpose mentioned in subsection (4) as the father of the child.

(2) If—

- (a) the child has been carried by W as a result of the placing in her of an embryo,
- (b) the embryo was not created at a time when W was a party to a marriage or a civil partnership but was created in the course of treatment services provided to W in the United Kingdom by a person to whom a licence applies,
- (c) a man consented in writing (and did not withdraw the consent)—
  - (i) to the placing of the embryo in W after his death, and
  - (ii) to being treated for the purpose mentioned in subsection (4) as the father of any resulting child,
- (d) the creation of the embryo was not brought about with the sperm of that man,
- (e) the man died before the placing of the embryo in W,
- (f) immediately before the man's death, the agreed fatherhood conditions set out in section 37 were met in relation to the man in relation to treatment proposed to be provided to W in the United Kingdom by a person to whom a licence applies,
- (g) W has elected in writing not later than the end of the period of 42 days from the day on which the child was born for the man to be treated for the purpose mentioned in subsection (4) as the father of the child, and
- (h) no-one else is to be treated—
  - (i) as the father of the child by virtue of section 35 or 36 or by virtue of section 38(2) or (3), or
  - (ii) as a parent of the child by virtue of section 42 or 43 or by virtue of adoption,

then the man is to be treated for the purpose mentioned in subsection (4) as the father of the child.

(3) Subsections (1) and (2) apply whether W was in the United Kingdom or elsewhere at the time of the placing in her of the embryo.

(4) The purpose referred to in subsections (1) and (2) is the purpose of enabling the man's particulars to be entered as the particulars of the child's father in a relevant register of births.

(5) ...

41 Persons not to be treated as father

(1) Where the sperm of a man who had given such consent as is required by paragraph 5 of Schedule 3 to the 1990 Act (consent to use of gametes for purposes of treatment services or non-medical fertility services) was used for a purpose for which such consent was required, he is not to be treated as the father of the child.

(2) Where the sperm of a man, or an embryo the creation of which was brought about with his sperm, was used after his death, he is not, subject to section 39, to be treated as the father of the child.

(3) Subsection (2) applies whether W was in the United Kingdom or elsewhere at the time of the placing in her of the embryo or of the sperm and eggs or of her artificial insemination.

Cases in which woman to be other parent

42   Woman in civil partnership or marriage to a woman at time of treatment

(1) If at the time of the placing in her of the embryo or the sperm and eggs or of her artificial insemination, W was a party to a civil partnership or a marriage with another woman, then subject to section 45(2) to (4), the other party to the civil partnership or marriage is to be treated as a parent of the child unless it is shown that she did not consent to the placing in W of the embryo or the sperm and eggs or to her artificial insemination (as the case may be).

(2) This section applies whether W was in the United Kingdom or elsewhere at the time mentioned in subsection (1).

43   Treatment provided to woman who agrees that second woman to be parent

If no man is treated by virtue of section 35 as the father of the child and no woman is treated by virtue of section 42 as a parent of the child but—

    (a) the embryo or the sperm and eggs were placed in W, or W was artificially inseminated, in the course of treatment services provided in the United Kingdom by a person to whom a licence applies,

    (b) at the time when the embryo or the sperm and eggs were placed in W, or W was artificially inseminated, the agreed female parenthood conditions (as set out in section 44) were met in relation to another woman, in relation to treatment provided to W under that licence, and

    (c) the other woman remained alive at that time,

then, subject to section 45(2) to (4), the other woman is to be treated as a parent of the child.

44   The agreed female parenthood conditions

(1) The agreed female parenthood conditions referred to in section 43(b) are met in relation to another woman ('P') in relation to treatment provided to W under a licence if, but only if,—

    (a) P has given the person responsible a notice stating that P consents to P being treated as a parent of any child resulting from treatment provided to W under the licence,

    (b) W has given the person responsible a notice stating that W agrees to P being so treated,

    (c) neither W nor P has, since giving notice under paragraph (a) or (b), given the person responsible notice of the withdrawal of P's or W's consent to P being so treated,

    (d) W has not, since the giving of the notice under paragraph (b), given the person responsible—

        (i) a further notice under that paragraph stating that W consents to a woman other than P being treated as a parent of any resulting child, or

        (ii) a notice under section 37(1)(b) stating that W consents to a man being treated as the father of any resulting child, and

    (e) W and P are not within prohibited degrees of relationship in relation to each other.

(2) A notice under subsection (1)(a), (b) or (c) must be in writing and must be signed by the person giving it.

(3) A notice under subsection (1)(a), (b) or (c) by a person ('S') who is unable to sign because of illness, injury or physical disability is to be taken to comply with the requirement of subsection (2) as to signature if it is signed at the direction of S, in the presence of S and in the presence of at least one witness who attests the signature.

45   Further provision relating to sections 42 and 43

(1) Where a woman is treated by virtue of section 42 or 43 as a parent of the child, no man is to be treated as the father of the child.

(2) In England and Wales and Northern Ireland, sections 42 and 43 do not affect any presumption, applying by virtue of the rules of common law, that a child is the legitimate child of the parties to a marriage.

(3) ...

(4) Sections 42 and 43 do not apply to any child to the extent that the child is treated by virtue of adoption as not being the woman's child.

46 Embryo transferred after death of civil partner or wife or intended female parent

(1) If—

(a) the child has been carried by W as the result of the placing in her of an embryo,

(b) the embryo was created at a time when W was a party to a civil partnership or marriage with another woman,

(c) the other party to the civil partnership or marriage died before the placing of the embryo in W,

(d) the other party to the civil partnership or marriage consented in writing (and did not withdraw the consent)—

(i) to the placing of the embryo in W after the death of the other party, and

(ii) to being treated for the purpose mentioned in subsection (4) as the parent of any resulting child,

(e) W has elected in writing not later than the end of the period of 42 days from the day on which the child was born for the other party to the civil partnership or marriage to be treated for the purpose mentioned in subsection (4) as the parent of the child, and

(f) no one else is to be treated—

(i) as the father of the child by virtue of section 35 or 36 or by virtue of section 45(2) or (3), or

(ii) as a parent of the child by virtue of section 42 or 43 or by virtue of adoption,

then the other party to the civil partnership or marriage is to be treated for the purpose mentioned in subsection (4) as a parent of the child.

(2) If—

(a) the child has been carried by W as the result of the placing in her of an embryo,

(b) the embryo was not created at a time when W was a party to a marriage or a civil partnership, but was created in the course of treatment services provided to W in the United Kingdom by a person to whom a licence applies,

(c) another woman consented in writing (and did not withdraw the consent)—

(i) to the placing of the embryo in W after the death of the other woman, and

(ii) to being treated for the purpose mentioned in subsection (4) as the parent of any resulting child,

(d) the other woman died before the placing of the embryo in W,

(e) immediately before the other woman's death, the agreed female parenthood conditions set out in section 44 were met in relation to the other woman in relation to treatment proposed to be provided to W in the United Kingdom by a person to whom a licence applies,

(f) W has elected in writing not later than the end of the period of 42 days from the day on which the child was born for the other woman to be treated for the purpose mentioned in subsection (4) as the parent of the child, and

(g) no one else is to be treated—

(i) as the father of the child by virtue of section 35 or 36 or by virtue of section 45(2) or (3), or

(ii) as a parent of the child by virtue of section 42 or 43 or by virtue of adoption,

then the other woman is to be treated for the purpose mentioned in subsection (4) as a parent of the child.

(3) Subsections (1) and (2) apply whether W was in the United Kingdom or elsewhere at the time of the placing in her of the embryo.

(4) The purpose referred to in subsections (1) and (2) is the purpose of enabling the deceased woman's particulars to be entered as the particulars of the child's other parent in a relevant register of births.

(5) …

47   Woman not to be other parent merely because of egg donation

A woman is not to be treated as the parent of a child whom she is not carrying and has not carried, except where she is so treated—

    (a) by virtue of section 42 or 43, or

    (b) by virtue of section 46 (for the purpose mentioned in subsection (4) of that section), or

    (c) by virtue of adoption.

Effect of sections 33 to 47

48   Effect of sections 33 to 47

(1) Where by virtue of section 33, 35, 36, 42 or 43 a person is to be treated as the mother, father or parent of a child, that person is to be treated in law as the mother, father or parent (as the case may be) of the child for all purposes.

(2) Where by virtue of section 33, 38, 41, 45 or 47 a person is not to be treated as a parent of the child, that person is to be treated in law as not being a parent of the child for any purpose.

(3) Where section 39(1) or 40(1) or (2) applies, the deceased man—

    (a) is to be treated in law as the father of the child for the purpose mentioned in section 39(3) or 40(4), but

    (b) is to be treated in law as not being the father of the child for any other purpose.

(4) Where section 46(1) or (2) applies, the deceased woman—

    (a) is to be treated in law as a parent of the child for the purpose mentioned in section 46(4), but

    (b) is to be treated in law as not being a parent of the child for any other purpose.

(5) Where any of subsections (1) to (4) has effect, references to any relationship between two people in any enactment, deed or other instrument or document (whenever passed or made) are to be read accordingly.

(6) In relation to England and Wales and Northern Ireland, a child who—

    (a) has a parent by virtue of section 42, or

    (b) has a parent by virtue of section 43 who is at any time during the period beginning with the time mentioned in section 43(b) and ending with the time of the child's birth a party to a civil partnership with the child's mother,

is the legitimate child of the child's parents.

(7) In relation to England and Wales and Northern Ireland, nothing in the provisions of section 33(1) or sections 35 to 47, read with this section—

    (a) affects the succession to any dignity or title of honour or renders any person capable of succeeding to or transmitting a right to succeed to any such dignity or title, or

    (b) affects the devolution of any property limited (expressly or not) to devolve (as nearly as the law permits) along with any dignity or title of honour.

(8) …

References to parties to marriage or civil partnership

49   Meaning of references to parties to a marriage

(1) The references in sections 35 to 47 to the parties to a marriage at any time there referred to—

    (a) are to the parties to a marriage subsisting at that time, unless a judicial separation was then in force, but

    (b) include the parties to a void marriage if either or both of them reasonably believed at that time that the marriage was valid; and for the purposes of those sections it is to be presumed, unless the contrary is shown, that one of them reasonably believed at that time that the marriage was valid.

(2) In subsection (1)(a) 'judicial separation' includes a legal separation obtained in a country outside the British Islands and recognised in the United Kingdom.

50   Meaning of references to parties to a civil partnership

(1) The references in sections 35 to 47 to the parties to a civil partnership at any time there referred to—

(a) are to the parties to a civil partnership subsisting at that time, unless a separation order was then in force, but

(b) include the parties to a void civil partnership if either or both of them reasonably believed at that time that the civil partnership was valid; and for the purposes of those sections it is to be presumed, unless the contrary is shown, that one of them reasonably believed at that time that the civil partnership was valid.

(2) The reference in section 48(6)(b) to a civil partnership includes a reference to a void civil partnership if either or both of the parties reasonably believed at the time when they registered as civil partners of each other that the civil partnership was valid; and for this purpose it is to be presumed, unless the contrary is shown, that one of them reasonably believed at that time that the civil partnership was valid.

(3) In subsection (1)(a), 'separation order' means—

(a) a separation order under section 37(1)(d) or 161(1)(d) of the Civil Partnership Act 2004 (c. 33),

(b) a decree of separation under section 120(2) of that Act, or

(c) a legal separation obtained in a country outside the United Kingdom and recognised in the United Kingdom.

Further provision about registration by virtue of section 39, 40 or 46

51   Meaning of 'relevant register of births'

For the purposes of this Part a 'relevant register of births', in relation to a birth, is whichever of the following is relevant—

(a) a register of live-births or still-births kept under the Births and Deaths Registration Act 1953 (c. 20),

(b) ...

(c) ...

52   Late election by mother with consent of Registrar General

(1) The requirement under section 39(1), 40(1) or (2) or 46(1) or (2) as to the making of an election (which requires an election to be made either on or before the day on which the child was born or within the period of 42 or, as the case may be, 21 days from that day) is nevertheless to be treated as satisfied if the required election is made after the end of that period but with the consent of the Registrar General under subsection (2).

(2) The Registrar General may at any time consent to the making of an election after the end of the period mentioned in subsection (1) if, on an application made to him in accordance with such requirements as he may specify, he is satisfied that there is a compelling reason for giving his consent to the making of such an election.

(3) ...

Interpretation of references to father etc. where woman is other parent

53   Interpretation of references to father etc.

(1) Subsections (2) and (3) have effect, subject to subsections (4) and (6), for the interpretation of any enactment, deed or any other instrument or document (whenever passed or made).

(2) Any reference (however expressed) to the father of a child who has a parent by virtue of section 42 or 43 is to be read as a reference to the woman who is a parent of the child by virtue of that section.

(3) Any reference (however expressed) to evidence of paternity is, in relation to a woman who is a parent by virtue of section 42 or 43, to be read as a reference to evidence of parentage.

(4) This section does not affect the interpretation of the enactments specified in subsection (5) (which make express provision for the case where a child has a parent by virtue of section 42 or 43).

(5) Those enactments are—

(a) ...

(b) the Schedule to the Population (Statistics) Act 1938 (c. 12),

(c) the Births and Deaths Registration Act 1953 (c. 20),

(d) the Registration of Births, Deaths and Marriages (Special Provisions) Act 1957 (c. 58),

(e) ...

(f) the Congenital Disabilities (Civil Liability) Act 1976 (c. 28),

(g) the Legitimacy Act 1976 (c. 31),

(h) the Births and Deaths Registration (Northern Ireland) Order 1976 (S.I. 1976/1041 (N.I. 14)),

(i) the British Nationality Act 1981 (c. 61),

(j) the Family Law Reform Act 1987 (c. 42),

(k) Parts 1 and 2 of the Children Act 1989 (c. 41),

...

(6) This section does not affect the interpretation of references that fall to be read in accordance with section 1(2)(a) or (b) of the Family Law Reform Act 1987 or Article 155(2)(a) or (b) of the Children (Northern Ireland) Order 1995 (references to a person whose father and mother were, or were not, married to each other at the time of the person's birth).

Parental orders

54   Parental orders

(1) On an application made by two people ('the applicants'), the court may make an order providing for a child to be treated in law as the child of the applicants if—

(a) the child has been carried by a woman who is not one of the applicants, as a result of the placing in her of an embryo or sperm and eggs or her artificial insemination,

(b) the gametes of at least one of the applicants were used to bring about the creation of the embryo, and

(c) the conditions in subsections (2) to (8) are satisfied.

(2) The applicants must be—

(a) husband and wife,

(b) civil partners of each other, or

(c) two persons who are living as partners in an enduring family relationship and are not within prohibited degrees of relationship in relation to each other.

(3) Except in a case falling within subsection (11), the applicants must apply for the order during the period of 6 months beginning with the day on which the child is born.

(4) At the time of the application and the making of the order—

(a) the child's home must be with the applicants, and

(b) either or both of the applicants must be domiciled in the United Kingdom or in the Channel Islands or the Isle of Man.

(5) At the time of the making of the order both the applicants must have attained the age of 18.

(6) The court must be satisfied that both—

(a) the woman who carried the child, and

(b) any other person who is a parent of the child but is not one of the applicants (including any man who is the father by virtue of section 35 or 36 or any woman who is a parent by virtue of section 42 or 43),

have freely, and with full understanding of what is involved, agreed unconditionally to the making of the order.

(7) Subsection (6) does not require the agreement of a person who cannot be found or is incapable of giving agreement; and the agreement of the woman who carried the child is ineffective for the purpose of that subsection if given by her less than six weeks after the child's birth.

(8) The court must be satisfied that no money or other benefit (other than for expenses reasonably incurred) has been given or received by either of the applicants for or in consideration of—

(a) the making of the order,

(b) any agreement required by subsection (6),

(c) the handing over of the child to the applicants, or

(d) the making of arrangements with a view to the making of the order,

unless authorised by the court.

(9) For the purposes of an application under this section—

(a) in relation to England and Wales—

(i) 'the court' means the High Court or the family court, and

(ii) proceedings on the application are to be 'family proceedings' for the purposes of the Children Act 1989,

...

(10) Subsection (1)(a) applies whether the woman was in the United Kingdom or elsewhere at the time of the placing in her of the embryo or the sperm and eggs or her artificial insemination.

(11) An application which—

(a) relates to a child born before the coming into force of this section, and

(b) is made by two persons who, throughout the period applicable under subsection (2) of section 30 of the 1990 Act, were not eligible to apply for an order under that section in relation to the child as husband and wife,

may be made within the period of six months beginning with the day on which this section comes into force.

55   Parental orders: supplementary provision

(1) The Secretary of State may by regulations provide—

(a) for any provision of the enactments about adoption to have effect, with such modifications (if any) as may be specified in the regulations, in relation to orders under section 54, and applications for such orders, as it has effect in relation to adoption, and applications for adoption orders, and

(b) for references in any enactment to adoption, an adopted child or an adoptive relationship to be read (respectively) as references to the effect of an order under section 54, a child to whom such an order applies and a relationship arising by virtue of the enactments about adoption, as applied by the regulations, and for similar expressions in connection with adoption to be read accordingly.

(2) The regulations may include such incidental or supplemental provision as appears to the Secretary of State to be necessary or desirable in consequence of any provision made by virtue of subsection (1)(a) or (b).

(3) In this section 'the enactments about adoption' means—

(a) ...

(b) the Adoption and Children Act 2002 (c. 38),

...

...

General

58   Interpretation of Part 2

...

(2) For the purposes of this Part, two persons are within prohibited degrees of relationship if one is the other's parent, grandparent, sister, brother, aunt or uncle; and in this subsection references to relationships—

(a) are to relationships of the full blood or half blood or, in the case of an adopted person, such of those relationships as would subsist but for adoption, and

(b) include the relationship of a child with his adoptive, or former adoptive, parents, but do not include any other adoptive relationships.

(3) Other expressions used in this Part and in the 1990 Act have the same meaning in this Part as in that Act.

...

PART 3 MISCELLANEOUS AND GENERAL

General

...

63 Meaning of 'the 1990 Act'

In this Act, 'the 1990 Act' means the Human Fertilisation and Embryology Act 1990 (c. 37).

Children and Young Persons Act 2008

(2008 c. 23)

PART 2 FUNCTIONS IN RELATION TO CHILDREN AND YOUNG PERSONS

Well-being

7 Well-being of children and young persons

(1) It is the general duty of the Secretary of State to promote the well-being of children in England.

(2) The general duty imposed by subsection (1) has effect subject to any specific duties imposed on the Secretary of State.

(3) The activities which may be undertaken or supported in the discharge of the general duty imposed by subsection (1) include activities in connection with parenting.

(4) The Secretary of State may take such action as the Secretary of State considers appropriate to promote the well-being of—

(a) persons who are receiving services under sections 23C to 24D of the 1989 Act; and

(b) persons under the age of 25 of a prescribed description.

(5) The Secretary of State, in discharging functions under this section, must have regard to the aspects of well-being mentioned in section 10(2)(a) to (e) of the Children Act 2004 (c. 31).

(6) In this section—

'children' means persons under the age of 18; and

'prescribed' means prescribed in regulations made by the Secretary of State.

...

Education and training

20 Designated member of staff at school for pupils looked after by a local authority

(1) The governing body of a maintained school must designate a member of the staff at the school ('the designated person') as having responsibility for promoting the educational achievement of registered pupils at the school who—

(a) are being looked after by a local authority; or

(b) fall within subsection (6).

(2) The governing body must ensure that the designated person undertakes appropriate training.

(3) The appropriate national authority may by regulations make provision requiring the governing body of a maintained school to ensure that the designated person has qualifications or experience (or both) prescribed by the regulations.

(4) In excrcising its functions under this section a governing body of a maintained school must have regard to any guidance issued by the appropriate national authority.

(5) For the purposes of subsection (1)(a) a person is 'looked after by a local authority' if the person is—

(a) looked after by a local authority for the purposes of the 1989 Act . . .

. . .

(6) A person falls within this subsection if the person—

(a) is a relevant child within the meaning of section 23A of the 1989 Act . . .;

(b) is a former relevant child within the meaning of section 23C of the 1989 Act . . .; or

(c) . . .

(7) In this section—

'appropriate national authority' means—

(a) in relation to a governing body of a maintained school in England, the Secretary of State;

(b) in relation to a governing body of a maintained school in Wales, the Welsh Ministers;

'maintained school' has the same meaning as in Chapter 1 of Part 3 of the Education Act 2002 (c. 32) (see section 39(1) of that Act);

'registered pupil' has the same meaning as in the Education Act 1996 (c. 56) (see section 434(5) of that Act).

. . .

Education and Skills Act 2008

(2008 c. 25)

PART 1   DUTY TO PARTICIPATE IN EDUCATION OR TRAINING: ENGLAND

Chapter 1   Young persons

Duty to participate in education or training

1   Persons to whom Part 1 applies

This Part applies to any person who is resident in England and who—

(a) has ceased to be of compulsory school age,

(b) has not reached the age of 18, and

(c) has not attained a level 3 qualification (see section 3).

2   Duty to participate in education or training

(1) A person to whom this Part applies must—

(a) be participating in appropriate full-time education or training (see section 4),

(b) be participating in training in accordance with a contract of apprenticeship or an apprenticeship agreement, or

(c) both—

(i)   be in full-time occupation (see section 5), and

(ii) participate in sufficient relevant training or education in each relevant period (see sections 6 to 8).

(2) For the purposes of this Part, a person who is in full-time occupation is to be taken to be participating in sufficient relevant training or education at any particular time if—

(a) arrangements have been made (whether by means of enrolment on a course or courses, or otherwise) for the person to receive sufficient relevant training or education during the current relevant period, and

(b) where the arrangements call for the person to be participating in training or education at the time, the person is so participating.

Interpretation

3 Level 3 qualification

(1) In this Part, 'level 3 qualification' means a prescribed qualification, or a qualification of a prescribed description, at level 3.

(2) For this purpose, level 3 is the level of attainment (in terms of breadth and depth) which, in the opinion of the Secretary of State, is demonstrated by the General Certificate of Education at the advanced level in two subjects.

(3) A qualification, or description of qualification, prescribed under subsection (1) may be prescribed by reference to an assessment made by the Office of Qualifications and Examination Regulation (in this Part referred to as 'Ofqual') of the level of attainment demonstrated by a qualification; and for that purpose regulations under subsection (1) may confer a function (which may include the exercise of a discretion) on the Authority.

...

(5) The Secretary of State may by order amend subsection (2) so as to substitute a different qualification for the qualification for the time being referred to.

4 Appropriate full-time education or training

(1) In this Part, 'appropriate full-time education or training', in relation to a person, means full-time education or training which is suitable for the person, having regard—

(a) to the person's age, ability and aptitude, and

(b) to any special educational needs which the person may have,

and is provided at a school, at a college of further education, at an institution within the higher education sector or otherwise.

(2) Regulations may provide that a particular description of—

(a) education provided otherwise than at a school, or

(b) training,

is, or is not, to be treated as being 'full-time' for the purposes of this section.

5 Full-time occupation

(1) For the purposes of this Part, a person is in full-time occupation if the person works for at least 20 hours per week—

(a) under a contract of employment, or

(b) in any other way which may be prescribed,

otherwise than under a short-term contract or arrangement.

(2) The power conferred by subsection (1)(b) includes, in particular, power to prescribe the following ways of working—

(a) as a self-employed person,

(b) otherwise than for reward, or

(c) as the holder of an office.

(3) For the purposes of this section, the number of hours for which a person works per week is—

(a) the number of the person's normal weekly working hours, less

(b) the number of hours of actual guided learning—

(i) which constitute relevant training or education, and

(ii) in which the young person participates each week during normal weekly working hours.

(4) In subsection (3)—

'normal weekly working hours'—

    (a) in relation to a person employed under a contract of employment, means the person's normal working hours in a week, and

    (b) in relation to a person working in a way prescribed under subsection (1)(b), has the prescribed meaning;

'actual guided learning' has the meaning given by section 8(3).

(5) Section 234 of the Employment Rights Act 1996 (c. 18) (construction of references to normal working hours where employee entitled to overtime pay) applies for the purposes of the definition of 'normal weekly working hours' in subsection (4) as it applies for the purposes of that Act.

(6) Regulations may make provision for a person to be, or not to be, treated as working for at least 20 hours per week in cases where the number of hours for which the person works per week (calculated under subsection (3)) varies from week to week.

(7) Where a person works otherwise than under—

    (a) a single contract of employment, or

    (b) a single arrangement (in the case of a way of working prescribed under subsection (1)(b)),

the number of hours for which the person works per week is the aggregate of the amounts calculated under subsection (3) in relation to each of the contracts or arrangements under which the person works.

(8) For the purposes of subsection (1)—

    (a) a contract of employment is a short-term contract unless it—

        (i)   has a fixed term of 8 weeks or longer, or

        (ii) does not have a fixed term but has been, or can reasonably be expected to be, in force for at least 8 weeks;

    (b) an arrangement, in the case of a way of working prescribed under paragraph (b) of that subsection, is a short-term arrangement unless it has been, or can reasonably be expected to be, in force for at least 8 weeks.

6 Relevant training or education

(1) In this Part, 'relevant training or education' means training or education towards a regulated qualification provided by a course or courses.

(2) 'Regulated qualification' has the same meaning as in Part 7 of the Apprenticeships, Skills, Children and Learning Act 2009 (see section 130 of that Act).

7 Relevant period

(1) In this Part, 'relevant period', in relation to a person, means a period beginning with a start date and ending with the next end date.

(2) The following are start dates for the purposes of subsection (1)—

    (a) a date on which subsection (4) starts to apply to the person;

    (b) the date immediately following the end of a relevant period (if on that date that subsection still applies to the person).

(3) The following are end dates for the purposes of subsection (1)—

    (a) a prescribed date;

    (b) a date on which subsection (4) ceases to apply to the person.

(4) This subsection applies to a person at any time when—

    (a) this Part applies to the person, and

    (b) the person is not participating in education or training in accordance with section 2(1)(a) or (b).

8 Sufficient relevant training or education

(1) For the purposes of this Part, relevant training or education is 'sufficient' in relation to any relevant period if it amounts in aggregate to—

    (a) at least 280 hours of guided learning, in the case of a relevant period which is one year;

    (b) such number of hours of guided learning as is determined in accordance with regulations, in the case of any other relevant period.

    (2) For the purposes of this Part, a person participates in a particular number of hours of guided learning by—

        (a) participating in actual guided learning for that number of hours, or

        (b) completing a course or courses which can reasonably be expected to be adequate to enable persons completing it or them to achieve any standard required to attain a form of a regulated qualification to which that number of hours of guided learning has been assigned.

    (3) In subsection (2)—

'actual guided learning', in relation to a person, means time the person spends—

        (a) being taught or given instruction by a lecturer, tutor, supervisor or other appropriate provider of training or education, or

        (b) otherwise participating in education or training under the immediate guidance or supervision of such a person,

but does not include time spent on unsupervised preparation or study, whether at home or otherwise;

'assigned' means assigned by a recognised body in accordance with section 145 of the Apprenticeships, Skills, Children and Learning Act 2009;

'regulated qualification' has the same meaning as in Part 7 of the Apprenticeships, Skills, Children and Learning Act 2009 (see section 130 of that Act)

    (4) Regulations may make provision for attributing to any relevant period a number of hours of guided learning in which a person participates (or is treated by the regulations as participating) by virtue of subsection (2)(b) in cases where courses do not begin and end during a single relevant period.

…

Chapter 4   Parenting contracts and parenting orders

40   Parenting contracts

    (1) This section applies where a person to whom this Part applies ('the young person') is failing to fulfil the duty imposed by section 2.

    (2) A local authority in England may enter into a parenting contract with a parent of the young person—

        (a) if the parent is resident in England, and

        (b) the authority considers that entering into the parenting contract would be desirable in the interests of the young person's fulfilment of that duty.

    (3) A parenting contract is a document which contains—

        (a) a statement by the parent that the parent agrees to comply with such requirements as may be specified in the document for such period as may be so specified, and

        (b) a statement by the local authority that it agrees to provide support to the parent for the purpose of complying with those requirements.

    (4) The requirements mentioned in subsection (3) may include (in particular) a requirement to attend a counselling or guidance programme.

    (5) A parenting contract must be signed by the parent and signed on behalf of the local authority.

    (6) A parenting contract does not create any obligations in respect of whose breach any liability arises in contract or in tort.

41   Parenting orders

    (1) This section applies where a person to whom this Part applies ('the young person') is failing to fulfil the duty imposed by section 2.

(2) A local authority in England may apply to a magistrates' court for a parenting order in respect of a parent of the young person, if the parent is resident in England.

(3) If such an application is made, the court may make a parenting order in respect of the parent if it is satisfied that—

(a) the young person is failing to fulfil the duty imposed by section 2, and

(b) the making of the order would be desirable in the interests of the young person's fulfilment of that duty.

(4) A parenting order is an order which requires the parent—

(a) to comply, for a period not exceeding 12 months, with such requirements as are specified in the order, and

(b) subject to subsection (5), to attend, for a concurrent period not exceeding 3 months, such counselling or guidance programme as may be specified in directions given by the responsible officer.

(5) A parenting order under this section may, but need not, include a requirement mentioned in subsection (4)(b) in any case where a parenting order under this section or any other enactment has been made in respect of the parent on a previous occasion.

(6) A counselling or guidance programme which a parent is required to attend by virtue of subsection (4)(b) may be or include a residential course but only if the court is satisfied that the following two conditions are fulfilled.

(7) The first condition is that the attendance of the parent at a residential course is likely to be more effective than attendance at a non-residential course in the interests of the young person's fulfilment of the duty imposed by section 2.

(8) The second condition is that any interference with family life which is likely to result from the attendance of the parent at a residential course is proportionate in all the circumstances.

42   Parenting orders: supplemental

(1) In deciding whether to make a parenting order under section 41, a court must take into account (amongst other things)—

(a) any refusal by the parent to enter into a parenting contract under section 40 in respect of the person to whom this Part applies, or

(b) if the parent has entered into such a parenting contract, any failure by the parent to comply with the requirements specified in the contract.

(2) Subsections (3) to (7) of section 9 of the Crime and Disorder Act 1998 (c. 37) (supplemental provisions about parenting orders) apply in relation to a parenting order under section 41 as they apply in relation to a parenting order under section 8 of that Act.

43   Parenting orders: appeals

(1) An appeal lies to the Crown Court against the making of a parenting order under section 41.

(2) Subsections (2) and (3) of section 10 of the Crime and Disorder Act 1998 (appeals against parenting orders) apply in relation to an appeal under this section as they apply in relation to an appeal under subsection (1)(b) of that section.

44   Parenting contracts and parenting orders: further provisions

(1) Local authorities in England and responsible officers must, in carrying out their functions in relation to parenting contracts under section 40 and parenting orders under section 41, have regard to the extent to which any failure by, or anything done by, a parent of a person to whom this Part applies is affecting, or is likely to affect, that person's fulfilment of the duty imposed by section 2.

(2) Regulations may make further provision about the exercise by local authorities in England of their functions relating to—

(a) parenting contracts under section 40, or

(b) parenting orders under section 41.

(3) The provision that may be made under subsection (2) includes—

  (a) provision limiting the power of a local authority to enter into a parenting contract, or apply for a parenting order, in prescribed cases;

  (b) provision requiring one local authority to consult with another before taking any prescribed step;

  (c) provision requiring the provision of information by one local authority in England to another;

  (d) provision as to how the costs associated with parenting contracts under section 40 or parenting orders under section 41 (including in each case the costs of providing counselling or guidance programmes) are to be met.

(4) In this Chapter—

'parent', in relation to a young person, is to be construed in accordance with section 576 of the Education Act 1996 (c. 56), but does not include a person who is not an individual;

'responsible officer', in relation to a parenting order, means an officer of a local authority who is specified in the order.

...

Pensions Act 2008

(2008 c. 30)

PART 3 PENSION COMPENSATION

Chapter 1   Pension compensation on divorce etc.

107   Scope of mechanism

(1) Pension compensation sharing is available under this Chapter in relation to a person's shareable rights to PPF compensation.

(2) For the purposes of this Chapter, a right of a person to PPF compensation is 'shareable' unless it is of a description specified by regulations made by the Secretary of State.

108   Interpretation

In this Chapter—

'the Board' means the Board of the Pension Protection Fund;

'PPF compensation' means compensation payable under the pension compensation provisions;

'the pension compensation provisions' means—

  (a) Chapter 3 of Part 2 of the Pensions Act 2004 (pension protection) and any regulations or order made under it,

  (b) this Chapter and any regulations or order made under it, and

  (c) any provision corresponding to the provisions mentioned in paragraph (a) or (b) in force in Northern Ireland;

'prescribed' means prescribed by regulations made by the Secretary of State;

'the relevant order or provision' means the pension compensation sharing order, or provision contained in a qualifying agreement, which gives rise to the pension compensation sharing;

'the transfer day' means the day on which the relevant order or provision takes effect;

'the transferee' means the person for whose benefit the relevant order or provision is made;

'the transferor' means the person to whose rights the relevant order or provision relates.

109 Activation of pension compensation sharing

Section 111 applies on the taking effect of any of the following relating to a person's shareable rights to PPF compensation—

   (a) a pension compensation sharing order under the Matrimonial Causes Act 1973 (c. 18);
   (b) a pension compensation sharing order under Schedule 5 to the Civil Partnership Act 2004 (c. 33);
   (c) an order under Part 3 of the Matrimonial and Family Proceedings Act 1984 (c. 42) (financial relief in England and Wales in relation to overseas divorce etc.) corresponding to such an order as is mentioned in paragraph (a);
   (d) an order under Schedule 7 to the Civil Partnership Act 2004 (c. 33) (financial relief in England and Wales after overseas dissolution etc. of a civil partnership) corresponding to such an order as is mentioned in paragraph (b);
   (e) an order under any provision corresponding to a provision mentioned in any of paragraphs (a) to (d) in force in Northern Ireland.
   (f) ...
   (g) ...

...

111 Creation of pension compensation debits and credits

   (1) On the application of this section—
      (a) the transferor's shareable rights to PPF compensation that derive from rights under the specified scheme become subject to a debit of the appropriate amount, and
      (b) the transferee becomes entitled to a credit of that amount as against the Board.
   (2) For the purposes of subsection (1) 'the appropriate amount' means—
      (a) where the relevant order or provision specifies a percentage to be transferred, that percentage of the cash equivalent of the relevant compensation on the valuation day;
      (b) where the relevant order or provision specifies an amount to be transferred, the lesser of—
         (i)   that specified amount, and
         (ii) the cash equivalent of the relevant compensation on the valuation day.

   (3) For the purposes of subsection (2) 'the relevant compensation' means the payments or future payments to which, immediately before the transfer day, the transferor is entitled under the pension compensation provisions by virtue of the transferor's shareable rights to PPF compensation that derive from rights under the specified scheme.

   (4) The Secretary of State may by regulations provide for any description of payment to be disregarded for the purposes of subsection (3).

   (5) For the purposes of this section—
   'the specified scheme' means the pension scheme specified in the relevant order or provision;
   'the valuation day' means such day within the implementation period for the credit under subsection (1)(b) as the Board may specify by notice in writing to the transferor and transferee.

   (6) The credit to which the transferee becomes entitled under subsection (1)(b) is referred to in this Chapter as a 'pension compensation credit'.

112 Cash equivalents

   (1) The Secretary of State may by regulations make provision about the calculation and verification of cash equivalents for the purposes of section 111.

   (2) Regulations under this section may include provision for calculation and verification in a manner approved by the Board.

113   Reduction of compensation

(1) Where any of a person's shareable rights to PPF compensation are subject to a pension compensation debit, each payment or future payment—

    (a) to which the person is entitled under the pension compensation provisions by virtue of those rights, and

    (b) which is a qualifying payment,is reduced by the appropriate percentage.

(2) For the purposes of subsection (1) a payment is 'qualifying payment' if the cash equivalent by reference to which the amount of the pension compensation debit is determined includes an amount in respect of it.

(3) In this section 'the appropriate percentage', in relation to a pension compensation debit, means—

    (a) the percentage specified in the pension compensation sharing order or provision on which the debit depends; or

    (b) if the pension compensation sharing order or provision on which the debit depends specifies an amount to be transferred, the percentage which the appropriate amount for the purposes of subsection (1) of section 111 represents of the amount mentioned in subsection (2)(b)(ii) of that section.

114   Time for discharge of liability

(1) This section applies where the Board is subject to a liability in respect of a pension compensation credit.

(2) The Board must discharge the liability before the end of the implementation period for the credit.

(3) The Secretary of State may make provision by regulations as to circumstances in which the implementation period for the credit is extended for the purposes of this section.

115   'Implementation period'

(1) For the purposes of this Chapter, the implementation period for a pension compensation credit is the period of 4 months beginning with the later of—

    (a) the transfer day, and

    (b) the first day on which the Board is in receipt of—

        (i)   the relevant documents, and

        ((ii) such information relating to the transferor and transferee as the Secretary of State may prescribe by regulations.

(2) In subsection (1)(b)(i), 'the relevant documents' means copies of—

    (a) the relevant order or provision, and

    (b) the order, decree or declarator responsible for the divorce, dissolution or annulment to which it relates.

(3) Subsection (1) is subject to any provision made by regulations under section 117(2)(a).

(4) The Secretary of State may by regulations—

    (a) make provision requiring the Board to notify the transferor and transferee of the day on which the implementation period for the credit begins;

    (b) provide for this section to have effect with modifications where the credit depends on a pension compensation sharing order and the order is the subject of an application for leave to appeal out of time.

116   Discharge of liability

(1) This section applies where the Board is subject to a liability in respect of a pension compensation credit.

(2) The Board must discharge the liability by sending a notice to the transferee.

(3) On the sending of the notice the transferee becomes entitled, with effect from (and including) the transfer day, to compensation calculated in accordance with Schedule 5.

(4) For the purposes of that calculation, the initial annual rate of compensation is an amount determined by the Board.

(5) The Board must determine that amount in such a way as to secure that the cash equivalent value of the compensation to which the transferee becomes entitled under subsection (3) equals the amount of the credit.

(6) The Secretary of State may by regulations make provision about the calculation of cash equivalents for the purposes of subsection (5).

(7) The notice sent under this section must—

    (a) state that the transferee is entitled to periodic pension compensation calculated under Schedule 5, and

    (b) specify the amount determined under subsection (4).

(8) Where the transferee dies before liability in respect of the credit has been discharged—

    (a) subsections (2) to (7) do not have effect in relation to the discharge of liability in respect of the credit, and

    (b) liability in respect of the credit must be discharged in accordance with regulations made by the Secretary of State.

117   Charges in respect of pension compensation sharing costs

(1) The Secretary of State may by regulations make provision for the purpose of enabling the Board to recover from the parties to pension compensation sharing prescribed charges in respect of prescribed descriptions of pension compensation sharing activity.

(2) Regulations under subsection (1) may include—

    (a) provision for the start of the implementation period for a pension compensation credit to be postponed in prescribed circumstances;

    (b) provision enabling the Board to set off against any PPF compensation payable to a party to pension compensation sharing any charges owed to it by that party under the regulations;

    (c) provision, in relation to payments in respect of charges recoverable under the regulations, for reimbursement as between the parties to pension compensation sharing.

(3) For the purposes of regulations under subsection (1), the question of how much of a charge recoverable under the regulations is attributable to a party to pension compensation sharing is to be determined as follows—

    (a) where the relevant order or provision includes provision ('provision for apportionment') about the apportionment of charges under this section, there is attributable to the party so much of the charge as is apportioned to that party by that provision for apportionment;

    (b) where the relevant order or provision does not include provision for apportionment, the charge is attributable to the transferor.

(4) In subsection (1), the reference to pension compensation sharing activity is to activity attributable directly or indirectly to the application of section 111 by virtue of the relevant order or provision.

118   Supply of information about pension compensation in relation to divorce etc.

(1) The Secretary of State may by regulations—

    (a) make provision imposing on the Board requirements with respect to the supply of information relevant to any power with respect to—

        (i) financial relief under Part 2 of the Matrimonial Causes Act 1973 (c. 18) or Part 3 of the Matrimonial and Family Proceedings Act 1984 (c. 42) (England and Wales powers in relation to domestic and overseas divorce etc),

        (ii) financial relief under Schedule 5 or 7 to the Civil Partnership Act 2004 (c. 33) (England and Wales powers in relation to domestic and overseas dissolution of civil partnerships etc),

(iii) financial relief under any provision corresponding to a provision mentioned in sub-paragraph (i) or (ii) in force in Northern Ireland,

(iv) ... or

(v) provision as to pension sharing, or pension compensation sharing, that is contained in an agreement that is a qualifying agreement for the purposes of section 28(1)(b) and (c) of the Welfare Reform and Pensions Act 1999 (c. 30) (activation of pension sharing) or this Chapter;

(b) make provision about calculation and verification in relation to the valuation of PPF compensation for the purposes of regulations under paragraph (a);

(c) make provision for the purpose of enabling the Board to recover prescribed charges in respect of providing information in accordance with regulations under paragraph (a).

(2) Regulations under subsection (1)(b) may include provision for calculation and verification in a manner approved by the Board.

(3) Regulations under subsection (1)(c) may include provision for the application in prescribed circumstances, with or without modification, of any provision made by virtue of section 117(2).

...

Marriage (Wales) Act 2010

(2010 c. 6)

1 Application of this Act

(1) This Act applies only to parishes in the area subject to the Welsh Church Act 1914 and accordingly any reference to 'a parish' is to a parish within that area.

(2) In subsection (1), 'the area subject to the Welsh Church Act 1914' means the area in which the Church of England was disestablished by that Act.

2 Marriages solemnized in churches, etc in parishes with which a party has a qualifying connection

(1) A person intending to be married shall have the like, but no greater, right to have the marriage solemnized in a parish church of a parish with which he or she has a connection specified in subsection (3) (in this Act referred to as a 'qualifying connection') as that person has to have the marriage solemnized in the parish church of the parish in which he or she resides or which is his or her usual place of worship.

(2) Where a church or other building is licensed for the solemnisation of marriages under section 21(1) of the 1949 Act this section shall apply to such church or other building, while the designation is in force, as it applies to a parish church.

(3) For the purposes of this section a person has a qualifying connection with a parish in which the marriage is to be solemnized if—

(a) that person was baptised in that parish (unless the baptism took place in a combined rite which included baptism and confirmation) or is a person whose confirmation has been entered in the register book of confirmation for any church or chapel in that parish;

(b) that person has at any time had his or her usual place of residence in that parish for a period of not less than six months;

(c) that person has at any time habitually attended public worship in that parish for a period of not less than six months;

(d) a parent of that person has during the lifetime of that person had his or her usual place of residence in that parish for a period of not less than six months or habitually attended public worship in that parish for that period; or

(e) a parent or grandparent of that person has been married in that parish.

(4) For the purpose of subsection (3)(d) or (e) 'parent' includes an adoptive parent and any other person who has undertaken the care and upbringing of the person seeking to establish a qualifying connection and 'grandparent' shall be construed accordingly.

(5) A person who has the right to have a marriage solemnized in accordance with subsection (1) shall have the like right to have the banns of that marriage published in the parish church where the marriage is to be solemnized.

(6) The right to have banns published conferred by subsection (5) is additional to and not in substitution for the requirements of section 6 of the 1949 Act for banns to be published in the parish church of the parish where the parties to the marriage reside or of each parish in which one of them resides.

(7) Where a marriage is intended to be solemnized in accordance with subsection (1) following the publication of banns by virtue of subsection (5) subsections 11(2) and (4) of the 1949 Act shall apply as those subsections apply to a marriage of which the banns have been published in a parish or district in which neither of the persons to be married resides by virtue of section 6(4) of the 1949 Act.

(8) Subject to subsection (9), a person who wishes to have his or her marriage solemnized in accordance with subsection (1) shall provide such information, written or otherwise, as the minister of the parish in which the marriage is to be solemnized may require in order to satisfy himself or herself that that person has a qualifying connection, and—

(a) section 8 of the 1949 Act shall apply as if the reference in that section to a clergyman were a reference to the minister; and

(b) the minister shall be under a duty, when considering whether any information provided to him or her is sufficient to satisfy himself or herself under this subsection that the person wishing to have the marriage solemnized has a qualifying connection, to have regard to any guidance issued under section 4.

(9) If the minister considers that it is necessary to do so, in order to satisfy himself or herself that a person has a qualifying connection, he or she may require that person to supply or support any information required to be provided under subsection (8) by means of a statutory declaration.

(10) Where a public chapel is licensed by a bishop for the publication of banns and the solemnization of marriages under section 20 of the 1949 Act, this section shall apply as if that chapel were a parish church of the parish or of any parish the whole or part of which is within the district specified in the licence.

(11) In this section—

'church' does not include a cathedral;

'minister' means—

(a) where a special cure of souls has been assigned to any priest for the area in which the church where the marriage is to be solemnized is situated, whether in a Rectorial Benefice or otherwise, that priest; or

(b) where paragraph (a) does not apply, the incumbent of the benefice in the area of which that church is situated; or

(c) where neither of the above paragraphs apply, the priest in charge of that benefice; or

(d) where none of the above paragraphs apply, in the case of a Rectorial Benefice, the vicar who has held office for the longest period in that Benefice; or

(e) where none of the above paragraphs apply, the area dean of the deanery in which that church is situated;

'parish' includes a conventional district; and

any reference to baptism, confirmation, marriage or public worship shall be construed as a reference to baptism, confirmation, marriage or public worship, as the case may be, according to the rites of the Church in Wales.

(12) Where a parish has ceased to exist or the boundaries thereof have been altered and a person who wishes to have his or her marriage solemnized in accordance with subsection (1) can

establish a qualifying connection with a place situated within such a parish then, if that place is, at the time when the notice under section 8 of the 1949 Act is delivered, situated within the parish in which the church where the marriage is to be solemnized is situated, that person shall be deemed to have a qualifying connection with that parish.

(13) In relation to the establishment of a qualifying connection under subsection (3)(a) by virtue of confirmation the references in subsection (12) to a place shall be construed as a reference to the church or other place of worship in whose register the confirmation was entered.

3   Marriage by common licence

(1) Notwithstanding section 15 of the 1949 Act a common licence may be granted to a person for the solemnization of a marriage in any church or chapel in which that person may be married under section 2 of this Act, and section 16(1)(b) of the 1949 Act shall, where a common licence may be granted by virtue of this section, have effect as if it required one of the persons to be married to swear that one or both of those persons has a qualifying connection with a parish within the meaning of section 2(3) of this Act and to state the nature of that connection and section 2(8) of this Act shall apply as if the reference therein to the minister of the parish were a reference to the authority having power to grant the licence.

(2) Where an application has been made for the grant of a common licence under subsection (1), section 2(12) shall have effect as if the reference to the date on which the notice required under section 8 of the 1949 Act is delivered were a reference to the date of the application for the grant of the common licence.

4   Guidance

The Order of Bishops may from time to time issue guidance as to the exercise of any functions by a minister under section 2(8) or (9) or by the authority having power to grant a common licence under section 2(8) as applied by section 3.

5   Supplementary

(1) In this Act 'the 1949 Act' means the Marriage Act 1949 (c 76) and, unless the context otherwise requires, expressions used in this Act have the same meaning as in the 1949 Act.

(2) Where a marriage has been solemnized—

(a) in accordance with section 2(1), or

(b) on the authority of a common licence granted by virtue of section 3,

it shall not be necessary in support of the marriage to give any proof that either party had a qualifying connection with the parish in which the marriage was solemnized and no evidence shall be given to prove the contrary in any proceedings touching the validity of the marriage.

Equality Act 2010

(2010 c. 15)

PART 2 EQUALITY: KEY CONCEPTS

Chapter 1   Protected characteristics

4   The protected characteristics

The following characteristics are protected characteristics—

    age;

    disability;

    gender reassignment;

marriage and civil partnership;

pregnancy and maternity;

race;

religion or belief;

sex;

sexual orientation.

5 Age

(1) In relation to the protected characteristic of age—

    (a) a reference to a person who has a particular protected characteristic is a reference to a person of a particular age group;

    (b) a reference to persons who share a protected characteristic is a reference to persons of the same age group.

(2) A reference to an age group is a reference to a group of persons defined by reference to age, whether by reference to a particular age or to a range of ages.

…

8 Marriage and civil partnership

(1) A person has the protected characteristic of marriage and civil partnership if the person is married or is a civil partner.

(2) In relation to the protected characteristic of marriage and civil partnership—

    (a) a reference to a person who has a particular protected characteristic is a reference to a person who is married or is a civil partner;

    (b) a reference to persons who share a protected characteristic is a reference to persons who are married or are civil partners.

…

11 Sex

In relation to the protected characteristic of sex—

    (a) a reference to a person who has a particular protected characteristic is a reference to a man or to a woman;

    (b) a reference to persons who share a protected characteristic is a reference to persons of the same sex.

12 Sexual orientation

(1) Sexual orientation means a person's sexual orientation towards—

    (a) persons of the same sex,

    (b) persons of the opposite sex, or

    (c) persons of either sex.

(2) In relation to the protected characteristic of sexual orientation—

    (a) a reference to a person who has a particular protected characteristic is a reference to a person who is of a particular sexual orientation;

    (b) a reference to persons who share a protected characteristic is a reference to persons who are of the same sexual orientation.

Chapter 2 Prohibited conduct

Discrimination

13 Direct discrimination

(1) A person (A) discriminates against another (B) if, because of a protected characteristic, A treats B less favourably than A treats or would treat others.

(2) If the protected characteristic is age, A does not discriminate against B if A can show A's treatment of B to be a proportionate means of achieving a legitimate aim.

(3) …

(4) If the protected characteristic is marriage and civil partnership, this section applies to a contravention of Part 5 (work) only if the treatment is because it is B who is married or a civil partner.
…

19   Indirect discrimination

(1) A person (A) discriminates against another (B) if A applies to B a provision, criterion or practice which is discriminatory in relation to a relevant protected characteristic of B's.

(2) For the purposes of subsection (1), a provision, criterion or practice is discriminatory in relation to a relevant protected characteristic of B's if—

  (a) A applies, or would apply, it to persons with whom B does not share the characteristic,

  (b) it puts, or would put, persons with whom B shares the characteristic at a particular disadvantage when compared with persons with whom B does not share it,

  (c) it puts, or would put, B at that disadvantage, and

  (d) A cannot show it to be a proportionate means of achieving a legitimate aim.

(3) The relevant protected characteristics are—

age;
disability;
gender reassignment;
marriage and civil partnership;
race;
religion or belief;
sex;
sexual orientation.
…

Discrimination: supplementary

23   Comparison by reference to circumstances

(1) On a comparison of cases for the purposes of section 13, 14, or 19 there must be no material difference between the circumstances relating to each case.
…

(3) If the protected characteristic is sexual orientation, the fact that one person (whether or not the person referred to as B) is a civil partner while another is married to a person of the opposite sex is not a material difference between the circumstances relating to each case.

(4) If the protected characteristic is sexual orientation, the fact that one person (whether or not the person referred to as B) is married to a person of the same sex while another is married to a person of the opposite sex is not a material difference between the circumstances relating to each case.

24   Irrelevance of alleged discriminator's characteristics

(1) For the purpose of establishing a contravention of this Act by virtue of section 13(1), it does not matter whether A has the protected characteristic.

(2) For the purpose of establishing a contravention of this Act by virtue of section 14(1), it does not matter—

  (a) whether A has one of the protected characteristics in the combination;

  (b) whether A has both.

25   References to particular strands of discrimination

(1) Age discrimination is—

  (a) discrimination within section 13 because of age;

  (b) discrimination within section 19 where the relevant protected characteristic is age.…

(3) Gender reassignment discrimination is—
   (a) discrimination within section 13 because of gender reassignment;
   (b) discrimination within section 16;
   (c) discrimination within section 19 where the relevant protected characteristic is gender reassignment.
(4) Marriage and civil partnership discrimination is—
   (a) discrimination within section 13 because of marriage and civil partnership;
   (b) discrimination within section 19 where the relevant protected characteristic is marriage and civil partnership....
(8) Sex discrimination is—
   (a) discrimination within section 13 because of sex;
   (b) discrimination within section 19 where the relevant protected characteristic is sex.
(9) Sexual orientation discrimination is—
   (a) discrimination within section 13 because of sexual orientation;
   (b) discrimination within section 19 where the relevant protected characteristic is sexual orientation.

Other prohibited conduct

26 Harassment

(1) A person (A) harasses another (B) if—
   (a) A engages in unwanted conduct related to a relevant protected characteristic, and
   (b) the conduct has the purpose or effect of—
      (i)   violating B's dignity, or
      (ii) creating an intimidating, hostile, degrading, humiliating or offensive environment for B.
(2) A also harasses B if—
   (a) A engages in unwanted conduct of a sexual nature, and
   (b) the conduct has the purpose or effect referred to in subsection (1)(b).
(3) A also harasses B if—
   (a) A or another person engages in unwanted conduct of a sexual nature or that is related to gender reassignment or sex,
   (b) the conduct has the purpose or effect referred to in subsection (1)(b), and
   (c) because of B's rejection of or submission to the conduct, A treats B less favourably than A would treat B if B had not rejected or submitted to the conduct.
(4) In deciding whether conduct has the effect referred to in subsection (1)(b), each of the following must be taken into account—
   (a) the perception of B;
   (b) the other circumstances of the case;
   (c) whether it is reasonable for the conduct to have that effect.
(5) The relevant protected characteristics are—
   age;
   disability;
   gender reassignment;
   race;
   religion or belief;
   sex;
   sexual orientation.

27   Victimisation

(1) A person (A) victimises another person (B) if A subjects B to a detriment because—

    (a) B does a protected act, or

    (b) A believes that B has done, or may do, a protected act.

(2) Each of the following is a protected act—

    (a) bringing proceedings under this Act;

    (b) giving evidence or information in connection with proceedings under this Act;

    (c) doing any other thing for the purposes of or in connection with this Act;

    (d) making an allegation (whether or not express) that A or another person has contravened this Act.

(3) Giving false evidence or information, or making a false allegation, is not a protected act if the evidence or information is given, or the allegation is made, in bad faith.

(4) This section applies only where the person subjected to a detriment is an individual.

(5) The reference to contravening this Act includes a reference to committing a breach of an equality clause or rule.

PART 3   SERVICES AND PUBLIC FUNCTIONS

Preliminary

28   Application of this Part

(1) This Part does not apply to the protected characteristic of—

    (a) age, so far as relating to persons who have not attained the age of 18;

    (b) marriage and civil partnership.

(2) This Part does not apply to discrimination, harassment or victimisation—

    (a) that is prohibited by Part 4 (premises), 5 (work) or 6 (education), or

    (b) that would be so prohibited but for an express exception.

(3) This Part does not apply to—

    (a) a breach of an equality clause or rule;

    (b) anything that would be a breach of an equality clause or rule but for section 69 or Part 2 of Schedule 7;

    (c) a breach of a non-discrimination rule.

Provision of services, etc

29   Provision of services, etc

(1) A person (a 'service-provider') concerned with the provision of a service to the public or a section of the public (for payment or not) must not discriminate against a person requiring the service by not providing the person with the service.

(2) A service-provider (A) must not, in providing the service, discriminate against a person (B)—

    (a) as to the terms on which A provides the service to B;

    (b) by terminating the provision of the service to B;

    (c) by subjecting B to any other detriment.

(3) A service-provider must not, in relation to the provision of the service, harass—

    (a) a person requiring the service, or

    (b) a person to whom the service-provider provides the service.

(4) A service-provider must not victimise a person requiring the service by not providing the person with the service.

(5) A service-provider (A) must not, in providing the service, victimise a person (B)—

    (a) as to the terms on which A provides the service to B;

    (b) by terminating the provision of the service to B;

    (c) by subjecting B to any other detriment.

(6) A person must not, in the exercise of a public function that is not the provision of a service to the public or a section of the public, do anything that constitutes discrimination, harassment or victimisation.

(7) A duty to make reasonable adjustments applies to—

(a) a service-provider (and see also section 55(7));

(b) a person who exercises a public function that is not the provision of a service to the public or a section of the public.

(8) In the application of section 26 for the purposes of subsection (3), and subsection (6) as it relates to harassment, neither of the following is a relevant protected characteristic—

(a) religion or belief;

(b) sexual orientation.

...

31 Interpretation and exceptions

(1) This section applies for the purposes of this Part.

(2) A reference to the provision of a service includes a reference to the provision of goods or facilities.

(3) A reference to the provision of a service includes a reference to the provision of a service in the exercise of a public function.

(4) A public function is a function that is a function of a public nature for the purposes of the Human Rights Act 1998.

...

(6) A reference to a person requiring a service includes a reference to a person who is seeking to obtain or use the service.

(7) A reference to a service-provider not providing a person with a service includes a reference to—

(a) the service-provider not providing the person with a service of the quality that the service-provider usually provides to the public (or the section of it which includes the person), or

(b) the service-provider not providing the person with the service in the manner in which, or on the terms on which, the service-provider usually provides the service to the public (or the section of it which includes the person).

(10) Schedule 3 (exceptions) has effect.

...

PART 9 ENFORCEMENT

Chapter 1   Introductory

113 Proceedings

(1) Proceedings relating to a contravention of this Act must be brought in accordance with this Part.

(2) Subsection (1) does not apply to proceedings under Part 1 of the Equality Act 2006.

(3) Subsection (1) does not prevent—

(a) a claim for judicial review;

(b)–(d) ...

(4) This section is subject to any express provision of this Act conferring jurisdiction on a court or tribunal.

...

(7) This section does not apply to—

(a) proceedings for an offence under this Act;

(b) ...

Chapter 2   Civil courts

114   Jurisdiction

(1) The county court or, in Scotland, the sheriff has jurisdiction to determine a claim relating to—

    (a) a contravention of Part 3 (services and public functions);

    (b)–(e) ...

...

(5) For the purposes of proceedings on a claim within subsection (1)(a)—

    (a) a decision in proceedings on a claim mentioned in section 115(1) that an act is a contravention of Part 3 is binding;

    (b) it does not matter whether the act occurs outside the United Kingdom.

(6) The county court or sheriff—

    (a) must not grant an interim injunction or interdict unless satisfied that no criminal matter would be prejudiced by doing so;

    (b) must grant an application to stay or sist proceedings under subsection (1) on grounds of prejudice to a criminal matter unless satisfied the matter will not be prejudiced.

...

118   Time limits

(1) Proceedings on a claim within section 114 may not be brought after the end of—

    (a) the period of 6 months starting with the date of the act to which the claim relates, or

    (b) such other period as the county court or sheriff thinks just and equitable.

...

(6) For the purposes of this section—

    (a) conduct extending over a period is to be treated as done at the end of the period;

    (b) failure to do something is to be treated as occurring when the person in question decided on it.

(7) In the absence of evidence to the contrary, a person (P) is to be taken to decide on failure to do something—

    (a) when P does an act inconsistent with doing it, or

    (b) if P does no inconsistent act, on the expiry of the period in which P might reasonably have been expected to do it.

...

119   Remedies

(1) This section applies if the county court or the sheriff finds that there has been a contravention of a provision referred to in section 114(1).

(2) The county court has power to grant any remedy which could be granted by the High Court—

    (a) in proceedings in tort;

    (b) on a claim for judicial review.

...

(4) An award of damages may include compensation for injured feelings (whether or not it includes compensation on any other basis).

(5) Subsection (6) applies if the county court or sheriff—

    (a) finds that a contravention of a provision referred to in section 114(1) is established by virtue of section 19, but

    (b) is satisfied that the provision, criterion or practice was not applied with the intention of discriminating against the claimant or pursuer.

(6) The county court or sheriff must not make an award of damages unless it first considers whether to make any other disposal.

(7) The county court or sheriff must not grant a remedy other than an award of damages or the making of a declaration unless satisfied that no criminal matter would be prejudiced by doing so.

...

Chapter 5   Miscellaneous

136   Burden of proof

(1) This section applies to any proceedings relating to a contravention of this Act.

(2) If there are facts from which the court could decide, in the absence of any other explanation, that a person (A) contravened the provision concerned, the court must hold that the contravention occurred.

(3) But subsection (2) does not apply if A shows that A did not contravene the provision.

...

137   Previous findings

(1) A finding in relevant proceedings in respect of an act which has become final is to be treated as conclusive in proceedings under this Act.

(2) Relevant proceedings are proceedings before a court or employment tribunal under any of the following—

  (a) section 19 or 20 of the Race Relations Act 1968;
  (b) the Equal Pay Act 1970;
  (c) the Sex Discrimination Act 1975;
  (d) the Race Relations Act 1976;
  (e) section 6(4A) of the Sex Discrimination Act 1986;
  (f) the Disability Discrimination Act 1995;
  (g) Part 2 of the Equality Act 2006;
  (h) the Employment Equality (Religion and Belief) Regulations 2003 (SI 2003/1660);
  (i) the Employment Equality (Sexual Orientation) Regulations 2003 (SI 2003/1661);
  (j) the Employment Equality (Age) Regulations 2006 (SI 2006/1031);
  (k) the Equality Act (Sexual Orientation) Regulations 2007 (SI 2007/1263).

(3) A finding becomes final—

  (a) when an appeal against the finding is dismissed, withdrawn or abandoned, or
  (b) when the time for appealing expires without an appeal having been brought.

...

PART 11 ADVANCEMENT OF EQUALITY

Chapter 1   Public sector equality duty

149   Public sector equality duty

(1) A public authority must, in the exercise of its functions, have due regard to the need to—

  (a) eliminate discrimination, harassment, victimisation and any other conduct that is prohibited by or under this Act;
  (b) advance equality of opportunity between persons who share a relevant protected characteristic and persons who do not share it;
  (c) foster good relations between persons who share a relevant protected characteristic and persons who do not share it.

(2) A person who is not a public authority but who exercises public functions must, in the exercise of those functions, have due regard to the matters mentioned in subsection (1).

...

(9) Schedule 18 (exceptions) has effect.

150 Public authorities and public functions

(1) A public authority is a person who is specified in Schedule 19.

...

(3) A public authority specified in Schedule 19 is subject to the duty imposed by section 149(1) in relation to the exercise of all of its functions unless subsection (4) applies.

(4) A public authority specified in that Schedule in respect of certain specified functions is subject to that duty only in respect of the exercise of those functions.

(5) A public function is a function that is a function of a public nature for the purposes of the Human Rights Act 1998.

...

156 Enforcement

A failure in respect of a performance of a duty imposed by or under this Chapter does not confer a cause of action at private law.

...

PART 15 FAMILY PROPERTY

198 Abolition of husband's duty to maintain wife

The rule of common law that a husband must maintain his wife is abolished.

199 Abolition of presumption of advancement

(1) The presumption of advancement (by which, for example, a husband is presumed to be making a gift to his wife if he transfers property to her, or purchases property in her name) is abolished.

(2) The abolition by subsection (1) of the presumption of advancement does not have effect in relation to—

(a) anything done before the commencement of this section, or

(b) anything done pursuant to any obligation incurred before the commencement of this section.

...

SCHEDULE 3 SERVICES AND PUBLIC FUNCTIONS: EXCEPTIONS

PART 1 CONSTITUTIONAL MATTERS

...

Judicial functions

3.—(1) Section 29 does not apply to—

(a) a judicial function;

(b) anything done on behalf of, or on the instructions of, a person exercising a judicial function;

(c) a decision not to commence or continue criminal proceedings;

(d) anything done for the purpose of reaching, or in pursuance of, a decision not to commence or continue criminal proceedings.

(2) A reference in sub-paragraph (1) to a judicial function includes a reference to a judicial function conferred on a person other than a court or tribunal.

...

PART 3 HEALTH AND CARE

Care within the family

15.—A person (A) does not contravene section 29 only by participating in arrangements under which (whether or not for reward) A takes into A's home, and treats as members of A's family, persons requiring particular care and attention.

...

PART 6 MARRIAGE: GENDER REASSIGNMENT

Gender reassignment: England and Wales

24.—(1) A person does not contravene section 29, so far as relating to gender reassignment discrimination, only because of anything done in reliance on section 5B of the Marriage Act 1949 (solemnisation of marriages involving person of acquired gender).

(2) A person (A) whose consent to the solemnisation of the marriage of a person (B) is required under section 44(1) of the Marriage Act 1949 (solemnisation in registered building) does not contravene section 29, so far as relating to gender reassignment discrimination, by refusing to consent if A reasonably believes that B's gender has become the acquired gender under the Gender Recognition Act 2004.

(3) Sub-paragraph (4) applies to a person (A) who may, in a case that comes within the Marriage Act 1949 (other than the case mentioned in sub-paragraph (1)), solemnise marriages according to a form, rite or ceremony of a body of persons who meet for religious worship.

(4) A does not contravene section 29, so far as relating to gender reassignment discrimination, by refusing to solemnise, in accordance with a form, rite or ceremony as described in sub-paragraph (3), the marriage of a person (B) if A reasonably believes that B's gender has become the acquired gender under the Gender Recognition Act 2004.

PART 6A MARRIAGE OF SAME SEX COUPLES IN ENGLAND AND WALES

25A   Marriage according to religious rites: no compulsion to solemnize etc

(1) A person does not contravene section 29 only because the person—

(a) does not conduct a relevant marriage,

(b) is not present at, does not carry out, or does not otherwise participate in, a relevant marriage, or

(c) does not consent to a relevant marriage being conducted,

for the reason that the marriage is the marriage of a same sex couple.

(2) Expressions used in this paragraph and in section 2 of the Marriage (Same Sex Couples) Act 2013 have the same meanings in this paragraph as in that section.

...

Section 149   **SCHEDULE 18**

PUBLIC SECTOR EQUALITY DUTY: EXCEPTIONS

Children

1.—(1) Section 149, so far as relating to age, does not apply to the exercise of a function relating to—

(a) the provision of education to pupils in schools;

(b) the provision of benefits, facilities or services to pupils in schools;

(c) the provision of accommodation, benefits, facilities or services in community homes pursuant to section 53(1) of the Children Act 1989;

(d) the provision of accommodation, benefits, facilities or services pursuant to arrangements under section 82(5) of that Act (arrangements by the Secretary of State relating to the accommodation of children);

...

Judicial functions, etc

3.—(1) Section 149 does not apply to the exercise of—

(a) a judicial function;

(b) a function exercised on behalf of, or on the instructions of, a person exercising a judicial function.

(2) The references to a judicial function include a reference to a judicial function conferred on a person other than a court or tribunal.

SCHEDULE 19 PUBLIC AUTHORITIES

PART 1 PUBLIC AUTHORITIES: GENERAL

...

Court services and legal services

The Children and Family Court Advisory and Support Service.
The Judicial Appointments Commission.
The Legal Services Board.
...

Health, social care and social security

...

The Child Maintenance and Enforcement Commission.
...

Local government

A county council, district council or parish council in England.
A parish meeting constituted under section 13 of the Local Government Act 1972.
Charter trustees constituted under section 246 of that Act for an area in England.
The Greater London Authority.
A London borough council.
The Common Council of the City of London in its capacity as a local authority or port health authority.

The Sub-Treasurer of the Inner Temple or the Under-Treasurer of the Middle Temple, in that person's capacity as a local authority.

...

PART 2 PUBLIC AUTHORITIES: RELEVANT WELSH AUTHORITIES

...

Local government

A county council, county borough council or community council in Wales.

...

Other public authorities

...

The Commissioner for Older People in Wales or Comisiynydd Pobl Hyn Cymru

The Children's Commissioner for Wales or Comisiynydd Plant Hyn Cymru.

...

Crime and Security Act 2010

(2010 c. 17)

...

Domestic violence

24 Power to issue a domestic violence protection notice

(1) A member of a police force not below the rank of superintendent ('the authorising officer') may issue a domestic violence protection notice ('a DVPN') under this section.

(2) A DVPN may be issued to a person ('P') aged 18 years or over if the authorising officer has reasonable grounds for believing that—

   (a) P has been violent towards, or has threatened violence towards, an associated person, and

   (b) the issue of the DVPN is necessary to protect that person from violence or a threat of violence by P.

(3) Before issuing a DVPN, the authorising officer must, in particular, consider—

   (a) the welfare of any person under the age of 18 whose interests the officer considers relevant to the issuing of the DVPN (whether or not that person is an associated person),

   (b) the opinion of the person for whose protection the DVPN would be issued as to the issuing of the DVPN,

   (c) any representations made by P as to the issuing of the DVPN, and

   (d) in the case of provision included by virtue of subsection (8), the opinion of any other associated person who lives in the premises to which the provision would relate.

(4) The authorising officer must take reasonable steps to discover the opinions mentioned in subsection (3).

(5) But the authorising officer may issue a DVPN in circumstances where the person for whose protection it is is-sued does not consent to the issuing of the DVPN.

(6) A DVPN must contain provision to prohibit P from molesting the person for whose protection it is issued.

(7) Provision required to be included by virtue of subsection (6) may be expressed so as to refer to molestation in general, to particular acts of molestation, or to both.

(8) If P lives in premises which are also lived in by a person for whose protection the DVPN is issued, the DVPN may also contain provision—

(a) to prohibit P from evicting or excluding from the premises the person for whose protection the DVPN is issued,

(b) to prohibit P from entering the premises,

(c) to require P to leave the premises, or

(d) to prohibit P from coming within such distance of the premises as may be specified in the DVPN.

(9) An 'associated person' means a person who is associated with P within the meaning of section 62 of the Family Law Act 1996.

(10) Subsection (11) applies where a DVPN includes provision in relation to premises by virtue of subsection (8)(b) or (8)(c) and the authorising officer believes that—

(a) P is a person subject to service law in accordance with sections 367 to 369 of the Armed Forces Act 2006, and

(b) the premises fall within paragraph (a) of the definition of 'service living accommodation' in section 96(1) of that Act.

(11) The authorising officer must make reasonable efforts to inform P's commanding officer (within the meaning of section 360 of the Armed Forces Act 2006) of the issuing of the notice.

25 Contents and service of a domestic violence protection notice

(1) A DVPN must state—

(a) the grounds on which it has been issued,

(b) that a constable may arrest P without warrant if the constable has reasonable grounds for believing that P is in breach of the DVPN,

(c) that an application for a domestic violence protection order under section 27 will be heard within 48 hours of the time of service of the DVPN and a notice of the hearing will be given to P,

(d) that the DVPN continues in effect until that application has been determined, and

(e) the provision that a magistrates' court may include in a domestic violence protection order.

(2) A DVPN must be in writing and must be served on P personally by a constable.

(3) On serving P with a DVPN, the constable must ask P for an address for the purposes of being given the notice of the hearing of the application for the domestic violence protection order.

26 Breach of a domestic violence protection notice

(1) A person arrested by virtue of section 25(1)(b) for a breach of a DVPN must be held in custody and brought before the magistrates' court which will hear the application for the DVPO under section 27—

(a) before the end of the period of 24 hours beginning with the time of the arrest, or

(b) if earlier, at the hearing of that application.

(2) If the person is brought before the court by virtue of subsection (1)(a), the court may remand the person.

(3) If the court adjourns the hearing of the application by virtue of section 27(8), the court may remand the person.

(4) In calculating when the period of 24 hours mentioned in subsection (1)(a) ends, Christmas Day, Good Friday, any Sunday and any day which is a bank holiday in England and Wales under the Banking and Financial Dealings Act 1971 are to be disregarded.

27 Application for a domestic violence protection order

(1) If a DVPN has been issued, a constable must apply for a domestic violence protection order ('a DVPO').

(2) The application must be made by complaint to a magistrates' court.

(3) The application must be heard by the magistrates' court not later than 48 hours after the DVPN was served pursuant to section 25(2).

(4) In calculating when the period of 48 hours mentioned in subsection (3) ends, Christmas Day, Good Friday, any Sunday and any day which is a bank holiday in England and Wales under the Banking and Financial Dealings Act 1971 are to be disregarded.

(5) A notice of the hearing of the application must be given to P.

(6) The notice is deemed given if it has been left at the address given by P under section 25(3).

(7) But if the notice has not been given because no address was given by P under section 25(3), the court may hear the application for the DVPO if the court is satisfied that the constable applying for the DVPO has made reasonable efforts to give P the notice.

(8) The magistrates' court may adjourn the hearing of the application.

(9) If the court adjourns the hearing, the DVPN continues in effect until the application has been determined.

(10) On the hearing of an application for a DVPO, section 97 of the Magistrates' Courts Act 1980 (summons to witness and warrant for his arrest) does not apply in relation to a person for whose protection the DVPO would be made, except where the person has given oral or written evidence at the hearing.

28 Conditions for and contents of a domestic violence protection order

(1) The court may make a DVPO if two conditions are met.

(2) The first condition is that the court is satisfied on the balance of probabilities that P has been violent towards, or has threatened violence towards, an associated person.

(3) The second condition is that the court thinks that making the DVPO is necessary to protect that person from violence or a threat of violence by P.

(4) Before making a DVPO, the court must, in particular, consider—

    (a) the welfare of any person under the age of 18 whose interests the court considers relevant to the making of the DVPO (whether or not that person is an associated person), and

    (b) any opinion of which the court is made aware—

        (i) of the person for whose protection the DVPO would be made, and

        (ii) in the case of provision included by virtue of subsection (8), of any other associated person who lives in the premises to which the provision would relate.

(5) But the court may make a DVPO in circumstances where the person for whose protection it is made does not consent to the making of the DVPO.

(6) A DVPO must contain provision to prohibit P from molesting the person for whose protection it is made.

(7) Provision required to be included by virtue of subsection (6) may be expressed so as to refer to molestation in general, to particular acts of molestation, or to both.

(8) If P lives in premises which are also lived in by a person for whose protection the DVPO is made, the DVPO may also contain provision—

    (a) to prohibit P from evicting or excluding from the premises the person for whose protection the DVPO is made,

    (b) to prohibit P from entering the premises,

    (c) to require P to leave the premises, or

(d) to prohibit P from coming within such distance of the premises as may be specified in the DVPO.

(9) A DVPO must state that a constable may arrest P without warrant if the constable has reasonable grounds for believing that P is in breach of the DVPO.

(10) A DVPO may be in force for—

(a) no fewer than 14 days beginning with the day on which it is made, and

(b) no more than 28 days beginning with that day.

(11) A DVPO must state the period for which it is to be in force.

29   Breach of a domestic violence protection order

(1) A person arrested by virtue of section 28(9) for a breach of a DVPO must be held in custody and brought before a magistrates' court within the period of 24 hours beginning with the time of the arrest.

(2) If the matter is not disposed of when the person is brought before the court, the court may remand the person.

(3) In calculating when the period of 24 hours mentioned in subsection (1) ends, Christmas Day, Good Friday, any Sunday and any day which is a bank holiday in England and Wales under the Banking and Financial Dealings Act 1971 are to be disregarded.

30   Further provision about remand

(1) This section applies for the purposes of the remand of a person by a magistrates' court under section 26(2) or (3) or 29(2).

(2) In the application of section 128(6) of the Magistrates' Courts Act 1980 for those purposes, the reference to the 'other party' is to be read—

(a) in the case of a remand prior to the hearing of an application for a DVPO, as a reference to the authorising officer,

(b) in any other case, as a reference to the constable who applied for the DVPO.

(3) If the court has reason to suspect that a medical report will be required, the power to remand a person may be exercised for the purpose of enabling a medical examination to take place and a report to be made.

(4) If the person is remanded in custody for that purpose, the adjournment may not be for more than 3 weeks at a time.

(5) If the person is remanded on bail for that purpose, the adjournment may not be for more than 4 weeks at a time.

(6) If the court has reason to suspect that the person is suffering from a mental disorder within the meaning of the Mental Health Act 1983, the court has the same power to make an order under section 35 of that Act (remand to hospital for medical report) as it has under that section in the case of an accused person (within the meaning of that section).

(7) The court may, when remanding the person on bail, require the person to comply, before release on bail or later, with such requirements as appear to the court to be necessary to secure that the person does not interfere with witnesses or otherwise obstruct the course of justice.

31   Guidance

(1) The Secretary of State may from time to time issue guidance relating to the exercise by a constable of functions under sections 24 to 30.

(2) A constable must have regard to any guidance issued under subsection (1) when exercising a function to which the guidance relates.

(3) Before issuing guidance under this section, the Secretary of State must consult—

(a) the Association of Chief Police Officers, and

…

(c) such other persons as the Secretary of State thinks fit.

…

33   Pilot schemes

(1) The Secretary of State may by order made by statutory instrument provide for any provision of sections 24 to 32 to come into force for a period of time to be specified in or under the order for the purpose of assessing the effectiveness of the provision.

(2) Such an order may make different provision for different areas.

(3) More than one order may be made under this section.

(4) Provision included in an order under this section does not affect the provision that may be included in relation to sections 24 to 32 in an order under section 59 (commencement).

Legal Aid, Sentencing and Punishment of Offenders Act 2012

(2012 c. 10)

PART 1   LEGAL AID

...

Civil legal aid

8   Civil legal services

(1) In this Part 'legal services' means the following types of services—

    (a) providing advice as to how the law applies in particular circumstances,

    (b) providing advice and assistance in relation to legal proceedings,

    (c) providing other advice and assistance in relation to the prevention of disputes about legal rights or duties ('legal disputes') or the settlement or other resolution of legal disputes, and

    (d) providing advice and assistance in relation to the enforcement of decisions in legal proceedings or other decisions by which legal disputes are resolved.

(2) The services described in subsection (1) include, in particular, advice and assistance in the form of—

    (a) representation, and

    (b) mediation and other forms of dispute resolution.

(3) In this Part 'civil legal services' means any legal services other than the types of advice, assistance and representation that are required to be made available under sections 13, 15 and 16 (criminal legal aid).

9   General cases

(1) Civil legal services are to be available to an individual under this Part if—

    (a) they are civil legal services described in Part 1 of Schedule 1, and

    (b) the Director has determined that the individual qualifies for the services in accordance with this Part (and has not withdrawn the determination).

(2) The Lord Chancellor may by order—

    (a) add services to Part 1 of Schedule 1, or

    (b) vary or omit services described in that Part,

(whether by modifying that Part or Part 2, 3 or 4 of the Schedule).

10   Exceptional cases

(1)   Civil legal services other than services described in Part 1 of Schedule 1 are to be available to an individual under this Part if subsection (2) or (4) is satisfied.

(2)   This subsection is satisfied where the Director—

(a)   has made an exceptional case determination in relation to the individual and the services, and

(b)   has determined that the individual qualifies for the services in accordance with this Part, (and has not withdrawn either determination).

(3)   For the purposes of subsection (2), an exceptional case determination is a determination—

(a)   that it is necessary to make the services available to the individual under this Part because failure to do so would be a breach of—

(i)   the individual's Convention rights (within the meaning of the Human Rights Act 1998), or

(ii)   any rights of the individual to the provision of legal services that are enforceable EU rights, or

(b)   that it is appropriate to do so, in the particular circumstances of the case, having regard to any risk that failure to do so would be such a breach.

. . .

Contributions and costs

. . .

25   Charges on property in connection with civil legal services

(1)   Where civil legal services are made available to an individual under this Part, the amounts described in subsection (2) are to constitute a first charge on—

(a)   any property recovered or preserved by the individual in proceedings, or in any compromise or settlement of a dispute, in connection with which the services were provided (whether the property is recovered or preserved for the individual or another person), and

(b)   any costs payable to the individual by another person in connection with such proceedings or such a dispute.

(2)   Those amounts are—

(a)   amounts expended by the Lord Chancellor in securing the provision of the services (except to the extent that they are recovered by other means), and

(b)   other amounts payable by the individual in connection with the services under section 23 or 24.

(3)   Regulations may make provision for exceptions from subsection (1).

(4)   Regulations may make provision about the charge under subsection (1) including, in particular—

(a)   provision as to whether the charge is in favour of the Lord Chancellor or a person by whom the services were made available,

(b)   provision modifying the charge for the purposes of its application in prescribed cases or circumstances, and

(c)   provision about the enforcement of the charge.

(5)   Regulations under subsection 4(c) may, in particular, include—

(a)   provision requiring amounts recovered by the individual in proceedings or as part of a compromise or settlement of a dispute, and costs payable to the individual, to be paid to the Lord Chancellor or a person by whom the services were made available,

(b) provision about the time and manner in which the amounts must be paid,

(c) provision about what the Lord Chancellor or the person by whom the services were made available must do with the amounts,

(d) provision for the payment of interest on all or part of the amounts,

(e) provision for the payment to the individual concerned of any amount in excess of the amounts described in subsection (2), and

(f) provision for the enforcement of requirements described in paragraph (a).

(6) Regulations under this section may include provision requiring information and documents to be provided.

...

PART 2 LITIGATION FUNDING AND COSTS

...

Offers to settle

55 Payment of additional amount to successful claimant

(1) Rules of court may make provision for a court to order a defendant in civil proceedings to pay an additional amount to a claimant in those proceedings where—

(a) the claim is a claim for (and only for) an amount of money,

(b) judgment is given in favour of the claimant,

(c) the judgment in respect of the claim is at least as advantageous as an offer to settle the claim which the claimant made in accordance with rules of court and has not withdrawn in accordance with those rules, and

(d) any prescribed conditions are satisfied.

(2) Rules made under subsection (1) may include provision as to the assessment of whether a judgment is at least as advantageous as an offer to settle.

(3) In subsection (1) 'additional amount' means an amount not exceeding a prescribed percentage of the amount awarded to the claimant by the court (excluding any amount awarded in respect of the claimant's costs).

(4) The Lord Chancellor may by order provide that rules of court may make provision for a court to order a defendant in civil proceedings to pay an amount calculated in a prescribed manner to a claimant in those proceedings where—

(a) the claim is or includes a non-monetary claim,

(b) judgment is given in favour of the claimant,

(c) the judgment in respect of the claim is at least as advantageous as an offer to settle the claim which the claimant made in accordance with rules of court and has not withdrawn in accordance with those rules, and

(d) any prescribed conditions are satisfied.

(5) An order under subsection (4) must provide for the amount to be calculated by reference to one or more of the following—

(a) any costs ordered by the court to be paid to the claimant by the defendant in the proceedings;

(b) any amount awarded to the claimant by the court in respect of so much of the claim as is for an amount of money (excluding any amount awarded in respect of the claimant's costs);

(c) the value of any non-monetary benefit awarded to the claimant.

(6) An order under subsection (4)—

    (a) must provide that rules made under the order may include provision as to the assessment of whether a judgment is at least as advantageous as an offer to settle, and

    (b) may provide that such rules may make provision as to the calculation of the value of a non-monetary benefit awarded to a claimant.

(7) Conditions prescribed under subsection (1)(d) or (4)(d) may, in particular, include conditions relating to—

    (a) the nature of the claim;

    (b) the amount of money awarded to the claimant;

    (c) the value of the non-monetary benefit awarded to the claimant.

(8) Orders under this section are to be made by the Lord Chancellor by statutory instrument.

(9) A statutory instrument containing an order under this section is subject to annulment in pursuance of a resolution of either House of Parliament.

(10) Rules of court and orders made under this section may make different provision in relation to different cases.

(11) In this section—

'civil proceedings' means proceedings to which rules of court made under the Civil Procedure Act 1997 apply;

'non-monetary claim' means a claim for a benefit other than an amount of money;

'prescribed' means prescribed by order made by the Lord Chancellor.

Section 9

SCHEDULE 1

CIVIL LEGAL SERVICES

PART 1   SERVICES

Care, supervision and protection of children

1.—(1) Civil legal services provided in relation to—

    (a) orders under section 25 of the Children Act 1989 ('the 1989 Act') (secure accommodation);

    (b) orders under Part 4 of the 1989 Act (care and supervision);

    (c) orders under Part 5 of the 1989 Act (protection of children);

    (d) approval by a court under paragraph 19 of Schedule 2 to the 1989 Act (arrangements to assist children to live abroad);

    (e) parenting orders under section 8 of the Crime and Disorder Act 1998 ('the 1998 Act');

    (f) child safety orders under section 11 of the 1998 Act;

    (g) orders for contact under section 26 of the Adoption and Children Act 2002 ('the 2002 Act');

    (h) applications for leave of the court to remove a child from a person's custody under section 36 of the 2002 Act;

    (i) placement orders, recovery orders or adoption orders under Chapter 3 of Part 1 of the 2002 Act (see sections 21, 41 and 46 of that Act);

    (j) orders under section 84 of the 2002 Act (parental responsibility prior to adoption abroad).

(2) Civil legal services provided in relation to an order under an enactment made—
  (a) as an alternative to an order mentioned in sub-paragraph (1), or
  (b) in proceedings heard together with proceedings relating to such an order.

Exclusions

(3) Sub-paragraphs (1) and (2) are subject to the exclusions in Parts 2 and 3 of this Schedule.

Definitions

(4) In this paragraph 'children' means persons under the age of 18.
...

Community care

6.—(1) Civil legal services provided in relation to community care services.

Exclusions

(2) Sub-paragraph (1) is subject to the exclusions in Parts 2 and 3 of this Schedule.

Definitions

(3) In this paragraph—
'community care services' means services which a relevant person may provide or arrange to be provided under—
  ...
  (f) section 17 of the Children Act 1989 ('the 1989 Act') (provision of services for children in need);
  (g) section 20 of the 1989 Act (provision of accommodation for children);
  (h) sections 22A, 22B, 22C and 23 of the 1989 Act (accommodation and maintenance for children in care and looked after children);
  (i) sections 23B and 23C of the 1989 Act (local authority functions in respect of relevant children);
  (j) sections 24, 24A and 24B of the 1989 Act (provision of services for persons qualifying for advice and assistance);
  (k) section 2 of the Carers and Disabled Children Act 2000 (services for carers);
...
'relevant person' means—
  (a) a district council;
  (b) a county council;
  (c) a county borough council;
  (d) a London borough council;
  (e) the Common Council of the City of London;
  (f) a Primary Care Trust established under section 18 of the National Health Service Act 2006;
  (g) a Local Health Board established under section 11 of the National Health Service (Wales) Act 2006;
  (h) any other person prescribed for the purposes of this paragraph.
...

Inherent jurisdiction of High Court in relation to children and vulnerable adults

9.—(1) Civil legal services provided in relation to the inherent jurisdiction of the High Court in relation to children and vulnerable adults.

Exclusions

(2) Sub-paragraph (1) is subject to the exclusions in Parts 2 and 3 of this Schedule.

Definitions

(3) In this paragraph—

'adults' means persons aged 18 or over;

'children' means persons under the age of 18.

Unlawful removal of children

10.—(1) Civil legal services provided to an individual in relation to the following orders and requirements where the individual is seeking to prevent the unlawful removal of a related child from the United Kingdom or to secure the return of a related child who has been unlawfully removed from the United Kingdom—

    (a) a prohibited steps order or specific issue order (as defined in section 8(1) of the Children Act 1989);

    (b) an order under section 33 of the Family Law Act 1986 for disclosure of the child's whereabouts;

    (c) an order under section 34 of that Act for the child's return;

    (d) a requirement under section 37 of that Act to surrender a passport issued to, or containing particulars of, the child.

(2) Civil legal services provided to an individual in relation to the following orders and applications where the individual is seeking to secure the return of a related child who has been unlawfully removed to a place in the United Kingdom—

    (a) a prohibited steps order or specific issue order (as defined in section 8(1) of the Children Act 1989);

    (b) an application under section 27 of the Family Law Act 1986 for registration of an order relating to the child;

    (c) an order under section 33 of that Act for disclosure of the child's whereabouts;

    (d) an order under section 34 of that Act for the child's return.

Exclusions

(3) Sub-paragraphs (1) and (2) are subject to the exclusions in Parts 2 and 3 of this Schedule.

Definitions

(4) For the purposes of this paragraph, a child is related to an individual if the individual is the child's parent or has parental responsibility for the child.

(5) In this paragraph 'child' means a person under the age of 18.

Family homes and domestic violence

11.—(1) Civil legal services provided in relation to home rights, occupation orders and non-molestation orders under Part 4 of the Family Law Act 1996.

(2) Civil legal services provided in relation to the following in circumstances arising out of a family relationship—

    (a) an injunction following assault, battery or false imprisonment;

    (b) the inherent jurisdiction of the High Court to protect an adult.

Exclusions

(3) Sub-paragraphs (1) and (2) are subject to—

    (a) the exclusions in Part 2 of this Schedule, with the exception of paragraphs 3 and 11 of that Part, and

    (b) the exclusion in Part 3 of this Schedule.

Definitions

(4) For the purposes of this paragraph—

    (a) there is a family relationship between two people if they are associated with each other, and

    (b) 'associated' has the same meaning as in Part 4 of the Family Law Act 1996 (see section 62 of that Act).

(5) For the purposes of this paragraph, the Lord Chancellor may by regulations make provision about when circumstances arise out of a family relationship.

Victims of domestic violence and family matters

12.—(1) Civil legal services provided to an adult ('A') in relation to a matter arising out of a family relationship between A and another individual ('B') where—

    (a) there has been, or is a risk of, domestic violence between A and B, and

    (b) A was, or is at risk of being, the victim of that domestic violence.

General exclusions

(2) Sub-paragraph (1) is subject to the exclusions in Part 2 of this Schedule, with the exception of paragraph 11 of that Part.

(3) But the exclusions described in sub-paragraph (2) are subject to the exception in sub-paragraph (4).

(4) The services described in sub-paragraph (1) include services provided in relation to conveyancing, but only where—

    (a) the services in relation to conveyancing are provided in the course of giving effect to a court order made in proceedings, and

    (b) services described in that sub-paragraph (other than services in relation to conveyancing) are being or have been provided in relation to those proceedings under arrangements made for the purposes of this Part of this Act.

(5) Sub-paragraph (1) is subject to the exclusion in Part 3 of this Schedule.

Specific exclusion

(6) The services described in sub-paragraph (1) do not include services provided in relation to a claim in tort in respect of the domestic violence.

Definitions

(7) For the purposes of this paragraph—

    (a) there is a family relationship between two people if they are associated with each other, and

    (b) 'associated' has the same meaning as in Part 4 of the Family Law Act 1996 (see section 62 of that Act).

(8) For the purposes of this paragraph—

    (a) matters arising out of a family relationship include matters arising under a family enactment, and

    (b) (subject to paragraph (a)) the Lord Chancellor may by regulations make provision about when matters arise out of a family relationship.

(9) In this paragraph—

'adult' means a person aged 18 or over;

'domestic violence' means any incident of threatening behaviour, violence or abuse (whether psychological, physical, sexual, financial or emotional) between individuals who are associated with each other;

'family enactment' means—

    (a) section 17 of the Married Women's Property Act 1882 (questions between husband and wife as to property);

    (b) the Maintenance Orders (Facilities for Enforcement) Act 1920;

    (c) the Maintenance Orders Act 1950;

    (d) the Maintenance Orders Act 1958;

    (e) the Maintenance Orders (Reciprocal Enforcement) Act 1972;

    (f) Schedule 1 to the Domicile and Matrimonial Proceedings Act 1973 (staying of matrimonial proceedings) and corresponding provision in relation to civil partnerships made by rules of court under section 223 of the Civil Partnership Act 2004;

    (g) the Matrimonial Causes Act 1973;

    (h) the Inheritance (Provision for Family and Dependants) Act 1975;

    (i) the Domestic Proceedings and Magistrates' Courts Act 1978;

    (j) Part 3 of the Matrimonial and Family Proceedings Act 1984 (financial relief after overseas divorce etc);

    (k) Parts 1 and 3 of the Family Law Act 1986 (child custody and declarations of status);

    (l) Parts 1 and 2 of the Children Act 1989 (orders with respect to children in family proceedings);

    (m) section 53 of, and Schedule 7 to, the Family Law Act 1996 (transfer of tenancies on divorce etc or separation of cohabitants);

    (n) Chapters 2 and 3 of Part 2 of the Civil Partnership Act 2004 (dissolution, nullity and other proceedings and property and financial arrangements);

    (o) section 54 of the Human Fertilisation and Embryology Act 2008 (applications for parental orders).

    (p) section 51A of the Adoption and Children Act 2002 (post-adoption contact orders).

Protection of children and family matters

13.—(1) Civil legal services provided to an adult ('A') in relation to the following orders and procedures where the child who is or would be the subject of the order is at risk of abuse from an individual other than A—

    (a) orders under section 4(2A) of the Children Act 1989 ('the 1989 Act') (removal of father's parental responsibility);

    (b) orders under section 6(7) of the 1989 Act (termination of appointment of guardian);

    (c) orders mentioned in section 8(1) of the 1989 Act (child arrangements orders and other orders);

    (d) special guardianship orders under Part 2 of the 1989 Act;

    (e) orders under section 33 of the Family Law Act 1986 ('the 1986 Act') (disclosure of child's whereabouts);

    (f) orders under section 34 of the 1986 Act (return of child).

    (g) orders under section 51A of the Adoption and Children Act 2002 (post-adoption contact).

Exclusions

(2) Sub-paragraph (1) is subject to the exclusions in Parts 2 and 3 of this Schedule.

Definitions

(3) In this paragraph—

'abuse' means physical or mental abuse, including—

    (a) sexual abuse, and

    (b) abuse in the form of violence, neglect, maltreatment and exploitation;

'adult' means a person aged 18 or over;

'child' means a person under the age of 18.

Mediation in family disputes

14.—(1) Mediation provided in relation to family disputes.

(2) Civil legal services provided in connection with the mediation of family disputes.

Exclusions

(3) Sub-paragraphs (1) and (2) are subject to the exclusions in Part 2 of this Schedule, with the exception of paragraph 11 of that Part.

(4) But the exclusions described in sub-paragraph (3) are subject to the exception in sub-paragraph (5).

(5) The services described in sub-paragraph (2) include services provided in relation to conveyancing, but only where—

    (a) the services in relation to conveyancing are provided in the course of giving effect to arrangements for the resolution of a family dispute, and

    (b) services described in that sub-paragraph or sub-paragraph (1) (other than services in relation to conveyancing) are being or have been provided in relation to the dispute under arrangements made for the purposes of this Part of this Act.

(6) Sub-paragraphs (1) and (2) are subject to the exclusion in Part 3 of this Schedule.

Definitions

(7) For the purposes of this paragraph—

    (a) a dispute is a family dispute if it is a dispute between individuals about a matter arising out of a family relationship between the individuals,

    (b) there is a family relationship between two individuals if they are associated with each other, and

    (c) 'associated' has the same meaning as in Part 4 of the Family Law Act 1996 (see section 62 of that Act).

(8) For the purposes of this paragraph—

    (a) matters arising out of a family relationship include matters arising under a family enactment, and

    (b) (subject to paragraph (a)) the Lord Chancellor may by regulations make provision about when matters arise out of a family relationship.

(9) In this paragraph—

'child' means a person under the age of 18;

'family enactment' has the meaning given in paragraph 12.

Children who are parties to family proceedings

15.—(1) Civil legal services provided to a child in relation to family proceedings—
   (a) where the child is, or proposes to be, the applicant or respondent;
   (b) where the child is made a party to the proceedings by a court under rule 16.2 of the Family Procedure Rules;
   (c) where the child is a party to the proceedings and is conducting, or proposes to conduct, the proceedings without a children's guardian or litigation friend in accordance with rule 16.6 of the Family Procedure Rules.

Exclusions

(2) Sub-paragraph (1) is subject to the exclusions in Parts 2 and 3 of this Schedule.

Definitions

(3) For the purposes of this paragraph—
   (a) proceedings are family proceedings if they relate to a matter arising out of a family relationship,
   (b) there is a family relationship between two individuals if they are associated with each other, and
   (c) 'associated' has the same meaning as in Part 4 of the Family Law Act 1996 (see section 62 of that Act).

(4) For the purposes of this paragraph—
   (a) matters arising out of a family relationship include matters arising under a family enactment, and
   (b) (subject to paragraph (a)) the Lord Chancellor may by regulations make provision about when matters arise out of a family relationship.

(5) In this paragraph—
'child' means a person under the age of 18;
'family enactment' has the meaning given in paragraph 12.

Forced marriage

16.—(1) Civil legal services provided in relation to forced marriage protection orders under Part 4A of the Family Law Act 1996.

Exclusions

(2) Sub-paragraph (1) is subject to the exclusions in Parts 2 and 3 of this Schedule.
...

Loss of home

33.—(1) Civil legal services provided to an individual in relation to—
   (a) court orders for sale or possession of the individual's home, or
   (b) the eviction from the individual's home of the individual or others.

(2) Civil legal services provided to an individual in relation to a bankruptcy order against the individual under Part 9 of the Insolvency Act 1986 where—
   (a) the individual's estate includes the individual's home, and
   (b) the petition for the bankruptcy order is or was presented by a person other than the individual,
including services provided in relation to a statutory demand under that Part of that Act.

General exclusions

(3) Sub-paragraphs (1) and (2) are subject to the exclusions in Part 2 of this Schedule, with the exception of paragraph 14 of that Part.

(4) But the exclusions described in sub-paragraph (3) are subject to the exceptions in sub-paragraphs (5) and (6).

(5) The services described in sub-paragraph (1) include services provided in relation to proceedings on an application under the Trusts of Land and Appointment of Trustees Act 1996 to which section 335A of the Insolvency Act 1986 applies (application by trustee of bankrupt's estate).

(6) The services described in sub-paragraph (1) include services described in any of paragraphs 3 to 6 or 8 of Part 2 of this Schedule to the extent that they are—

  (a) services provided to an individual in relation to a counterclaim in proceedings for a court order for sale or possession of the individual's home, or

  (b) services provided to an individual in relation to the unlawful eviction from the individual's home of the individual or others.

(7) Sub-paragraphs (1) and (2) are subject to the exclusion in Part 3 of this Schedule.

Specific exclusion

(8) The services described in sub-paragraph (1) do not include services provided in relation to—

  (a) proceedings under the Matrimonial Causes Act 1973;

  (b) proceedings under Chapters 2 and 3 of Part 2 of the Civil Partnership Act 2004 (dissolution, nullity and other proceedings and property and financial arrangements).

Definitions

(9) In this paragraph 'home', in relation to an individual, means the house, caravan, houseboat or other vehicle or structure that is the individual's only or main residence, subject to sub-paragraph (10).

(10) References in this paragraph to an individual's home do not include a vehicle or structure occupied by the individual if—

  (a) there are no grounds on which it can be argued that the individual is occupying the vehicle or structure otherwise than as a trespasser, and

  (b) there are no grounds on which it can be argued that the individual's occupation of the vehicle or structure began otherwise than as a trespasser.

(11) In sub-paragraphs (9) and (10), the references to a caravan, houseboat or other vehicle include the land on which it is located or to which it is moored.

(12) For the purposes of sub-paragraph (10) individuals occupying, or beginning occupation, of a vehicle or structure as a trespasser include individuals who do so by virtue of—

  (a) title derived from a trespasser, or

  (b) a licence or consent given by a trespasser or a person deriving title from a trespasser.

(13) For the purposes of sub-paragraph (10) an individual who is occupying a vehicle or structure as a trespasser does not cease to be a trespasser by virtue of being allowed time to leave the vehicle or structure.

...

Presumption of Death Act 2013

(2013 c. 1)

Declaration of presumed death

1   Applying for declaration

(1) This section applies where a person who is missing—

    (a) is thought to have died, or

    (b) has not been known to be alive for a period of at least 7 years.

(2) Any person may apply to the High Court for a declaration that the missing person is presumed to be dead.

(3) The court has jurisdiction to hear and determine an application under this section only if—

    (a) the missing person was domiciled in England and Wales on the day on which he or she was last known to be alive,

    (b) the missing person had been habitually resident in England and Wales throughout the period of 1 year ending with that day, or

    (c) subsection (4) is satisfied.

(4) This subsection is satisfied if the application is made by the spouse or civil partner of the missing person and—

    (a) the applicant is domiciled in England and Wales on the day on which the application is made, or

    (b) the applicant has been habitually resident in England and Wales throughout the period of 1 year ending with that day.

(5) The court must refuse to hear an application under this section if—

    (a) the application is made by someone other than the missing person's spouse, civil partner, parent, child or sibling, and

    (b) the court considers that the applicant does not have a sufficient interest in the determination of the application.

(6) This section has effect subject to section 21(2).

2   Making declaration

(1) On an application under section 1, the court must make the declaration if it is satisfied that the missing person—

    (a) has died, or

    (b) has not been known to be alive for a period of at least 7 years.

(2) It must include in the declaration a finding as to the date and time of the missing person's death.

(3) Where the court—

    (a) is satisfied that the missing person has died, but

    (b) is uncertain at which moment during a period the missing person died,

the finding must be that the missing person is presumed to have died at the end of that period.

(4) Where the court—

    (a) is satisfied that the missing person has not been known to be alive for a period of at least 7 years, but

    (b) is not satisfied that the missing person has died,

the finding must be that the missing person is presumed to have died at the end of the period of 7 years beginning with the day after the day on which he or she was last known to be alive.

3   Effect of declaration

(1) A declaration under this Act is conclusive of—

    (a) the missing person's presumed death, and

    (b) the date and time of the death.

(2) A declaration under this Act is effective against all persons and for all purposes, including for the purposes of—

(a) the acquisition of an interest in any property, and

(b) the ending of a marriage or civil partnership to which the missing person is a party.

(3) But subsections (1) and (2) apply to a declaration only if—

(a) it has not been appealed against and the period for bringing an appeal has ended, or

(b) it has been appealed against and the appeal (and any further appeal) has been unsuccessful.

(4) For the purposes of subsection (3), an appeal has been unsuccessful if—

(a) it has been dismissed or withdrawn, and

(b) any period for bringing a further appeal has ended.

4   Other powers of court making declaration

(1) When making a declaration under this Act, the court may—

(a) determine any question which relates to an interest in property and arises as a result of the declaration, and

(b) determine the domicile of the missing person at the time of his or her presumed death.

(2) When making a declaration under this Act, the court may make such order as it considers reasonable in relation to any interest in property acquired as a result of the declaration.

(3) An order under subsection (2) may direct that the value of any interest in property acquired as a result of the declaration is not to be recoverable by virtue of an order made under section 7(2).

(4) It may, in particular, direct that the value of the interest—

(a) is not to be recoverable in any circumstances, or

(b) is not to be recoverable where conditions specified in the order are met.

Variation order

5   Varying and revoking declaration

(1) On an application by any person, a declaration under this Act may be varied or revoked by an order of the High Court (a 'variation order').

(2) The court must refuse to hear an application for a variation order if it considers that the applicant does not have a sufficient interest in the determination of the application.

6   Effect of variation order

(1) A variation order does not affect an interest in property acquired as a result of a declaration under this Act (but see section 7).

(2) A variation order does not revive a marriage or civil partnership that was brought to an end by virtue of a declaration under this Act.

(3) Except as otherwise required by subsection (1) or (2)—

(a) where a variation order varies a declaration, subsections (1) and (2) of section 3 have effect in relation to the declaration as varied by the order, and

(b) where a variation order revokes a declaration, those subsections cease to have effect in relation to the declaration.

(4) But subsection (3) applies only if—

(a) the variation order has not been appealed against and the period for bringing an appeal has ended, or

(b) the variation order has been appealed against and the appeal (and any further appeal) has been unsuccessful.

(5) For the purposes of subsection (4), an appeal has been unsuccessful if—

(a) it has been dismissed or withdrawn, and

(b) any period for bringing a further appeal has ended.

7   Other functions of court making variation order

(1) When making a variation order, the court may—

    (a) determine any question which relates to an interest in property and arises as a result of the variation order, and

    (b) determine the domicile of the missing person at the time of his or her presumed death.

(2) When making a variation order, the court must make such further order (if any) as it considers reasonable in relation to any interest in property acquired as a result of the declaration varied or revoked by the order ('the original declaration') (but see subsections (3), (5) and (6)).

(3) The court must not make an order under subsection (2) if the application for the variation order was made after the end of the period of 5 years beginning with the day on which the original declaration was made, unless it considers that there are exceptional circumstances which make it appropriate to do so.

(4) In considering what order to make under subsection (2), the court must, as far as practicable, have regard to the principles in section 8.

(5) An order under subsection (2) does not affect income that accrued in the period—

    (a) beginning with the day on which the original declaration was made, and

    (b) ending with the day on which the variation order was made.

(6) An order under subsection (2) does not affect or provide grounds to challenge—

    (a) a related good faith transaction, or

    (b) an interest in property acquired under such a transaction.

(7) A 'related good faith transaction' is a transaction under which a person acquires an interest in the property that is the subject of the order (or any part of it) in good faith and for value from—

    (a) a person who acquired an interest in the property (or any part of it) as a result of the original declaration, or

    (b) a person who acquired an interest in the property (or any part of it) from a person described in paragraph (a), whether directly or indirectly.

(8) Where a person has entitlement under a trust by virtue of an order under subsection (2), the trustee is liable to that person for any loss suffered by that person on account of any breach of trust by the trustee in the administration or distribution of all or part of the property that is the subject of the order.

(9) Subsection (8) does not apply to the extent that the trustee's liability is restricted under any enactment or by any provision in a deed regulating the administration of the trust.

(10) In subsection (9) 'enactment' includes an enactment contained in—

    (a) an instrument made under an Act, or

    (b) an Act or Measure of the National Assembly for Wales or an instrument made under such an Act or Measure.

8   Principles

(1) These are the principles referred to in section 7(4).

(2) The first principle is relevant where property ('the relevant property') is being or has been administered under a trust.

(3) The first principle is that—

    (a) a person who, but for section 6(1), would have an interest in the relevant property by virtue of a variation order, and

    (b) a person who, but for section 6(1), would have acquired an interest in the relevant property from a person described in paragraph (a),

should be entitled to have made over to him or her by the trustee in full satisfaction of that interest the things listed in subsection (4).

(4) Those things are—

    (a) the interest in the relevant property or an equivalent interest in property representing the relevant property, to the extent that such property is still in the hands of the trustee when the variation order is made, and

(b) the value of the interest in the relevant property, to the extent that such property has been distributed.

(5) The second principle is relevant where an insurer has paid a capital sum as a result of a declaration varied or revoked by a variation order.

(6) The second principle is that the capital sum, or any part of the capital sum, should be repaid to the insurer if the facts in respect of which the variation order was made justify such repayment.

(7) The references in subsections (5) and (6) to a capital sum do not include a capital sum distributed by way of an annuity or other periodical payment.

Further provision about declarations and orders

9 Giving notice of application

(1) A person who makes an application under this Act for a declaration or a variation order must send to the persons specified by rules of court—

(a) notice of the application, and

(b) any other information specified by rules of court.

(2) An application under this Act for a declaration or a variation order must be advertised in accordance with rules of court.

(3) The court must refuse to hear an application under this Act for a declaration or a variation order if the requirements in this section have not been met.

10 Attorney General

(1) In proceedings on an application under this Act for a declaration or a variation order, the court may at any stage direct that papers relating to the matter be sent to the Attorney General.

(2) It may do so on the application of a party to the proceedings or without such an application being made.

(3) Where the Attorney General incurs costs in connection with an application under this Act for a declaration or a variation order, the court may make such order as it considers appropriate as to the payment of the costs by parties to the proceedings.

(4) Subsection (3) applies whether the costs are incurred by virtue of a direction under subsection (1), an intervention under section 11(2) or otherwise.

11 Right to intervene

(1) The missing person's spouse, civil partner, parent, child or sibling may intervene in proceedings on an application under this Act for a declaration or a variation order.

(2) The Attorney General may intervene in such proceedings, whether or not the court directs papers relating to the application to be sent to the Attorney General.

(3) Any other person may intervene in such proceedings only with the permission of the court.

(4) References in this section to intervening in proceedings include—

(a) arguing before the court any question in relation to the application which the court considers it necessary to have fully argued,

(b) in proceedings on an application for a declaration under this Act, seeking a determination or order under section 4, and

(c) in proceedings on an application for a variation order, seeking a determination or order under section 7.

12 Information

(1) In proceedings on an application under this Act for a declaration or a variation order, the court may by order at any stage require a person who is not a party to the proceedings to provide it with specified information that it considers relevant to the question of whether the missing person is alive or dead.

(2) It may do so only where it considers it necessary for the purpose of disposing of the proceedings.

(3) It may do so on the application of a party to the proceedings or without such an application being made.

(4) The order may not require the provision of information—

    (a) which is permitted or required by any rule of law to be withheld on grounds of public interest immunity,

    (b) which any person would be entitled to refuse to provide on grounds of legal professional privilege, or

    (c) whose provision might incriminate the person providing it, or that person's spouse or civil partner, of an offence.

(5) Before making an order under this section, the court must send notice of its intention to make the order to any person who, in its opinion, is likely to be affected by the order.

(6) The court may discharge or vary an order made under this section on an application made by any person who, in the opinion of the court, is affected by it.

(7) In this section 'specified' means specified in an order under this section.

13 Insurance against claims: trustees

(1) If the court so directs, the trustee of a trust affected by a declaration under this Act must as soon as reasonably practicable take out an insurance policy in respect of any claim which may arise by virtue of an order under section 7(2).

(2) For the purposes of this section, a trust is affected by a declaration under this Act if—

    (a) it arises as a result of the declaration, or

    (b) property held under the trust is affected by the declaration.

(3) A premium payable by the trustee in accordance with a direction under this section may be paid out of money or other property held under the trust.

14 Insurance against claims: insurers paying capital sums

(1) Before paying a capital sum to a person as a result of a declaration under this Act, an insurer may require the person to take out an insurance policy in respect of any claim which the insurer may make in the event of a variation order being made.

(2) The policy must be taken out—

    (a) in the person's own name, and

    (b) for the benefit of the insurer.

(3) Subsection (1) does not apply where the sum is paid in respect of an annuity or other periodical payment.

(4) In this section 'insurer' means any person who provides for the payment of a benefit on a person's death.

Register of Presumed Deaths

15 Register of Presumed Deaths

(1) The Registrar General must maintain a register which is to be called the Register of Presumed Deaths.

(2) The register must be maintained in the General Register Office.

(3) The register may be maintained in any form the Registrar General considers appropriate.

(4) Schedule 1 (further provision about Register of Presumed Deaths) has effect.

Other determinations

16 Other determinations about death of missing person

(1) No declaration which may be applied for under section 1 may be made otherwise than under this Act.

(2) Where a court or tribunal makes a declaration that a missing person is presumed to be dead (other than on an application under this Act), subsections (2) to (4) of section 2 apply to the court or tribunal as they apply to the High Court when it makes a declaration under this Act.

(3) Schedule 2 (amendment of provisions about presumption of death) has effect.

(4) Apart from subsections (1) to (3) and Schedule 2, nothing in the preceding provisions of this Act affects any power or duty that a court or tribunal has other than under this Act to determine a question relating to the death of a missing person.

20 Interpretation

(1) In this Act—

'the court' means the High Court (except in section 16(2));

'interest in property' means an interest in property of any description, including an estate in land and a right over property;

'the missing person', in relation to a declaration under this Act or an application, determination or order made in connection with such a declaration, means the person who is or would be the subject of the declaration;

'the Registrar General' means the Registrar General for England and Wales;

'sibling' means a sibling of the full blood or the half blood;

'trustee' includes an executor, administrator or personal representative;

'variation order' has the meaning given in section 5.

(2) References in this Act to a party to proceedings include a person intervening in the proceedings in accordance with section 11.

SCHEDULE 1 REGISTER OF PRESUMED DEATHS

Entries in Register of Presumed Deaths

1.—(1) When a declaration under this Act satisfies section 3(3)(a) or (b), the court must send to the Registrar General—

(a) a copy of the declaration, and

(b) any prescribed information.

(2) On receipt of a copy of a declaration in accordance with sub-paragraph (1), the Registrar General must—

(a) make an entry in the Register of Presumed Deaths containing the name of the missing person and such other information as may be prescribed in relation to that person's presumed death,

(b) secure that the entry made in the Register of Presumed Deaths is included in the Index of the registers of deaths, and

(c) make traceable the connection between the entry in the Register of Presumed Deaths and the index of the registers of deaths.

(3) In this paragraph 'prescribed' means prescribed by regulations made by the Registrar General with the approval of the Secretary of State.

Amendment and cancellation of entries in Register

2.—(1) When a variation order satisfies section 6(4)(a) or (b), the court must send to the Registrar General—

(a) a copy of the order, and

(b) any prescribed information.

(2) Where the variation order varies a declaration, on receipt of a copy of the order in accordance with sub-paragraph (1), the Registrar General must—

(a) amend the entry in the Register of Presumed Deaths in relation to the missing person, and

(b) amend any entry relating to that person made in the index of the registers of deaths in accordance with paragraph 1(2)(b).

(3) Where the variation order revokes a declaration, on receipt of a copy of the order in accordance with sub-paragraph (1), the Registrar General must—

(a) cancel the entry in the Register of Presumed Deaths relating to the missing person, and

(b) cancel any entry relating to that person made in the index of the registers of deaths in accordance with paragraph 1(2)(b).

(4) In this paragraph 'prescribed' means prescribed by regulations made by the Registrar General with the approval of the Secretary of State.

Searches and certified copies

3.—(1) Any right to search the index of the registers of deaths includes the right to search entries included in it in accordance with paragraph 1(2)(b).

(2) Any person is entitled to have a certified copy of an entry in the Register of Presumed Deaths (but see paragraph 6).

(3) The Registrar General must cause a certified copy of an entry in the Register of Presumed Deaths to be sealed or stamped with the seal of the General Register Office.

(4) No certified copy of an entry in the Register of Presumed Deaths is to be of any force or effect unless it is sealed or stamped in accordance with sub-paragraph (3).

(5) Section 34(5) of the Births and Deaths Registration Act 1953 (certified copy on form different from original entry deemed to be true copy) applies in relation to a copy of an entry in the Register of Presumed Deaths as it applies in relation to a copy of an entry in a register made under that Act.

Proof of death

4.—A certified copy of an entry in the Register of Presumed Deaths in relation to a person is to be received as evidence of the person's death, without further or other proof, if it purports to be sealed or stamped in accordance with paragraph 3(3).

Correction and annotation of Register

5.—(1) Where it appears to the Registrar General that there is a clerical error in the Register of Presumed Deaths, the Registrar General may authorise a person to correct the error.

(2) Where it appears to the court that there is an error in the Register of Presumed Deaths, the court may direct the Registrar General to secure that the error is corrected.

(3) The Registrar General may annotate, or cancel the annotation of, any entry in the Register of Presumed Deaths.

(4) Sub-paragraph (5) applies where it appears to the Registrar General that the death of a missing person to whom an entry in the Register of Presumed Deaths relates—

(a) has been registered in a register of deaths made under the Births and Deaths Registration Act 1953, or

(b) has been recorded in a register kept or maintained under the law of a country or territory outside England and Wales corresponding in nature to a register described in paragraph (a).

(5) The Registrar General must annotate the relevant entry in the Register of Presumed Deaths accordingly.

Fees

6.—(1) A fee of a prescribed amount is payable to the Registrar General for a certified copy of an entry in the Register of Presumed Deaths.

(2) The Registrar General may refuse to provide such a copy until the prescribed fee is paid, except as otherwise prescribed.

(3) In this paragraph 'prescribed' means prescribed by regulations made by the Secretary of State.

Interpretation

7.—In this Schedule 'the index of registers of deaths' means the index kept in the General Register Office of certified copies of entries in the registers of deaths made under the Births and Deaths Registration Act 1953.

Marriage (Same Sex Couples) Act 2013

(2013 c. 30)

PART 1 MARRIAGE OF SAME SEX COUPLES IN ENGLAND AND WALES

Extension of marriage

1 Extension of marriage to same sex couples

(1) Marriage of same sex couples is lawful.

(2) The marriage of a same sex couple may only be solemnized in accordance with—

(a) Part 3 of the Marriage Act 1949,

(b) Part 5 of the Marriage Act 1949,

(c) the Marriage (Registrar General's Licence) Act 1970, or

(d) an Order in Council made under Part 1 or 3 of Schedule 6.

(3) No Canon of the Church of England is contrary to section 3 of the Submission of the Clergy Act 1533 (which provides that no Canons shall be contrary to the Royal Prerogative or the customs, laws or statutes of this realm) by virtue of its making provision about marriage being the union of one man with one woman.

(4) Any duty of a member of the clergy to solemnize marriages (and any corresponding right of persons to have their marriages solemnized by members of the clergy) is not extended by this Act to marriages of same sex couples.

(5) A 'member of the clergy' is—

(a) a clerk in Holy Orders of the Church of England, or

(b) a clerk in Holy Orders of the Church in Wales.

Religious protection

2 Marriage according to religious rites: no compulsion to solemnize etc

(1) A person may not be compelled by any means (including by the enforcement of a contract or a statutory or other legal requirement) to—

(a) undertake an opt-in activity, or

(b) refrain from undertaking an opt-out activity.

(2) A person may not be compelled by any means (including by the enforcement of a contract or a statutory or other legal requirement)—

(a) to conduct a relevant marriage,

(b) to be present at, carry out, or otherwise participate in, a relevant marriage, or

(c) to consent to a relevant marriage being conducted,

where the reason for the person not doing that thing is that the relevant marriage concerns a same sex couple.

(3) In this section—

'opt-in activity' means an activity of the kind specified in an entry in the first column of the following table which falls to be undertaken for the purposes of any enactment specified in the corresponding entry in the second column;

'opt-out activity' means an activity which reverses, or otherwise modifies, the effect of an opt-in activity.

Activity	Enactment
Giving consent	— Any of these provisions of the 1949 Act: (a) section 26A(3); (b) section 26B(2), (4) or (6); (c) section 44A(6); (d) section 46(1C) — Regulations under section 70A(5) of the 1949 Act (as mentioned in section 70A(6)(c) of that Act) relating to an application for registration — Section 1(3) of the Marriage (Registrar General's Licence) Act 1970 — An armed forces overseas marriage Order in its application to marriages of same sex couples (as mentioned in paragraph 9(5) of Schedule 6)
Applying for the registration of a building	Section 43A of the 1949 Act
Authorising a person to be present at the solemnization of marriages of same sex couples in a building registered under section 43A of the 1949 Act	Section 43B of the 1949 Act
Being authorised to be present at the solemnization of marriages of same sex couples in a building registered under section 43A of the 1949 Act	Section 43B of the 1949 Act
Giving a certificate, giving a copy of a consent, or certifying any matter	Any of these provisions of the 1949 Act: (a) section 43A(3); (b) section 43B(2); (c) section 44A(7)

(4) In this section—

'1949 Act' means the Marriage Act 1949;

'armed forces overseas marriage Order' means an Order in Council under Part 3 of Schedule 6;

'person'—

    (a) includes a religious organisation;

    (b) does not include a registrar, a superintendent registrar or the Registrar General;

'relevant marriage' means—

    (a) a marriage of a same sex couple solemnized in accordance with—

        (i) section 26A or 26B of the 1949 Act (marriage in a place of worship or in another place according to religious rites or usages),

        (ii) Part 5 of the 1949 Act (marriage in a naval, military or air force chapel),

        (iii) section 1 of the Marriage (Registrar General's Licence) Act 1970 (deathbed marriage), where the marriage is according to religious rites or usages, or

        (iv) an armed forces overseas marriage Order, where the marriage is according to religious rites or usages,

    including any ceremony forming part of, or connected with, the solemnization of such a marriage; and

    (b) a marriage ceremony read or celebrated in accordance with section 46 of the 1949 Act in respect of a same sex couple (religious ceremony after registrar's marriage of same sex couple);

and a reference to conducting a relevant marriage is to be read accordingly.

    ...

The Church in Wales

8   Power to allow for marriage of same sex couples in Church in Wales

(1) This section applies if the Lord Chancellor is satisfied that the Governing Body of the Church in Wales has resolved that the law of England and Wales should be changed to allow for the marriage of same sex couples according to the rites of the Church in Wales.

(2) The Lord Chancellor must, by order, make such provision as the Lord Chancellor considers appropriate to allow for the marriage of same sex couples according to the rites of the Church in Wales.

(3) The provision that may be made by an order under this section includes provision amending England and Wales legislation.

(4) In making an order under this section, the Lord Chancellor must have regard to the terms of the resolution of the Governing Body mentioned in subsection (1).

(5) If it appears to the Lord Chancellor—

    (a) that a reference in this section to the Governing Body has ceased to be appropriate by reason of a change in the governance arrangements of the Church in Wales, the reference has effect as a reference to such person or persons as the Lord Chancellor thinks appropriate; or

    (b) that a reference in this section to a resolution has ceased to be appropriate for that reason, the reference has effect as a reference to such decision or decisions as the Lord Chancellor thinks appropriate.

...

Other provisions relating to marriages of same sex couples

9   Conversion of civil partnership into marriage

(1) The parties to an England and Wales civil partnership may convert their civil partnership into a marriage under a procedure established by regulations made by the Secretary of State.

(2) The parties to a civil partnership within subsection (3) may convert their civil partnership into a marriage under a procedure established by regulations made by the Secretary of State.

(3) A civil partnership is within this subsection if—

    (a) it was formed outside the United Kingdom under an Order in Council made under Chapter 1 of Part 5 of the Civil Partnership Act 2004 (registration at British consulates etc or by armed forces personnel), and

    (b) the part of the United Kingdom that was relevant for the purposes of section 210(2)(b) or (as the case may be) section 211(2)(b) of that Act was England and Wales.

(4) Regulations under this section may in particular make—

    (a) provision about the making by the parties to a civil partnership of an application to convert their civil partnership into a marriage;

    (b) provision about the information to be provided in support of an application to convert;

    (c) provision about the making of declarations in support of an application to convert;

    (d) provision for persons who have made an application to convert to appear before any person or attend at any place;

    (e) provision conferring functions in connection with applications to convert on relevant officials, relevant armed forces personnel, the Secretary of State, or any other persons;

    (f) provision for fees, of such amounts as are specified in or determined in accordance with the regulations, to be payable in respect of—

        (i)   the making of an application to convert;

        (ii) the exercise of any function conferred by virtue of paragraph (e).

(5) Functions conferred by virtue of paragraph (e) of subsection (4) may include functions relating to—

    (a) the recording of information on the conversion of civil partnerships;

    (b) the issuing of certified copies of any information recorded;

      (c) the conducting of services or ceremonies (other than religious services or ceremonies) following the conversion of a civil partnership.

(6) Where a civil partnership is converted into a marriage under this section—

      (a) the civil partnership ends on the conversion, and

      (b) the resulting marriage is to be treated as having subsisted since the date the civil partnership was formed.

(7) In this section—

'England and Wales civil partnership' means a civil partnership which is formed by two people registering as civil partners of each other in England or Wales (see Part 2 of the Civil Partnership Act 2004);

'relevant armed forces personnel' means—

      (a) a member of Her Majesty's forces;

      (b) a civilian subject to service discipline (within the meaning of the Armed Forces Act 2006);

and for this purpose 'Her Majesty's forces' has the same meaning as in the Armed Forces Act 2006;

'relevant official' means—

      (a) the Registrar General;

      (b) a superintendent registrar;

      (c) a registrar;

      (d) a consular officer in the service of Her Majesty's government in the United Kingdom;

      (e) a person authorised by the Secretary of State in respect of the solemnization of marriages or formation of civil partnerships in a country or territory in which Her Majesty's government in the United Kingdom has for the time being no consular representative.

10 Extra-territorial matters

(1) A marriage under—

      (a) the law of any part of the United Kingdom (other than England and Wales), or

      (b) the law of any country or territory outside the United Kingdom,

is not prevented from being recognised under the law of England and Wales only because it is the marriage of a same sex couple.

(2) For the purposes of this section it is irrelevant whether the law of a particular part of the United Kingdom, or a particular country or territory outside the United Kingdom—

      (a) already provides for marriage of same sex couples at the time when this section comes into force, or

      (b) provides for marriage of same sex couples from a later time.

…

Effect of extension of marriage

11 Effect of extension of marriage

(1) In the law of England and Wales, marriage has the same effect in relation to same sex couples as it has in relation to opposite sex couples.

(2) The law of England and Wales (including all England and Wales legislation whenever passed or made) has effect in accordance with subsection (1).

(3) Schedule 3 (interpretation of legislation) has effect.

(4) Schedule 4 (effect of extension of marriage: further provision) has effect.

(5) For provision about limitations on the effects of subsections (1) and (2) and Schedule 3, see Part 7 of Schedule 4.

(6) Subsections (1) and (2) and Schedule 3 do not have any effect in relation to—

      (a) Measures and Canons of the Church of England (whenever passed or made),

      (b) subordinate legislation (whenever made) made under a Measure or Canon of the Church of England, or

    (c) other ecclesiastical law (whether or not contained in England and Wales legislation, and, if contained in England and Wales legislation, whenever passed or made).

(7) In Schedules 3 and 4—

'existing England and Wales legislation' means—

    (a) in the case of England and Wales legislation that is primary legislation, legislation passed before the end of the Session in which this Act is passed (excluding this Act), or

    (b) in the case of England and Wales legislation that is subordinate legislation, legislation made on or before the day on which this Act is passed (excluding legislation made under this Act);

'new England and Wales legislation' means—

    (a) in the case of England and Wales legislation that is primary legislation, legislation passed after the end of the Session in which this Act is passed, or

    (b) in the case of England and Wales legislation that is subordinate legislation, legislation made after the day on which this Act is passed.

PART 2   OTHER PROVISIONS RELATING TO MARRIAGE AND CIVIL PARTNERSHIP

12   Change of gender of married persons or civil partners

Schedule 5 (change of gender of married persons or civil partners) has effect.

13   Marriage overseas

(1) Schedule 6 (marriage overseas) has effect.

(2) The Foreign Marriage Act 1892 is repealed.

14   Marriage according to the usages of belief organisations

(1) The Secretary of State must arrange for a review of—

    (a) whether an order under subsection (4) should be made permitting marriages according to the usages of belief organisations to be solemnized on the authority of certificates of a superintendent registrar, and

    (b) if so, what provision should be included in the order.

(2) The arrangements made by the Secretary of State under subsection (1) must provide for the review to include a full public consultation.

(3) The Secretary of State must arrange for a report on the outcome of the review to be produced and published before 1 January 2015.

(4) The Secretary of State may by order make provision for and in connection with permitting marriages according to the usages of belief organisations to be solemnized on the authority of certificates of a superintendent registrar.

(5) An order under subsection (4) may—

    (a) amend any England and Wales legislation;

    (b) make provision for the charging of fees.

(6) An order under subsection (4) must provide that no religious service may be used at a marriage which is solemnized in pursuance of the order.

(7) In this section 'belief organisation' means an organisation whose principal or sole purpose is the advancement of a system of non-religious beliefs which relate to morality or ethics.

15   Review of civil partnership

(1) The Secretary of State must arrange—

    (a) for the operation and future of the Civil Partnership Act 2004 in England and Wales to be reviewed, and

    (b) for a report on the outcome of the review to be produced and published.

(2) Subsection (1) does not prevent the review from also dealing with other matters relating to civil partnership.

(3) The arrangements made by the Secretary of State must provide for the review to begin as soon as practicable and include a full public consultation.

...

Section 10

SCHEDULE 2

EXTRA-TERRITORIAL MATTERS

PART 1 ENGLISH AND WELSH MARRIAGES OF SAME SEX COUPLES: TREATMENT IN SCOTLAND AND NORTHERN IRELAND

Scotland

1.—(1) The Secretary of State may, by order, provide that, under the law of Scotland, a marriage of a same sex couple under the law of England and Wales is to be treated as a civil partnership formed under the law of England and Wales (and that, accordingly, the spouses are to be treated as civil partners).

(2) The Secretary of State may by order—

(a) provide for the treatment of a marriage as a civil partnership (by virtue of an order under sub-paragraph (1)) to have effect subject to provision made by the order;

(b) specify cases in which a marriage is not to be treated as a civil partnership by virtue of an order under sub-paragraph (1).

(3) The power conferred by sub-paragraph (1) may only be exercised if marriage of same sex couples is not lawful under the law of Scotland.

(4) If marriage of same sex couples becomes lawful under the law of Scotland, that does not—

(a) affect the validity of any order made under this paragraph; or

(b) prevent the revocation of any such order (with or without transitional, transitory or saving provision being made) using the powers conferred by this paragraph.

Northern Ireland

2.—(1) Under the law of Northern Ireland, a marriage of a same sex couple under the law of England and Wales is to be treated as a civil partnership formed under the law of England and Wales (and accordingly, the spouses are to be treated as civil partners).

(2) The Secretary of State may by order—

(a) provide for the treatment of a marriage as a civil partnership (by virtue of sub-paragraph (1)) to have effect subject to provision made by the order;

(b) specify cases in which a marriage is not to be treated as a civil partnership by virtue of sub-paragraph (1).

...

PART 2 MARRIAGE TREATED AS CIVIL PARTNERSHIP: DISSOLUTION, ANNULMENT OR SEPARATION

Order made in relation to civil partnership: validity in relation to marriage

4.—(1) This paragraph applies in a case where a marriage of a same sex couple under the law of England and Wales is—

(a) by virtue of an order under paragraph 1, treated under the law of Scotland as a civil partnership, or

(b) by virtue of paragraph 2, treated under the law of Northern Ireland as a civil partnership.

(2) If—

    (a) a final order is made in relation to the deemed civil partnership, and

    (b) the validity of that order is recognised throughout the United Kingdom,

that order has, throughout the United Kingdom, the same effect in relation to the actual marriage that it has in relation to the deemed civil partnership.

(3) If—

    (a) a separation order is made in relation to the relevant couple as parties to the deemed civil partnership, and

    (b) the validity of that order is recognised throughout the United Kingdom,

that order has, throughout the United Kingdom, the same effect in relation to the couple as parties to the actual marriage that it has in relation to them as parties to the deemed civil partnership (and has effect in relation to any other persons accordingly).

(4) In this paragraph—

'actual marriage' means the marriage of the same sex couple under the law of England and Wales;

'deemed civil partnership' means the civil partnership which the actual marriage is treated as being;

'final order' means—

    (a) the dissolution or annulment of a civil partnership obtained from a court of civil jurisdiction in any part of the United Kingdom;

    (b) an overseas dissolution or annulment;

'relevant couple' means the same sex couple who are parties to the actual marriage;

'separation order' means—

    (a) a legal separation of the parties to a civil partnership obtained from a court of civil jurisdiction in any part of the United Kingdom;

    (b) an overseas legal separation of the parties to a civil partnership.

…

Section 11

SCHEDULE 3

INTERPRETATION OF LEGISLATION

PART 1 EXISTING ENGLAND AND WALES LEGISLATION

Interpretation of existing England and Wales legislation

1.—(1) In existing England and Wales legislation—

    (a) a reference to marriage is to be read as including a reference to marriage of a same sex couple;

    (b) a reference to a married couple is to be read as including a reference to a married same sex couple; and

    (c) a reference to a person who is married is to be read as including a reference to a person who is married to a person of the same sex.

(2) Where sub-paragraph (1) requires a reference to be read in a particular way, any related reference (such as a reference to a marriage that has ended, or a reference to a person whose marriage has ended) is to be read accordingly.

(3) For the purposes of sub-paragraphs (1) and (2) it does not matter how a reference is expressed.

Interpretation of legislation about couples living together as if married

2.—(1) In existing England and Wales legislation—

    (a) a reference to persons who are not married but are living together as a married couple is to be read as including a reference to a same sex couple who are not married but are living together as a married couple;

(b) a reference to a person who is living with another person as if they were married is to be read as including a reference to a person who is living with another person of the same sex as if they were married.

(2) Where sub-paragraph (1) requires a reference to be read in a particular way, any related reference (such as a reference to persons formerly living together as a married couple) is to be read accordingly.

(3) For the purposes of sub-paragraphs (1) and (2) it does not matter how a reference is expressed.

3.—(1) This paragraph applies to existing England and Wales legislation which deals differently with—

(a) a man and a woman living together as if married, and

(b) two men, or two women, living together as if civil partners.

(2) If two men, or two women, are living together as if married, that legislation applies to them in the way that it would apply to them if they were living together as civil partners.

General

4.—This Part of this Schedule does not limit section 11(1) or (2).

PART 2 NEW ENGLAND AND WALES LEGISLATION

5.—(1) This paragraph applies to provision made by—

(a) this Act and any subordinate legislation made under it, or

(b) new England and Wales legislation,

including any such provision which amends existing England and Wales legislation.

(2) The following expressions have the meanings given—

(a) 'husband' includes a man who is married to another man;

(b) 'wife' includes a woman who is married to another woman;

(c) 'widower' includes a man whose marriage to another man ended with the other man's death;

(d) 'widow' includes a woman whose marriage to another woman ended with the other woman's death;

and related expressions are to be construed accordingly.

(3) A reference to marriage of same sex couples is a reference to—

(a) marriage between two men, and

(b) marriage between two women.

(4) A reference to a marriage of a same sex couple is a reference to—

(a) a marriage between two men, or

(b) a marriage between two women.

(5) A reference to a same sex couple who are not married but are living together as a married couple is a reference to—

(a) two men who are not married but are living together as a married couple, or

(b) two women who are not married but are living together as a married couple.

(6) This Part of this Schedule does not limit section 11(1) or (2).

Section 11

SCHEDULE 4

EFFECT OF EXTENSION OF MARRIAGE: FURTHER PROVISION

PART 1 PRIVATE LEGAL INSTRUMENTS

Existing instruments

1.—(1) Section 11 does not alter the effect of any private legal instrument made before that section comes into force.

(2) In this paragraph 'private legal instrument' includes—
   (a) a will,
   (b) an instrument (including a private Act) which settles property,
   (c) an instrument (including a private Act) which provides for the use, disposal or devolution of property, and
   (d) an instrument (including a private Act) which—
      (i) establishes a body, or
      (ii) regulates the purposes and administration of a body,
      (whether the body is incorporated or not and whether it is charitable or not);
but (with the exception of the kinds of private Act mentioned above) it does not include England and Wales legislation.

PART 2 PRESUMPTION ON BIRTH OF CHILD TO MARRIED WOMAN

Common law presumption

2.—(1) Section 11 does not extend the common law presumption that a child born to a woman during her marriage is also the child of her husband.

(2) Accordingly, where a child is born to a woman during her marriage to another woman, that presumption is of no relevance to the question of who the child's parents are.

...

PART 7 PROVISIONS WHICH LIMIT EQUIVALENCE OF ALL MARRIAGES ETC

Contrary provision

27.—(1) The relevant enactments are subject to—
   (a) the preceding provisions of this Schedule, and
   (b) any order under sub-paragraph (3).
(2) The relevant enactments are subject to any other contrary provision made by—
   (a) the other provisions of this Act,
   (b) any other subordinate legislation made under this Act, and
   (c) any new England and Wales legislation,
including any such contrary provision contained in amendments of existing England and Wales legislation.
(3) The Secretary of State may by order—
   (a) provide that a relevant enactment has effect subject to provision made by the order, or
   (b) specify cases in which a relevant enactment does not apply.
(4) In this paragraph 'relevant enactment' means—
   (a) section 11(1) and (2) and Schedule 3 (equivalence of all marriages in law), or
   (b) section 9(6)(b) (marriage arising from conversion of civil partnership treated as having subsisted from formation of civil partnership).

...

Children and Families Act 2014

(2014 c. 6)

...

PART 2 FAMILY JUSTICE

10 Family mediation information and assessment meetings

(1) Before making a relevant family application, a person must attend a family mediation information and assessment meeting.

(2) Family Procedure Rules—

(a) may provide for subsection (1) not to apply in circumstances specified in the Rules,

(b) may make provision about convening a family mediation information and assessment meeting, or about the conduct of such a meeting,

(c) may make provision for the court not to issue, or otherwise deal with, an application if, in contravention of subsection (1), the applicant has not attended a family mediation information and assessment meeting, and

(d) may provide for a determination as to whether an applicant has contravened subsection (1) to be made after considering only evidence of a description specified in the Rules.

(3) In this section—

'the court' means the High Court or the family court;

'family mediation information and assessment meeting', in relation to a relevant family application, means a meeting held for the purpose of enabling information to be provided about—

(a) mediation of disputes of the kinds to which relevant family applications relate,

(b) ways in which disputes of those kinds may be resolved otherwise than by the court, and

(c) the suitability of mediation, or of any such other way of resolving disputes, for trying to resolve any dispute to which the particular application relates;

'family proceedings' has the same meaning as in section 75 of the Courts Act 2003;

'relevant family application' means an application that—

(a) is made to the court in, or to initiate, family proceedings, and

(b) is of a description specified in Family Procedure Rules.

(4) This section is without prejudice to sections 75 and 76 of the Courts Act 2003 (power to make Family Procedure Rules).

...

13 Control of expert evidence, and of assessments, in children proceedings

(1) A person may not without the permission of the court instruct a person to provide expert evidence for use in children proceedings.

(2) Where in contravention of subsection (1) a person is instructed to provide expert evidence, evidence resulting from the instructions is inadmissible in children proceedings unless the court rules that it is admissible.

(3) A person may not without the permission of the court cause a child to be medically or psychiatrically examined or otherwise assessed for the purposes of the provision of expert evidence in children proceedings.

(4) Where in contravention of subsection (3) a child is medically or psychiatrically examined or otherwise assessed, evidence resulting from the examination or other assessment is inadmissible in children proceedings unless the court rules that it is admissible.

(5) In children proceedings, a person may not without the permission of the court put expert evidence (in any form) before the court.

(6) The court may give permission as mentioned in subsection (1), (3) or (5) only if the court is of the opinion that the expert evidence is necessary to assist the court to resolve the proceedings justly.

(7) When deciding whether to give permission as mentioned in subsection (1), (3) or (5) the court is to have regard in particular to—

    (a) any impact which giving permission would be likely to have on the welfare of the children concerned, including in the case of permission as mentioned in subsection (3) any impact which any examination or other assessment would be likely to have on the welfare of the child who would be examined or otherwise assessed,

    (b) the issues to which the expert evidence would relate,

    (c) the questions which the court would require the expert to answer,

    (d) what other expert evidence is available (whether obtained before or after the start of proceedings),

    (e) whether evidence could be given by another person on the matters on which the expert would give evidence,

    (f) the impact which giving permission would be likely to have on the timetable for, and duration and conduct of, the proceedings,

    (g) the cost of the expert evidence, and

    (h) any matters prescribed by Family Procedure Rules.

(8) References in this section to providing expert evidence, or to putting expert evidence before a court, do not include references to—

    (a) the provision or giving of evidence—

        (i) by a person who is a member of the staff of a local authority or of an authorised applicant,

        (ii) in proceedings to which the authority or authorised applicant is a party, and

        (iii) in the course of the person's work for the authority or authorised applicant,

    (b) the provision or giving of evidence—

        (i) by a person within a description prescribed for the purposes of subsection (1) of section 94 of the Adoption and Children Act 2002 (suitability for adoption etc.), and

        (ii) about the matters mentioned in that subsection,

    (c) the provision or giving of evidence by an officer of the Children and Family Court Advisory and Support Service when acting in that capacity, or

    (d) the provision or giving of evidence by a Welsh family proceedings officer (as defined by section 35(4) of the Children Act 2004) when acting in that capacity.

(9) In this section—

'authorised applicant' means—

    (a) the National Society for the Prevention of Cruelty to Children, or

    (b) a person authorised by an order under section 31 of the Children Act 1989 to bring proceedings under that section;

'child' means a person under the age of 18;

'children proceedings' has such meaning as may be prescribed by Family Procedure Rules;

'the court', in relation to any children proceedings, means the court in which the proceedings are taking place;

'local authority'—

    (a) in relation to England means—

        (i) a county council,

        (ii) a district council for an area for which there is no county council,

        (iii) a London borough council,

        (iv) the Common Council of the City of London, or

        (v) the Council of the Isles of Scilly, and

    (b) in relation to Wales means a county council or a county borough council.

(10) The preceding provisions of this section are without prejudice to sections 75 and 76 of the Courts Act 2003 (power to make Family Procedure Rules).

...

Anti-social Behaviour, Crime and Policing Act 2014

(2014 c. 12)

...

PART 10   FORCED MARRIAGE

121   Offence of forced marriage: England and Wales

(1) A person commits an offence under the law of England and Wales if he or she—

    (a) uses violence, threats or any other form of coercion for the purpose of causing another person to enter into a marriage, and

    (b) believes, or ought reasonably to believe, that the conduct may cause the other person to enter into the marriage without free and full consent.

(2) In relation to a victim who lacks capacity to consent to marriage, the offence under subsection (1) is capable of being committed by any conduct carried out for the purpose of causing the victim to enter into a marriage (whether or not the conduct amounts to violence, threats or any other form coercion).

(3) A person commits an offence under the law of England and Wales if he or she—

    (a) practises any form of deception with the intention of causing another person to leave the United Kingdom, and

    (b) intends the other person to be subjected to conduct outside the United Kingdom that is an offence under subsection (1) or would be an offence under that subsection if the victim were in England or Wales.

(4) 'Marriage' means any religious or civil ceremony of marriage (whether or not legally binding).

(5) 'Lacks capacity' means lacks capacity within the meaning of the Mental Capacity Act 2005.

(6) It is irrelevant whether the conduct mentioned in paragraph (a) of subsection (1) is directed at the victim of the offence under that subsection or another person.

(7) A person commits an offence under subsection (1) or (3) only if, at the time of the conduct or deception—

    (a) the person or the victim or both of them are in England or Wales,

    (b) neither the person nor the victim is in England or Wales but at least one of them is habitually resident in England and Wales, or

    (c) neither the person nor the victim is in the United Kingdom but at least one of them is a UK national.

(8) 'UK national' means an individual who is—

    (a) a British citizen, a British overseas territories citizen, a British National (Overseas) or a British Overseas citizen;

    (b) a person who under the British Nationality Act 1981 is a British subject; or

    (c) a British protected person within the meaning of that Act.

(9) A person guilty of an offence under this section is liable—

    (a) on summary conviction, to imprisonment for a term not exceeding 12 months or to a fine or both;

    (b) on conviction on indictment, to imprisonment for a term not exceeding 7 years.

(10) In relation to an offence committed before the commencement of section 154(1) of the Criminal Justice Act 2003, the reference to 12 months in subsection (9)(a) is to be read as a reference to six months.

International Conventions

For the European Convention for the Protection of Human Rights and Fundamental Freedoms (1950), see the Human Rights Act 1998 (1998 c. 42)

United Nations Convention on the Rights of the Child (1989)

PART I

Article 1

For the purposes of the present Convention, a child means every human being below the age of eighteen years unless, under the law applicable to the child, majority is attained earlier.

Article 2

1. States Parties shall respect and ensure the rights set forth in the present Convention to each child within their jurisdiction without discrimination of any kind, irrespective of the child's or his or her parent's or legal guardian's race, colour, sex, language, religion, political or other opinion, national, ethnic or social origin, property, disability, birth or other status.

2. States Parties shall take all appropriate measures to ensure that the child is protected against all forms of discrimination or punishment on the basis of the status, activities, expressed opinions, or beliefs of the child's parents, legal guardians, or family members.

Article 3

1. In all actions concerning children, whether undertaken by public or private social welfare institutions, courts of law, administrative authorities or legislative bodies, the best interests of the child shall be a primary consideration.

2. States Parties undertake to ensure the child such protection and care as is necessary for his or her well-being, taking into account the rights and duties of his or her parents, legal guardians, or other individuals legally responsible for him or her, and to this end, shall take all appropriate legislative and administrative measures.

3. States Parties shall ensure that the institutions, services and facilities responsible for the care or protection of children shall conform with the standards established by competent authorities, particularly in the areas of safety, health, in the number and suitability of their staff, as well as competent supervision.

…

Article 6

1. States Parties recognise that every child has the inherent right to life.

2. States Parties shall ensure to the maximum extent possible the survival and development of the child.

Article 7

1. The child shall be registered immediately after birth and shall have the right from birth to a name, the right to acquire a nationality and, as far as possible, the right to know and be cared for by his or her parents.

2. States Parties shall ensure the implementation of these rights in accordance with their national law and their obligations under the relevant international instruments in this field, in particular where the child would otherwise be stateless.

...

Article 9

1. States Parties shall ensure that a child shall not be separated from his or her parents against their will, except when competent authorities subject to judicial review determine, in accordance with applicable law and procedures, that such separation is necessary for the best interests of the child. Such determination may be necessary in a particular case such as one involving abuse or neglect of the child by the parents, or one where the parents are living separately and a decision must be made as to the child's place of residence.

2. In any proceedings pursuant to paragraph 1 of the present article, all interested parties shall be given the opportunity to participate in the proceedings and make their views known.

3. States Parties shall respect the right of the child who is separated from one or both parents to maintain personal relations and direct contact with both parents on a regular basis, except if it is contrary to the child's best interests.

4. Where such separation results from any action initiated by a State Party, such as the detention, imprisonment, exile, deportation or death (including death arising from any cause while the person is in the custody of the State) of one or both parents or of the child, that State Party shall, upon request, provide the parents, the child or, if appropriate, another member of the family with the essential information concerning the whereabouts of the absent member(s) of the family unless the provision of the information would be detrimental to the well-being of the child. States Parties shall further ensure that the submission of such a request shall of itself entail no adverse consequences for the person(s) concerned.

Article 10

1. In accordance with the obligation of States Parties under article 9, paragraph 1, applications by a child or his or her parents to enter or leave a State Party for the purposes of family reunification shall be dealt with by States Parties in a positive, humane and expeditious manner. States Parties shall further ensure that the submission of such a request shall entail no adverse consequences for the applicants and for the members of their family.

2. A child whose parents reside in different States shall have the right to maintain on a regular basis, save in exceptional circumstances, personal relations and direct contacts with both parents. Towards that end and in accordance with the obligation of States Parties under article 9, paragraph 1, States Parties shall respect the right of the child and his or her parents to leave any country, including their own, and to enter their own country. The right to leave any country shall be subject only to such restrictions as are prescribed by law and which are necessary to protect the national security, public order (ordre public), public health or morals or the rights and freedoms of others and are consistent with the other rights recognised in the present Convention.

...

Article 12

1. States Parties shall assure to the child who is capable of forming his or her own views the right to express those views freely in all matters affecting the child, the views of the child being given due weight in accordance with the age and maturity of the child.

2. For this purpose, the child shall in particular be provided the opportunity to be heard in any judicial and administrative proceedings affecting the child, either directly, or through a representative or an appropriate body, in a manner consistent with the procedural rules of national law.

...

Article 18

1. States Parties shall use their best efforts to ensure recognition of the principle that both parents have common responsibilities for the upbringing and development of the child. Parents or, as the case may be, legal guardians, have the primary responsibility for the upbringing and development of the child. The best interests of the child will be their basic concern.

2. For the purpose of guaranteeing and promoting the rights set forth in the present Convention, States Parties shall render appropriate assistance to parents and legal guardians in the performance of their child-rearing responsibilities and shall ensure the development of institutions, facilities and services for the care of children.

3. States Parties shall take all appropriate measures to ensure that children of working parents have the right to benefit from child-care services and facilities for which they are eligible.

...

Article 22

1. States Parties shall take appropriate measures to ensure that a child who is seeking refugee status or who is considered a refugee in accordance with applicable international or domestic law and procedures shall, whether unaccompanied or accompanied by his or her parents or by any other person, receive appropriate protection and humanitarian assistance in the enjoyment of applicable rights set forth in the present convention and in other international human rights or humanitarian instruments to which the said States are Parties.

2. For this purpose, States Parties shall provide, as they consider appropriate, co-operation in any efforts by the United Nations and other competent intergovernmental organisations or non-governmental organisations co-operating with the United Nations to protect and assist such a child and to trace the parents or other members of the family of any refugee child in order to obtain information necessary for reunification with his or her family. In cases where no parents or other members of the family can be found, the child shall be accorded the same protection as any other child permanently or temporarily deprived of his or her family environment for any reason, as set forth in the present Convention.

...

Article 40

1. States Parties recognise the right of every child alleged as, accused of, or recognised as having infringed the penal law to be treated in a manner consistent with the promotion of the child's sense of dignity and worth, which reinforces the child's respect for the human rights and fundamental freedoms of others and which takes into account the child's age and the desirability of promoting the child's reintegration and the child's assuming a constructive role in society.

2. To this end, and having regard to the relevant provisions of international instruments, States Parties shall, in particular, ensure that:

(a) No child shall be alleged as, be accused of, or recognised as having infringed the penal law by reason of acts or omissions that were not prohibited by national or international law at the time they were committed;

(b) Every child alleged as or accused of having infringed the penal law has at least the following guarantees:

(i) To be presumed innocent until proven guilty according to law;

(ii) To be informed promptly and directly of the charges against him or her, and, if appropriate, through his or her parents or legal guardians, and to have legal or other appropriate assistance in the preparation and presentation of his or her defence;

(iii) To have the matter determined without delay by a competent, independent and impartial authority or judicial body in a fair hearing according to law, in the presence of legal or other appropriate assistance and, unless it is considered not to be in the best interest of the child, in particular, taking into account his or her age or situation, his or her parents or legal guardians;

      (iv) Not to be compelled to give testimony or to confess guilt; to examine or have examined adverse witnesses and to obtain the participation and examination of witnesses on his or her behalf under conditions of equality;

      (v) If considered to have infringed the penal law, to have this decision and any measures imposed in consequence thereof reviewed by a higher competent, independent and impartial authority or judicial body according to law;

      (vi) To have the free assistance of an interpreter if the child cannot understand or speak the language used;

      (vii) To have his or her privacy fully respected at all stages of the proceedings.

3. States Parties shall seek to promote the establishment of laws, procedures, authorities and institutions specifically applicable to children alleged as, accused of, or recognised as having infringed the penal law, and, in particular:

      (a) The establishment of a minimum age below which children shall be presumed not to have the capacity to infringe the penal law;

      (b) Whenever appropriate and desirable, measures for dealing with such children without resorting to judicial proceedings, providing that human rights and legal safeguards are fully respected.

4. A variety of dispositions, such as care, guidance and supervision orders; counselling; probation; foster care; education and vocational training programmes and other alternatives to institutional care shall be available to ensure that children are dealt with in a manner appropriate to their well-being and proportionate both to their circumstances and the offence.

...

Index

Blackstone's Statutes on

Family Law